A History of
Russian Literature

A History of Russian Literature

Victor Terras

Yale University Press

New Haven and London

This publication has been supported by a grant
from the National Endowment for the
Humanities, an independent federal agency.

Set in ITC Garamond by Asco Trade Typesetting
Ltd., Hong Kong.
Printed in the United States of America by
Hamilton Printing Co., Castleton, New York.

Library of Congress Cataloging-in-Publication
Data

Terras, Victor.
A history of Russian literature / Victor Terras.
p.   cm.
Includes bibliographical references and index.
ISBN 0-300-04971-4 (cloth)
        0-300-05934-5 (pbk.)
1. Russian literature—History and criticism.
I. Title.
PG2950.T43   1991
891.709—dc20   91-13337 CIP

The paper in this book meets the guidelines for
permanence and durability of the Committee on
Production Guidelines for Book Longevity of the
Council on Library Resources.

10 9 8 7 6 5 4 3 2

Contents

Preface

Through much of its history, Russian society has been different from the societies of Western Europe, although never, except perhaps during the Soviet period, so different that the Russian institutions, social relations, and general way of life could not be explained in terms familiar to the Western reader. A translation of Russian facts into our own conceptual system will skew them somewhat. Serfdom in Russia was not the same as serfdom in Western Europe or slavery in America, but "serf" as a translation of Russian *krepostnoi* and "slave" as a translation of Russian *rab*, a word used by some serf-owners as its synonym, convey the idea well enough. Likewise, Russian literature in translation has spoken to Westerners—indeed, thrived in the West—despite the disparities of Russian and Western culture.

Addressed to Western readers, this history tries to present Russian literature as it was perceived by Russian readers. It also seeks to convey to a general reader a scholar's view of the subject. The emphasis is on producing a maximum of information rather than on structuring that information to support any particular conception of its meaning.

The method used in this history is eclectic and is based on several compromises. The presentation is conventionally chronological, but literary trends, authors, and works are viewed not only as they may have appeared to contemporaries, or as links in an ongoing evolution, but also in terms of the understanding and sensibility of later periods and even of our own age. Thus, Pushkin will be a ubiquitous presence in much of this history. Literature is seen as a collective effort, but important authors are singled out and discussed. Biographical data have been introduced insofar as they seemed relevant to an understanding of the author's work or its impact.

This history concentrates on "serious" or "high literature," authors and works appreciated by an educated elite in their own time and later, rather than literature serving to entertain or edify a mass audience (although some information concerning the latter has been introduced). A concentration on high literature seems appropriate because it is this part of Russian literature that is of primary interest to the foreign reader. For the same reason, more attention was paid to the intrinsic aesthetic content of literature than to its social value and historical importance or to reader response at the time of a work's appearance.

If there is one trait of Russian literature that distinguishes it from the major literatures of the West, it is its persistent claim to a social function. Medieval literature, whenever it was not directly a part of religious life, tended to have a political function, as in the chronicles and war tales. In the seventeenth and eighteenth centuries literary activity was centered in the imperial court, serving it in various functions. After a generation of creative independence during the Golden Age of Russian poetry in the 1820s and 1830s, Russian literature became a forum of social and political debate. The novels of Turgenev, Dostoevsky, Tolstoi, and their contemporaries were perceived by their readers as partisan statements on Russian society and its future. After a brief interval of emancipation from social and political concerns, provided by the Silver Age of Russian poetry at the turn of the twentieth century, literature became completely politicized during the Soviet period, and the history of literature was incorporated into political history. Russian critics and literary historians, with few exceptions (among whom the formalists of the 1920s were the most notable), have seen literature as inseparable from social history. Even those who did insist on its creative autonomy assumed that art, if true to its calling, would without fail serve the cause of social justice and progress. The facts of Russian literature as presented in this history disprove this conception.

Only directly observable reflections of ideas, ideologies, and modes of thought on literature are dealt with. No attempt is made to find a "deep structure" or teleology beneath the surface of the literary facts presented.

Russian literature originated from three sources, each of which retained its distinct identity within the mainstream of Russian life. What in modern times has been known as "folk culture" and "folk literature" (*narodnaya literatura*) has its roots in the pre-Christian culture of East Slavic tribes living in what in later times would be western Russia.[1] With the coming of Christianity in the tenth century, Russia joined *Slavia orthodoxa*, a group of South and East Slavic nations that were culturally dependent on Byzantium.

Medieval Russian literature was dominated by the religious and ritual needs of the Orthodox church. Byzantine in style as well as substance, it merged to some degree with secular literature, which began to develop in the seventeenth century, but its elements

---

1. The Russian Primary Chronicle presents this vivid picture of tribal life before the coming of Christianity: "The Radimichi, the Vyatichi, and the Sever all had the same customs, living in the woods like animals, eating all kinds of unclean food, and using foul language before their fathers and daughters-in-law; nor were there marriages among them, but games played halfway between their villages, where they would get together for these games, dancing, and all kinds of devilish songs; and here they would abduct wives for themselves, each taking the one with whom he had an agreement beforehand, and they would also have two and three wives. And when one of them would die, they would have a funeral feast for the deceased and make a huge pyre and lay him on it and burn the corpse, and then they would gather his bones in a small vessel which they would then place on a post by the roadside, which the Vyatichi are doing to this day." (*Povesti drevnei Rusi XI–XII veka* [Leningrad: Lenizdat, 1983], 28–29. My translation.)

remained ideologically and linguistically recognizable even after Russian literature had become thoroughly westernized.

Modern Russian literature got its start in the seventeenth century, from an effort of Orthodox churchmen in western Russia, then under Polish rule, to transplant the literary culture of the Polish Catholic baroque to Russian soil. But only in the early eighteenth century did Russian literature join the mainstream of Western literary life through translation and imitation of works then current in France, England, Germany, and other countries of Western Europe. Before the century was over, works had been produced whose intellectual and aesthetic value equaled anything produced in the West, and Russian literature began to be translated into the languages of Western Europe.[2]

Russian folk literature must be observed in the light of comparative folklore. Medieval Russian literature can be understood only in the context of its Byzantine origins. Modern Russian literature requires constant attention to the influence of Western ideas, trends, and styles. And a good deal of cross-referencing among the three branches of Russian literature is necessary.

The subject matter of this history is not homogeneous. Following standard practice, religious genres, such as the saint's life and the homily, are dealt with extensively in the chapters on the medieval period but are abandoned at the point when Peter the Great decreed that religious and secular literature should be separate. The reason for

2. Some translations of Russian poetry appeared in England and Germany even in the eighteenth century. But only Sir John Bowring's *Specimens of the Russian poets* (1821–23) created a genuine interest in Russian literature in the English-speaking countries.

this practice is that medieval Russia produced few secular works, hardly enough to form a "literature." For similar reasons the chapters on sixteenth- and seventeenth-century literature deal with some works that later descended to the level of folk literature or folklore, treated only marginally in subsequent chapters.

The literature of the early period arose mostly in regions that are today a part of the Ukraine and Belorussia. Much of seventeenth-century Muscovite literature was generated by Ukrainian and Belorussian immigrants to Muscovy. It stands to reason that Ukrainian and Belorussian literatures have as good a claim, or better, to some of the authors and works dealt with in the first four chapters of this history of Russian literature. The controversy over the beginning of Ukrainian and Belorussian as separate languages and literatures has not been broached in this history. Inclusion of such authors as Feofan Prokopovich, Saint Dimitry of Rostov, and Stefan Yavorsky does not necessarily imply that they were "Russian" authors. It suggests only that they were important for the development of Russian literature.

This history claims the traditional privilege of academic historians to stop a generation short of the present. A certain detachment and perspective are needed in a work that is meant to be in use for some years. Selection and assessment of authors and works to be included in a historical treatment is difficult without the help provided by the selection process of history. Distance from events protects the historian from the intrusion of developments that overturn his or her judgments. Dealing with authors who are still active is difficult. An academic historian is rarely equipped to make the intuitive judgments that are the prerogative of the literary critic of contemporary literature.

The survey form of history takes a bird's-eye view of its subject and therefore has no eye for details. Since in literature the adage "God is in the detail" may well apply, this may cause a survey to miss the very essence of its subject. The best that can be done is to introduce an occasional highlight and to suggest that many more are there to reward the reader who will proceed from this survey to the literature itself.

The manuscript of this book was completed in the fall of 1989, at a time when developments in the Soviet Union and Eastern Europe made it clear to me that an attempt to integrate a historical treatment of Russian literature with an analysis of its present condition would be futile. Subsequent events, which indicate that the situation in the Soviet Union is still very much in flux, have confirmed me in this view. Regretfully, therefore, I refrain in these pages from reacting as much as I might have to the stimulation that I received from exchanges of ideas, understandably relating to the contemporary scene for the most part, with scholars from all over the world, including many from the Soviet Union, during my association with the Kennan Institute for Advanced Russian Studies as a fellow of the Woodrow Wilson International Center for Scholars in 1988–89. But then, the progress of my work owes much to the ready access to the riches of the Library of Congress that my fellowship entailed.

I owe a debt of gratitude to Edward Tripp of Yale University Press, Frank R. Silbajoris of Ohio State University, and my colleagues at Brown University, Sam Driver, Alexander Levitsky, and Robert Mathiesen, who read the manuscript, made corrections in it, and provided me with valuable suggestions. Richard Miller, the manuscript editor, patiently smoothed out the rough edges and many solecisms of the text. I also thank my students and colleagues, many of whom will recognize their own ideas in this book, for the fruitful discussions we have had over the years. Of course, I alone am responsible for the shortcomings of this book.

A History of
Russian Literature

Chapter 1

Russian Folklore

Early records of Russian folklore are rare, because the Russian Orthodox church, well aware of its pagan origins, was inveterately opposed to it. The church recognized that the illiterate peasantry persisted in a dual faith (*dvoeverie*), embracing elements of Christianity and observing its ritual yet continuing to practice an animistic religion. Throughout the Middle Ages we are limited to occasional hostile mention of what was clearly a vigorous strain of Russian culture, especially among the lower classes. Abbot Panphilius (Panfily), an early sixteenth-century churchman, for example, complains about the pagan celebration of Saint John's Eve with indecent songs as well as provocative dancing and gestures by women, "a grave temptation to married men and youths." He also reports that on this night people gathered herbs that they believed had magical properties. Panphilius denounces these goings-on as thoroughly pernicious and diabolic.[1] A pastoral letter by

Daniel (Daniil), metropolitan of all Russia (1522–39), directed against worldly temptations that distract not only laymen but even the clergy from a godly life, contains a catalog of diabolic pastimes indulged in by the Russian people: attending to minstrels (*skomorokhi*) and dancers, playing chess and checkers, indulging in irreverent jests, "devilish songs, and huge and inordinate drinking bouts," and consulting soothsayers and astrologers as well as "so-called cloud-chasers, wizards, charmers, and magicians."[2]

Nevertheless, occasional themes and phrases from Russian folklore entered medieval literature, the chronicles in particular. In some instances local legends and traditions found their way into saints' lives, such as the fifteenth-century life of Saint Mercurius (Merkury) of Smolensk, who walked home from a battle against the invading Tatars carrying his severed head under his arm.

Only since the seventeenth century do we have texts that are either outright tran-

1. *A sermon of instruction on the day of John the Baptist, to the Christ-loving city of Pskov and all Orthodox Christendom, by Panphilius, abbot of Elizarov Hermitage.*

2. *Instruction of Daniel, Metropolitan of All Russia.*

scriptions of works from oral tradition or fairly close paraphrases. Richard James, chaplain of the British embassy in Moscow, recorded a number of songs in 1619–20. Samuel Collins, a British physician to Tsar Alexis in the 1660s, recorded ten folktales (published in 1671). Prose paraphrases of several epic songs (*The Tale of Sukhan*, *Mikhail Potok*, *The Tale of the Seven Heroes of Kiev*) found in seventeenth-century manuscripts suggest that the epic tradition that had started in Kiev had by then established itself in Muscovy. A modest number of satirical tales and fables reflect Russia's developing connections with the West, as many of the themes featured here seem to have come to Russia from such Western sources as the *Facetiae* of Poggio Bracciolini.

The first major manuscript collection of epic songs dates from the mid-eighteenth century. These songs, attributed to a Cossack named Kirsha Danilov, were apparently recorded in western Siberia. By the 1770s and 1780s printed songbooks (which contained old as well as recently composed songs) and collections of Russian folktales were a commercial commodity. Parallel to the westernized literature of the elite, there now developed a popular literature of chapbooks (*lubochnaya literatura*), which became a receptacle for folk traditions mixed with elements of traditional religious literature and of high literature. Chapbooks were directed at the growing number of literate members of the lower classes, mostly in the cities. Sold at fairs and in the marketplace, they represented a flourishing industry until the revolution of 1917. During the last quarter of the eighteenth century Russian folk songs and dances, as well as other elements of Russian folklore, began to appear onstage, used by authors of comic operas and vaudevilles, which were otherwise close imitations of French and Italian

examples. This practice continued in the nineteenth century.

Only with the advent of romanticism in the 1820s was a real effort to collect Russian folklore launched and its scholarly study initiated. Since the romantic period Russian poets have occasionally written poetry in the manner of the folk song. Pushkin's "Tale of the She-Bear" (1830) and Lermontov's "Song of the Merchant Kalashnikov" (1837) are early examples. Starting with Aleksei Koltsov (1809–42), Russian poets have often written in the style and meter of the folk song. Some, such as Nikolai Nekrasov (1821–77) and Nikolai Klyuev (1887–1937), developed a style that combined a popular ethos and elements peculiar to the folk song with the formal structure and sensibility of *Kunstdichtung*. Similarly, the Russian folktale has found a reflection in Russian high literature, both in the form of direct imitation, as in some of Lev Tolstoi's "tales for the people," and in combination with literary forms, as in Pushkin's fairy tales in verse or the folkloristic novels of Aleksandr Veltman (1800–1870).

The populist mystique that affected the conservative Russian Slavophiles no less than progressive circles of the nineteenth-century Russian intelligentsia produced the side effect of an active interest in folk culture. A lively collecting effort by dedicated amateurs in the educated public led to the establishment of a large corpus of recorded songs, tales, legends, proverbs, riddles, and other forms of folklore. The most important collections were, for lyric songs, *Songs*, collected by Pyotr Kireevsky (10 vol., 1860–74); for epic songs, *Songs*, collected by Pavel Rybnikov (4 vol., 1861–67), and *Byliny of the Onega Region*, by Aleksandr Hilferding (3 vol., 1873); for prose tales, *Russian Folktales*, collected by Aleksandr Afanasyev (1855–64); for legends, *Itiner-*

ant Beggars,[3] by Pyotr Bessonov (2 vol., 1861–63); and for proverbs, *Proverbs of the Russian People*, by Vladimir Dahl (1862). Much further work was later done by academic as well as amateur collectors.

Russian folklorists of the nineteenth and early twentieth centuries followed trends in international folklore studies. The mythological school, developed in Germany by the brothers Grimm, sought to reduce the plots of folk songs and folktales to primeval cosmological myths. The Russian folklorist Fyodor Buslaev (1818–97), an adherent of this school, saw for example in the feats of Ilya of Murom, the great hero of the Russian folk epic, vestiges of ancient myths of Perun, the Slavic god of thunder. The mythological school was superseded by a historical school, which strove to link a given theme or plot to a specific historical event or period, and a comparative school, which followed the migrations of themes, plots, and other elements of folklore across cultural and linguistic boundaries to their source. A leading exponent of the historical school was Vsevolod Miller (1848–1913) and of the comparative school Aleksandr Veselovsky (1838–1906).

After the Revolution of 1917 the study of Russian folklore soon became politicized, as Soviet scholars tried to see folklore in terms of social relations and class struggle. Attention was now devoted to contemporary forms, such as urban and workers' folklore, to satirical songs and tales, and to epic songs about outlaws and rebels, such as Stepan Razin (seventeenth century) and Emelyan Pugachov (eighteenth century). Interest in traditional forms like religious legends dwindled. Soviet folklorists made a point of

crediting the simple Russian people, rather than the minstrels of medieval princely courts, with the creation of the heroic epic.[4] Twentieth-century Russian folklorists have done some important theoretical work. Vladimir Propp (1895–1970), in his *Morphology of the Folktale* (1928), concluded that all Russian magic tales, however different their dramatis personae and plots, have an identical basic mechanics readily reduced to a limited number of functions, such as "obstacle" and "helper," which unfold in predictable sequences. Propp's insights in this and other studies have had an impact on international folklore studies, as has the work of Russian structuralists including Vladimir Toporov (b. 1928) and Vyacheslav Ivanov (b. 1929).

Most forms of Russian folklore were vigorous in the eighteenth century, as a part of a peasant culture that existed independently of the culture of the Westernized upper classes. But in the course of the nineteenth century all folk song genres gradually became crystallized—that is, their tradition came to rely on mechanical memory instead of creative improvisation. The only genre remaining alive was the *chastushka*, a rhymed ditty of recent origin. In the 1930s some futile efforts were made to revive the old folk song and press it into the service of communist propaganda and the glorification of Stalin. With universal literacy there was no longer a raison d'être for an oral tradition. Moreover, since the old peasant culture, with its architecture, art, and music, fell victim to urbanization and the collectivization of agriculture, the traditions of folk song and folktale lacked a proper cultural setting.

---

3. The Russian title is *Kaliki perekhozhie*, referring to blind or lame wanderers who spread legends from town to town.

4. See Felix J. Oinas, "The Problem of the Aristocratic Origin of Russian *Byliny*," *Slavic Review* 30 (1971): 513–22.

The Folk Song

The formal structure of the Russian folk song is different from anything found in Russian literary poetry, except in the instances when poetry imitates the folk song. It has been observed that the rhythm of a Russian folk song disintegrates in spoken recitation, suggesting that a folk song's natural rendition is musical. Nevertheless, certain persistent rhythmical patterns appear, especially in the epic songs. Russian, a stress-timing language (like English) rather than a syllable-counting language (like French), lacks the equisyllabic lines found in the folk song in other Slavic languages, such as Serbian, but tends to favor a trochaic rhythm (x́x) with a constant number of stresses (often three) per line and a dactylic clausula (x́xx).

The old folk song has no rhyme whether it is sung (lyric songs) or recited (epic songs and laments). Only so-called spoken verse (*skazovy stikh*, also *rayoshny stikh*), used in short forms—proverbs, sayings, wisecracks, riddles, speeches of the master of ceremonies at a folk wedding, cries of hucksters and traders—has rhyme, as does the *chastushka* (from *chasty*, "fast"), a short (usually four-line) lyric or satirical song performed to the accompaniment of an accordion or balalaika. The chastushka, apparently a young genre (dating from no earlier than the eighteenth century), may have developed under foreign or literary influence.

The singer of songs is basically an improviser. Folk singers have at their disposal certain traditional themes, plots, and images, a large number of formulaic expressions, and a certain style of performance. The language of the folk song and folktale is distinct from normal speech lexically, morphologically, and syntactically. It features many archaisms, standard epithets (Duke Vladimir of Kiev, for example, is routinely called Vladimir the Fair Sun), and formulaic noun-adjective combinations: the sea is always blue, the steppe clear, the earth always damp Mother Earth. The language of the folk song is fond of pleonasms, such as tautological compounds ("plight-misfortune"), emphatic reduplication ("she cried-cried"), and paronomasia ("living a life"). It includes many compounds which in ordinary speech are perceived as quotations from poetry or fairy tales: copulative compounds ("father-mother" instead of "father and mother"), determinative compounds ("woe-peasant" meaning "luckless peasant"), and descriptive compounds ("first daughter, serve-a-cake, second daughter, close-your-fist"). The language of folk poetry seeks out parallelism, sometimes enhancing it by grammatical rhyme ("he took to drinking, took to thinking") and often against normal usage, as when a preposition is pleonastically repeated ("in the capital city, in Kiev" instead of "in the capital city of Kiev"). A simile or metaphor is often presented in several (ordinarily three) parallel images: "It wasn't a hawk that fluttered by, it wasn't a stoat that leaped by, it wasn't a falcon that flew by, it was a valiant good lad that rode by." The negative simile seen in this example is very common. Russian folk poetry uses tropes and figures sparingly, and they are always formulaic—the mark of oral improvisation. Some literary attempts at re-creating folk poetry have failed precisely because they were overladen with imagery and poetic devices.

Lyric Genres

Musically, a song is either fast (*chastaya*) or drawn out (*protyazhnaya*). Its function determines whether it is ritual (ceremonial) or nonritual. Depending on the singer's persona, it is a soldier song, a robber song, a barge hauler song, and so on. It may be a "male" or a "female" song. Each division has its genres.

Russian folk culture was highly ritualized, and most rituals were accompanied by appropriate songs. There were work songs, seasonal songs for Christmas, Shrovetide, spring, and harvest, and songs for important family occasions, such as weddings and funerals.

A Russian peasant wedding was, to borrow Aleksandr Veselovsky's term, a free mystery play—a sequence of choral and mimetic actions integrated by their subject, the battle and ultimate reconciliation of the sexes. At the bridegroom's house a martial atmosphere is created, as a raiding party under the leadership of a colonel or flag bearer prepares to abduct the bride. The bridegroom, called "duke," and his friends, called "warriors," all carrying wooden swords, set out for the bride's house. The bride's party places gates or roadblocks in their way. All of this action follows a fixed pattern; the words and songs are traditional, though used in free variations. In the end the storming of the bride's home is enacted, and peace is made. Gifts are exchanged and the feast begins. After the meal the bride says farewell to her bridesmaids, as laments are sung and tears shed. The whole party now moves on to the groom's house. As the feast continues, the couple's bed is made in the barn or stable, often with a sack of corn as a pillow—all for fertility. The bride is dressed in a white shirt as her bridesmaids sing love songs. The bride and groom retire while the guests continue the feast. Immediate defloration of the bride is expected of the groom, and the bloody shirt is displayed triumphantly by the bride's mother. If the bride turns out not to be a virgin, she and her parents suffer ribald jests and songs (formulaic like the rest).

The lament (*plach*) expressed grief in a conventional, socially approved form. There were formulas for every occasion: a funeral lament for a breadwinner would of course be different from one for a mother or a child. Laments of the bride about her loss of a happy maidenhood in the bosom of a loving family were a part of the wedding ceremony. Other laments were recited when a young man was leaving the village for military service. There were laments occasioned by calamities that affected the community, such as fires or floods. Laments were often recited by professional wailers, usually older women who were paid for their services. The formal structure of the lament resembles that of the epic song. Like the epic song, the lament was performed as a recitative and was improvised from a set of formulaic expressions, following an established sequence of images appropriate to the progress of the funeral or other occasion.

Nonritual songs display a variety of topics and moods. They were often performed by a chorus with a lead singer, particularly game and dance songs. Game songs (*khorovodnye pesni*) are stylized vignettes of the joys and sorrows of village life. Dance songs (*plyasovye pesni*) typically present brief dramatized pictures of the battle of the sexes. A common genre is that of songs of grief, such as those about an orphan's hard lot or a young wife who dreams of the easy life at her parents' house. There are also love songs and lullabies. At the other end of the emotional scale are satirical songs, humorous songs (sometimes with a fine sense of the absurd), and so-called daring songs (*udalye pesni*), boasting of an outlaw's free and happy life. In robber songs (*razboinich'i pesni*) the outlaw finds himself in prison, awaiting execution, and likens himself to a captive eagle or falcon dreaming of happiness and freedom.

Epic Genres

The Russian epic song (*bylina*) was chanted to a simple melody. There were more songs than melodies, so that the same melody would be used for different songs. Some performers would insert brief spoken comments between chanted lines. Performers, male or female, had extensive repertoires which they could vary and recombine. No song would ever appear in exactly the same form twice. An epic song can vary in length from less than a hundred to several hundred lines. It features a formulaic prelude (*zachin*) and a formulaic close (*kontsovka*). There is no stanzaic structure. Lines are of uneven length but are made to fit the basic rhythm of the recitative through insertion of filler particles, shifting stress, syncope, and other devices. The plot of a bylina unfolds slowly. There is a great deal of descriptive detail but little narrative strategy. Episodes are often developed triadically (for example, the hero may have to overcome three successive obstacles), and the climax is sudden. Psychological motivation is absent: the heroes speak and act but do not think.

There are two types of byliny, historical and mythical. Historical byliny deal with the exploits of such historical personages as Ivan the Terrible, Peter the Great, Stepan Razin, and Emelyan Pugachov and reflect the people's reaction to events associated with these figures. The image of Ivan the Terrible is positive, whereas Peter the Great comes off rather badly. The singer unequivocally sides with the outlaws Razin and Pugachov. Historical byliny may be likened to folk ballads of the English-speaking world.

Mythical songs form several distinct cycles. Some byliny are apparent vestiges of Slavic cosmological and totemic myths, celebrating culture heroes rather than warriors. In this group are several songs about Svyatogor (Holy Mount), a giant so huge that Mother Earth cannot bear him. In one of these songs Svyatogor boasts that he could lift the whole world if only he could find a point of support. As he rides through the steppe, he comes across a small bag, which he finds too heavy to lift from the saddle. When he dismounts and tries to lift the bag, it will not budge even though the giant has strained so mightily that he is up to his knees in the ground. He makes one more frantic effort and is swallowed by Mother Earth. Mikula Selyaninovich (Nicholas, the Peasant's Son) is a mighty plowman who plows so fast that Duke Volga Svyatoslavovich (probably an allusion to Duke Oleg of Kiev) can barely overtake him on horseback. Volkh Vseslavovich (from *volkhv*, "sorcerer," and Vseslav, an eleventh-century duke of Polotsk whom the Russian Primary Chronicle reports to have had a werewolf's magical powers) can change himself into a variety of animals at will and performs incredible feats of magic and cunning.

By far the most important set of mythical songs is the Kiev cycle, in which Vladimir the Fair Sun, clearly identical with Vladimir I, grand duke of Kiev (979–1015), plays the role that King Arthur or Charlemagne play in the epic tradition of the West. At least one of the main heroes of this cycle, Dobrynya Nikitich, may have an identifiable historical prototype in Dobrynya, an uncle and general of Vladimir's. There is also a Novgorod cycle, in which the wealth and unruly freedom of the great northern trading city are well remembered.

The heroes (*bogatyri*) of the Kiev cycle are engaged in constant battles against the infidel Tatars, a substitute for the historical Pechenegs and Polovetzians. Contrary to historical truth, the Russian heroes are always victorious. Many byliny feature familiar international themes. Dobrynya Nikitich, accomplished in all the knightly arts and in music, clearly the aristocrat among the bogatyri, is the Russian dragon slayer. He also appears in the familiar role of guest at his wife's wedding. Alyosha Popovich (the Parson's Son), another popular hero, has persuaded Dobrynya's wife to marry him after her husband has not been heard from in six years. But Dobrynya appears at the wedding disguised as a minstrel and claims his wife. Alyosha, a crafty sort, talks his way out of this tight spot. Yet Alyosha has his heroic exploits, too. It is he who slays the formidable Tatar prince Tugarin Zmeevich (echoing the historical Tugorkan, a Polovetzian khan; Zmeevich is from *zmei*, "dragon").

The hero of heroes is Ilya of Murom, who is featured in many byliny, alone and with other heroes. Like the other bogatyri, he fights the Tatars, but he also appears in a number of plots found in epic tales throughout the world. In one bylina, for example, Ilya is captured by the giant Svyatogor, who ties him up and sticks him in his pocket. On his belt the giant carries a glass cage in which he keeps a beautiful princess whom he has kidnapped. When Svyatogor lies down to sleep, the princess promises Ilya that she will let him flee if he will make love to her. After it is done, she demands that he give her his ring, which she puts on a string on which she already has thirty-three other rings. The Russian folk epic and folktale tend to be quite negative about feminine virtue.

Ilya of Murom is the son of a peasant (Cossack singers make him a Cossack), a simple soul whose straightforward manner often gets him in trouble with Duke Vladi-mir and his court. Ilya spent the first thirty-three years of his life immobile, without the use of his legs, until miraculously healed and given prodigious strength by two holy pilgrims. They come to his house and ask for a drink of water. When Ilya responds that he cannot move, they order him to get up. He does and immediately feels great strength rising through his body. He sets out for Kiev to serve Duke Vladimir. Along the way Ilya defeats and captures the terrible highwayman Solovei (Nightingale), whose shrill whistle alone can kill a man.

The bogatyri of the Kievan cycle, but especially Ilya of Murom, have been and still are a part of the Russian national consciousness. When in *The Brothers Karamazov* Dostoevsky calls a boy hero Ilya, he is pointing at Ilya of Murom.

The epics of the Kievan cycle present a heroic world through peasant eyes. (This is reflected in the language of the epic, which mixes highly stylized poetic diction with crude vulgarisms.) A sense of the tragic, which may have played a greater role in earlier versions (there is evidence for this in the case of *The Tale of Sukhan*, of which there exists a seventeenth-century paraphrase), is generally absent. The bylina as sung by the peasant singers of the Russian north is basically optimistic and materialistic. It has been assumed that the heroic epic originated at the princely courts of the Kievan era. (These courts probably employed minstrels.) When Kievan Russia collapsed in the thirteenth century, the epic songs moved north with the *skomorokhi*, traveling entertainers at whose hands the songs were adjusted to a new, Muscovite ethos, though they retained their Kievan setting. In the sixteenth and seventeenth centuries the skomorokhi periodically suffered persecution by ecclesiastical and secular authorities and gradually drifted to the northern and northeastern frontiers, where the arm of the government could not reach them. In the Russian north, where Karelian peasants with a rich epic tradition were neighbors, the heroic epic became the property of peasant singers. The texts of Kirsha Danilov's collection suggest that by the eighteenth century the mythical bylina had become more or less crystallized and that active songmaking was limited to new historical songs like the cycle concerning the Pugachov rebellion of 1773. Singers were active in the north and in Siberia well into the twentieth century, but these were performers, not creators. Nevertheless, Russia is one of only a few modern nations to have boasted a living epic tradition.

A special genre of Russian folk poetry is the *dukhovny stikh* (literally, "spiritual rime"), formally similar to the bylina but based on Scripture (episodes from the lives of Jesus and the Virgin Mary, for example), saint's lives (Boris and Gleb, Alexis, George, and others), religious legends, and apocrypha. A dukhovny stikh may be several hundred lines long, though most are shorter. The dukhovny stikh represents a fusion of Russian folklore and Russia medieval literature. Whereas the world of the bylina and fairy tale is largely of pre-Christian origin, that of the dukhovny stikh is Christian. Its bearers were mostly pious pilgrims, and their songs were meant to be primarily edifying, though some are quite entertaining. The earliest recorded dukhovny stikh is the *Tale of Woe and Misfortune, how Woe-Misfortune led a youth to a monk's station*, extant in two early eighteenth-century manuscripts but believed to have been composed in the seventeenth century. In its language and general manner it is somewhat more literary than *dukhovnye stikhi* recorded later. It is also much longer (almost five hundred lines).

Dukhovnye stikhi also contain a Russian peasant's cosmology and cosmogony. "The Book of the Dove" (the dove is of course the Holy Ghost), a dukhovny stikh in dialogue form, answers a long series of questions like "Whence came our bodies?" ("Our bodies come from damp earth") and "Whence came our red blood?" ("Our red blood comes from the black sea.") "The Book of the Dove" has unmistakable echoes from medieval texts, such as the *Hexaemeron* (*Shestodnev*) of John, exarch of Bulgaria, manuscripts of which circulated in Russia at least as early as the thirteenth century.[5]

The dukhovny stikh was still alive in the nineteenth century and entered a number of important works of modern Russian literature. Alexis, Man of God, figures prominently in Dostoevsky's *Brothers Karamazov*. Echoes of several dukhovnye stikhi appear in Lev Tolstoi's cycle of "tales for the people." Several major writers, including Vladimir Odoevsky, Vsevolod Garshin, Nikolai Leskov, and Aleksei Remizov, utilized themes from dukhovnye stikhi in their prose tales.

The Folktale

The Russian folktale has many subgenres. There are magic tales (*volshebnye skazki*), tales of everyday life (*bytovye skazki*), satirical tales, animal fables, allegorical tales, religious tales (legends), and soldiers' tales. A folktale may be brief (ten to fifteen lines) or the length of a short story (ten pages or more). The teller of tales is an improviser working almost like the singer of songs.

5. *Shestodnev*, like *hexaemeron*, means "the six days [of Creation]." John the Exarch's work was based on the *Hexaemeron* of Basil the Great (329–79), a work combining biblical cosmology and cosmogony with elements of the Hellenic tradition (Plato, Aristotle, and others).

Tellers use much the same language: the language of a magic tale is close to that of an epic song, the language of a satirical tale is close to that of a satirical song, and so on. There were, of course, good tellers of tales, as well as not-so-good ones. Some would enrich the text with their improvisations; other would stay within the bare outline of the plot. Skilled tellers of tales would add a running commentary, in colloquial language, to their stylized narrative.

The Russian folktale, like the epic song, has a formulaic beginning and close. It often features inserted verse lines. Most of the themes found in the Russian folktale have international equivalents.

The magic tale creates an unreal, supernatural world of evil spirits, vampires, witches (such as the cruel, man-eating Baba Yaga), ogres, dragons, enchanted animals (such as the firebird, made famous by Igor Stravinsky's ballet), spirits in bottles, talking fish, and magic swords and tablecloths. The plot of the magic tale is simple and stereotypical. The hero is usually a young prince (*Ivan tsarevich*) or Johnny the Fool (*Ivanushka durachok*, often a much-maligned third son). Heroines, somewhat rarer, are usually princesses or poor orphans. In the course of the story the hero or heroine goes through a sequence of trials and adventures, often arranged in triads, as when the hero vanquishes in succession knights wearing bronze, silver, and golden armor. There is always a happy ending.

The personages of the magic tale are conventional. Their character is determined by their function, and their actions have little or no psychological motivation. The magic tale is of prehistorical and pre-Christian origin. Particular stories, however, may have a literary source, such as one of the medieval romances of chivalry which reached Russia, usually via Poland, in the seventeenth century. In the nineteenth and twentieth centuries some stories were recorded whose source was Pushkin's fairy tales in verse or Gogol's Ukrainian tales. Animist and totemic details are easily gleaned from many of the magic tales. The witch who keeps the bird of spring in a cage, the magic doll of Vasilisa the Beautiful, Red-nosed Grandfather Frost (malevolent and treacherous, not friendly at all), Koshchei the Deathless, whose death is concealed in a Chinese box of absurdities, Ivanko the Bearlet, son of a peasant woman and a bear, and other popular characters of the magic tale can be readily traced to earlier myths. Stories whose central theme is a journey to the land of the dead are assumed to have descended from pre-Christian maturation rituals featuring the youths' death and rebirth. It must be emphasized that modern storytellers do not believe in their story. In fact, they address it with irony and blatant disrespect.

The magic tale played a significant role in Russian social life until fairly recently. Princes and nobles kept professional storytellers to entertain them, and the teller of tales was a popular figure among the lower strata of society, too. The great writers and poets of the nineteenth century, notably Pushkin, grew up on fairy tales told them by their nurses and servants. Many tales have been recorded even in the twentieth century. The Russian magic tale has surfaced in literature, opera, and ballet. Some examples are Pushkin's fairy tales in verse, Gogol's Ukrainian tales, the opera *The Snow Maiden* by Ostrovsky and Rimsky-Korsakov, Stravinsky's ballet *The Firebird*, and Prokofiev's ballet *The Joker*.

Tales of everyday life usually have a transparent moral message. They deal with family relations (often in a nasty, misogynist manner), with peasant-landlord relations (from the peasant's point of view, naturally), and with such topics as the cheater cheated and the evildoer brought to justice. Satirical tales treat universal complaints—about greedy and lecherous priests, venal judges, and various forms of social injustice. Some of the best-known satirical tales are on record in manuscripts dating from as early as the seventeenth century. They are all based on international themes and plots. An example is the story of Karp Sutulov's virtuous and clever wife, who foils three local dignitaries trying to seduce her in her husband's absence. She lets them come to her house at short enough intervals so that each is surprised by the next and has to hide in a trunk, the last as she pretends that her husband has returned. Having locked her confessor, the local bishop, and a rich merchant safely in separate trunks, she reports them to the governor and wins everybody's praise. In the *Tale of Shemyaka's Judgment* the judge pronounces an absurd judgment in the hope of a bribe, only to learn that he has been cheated. A poor peasant borrows a rich man's horse. Too bashful to ask for a harness, he ties his plow to the horse's tail and tears it off. The rich man takes him to court. On their way to town they stop at a priest's house. The poor man falls off the stove in his sleep and crushes the priest's infant child to death. The priest joins the rich man as they proceed to town the next morning. Along the way they see the poor man jump off a bridge to end it all, but he lands on the neck of a man standing under the bridge, killing him. The victim's brother joins the other two as they proceed. Desperate, the poor man picks up a rock, which he hides under his shirt. As the three plaintiffs present their cases, the poor man, having caught the judge's attention, keeps pointing at the heavy object under his shirt. Having heard

the testimony, the judge pronounces his judgment: the defendant is to keep the plaintiff's horse until it has grown a new tail; the defendant shall sleep with the priest's wife until she has borne a new baby; the dead man's brother can have his revenge by jumping off the same bridge while the defendant stands under it. Now the judge orders the poor man into his chambers and commands, "Give me the money you showed me in the courtroom!" The poor man replies, "I have no money, just this rock, which would have smashed your skull if you had pronounced me guilty!" The judge answers: "Well, you can't win 'em all—at least I'm safe."

A subgenre of the satirical tale is the tale of the cheated devil, conceivably inspired by the rivalry between the old and the new religion. The old deities are reduced to clumsy and stupid losers, ever vulnerable to the sign of the cross. Another genre is the soldier tale, usually picaresque: a worldly-wise veteran cheats an unsuspecting civilian, often a woman. The storyteller is quite class-conscious: his sympathy is with the enlisted man, not the officer. A soldier finds a purse full of gold pieces. He reports the find to his captain, who promptly demands half of the reward. When the colonel whose purse it was asks the soldier what he would like as a reward, the soldier requests a hundred lashes—fifty for himself, fifty for the captain. The colonel orders that all hundred lashes be given to the captain, and he gives the soldier ten gold pieces.

Religious allegorical tales and legends left a lasting mark on Russian literature, entering it directly or through imitation. Vladimir Odoevsky, Dostoevsky, Tolstoi, Leskov, and Remizov were among the many writers who used this genre in their works. Grushenka's tale of the onion in *The Brothers Karama-*

zov is perhaps the most famous example. In the tale "Three Elders" (1886), included by Tolstoi in his *Fourth Russian Reader*, a bishop is visiting his parishes on the White Sea. As his boat sails along, his crew tell him of three elders living on a desert island. The ·bishop decides to visit them. He finds them living in a cave, barely dressed, almost speechless, but fervently repeating the same prayer again and again: "We are three, Thou art three, God have mercy on us!" The bishop decides to do something for the holy fools and spends the entire day teaching them the Lord's Prayer. By nightfall they can recite it, and the bishop leaves. But no sooner is his boat a few hundred yards offshore than he hears the three elders shouting, "We have forgotten it again!" as they come running across the water toward his boat. The earliest record of this tale on Russian soil is Prince Kurbsky's "Legend of the Apparitions to Saint Augustine, Bishop of Ionia," which goes back to a West European legend told to Kurbsky by Maximus the Greek. The great authority of Maximus among Russian Old Believers may have brought the legend renown in their settlements on the Volga— hence Tolstoi's subtitle, "From Folktales on the Volga."

Folk Drama

Russian folk drama has several independent sources. The elaborate and dramatic wedding ritual, as well as some types of holiday mummery, especially at Shrovetide, are theatrical performances based on more or less fixed texts. It is likely that the skomorokhi gave theatrical performances, but there is no direct evidence for this before the early seventeenth century, and we have no texts. The earliest attested theatrical performances in Russia were brief religious scenes staged on church porches. It is possible that Russian churchmen attending the Council of Florence in 1439 saw such performances and initiated similar events in Muscovy. By far the most popular of these scenes was the "Action of the Furnace," enacting the miraculous rescue of three Hebrew youths from death in King Nebuchadnezzar's fiery furnace (after Daniel 3:12–30). For a long time the popular word for actor was Chaldean (*khaldei*). There seems to be no direct link between these performances and biblical plays with comic interludes, staged in the seventeenth century by Ukrainian churchmen in the Ukraine and in Muscovy, which came from the tradition of the Jesuit school drama.

Another source of the folk drama was the vertep puppet theater, which entered Muscovy from Poland via the Ukraine. It was called *vertep* (den, cave) because of its main attraction, a nativity play set in the "den" in which the Savior was born. Its highlight was a lurid scene in which the devil appeared to take the wicked king Herod down to hell. The main attraction was followed by burlesque scenes with song and dance, analogous to the intermedia of the school drama. The vertep was done by a single puppeteer, who also did all the talking. The language of the vertep is prose vernacular with a good dose of biblical Slavonic.

Another version of the popular puppet theater was described by the German diplomat Adam Olearius, who traveled through Muscovy in 1633–39. The puppeteer performed while carrying his theater on his head. The main personage of this type of theater, popular in Russia into the twentieth century, was Petrushka (Pierrot), a gruff brawling brute whose rapid-fire encounters with his wife, a gypsy, a doctor, a German clown, a policeman, and a vicious dog have him alternately dishing out and absorbing punishment. The action features Petrushka's wisecracks and comic misfortunes, as well as his heavy club, ever ready to spring into action. The language of Petrushka is a colorful vernacular, with occasional sorties into spoken verse. There is also some song and dance inserted into the program.

In the second half of the seventeenth century the school drama came to Muscovy from the Ukraine. A court theater was started in 1673, and foreign troupes began to visit Russia during the reign of Peter the Great, giving public performances. Some private theaters were started as early as in the first half of the eighteenth century, and they often employed serf actors and actresses. Through all these developments the common people acquired a flair for the theater, and a folk theater came into existence concurrently with the wholly westernized imperial stage in Petersburg and Moscow. The folk theater, manned by amateur actors from the urban lower classes, gave performances in many cities during the holiday seasons, especially at Shrovetide. Properties, stage decorations, and costumes were simple and functional. Delivery was stiff and exaggerated. Female characters were played by young men. The language was the vernacular, laced with puns, folksy humor, and song. The audience was composed of anybody who would happen to be in the marketplace or fairgrounds at the time.

The oldest and most popular folk plays are the *Comedy of Tsar Maximilian and His Rebellious Son Adolphe*, ostensibly a dramatized saint's life, and *The Boat*; both are apparently from the first half of the eighteenth century, though recorded only in the nineteenth. The pagan tsar Maximilian, having recently taken a second wife, also

a pagan, orders the execution of his son, Adolphe, a Christian, as the young man steadfastly refuses to betray his religion. But the story of Adolphe's martyrdom is overlaid with all kinds of versions—songs, wisecracks, and buffoonery. It is likely that the audience recognized in Tsar Maximilian none other than Peter the Great, who, having married a Lutheran, the future tsarina Catherine I, had his son Alexis executed. Alexis was seen by many as a martyr to the cause of true Orthodoxy.

The Boat is clearly a dramatic version of the songs celebrating the seventeenth-century outlaw Stepan Razin. Its cast features a band of outlaws on a boat on the Volga. A stranger appears and tells his story: he and his brother were highwaymen; they were caught and put in prison; his brother died there but he escaped, having killed a prison guard. The stranger is welcomed with open arms. The next scene shows the outlaws sacking the estate of a rich landowner. The action is repeatedly interrupted by the singing of robber songs. The main stage effect is created by the actors' sitting on the floor and making the motions of rowing a boat. "The Boat," like the epic songs on the same subject, is explicit in its sympathy for the outlaws and in its hatred for landowners and government authorities. The story of the stranger inspired Pushkin to write his narrative poem "The Brigand Brothers" (1821–22), and echoes of *The Boat* are found in Ostrovsky's play *The Governor* (1864). In Lev Tolstoi's *Youth* (1857) a group of students at a party enact *The Boat*.

Russian vaudeville, staged since the 1770s, developed as an imitation of French vaudeville, but early on it incorporated Russian songs and dances. It soon spilled over into folk theater, which also used the lyrics of such "literary" poets as Lomonosov, Derzhavin, and Pushkin. Dostoevsky's *Notes from the House of the Dead* (1861) has a vivid description of a theatrical performance in a Siberian prison. The prisoners are doing their version of a vaudeville that Dostoevsky, a nobleman, had seen on the stage of one of the imperial theaters in Saint Petersburg.

2

Old Russian Literature: Eleventh to Thirteenth Centuries

The entry for the year 852 in the Russian Primary Chronicle begins with these words: "In the year 6360, when Michael began his reign [in Byzantium], the Russian land first let itself be known.[1] We learned of this because under that emperor Rus made a raid on Constantinople, as it says in the Greek chronicle [of George Hamartolus]." Kievan Russia was an economic and military power of some importance before it became Christian and literate. What we know about Russia in the ninth and the first half of the tenth centuries comes from Byzantine, Arabic, West European (Latin), and Jewish sources, as well as from oral traditions that entered into the Russian chronicles.

Kievan Russia (Rus)[2] was founded by Scandinavian traders, called *vaeringer* in Old Norse, *varangoi* in Greek, and *varyagi* in Russian. Having discovered waterways

from the Baltic Sea to the Caspian and the Black seas, they established trading posts and forts along them and by the second half of the ninth century had become permanent settlers. The waterway most important for Kievan Russia was "the way from the Varangians to the Greeks," which went from the Baltic Sea to the Black Sea with a single portage along the route. On this waterway there lay the great cities of early Russia— Novgorod, Smolensk, and Kiev. The Varangians traded the products of the northern forests, such as furs, wax, honey, and tar, for Mediterranean textiles, luxury goods, weapons, and wines. More than a few Varangians, as well as Slavs and Finns who manned their boats, chose to stay in Constantinople, mostly as the emperor's mercenaries. By the tenth century some Varangians were Christians and there was at least one Christian

1. Pre-Petrine Russia counted years from the creation of the world, dated 5508 B.C.

2. The origin of the name *Rus* is controversial. The most likely explanation is that it is identical with the Finnish word for Swede, *rōtsi* or *ruotsi*. Phonologically the match is perfect, as *ts* would

have to become *s* in Slavic. There is much evidence that the name *Rus* (Greek *Rhōs*, Arabic *Ros*) was initially applied to the Scandinavian intruders only. Constantine Porphyrogenitus deliberately distinguishes the "Russian" language from the "Slavic."

church in Kiev. The first reported Christian martyrs on Russian soil were two Varangians massacred by a pagan mob in 983. In 957 Olga, dowager duchess of Kiev (her husband Igor was killed in battle in 945), had herself baptized on the occasion of a state visit to Constantinople, an event attested in Russian and Greek sources.[3] Her son Svyatoslav (945–72), the first duke of Kiev to bear a Slavic name,[4] remained a pagan, as did his son Vladimir (Scandinavian Valdimar) until 988, when he and his nation formally embraced the Greek Orthodox religion.

The transition from paganism to Christianity was remarkably smooth and swift, at least for the upper classes. Being a Christian ruler helped Vladimir and his successors politically, giving prestige and legitimacy to their rule. To Vladimir it meant that he would have a Byzantine princess as his wife. (The pagan Vladimir had already taken several wives.) Hence the Kievan rulers eagerly promoted the new religion. Byzantium was then flourishing, and Byzantine culture, strongly focused in the pomp and ceremony of religious ritual, attracted the northern barbarians. Many of them were familiar with Christian culture, and some were already Christians.

The fact that Christianity came to the eastern Slavs from Byzantium, whereas the western Slavs received it from Rome, was fateful. Russia remained culturally in the orbit of Byzantium until the seventeenth century. For half a millennium Russian culture and the Russian language were exposed to Greek, rather than Latin, influence. Russia inherited from Byzantium an attitude of profound hostility, scorn, and suspicion not only toward the Roman church but also toward everything Western. A dependance on Byzantium and isolation from the West, not calamitous so long as Byzantium was culturally the West's superior or equal, became a serious obstacle to Russia's cultural progress when Byzantine culture stagnated and the West became vigorously creative in the High Middle Ages.

A religious schism between East and West developed over the centuries. Aside from relatively minor theological disagreements, the primacy of the pope, which the Eastern church did not recognize, was a stumbling block. What really made the schism insurmountable were the profound differences in ritual, custom, and religious culture (architecture, art, music) that developed over the centuries. Thus, the Eastern church allowed the liturgy to be conducted in the vernacular (Slavonic in Russia), whereas the Roman church insisted on the Latin liturgy everywhere. The Eastern church allowed parish priests to marry; the Roman church insisted that they practice celibacy. The icon played a greater role in the Eastern church, since it held that the human face had retained a likeness to the face of God in spite of the Fall. Eastern church music was vocal and homophonic; polyphonic music came to the Russian church only in the seventeenth century, from the West.

An important reason for Russia's rapid Christianization lay in its Bulgarian connection. By the time Russia became a Christian nation, Bulgaria had been one for over a century. The "apostles of the Slavs," the Greek brothers Cyril (d. 869) and Methodius (d. 885), had created a literary language based on Bulgarian, in which a substantial number of religious and some secu-

3. Constantine Porphyrogenitus, *De ceremoniis aulae byzantinae*, 2:15.

4. The name Olga derives from the Scandinavian Helga, and Igor from the Scandinavian Ingvar. The Greek sources call him Ingor.

lar texts were available by the end of the tenth century.[5] Most of these texts were required in the conduct of church services: the New Testament, the Psalter and some other books of the Old Testament, the Holy Liturgy, euchologia (prayer books), and the Nomocanon. The lives of Byzantine calendar saints, being an integral part of the service, were also translated early. Some Bulgarian vitae, those of saints Cyril and Methodius in particular, soon joined them. The sermons of John Chrysostom and a few other Fathers of the Eastern church were also indispensable. Some Bulgarian sermons by Saint Clement and Presbyter Cosmas were added to these. John, exarch of Bulgaria, translated some theological works by Basil the Great and John Damascene. A fairly rich apocryphal literature also existed, some of it reflecting the doctrines of the Bogomil heresy, which had its start in Bulgaria.

In the tenth century South and East Slavic were still mutually intelligible languages. Bulgarian books could be read by a Russian with little difficulty, although a copyist might change Bulgarian forms to their Russian equivalents.[6] It is likely that Russians had used Bulgarian Cyrillic script for official documents even before 988. With Christianity, there came books from Bulgaria, and since it was simpler to copy them verbatim than to change the text to Russian, the language created by Cyril and Methodius, called Slavonic, became the language of the Russian church. Slavonic played the same role in *Slavia orthodoxa* as Latin did in the Catholic West. Centuries later, when Serbian, Bulgarian, Ukrainian, and Russian were no longer mutually intelligible, the Orthodox clergy was still using the same language, with slight local modifications. This meant that not only books but writers too could cross national boundaries within the Orthodox Slavic world. Some major writers of Old Russian literature were immigrants from the Balkans.

Many manuscripts that circulated in Kievan Russia, were of Bulgarian or Serbian origin. The first complete manuscript of the homilies of John Chrysostom, dating from the thirteenth century, is Bulgarian. The oldest extant copy of the *Hexaemeron* of John the Exarch is of Serbian origin. The second- and third-oldest Russian manuscripts are the *Miscellanies* of Svyatoslav, dated 1073 and 1076. They contain mostly excerpts from the writings of the church fathers, but also a few secular pieces, including a tract *On Signs* by George Choeroboscus, which lists the principal tropes and figures of classical poetics and rhetoric. The *Miscellanies* were based on texts initially translated from the Greek for Tsar Symeon of Bulgaria nearly two hundred years earlier (in fact, the scribe neglected to change "Symeon" to "Svyatoslav" in one passage).

The smooth transition to a Christian and literate culture came at a price. The Eastern church, unlike the Roman church, allowed its member nations to have the Scriptures, the liturgy, and their entire religious culture and literature in their own language.[7] The Russian clergy, with very few exceptions,

5. On the Cyrillo-Methodian tradition, see Roman Jakobson, *Selected Writings*, vol. 6, *Early Slavic Paths and Crossroads*, ed. Stephen Rudy, pt. 1, *Comparative Slavic Studies: The Cyrillo-Methodian Tradition* (The Hague: Mouton, 1987).

6. For example, Bulg. *brěgŭ* (river bank) to Russ. *beregŭ*; Bulg. *pragŭ* (threshold) to Russ. *porogŭ*; Bulg. *noshtǐ* (night) to Russ. *nochǐ*; Bulg. *vizhdǐ* (see) to Russ. *vizhǐ*. These and other transformations are regular and predictable.

7. First Corinthians 14:10–14 was often cited in justification of this policy—by George Hamartolus, himself a non-Hellene, for example.

remained ignorant of Greek and had no access to Greek literature. In fact, the quality of translations from the Greek rarely reached the standard established by Cyril and Methodius. Their translations were literal, introducing a good deal of Greek syntax into the Slavic text, but they were based on a text perfectly understood and conscientiously rendered. Later translators often translated without really understanding the original. The *Miscellanies* of Svyatoslav are a case in point.

There were exceptions, however. The *Bellum iudaicum* of Josephus Flavius, for example, the only pre-Christian classic known in medieval Russia, reads well in what is considered to be a twelfth-century translation prepared in Russia. The Russian text makes some judicious omissions and has several insertions based on the New Testament which are not found in Greek manuscripts. The *Bellum iudaicum* is quoted or referred to frequently in Old Russian literature, and it became a model for Russian writers dealing with martial topics.

A catalog of texts available to a Russian cleric in the Middle Ages shows that Russia received Byzantine literature in its standard and utilitarian form, and that none of the intellectual excitement, controversy, and sophistication of which Byzantine culture was capable until its end ever reached Russia. In matters of doctrine the Russian church followed whatever happened to be the conservative line in Constantinople. Russia certainly did not take part in any of the revivals of classical literature and philosophy that enlivened Byzantine cultural life.[8] Yet medieval Russian architecture, icon painting, and mosaic reached a high level of accomplishment, following their Byzantine examples not at all slavishly, and the same is true of Russian church music. Hence it stands to reason that the intellectual sterility and conservatism of Russian medieval literature are linked to Russia's linguistic autonomy.

The literatures of *Slavia orthodoxa* developed a language and a rhetoric which, at least in their best examples, equaled what the Byzantines had to offer. But we look in vain for the intellectual ferment, subtlety, and boldness found in the writings of the Western schoolmen and mystics. Russian medieval thought was guided by traditional authority and prescribed emotion. We encounter few expressions of personal mystic experience, although medieval Russian churchmen were at least as credulous of miracles as their Western counterparts. Christian faith during the Kievan period was uncomplicated and appeared to pose no problems. Medieval Russian literature was essentially utilitarian, a vehicle of ritual, devotion, and edification. Literature as entertainment or as self-expression was slow to develop, with no examples to emulate except folklore, which was held in low regard. Russian medieval texts have a literary character and a formal tradition, but they are not autonomous works of art in the modern sense.[9] They have to be viewed in the context of their function in religious and social life, together with religious art and music.

Functionality also ruled authorship. An author's name was important only if it could add to the authority of his work. If not, anonymity was in order. Even a patently corrupt text might remain unchallenged simply because of the authority of its author

8. See A. P. Kazhdan and Ann Wharton Epstein, *Change in Byzantine Culture in the Eleventh and Twelfth Centuries* (Berkeley and Los Angeles: University of California Press, 1986).

9. See *Gattungsprobleme der älteren slavischen Literaturen*, ed. Wolf-Heinrich Schmidt (Wiesbaden: Harrassowitz, 1984).

or alleged author. On the other hand, a text not protected by such authority might be freely altered by a scribe according to the needs of the moment. Thus when Josephus Flavius mentions the veil of the Temple, the Russian text adds, following Matthew 27:51 and Luke 22:45, "This veil was whole a generation earlier, for people were pious then, but now it offered a pitiful sight, as it was suddenly rent from top to bottom when a man of good works and in fact no mere man was delivered to his death for pay."[10] Similar instances are common in medieval Russian historiography.

A medieval writer was author (or compiler or translator) and scribe at the same time. He prided himself on his calligraphic and illuminating skills as much as on his learning and devotion. His work, once finished, was a useful and indeed a precious commodity, which would serve a religious community for many generations. The distinction between author and copyist was fluid and hardly important. In fact, there seems to have been little awareness of it.

A catalog of extant manuscripts dating from the eleventh to the fourteenth centuries contains 1493 titles.[11] (One can only guess how many manuscripts were in circulation in Kievan Russia.) Of these, thirteen (all dating from the eleventh to early twelfth centuries) are classified as Slavonic, 960 as Russian, 185 as Bulgarian, 299 as Serbian, and 36 as "others." All but 178 are on parchment. Paper began to appear commonly only in the fourteenth century.

Virtually all of the manuscripts comprise functional literature. Gospel texts naturally dominate, and most of the manuscripts are of the *aprakos* (Greek *apractos*) type, that is, the Gospel text is organized as a sequence of Sunday readings over a calendar year. *Tetraevangeliya*, with the four Gospels in the traditional order, are rarer. The oldest extant Russian manuscript, the Ostromir Gospel of 1056–57, is an aprakos. It was copied from a Slavonic original by Gregory (Grigory), a deacon, for Ostromir, governor of Novgorod. The manuscript has elaborate miniatures of the evangelists, richly ornamented chapter headings, and large golden initials. The Epistles of the New Testament, known as *Apostol*, were also in circulation early, usually in aprakos form. The Psalter is represented by a number of early manuscripts, including one with a commentary by Theodoret of Cyrrhus. The Book of Revelation is extant in a twelfth-century manuscript. The earliest extant manuscript of a book of the Old Testament is Isaiah, from the late twelfth or early thirteenth century, closely followed by the Song of Solomon, with a theological commentary. Throughout the Middle Ages a complete translation of the Old Testament was unavailable in Russian. What was known as the *Paleya* (from Greek *palaia diathece*, "old testament") was the Book of Genesis with a variety of apocryphal additions.[12]

---

10. *La Prise de Jérusalem de Josèphe le Juif: Texte vieux-russe publié integralement*, ed. V. Istrin, 2 vols. (Paris: Institut d'études slaves, 1934–38), 2:82.

11. "Predvaritel'nyi spisok slavyano-russkikh rukopisei XI–XIV vv., khranyashchikhsya v SSSR," *Arkheograficheskii ezhegodnik za 1965 god* (Moscow, 1966), 177–272, and L. P. Zhukovskaya, "Pamyatniki russkoi i slavyanskoi pis'mennosti XI–XIV vv. v knigokhranilishchakh SSSR," *Sovetskoe slavyanovedenie*, 1969, no. 1:5–71.

12. The Russian Middle Ages had a decided bias against the Old Testament. The *Kiev Patericon* tells the story of a monk who knew all the books of the Old Testament but could not stand the sight or sound of the gospels and epistles of the New Testament. Through the prayers of his brothers in Christ he eventually forgets the Old Testament entirely, so that he has to learn how to read again. He becomes meek and obedient and is rewarded by being made bishop of Novgorod.

Among the oldest extant manuscripts are saints' lives for liturgical use (*sluzhebnye minei*, Gr. *leitourgica menaia*); the so-called *Sinai Paterikon* (really the *Leimon pneumaticos* of John Moschus, a miscellany of edifying tales about sixth-century monastic life); different versions of the Nomocanon (*Kormchaya*, a guidebook of monastic rule), among which a copy of the stern rule of Theodore the Studite dates from the late twelfth century; texts covering the various liturgies and liturgical prayers;[13] the *Pandectae* (didactic commentary on the Holy Scriptures) of Antiochus of Jerusalem, as well as those of Nicon of Mount Mauros; the *Theology* of John Damascene, translated by John the Exarch; collections of homilies by Fathers of the Church, such as John Chrysostom, Gregory of Nazianzus, Ephraim Syrus, Cyril of Jerusalem, and others; the *Climax* of John Climacus; and a variety of saint's lives not directly linked to the liturgy, some of them apocryphal. The earliest extant manuscript of a Russian work (from the thirteenth century) has two fragments of prayers by Cyril of Turov. Some of his homilies are contained in a thirteenth-century collection of homilies which also includes sermons by Cyril of Jerusalem, John Chrysostom, and Basil the Great.

Byzantine church music came to Russia as an integral and inexpendable part of the liturgy. The Byzantines strictly distinguished sacred from secular music. Sacred music was homophonic and vocal; it was the only music set down in notation. Russia followed the Byzantine example. Liturgical singing was called sign singing (*znamenny raspev*), thus distinguishing it from the oral tradition of secular music, which could be polyphonic and used musical instruments. A good number of liturgical texts and hymns with musical notation are extant from the Kievan period. A holiday *Sticherarion* (114 sheets) is dated 1156–63, and a *Sticherarion* for the Lenten season comes from the late twelfth century. Several *heirmologia*, *trioidiai*, and *kontakaria* are also from the twelfth century. The Greek originals of these texts were versified, and the Slavonic translations were in rhythmic prose adapted to the musical score.

The only work that gave the Russian reader some contact with classical antiquity was the *Melissa* (*Bchela* or *Pchela*), an eleventh-century anthology of sayings, quotations, anecdotes, and moral dicta organized by topic, mostly assorted virtues and vices ("On Humility," "On Vanity"). It was compiled by a monk, Antonius, who used mainly the *Florilegium* of John Stobaeus and a miscellany by Maximus Confessor. There he found a large number of dicta attributed to rulers, philosophers, orators, and historians of antiquity—Plutarch, Socrates, Herodotus, Aristotle, Diogenes, Epictetus, Philip and Alexander of Macedon, Demosthenes, and others, collectively called external philosophers, as against the church's own apostles, saints, and fathers. The popularity of *Melissa* in medieval Russia meant that a well-read Russian would at least have heard the names of the great men of ancient Greece.

Byzantine natural science relied mostly on the classical tradition, diluted by a few later authors. The works that reached Russia were few. They included the cosmology of the *Hexaemeron* (with quotations from Plato, Aristotle, and other Greek philosophers) and the *Paleya*, as well as the *Physiologus*, a compilation of the late Hellenistic period, containing information, much of it fantastic and absurd, about birds and other animals.

13. The *sluzhebnik* (from *sluzhba*, "liturgy"), the *trebnik* (from *treba*, "sacrament"), the *paremeinik* (from *paremiya*, "parable"), the *chasoslov* (book of hours), the *prolog* (Greek *synaxarion*, a book of liturgic saint's lives), and so on.

Medieval Russian geography is a mixture of observed fact and uncritical fiction. The Russian chroniclers have an accurate picture of the vast territory from Constantinople to the Baltic Sea and even to the Arctic Ocean (called the Breathing Sea on account of its strong tides), and their ethnology is well informed as far as eastern and northern Europe are concerned. Slavic, Germanic, Baltic, and Finnish nations and tribes are correctly placed. But whenever distant lands enter the picture, the mythical and the miraculous take over. The *Christian Topography* of Cosmas Indicopleustes, known in Russia as early as in the twelfth century, is a work about India (which Cosmas never saw) as well as mythical regions. It also contains a fantastic anti-Ptolemaic cosmology in which angels regulate the movement of the heavenly bodies.

The *Legend of the Kingdom of India*, which originated in Byzantium in the twelfth century, came to Russia in the thirteenth or fourteenth century. Known in the West as the *Epistle of Presbyter John*, it is a fictitious missive addressed to Emperor Manuel, or western Christendom at large, by the ruler of a mythical Christian kingdom in the East. It tells of the many marvels of India, the power, splendor, and virtues of its ruler and his realm, and the exemplary organization of his domain. This medieval utopia contains some material also found in the *Alexandriad*, the *Physiologus*, and Christian apocrypha. The *Legend of the Kingdom of India* gained wide popularity in Russia, entering Russian folklore in the "Bylina of Dyuk Stepanovich," for example. It also left echoes in Russian literature, as in Vyacheslav Ivanov's *Tale of Tsarevich Svetomir.*

The chronicles are probably the finest achievement of Old Russian literature. This distinction is remarkable since the Byzantine examples known to the Russian chroniclers were mediocre monkish compilations which had lost all meaningful contact with classical historiography. Even major events and personages, like Alexander the Great, Julius Caesar, and Caesar Augustus, about whom accurate information was on hand, were badly distorted in these works. The chronicle of George Hamartolus (up to A.D. 864), continued by Symeon Logothete (up to 948), was known in Russia already in the eleventh century and was used by the author (or authors) of the Russian Primary Chronicle. The chronicle of John Malalas of Antioch (sixth century), which like that of George Hamartolus came to Russia via Bulgaria, was also used by the Russian chroniclers. Only in the fifteenth century did the chronicles of John Zonaras and Constantine Manasses reach Russia. Excellent Byzantine historians such as Procopius of Caesarea, Theophylact Simocatta, Leo Diaconus, Constantine Porphyrogenitus, and others remained untranslated and unknown, not to speak of the great historians of antiquity.

Apocrypha, works of religious content not included in the canon of the church, entered Russia together with canonic literature (again usually through Bulgaria.) There existed, for example, several apocryphal gospels in addition to the four canonical ones. In some instances the dividing line was vague, and Russian churchmen would at times use the authority of an apocryphal work in a theological debate.[14] Furthermore, the status of some works, like Revelation, changed over the centuries. The

14. In his homily *On the Heresy of the Heretics of Novgorod*, for example, Joseph Volotsky refers to John the Divine's victory over the sorcerer Cynops on the island of Patmos, when the sorcerer was flung "into the chasm of the sea," thus justifying drastic action against Russian heretics. This story is taken from an apocryphal vita of John the Divine.

Orthodox church distinguished permitted (*homologoumena*) and prohibited (*aporrheta*) works. An index of prohibited books existed as early as the eleventh century (there is a list in the *Miscellany* of Svyatoslav of 1073). Later *Nomocanones* contain such lists.

Apocrypha came not only from the Orthodox Christian tradition but also from heretical sects like the Manichaean Bogomils of Bulgaria, from the Latin West, and from Buddhist, Talmudic, Moslem, and pagan (Persian, Egyptian, and Hellenic) sources. Apocrypha cover a wide range of topics—theology, cosmogony, cosmology, eschatology, human nature, biblical history, the good life, and general wisdom. As for genres, there are dialogues, parables, stories, anecdotes, riddles, and various mixed forms. A few cycles can be discerned, such as anecdotes about the wisdom of King Solomon, originating in the Jewish tradition (only some of it scriptural) but widely known even in the gentile tradition. Renowned were apocrypha about Solomon, Kitovras (from Greek *kentauros*), a half-human creature, and the shamir stone (from Hebrew *shamir*, "diamond"). The popular *Tale about How God Created Adam* departs from Genesis in that it lets Satan participate in Adam's creation, an apparent echo of the Manichaean doctrines of the Bogomils. Some of the apocrypha are also known in the Catholic West, and only a few seem to have arisen on Slavic soil.

Eventually some of the apocrypha entered the oral tradition of folklore and surfaced as popular legends or dukhovnye stikhi centuries after they are first attested in Old Russian literature. The *Dialogue of Three Prelates* (John Chrysostom, Basil the Great, and Gregory the Divine) was known in Russia as early as the eleventh century. It is an apocryphal compilation of popular wisdom often assuming the form of a riddle: "What two enemies fight on earth day and night? Life and death." It covers a variety of theological, cosmological, and anthropological questions, such as "What were angels made of? Of God's spirit, of light and fire."

The *Legend of Our Father Agapius* takes the holy man on a tour of paradise. The notion that the Garden of Eden still exists on earth was widespread in the Middle Ages, although it was contested by some churchmen, who preferred to believe in an "ideal" paradise.

The Holy Virgin's Tour of Torments, made famous in the Grand Inquisitor chapter of Dostoevsky's *Brothers Karamazov*, takes the Virgin Mary on a tour of hell, with the Archangel Michael as her guide. The catalog of sinners and the torments meted out to them is rather unimaginative, and the Virgin's reactions naively reflect the prejudices of a Byzantine cleric. The Virgin sheds many tears over the torments of the damned, but when told of their sins she finds that the punishment fits the crime. Among those to whom she shows no mercy are "the Jews who tortured our Lord Jesus Christ." But in the end the Virgin and her Son obtain from the Lord an annual period of respite for the sinners, from Maundy Thursday to Pentecost. The Russian version features an insertion that has certain sinners suffer for having venerated the Slavic pagan gods Troyan, Khors, Veles, and Perun.

The *Tale of Barlaam and Joasaph*, which originated in India, contains elements of the legend of Buddha and became widely known in Europe.[15] The Russian text was translated from the Greek in the late

15. The full title is *Books of Barlaam, an edifying tract from the eastern land of Ethiopia called India, brought to the Holy City by John, a monk and honest and virtuous man of the monastery of Saint Sabbas.*

eleven or early twelfth century. It gained wide popularity, and excerpts from it were used by many writers—Cyril of Turov, for example. The legend tells the story of Joasaph, an Indian prince who is shielded from the outside world until he meets the sage Barlaam, who introduces him to evil and suffering. The story then turns into a miscellany of parables, all familiar in Oriental as well as Western literature. In one, a man pursued by a unicorn falls into a well, barely managing to hold onto the roots of a tree inside the well. He sees that a dragon is waiting for him at the bottom and four serpents eye him from the top. A white mouse and a black mouse are gnawing at the roots of the tree. But when the man spies some honey dripping from the tree, he forgets the danger he is in and starts eating the honey. The medieval text sees this as a parable of human folly: a person ignores death (the unicorn), hell (the dragon), the perishability of the material elements of which the human body is composed (the four serpents), and the passage of time (day and night gnawing away at the tree of life), thinking only of earthly pleasures. To a modern writer like Tolstoi (in his *Confession*), it is a metaphor of the human condition from an Epicurean's viewpoint. The "Tale of Barlaam and Joasaph" also contains a competent refutation of religions rivaling Christianity: the Chaldean, which falls into the error of venerating the elements instead of their creator; the Hellenic, which venerates gods who have all the human vices (a catalog of Greek gods is given); and the Egyptian, which elevates dumb animals to gods. A brief history of the Jews is then given, ending in their rejection of Jesus Christ. The text concludes with a summation of the Christian creed.

Little secular fiction can be assumed to have circulated in Kievan Russia. The Trojan War was known only through the chronicle of John Malalas. The *Alexandriad* of pseudo-Callisthenes appears to have been known since the eleventh or twelfth century, although no early versions are extant. The Byzantine romance of Digenis Acritas, a tenth-century work known in the original Greek only in fifteen-century copies, somehow found its way to Russia. A single copy of the *Action of Devgeny* was discovered in the miscellany that also contained the *Igor Tale*. Only in 1856 was another, much later copy found. There is evidence that the *Action of Devgeny* was known in Russia early, as a couple of chronicle passages and the *Life of Alexander Nevsky* apply Greek epithets of Devgeny to their heroes. Devgeny is the son of the Saracen king Amir and a Greek princess kidnapped by him. The rather repetitious episodes of the romance tell of Devgeny's wondrous feats of strength, valor, and chivalry. None of them seems very imaginative, nor are they well told, but they show a command of the sentimental high style of popular romance. The incredible feats of Devgeny and his uncles are laced with pious assertions of faith in the Lord, who is always credited with aiding his Christian champions. Fourteen-year-old Devgeny, having already killed a bear with his hands and run down a stag and torn it in half, now faces a lion (this time he is armed with a sword) and says, "Sir, I place my hope in the Creator and in the greatness of God and in the prayers of my mother who bore me." The narrator likewise inserts pious phrases quite frequently.

The *Tale of Akir the Wise*, also in the miscellany with the *Igor Tale* but known in many other copies, is one of the few works of Old Russian literature translated from a language other than Greek (possibly Armenian). It was known in Russia as early as the twelfth century. The tale relates how Akir, vizier to King Sinagrip (possibly Sennacherib of Assyria, r. 704–681 B.C.), is denounced by his own adopted son Anadan, uses his wits to escape execution, regains the good graces of his sovereign by performing successfully as his ambassador to the pharaoh of Egypt, and gets his revenge on Anadan. Much of the text is devoted to Akir's fatherly advice to his son before and after Anadan's crime. Some of it is delightfully cynical: "If a rich man's son eats a snake, people say that he took it as medicine; if a poor man does the same, they say he ate it because he was hungry."

The animal fables of *Stephanites and Ichnelates* come from the Indian miscellany *Hitopadeshah* (Sound Advice), via the Persian, Arabic, and Greek.[16] The Bulgaro-Russian version (thirteenth or fourteenth century) is based on an eleventh-century Byzantine text. It was apparently perceived as another *Melissa* rather than as an entertaining storybook. The translation is awkward and often misses the point. The two jackals Stephanites and Ichnelates, councillors to the lion, king of the beasts, are called *neki zver*, "a certain animal" (or simply *zver*) in the Slavic version, as there was no Slavic word for jackal. In one of the fables the Greek word for swan (*kyknos*) is replaced by the Slavic word for crane (*zherav*), apparently because in Slavic folklore the swan has a noble, poetic image unfit for the satirical role in this fable. Elsewhere the translator misread Greek *pas* (all) as *pais* (boy) and had to invent a small parable to make some sense out of the passage. There are also moral-didactic insertions not found in any of the Greek manuscripts. *Stephanites and Ichnelates* presents a world of ruthless

court intrigue. The two jackals are involved in a chain of incidents each of which is introduced by a fable in support of whatever the narrator seeks to accomplish. The ruses contemplated and foiled in the framing narrative as well as in the fables are often ingenious. When a hungry lion demands food from his courtiers—the raven, the fox, the wolf, and the camel—they make a pact for each of them to offer himself to be eaten, but to then be saved by an objection raised by the other three. The raven is found to be too thin and puny, the fox's flesh has a foul smell, the wolf is only "dog meat." When it is the camel's turn, his friends shout in unison that he is good eating and help the lion devour him. The ethos of *Stephanites and Ichnelates* is expressed in this dictum by Ichnelates: "A cowardly man dislikes these three things: serving a king, sailing the seas, and standing up to an enemy. But there are two places destined for the high-minded: a royal court and a hermitage in the desert." *Stephanites and Ichnelates* enjoyed considerable popularity well into the seventeenth century. Eventually it was displaced by Aesop's fables and the fables of the modern literatures of the West.

The *Tale of Eustachius Placidus*, a Byzantine Christian romance, reached Russia in the twelfth century. It was eventually incorporated into the *Martyrologue* of Metropolitan Macarius, but its plot is that of a late Hellenistic romance of the type of Heliodorus's *Ethiopian Journeys*. The members of a loving family are separated, experience all kinds of adventures, and are finally reunited. The Christian ingredient is provided by the circumstance that the hero's miraculous conversion to the Christian faith triggers these events. Placidus, a Roman general under Trajan and Hadrian, pursues a stag on a hunt. Suddenly he perceives a luminous cross and a brilliant image of Jesus Christ

16. *A writ* [spisanie] *by Seth of Antioch, while others say by John Damascene, the eminent hymnist, about beasts called Stephanites* [and] *Ichnelates.*

between the horns of the stag and hears the Savior's voice. The stag motif is familiar from other legends, for example, the legend of Saint Julian the Hospitaler and the legend of Saint Eustace.[17]

Russian Hagiography

Medieval literature was largely written by monks, for monks, and about monks. The saint's life (Latin *vita*, Slavonic *zhitie*) is its central genre. It expresses the monastic ideal of the godly life. The God-fearing prince, the martyr, the missionary, and the ascetic are its heroes. The canonic form of the saint's life was established in the fourth century. A famous early example is the vita of Saint Anthony by Athanasius of Alexandria, which features one of the central themes of hagiography, an ascetic's struggle with the demons of temptation. Early Byzantine vitae, well known in Russia, are full of violent conflict with pagan rulers, heresiarchs and their patrons, and demons in human and other shapes. Russian vitae usually are less tense, more peaceful and serene. Their demons are rarely terrible. There is nothing in the Old Russian tradition that would approach the stark horror of Tolstoi's modern version of the ascetic's struggle with temptation in "Father Sergius."

The saint's life is the heroic epic of the church. Its hero is perfect. The evil forces against which the saint fights are presented as being outside of him or her. The outcome

17. The Saint Eustace legend was widely popular in the West as well as in the Orthodox East. The Latin version is *Passio Sancti Eustachii cum sociis suis* (tenth century), the French *La vie de Saint Eustace* (thirteenth century). An Anglo-Saxon version is extant from the tenth century. See Holger Petersen, *La vie de Saint Eustache* (Paris, H. Champion, 1928). On the stag, see Marcelle Thiébaux, *The Stag of Love: The Chase in Medieval Literature* (Ithaca: Cornell University Press, 1974), 61–63.

of the struggle is predictable. The devil and his cohorts are fighting a hopeless battle. The plot and structure of the saint's life are schematic, although there is variety in the details: saints may perform different feats and miracles, meet different foes, and die in different ways. In some instances pre-Christian myths have entered hagiography. The vita of Saint George the Dragon Slayer echoes the classical myth of Perseus and Andromeda. Saint Basil the New, a ninth-century saint, is flung into the sea and saved by dolphins like Arion in Herodotus's story. By the time the saint's life reached Russia its form was crystallized and functional. Saints' lives were recited in church, in short versions from the Lectionary (Gr. *synaxarion*, Russ. *prolog*) or longer versions from the *Martyrologue* (*Chet'i minei*, readings arranged by month). There also existed independent saints' lives, some of them apocryphal.

A saint's life starts with an introduction in which the author invokes the Lord's assistance and may present himself, always employing the *topos* (rhetorical cliché) of humility and giving the reason for having embarked upon so lofty an enterprise. The introduction also contains a first eulogy of the saint. The encomium then relates the saint's life, achievements, and death. In most instances a saint's biography is stereotypical. The saint, often an only or a last child, comes from a good, God-fearing family. In some vitae there is an aura of miracle about the saint's conception and birth; his or her mother may have had prophetic dreams. The saint's parents may refrain from sexual intercourse after conception and even join their son or daughter in taking holy vows. Future saints are quiet, obedient, and studious children who shy away from the rough games of other children. They develop an early interest in the religious life and in holy books, showing outstanding qualities of mind and spirit. They eagerly seek holy vows and start their religious career under the guidance of a holy man. The saint's feats as a martyr, ascetic, missionary, bishop, founder of a monastery, and so forth are more specific than the rest of his or her biography. Yet the qualities of humility, simplicity, unswerving faith, courage in the face of adversity and persecution, and love of the religious life dominate and determine all actions. The saint's feats are often likened to those of a celebrated predecessor. The saint's death, whatever its circumstances, is presented as a blessed event for which the saint is well prepared. It is obligatory that miracles such as spectacular cures take place at the saint's grave and that a heavenly fragrance waft from it. The epilogue consists of another, more lengthy eulogy of the saint and his or her accomplishments. Touching anecdotes may offer occasional relief from the multitude of scriptural quotations and rhetorical flourishes.

The first and most popular Russian saint's life is that of Boris and Gleb, two young princes assassinated at the instigation of their brother Svyatopolk in the course of the struggle for succession to Vladimir I in 1015. This fratricidal strife ended in the victory of Yaroslav the Wise. The vita exists in two versions, and there is also a detailed account of the events in the Primary Chronicle. The first version is ascribed to a monk named Jacob, the second to Nestor, a monk of the Kiev Cave Monastery.[18] The first does not quite follow the canon of Byzantine hagiography, for it tells the story of the

princes' violent death without a proper introduction and with little preliminary encomiastic detail. It also replaces the conventional epilogue with an account of Svyatopolk's miserable death. But it has most of the other traits of a conventional saint's life. Boris and Gleb are presented as gentle, meek, and devout youths—hardly true to historical fact—whereas Svyatopolk has all the traits of a traditional villain. He is given a monologue in which he lays out his nefarious plans. Boris, the older, is a marvel of filial piety (a lengthy prayerful lament at receiving the news of his father's death is inserted) and brotherly love (he refuses the call of his men who want to fight for him against Svyatopolk). He would rather die than shed Russian blood. Pious tirades and prayers are put into the mouths of both princes. Gleb, almost a child, launches into an elaborate lament at hearing that his brother has been slain. The princes pray tearfully before their deaths, and witnesses cry bitterly and utter words of lamentation. The author has a sense of drama, and he carefully builds the tension before each murder. Gleb's death is given added pathos: the young prince believes that an approaching boat, sent by his brother, carries friends, and he is preparing to embrace his assassins when they pull their swords to kill him. The bodies of the martyred princes do not decompose, but emit a heavenly perfume—signs of the princes' holiness. Angelic voices are heard in the air over Gleb's body, and a bright light shines over it in the darkness. Added to the vita is a brief portrait and character sketch, an example of verbal iconography: "This faithful Boris, being of good stock, was obedient to his father, following him in everything. He was handsome of body and tall, round of face, powerful in the shoulders, slim in the loins, with gracious eyes, a cheerful mien, his

18. The version ascribed to Jacob, known as the *Legend and passion and eulogy of the holy martyrs Boris and Gleb*, is contained in a late twelfth-century miscellany known as *Uspenskii sbornik*. Nestor's version is known as *Nestor's lection on the life and wrongful death of the blessed martyrs Boris and Gleb*.

beard and whiskers short, for he was still young; shining with imperial lustre, strong in body, adorned in all ways, like a flower in the bloom of his youth, brave in battle, wise in council, and with understanding in all things, and God's grace was in full bloom upon him."

The *Life of Saints Boris and Gleb* ascribed to Nestor relates the same story, but with more restraint and in keeping with the structure and style of a Byzantine saint's life. Both versions do their best to put their heroes into a hagiographic frame. Jacob's version compares the fate of the Russian princes to that of Saint Wenceslaus of Bohemia and Saint Nicetas, a fourth-century martyr, whereas Nestor's brings in Saint Eustace, Romanus the Melode (a Byzantine hymnographer—Boris's Christian name was Roman), Julian the Apostate, and others.

The legend of Boris and Gleb pursued a political as well as a religious end. Their canonization enhanced the authority of Yaroslav the Wise and was important to his successors, giving the dynasty and Russia their own patron saints. The legend circulated in hundreds of copies and became a part of Russian popular mythology (a widely known dukhovny stikh derives from it). The vita of Saints Boris and Gleb served as a model for a number of later vitae of Russian princes.

Nestor is also the author of a vita of Saint Theodosius, first abbot of the Kiev Cave Monastery, who died in 1074 and was canonized in 1108. The *Life of Saint Theodosius*, an exceptionally lengthy example of the genre (some fifty printed pages), follows the familiar pattern of Byzantine hagiography. After a brief invocation to the Lord, the writer identifies himself and launches into a declaration of his "crudeness and lack of understanding" mitigated only by his love for the blessed Theodosius. After

once more addressing the Lord in a brief prayer for assistance in his pious labor, Nestor starts his encomium. The hero is born of good Christian parents. He shows an early inclination for a scholarly and religious life, preferring holy books to childish games and beggarly rags to the fine clothes of his playmates. These are clichés, but what follows is not. The holy youth's mother, an energetic and domineering woman widowed when Theodosius was thirteen, is opposed to her son's religious aspirations. There develops a painful struggle between her and the equally single-minded Theodosius. Eventually he takes holy vows. His mother finally makes her peace with him, and herself enters a nearby convent. As a monk, Theodosius excels in all the monastic virtues and ascetic feats. He overcomes diabolic visitations and withstands excruciating pain and mental suffering. (All of this is quite conventional.) He is rewarded by being made abbot of the growing monastery. Theodosius clearly appeared to be an eccentric even to his devoted followers. Nestor reports with awe how the abbot would steal away from the monastery at night to do missionary work among the Jews of Kiev, fully expecting to be killed by them, and how he would spend the Lenten season in a lonely and wretched cave fasting and praying.

The vita of Theodosius is also the story of the growth of a community of cave-dwelling hermits into a stately monastery of economic and political importance. The humble novice ascetic develops into a capable administrator and a man of far-reaching authority, an authority so great that Theodosius could actually support the losing cause of Duke Izyaslav in 1073 and yet be courted by the winner, Svyatoslav. Grand Duke Izyaslav of Kiev (r. 1054–73) emerges as a pious and God-fearing ruler, a friend of the monastery who liked to share a frugal meal with the monks. The Primary Chronicle shows Izyaslav from a different side. It eulogizes him at his death but also reports his evil deeds, such as when he broke an oath to Duke Vseslav of Polotsk, repeatedly sought the help of King Bolesław of Poland,[19] and shed much Russian blood in the fratricidal feuds of the time. The miracles with which Theodosius is credited are mostly mundane. His confidence that the monastery's depleted supply of flour, oil, or wine will somehow be replenished is rewarded with miraculous speed and munificence.

Nestor is a remarkable writer. He employs an eminently literate Slavonic, accurately managing its elaborate Greek syntax. He cites Scripture frequently and aptly. Yet his style is never stilted or mannered. He retains control over his narrative while inserting the expected rhetorical digressions, apostrophes, and musings. He shows consummate tact in handling politically or otherwise delicate episodes and preserves his hero's dignity without sacrificing the truth of the matter. Nestor's narrative has a wonderful warmth which reflects his genuine affection for his hero, his monastery, and the Russian lands. The details of the vita are partly stereotypical (the inevitable temptation by hellish forces victoriously overcome) and partly idiosyncratic, as in the detailed account of the holy man's last days and death, which surely served as a model for Father Zosima's death in Dostoevsky's *Brothers Karamazov*.

The *Life of Saint Theodosius* became a model, too, for many later Russian vitae. One example is the *Life of Saint Abraham of Smolensk*, written by his disciple Ephraim at the time of the Tatar invasion.[20]

It resembles the *Life of Saint Theodosius* but has fewer idiosyncratic traits and more formulaic elements, although the text shows Abraham to have been a man of extraordinary gifts, famous for his wisdom and erudition, and admired for his exegesis of sacred texts and for his icon painting. The *Life of Saint Abraham* makes a point of inserting material from the vitae of other saints (John Chrysostom, Ephraim Syrus, Anthony, Sabbas, Euthymius, and of course Theodosius). The formal parts of this saint's life are longer and more elaborate than in Nestor's work. The eulogy at the end is two printed pages long, and the humility topos acquires a life of its own, as Ephraim produces a catalog of his own vices, to which he opposes the lofty virtues of his teacher.

Related to hagiography are edifying tales or anecdotes from monastic life, gathered in a *paterikon*, a miscellany also containing other (usually brief) edifying tracts like exhortations, epistles, and vitae, all of which are linked by their common association with a celebrated monastic community. In medieval Russia the *Paterikon of Mount Sinai* was known from the very beginning. Later the Egyptian, Roman, and Jerusalem paterika were translated from the Greek. The first Russian paterikon arose at the Kiev Cave Monastery, founded early in the eleventh century.[21] The Kiev Cave Monastery was the parent of all Russian monasteries, of which there were fewer than a hundred at the time of the Tatar invasion. When the *Kiev Paterikon* was started in the 1220s,

19. He also turned for help to Emperor Henry IV and Pope Gregory VII.

20. *Life and passion of our blessed Abraham of the city of Smolensk, sainted by much suffering.*

21. One of the titles under which it is known is *Paterikon of the caves, viz. on the erection of a church, may it be understood by all, erected by the providence and will of the Lord Himself and the prayers and wish of His most pure Mother and achieved pleasing to God, like the Heavens, [our] great Church of the Holy Virgin, viz. The monastery of our holy and great Father Theodosius.*

the monastery already had to its credit a rich tradition of canonized brethren, ascetic feats, moral leadership, and cultural achievement. It also possessed a rich oral tradition. According to the frame narrative of the paterikon, it got its start when Simon, bishop of Vladimir, who was tonsured at the Kiev Cave Monastery, addressed an admonitory epistle to Polycarp, a monk of that monastery, who in the bishop's opinion had shown inordinate ambition and insufficient humility in his pursuit of high ecclesiastical office. The epistle was accompanied by nine accounts of ascetic feats by monks of the Kiev Cave Monastery bearing the message that humility and self-effacement were the cardinal monastic virtues. Polycarp, following Simon's example, collected eleven stories, accompanying these with a missive to Acyndinus, abbot of the monastery. Some further pieces were added (also in the thirteenth century) including excerpts from the chronicles related to the history of the monastery. All the stories in the paterikon concern individuals and events of the eleventh and twelfth centuries. The *Kiev Paterikon* was revised many times. It is extant in several manuscripts, the oldest of which dates from 1406 and was prepared by Bishop Arsenius of Tver, as well as in later printed editions from the seventeenth century on.

Many of the stories of the *Kiev Paterikon*, though pious and edifying, are close to the genre of the novella. In one such story Moses the Hungarian, as a prisoner of war in Poland, heroically resists the advances of a Polish magnate's widow; he eventually takes refuge in the monastery and dies there of the wounds he suffered at the hands of the lady's servants. This story, like many others, has a verifiable historical setting. Duke Mstislav Svyatopolchich stabs the monk Basil with an arrow. Mortally wounded, Basil

prophesies that the duke will meet his death from that same arrow. In fact, Mstislav Svyatopolchich did die of an arrow wound, during the siege of Vladimir in 1099. Sometimes the same event is portrayed in a different light in different texts. In the *Kiev Paterikon* the drowning of Duke Rostislav Vsevolodovich and his men in 1093 is reported together with the story of Gregory, a monk who, when taunted by the duke's soldiers, prophesied that they would all meet their death by drowning (whereupon the duke had the monk drowned). The Primary Chronicle describes the battle and the drowning of the duke and his soldiers objectively. What guilt there may have been is with the Russian leaders for refusing to listen to the advice of those who warned them not to attack the Polovetzians with insufficient forces. The *Igor Tale*, by contrast, gives a poetic version of the event tenderly sympathetic to the young duke.

Diabolic deception, such as when the devil assumes the shape of a monk to create confusion and false suspicions, is a frequent theme. The vindication of the righteous may be slow or even delayed until after death, as in the story of Basil and the arrow. There Basil and another monk, Theodore, suffer cruel deaths when Duke Mstislav tries to extort from them the secret of a hidden treasure, which the devil, having assumed Basil's shape, had told him that Theodore had found.

Many of the stories feature miracles, some of which a modern reader might perceive as apt novelistic invention. An example is the story of the icon painter Olympius. When his mortal illness prevents him from fulfilling his last commission, an angel sent by God paints the icon for him. (Miracles connected with icons are a commonplace of Old Russian literature.) In several instances evildoers meet their punishment through a monk's miraculous powers. A monk named Gregory repeatedly stops thieves by uncanny means. He prophesies to one of them that he will die by strangulation. When the man comes back at night to plunder the monastery's fruit trees, he falls from a broken branch and is choked by a necklace he is wearing. In some of the stories a dead person comes back to life in response to a challenge. When the gravedigger Marko improperly buries some corpses, they return to life in order to secure their proper burial.

A monkish ethos and the formulaic and ritualistic patterns of medieval thought are dominant in the *Kiev Paterikon*. But it also offers more than mere glimpses of other aspects of Russian medieval life. Political partisanship and intrigue in which the monastery is involved appear often. Some of the stories are, from a modern reader's viewpoint, starkly realistic case histories of individuals suffering from severe physical handicaps, chronic illness, mental retardation, or psychosis. The saints among the monks are distinguished by their capacity to put up with the hideous sight, awful stench, and quirky behavior of their afflicted brothers. Altogether, the *Kiev Paterikon* gives us a fascinating picture of medieval monastic life, and a good deal of secular life too.

After the encomium of Saints Boris and Gleb, the most important example of the princely vita is the *Life of Alexander Nevsky*, written in the 1280s. Significantly, an episode in this vita reports the vision of a Finnish convert in which Boris and Gleb come to Alexander's aid in the battle on the Neva River. The *Life of Alexander Nevsky* is extant in some fifteen variants. In two of the manuscripts it is preceded by the *Orison on the Ruin of the Russian Land*, decidedly a secular text. Hence there exists a theory that the *Life* as we have it is a revision of what was initially a secular work close to the genre of the war tale.[22]

The *Tale of the Life and Valor of the True Believer and Grand Duke Alexander* celebrates Aleksandr Yaroslavich (1220–63), duke of Novgorod and (after his father's death) grand duke of Vladimir and all Russia. As a young man he won two great victories, over the Swedes on the Neva (hence his epithet, Nevsky) in 1240 and over the Livonian Order on the ice of Lake Peipus in 1242. His *Life*, written by an unidentified younger contemporary who had heard of these feats "from his fathers," became a document of national significance as it charted the course of Russia's political future. The victories over the Catholic Swedes and Germans are triumphantly celebrated and ascribed to the intervention of a host of angels fighting on the Russian side. The grand duke's submission to the Tatar yoke is presented as not only wise but also honorable.

The *Life of Alexander Nevsky* is a mixture of war tale and saint's life. The heroics of six soldiers (identified by name) in the battle on the Neva are graphically described. On the other hand, Alexander's piety and his love of church and clergy are given a great deal of attention, and he is shown in prayer as often as in battle. His death (of an unspecified illness) and burial are presented quite in the manner of a saint's life. A miracle is performed by his body as he lies in state. Alexander was canonized by the Orthodox church, and his *Life* came to serve a liturgical function.

The *Life of Alexander Nevsky* shows that by the end of the thirteenth century the image of the ideal prince was well established in Russia. There is little to learn about

22. The text of the *Life of Alexander Nevsky* suggests that its author was familiar with the work of Josephus Flavius.

the real Alexander from the *Life*. We see a God-fearing, pious, humble, but entirely faceless ruler. That a battle may have raged in Alexander's heart between his honor as a warrior and the political advantage of being on good terms with the khan never occurs to the writer. The embarrassing details of Alexander's vassalage are slurred over. Batu Khan is not even called by name, much less labeled a godless pagan, but is identified vaguely as "a certain powerful tsar of the eastern parts." When the principality of Alexander's younger brother is invaded and sacked by the Tatars, his reaction, praised by the writer, is merely to rebuild destroyed churches and give aid to the victims.

The influence of hagiographic literature on the development of the Russian national consciousness can hardly be overestimated. Saints' lives were for many of the literate almost the only narrative literature they ever became acquainted with. To some writers of the eighteenth and nineteenth centuries, saints' lives were still the first literary texts they encountered. With church attendance mandatory for students, all educated Russians, even in the nineteenth century, were exposed to saints' lives during their most impressionable years. In one way or another, saints' lives entered the writings of almost every major Russian writer before the Soviet period. Gogol's famous story "The Overcoat" is on one level a travesty of the vita of Saint Acacius. Dostoevsky's *Brothers Karamazov* contains the vita of Father Zosima. Leskov wrote a cycle of stories based on the *Lectionary*. Several of Tolstoi's works have strong connections with the saint's life; "Father Sergius" is the most striking example. Among twentieth-century writers Vyacheslav Ivanov, Aleksei Remizov, Boris Zaitsev, Ivan Shmelyov, and others have written works drawing on the hagiographic tradition.

Much of the hagiographic tradition entered Russian folklore, especially in the form of legends or dukhovnye stikhi. Saint George as the protector of cattle, Saint Nicholas as intercessor in the trials and tribulations of daily existence, the prophet Elijah as the peasant's friend, and many other figures from the saints' calendar were a part of the daily life of the Russian people well into the twentieth century.

Pilgrimages

The pilgrimage (*khozhdenie*) is a genre closely related to hagiography. The traveler's description of holy or otherwise noteworthy places, a genre of classical literature, carried over into Byzantine literature and appeared early in Russian literature. In 1062 Barlaam, a monk of the Kiev Cave Monastery, visited Palestine, though he left no travelogue. Daniel (Daniil), abbot of an unidentified Russian monastery, was the first Russian to produce an extant travelogue of a pilgrimage to Jerusalem and the holy places in 1104–6.[23] His *Pilgrimage* must have been popular—it is extant in some 150 manuscripts, the oldest of which is included in a fifteenth-century version of the *Kiev Paterikon*.

Daniel may have been the cleric who in 1113 was named bishop of Yuryev in southern Russia and died in 1122. He probably made his pilgrimage with a group of Russian pilgrims in 1104–6, when the Holy Land was held by the Crusaders under King Baldwin, who is reported by Daniel to have treated the pilgrims with kindness and respect.

Daniel's *Pilgrimage* is introduced by the usual humility topos, as he declares that he,

23. *Life and pilgrimage of Daniel, an abbot of the Russian land.*

"worst of all monks, burdened by many sins and lacking in any good works, wanted to see the holy city of Jerusalem and the promised land driven by his own intent and impatience." Daniel's narrative follows the route of his journey. Stops en route to the Holy Land are mentioned briefly, almost always for their religious interest: Ephesus, Patmos, Cyprus, Rhodes, and other places known from the Acts of the Apostles or from saint's lives. Daniel must have spent more than a year in the Holy Land, where he visited many places known from the Old and New Testaments: Bethlehem, Nazareth, Cana, Capernaum, and Emmaus, as well as Melchizedek's cave, the oak of Mamre, Jacob's well, the graves of Rachel, Joseph, and many other biblical personages, the spot where David slew Goliath, the cave where Jesus was tempted by the devil, and Matthew's custom station. Although he makes mistakes, he shows himself well read in the Bible. Occasionally he enlivens his topography by comparing what he sees with things back home. The Jordan reminds him of the Snov (a tributary of the Desna), a certain tree looks like a Russian alder, and so on.

Daniel's journal ends with a detailed description of the celebration of Easter in Jerusalem. King Baldwin graciously permits the Russian abbot to place his lamp alongside the others over the Lord's sepulchre. Daniel worries whether the miracle of spontaneous ignition by the light emanating from the holy sepulchre will be granted to his lamp and reports, without malice, that his and other lamps set up by the Eastern church were ignited, whereas three Frankish lamps were not. The bitter hostility against the Western church which will be felt in Russia a century later is absent here. Daniel further reports that he has inscribed the names of the reigning Russian princes (in order of seniority!) in the Church of Saint Sabbas and

that he has said sincere prayers for everybody in Russia he could think of.

Daniel's narrative, rather laconic and matter-of-fact, is competent and intelligent, covering a lot of ground in about a hundred pages. It compares favorably with medieval Western and Arabic travelogues and started a tradition that extended into modern times.[24] Throughout the twelfth century pilgrimages to the holy places seem to have been common, and pilgrims traveled in large groups, a fact that impressed itself upon the memory of Russian folklore. Late in the twelfth century, Anthony, who subsequently became archbishop of Novgorod, reported on his pilgrimage to Constantinople. After the collapse of Kievan Russia in the thirteenth century, when the route to the holy places led down the Don River to the Crimea, Russians continued to find their way to Constantinople, where a Russian colony seems to have existed even in the fourteenth century, as we learn from the travelogue of Stefan of Novgorod, who visited the imperial city in 1348 or 1349.

Homiletics

A number of Byzantine and a few Bulgarian homilies were available to Russian churchmen in Slavonic early on. Collections of homilies by Anastasius of Sinai, Basil the Great, Cyril of Jerusalem, Isaac of Nineveh, Gregory of Nazianzus, John Chrysostom, Gennadius of Constantinople, Clement of Bulgaria, and others, as well as miscellanies of homilies by various authors, are common

24. *Tale of his travels and pilgrimages through Russia, Moldavia, Turkey, and the Holy Land, by Parfeny, a monk, tonsured at Holy Mount Athos*, 2d ed. (Moscow, 1856), written entirely in the manner of Daniel's *Pilgrimage*, was a best-seller of sorts and was used extensively by Dostoevsky in his *Brothers Karamazov*.

among extant manuscripts. Russian church-men at cathedral churches followed these traditions. But we can only surmise what a parish priest, probably barely literate and having few if any books, may have told his congregation in his Sunday sermon. Short homilies by Luke (Luka) Zhidyata, archbishop of Novgorod (1036–61); Saint Theodosius, abbot of the Kiev Cave Monastery; Elijah (Ilya), a Novgorod cleric (dated 1165), and Gregory (Grigory) "the Philosopher," bishop of Belgorod (thirteenth century), all are pieces of routine biblical exegesis, and hence are of little literary interest. It is a single sermon by Hilarion (Ilarion), written before 1051, the year he was named metropolitan of Kiev, that evinces the rapid pace of Russia's acquisition of Byzantine culture—the *Sermon on Law and Grace.*[25]

Hilarion, a Russian, was created metropolitan by Grand Duke Yaroslav against the wishes of the Constantinople patriarchate. Metropolitans before and after him were Greeks. His *Sermon on Law and Grace* gives eloquent testimony of his loyalty to his secular ruler. It is addressed to Yaroslav, congratulating him on the flourishing condition of Christianity in his realm and eulogizing his late father Vladimir as Russia's "teacher and preceptor," equal to Saints Peter and Paul in Rome, Saint Thomas in India, or Saint Mark in Egypt. The panegyrical conclusion of the sermon is preceded by a skillful and vigorous paraphrase of the allegory of Hagar and Sarah (Galatians 4:22–31), showing how the law of Moses is but a preparatory stage leading to the grace and freedom of Holy Baptism, which in turn opens the gate to eternal life. "It was the law, not grace, that Moses brought down from Mount Sinai, not

the truth but a shadow" (where "shadow" means "promise," as in Hebrews 10:1).

Although popular in medieval Russia, Hilarion's *Sermon* is extant in relatively late copies only, and it is likely that some scriptorial revisions have been made in the text. Hence its accurate and elegant Slavonic should not be credited to Hilarion alone. Yet the composition and rhythmic cadences of the panegyric must be his alone. They testify to the fact that only two generations after Vladimir had embraced Christianity a native Russian could come up with a rhetorical and intellectual performance of which no Byzantine or Latin preacher would have been ashamed. Moreover, Hilarion must have had at least a small audience that could appreciate his theological learning and rhetorical skill.

The following two centuries provide enough examples of divine eloquence to make it certain that educated Russian churchmen possessed the same rhetorical skills as their Byzantine masters. The most famous scholar and philosopher of the twelfth century was Clement (Klimenty) of Smolensk, metropolitan of all Russia (1147–54). Of his many works only one is extant, the *Epistle to Presbyter Thomas*, written in the manner of an oral discourse.[26] In it Clement defends himself against charges of vainglory and ambition and rejects the notion that in his desire to gain the reputation of a "philosopher," he uses "Hellenic" (that is, pagan) authors in his exegesis of the Bible, "writing not from the Holy Fathers but from Homer, Aristotle, and Plato." (In fact, there is nothing in Clement's *Epistle* that suggests that his learning went beyond patristic texts available in Slavonic.) Cle-

---

25. *Homily of Metropolitan Hilarion on the Law given to Moses and on the Grace and Truth that was Jesus Christ.*

26. The epistle must be considered an established literary genre since the beginning of Russian literature. The epistles of the New Testament and of several church fathers served as examples.

ment also defends his exegetical style, which reads the Bible not literally but allegorically. The examples of Clement's exegesis produced in the *Epistle* indeed amount to an arbitrary and mechanical assignment of allegorical meaning to biblical passages, such as when he explains that "the woman of Samaria [John 4:7–29] is the soul, her five husbands are the five senses, and her sixth is the mind." Clement's defense is simple: he can justly say that these allegorical interpretations are not his own but are gleaned from one of the Holy Fathers (Nicetas of Heracleia in the instance cited). It appears that Clement refers back to Hilarion's *Sermon*, for the juxtaposition of the law of the Old Testament to the grace of the New Testament is one of the main themes of the *Epistle*, too.

Saint Cyril of Turov (1130–82), an ascetic and bishop of Turov (c. 1169–82), was a prolific writer who earned a reputation as the Russian Chrysostom. He wrote homilies (*slovesa*), epistles to ecclesiastical and secular authorities, colloquies (*besedy*), liturgical texts devoted to several saints, and prayers to Jesus Christ, the apostles, and the archangels. Cyril humbly calls himself "a gatherer of ears, who preaches from the books." Indeed, his works make ample use of Gregory of Nazianzus, John Chrysostom, Basil the Great, and other church fathers. In his *Parable on the Human Soul and Body*[27] Cyril declares: "Let us not advance our thoughts in our individual uninstructed language, but let us draw on the Holy Scriptures." This attitude is of course characteristic of the Middle Ages. But then, too, the boundary between scriptural text

and the author's imagination is more fluid than in modern theology. In the same work Cyril tells a parable which begins by following Matthew 21:33 but then veers onto a different path. In Cyril's parable a husbandman (God) hires two laborers, a blind man (the soul) and a lame man (the body), to guard his vineyard (the world), which is surrounded by a fence (God's commandments). The laborers turn out to be unfaithful and steal the owner's fruit. The husbandman returns and discovers their transgression. They blame each other, and he casts them out of his vineyard to be judged when the time comes. The story is lively, and its message is explained in a vigorously direct manner.

Cyril's sermons have the same allegorical quality as the *Parable* and the same imaginative approach to the biblical text. In a sermon based on the scriptural account of the deposition of Christ's body from the Cross, its burial by Nicodemus and Joseph of Arimathea, and Christ's resurrection (Luke 23:50–24:6),[28] the preacher uses his imagination to build up the spare account of the Gospel into a detailed narrative. Joseph delivers one oration before Pilate and another as he faces Christ's body. He gives each detail of his narrative an allegoric meaning: Christ's body was entombed to give life to those entombed for ages; His tomb was secured with a sealed stone to destroy the gates and bolts of hell; He was guarded by soldiers visible to all and invisibly descended to hell to put Satan in chains. The sermon concludes with an elaborate tribute to Joseph composed of a series of allegorical conceits culminating in a prayer

27. *Parable of Cyril, a monk, on the human soul and on the body, and on transgression of God's commandment, and on the resurrection of the human body, and on the judgment that will be, and on torments.*

28. *Homily of Saint Cyril, a monk, on the deposition of Christ's body from the Cross and on the bearers of myrrh, according to the Gospel, and a eulogy to Joseph on the third Sunday after Easter.*

addressed to him. The narrative text of the sermon alternates with lyric passages that can be broken down into lines, each consisting of two cola (rhythmic units). If proper pauses are observed, the text acquires a regular rhythm. The rhythm is enhanced by consistent parallelism and outright repetition: "The heavens were horrified, and the earth trembled, / Refusing to suffer godless Jewish audacity, / The sun went dark, the rocks burst, / Denouncing Jewish godlessness."

Cyril's most famous sermon, the *Sermon for the Sunday after Easter*, follows the paschal sermon of Gregory of Nazianzus. Its theme is a joyous recognition of the mysteries of religion in the awakening of nature in springtime. In a series of similes Easter is identified with spring, the resurrection of nature. The plowman bends the verbal steer to the spiritual yoke, buries the plow of the cross into the furrows of the mind to sow the seed of penitence, and rejoices in the hope of a harvest of salvation.

Christ's resurrection and his triumph over Satan is at the center of Cyril's theology. In his sermon on the Ascension he paints a magnificent picture of Christ on the day of Ascension, surrounded by the saints of the Old and the New Testaments, the angels and archangels, and even the "heathen" church. Christ rises to heaven to present his human soul to the Father. At the gates of heaven it is Christ's voice that reveals the godhead in the "slave's image" of man vested in flesh, saying, "Open to me the gates of righteousness" (Psalm 118:19).

Cyril's colloquies and sermons are admirable, given that originality was not considered a virtue in the Middle Ages. They are carefully structured, ingeniously developed from an imaginative reading of the Bible, and artful in their phrasing. Cyril has a command of every figure and trope of classical rhetoric, controls a syntax as difficult as that of his Byzantine examples, and possesses a rich vocabulary.

Cyril's prayers are lengthy lyric poems in prose, saturated with rhetorical figures, tropes, and artful conceits. Thus Saint Peter is addressed not only as "the unshakable foundation of the Church" and "the holder of the keys of heaven," but also as "the fisherman in the depths of foolishness" who is asked to "capture us in his divine net." Cyril was the first Russian to cultivate the Byzantine canon sung during the liturgy. Two of these, a *Penitential Canon* and a *Canon of Supplication*, are extant. These canons are as close to poetry as anything in Old Russian literature. They have none of the rhythm-creating elements of modern Russian poetry (meter, rhyme), but that is compensated for by the fact that they were sung—the melody carried the rhythmic element of the composition.

The homilies of Saint Cyril are remote from "real life," as are other extant examples of the homiletics of his age.[29] The Tatar invasion put the faith of Russian Christendom to a severe test, causing Russian clerics to direct their thoughts to the moral implications of this calamity. An outstanding preacher of the period was Serapion (d. 1275), bishop of Vladimir, five of whose sermons are extant. In each he urges Russian Christians to heed the warnings sent them by the Lord, to do penance, and to mend their ways. Serapion perceives the Tatar invasion as divine punishment for Russia's

29. For example, a sermon by Moses (Moisei), Abbot of Vydubichi Monastery near Kiev, delivered in 1198 on the occasion of the dedication of a wall supporting the monastery, concentrates on giving thanks to Grand Duke Ryurik Rostislavovich, who provided funds for the structure. The address is decidedly panegyrical, liberally embroidered with quotations from and allusions to the Bible and several church fathers.

sins: miscarriage of justice by wicked and merciless judges, bribery, extortion, murder and robbery, lechery and adultery, calumny, lying, slander, false oaths and deception, sorcery, and "all kinds of satanic practices." He sadly observes that the misfortunes which have struck the Russian people have not made them repent. Serapion's position is that of an earnest, enlightened, and humane churchman. His sermons are no mere rhetorical exercises: they ring sincere and fit the occasion. When he speaks of sin, he has specific crimes in mind. Thus he condemns the practice of testing a woman charged with witchcraft by flinging her into deep water (her staying afloat being proof of her guilt), a practice common in the Middle Ages even in the West. Serapion suggests that the devil could cause an innocent victim to float precisely in order to make murderers of her accusers. He insists that guilt in capital cases should be determined on the basis of evidence by many witnesses.

The sermons of Serapion are structured according to the familiar pattern of classical rhetoric: exordium, narration, argumentation, refutation, and peroration. They obviously pursue the creation of rhythmic cadences and feature an array of rhetorical devices, including climax, apostrophe, rhetorical question, parallelism, metaphor, and simile. Serapion quotes freely from the Old and New Testaments (especially Psalms) and displays an erudition that goes beyond Scripture and the Fathers of the Eastern church. As he reminds his flock of calamities visited on sinful humanity before the earthquakes, crop failures, and invasions of his own time, he mentions antediluvian giants consumed by fire, the Great Flood, Sodom destroyed by fire and brimstone, the ten plagues of Egypt, the Canaanites killed by stones from heaven (Joshua 10:11), the battles of the judges, the pestilence under

David (2 Samuel 24:13), and the capture of Jerusalem by Titus. The lively language and down-to-earth imagery of Serapion's sermons contrast with the abstract and solemn spirituality of Hilarion and Cyril.

Chronicles

The Russian chronicles (*letopisi*) may be likened to a tree with many branches. Many regional chronicles were started as continuations of the Primary Chronicle of Kiev, often called the *Tale of Bygone Years* after its preamble: "These are the tales of bygone years, whence the Russian land took its beginning, who was first to reign in Kiev, and how the Russian land came into being." The Primary Chronicle was written in or near 1113, possibly by Nestor, a monk of the Kiev Cave Monastery known as the author of the vitae of saints Boris and Gleb and of Saint Theodosius. The textual history of this chronicle is exceedingly complex. A series of scholars, among whom A. A. Shakhmatov (1860–1920) and D. S. Likhachev (b. 1906) are the most meritorious, have tried to unravel it. Only the barest outline of their findings is presented here, and the often ingenious reasoning behind them must be omitted. The Primary Chronicle was based on an earlier text, probably composed in 1093, perhaps under the impression of a recent crushing defeat of the Russian princes at the hands of the Polovetzians. The First Novgorod Chronicle, by far the oldest extant chronicle manuscript (written in the thirteenth and fourteenth centuries), was apparently based on this version, not on Nestor's. There is reason to believe that the version of 1093 was preceded by two earlier versions, the first composed as early as the 1040s. Some episodes—such as the story of Olga's journey to Constantinople and her baptism, and the account of Vladimir's conversion to Christianity—may have existed in written form even earlier.

The *Tale of Bygone Years* served as a basis for regional chronicles, as a local chronicler would copy it and then add his own entries. It is best preserved in the Laurentian Chronicle of 1377 and the Hypatian Chronicle of circa 1420. The Laurentian includes an account of Russian history up to 1305, with a focus on northern Russia; the Hypatian covers mainly Kievan and Galician-Volhynian Russia until 1289.

The Primary Chonicle reflects the use of several written sources: texts of treaties from the archives of Kiev, the Byzantine chronicles of George Hamartolus (continued by Symeon Logothete) and John Malalas,[30] Byzantine saint's lives, Byzantine apocrypha like the *Revelation of Methodius of Patara* (sub anno 1096), a *Tale of the Origin of Slavonic Writing* (s.a. 898), Nestor's *Life of Saints Boris and Gleb* (s.a. 1015), and of course the Bible. It resembles Byzantine universal chronicles in that it begins with a brief geography of the known world based on its partition among the sons of Noah—Shem, Ham, and Japheth. The Rus-

---

30. *Chronikon syntomon ek diaphoron chronographon te kai exegeton syllegen kai syntethen hypo Georgiou Hamartolou Monachou*, in seven books, and *Ioannou Malala Chronographia*, in eighteen books, are both attempts to integrate the Bible and assorted works by church fathers with what little the authors knew about history from classical sources. Their chronology is unreliable and their credulity unlimited. Malalas, for example, tells us that Nero, having heard of Jesus Christ before he became emperor and having gained the impression that He was "a great philosopher and miracle worker," ordered Him brought to Rome. When told that Christ had been crucified a long time age, Nero got angry and ordered Annas and Caiaphas brought to Rome, as well as Pilate, who had been living in Palestine after having been relieved of his post as procurator. Annas and Caiaphas win their release by blaming Pilate for the crucifixion. We hear nothing of Pilate's further fate.

sian chronicler adds a section on his own part of the world, extending the catalog of nations found in Greek sources to include a number of Slavic, Finnish, and Germanic peoples. From here until the entry for 852, when George Hamartolus reports the first Russian raid on Constantinople, the Russian chronicler was on his own. He had no help from Greek sources, since those accessible to him paid almost no attention to Russia. His introducing the text of two treaties (912 and 945) between Russia and Byzantium suggests that he may have had some other archival material at his disposal.

But basically the author of the Primary Chronicle must have been working with oral traditions, less reliable the further they are removed from his own time. The episodes covering the reign of the first dukes of Kiev—Ryurik, Oleg, and Igor (d. 945)—resemble Old Norse sagas, and much in them is fiction, featuring themes identified as far back as Herodotus. In one of these episodes Olga avenges the death of her husband, Duke Igor, at the hands of Derevlyane tribesmen by tricking them into thrice misinterpreting an ambiguous message. A party of their leaders is buried alive in their boat when Olga "honors" them by letting her men carry them into her courtyard, where a deep ditch has been dug for them. A second party is burned alive in a bathhouse preparing for a feast at her invitation. A third is cut down after having been made drunk at what the men take to be Igor's funeral feast. Scandinavian and Slavic warriors were buried in their boats, the dead were washed before being burned on a funeral pyre, and the funeral feast was the tribesmen's own. Olga then lays siege to the Derevlyane's last stronghold and captures it, again by trickery. She promises them peace for a nominal tribute of pigeons and sparrows; then she has the birds fitted with tinder, which is set on fire, and released to fly back to the thatched roofs of the fort. (This particular stratagem is found in Herodotus, and the story may have come to Russia from Byzantium.)

The initial episode of the Primary Chronicle is controversial. It reports that the original Rus were Varangians, whom the Slavs of Novgorod invited to come and create order in their vast, rich, and unruly land. Although the story is clearly fictitious, the fact remains that the names of the first dukes of Kiev are Scandinavian, as is the name of Duke Igor's wife, Olga. The chronicle tradition according to which Rus was founded by Scandinavians is supported by evidence from Byzantine, Arabic, and Western sources, but it has been challenged by Russian scholars ever since Mikhail Lomonosov in the eighteenth century, often with ingenious arguments. The controversy, however, is hardly relevant to the history of Russian literature, because Old Russian literature depends entirely on Byzantine models. What role the Varangians played in the development of the Russian polity and of Russian law is a question that does not concern the literary scholar.

Beginning with the reign of Svyatoslav Igorevich (945–72) the Russian chronicle moves on firmer historical ground. Svyatoslav's campaigns in Bulgaria and his battles with Emperor John Tzimisces (969–76) are well attested even in such Byzantine sources, as the chronicle of Leo Diaconus, where a rather striking description of the Russian duke is found. Yet the Russian chronicle is still laced with legend and fiction. This is true of the lengthy account of how Vladimir Svyatoslavich (980–1015) chose to embrace the Greek Orthodox faith over the Latin, the Muhammadan, and the Jewish. It mixes authentic fact (verified by Greek sources) with the obviously anecdotal, as when Vladimir rejects Islam,

offered him by the Volga Bulgars, on the grounds that Russians like pork and wine, and Judaism, presented by the Jewish Khazars, because he cannot trust the law of a people driven from their homeland and scattered throughout the world by their God.

The chronicle deals primarily with the almost continuous wars of the Russian princes against the Turkic nomads of the southern steppes—first the Khazars, then the Pechenegs, and later the Polovetzians—as well as with their internecine feuds. The princes battled over the succession to Vladimir's throne, then over the succession to that of his son, Yaroslav the Wise (1016–54), after whose death these feuds became almost incessant. Often Russian princes allied themselves with the Polovetzians, the Poles, and the Hungarians against their own brothers. The Primary Chronicle is a chronicle of the princely families, whose births and deaths are duly reported. Events relating to Christian life, like the building of churches and the founding of monasteries, the appointment of important clerics, or the suppression of vestiges of paganism, are also recorded, as are such natural phenomena as comets, eclipses, floods, and earthquakes. The chronicle says little about the life of the common people or about economic, legal, and social developments.

The style of the Primary Chronicle is distinct from the more devoutly formulaic style of the saint's life. Still, the monk in the narrator shows through. When he reports, in 1097, that the warring princes had for once come to an agreement, he comments: "All the people were glad; only the devil was peeved by their love." There is never any doubt as to the moral meaning of historical events. A Russian defeat at the hands of the infidels is always seen as God's punishment for the Christians' transgressions.

The chronicler has a story to tell, and he

usually tells it well. Dialogue quoted is always laconic and often pithy. When the Polotsk princess Rogneda rejects the marriage proposal of Vladimir of Kiev, she says, "I will not unshoe the slavewoman's son, but I will marry Yaropolk." She will perform the symbolic act of a bride's submission to her husband for Yaropolk, born by Svyatoslav's royal consort, but not for Vladimir, son of Malusha (also Malfred), Olga's housekeeper. The narrative is seasoned with proverbial sayings, in addition to biblical quotations. In some episodes the reader senses the presence of a narrator who will report what he has heard himself from eyewitnesses, in particular one Yan Vyshatich (d. 1106), a councillor to the grand dukes of Kiev who was the grandson of Ostromir, governor of Novgorod, patron of the Ostromir Gospel, and a direct descendant of Sveneld, trusted lieutenant of Igor and Svyatoslav.

The chronicles are of great importance for the history of Russian literature, for several reasons. Although portions of them are dry annals of no literary merit, they also contain episodes that are as interesting to read as anything in Herodotus. The chronicles served as a receptacle for writings that had little or no historical relevance, like the *Instruction to His Children* by Grand Duke Vladimir Monomachus, a didactic work, or Afanasy Nikitin's fifteenth century account of his journey to India. The chronicles were from the beginning politically committed documents instrumental in creating a national or regional mythology. There are instances in which the same events are presented in a wholly different light by various chronicles; some, for example, represent the position favoring a strong central authority (Moscow, in later centuries), whereas others speak for the democratic city-states of Novgorod and Pskov. There is evidence that chronicles—even the Kiev Primary Chronicle—were rewritten after a change of ruler. Pushkin's image of the chronicler Pimen in *Boris Godunov*, which presents him as a stern and incorruptible reporter of the princes' good and evil deeds, rarely applies to the medieval chronicler.

The language of the chronicles varies from one to the next, as well as within each—understandable in view of multiple authorship and the frequent insertion of extraneous material. Basically, the language of the chronicles is Russian, with a strong seasoning of Slavonic both in the form of biblical and other quotations and in the form of Slavonic loanwords and phrases. On occasion there is a breath of the vernacular, in idiomatic expressions, proverbs, and sayings. The chronicle can be eloquent and moving, as when reporting the misery of Russians led away into captivity by the Polovetzians in 1093. It certainly can tell a good story, for example, the account of the blinding in 1097 of Duke Vasilko of Terebovl by dukes Svyatopolk of Kiev and David of Volhynia. It can write history with a political cast, protecting the interests of the Orthodox church.

Among the sequels to the *Tale of Bygone Years* the Galician-Volhynian Chronicle, dealing mainly with events in southwestern Russia, is of the greatest literary interest. It has been preserved in several versions, the oldest of which is the Hypatian Chronicle. The Galician-Volhynian Chronicle covers the period from 1201 to 1289, telling of countless major and minor campaigns, sieges, raids, and battles as the princes of the region engaged in constant internecine feuds. Since they had many links through intermarriage and alliances with royalty and magnates of Hungary, Poland, Lithuania, and Germany (not to speak of the Polovetzians to the East) the armies of these neighbors were on Russian soil almost continually;

Russian princes, meanwhile, led their troops as far west as Bohemia and Silesia. The Galician-Volhynian chronicle has an international flavor, as we hear about dynastic struggles of the Holy Roman Empire, a disastrous flood on the coast of the North Sea, and the good works of the sainted Elizabeth (a Hungarian princess), wife of the landgrave of Thuringia. The central event is of course the Tatar invasion.

The hero of the Galician-Volhynian Chronicle is Grand Duke Daniel (Daniil Romanovich, 1201–64) of Galicia, a mighty warrior, sage ruler, and builder of towns and churches. As a young man, he is described as "bold and valiant, without a blemish from head to foot." After his death he is remembered as virtuous, brave, and wise, "a second Solomon." Daniel also emerges as a human being, such as when he must make the humiliating journey to Batu's camp to be confirmed in his vassalage to the Tatar khan. Batu makes him take a draught of koumiss (fermented mare's milk), and Daniel empties the bitter cup as a sign of submission. Later Batu sends him a beaker of wine—for the khan is human, too.

The Galician-Volhynian Chronicle, compiled by four different clerics, is like other chronicles not a work of objective historiography but an expression of strong partisan interests and sympathies. The chroniclers have obvious literary ambitions, stimulated perhaps by the example of Josephus Flavius. Some sections of the chronicle clearly have literary merit, such as this concise yet graphic passage on the siege of Kiev in 1240: "Batu came to Kiev with a powerful host, a great multitude of his force, and surrounded the city, and his forces were all around it, and the city was under heavy siege. And Batu stood in sight of the city, his men camped around it. And you could not hear a voice for the creaking of his carts, the bellowing of his many camels, and the neighing of his herds of horses, and the whole Russian land was crowded with soldiers."

The Igor Tale *and Other War Tales*

The *Igor Tale*,[31] by far the most famous work of Old Russian literature, is a lyric-rhetorical composition by an unknown author, occasioned by the defeat of Duke Igor of Novgorod-Seversk and three other Russian princes by the Polovetzians on May 12, 1185. The fact that Duke Igor's father-in-law, Yaroslav of Galich, who died October 1, 1187, is referred to as still living suggests that it was composed before that date. The actual events in question are related in the Hypatian chronicle in somewhat greater detail. Igor's ill-advised raid deep into the Polovetzian steppes between the Dnieper and the Don led to an initial success, the capture of a Polovetzian encampment and rich booty. But when the Russians decided to stay the night rather than retreat under the cover of darkness, they found themselves surrounded by the enemy's main force and cut off from water. They fought back for the better part of two days but in the end were overwhelmed. Igor was wounded and taken prisoner. He escaped five months later. His son Vladimir married a daughter of the Polovetzian khan Konchak while in captivity.

The *Igor Tale* survived in a single sixteenth-century copy, bound together with several other works of Old Russian literature including the rare *Action of Devgeny*. It was discovered by Count A. I. Musin-Pushkin in 1795 and published in 1800. The manu-

31. *The tale of the host of Igor, son of Svyatoslav, grandson of Oleg (Slovo o plŭku Igorevĕ, Igorya syna Svyatŭslavlya, vnuka Olĭgova).*

script was destroyed in the Moscow fire of 1812, but a copy prepared for Catherine II remained (it was discovered only in 1864). Both the scribe who copied the sixteenth-century text and the scholars who prepared Catherine's copy and the edition of 1800 had considerable difficulty reading the manuscript. A number of passages have remained impenetrable to this day.

The *Igor Tale*'s generic and stylistic uniqueness has caused some scholars to doubt its authenticity. It has been suggested that the *Igor Tale* was an eighteenth-century fabrication analogous to James McPherson's Ossian and Václav Hanka's "old Czech" manuscripts. The philological evidence for authenticity, however, is conclusive. The later *Zadonshchina*, definitely authentic, is undoubtedly derived from the *Igor Tale*. The language of the *Igor Tale* is genuinely Old Russian, and it contains some realia, such as Turkic words, with which no eighteenth-century scholar could have been familiar.

The *Igor Tale* as a whole is different from any other Old Russian work, though it contains many elements familiar from other texts. The military phraseology is, at least in part, that of Josephus Flavius and the war tales. The author's bitterness at the Russian princes' fratricidal feuds, which prevented them from defending the Russian lands against the common enemy, is shared by other medieval writers. The syntax and rhythmic cadences of the *Igor Tale* are similar to those of the sermons of Cyril of Turov. Some of the proverbial and formulaic expressions found in the text have their parallels in the chronicles. Most of the three-hundred-odd personal and place names found in the tale can be verified from other sources. But there are other elements that are quite unique. The most striking of these is the pervasive introduction of pagan

mythology and its deities, which almost surely excludes the authorship of a cleric.

The *Igor Tale* has many formulaic expressions evidently belonging to the domain of oral poetry, not necessarily Russian: the singer's "tree of thought" linking heaven and earth suggests an Old Norse connection. It also has massive accumulations of devices characteristic of oral poetry—parallelism, repetition acting as a refrain, negative simile ("It wasn't ten falcons he set on a flock of swans, but his wise fingers touching live strings, which of themselves sang the princes' glory"), formulaic epithets, triadic phrasing, metaphoric nature imagery (more than twenty animal and bird species appear, almost always figuratively), the pathetic fallacy (even the Donets River speaks to Igor as he swims across it "like a white drake"), and frequent alliteration. Although all of these devices are found in Russian oral poetry, there are not many instances of direct coincidence between *Igor Tale* and folk poetry as regards specific images, formulaic expressions, or epithets—understandable in view of the fact that the oldest surviving texts of Russian oral poetry were recorded more than four centuries later. Nor are the spirit and style of the *Igor Tale* those of Russian folk poetry. Its point of view is aristocratic rather than popular. Stylistically it is mannered, overladen with verbal ornament and ingenious conceits, whereas the Russian folk song uses its devices sparingly. The *Igor Tale* is a literary work, not recorded oral prose or poetry.

The *Igor Tale* has some epic traits, though it is in prose. In fact, the preamble prepares the reader for an epic, as it invokes the memory of an ancient bard, Boyan.[32] But the many lyric digressions, the absence of con-

---

32. Boyan is generally considered to be a proper name; but in fact it is a *nomen agentis* from *bayati*, "to tell a tale," hence "teller of tales."

tinuous action, and the density of the text are not epic, certainly not in the manner of the oral epic as it has been known since the seventeenth century. Nor does the *Igor Tale* much resemble the war tales, which present episodes from the struggle against the invading Tatars in the manner of the chronicles. The *Igor Tale* is called a *slovo* by its author (or by the scribe who copied it). A *slovo* (literally, "word") is in Old Russian usage any discourse, pamphlet, orison, sermon, or speech—a rhetorical work addressing itself to a specific topic. The topic of the *Igor Tale* is a call for unity among the Russian princes, triggered by yet another crushing defeat caused by the lack of it. But the message is not well focused and is overshadowed by the work's epic and lyric elements.

To borrow a term from modern Russian literature, the *Igor Tale* is a lyric *poema* in rhythmic prose. It has only snatches of narrative relating to Igor's campaign, capture, and escape. It often launches into emotional lyric apostrophes, like "O Russian land, now you have disappeared behind the hills," when Igor's army has reached the point of no return. Many times the narrator digresses to relate the glorious—and the not so glorious—deeds of Igor's ancestors, all verified by the chronicles. Sometimes these digressions relate to the narrator's main concern, the decline of the former authority and glory of the grand dukes of Kiev. The narrator remembers the long-lasting and fateful enmity between the descendants of Yaroslav the Wise and those of Izyaslav of Polotsk and shifts to the uncanny story of Vseslav of Polotsk (1044–1101), who "touched the golden throne of Kiev with his spear" (Vseslav was briefly grand duke of Kiev in 1068) after he had "unlocked the gates of Novgorod, shattered Yaroslav's glory, and leaped like a wolf from Dudutki to the Nemiga River" (where he suffered defeat in 1066).

After a few formulaic lines on the battle on the Nemiga, we learn that "Duke Vseslav sat in judgment over people, governed cities for princes, but himself scoured the land as a wolf at night: he would rove all the way from Kiev to Tmutorokan [a distance of several hundred miles] before the cock would crow, crossing the path of the great Khors [a pagan deity, apparently the sun god] as a wolf, for they would ring the matins at Saint Sophia's in Polotsk and he would hear the bells in Kiev." The *Igor Tale* is addressed to readers who were familiar with the genealogy of Russia's princes and with Russia's past.

Perhaps the most famous passage of the *Igor Tale* is the lament of Yaroslavna, Igor's wife. She fancies herself flying to her husband's side as a seagull "to wash his bloody wounds." In three parallel apostrophes she addresses the wind, the Dnieper River, and the sun, asking them to help her to be reunited with her husband. The intimate connection between human events and natural phenomena seen here permeates the entire text, which gives a sense of the landscape—its hillocks, ravines, rivers, streams, swamps, and lakes. The sky too is alive, with rain and mist, stormclouds and waterspouts, thunder and lightning, and even an eclipse (there was one on May 1, 1185). The *Igor Tale* creates a world that is wholly different from that of the religious literature of medieval Russia, a world which to some extent survived in Russian folk poetry.

The *Igor Tale* is evidence of the wealth, sophistication, and elegance of the secular poetic idiom that existed in Kievan Russia and which, but for the *Igor Tale*, would essentially be lost to us. Whether the *Igor Tale* is a literary masterpiece is a different question. In spite of its relative brevity (about ten printed pages) it has little structure. Its hero hardly emerges as a character, remaining hidden behind an array of poetic commonplaces. The unresolved contradiction between censure of Igor's rash and wrongful action (as seen by Grand Duke Svyatoslav of Kiev in one of the digressions) and sympathy with him does not develop into anything like a tragic conflict. The unity of the *Igor Tale* is stylistic, as the entire text is carried by the same intensity and loftiness of feeling and imagination. There is also a deep and pervasive concern for the Russian land, not any particular region or principality, which finds expression in scornful censure of the Russian princes' attitude where "one brother says to another, 'This is mine, and that is mine too!'" The Russian land, its beauty and plenitude and its distress and sorrow, is the real subject of the *Igor Tale*.

The secondary literature on the *Igor Tale* would fill a library. The tale has been a school text for many generations, and it is a part of the Russian cultural heritage. Aleksandr Borodin's opera *Prince Igor* (1890), with its popular *Polovetzian Dances*, has made the *Igor Tale* internationally known.

The closest thing to the *Igor Tale* that we have from the early period of Russian literature is several thirteenth-century war tales (*voinskie povesti*) about the Tatar invasion. They differ from chronicle passages dealing with the same events not so much by their content as by their composition. The language of the war tales is closer to Slavonic than that of the chronicles and has more biblical quotations. There are more inserted speeches, by princes and others, more pathetic apostrophes to the reader, and more similes and metaphors. Even more than in the chronicles the image of a Russian prince is an idealized stereotype. He is pious, God-fearing, and valiant—a Christian warrior. The battle scenes are also stereotypical, giving no details regarding strategy, weaponry, or troop movements. Victory is always sent by God; defeat is "God's punishment for our sins."

The Tatar invasion was perceived quite differently from the raids of the Polovetzians, with whom Russia had learned to live. Russian princes often allied themselves with Polovetzian khans and married their daughters. The Tatars were an alien, terrifying, and intractable race. The Novgorod Chronicle says, "There came [to the Russian lands] unknown heathens, and nobody knows for sure who they are or whence they came, and what their language be or of what tribe they are, and what their faith is; and they are called Tatars, while others call them Taurmens, and still others Pechenegs" (s.a. 1224). The Tatar invasion is seen as a divine visitation, like a flood or an earthquake, and the struggle against the Tatars is conceived as an opportunity for sacrifice and martyrdom.

The *Orison on the Ruin of Russian Land and on the Death of Grand Duke Yaroslav*, from the 1230s or 1240s, is a fragment of a longer work on the invasion of Russia by the Tatars. It is extant in two copies, both attached to the *Life of Alexander Nevsky*. The *Orison* is a rhetorical invocation to the glory of the Russian lands, describing the beauty of the country, sketching its limits by listing its many neighbors, and telling how they all lived in fear and respect of Russia until the calamity occurred. Here the text breaks off. The rhetoric of this piece resembles that of the *Igor Tale*, but it is too short to allow any further conclusions. Significantly, here as elsewhere the Russian land is defined by its religion: "You have a plenitude of all things, Russian land, O true-believing Christian faith!"

The *Tale of the Destruction of Ryazan by Batu* relates events reported in the chronicles but adds an epic flair by introducing emotionally charged detail, biblical symbolism (such as the "cup of death" [cf. Luke 22:42] to be drained by the faithful), dramatic dialogue, and lengthy laments over the dead. It also contains the story of the heroic battle of a small Russian detachment led by one Evpaty Kolovrat (apparently a fictitious personage, since there is no mention of him in any other source) against the whole Tatar army. The "Tale" is told in the ornate yet vigorous manner of Josephus Flavius.

A Book, Called the Chronicler, written on the fifth day of September, 1237, reports the events of the Tatar invasion from a broad historical perspective extending back to Vladimir I. It refers to several other texts dealing with the Tatar invasion, including the tales of Mercurius of Smolensk and Duke Michael of Chernigov, and adds a story of its own: the legend of the town of Kitezh, which vanished at the time of the Tatar invasion and will remain invisible until the Second Coming of Christ. This particular legend became widespread among Russian Old Believers in northeastern Russia. The text of *A Book, Called the Chronicler* was composed at a much later date than 1237, but the legend contained in it must have originated at the time of the Tatar invasion.

The *Orison on the Recently Sainted Martyr Michael, a Russian Prince, and Theodore, a General of the Former* tells of the martyrdom of Duke Michael of Chernigov and his lieutenant Theodore, who refused to submit to a pagan ritual during an audience with Batu Khan in 1245 and were therefore killed. The story is told in the pathetic style of a eulogy, with ample rhetorical embellishments. Nothing is known about the author, who identifies himself as Father Andrew. He may have accompanied the duke on his fateful journey and witnessed his death.

The earliest extant written version of the *Legend of Mercurius of Smolensk* is from the second half of the fifteenth century, but

the legend is assumed to have arisen in the thirteenth. It is a fusion of folklore, history, and hagiography. The Russian saint shares his day in the calendar with a Byzantine saint of the same name, whose story is similar to his. Mercurius, a virtuous and pious youth, has a vision of the Virgin, who instructs him to attack and rout the host of the approaching Batu Khan. After his victory, he will meet a "beautiful warrior" to whom he is to surrender his arms and who will then behead him. Mercurius will take his head under his arm and walk back to Smolensk. The vision comes true. On his return journey, the headless warrior is jeered at by a young woman. He then dies. His body resists burial until the archbishop of Smolensk has a vision telling him that "whoever sent him out to victory will also bury him," and the warrior-saint's body is miraculously transferred to the local cathedral. The triumphant march of a headless hero is a theme of international folklore; Saint Denis, patron saint of France, is the best-known example. The legend has a historical basis in the fact that Smolensk was never attacked by the Tatars. The language of the legend is that of a saint's life.

Other Works

The *Instruction to His Children* by Vladimir Monomachus (1053–1125),[33] grand duke of Kiev (1113–25), is found in the Laurentian Chronicle, s.a. 1096. A didactic work, it apparently follows the example of the *Instruction* of Xenophon and Mary, found in the *Miscellany* of Svyatoslav of 1076. The *Instruction* was probably written not long before 1125, the year of the grand duke's

33. Vladimir Monomachus was a son of Grand Duke Vsevolod and his wife Anna, daughter of Emperor Constantine Monomachus. Vsevolod's second wife was a Polovetzian princess.

death, since the author says that he is writing it while seated in a sleigh (the dead were transported to their grave by sleigh). The *Instruction* has two rather different parts. In the first, Vladimir, after a perfunctory humility topos, dispenses the conventional wisdom of his religion. Initially he praises the beauty and order of God's world, marveling that God, having created man from dust, still gave each human face a distinctive form and filled forest and steppe with such a variety of animals and birds for man's sustenance and joy, even causing some birds "to migrate to our land from southern climes and into our hands." Vladimir then urges his sons always to thank and praise God and to persist in prayer, even during a wearying ride on horseback, not to forget the poor, not to kill any Christians, not to swear an oath gratuitously (but never to break an oath once sworn), "to treat bishops, priests, and abbots with love, seeking their benediction," and never to yield to the sin of pride. All in all, the spiritual part of the *Instruction* sounds like the work not of Vladimir, a warrior, but of a ghostwriting cleric.

In the second part Vladimir proceeds to things more mundane, though still in the same Christian spirit. He encourages his sons to be affable ("never let a man pass by without giving him a kind word"), to visit the sick, to honor the dead ("for we are all mortal"), and to love their wives without yielding them power over themselves. Most of all, Vladimir warns against sloth, "the mother of all evil." There are some practical details which show that Vladimir is speaking from experience. He advises his sons always to set up their own guards, never to lie down to rest before making sure that their camp is well protected, and to be the first to rise. When urging his sons not to forget any of the good they know and to learn what they do not know, he remembers that his own father had learned five languages (no doubt Greek and Polovetzian were two of them), "for this gives you honor in foreign lands."

The concluding section of the *Instruction* is the most interesting, for in it we seem to hear the old warrior's own voice as he reminisces about the many battles he has fought (he counts eighty-three major campaigns and twenty peace treaties with the Polovetzians) and the injuries he has incurred on his hunting parties. He observes, not without pride, that he has been a ruler who did things himself instead of letting his men do them for him, in war and on the hunt. He has been a ruler who kept a close eye on his governors and officials, "not allowing the powerful to do injustice to any poor peasant or poor widow," keeping his own house in order, and seeing to it that church services were properly performed. The *Instruction* ends with an appeal to put all one's trust in the Lord and to accept the trials of life, and even death, with equanimity.

Vladimir's *Instruction* is not a great work of literature, but it gives evidence of the literacy and the moral ideals of the Kievan upper class. Vladimir always carried his psalter with him (he quotes from it in his *Instruction*) and certainly was imbued with the values of the church. Russians, Christians for less than a hundred years, were no longer barbarians.

The *Supplication of Daniel the Exile*, addressed to Duke Yaroslav Vladimirovich of Pereyaslavl (1213–36), is more important as a document of Russian cultural history of the Kievan period than as a work of verbal art. Its author has not been identified, nor is the purpose of its composition clear. Daniel, in flowery language and with many artful similes and metaphors, sings the praises of a generous prince and complains about his own poverty. He then dispenses words of wisdom on a variety of topics, but mostly on the sorry lot of a man who is afflicted with a wicked wife. Daniel's aphorisms, and particularly those of a misogynous nature, are of the kind found in collections of apothegms such as the Book of Ecclesiastes or the *Tale of Akir the Wise*, the latter of which is also misogynous. Yet Daniel's aphorisms have an added dimension of buffoonery, such as is found in the *ioci monachorum* (monks' jokes) of the West. In fact, he seems to be intentionally misquoting scriptural wisdom or applying it in an absurd context.

The *Supplication* may be read as a rhetorical or even poetic exercise. It breaks down into isocolic lines, often forming a parallelism or an antithesis: "A rich man is known everywhere, even in a strange city, / But a poor man walks unrecognized, even in his own city." As in the case of the *Igor Tale* it is unclear whether the *Supplication* is an exhibit of a literary culture lost to us or merely an isolated individual effort that has reached us by accident.

3

Old Russian Literature: Fourteenth to Sixteenth Centuries

The decline of Kiev started before the Tatar invasion. Andrew (Andrei) Bogolyubsky (r. 1157–74) of Suzdal transferred the site of the grand duchy to Vladimir, one hundred miles east of Moscow. The reasons for the decline of Kiev were manifold. The commerce with Byzantium and the Mediterranean was much reduced, less important than the trade with the Hanseatic League run by the northern cities of Novgorod, Pskov, and Smolensk. Byzantium was now in decline, and relative proximity to it meant less. The Polovetzians controlled the lower course of the Dnieper and periodically raided the Russian lands, causing Russian peasants to seek the safety of the northern forests. The incessant feuds of the Russian princes, who often allied themselves with the Polovetzians, made a shambles of central authority.

The Tatar invasion of the 1230s and the so-called Tatar yoke that followed it caused the Russian north, parts of which the Tatars never reached, to gain in importance at the expense of the devastated south. The duchy of Moscow, insignificant before the fourteenth century, quickly rose to a position of

leadership. In 1325 the see of the metropolitan of all Russia was moved from Vladimir to Moscow.

Moscow's drive for hegemony was nurtured by the memory of Russian unity under Yaroslav the Wise and Vladimir Monomachus of Kiev. Muscovite rulers always insisted that they represented the main line of the dynasty started by Ryurik the Varangian. Not a few other princes could and did raise the same claim. Moscow's quest for supremacy gained momentum when Grand Duke Ivan III (r. 1462–1505) married Zoe Palaeologue, niece of the last emperor of Byzantium, in 1472 and the idea that Moscow was the third Rome, destined to succeed Constantinople as the leader of Orthodox Christendom, became official doctrine. The transformation of the Russian lands into a despotic monarchy under one supreme ruler was made complete by Ivan IV (r. 1533–84), who was the first Russian ruler officially to assume the title of tsar (caesar).

Another development caused by the Tatar invasion was the ascendancy of the grand duchy of Lithuania, whose warrior aristocracy was Lithuanian and pagan into the fourteenth century, but most of whose subjects were Orthodox Russians. In 1386 Jagiello, grand duke of Lithuania, married Jadwiga, heiress to the throne of Poland, and henceforth Poland and Lithuania formed a commonwealth. It is at this stage that one can begin to distinguish three distinct East Slavic nations: the Muscovite (also called Great Russian), the Ukrainian (Little Russian), and the Belorussian (White Russian). The cultures of the Ukraine and Belorussia were now exposed to the ever-increasing influence of the Catholic West, while Muscovy considered itself to be the only rightful guardian of Orthodoxy.

The Hesychast movement in Byzantium,[1] launched in the first half of the fourteenth century and centered in the monasteries of Mount Athos (which housed a colony of Russian monks), resulted, after some sharp controversy, in a decisive victory for conservative Orthodoxy and the monastic ideals of Mount Athos. It also led to a general revival of religious life. Such a revival was very much in evidence in Muscovy, where cultural and economic progress depended largely on the monasteries. The founding of the Monastery of the Holy Trinity in the woods northeast of Moscow by Saint Sergius of Radonezh, who became abbot in 1353 or 1354, was a milestone in a movement that resulted in the founding of eighty monasteries in northeast Russia alone in the fourteenth century (some seventy more were added in the first half of the fifteenth). Many of these monasteries became the nuclei of cities and townships, and they served as a vehicle of Muscovy's eastward expansion.

Through the sixteenth century the monasteries continued to be the only bearers of a literate culture. The Monastery of Saint Cyril on White Lake, founded in 1397, had a library of 212 books in 1489 (a catalog is extant), and that of the Holy Trinity Monastery, probably the richest, had about three hundred volumes. Half the books at Saint Cyril's were liturgical. The Scriptures were represented by eleven volumes, only one of these a book of the Old Testament (Jeremiah). Saints lives, ascetic treatises, the writings of the church fathers, and miscellanies of religions texts comprised the balance. No secular, historical, or scholarly work is listed in the catalog—probably an intentional omission, since we know of several secular texts that were copied at Saint Cyril's at about that time. Almost all the works listed are translations from the Greek.

The Ottoman Turks conquered the Balkan peninsula in the fourteenth century. The Orthodox Serbs and Bulgarians were now under the rule of Muslim infidels, and some of their clergy sought refuge in Russia, where the Tatars did not interfere in religious life and exerted little cultural influence. These South Slavic churchmen were strongly affected by the Hesychast movement and brought with them a new literary style, based on the notion that words are no mere signs but are deeply meaningful in themselves. The leading Bulgarian writer of the fourteenth century was Euthymius (Evfimy), who became patriarch of Trnovo in 1375. Closely associated with the Greek leaders of conservative Hesychasm—Gregory of Sinai, Gregory Palamas, and Philotheus, patriarch of Constantinople, who like Euthymius were at one time monks at Mount Athos—he created models of a new hagiographic style which was soon carried to Russia by his

---

1. From Greek *hesychia*, "silence, quiet, speechlessness." The movement has as its goal full unity with God and saw complete seclusion from the world as the only way to attain it.

disciples Gregory (Grigory) Tsamblak (c. 1364–1450), who became metropolitan of Kiev in 1416, and Cyprian (Kiprian, d. 1406), metropolitan of Moscow since 1390. Gregory wrote the vita of Euthymius and was celebrated for his eloquent sermons. Cyprian created a precedent by rewriting the vita of Peter, first metropolitan of Moscow, originally composed in the old formulaic and austere manner by Prochorus (Prokhor), metropolitan of Rostov (d. 1327).

The new style consciously pursued solemnity, artful complexity, a wealth of metaphor and rhetorical figures, and a high pathos while pointedly neglecting factual biographical detail. This manner was to convey the emotional exaltation and other-worldliness of the Hesychast sensibility. It could easily degenerate into thoughtless rhetorical formalism, as is suggested by the term applied to the new style—*weaving of words* (*pletenie sloves*). The Euthymian style dominated Russian literature during the fifteenth and sixteenth centuries.

Byzantine influence never halted even under the Tatar yoke and in spite of the decline of Byzantium. Greek clerics continued to occupy high positions in the hierarchy of the Russian church, and Russians continued to travel to Constantinople across the Black Sea, now controlled by the Genoese and Venetians. The decisive break that caused Moscow to declare its doctrinal and moral independence from the patriarchate of Constantinople came in connection with the Ecumenical Council and resultant Union of Florence (1439). The head of the Russian delegation to the council, Isidore, metropolitan of Kiev (1437–41), a Greek, was one of the signatories of the union. On his return to Russia Isidore was accused by the Muscovites of having sold out (literally) to the Latins and of having coerced his

Russian colleagues, including Bishop Abraham (Avramy) of Suzdal, to acquiesce in his betrayal. He was deposed and put in prison, and eventually he escaped to the West. When Constantinople fell in 1453, Moscow was ready to declare itself the third Rome and the one remaining bastion of unerring Orthodoxy.

We have several Russian accouts of the Council of Florence. The most interesting of these is a journey (*khozhdenie*) by an anonymous member of the delegation, in the manner of traditional pilgrimage literature. The Russian's wonder at the wealth and beauty of the cities of Western Europe is frank, and there is in his account no trace of the bitterness that accompanied the establishment of the Florentine Union. Bishop Abraham of Suzdal also recorded some of his impressions, specifically a description of religious theater that he had seen in Florence. Another delegate, a monk from Suzdal named Simon, sharply denounced the union in his *Account of the Eighth Council*. It appears from all these accounts and from other Russian sources of the period that the Russian clerics, who knew little Greek and no Latin, hardly understood the theological subtleties brought up in Florence and were mainly concerned with the status and dignity of their church. The Greeks, in mortal danger of being overrun by the Turks, who were closing in on Constantinople, were cast in the role of petitioners. The Muscovites had no reason to join them in this attitude. The author of the *Journey* ingenuously concentrates on reporting how the Russian delegation was respected and honored by secular as well as ecclesiastical authorities.[2]

---

2. See I. Ševčenko, "Intellectual Repercussians of the Council of Florence," *Church History* 24 (1955): 291–323.

The Renaissance and humanism, which had a powerful impact on Poland and significantly affected the Orthodox population of the grand duchy of Lithuania, hardly penetrated to Muscovy. Some individuals came to Muscovy from the West, such as the Italian Aristotele Fioravanti, who brought Renaissance architecture to the Moscow Kremlin in the 1470s, or Maximus (Maksim), a Greek humanist, who was brought to Moscow by Ivan III to serve as a librarian and translator. In general the intellectual gap between Russia and the West was widening, as Russia remained culturally medieval, even though its civil administration and military forces were efficient enough to implement the expansion of the Muscovite state in every direction. Educated Russian churchmen occasionally seem to have realized the backwardness of Russian intellectual life. When Gennadius, archbishop of Novgorod (1485–1505), decided to assemble a Slavonic version of the Old Testament, he had to allow parts of it to be translated from the Vulgate. In an epistle to another cleric, Joasaph, former archbishop of Rostov and Yaroslavl, written in 1489, Gennadius inquires about the availability of a series of texts, noting that "the Latins have got them all."

Poland, until the seventeenth century, was remarkably tolerant of religious minorities and became a refuge to members of the Bohemian Brotherhood and other Protestants. Some Protestant ideas made their way to Russia, and analogous movements seem to have developed spontaneously. There were the *strigolniki* (shearers, allegedly named after the trade of their founder, Deacon Karp) and the *zhidovstvuyushchie* (Judaizers). The shearers were suppressed in 1427; the Judaizers were active during the last quarter of the fifteenth century and were definitively suppressed only in 1504. The center of their activities lay in northwestern Russia (Novgorod and Pskov). They were anticlerical, democratic, and fundamentalist.[3] We know them only through the writings of the churchmen who condemned them.

The basic conflict that dominated Russian public and spiritual life was that between the emerging absolutist state, supported by a church eager to be its willing instrument, and the previously independent city-states and appanage princes, gradually reduced to the status of boyars (feudal lords). These princes were in alliance with a less worldly and more spiritual strain within the church, spearheaded by the hermits beyond the Volga (*zavolzhskie startsy*). The hermits were also identified as the "non-possessors" (of property and secular power). They relied on the authority of Nilus (Nil) Sorsky while the "possessors" followed Joseph (Iosif) Volotsky.

In spite of the destruction wrought by the Tatars and the continuing internecine feuds of the Russian princes, the fourteenth and fifteenth centuries were not culturally regressive or sterile. This is attested not only by the spectacular development of church architecture and fresco as well as icon painting,[4] but also by literature. More trans-

3. A nine-line gnomic poem, signed "Fedor Kuritsyn, deacon" in numerical code, may be a heretical text of the Judaizers. It starts with the words "The soul is free, faith is its bastion." See Ya. S. Lur'e, " 'Laodikiiskoe poslanie' Fedora Kuritsyna," in *Pamyatniki literatury drevnei Rusi: Vtoraya polovina XV veka* (Moscow: Khudozhestvennaya literatura, 1982), 538–39, 675–78.

4. Andrei Rublyov, a monk of the Holy Trinity Monastery who is considered the greatest icon painter ever active in Russia, flourished in the first quarter of the fifteenth century. His fame is rivaled only by that of his older contemporary

lations from the Greek were made, some reaching Russia via the Balkans. The lengthy *Dioptra*, a prose translation of Philip Mono-tropus's eleventh-century verse dialogue, came to Russia from the Balkans in the fourteenth century. Since it is extant in at least 160 manuscripts, with some of the Russian copies dating from the last quarter of the fourteenth century, it may be assumed that it is representative of the intellectual capability of a well-read Russian at the time.

The main section of the *Dioptra* (*Mirror*) is a dialogue of the body and the soul, which argue about their respective importance. The body, which does most of the talking, asserts that without it—lowly and mortal though it may be—the soul could not possibly manifest itself. The body contends that the mind is a bodily organ, its three faculties (memory, imagination, and intellect) localized in the back, the front, and the middle of the brain. When the brain is diseased or ages, the soul loses these faculties. The basic virtues of justice and wisdom, chastity, and courage depend on the drives generated by these faculties. The soul, astonished at the power of the body's arguments, asks the body where it has acquired such knowledge. The body replies that it came into this world a tabula rasa, but followed the precept of Matthew 7:7: "Ask, and it shall be given you; seek, and ye shall find; knock, and it shall be opened unto you." At this stage the body acknowledges that its materialist argument is based on such pagan authorities as Aristotle, Hippocrates, and Galen, and remembers that Gregory of Nyssa, a church father, objected that the mind, an incorporeal entity,

cannot be localized. Only God knows the origin and nature of the soul, which is not made of any of the elements or humors.

The next question asked is, which came first, body or soul? According to Genesis, God first created the body, then planted a soul into it. A parable told by the body illustrates the relationship of God, soul, and body. A king found a naked, feeble, wretched beggar and gave him fine clothes, health, and wealth. But the beggar betrayed his benefactor and began plotting against him. The king punished him by turning him out into a desolate place where he would die, his rags having fallen off him, leaving him totally naked. The beggar is the soul, the king is God, and the clothes are the body. The soul is indeed the real I, created in the image of God, who has given man the capacity to be godlike: "Be ye therefore perfect, even as your Father which is in heaven is perfect" (Matthew 5:48). The principle of the unmoved mover is advanced and the soul defined as "self-moving." A soul that has kept itself pure joins the light of angels once it has left its body, whereas a corrupt soul is cast into the darkness of fallen angels led by Lucifer.

The dialogue then turns to the question of whether Adam was created mortal or immortal. If man were mortal, death could not be the wages of sin (Romans 6:23). But then what about the resurrection of the body? The answer is provided in 1 Corinthians 15:42–44, quoted by the body: "There is a natural body, and there is a spiritual body." There follows an eloquent description of life after the Second Coming, when the bodies of the righteous will lose their infirmities and carnal passions, their sex and age differences, and all hostile feelings, and when men will be like angels. The fate of the wicked is presented in a variant of the para-

---

Theophanes (Feofan) the Greek and Dionysius (Dionisy), a Russian master active toward the end of the fifteenth century.

ble of the wicked husbandmen' (Matthew 21:33–41).

The wide distribution of the *Dioptra* shows that the great philosophers of antiquity were known at least by name,[5] and that by the fourteenth century educated Russians possessed an impressive philosophical vocabulary. It also suggests that medieval Russians had the tools to make basic philosophical discriminations, such as between the noumenal (*mysleny*) and the phenomenal (*vidimy*) world, a materialist and an idealist view of the mind, and principles like the argument of the unmoved mover and the moral ambivalence of human faculties and drives. These very discriminations and principles, however, may be found in the works of the church fathers. Philip Monotropus consistently corroborates his main theses with quotations from Gregory of Nyssa, Gregory of Nazianzus, John Damascene, Basil the Great, and of course Saint Paul.

A much less popular and considerably later source of anthropological speculation is the *Secret of Secrets* (*Tainaya tainykh*), known in the West as the *Secretum secretorum*. Its origins are in an Arabic text of the eighth or ninth century. The Russian translation was made (apparently from the Hebrew) in the late fifteenth or early sixteenth century in western Russia, judging by its language. The work is addressed to Alexander the Great by his teacher Aristotle and is offered as a manual to a successful ruler. We meet here, in spite of many awkward formulations, the basic terms and concepts found in the *Dioptra*:

At first God created free will [*samovlast*, Gr. *autexousia*], spiritual, most complete, and most particular, and made emplastic in it all that is, and called it mind [*um*, Gr. *nous*]. And from the same entity he created its subject, called the soul [*dusha*], also possessing free will in the highest degree. And then in his wisdom he attached it to a sensual body. And he arranged for the body to be like the land, and the mind like a king, and the soul like a governor who travels across the land observing its behavior.

The *Secret of Secrets* ends with a catalog of desirable and undesirable traits, surveying the body from head to foot. Thus Aristotle warns Alexander against any man who is fair-skinned and blue-eyed. "Many Germans are like this," he notes.

An epistle by Basil (Vasily), archbishop of Novgorod, to Theodore (Feodor), bishop of Tver, written in 1347, shows that Russian churchmen gave thought to questions of dogma and could themselves make the discriminations found in the *Dioptra*. Basil instructs Theodore on a point of faith that has been hotly debated in Theodore's diocese. The question is that of the nature of paradise: is it actually a place on earth, or is it an ideal entity? Basil produces a great deal of evidence which satisfies him that the former is true. He quotes from the Bible, the Holy Liturgy, the Lectionary, the works of several church fathers, and such apocryphal texts as the *Book of Enoch*, the *Life and Journey to Paradise of Saint Agapius*, and the *Tale of Macarius of Rome*. He adds some firsthand evidence. On his pilgrimage to Jerusalem he was shown the relics of Adam. It is common knowledge, he declares, that reflections of hellfire are seen often by those who sail the Breathing Sea (the Arctic Ocean with its

5. A *Tale of Aristotle the Wise, Hellenic Philosopher*, containing excerpts mostly from Diogenes Laertes, is attached to some copies of the *Secret of Secrets*. It is purely anecdotal.

frequent displays of the aurora borealis). Moreover, only a generation ago two Novgorod ships, commanded by one Moislav and his son Yakov, returned from a voyage reporting that a storm had carried them to some high mountains of a marvelous azure and shaped like an iconostasis, from behind which a wondrous light shone and joyous singing and rejoicing were heard. Those of the crew who scaled the mountain did not return, and one who was pulled back by his crewmates was dead.

Basil concludes his argument by suggesting that "ideal paradise" exists only for saints who have departed this life, not for saints still in the flesh. Ideal paradise will come to mankind only with the Second Coming of Christ. Basil's brief treatise gives us an insight into the mind of a cultured, well-read, and obviously intelligent cleric. His world is medieval, the boundaries between fact and fiction fluid; sacred texts, and one suspects almost anything in writing, enjoy absolute authority, although subject to interpretation. Basil's empirical knowledge, geographical in this case, is severely limited. It must be understood that the Russian churchman shares these limitations with the best of the Byzantine writers like Michael Psellos.

A collection of miscellaneous tracts from the library of Saint Cyril (1337–1427) of the White Lake (Belozersk) Monastery, possibly compiled by Cyril himself, contains a piece entitled *By Galen, from Hippocrates* (*Galinovo, iz Ipokrata*). It features the theory of the four elements and the four humors, and a system by which the seasons, the ages of man, the basic components of the human mind, and the structure of the universe are derived from these entities. As far as anthropology is concerned, this text largely coincides with the *Dioptra*, even in

its terminology, but it covers more ground. From Alexander of Aphrodisia, for instance, it has a description of the action of semen in the womb and an embryology, including even a mechanism for sex determination.

In a section on cosmology the reader is informed that the universe is like an egg, with the earth the yolk, the air the white, and the heavens the shell. The writer does not see a contradiction between this view and a description of the Ocean River (*reka glagolemaya Okean*), which flows around all of terra firma—"beyond it there is no land." Exact figures are given for the distance from earth to heaven (3,650,000 miles), from north to south, and from east to west. Clouds, earthquakes, the four seas, thunder and lightning, and other natural phenomena are discussed.

Medieval Russia seems to have adopted the Byzantine view of the natural world, essentially still that of Plato's *Timaeus*. The notion that a person's health depended on a proper balance of humors and elements entered the medieval Russian worldview as well. (We know from various sources that a medical profession existed in medieval Russia.) Russians in the Middle Ages sought to synchronize this classical wisdom with Scripture, as the present text does, instead of developing or verifying it through their own observations.

Hagiography

Russian hagiography underwent a distinct change of style in connection with the so-called second South Slavic influence, that is, the ascendancy of the Euthymian style introduced by South Slavic immigrants like Cyprian and Gregory Tsamblak, and later Pachomius Logothete. The principal exponent of the new style was Epiphanius the Wise (Epifany premudry), a contemporary of Cyprian and Gregory. Some of his works were probably edited and revised after his death by Pachomius.

Epiphanius (d. between 1418 and 1422) is known only from his works, the most important of which are the vitae of his teachers, Saint Sergius of Radonezh (c. 1314–92), founder of the Holy Trinity Monastery, and Saint Stephen of Perm (d. 1396). He spent most of his life at the Holy Trinity Monastery, where he must have arrived before the death of Sergius. Before this he apparently was a monk at the Monastery of Gregory the Divine in Rostov, where he met Stephen of Perm. Epiphanius was a well-traveled monk who had been to Mount Athos, Constantinople, and Jerusalem. In his *Life of Saint Stephen of Perm* he says that he "was not brought up in Athens, nor did he learn the weaving of artful rhetorical figures or poetic words from philosophers, nor did he study the dialogues of Plato or Aristotle." But this is part of the obligatory humility topos. Actually, Epiphanius was well read and must have known Greek. Moreover, his style is that of the school of Euthymius, featuring long and convoluted periods (which are, however, grammatically flawless), emotion-laden exclamatory phrases, rhetorical questions, parallelism and antithesis, pleonastic accumulation of images and similes, and what D. S. Likhachev has termed abstract psychologism—elaborate description of the saint's inner life by means of familiar clichés: "And thus he exhausted his body with much abstinence and many labors, and whenever the devil would cause carnal desires to stir in his mind, he would perform even greater ascetic feats and devote all his care to the welfare of that place, so that his labors might be pleasing to God." The narrative is frequently interrupted by rhetorical flourishes in rhythmic prose marked by anaphoric repetition, parallelism, and climactic arrangement. It is saturated with quotations from the Bible and the church fathers, with prayers, and with elaborate metaphors: "He easily sailed across the dark ocean of life and took the ship of his soul to port safely, loaded with spiritual riches, reaching a quiet haven unharmed. On his spiritual wings he soared to the heights of reason, adorning himself with the crown of chastity, and presented himself to the Lord, arriving from death to life."

The *Life of Saint Sergius of Radonezh* combines the traditional encomiastic schema with an unusual amount of factual information (still more may have been edited out by Pachomius Logothete). It has its share of miracles, most of which are remarkable only to a reader who has not read many saints' lives. We hear that the future saint cried in his mother's womb, that he refused to suckle her breast when she had eaten meat, and that he would not drink her milk on Wednesdays and Fridays. In a precise allegorical exegesis of these miracles Epiphanius (or his editor) displays an amazing erudition on miracles performed by saints in their infancy.

The saint was born into a noble family impoverished by the civil strife of the age, was a slow learner (it took a miracle for him to master the art of reading), but had a burning desire to become a monk. He walked deep into the wilderness and built himself a solitary hermitage with his own hands. Initially he had to fight off not only evil spirits but wild animals as well. A bear whom he fed was his only companion for a time. Later Sergius was joined by a few other hermits. Eventually the hermitage became a monastery—the famous Monastery of the Holy Trinity (Troitskaya Lavra), a structured religious community with a well-defined distribution of duties. In the course of its growth Sergius labored diligently not only as its spiritual leader but also as a carpenter, farmer, baker, and tailor. The Holy Trinity Monastery became the model for many other monasteries, several of which were headed by Sergius's disciples. Sergius's actual authority and influence belie the prolific assertions of his reticence and humility found in his vita. He energetically supported the ascendancy of Moscow and encouraged Grand Duke Dimitry to stand up to the Tatars. After victory at the battle of Kulikovo the grand duke rewarded Sergius by establishing yet another monastery. A significant episode is reported toward the end of the holy man's life. A visiting bishop from Constantinople was struck blind when he refused to believe in what others told him about Sergius's great holiness. Sergius himself restored the Greek's eyesight. The self-assertion of Muscovite Russia is obvious here. The Russians were proud to have among themselves as great a luminary as any of the Byzantine saints of old.

Sergius's death, briefly reported, is followed by the usual miracles. His body emits a heavenly perfume, his face shines brightly like snow, and numerous miraculous cures occur immediately. The vita concludes with a long and flowery eulogy. The *Life of Saint Sergius of Radonezh* is a work of huge political and cultural importance. Sergius became the patron saint of Muscovy. In spite of his ascetic life he was a strong precursor of Joseph Volotsky and a mainstay of the ideology of the possessors and of Moscow as the third Rome.

The *Life of Saint Stephen of Perm*, devoted as it is to a lesser figure than Sergius of Radonezh, also shows less of a personal involvement on the part of Epiphanius. Apparently he knew Stephen less intimately than Sergius. Stephen, a missionary who worked among the pagan Finnish tribes of

the northeast, hardly emerges as a person. The *Life of Saint Stephen* contains a good geographic survey of the northeast including its rivers, towns, and ethnic groups. Stephen is credited with having mastered three languages—Russian, Greek, and Permian. For the Permians he created a special alphabet, which is given in the text of the vita. Stephen's duel of wits with a local shaman is reported with humor. The shaman dares the missionary to walk thrugh a fire and to dive under the ice of a frozen river. Stephen calls his bluff by suggesting that they pass the test holding hands. The rhetorical passages of the *Life of Saint Stephen* are, if anything, even more elaborate than those of the *Life of Saint Sergius*. The eulogy is close to being a strophic poem, each strophe devoted to one of the roles played by Saint Stephen—prophet, apostle, baptist, lawgiver, preacher, evangelist, prelate, teacher, and martyr.

Russian hagiography became a vehicle of local traditions and political aspirations, promoting saints reluctantly or never recognized by central authorities (as in the case of Mercurius of Smolensk). The city of Novgorod, fighting for its independence from Moscow, was intent on maintaining a local tradition of religious feats. In the vita of Jonah (Iona), archbishop of Novgorod, written shortly after his death in 1471, we hear that the archbishop made a vigorous effort to engage the services of the Serb Pachomius Logothete to write the vita of Barlaam (d. 1192), founder of the Khutyn Monastery near Novgorod, a saint around whose person a cycle of legends grew. The text lists other vitae commissioned by Jonah and points out that the archbishop "did not spare great expense [in gold and sables] for the sake of the glorious memory of God's saints."

The vita of Jonah shows a prelate actively

engaged in secular politics. In 1463 Jonah traveled to Moscow to defend the freedom of Novgorod before the grand duke and the metropolitan of Moscow. His oration before the grand duke is paraphrased. The conclusion of the vita is more traditional. We hear that after Jonah's death his grave was left open for forty days while requiem services were performed and that during this time the corpse emitted no odor. Therefore the grave was not filled with earth but merely covered with planks. No odor ever developed, and many healings were reported at the gravesite.

Another local favorite of Novgorod was John (Ioann), archbishop of Novgorod from 1167 until his death in 1186. Around his person there developed legends of various miracles which took written form in the fourteenth century. The most famous is the tale of John's trip to Jerusalem on the back of a devil, whom he captured by expert use of the sign of the cross.[6] The devil gets his revenge when he shows himself at the holy man's residence in the shape of a lewd woman.[7] The good people of Novgorod decide to deport their archbishop and put him on a raft that will carry him down the Volkhov River and out of town. John is saved by another miracle: the raft moves up the river instead of down. John's airborne journey is the first record of a theme that is common in Russian folklore, appearing again in the seventeenth-century *Tale of Savva Grudtsyn* and in Gogol's Ukrainian tales.

Whereas most hagiographic works of Novgorod and Pskov back the freedom of these republics, the *Life of Michael of Klopsk* takes a pro-Muscovite position. Michael was a holy fool (*yurodivy*) who lived in the Klopsk Monastery (near Novgorod) for fifty years (c. 1400–1450). His vita is not a conventional saint's life but a series of vignettes from the life of the holy fool. Assorted miracles linked to Michael's presence are reported. His vita, dating from the 1470s, has a clear antiboyar, pro-Moscow bias.

Much as in the West, some of the local saints were of dubious historical credibility, and their formal vitae were based entirely on local traditions instead of on authentic biographic facts. Such is one of the most interesting pieces of Russian hagiography, the *Life of Peter and Fevroniya*, attributed to Erasmus, a monk, initially in Pskov and later in Moscow (fl. 1540–70).[8]

The content of the *Life of Peter and Fevroniya* is unlike that of the usual saint's life except for the introduction and the eulogy. Its plot is a concatenation of a series of themes widely recorded in folk traditions east and west. Duke Paul of Murom learns that his virtuous wife is visited by a dragon who can assume human shape. When Peter, the duke's brother, kills the dragon with a magic sword, some of the dragon's blood spills on him, causing his body to break out

6. *A second tract (slovo) on that same great prelate John, archbishop of Great Novgorod, how he went from Novgorod to Jerusalem in a single night and returned to Novgorod that same night.*

7. The theme occurs elsewhere in Old Russian literature. In a legend told *On the city of Murom and its bishop, how he left for Ryazan*, by Erasmus, author of the *Life of Peter and Fevroniya*, we hear how Basil, a holy man, was framed by the Devil, who was seen leaving his residence in the shape of a woman. When taken down to the Oka River to be put on a boat and sent away into exile, the holy man spread his cloak on the water, stepped on it, and flew away, covering the two hundred miles to Ryazan in six hours.

8. *Tale (povest) of the life of the two new miracle-working saints of Murom, the true-believer, blessed and praiseworthy duke Peter, named David in his monastic state, and his spouse, the true believer, blessed and praiseworthy duchess Fevroniya, named Euphrosyne in her monastic state.*

in sores. All efforts to cure the prince fail until one of his servants comes upon Fevroniya, a young peasant woman, who offers to cure Peter if he will marry her. At this point the theme of the wise woman takes over. Fevroniya, adept at posing and solving riddles, is always a step ahead of her opponent. She instructs Peter to use the ointment that she has prepared on all his sores save one. When the treated sores have all disappeared, he goes back on his promise and promptly suffers a relapse. This time he does marry Fevroniya and is cured for good. After Paul's death Peter succeeds him to the throne of Murom. His boyars, unwilling to have a peasant woman for their duchess, promise Fevroniya anything she wants if she will only renounce her claim to the throne. She asks for only one thing—her husband. Peter prefers exile with his wife to ruling without her. Soon both are recalled to the throne in Murom. After a few further edifying and miraculous episodes, all based on familiar migratory themes, Peter and Fevroniya die on the same day, having taken holy vows and changed their names to David and Euphrosyne. The greatest miracle happens after their death. When Euphrosyne is refused burial in the Murom cathedral and is interred separately from her husband at the local nunnery, their bodies miraculously keep returning to a common sepulchre until allowed to rest there.

The legend of Peter and Fevroniya has little or no historical basis. The inclusion of outright fiction in the vitae of saints, (particularly local saints) was common in Russia as well as in the West. The *Life of Peter and Fevroniya* testifies to the presence in medieval Russia of a rich oral tradition similar to that which in the West led to the *Decameron* and the *Canterbury Tales*.

The hagiographic works just discussed differ from the typical canonical vita in the inordinate role of the fantastic in them. But at least one work diverges from the canon in the opposite direction. It is the account of the last days and the death of Saint Paphnutius (Pafnuty) of Borovsk by his disciple Innocent (Innokenty), which was eventually incorporated into the *vita* of Paphnutius by Vassian Sanin, another disciple.[9] Innocent meticulously records his teacher's every word and move (some of the prayers may have been touched up), every bit of food he takes or refuses. The pathos of the holy man's last days is created by the circumstance that he cannot escape the worldly concerns of his office and for once be alone with God after sixty years of obliging princes and boyars in vain. He expresses his feelings to Innocent when the latter conveys to him the wish of emissaries from the grand duke and other dignitaries to see him and express their concern for his health: "Has not the Lord in his mercy, wishing not to let me, a sinner, die unrepentant, granted me six days for repentance? Will you not grant me peace for one hour, but rather inflict these laymen upon me?" Paphnutius, who in many ways anticipated his disciple Joseph Volotsky, was an ascetic much admired for combining great energy in practical economic activities with genuine spirituality.

The princely vitae of the Muscovite period show less variety and are less interesting than the monastic vitae. The image of the prince is frozen in the abstract Byzantine ideal of the pious autocrat. The *Life of Dimitry Ivanovich, Grand Duke* appears under the year 1389, the year of his death, in several chronicles, but was composed between 1430 and 1450, apparently for polit-

9. Innocent's account was written soon after the saint's death in 1477. Vassian, a brother of Joseph Volotsky, wrote the vita a quarter of a century later.

ical propaganda in the dynastic struggles of that period. The didactic and ideological purpose of the encomium is laid bare at the outset: "I shall make bold to speak without shame of the life of this our Tsar Dimitry, so that you who hear it, tsars and dukes, will learn to emulate his example." The grand duke of Moscow and all Russia, called Donskoi for his victory over the Tatars on the Don River in 1380, hardly emerges as an individual. The emphasis in the vita is entirely on his extraordinary piety. In an extended set of imaginative antitheses the point is made that the grand duke "wore the imperial purple and crown, yet wished every day to wear a monk's habit instead."

Dimitry's military exploits are given brief, almost perfunctory treatment, and the embarrassing failure to prevent the sack of Moscow in 1382 is never mentioned. His last will and testament are presented in the form of a deathbed oration. It is followed by his widow's lament, a rich poetic mixture of popular formulaic phrases and biblical rhetoric. The vita ends with a florid panegyric of the grand duke's many and high virtues, just as a Byzantine writer would eulogize an emperor. In a long tirade the late grand duke is likened to the sun (in an elaborate simile), to an angel, and to many biblical characters (Adam, Seth, Enoch, Noah, Eber, Abraham, Isaac, Joseph, and Moses). In each instance an elegant conceit is allowed to work to Dimitry's advantage. A passage from the eulogy demonstrates the total separation from reality characteristic of the princely vita:

> I believe that he was in no way inferior to a bee dispensing honeyed words, weaving together honeycombs of flowery words to fill the cells of one's heart with sweetness; the wisdom of his words convinced his teachers, and his vision stopped the

mouths of philosophers. No interlocutor was his equal, for he kept God's wisdom in his heart and was His secret interlocutor. He refused to utter harsh words. He spoke little, but understood much. He walked a path worthy of a ruler.

An almost contemporaneous work eulogizing the main rival of Basil (Vasily) II of Moscow (1425–62), Duke Boris Aleksandrovich of Tver (1425–61), strikingly demonstrates the political nature of the princely vita. Written around 1453—that is, in its subject's lifetime—the *Eulogy of the True Believer Grand Duke Boris Aleksandrovich, by Thomas [Foma], a Humble Monk*, clearly promotes Boris's visions of empire. The document consists of six separate pieces, each concentrating on a different aspect of Boris's reign, but all equally adulatory. The first of these makes an effort to establish Boris as a figure of ecumenical renown, quoting diplomatic correspondence between him and Emperor John VIII of Byzantium (1425–48) and reporting on the Florentine Council, at which Russian clerics (among them one Thomas of Tver, conceivably the author himself) were present. Thomas is reported to have read a letter from Boris to the gathered prelates, whereupon each of them gave a florid response praising the Christian virtues, the fame, and the power of the Russian prince. We hear messages, surely fabricated by Thomas himself, from the emperor of Byzantium, from the ecumenical patriarch Joseph, and from some twenty metropolitans including those of Trebizond, Nicomedia, and Nicaea.

Later in the encomium the point is driven home that the excellence of Boris Aleksandrovich as a ruler is such that he can be compared only to the greatest rulers of old—Solomon for wisdom, Tiberius for justice, Leo the Wise for erecting glorious edifices, Caesar Augustus for conducting a census of all his people, Tsar Symeon of Bulgaria for his love of letters, Emperor Constantine for his support of the church. Thomas goes on to discover further virtues in his prince, which he expresses by likening him to various biblical personages. In the section dealing with the military, political, and administrative achievements of the duke's reign, Thomas uses the same panegyric style. Boris is likened to Justinian and to Theodosius the Great. All his actions are shown to have been inspired by the noblest of motives. The duke's enemies—in particular his rival, Duke Dimitry Shemyaka of Moscow—are presented as treacherous villains. The whole document (some thirty printed pages) seems servile and sycophantic to a modern reader; unsympathetic contemporaries probably saw it that way too. But we must keep in mind that much of its manner was formulaic, inherited from Byzantium, and that it was a public relations job rather than a free composition. Because Tver was defeated in the power struggle with Moscow, the eulogy of Duke Boris Aleksandrovich never entered into an official chronicle and is extant in a single copy.

The Pskovian Chronicle contains a *Legend of the True Believer Duke Dovmont and His Valor*, composed toward the end of the fourteenth century. Dovmont, a Lithuanian prince, fled his country after the assassination of Grand Duke Mindovg in 1263. He came to Pskov in 1266, where he let himself be baptized, was elected duke, married a granddaughter of Alexander Nevsky, and was victorious in a long series of campaigns against "heathen Germans, Lithuanians, Estonians, and Karelians." After his death in 1299, he became a legend in Pskov and was venerated there as a local saint. His vita,

in the manner of Alexander Nevsky's, paints the familiar icon of an ideal Christian warrior-prince, with obligatory—though in this case unconvincing—emphasis on Duke Dovmont's exemplary piety.

Josephites and Hermits beyond the Volga

Joseph (Iosif) Sanin, later called Volotsky (1439–1515), came from a prominent family of boyars. Tonsured at Borovsk Monastery by Paphnutius, he succeeded him as abbot, then founded his own monastery at Volokolamsk. A protégé of Grand Duke Ivan III (1462–1505), Joseph was able to obtain ample gifts, land grants, and special privileges for his monastery. As an administrator, churchman, and writer, Joseph stood for the purity of the Orthodox faith, strict adherence to the ritual, a church as the right hand of the monarchy, and church participation in economic, political, and administrative affairs. Joseph had great influence at court and saw to it that Josephites (*iosiflyane*) were appointed to important ecclesiastical and secular positions.

Among Joseph's concerns was the eradication of heresies that were then arising in Muscovy. There was considerable religious and social ferment toward the end of the fifteenth century as the year 7000 from the creation of the world (A.D. 1492) approached: many, including some leading churchmen, thought it would bring the end of the world, whereas others, including the Judaizers, scoffed at this idea.[10] Joseph

10. Archbishop Gennadius of Novgorod (1484–1504), in an epistle addressed to Joasaph, formerly archbishop of Rostov, in 1489, goes into a detailed discussion of millennial chronology, denouncing the Judaizers and others who would not believe that the Second Coming would occur

combatted all heretics, and specifically the Judaizers, with the zeal and the methods of the Spanish Inquisition, of which he approved. Joseph's main work, *The Enlightener* (1494–1506, revised 1510–11), consists of sixteen sermons on heretical doctrines and official measures against heretics. *The Enlightener*, a work of rare power and conviction, had great influence on the subsequent development of the Russian Orthodox church.

In *The Enlightener* Joseph shows himself to be extremely well read. He lists a spate of instances in which men of the church had heretics killed to protect the faithful. His sources are the Bible, patristic literature, and church history, as well as some apocryphal texts.[11] Joseph insists that it is the duty of rulers to suppress heresy. He produces a number of examples where a ruler heeded the urging of the clergy to take such action; in others a ruler's failure to do so had detrimental consequences, starting with King Saul, who spared the life of Agag, king of the Amalekites, a mistake corrected by Samuel (1 Samuel 15:10–33). Joseph is able to produce an impressive array of butchery and torture for the sake of the true faith. His sermons are as remarkable for their erudition and eloquence as they are for their cold bigotry. They are not the work of a naive or crude mind but are quite comparable to antiheretical documents in the West.

Joseph's other major work is a monastic Rule written shortly before his death and hence called his *Spiritual Testament*. It deals mostly with the formal aspects of monastic life. Joseph appears as the same stern and dour man in his epistles, extant in mid-sixteenth-century copies. For example, in a response to a noble lady who had complained about excessive charges for memorial masses for her late husband, declaring that the monastery had been negligent in meeting its obligations, Joseph matter-of-factly gives a precise account of all the expenses incurred by the monastery. He limits moral edification to a minimum and blatantly deals with masses as though they were a commodity.

The party of the Josephites or possessors (*styazhateli*) met with some opposition from the hermits beyond the Volga, whose leader was Nilus (Nil) Maikov, later named Sorsky (1433–1508). The hermits called themselves nonpossessors (*nestyazhateli*).

Nilus was tonsured at the Monastery of Saint Cyril on the White Lake at an early age, spent some time on Mount Athos, and visited Constantinople, where must have been exposed to Hesychast doctrine. Upon his return to the White Lake, Nilus retired to a hermitage on the Sora River (hence Sorsky). He was eventually joined there by other monks, and they became known as the hermits beyond the Volga. Nilus refused to engage in any public activity. But at the church council of 1503 he did speak out on two issues. Although he condemned any heresy as vigorously as Joseph Volotsky, he advocated persuasion instead of persecution as a remedy. He was overruled, and the heretics were violently suppressed in 1504.[12] Nilus also raised the issue of posses-

---

in the year 7000 (A.D. 1492). Gennadius's epistle is characteristic of the medieval attitude still firmly entrenched in Russia. Gennadius was an erudite man, an "intellectual" no doubt, but his thinking was stymied by the letter of the texts he had studied, and he never managed to break through to the factual core of his subject.

11. See chap. 2, n. 14.

12. An extant epistle of the hermits of Saint Cyril's monastery addressed to Grand Duke Vasily Ivanovich in 1504 refutes Joseph's uncompromisingly harsh policy with regard to heretics. It produces counterexamples to those adduced by Joseph and explains that even the harsh measures

sion of land by the church, to which he was opposed. On this issue, too, the position of the hermits beyond the Volga failed to prevail.

Nilus disagreed with Joseph regarding monastic discipline, as a comparison of his *Monastic Rule* with Joseph's shows. Nilus's *Monastic Rule*, usually entitled *Chapters on Mental Activity*, instructs his disciples in both the theory and practice of spiritual purification, whose ultimate aim is to reach the state of spiritual tranquillity (*bezmolvie*, Gr. *hesychia*) that allows divine contemplation. Nilus is less concerned with ritual than with the psychology of ascetic discipline, allowing every monk to choose his own way to salvation. His basic principles are, "Physical action is only the leaf, whereas mental [action] is the fruit" and "He who prays with his lips only, neglecting the mind, prays to the air."

Nilus and his disciples differed from their opponents in other significant respects. Nilus sought the truth in Scripture, specifically in the New Testament, and stood ready to challenge the authority of other texts. Meanwhile the Russian Orthodox church was all too willing to embrace spurious patristic and hagiographic works, even apocryphal ones. Furthermore, the hermits beyond the Volga were apt to write in a Slavonic untouched by the ornamental manner of Pachomius Logothete.

The controversy between the Josephites and the hermits beyond the Volga continued after the death of Joseph and Nilus. The Josephites prevailed and dominated the Russian church during the reign of Ivan IV (1533–84). Macarius, metropolitan of all Russia (1542–63), was a staunch Josephite. Yet the hermits beyond the Volga had created a tradition of asceticism and piety, as well as a distinct literary style, that never quite disappeared from Russian life. Although Nilus was officially canonized only in 1903, the religious sensibility for which he stood had remained alive through the intervening centuries. Dostoevsky's Father Zosima in *The Brothers Karamazov* owes much to Nilus and the tradition he started.[13]

Among the writers who belong to the school of the hermits beyond the Volga, Vassian Patrikeev (d. before 1545), a disciple of Nilus, Maximus the Greek (c. 1475–1556), and Andrew (Andrei) Kurbsky (1528–83) are the most prominent. Vassian, who came from a boyar family, led the opposition to Joseph Volotsky and the possessors. He paid for his action by being sent to Volokolamsk Monastery in 1531, where he died a prisoner of his ideological enemies. Few of his works are extant, all of them polemic tracts under such titles as *A Response to Those Who Slander the Truth of the Gospel, on monastic life and the organization of the church; A Selection from Many Chapters of the Holy Niconian Rules,*[14] *against Joseph Volotsky, by Vassian, a disciple of Nilus Sorsky; and A Selection of Holy Rules, gathered from many books, against Joseph, Abbot of Voloko-*

---

attested to in the Bible were taken under more serious conditions than those now existing in Russia. The most telling argument is that Joseph is neither Moses, nor the prophet Elijah, nor Peter or Paul. The epistle recommends to use prayer instead of resorting to killing in dealing with heretics. The epistle was apparently written (possibly by Vassian Patrikeev) after the church council of 1504 had condemned the heretics, but before they had been executed.

13. Nilus's *Monastic Rule* and the writings of some of the bearers of his ideals, such as Saint Tychon (Tikhon) of Zadonsk (1724–83), are found in George P. Fedotov, *A Treasury of Russian Spirituality*, vol. 2 of his *Collected Works* (Belmont, Mass.: Nordland, 1975).

14. Nicon of Mount Maurus, a Byzantine cleric.

lamsk and his disciples, and answers to various questions, gleaned from books, by that same hermit monk Vassian. The argument, usually conducted in the form of a dialogue between Joseph and Vassian, deals with the meaning and proper form of monastic life. Vassian denounces the secular ambitions of Russian monks, their greed, their lack of compassion for the poor, their practice of usury and exploitation of peasant labor, and their lack of charity and selflessness. Vassian's style is always concretely polemical, not contemplatively abstract as that of his teacher can sometimes be. Yet it is well within the framework of Byzantine rhetoric.

Maximus the Greek (Maksim Grek, c. 1475–1556; his secular name was Michael Trivolis) came to Moscow from Mount Athos in 1518 at the invitation of Grand Duke Basil III, to be his librarian and to help in the revision of translations of sacred texts. He had previously spent years in Italy and was imbued with the spirit of Italian humanism. In Florence he had witnessed the triumph and death at the stake of Girolamo Savonarola in 1498, which left a deep impression on him. In spite of his exposure to humanism Maximus retained a stern dogmatic and ascetic outlook on life. His was definitely a medieval mind. In Russia Maximus quickly acquired a command of Slavonic, though his style remained awkward and his grammar flawed. Apparently he continued to think in Greek. A competent philologist, he soon discovered errors in the texts he had been asked to review. (He had the temerity to make fun of howlers that he found in venerable Slavonic texts.) He was an outspoken opponent of the Muscovite doctrine of the third Rome and voiced the opinion that Moscow had no right to declare itself independent from the patriarchate of Constantinople. This position, as well as the

fact that he had joined the party of the hermits beyond the Volga, soon caused Maximus to fall into disfavor with his ecclesiastical superiors. In 1525 he was tried for heresy by an ecclesiastical tribunal and exiled to Volokolamsk Monastery, a prisoner of the Josephites. In 1531 he was on trial again, this time together with a group of other nonpossessors headed by Vassian Patrikeev. He was charged not only with heresy but also with lese majesty, having insulted the grand duke in his writings. Maximus spent the next seventeen years in chains in various monastery dungeons. Only in 1548, when Macarius replaced Daniel as metropolitan, was his condition alleviated.

Maximus was a prolific writer and translator. He contributed to the *Martyrologue* of Macarius by translating homilies and saints' lives by Symeon Metaphrastes. He wrote a number of didactic tracts on matters of topical interest, for example, one in which he exposed astrology and fortune-telling manuals as frauds.[15] But his primary concerns were the monastic ideal and the Russian polity. He was remarkably outspoken on both.

In a dialogue, *A Dispute on the Essence of Monastic Life, the disputants being Philoctemon and Actemon, viz. a lover of possessions and a nonpossessor*, Maximus vigorously exposes the hypocrisy of the possessors, who offer the excuse that their monastery's land does not belong to them but to the monastic community. He likens the wealth accumulated by monasteries through the exploitation of poor peasants to a harlot who corrupts their spirit.

In a rambling *Terrible and Memorable Tale, by that same monk, Maximus the*

---

15. *A missive (poslanie) by that same monk, Maximus the Greek, to a certain monk, formerly an abbot, on a foreign enticement, called Fortune, and her wheel.*

Greek, on the perfect monastic life Maximus uses his Western experience to present his position on the monastic ideal. Early in this work he tells the story of Saint Bruno and the founding of the Carthusian order. A fairly detailed description of a Carthusian monastery is also given. His description of Carthusian austerity is clearly directed at the Russian possessors. Maximus then tells the story of Savonarola, whose follower he had been as a Dominican monk at San Marco's in Florence. He sees him as a martyr, put to death by the evil Pope Alexander VI. Maximus, passionately devout, must have seen the mundane concerns of Joseph Volotsky as analogous to the power politics of Renaissance popes. Savonarola is presented as a saint and given a lengthy eulogy. The three friars executed in Florence are likened to "ancient defenders of the faith, if only they had not been of the Latin faith." Maximus then points out that he is not telling his story to show the purity and perfection of the Latin faith but merely to demonstrate that a zeal to follow the faith of Christ exists there too. The moral of the story is, "The divine paradise will not admit those who secretly, through extortion and inhumanity, gather themselves treasures of gold and silver here on earth, but will reject them, saying: 'Begone, dogs, sorcerers, fornicators, murderers, and idolators, and all who love and commit falsehood'."

A Homily of Maximus the Greek, expounding at length and with sorrow the Disorders and Unlawful Acts of Rulers and Authorities in Recent Times is an allegory featuring a dialogue between a wanderer "on a hard and woeful journey" and a woman dressed in widow's black sitting by the wayside and weeping bitterly, threatened by ferocious beasts closing in on her. Upon much urging, she tells him of her woes: "My name is not one, but I have many,

for I am called leadership, and power, and rule, and sovereignty, yet my real name, including all these others, is Basileia.[16] I have received this excellent name from the Almighty, because those who hold me ought to be the strength and support of the people under them, and not their destruction and constant peril." She explains that the cause of her sorrow is the abuse of her authority "by earthly powers who are dominated by greed, who practice extortion and torment their subjects by exacting from them money as well as the erection of sumptuous edifices, which are of no use to the assertion of their authority, but merely serve the excessive whims and pleasures of their mischievous souls." She goes on to produce a catalog of crimes committed by the rulers and the mighty of the earth and predicts that they will be punished for their misdeeds. Basileia concludes her diatribe by complaining that she does not have the support of men of God who would stand up for her before earthly rulers—no Samuel, Elijah, Basil the Great, or John Chrysostom, all champions of justice.

Maximus was considered a saint by many of his party, and his memory persisted in spite of the ban imposed on him by the official church. Duke Andrew Kurbsky considered himself Maximus's disciple, and the monk was well regarded by the Old Believers of the seventeenth century and after. His life and works are a melancholy document of the best and the worst in the Muscovy of his age.

Pilgrimages

The pilgrimage (*khozhdenie*) continued as a genre of Russian literature throughout the Moscow period. After the fall of Kiev the

16. Gr. "sovereignty, royal authority."

road to Constantinople went down the Don River to Azov, then on to Kafa (Kerch) and Surozh (Sudak), across the Black Sea to Sinope, and on to Constantinople, which had a permanent Russian colony and a Russian church.[17] Muslim authorities by and large let pilgrims pass unmolested.

Toward the end of the fourteenth century Archimandrite Agraphenius (Agrafeny) of Smolensk visited Jerusalem and left a record of his pilgrimage. In 1389 Ignatius, also of Smolensk, who accompanied Metropolitan Poemen (Pimen) to Constantinople, gave a detailed account of the journey and points of interest in the imperial city. The journey is described as a routine venture. The "Frankish" (Venetian) captain who takes the Russian party across the Black Sea arrests the metropolitan for a debt he had incurred on an earlier trip, but the matter is soon settled amicably. The sight-seeing in Constantinople, led by a tour guide, is portrayed as something less than exciting.

Pilgrimages to the holy places continued in the fifteenth and sixteenth centuries. In 1420 Zosima, a monk of Trotsk in western Russia, traveled to Mount Athos, Constantinople, and Jerusalem and wrote a vivid account of his journey. In 1465–66 a merchant named Vasily visited the holy places and left an interesting travelogue. There were others, too, in the fifteenth century.

In 1558 Archdeacon Gennadius, accompanied by one Vasily Poznyakov and Vasily's son, traveled to Alexandria in response to a visit to Russia by a delegation from Joachim, patriarch of Alexandria, and Macarius, archbishop of Mount Sinai. The account of this journey was written by Poznyakov, since Gennadius had died in Constantinople

on the return to Russia. The most popular of all pilgrimages were those of Trifon Korobeinikov in 1582 and 1593. The first journey took his party to Constantinople and Mount Athos with gifts from Ivan IV for masses to be served for the soul of Tsarevich Ivan Ivanovich, killed by his father. The second trip took Korobeinikov to Palestine to distribute alms in celebration of the birth of Tsarevna Feodosia Feodorovna. For his travelogue Korobeinikov relied on Poznyakov's. It became the definitive pilgrimage, was copied innumerable times, and later went through many printings as a chapbook. More pilgrimages continued to appear in the following centuries.

Afanasy Nikitin's *Journey beyond Three Seas* is extant in three versions, each incorporated into a chronicle. Afanasy, a merchant of Tver about whom we know only what he tells us in his travelogue, traveled widely in the Near East and India from 1468 to 1474. His journey started as a commercial venture with some other Russian merchants. But he lost his goods to river pirates near Astrakhan and instead of returning to Russia went on to Persia across the Caspian Sea. He then traveled to India, where he visited Bidar, Raichur, Gulbarga, and other cities in southern India, and possibly Ethiopia and Muscat in Arabia. He then returned to Persia and home through Anatolia, Trebizond, the Black Sea, and the Crimea. Afanasy died shortly after his return to Russia. Afanasy describes aspects of the life and customs of the places he visited, including dietary and sexual habits, religious ceremonies, rites, festivals, agriculture, and the products of the local economy (fruit, silk, precious stones). Peculiar to Afanasy's travelogue are numerous phrases and whole passages in Turkic and Persian, some of which conceal things he may have wanted to keep private, such as a passage on prostitution in India or his

17. See M. N. Tikhomirov, "Puti iz Rossii v Vizantiyu v XIV–XV vv.," in *Vizantiiskie ocherki*, ed. M. N. Tikhomirov (Moscow: Akademiya nauk SSSR, 1961), 3–33.

expression of dismay at falling into Islamic habits.

Afanasy's travelogue is not a work of art, but it is a remarkable document. Written in a vigorous vernacular, it shows that a fifteenth-century Russian merchant could be quite literate—literate enough to transliterate intelligibly a foreign language into Cyrillic. Afanasy mentions that he lost all his books when he was robbed.[18] His travelogue shows a man keenly interested in foreign ways, without any glaring prejudice, and capable of real religious soul searching.

The Zadonshchina *and Other Works on the Battle of Kulikovo*

On September 8, 1380, a coalition of Russian princes led by Grand Duke Dimitry Ivanovich of Moscow defeated Mamai Khan of the Golden Horde in the battle of Kulikovo (Sandpiper Field) on the Don River. The battle was of no great military significance since the Tatars returned and retained their suzerainty over Russia for another one hundred years, but its moral effect was huge. Thus it was only natural that it became the focus of a cycle of literary works. (Subsequent defeats and humiliations at the hands of the Tatars were reported routinely and matter-of-factly in the chronicles.)

Several brief factual accounts of the battle along with some literary sources were used by a mid-fifteenth-century annalist to write the so-called chronicle tale (*letopisnaya povest*) about the battle. The chronicle tale is filled with biblical quotations and embellished by florid rhetorical figures, imagery,

and emotional apostrophes. It describes the course of the battle with precision up to the point when the Tatars broke through the left wing of the Muscovite army. But the turning point of the battle and the eventual victory of the Muscovites are attributed to a divine miracle: angels shooting fiery arrows came to the aid of the Christian host and saved the day.

A contemporary of the battle, possibly one Sofony of Ryazan, wrote the *Zadonshchina* ("battle beyond the Don") within no more than a few years after the event. Sofony, otherwise unknown, is named as the author in two of the extant copies, whereas the text itself suggests that he may have been the author of a work, now lost, that was used by the actual writer. According to Roman Jakobson's plausible conjecture, the author of the *Zadonshchina* was inspired by the *Igor Tale*, which he had finished copying before he set about writing his own work. Only this supposition can account for the many direct and often clumsy borrowings from the *Igor Tale*. The author made an effort to present his account of a great Russian victory as an antiphon to the defeat of two hundred years earlier, but for the most part he produced a travesty of the original owing to frequent misunderstanding of the historical ambience and poetic spirit of the *Igor Tale*. What poetry there is left is deflated by the insertion of pedestrian facts and religious clichés. The *Zadonshchina*'s principal importance for the study of Old Russian literature is that it provides incontrovertible evidence of the *Igor Tale*'s authenticity.

The *Tale of the Battle with Mamai*,[19]

---

18. The literacy of the Russian merchant class in the Middle Ages is proven by rich finds of birchbark scrolls, particularly in Novgorod. They show that Novgorod burghers routinely communicated among themselves in writing.

19. The text begins with these words: "Here begins the tale of how God granted the Sovereign Grand Duke Dimitry Ivanovich a victory over the heathen Mamai [in a battle] beyond the Don and [of how], through the prayers of the most pure

written during the first quarter of the fifteenth century, when the memory of the event was still alive, gives the most complete account of the battle. It is not a simple historical narrative but an emotion-laden rhetorical composition in which political and military events are presented as a battle of good and evil. The enemy—the infidel Mamai, of course—but also Grand Duke Olgerd of Lithuania (who had died in 1377 but was introduced into the narrative anyway), whose forces were largely Russian, and Duke Oleg of Ryazan are all presented as possessed by Satan and bent upon destroying the Christian faith. The narrator's moral viewpoint is projected onto the speeches of his heroes and villains. In an extended dramatic monologue Duke Oleg reveals his evil designs. He calls himself "accursed" and "worse than the Lithuanian Olgerd," who is of the heretical Latin faith, whereas he, being of the Orthodox faith, should have known better than to withdraw his support from Grand Duke Dimitry. Oleg fears that he will be swallowed by the earth like Svyatopolk of old, murderer of Saints Boris and Gleb, but in the end decides to join the side that is more likely to win.

The narrator uses other artful devices. He invents letters allegedly sent to Mamai Khan by Oleg and Olgerd, as well as the Khan's reply, in which he boasts that even without their help he could "take ancient Jerusalem as did the Chaldeans of old." The narrative is interspersed with many long prayers, exhortations to the Russian princes by Sergius of Radonezh and Metropolitan Cyprian (whom the Grand Duke had actually banned from coming to Moscow), and orations by Grand Duke Dimitry and other princes.

The actual narrative is remarkably close in manner to classical historiography. Omens are reported, the leaders address their troops, and the battle itself is described with many metaphors, similes, and rhetorical embellishments.

Yet another account of the battle of Kulikovo is found in the *Life of Dimitry Ivanovich*, discussed earlier.[20] It is derivative and perfunctory.

Moscow, the Third Rome

The idea that Russia, and Moscow in particular, should assume leadership of the Orthodox world after Constantinople, the second Rome, had betrayed the true faith by entering the Florentine Union (in 1439) and had fallen to the Turkish infidels (in 1453) was a logical corollary of the doctrine, central to Byzantine ideology, that Constantinople was the legitimate heir of the Roman Empire. With Muscovy growing in territory and military might, the continued presence of a strong Byzantine tradition made the thought of empire manifest and attractive. The idea of Russia's succession to imperial power became the subject of several major works of the Muscovite period.

The first work in which the theme of a transfer of imperial regalia appears is known as the *Legend of the Kingdom of Babylon*,[21] which originated in the late fourteenth or early fifteenth century. It tells of the journey of a Greek, an Abkhazian, and a Russian to Babylon, where they enter the royal palace and find the crowns of Nebuchadnezzar.

---

20. See p. 57.

21. *A Tale about Babylon, [and] about three youths. The embassy of King Levky, named Vasily in baptism, which he sent to Babylon to ask for an omen from three holy youths, Ananiah, Azariah, and Meshach.* The "three holy youths" are from Daniel 3: 12–30.

Virgin and the Orthodox Christianity of Russian miracle workers, God exalted the Russian land and put to shame the godless sons of Hagar."

They take these back to King Vasily, who had dispatched them.[22] The story became popular in Russia, and many copies dating from as early as the sixteenth century are extant. In later versions the imperial regalia are explicitly reported to have been taken to Russia. The *Legend of the Kingdom of Babylon* also entered folklore and is known in the form of a folktale.

In the *Legend of the Grand Dukes of Vladimir of Great Russia* the idea of Moscow's ascendancy to imperial power is made explicit. It has been surmised, without actual proof, that the *Legend* was first composed by Pachomius Logothete,[23] sometime in the second half of the fifteenth century. A first short version of the *Legend* appears in an *Epistle* by Spiridon-Sabbas of the 1510s, and the first complete version dates from about 1527. It was included in the official Moscow chronicles and in the *Book of Generations*. The episode about the acquisition of the imperial regalia by Vladimir Monomachus was recited at the coronation of Ivan IV in 1547. The complete *Legend* was used in Muscovite diplomacy.

The narrative begins with Noah and quickly advances to Alexander the Great, who is the son of Nectanab (Nektanav), an Egyptian sorcerer, and Olympias (Alimpiyada), daughter of the king of Ethiopia and consort of Philip of Macedon. Olympias married Byz (Viz), a relative of Nectanab, and bore him a daughter, Antium (Antiya), whereupon Byz founded a city, Byz-Antium (Viz-Antiya), "which is now called Tsargrad."[24]

The next episode has Cleopatra, queen of Egypt, seduce Antony, a Roman general dispatched to Egypt by "Julius, Roman Caesar." Julius then sends his brother Augustus to conquer Antony and Cleopatra's Egypt. Antony is killed, and Cleopatra commits suicide. In the meantime Julius is killed by his generals Brutus (Vrutos), Pompey (Pomply), and Crassus (Kras). The people of Egypt now proclaim Augustus their sovereign. He is invested with the regalia of Sesostris, king of Egypt, the miter of Porus, king of India (which was captured by Alexander), and the mantle of Felix, ruler of the universe (*tsarya Filiksa, vladushchago vselennoyu*).

Augustus had a relative, Prus, to whom he gave the cities of Marborok, Turn, Gdansk, "and many other cities along the river called Neman, which flows into the sea." The "Prussian land," according to the *Legend*, took its name from Prus. A Novgorod "commander" (*voevoda*) named Gostomysl, before his death, asked the people of Novgorod to get themselves a new leader from Prussia. The chosen one was Ryurik, "a descendant of the Roman Caesar Augustus," who came to Novgorod with his brothers Sineus and Truvor and a nephew, Oleg.

From here on the *Legend* is a bird's-eye view of the Russian chronicles. It is reported that Emperor Constantine Monomachus, at war with the Persians and Latins and seeing

---

22. "King Levky, named Vasily" is Leo VI Basileus ("the Philosopher"), of the Greek version of the legend.

23. Pachomius Logothete (Pakhomy Logofet) came to Russia from Mount Athos between 1429 and 1438. He was active first in Novgorod, then at the Holy Trinity Monastery (in the 1440s and 1450s), in Moscow (in the 1460s), and at Saint Cyril's on the White Lake (1462–63). Pachomius was the first professional writer in Russian literature. Though a monk, he was apparently paid handsomely for his work. He was the author of the first version of the *Russian Chronograph*, many saints' lives (Nicon, Metropolitan Alexis, Barlaam of Khutyn, Cyril of the White Lake, and others), eulogies (*pokhvaly*), and liturgies (*sluzhby*), for example, the *Liturgy for Peter and Fevroniya*.

24. The Slavic name of Constantinople, lit. "Imperial City."

his province of Thracia invaded by Vladimir Vsevolodovich, decided to send a delegation to the Russian prince to sue for peace and offer precious gifts: a cross made from the cross on which Christ was crucified, Constantine's own imperial crown on a golden platter, a heart-shaped cup from which Augustus, emperor of Rome, had drunk wine, a necklace that Augustus had worn on his shoulders, and a chain "forged from Arabian gold, and many other imperial gifts." The point is stated clearly: "Since that time and so to this day the grand dukes of Vladimir are crowned with the imperial crown which the Greek emperor Constantine Monomachus sent [to Russia], when [the duke of Vladimir] is made grand duke of all Russia."

The document contains flagrant errors even concerning relatively recent events. Vseslav, not Svyatoslav Igorevich, is reported to have battled the Greeks. Vladimir Vsevolodovich Monomachus is reported as adversary and then friend of Constantine Monomachus, yet he was two years old when the emperor died. The *Legend* ends with a denunciation of the Latin heresy and a declaration of the Orthodox faith: "But we Orthodox Christians profess the Holy Trinity of an eternal [*beznachalny*, "without beginning," Gr. *achronos*] God with His only-begotten Son and the most holy, consubstantial and life-giving Spirit, Whom we believe in and praise and revere as a single deity."

If the *Legend of the Grand Dukes of Vladimir* brings the imperial purple to Russia, the *Tale of the White Cowl of Novgorod* does the same for the symbol of church power. A. V. Cherepnin has suggested that this piece was penned by Demetrius Trachaniotes, a Greek, who had been to Rome as an emissary of Archbishop Gennadius of

Novgorod.[25] Gennadius was suspected, not without reason, of having pro-Latin sympathies. The *Tale of the White Cowl of Novgorod*, intended to clear him of such charges, was a political document. It was also tremendously popular, being extant in some 250 copies.

The involved narrative tells of the peregrinations of the white cowl, emblem of supreme ecclesiastical authority. Pope Sylvester is its first bearer. Pope Tharmus (who must be Formosus, 891–96), installed by King Karul (who must be Charlemagne, 768–814), having embraced the Apollinarian heresy,[26] allows the cowl to fall into oblivion. Another pope orders it burned, but he is prevented from executing his plan and instead has it shipped abroad. After its return to Rome, the pope has more evil designs on the white cowl, but he is stopped by an angel who orders him to ship it to Constantinople. Once there the cowl is in the custody of Patriarch Philotheus (1353–55 and 1364–76). Now the ghosts of Pope Sylvester and Emperor Constantine appear to Philotheus and declare:

Upon the third Rome, which is in the Russian land, the grace of the Holy Spirit has begun to shine. And know you, Philotheus, that all Christians will in the end come together in a single Russian empire, on account of [its] Orthodoxy. For in the years of old, by the will of the earthly emperor, Constantine, of this imperial

25. A. V. Cherepnin, "K voprosu o russkoi publitsistike kontsa XV v.", in *Literatura i obshchestvennaya mysl' drevnei Rusi* (Leningrad, Nauka, 1969), 151–54.

26. The doctrine of Apollinaris (d. A.D. 390), bishop of Laodicea in Syria. He taught that the body of Christ was a spiritualized and exalted form of humanity and also that the logos assumed the place of the human mind in Christ. He was condemned by several synods.

city, the imperial crown was presented to the Russian tsar. But the white cowl shall by the will of Christ the heavenly ruler now be presented to the archbishop of Novgorod.

The recipient of the white cowl is Basil (Vasily), archbishop of Novgorod (1330–42), so the chronology is off by at least a decade even here. The plot of the *Tale of the White Cowl* is, to a modern reader, embarrassingly unimaginative and strained. Its purpose is neither history nor entertainment, nor even moral edification, but political ideology.

The *Epistle to Grand Duke Basil*, by Philotheus (Filofei), a monk from Pskov, opens with an elaborate salutation:

For the church of old Rome fell through the unbelief of Apollinarian heresy; the doors of the church of Constantinople, the second Rome, were smashed open by the poleaxes and hatchets of the sons of Hagar. But now the holy conciliar apostolic church of the third, new Rome of your sovereign empire shines forth brighter than the sun in all the ends of the *oecumene*, proclaiming the Orthodox Christian faith to the whole world.[27]

Then in the exordium we read: "See and hear, pious tsar, how all Christian kingdoms have come together in yours, how two Romes have fallen, while the third stands, and there will not be a fourth." The purpose of the epistle is to urge the grand duke to take action against heretics who do not adhere to the ritual of the church and against sodomites among laymen, "as well as

others, about whom I shall remain silent, but let the reader understand what he will."

Another epistle by Philotheus, this one addressed to the Muscovite governor of Pskov, tells us much more about the ideology of the third Rome. After having responded to his correspondent's question regarding some astrologers' prediction of the impending end of the world, which he dismisses as "blasphemy and idle fancy," he gets to discussing the East-West schism and makes some significant observations. His pièce de résistance is the question of whether the host should be prepared from leavened or unleavened dough. He links the latter (Western) practice directly to the Apollinarian heresy, because it implies that "our Lord Jesus Christ did not receive a human body from the Holy Virgin, but rather passed through her virgin womb as through a chimney, with a ready heavenly body."

In attacking the Latins, Philotheus calls them partners in crime of the Jews, for wasn't Pilate a Latin, as were the soldiers who mocked and tortured Christ? He finds a way to link this accusation to a detail of ritual: "Do not the Latins to this day, when doing their prayers, merely make a small genuflection instead of bowing their head?" (The allusion is to the mock genuflections of Roman soldiers before Christ [Matthew 27:29]).

The epistle concludes with another forceful assertion of the third Rome. Philotheus was well read, and his thinking is not devoid of logic. But his was still a deeply medieval mind.[28] His writings are a striking exhibit of

27. The full title of the work is *An epistle to Grand Duke Basil, on the [correct] execution of the sign of the cross and on Sodomite fornication*. Philotheus lived c. 1465–1542. This epistle was written between 1514 and 1521.

28. Philotheus has a basic knowledge of medieval astronomy and rejects astrology ("under what star a man was born, at a good or at a bad time"). He does so, however, not by using scientific or logical reasoning, but on the authority of Scrip-

the ritualism that was characteristic of Muscovite religious and secular life.

The *Book of Generations of the Imperial Genealogy* was another project initiated by Metropolitan Macarius. It was composed by Athanasius (Afanasy), confessor to Tsar Ivan IV, and completed around 1563. Fourteenth-century panegyrical biographies of Serbian kings, which were known in Russia, may have provided the idea for this work. Its schema is that of a ladder, whose first rung is Ryurik (Ivan IV is the twentieth rung) and which ultimately leads to God.

The preamble sets the tone of the work: "The book of generations of the imperial genealogy of the God-anointed holders of the scepter, who shone in the Russian land in piety, planted by God like trees of paradise near a spring, watered by the right faith, nurtured by godly wisdom and grace, illuminated by divine glory," and so on. The *Book of Generations* is a panegyric recapitulation of the Russian chronicles with an emphasis on genealogical detail—princely marriages, conceptions (sometimes effected through prayer and divine intervention), births, and deaths. The virtues of the rulers introduced in the *Book of Generations* are stereotypical. They are "lovers of Christ," "kind and gracious," "staunch defenders of Orthodoxy," "eradicators of all heresy." The Russian tsar should "unite the domains of neighboring rulers under his rule, while

seeking relations of brotherly love with the most exalted distant monarchs."

The longest and by far the most interesting "generation" is of course that of the reigning sovereign, Ivan IV. The tsar's enemies are duly exposed as power-hungry, greedy, and corrupt, whereas the tsar possesses all conceivable royal and Christian virtues. A remarkable episode is devoted to the miracle-working holy fool Vasily, who walked naked through the streets of Moscow in the heat of summer and in the cold of winter. Terrible fires that destroyed large sections of Moscow are described with great poignancy. Several miracles are reported in connection with the fire of June 21, 1547—the miraculous preservation of the miracle-working icon of the Virgin, known as the Mother-of-God of Vladimir, and her appearance as a vision in the sky above the city.

The language of the *Book of Generations* is in the best tradition of the Euthymian school. Its style is polished, featuring long, virtuosically balanced periods and frequent rhythmic passages. The panegyrical rhetoric often sounds official and even perfunctory, but sometimes a warm pathos breaks through, as in the touching, though wholly imaginary, story of Igor's courtship of Olga. The future grand duchess is presented as a simple maiden who possesses the qualities of courage and dignity that would make her a saint of the Russian Orthodox church. The *Book of Generations* is a masterpiece of political propaganda.

Historiography

The writing of chronicles continued and even expanded in the fifteenth and sixteenth centuries as the chronicle became a consciously and systematically implemented instrument of political power struggles. The

---

ture, 1 Corinthians 15: 40–41 in particular. He says that the apostle, "having been in the very middle of the stars, saw there those very angelic forces, how they maintain an incessant service for man's benefit: some carry the sun, others the moon, still others the stars, while some give direction to the air, winds, clouds, thunder, some carrying water from earth to the clouds, and angels also direct the seasons on earth, so plants may grow, spring and summer, fall and winter." No angels are mentioned by Saint Paul.

grand dukes of Muscovy literally carried their chronicles with them on their expeditions to bolster claims of what they considered their patrimony (*votchina*). In the chronicles they found or fabricated support for those claims. The other side, whether it be Tver or Novgorod or Pskov, justified its claim to independence by its own chronicle. Chronicle writing also continued in western Russia, now part of the grand duchy of Lithuania. A chronicle written in Smolensk in 1446 sees Russian history from the Lithuanian vantage point. Local urban chronicles were kept at various times even in smaller provincial centers like Vitebsk, Mogilev, and Slutsk.[29] In the West Russian chronicles the influence of such Polish historians as Marcin Bielski (1495–1575) was a factor. Bielski's *Universal Chronicle* (*Kronika wszystkiego świata*, 1551) was translated into Russian as early as 1584.

More Byzantine historical works reached Russia, via the Balkans, in the fifteenth century. John Zonaras's twelfth-century manual of world history up to the accession to the throne of John Comnenus in 1118 is based on better sources than the chronicles of Malalas and Hamartolus. The versified chronicle of Constantine Manasses (twelfth century), which goes up to the ascension to the throne of Alexius Comnenus (1081), is unreliable as to its facts,[30] but it has literary qualities. Manasses is fond of elaborate circumlocutions and rhetorical flourishes. He is fascinated by the anecdotal and the lurid and likes to pass summary judgment on historical personages in unctuous moral tirades. He has abandoned the annalistic principle of earlier historians and tells the whole story of a ruler in a single episode. The Slavic text has a number of insertions by the translator relating events of Bulgarian history. Manasses' style apparently influenced a number of authors and works of Bulgarian, Serbian, and Russian literatures: Gregory Tsamblak, Pachomius Logothete Philotheus of Pskov, the *Tale of the Kingdom of Kazan*, the *Tale of the Capture of Pskov*, and others.[31]

With the aid of these additional sources Russia was now ready to compile its own Orthodox world history. A first version was prepared by Pachomius Logothete in 1442. It was followed by several ever-expanding codices. The *Russian Chronograph* of 1512, apparently created at Joseph's Volokolamsk Monastery, is a compilation of biblical history, the *Hellenic and Roman Annalist* (itself a compilation from several sources), the works of Constantine Manasses and John Zonaras, the *Alexandriad* and the *Gesta troianorum* (both in Serbian translations), the vitae of several Serbian kings and archbishops, and existing Russian chronicles. Besides Russia, it covers the ancient Orient, Greece and Rome, Byzantium, Serbia, and Bulgaria—and in connection with

---

29. On West Russian chronicles, see N. N. Ulashchik, *Vvedenie v izuchenie belorussko-litovskogo letopisaniya* (Moscow: Nauka, 1985).

30. We hear, for example, that Priam of Troy sent for help to King David, who declined because he would rather not let his men mingle with "Hellenes and barbarians, people with no knowledge of God, and idolators, fearing that his Jews might be tempted by them, being by nature inclined to such vice."

31. There is a chance that the author of the *Igor Tale* was familiar with Manasses. His preamble, in which he praises the singer of old, Boyan, and regretfully resigns himself to a different mode, has a striking parallel in Manasses, who says that he will not describe the Trojan War as Homer did. For the Slavic version, see *Die slavische Manasses-Chronik*, ed. Joan Bogdan, Slavische Propyläen, 12 (Munich: Fink, 1966), 36. The narrative style of the *Igor Tale* is rather similar to that of Manasses.

these a good deal of Ottoman history. Organized by the reigns of rulers (instead of year by year), it aims at a continuous narrative and achieves this end impressively. The *Russian Chronograph* was copied and expanded well into the seventeenth century. About five hundred copies are extant. Elements of the *Chronograph* were included in the authoritative Nicon chronicle, which reached the year 1558, and the monumental *Illustrated Chronicle* (*Litsevoi letopisnyi svod*), prepared in the 1560s and 1570s.

The concluding chapter of the *Russian Chronograph* of 1512 is a detailed account of the capture of Constantinople by the Turks in 1453.[32] Like other episodes of the Russian chronicles, it was originally an independent work. A postscript names one Nestor Iskander as the author. The *Tale of the Capture of Constantinople* is assumed to be a Russian original. It is written in the familiar idiom of the war tale, with some modern vocabulary (cannons, arquebuses), many Turkish terms, and some Greek words and Grecisms. The narrative is vivid, the inserted prayers and orations eloquent. The conclusion of the *Tale* turns to eschatology, specifically the apocryphal revelations of Methodius of Patara, Leo the Wise, and Daniel the Prophet (not the biblical Book of Daniel), predicting the defeat of the Ishmaelites by a "russet people" (Russian *rusyi*, "light brown, russet," puns with *Rus'*, "Russia"). The *Tale of the Capture of Constantinople* emphasizes that Constantinople fell because of its many sins. It sets the stage for the doctrine of the third Rome.

Chronicle writing, insofar as it dealt with

32. There are other instances in which Byzantine history is incorporated into Russian chronicles. The First Novgorodian Chronicle contains a rather detailed account of the capture of Constantinople by the Crusaders in 1204, apparently based on a Russian eyewitness's story.

contemporary events, became more openly political in the fifteenth century. The official Moscow version of Ivan III's campaign against Novgorod in 1471 summarizes the proceedings at the Novgorod *veche* (popular assembly) in crassly ideologized terms. Those who stand for the ancient freedom of the republic are reported to have said that they would like to be ruled by King Casimir of Poland and are called "traitors, taught by the devil, worse than devils and tempters themselves, inviting the downfall of their own land," as well as "depraved heretics." Their opponents are made to quote almost literally a letter of the grand duke in which he flatly asserts that he owns Novgorod by virtue of his descent from Ryurik and Vladimir. The grand duke's campaign against Novgorod is likened to his great-grandfather's campaign against Mamai Khan, the situation in Novgorod to that in Jerusalem under siege by Titus. Muscovite atrocities (Novgorodian prisoners are forced to cut off each other's noses, lips, and ears, then are sent back to Novgorod as a warning) are reported calmly, without disapproval.

The Novgorodian version of the same events is found in the Fourth Novgorodian Chronicle (the only Novgorodian Chronicle to go beyond 1448). It differs fundamentally from the Muscovite version. Thus the Novgorodians sent for help to the king of Poland only after the Muscovites had launched their attack, and their messenger never reached his destination. This version is the historical truth; the Muscovite version is a fabrication. But when the Novgorodian annalist reports the execution of a traitor who had spiked five Novgorodian cannons, he too observes that the man had fallen prey to the devil's tempting lures.

The North Russian Chronicle of 1472, whose patron was Duke Yury Vasilievich of

Dmitrov (with whose death on 12 September 1472, it ends), is sharply critical of Moscow. Having described an instance of the horrible atrocities ordered by Grand Duke Basil, the annalist observes: "But the multitudes of the people, from boyars and great merchants and clergy down to simple folk, seeing this, were in great fear and awe at this pitiful spectacle, so that the eyes of all were filled with tears, because they had never heard or seen such a thing from a Russian prince, since it was unfitting for a great Orthodox ruler, the only one in the whole world, to mete out such punishment and to shed blood during the High Lenten season." Yet a few lines later we read: "That same year, on March 27, the true believer and Christ lover Duke Basil passed on to his reward." This comment may be ironic, for there are several obvious instances of wry irony found elsewhere in the chronicle. Thus after having talked about a miracle-working prince, at whose grave many people were healed, the annalist tells the story of another "miracle worker," a governor of the city of Yaroslavl, who performed miracles of transforming local land and property into possessions of the grand duke of Moscow.

In 1510 the ancient free city of Pskov was annexed by Moscow without a fight. The people of Pskov had to suspend their veche and surrender the veche bell, symbol of their freedom, to the Muscovites. Three hundred leading citizens of Pskov were deported to Moscow with their families. The city was henceforth to be governed by officials appointed by the grand duke. They ruled the city with brutal force, exacted steep bribes, and disregarded the promises that the Grand Duke had given to the Pskovians. Many citizens became monks and nuns for fear of further reprisals. The chronicler of the Third Pskovian Chronicle reports the events with sorrow and bitterness. He does not recognize the grand duke's right to rule over Pskov and believes that Pskov fell victim to Muscovite treachery. The First Pskovian Chronicle is more restrained, but still does not conceal the sorrow of the people:

> The Pskovians bowed down to the ground and could not give an answer, for their eyes were as full of tears as a mother's breast is with milk, and only the young and senseless were not weeping. Finally they said: "Envoy of the sovereign, with God's help we shall think it over among ourselves and give you an answer tomorrow." And here they fell to weeping bitterly. How didn't their eyes fall to the ground together with their tears, how didn't their hearts burst, torn from their roots!

The *Tale of the Kingdom of Kazan*[33] is, besides the *Zadonshchina*, the only work of pre-seventeenth-century Muscovite literature that shows any inclination toward the heroic. Perhaps this reflects the facts of Muscovy's history.[34] Its anonymous author was a Russian, who according to his own evidence had for many years been a prisoner of the khan of Kazan.[35] The *Tale* presumably was written around 1564, twelve years after the

33. The full title is *A brief account of the beginning of the Kingdom of Kazan, and of the battles and victories of the grand dukes of Moscow over the kings of Kazan, and of the capture of Kazan, recently occurred.*

34. The successes of Muscovy and in particular the lifting of the Tatar yoke took place in a singularly unheroic manner. When Khan Akhmat invaded Muscovy in 1480, the grand duke met him on the Uhra River, a tributary of the Oka. After some indecision both armies retreated, afraid to do battle.

35. This may be a literary invention. His story does not sound convincing.

fall of Kazan in 1552. Some 240 copies are extant under various titles.

Basically a history, the *Tale of the Kingdom of Kazan* generally follows the style of the Russian chronicles. A number of lyric passages, however, place it among the more poetic and rhetorical war tales. The author may have been influenced by Nestor Iskander's *Tale of the Capture of Constantinople*. The passages relating to Muscovy and Ivan IV are entirely in the spirit of the *Legend of the Grand Dukes of Vladimir* and the *Book of Generations*.

The story consists of several loosely connected episodes whose point of view shifts from the Tatar Muslim kingdom of Kazan to Orthodox Muscovy and back. This split point of view extends even to the author's emotional involvement. Tatar atrocities are described sorrowfully and in graphic detail, and the ultimate victory of Russian arms is greeted with pride and joy. Yet the lyric centerpiece of the *Tale* is a lament of the captive queen of Kazan as she is taken away to Moscow. A special episode is devoted to the futile attempt of three thousand Tatar soldiers to break through the Russian lines. Their valor meets with the narrator's sympathy and admiration.

The *Tale of the Kingdom of Kazan*, although it may contain some folkloric elements, is a learned work by the standards of its time. It borrows details from the chronicles (for example, when boasting that Svyatoslav Igorevich had often exacted tribute from "those noble Greeks, who had vanquished illustrious Troy and proud King Xerxes of Persia") and from saints' lives. It is also an eminently political work, as the glory of the tsar is promoted in every possible way. Toward the end there is a striking iconic presentation of the triumphant tsar returning to his capital city: "He was adorned in his full imperial regalia, as on the glorious day of Christ's resurrection, wearing his silver armor and a golden crown, decorated with many pearls and precious stones, and the imperial purple about his shoulders. And there was nothing to be seen at his feet but gold and silver and pearls and precious stones. And no man has ever seen such precious things anywhere, and they astound the minds of all who perceive them."

The *Tale* remained a beacon not only in Russian literature but in the Russian national consciousness as well. It served as the source of Kheraskov's epic, *The Rossiad* (1779), and helped establish the self-image of Muscovite Russia. The following passage curiously anticipated the image of the Russian nation as developed by nineteenth-century Slavophiles:

> The Ishmaelites are skilled [at war]. They learn to fight early on; from childhood do they develop these ways, which is why they were hard and fearless and eager, while we were meek; for they were so blessed by their forefathers Ishmael and Esau the Proud to live by their arms, while we are descended from our kind and meek forefather Jacob. Hence we cannot resist them by force, but meet them with meekness, like Jacob before Esau; but we defeat them with the arms of the Cross.

The *Tale of the Coming of the Lithuanian King Stephen to Pskov*,[36] by an anonymous author, relates the siege of Pskov in 1581 rather in the same manner of the earlier *Tale of the Kingdom of Kazan*, but without that tale's attractive traits. The

36. The full title is *The tale of the coming of the Lithuanian king Stephen, with a a great and prideful host, to the great and glorious city of Pskov, protected by God, and how God saved the city of Pskov, protected by him, from the hands of our enemies, who barely made their escape, by the Grace of the most Eternal Trinity.*

whole account is the most unpleasant propaganda. The enemy is likened to "insatiable hell opening its chasmlike jaws" and is presented as evil incarnate. The absent tsar is glorified ad nauseam in the by now familiar formulaic style. The valiant efforts of his soldiers, described well and in some detail, yield time and again to elaborate hagiographic passages featuring prayers and miracles that saved the city. The fact that the campaign was really an inglorious defeat for Ivan IV is glossed over and has to be retrieved from between the lines: "You are not overpowering us with your force, rather, we are humbled for our sins! For it is said in the *Tale of the Capture of Jerusalem by Titus, Emperor of Rome*, 'Not because God loved Titus, but to punish Jerusalem.'"

Fiction

The fifteenth and sixteenth centuries showed no significant increase in written fiction, either translated or original. Nevertheless, certain additions were made to the list of works known to at least some literate Russians. One of these was the *Alexandriad*, a Hellenistic romance attributed falsely to Callisthenes, a historian who lived c. 370–327 B.C.[37] This work led to several Latin imitations, as well as to medieval *Alexandriads* in many other languages (including Provençal, French, German, and Czech). One version developed in southeastern Europe and reached Russia via Serbia. Some Russians may have known Pseudo-Callisthenes already in the eleventh century, since the chronicles of the twelfth and thirteenth centuries contain formulaic expressions taken from it; but it became widely known only in the fifteenth century.

The Russian version is more muddled than the Serbian, as more errors have crept into the text. The scribe is utterly ignorant of classical antiquity and mauls even the names of major mythological figures like Hermes, Poseidon, Achilles and Ajax. The Greek text had Alexander encounter "monkey-men" (*pithekoi*, Serbian *pitiki*). In the Russian text they became "bird-men" (*ptitsi*) and the manuscript properly shows men with the faces of ducks. There are also ants (*mravii*) large enough to swallow a horse, based on a similar misunderstanding (the Greek word, *myrmex*, has a dual meaning).

In spite of its Christian veneer the *Alexandriad* cannot conceal the fact that its brave, generous, and righteous hero is a "Hellene," a pagan. The church viewed it with misgivings. Even Maximus the Greek, a humanist, warned against it. It was nevertheless popular and was copied many times.

Alexander is the son of the exiled Egyptian king Nectonab, who seduces Philip's spouse Olympias by appearing to her in the disguise of the Egyptian god Ammon.[38] Young Alexander studies the "Iliid" and the "Diosy" (*Iliidu i Diosiyu*) under the tutelage of Aristotle and Menander.[39] The historical facts of his career are badly distorted. The Scythians become *kumane*, that is,

---

37. The Greek text is entitled *Praxeis Alexandrou*, in three books. It may have been inspired by a desire to establish a strong link between the Ptolemaic dynasty of Egypt and the royal house of Macedon. The Russian *Alexandriad* is entitled *The familiar tale of Alexander, King of Macedon and Great Monarch, an example for brave knights to bear*. See *Roman ob Aleksandre Makedonskom po russkoi rukopisi XV veka*, ed. M. I. Botvinnik, Ya. S. Lur'e, and O. V. Tvorogov (Moscow: Nauka, 1965).

38. We know this motif even from the Indian *Panchatantra*.

39. Menander (c. 342–291 B.C.), the leading playwright of the younger Attic comedy, was known through the *Melissa* and other anthologies.

Polovetzians. Alexander goes to Rome, which opens its gates to him voluntarily. In Jerusalem he is greeted by the prophet Jeremiah, who plays a significant role in the narrative. When Alexander seats himself on the Persian throne, he crowns himself with King Solomon's crown.

Alexander visits the Islands of the Blessed, which are populated by the descendants of Seth. Their king is Ivant,[40] a "Rakhman teacher."[41] His subjects are naked, live separate from their women, eat only fruit, and drink only spring water. They display great wisdom and virtue. The Garden of Eden is located there; it is surrounded by a copper mountain and guarded by seraphim wielding fiery swords.

Alexander's action to lock the savage nations (Gog and Magog, and a host of others) out of the *oecumene* is borrowed from the *Revelation of Methodius of Patara*, an apocryphal work falsely attributed to Bishop Methodius and known in Russia as early as the eleventh century. In the account of Alexander's battle with Porus the Russian text lets the Indian king use "one hundred thousand leopards, viz. elephants." (The Serbian text has simply "elephants.") The Russian scribe did not know the Greek word *elephas* and substituted a word he was familiar with, though he did not know its exact meaning. It appears that he, as well as the author of the original, had a rather fuzzy notion of large numbers. The geography of the *Alexandriad* too is vague. The land of Queen Candace, featured in an inserted novella, is located alternately in Ethiopia and in Asia Minor. Alexander is said to have

died "in the land of the Chaldeans near Egypt, in northern Mesopotamia on the river Nile."

The Trojan War was at first known only through John Malalas, and somewhat later through Constantine Manasses. In some copies of Manasses a separate text is inserted, apparently from the Latin, known as the *Parable of the Kings*. It repeats the story of Troy in more detail, carefully eliminating its Hellenic essence. The three goddesses in the judgment of Paris are made into three water nymphs (*vily*); Eris becomes "a very wicked, quarrelsome lady" named Dievoshkordia (Lat. Discordia). The *Parable of the Kings* was probably composed in Croatia.

The Russian *History of Troy (Troyanskaya istoriya)* came to Russia from Serbia. It covers not only the siege of Troy but also a wide range of other myths, like the story of the Argonauts, in the manner of medieval romances. The role of the Olympic gods is reduced almost to nil; Thetis becomes a simple queen (*tsaritsa*). The sources of these medieval versions of the Trojan War, which reached Russia in the fifteenth century, were not the Homeric epics but Hellenistic fabrications attributed to legendary participants of the Trojan War.[42]

The work that finally introduced a broader public to the Trojan War was *Historia destructionis Troiae*, by Guido de Columnis (thirteenth century), a work of great influence in the West. Apparently a complete

---

40. Greek *Euanthes*; Russian Ivant apparently is contaminated with the name of Presbyter John.

41. The *rakhmane* (Brahmins), on whom there is a chapter in the chronicle of George Hamartolus, seem to have captured the Russian imagination early. They became a part of folklore.

42. One was Dictys, a companion of Idomeneus of Crete, whose "manuscript" was "discovered" during the reign of Nero, when an earthquake opened his tomb. See Dictys Cretensis, *Ephemeridos belli troiani libri a Lucio Septimo ex graeco in latinum sermonem translata*, ed. Werner Eisenhut (Leipzig; Teubner, 1958). The other was Dares, a defender of Troy, mentioned by Homer as a priest of Hephaestus. See Dares Phrygius, *De excidio Troiae*, ed. F. Meister (Leipzig; Teubner, 1873).

translation existed in Russia in the early sixteenth century. Almost the complete text was incorporated into the *Illustrated Chronicle* under Ivan IV. The translation was bad—slavish and often missing the correct meaning. But the work soon found Russian imitators nevertheless.

The fifteenth century produced the first examples of what may be considered literature of entertainment, although a moral tendency is always in evidence. This is true of the *Tale of Dracula*, a work of the late fifteenth century. There is a good chance that it was written by Fyodor Kuritsyn, who in 1482–84 led a Russian embassy to Matthias Corvinus, king of Hungary (1458–90). He also saw Stephen the Great, hospodar of Moldavia. The story is told as if by a person who has visited the lands where the action takes place. Events and persons seem real, although the facts are often distorted.

Dracula was Vlad, called Tsepesh, "the Impaler," ruler of a region of Romania identified as Muntenia ("Mountain Country," that is, eastern Walachia) from 1456 to 1462 and again in 1477. Between his two terms he was a prisoner of King Matthias. Reports of Dracula's cruelty reached the West as well as the East. He is mentioned in anonymous German brochures like *On the Great Monster Drakola Waida*, by the Meistersinger Michael Beheim, and in *Hungarian Chronicle*, by the Italian humanist Antonio Bonfini. The Russian story gives no dates, and its readers probably had no idea where the land of Muntenia was located. The horrible cruelties of the Impaler are reported casually. In fact, the impression conveyed is that Dracula is a just ruler and that there is method even in his mad-dog brutality. The modern reader is astonished to read that when the members of a Turkish embassy kept their hats on in Dracula's presence, following the custom in their own land, the Walachian

ruler ordered their headgear nailed to their heads. (Ivan the Terrible was falsely credited with the same feat.) Dracula, according to the tale, lost his soul when he could not bear the "temporal darkness" of his prison (where he amused himself by impaling mice) and embraced the Latin faith to be set free—apparently his cruelties did not stand in the way of "eternal light."

The *Tale of Dracula* is remarkable for the absence of a specific moral or didactic message. It reads as if the writer conceived it as a curiosity that his readers might enjoy. Later the figure of Dracula merged with that of Ivan IV, and the message of calculated cruelty as a necessary element of statecraft became explicit, as in the writings of Ivan Peresvetov.

The *Tale of Three Kings: Arcadius, King Nesmeyan [Laugh-Not] the Proud, and King Borzomysl [Quick-Think] Dmitrievich* is extant in seventeenth-century copies only, but textual evidence suggests that it was composed in the fifteenth century, apparently in Russian, as a version of a widely known anecdote. A simpleton (a boy in this case) solves two riddles posed by a cruel ruler, saving his and his father's lives, and anticipates the third by tricking the king into handing him his sword and regalia, and killing him. The peculiarity of the Russian version lies with the setting of the story. The cruel king of Antiochia is forcing his Orthodox subjects to convert to the Latin faith. They are freed by young Borzomysl, son of Dmitry, a merchant from Constantinople. The story, like other texts of pre-Petrine Russia, displays a shocking ignorance of Catholicism.

More interesting and more modern is the *Tale of a Presbyter Who Fell into Heavy Sin*, a legend which the narrator says was passed on by word of mouth for a long time before he put it down. In fact, it is close in genre to the novella. Timothy, a priest of Vladimir, abuses the confessional to seduce a young woman of good family and flees to Kazan, where he embraces Islam and joins the khan's service. He rises to a high position, inflicting much evil on the Russian people. On one of his expeditions he rides behind his unit and inadvertently starts the hymn "All Creation Rejoices." A Russian youth hiding nearby takes him to be a Russian and leaves his hiding place. Timothy almost kills him but, when the youth pleads for his life, is suddenly overcome by remorse, tells him his story, and asks the youth to act as his messenger to the metropolitan and the grand duke. He would be willing to return to Muscovy if granted a full pardon verified by the grand duke's official seal. When the youth returns with the pardon, Timothy utters more words of remorse and gratitude, collapses, and dies. The youth returns to Moscow to report the edifying ending of the story and is richly rewarded by the grand duke. The tale seems to be an original Russian composition on the theme that the church rejoices more over one repentant sinner than over a hundred righteous men.

The late fifteenth and the sixteenth centuries produced a number of other pieces of fiction based on oral traditions. The *Tale of Luke of Koloch*, was eventually incorporated into several chronicles and into the *Book of Generations*, but it is decidedly novelistic. It tells of the miraculous discovery of a wonder-working icon by a poor peasant named Luke. (Miracle-working icons are a common theme in Old Russian literature.) Luke now travels all over the country with his icon, effecting cures. He acquires great wealth, a mansion, and many servants and starts living the life of a gentleman. He is not afraid to antagonize the men of the local duke. One of them, a bear handler, sets his bear on him. Badly mauled, Luke

repents his pride and lives out his life as a monk in a monastery that he founds with his amassed wealth.

The earliest manuscript of the *Tale of the Hermit who asked for the hand of the King's Daughter* dates from the first third of the sixteenth century. The work is a fusion of a play on Matthew 7:7 ("Ask and it shall be given you") and the familiar theme of the demon in a bottle who is tricked into returning into the bottle after having fulfilled his liberator's wish.

The *Tale of Queen Dinara* is a fictionalized biography of Queen Tamara of Georgia (r. 1184–1212), contaminated with traditions about another queen of Georgia, Dinara (tenth century). It was composed during the first half of the sixteenth century, apparently form stories heard either from Georgian envoys or from monks of the Georgian monastery on Mount Athos. Queen Dinara combines the martial ardor of an Amazon with the prayerful piety of an Orthodox ruler, defeats the king of Persia in battle, decapitates him, and carries his head on her lance to Tabriz, a Persian city. There she captures rich booty, "precious stones and a dish from which they say King Nebuchadnezzar had eaten, and precious pearls, and a large quantity of gold."

Among these and other texts representing a trend toward secular fiction, a *Homily on Hops, by Cyril, a Slavonic Philosopher* stands out on account of its form.[43] Hops (Khmel', the Slavic Bacchus) is made to speak for himself: "I am stronger than any other plant on earth, coming from powerful roots, from a great and multiple family, and my mother was created by God himself. I

43. One of the oldest copies was made by Efrosin, a monk of the monastery of Saint Cyril on the White Lake, in the 1470s. Efrosin copied a number of important texts, including several secular ones, such as the *Tale of Dracula.*

have fine feet and an insatiable belly, my hands embrace the whole earth, and I have a high-minded head and nobody is equal to me in wisdom." This satirical diatribe on the ravages of drunkenness is apparently the earliest example of a secular prose text with inserted rhymed lines, a stylistic trait characteristic of popular narrative.[44]

The Synthesis of Muscovite Culture under Ivan IV

The long reigns of Ivan III (1462–1505), Basil III (1505–33), and Ivan IV (1533–84) were marked by a steady and conscious pursuit of well-defined goals inherited from Byzantium. The monolithic ideological stability of Muscovy under these rulers remained intact through endless, mostly expansionist wars and equally pervasive inner turmoil. The church played a central role in the consolidation of the Muscovite state. It had its hands full with various heresies during much of this period.[45] But they were all suppressed, and conservative Orthodoxy prevailed. The movement of Nilus Sorsky and the hermits beyond the Volga was too purely spiritual and disinterested in worldly affairs to be more than an occasional nui-

sance. Meanwhile church architecture, fresco and icon painting, and church music all flourished, as did religious literature of a conservative encyclopedic kind.

The great literary enterprises of the sixteenth century were initiated by Metropolitan Macarius (1482–1563, metropolitan 1542–63), an active and capable churchman. He also arranged for the first printing press to be established in Muscovite Russia. It produced the first book known to have been printed in Muscovy, the Epistles of the New Testament, in 1564. But the press was destroyed by a Moscow mob soon afterward, and the printers, Ivan Fyodorov and Pyotr Mstislavets, fled to Poland. No more books were printed in Muscovy until the end of the century. The great encyclopedic works initiated by Macarius had to remain in manuscript.[46]

Macarius's finest achievement was the *Great Martyrologue* of 1552, twelve volumes in folio, close to thirty thousand pages in all, and prepared in several copies. It was conceived as analogous to the work of Symeon Metaphrastes (tenth century), much of which was translated. Before its appearance a vast number of local vitae had been used without much discrimination. Now there was a canon upon which later, printed collections were based. The style of the *Great Martyrologue* is polished, ornate,

44. On spoken verse (*skazovy stikh*), see p. 4 above. An example from *Homily on Hops*: Lezha ne moshchno Boga umoliti / chesti i slavy ne poluchiti (Lying down one cannot God's grace obtain, / nor honor and glory gain).

45. From the polemical writings of Zenobius (Zinovy) Otensky, a monk of Otnyaya Pustyn near Novgorod (d. c. 1570), we can gather some information on the heresy of Theodosius (Feodosy) Kosoi (the Cross-eyed), who preached the idea of full equality, rejected the hierarchy of the Church, the Trinity, the sacraments, icons, and even churches—obviously influenced by the doctrines of the Taborites and the Anabaptists. Zenobius, a disciple of Maximus the Greek, is remarkable also for his vivid descriptions of the plight of the common people: crop failures, famine, abuses by corrupt officials, and so on.

46. Meanwhile Russian books had been printed in the West for some time. As early as 1517 Frantsisk Skorina of Polotsk (1490–1541), who had studied medicine in Cracow and Padua, printed in Prague twenty-three books of the Old Testament, under the title *A Russian Bible, produced by Doctor Frantsisk Skorina from the famous city of Polotsk, to the glory of God and to properly instruct all people*. He later added other texts. Skorina's books were burned in Moscow. The first complete Slavonic Bible appeared in Ostrog, in the grand duchy of Lithuania, in 1581.

and rhetorical, Byzantine in the highest degree.

In addition to saints' lives the *Great Martyrologue* contains a variety of devotional readings and other texts that the compilers felt were of religious importance, including the *Emerald* and the *Golden Chain*, collections of excerpts from the church fathers,[47] the *Christian Topography* of Cosmas Indicopleustes, and the polemical writings of Joseph Volotsky. Only about one-half of the sixteenth-century *Martyrologue* has ever been printed. The most notable later edition of the work was prepared by Saint Dimitry of Rostov (1689–1705).

The verbal culture of the age of Macarius corresponds to the style developed by Muscovite culture at large: the heavy, elaborately embroidered robes of the boyars, the intricate court ceremonial, the extremely formalized hierarchy of social relations, even a style of sacred music which had developed from simple psalmody into flowery bel canto with a wide amplitude of pitch and complex rhythmic structure.

Macarius was the initiator of several church councils, of which the council of 1551 was the most important. It produced the *Code of Laws* and the *Stoglav* (*Book of a Hundred Chapters*). The *Stoglav* was composed under the direct supervision of the metropolitan and had been initiated by the grand duke himself: his specific questions, addressed to the assembled council of churchmen, are answered in meticulous detail. The result is a code of religious and ritual rules and moral teachings. One learns from it a great deal about a variety of heresies, superstitions, and folk traditions that the church found it necessary to condemn. One also learns interesting details about the

performance of church services and church music, as well as about iconography and other aspects of religious life.

Muscovite encyclopedic writing extended to the secular sphere. The *Azbukovnik* (from *azbuka*, "alphabet") is an encyclopedia of secular knowledge of the kind a Muscovite needed to be a model subject of the tsar, and the *Domostroi* (a loan translation of Greek *oikonomos*) is a didactic work dealing with the obligations of a paterfamilias.

The *Domostroi* apparently was first composed in Novgorod in the early sixteenth century and later copied, with appropriate modifications, by Sylvester, a monk who was the tsar's confessor and advisor from 1547 to 1553. It may well have arisen in imitation of didactic works by Western humanists, whose ultimate model was Xenophon's *Oeconomicus*. The *Domostroi* is, however, well adapted to Russian life and gives a graphic description of a wealthy Russian household of the time. *Domostroi*'s sixty-four chapters deal with three areas of a paterfamilias's duties: those to ecclesiastical and secular authorities, those to his family, and those related to the management of his household. Its utilitarian quality is emphasized by the preamble: "I, (insert name), bless, and teach, and instruct and enlighten my son, (insert name), and his wife and their children and members of their household to be obedient to all Christian law and to live in justice and purity of conscience." It was thus meant to be copied with proper names inserted.

The *Domostroi* became proverbial as a symbol of the evils of Muscovy as perceived by progressive nineteenth-century ideologues, for some of its admonitions seemed unbearably oppressive. The advisee is asked to "humbly speak the truth before the tsar, as though he were God Himself, and obey

47. From the Byzantine tradition of the *Catenae patrum.*

him in everything" and is authorized to "beat his wife with a whip, having removed her shirt and holding her hands, in accordance with her guilt." But it is also said, in the chapters in question, that a man ought to "honor and pay obeisance to his superiors, respect the middling ones like brothers, treat the feeble and sorrowful with love, love those younger than himself like children, do no evil to any creature of God." Punishment should be inflicted only "for great guilt and calamitous deeds, or for great and terrible disobedience or neglect." The general picture drawn of an ideal household is an attractive one, particularly since it envisages an active paterfamilias who knows his domain well and runs it with care and diligence. The language of the *Domostroi* is close to the vernacular, with enough Slavonic to give it a certain air of authority. It is fluently written and makes for interesting reading.

The great compilations of the age of Ivan IV (The *Book of Generations* and the great sixteenth-century chronicles belong with the texts mentioned here) were a conservative bastion erected against a flood of Western influences: the Reformation, which had found many adherents in neighboring Poland, the Catholic Counter-Reformation, which was then beginning, and the secular humanism of the Renaissance. They defended the values and beliefs of old Russia. Their spirit as well as their style were late Byzantine, of a conservative and ecclesiastical variety.

The sixteenth century saw the first examples of publicistic writing by laymen.[48] One

such writer was Fyodor Karpov, a courtier and diplomat, whose epistles to Maximus the Greek, Metropolitan Daniel (d. 1547, metropolitan 1522–39), and Philotheus of Pskov are extant. Karpov's correspondence with Maximus deals with philosophical and philological topics. In an epistle to Metropolitan Daniel, Karpov energetically champions the duty of the state to take strong action against the lawless (meaning heretics) rather than practice tolerance, quoting Romans 1:32 and Ezekiel 33:5–6 to make his point. He suggests that man has always lived under the law, first that of Nature, then that of Moses, then that of Christ. Hence, without rejecting tolerance outright, Karpov insists on the need for a strong government to protect the weak and the innocent. Karpov's writings are remarkable for frequent references to classical authors, including some awkwardly translated lines from Ovid.[49]

The secular aspect of Muscovite ideology was formulated most forcefully by Ivan Semyonovich Peresvetov, allegedly a Russian nobleman from Lithuania, who came to Moscow around 1538 hoping to make his fortune. There is some doubt as to the reality of Ivan Peresvetov as a person, at least as he presents himself in his writings. An impoverished nobleman and soldier of fortune from what was then Lithuania, he claims to have served Ferdinand I, king of Hungary

48. Clerics too were now more inclined to write on secular affairs. Erasmus, author of the *Life of Peter and Fevroniya*, also wrote a socioeconomic treatise entitled *A directive and geometry to rulers, if they want one* (*Ashche voskhotyat tsarem pravitel'nitsa i zemlemerie*), in which he discusses unfair taxation, excessive burdens imposed on the peasantry, and the evils of drinking. Among his suggestions is one to close all public drinking places since they promote brawls and murder as well as adultery and fornication. These are also places, he writes, where players gather to sing lewd songs and play devilish tunes.

49. D. Freydank, "Zu Wesen und Begriffsbestimmung des russischen Humanismus," *Zeitschrift für Slawistik* 13 (1968), suggests that Karpov had read the *Nicomachean Ethics* and the *Politics* of Aristotle in Latin. Karpov translates *res publica* as *dĕlo narodnoe*, *civitas* as *grazhdanstvo*, and so on.

and Bohemia (1527–38), and Peter IV, hospodar of Walachia (1541–46). There is no record of his service. He also claims to be a descendant of a certain Peresvet, mentioned in the *Tale of the Battle with Mamai*. Peresvetov's Russian shows none of the West Russian traits that by then showed up in the writings of the less literate in the grand duchy of Lithuania. But his works are extant in seventeenth-century copies only, so their language may have been adjusted to Muscovite usage.

Peresvetov's writings have come to us in several collections, the oldest of which is from the 1630s. The most nearly complete includes a *Tale of the Founding of Constantinople*, a *Tale of the Capture of Constantinople* (by Nestor Iskander, not Peresvetov), a *Tale about Books*, a *Tale about Sultan Mahmet*, a first and second *Prophecy of Philosophers and Doctors*, a *Tale about Emperor Constantine*, and two petitions addressed to Tsar Ivan IV. The more interesting of these are the *Tale about Sultan Mahmet* and the petitions, one "small," the other "great". The *Small Petition* offers the tsar military advice, specifically suggesting the introduction of "hussar shields" which will "stop an arrow at close range and a bullet at long range." Peresvetov offers to start production of these shields immediately if the tsar will give him carpenters and other craftsmen to do the job. The *Great Petition* offers the tsar unsolicited advice of a more general nature which more or less corresponds to Ivan's policies: maintaining a standing, well-paid and well-supplied army, substituting appointed judges for hereditary ones, replacing feudal lords with loyal servants, and using draconian measures to put an end to corruption. Peresvetov repeatedly sets the "Turkish Sultan Muhammad" as an example to be emulated—hardly a tactful

way to put his message across. Nonetheless, Peresvetov's *Great Petition* comes close to presenting a synthesis of Muscovite ideology.

Peresvetov's *Tale about Sultan Mahmet* (written c. 1547) begins with the sultan's observations on the cause of the downfall of Emperor Constantine: he was a victim of the greed and corruption of the Greek magnates, whose betrayals and heresies broke the emperor's valor. He recommends harsh punishment for corrupt judges and harsh trials by ordeal or single combat. In the case of single combat the contestants are pushed naked into a dark room in which a single razor is placed: "He who finds it is in the right." The sultan believes that "a ruler cannot sustain his rule without fear."

The sultan's main concern is to keep his army of forty thousand janissaries happy by paying them well. Therefore he makes sure that his treasury is always full, and to that end he keeps his tax collectors happy and honest. Having observed that slaves make poor soldiers, the sultan gave the men who had previously served the emperor reluctantly their freedom and good pay—and they became willing fighters.

Peresvetov leaves no doubt as to the purpose of his essay. He hopes that Ivan IV's Russia will give Orthodoxy a powerful secular arm which will restore the Christian Empire lost by the Greeks. Peresvetov's ideas, not so far removed from Machiavelli's, were of course too blunt to ever serve as official ideology. We have the official version from Ivan IV himself, in his correspondence with Duke Andrew Kurbsky.

After suffering a defeat against the Polish-Lithuanian forces on April 3, 1564, Duke Andrei Mikhailovich Kurbsky (1528–83), a general (*voevoda*) under Ivan IV, defected to the enemy. He entered the service of

King Sigismund of Poland and became active as a publicist attacking Ivan's despotism. Kurbsky, himself of royal lineage, felt at home in the Polish-Lithuanian common-wealth, where the magnates enjoyed full freedom of action and the king's power was severely curtailed. His political views were theirs, particularly since he and his peers had been victims of the *oprichnina*, Ivan's program to convert the domains of the old aristocracy into the tsar's personal posses-sions, which he then redistributed to his loyal servants.

In the West Kurbsky wrote a *History of the Grand Duke of Muscovy* (1576–78), the first Russian historical work governed by a systematically executed plan. But his fame rests with his correspondence with Ivan IV, extant in seventeenth-century copies. Soon after his defection Kurbsky addressed a let-ter to the tsar, in which he accused him of ungodly arrogance and unlawful and unwar-ranted persecution of his most loyal sub-jects. Kurbsky's letter, relatively short and moderate in tone, elicited a lengthy and ferocious response, penned (or dictated) by the tsar. In this rambling and stylistically uneven epistle (it ranges from pompous Sla-vonic to outright vulgarisms) Ivan vigorous-ly stated his position. He believes himself to have received his authority as tsar from God. The empire is his patrimony. It is his sacred duty to preserve the integrity of Orthodoxy and to expand his empire. His subjects, and this includes the boyars, are his servants (the Russian word *rab* used here doubles for "slave"), who owe him unquestioning obedience. Hence, "If you are indeed a righteous and pious man, why did you not choose to accept the suffering which I, a severe ruler, would inflict on you and [thereby] earn the crown of [eternal] life?" He goes on to chide Kurbsky with the exam-

ple of Vasily Shibanov, Kurbsky's servant, who was not afraid to deliver his master's letter to the tsar, knowing that a cruel death awaited him.

Ivan pours out all the venom of his bitter-ness at the humiliations he professes to have suffered from the boyars when still a child (he inherited the throne when only three years old). He concludes the letter with another vituperative tirade in which he final-ly charges that his opponent has left his senses and become "like a rotten vessel which cannot hold anything and is therefore bereft of any wisdom." In spite of its collo-quialisms and even vulgarisms, Ivan's style is an example of "weaving of words" in the manner of Pachomius Logothete. It is convo-luted, florid, emotional, and pompous. There is a tendency to form long periods with multiple embedded sentences resembling Chinese boxes. The tone of Ivan's letters is subject to abrupt shifts from tearful self-pity to righteous wrath, from sanctimonious ex-pressions of piety to bitter sarcasm, from unctuous moralizing to crude invective.

Kurbsky came from the school of Max-imus the Greek and, for this among other reasons, was averse to florid rhetoric. Once in the West, he quickly acquired a Cicero-nian taste for simple elegance and wise mod-eration in the use of rhetorical figures. One of his charges against Ivan is that of illiteracy and barbarity: "[Your letter is composed] so barbarously that it has become a subject of wonder and a laughingstock not only among men of learning and experience but even to any child, particularly since you have dis-patched it to a foreign country, where some men are found who are instructed not only in grammar and rhetoric but in dialectic and philosophical studies as well." Here, for the first time, a Russian writer was expressing a preference for Western learning over traditional Muscovite piety. Duke Andrew Kurbsky was the first Russian "westernizer."

Five letters were exchanged altogether, two by the tsar and three by Kurbsky. Since they have survived only in seventeenth-century copies, presumably edited, this celebrated correspondence ought to be viewed as a statement of warring ideologies as much as an expression of two idiosyncratic personalities. On one side we have autocracy, supported by the Josephite church, and on the other the boyar aristocracy, allied with the movement of the hermits beyond the Volga.

The Muscovite polity and its culture were an imposing achievement. Muscovy had made Byzantine religious culture fully its own and had given it its peculiar Russian imprint. Literature, along with every other aspect of creative endeavor, was like in Byzantium integrated into a stable religious and political system.

Muscovite Russia was now in every way, and most of all culturally, more removed from the West than it had been during the Kievan period. From a Western viewpoint Russia was now decidedly exotic and backward. Russian literature even at the end of the sixteenth century had not progressed beyond its Byzantine heritage. It would take a powerful influx of Western ideas to make Russia and its literature rejoin the mainstream of Western civilization.

Chapter 4

The Seventeenth Century

The Muscovy of Ivan IV had seemed stable and remained so under his son Fyodor (1584–98), the last ruler of the Ryurik dynasty. He was succeeded by Boris Godunov, the tsarina's brother, who was rumored to have hired the assassins who killed the tsarevich, Dimitry, another son of Ivan IV, in 1591. In 1603 a runaway monk from Moscow, Grigory Otrepyev, appeared in Poland declaring himself to be the tsarevich miraculously saved from his assassins. Supported by some Polish magnates, the pretender invaded Muscovy in 1604 at the head of some fifteen hundred Cossacks, Polish soldiers of fortune, and other adventurers. When Godunov died unexpectedly in April 1605, the pretender was recognized by many as the legal successor to the throne; he entered Moscow in triumph on June 20, 1605, and was crowned tsar. He soon made himself unpopular by marrying a Polish noblewoman, surrounding himself with foreigners, and cultivating Western habits. His assassination in a palace revolt in 1606 signaled the beginning of the Time of Troubles, which saw the disintegration of central au-

thority, peasant uprisings, Cossack raids, a Polish invasion that led to the occupation of Moscow, a Swedish force in Novgorod, a collapse of law and order, famine, and general misery. The interregnum and Time of Troubles ended with the election of Michael Romanov as tsar in 1613. The Romanov dynasty was to rule Russia for the next three hundred years.

During the rest of the seventeenth century the Romanovs continued the expansionist policies of Ivan IV, smothered inner dissent, overcame a schism within the Russian church, survived several major urban and peasant revolts, and cautiously led Russia toward its future as a major European power. Under the first Romanovs Russia developed the social structure that one meets even in the literature of the first half of the nineteenth century. The church was now fully under the tsar's control. The old boyar aristocracy was ceding its place to a new class of nobles (*dvoryanstvo*), who had been granted their land by the tsar and were obliged to serve him at his discretion. The peasantry was definitively reduced to serfdom by the Law Code of 1649. The peasant commune (*mir*) became institutionalized, largely because the village community, not the individual household, was now held responsible for the payment of taxes and other obligations. As the condition of the peasantry deteriorated, peasant discontent led to uprisings, like the one headed by Stepan Razin on the Volga in 1667–1671, and to the flight of peasants to the fringes of the empire, where they would join Cossack settlements, which were free of government control. The Old Believer movement late in the century caused large groups of people to flee to remote areas of the northeast. The persecution of *skomorokhi* (traveling players) under Tsar Alexis also drove them into the virgin forests of the north, where they preserved the epic tradition started in Kiev centuries earlier.

Urban life was changing as well. There was more taxation and more government control of the crafts and trades. In Moscow Russian merchants and artisans now had to compete with a sizable community of immigrants from the West, mostly German but also Swiss and Scottish. The "German suburb" (*nemetskaya sloboda*, literally, "German liberty") of Moscow was a permanent focus of Western influence. It was here that Tsarevich Peter became a determined westernizer. The tsar's standing army of mercenaries had many foreign officers.

Russia now had permanent diplomatic relations with the West. The presence of foreign diplomats in Moscow and foreign travel by Russian delegations led to the presence of bilingual or multilingual individuals in Muscovy. Lithuania had entered into even closer ties with Poland in the Union of Lublin (1569), and the upper and middle classes of this area were becoming progressively Polonized. The Union of Brześć-Litewsk (1596) created the Uniate church, which

recognized the primacy of the pope while retaining the Slavonic liturgy, married parish priests, and other elements of the Orthodox tradition. Polish culture spread across the border into Muscovy. This process was enhanced by the migration to Muscovy of many Ukrainian and Belorussian clerics who had been educated at the Kiev Academy or at other schools outside Muscovy. These men spoke and wrote Latin and Polish besides Slavonic and their native tongue. Since they were in the forefront of the nascent modern Russian literature, their linguistic usages were reflected in the development of literary Russian.

The seventeenth century saw the founding of the first schools in Muscovy. In 1648 Fyodor Rtishchev, a boyar, organized a short-lived school of the Kievan type at Saint Andrew's Church near Moscow. In the 1650s Patriarch Nicon had his protégé Arsenius, a Greek monk educated in Italy, establish a school, also short-lived, in which Greek and Latin were taught. In 1665 Symeon Polotsky founded the Zaikonospasskaya School,[1] which taught Latin, rhetoric, and poetics, among other subjects. The school was attended by some government clerks, among them Sylvester Medvedev. Although closed in 1668, it reopened at the same location in 1682, with Medvedev in charge, and by 1686 he had twenty-three students. Polotsky and, after his death in 1680, Medvedev actually planned to start a school of higher learning. Nothing came of the projected "university," as Medvedev's patron, Tsar Fyodor, died in 1682. But Medvedev continued to teach at his school, in the "Latin" style. Greek was taught at a school founded at the government printing house in 1681. Its first teacher was Timothy,

1. The school was named after its location, Our Savior Monastery behind the Icon Shops (*Spasskii monastyr' za ikonnym ryadom*).

a Russian monk, who had spent years at Mount Athos and in Palestine. In 1685 the brothers Ioannikios and Sophronios Lichudis arrived in Moscow from Venice and soon opened their Greek school with Patriarch Ioakim's strong support. It was perceived as a counterweight to the burgeoning Latin influence. The Lichudis' school eventually merged with Medvedev's and became the Slavonic-Greco-Latin Academy (a seminary, really), which well into the eighteenth century was Muscovy's leading educational institution. Trediakovsky and Lomonosov were among its alumni. It taught Latin, which allowed its graduates to embark on academic studies in the West, where academic lectures were still conducted in Latin.

The seventeenth century shows the influx of Western culture on a broad front. In church music polyphony was introduced, though not without objection from conservative churchmen. Russian icons began to resemble religious paintings of the Western baroque. Painters of the official, Niconian school, such as Simon Ushakov, court painter to Tsar Alexis, consciously pursued "well-shaped painting of holy icons" and the art of painting "lifelike" human likenesses, obtaining a "well-formed image."[2] Polotsky was a strong supporter of the new style and closely collaborated with Ushakov, who also illustrated his *Psalter.* He may have coauthored, with Ushakov, *A Tract Addressed to a Conscientious Lover of Icon Painting*, which energetically advocates the new "beautiful" style. The new style was violently attacked by churchmen of the old school, Old Believers in particular, who saw it as a betrayal of the ascetic ideals of the Orthodox church.

Through virtually all of the seventeenth century Russian literature remained in manuscript. A permanent printing house was established in Moscow under the first Romanov. It was operated as a government agency, called *pechatny dvor* (literally, "printing court"). In the entire seventeenth century a total of 483 books was printed. Of these, fourteen were secular, including eight primers (the first in 1634), the Slavonic grammar of Melety Smotritsky (1648), and the Law Code of 1649. In the late 1670s Polotsky established a special printshop (the "upstairs printshop"), which produced six books between 1677 and 1683, all either written or sponsored by him, among them his *Versified Psalter* (1680) and his prose works *Spiritual Dinner* (1681) and *Spiritual Vesper* (1683).[3]

In spite of these advances Russia still appeared to be an exotic and barbarian

2. A. N. Robinson, *Bor'ba idei v russkoi literature XVII veka* (Moscow: Nauka, 1974), 290.

3. A. M. Panchenko, *Russkaya stikhotvornaya kul'tura XVII veka* (Leningrad: Nauka, 1973), 146–47. An undated and anonymous manuscript, *An Account of the Production of Printed Books* (*Skazanie izvestno o voobrazhenii knig pechatnogo dela*), assumed to have been composed during the reign of the first Romanov, gives little factual detail and a great deal of panegyrics to tsars Ivan IV and Michael. It presents the history of Muscovite printing as if it continued without interruption from 1561 until the press was destroyed by the Poles in 1611. In 1613, it is then reported, a small printing shop operated in Nizhny Novgorod by one Nikita Fofanov was transferred to Moscow by order of the tsar. It is indicated that Fofanov had fled to Nizhny Novgorod from Moscow. Ivan Fyodorov, who had started a printing press in Moscow under Ivan IV but left in 1565 to continue his work in the Polish-Lithuanian commonwealth, also wrote a brief *Account which explains where this printing press had its beginning and how it came to fruition* (*Siya ubo povest' iz"yavlyaet, otkudu nachasya i kako s"vershisya drukarnya siya*), which he attached as an afterword to an edition of the Epistles printed in Lwów in 1574. Fyodorov's main achievement was the Ostrog Bible of 1581.

country to the Western traveler. Adam Olearius, member of a Holsteinian diplomatic mission from 1635 to 1639, wrote: "If one observes the Russians with regard to their mentality, customs, and life-style, one must properly count them among the barbarians. Nor can one credit them with what has been held to be true of the Greeks of old, with whom they boast to be linked by origin and culture, while having accepted neither their language nor their art, namely, that they were the only intelligent and refined nation, while all others, not being Greek, were barbarians. For the Russians have no liking for the liberal arts and sciences and have little desire to engage in their pursuit."[4] Olearius. was a sharp and sympathetic observer. At the time when he visited Russia, the gap between Russia and the West was wider than ever, owing as much to the rapid progress of the West as to the much slower pace at which Russia was moving in the same direction. The West had universities, science, literature in the vernacular, secular music, and theater. Russia had none of these. Slavonic was still used in literary discourse, while the Russian vernacular prevailed in the officialese of the tsar's chancelleries.

Russia was still leaning on its Byzantine traditions. The schism in the Russian church occurred when Patriarch Nicon sought to make the Russian liturgy and ritual conform to the practices of the Greek church. The Greeks, however, were now themselves culturally behind the times and had little to offer to the Russians.

Russian xenophobia did not extend to things practical (the military, commerce, technology, tobacco, hard liquor), but it was

4. Adam Olearius, *Vermehrte neue Beschreibung der Muscowitischen und Persischen Reyse* (Schleszwig: Johan Holwein, 1656), 184 (my translation).

strong in the cultural sphere. It was Russia's aversion to embrace the humanistic culture of the West that caused Olearius to call Russians "barbarians." The Romanovs had a military, administrative, and fiscal organization that allowed them to control a huge territory and to conduct an aggressive foreign policy. Politically, Russia was ready to join absolutist Europe. Developments in Russian religious life showed some remarkable parallels to the West. But in the area of humanistic culture Russia was appallingly backward. The first pieces of Western secular literature to reach the Russian upper classes, and specifically the tsar's court, were romances of the kind that in the West had been folk literature for some time. The first court theater established under Tsar Alexis had a repertoire that would have made it folk theater in the West. Much of the poetry of Symeon Polotsky, Russia's first court poet, was of the kind that in the West would have been addressed to the people rather than to an educated elite. The reasons for Russia's cultural backwardness were the near absence of schools of any kind and the total absence of secular learning, xenophobia nurtured by the bigotry of most of the leaders of the church, and the church's negative attitude toward secular art and literature. Having had no Renaissance, no humanist movement, and no Reformation, Russia had remained culturally medieval.

The Byzantine Heritage

Throughout the seventeenth century the traditional genres of Old Russian literature continued to be cultivated, though with somewhat diminished vigor and not without contamination by Western influences. New collections of saints' lives were produced, with an emphasis on native saints. Saint Dimitry of Rostov, a Ukrainian cleric active in Muscovy, compiled, edited, and prepared for print a twelve-volume edition of the *Martyrologue* (1689–1705). Its language is basically the Slavonic taught at the Kiev Academy, of which he was an alumnus. It was based on the *Martyrologue* of Macarius as well as on the Russian *Lectionary*, but Dimitry also used Catholic Polish sources. The *Kiev Paterikon* received its final, printed redaction in 1661 under the editorship of Innocent (Innokenty) Gizel, abbot of the Kiev Cave Monastery from 1656 until his death in 1683.

The saint's life was now developing offshoots that pointed toward a secularization of the genre. The vita of Yulianiya Osoryina-Lazarevskaya (d. 1604), written by her son Kallistrat Osoryin in the 1620s or 1630s, is a mixture of family saga and saint's life. Osoryin, a boyar layman, tells the story of a saintly woman who since her childhood possessed all the virtues of an ascetic. She was married, though, and bore her husband sons and daughters. As the mistress of a large household Yulianiya selflessly helped the poor in times of famine and pestilence. After her husband's death she continued her charitable work and added to it various ascetic practices, such as wearing only light clothes in the coldest winter and mortifying the flesh by self-inflicted pain. True to the tradition of the saint's life, Yulianiya is reported to have had heavenly visions, but also to have suffered several diabolic visitations, which she triumphantly repulsed. Her death and burial were accompanied by the familiar phenomena recorded in saints' lives, such as a sweet perfume emitted by a body that refused to decay. The language of the *Life of Yulianiya Lazarevskaya* is Slavonic, and it has all the ingredients of a canonical saint's life. But it is also a biography, albeit idealized, and depicts the reality of the secular world in which Yulianiya lived. The vita of Yulianiya was only one of several seventeenth-century works combining vita and biography. More examples will be discussed in connection with Old Believer literature.

The genre of the pious pilgrimage stayed alive. Existent texts continued to be copied, and some new ones were added, such as the *Proscynetarium* of Arsenius Sukhanov, a Greek monk who was sent to the holy places by Patriarch Nicon to research the liturgical and ritual practices of the Greek church. Arsenius's career was not atypical for a seventeenth-century Russian cleric. He was educated in Italy in the Catholic faith, converted to Orthodoxy and made a career in the Russian Church under Nicon, then fell into disgrace together with him.

The sermon, which had become neglected in the fifteenth and sixteenth centuries, experienced a strong revival in western Russia, stimulated by the need to defend Orthodoxy against the inroads made by active Catholic proselytizing. Such Ukrainian and Belorussian clerics as Symeon Polotsky, Stefan Yavorsky, and Feofan Prokopovich brought the art of religious eloquence with them when they took up high ecclesiastical positions in Muscovy.

Historical Works

The tradition of chronicle writing also continued in the seventeenth century. It was terminated only by a ukase of Peter the Great. One of the principal chronicles, the Niconian, takes its account as far as 1630. As late as 1678 Tychon (Tikhon), archimandrite of Saint Macarius Monastery, completed an updated version of the *Book of Generations.* The government kept its own official *Record of the Grand Dukes and Tsars of Russia, Whence Came the Roots of Their Sovereignty*, also referred to as the *Great Book of State*, composed by Artamon

Matveev, closest adviser to Tsar Alexis. It was in official use with the foreign service (*posolsky prikaz*). At any rate, seventeenth-century chronicle writing was even more political than ever before. The West, however, was making inroads even here. The *Russian Chronograph* of 1512 had ignored Western history. The second (1617) and third (1620) versions use some Polish sources and include events of Western history.

The Time of Troubles produced a series of historical, publicistic, and memoiristic works which in one way or another differed from the medieval models of the chronicle and the war tale. The *Lament on the Ultimate Ruin of the Most Exalted and Most Glorious Muscovite State, to the profit and instruction of those who would listen*, written around 1612 by an anonymous author, is similar in structure and spirit to Serapion's sermons on the Tatar invasion. The prophet Jeremiah may have served as a model. The *Lament* praises the wealth and glory of Muscovy before the Time of Troubles, then gives a bird's eye view of the events that caused Muscovy's ruin at the hands of foreign invaders, precipitated by domestic treason. The *Lament* ends in a prayer of thanksgiving to the Lord, who will not allow His flock to be utterly crushed. The events of the Time of Troubles are seen entirely in religious terms. It is the Orthodox faith that is under attack. Pseudo-Dimitry (the pretender) is said to have "wanted to destroy the Orthodox Christian faith and holy churches, and to set up Latin churches and establish the Lutheran faith."[5] The language of the *Lament* is flowery, ornate, and highly emotional.

5. Russians call an Orthodox, a Catholic, and a Protestant church each by a different name: *tserkov'*, *kostel*, and *kirka*, respectively.

More remarkable, but in the same spirit, is the much longer *History to Be Remembered by Future Generations*, by Abraham (Avraamy) Palitsyn, completed in 1620 (though most of it was apparently written in 1611–12). Palitsyn, a monk of the Holy Trinity Monastery, had been an active participant in the defense of that monastery against a Polish force led by Hetman Piotr Sapieha in 1608. His description of Polish and Cossack atrocities seems to partake of the international repertoire of horrors allegedly committed by a hated enemy: babies smashed against walls, impaled, or roasted before their mothers' eyes, virgins gang-raped on the dead bodies of their protectors, churches desecrated. Palitsyn gives highly emotional, graphic, and certainly exaggerated descriptions of the anarchy, suffering, and cruelty of the Time of Troubles:

> Then people were hiding in impassable thickets and in the wilderness of dark forests and in unexplored caves and in the water behind some bushes and praying to their Creator with tears that night might fall, allowing them to rest even a little on dry ground. But there was no relief or place to hide and rest either at night or in the daytime, and instead of the moon many fires lit up fields and forests at night, and nobody was able to move from the spot he found himself at, for there were men awaiting people to come out of the forest as though they were hunted animals.

Palitsyn, too, sees the calamities that have descended upon Russia as divine chastisement for the people's greed, cupidity, hypocrisy, lechery, drunkenness, and selfwill. "Slaves," he says, "wanted to be lords, the unfree leaping into freedom, while the military estate began to act like boyars." Palitsyn is a skillful stylist with an excellent command of solemn pathos, righteous wrath, sarcasm, and emphasis through parallelism sometimes amounting to grammatical rhyme.

The title of the work known as *The Other Relation* was derived by nineteenth-century scholars from its long and convoluted preamble, which identifies it as the companion piece of a "first history," presumably Palitsyn's. It relates events from the death of Ivan IV in 1584 to the death of Michael in 1645. Its six sections were apparently written by several authors. Included in the narrative are the texts of some official documents. The work is ideologically homogeneous—pro-Shuisky and pro-Romanov,[6] as well as conservative, patriotic, and xenophobic. Ivan IV is called a "monarch brightly resplendent in piety." The main charge against the pretender is that he wanted to "trample into the dust our Christian faith, destroy our churches, and establish Roman churches instead." Marina Mniszek, the pretender's Catholic consort, is called a "Lutheran" and a "woman of the Moslem faith" in the same breath.[7] The spirit of *The Other Relation* is still medieval and Byzantine, although sections of the work have literary merit. The account of the pretender's body lying naked in the marketplace for three days is not without a somber power: "And as he lay there, many people heard at midnight, and all the time until the cock crowed, over his accursed corpse a great hubbub of voices, and tambourines and pipes and other devilish play: for Satan

rejoices at the arrival of his faithful servant." The language of *The Other Relation* varies from formulaic chronicle entries to highly figurative poetic diction. For the most part the historical facts reported are drowned out by the narrator's rhetorical effusions.

The *Tale of This Book of Bygone Years*, whose preamble ends with the words "this book was written on June 28, 1626," was for a long time attributed to Duke I. M. Katyrev-Rostovsky (d. 1640), a courtier who had a part in the events of the Time of Troubles, but has now been proven to be the work of Duke Semyon Ivanovich Shakhovskoi (d. 1653), one of the first Russians to write verse. Shakhovskoi's work is in many ways different from those mentioned earlier. It is ideologically less conservative. The author is cautiously ambivalent about Ivan IV. He praises him for his victories over "Kazan and many other Moslem kingdoms" but does not conceal the tsar's evil deeds: "But [as punishment] for the growing multitude of the sins of Orthodox Christendom, he turned contrary and full of wrath and fury and began to persecute people cruelly and mercilessly and to shed the blood of his subjects." The invasion of Russia by King Stefan Batory of Poland is perceived as God's punishment of the tsar, who is, moreover, presented as frightened and meekly seeking to plead with the invader to desist. On the other hand, we are not told that Ivan IV murdered his son Ivan; the text simply says that he "passed away."

Shakhovskoi's moralizing character sketches—for example, his account of how Boris Godunov, a man remarkable for "the beauty of his face and the subtlety of his mind, charitable and pious, skilled in debate and magniloquent, who accomplished many wonderful things in the imperial city while

---

6. The Shuisky family played a major role in the events of the Time of Troubles. Vasily Shuisky was tsar from 1606 to 1610.

7. *Zhena bezarmenskie very*; Russian *basurman* is a corrupted form of *musulman* (Muslim).

in power," became a murderer and a tyrant—as well as the emotional apostrophes to these characters are quite in the manner of Constantine Manasses. Shakhovskoi's battle scenes are more detailed than those in earlier works. The battle of Klushino (1610) is described in strategic detail, though it falls far short of the description provided by the Polish general, Hetman Stanisław Żółkiewski (1547–1620), in his classic *Beginning and Progress of the Moscow War* (*Początek i progres Wojny moskiewskiej*, 1612).[8] A closer examination of Shakhovskoi's battle scenes reveals that their details are often lifted verbatim from Guido de Columnis's *Historia destructionis Troiae*.[9] Moreover, Shakhovskoi's famous poetic rendering of the arrival of spring in 1607 is largely taken from Guido's descriptions of the changing seasons. At the conclusion of Shakhovskoi's history is a *Brief Description of the Tsars of Muscovy, Their Appearance, Their Stature, and Their Habits.* Even these descriptions contain many details taken from Guido's portraits of the heroes of the Trojan War. In particular, Shakhovskoi's much praised portrait of Xenia Godunov largely coincides with Guido's description of Priam's daughter Polyxena. Shakhovskoi adds to each physical portrait a moral assessment, much in the manner of Constantine Manasses. Here, for example, is the portrait of Ivan IV:

> Tsar Ivan was not handsome, having gray eyes and an elongated aquiline nose. He

was of tall stature, with a lean body, high-shouldered and broad-chested, thickly muscled. A man of marvelous understanding, well versed in book learning and most eloquent, boldly inclined toward the military and eager to advance his patrimony; most hard-hearted toward the servants given him by God and bold and merciless in bloodshed and killing, he caused a multitude of people, high and low, to perish under his rule, sacked many of his own cities, had many prelates of the church imprisoned and killed without mercy, and inflicted many other ills on his servants, and he also defiled many women and maidens by fornication. That same Tsar Ivan did many good things, was very fond of his soldiers and never failed to provide for them from his treasury as they would demand. Such was Tsar Ivan.

The portraits are followed by a thirty-line epilogue in rather awkward presyllabic verse.

Several works dealing with the Time of Troubles are close to the genre of the memoir, then popular in the West including Poland. Such are the *Annals* of Ivan Timofeev (d. 1629), a *dyak* (official in charge of an office of the tsar), who wrote this work between 1616 and 1619. The *Annals* tell the history of Russia from Ivan IV to the ascension of Michael Romanov to the throne. They are written in the familiar propagandistic Byzantine style and end in a panegyric effusion celebrating the new tsar and his ancestry. But the *Annals* also contain some specific details that only an eyewitness could have known and have the immediacy of an account by one who was close to the foci of power.

The same is true of the *Account of the Days of the Tsars and Prelates of Muscovy*,

8. Żółkiewski appears as Zheltovsky in Shakhovskoi's narrative.

9. Many Latin idioms are translated literally, often senselessly. For instance, *ore gladii persequuntur*, "pursue at sword's point," becomes *usty mecha gonyat*, literally, "chase with the lips of the sword."

by Duke Ivan Andreevich Khvorostinin (d. 1625), a relative of Duke Shakhovskoi. Khvorostinin had been close to Pseudo-Dimitry (he held the court position of "carver" to the tsar), and his work may have been an attempt at personal rehabilitation. Khvorostinin was often in trouble with the authorities on account of his westernizing and freethinking views. His work is kept in the conventional rhetorical manner, but he has interesting character studies of such major historical personages as Tsar Boris and Duke Dimitry Pozharsky, hero of the resistance to the Polish occupation. Khvorostinin was also one of the first Russians to write verse.

Among the many works about the Time of Troubles the anonymous *Writ on the Demise and Burial of Duke Mikhail Vasilievich Shuisky, called Skopin* (1612) stands out linguistically and stylistically.[10] Shuisky, at the age of twenty-four, was allegedly poisoned by Mariya, wife of Dimitry Shuisky, his uncle. Mariya was the daughter of the infamous Malyuta Skuratov, the most feared of Ivan the Terrible's henchmen. After a genealogical preamble, the story tells, how the hero was invited to be godfather to a son born to Duke Ivan Mikhailovich Vorotynsky (Mariya Shuisky was the godmother), became violently ill at the christening party, was taken home and died the following morning. "German" doctors sent by a friend, the Swedish general Jacob de la Gardie, could not save him. The major part of the piece (about seven of nine pages) is devoted to Shuisky's funeral. An argument develops about a proper burial site, and then it is difficult to find a coffin to fit the hero's huge body. There is an incident

when de la Gardie is first refused, then granted permission to approach the duke's bier. The whole piece has many elements of the language and style of Russian folklore: pleonastic repetition, paronomasia, formulaic phrases, similes and metaphors known in folk poetry, and the rhythm of a folktale. Much of the narrative is still literary, even Slavonic, and a number of biblical parallels are developed. But there are passages that are close to the manner of the popular lament.

The many historical, rhetorical, memoiristic, and polemical prose works of the first half of the seventeenth century (only a few of which have been mentioned here) exhibit a tendency to go against the conventional Slavonic rhetoric of religious literature. This is true even in those instances when the writer defends perfectly conservative values. The administration of the Russian Empire now included a sizable number of literate bureaucrats. Being men of affairs, they had learned to think in pragmatic secular terms and to express themselves in prose appropriate to the occasion. A standard officialese developed under the first Romanovs. A historical accident has preserved a lengthy product of this ambience, written in its natural idiom. Grigory Karpovich Kotoshikhin (c. 1630–67), a clerk in the foreign office, defected to the Swedes in 1664. He was sent to Stockholm, where Magnus de la Gardie, royal chancellor of Sweden, commissioned him to write a detailed description of contemporary Muscovy. The untitled manuscript was translated into Swedish and remains to this day in the library of the University of Uppsala. It was discovered there and published in Russia only in 1840. It provoked lively discussions and attracted many comments, particularly by "progressives" who believed

10. There exists another tale about the duke, which deals more with his military exploits.

that it discredited the Slavophiles' positive image of pre-Petrine Russia.[11]

Kotoshikhin's work is written in the Russian vernacular with a heavy admixture of officialese. In thirteen chapters it deals with the tsar, his family, and his court; the various officials and servants of the tsar; the Muscovite diplomatic service and foreign diplomats in Moscow; the service departments of the tsar's court (finance, provisions, stables, and so on); the imperial administration of the Russian lands, altogether thirty-six offices; the recruitment of troops; commerce and trade; various classes of peasants (the tsar's, those belonging to monasteries and to landowners); state-operated industries and commerce; and the life of boyars and other classes of people. Kotoshikhin manages to provide a tremendous amount of information in the form of a fluent narrative which at times resembles a sociological study. In discussing the tsar's mint, he gives a detailed and perhaps overly lurid account of the "copper rebellion" of 1662. The minting of an excessive amount of copper money had caused a disastrous inflation, which led to widespread unrest and rioting. The most serious of these riots, in July 1662, was cruelly suppressed: several thousand citizens were killed on the spot, arrested and summarily executed, or punished by

amputation of a limb, branding, and exile to Siberia. In the last chapter Kotoshikhin carefully records Muscovite upper-class marriage customs (an imperial wedding is described in chapter 1). The crassly mercenary and sometimes fraudulent practices of Muscovite matchmaking, concealed by elaborate ritual piety, appeared outrageous to liberal nineteenth-century readers, as did the segregation and enforced ignorance of upper-class women.

It has been suggested that Kotoshikhin, in seeking to accommodate his Swedish employers, told them what they wanted to hear and described Muscovy as more backward, cruel, and barbarian than it really was. It seems that such supposition is unfounded. Much of the information provided by him coincides with what is reported by Olearius and other Western sources. His work is important not only as a historical document. It shows that a literate Russian could write about real life directly and expressively.

A somewhat earlier document of literary fame demonstrates that literacy was penetrating even into the life of Russians outside the direct reach of secular and ecclesiastical authorities. In October 1642 a delegation of Don Cossacks came to Moscow asking Tsar Michael to assume suzerainty over the port of Azov, which the Cossacks had taken in 1637 and defended against a strong Turkish assault and subsequent siege in 1641. The document that describes these events and asks the tsar to take Azov under his protection was prepared by a Cossack captain, Fyodor Poroshin. The petition was refused, as the tsar was unwilling to go to war against the sultan, but the document went on to become "literature." It was copied many times and generated a folkloric fairy-tale version. The *Tale of the Siege of Azov* is a curious mixture of chronicle (an outright chronicle account of the events also exists),

11. The radical critic Nikolai Dobrolyubov wrote, "His views were broader, more humane than those of any Russians who wrote about Russia before him, even in a negative sense. He is an educated representative of the interests of the middle class, oppressed by the old aristocracy's ignorance and arrogance . . . advanced enough to deplore the coarseness of family relations, the ignorance of the upper class, administrative fraud, the cruelty of torture, and Russia's alienation from Europe" (N. A. Dobrolyubov, *Sobranie sochinenii*, 9 vols. (Moscow and Leningrad: Gosizdat khud. lit., 1961–64), 2:248.) Similar reactions came from Alexander Herzen, Vissarion Belinsky, and Nikolai Chernyshevsky.

of war tale, and folk epic. The forces of the enemy and the progress of military operations are described in detail, but the numbers of the enemy are greatly exaggerated—a characteristic of the war tale. The battle scenes combine accurate factual detail with the poetic figures and tropes of Russian folk poetry and even the lilt of bylina verse. The trait that makes it most different from every similar work preceding it is its popular ethos: an edge of cocky defiance (the Cossacks freely admit that they are refugees from oppression suffered at the hands of Muscovite landowners and officials), "cool" bravado, coarse invective for the enemy, a show of proper piety and righteousness (hardly convincing in view of the Cossacks' known lawlessness), and effusive self-pity. It lacks the staid corrrectness and controlled pathos of the literary texts of the same period. The *Tale of the Siege of Azov* clearly displays the sentimental high style of the uneducated sensibility.

The Niconian Reforms and their Consequences

In 1654 Patriarch Nicon (1652–56) began instituting church reforms that from today's vantage point appear minor. They were to remove some discrepancies that had developed between the Greek and Russian versions of the church ritual. The one that created the greatest uproar pertained to the position of fingers when making the sign of the cross. The old way, as described by Avvakum, a leader of the Old Believers, was, "Put together thumb, little finger, and ring finger (for a symbol of the Holy Trinity), and index finger and middle finger (Father and Son), with the middle finger inclined downward (to indicate Christ's care for man on earth)." Nicon instructed his flock to put together thumb, index, and middle finger for

a symbol of the Holy Trinity. Avvakum said that the new way could stand only for the unholy trinity of unclean spirits in Revelation 16:13. There were some other details of the same order and some adjustments in the text of the liturgy. The fact that these reforms caused a fateful schism in the Russian church and made millions of Russian Old Believers persecuted outcasts for centuries to come is difficult to understand, and hence scholars have sought to find deeper causes of the schism.

Initially Nicon and his supporters were of one mind with those who were going to become their bitter enemies, both equally intent upon a moral regeneration of the Russian church, a program heartily approved by Tsar Alexis. Later the patriarchate and the tsar were quite willing to receive the rebels back into the fold and resorted to violent repression of the schismatics with some reluctance. But the patriarchate and the tsar wanted a church that was orderly and disciplined, with learned and cultured preachers such as the Kiev Academy was sending to Muscovy, whereas the leaders of the Old Believers were activists who would carry their message into the homes and even into the marketplaces of their parishes. Avvakum denounced his learned opponents, who knew Latin, Greek, and Hebrew but in his opinion lacked "the love and other virtues that the Lord wants of us." He also denounced those Russian icon painters who depicted the Savior "after the Frankish, namely the German fashion," with "a full face, red lips, curly hair, strong hands and muscles, thick fingers, also with strong thighs, altogether well fed and fat, like a German."

The upheaval that accompanied the schism is interpreted by Soviet historians to have been basically social in nature, although both parties acted as if they were concerned only with religious issues. The Old Believers, so the theory goes, were supported primarily by the peasantry and the suburban lower class of the cities, who projected their grievances against landowners, church, and government into their refusal to accept the "new" religion. Avvakum's catalogue of martyrs, however, includes men of diverse backgrounds—monks, holy fools, and artisans, but boyars, too. Soviet scholars have pointed out connections between the Old Believer movement and peasant uprisings like the one led by Stepan Razin.[12] Although this theory may apply in a broad historical context, it appears as no more than a subtext in the writings of the Old Believers. The writings of Avvakum and his followers suggest that their primary concern was to maintain the ideal of a penitential Orthodox spirituality in the face of an incipient takeover of the Russian church by Western scholastic humanism.[13] The fact that the Old Believers developed a special fondness for the traditions of Maximus the Greek and the hermits beyond the Volga corroborates this view. Although there are similarities between the Old Believer movement and Protestant sectarian movements in the West, no significant direct connections have been found so far. The passion with which details of ritual were defended by the Old Believers, while the Niconians maintained that these were immaterial per se and that what really mattered was obedience to the church,

places the Old Believers with the old Muscovite tradition, which gave a deep spiritual significance to these details.

The struggle between Niconians and Old Believers had a precedent two generations earlier in the Orthodox Ukraine and Belorussia. The creation of the Uniate church led to a flurry of impassioned polemic. Opponents of the union, such as Ivan Vyshenskyj (d. 1620s), assumed a position analogous to that of the Muscovite Old Believers, realizing the conventional humility topos and presenting themselves as ignorant simple souls who loved their Russian (or Slavonic) language and abhorred the clever rhetoric of their Latinate adversary. In fact, Vyshenskyj was anything but ignorant. A monk from Mount Athos, he knew Greek and could hold his own against that redoubtable champion of the Polish Counter-Reformation, the Jesuit Piotr Skarga (1536–1612).

The Old Believers produced the most striking personality and most remarkable writer of the seventeenth century, Protopop Avvakum (1621–1682). An ordinary parish priest in the Nizhny Novgorod region, Avvakum acquired an early reputation as a moral zealot. He was repeatedly manhandled and expelled by his parishioners, who resented his outrageous meddling in what they felt were their private affairs. However, Avvakum had the sympathy and protection of the Moscow "zealots of piety" and of the tsar.[14] In 1652 Nicon, himself a "zealot of piety," became patriarch and almost immediately embarked upon his reforms. Avvakum, along

---

12. The siege and fall of Solovki Monastery, held by Old Believers against the tsar's forces, became the subject of a folk epic in which the fall of the stronghold on January 22, 1676, is linked with the death of Tsar Alexis (on January 30 of that year), described in lurid detail and declared as God's punishment. See Robinson, pp. 212–214.

13. Priscilla Hunt, "Samoopravdanie protopopa Avvakuma," *Trudy otdela drevnerusskoi literatury*, 32 (1977): 70–83.

14. In the 1640s there existed in Moscow a circle of "zealots of piety" (*revniteli blagochestiya*). Nicon, then an archimandrite, Ivan Neronov, *protopop* of Kazan Cathedral in Moscow, and Stefan Vonifatyev, the tsar's confessor, belonged to it, and it had the blessings of the tsar himself. Avvakum received benevolent encouragement from the circle.

with some others, promptly announced his noncompliance. In 1653 he was exiled to Tobolsk in western Siberia, where he continued to preach dissent. He was punished by exile to the far east but allowed to return when Nicon fell from grace. Back in Moscow in 1663, Avvakum refused to compromise, although the tsar made a gracious offer of reconciliation. He was exiled to the far north, returned to Moscow once more in 1666, but then spent the rest of his life in prison at Pustozersk on the White Sea. Kept under inhuman conditions, he managed not only to write prolifically, but also to make himself the spiritual leader of the Old Believer movement. Many of his followers were executed or cruelly mutilated, but Avvakum was spared until 1682, when he was burned at the stake with some other Old Believers. He was even then thought by many to be a saint. Surviving Old Believers carefully preserved his works and prepared numerous copies. About eighty separate pieces are extant, some of them in Avvakum's own hand. They include petitions to the tsar, epistles, colloquies on religious topics, letters of instruction, exegetical and theological writings, polemical tracts, and notes on various events and individuals. His main work, however, is his famous *Life of Protopop Avvakum, Written by Himself* (probably in 1672–73), of which two autographs are extant.[15]

Avvakum's autobiography was not unprecedented (there is of course the example of Saint Augustine), even in Russia. There was the earlier autobiography of his associate Epiphanius, a monk of Solovki Monastery, who no doubt was aware of an autobiographic tradition that existed there.[16] Avva-

kum's predecessors are often just as robustly down-to-earth as he is. The difference, a huge one, is in the author's personality and talent. Avvakum, a man of boundless energy, has a story to tell and does it well, unlike Epiphanius and those who preceded him.[17]

Avvakum's *Life* is certainly informed by the canonical vita. Its hero is devout, a zealous cleric, a martyr, and a miracle worker. He exorcises evil spirits and credits himself with a number of miraculous cures and conversions. He reports several divine visions as well as bouts with evil spirits. He is well read and quotes the Bible, the *Margarites* (a collection of sermons by John Chrysostom), the Nomocanon, the *Azbukovnik*, Dionysius Areopagita, Basil the Great, Nicon of Mount Maurus, and other church fathers. In defending the old way of making the sign of the cross, he adduces not only ancient fathers (Theodoret of Cyrrhus and Peter Damascene) but also Maximus the Greek. Many of the similes and images used by Avvakum are from the *Martyrologue* and other religious works.

But in other ways Avvakum's *Life* is quite different from a saint's life. The narrative is mostly in the living vernacular, with only religious and abstract terms and phrases in Slavonic. (Quotations from the Bible and other religious texts are in Slavonic, of course.) From the text there emerges a complex and fascinating individual: religious zealot and paterfamilias, simple parish priest and visionary, spiritual and bigoted,

15. *Pustozerskii sbornik: Avtografy sochinenii Avvakuma i Epifaniya*, ed. N. S. Demkova et al. (Leningrad: Nauka, 1975).

16. Robinson, *Bor'ba idei*, 369.

17. The hermit Epiphanius (*Pustozerskii sbornik*, 80–91, 112–38) was clearly a yurodivy, that is, a mentally deranged fool-in-Christ, who was plagued by hallucinations. He reports how he frequently had to battle demons in his wilderness retreat. A lengthy episode tells of the infestation of his cell by ants, which kept attacking his private parts until he found the proper prayer to make them disappear. Still, his vita gives us an idea of a hermit's life.

stubborn and self-righteous but also humble and ready to do severe penance for sins committed, capable of rabid fits of violence but also of tenderness and gentle sympathy.

After a terrible whipping from Pashkov, the captain who escorts him to his Siberian exile, Avvakum at first likens himself to Job, then has an afterthought. Job, he says, was born of the bad branch of Abraham (apocryphal commentaries to the Book of Job made him a descendant of Esau) and was an unlettered man in a foreign land. How could he, Avvakum, in possession of the wisdom of the Old and New Testaments, be so blind as not to see that the Lord's chastisement was all to the good? He humbles himself in his heart and immediately feels refreshed and without pain. Of Pashkov, his tormentor, he says later, "He tortured me for ten years, or I him—I don't know, God will sort it out." (Avvakum was capable of a grim self-irony.)

In a flashback to the distant past Avvakum relates how he once came home feeling low and found his wife having a fight with their maid. Angered, he gave both a beating: "For I am always prone to losing my temper, accursed that I am, and all too ready to use my fists." Then, remorseful, he begged the women's forgiveness and made each member of his household give him five lashes with a whip—which they did, though not without many tears. Or this powerful passage of penitential self-abasement:

I am possessed by unreason and hypocrisy, steeped in lies, clothed in hatred of my brethren, and self-love, and I am perishing, by all human judgment. And lest I think that I am something, I am dirt and putrefaction, accursed—simple shit. And I stink from everywhere, body and soul. I ought to live with dogs and pigs in a pen, since they also stink, but dogs and pigs stink by nature, while I stink because

of my sins beyond nature, like a dead dog flung into a city street.

Avvakum, with all his ritualism and superstitions, has a deep and clear understanding of the Gospel message as interpreted by Saint Paul. He can be understanding and generous. Having reported, without rancor, that his two sons caved in under threat of execution and betrayed the cause, he recalls that Saint Peter, too, betrayed the Lord and expresses the hope that they will be forgiven. Having related how the tongue of an Old Believer, cut out by the tsar's executioner, miraculously grew back, Avvakum says that the faithful believe even without a miracle, but that those of weaker faith would be fortified by it.

Avvakum is a dyed-in-the-wool conservative from whom we hear the old argument of the third Rome, which should need neither the first, "which fell a long time ago," nor the second, "which has allowed Orthodoxy to be corrupted while in the hands of the Turkish Muhammad." Old anti-Latin biases flare up. Avvakum tells the story of Pope "Farmos," a semifictitious personage well known from earlier authors, whose body, he relates, was exhumed by Pope Stephen, who had his three fingers chopped off, each causing the earth to open a chasm from which an awful stench arose. Only after Farmos's corpse was flung into the Tiber and Pope Stephen made the sign of the cross in the correct manner did the chasms close. To Avvakum, Russia and Orthodoxy are synonymous. The upper classes were the most inclined to fall prey to the seductions of the West, and hence Avvakum appeared to be hostile to them. But he was no social revolutionary.

Avvakum's *Life* is a kaleidoscope of Russian daily life with its mundane worries; Avvakum's trials and tribulations; quixotic, even comic scenes showing Avvakum trying to force his sense of right and justice on an unwilling community; scenes of horrible violence and suffering; miracles, visions, and diabolic visitations; and passages of deep introspective analysis. Avvakum can tell a story with a power and concision unparalleled in Russian literature. There is, for example, this account of his return home from ice fishing one Siberian winter night: walking, then stumbling along as he pulls a sled with the catch, then tiring and abandoning the sled, walking ever more slowly, falling and getting up again, then crawling, finally pushing himself along in a sitting position—and making it home to safety toward morning. It would take nearly two hundred years until Tolstoi would achieve the immediacy and plasticity of expression that came naturally to Avvakum.

Other than the narrative passages of Avvakum's *Life*, the writings of the Old Believers were still medieval. Avvakum and his associates were well read, but in works that had been a staple of the literate clergy since the Kievan period. Their cosmology was that of the *Paleya*. "God commanded that the earth rest on water, and not on whales," says a tract in a Pustozersk miscellany that includes the lives of Avvakum and Epiphanius. The writer was aware of the Russian folk belief according to which the earth is supported by four giant whales swimming in the ocean. He refuted this notion by referring to John Damascene, who had said, "Thou hast fixed the earth upon nothing by Thy command."

The Old Believer movement produced some other remarkable works. The best known of these is the *Life of Boyarynya Morozova, Duchess Urusova, and Marya Danilova*, written by an anonymous contemporary. Morozova and Urusova belonged to the high aristocracy of Moscow and their

martyrdom immediately became a legend. Their *Life* is structured like a canonical vita and features many of the same traits. The life of the two noble ladies before their martyrdom is presented in conventional formulaic terms. The *Life* is analogous to Avvakum's in the shocking realism of the description of the many tortures inflicted on the women. Moreover, its general ethos is as defiant and unsentimental as Avvakum's.

The polemical literature produced by the supporters of Nicon and the official church, though ample, is of lesser literary interest. A life of Nicon was written soon after his death by Ivan Shusherin, an ardent supporter.[18] Quite conventional in every way, it failed to bring out the pathos of Nicon's meteoric rise and abrupt fall, nor did it do justice to his energetic and attractive personality or his ambitious plans of a Russian theocracy.

Although Nicon fell from grace, his reforms and the course he gave to the Russian church survived. The most eloquent defense of Nicon's reforms and the ideas underlying them was made by Symeon Polotsky in his *Scepter of Government* (1667), a substantial volume printed in the name of the church council of 1666. Symeon explicitly seeks to refute the positions of the Old Believers, quoting their spokesman of the moment, Lazarus, a priest and friend of Avvakum, who had recently addressed the tsar in a denunciatory "scroll." Symeon defends the position of the absolutist ruler who demands unquestioning obedience for the sake of the unity and stability of church and empire. The Old Believers openly said that God's law was above the tsar's law and that Alexis did not deserve the epithet "most quiet and

---

18. *Relation of the birth and education and life of the Most Holy Nicon, patriarch of Moscow and of all Russia* (*Izvestie o rozhdenii i vospitanii i o zhitii svyateishego Nikona, patriarkha moskovskogo i vseya Rossii*, Moscow, 1871).

most gentle" (*tishaishii i krotchaishii*) given him by the official church. They also held that it was improper to include the tsar as a person in the liturgy, as Nicon had ordered. Symeon carried the day, however, both politically and in a literary context. The tsar's power over the church would grow even stronger, and for a long time to come Symeon's language and style would dominate educated literary expression. Tsar Alexis was in more ways than is commonly acknowledged a precursor of his son Peter.

The Literature of Western Russia

Until the middle of the seventeenth century the Ukraine and Belorussia were a part of the Polish-Lithuanian commonwealth. The Cossack wars that began in 1648 led to the creation, in 1654, of a semi-independent Ukraine, now a vassal state of Muscovy. The peace treaty of Andrusovo (1667) brought Kiev and Smolensk under Muscovite rule. These political developments opened the doors to an influx of Western baroque culture and to the migration to Muscovy of clerics educated in the Latin scholastic tradition.

Poland fully participated in every aspect of Renaissance and baroque culture. Architecture, art, music, literature, and scholarship were entirely on a European level. Major works of the literatures of Western Europe were almost immediately translated. Religious life was vigorously active, especially owing to the manifold activities of the Jesuit order. The Union of Brześć-Litewsk, which caused large numbers of Orthodox Ukrainians and Belorussians to move to the Catholic camp, alerted the Orthodox church to the danger of losing even more of its flock and forced it to take some action to become competitive with the Catholic church. A better education for

its priests in particular was a concern in an age of bitter polemical battles between supporters and opponents of the Union. Providing schools for the children of the gentry was of the essence, since the Orthodox gentry, especially its more wealthy and powerful families, was converting to Catholicism and becoming culturally Polonized, with Polish Jesuit schools a powerful instrument of proselytizing. The founding of the school of the Confraternity of the Epiphany (*Bogoyavlenskoe bratstvo*) in Kiev in 1615 was a milestone in the history of Ukrainian as well as Russian culture. In 1632 the metropolitan of Kiev, Peter Mogila (Ukrainian Mohyla), united this school with the recently established gymnasium of the Kiev Cave Monastery, elevating it to the status of an academy and giving it a Latinate scholastic curriculum patterned after Polish Jesuit academies.

The lower classes of the Kiev Academy taught primarily Latin grammar; the intermediate, rhetoric and poetics; and the higher, philosophy and theology. The languages taught were Slavonic, Polish, Latin, Greek, and Hebrew. Music, art, and geometry were also in the curriculum. The academy's program featured lectures, declamations, disputations, and theatrical performances. Although not a progressive institution, the Kiev Academy was a huge step toward a cultural rapprochement between Orthodox East and Catholic West. A graduate of the academy was fluent in Latin and could read Greek, so that Western philosophy and science were accessible to him. He could communicate with Western scholars and was qualified to study in the West. The Kiev Academy became a model for other schools, at first in western Russia and later in Muscovy. Russian Orthodox divinity schools followed its Latinate model well into the nineteenth century.

The Kiev Academy was the cradle of Ukrainian literature and indirectly of modern Russian literature as well. The literature that developed there was essentially baroque, as were the architecture, art, and sacred music that flourished in the Ukraine in the seventeenth century. Much as in the West, sacred eloquence was energetically revived and eventually transplanted to Muscovy by Ukrainian clerics. The polemical literature of the seventeenth century featured skilled and fiery defenders of both the Orthodox and the Uniate positions. A new form of historiography, patterned after Western baroque examples, superseded the old chronicles. From these works nineteenth-century Ukrainian writers and poets gathered the material for their image of the past glory of a free Ukraine. These works also inspired Nikolai Gogol to write his historical novel *Taras Bulba* and other fiction set in the Ukrainian past.

Under the influence of Latin and Polish poetry the Kiev Academy developed a rich tradition of predominantly religious poetry in rhymed syllabic verse. (The Polish system of versification is syllabic, analogous to that of the Romance languages.) As many as 150 different strophic patterns, including familiar classical strophes such as the Sapphic, occur in seventeenth-century Ukrainian poetry. Its principal religious genres were the hymn, the ode (to the Virgin, various saints, church holidays, icons, and miracles), lyrics of personal religious experience, and songs of penitence, death, and the Last Judgment. Secular genres were emblematic and heraldic verse, the elegy, the lament, the epigram, the patriotic ode, and the love song—in a word, most of the genres current in Western baroque poetry. Furthermore, the poets of the Ukrainian baroque employed all the graphic devices known in the West: the acrostic, the rebus, alphabet verse,

the palindrome, and various forms of figured verse (that is, poems printed in the form of a cross, a chalice, a crescent, and so on).[19]

The example of the Jesuit school drama led to the development of Ukrainian baroque drama: Christmas and Easter plays, plays about saints, and morality plays. Like their Western models, Ukrainian religious spectacles featured burlesque interludes. The main text of religious drama was in Slavonic, partly adapted to Ukrainian; the interludes were in the pure vernacular.

The achievements of Ukrainian baroque literature were carried to Muscovy by Ukrainian and Belorussian clerics who rose to important positions in the Russian church and the Muscovite civil administration. This development played a decisive role in the formation of literary Russian, the beginnings of organized formal education, and the creation of a new, Western-style literature.

The Beginnings of Poetry

Russian literary poetry developed under the influence of Western examples. Liturgic and hymnal texts, though adapted to the rhythm of their music, were nonsyllabic and unrhymed (the Greek originals were in regular verse, but the Russian translators made no effort to duplicate it), as was Russian folk verse. In some texts from the sixteenth century on, lines of irregularly rhymed prose (*skazovy stikh*) occasionally appear. All of these forms lack the metric principle that informs syllabic and syllabotonic poetry.[20]

19. Dmytro Čyževs'kyj, *A History of Ukrainian Literature* (Littleton, Colo.: Ukrainian Academic Press, 1975), 278–307.

20. The difference between rhymed prose and poetry is that in rhymed prose the interval between rhymes is not defined by any rule, whereas in poetry it is defined in terms of stressed syllables or a count of syllables.

Seventeenth-century texts show that Russians learned to write regular syllabic verse with difficulty, often slavishly following Polish examples to the point of stressing Russian words incorrectly in order to get the feminine rhymes required in Polish, where the stress always falls on the penultimate syllable of a word (stress is free in the East Slavic languages—Russian, Ukrainian, and Belorussian). Moreover, throughout the seventeenth century we find in much of the extant poetry obvious violations of the syllabic meter and of the most elementary principles of rhyme, suggesting that Russian versifiers hardly felt at home in the prosodic system borrowed from Polish.[21]

The first substantial body of Russian verse is extant in various occasional texts (album verse, petitions, epistles, gnomic pieces, polemics) produced by clerks in the tsar's service, the government printing press in particular. For example, one Aleksei Romanchenkov, a member of the Russian embassy that traveled to Persia together with the Holsteinian embassy in 1637–39, entered a few cordial lines into the album of a Holsteinian colleague on January 15, 1638. Heraldic verse also came to Muscovy from the West. The first Russian example dates from 1659 and describes the (imaginary) seal of the patriarch of Moscow.[22]

Clerics as well as laymen composed religious and moral-didactic verse that may be termed pre-syllabic. Pre-syllabic verse has lines of varying length, though an effort is made to keep them balanced, and no stanzaic structure. Its rhymes, mostly of grammatical endings, are often inexact, that is, they do not qualify as rhymes under the rules of later syllabic poetry. On the other hand, some of these pieces have artifices popular in baroque poetry, such as acrostic and serpentine verse. Known authors (there are many anonymous pieces) belong to a wide range of social groups. There are the dukes Katyrev-Rostovsky, Shakhovskoi, and Khvorostinin, also known for their historical prose. Khvorostinin may have penned his virulently anti-Catholic versified diatribes in an effort to refute charges of Arian heresy (neighboring Poland was then a refuge to many Arians). Monks of Patriarch Nicon's New Jerusalem Monastery cultivated the singing of hymns after the Polish-Ukrainian fashion, and some hymns composed by one of them, a monk named German (d. 1682), are extant. German also composed two versified epitaphs to Nicon. Even Old Believer rebels have left some versified texts. A polemical miscellany edited by Avraamy, a monk, contains prose texts by Avvakum, Ivan Neronov, Deacon Fyodor, and Avraamy himself. Some of Avraamy's anti-Nicon diatribes are in pre-syllabic verse.

The father of Russian syllabic poetry, Symeon Polotsky (1629–80),[23] a native of Polotsk in Belorussia and an alumnus of the Kiev Academy, came to Moscow in 1664, where he was active as a churchman (he was a monk), pedagogue, publicist, and poet. Symeon had written Latin, Polish, and Slavonic verse and prose before moving to Moscow, where he developed an archaizing Russo-Slavonic idiom with an admixture of

21. Early attempts by Ukrainian and Belorussian scholars to develop a manual of versification for the East Slavic languages remained fruitless. Mele ty Smotritsky's celebrated grammar (1619) has a chapter on versification, but, following Greek and Latin prosody, it operates with long and short syllables, which rendered it useless because in the East Slavic languages quantity (vowel length) is not a distinctive feature.

22. On the subject of heraldic verse, see Nils Åke Nilsson, *Russian Heraldic Virši from the Seventeenth Century*, Acta Universitatis Stockholmiensis, 10 (Uppsala, 1964).

23. His secular name was Samuil Emelyanovich Petrovsky-Sitnyanovich.

Ukrainian elements. His syntax is Latinate, as was that of the literary Polish of his age. Symeon actively participated in church affairs. He played a leading role in formulating the resolutions of the church council of 1666–67, and wrote topical, cautiously moralizing sermons as well as a book, *The Scepter of Government* (1667), in which he asserted the ruler's absolute authority and fiercely attacked all dissenters. Significantly, Symeon addressed his panegyrics not only to the tsar and the imperial family but also to patriarchs Ioasaph and Ioakim.

Symeon was the first of the great Russian court poets, as close to real power as any of his successors. A tireless and extraordinarily capable man, he served the ideals in which he believed well and with success. As a court poet, he wrote dedicatory poems addressed to tsars Alexis and Fyodor, some of them in the name of members of the tsar's family, including the future Tsar Peter I. But panegyrical poetry represents only a small part of Symeon's immense output, gathered in two large collections, *The Garden of Many Flowers* (1678, extant in three copies) and *Rhythmology* (1678–79, extant in a single copy). In addition to panegyrical poems like "The Russian Eagle," some of which are artfully arranged on the page in graphic symbols (a star, a cross) they contain versified paraphrases from such familiar miscellanies as the *Legenda aurea*, the *Gesta romanorum*, the *Melissa*, the *Leimon pneumatikon* of John Moschus, and the *Speculum historiale* of Vincent de Beauvais; tidbits from Pliny's *Historia naturalis*; moral reflections on marriage, widowhood, old age, maidenly virtue, greed, drunkenness, friendship, moderation, and other topics; and satirical character studies on various stations in life ("The Monk," "The Merchant," "The Administrator," "Married Life"). Some of the poems are organized into cycles—"Pride," "Lust," "Slander," "Fame," "Death," "Conscience," "Learning," "Youth"—an arrangement also found in some of Symeon's sources, such as the *Melissa*.

Symeon's rhymed Psalter, published in 1680, is one of the finest exhibits of Muscovite printing. Its frontispiece, an engraving showing King David, would have graced any Western book of the time. It was, if nothing else, a courageous enterprise. In Russia any departure from the canonical text of the Bible was thought to be sacrilegious. When Symeon undertook this task, following the example of Western poets and the Pole Jan Kochanowski in particular, he was taking a risk. In his preface, in prose and in verse, he tried to justify his project by pointing out that the Hebrew original was a work of poetry, that other nations possessed poetic versions of the Psalter, and that "sweet and harmonious singing of the Polish Psalter, translated in verse" was widespread not only in the Ukraine and Belorussia but even in Muscovy. In spite of vociferous denunciations by the Grecophile opposition, which included even Patriarch Ioakim, Symeon's Psalter was set to music by V. P. Titov and enjoyed a wide currency for a long time.[24] It started a tradition, as virtually every major poet of the following century tried his hand at a versified Russian Psalter.

Symeon's verses fully answer a description of West European baroque poetry. His meters are the thirteen-syllable alexandrine with a caesura after the seventh syllable and feminine rhyme, the hendecasyllable with a caesura after the fifth syllable, and some other meters common in the West, includ-

24. I. P. Eremin, "Simeon Polotskii—poet i dramaturg," in Simeon Polotskii, *Izbrannye sochineniya* (Moscow and Leningrad: AN SSSR, 1953), p. 241.

ing a syllabic Sapphic strophe.[25] Symeon's poetic world, too, is that of the religious Western baroque. He is familiar with classical mythology and uses it on occasion. But he still draws the bulk of his imagery from the Bible, the Psalter in particular. Like prose panegyrists of the two preceding centuries, Symeon concentrates on his sovereign's Christian virtues.[26]

Symeon Polotsky wrote about fifty thousand lines of verse. Some of them have been published only recently, some not at all. It stands to reason that a poet who writes thousands of lines will produce a few good lines even if he has little talent. An aesthetic assessment of Symeon and other Russian poets who wrote syllabic verse is difficult. They are at a disadvantage with post-syllabic readers because the leisurely recitative of their verse differs radically from the driving rhythms of syllabotonic verse. Their baroque imagery appears artificial. The religious verses of Symeon and his disciples—clearly their best—seem contrived to a reader who expects the immediacy and warmth of Protestant hymns. Nevertheless, Symeon created a form and a style capable of further development. His Psalter, though lacking in poetic grace, has a solemn dignity which was not lost upon his eighteenth-century successors.

Sylvester Medvedev (1641–91), a native

of Kursk, became a disciple of Symeon Polotsky in 1665 while a clerk in the tsar's secret chancery (*prikaz tainykh del*). He took holy vows only in 1677. Medvedev succeeded his mentor in most of his functions at Symeon's death in 1680 and also served as an editor and proofreader at the government printing house. He was close to Tsarevna Sophia, regent during the minority of Peter I, and paid for it with his life. When Peter assumed power in 1689, Medvedev was arrested on what seem to have been trumped-up charges, was tortured repeatedly, and was executed in 1691. Medvedev, active as an organizer and pedagogue, was less of a poet than Symeon, although he had great linguistic ability. He wrote creditable Latin verse. His Russian verse, panegyrical, moral-didactic, and religious, is weaker than Symeon's. His "Epitaph" to Symeon in twelve quatrains of alexandrines is pedestrian as well as awkward.

Medvedev's successor was Karion Istomin (c. 1650–1717), a relative of his, also a monk, who came to Moscow around 1679. He acted as an associate of Medvedev's both at court (as a tutor, translator from the Latin, preacher, and court poet) and at the printing house. More cautious than Medvedev, he survived the upheaval of 1689 and subsequently made a modest career as secretary to Patriarch Adrian. He was head of the printing house from 1698 to 1701. As a poet, Istomin was somewhat more skillful than Medvedev, but equally pedestrian. He wrote a number of rhymed didactic works: two primers, an encyclopedic work entitled *Polis* containing a synopsis of the sciences in a scholastic curriculum—grammar, syntax ("transformation of words into thoughts"), poetics, arithmetic, astrology— and an untitled didactic poem in fourteen stanzas of twelve lines each, outlining the day of a dutiful youth or servant, with the

25. It appears that whenever his meter required it, Symeon would place the stress of a word on the penultimate syllable even if the natural stress lay elsewhere. For example, *égo / svoégo* is treated as a feminine rhyme at line's end, although the vernacular pronunciation is *egó / svoegó*. There was support for such practice in the fact that the stress of Slavonic words, as established by tradition, often differed from the stress of the same words in Russian.

26. For further information, see Anthony Hippisley, *The Poetic Style of Simeon Polotsky*, Birmingham Slavonic Monographs, 16 (Birmingham: University of Birmingham, 1985).

last line of each stanza giving the number of lashes (from three to twenty) to be received for noncompliance with the instructions in point.

Toward the end of the seventeenth and well into the eighteenth century an ability to produce and to appreciate rhymed syllabic verse was a part of general culture among certain social groups. A body of syllabic verse, much of it anonymous, is extant in manuscript. Its topics, moral and religious, panegyrical and patriotic, suggest that its authors as well as readers were mostly clerics and government officials. In some instances the question arises whether a given piece ought to be assigned to Russian or to Ukrainian literature. Even if there is linguistic evidence favoring Ukrainian (such as rhyming etymological *ě* and *i*, which are pronounced identically in Ukrainian but remain different vowels in Russian), it is not necessarily conclusive since a Russian poet may have simply followed established patterns. In the case of identified authors a similar dilemma exists because some Ukrainian clerics, such as Stefan Yavorsky, Saint Dimitry of Rostov, and Feofan Prokopovich, started their careers in the Ukraine, but flourished for many years in Muscovy.

To what extent can it be deduced from extant texts that aside from formal traits a genuine baroque sensibility existed in Russia in the seventeenth century? No such sensibility seems to have informed Symeon Polotsky and his disciples. But there are several minor and at least two major poetic works of the late seventeenth century that are thoroughly baroque in their preoccupation with mortality, images of decay and corruption, and visions of hell, but also in their allegorical depictions of the heavens and the heavenly host. The anonymous "Ladder to Heaven" (more than a thousand lines) has some Ukrainianisms and may not

be an original work, although no specific source has been discovered. The author of the "Pentateugum," Jan (Andrei, after his conversion to Orthodoxy) Biełobocki (Belobotsky), was a Polish scholar educated at several European universities who came to Russia in 1681 hoping to obtain a teaching position with the academic institution then planned by Medvedev and Istomin.

Soon after his arrival in Moscow Belobotsky converted to Russian Orthodoxy and began to write in Russo-Slavonic. His academic position never materialized, and instead he made a modest career in the diplomatic service, participating in a mission to China. He prepared a translation of Thomas à Kempis's *Imitatio Christi* (1684–85) and some other works. His "Pentateugum," extant in a single late seventeenth-century copy, deals with death, the Last Judgment, hell and eternal torments, the glory of those who live in eternal bliss, and human life as a dream (or its vanity), all in 166 octaves. The entire text of this poem has been traced to the works of German Jesuit poets, which existed in Latin and German versions and had been translated into Polish by the Polish Jesuit Zygmunt Brudecki (1610–47).[27] The anonymous "Ladder to Heaven" has a similar structure and apparently the same general

27. A. Kh. Gorfunkel', "Andrei Belobotskii—poet i filosof kontsa XVII–nachala XVIII v.," *Trudy otdela drevnerusskoi literatury* 18 (1962): 188–213. The source of the first four sections is *Quatuor hominis ultima*, by Ioannes Niess (1588–1629) and Matthaeus Rader (1561–1634); that of the fifth is *Ode Nova dicta Hecatombe de Vanitate Mundi*, by Jacob Balde (1604–68). It is conceivable that some direct contacts existed between German baroque poets and Russian versifiers of the seventeenth century. Paul Fleming (1609–40), a leading German poet, visited Muscovy as a member of the Holsteinian mission recorded by Olearius. Quirin Kuhlmann (1651–89), another leading poet, was burned at the stake in Moscow as a heretic. Pastor Johann Gregorii was a competent amateur poet.

source. It deals with death, body and soul, hell, the seven mortal sins, the kingdom of heaven, and the nine beatitudes.

Both poems exhibit a more mature poetic sensibility than may be found in Medvedev or Istomin. That both contain some elegant verses and relatively few awkward ones suggests that a certain technical routine had developed by the end of the century. Technically the anonymous work is stronger: the vast majority of its rhymes are flawless, and its rhythm is frequently enhanced by regular syllabotonic stress patterns. Belobotsky's poem has some irritating Polonisms, such as rhymes that would be good in Polish but are poor in Russian or Slavonic.[28] Yet he manages to create some striking imagery of pain, horror, and putrefaction. The "Pentateugum" and the "Ladder of Heaven" are a curious episode in the history of Russian literature, but essentially a dead end. A Catholic baroque sensibility does not seem to have ever gained a foothold in Muscovy.

The Beginnings of Drama

The seventeenth century witnessed some sporadic theatrical activity, which linked up with the continuous tradition that began in the mid-eighteenth century. The Kiev Academy and its daughter institutions played a role similar to that which they played in the history of Russian poetry. Early manuscripts suggest that there was dialogical declamation instead of theater, but as early as 1631 there appeared in print a genuine play,

Meditations on the Passion of Christ, by Ioanniky Volkovich. It is composed on the pattern of Byzantine religious drama. But later Kievan religious school drama followed Polish Jesuit school drama. It featured Christmas plays, Easter plays, eschatological plays (on the Last Judgment, hellfire), hagiographic plays (on Saint Alexis, Saint Catherine), and allegorical morality plays (*The Prodigal Son*, *The Rich Man and Lazarus*). Following the example of Polish school drama, the Ukrainian theater developed burlesque interludes (intermedia) within these religious plays. The Ukrainian school drama was transplanted to Muscovy by Symeon Polotsky and Saint Dimitry of Rostov. It also stimulated the Ukrainian puppet theater (*vertep*) and the Russian Shrovetide folk theater.

Symeon Polotsky was Muscovy's first dramatist, and his *History or Action of the Gospel Parable of the Prodigal Son, performed in the Year of Our Lord 1685* the first dramatic text printed in Muscovy. Symeon's *Tragedy of King Nebuchadnezzar, the Golden Calf, and Three Youths Not Burnt in a Furnace* is extant in manuscript. Symeon was familiar with the school drama from his student days at the Kiev Academy. In the Kievan school drama the main dialogue was in Latin or Slavonic, the interludes in the local vernacular. The texts of Symeon's plays are in Russo-Slavonic. No text is given for interludes, but their place is explicitly indicated; presumably they were improvised. Symeon's plays are creditable as school drama goes. The verse is smooth yet flexible enough to permit fluent dialogue. In *The Prodigal Son* the combination of stilted Slavonic diction and mundane action creates an effect of ironic estrangement which may not have been entirely unintentional. It has the charm of allowing the viewer to recognize things familiar in "real life" in a

---

28. Belobotsky's verse is basically trochaic tetrameter with a crossing rhyme scheme (*ababcdcd*), but in the manuscript two tetrameters are combined in a single line, and the tendency toward an inexact rhyme is stronger in the middle of the line; hence the effect is that of a Latin sixteen-syllable octonarius. Jacob Balde's poem is in octaves, too, but is iambic. The rhyme scheme is the same as Belobotsky's.

form removed from real life by language, stage setting, and verse. It is likely that *The Prodigal Son* bore a message to young Russians who were intent on leaving Muscovy for the freedom of the West.

The *Tragedy of Nebuchadnezzar* was a revival of the well-known *Furnace Action*, which had been regularly performed at some Russian churches on December 17 in the sixteenth and early seventeenth centuries but had been banned, along with the skomorokhi who acted in it, by the middle of the seventeenth century.[29] Symeon's play suggests how art can stand separate from life: he wrote this tragedy, about three youths who dared a despot to burn them to death for their faith, while his own sovereign was letting religious dissenters be burned at the stake.

Dimitry Tuptalo (1651–1709), metropolitan of Rostov, who was canonized as a saint of the Orthodox church in 1751, is best known as the compiler of an authoritative multivolume edition of the *Martyrologue*. But he also established the first Orthodox seminary in Muscovy, where he cultivated the school drama, and was a major religious poet. While Saint Dimitry's poetry is considered as belonging to Ukrainian literature, his plays cannot be overlooked in a history of Russian drama. The most popular of them, *The Repentant Sinner*, was performed well into the eighteenth century. However, only the texts of two other plays, a Nativity play and a Dormition play, are extant. Both follow the canon of the Jesuit school drama. In the Nativity play

dramatic action is provided by Herod's futile persecution of the Jesus child and the tyrant's wretched end; in the Dormition play it is supplied by Jacob's dream of the ladder (the connection to the Virgin's Dormition lies with her role as a "ladder" from man to God). Much of both plays is devoted to the appearance of allegorical figures: Peace, Love, and Humility; Faith, Hope, and Charity; Conscience and Clemency. The school drama was cultivated at some other educational institutions, including the Slavonic-Greco-Latin Academy in Moscow.

The other beginning of the Russian theater, although independent of the Kievan school drama, led to a similar type of theater. Johann Gottfried Gregorii (1631–75), a German pastor who went to Muscovy to make his fortune, was an amateur poet of sorts and became a playwright by accident. Tsar Alexis had taken young Nataliya Naryshkin as his second wife, and the fun-loving young empress was eager for Western-style entertainment. Boyar Artamon Matveev of the Foreign Office was instructed to provide some and produced a German orchestra and a court theater. A wooden building was erected, and Pastor Gregorii was charged with staging a play. He did so in four months, and the play was presented before the tsar and his court on October 17, 1672. Gregorii wrote the play in German verse, and it was translated into Russian prose (with occasional grammatical rhyme). The Russian of the translation is wooden, stilted, heavily Slavonic, but grammatically correct. There are occasional calques from the German. The actors, mostly German, were members of the foreign colony. The female parts were played by young men. The play, known as the *Action of Artaxerxes* (*Artakserksevo deistvo*), is terribly long and unwieldy, as Gregorii prudently followed the text of the Book of

29. Olearius has a description of the antics of the "Chaldeans" who enacted this spectacle. See his *Vermehrte neue Beschrebung*, 284. There were two other "actions" known in Muscovy: *Action of the Terrible Judgment* (enacted on the Sunday before Shrovetide) and *Procession on the Ass* (enacted on Palm Sunday).

Esther to the letter. The performance took ten full hours. It is uncertain whether the first performance was in German or in Russian.[30] Unlike the plays that followed it, *Artaxerxes* has little comedy. The only outright comic scene shows the hangman getting ready to hang Haman and mocking his victim. But an extant plan for the play indicates comic interludes.

Gregorii went on to write five more plays: *Judith, Joseph* (*A Small Cool Comedy about Joseph*), *Bayazed and Tamerlane* (the only nonbiblical play of the lot), *A Pitiful Comedy of Adam and Eve* (an allegory in the manner of the German *Paradeisspiel*, featuring God, the serpent, archangels, and personified virtues), and *Young Tobias* (the text of this play is lost). These plays differ significantly from *Artaxerxes*. *Judith*, in particular, features extensive comedy, delivered by the soldier Susakim and Judith's maid, Abra. *Bayazed and Tamerlane* features Pickelhäring and Tölpel, stock characters of the German folk theater.

After Gregorii's death, Georg Hübner, an interpreter in the Foreign Office, staged *Bayazed and Tamerlane* and a *Comedy about Saint George* (*Egor'evskaya komediya*, now lost). He was in turn replaced by the Kievan Stefan Chizhinsky, who staged two plays, *David and Goliath* and *Bacchus and Venus* (both lost). After the death of Tsar Alexis in 1676, the theater was closed. The theater of Tsar Alexis was largely a dead end, though it was not totally forgotten. Some of Gregorii's plays were staged in the eighteenth century. The whole episode demonstrated Russia's readiness to embrace

Western culture and highlights the role of foreigners in Russian cultural life. Among Gregorii's actors was Lorenz Blumentrost, the court physician. His son Lorenz, also a physician, was to become the first president of the Imperial Academy of Sciences.

Early Recordings of Folk Poetry

The seventeenth century produced the first substantial records of Russian folk poetry, both epic and lyric. The first major collections date from the second half of the eighteenth century. The pieces recorded in the seventeenth century suggest that most—if not all—of the mythical epic songs recorded in the nineteenth century were already extant in seventeenth-century versions. New epic songs, however, were still being composed. Songs about Ivan the Terrible were recent additions, songs about the outlaw Stepan Razin were coming into existence, and songs about Peter the Great and Emelyan Pugachov were yet to come.

Five brief epic songs on events of the Time of Troubles were recorded in a miscellany brought back to England in 1620 by Richard James, chaplain of the British embassy in Moscow. Two of these are laments in the name of Xenia Godunov, daughter of Tsar Boris, speaking as a bird fearful of being captured by the wicked Grishka Otrepyev and put in a cage. One song deals with the death of Michael Skopin-Shuisky, an event related in greater detail both in a more literary historical account (*Writ on the Demise and Burial of Duke Mikhail Vasilievich Shuisky*) and in a bylina found in Kirsha Danilov's collection. One song describes a raid by the Crimean Tatars, and one sings of Tsar Michael's ascent to the throne.

A fairly long and well-composed bylina about the pretender and his consort is ex-

30. André Mazon has produced some good arguments in favor of a Russian presentation. André Mazon and Frédéric Cocron, *La Comédie d'Artaxerxès* (*Artaxerxovo děistvo*) *présentée en 1672 au Tsar Alexis par Gregorii le Pasteur* (Paris: Institut d'études Slaves, 1954), 32–33.

tant in a late seventeenth-century manuscript. A variant close to it is found in Kirsha Danilov's collection. No seventeenth- or even eighteenth-century records have survived of any songs about Stepan Razin because they were strictly forbidden, even under penalty of death.

Some older songs of the mythical type are also extant in seventeenth-century manuscripts—some close to the oral text, some in simple prose paraphrase, and some in a literary version. The *Tale of Sukhan* (*Povest' o Sukhane*), for example, is a work of literature based on a bylina, much as many works of medieval French and German literature are founded in the folk tradition. Ilya of Murom is represented by several different texts, among which the bylina *Ilya of Murom and the Robber Nightingale* appears in many copies. Alyosha Popovich, Mikhail Potok, Sukhan, and other heroes also have at least one text devoted to each of them.

The most remarkable among the works of the seventeenth century that must be assigned to the domain of folk poetry is the *Tale of Woe-Misfortune*. Its moral sensibility is that of the conservative middle class, its style that of the spiritual rime (*dukhovny stikh*). The tale starts literally from Adam and Eve, develops a general view of the human condition where man, inveterately sinful, disobedient, and rebellious, is punished by God with various misfortunes, and then tells the story of an anonymous youth of God-fearing parents who, "being young and foolish at the time, was ashamed to submit to his father and to bow to his mother, and who wanted to live after his own desire." What follows at first resembles the parable of the prodigal son but then takes a different turn. The youth builds a new life abroad and is ready to start a family when he makes the mistake of boasting that

he has made himself a better fortune than the one he lost. Now Woe pursues him relentlessly wherever he turns. He abandons his betrothed and returns to his former dissipated life. He finds himself penniless and hungry at a river crossing, unable to pay the ferryman. Desperate, he wants to drown himself, but Woe appears from behind a rock, gives him a stern lecture, and asks him to submit to her, his only salvation, "for there is nothing wiser in this world than Woe-Misfortune." The young man now makes a desperate attempt to escape Woe by returning to his parents, but Woe will not let him: "If you will fly to the sky like a bird or swim in the blue sea like a fish, I will still be at your right hand!" The narrative now accelerates. The young man "takes to the sky as a steel-blue dove, Woe-Misfortune after him as a gray hawk, he runs away as a gray wolf, she after him as a pack of greyhounds." Always at his side, Woe tempts him to commit robbery and murder so he would end his life on the gallows, but the young man finally finds a safe haven: he enters a monastery, where Woe-Misfortune cannot follow him. The tale ends with a brief prayer.

The *Tale of Woe-Misfortune* is written in the verse of the bylina and uses its tropes and figures, such as tautological compounds ("Woe-Misfortune" and many others), paronomasia ("seduced him with seductive words"), and copulative compounds ("naked-barefoot"). The familiar formulaic phrases of the folk epic appear consistently, as does its imagery. But the *Tale* also contains strong elements of religious literature. The proem is styled in the manner of medieval cosmology. The parable of the prodigal son is a strong presence, and the personification of Woe-Misfortune falls in line with religious allegories found in Byzantine as well as Western literature. The *Tale* also has elements of a realistic or picaresque tale: the drunken youth is robbed of his fine clothes and footwear and finds himself wearing rags and torn bast shoes when he comes to his senses. The *Tale of Woe-Misfortune* shows that the native resources of the Russian folk tradition, if combined with those of religious literature, were sufficient to create literature comparable in quality to analogous creations of Western baroque literature.

Some lyric poetry is extant in seventeenth-century manuscripts, including the miscellany of Richard James. Manuscripts have also been found that reveal efforts by literate noblemen to compose lyric poetry in the manner of the folk song instead of after the fashion of Symeon Polotsky's syllabic verse.

The Beginnings of Prose Fiction

In the seventeenth century the Russian elite, headed by the tsar and his court, began to develop a taste for literary fiction. The fact that more than a few members of the upper classes now knew Polish, and a few even Latin, surely had something to do with it. Manuscript miscellanies of fiction now became more common. Most of the fiction was translated from Polish, though some pieces were translated from South Slavic and Czech. Along with collections of tales from the Byzantine tradition like the *Melissa* and *Stephanites and Inchnelates*, collections translated from Western sources were now circulating in manuscript. Such were excerpts from the *Speculum magnum exemplorum*, a huge collection of moral parables and tales. It reached Russia in a Polish version (printed in Cracow in 1633), parts of which were repeatedly translated and collected, "by the wish and command of Tsar

Alexis," in 1667. The heterogeneous material of the collection (anecdotes, tales, novellas, parables, legends, fables, jokes) is organized into rubrics by the moral message of the piece—"On Honoring One's Parents," "On Temptations of the Flesh," "On Patience." Didactic comments and even dogmatic exegesis accompany the narrative.

Another such collection was the *Gesta romanorum*, first printed in Cologne in 1473 but containing tales known even in classical antiquity. In this collection, as elsewhere, stories of patently profane content were given a pious or even religious allegorical interpretation so that they could be used as material for Sunday sermons. The Russian manuscript version of 1681, translated from the Polish, has only part of the Latin collection. Some of the tales of the *Speculum magnum* and the *Gesta romanorum* entered Russian folklore and the Russian chapbooks. One such piece is the "Tale of Tsar Agei and How He Suffered for His Pride," which also served as the source of Vsevolod Garshin's story "The Legend of Agei the Proud" (1886).[31] Tsar Agei is cured of his pride when he strips off his clothes to swim a river in pursuit of a stag and an angel takes them, assuming his shape and position; Agei is left to continue his life as a naked beggar.

The *Speculum magnum*, the *Gesta romanorum*, and some other collections of tales ostensibly served to inculcate Christian morality. The popular *Historia septem sapientum Romae*, which appears in Russia in several versions beginning in the early seventeenth century (at least seventy copies are extant), hardly reflects a Christian sensibility. Of oriental origin, the *Tale of the*

31. The story appears under various titles in several Western literatures, e.g., *L'Orgueil et présumption de l'empereur Jovinien* (Lyon, 1581).

Seven Sages appeared in a Latin translation (from the Hebrew) in the early Middle Ages, and later in all of the major European languages. The Russian versions were derived from a Polish translation. The *Tale of the Seven Sages* has an artful frame. The wicked stepmother of a young prince is plotting his death, taking advantage of his temporary loss of the power of speech. She denounces him to his father, whom she urges to have his son executed. She tells him a parable, to the effect that failing to cut down a rotten tree will only harm the good trees. One of the seven sages, who are the prince's tutors, responds with his own parable, the story of the faithful hound who saved his master's baby from a vicious hawk but knocked over the baby's cradle as he did so. His master, arriving on the scene, rashly killed the hound and discovered, too late, that the baby was alive and well. The wicked queen answers with another parable—and so it goes until the prince recovers the power of speech and exposes the queen's evil designs. In the process readers hear many tales, some of which they could have found even in *Stephanites and Ichnelates*, the *Gesta romanorum*, and other collections. The *Tale of the Seven Sages* was used by Boccaccio in the *Decameron*, by Chaucer in the *Canterbury Tales*, and by others.

Further collections translated from the Polish and widely circulated in Russia were Aesop's fables, the *Facetiae* of Poggio Bracciolini, and the *Apophthegmata* (witty repartees and aphorisms attributed to illustrious historical personages) by Bieniasz Budny. It all meant that beginning in the seventeenth century, much more than before, Russians would become familiar with the same conceits, plots, and literary imagery that were current in the West.

The seventeenth century saw numerous additions to medieval romances like the *Alexandriad* that were previously known in Russia.[32] The romances that reached Russia in the seventeenth century were no longer high literature in the West but had experienced the fate of so many works and genres once fashionable: they had become popular entertainment. The most popular by far of these romances was the *Tale of Prince Bova*, extant in a large number of copies, none of which predates the seventeenth century. But there is extraliterary evidence that the tale was known earlier: the names of some of its characters appear as given names in Russia in the late sixteenth century. The tale goes back to the Italian romance in verse *Buovo d'Antona* (first printed in 1491), probably via a Serbo-Croatian translation.[33] Although the plot and most of the names of the romance coincide with the Italian original, the Russian text is far removed from the Italian, so it must have had a life of its own for some time. Prince Bova is the son of Queen Militrisa (a Russian distortion of Italian *meretrice*, "harlot"), who has murdered his father and is now married to King Dodon (It. Duodo). Militrisa tries to kill Bova as well, but he escapes and enters the service of King Zenzevei (It. Sansimone, the name of Drusiana's principality), with whose daughter Druzhevna (It. Drusiana) he falls in love. After many exciting adventures Bova is finally united with Druzhevna and returns home to inflict just punishment on Dodon and Militrisa. The *Tale of Prince Bova* became a Russian folktale and a popular chapbook. It returned to high literature

32. The catalog presented here is incomplete, as only the more popular of them, circulated in more than a few copies, will be mentioned.

33. The Italian romance, in turn, goes back to a thirteenth-century French romance, *Beuves d'Hanstone*, by Pierre du Ries.

as Pushkin's fairy tale in verse, "The Tale of Tsar Saltan."[34]

Almost as popular as *Bova* was the *Story of Brave Duke Peter of the Golden Keys*. It was a translation from the Polish, whose ultimate source was the French *Roman de Pierre de Provence et de la belle Maguelonne de Naples* (first printed in 1490). It is a tale of two lovers separated by fate and finally reunited when Peter happens to be taken to a hospital for sick mariners that is founded and run by the beneficent Magilena. This romance features many touching scenes. Russian popular taste tended to run to a sentimental high style and moving, doleful peripeteias—particularly if the subjects were exalted personages. The adventures of Peter and Magilena met all these requirements. Their story also became a popular chapbook.

Other romances translated from the Polish were *The Fair as well as Edifying and Entertaining Tale of Otto, Roman Emperor, and His Spouse, Empress Olunda, whom he exiled to a most desolate and remote desert with her two children* (the title continues for several more lines), known in France as *L'Histoire de Florent et Lyon, enfants de l'empereur de Rome* and in Germany as *Das Volksbuch vom Kaiser Octavianus*; the *History of Apollo, King of Tyre* (originally from the Greek, often the last chapter of the *Gesta romanorum*); the *History of Melusine* (the familiar tale of Count Raimond de Poitou and his wife, who changes into a snake on Saturdays); the *Tale of Bruntsvig, a Prince of the Czech Land* (it originally appeared in Czech in 1565, but the Russian version is from the Polish), a tale of fantastic travel taking the hero to Magnet Mountain,

Diamond Mountain, and the wonders of Arabia; the *Tale of Vasily, Golden-haired Prince of the Czech Land, and Polimestra, His Beautiful French Princess* (a presumed Czech original has not been found), a courtly version of *The Taming of the Shrew*. The *Tale of Prince Valtasar, how he served a certain king* may not be an outright translation, but rather a compilation from several romances. It also contains some pieces known from the *Facetiae* and other miscellanies.

A single Russian romance came from the East, the *Tale of Eruslan Lazarevich*, whose source is Firdausi's epic *Shah Namah* (The Book of Kings). Its hero's name is derived from Persian *uruslan* (lion), epithet of Rustem, one of Firdausi's heroes. Rustem's father was Zalazar—hence Lazarevich. The Persian epic apparently reached the anonymous author of the Russian version via a Turkic paraphrase, as evidenced by a number of Turkic words in the text. *Eruslan Lazarevich* became almost as popular as *Bova* and was also made into a chapbook.

The texts of most of these romances show the hand of translators wholly unskilled in the art of fiction. Their language reeks of the chancery or the consistory and is wooden, awkward, and incoherent. The Russian clerks who were ordered to translate Polish romances for the tsar and his court had the greatest difficulty with the courtly and amatory phraseology of the originals. They might have sought the help of the language of folk poetry but were not prepared to use it in writing.

The romances mentioned here—and a host of similar ones—continued to be read and copied well into the next century and actually coexisted with the printed literature of classicism and sentimentalism. Still, like much of the other literature of the seventeenth century, they were largely a

---

34. Pushkin wrote an incomplete verse epic, *Bova*, while still a student. Other Russian poets, including Karamzin and Radishchev, also used the story.

dead end as far as the living mainstream of Russian literature was concerned.

A desire to put to paper the secular and private concerns of contemporary Russian life was beginning to develop in the seventeenth century. The evidence for this is a body of prose satires and two works of fiction that are close to the Western picaresque novella. The *Tale of Savva Grudtsyn*,[35] written toward the end of the seventeenth century, lets its story begin in 1606. The plot visits several Russian cities, including Moscow. Savva is sent on a business trip by his father, a merchant. He is seduced by the wife of the merchant whom he was sent to have business with. She makes him drink a love potion, causing him to sell his soul to the devil for her love. Savva then travels— airborne—all over Russia in the devil's company and distinguishes himself in the siege of Smolensk by the Poles. But then he falls gravely ill and is severely tormented by the devil, although he has confessed and repented his sins. Even the tsar shows his concern. Finally the Virgin appears to Savva and announces that she will perform a miracle at Moscow's Kazan Cathedral on the day of the Virgin of Kazan. The miracle actually happens: a voice from heaven is heard, and the paper that Savva had signed for the devil drops on the cathedral floor with his signature deleted. Savva then gives all his property to the poor and withdraws to a monastery. The story, comprising about fifteen printed pages, is told artlessly, mostly in the present tense, and rather awkwardly. The narrator seems to be groping for a proper

style and is at ease only when he deals with the moral and religious part of his tale. The language is basic Russo-Slavonic, laced with vernacular words and phrases. It is more readable than most of the translated romances.

Whereas the *Tale of Savva Grudtsyn* is composed of several fantastic motifs implanted into a real-life ambience, the *Tale of Frol Skobeev, a Russian Nobleman* is a realistic story of picaresque adventure. The start of its plot is dated 1680, but its language and descriptive detail suggest that it was written around the turn of the century. It is about as long as *Savva Grudtsyn*, and hence may be considered a novella. Frol Skobeev, a poor nobleman from the provinces who ekes out a living as an informer and shyster, decides to make his fortune by marrying Annushka, the daughter of an important official. He joins Annushka's Christmas party disguised as a girl and bribes her nurse to arrange a game of nuptials in which Annushka will be the bride and Frol the bridegroom. The nurse then makes the other girls sing at the top of their voices so that Annushka's screams cannot be heard when Frol has his way with her. Frol now quickly presses his advantage. He secretly marries a willing Annushka. Her parents, after some futile bluster, give the couple their blessings. Frol Skobeev is set up as a man of property and eventually inherits his father-in-law's fortune. The *Tale of Frol Skobeev* is clearly a satire, conceivably aimed at a particular person: even the names of its characters may be thinly disguised real names. Its language and way of thinking are secular. Frol Skobeev, a rogue with no redeeming traits, is rewarded for his trickery. The story may have been conceived as an ironic comment on the new (Petrine) age by a person indignant about the cynicism and moral decline of Russian society under

---

35. The manuscript title is *Most wonderful and veracious tale, which occurred in this time, how merciful God shows His mercy to Christian people* (*Povest' zelo predivna i istinna, yazhe byst' vo dni siya, kako chelovekolyubivyi Bog yavlyaet chelovekolyubie svoe nad narodom khristianskim*).

Peter the Great. It has been preserved in several copies and was probably read as pure entertainment by many readers. The episode of the lover disguised as a woman is of course an ancient and widely known theme of fiction.

The *Tale of Frol Skobeev* is one of a number of satirical works showing that Russians under the Romanovs were quite capable of an irreverent, cynical, and irreligious view of life. The *Kalyazin Petition* contains the names of some real people. In it the monks of Kalyazin Monastery address Symeon, archbishop of Tver (1676–81), asking for relief from what they perceive as the injustices they suffer at the hands of their abbot, Gabriel. As they complain about what is clearly Gabriel's strict enforcement of the monastic rule, they sadly recall the idle, dissolute and drunken life that they were allowed to lead before he was made abbot and that they take to be their rightful privilege. The satire is racy, graphic, and thoroughly irreverent. Its irony is sharp and witty. Several other anticlerical satires of this kind are extant, for instance, the *Tale of Sabbas the Priest*, on the misadventures of a provincial candidate for the priesthood in Moscow, and the *Tale of the Drunk Who Entered Paradise*, a parody of the pious pilgrimage genre. *Service to the Tavern*, also known as *Holiday of the Tavern Drunks*, is a spirited parody of Holy Mass, the saint's life, and other elements of religious life. The milieu of a Russian tavern is vividly presented in the formulaic language of the church. Satire of this type (*parodia sacra*) was common in Western Europe throughout the Middle Ages and does not necessarily evince antireligious sentiment.

Other satirical stories have the judiciary for their target. The *Tale of Yorsh Yershovich* ("Ruff Ruffson") reports on the trial of the ruff before a court of other fishes, with the bream and other large fishes serving as plaintiffs and accusers. The ruff is clearly a poor nobleman who tries to make a living by his wits. The big fishes are boyars and large landowners. The court is openly corrupt and the whole proceedings a travesty of justice. (The *Tale of Shemyaka's Judgment* is another such satire.) Seventeenth-century satire reflects a movement toward modernity, a secular worldview, and the West. By that time there had developed a class of literate laymen who were socially mobile, took a critical view of the world, and expressed that view in the vernacular. Slavonic had acquired a new function: it was used for ironic and parodic effect.

5

The Eighteenth Century

The reforms of Peter the Great (r. 1682–1725) changed Russia from a semi-Asiatic despotate into a socially and culturally backward European power. Military or civil service, often under superiors who were foreigners or Germans, Poles, or Ukrainians from the recently conquered western provinces, thoroughly Europeanized the gentry within a generation or two. Though there was some opposition to it, the new life-style appealed to most. It meant adopting European-style dwellings and clothes; smoking tobacco and drinking hard liquor or imported wines instead of native beer and mead; allowing women to participate in social events (balls, dinner parties, receptions); and being conversant in at least one foreign language, usually French or German.

Peter's modern army, navy, and civil service created a new middle class. Nobility could now be attained by rising through the "table of ranks." The new nobles, largely urban, pursued an even more westernized life-style than did the hereditary rural gentry. Peter the Great promoted commerce and industry and granted the merchant class

ample privileges, such as exemption from military service, land grants, and self-administration of trade organizations and guilds. The merchant class remained unwesternized well into the nineteenth century, however, and its culture continued to be linked to the church and Russian folk traditions. Russian literature views the merchant class almost always from the outside, if at all.

The reorganization of the Russian state and Russian society was costly. It was paid for by a serious deterioration of the condition of the Russian peasantry and the eighteenth century saw serfdom at its worst. It also saw much peasant unrest, culminating in the Pugachov rebellion of 1773.

Under the three empresses, Anna (1730–40), Elizabeth (1741–62), and Catherine II (1763–96), and most notably under Peter III (1762), the gentry was allowed gradually to increase its privileges and rid itself of all duties. The reign of Catherine II, in particular, was a golden age for the great nobles who owned thousands of serfs. They could afford to build elegant manor houses with beautiful parks, kept large numbers of live-ried servants, entertained hundreds of guests at hunting parties and balls, and had private orchestras and even theaters man-ned by serfs, some of them trained at their owner's expense in the capital cities or even abroad. These nobles also hired French tutors for their children, assembled libraries of books in Western languages, and bought European art and musical instruments. Many traveled widely in Europe, and some stayed there for years on end.

The Russian aristocracy soon developed a taste for literature and the theater. More than a few high dignitaries earned them-selves at least a modest place in Russian letters. Some major poets and writers were of the aristocracy and held high government office, for example, the satirist Kantemir, the dramatists and poets Sumarokov and Kheras-kov, and the versatile poet and writer Nikolai Lvov. Others, like Derzhavin, Karam-zin, and Zhukovsky, acquired high status largely through their literary work.

Peter the Great put an end to the role of the clergy in Russian literature. In 1701 the boyar Ivan Alekseevich Musin-Pushkin was instructed "to take charge of the Holy Pat-riarch's house, the bishoprics, and matters pertaining to monasteries." Musin-Pushkin immediately ordered that "monks should write nothing at all when alone in their cells, nor should they keep ink or paper; and if they are to write, then only in the refectory, with the permission of their superiors and in compliance with the traditions of the church fathers." In 1708 "civil script," which had a Latin ductus, was introduced for use in all secular affairs; Cyrillic was retained for use in religious texts. Secular and religious literature now went their sepa-rate ways. In 1721 the Russian church was officially made on organ of the state, run by the Holy Synod, which was headed by a lay

procurator appointed by the tsar. In this, too, Peter followed the example of Euro-pean Protestant monarchies. Feofan Pro-kopovich, archbishop of Novgorod and a leading poet, man of letters, and preacher of his age, was the father of the "Clerical Reg-ulations," which in effect severed the ties between the Russian church and Russian literature. In the West, even in modern times, many clergymen were also important men of letters. In Russia no member of the clergy ever entered secular literature with any success. Eighteenth-century Russian poets, however, continued the tradition started by Symeon of Polotsk in that almost all of them wrote religious poetry and tried their hand at versified renditions of the Psalter.[1]

Under Peter the Great education became independent of the church. Peter founded a number of technical schools, including a naval academy and an engineering school, and in 1714 issued a ukase to open grammar schools throughout the empire. He also made arrangements for the establishment of the Academy of Sciences and Fine Arts, which was officially opened by his widow, Catherine I, in 1725.

The Imperial Academy immediately attracted some first-rate scientists and scho-lars, mostly from German-speaking coun-tries: the mathematicians Daniel Bernoulli and Leonhard Euler, the physicist Friedrich Wilhelm Richmann, the historian Gerhard

---

1. The total number of versified psalms com-pleted by the end of the century exceeds one thousand separate texts. Other texts of the Old Testament and New Testament, religious hymns and chants, and parts of the liturgy were also versified. Spiritual odes were written by many eighteenth-century poets. The spiritual ode sur-vived much longer (well into the nineteenth century) as a major poetic genre than did the panegyrical ode addressed to a ruler or benefactor.

Friedrich Müller (1705–83),[2] and others. Some of the members of the academy also wrote verse or composed music. At a convocation the empress would be greeted by an academician's original cantata and panegyrical declamations, and the academy would be responsible for the arrangement of fireworks, illuminations, concerts, and spectacles for the empress and her court. The academy played a decisive role in the growth of Russian literature. Vasily Trediakovsky, secretary of the academy and later a professor of eloquence, and Mikhail Lomonosov, scientist, grammarian, historian, and a leading academician, were the founders of modern Russian poetry. Their epoch-making treatises on Russian versification were written as reports to the academy. Until the appearance of the first Russian journals in the 1760s, the academy provided the only outlet for serious literary publications: *Notes to the News* (1728–42), printed as a supplement to the newspaper *Saint Petersburg News* (published by the academy beginning in 1727), and later *Monthly Essays Serving the Public Weal and Entertainment* (1755–64).

In 1732 the Cadet Academy, later called the Corps of Infantry Cadets, was founded in Petersburg. Its graduates were given officer's rank, a way to circumvent Peter's decree by which even nobles had to rise through the ranks. Circles of lovers of poetry and drama were soon active at this school. Aleksandr Sumarokov, the father of modern Russian drama, was a member of its first graduating class. Mikhail Kheraskov, class of 1751, went on to become a leading man of letters.

In 1755 Moscow University was founded, largely through the efforts of Lomonosov, and in the following year it began to publish a newspaper, *The Moscow News*. In 1760 a journal, *Profitable Entertainment*, was initiated there by Kheraskov.

Gradually secondary education also began to spread across the empire. In 1758 a secondary school (*gimnaziya*) was established in Kazan, a city which in 1804 became the site of a university. The great poet Gavrila Derzhavin was among the school's first alumni. Russian education developed from the top down. Russia had a distinguished academy before it had a university; it had a university before it had a network of secondary schools; and it had adequate secondary schools long before it had any organized elementary education.

The first groupings of literati arose in the second half of the century. The court of Catherine II and Moscow University were centers of literary activity. Catherine, who had serious literary interests and was herself a prolific playwright (in Russian and French), encouraged literary activities. Her secretary and editorial assistant, Ivan Elagin (1725–94), headed a circle of playwrights that included Denis Fonvizin and Vladimir Lukin. Nikolai Lvov (1751–1803), a man of broad culture and diverse interests as well as a competent minor poet and collector of folk songs, was the central figure of a circle including his brother-in-law Derzhavin, Vasily Kapnist, Mikhail Muravyov, and several minor poets and men of letters. Mikhail Kheraskov was the focus of literary activities around Moscow University for many years. The tireless Nikolai Novikov gathered collaborators for his journalistic and book-publishing activities first in Petersburg (from 1769 to 1779) and then in Moscow. In the 1790s Nikolai Karamzin assumed a position of leadership both by his example and by his editorial initiative.

---

2. See J. L. Black, *G.-F. Müller and the Imperial Russian Academy* (Kingston and Montreal: McGill-Queen's University Press, 1986).

Peter the Great launched a program to make Western thought and knowledge available in Russian. Even some of his high-ranking aides were pressed into service as translators. Most of the works translated during Peter's reign were of a scientific or technical nature, but some famous works in history, law, and political science were also translated and printed,[3] as were some works acquainting the Russian public with Western manners and etiquette, classical mythology, and the emblems, clichés, and anecdotes current in sophisticated Western society.[4] The translators of all these works were a motley crowd: Muscovite officials and clerks, Ukrainian clerics, Polish noblemen, Swedish prisoners of war, and Germans from the Moscow "German suburb." Their lexicon was a chaos of Slavonic high style and vulgarisms, Ukrainianisms and Polonisms, loan translations from the German, French, or Latin, and thousands of outright borrowings. The grammar was anarchic, mixing Slavonic, Muscovite, and Ukrainian forms and syntax. Subsequently Russian literature, in particular the theoretical and poetic works of Trediakovsky, Lomonosov, and Sumarokov, played a decisive role in transforming the chaotic language they faced as young men into the

serviceable literary idiom they left to their successors.

Translations of works of imaginative literature gradually became available. Trediakovsky's translation of Paul Tallement's *Voyage à l'isle d'Amour ou La Clef des coeurs*, presented to the academy in 1730, was the first modern work of fiction to appear in Russian translation. Trediakovsky also translated Horace's *Ars poetica*, Boileau's *Art poétique*, John Barclay's *Argenis*, and Fénelon's *Aventures de Télémaque*. In the course of the eighteenth century most major Latin and Greek classics were translated. French literature, often read in the original, was translated as well as imitated. Echoes of Malherbe, Boileau, Racine, Corneille, Molière, Jean-Baptiste and Jean-Jacques Rousseau, and especially Voltaire appear constantly. Some influential German authors were Johann Christian Günther, admired and imitated by Lomonosov, Johann Wilhelm Ludwig Gleim, whose Anacreontic odes influenced Sumarokov's, Christian Fürchtegott Gellert, whose fables were paraphrased by Ivan Chemnitzer, among others, and Friedrich Gottlieb Klopstock, an influence (along with Milton) on Kheraskov's metaphysical poems. Among the English, Milton, Pope, Addison, Young, and Thomson were well known. Shakespeare met with the Russians' full approval only since the 1770s. Among the Italians, Ariosto, Tasso, and Metastasio were the best known.

Toward the end of the century enough of a reading public existed to make the translation of novels commercially profitable. Lesage's *Gil Blas* was translated in 1754, his *Le Diable boiteux* in 1763, Voltaire's *Micromégas* and *Memnon* in the academy's *Monthly Essays* in 1756, and his *Zadig* in Sumarokov's *Busy Bee* in 1759. From the 1760s to the 1780s all of Voltaire's known works

3. For example, *De iure belli et pacis* (1625), by Hugo Grotius, *De iure naturae et gentium* (1672), by Samuel Pufendorf, and *Money and Trade Considered* (1705), by John Law.

4. Baroque emblems and symbols came to Russia with the triumphal arcs, gates, obelisks, statuary, and fireworks and illuminations celebrating Peter's victories. Printed texts explained the symbolism of these artifacts or described and commented on a particular structure or celebration, under such titles as *Triumphal Gates to the Temple of Immortal Glory* (Moscow, 1703), *Glorious Triumph of the Liberator of Livonia, Captor and Conqueror of the Proud Swedish Lion* (Moscow, 1704), and *Politico-Majestic Apotheosis of the Glorious Valor of Our All-Russian Hercules* (Moscow, 1709).

were translated, some repeatedly. Defoe's *Robinson Crusoe* was translated between 1762 and 1764, Cervantes's *Don Quixote* and Rousseau's *La Nouvelle Héloïse* in 1769, Goethe's *Werther* in 1781, and Prévost's *Manon Lescaut* in 1790. In the 1790s the novels of Richardson, Sterne, Fielding, Smollett, Rousseau, and others were routinely translated and soon were imitated. Fourteen novels by Ducray-Duminil appeared in Russian between 1794 and 1809, and ten novels by Ann Radcliffe were published during the same time span.

From the 1730s Russian literature begins to develop in step with the literature of the West. Trediakovsky and Lomonosov still followed an aesthetic that was substantially baroque, although their philosophical worldview was that of the Enlightenment. Elements of a baroque sensibility can be detected even as late as Derzhavin. Sumarokov and his many followers were vintage classicists who saw a marked contrast between their own poetic practices and those of Lomonosov. Sumarokov preached and practiced classicist *vraisemblance* (verisimilitude), *bienséance* (propriety), and a "natural" and lucid style of expression and castigated what he saw as Lomonosov's pompous imagery and turgid diction. Sumarokov's classicism was in turn superseded in poetry by the preromantic style and sensibility of Edward Young, James Macpherson's Ossian, and the German Storm and Stress (*Sturm und Drang*), which informed Kheraskov, Derzhavin, and Karamzin, and in drama by the manner of the *comédie larmoyante*. Sentimentalist prose fiction in the manner of Rousseau and Sterne also made its appearance in Russia without much delay.

Russian journalism, which was later to become the lifeblood of Russian literature, was slow in starting. The first newspaper, *The News* (*Vedomosti*), was founded by Peter in 1703. In 1727 it became *The Saint Petersburg News*, published by the Academy of Sciences. Only in 1759 did the first journals that owed their existence to private initiative appear: Sumarokov's *Busy Bee* and *Idle Time Put to Good Use*, published by alumni of the Corps of Infantry Cadets. Both were short-lived. The 1760s and 1770s saw the appearance of a series of equally ephemeral satirical journals patterned after *The Tatler* and *The Spectator*, some of them edited and published by Nikolai Novikov, the father of Russian journalism, and some by Catherine II herself.

In 1779 Novikov moved from Petersburg to Moscow, where he published the daily, *Moscow News* (1779–89), with a weekly supplement for children (1785–89), several journals, and a series of translations of works by Western authors: Shakespeare, Rousseau, Diderot, Beaumarchais, Lessing, and many others. The events of 1789 put an end to all these activities. Novikov, an active Freemason and advocate of social reform, was arrested in 1792 and kept in prison until Catherine's death in 1796. He was succeeded as the leader of Russian journalism by Nikolai Karamzin, whose *Moscow Journal*, though also short-lived (1791–92), became the prototype of the encyclopedic "thick journals" of the next century. Subsequently Karamzin initiated the publication of several more journals and almanacs, including *Aglaia* (1794–95) and *The Aonids* (1796–99).

The age of Catherine II saw the first great flowering of Russian poetry. The writing of occasional poetry was now a common practice among members of the educated upper class. Even some society ladies (Kheraskov's wife, Elizaveta, for example) wrote verse. The quality of Russian poetry was now on a par with European poetry in all the major genres.

The Russian theater developed slowly during the first half of the century. Peter's efforts to establish a public theater with the aid of a German traveling troupe ended in failure, but they caused some private theaters to spring up. The school drama, brought to Muscovy from the Ukraine, was cultivated at several divinity schools. Some foreign troupes visited Russia in the 1730s and 1740s, and in later years these visits became frequent and regular. The imperial theaters, which were to hold a monopoly on Russian theatrical performances in the two capitals for more than a century, developed from amateur performances by students of the Corps of Infantry Cadets, led by Sumarokov, who also provided the Russian stage with a repertory of classicist tragedies and comedies. Elizabeth established the first permanent public theater in Saint Petersburg in 1756.

Catherine II, who wrote Russian comedies in her leisure hours, also showed interest in the progress of the Russian stage. In 1773 she had a theater, the Bolshoi, built in Saint Petersburg, and in 1779 she founded a school for the training of actors, dancers, and singers. During her reign several public theaters in Saint Petersburg and Moscow were placed under government management, and eventually government monopoly was established over all theatrical activities in the capital cities.

By the last quarter of the century Russians, particularly in the capital cities, had become avid theatergoers. Tragedy and comedy, tragic and comic opera, and ballet all reached a European level. A large number of French, Italian, and German plays of all genres was translated. Much as in the West, the lighter genres, especially comic opera and vaudeville, were the money-makers, both in the capitals and in the provinces. In

tragedy, Sumarokov's plays were still staged, but he was plainly bested by Nikolai Nikolev, Yakov Knyazhnin, and Vladislav Ozerov. In comedy, Denis Fonvizin, Vasily Kapnist, Vladimir Lukin, and others fully succeeded in imparting to that genre a Russian ethos and attacking some real ills of Russian life—even serfdom. In comic opera, such as Mikhail Popov's *Anyuta* (1772), Aleksandr Ablesimov's *Miller, Sorcerer, Cheat, and Matchmaker* (1779), and Mikhail Matinsky's *Arcades of Saint Petersburg* (1792), Russian folk tunes, dances, and customs were introduced to the applause of the public.

Prose fiction, the novel in particular, grew more slowly than poetry and drama. Two separate strains, a "high" and a "low," developed side by side. Literacy now extended to the urban lower-middle and servant class, and there was a market for pulp fiction and songbooks. Romances that had circulated in manuscript in the seventeenth century, like *Prince Bova* or *Peter of the Golden Keys*, as well as new tales of adventure, romantic brigandage, and genteel love, went through many printings as chapbooks well into the nineteenth century.

In the meantime, high fiction followed the trends of Western literature. Fyodor Emin was the first Russian novelist. His novels of the 1760s pioneered the moral tale (*conte moral*), the philosophical tale (*conte philosophique*), and the sentimental epistolary novel, all of which became widespread and popular toward the end of the century.

Nikolai Karamzin was the first great Russian man of letters whose fame and influence rested with his prose, discursive as well as imaginative. His *Letters of a Russian Traveler* (1791–1801), patterned after Sterne's *Sentimental Journey*, lacked Sterne's wit and whimsy. But the letters' urbanity and easy intimacy with European intellectual life, together with the Russian traveler's quiet self-assurance, demonstrated that an educated Russian was now fully a European.

Poetry

During the first quarter of the eighteenth century, writing in verse was a widespread practice. Most of the time it had little in common with poetry. The verse was on the whole religious or didactic. Figured and emblematic verse was very popular. In 1707, in Chernigov, Archbishop Ioann Maksimovich published a book entitled *O Virgin, Mother of God*, written entirely in verse (even the title)—a total of twenty-four thousand lines. Laymen had also acquired the habit. In 1717 Prokopovich observed in a private letter: "Everybody now writes verse ad nauseam." The verse was syllabic until the epoch-making innovations of Trediakovsky and Lomonosov in the 1730s.

In the age of Peter the Great some members of the Moscow German community wrote Russian syllabotonic verse after the German fashion. Willim Mons (1688–1724), brother of Anna Mons, at one time the tsar's mistress, wrote love songs in German and Russian. Two German pastors, Ernst Glück (1652–1705) and Johann Werner Paus (1670–1735), translated German hymns into Russian. When Lorenz Blumentrost (1692–1755) became the first president of the Academy of Sciences, he hired Paus, who had been his teacher, to work for the academy as a translator. There may well have been a connection between Paus's efforts and Trediakovsky's eventual move to syllabotonic versification.

Meanwhile the genres of poetry that had come to Muscovy from the Kiev Academy continued to be cultivated, mostly at the Moscow Slavonic-Latin ("Greco" had been dropped) Academy and several divinity schools. Secular didactic works were often composed partly or entirely in verse. Fyodor Polikarpov (d. 1731), a grammarian, lexicographer, and historian, and Leonty Magnitsky (1669–1739), author of a famous arithmetic text, both alumni of the Slavonic-Latin Academy, wrote their works in verse.

Three important churchmen under Peter the Great, to whom Ukrainian literature may have a better claim than Russian literature does, continued the tradition of syllabic religious and panegyrical verse. Stefan Yavorsky (1658–1722), a Galician, became caretaker of the patriarchate after the death of Adrian, last patriarch of Moscow, in 1701 and subsequently president of the newly founded Holy Synod. He left a voluminous legacy of theological works, sermons, and poetry. Yavorsky wrote verse in Latin, Polish, and Slavonic with equal facility. Among his Russo-Slavonic verse, his patriotic "Verses on Mazepa's Treason, Published in the Name of All Russia" (1709) appear labored and uninspired, whereas the cycle "Emblemmata et Symbola" (1707), in memory of a Kievan prelate, reveals Yavorsky's true worth. These gnomic stanzas on the perishability of the body and the immortality of the soul, a believer's serene faith through all trials and tribulations, and other such topics have a mature dignity and the polished form worthy of a poet laureate, an honor Yavorsky earned for his Latin verse. Yavorsky's rhymes show that he pronounced his Slavonic as a Ukrainian would.

Feofan Prokopovich (1681–1733), a Kievan, had (like Yavorsky) at one time embraced the Uniate faith as he pursued his studies in Poland and in Rome. But unlike the scholarly Yavorsky, his ideological antagonist, he was politically ambitious and unscrupulous. Though nominally Yavorsky's subordinate, he played a major role in drafting and implementing Peter's reform of the Russian church over Yavorsky's objections. Prokopovich, a professor of poetics and rhetoric at the Kiev Academy early in his life, was a prolific author. He wrote many theological tracts, as well as a number of works on the administration and reorganization of the Russian church. He was famous for his sermons, and also composed a fair amount of poetry—religious, panegyric, occasional, and even satirical and Anacreontic. His "Epinikion," a lengthy celebratory ode on the Russian victory over the Swedes at Poltava, is close to similar efforts by French and German panegyrists of the period.

Dimitry Tuptalo (1651–1709), metropolitan of Rostov, was yet another Ukrainian cleric to become a Muscovite prelate. His remarkable poetry has even stronger Ukrainian traits than that of his compatriots Yavorsky and Prokopovich and should rightfully be considered within the context of Ukrainian literature.[5]

The best example of Russian syllabic religious poetry belongs to Pyotr Buslaev, of whom it is only known that he was a graduate of the Moscow Slavonic-Latin Academy and a deacon of the Kremlin Cathedral of the Dormition. He left a long poem in alexandrines (two parts, each with a hundred couplets), entitled "Spiritual Contemplation, Rendered in Verse, on the Transmigration to Eternal Life of Her Excellency, Baroness Mariya Yakovlevna Stroganova" (1734). The baroness (1677–1733), heiress to her husband's millions, was also an imperial lady-in-waiting and a major philanthropist. She may have been the poet's personal benefactress. The poem gives an austere account of the fifty-six-year-old matron's death and burial in the first part and reports her ascent to and reception in heaven in the second. Mystical and allegorical figures accompany the baroness on her progress. Christ the Crucified and the Holy Virgin, assisted by angels, are present in her hour of death. When she ascends the ladder to heaven, her virtues (faith, a clear conscience, charity, continence, and love) accompany her in the shape of beautiful maidens. The poem is as strong in its starkly realistic depiction of the dying woman and the grief in her house as it is in its ideal images of religious allegory. The serious dignity and warm pathos of the poem never seem pompous or insincere. The verse is polished, and there are many rhymes that even a poet of the golden age would have considered good. The language is Russian, with no more Slavonic than is found in Lomonosov's odes. A moderate number of Latin loanwords appears: *instrument, fundament, element, kontsert, triumf.* The imagery and symbolism of the poem, essentially of the kind typical of a religious hymn, are simple enough. They are, however, meticulously explained in footnotes, a practice also continued by some later Russian poets and not uncommon in the West. The general impression is decidedly one of Catholic or Protestant baroque, although no outright violations of Orthodox theology are apparent. Buslaev's poem shows that Russian syllabic verse had reached a level where it was capable of imaginative yet controlled expression of feeling without having to lean on foreign examples or depend on clichés. Buslaev was a poet, not a rhymester.

Kantemir

Antiokh Dmitrievich Kantemir (1709–44) is one of the several surprises served up by Russian literature. He was the son of the hospodar (viceroy) of Moldavia, also an im-

5. See p. 107.

portant man of letters, who cast his lot with the Russians and had to flee his country when Peter's campaign against the Turks collapsed in 1711. Kantemir received an excellent, mostly private education, began to write verse while still in his teens, and was befriended by leading Russian literati like Prokopovich and the historian Vasily Tatishchev. He wrote his first satires around 1730, the year when, as an officer of the guards, he took part in the palace revolt that put Anna Ioannovna on the throne. In 1731 he was dispatched to London as the empress's resident. He became her ambassador to France in 1738. In London and in Paris he associated with leading men of letters and always found time from his official duties to do some literary work. He translated Horace, Juvenal, Cornelius Nepos, Anacreon, Montesquieu's *Lettres persanes*, Fontenelle's *Discours sur la pluralité des mondes*, and parts of Boileau's satires. He corresponded with the Petersburg Academy of Sciences and wrote fables, epigrams, and some erotic verse, as well as starting an epic poem, the *Petride*. But his fame rests on his satires, which appeared in print as late as 1762 (a French translation had appeared in 1749) but were widely circulated in manuscript.

In the nine satires, amply annotated by the author, Kantemir follows the example of and acknowledges a debt to Horace, Juvenal, Boileau, La Bruyère, Pope, and others. Kantemir's second satire, on the arrogance of old nobility, follows Boileau's fifth; his fourth, on the hazards of being a satirist, is close to Boileau's ninth. The third features a series of character sketches à la La Bruyère: the miser, the spendthrift, the gossip, the bore, the hypocrite, the lickspittle, the drunk, and so on. The sixth contains some variations on Horace's second epode, "Beatus ille, qui procul negotiis," and has a

number of quotes from Horace's epistles and satires. The first, "To My Reason" (or "On the Detractors of Education") and the seventh, "On Education," contain the kernel of Kantemir's enlightened moral and social views. Contemptuous of all class or other prejudices—an attitude more admirable in a man of royal blood (Kantemir's mother came from the imperial Kantakuzen family) than in the bourgeois Boileau—Kantemir measures a man's worth solely by his good works and service to society. He firmly believes that education helps a man to be a better human being and to take better care of his public and private affairs. He asserts that impressionable childhood and adolescence are best suited to implanting humane ideas and civilized habits in men, as well as that well-tempered love, careful attention to a child's progress, proper understanding of a young mind and soul, and a willingness to praise are more effective than stern rules or severe discipline. A hundred years later, Belinsky said that Kantemir's ideas on education were "so sane and humane that they ought to be printed in golden letters" and suggested that every newlywed couple should learn Kantemir's lines by heart. Kantemir's championing of education is by no means facile. He introduces into the seventh satire its many formidable enemies and is not at all sure that they will be vanquished. Their individual voices belong to familiar types: Criton, the obscurantist; Sylvan, the hidebound materialist; Philaret, the narrow man of virtue; Luke, the drunken Epicurean; Medor, the frenchified fop.

Kantemir draws remarkably sharp pictures of life in Petrine Russia. In the sixth satire he graphically describes the arduous and humiliating activities of a Russian who wants to get ahead in the world, and also the particular hardships to be endured by a Petersburg courtier. The vices castigated reflect unmistakably Russian traits: widespread drunkenness, pettifoggery and obfuscation in official places, bigotry and obscurantism among the upper classes, and crude superstition among the uneducated are illustrated by examples that have the ring of real life.

Kantemir's language is decidedly Russian, not Slavonic, yet it is urbane, supple, and modern. His translations of Boileau's satires put his Russian to a crucial test, which they pass most creditably. The translations simplify the original and fail to render some of the finer nuances, puns, and witticisms, but on the whole they show that the Russian language can do the job. Kantemir's syntax is often Latinate after the fashion of his times, but this is compensated by many idiomatic turns and colloquialisms. Sumarokov's deprecating comments in his second epistle ("On Poetry") to the effect that Kantemir, "being a foreigner, did not know the true beauty of our language" are quite groundless. Kantemir's satires are as lively and casual as anything by Sumarokov, and certainly more graceful.

Kantemir's syllabic alexandrines, with a caesura after the seventh or fifth syllable and feminine-rhyme couplets, read smoothly. His caesura, which often does not coincide with a syntactic pause, creates an unobtrusive rhythm unlike that of syllabotonic verse; but it is verse nevertheless. Kantemir's rhymes are correct—often ingenious. Altogether, there is ample reason to agree with Belinsky, who said that modern Russian literature began with Kantemir.

Trediakovsky

Vasily Kirillovich Trediakovsky (1703–69), the son of a village priest, left his home near Astrakhan at the age of twenty to attend the Moscow Slavonic-Latin Academy, where, in his words, he "went straight into rhetoric," having learned some Latin from Catholic missionaries in Astrakhan. At the academy he was taught to write syllabic verse. In 1726 he made his way to Holland, whence he traveled to Paris on foot. Supported by the Russian ambassador, he was able to attend the Sorbonne. Having received his diploma, he returned to Russia in 1730, an erudite humanist who could write bad but correctly versified French, Latin, and Russian verse. His "Celebratory Verses to the City of Paris" (c. 1728) follow the conventions of a *laus urbis* but ring true, as they conclude:

> Beautiful city! dear banks of the Seine!
> Who does not love thee? Only a brutish
>   mind would not!
> But I will not ever be able to forget thee
> So long as I live on earth.

Trediakovsky's verse translation, still syllabic, of Abbé Tallement's *Voyage à l'isle d'Amour ou La Clef des coeurs* (1730), awkward and graceless though it was, still was the first published attempt to bend the Russian language to the requirements of modern belles lettres. It earned Trediakovsky a position as a secretary-translator with the academy.

In 1735 Trediakovsky presented to the academy a treatise, *A New and Brief Method of Composing Russian Verse, with Definitions of the Pertinent Terms*, in which he correctly described the natural prosody of Russian and drew from it a new system of versification, the syllabotonic, used in German and English poetry. In this system a line of verse is defined by a constant number of syllables and by rules that determine stressed and unstressed positions in the line. In a trochaic line, for example, only the odd-numbered syllables may be stressed, and all even-numbered syllables must be unstressed. Trediakovsky added to his treatise various examples of his own poetry, written according to the new rules. Trediakovsky's insights were substantially correct, and his suggestions pointed in the right direction, but his cautiously worded paper is so poorly focused and so badly organized that its important message almost gets lost. A comparison with Lomonosov's lucid and vigorous presentation of the subject, which goes further than Trediakovsky's, shows Lomonosov to be much the superior theorist.[6] Trediakovsky's system was soon amplified by Lomonosov, and since the 1740s both, along with a rapidly increasing number of other poets, wrote verses whose versification was essentially the same as that of most Russian poetry to this day.

In 1745 Trediakovsky was appointed professor of eloquence at the academy. A tireless worker, he produced further grammatical and philological treatises,[7] many volumes of translations in verse and in prose, some plays, and a great deal of secular and spiritual verse, including a complete version of the Psalter. He also fulfilled the functions of a court poet, a position that was not highly regarded at the time. In 1740 Trediakovsky, after a run-in with a minor court aide, was taken to the guardhouse and given a severe flogging by order of Empress Anna's court minister. Trediakovsky's modest success was also short-lived. He was soon superseded as court poet by Lomonosov. In the 1750s his poetic efforts were no longer taken seriously or even printed. He

lost his position with the academy in 1759 and died forgotten and in poverty.

Trediakovsky's panegyrical verse, syllabotonic or syllabic, hardly rises above the level of Symeon Polotsky and his school. Both versions of his "Solemn Ode on the Surrender of the City of Gdansk" (the syllabic version of 1734 and the syllabotonic of 1742) are clumsy and wooden, lacking any sustained rhythm. This ode, inspired by Boileau's "Ode sur la prise de Namur," from which it borrows metric and strophic structure, much of the imagery and phraseology, as well as whole lines verbatim, drastically exhibits the characteristic deficiencies of Trediakovsky's poetry. He needlessly expands his own work beyond the limits of the original. He turns the elegant conceits of the original into ludicrous bathos: "Quelle docte et sainte ivresse" becomes "What sober drunkenness." A tortuous Latinate syntax often makes comprehension difficult. On the positive side, the Russian poet clearly understands Boileau's conceits and adds many of his own from a rich arsenal of classical mythology.

Trediakovsky also wrote elegies, sonnets, epigrams, fables, madrigals, and songs. Some of the songs have poetic merit. Quite a few were set to music and survived their creator. Trediakovsky's more ambitious longer poems contain some sonorous lines and felicitous images but are invariably spoiled by his tone-deafness, which let him allow grotesque tongue-twisters to stand, destroy his tonic rhythm by putting heavy syllables in the upbeat, and mix pompous Slavonicisms with prosaic vulgarisms. Trediakovsky tended to lapse into profusion and verbosity, and numbing accumulations of tautologies. This is true even of his more successful efforts, such as the ode "Praise to Ingermanland and the Imperial City of Saint Petersburg" (1752), which launched a long tradi-

6. A new edition of Trediakovsky's work, *A Method of Composing Russian Verse, corrected and amplified from that published in 1735* (1752), adopted Lomonosov's suggestions.

7. For example, Trediakovsky's *Discourse on Old and New Orthography* (1748) demands that Slavonic spelling be replaced by Russian, partly anticipating Lomonosov.

tion of verse and prose devoted to that city. The ode has some good lines, and its dozen quatrains in iambic pentameter flow smoothly; but it also has some cacophonous, awkward, and pedestrian lines that spoil the whole.

Trediakovsky's complete versified rendition of the Psalter is his finest poetic achievement. The sacred text forced him to refrain from unwarranted improvisation. His version is simple and dignified, borne by genuine religious feeling.

Trediakovsky's *Theoptia* (1750–54), inspired by Pope's *Essay on Man*, which he read in French translation, consists of six epistles in alexandrines, altogether some five thousand lines. It was an attempt to formulate a worldview consistent with modern science and Deist philosophy, yet acceptable to an only moderately enlightened Orthodox church. The *Theoptia* is not without merit. It shows an erudite mind familiar with Plato and Lucretius, Descartes and Newton, and a host of ancient and modern philosophers. But the whole is vitiated by awkward formulations, as well as lapses into crude materialism and literalism when Trediakovsky introduces examples and observations of his own.

Trediakovsky's *Telemachis* (printed in 1766), a heroic epic in hexameters based on Fénelon's *Aventures de Télémaque*, a work which earned him mostly vituperation and ridicule, was in fact of considerable merit. It introduced the dactylic-trochaic hexameter to Russian poetry, having enough well-formed lines to show that this was an attractive addition to a Russian poet's repertory. The translation of Fénelon's thoughts and conceits is often vigorous. It is likely that the reasons Catherine II and her courtiers heaped scorn on Trediakovsky's *Telemachis* were similar to those that caused Louis XIV and his court to reject Fénelon's work. The

moralizing tone of the *Telemachis* and its direct attacks on tyranny, favoritism, and court intrigue hardly appealed to Catherine. An episode in which crazed King Pygmalion of Tyre is first poisoned and then strangled by his consort, who wants to elevate her young lover to the throne, must have elicited unpleasant associations. On balance the *Telemachis* deserved a better fate. The idea of versifying Fénelon's novel was in itself a good one. Even as a poem the *Telemachis* is not as bad as it was made out to be by Trediakovsky's enemies. Its moral message was certainly in tune with the spirit of the Enlightenment. It has many lines of which no poet would have to be ashamed, though just as many are spoiled by awkward versification or infelicitous phrasing.

Lomonosov

Whereas Trediakovsky represented the expected progress of Russian literature, Mikhail Vasilievich Lomonosov (1711–65) was, like Kantemir, an unexpected surprise. He was born the son of a well-to-do free peasant near Kholmogory in the extreme north, learned to read only in his late teens, and enrolled in the Slavonic-Latin Academy at nineteen. In 1735 he was sent to the Petersburg Academy to continue his studies and thence to Germany, in 1736, to study mining engineering. There he spent five years, first in Marburg and later in Freiberg, the site of a school of mining, and returned to Russia as a scientist who was fully abreast of the most recent theoretical and experimental advances in physics and chemistry. He continued to do important scientific work until the end of his life.

Lomonosov had also developed an interest in the humanities and in poetry. He carried with him to Germany Trediakovsky's *New and Brief Method of Composing Rus-*

sian Verse. In Germany he became acquainted with German syllabotonic poetry. In 1739 he sent to the Petersburg Academy his own *Epistle on the Rules of Russian Versification,* accompanied by a practical exhibit, his "Ode' on the Capture of Khotin."[8] Issuing from the premise that "Russian verses should be composed according to the native quality of our language, while such elements as are quite alien to it should not be introduced to it from foreign languages," Lomonosov's epistle, a mere eight pages long, contains a complete description of Russian syllabotonic versification as it has been practiced ever since. It establishes the basic meters and rhyme types, doing away with all the limitations imposed on these by Trediakovsky. Lomonosov's *Epistle* bears the mark of genius: it only says the obvious in exceedingly simple terms—yet no one had said it before. It gets directly to the heart of the matter, and stays there.

Upon his return to Russia Lomonosov joined the Petersburg Academy as an adjunct in physics, and in 1745 he was appointed to a professorship in chemistry. He continued to pursue his other interests, too. He quickly took over the position of court poet from Trediakovsky, and wrote some excellent spiritual poetry, two passable tragedies, commissioned by Empress Elizabeth, and poetry in a lighter vein. He also excelled as a linguist and theorist of language. His *Brief Manual of Eloquence* (1748) does not introduce any new ideas but is exemplary in its clarity and concision. His *Russian Grammar* (1755) is admirable

for its precision, its logical organization, and its judicious discrimination of the different social levels of the Russian language. Lomonosov's celebrated essay *"Preface* on the Utility of Religious Books" (1758) suggested an intelligent solution to the then still chaotic condition of the lexicon of literary Russian.[9] Recognizing that literary Russian was a hybrid of Slavonic and the Russian vernacular, Lomonosov suggested that the traditional three styles of literary discourse (*stylus sublimior, stylus mediocris, stylus inferior*) be determined by their respective use of Slavonic words, which were to be eliminated from the genres of the low style.

Lomonosov dabbled in history as well. When his colleague, the historian G. F. Müller, asserted, in a treatise entitled *The Origin of the Russian Nation and Its Name* (1749), that Kievan Russia was founded by Norman invaders, Lomonosov vigorously objected, thus becoming the first "anti-Normanist." On top of it all, Lomonosov was an energetic and competent administrator, who played a decisive role in the founding and development of Moscow University, as well as in the establishment of the Monthly Essays series of the Academy. It would seem incredible that this superbly capable man of action (Lomonosov was also an astute courtier who earned for himself high rank and the ownership of several hundred serfs) should also have been a great poet.

Lomonosov is a poet who knows no technical difficulties: he is always in command of his devices and never lets his form lead him. He is well aware of euphony and sound symbolism (he discusses these in his *Brief Manual of Eloquence*). His baroque poetics, which caused his classicist successors,

8. Lomonosov's ode, written in iambic tetrameter, follows the metric and strophic structure, as well as the rhyme scheme of Johann Christian Günther's ode "Auf den zwischen Ihro Kaiserl. Majestät und der Pforte an 1718 geschlossenen Frieden" (1718), whose subject was also similar.

9. This preface was written for a book, *A Collection of Various Works in Verse and in Prose,* by Mikhailo Lomonosov (Moscow, 1757), printed before the preface was finished.

from Sumarokov to Pushkin, to find him stilted and foreign, is based on the principles of conceit (*vymysel*), ingenious tropes, "metaphysical" similes, hyperbole, and controlled exaltation (*vostorg*). Lomonosov's poetic syntax features a great deal of hypallage (Sumarokov would quibble about phrases like "the heights of Parnassus heaved a sigh," instead of "sighs were heard on the heights of Parnassus"), semantic fuzziness ("be silent, fiery sounds!"), metonymic displacement (Sumarokov would find fault with with "the bow flies amidst the watery depths"—it is the whole ship, he said).

Lomonosov wrote emblematic and panegyrical verse for coronations, illuminations, ship launchings, balls, imperial arrivals and departures, name days, birthdays, anniversaries, and other celebrations. His main genre was the triumphal or panegyrical ode of the baroque, which he mastered to perfection even in his first great ode, "On the Capture of Khotin." Its poetics is essentially that of Horace's "Ad urbem Romam" (*Odes* 4.4). The ode is a free kaleidoscopic sequence of scenes and images. It features a great deal of mythology (mostly Greek, but biblical, too),[10] excursions into the glories of Russian history, imperial genealogy, and nature imagery of a classical landscape à la Poussin. Like Boileau and Günther, his examples, Lomonosov was addressing a noncombatant crowned sovereign, who is elevated to heroic stature. Here are some lines from "Ode on the Capture of Khotin"

that are typical of Lomonosov's treatment of battle scenes:

> Is it not bronze seething in Aetna's womb,
> Its gurgling mixed with boiling sulphur?
> Is it not hell tearing at its heavy chains,
> Threatening to open its gaping jaws?
> It is the progeny of that outcast slave[11]
> Who, having filled the mountain gorges
>   with fire,
> Flings flames and metal into the valley
>   below,
> where our men, chosen for this arduous
>   task,
> In full sight of the enemy and over
>   swampy ground
> Boldly advance to cross a rapid stream
> And attack the fire.

In typical baroque fashion Lomonosov can be brutally graphic:

> Mixed with dust, blood seethes here.
> A helmet with a head lies here, and there a
>   corpse,
> And here a sword held by a severed hand.

Later in the ode Lomonosov conjures the spirits of both Peter the Great and Ivan the Terrible, having them inspire the Russian soldiers to even greater valor. (Horace and Günther, too, let the spirits of ancient heroes join the fray.) Lomonosov's compositions are, if anything, more compact, more energetic, and nobler—and have fewer lapses into unintentional bathos—than his modern examples. They are sonorous, sure in their rhythm, and semantically challenging. A peculiarity of Lomonosov's poetic manner is a preference for vertical, soaring imagery, especially at the beginning of a poem. In his ode "On the Arrival of Elizaveta

10. For example, in an ode to Peter the Great (1743) Lomonosov calls Peter's mother "blessed thou among women" (after Luke 1:28) and says of Peter: "Neptune has recognized his reign, / While Minerva and strong Mars declare: / "He was a god, he was your god, o Russia, / In you he assumed flesh and blood, / Having descended to you from lofty heights."

11. The line alludes to the myth that made all Mohammedans descendants of Ishmael, son of Hagar, Abraham's slave. Günther also refers to it in his ode.

Petrovna from Moscow to Saint Petersburg after her Coronation" (1742) the charge of the Russian fleet is likened to the march of a giant stepping from the top of one hill to the next, leaving the valleys deep below him. Or, the poet will assume a cosmic perspective and let Russia rise to the clouds and see her domain reaching all the way from the great Chinese wall to the mountains of the Caucasus (this conceit appears in various forms in this and some other odes).

In 1743 Trediakovsky, Lomonosov, and Sumarokov engaged in a competition to translate Psalm 143. All three poets, as well as virtually every other major eighteenth-century Russian poet, composed versions of the Psalms as well as spiritual odes (*ody dukhovnye*) more or less in the manner of the Psalter. The tradition of the Russian spiritual ode has some direct links to the Psalter of Symeon Polotsky, to the hymns and canons of the Orthodox church, and to the eloquence of John Chrysostom, Gregory Narianzus ("the Divine"), and Ephraim Syrus.[12] Lomonosov's spiritual odes, by far the best of his generation, served as a point of departure to the poets who followed him—Sumarokov ("Ode on the Majesty of God"), Kheraskov ("Ode on the Majesty of God"), Maikov ("Ode on the Immortality of the Soul"), Derzhavin ("God"), and others.

Lomonosov's celebrated odes "Vespertine Meditation on the Majesty of God occasioned by a Great Display of Northern Lights" and "Morning Meditation on the Majesty of God" (both 1743) are admirable in every respect. Their cosmic panorama unfolds in a series of magnificent images, such as the famous chiasmus describing nightfall:

12. In his *Manual of Eloquence* Lomonosov uses many examples of tropes chosen from religious texts.

An abyss opens up, full of stars,
The stars countless, the abyss bottomless.

The voice of the scientist, curious about the unsolved mysteries of science and armed with the most advanced knowledge, effortlessly blends into that of the Deist thinker who profoundly believes in the order and harmony of the universe, and the inspired poet overwhelmed by the beauty of God's creation. Lomonosov's conceits are ingenious, yet they are also marvelously graphic, and what is more, they are good science. The sun is

An eternally burning ocean,
Where waves of fire rush about
Without ever finding a shore,
Where flaming vortices whirl around
Tumultuously for many centuries,
Where stones boil like water
And fiery rains fall thunderously.

The two cantos of Lomonosov's unfinished verse epic in alexandrines, *Peter the Great* (1756–61), follows the genre of Voltaire's *Henriade*. It is decidedly a learned work, as various historical reminiscences of which only a historian could have knowledge are introduced. In the first canto Peter relates the whole history of the *streltsy* mutiny of 1682, and there are excursions into earlier history: the murder of Dimitry Ioannovich, the Time of Troubles, the siege of Solovki Monastery in 1666–76. At the start of the second canto the poet celebrates the recent victories of Russian arms against Prussia, then goes on to describe the siege and storming of Noteburg on Lake Ladoga by Peter. Here Lomonosov uses the occasion to bring up Alexander Nevsky's victory over the Swedes and make him intervene to support the Russian effort.

Peter the Great features much classical

mythology. There is, for instance, an artful description of the palace of Neptune, who appears before the Russian tsar to apologize for having inconvenienced him by starting a storm. Lomonosov's epic is borne by the spirit of the Enlightenment. In the preamble he actually invokes "infinite wisdom" (*premudrost' beskonechna*), asking her "to shed her light on him."[13] Although the epic concentrates on Peter's military exploits, his works of peace also receive due attention. Moreover, Lomonosov introduces many formulaic expressions of traditional piety deploring the ravages of war. The epic has its valleys, some of which are caused by the court poet's bows in the direction of the reigning empress, but it also has its felicitous heights. The heroic epic was even then an anachronism, and Lomonosov did as well as possible under the circumstances. His language, imagery, and pathos are always appropriate to the subject.

Lomonosov's long didactic poem "Epistle on the Usefulness of Glass" (1752) is not only the best example of this genre in Russia but also a charming and most entertaining poetic composition which can be read with pleasure even today. As the various uses of glass are described, the reader is given a series of brief lectures in the physical sciences, as the telescope leads to a discussion of astronomy, the microscope to microbiology, and so on. The poem projects Lomonosov's Deist philosophy and his faith in human reason, science, and progress.

Lomonosov also wrote Anacreontic odes, fables, epitaphs, songs, epigrams, satires, an idyll, "Polydorus" (celebrating Duke Razumovsky, the empress's favorite), the humorous "Hymn to the Beard," and a number of

verse translations from French, German, and Latin.

Sumarokov

Aleksandr Petrovich Sumarokov (1718–77), the father of modern Russian drama, was a prolific poet as well. He was the first Russian nobleman to make literature his vocation. Educated at the Corps of Infantry Cadets, he learned French and German, not Slavonic (as Trediakovsky and Lomonosov had at the Slavonic-Latin Academy). He owed little to the tradition of Symeon Polotsky, which was certainly present in the spiritual odes of Trediakovsky and Lomonosov. And whereas Lomonosov's disciples tended to be of humble, often clerical origins, the circle of men of letters who gathered around Sumarokov was formed by educated nobles. The poetic language of Sumarokov and his disciples moved perceptibly away from Slavonic and toward the language spoken by educated Russian laymen.

From the beginning of his career Sumarokov was in competition with Trediakovsky and Lomonosov. The three were also each other's main critics. Sumarokov never became a court poet, although he did present his panegyrics to Elizabeth and Catherine II. He took pride in his ancient lineage and was too independent and too much under the sway of the liberal ideas of the Age of Reason to be a successful courtier and civil servant. His tenure as director of the imperial stage was brief and unhappy. The position of court poet to Catherine II went to Vasily Petrov (1736–99), a careerist of humble origins, who skillfully imitated the style of his master Lomonosov.

Sumarokov charted the course of his poetic career in his *Two Epistles, in the First of*

13. Russian *premudrost'*, like Greek *sophia*, is feminine.

which the Russian Language is dealt with, and in the Second, Versification (1747), essentially an abbreviated paraphrase of Boileau's *Art poétique*, some consecutive lines from which are translated verbatim, as Trediakovsky charged. The *Epistles* however, contained a good deal of Sumarokov's own thought and did address themselves to Russian literature. Sumarokov practiced virtually every form of poetry known in his age: panegyrical, spiritual, and Anacreontic ode, elegy, sonnet, ballad, rondeau, stanza, madrigal, epigram, eclogue, fable, satire, fairy tale, and epistle. Like Trediakovsky, he is at his best in the lyric song, when it approaches the Russian folk song in mood, imagery, and language. Sumarokov also tried every conceivable form of metric structure, including rhymeless verse, lines of unequal length, and Russian folk verse.

Sumarokov gathered around himself a school of younger poets who shared his theoretical views and his poetic style. Nevertheless, he is a pathetic figure. An intelligent and capable man, he misjudged his own talent, or perhaps the nature of poetic talent in general, and staked his life on his poetry. When his overestimation of his importance caught up with him, he became bitter and vindictive. He finished his days as a poor alcoholic. Posterity judged him harshly, seeing only the mediocrity of his talent and ignoring his huge merits in establishing solid standards of Russian poetry and drama.

Maikov

Vasily Ivanovich Maikov (1728–78), more talented than Sumarokov, remained an amateur poet, holding important civil service posts after initially serving in the guards. Maikov practiced most of the forms of poetry that Sumarokov did: panegyrical and spiritual odes, epigrams, fables, and a great deal of occasional poetry. He also wrote two tragedies. The most remarkable of these works are his spiritual odes and his versions of psalms, in particular an ode "On the Last Judgment" (1763), which has a magnificently graphic description of the cosmic catastrophe preceding the Last Judgment.

Maikov is, however, best known and remembered for his mock-heroic epics "The Ombre Players" (1763) and "Elisei, or Bacchus Enraged" (1769). Both explicitly follow the example of Scarron's *Virgile travesti* and Boileau's *Le Lutrin* but have enough recognizably Russian detail and earthy Russian vernacular diction to make them robustly alive. They are addressed to a reader who is familiar not only with Greek mythology but also with its parodic treatment in French literature and with the Russian literary scene. The amorous and other adventures of Elisei, a drunken Russian coachman, mix ribald humor with spirited satire of the corruption, injustice, and lechery rampant in Catherine's Petersburg, and with ample literary allusions. An insouciantly fantastic plot is developed with graphic realism, such as when Elisei, invisible under a Fortunatus cap, makes love to a tax farmer's wife in the presence of her puzzled husband.

Kheraskov

Mikhail Matveevich Kheraskov (1733–07) was the leading poet to emerge from the school of Sumarokov. Like Kantemir, he was descended from a Romanian nobleman who had joined Peter the Great during his unsuccessful campaign in Bessarabia. He attended the Corps of Infantry Cadets for eight years, graduating in 1751. Kheraskov resigned his commission after a few years and joined the civil service, where he was associated with Moscow University from its inception in 1755, with a ten-year hiatus (1770–79), to the end of his life. He was appointed curator of the university in 1779. A kindly, selfless, and generous man, Kheraskov did great service to the cause of Russian education, literature, and journalism. An active contributor to Russia's first journals, he published several himself, including *Useful Entertainment* (1760–62), Russia's first journal devoted entirely to literature. Kheraskov was an active Freemason, and his Masonic ideals are amply reflected in his works.[14]

Kheraskov won his greatest fame with his verse epics. His *Battle of Chesmen* (1771), in five cantos, describes the naval battle of 1770 in which a Russian squadron under Alexis Orlov routed a strong Turkish force under Hassan-Bey Pasha. It compares favorably with any similar effort in French or German literature. (It was translated into both languages.) The account of the engagement is slightly encumbered by mythological frills, the inevitable bows in the direction of the empress, and conventional epic metaphors, but it has long stretches of lively battle detail and reflects a warm concern for the death and suffering of brave Russians and Turks. It is stronger than the celebrated

Rossiad, which for lack of concrete subject matter is often remote and anemic.

Kheraskov's *Rossiad* (1771–79), which in twelve cantos relates the siege and capture of Kazan in 1552, was the first successful and complete attempt at creating a Russian national epic. It remained unsurpassed, if only for the reason that the genre was even then obsolete. In a preface Kheraskov shows that he is familiar not only with classical epic poetry but also with the modern epics of Tasso, Camões, and Voltaire, as well as with Milton's *Paradise Lost.* His own epic combines imagery and poetic devices from this entire tradition. Some clear borrowings from Virgil, Tasso, and Voltaire do appear. Christian and even specifically Russian Orthodox themes are found side by side with classical imagery and mythology. Saint Sergius of Radonezh and a host of Russian princes, some of them sainted, appear, but so do nymphs and naiads and the heroes of the Trojan War; the Volga and the Tiber both have a place in the poem. God the Lord dispatches His angels much as Zeus dispatched Hermes or Iris, and like Zeus, He uses a scale that raises Russia's lot heavenward and lowers that of the Mongol Horde to destruction. As in Homer and Virgil, the elements are made actants in the plot by placing them in the service of interested parties. A Tatar sorcerer tries to freeze the Russians into abandoning the siege but is foiled by a solemn supplication of the assembled Russian clergy.

The action of the *Rossiad* begins as God the Lord sends one of His angels, who is Ivan IV's ancestor Alexander, duke of Tver, who suffered a martyr's death at the hands of the Tatars, to instruct the tsar to launch his campaign against the infidels. (Kheraskov conveniently ignores another of the tsar's ancestors, Ivan Kalita, duke of Moscow, who may have been responsible for Alexander's

14. Here is an illustrative passage from Kheraskov's *Rossiad*: "Open for me, Eternity, the gates of those habitations / Where all earthly vanity is cast off, / Where the souls of the righteous earn their reward, / Where glory, where crowns are held to be worthless, / Where before an altar strewn with stars / The last slave will stand next to a king, / Where the poor will forget poverty, the miserable their plight, / Where every man will be every other's equal." The "altar strewn with stars" suggests Masonic rites. The emphasis on equality reflects the Masonic ideal of universal brotherhood. The Masons' altruistic concern for the poor and downtrodden is also in evidence.

death and certainly profited from it.) Alexander's shadow, which appears to Ivan in a dream, is patterned after similar figures in Homer and Virgil, as is the speech he delivers. To encourage the tsar to take speedy action, God lets him have a vision of all the martyred Russian princes, whereupon Alexander's shadow resumes his diatribe. This episode (about one hundred lines) and some others, too, are very well composed, showing a sensibility appreciative of Virgil and modern imitators of his art. With the advent of romanticism, this sensibility disappeared in Russia, and Kheraskov's epic was perceived as quaint at best.

Kheraskov's idealized image of Ivan the Terrible has its roots in the sixteenth-century *Tale of the Kingdom of Kazan* but seems strained in view of the tsar's later reputation. The *Tale*, Kheraskov's principal source, provided him with a heroine, the Tatar queen who surrendered to the Russian tsar. Kheraskov builds up this episode in three full cantos with elaborate lyric effusions. The martial details of the siege and capture of Kazan are kept in the baroque manner developed by Lomonosov, a mixture of gory carnage, soaring valor of idealized leaders, and a wealth of metaphor and mythological simile (Andrei Kurbsky is likened to Achilles, for example). There is hardly any effort made to re-create the actual military events of 1552.

Kheraskov's verse is the alexandrine couplet, with alternating masculine and feminine rhymes and a caesura after the sixth syllable. It is generally smooth, but rarely does it sustain the drive of its rhythm for more than a few lines. Kheraskov's language is appropriate to the heroic poem of the baroque: intensely metaphorical, bristling with tropes and figures, syntactic inversion, and hypallage. It appears unbearably stilted to a post-baroque sensibility.

Kheraskov continued the tradition, started by Trediakovsky, of the philosophical epic. His *Vladimir* (1785), *The Oecumene* (1790), and *The Pilgrims* (1795) follow the example of Milton, or more specifically, of Klopstock's *Messias.* They are full of lofty sentiment and contain many well-turned phrases, but lack the splendor of Lomonosov's and Derzhavin's spiritual and philosophical odes. Kheraskov also wrote a number of moral-didactic poems, such as "On Happiness," "On Wealth," and "On Desires." The last line of Kheraskov's "Thoughts Gathered from Ecclesiastes" (1765), forty stanzas on the vanity of life, became proverbial: "Fear nobody, o mortal, fear only God!"

Kheraskov's Anacreontic odes are pleasing, though they lack real charm or invention. Like his predecessors, he wrote some simple songs, patterned as much after foreign (German) as after Russian folk songs.

Bogdanovich

Ippolit Fyodorovich Bogdanovich (1743–1803) was, like Maikov, a poet of talent who was able to concentrate on his poetry only intermittently. He, too, was a moderately successful civil servant, most of whose literary efforts were translations that he made in his official capacity. He practiced various genres of poetry, including the spiritual, with remarkable success, but is remembered for a single work, *Dushenka, an Ancient Tale in Free Verse* (1783), an adaptation in three cantos of La Fontaine's *Amours de Psyché et de Cupidon.* "Free verse" here means iambic lines of frequently varying length and irregular rhyme schemes. Bogdanovich's versification is masterful and is consistently in tune with the progress of the plot.

The name Dushenka is the diminutive of

dusha (soul), hence an accurate translation of *psyche*, but it is also a colloquial term of endearment. This felicitous double meaning is characteristic of the whole composition. It tells the old story of Apuleius in the precious form given it by La Fontaine, yet Bogdanovich gives it a Russian air by introducing elements of Russian folklore, proverbial turns of speech, and sly, folksy humor. *Dushenka* showed that Russian poetry was now capable of being as daring, elegant, and sophisticated as anything in the West, and this without being entirely imitative. It now could convey a sense of a specifically Russian sensibility.

Bogdanovich is able to express serious philosophic thought in appropriate Russian verse. His translation of Voltaire's "Poème sur le désastre de Lisbonne" (1763) deliberately tones down Voltaire's acrimony but expresses his thoughts with vigor and precision. Nevertheless, of all the works of this talented poet only *Dushenka* survived into the next century. Pushkin remembers Bogdanovich fondly in *Eugene Onegin*, and his "Ruslan and Lyudmila" is not far removed from *Dushenka* in style and spirit.

Derzhavin

Gavrila Romanovich Derzhavin (1743–1816) was yet another anomaly in an otherwise normal development of Russian literature as it moved to join the mainstream of European literature. While staying well within the poetic genres cultivated by his predecessors, he released a cornucopia of sonorous verses bursting with exuberant wealth of invention, magnificently vivid imagery, and an indomitable vigor of expression. Within his range of the imagination Derzhavin as a poet is second to none, in Russia or elsewhere. Even the perceptive Belinsky underestimated him, because such

greatness seemed premature from his historicist vantage point.

Derzhavin's career was as incredible as Lomonosov's. He was born in Kazan, the son of an impoverished country squire of Tatar descent, lost his father early, and did not complete what little formal education he could get at the newly founded Kazan gymnasium. He could consider it his good fortune when he was sent to Petersburg to serve in the guards as a private, though he had to wait until 1772 to get his commission. He distinguished himself in the Pugachov campaign of 1773 and by then had begun to make a name for himself as a poet. His career accelerated when he switched from the military to the civil service in 1779 and advanced steeply after his ode "Felitsa" (1782), in which he artfully mixed satire (directed at Catherine's courtiers) with homage (directed at Catherine), met with the empress's approval. Derzhavin eventually attained high rank (he was governor general of a province, senator, and briefly minister of justice), considerable wealth, and a leading position in the world of Russian letters.[15]

Derzhavin's best poetry combines power of thought and invention with vivid and varied imagery and with supreme mastery of rhythm and euphony. His iambic verse has great rhythmic variety, much enhanced by intensive use of euphonic devices: alliteration in every conceivable pattern, vowel assonance, and vowel modulation. Derzhavin was superior to his predecessors in every genre. His Anacreontic poetry,

15. In the 1770s and 1780s Derzhavin belonged to a literary circle among whose members were Nikolai Lvov and Vasily Kapnist (his brothers-in-law: the three were married to three sisters Dyakov), Ivan Chemnitzer, and some others. In his old age Derzhavin was an active member of Admiral Shishkov's Colloquy (see pp. 164–65).

polished and graceful, has that extra touch of a concrete Russian detail, vivid nature scene, or flash of genuine emotion. His martial and patriotic panegyrics are as sonorous and rich in ingenious conceits as Lomonosov's, but have more of a sustained and structured flow of thought and more natural imagery. More inclined toward Horace than Pindar (according to his own assertion), he skillfully mixed the panegyrical and solemn with verses in a lighter, satirical, or idyllic vein. Derzhavin's grand ode "On the Capture of Izmail" (1790–91) offers not only a kaleidoscope of magnificent battle scenes but also a rousing hymn to the growing Russian Empire. It concludes, however, with some stanzas in praise of peace over war.

Like most other poets of his century, Derzhavin wrote religious odes and translated the Psalter. His greatest glory is his philosophical odes, such as "On the Death of Duke Meshchersky" (1779), "God" (1784), "On the Death of Countess Rumyantseva" (1788), and "The Waterfall" (1791–94). The thoughts expressed here are not original or profound. They are those of a Deist who marvels at the beauty of God's creation and bows his head before its mysteries, of a man of the Enlightenment who believes in the strength and dignity of the human spirit. Derzhavin is also much concerned with human mortality and the transience of all temporal glory. His famous last poem, "The River of Time"—really the first and only stanza of an ode "On Perishability," also called the "Slate Pencil Ode" (the poet's autograph was preserved on a slate board for years after his death)—contains the acrostic "Ruin of Glory." The exhilarating effect of Derzhavin's philosophical-religious odes comes from the fullness of life and nature that they project. The ode "God" expresses man's grateful sonhood, a belonging to and sharing in God's power and glory,

through magically vivid visions of God's world: the macrocosm of a luminous stellar universe and the microcosm of vibrant specks of hoarfrost glistening in the winter sun. Derzhavin's capacity for turning abstract concepts into poetic images is rivaled only by the greatest, a Milton or a Goethe.

In "The Waterfall" Derzhavin brilliantly develops his vision of the human condition from a description of a Karelian waterfall. He muses on the sudden and spectacular reverses in the fortunes of the high and the mighty of this world and arrives at the melancholy sight of the body of Generalissimo Potemkin, proud conqueror of the Crimea, laid out on the ground along a desert trail, his eyes covered by two copper coins. The conclusion developed in the last five stanzas, in returning to the waterfall, leads to the insight that only pure truth will flow on forever like the crystal-clear waters of the northern waterfall.

In Derzhavin's later poetry, including "The Waterfall," the influence of preromantic themes and sensibilities is felt. A prose translation of Macpherson's Ossianic poems (via the French) by Ermil Kostrov appeared in 1792 and in 1793 Nikolai Lvov published his translation of a Skaldic poem (also via the French). These had a significant influence on Derzhavin and other Russian poets of the period, but also acted as a stimulus toward a greater and more immediate use of Russian folklore.

The old Derzhavin, after his forced resignation as minister of justice in 1803, became one of the "archaists" around Admiral Aleksandr Shishkov and developed a poetic style that was different from that of his heyday under Catherine II. He tried new genres: the cantata ("Perseus and Andromeda," 1807), the oratorio ("The Healing of Saul," 1809), and the dithyramb ("Orpheus Meeting the Sun," 1811). His themes and imagery moved closer to classical antiquity as well as to the Bible. His language became pointedly "difficult" through Slavonicisms, neologisms (compounds of his own creation, in particular), and solecisms, his rhythms ponderous, mainly through the use of many spondees. Derzhavin's later poetry is generally little known and is considered inferior to that of his prime. This reputation may be due in part to the relative neglect of religious and philosophical poetry by Russian literary critics and historians. Derzhavin's late ode "Christ" (1814) may yet be recognized as a worthy counterpoint to the early ode "God."

Derzhavin's poetry is a mirror of the flowering of the Russian gentry under Catherine II. A bard of the golden freedom and lavish life-style of the Russian nobleman, Derzhavin loved his country as it was (he was at all times a staunch defender of the monarchy and of serfdom), its nature, its traditions, and its holidays and feasts. What Horace was to Caesar Augustus, Derzhavin was to the age of Catherine the Great. It was only fitting that he wrote a noble and eloquent "Exegi monumentum" of his own.[16]

Kapnist, Karamzin, Muravyov

Vasily Vasilievich Kapnist (1758–1823), a Ukrainian nobleman of Greek descent, belonged to the literary circle of Nikolai Lvov and was a friend of Derzhavin's. He was director of the imperial theaters under Tsar Paul. Although his fame is based on his

---

16. See p. 144 for Derzhavin's dramatic works. His theoretical and critical essays are not distinguished, but his "Explication of my own Poems" (*Ob"yasnenie k svoim stikhotvoreniyam*) offers some informative comments. Derzhavin's autobiographical *Notes* (*Zapiski*, finished 1812, published 1859) are naively sincere and therefore of great interest.

satirical comedy *Chicane*, Kapnist was also a prolific poet of remarkable talent.

Kapnist wrote panegyrical and religious odes (including some excellent versions of psalms). His Anacreontic odes and occasional poetry have a fresh immediacy, and the better among them are hardly inferior to Derzhavin's. Kapnist also translated Horace (very well) and wrote imitations of a number of Horatian odes. While Kapnist's poetry, excellent though it is, lacks a distinct voice of its own, he has the distinction to have been the first Russian poet to be inspired by the idea of civic freedom. His "Ode on Slavery" and "Ode on the Abolition in Russia of the Calling 'Slave' by Catherine II on February 15, 1786" are sincere expressions of the poet's noble sentiments, even though they seem ironic in historical retrospect.

Nikolai Karamzin, the prime prose writer of the eighteenth century, also wrote a great deal of poetry. It is technically smooth and does not lack wit, but it often lapses into prosiness and is rhythmically and euphonically wooden. Karamzin's most interesting poems are philosophical odes in the manner of Schiller, whose direct influence is obvious. "Talents" (1796), a five-hundred-line ode, combines the ideas of Schiller's "Eleusinian Festival" and "Artists" (*Die Künstler*), praising the victory of Phoebus over primeval savagery and the various ways in which the arts and poetry contribute to the education of mankind, overcoming the darkness of evil and spreading the light of truth. Other odes in the same vein are "To Virtue" (1802), "To Mercy" (1792), and "Epistle to Women" (1795).

Mikhail Nikitich Muravyov (1757–1807), like his friend Derzhavin, owed his brilliant career (at his death he was deputy minister of education and curator of Moscow University) to his literary reputation: in the

1780s and 1790s he tutored the young grand dukes Alexander and Constantine in Russian letters. Muravyov's poetry lacks originality, but it is polished and in good taste. He cultivated the familiar genres of eighteenth-century poetry, tending toward a sentimentalist mode, extolling friendship, family happiness, and the pleasures of rural life with more of a personal note than his predecessors. Many of his poems are addressed to friends (Maikov, Chemnitzer, Petrov, Bogdanovich, Kheraskov, and others). Melancholy moods, with echoes of Edward Young's *Night Thoughts*, are frequent. Muravyov was also an excellent translator of classical and modern poets.

Fabulists

The fable, one of the favorite genres of classicism everywhere, reached a high level of accomplishment in Russia. The animal fable in prose had been a part of the literary tradition since the Middle Ages. Symeon Polotsky, Trediakovsky, Lomonosov, Sumarokov, Kheraskov, Maikov, Bogdanovich, and Derzhavin all wrote fables. Three poets, Chemnitzer, Dmitriev, and Krylov, are remembered primarily for their fables, although all three excelled in other genres as well.

Ivan Ivanovich Chemnitzer (Khemnitser, 1745–1784), the son of a German immigrant military surgeon, served in the military and civil service with little success. He died as Russian consul general in Smyrna, Turkey. Chemnitzer belonged to the literary circle of Nikolai Lvov and was on friendly terms with Kapnist and Derzhavin.

Most of Chemnitzer's fables are adapted from La Fontaine or Gellert. Their language and versification are those used later by Krylov: a vigorous colloquial vernacular and varied rhyme schemes in lines of frequently changing length. The moral of Chemnitzer's fables is that of a liberal enlightener. His peculiar contribution is a wry irony which at times turns to bitterness, especially with regard to the fair sex and marriage.

Chemnitzer's satires, in alexandrines, are the work of an angry young man. His satire, "On Bad Judges," attacks the incredible ignorance, stupidity, and hopeless incompetence of those Russian judges who are at least honest, and the shameless venality and utter cynicism of the rest. In his satire, "On the Bad Condition of the Civil Service and on How even Appointments to Government Posts are at the Pleasure of Corruption," Chemnitzer describes his own experiences as an office seeker: the long hours spent in the antechambers of potential employers or patrons, rude lackeys, supercilious magnates, brief hopes soon shattered, corruption in high places and low, and the impossibility of an honest man being accepted into a corrupt bureaucracy.

Chemnitzer wrote verse in other genres (ode, song, epigram, epistle), none of it distinctive. He also wrote a good deal of German verse (undistinguished) and some French verse (bad). As a fabulist, Chemnitzer lacks Dmitriev's suave urbanity or Krylov's homespun humor. His satire has none of Kantemir's polish and patrician equanimity. But it is alive in the sense of Juvenal's dictum: *Si natura negat, dat indignatio verbum.*

Ivan Ivanovich Dmitriev (1760–1837) was a talented amateur poet who held important posts in the civil service, lastly that of minister of justice. He was a close friend and associate of Karamzin, whose aesthetic preferences he also shared. His poetry bears sentimentalist and Ossianic traits. Like Karamzin, he withdrew from the literary scene after the turn of the century but was highly regarded by his contemporaries. His fables earned him a reputation as the Russian La Fontaine, though they were eventually superseded by Krylov's.[17] Polished in a casual way, they lack the native vigor of Krylov's fables, or even Chemnitzer's.

Ivan Andreevich Krylov (1769–1844) was a prominent journalist, critic, and playwright in the 1790s and 1800s. He turned to the fable rather late in his career, completing his translation of La Fontaine's fables in 1805 and publishing his first collection of original fables in 1809. Having secured a post, practically a sinecure, with the Petersburg Public Library in 1812, Krylov went on to write fables at a leisurely pace. As a fabulist, he was hailed as a classic even in his lifetime. Krylov's fables soon entered school primers, and many of them are to this day ingrained in every literate Russian's mind. Such lines as "an obliging fool is more dangerous than an enemy" have become proverbial.

A bold and witty satirist before he became a fabulist, Krylov addressed himself to Russian reality, often in a poignant manner. The form of the animal fable protected him against censorship—even when he would attack censorship itself, as in a fable, "Cat and Nightingale" (1824), with the moral: "A nightingale will not sing well in a cat's claws." In Krylov's sheep one is tempted to see the downtrodden peasants of Russia; the wolves are the gentry. Topics of the day were mirrored in many of Krylov's fables. "The Quartet" (1811), for example, which has a bear, a monkey, an ass, and a goat trying to produce harmonious music, with expected results, was aimed at a set of new ministerial appointments by Alexander I. (Krylov, a conservative, was opposed to the young tsar's liberal reforms and heartily disliked the bright young men who were implementing them.) Most of these pieces, however, retained their charm and vigor even after they had lost their topical edge.

Krylov's fables follow the form of La Fontaine's but are Russian to the core. Even Krylov's verse, ostensibly conventional iambic or trochaic lines of changing length and varied rhyme patterns, often take on the rhythm of folk verse (*skazovy stikh*). The ethos of Krylov's fables is that of a conservative middlebrow Russian: wary of academic learning and highfalutin rhetoric; suspicious of foreign ideas and manners; resentful of bureaucratic and police tyranny; supportive of common civic virtues, simple good sense, and a quiet patriotism; and fond of life's simple pleasures. It is also the ethos of a man who has seen the world and knows all human sins and foibles, but who still believes in justice and virtue. Krylov's tone is that of a solid bonhomie, behind which there lurks a sly humor—worldly-wise, even cynical, but never malevolent. Krylov's language is vigorous, precise, and idiomatic. His fables are among the top achievements of Russian literature.

Drama

As early as 1702 Peter the Great renewed his father's effort to establish a Russian theater. Johann Kunst, head of a German traveling ensemble, was commissioned to train some twenty Russian actors. A theater was ordered to be built, and the first spectacle took place in Moscow on December 14, 1702. The repertoire was European, translated from German versions of Italian and French plays: Molière's *Amphitryon* and *Les Précieuses ridicules*, a version of *Don Juan* (not Molière's), Thomas Corneille's *Le Geôlier de soi-même*, and other readily identified titles. Some of the Russian texts

---

17. As late as 1821 Pyotr Vyazemsky, in an essay, "The Poetry of I. I. Dmitriev," gives preference to Dmitriev over Krylov.

are extant. The translations were quite poor, though some comic scenes are well adapted to Russian mores. Performances were regularly given, twice a week, but failed to attract good audiences, probably because of resistance by the clergy and other conservative elements. The Red Square Theater lasted until 1706. Simultaneously, theatrical performances went on at the Slavonic-Latin Academy in Moscow and at several divinity schools in the provinces. All these theaters were instructed to stage "triumphal comedies" to celebrate Peter's victories: *On the Taking of Noteburg* (1703), *On the Liberation of Livonia and Ingermanland* (1705), and *On the Divine Destruction of Proud Destroyers* (1710), celebrating the victory of Poltava. These spectacles were a mixture of biblical scenes (the victory of Moses over Pharaoh), classical mythology (Jupiter and Phoebus make appearances), heraldic emblems (the Swedish lion defeated by the Russian eagle), and moral allegory (Virtue, Wisdom, Jealousy, Rapacity, et cetera, appear personified). They also featured music, ballet, pageantry, and fireworks.

In 1707 Nataliya Alekseevna (1673–1716), the tsar's sister, founded a court theater at her residence in Preobrazhenskoe near Moscow. She used the props, costumes, and texts of Kunst's theater. When she moved to Saint Petersburg, she organized a theater there, too. She also wrote some plays herself, dramatized versions of saints lives and of the popular *Tale of Otto, Roman Emperor.* The widow of Tsar Ivan, Praskovya Fyodorovna, had her own theater, and so did Ekaterina Ivanovna, his daughter. More theaters were soon founded, even in the provinces. The plays were mostly hybrids of dramatized versions of courtly romances, such as the "Comedy of the Beauteous Melusina," and the allegoric school drama, with the burlesque interludes of the latter some-

times retained. Some of Pastor Gregorii's plays were also staged.

The Kiev school drama, transplanted to Muscovy by Ukrainian clerics (who formed the teaching staffs of seminaries that since the late seventeenth century were an obligatory step to the priesthood), continued well into the middle of the eighteenth century. Only a few of the texts have survived.[18] *A Terrifying Representation of Our Lord's Second Coming*, enacted at the Moscow Slavonic-Latin Academy on February 4, 1702, is a hybrid of the panegyric and the religious spectacle. A plethora of allegorical figures, such as the Church, the seven Virtues, the World, God's Glory, Omnipotence, Wisdom, Justice, Wrath, Sufferance, and Grace, appear, along with Nebuchadnezzar and Daniel, the devil, and many angels, but also a Russian Mars, the Russian Eagle, Fortune, and Victory. The spectacle's anonymous author apparently sought to present a safe and loyal view of a world in crisis. (An apocalyptic mood was widespread in Russia at the time, and many took Peter to be the Antichrist.) In the course of the spectacle the enemies of the Church, specifically the Kingdom of Poland, are vanquished and dispatched to hell, while her righteous sons are rewarded. The spectacle ends in a monologue by a triumphant Church. It is written in smooth syllabic verse. The language has some Ukrainianisms but is vigorous and fits the occasion. The author knew his rhetoric and poetics, which he probably taught at the academy. This and other allegorical spectacles presented by students of the Moscow Slavonic-Latin Academy and seminarians at Novgorod, Tver, Rostov, and elsewhere were quite similar to analogous spectacles

18. See I. M. Badalich and V. D. Kuz'min, *Pamyatniki russkoi shkol'noi dramy XVIII veka* (*po zagrebskim spiskam*) (Moscow: Nauka, 1968).

enacted in Western Europe on important state occasions.

The last school drama of the panegyrical type produced by the Moscow Academy was occasioned by the palace revolution that put Elizabeth (r. 1741–62) on the throne. It was entitled "Image of a Russian Triumph" and featured a variety of allegorical figures, biblical (Abraham and Melchizedek) as well as classical (Hercules, Fortune, Glory), presided over by Russia herself. In the provinces the school drama survived even longer.

During the reign of Empress Anna (1730–40) foreign troupes began to visit the Russian capitals (Saint Petersburg and Moscow)—first Italian opera and ballet, and even commedia dell'arte. French and German troupes soon followed. In 1739–40 Petersburg saw a series of performances by the German ensemble of Caroline Neuber (who was not present herself), which played Racine, Corneille, and Voltaire in German translation, as well as German tragedies by Johann Christoph Gottsched and Johann Elias Schlegel, all in the style of high classicism. Russian classicist drama as developed by Sumarokov followed Gottsched's *Die deutsche Schaubühne* as much as Boileau's *Art poétique.*

After Anna's death the Francophile Elizabeth asked the German troupe to leave, and in 1742 she invited Sérigny's French troupe, which stayed on for several years, playing the French tragedies as well as comedies by Molière, Regnard, and Destouches. Even during Elizabeth's reign further German troupes visited Russia, and subsequently Petersburg's strong German colony was always able to support a German theater.

In the meantime students of the Corps of Infantry Cadets had developed an amateur theater staging French classicist plays. Aleksandr Sumarokov, an alumnus of the corps who had already established himself as a poet competing with Trediakovsky and Lomonosov, wrote the first Russian classicist tragedy, *Khorev* (1747), and had it performed by a cadet ensemble in 1749. The empress heard of the performance (Sumarokov was adjutant of Elizabeth's favorite, Duke Razumovsky) and had it repeated at her court. She liked it so well that she decided to establish a Russian theater and ordered Trediakovsky and Lomonosov to write plays for it, too. Sumarokov's first five tragedies, written between 1747 and 1751, became the nucleus of the theater's repertoire. Altogether, Sumarokov wrote eleven tragedies and twelve comedies.

Initially Sumarokov's plays were enacted by students of the Corps of Infantry Cadets. In 1751 a successful amateur theater led by a young merchant, Fyodor Volkov (1729–63), was brought to Saint Petersburg from Yaroslavl (near Moscow) to perform before the empress. Volkov and two of his leading actors became the nucleus of a public theater founded in 1756, with Sumarokov as its first director.

Sumarokov's plays were mechanical imitations of French and German classicist drama. The plots of his tragedies featured a conflict between love and some form of duty—moral, filial, or patriotic. *Hamlet*, which Sumarokov knew in a French prose paraphrase, became an exemplary classicist tragedy, printed in 1748 and first produced in 1750 with great success. Claudius, with the aid of Polonius, an ambitious courtier, has murdered his brother and married Gertrude, his wife. Hamlet has a dream that tells him what has happened (a ghost would have been in violation of classicist *vraisemblance*). Claudius is torn by pangs of conscience, but Polonius reassures him, and they plot to kill both Hamlet and Gertrude, who has now renounced Claudius. Ophelia is to marry Claudius. Hamlet raises the torch of revolt against Claudius and Polonius, and Ophelia firmly refuses to yield to Claudius. Condemned to death, she is saved by the arrival of Hamlet, who earlier was reported dead. Ophelia pleads for her father's life, and Hamlet is saved from a painful dilemma when Polonius commits suicide. It has been pointed out that Sumarokov introduced elements of plot from Corneille's *Le Cid* and Racine's *Britannicus* into Shakespeare's plot, thus creating for Ophelia the familiar conflict of love and filial duty.[19]

Sumarokov's only tragedy to survive on stage into the nineteenth century was *Dimitry the Pretender* (1771), less purely classicist and perhaps affected by an incipient interest in Shakespeare. It contains a good deal of straightforward "ideology," as the despot Dimitry is set up as a foil to an ideal enlightened monarch: "Blest be on earth the purple-bearing man/who won't restrain the freedom of our souls," exclaims Xenia, heroine of the play. There are other harangues in the spirit of enlightened philosophy. *Dimitry the Pretender* has little dramatic suspense. Dimitry reveals himself in all his villainy in the opening scene, declaring that he has no love for Russia but owes a debt of gratitude to Poland and recognizes the authority of the pope. Dimitry's monologue at the end of act 2 lets the usurper—absurdly, to a modern sensibility—envisage his imminent fall and certain death as just punishment for his crimes and relief for the victims of his tyranny. What little plot there is, is generated by the pretender's passion for Xenia Shuisky, daughter of the man who will lead the uprising against the pretender. Nevertheless, the play has a

certain (albeit naive) logic, and the character of Dimitry, though bluntly contrived, stands for an idea eloquently stated in a monologue at the beginning of act 4. Like Richard III, Dimitry is evil of his own free will:

> On earth all live to their own selfish ends,
> And in a world both baneful and depraved
> I chose to be a tyrant. Virtue is praised,
> But surely non-existent here on earth.
> If Hell to mortal men will hold no fear,
> Then let Dimitry justly strike them here!

In a way, Sumarokov has stumbled upon a sense of human capacity for active, self-conscious evil that looks forward to the German Storm and Stress, as in Schiller's *Die Räuber*, a play that appeared ten years after *Dimitry the Pretender.*

Sumarokov's tragedies share the traits found in their French models. The unities of time, space, action, and style are scrupulously observed. The dialogue is rhetorical, without any pretense to psychological or historical verisimilitude. All characters, male and female, talk alike. Monologues and asides are frequent. Russian classicist tragedy was declaimed by the actors, facing the audience, rather than acted. In keeping with the staging (in contemporary costume and with few props), there was no attempt at historical, national, or local stylization. To later readers the tragedies of Sumarokov appeared stilted, vacuous, and wholly devoid of life. But contemporary audiences, who had a greater capacity for suspending disbelief, were moved by their pathos and lofty diction. Although Sumarokov had none of Racine's poetic genius, the effect of his tragedies justified his claim to the title of the Russian Racine.

Sumarokov's comedies were rather straightforward imitations of Molière and "immortal" Philippe Destouches (so called

---

19. Simon Karlinsky, *Russian Drama from Its Beginnings to the Age of Pushkin* (Berkeley and Los Angeles: University of California Press, 1985), 69.

in Sumarokov's second epistle). Even their titles—*The Imaginary Cuckold, The Usurer, A Dowry by Deception*—suggest their conventional nature. The first of them, the one act *Tressotinius* (1750), was a lampoon of the hapless Trediakovsky, presented in the manner of Molière's ludicrous pedants.

Lomonosov, ordered by Elizabeth to write plays for her theater, obliged with two tragedies. Even in this genre, alien to him, he did better than Sumarokov. Poor Trediakovsky, as expected, did worst. Lomonosov's *Tamira and Selim* is built around an incident of Russian history. After the battle of Kulikovo, Khan Mamai fled to the Crimea, where he was soon recognized and killed. Lomonosov lets him appear at the court of the Crimean Khan Mumet ahead of the news of his defeat and try to improve his fortunes by marrying Mumet's daughter, Tamira, who loves Selim, prince of Bagdad. The drama has a happy ending. The wicked Mamai suffers just punishment at the hands of Selim, and the lovers are united. The play is written in smooth alexandrines. Its dialogue is spirited as classicist drama goes. The plot is suspenseful, but it is based on external circumstance and lacks ideal, moral, or psychological interest. A Russian audience would be intrigued by the references to Russian history in this oriental setting. *Tamira and Selim* is a credit to Lomonosov's intelligence and ingenuity, but it is no more than a competent fabrication. Lomonosov's other tragedy, *Demophon*, has its merits, too. Demophon, son of Theseus, returning from the capture of Troy, finds himself fatefully torn between Phyllis, a Thracian princess, and Illione, a captive daughter of Priam. He perishes after a series of violent peripeteias. The play displays flashes of psychological interest and warm pathos, and the female antagonists are well drawn. But the resolution of the play is unconvincing and,

moreover, is feebly reported by a messenger.

Throughout the eighteenth century and after, the repertoire of Russian theaters consisted largely of translated or adapted foreign plays. In the 1760s the classics of the French classicist theater were joined by the middle-class tragedy (*meshchanskaya tragediya*), of British origin,[20] and the French *comédie larmoyante* (*sleznaya* or *slezlivaya komediya*). Ivan Elagin (1725–94), director of the Saint Petersburg court theater from 1766 to 1779, led a group of competent translators and playwrights, among them Bogdan Elchaninov (1744–70), Denis Fonvizin, and Vladimir Lukin, who adapted many foreign plays for the Russian stage.[21]

Once the theater had become an institution supported by the court, more playwrights emerged, producing plays in the manner of the European theater in vogue at the time. As early as 1758 the versatile Kheraskov produced a three-act tragedy, *The Nun of Venice*, which was a departure from the classicist canon in that its characters were not royal personages, the action could be perceived as contemporary, and the plot had possible political implications.

20. George Lillo's *London Merchant, or the Adventures of George Barnwell* (1731) was translated and performed in 1764, Edward Moore's *The Gamester* (1753) in 1773.

21. Among the foreign playwrights whose plays in the manner of the *comédie larmoyante* appeared in Russia were Voltaire, Diderot, Beaumarchais, Louis-Sebastien Mercier, Michel-Jean Sedaine, Bernard-Joseph Saurin, Christian Fürchtegott Gellert, August Friedrich Kotzebue, and others. Original "tearful comedies" began to appear in the 1770s. Karlinsky, *Russian Drama*, 103, considers Elchaninov's *The Giddypate Undone* (1767), which combines elements of *La Coquette corrigée* (1756) by Jean-Baptiste de la Noue with the dénouement of Molière's *Le Misanthrope*, by far the best of these "adaptations to our customs."

But mainly it was aimed at moving the audience to tears. Corance, the hero of the play, is arrested on the grounds of a foreign embassy, an offense punishable by death. He had stolen into the chapel of the adjoining convent where Zanetta, once his promised bride, is now a nun. Rather than revealing that he has met her, he admits to being a spy and is condemned to death. Zanetta, in desperation, blinds herself, and after some further peripeteias dies of a broken heart. Corance kills himself.

Kheraskov went on to write nineteen more plays, including eight more tragedies and five plays in the style of the *comédie larmoyante*. His tragedies follow the classicist canon, but his plots are livelier and more believable than Sumarokov's and his dialogue more natural. He also followed the trend toward greater national awareness. In his late tragedy *Moscow Liberated* (1798), Sofya, sister of Duke Pozharsky, the liberator of Moscow from Polish invaders, falls in love with the son of the Polish general, Hetman Zhelkovsky, and tragically slips into becoming a traitress to her country. When her lover is killed by the Russians, she commits suicide.

Yakov Borisovich Knyazhnin (1742–91), Sumarokov's son-in-law, is remembered through Pushkin's line (from an excursus on the Russian stage in *Eugene Onegin*) as "imitative Knyazhnin." In fact, Knyazhnin adapted several plays by Metastasio, Racine, and Voltaire for the Russian stage. His biography and his oeuvre are of considerable interest and have been the subject of scholarly controversy. His tragedies *Rosslav* (1784) and *Vadim of Novgorod* (1789) survived him by many years. *Vadim* became a cause celèbre of Russian censorship and was an inspiration to the Decembrists of 1825. It is a tragedy à la Voltaire rather than Racine, with a lively plot set in motion by political

passions. The action takes place in mythical Novgorod. The antagonists are Rurik, who has established monarchical rule, and Vadim, who fights to maintain the republican traditions of the city. Ramida, Vadim's daughter, loves Rurik, but in the end kills herself as a token of her loyalty to her defeated father, who also kills himself. The republican message is explicit:

> What matter if this Rurik was a hero
> born—
> What hero is uncorrupted once he wears
> the crown?
> Intoxicated by the poison of his grandeur,
> What ruler was not soon depraved by the
> purple?
> Autocracy is everywhere the cause of evil,
> As it corrupts even the purest virtue,
> And as it gives free rein to human passion,
> Gives license to a king to be a tyrant.

Whether Knyazhnin actually meant to attack Russian autocracy remains a subject of debate, as does whether Knyazhnin's sudden death had anything to do with the anger of the aging empress, who had the work (printed in 1793) publicly burned. Knyazhnin also wrote comedies and libretti for comic operas. One of the operas, *Misfortune from a Carriage* (1779), features sentimental arias and duets sung by a peasant hero and heroine and may have been a frontal attack on serfdom. Lukyan, a young peasant, is about to be sold into the army and separated from his fiancée Anyuta because his master needs money to buy a fancy French-style carriage. Only the trickery of a jester (*shut*) saves him.

Among a number of other playwrights who wrote tragedies, Nikolai Petrovich Nikolev (1758–1815), adopted son of Duchess Dashkova, Catherine's intimate friend, was the most prominent in the 1780s and 1790s. Blind for much of his life,

Nikolev was nevertheless a prolific playwright who wrote tragedies as well as comedies. His greatest success was *Sorena and Zamir* (1785), essentially an adaptation to a Russian setting of Voltaire's *Alzire, ou les américains.* The role of Voltaire's noble Indians is given to the Polovetzians of Kievan Russia, as a result of which the play in effect promotes a tribal democracy against monarchy, and pagan mores against Christianity. There were some problems with its staging, but eventually Catherine let it pass. After the French Revolution Nikolev stayed with tamer topics.

Vladislav Aleksandrovich Ozerov (1769–1816), another alumnus of the Corps of Cadets, was the last major tragic dramatist in the classicist tradition. His career was cut short by mental illness. Some (albeit isolated) critics credit him with true greatness. Osip Mandelshtam spoke of the "flowering of solemn pain" in Ozerov's theater and called it "the last ray of a tragic sunset." More recently, Simon Karlinsky has given a sympathetic and convincing assessment of Ozerov's plays.[22]

Ozerov's first play, *Yaropolk and Oleg* (1798), was still in the manner of Knyazhnin or Nikolev, although Ozerov shows himself as the superior versifier. His alexandrines flow smoothly, and their rhymes come effortlessly. Ozerov scored a major success with *Oedipus in Athens* (1804), based on Sophocles' *Oedipus in Colonus* and other plays dealing with the Oedipus myth. Its effect is based on the moving tirades of an Oedipus wiser, but his spirit unbroken, by suffering, Antigone's self-sacrificing loyalty to her father, and the desperate pleas of Polynices for his father's forgiveness. The pathos of *Oedipus in Athens* has genuine

warmth, and its poetic truth is not diminished by its rhetoric.

Fingal, a Tragedy in Three Acts in Verse, with Choruses and Pantomime Ballet (1805) was derived from Ossian (the choruses are those of bards, priests, and maidens). With Ossianic moods still in fashion, *Fingal* was a success, but it is decidedly weaker than *Oedipus in Athens.* Ozerov scored his greatest success with his patriotic tragedy *Dimitry Donskoi* (1806), in which he managed to invent a conventional—and historically absurd—conflict of love and duty for the fourteenth-century grand duke. The patriotic tirades of the play delighted Russian audiences (Russia was at war with Napoleon at the time). Ozerov's last play, *Polyxena* (1808–9), returned to a classical theme and to the "solemn pain" of *Oedipus in Athens.*

Derzhavin, in his declining years, wrote a number of plays and opera libretti. *Herod and Mariamne* (1807) is based on Josephus Flavius, *Evpraksiya* (1808) on the *Tale of the Invasion of Russia by Batu*, [*Vasily*] *the Blind* (1808) on the Moscow chronicles, and *Pozharsky* (an opera, 1807) on several sources from the Time of Troubles. Derzhavin wrote his plays in response to the successful "modern" plays of Ozerov, considered falsely sentimental by Derzhavin and his conservative friends. Derzhavin's plays, however, were considered by everybody, including his friends and admirers, to be quite unsuited for the stage. They stay close to their historical sources, use an archaizing language to convey the spirit of the period, and are awkwardly constructed and difficult to follow. They are loaded with political allusions. Still, one finds in them many magnificent verses.

Russian comedy succeeded earlier than tragedy in bringing Russian characters and

22. Karlinsky, *Russian Drama*, 195–216.

Russian mores to the stage. To be sure, the comic repertoire depended largely on translations of Molière, Destouches, Regnard, Campistron, Legrand, Holberg, Gellert, and others. Early Russian efforts, specifically those of Sumarokov, were uninspired adaptations of familiar plots. The first Russian playwright to give such adaptations a genuine Russian flavor was Vladimir Lukin (1737–94). His play *The Trinket Vendor*, adapted from Robert Dodsley's *The Toy Shop* (via the French), consists of a series of short scenes in which the trinket vendor figures as a satirist and his customers as targets of his wit. Among his victims are Lukin's rival playwrights, Sumarokov and Aleksei Rzhevsky (1737–1804). The play is remarkable for various artful conceits and playful ambiguities that permeate its structure and its dialogue, in particular a clever complexity of frames surrounding the actual stage. Lukin also wrote the first Russian comedy recognizably set in Russia, specifically since a serf has a key role in the play: *The Spendthrift Corrected by Love* (1765) is an early example in Russia of the *comédie larmoyante* and introduces merchants, moneylenders, and gamblers from Lukin's own milieu.

Denis Ivanovich Fonvizin (1744–92), a Moscow nobleman of German origin educated at Moscow University and a moderately successful government official, produced several plays, two of which established him as the best comic playwright of the eighteenth century. *The Brigadier* (1769) is a satire on the Gallomania of the Russian gentry and the loose morals that it engendered. The brigadier abuses his wife, a good but old-fashioned and terribly naive Russian woman, and courts the wife of his friend, a state councillor. His son, recently back from Paris, is expected to marry Sofya, the coun-

cillor's virtuous and intelligent daughter, but instead makes advances to her all-too-willing stepmother. In the end the adulterers are shamed, and Sofya can marry Mr. Dobrolyubov (Goodlove), a young nobleman worthy of her. The plot is static and hardly original, but the dialogue is racy and often funny. The characters are drawn rather well. The brigadier's wife, utterly devoid of social sophistication, vanity, or amorous inclinations, has a scene with that lecherous hypocrite, the councillor, that a Gogol could have been proud of: she honestly does not catch the drift of the councillor's progressively bolder innuendos, nor does she get the meaning of his direct declaration of love—not even when he goes down on his knees before her and her son shouts *bravissimo!* as he interrupts their tête-à-tête.

The Minor (1782) has a more complicated plot, set in motion by the domineering Mrs. Prostakov (Simpleton), née Skotinin (Brute), who tries to gain control of the estate of an orphaned neighbor, Sofya, by marrying her, first to her crude and brutish brother, then to her son Mitrofanushka (the minor), a good-for-nothing, spoiled brat of sixteen. There is a happy and moral ending. A government inspector, traveling incognito, has gathered enough evidence to relieve the Prostakovs of their jurisdiction over their estate. Mitrofanushka turns against his mother. Sofya marries the man she loves.

Both plays carry an "enlightened" message. Swipes are taken at official corruption, the ignorance and crude manners of the rural gentry, and the abuses of serfdom. The characters of *The Brigadier* are still essentially those of French classicist comedy. Mrs. Prostakov, her brother, and her son, a meek serf woman, and an uppity serf who talks back to Mrs. Prostakov give *The Minor* enough local color to make it a genuinely Russian play. Some of its scenes are funny to almost any audience. *The Minor* soon became, and has remained, a permanent fixture not only of the Russian stage but of Russian cultural consciousness as well. Some of its lines became proverbial.

The 1780s and 1790s saw the vigorous development of Russian comedy and comic opera. Though most texts were patterned after French examples and the music, too, was largely foreign, Russian themes, Russian customs, and Russian songs and dances entered the lighter dramatic genres more and more often. *The Miller, Sorcerer, Cheat, and Matchmaker*, by Aleksandr Ablesimov (1742–83), staged in 1781, was derived from Rousseau's *Le Devin du village* and had a plot that was implausible for Russian conditions, but it was a huge success because of some racy dialogue and many Russian folk tunes. *The Arcades of Saint Petersburg*, by Mikhail Matinsky (1750–c. 1820), staged in 1792, has a plot that has not been traced to a foreign source and is set in the milieu of the tradition-bound merchant class. It features a colorful Russian wedding.

Pyotr Alekseevich Plavilshchikov (1760–1812), an actor and playwright, wrote a sequel to Ablesimov's *The Miller*, a one-act comedy entitled *The Miller and the Hot-Mead Vendor as Rivals*, as well as a spin-off from Fonvizin's *The Minor* (he had been a member of its original cast), *Kuteikin's Engagement Party*, which features some of the characters of Fonvizin's play. Plavilshchikov's *The Landless Peasant* (1790), a *comédie larmoyante*, is even closer to Russian reality. Plavilshchikov came from the merchant class but was an educated man (he was a graduate of Moscow University). He wrote prefaces for his plays, in which he

developed his ideas on acting and the theater and advocated a Russian national theater.

Vasily Kapnist's comedy in verse *Chicane* (staged 1798) can stand comparison with Fonvizin's two fine prose comedies. Kapnist's smooth alexandrines do not take away from the expressiveness of his dialogue, but rather enhance its mordant satire. Nor do the conventional classicist plot and the "talking" names of the characters (judges with names like Hook and Crook) conceal the fact that the action is about real people and events in a provincial Russian town. The plot is generated by the refusal of Major Pryamikov (Straight) to bribe the presiding judge in order to get a favorable decision in a wholly groundless suit against him, and it is complicated by the defendant's being in love with the crooked judge's virtuous daughter. The obligatory happy ending is obtained through a deus ex machina like that in *Tartuffe*: a ukase by the Senate (Russia's high court under the tsars) restores justice. The ending is as ambiguous as that of Gogol's *Inspector General*, for it could mean that justice will ultimately prevail, even in Catherine's Russia, or that it is extremely unlikely that it will (how often will the Senate even hear a case?). Even bolder are the details of the plot, which has legal procedures serve flagrant injustice in a wholly plausible way. Its highlight is a scene in which the judge's innocent daughter sings a hymn in praise of the virtue and charity of the empress (to the accompaniment of a harp, yet!), while her father's rapacious legal cohorts chime in with a cynical hymn to bribe taking. Staging of the play was made possible only by the fact that Tsar Paul approved of almost anything that would make his mother look bad.

Ivan Krylov, a journalist and playwright before he became a fabulist, translated several foreign plays and wrote some original comedies—the first of these, *The Fortune Teller from Coffee Grounds*, the text for a comic opera, when he was only sixteen. Krylov, a protegé of Knyazhnin's in his youth, went on to lampoon his benefactor as Mr. Rifmokrad (Rhyme Stealer) in a skit entitled *The Mischief Makers.* He parodied Knyazhnin's best-known tragedy, *Dido*, in a spirited comedy, *Trumf* (1800), where the role of Aeneas falls to Trumf, a stupid and cowardly German prince who speaks Russian with a Saxon accent.

Duke Aleksandr Aleksandrovich Shakhovskoi (1777–1846) served in the guards but was attracted to the theater early. His first play was staged in 1795. In 1802 he resigned his commission and joined the management of the imperial theaters, whose director he became eventually, holding this post (with some interruptions) until 1826. A political and literary conservative, Shakhovskoi was an active member of Admiral Shishkov's Colloquy of Amateurs of the Russian Word and lampooned his sentimentalist and romantic contemporaries in his satires and plays. He was, however, a progressive linguistically. His Russian is essentially that of Griboedov's *Woe from Wit* and of Pushkin.

Shakhovskoi was a prolific writer and translator of serious dramatic works, comedies, and vaudevilles, providing his theaters with much of their repertoire. Shakhovskoi's first play after his early debut of 1795 was *The Intrigue Monger* (1804), an adaptation of Gresset's *Le Méchant.* It was a failure. But the next year he had his first hit with *A New Sterne* (1805), a perceptive and witty lampoon of the Russian sentimentalists and their precious and flaccid style. Karamzin himself was the main target. A later play, *A Lesson to Coquettes, or the Spa of Lipetsk*

(1815), resumed the attack, with Zhukovsky now the principal target as Mr. Violet, who recites ludicrous sentimental verses while accompanying himself on the guitar. The main plot of that comedy is about the comeuppance of Countess Lelev, an egotistical but clever and spirited coquette, who resembles Célimène of Molière's *Le Misanthrope.* Among Shakhovskoi's many plays, *The Futile Planners* (1818) was the most controversial and the most reactionary. The target of its satire is progressive landowners who ruin themselves by attempting new agricultural and industrial techniques and consort with professorial types who have foreign-sounding names and liberal ideas.

Shakhovskoi continued to write plays and poetry until his death. His comedies of the 1820s and 1830s contain vivid reflections of the literary feuds of that period. At one time he collaborated with Griboedov on a comedy, *All in the Family* (1818), and was a friend of Pushkin's, who immortalized him in an excursus on the Russian stage in the first chapter of *Eugene Onegin*:

> Here did the mordant Shakhovskoi
> His comedies' noisy swarm deploy.

Shakhovskoi was successful both as a playwright and as an administrator. Under his direction the imperial stage became a thoroughly professional institution and developed some fine actors and actresses.

Prose Fiction

Under Peter the Great many works that forced their translators to create a vocabulary for European institutions, public affairs, and social relations were translated. As early as 1708 there appeared a book entitled *Examples of How Various Compliments Are to Be Written.* It was reprinted many times and taught a generation of Russians the polite epistolary style of educated Europe. In 1725 *On the Gods*, by the Greek antiquarian Apollodorus, appeared with a preface by Feofan Prokopovich. It taught literate Russians classical mythology and emblematics, which henceforth began to appear in Russian literature alongside biblical images and symbols. Peter the Great took an interest in history and had several historical works translated. He also commissioned the compiling of a history of Russia. A first effort, by the court poet and translator Fyodor Polikarpov, failed to meet with the tsar's approval. The first modern history of Russia, a brief survey, was compiled by A. I. Mankeev, a secretary of the Russian embassy in Stockholm, while interned in Sweden during the Northern War. The first scholarly history of Russia was written by Vasily Nikitich Tatishchev (1686–1750), initially a geographer, geologist, and surveyor, who over the years had gathered a large collection of chronicles, lives, documents, and miscellanies, from which he eventually compiled a history of Russia. It was not elegantly written, but its scholarship was up to European standards. Tatishchev's work appeared posthumously (three volumes in 1768–74, a fourth in 1784, and an incomplete fifth volume in 1843). Tatishchev's is by all means a modern mind: he is a freethinker, rationalist, and pragmatist. Tatishchev's language can be called modern Russian, though it still contains a great deal of Slavonic.

Ivan Tikhonovich Pososhkov (1652–1726), a man of humble origins, rose to a position of wealth and influence by serving Peter's mercantile projects. Toward the end of his life he wrote several works in which he set down his ideas, developed over years of experience in commerce, manufacturing, and mining. The best known of these are *A Fatherly Testament* (1718) and *On Poverty and Wealth*, which was presented to the tsar in 1724 but earned Pososhkov no laurels. He was arrested after Peter's death and died in prison. In this book Pososhkov discusses every stratum of Russian society, as well as various trades and crafts, even "robbery," (that is, crime), and—with "the tsar's interest" in mind—advocates various liberal policies. Pososhkov writes a vigorous vernacular Russian, thus remaining outside the mainstream of literary Russian, which continued to carry a heavy strain of Slavonic and was strongly influenced by foreign (Latin, German, or French) syntax and style.

The age of Peter the Great produced a number of public figures who wrote their personal memoirs, accounts of their journeys or of their times. Count Pyotr Andreevich Tolstoi (1645–1729) wrote a perceptive travelogue, *Journey of Stolnik Pyotr Andreevich Tolstoi through Italy in 1697–1699*, and Count Boris Petrovich Sheremetev (1652–1719) described his travels through Poland, Austria, and Italy. Russian travelers in Western Europe, of whom there were now many,[23] viewed the West much as European travelers viewed Russia, with curiosity but without hostility. They liked European universities, European courts of law, and the position of women in European society, but they did find things to criticize. Tolstoi, for instance, noted the lax morals of the upper class and the foppishness of impecunious Italian nobles.

Prose fiction remained in manuscript and occupied an inferior position well into the eighteenth century. Sumarokov still spoke disparagingly of the novel. Only the second

23. See, for example, Fred Otten, *Der Reisebericht eines anonymen Russen über seine Reise nach Westeuropa im Zeitraum 1697/1699*, Slavistische Veröffentlichungen des Osteuropa-Instituts der Freien Universität Berlin, 59 (Wiesbaden: Harrassowitz, 1985).

half of the century saw the emergence of prose fiction generated by immediate contact with contemporary European literature. The eighteenth century also saw a split of Russian literature along class lines: a wholly westernized high literature and a literature aimed at the literate middle-and lower-class reader, under some Western influence but nurtured to a large extent by the traditions of religious and oral literature. A lowbrow readership was now catered to by the *lubok*, printed single sheets and chapbooks hawked at fairs and in the market place. The literature of lubok included songbooks, collections of folktales under such titles as *Grandfather's Promenades* (1786, with many subsequent editions) or *Medicine against Melancholy and Sleeplessness* (also 1786, with subsequent editions published well into the nineteenth century), popular versions of tales of chivalry, and popular versions of the narrative genres of high literature, such as the sentimental novel.[24]

During the Petrine period prose fiction, still in manuscript only, continued in the style established in the seventeenth century. Among the most popular was the *Story of the Russian Sailor Vasily Koriotsky and the Beautiful Princess Irakliya of the Land of Florence*, which circulated in many copies and eventually surfaced as a bylina and as a chapbook. The tale's ethos is modern: a young Russian nobleman leaves misery be-

hind at home and finds success in the world. Vasily succeeds because he is clever, self-reliant, and possesses expert knowledge. The love intrigue is also modern: it is about romantic love. The language is an odd mixture of vernacular, Slavonic, and new loanwords, the sensibility a mixture of folktale, romance of chivalry, didactic parable (Vasily prays a lot), and adventure thriller.

The *Story of Alexander, a Russian Nobleman*, three times as long as the *Story of Vasily Koriotsky*, is even more of a hybrid. It contains elements of *Peter of the Golden Keys*, a tale of chivalry (the combat scenes are medieval, for they do not feature firearms), but also episodes of gallant love in the manner of the *roman precieux*. The story ends with Alexander's death by drowning. His beloved stabs herself to death. A former ladylove of his, upon hearing that Alexander lies buried next to another woman, exhumes his body and, with it, flings herself into a deep ravine. The tale contains love letters, flowery dialogues, and lyric effusions.

The *Tale of John the Merchant* has the son of a prosperous Petersburg merchant for its hero. John goes to work for a merchant in Paris and has a torrid love affair with his daughter Eleonora. The story mixes gallant love with some coarse buffoonery. It is closer to the popular narrative style than most other stories of its kind. Like some of the other stories, it has some crudely versified inserts.

Only toward the middle of the century did prose fiction finally break into print. There were some translations in the 1750s and 1760s: Le Sage's *Gil Blas* (1754–55), Defoe's *Robinson Crusoe* (1762, first edition of twelve hundred copies, unusually high), Scarron's *Roman comique* (1763). By the 1770s scores of foreign novels were being translated. By the end of the century

24. One of the earliest and most interesting pieces of *lubok* is a print, with captions entitled *Mice Burying the Cat*. It shows a funeral procession in which the corpse of the cat, well tied with strings lest he—heaven forbid!—arise, is driven on a sleigh by eight mice and followed by a crowd of rats and mice. The details of the picture and the captions make it clear that the cat is Peter I. Some of his enemies, such as Metropolitan Stefan Yavorsky, are also readily recognizable. The captions, in *rayoshnik*-type verse, gleefully vent the relief and schadenfreude of Peter's many enemies.

most major foreign novels, and many second-and third-rate novels, had found their way to the Russian reader. For instance, as many as thirty-two titles by François Thomas Marie de Baculard d'Arnaud (1718–1805), who tended to take his themes from contemporary English literature, were available in Russian by 1800. Eventually, some Russians thought of making literature a commercial venture and using native material in the process.

Mikhail Dmitrievich Chulkov (c. 1742–92) attended the Moscow gymnasium for commoners (*raznochintsy*), was for several years an actor at the court theater in Saint Petersburg, then served as a lackey at court, and finally made a successful civil service career in the College of Commerce, earning rank and nobility. As a littérateur, he remained an outsider, and what contacts he had with Sumarokov, Novikov, and other exponents of high literature were less than cordial. More of a professional writer than any of his contemporaries, Chulkov was a prolific author of fiction and nonfiction. He published five volumes of a miscellany, *The Mocker* (1766–68, 1789), rather in the manner of Scarron's *Roman comique*, from which he borrowed some items. *The Mocker* contains picaresque and genre tales, some quite realistic, almost in the manner of Restif de la Bretonne, as well as tales of chivalry, all told skillfully in a style close to that of the chapbooks.

Chulkov's best-known work is the incomplete story "The Comely Cook" (1770). The story breaks off at a suspenseful juncture, but a sequel was never published. It is told by the heroine, Martona, a Russian Moll Flanders. Contrary to traditional interpretations, "The Comely Cook" is not a satirical or realistic period piece but rather an entertainment, whose plot, setting, and sensibility are those of a European picaresque novel.

Like Chulkov's other tales, it is uninhibited erotically. Martona, though amorous and easily moved to tears, has a carnal and even cynical view of life, consistently contrasted with the "official" moral code and the heartless hypocrisy of those who pretend to live by it. Chulkov's ethos and style are quite different from the sensibility of aristocratic literati like Kheraskov and Karamzin.

Among Chulkov's other literary ventures were two short-lived magazines, *The Parnassian Bijoutier* (1770), a monthly, and *This and That* (1769), a weekly; a *Collection of Various Songs* (4 vols., 1770–74), which later appeared in several expanded editions; several versions of a mythological dictionary (1766–69); a *Dictionary of Russian Superstitions* (1782); and several works on Russian commerce.

Vasily Alekseevich Lyovshin (1746–1826), of ancient but impoverished nobility, served in the military and later in the civil service, advancing slowly through the table of ranks. An incredibly prolific writer, he published some ninety books of fiction and nonfiction, many of the former translations, mostly from the German, the latter for the most part compilations on economics, industry, and agriculture. Lyovshin's fiction belongs, like Chulkov's, to the "low" popular genres, particularly that of the tale of chivalry. But like several of his contemporaries, including Emin, Kheraskov, and Chulkov, he also produced a utopian novel, *A Most Recent Voyage* (1784), which has men fly to the moon and "lunatists" visit the earth. Like other Russian eighteenth-century utopists, Lyovshin depicted a utopia of patriarchal and rural Slavic life, uncorrupted by Western science and industry. Lyovshin's most memorable contribution to Russian literature was his *Russian Fairy Tales* (10 vols., 1780–83). Some of these are authentic Russian folktales, retold in the compiler's middlebrow idiom, others are taken straight from *Arabian Nights*, and still others are essentially tales of chivalry. Some appear to be Lyovshin's own inventions.

Mikhail Ivanovich Popov (1742–90), who at one time collaborated with Chulkov, published a three-volume work entitled *Slavic Antiquities* (1770–71), reissued in 1778 under the title *Ancient Curiosities, or Adventures of Russian Princes*. The tales told by Popov are tales of chivalry, with Slavic names introduced for local color.

Adventures of Ivan, a Merchant's Son (in two parts, 1785–86), by Ivan Novikov, is a miscellany of picaresque adventure and romantic brigandage, the latter an import from the West that took root quickly in Russian popular literature. Among other episodes, it contains the familiar *Tale of Frol Skobeev* and another that is clearly an imitation of Chulkov's "The Comely Cook." The anonymous *Luckless Nikanor, or Adventures of G., a Russian Nobleman* (three parts, 1775–89) tells of the misadventures of a poor hanger-on of a nobleman. It is awkwardly told, but introduces more specifics of Russian life than can be found in either Chulkov or Lyovshin.

Russian fiction addressed to the lowbrow reader shares its basic traits with its Western counterpart. In Russia, too, tales of romantic brigandage became popular in the eighteenth century and remained so until Soviet literary policies stopped them, as did tearjerking romances about the trials and tribulations of a noble hero (often a count) and his ladylove. A certain Matvei Komarov (nothing is known about him) created a classic of sorts in his "Detailed and True Description of the Good and Evil Deeds of the Russian Crook, Thief, Brigand, and Former Moscow Police Agent Vanka Kain, of His Entire Life and Adventures" (1779). The story was reprinted many times well into

the nineteenth century. (Vanka Kain, by the way, was a real person, who in 1748 created a sensation when after a series of robberies he offered his services to the Moscow police.) Komarov's "Romance of Milord George" (1782) tells of the lord's undying love, which after many trials leads to lawful wedlock. It was reprinted innumerable times, the last in 1918.

Only since the 1760s did Russian prose fiction begin to respond directly to contemporary Western examples. The *conte moral*, the *conte philosophique*, and the sentimental novel were the first genres to enter Russian high literature. Crébillon-fils, Voltaire, Rousseau, Richardson, and Sterne were among the principal examples. Since Russian writers lacked the social and literary context of their Western models, the traits characteristic of eighteenth-century fiction often appear lifeless and unmotivated in their works. In the West sentimentalism made sense as an antithesis to the sober rationalism of the early Enlightenment. The appeal of "night thoughts," graveyards, and apparitions, a penchant for naive religious faith, natural virtue, and the simple life, a pessimistic view of the progress of human society along with a cult of the creative individual ("genius") were all an inevitable reaction to what had preceded them. In Russia this context was barely present. Russian men of letters who expressed Western ideas and sensibilities in their writings had only a tenuous connection with the political, public, and social realities of Russian life. It is impossible to gain a true picture of Russian life from eighteenth-century Russian prose fiction.

Fyodor Aleksandrovich Emin (c. 1735–70) straddled the fence between the low prose entertainments of Chulkov or Popov and the more genteel novels of Kheraskov and other aristocratic literati. Emin apparently was born in the Ukraine and may have attended the Kiev Academy. But he came to Petersburg via London, where he had presented himself to the Russian embassy as a moslem ex-janissary desiring to convert to the Russian Orthodox faith. He then worked as a language teacher at the Corps of Infantry Cadets and soon became a professional littérateur. He translated a great deal from several languages and wrote seven original novels (or romances) as well as three volumes of a wholly unscholarly *History of Russia* (up to the year 1213). He also published the satirical journal *Hell's Post* (1769) and contributed to Novikov's journal *The Drone.*

Emin's romances differ from the popular entertainments of his age by the presence of some moral philosophizing, attempts at enlightening the reader on points of history, distant countries, and alien cultures, and a somewhat more genteel diction. The most popular of Emin's novels, *Fickle Fortune, or the Adventures of Miramond* (1763) features a noble young Turk's fantastic journeys through various exotic lands. *The Adventures of Themistocles* (also 1763), set in an imaginary classical antiquity, was the first Russian novel to pursue the expression of a moral and political philosophy after the fashion of Fénelon's *Les Aventures de Télémaque,* preceding Trediakovsky's versified translation of Fénelon (1766) as well as Kheraskov's *Numa, or Flourishing Rome* (1768). Emin's epistolary novel *The Letters of Ernest and Doravra* (four volumes, 1766), rather in the manner of Rousseau's *La nouvelle Héloïse,* is the first Russian novel to bear a clear imprint of sentimentalism.

Emin's novels must have been hastily written, are indiscriminately derivative, and feature no characters who are really alive. Their plot construction is elementary. But

they are a move in the direction of launching the nascent genre of the modern novel into the mainstream of Russian literature. There is a direct connection, usually parodic, between Emin's *Miramond* and the adventure novel of the romantic period (Veltman, Senkovsky), as well as between *Ernest and Doravra* and the "sentimental humanitarianism" of the natural school— also parodic, as in the case of Dostoevsky's *Poor Folk.*

Kheraskov was the only major figure of eighteenth-century Russian literature to be active as a poet and dramatist and also as a writer of prose fiction. His first novel, *Numa, or Flourishing Rome* (1768), a *conte philosophique,* creates a utopian dream of an enlightened monarchy under Numa Pompilius, mythical king of Rome. Kheraskov's second novel, *Cadmus and Harmony* (1786), is set in mythical Thebes and is an adventure novel with an allegorical subtext. The story of the hero's many trials, repeated fall, and eventual redemption is to be understood in terms of Kheraskov's Masonic convictions. His third novel, the lengthy *Polydorus, Son of Cadmus and Harmony* (1794), its sequel, is an allegorical denunciation of the French Revolution and its godless leaders. Kheraskov's novelistic style is ornate and intricate. Exceedingly "literary," it lacks a natural storyteller's unselfconscious grace.

Around the turn of the century a number of sentimental novels and stories appeared, all more or less imitative of Western models, as even their titles indicate. *Werther's Sentiments, or Unfortunate M——v* (1793), by Aleksandr Klushin (1763–1804), who also wrote satirical comedies, poetry, and criticism, follows the plot of Goethe's novel but touches its content only on the surface. Two novels by Nikolai Fyodorovich Emin (1760–1814), son of Fyodor Aleksandrovich, were also patterned after Goethe's *Werther: Roza* (1786) and *Play of Fate* (1789). Pavel Yurievich Lvov (1770–1825) produced *A Russian Pamela, or the Story of Maria, a Virtuous Peasant Girl* (1789), following Richardson, who was extremely popular in Russia. Aleksandr Benitsky (1780–1809) and Aleksandr Izmailov (1779–1831) wrote philosophical Oriental tales in the manner of Voltaire. Izmailov also produced *Poor Masha, a Russian Tale, Partly True* (1801) and *Eugene, or the Detrimental Effects of Bad Upbringing and Company* (1799–1801), a *conte moral.*

Aleksandr Nikolaevich Radishchev (1749–1802) owes his great fame to a single work, his *Journey from Petersburg to Moscow* (1790). His other prose writings are either short, such as his "Life of Fyodor Vasilievich Ushakov" (published in 1789 but apparently written soon after Ushakov's death in 1770), or deal with scientific or philosophical topics. His poetry, including a celebrated ode, "Freedom," while expressing lofty ideals, shows little talent. Radishchev, of provincial nobility, served as a page at the imperial palace from an early age and was sent, with a group of other pages, to the University of Leipzig to study law. His stay there from 1766 to 1771, described in the "Life of Ushakov," a fellow student, made Radishchev a well-read philosophe and a passionate adept of the liberal Enlightenment. Upon his return to Russia, Radishchev served as a military prosecutor and later as a middle-echelon civil servant. It seems likely that Radishchev published his *Journey* in the hope of getting some relief from his straitened circumstances. It nearly cost him his life. His death sentence was commuted by Catherine to ten years' exile in Siberia, from which he was allowed to return after the empress's death. Radishchev committed suicide in 1802. His posthumous fame as a martyr and visionary grew steadily throughout the nineteenth century.

Radishchev's *Journey* is an utter surprise if viewed solely in the context of Russian literature: a truly revolutionary document from the reign of Catherine II, more than a generation before similar ideas would be voiced by the Decembrists. But it is no surprise if viewed in the context of the European Enlightenment, written as it was on the eve of the French Revolution, by a man who had studied in the West and was well versed in the works of the leading philosophes of the age. Radishchev's violent reaction to the abuses of Russian serfdom is the same as is found in works by European writers of his education and frame of mind who came in contact with serfdom, for example in Garlieb Merkel's *Die Letten, vorzüglich in Liefland, am Ende des philosophischen Jahrhunderts* (1796).

Radishchev's *Journey* is an artless mixture of observed Russian fact, sometimes poignantly described, and humanitarian and libertarian rhetoric entirely in the manner of Helvétius or Rousseau. It has none of the charm and wit of Sterne's *Sentimental Journey*, which served as its formal model. The journey itself is uninteresting. Passing through Novgorod gives the traveler a chance to dwell on the ancient freedom of the republic of Novgorod. The loose maidens of Valdai, who seek to lure the traveler into a bathhouse, where his morals and his purse will suffer, offer some relief from the generally somber mood of the *Journey*. There are some good genre scenes: an accurate description of the interior of a peasant hut and the grinding poverty of its inhabitants; a blind minstrel singing a spiritual ballad, the *Tale of Alexis, Man of God*; army recruits tearfully taking leave of their families—among them a Frenchman down on his luck. Other episodes are clearly introduced to deliver a message. There is the landowner who has deflowered as many as sixty peasant girls: here Radishchev discourses on the corruption of peasant mores by depraved landowners and sings a paean to the purity of the peasant maiden. Episodes about a landowner who was murdered by his serfs after having abused them mercilessly for years, and about an auction at which some serfs are sold, contain impassioned diatribes on the horrors of such practice.

Radishchev lets his traveler and various characters whom he meets on his way discuss a variety of subjects and deliver some fiery tirades against aristocratic landownership, the hubris and reckless luxury of rulers, the white man's murder of Indian natives, the evils of slavery, and other such topics. In a lengthy excursus on censorship Radishchev asserts that freedom of thought is the best way to support true faith and that any form of censorship is counterproductive. Elsewhere, Rousseau's ideas on education are expounded with vigor and conviction.

Catherine's wrath at reading Radishchev's *Journey* was well founded, particularly since we know from her own dramatic and other writings that she was well informed about the actual condition of her empire and could see the crying disparity between her enlightened ideas and Russian reality. Radishchev's charges were true, and therefore dangerous.

Nikolai Ivanovich Novikov (1744–1818), not a major writer, nevertheless is among the most important figures in the history of Russian literature. The son of a wealthy landowner, he attended the gymnasium attached to the newly founded university in Moscow, served in the guards, and worked for Catherine's legislative commission from 1767 until its dismissal in December 1768. In 1769

Novikov founded the satirical journal *The Drone* and after its demise in 1770 several successors: *The Tatler* (1770), *The Painter* (1772–73), and *The Purse* (1774). From here on Novikov devoted himself full-time to journalistic and literary endeavors.

The Drone soon found itself engaged in a spirited polemic with *All and Sundry*, a satirical journal founded and run by the empress herself. *The Drone* attacked government inefficiency and corruption, judicial misconduct, and the inordinate luxury and lax morality of Catherine's courtiers. *All and Sundry* found the severity of these attacks excessive and uncharitable. Novikov's journals could be very outspoken. Among a selection of "advertisements" we read: "A young Russian piglet, who journeyed to foreign parts to improve his mind and did so with profit in that he returned a full-grown swine, may be seen free of charge in any street of the city." Another "advertisement" offers the services of a Frenchman who will teach Russians how to successfully cheat at cards, for the modest remuneration of playing with him for cash. Catherine's journal advocated a more decorous tone. In particular, it was opposed to any personal attacks—understandably, since *The Drone* went so far as to bring up the topic of "foreign ladies" of mature age with a fondness for young men—many young men.

In 1772 Novikov published his *Outline of a Historical Dictionary of Russian Writers*, containing 317 entries,[25] a major step toward the writing of a history of Russian literature. A great bibliophile, Novikov pub-

---

25. Novikov's work was to some extent a response to an anonymous article, "Nachrichten über einige russische Schriftsteller," in the Leipzig *Neue Bibliothek der schönen Wissenschaften und freien Künste* (1768), which let Russian literature begin with Peter the Great and listed a mere forty authors. Novikov could list fifty-four pre-Petrine authors.

lished some valuable source material in a series, *Old Russian Library* (1773–75). He also started a scholarly journal, *The Saint Petersburg Learned News* (1779). In 1779 Novikov moved to Moscow, where he published a newspaper, *The Moscow News* (1779–89), several journals, and a large number of important books including translations of works of world literature (Shakespeare, Rousseau, Lessing, Diderot, Beaumarchais, and others).[26]

An active Freemason and close friend of Johann Georg Schwarz (1751–84), the leader of the Russian Rosicrucians, Novikov also engaged in a variety of philanthropic activities, founding and supporting schools, scholarships, orphanages, and hospitals, and gathered a remarkable library organized according to Masonic principles.

Novikov wrote essays on a variety of topics (education, commerce, morality, history) and critical reviews of contemporary literature, all in the spirit of the liberal Enlightenment. His activities elicited the displeasure of the empress, who lampooned him and Russian Freemasonry in a dialogue, "Le Secret de la Société Anti-Absurde, devoilé par quelqu'un qui n'en est pas" (1780), and in a trilogy of Russian comedies, *The Fraud, The Deluded*, and *The Siberian Shaman* (1785–86). In 1792 Novikov was arrested and imprisoned, although there was no evidence of any subversive intent on his part and his reputation was that of a kindly man and good Christian. He was released by Tsar Paul after Catherine's death, but never resumed his publishing activities and died a broken and impoverished man.

Novikov and Radishchev tried to deal with Russian life in terms of ideas current in the West and demonstrated that the Russian language was rapidly becoming a suitable medium for the discussion of social, moral, and political questions aired in the West. Neither Radishchev nor Novikov had extraordinary literary talent. But their generation was able to hand over to Karamzin a functional though irregular prose style, which he developed into the first stage of standard literary Russian, the language used by the great writers of the nineteenth century.

Nikolai Mikhailovich Karamzin (1766–1826), a man of no extraordinary talent, dominated the world of Russian letters like no Russian writer before or after him and left an important legacy to the writers who followed him, and this although he abandoned his literary activities in 1803, when he was appointed Imperial historiographer by Tsar Alexander I. Karamzin's monumental *History of the Russian State* (11 vol., 1818–24; a twelfth volume, dealing with the Time of Troubles, was incomplete at Karamzin's death), besides its great scholarly and political importance, significantly affected the development of Russian literature. Still, Karamzin before 1803 is the more important writer.

Karamzin came from the provincial gentry, was educated at J. M. Schaden's boarding school in Moscow (1779–83), served briefly in the guards, and in 1784 joined the circle of Moscow Freemasons led by Novikov. He was soon drawn into the lively literary activities of Novikov's group, did a great deal of translating from the German and English,[27] and wrote some derivative and rather cerebral poetry. A lengthy programmatic ode, "Poesy" (1787), advocates

---

26. In 1779 Novikov leased the facilities of Moscow University Press for ten years.

27. Karamzin translated Lessing's *Emilia Galotti* (1788), Shakespeare's *Julius Caesar* (1787), the first canto of Klopstock's *Messias*, parts of *The Seasons* by James Thomson, and some other works of French and German literature.

an orphic view of poetic creation and extols classical, English, and German (but no French) poets. Its sensibility is that of German Storm and Stress, one of whose leading figures, Jakob Michael Reinhold Lenz (1751–92), Karamzin met at Novikov's house. In 1789–90 Karamzin made a journey through Western Europe. It led to his *Letters of a Russian Traveler*, which appeared in *The Moscow Journal* (founded upon his return) and made him famous. Karamzin then proceeded to publish several other journals and almanacs in which appeared his short prose fiction, essays, and reviews.

Karamzin's *Letters of a Russian Traveler* were for several generations of educated Russians their main source of information about Western Europe. Echoes from the *Letters* may be found as late as in Dostoevsky's *The Brothers Karamazov*. The *Letters* were based on notes taken by Karamzin during his journey through Germany, Switzerland, France, and England, but were written entirely upon his return to Russia. They are a work of literature, not a personal document. Karamzin digested a great deal of material from travel guides, newspapers and journals, and literary and scholarly works, presenting it as immediate experience.

The portion of the *Letters* that took Karamzin through Germany and Switzerland to Lyon in France appeared in the *Moscow Journal* (1791–92), a part of the letters from England in the almanac *Aglaia* (1794–95). The portions dealing with Paris in 1790 were left out as apparently too risky. A separate edition (1797) remained incomplete because of difficulties with censorship. A complete edition finally appeared in 1801. Several more editions appeared in Karamzin's lifetime, the last in 1820.

Karamzin's *Letters* are patterned after Sterne's *Sentimental Journey through France and Italy*, many direct quotes and echoes of which appear throughout Karamzin's text.[28] But Karamzin pursued a broader aim than Sterne. He reports his experiences and impressions in a self-effacing but dignified tone, with occasional lyric effusions in poetry and prose, sometimes melancholy and sometimes enthusiastic. Karamzin lacks Sterne's elusive irony, though he tries at times to imitate Sternian anticlimax and bathos. When he digresses into melancholy contemplations in the manner of Edward Young's *Night Thoughts* (which his friend A. M. Kutuzov had translated) he is unconvincing. He is, however, an entertaining raconteur who tells a touching story or an amusing anecdote well. But more than anything else, he conveys to his reader a cultured Russian's understanding and appreciation of Western culture: literature, of course, but also political and economic life, popular life and social structure, art and architecture, and music and theater.

Karamzin admires Shakespeare above all, a sure sign of a pre-romantic sensibility. His comments, though not original, are certainly pertinent: Shakespeare's bombast, he observes, is part of the fashion of Shakespeare's times; his revelations of the human heart and profound thoughts are timeless. Karamzin's survey of recent English poets, writers, and historians is cursory but knowledgeable. He admires the wealth, power, and expressiveness of the English language, but faults its prosody, finding it "crude and unpleasant to the ear." Karam-

---

28. Hans Rothe has suggested that Karl Philipp Moritz's novel *Anton Reiser* and his travelogues *Reisen eines Deutschen in England* and *Reisen eines Deutschen in Italien* may have served as examples to Karamzin, who visited with Moritz in Berlin. See Hans Rothe, *N. M. Karamzins europäische Reise: Der Beginn des russischen Romans* (Bad Homburg: Gehlen, 1968), 139–40.

zin's view of French literature seems to be influenced by his German mentors. Rousseau is treated as a cult figure as the Russian traveler traces the great man's footsteps in Switzerland and in Paris. But Voltaire is denied "the genius of nature," and the great tragedians are credited with having created fine poetry but little dramatic action. Karamzin's attitude toward contemporary French literature and theater is one of interested detachment. He finds André Chénier's tragedy *Charles IX* "cold as ice," except for some allusions to contemporary events: too little action and too many boring monologues. As so often, he uses the occasion to stress Shakespeare's superiority to all that the French can offer. The only Francophone celebrity with whom he had a personal interview was the Swiss philosopher and naturalist Charles Bonnet (1720–93).

Well versed in contemporary German literature and philosophy, Karamzin reports cordial interviews with Immanuel Kant in Königsberg, Christoph Friedrich Nicolai and Karl Philipp Moritz in Berlin, and Herder and Wieland in Weimar. He attends Ernst Platner's lectures in Leipzig and is invited to dinner by the famous professor. In Zurich he visits the celebrated moralist and physiognomist Johann Kaspar Lavater, with whom he had previously been in correspondence. His constant companion in Paris is Wilhelm von Wolzogen, Schiller's brother-in-law. Presumably he also spoke German with his other travel companions, Count Adam Gottlob von Moltke and Jens Baggesen, a Danish poet and writer. Karamzin's references to German literature are both numerous and well informed.

Karamzin had to be careful in his comments on social and political matters, especially—though not only—in revolutionary Paris. But he likes to comment on local trade, industry, agriculture, and road conditions. He is obviously critical of Prussia, both between the lines (when he casually describes the obtuse arrogance of some Prussian officers) and in explicit comments on the quality of roads, restaurants, and customs service. Karamzin likes Saxony much better. In Frankfurt he is shocked by the squalor of the Jewish ghetto. He is delighted with Swiss democracy, industry, and virtue. He clearly enjoys the exuberant, easygoing, fun-loving life-style of the Parisians but is appalled by the gulf that separates the rich from the poor and by the squalid poverty found in France, a country blessed by nature. He sympathetically reports the story (taken from a newspaper but reported with some psychological details freely added by Karamzin) of a young man who took his own life when he realized that in spite of his education and his gifts he would never rise above the servant class. Karamzin's reportage lets us forget, most of the time, that he is in revolutionary Paris. He does describe a visit to the National Assembly, though. All the changes brought about by the Revolution are matter-of-factly reported to be for the worse.

England fascinates the Russian traveler more than continental Europe. He finds much to admire: the comfortable homes of the British, their evenly distributed wealth, their freedoms, and their institutions (he witnesses a parliamentary debate and a day's proceedings at the trial of Warren Hastings). He praises the wholesome beauty of their women (few Frenchwomen are beautiful, he adds). He esteems their good sense and the boldness and wit of their poets. But he is also appalled by the hideous faces of their beggars and rampant vice in the streets of London. He wryly observes that the British willingly sacrifice some of their safety from thieves and robbers to be safe from the importunities of a too powerful police force.

He mentions, with a note of sarcasm, that in Britain poverty has been declared a vice, and with surprising vehemence he declares that the British, who at home so insist on their human rights, treat their colonial subjects as animals.

With their wealth of literary and extra-literary material, their variety of moods from the dryly factual to the unabashedly lyrical, from the casual journalistic to the philosophical, and from that of the detached reporter to that of intimate personal revelation, Karamzin's *Letters* contain all the narrative, stylistic, and dialectical tools required for the writing of a modern novel. The sentimental, the psychological, the gothic, and the social novel are all there, and so are the main themes of the modern novel: the futile quest of self-conscious modern man for communion with nature, a social role in which he could feel at home, and a philosophy in which he could believe. Karamzin's *Letters* were not only immensely important as a stepping stone for the great literature of the nineteenth century. They are a masterpiece in their own right, remarkably fresh and interesting reading even today.

After the Letters Karamzin's imaginative prose is, at least from today's vantage point, a terrible letdown. "Poor Liza," which appeared in the June 1792 issue of the *Moscow Journal*, is the most striking example in all of Russian literature of a discrepancy between the fame and influence of a work and its intrinsic worth. This brief story tells of the seduction of Liza, a trusting peasant maiden, by Erast, a wealthy and dissolute young nobleman. Abandoned by Erast, who marries a rich widow for her money to clear his gambling debts, Liza drowns herself in the pond that had witnessed their love trysts. The story is embroidered with idyllic descriptions of the countryside near Moscow. The theme of "Poor Liza" was a favo-

rite of the German Storm and Stress movement. Karamzin transplanted it into Russian literature without bothering to adapt it to his Russian setting—no inkling of serfdom appears anywhere in the story. It is told, smoothly enough, in the effusively emotional and moralizing tone of sentimentalism. This wholly derivative and insipid literary exercise became the cornerstone and point of departure for serious Russian prose fiction because, however clumsily, it tried to motivate its plot psychologically, found the language to express the emotions of its characters, and placed the action into a recognizable Russian locale.

Karamzin wrote a number of other short stories, several of them almost as important as "Poor Liza," though none of them artistically superior to it. "Martha the Governor, or the Subjugation of Novgorod" (1803), published in the *Herald of Europe* after some difficulties with the censor, is a historical novella whose heroine, a historical personage, inspires the people of the republic of Novgorod to take a last stand against the conquering grand duke of muscovy, Ivan III. It is historically inaccurate, makes only feeble attempts at historical stylization, and features long speeches but little action. It tries to compromise between an obvious sympathy with the ancient freedom of Novgorod and a recognition of the inevitable historical necessity of the Moscow autocrat's victory. "Martha the Governor" seems feeble to anyone who, like the historian Karamzin, has read the stark yet emotion-laden chronicle accounts of the events of 1471.

Some fragments of stories, like "The Island of Bornholm" (1794) and "Sierra Morena" (1795), introduced the gothic manner into Russian literature—not that it needed an introduction, for the novels of Ann Radcliffe enjoyed wide popularity. More interesting are Karamzin's psychological vignettes, such as "My Confession: A Letter to the Editor of this Journal" (1802), "A Knight of Our Age" (1802–3), and "The Sentimental and the Cold" (1803). "My Confession" is remarkable for its unequivocally negative hero, an amoral and unscrupulous sensualist who is allowed to prosper to the end. "A Knight of Our Age" is the beginning of an *éducation sentimentale*, and "The Sentimental and the Cold" tries to draw a balance sheet of the advantages and disadvantages of spontaneity and native talent versus deliberate action and hard work. Although these pieces are brief, fragmentary, and hardly original from a European viewpoint, they are nevertheless a step in the direction of the world of Pushkin's *Eugene Onegin* and the society tale of the 1830s.

Criticism

Until the end of the eighteenth century Russian literature developed no coherent or consistent body of criticism. When it finally did, criticism was decidedly its weakest link, as Pushkin observed in 1825. Whenever critical opinions were expressed, they were hardly based on structured aesthetic thought. Russians were familiar with the writings of the most important literary theorists, but few such works were translated. Aristotle's *Rhetoric* and *Poetics* were translated in the Petrine period, and so was Horace's *Arts poetica*. Feofan Prokopovich's *Poetics*, based on these, was published only in 1786 but was widely read before then in manuscript. Boileau's *Art poétique* was translated by Trediakovsky in 1752, and an abridged translation of Voltaire's *Essai sur la poésie épique* appeared in 1763. *Les Beaux Arts réduits à un même principe* (1746), by Abbé Charles Batteux, was im-

mensely influential, but readers had to wait until 1808 for a Russian version. La Harpe's *Lycée, ou Cours de littérature ancienne et moderne* (1799–1805) appeared in Russian translation in 1810–14. The aesthetic theories of Lessing, Herder, and Kant were known to some Russians, but their works were translated only much later.[29] A brief Russian summary of Kant's aesthetic theory appeared in 1812, and it began to have a real influence on Russian criticism during the romantic period. The emotionalist and sensualist aesthetics of Rousseau and the British became an active influence in the 1790s. German and English romantic thought reached Russia in the 1820s.[30]

The first aesthetic doctrine to establish itself in Russia was that of classicism. Kantemir was a full-fledged classicist who routinely employed such key phrases as "usefulness and entertainment" (*pol'za i zabava*), "improving human mores" (*ispravlyat' nravy chelovecheskie*), "healthy good sense" (*zdravyi smysl*), and "imitating the [classical] models" (*podrazhanie obraztsam*). Trediakovsky, Lomonosov, Sumarokov, and their followers were in theory all classicists, but they had their philosophical differences. Trediakovsky charged Sumarokov with sensualism and Hobbesian materialism while placing himself with those who, like the seventeenth-century Dutch humanist Hugo Grotius, defined man not by his selfish and sensual instincts but by his rational and

29. Herder and Kant had direct connections to Russia. Herder had spent some years in Riga (1764–69) and took a lively interest in Slavic and Baltic folklore. The first edition of Kant's *Critique of Pure Reason* appeared in Riga in 1781.

30. Wackenroder and Tieck's *Herzensergiessungen eines kunstliebenden Klosterbruders* (1797) appeared in a translation by Stepan Shevyryov and others in 1826, under the title *On Art and Artists: Meditations of a Hermit, a Lover of Beauty*.

altruistic ones. Actually, Sumarokov's position was that of rationalist psychologism in the spirit of John Locke. His poetic objective was to represent the various emotional states of normal human beings. Accordingly, he saw Lomonosov's pursuit of the exalted, the heroic, and the sublime as a violation of the natural, of reason, and of *vraisemblance*.

Trediakovsky's occasional critical observations did not originate from any systematic doctrine, though he was of course conversant with the canon of classicism. He started the practice of grammatical and stylistic criticism of detail, which Gogol and Belinsky were still combatting in the 1830s for the sake of "organic" criticism of the work as a whole.

Lomonosov, with his hierarchy of styles and genres, his emphasis on clarity, and his command of rhetorical devices, was, as a critic and theorist, certainly a classicist. His criticism is concerned with bad grammar, poor thinking, "wrong style," improper diction, and cacophony. Lomonosov, unlike Trediakovsky, did have a sure sense of style: colloquial versus literary (even with regard to phonetics), rhetorical, poetic, historical, and even official (*prikazny*). He also had a feel for rhythm (*techenie slov*) and euphony: in his *Rhetoric* he actually sought to define the psychological "color" of each speech sound. Lomonosov left an unfinished essay, "On the Present Condition of the Letters in Russia," written in the early 1750s, apparently in response to the polemical literary atmosphere of those years, when Sumarokov and his followers were attacking the principles and the poetic practice of Lomonosov and his school.[31] If finished, it would have become the first work of Russian literary criticism.

Sumarokov stated his critical principles early, in his *Two Epistles, The First Dealing with the Russian Language and the Second with Versification* (1747).[32] They follow Boileau and in general express all the basic tenets of classicism: *vraisemblance*, on the grounds that art is representation of nature; imitation of classical models, on the grounds that eternal and universal rules of poetic creation were known to the ancients; the notion that literature has a moral-didactic function; strict adherence to the theory of genres; and a simple and "natural" diction, which to Sumarokov meant avoidance of most of the Slavonic elements recommended by Lomonosov.[33] Vasily Maikov, in his "Ode on Taste, to Aleksandr Petrovich Sumarokov" (1776),[34] summarized all these principles succinctly:

I will always find pleasing a taste
That is dignified, pure, and intelligible.
It is not bombast that appeals in verse;
What pleases is its purity.
Not thunder is beautiful,
But the riches of reason in a weighty
    discourse.

32. A second version of this work came out in 1774, under the title *Instruction to Those Who Want to Become Writers* (*Nastavlenie khotyashchim byti pisatelyami*).

33. It has been observed that Sumarokov differed from Lomonosov in giving more attention to the emotional side of poetic expression, as he demanded that the poet express emotions he had himself experienced: "He labors in vain / Who with reason alone seeks to affect reason: / He is no poet yet who expresses only thought / And whose blood flows cold, but he who affects the heart, / Who expresses feeling and whose blood is warm." However, the same recommendation could be gathered from Horace: "Si vis me flere, dolendum est primum ipsi tibi" (*Ars poetica* 102–3). Lomonosov, no less than Horace and Boileau, was well aware that it took inspiration, as well as intelligence and desire, to be a poet.

34. Sumarokov replied to it with "A Response to the Ode of Vasily Ivanovich Maikov."

31. I. Z. Serman, *Poeticheskii stil' Lomonosova* (Moscow and Leningrad: Nauka, 1966), 234–35.

Your language should be pure and clear:
It is such taste that is in accord with
     nature.

With all this theoretical equipment, Sumarokov's practical criticism remained a critique of stylistic and grammatical details, with aesthetic comments limited to phrases like "beautiful strophes" or "a very good line." Sumarokov's few comments on his rivals in the *Two Epistles* are positive as regards Lomonosov, still a friend at the time, negative as regards Trediakovsky, who lodged a formal complaint, and quite unfair to Kantemir.

The satirical journals of the 1760s and 1770s, as well as the mock-heroic epics and some comedies of the same period, contained a good deal of literary parody, satirical lampooning of literary rivals, and outright bickering and invective. Chulkov's satirical journals, for example, featured spirited attacks on his competitors.[35] The longest of these, "The Poets' Sad Downfall," close to a thousand lines, parodies some of the major contemporary poets (Lomonosov, Sumarokov, Maikov). Its principal target is Chulkov's successful rival Fyodor Emin, but others can be recognized, too—Sumarokov in particular, who appears as a blustering Jupiter. The journals of Emin and Novikov responded to these attacks in kind.

Novikov's *Outline of a Historical Dictionary of Russian Writers* (1772) contains much useful biographical information, but little more than the titles of each author's more important works, with an occasional word of praise or appreciation. Novikov's journals and especially his *Saint Petersburg Learned News* printed reviews of newly published books, original as well as translations, and some theatrical reviews. These

reviews, including those written by Novikov himself, tended to be descriptive rather than critical, and what criticism they contained was impressionistic and anecdotal.

Karamzin was justly called the first Russian critic by Belinsky. His *Letters of a Russian Traveler* contain much literary causerie and criticism. The *Moscow Journal* and other journals in which he had a hand carried many literary and theatrical reviews by him. He was the first Russian writer to devote an essay to assessing a contemporary ("On Bogdanovich and His Works," 1803). His *Pantheon of Russian Authors* (1801–2) provided not only biographical information but also a solid critical evaluation of many Russian authors from Nestor and the mythical Boyan to Sumarokov, Maikov, and Popov. Karamzin wrote several theoretical essays as well, such as "What Does an Author Need?" (1793).

A convinced westernizer, certainly in the first half of his life, Karamzin read all of the major European literatures in the original and knew them well. He was also philosophically educated, knowing Hume, Locke, Condillac, Bonnet, Rousseau, Kant, Herder, and others. He was the first Russian to use the adjective *aesthetic* (*esteticbesky*) and to be abreast of the aesthetic thought of Lessing, Schiller, and Kant.

The criticism of Karamzin and his followers retained many of the criteria of classicism: imitation of nature ("beautiful nature," in particular),[36] propriety,[37] the didactic

---

35. Three of these satirical pieces appeared as a separate booklet in 1775.

36. "What are the arts? Imitation of nature. Dense, intertwined tree branches were the model of the first hut and the foundation of architecture; the wind blowing into a hole in a broken reed or on the string of a bow taught us music; the shadows of objects taught us drawing and painting. The dove, perched on a branch and mourning her dead mate, was the teacher of the first elegiac poet" (*Aglaia*, 1:42).

37. The Karamzinist critic V. V. Izmailov attacked

function of art, and "good taste." The criticism of Karamzin and his school was predominantly a *critique de beautées*, seeking to find the good and beautiful in everything. Some new dimensions, however, were also in evidence. Karamzin refused to recognize the superiority of classical examples. He took a historical view, recognizing that literature, like society, was subject to change. Classicism's narrow rules regarding the social identity of genres, characters, and themes were greatly liberalized. Karamzin and his followers embraced an emotionalist aesthetic, considering natural, immediate, and sincere expression of emotion to be the principal task of literature. In fact, Karamzin believed that the poet, no matter what his subject, was really expressing *himself*, and he encouraged poets to take advantage of this fact. Hence an author needed a kind and tender heart as much as a sharp mind and a vivid imagination. In a sense, Karamzin was an aesthetic agnostic, as he believed that art cannot reveal anything about the objective world but merely reveals the artist's mind and soul: the reality created by a work of art is illusory, a deception (*obman*).

The central concepts of romantic criticism were decidedly absent from the views of Karamzin and his school. He was too much of a westernizer and former Mason to be a populist or to have any real understanding of folk poetry. His criticism is still essentially one of details and formal devices, with no trace of the "organicism" of German and British romantic critics. He deals with "man" in the abstract, not with historical

and national types. Language is to Karamzin an artifact controlled by its creator. His conception of style is based on the notion that a literary text should create certain effects and elicit certain emotions. Hence he is also a proponent of freedom of style. Karamzin greatly helped, through his example and his criticism, to erase the boundary between poetry and prose, between high style and middle style.

When Karamzin founded the *Herald of Europe* (1802–30), he had renounced some of his liberal and cosmopolitan ideas and moved toward a more conservative patriotic position. In a programmatic "Letter to the Editor" in the first issue of that journal, he placed the emphasis of his editorial policy on the political and moral education of his readership. Literary criticism was to be reduced in scope. In a letter to the editor that served as a preface to the *Herald of Europe* for 1808, Vasily Zhukovsky, who became editor of the journal that year, echoed an opinion expressed repeatedly by Karamzin: "Criticism and luxury are daughters of wealth; but at this point we are far from being Croesuses in literature!" Although Karamzin and his collaborators greatly enriched the intellectual equipment of Russian criticism, they did not advance far beyond their predecessors as practicing critics.

Karamzin stated his position on language usage in an essay, "On Love of the Fatherland and National Pride" (1802). He held that the language of high society (*bol'shoi svet*), and society ladies (*prelestnye damy*), in particular ought to be the nucleus of the literary idiom. The popular vernacular should be used in moderation, especially as a means to enrich the expression of emotions. The language of high society, to which Karamzin belonged, was thoroughly frenchified. Karamzin himself had contributed to

---

Nikolai Ilyin's play *Magnanimity, or the Recruit Draft* (1804) on the grounds that the depiction of the coarse manners of the peasantry could not be proper or profitable, as well as that the playwright's attempt to idealize his peasant heroes and to soften the coarseness of their language violated the principle of *vraisemblance*.

this condition by introducing a number of calques from the French.

As imperial historiographer, Karamzin became more and more conservative. In an essay of 1811, "A Note on Old and New Russia," he revised his earlier glorification of Peter the Great, accusing Peter's reforms of having deprived Russia of its firm moral traditions and forced it to adopt foreign mores. "We became citizens of the world, but in some instances ceased being citizens of Russia," he wrote. However, Karamzin still firmly believed that there was no turning back the wheel of history. As far as literature was concerned, he stated in a speech given in 1818 on the occasion of his election to the Russian Academy: "*Particular* beauties, which inform the character of *popular* poetry, must yield to *universal* beauties: the former change; the latter are eternal. It is good to write for Russians; it is still better to write for all humanity."

With all their basic conservatism and loyalty to the monarchy, Karamzin and his followers were westernizers who approved of the turn Russian society and Russian culture had taken since Peter the Great. But there were educated Russians even in the eighteenth century who thought otherwise. A conservative—one might say proto-Slavophile—undercurrent existed in Russian intellectual life and was to surface in the Shishkov-Karamzin controversy of the 1800s.[38] A moderate reaction against the progressive westernization of Russian life made itself felt on the Russian stage in the 1780s and 1790s, when a school of playwrights, headed by Lukin, Fonvizin, and Krylov, promoted the introduction of native Russian themes and types, as well as Russian songs, dances, and manners, on the Russian stage.

Pyotr Plavilshchikov, a friend and associate of Krylov's, with whom he coedited the journal *The Viewer*, in an essay entitled "On the Theater" (1792) and in several prefaces to his plays endorsed most of the positions of the classicist scene (didacticism, verisimilitude, propriety) but challenged others, specifically the doctrine of the three unities (on the grounds that they are "unnatural") and explicitly demanded that "Russian taste" take precedence over "foreign taste." Plavilshchikov, himself of merchant-class origin, preferred the "bourgeois or civic tragedy" to the "heroic tragedy."

Ivan Krylov, the fabulist and playwright, was also an active critic. In his reviews and essays, published in his own journals, *Mail of Spirits* (1789), *The Viewer* (1792), and *Saint Petersburg Mercury* (1793), he dealt primarily with the Russian theater. An enlightened classicist, he polemicized with the sentimentalists and preromantics from a position of common sense, *vraisemblance*, order, and good taste. He points at the prose of life lurking behind the sentimentalists' idyllic facade, makes fun of the preromantics' penchant for taking liberties with poetic form, but ridicules the traditional panegyrical ode, suggesting that it must almost inevitably turn into a lampoon. In the 1800s Krylov, as coeditor of the *Moscow*

38. Duke Mikhail Mikhailovich Shcherbatov (1733–90), a man of letters, poet, publicist, and historian, may be presented as a case in point. As a member of the legislative commission of 1767–68, he defended the privileges of the nobility. His utopian novel, *A Journey to the Land of Ophir, by Mr. S., a Swedish Nobleman* (1783–84, incomplete, published in 1896), envisages a strictly regimented society in which order and virtue reign supreme. At its head is a hereditary monarch, supported by a hereditary nobility. Shcherbatov's pamphlet *On the Deterioration of Morals in Russia* (1786–89, published by Herzen in London in 1858) denounces the loose morals at the court of Catherine II and the other eighteenth-century empresses.

Viewer (1806) and the *Dramatic Herald* (1808), was a staunch supporter of the conservative nationalist ideas of Admiral Shishkov and his Colloquy of Amateurs of the Russian Word.

The 1790s and early 1800s saw debates on the subject of the introduction of low style into Russian comedy and vaudeville. Ivan Dmitriev, Karamzin's friend and ally, in his essay "On Russian Comedy" (1802), castigated the alleged vulgarity of the plays of Plavilshchikov and other playwrights of his school. Nikolai Ilyin, a member of Shishkov's Colloquy, was attacked by some reviewers for bringing the "lowest class" on stage in his play *Magnanimity or the Recruit Draft* (1804). Significantly, he was defended by Krylov's *Dramatic Herald*.

In 1803 Admiral Aleksandr Semyonovich Shishkov (1753–1841), a relatively minor amateur man of letters whose conservative views had temporarily sidetracked his naval career (later he went on to become minister of education and president of the Russian Academy of Letters), published his treatise, "Discourse on the Old and New Style of the Russian Language." It was clearly a response to Karamzin's "On Love of the Fatherland and National Pride" and to the drift of Karamzin's linguistic and stylistic practices. Shishkov attacked what he saw as the euphuism, stiltedness, and affectation of Karamzin and his school, who while "thinking that they were Ossians and Sternes" produced ridiculous and barely comprehensible verse and prose. Shishkov was able to offer some good examples in support of his point. But more important, he charged that the Russian literary idiom itself had become corrupted by the excessive influx of foreign loans, calques, and stylistic traits: "Whence came to us the absurd thought that we must abandon our indigenous, ancient, and rich language and base a new

one on the rules of a foreign language, the French, which is uncongenial to us and is itself poor?"

Shishkov demanded that any enrichment of the Russian language should originate from its own native treasury, such as medieval chronicles, religious literature, and folk poetry. A determined purist, he asked for the elimination of outright loans as well as loan translations. He drew attention to the fact that Church Slavonic had most of the abstract terms that Karamzin and his followers were now lifting from the French.[39] Shishkov's arguments in favor of using Slavonic had political overtones: separating the Russian language from its Slavonic roots was tantamount to separating the Russian nation from its church.

Karamzin never responded to Shishkov (his own views were getting progressively more conservative, and he may have been quite sympathetic to some of Shishkov's positions). But his followers immediately reacted to the admiral's "Discourse." Rebuttals appeared in the Karamzinist journals *Moscow Mercury* (1803) and *Northern Herald* (1804). They declared that there was no need to return to the manners of "our forefathers," since contrary to the assertions of "certain severe judges" manners were improving, not deteriorating, and that there was no need to return to their language either, since "language always followed the progress of the sciences, the arts, and education."[40] Shishkov responded to

39. For example, Shishkov condemned the word *razvitie*, formed after French *développement*, and recommended the Slavonic *prozyabanie*, from *prozyabati*, "to grow" (of a plant).

40. P. I. Makarov (1765–1804), in a review article, "A Critique of the Book entitled *Discourse on the Old and New Style of the Russian Language*," *Moskovskii Merkurii* 4, on. 12 (1804): 155–98. See Rothe, *Karamzins europäische Reise*, 417, for further reviews.

these reviews in a separate "Appendix to the Treatise entitled 'Discourse on the Old and New Style of the Russian Language'" (1804). The lengthy controversy that ensued lasted well into the following decade and carried over into imaginative literature. Aleksandr Shakhovskoi lampooned the Karamzinists in a comedy, *The New Sterne* (1805), and in a mock-heroic epic *The Plundered Furcoats* (1813), while Konstantin Batyushkov satirized the purported obscurantism and ignorance of the Shishkovians in such parodic poems as "A Vision on the Shores of Lethe" (1809) and "The Singer in the Colloquy of Amateurs of the Russian Word (1813).

The Shishkovians were the first to organize. Their group, the Colloquy of Amateurs of the Russian Word, held regular meetings for a number of years and published a journal under that title (1811–16). Among the members of the Colloquy were Derzhavin, Krylov, Shakhovskoi, Duke Sergei Shirinsky-Shikhmatov, Count Dmitry Khvostov, and close to fifty other men (and a few women) of letters, many of them holding high rank in various branches of the government. The group also included some younger men, such as Nikolai Gnedich (1784–1833), translator of the *Iliad*.

The Karamzinians eventually formed their own literary society, Arzamas (named after a town in central Russia proverbial for homespun Russianness, near which Karamzin's estate was located). Arzamas met irregularly from 1815 to 1817. It lacked the firm structure of Shishkov's Colloquy and never had on official organ, but its individual members were assiduous in defending the notion that linguistic usage had nothing to do with morals or patriotism, and in mocking the reactionary archaist practices of the Shishkovians. Among the most active Arzamasians were Dmitriev, Batyushkov, Duke Pyotr Vyazemsky, Zhukovsky (who

kept minutes of their meetings in mock-heroic hexameters), and Vasily Pushkin (1767–1830) and his young nephew Aleksandr Sergeevich, whose satirical poem "Fonvizin's Shadow" (1815) lampooned the whole gallery of the Colloquy, not sparing even Derzhavin.

As far as language usage was concerned, the purist campaign of the Shishkovians was a total failure. The language of Karamzin became the standard idiom of literary Russian.[41] But in some other ways the outcome of the controversy was far less conclusive. The nationalist ethos of the Shishkovians lived on in such writers of the Decembrist generation as Katenin, Griboedov, and Küchelbecker. The link between the ideas of the Colloquy and the first generation of Slavophiles is well documented.[42] (In fact, the Shishkovians were dubbed *slavenofily* by their opponents, an allusion to their regard for the Slavonic language.) By 1820 Karamzin, Dmitriev, and the Karamzinists around the *Herald of Europe* found themselves allied with conservative classicists against the surge of romanticism and embraced the positions of Shishkov's Colloquy. The *Herald of Europe* published a scathing review of Pushkin's "Ruslan and Lyudmila" (1820). Professor Kachenovsky, editor of the *Herald of Europe*, carried on a running

---

41. A telling blow to Shishkov's notion of Slavonic as a treasure house of Russian was struck by Professor M. T. Kachenovsky (1772–1842), himself a conservative, who demonstrated in an essay, "On the Slavonic Language in General and Church Slavonic in Particular" (1816), that Slavonic was not an older form of Russian, but a South Slavic dialect (he thought Serbian, but A. Kh. Vostokov, in his "Discourse on the Slavonic Language" [1820], showed it was Bulgarian).

42. See Mark Altshuller, *Predtechi slavyanofil-'stva v russkoi literature* (*Obshchestvo "Beseda lyubitelei russkogo slova"*) (Ann Arbor: Ardis, 1984).

feud with Pushkin and his romanticist contemporaries.

Classicism died as hard in Russia as it did in France. Aleksei Merzlyakov (1778–1830), a professor at Moscow Univeristy who was a minor poet but the leading Russian critic between Karamzin and the romantic period, was basically a classicist. His *Brief Rhetoric* (1817) is essentially classicist in its outlook, with some concessions to an emotionalist aesthetics.[43] Merzlyakov, however, reassessed the Russian "classics," debunking Sumarokov, trying to save the reputation of Kheraskov, and extolling Derzhavin, Dmitriev, and Ozerov.

Russia's relative backwardness in aesthetics, literary theory, and criticism was conditioned by the fact that Russian literature since Sumarokov had aligned itself with French literature, where the canon of classicist poetics was seriously challenged only in the 1820s. Although eighteenth-century Russian literature produced some masterpieces and in general reached a European level, theoretical thought remained derivative and for the most part second-rate. This situation would change in the romantic period, which arrived in Russia belatedly (as in France) but initiated a lively interest in the philosophy of art, the relation between literature and society, and the historical mission of Russian literature.

43. Merzlyakov was greatly influenced by J. G. Sulzer's *Allgemeine Theorie der schönen Künste* (1771–74, 2d ed. 1792), an encyclopedia of aesthetics that presents a mixture of sentimentalist and pre-Romantic ideas with classicist *vraisemblance*, intellectualism, utilitarianism, and formalism.

6

The Romantic Period

The continued growth of the Russian Empire under Catherine II and her son and grandsons affected the development of Russian literature in several ways. The incorporation of a major part of Poland into the empire caused many Poles to enter the tsar's service or to join Russian cultural life. Two important writers of the period were Polish: Faddei Bulgarin (Tadeusz Bułharyn) and Osip Senkovsky (Józef-Julian Sękowski). Some Russian poets were influenced by Polish literature—Ryleev and Vyazemsky, for example. Polish writers who were exiled or otherwise displaced to Russia came in contact with Russian men of letters. The friendship between Pushkin and the great Polish poet Adam Mickiewicz, established during Mickiewicz's Russian exile and ruined by the futile Polish uprising of 1830, was fruitful for both parties.

Livonian Germans, reinforced by many immigrants from Germany, continued to play a role in Russian public life disproportionate to their small number, especially at court (the Russian court's dynastic ties were largely German) and in the higher echelon of military and civil service. German names also abound in the annals of Russian cultural life in the nineteenth century. Although French remained the language of the elite and the first foreign language taught in schools, Russian secondary and higher education continued to follow German examples. One of Russia's new universities, in Dorpat (now Tartu), Livonia, was in fact a German university, though it was attended by some Russians, such as the poet Yazykov. (The University of Dorpat had ceased to exist when the city was virtually destroyed by the Russians in the Northern War. It was reopened by Alexander I in 1802.) Russian literature reached readers in Germany earlier and on a broader front than in France or England. There were, however, some early admirers of Russian poetry even there. Sir John Bowring's *Specimens of the Russian Poets* (1821–23), which included works of Lomonosov, Derzhavin, Karamzin, Zhukovsky, Krylov, and Vyazemsky, created some genuine interest in Russian literature in the English-speaking world. The mutual interest that Pushkin and Prosper Mérimée showed in each other's work generated the first significant literary exchange between France and Russia. Mérimée also acquainted the French public with Gogol and Turgenev.

The conquest of the Crimea, Bessarabia, the Caucasus, and Finland gave Russian writers exotic locales admirably suited for the development of romantic plots. Pushkin, for example, used the former three in his verse epics, and Baratynsky's "Eda" is set in Finland. The locales of classical antiquity, medieval Europe, the ever-attractive world of the Mediterranean, and romantic Scotland were a frequent presence in the Russian literature of this period.

Now a dominant European power, Russia discovered the challenge of belonging to the European community. Economically and socially Russia was not catching up to the West, as it had seemed to be in the eighteenth century, but was actually losing ground. While the West was starting the industrial revolution, Russia failed to continue on the promising course which its metallurgical industry had taken in the eighteenth century. Although Russia was an exporter of grain, its agriculture remained primitive. Serfdom had been abolished throughout Europe, even in Prussia, but continued in Russia until 1861. An anachronistic class structure excluded the nobility from the pursuit of business and made it difficult for members of the other classes to get an education. The imperial bureaucracy was corrupt and inefficient. A Russian who had occasion to compare the condition of his country to that of Western Europe had to be ashamed of Russia's backwardness. Moreover, European public opinion, of which Russians were keenly aware, now began to matter.

Tsar Alexander I (r.1801–25), guided by his able minister Mikhail Speransky (1772–1839), undertook a series of reforms. A Council of State and European-style ministries were introduced. The whole legislative and administrative systems were revamped. Thanks to Speransky's efforts, Russia's new code of laws was quite up to European standards. The new judiciary and administrative systems set limits to the private arrogance, willfulness, and cruelty of rich landowners, though often replacing it by bureaucratic corruption and malfeasance. Such horrors of a sadistic landowner's reign of terror as described in Sergei Aksakov's *Family Chronicle* would go unchecked under Catherine II but might well have been stopped under Nicholas I.[1]

Also under Alexander I, a state school system and several universities were founded. Plans for elected local government and representative assemblies were made, and the emancipation of all serfs was considered (in fact, serfs were freed in the provinces of Estonia [1816] and Livonia [1819]).

In the second half of his reign Alexander I turned reactionary. Speransky fell from grace, though he was allowed to continue work on the Code of Laws. The response to Napoleon's invasion of Russia in 1812 was one of patriotic fervor, even among Russians who might have had reason to sympathize with the achievements of the French Revolution. There was a good deal of peasant unrest, as described in an episode of Tolstoi's *War and Peace*, but by and large the Russian people stood firm behind their tsar. The victory over Napoleon did much to enhance Russian self-respect. In fact, a certain nationalist swagger, previously unknown, may be detected in some works of Russian literature in the aftermath of the Napoleonic Wars.

The young men who returned from the

1. The natural father of the poet Aleksandr Polezhaev was exiled to Siberia for fatally flogging a serf.

wars or had witnessed the heroic years as teenagers expected that the tsar would reward his nation with progressive policies. When Alexander instead turned to arcane mysticism in his private life and to political reaction in his public policies, making Russia a pillar of the reactionary Holy Alliance, the young generation responded with widespread resentment. This led to the formation of a network of conspiratorial groups, the most active of which were responsible for the attempted coup of December 14, 1825. The aim of the Decembrists (*dekabristy*), as the rebels got to be called, was to depose Nicholas I, known as a conservative (he had succeeded his brother Alexander), then enthrone his brother Constantine, reputed to be more liberal, and have him grant Russia a constitutional government. Many of the Decembrists were men of letters; Ryleev (executed), Küchelbecker, and Bestuzhev (both exiled to Siberia) were the most prominent. Other literary figures, headed by Pushkin and Griboedov, were close to the Decembrists and were prevented from participating in the coup only by their absence from the capital.

The December coup, though crushed within a day, had far-reaching consequences. By almost any standards, Nicholas was lenient in punishing the rebels: only five were executed, after a lengthy and reasonably fair trial. But they were hanged instead of being shot, as should have befit officers and gentlemen, a disgrace bitterly resented by their friends. The Decembrist coup and its aftermath permanently alienated the progressive part of the Russian elite from the tsar and his government. The feeling persisted that the Decembrists were better men than those who suppressed the uprising. A legend soon arose about them and their wives, who followed them into exile in Siberia. They remained a subject of literary inspiration from Pushkin to the twentieth century.[2]

The reign of Nicholas I (1825–55) was a period of political and economic stagnation. The evils of serfdom, bureaucratic corruption, brutality in the army, stifling regimentation of intellectual life through censorship and goverment control of educational institutions—all these things were probably no worse under Nicholas than before, and in some ways even his government was slowly headed in the right direction. But the general mood in the country was dispirited. A widespread feeling that things were not well in Russia was confirmed by its humiliating defeat in the Crimean War of 1855–56.

Meanwhile Russian society was changing even without government initiative. The growing bureaucracy was generating a middle class whose life-style was substantially European. More and more of its members no longer came from the landed gentry but were *raznochintsy*, literally, men from various classes: the sons of parish priests, merchants, shopkeepers, and artisans. The growing middle class constituted a reading public which made journalism and the book trade profitable. By the 1820s literature could provide a writer with a living. After 1830 literature, concentrated in competing "thick journals," which featured novels (printed in installments), stories, poetry, articles on various topics of general interest, humor, and fashions, was rapidly becoming an industry. By the 1840s Russian literature was a forum of public opinion, a clearinghouse of ideas, and a national institution crucial to Russia's further development.

The oppressive reign of Nicholas I coincided with the golden age of Russian poetry.

2. Some examples are Nekrasov's "Russian Women," Mandelshtam's "Decembrist," and Olga Forsh's *Firstborn of Freedom*. Lev Tolstoi at one time worked on a novel about the Decembrists.

In prose, it produced Gogol and the "natural" school. The big three among the novelists of the nineteenth century, Turgenev, Dostoevsky, and Tolstoi, launched their careers during the reign of Nicholas. Herzen's observation that the age of Nicholas I, although intensely oppressive externally, was also an age of unprecedented inner freedom may offer a partial explanation of this historical paradox. Like eighteenth-century Germans, idealistic Russians of this period could not apply their energies to public affairs or other practical endeavors. Hence, as Chernyshevsky was to note later, they turned to literature as the only outlet for their aspirations, hopes, doubts, resentment, and anger.

The cultural and intellectual life of Russia continued to progress, but with few achievements of brilliance or originality (literature excepted). The theater produced some actors who, legendary in their lifetime, left a mark on literary history: the tragic actors Pavel Mochalov (1800–48) and Katerina Semyonova (1786–1849), and the great character actor Mikhail Shchepkin (1788–1863), who played the mayor in Gogol's *Inspector General*.[3] But there was little original, innovative, or creative stagecraft. Russian ballet had already reached the level of excellence for which it is known to this day; but it, too, merely continued in an established style.

Russian composers remained amateurs or were foreign-taught well beyond mid-century. (The Saint Petersburg Conservatory of Music was founded in 1862, the Moscow Conservatory in 1864.) Russian grand opera arrived in the 1830s. *Ascold's Grave* (1835), by A.N. Verstovsky (1799–1862), was the first of that genre to become

a permanent part of the repertoire. It was followed in 1836 by *A Life for the Tsar*, by M. I. Glinka (1804–57). Glinka's *Ruslan and Lyudmila* (1842) was the first Russian opera to conquer the international stage. Although these composers used some Russian folk tunes and rhythms, their operatic style was Italian, with some French and German influence.

In the visual arts, too, the Russians had become competent practitioners of Western styles. The Academy of Fine Arts, founded in 1757 in Saint Petersburg, produced generations of academic painters whose efforts were indistinguishable from those of their European colleagues. K. P. Bryullov (1799–1852) and A. A. Ivanov (1806–58) in particular had an impact on literature, where they are mentioned often (both were subjects of essays by Gogol).

The young Russian universities, perhaps with the exception of Moscow University, the oldest, were hard pressed to reach a European level, what with frequent harassment by overzealous bureaucrats, absurd restrictions imposed on curricula by the government, and poor preparation of students and professors. Gogol, at age twenty-five, with no academic background and no credentials other than his fiction, served as an adjunct professor of medieval history at Saint Petersburg University in 1834–35. Many professors, especially in the sciences, were foreigners, mostly Germans. Nevertheless, the writings of Herzen, Goncharov, Belinsky, Stankevich, Grigoryev, and many other graduates of Moscow University show that at least students of that institution received a good humanistic education. The Imperial Academy of Sciences continued as a first-rate research institution. The Russian Academy, founded in 1783 with Duchess Ekaterina Dashkova as its first president, specialized in the cultivation and regulation of

3. Shchepkin was born a serf. His freedom was bought in 1818, when the sum to obtain it was raised by public subscription.

the Russian language, publishing dictionaries and grammars. Many leading poets and writers were members. After the death in 1841 of its last president, Aleksandr Shishkov, it was incorporated into the Imperial Academy of Sciences as its department of Russian language and literature. It produced some excellent scholars. Aleksandr Vostokov (1781–1864), a curator of the manuscript section of the Imperial Public Library since 1815 and a member of the Russian Academy since 1820, did pioneering work in Slavic philology, published several important Old Russian and Church Slavonic manuscripts, and was also an outstanding grammarian and lexicographer. An academic edition of Derzhavin's works by Yakov Grot (1812–93) was exemplary for its time.

The first half of the nineteenth century was marked by intellectual ferment and controversy, which by the 1840s was beginning to show the outlines of the ideological spectrum that would describe educated Russia for the rest of the nineteenth century. The first half of the century was dominated by a search for an identity and for Russia's place in the family of nations and in history. Pre-Petrine Russia had defined itself through Orthodoxy. Throughout the eighteenth century Russia existed and grew without a historical self-awareness. The search for a definition of what Russia stood for crucially affected Russian literature.

The Karamzin-Shishkov controversy, the rise of nationalism in opposition to the westernizing policies of Alexander I, the wave of national solidarity in 1812, and Karamzin's *History of the Russian State* (12 vols. 1818–26) left no doubt as to Russia's self-definition as a nation-state. Little attention was paid to the fact that Russia was a multinational empire. Thus, even such progressive Russian intellectuals as the critic

Belinsky had little sympathy for Ukrainian aspirations to cultural, if not political, autonomy, and the government nipped such aspirations in the bud. Romantic ideas, which began to enter Russia in the 1810s, were grist for the mill of Russian nationalism.

The direction taken by Karamzin, later by Zhukovsky, and, most important, by Pushkin and his pleiad had Russian literature join the family of European literatures without any preconceived program or concern for national originality. But some Russians did not abandon the Shishkovian position that in order to express the Russian national spirit, literature should reach back to medieval Russian history and to Russian folk poetry. Romantic poets such as Katenin and Küchelbecker professed and practiced this doctrine.

The Decembrists were of the opinion that literature had a civic mission—to inculcate patriotism and civic responsibility. This meant that literature should concentrate on serious and lofty topics and cultivate genres appropriate to them, such as the patriotic ode. Ryleev and Bestuzhev, among others, held this view and practiced it in their poetry.

With the advent of German idealist philosophy, spread by Russians who had studied in Germany as well as by German professors teaching in Russia, the question of Russia's place in the evolution of the human spirit became paramount. It was debated in terms of Schelling's philosophy beginning in the 1820s and in terms of Hegel's philosophy of history beginning in the late 1830s. There was a consensus that Russia was a young nation whose days of glory lay ahead in the future. Westernizers like Chaadaev, Herzen, and Belinsky saw Russia as an as yet "ahistorical" nation getting ready to join the family of those great nations who had already contributed to the cumulative achievement of the human spirit. Russia's present task was to acquire the tools to make its contribution. The Westernizers' position implied a low opinion of the value of contemporary Russian literature—even Pushkin—relative to the great Western literatures. "Slavophiles" like Khomyakov, the brothers Kireevsky, and the Aksakovs believed that Russia already possessed a distinct historical identity, formed by the implantation of Byzantine Orthodox civilization into the fertile soil of Slavic folk culture. The westernization of Russia initiated by Peter the Great was a historical aberration that ought to be reversed. Russia should develop its culture from its native resources. Slavophiles also believed that it was Russia's historical mission to regenerate and perhaps supersede an aging European civilization.

Beginning in the 1830s some Russian writers, following French examples of *socialité*, engaged (so far as permitted by the censorship) in a more or less explicit campaign against the existing social order. Serfage, the inequities of the social class structure, and bureaucratic corruption were under attack in the works of Gogol, Pavlov, Panaev, Grigorovich, Dostoevsky, and other writers of the natural school championed by the critic Belinsky. In the 1840s French positivism and utopian socialism, as well as some German left-Hegelian ideas, began to reach Russia. The circle of M. V. Butashevich-Petrashevsky (1821–66), routed by the tsar's secret police in 1849, was propagating the ideas of Fourier and other utopian socialists. Among its members were several poets and writers, including Fyodor and Mikhail Dostoevsky.

The position of literature in society changed considerably in the course of the first half of the century. Karamzin had shown the way to literary professionalism. Zhukovsky and Pushkin were associated with the court, but they were men of letters first and foremost. Some poets and writers held high rank in the civil service or belonged to high society, or both, but by and large literature was becoming independent of direct patronage, and the connection between a writer's position in literature and in society tended to be coincidental. Still, censorship, the court's control of the stage in the capitals, and the tight regulation of journalism by the government (for instance, most periodicals were not allowed to print political news) gave an edge to authors approved by the government. Pushkin once said facetiously that he and Baratynsky were the only "nonapproved" (*neodobrennye*) writers around. (This was before he had to accept an appointment to the court of Nicholas I.)

Various literary groupings and schools sprang up in the course of the first decades of the century. Often, though not always, they would form around a journal or almanac—Baron Delvig's *Northern Flowers* (1825–32), for example. The Free Society of Amateurs of Letters, Sciences, and Arts, in Petersburg (1801–12), was politically liberal, but neoclassical in the sense that it advanced the introduction of classical themes and classical meters. It cultivated a preromantic enthusiasm for free nature in the mode of Ossian, strong passions, and creative genius. Opposed to the formally constituted Colloquy of Amateurs of the Russian Word was the informal Arzamas (1815–17). Whereas the Colloquy was conservative, nationalist, and purist, Arzamas followed Karamzin's moderate, liberal, and westernizing ideas. The Free Society of Amateurs of Russian Letters (1816–25), headed by the poet Fyodor Glinka, became a focus for politically inclined romantics, some of them (Küchelbecker, Bestuzhev, Ryleev) future Decembrists. The Free Society published a journal, *The Champion of Enlightenment and Philanthropy*.

The men who eventually became known as Decembrists formed several groups, such as the secret Union of Prosperity. Their public activities were focused in the almanacs *Pole Star* (1823–25) and *Mnemosyne* (1824–25). Simultaneously, a group of youthful Moscow poets and philosophers (called the "archivist youths" in *Eugene Onegin*, since some of them held minor pro forma posts at archives in Moscow), formed the Society of Wisdom Lovers. Among its members were Venevitinov, Vladimir Odoevsky, and Shevyryov. The *lyubomudry* (wisdom lovers) disbanded after the Decembrist coup but regrouped two years later around a journal, *The Moscow Herald*. Eventually this group developed into the first generation of Slavophiles.

The Slavophile Ivan Kireevsky's attempt in 1832 to found a journal, *The European*, failed, as publication was almost immediately suspended by the authorities. Subsequently, the Slavophiles published in *The Moscow Herald* and other journals until they had their own, *The Muscovite* (1841–56). The westernizers were not similarly organized, but in the 1840s Kraevsky's *National Annals* and, after 1846, *The Contemporary* were focal points of their journalism.

An informal circle of students of Moscow University grouped around Nikolai Stankevich (1813–40) in the early 1830s. Some of its members would later be famous: anarchist Mikhail Bakunin, historian Timofei Granovsky, critics Vissarion Belinsky and Vasily Botkin, and Slavophile critic and ideologue Konstantin Aksakov. The ideas of this circle were derived mostly from Fichte and Schelling. The romantic idealism of Stankevich and his friends is described in

Turgenev's novel *Rudin* (1856), in a flashback to the hero's student days. Simultaneously, another circle of Moscow University students, headed by Aleksandr Herzen and Nikolai Ogaryov, was debating more "progressive" (mainly utopian socialist) ideas.

By the late 1820s there had developed a rather clear demarcation line between literary plebeians and literary aristocrats, though both could be progressive or reactionary. Polemical skirmishes between Polevoi's *Moscow Telegraph* and Delvig's *Literary Gazette* had explicit class overtones. Plebeian publishers and writers, such as Bulgarin, Grech, and Senkovsky, were addressing a growing middle-class audience that included the provincial landowning gentry. Guided by the profit motive, they catered to the tastes of their public and steered clear of topics that might cause trouble with the censors. By 1830 a number of journals and newspapers were competing for subscribers. In 1830 six journals were appearing in Moscow alone, and three years later both Moscow and Petersburg had that many. Most journals expired after a brief run, but some established themselves as profit-making enterprises.

Karamzin's *Herald of Europe*, in the 1820s a bastion of literary conservatism from which professorial critics lambasted romanticism, lasted until 1830. Bulgarin's newspaper, *The Northern Bee* (1825–64), followed a wary political course and catered to unsophisticated middle-class tastes. Bulgarin was heartily hated by Pushkin and his pleiad and responded in kind. Polevoi's *Moscow Telegraph* (1825–34) was the self-proclaimed organ of Russian (French-style) romanticism. *The Moscow Herald* (1827–80) was founded by a group of romantic thinkers and poets influenced by German idealist philosophy. Delvig's *Literary Gazet-*

te (1830–31) was the first organ of Pushkin and his friends, preceding his own journal, *The Contemporary* (1836–66), which later, under the editorship of Nekrasov and Panaev, became the organ of the radical intelligentsia. Nadezhdin's *Telescope* (1831–36), which gave Belinsky his start, had the misfortune to publish Chaadaev's first "Philosophical Letter," for which it was promptly closed. For years Senkovsky's *Reading Library* (1834–65), whose principal contributor was its publisher (under the pen name of Baron Brambeus), had the largest circulation. Pushkin's "Queen of Spades" appeared in it. *National Annals* (1820–30, 1839–84) had its first heyday under Kraevsky, when Lermontov and the best writers of the natural school (Dostoevsky, Grigorovich, Butkov) published there. Later it succeeded *The Contemporary* as the organ of the radicals.

A major part of the fiction printed by Russian journals, or as separate books, was still translated, mostly from the French. Works by English authors often reached Russia via a French version. Authors popular in the West would promptly appear in Russian. Hugo, Lamartine, George Sand, Balzac, Janin, Sue, and a host of other French writers were routinely reviewed and discussed in Russian journals, as were Jean Paul, Hoffmann, Heine, and other German writers. Walter Scott, James Fenimore Cooper, Frederick Marryat, and Charles Dickens were as much standard fare of Russian readers as they were of English and Continental readers.

Russian literature developed the Gothic tale, the Byronic verse epic, the Waverley novel, the society tale, the romantic historical drama, the ballad, and other romantic genres, much as it had earlier developed the triumphal ode or the classicist tragedy. When the natural school turned to topics of Russian everyday life with angry sarcasm for the high and the mighty, and humanitarian sentiments for the underdog, it was following the example of Dickens's *Sketches by Boz*, the French physiological sketch, and the *socialisant* roman-feuilleton. When it turned to the grotesque, it was following the French *école phrénétique*. Nevertheless, Russian romanticism and romantic realism produced not only an impressive array of works comparable to the best Europe had to offer (for example, Pushkin's *The Captain's Daughter* is as good a Waverley novel as any by Walter Scott himself) but also some masterpieces of evident originality. *Eugene Onegin*, in spite of its debt to Sterne and Byron, is a work that is as unique as it is brilliant. Gogol's *Dead Souls*, ostensibly a conventional picaresque novel, is ultimately a work that defies assignment to any known genre. Gogol and the young Dostoevsky manipulated point of view, context, and subtext with a virtuosity hardly known in the West. Russian literature had arrived earlier than believed possible even by those who were confident that it would someday in the future. Even Belinsky, who fought for Gogol throughout his career, did not suspect that he was championing one of the great writers of world literature.

Philosophical Ideas, Aesthetic Theory, and Criticism

The words *romanticism* and *romantic*, in Russia as elsewhere, had three basic meanings (disregarding the colloquial). The poets who called themselves romantics perceived romanticism as a new school opposed to the conventions of classicism. This meaning was peculiar to French romanticism and was the one that Pushkin adopted. In Germany, and less so in England and in France, romantic literature, art, and culture in general were seen as a historical countercurrent to classical civilization, hence Christian and ethnically Celtic or Germanic—or, for a Russian, Slavic. In an even broader sense the dichotomy of romantic versus classical stood for complementary attitudes of human creativity, classical denoting objective, impersonal art, romantic meaning subjective art tending toward topics of current interest, tendentiousness, mannerism, ambiguity, and irony.

Russian romanticism is analogous to romantic movements in the West and was triggered by their influence. It was, however, different from them in certain ways. It was part of a reaction against an entrenched literary tradition, and it was associated with events in the sociopolitical sphere like the Decembrist uprising. But Russian romanticism was less a reaction against the Age of Reason and whatever else the eighteenth century stood for than was romanticism in the West.[4] The ideas of the Enlightenment, more recent in Russia, continued to be perceived as something positive by many Russian romantics.

The notion that in Germany the French Revolution was diverted to regions of the spirit, with "inner freedom" substituting for political freedom, applies to Russia as well. Some Russian romantics (Zhukovsky, Tyutchev, Vladimir Odoevsky) and the Slavophiles were not only mystical idealists but also political conservatives. Others would have no part of Teutonic philosophizing and were politically liberal—Pushkin and some of the Decembrists, for example. Soviet

scholars have divided all romanticism, including Russian, into two groups: reactionary (Zhukovsky, Odoevsky) and progressive (Pushkin, the Decembrists). Most German romantics, along with Coleridge, Wordsworth, and Walter Scott, are also called reactionary romantics, whereas Byron, Hugo, and Shelley are considered progressive romantics.

There was substantial agreement, however, on some important points between these groups. All romantics thought of nationality (*narodnost'*, from *narod*, "people," a calque from French *nationalité*, possibly via Polish *narodność*) as a major aesthetic phenomenon, although not all unequivocally considered it a cardinal virtue or indispensable quality of great art. The concept of *narodnost'* in art and literature is a corollary of the idea of a national spirit, basic to romantic thought.[5] In Russia, where the rift between the westernized educated class and the largely illiterate common people was huge and where a a living and attractive popular culture still existed, nationality could not fail to acquire a connotation of populism (*prostonarodnost'*, from *prostoi narod*, "the simple people").

Romantic individualism was also a pervasive trait. A preoccupation with the solitary hero (often the poet), the poet's position in society, and the clash between "poet and

4. The image of a shallow, frivolous, and lascivious eighteenth century is, however, not entirely absent in Russian literature. Some passages in *Eugene Onegin* give this impression. Mandelshtam, in the essay "Some Notes on Chénier," likened the eighteenth century to a dried-out lake which reveals all the hills and valleys of its bottom.

5. The idea of a national spirit (e.g., *dukh naroda* in Venevitinov) goes back at least to Herder. But its direct sources for Russian romantics were Madame de Staël's *De l'Allemagne* (1813) and Johann Peter Friedrich Ancillon's *Analyse de l'idée de littérature nationale* (1817). Ancillon, a Prussian statesman, tried to prove that only fully developed nations are capable of creating a truly national literature. Apparently he was trying to refute Sismondi and Madame de Staël, who looked for the origins of poetry in primitive societies. Ancillon also insisted on an organic link between literature, philosophy, and political life.

crowd" (the title of a poem by Pushkin) are dominant themes in Russian no less than in European romanticism. Romantic individualism led to a demand for freedom from the constraints of conventional genres, a broader linguistic basis, a search for local color and exotic settings, and a positive attitude toward new or unconventional forms. Such Romantic theorists of the 1820s and 1830s as Odoevsky, Venevitinov, and Polevoi attacked the positions of Batteux (among the French) and Merzlyakov (among the Russians)—"imitation of nature" (which the romantics countered with "self-expression"), "beautiful nature," normative poetics, the theory of taste, and *bienséance* (to all of which the romantics opposed "the truth of nature").

Romantic individualism was accompanied by a belief in the poet's intuitive powers, which allow him to see and understand reality more deeply than can most people. Different poets addressed their intuitions to different aspects of life—for example, Ryleev to the political, Küchelbecker to the prophetic, Baratynsky to the psychological, Zhukovsky to the metaphysical.

Although historicism, in the sense of a belief in a historical teleology and in a hypostatized zeitgeist (*dukh vremeni*), with both meanings accessible to the poet's intuition, was much a part of the thought of some Russian romantics (like Venevitinov, Ryleev, Bestuzhev, and Küchelbecker), it was by no means embraced by all of their contemporaries. Pushkin in particular refused to concede that poetry was subject to any laws of history. He too, though without a theoretical basis, was perhaps closest to an attitude of pervasive romantic irony, which makes the poet admit to himself and to his audience that the beautiful world of his creation is only an illusion, a futile escape from real-

ity. With the advent of a Hegelian philosophy of history in the late 1830s, historicism as preached and applied in literary criticism by Belinsky becomes dominant in Russian literary criticism and in Russian thought at large. Optimistic Hegelian historicism was partly balanced by the pessimistic anti-utopianism of conservative romantics such as Vladimir Odoevsky.

The mystical and metaphysical aspects of romanticism found an echo in only a few Russian poets. The romantic poet between two worlds—that of sensual reality and that of mysterious yearnings, dreams, and epiphanies—is not in the mainstream of the golden age of Russian poetry. Zhukovsky and Tyutchev, who represent this type of poet, both had exceptionally strong German connections. The poetry of a dual world (*dvoemirie*) eventually resurfaced in Russian symbolism, which also rediscovered Tyutchev.

The association of art and poetry with religion, so important in German romanticism, remained sporadic in Russia (until Vladimir Solovyov and the symbolists). Fyodor Glinka, a major religious poet, remained a marginal figure. But even Russian poets whose general orientation was far from religious (like Pushkin and Lermontov) wrote poetry on religious themes, and sometimes in religious forms.

The conception of the work of art as symbol and an awareness of its mythmaking potential, both central to romantic aesthetics, gained a strong foothold in Russia. Ryleev conceived his *Meditations* with this notion in mind as did Zhukovsky his *Ahasuerus* and Küchelbecker his epic poem of the same title. Gogol interpreted his own work in these terms, and Belinsky dealt with the works of Pushkin, Gogol, and Lermontov from this perspective.

The Arrival of Romanticism in Russia

In the 1800s and 1810s a renewed influence of classicist ideas, those of Batteux and La Harpe in particular, was felt in Russia.[6] Such members of the younger generation as S. S. Uvarov, I. M. Muravyov-Apostol, and N. I. Gnedich showed the influence of eighteenth-century German thought, especially of Winckelmann, Lessing, and Herder. They followed these Germans in demanding that Russians should follow the ancients, particularly the Greeks, rather than the French. The ideas of German Storm and Stress had by then reached Russia, but romanticism proper was slow in arriving. The first definition of romanticism attested in Russia was in an essay, "On Opera," by Jean Paul, translated in *The Northern Herald* (1805): "The romantic [*romanicheskoe*] is per se miraculous, and all that is miraculous is per se poetic [*stikhotvorcheskoe*]." The translation suggests that the translator missed Jean Paul's point, for *stikhotvorcheskoe* (from *stikhotvorets*, "versifier") does not transmit the meaning of the original.

Whereas Jena romanticism was the main source of Russian romantic thought, romantic ideas initially reached Russia through Madame de Staël's *De l'Allemagne* (1810) and J. C. L. Sismondi's *De la littérature du midi de l'Europe* (1813, revised in 1817, translated into Russian in 1823). Batyushkov's essay "On the Impressions and Life of the Poet," in *The Herald of Europe*, uses their ideas in interpreting poems by Lomonosov, Derzhavin, and Zhukovsky as products of the Russian national genius. But for the most part, Russian journals of the 1810s published sharply worded but poorly informed attacks against romanticism, including Madame de Staël's book. Romantic poetry was called barbarian, schismatic, and immoral.

The first news of Byron reached Russia in 1815, when V. V. Izmailov's *Russian Museum* printed excerpts of a Russian translation of "The Corsair." Byron was soon recognized as immoral and dangerous by Russian conservatives, and was deified by progressives.[7]

Zhukovsky was perhaps the purest Russian romantic. He began his career as a critic in the Karamzinian vein. The key concepts of his reviews and essays in *The Herald of Europe*, which he edited from 1808 to 1810, were still imitation of beautiful nature, refined taste, good sense, and morality, though in an essay "On the Moral Usefulness of Poetry" (1809) he expressed the notion that neither direct moralizing nor ratiocination had a place in poetry. Until about 1810 Zhukovsky's criticism was informed by Batteux, La Harpe, Johann Georg Sulzer (whose *Allgemeine Theorie der schönen Künste* was available in Russian since 1777), Lord Kames (Henry Home), and other outdated aesthetic theorists. Thus, Sulzer still had no place in his system for the novel, and Zhukovsky accordingly denied the novel any aesthetic or moral value. But around 1810 Zhukovsky had begun to read Schiller, Goethe, Herder, the Schlegels, Friedrich

6. In 1809 Shishkov published, with his own preface and notes, two essays by La Harpe, "On Eloquence" and "A Comparison of the French Language with the Ancient Languages," which contained ideas close to his own.

7. Here are some lines from Ryleev's poem "On the Death of Byron" (1824): "He lived for England and the world, / He was to his admiring age / a Socrates in wisdom, a Cato in spirit, / and Shakespeare's conqueror. / He solved all the mysteries under the sun, / Was indifferent to all blows of fate, / Obeyed only his own genius, / And recognized no other powers."

Bouterwek,[8] and Novalis and was converted to a romantic philosophy of art which sees the poet as a catalyst of ideas, a visionary, and a diviner of the ineffable. This development found expression in Zhukovsky's poetry, original and translated, rather than in any theoretical writings. Zhukovsky was also one of the first to introduce Byron to the Russian public. His masterful translation of "The Prisoner of Chillon" (1822) was greeted with enthusiasm by the young generation.

Zhukovsky's romantic works and ideas were almost immediately attacked for their Germanophile and mystical tendencies. Ridiculed and labeled immoral, absurd, and harmful by classicists, his works were also criticized for their lack of authentically Russian traits and social relevance by budding romantics of a nationalist and populist persuasion, such as Katenin and Küchelbecker.[9]

Katenin, Zhukovsky's rival for the honor of having been Russia's first romantic, was influenced by Sismondi and Madame de Staël more than by the Germans. He saw romanticism not so much in terms of themes, subjects, and ideas as in terms of the originality of their expression. This he pursued through the introduction of local color (*mestnost*), folkloric and archaic language and imagery, and a search for the native vigor and "distinctive quality" of the "primeval virgin poetry" of the Russian people. Katenin felt that Zhukovsky's elegant and polished poetry was hardly Russian at

all. Katenin followed this course in his programmatic writings as well as in his poetic practice. His ballad "Olga" (1816) was written to counter Zhukovsky's "Lyudmila" (1808) and "Svetlana" (1813); all three were versions of G. A. Bürger's "Lenore." Its language made a display of what a conservative critic such as Gnedich would perceive as "common folk coarseness" (*prostonarodnaya grubost*) and poor taste. Katenin's rather than Zhukovsky's manner, however, prevailed in the ballads of Pushkin and those who followed him.

Duke Pyotr Vyazemsky (1792–1878), a poet and man of letters with whom virtually all of his literary contemporaries, including Pushkin, had intensive and lasting connections, fashioned himself as a pioneer of romanticism. Having lost his father when he was fifteen, Vyazemsky grew up under the tutelage of Karamzin, who was married to his older sister. He began to publish in *The Herald of Europe* in 1808, developed friendships with Zhukovsky, Batyushkov, and other Karamzinists, and was an active member of Arzamas. Vyazemsky's first major critical essays, "On Derzhavin" (1816) and "On the Life and Works of V. A. Ozerov" (1817), dealt with their subjects in largely romantic terms, while retaining the enlightened and progressive principles of the eighteenth-century philosophes. Derzhavin was called "a genius formed by Nature herself" and was credited with inimitable originality, but also with universality as "a singer of all ages and all nations." Significantly, too, Vyazemsky called Derzhavin a "poet" and Lomonosov an "orator." Vyazemsky's effort to credit Ozerov with the virtues of a romantic poet was later refuted by Katenin and Pushkin.

In his essay on I. I. Dmitriev (1821, published in 1823 as a preface to Dmitriev's *Collected Works*) Vyazemsky used the

8. Friedrich Bouterwek, *Ästhetik* (1806), presents an eclectic system based on Kantian epistemology and a romantic philosophy of art.

9. See pp. 164–165 for Shakhovskoi's parodies. As early as 1812 Batyushkov wrote: "Under the banner of Cypris, / This new Don Quixote / Spends his life in daydreams: / He lives with chimeras, / Converses with spirits, / With a pensive moon, / And makes a laughingstock of himself!"

biography of this high-ranking government official and talented poet to express his own liberal political views, including even a hope that serfdom would soon be totally abolished. This may explain in part why Vyazemsky presented Krylov, who belonged to the conservative camp, as an imitator of Dmitriev and minimized Krylov's achievement in comparison to Dmitriev's. Vyazemsky was set straight on this score not only by Pushkin but even by Bulgarin.

In these and other essays and reviews Vyazemsky advanced the principal tenets of a romantic philosophy of art: nationality (he was the first Russian to use the word *narodnost'* as a literary term and praised Derzhavin for being *narodnyi*) historicism (in a Herderian, though not yet in a teleological Hegelian sense), individuality (in the form of a demand for originality), and the mixing of genres.

In the 1820s Vyazemsky's essays on Pushkin's verse epics were the first outright endorsement of romanticism in Russia. His essay "In Lieu of a Foreword to 'The Fountain of Bakhchisarai': A Conversation between the Publisher and a Classicist from the Viborg Side or from Vasiliev Island," written at Pushkin's invitation, was an impassioned call for national originality. In it he asserted that every earlier movement of modern Russian literature (Lomonosovian classicism, Karamzinian sentimentalism, and Zhukovskian romanticism) had amounted to no more than imitation of German examples. When Vyazemsky's position was attacked, he responded, and the whole polemic was perceived as the decisive battle between classicism and romanticism.

In 1830 Vyazemsky was one of the stalwarts of Delvig's *Literary Gazette* and now sparred not only with the conservatives Bulgarin and Grech but also, as one of the "aristocrats," with Polevoi's *Moscow Tele-*

graph. He was a major contributor to Pushkin's *Contemporary*, where he placed a well-reasoned favorable review of Gogol's *Inspector General*. Vyazemsky was one of the first admirers of French realism in Russia. He translated Benjamin Constant's *Adolphe* and voiced a high opinion of Stendhal, Balzac, and de Musset's *Confessions d'un enfant du siècle*. In the 1840s Vyazemsky turned conservative. He defended Gogol's *Selected Passages from a Correspondence with My Friends* and was strongly opposed to Belinsky and his followers.

"On Romantic Poetry" (1823), an essay by Orest Somov (1793–1833) initially published in *The Champion of Enlightenment and Philanthropy* and based excessively on Sismondi and Madame de Staël, was a plea for national poetry, the cultivation of popular traditions, and emphasis on local color. Somov found French classicist poetry "frigid and emaciated, because it was alien to the people that adopted it" and identified romantic poetry with the native traditions of Western Europe, starting with the Spanish Moors. He contends that "Shakespeare, father of the English theater, established romantic taste in British poetry." The Germans are given credit for having "invested the exalted truths of faith and philosophy in the rainbow colors of their poetry." Somov gives an outline of Russian folklore and folk poetry, chronicles, and heroic history, as well as modern Russian poetry. He finds the "dreary Teutonic rhapsodies" of contemporary Russian poets (viz. Zhukovsky) wholly uncongenial to "our lively and ardent Russian people" and inveighs against the affected manner introduced by Karamzin and his school. Somov's essay shows him poorly read in European literature (there is a disastrously bungled paragraph on Dante) and vague as to a program for Russian literature. But it was a beginning.

Decembrists

The Decembrists, insofar as they were men of letters (many were), tended toward a dynamic, progressive, civic-minded romanticism like Shelley's or Hugo's. They were equally opposed to Zhukovsky's mysticism and Pushkin's ironic outlook on life. Their attitude was well stated by Nikolai Gnedich (1784–1833), who wrote in *The Champion of Enlightenment and Philanthropy* (1821): "Let the pen in a writer's hand be what the scepter is in the hand of a tsar: firm, noble, and majestic! The pen writes of that which is inscribed upon the hearts of contemporaries and posterity. It serves the writer as a weapon against shameless ignorance and potent vice. It summons the high and the mighty of this Earth from their mute graves before the tribunal of posterity."

The famous line, "I am not a poet, but a citizen," belongs to Kondraty Ryleev (1795–1826), one of the leaders of the Decembrist revolt. It is the last line of his dedication of "Voinarovsky," addressed to Aleksandr Bestuzhev, another Decembrist. Ryleev, a minor poet, represents the civic strain of Russian romanticism most clearly and forcefully. He rejected the division of poetry into classical and romantic, asserting that there should be only one "true, national poetry," the laws of which are immutable.[10] Poetry should serve the people by embodying the loftiest ideas, feelings, and truths of an epoch. The people (*narod*) were to Ryleev an idealized body possessed of virtue, nobility, and strength. Nationality (*narodnost'*) meant identification with the people and with the national past. Ryleev prefaced his collection of *Dumy*,[11] ballads

on heroic personages from Russian history, with this quotation from the Polish poet Julian Niemcewicz's *Śpiewy historiczne*: "To remind the young generation of the deeds of their ancestors, acquaint it with the most shining epochs of national history, create a link between love of the fatherland and the first impressions of memory—such is a sure way to give a nation a strong sense of attachment to its motherland: nothing can later eradicate these first impressions and early concepts. They grow stronger with the years and produce valiant soldiers in battle and outstanding men in council." Vyazemsky found Ryleev's *Dumy* admirable. Pushkin called them "trash" and said that *dumy* was derived from German *dumm*, "stupid."

Wilhelm Küchelbecker, a Decembrist who barely escaped Ryleev's fate, shared Ryleev's ideals and his belief in the poet's mission. Like Ryleev, he emphasized the mythmaking power of poetry and explicitly demanded that classical mythology be replaced by a new, romantic mythology.[12] Küchelbecker's romantic ideas, however, had a sounder philosophical basis: he knew German romanticism well and understood its philosophical underpinnings.[13] As a critic, he consistently championed the organicist aesthetic of romanticism, demanding that art be a synthesis of the ideal and the real, and hence of

10. K. F. Ryleev, "Some Thoughts on Poetry," *Son of the Fatherland*, no. 22 (1825): 145–54.

11. *Dumy* means "meditations" (Lamartine's *Meditations* may have had some influence), but is also the Ukrainian term of a popular ballad about a hero of the past.

12. See the preface to Küchelbecker's play *Shakespearean Spirits* (1825).

13. During his stay in Western Europe (1820–21) Küchelbecker met Ludwig Tieck, with whom he discussed Goethe and Novalis, among others. In Paris he made the acquaintance of Benjamin Constant, then a leader of the liberal opposition, and Joseph-Étienne Jouy (1764–1846), a playwright and satirist. In May 1821 he delivered a series of lectures on Russian literature at the Athénée Royal. Upon returning to Russia, he published a summary of these lectures in the *Herald of Europe*.

the typical and the individual. He believed in the poet's visionary power and often made it the subject of his poetry.

Küchelbecker's article "On the Direction of Our Poetry, Lyric Poetry in Particular, during the Past Decade" presented an intelligent and challenging program of romanticism.[14] In it Küchelbecker asked Russians to reevaluate world literature in romantic terms. He regretfully pointed out the derivative and imitative quality of recent Russian poetry and suggested that it at least imitate worthier examples—Goethe rather than Schiller. It expressed the hope that Russian poetry would abandon its favored elegiac, idyllic, and epistolary genres and return to the heroic ode,[15] and that it would grow from Russia's own cultural resources, "the faith of our forefathers, our chronicles, songs, and tales of the people."

Küchelbecker was an opinionated but intelligent practicing critic. He recognized that both Shishkovians and Karamzinists had "romantics" among them. He welcomed Katenin's epic poem "Song about the First Battle between Russians and Tartars on the Kalka River under the leadership of Mstislav Mstislavich the Brave, Duke of Galicia" (1820) as a step in the right direction, but found it hard (*zhestkii*) and sometimes in bad taste. He felt that meter ought to be in accord with content and hence that mixing Russian folk verse, syllabotonic verse (borrowed by Lomonosov from the Germans), and classical meters was tantamount to mixing Russian with French and Latin phrases. Küchelbecker noticed and deplored Byron's influence in Pushkin's verse epics and found the immensely successful "A Prisoner of the Caucasus" quite weak—rightly so, as Pushkin himself would later admit.

Aleksandr Bestuzhev (1797–1837), one of the leaders of the Decembrist uprising, became famous as a prose writer after 1830. Before December 1825 he was better known as a poet and critic. Bestuzhev came from a literary family,[16] but also moved in high society. He started his literary career early, with essays and reviews in *Son of the Fatherland, The Loyalist*, and *The Champion of Enlightenment and Philanthropy*. He came to romanticism via Karamzin and was usually at odds with the archaist and folkloric manner of Katenin, Griboedov, and Küchelbecker. He was also opposed to the Teutonic mysticism of Zhukovsky. A political activist, he resented Pushkin's casual superciliousness in chapter 1 of *Eugene Onegin*. A lively and volatile spirit, Bestuzhev was the first Russian critic to use criticism consistently as a vehicle for his ironic wit. His review of Katenin's translation of Racine's *Esther* ("a paragon of quibbling, pseudo-witticisms, and ignorance," according to Küchelbecker) almost led to a duel. His judgment was often rash or simply uninformed. Pushkin's letters to him on more than one occasion set him straight. In a "Survey of Russian Literature in the Course of the Year 1824 and the Beginning of 1825" (*The Pole Star*, 1825) Bestuzhev said that

14. *Mnemosyne* 2 (1824): 29–44.

15. Here the influence of Ancillon's *Nouveaux essais de politique et de philosophie* (1824) is felt. Ancillon extolled the ode as the highest form of poetry and spoke highly of the rapture of inspiration that produces it. Pushkin, who leaned toward "emotion recollected in tranquillity," opposed this view. He and Delvig felt that Küchelbecker, recently still a Karamzinist, had been won over to the archaizing Shishkovian side by Griboedov. It is characteristic that Küchelbecker now found Dutch and Flemish genre painting banal and exceedingly mundane, lacking in the ideal, inspired quality which he sought in art, while Pushkin was about to descend with gusto to "the colorful trash of the Flemish school."

16. His father, A. F. Bestuzhev, together with I. P. Pnin, published the *Saint Petersburg Journal* (1798), the most progressive journal of its day.

Russia had "criticism, but no literature as yet." Pushkin, in a letter of June 1825, justly observed that the exact opposite was true.

Like his Decembrist friends, Bestuzhev identified romanticism with his political ideals and could not conceive of the poet as other than a lover of freedom and a bearer of ideals. Hence he appreciated Pushkin's "southern poems," which at least featured "love of freedom," but could never make himself accept *Eugene Onegin.*

Unlike his friends Ryleev and Küchelbecker, Bestuzhev was able to return to literature in an active role. His post-1830 theoretical and critical essays show a more extensive familiarity with romantic aesthetics and philosophy of history. By this time, however, Bestuzhev's theorizing was beside the point. Belinsky was waiting in the wings to debunk his fiction using precisely the concepts and language that Bestuzhev could handle only in the abstract.

Pushkin

Aleksandr Pushkin, notwithstanding occasional protestations to the contrary, was a professional man of letters who took a great interest in and had a profound understanding of criticism. We often hear him complain about the sorry state of Russian criticism.[17] He was the soul of *The Literary Gazette,* and when he finally had his own journal, *The Contemporary,* in 1836, he ran it with an experienced editor's professional savvy. Throughout his career Pushkin was involved in literary feuds, some of them, like that with Bulgarin, acrimonious. He fought his battles with gusto and was not above hitting below the belt. Pushkin's critical essays, reviews, and correspondence, in combination with material found in his poetry and fiction, allow one to get a fairly clear image of his theoretical views. Having grown up in the Karamzinist camp, Pushkin even as a mature writer retained some of its conservative views. He believed in good taste, which he saw as "a feeling of symmetry and appropriateness" (*chuvstvo sorazmernosti i soobraznosti*). He respected order, consistency, and precision of form. He took a moderate position on *narodnost'*. A believer in the "national spirit," he also believed that only civilized nations were capable of creating a national literature, and he did not entirely reject the Karamzinian notion of a language and literature developed in the ambience of high society.[18] Pushkin's distinction between poetry and prose—he saw precision and succinctness as the principal virtues of prose and reserved the play of emotions for poetry—was antiromantic. He never embraced the aesthetic organicism of his contemporaries, but stayed close to a Karamzinian emotionalist aesthetic that makes poetry an expression of subjective emotions, without pretense to cognitive powers: "An illusion which exalts us is dearer to us / Than a multitude of lowly truths" ("The Hero," 1830).

The notion that poetry is play, pursuit of pure harmony, that art is in fact something to be created for its own sake, was evidently attractive to Pushkin—a trait that alienated him from many of his contemporaries. Moreover, Pushkin would have none of the historicism that was beginning to dominate Russian thought.

Pushkin's position on romanticism was ambiguous (not neutral, as Vyazemsky was later to suggest in his memoirs). Pushkin

17. "If you were to read our journals, you would see that all that is called criticism here is uniformly stupid and ludicrous" (letter to P. V. Nashchokin, July 21, 1831).

18. According to Boris Tomashevsky, Pushkin's essay on *narodnost'* was strongly influenced by Ancillon's *Analyse.*

correctly suspected that the romantic zealots among his friends ("even Küchelbecker") had "a most obscure conception of romanticism."[19] He generally ignored the Neoplatonic philosophizing and religious mysticism that came to Russia from Germany, reacting to it parodically, and peripherally at that.[20] He would soon enough present his own "romantic" period as a mere youthful escapade, as when he has his "romantic Muse" galloping with him about the cliffs of the Caucasus, "on horseback, like Lenore in the moonlight" (*Eugene Onegin*, Chap. 8, sts. 4–5).

Nevertheless, Pushkin's theory and practice of poetry have enough romantic traits to fit the general mold of a romantic sensibility. First and foremost, he welcomed the romantic notion of the poet's free choice of form and went along, more radically than some romantic zealots, with the romantic abolition of fixed genres. Romantic stylization, exoticism, fragmentariness, and ellipticism, and in particular romantic irony, were the practical effect of this attitude. Even Pushkin's realism, his readiness to find poetry everywhere, especially in the prose of life, is a romantic trait.

Pushkin fully embraced the romantic theory of drama, rejecting the classicist dramatic canon and making Shakespeare the model of his own dramatic art. He agreed with Friedrich Schlegel's observation that the theater of Molière presents mere "types," whereas in Shakespeare the typical

19. Letter to Vyazemsky and L. S. Pushkin, May 25, 1825.

20. In *Eugene Onegin*, one of the "archive youths" ("a single melancholy joker") finds Tatyana "ideal" and promptly writes her an elegy. In "The Journeys of Eugene Onegin" we read, "My ideal is now the housewife, / My desire— peace / and a pot of cabbage soup." The romantic ideal is thus pulled down to the level of the mundane. The word itself becomes colloquial.

is wed to the individual, producing characters instead of types.

Like other poets since Horace, Pushkin devoted much thought and several of his most serious poems to the image and condition of the poet. This leitmotiv appears as early as 1818, in an epistle to Zhukovsky: "You are right, you create for the few" (alluding to the title of Zhukovsky's collection *Für Wenige*). In spite of what was really a favorable climate for poetry, Pushkin early on sensed the poet's isolation and complained that "our age is not an age for poets" (letter to Vyazemsky, April 20, 1820). With self-lacerating sarcasm he kept reiterating that he looked at his poems "much as a shoemaker looks at a pair of boots: I'm selling them at a profit" (letter to Vyazemsky, c. March 1823). In "Conversation of a Bookseller and a Poet" (1824) the bookseller finds a seemingly happy solution: "Inspiration is not for sale, / But one can sell a manuscript." In good romantic fashion, Pushkin distinguished inspiration (*vdokhnoven'e*) from rapture (*vostorg*, Lomonosov's trademark) and defined it as "an inclination of the soul toward a living acceptance of impressions, and hence toward a rapid grasp of concepts"—in other words, intuition. Although Pushkin asserts that inspiration is just as important in geometry as in poetry, he certainly perceives the poet's gift as something special. Pushkin's cycle on the poet ("The Poet," "To a Poet," "Poet and Crowd," "Arion," and others) unequivocally establishes that the poet is born

> Not for the travails of daily life,
> Not for gain, not for battles,
> But for inspiration,
> For sweet sounds and prayers.
> ("Poet and Crowd," 1828)

The poem "Arion" (1827), which has the poet, sole survivor of a shipwreck, "dry his wet clothes and sing his songs" (a transparent allegory of the fate of Pushkin and his Decembrist friends), makes the point that the poet's lot is independent of the course taken by the ship of state. The one poem that has been interpreted as charging the poet with a mission, "The Prophet" (1826), is a close paraphrase of Isaiah and must not be read as related to the poet's condition., It is a brilliant treatment of a poetic theme (a visionary getting the call) whose aesthetic potential Pushkin exploited to the hilt. Among all of Pushkin's statements on the poet, the following is perhaps the most damaging to the notion that Pushkin saw the poet as a leader and prophet: "Your verses. . . . are too clever. Poetry, may the Lord forgive me for saying this, must be a bit on the stupid side" (letter to Vyazemsky, May 24, 1826). Goethe, in a famous letter to Schiller, said much the same thing.

Belinsky responded to Pushkin's cycle on the poet with some sadness: "Pushkin forever locked himself into the proud majesty of an artist misunderstood and insulted [by the unhallowed crowd]." Plekhanov tried to undo the damage by claiming that by "the crowd" Pushkin meant "the high-society crowd," not the people at large. Yet Pushkin remained forever a beacon of light for those Russians, poets in particular, who would see poetry as an end in itself, as a pursuit of beauty and harmony, and nothing else. Aleksandr Blok's discourse "On the Poet's Calling" (1921) is the most eloquent expression of this view.

The Wisdom Lovers

Küchelbecker's familiarity with German romanticism was an accident of his birth. Almost simultaneously, though, more than a few young Russians became directly acquainted with German idealist philosophy,

some in the course of academic studies in Germany, others through German professors active in Russia. Pushkin let his romantic poet Lensky, in *Eugene Onegin*, study in Germany, rhyming "Lensky" and "Göttingensky."[21] By the mid-1820s Schelling's transcendental idealism had reached Russia,[22] and a group of young Muscovite poets and scholars led by Duke Vladimir Odoevsky (1804–69) formed the Society of Wisdom Lovers (1823–25), which tried to apply Schelling's philosophy to the Russian scene. Among its members and associates were Dmitry Venevitinov, Stepan Shevyryov, Mikhail Pogodin, Aleksei Khomyakov, and Ivan Kireevsky.

Much of Russian poetry and criticism since the 1820s and well into the 1850s was informed by Schelling's transcendental idealism and its "principle of identity." With all phenomena of nature an emanation and hence a symbol of the world spirit, their diversity was a matter of intensity rather than quality. With the perceiving (and thinking) subject identical to the perceived object, and with "becoming" rather than "being" the permanent condition of the universe, human history could be viewed as a process of self-cognition, in the course of which the human spirit generates symbols that bring it progressively closer to full identity with the world spirit. Creative intuition, as an organ of the national and through

21. Pushkin's own teacher at the Lyceum, A. I. Galich (1783–1848), later a professor at Petersburg University, had studied in Germany (1808–12) and was one of the first Russians to deal with art and poetry in modern "scientific" (German idealist) terms. He published a manual of aesthetics, *An Outline of the Science of the Beautiful* (1825).

22. For details, see Wsewolod Setschkareff, *Schellings Einfluss in der russischen Literatur der 20er und 30er Jahre des XIX. Jahrhunderts* (Leipzig: Harrassowitz, 1939).

it the human spirit, was credited with a key role in the creation of these symbols. This conception informed and influenced not only the Moscow wisdom lovers but also the Slavophiles, Gogol, Belinsky, Apollon Grigoryev, and even Dostoevsky.

Venevitinov popularized Schelling's philosophy in several brilliant prose pieces, including "Anaxagoras" (a dialogue), "Morning, Midday, Evening, and Night," and "Sculpture, Painting, and Music," which concludes with these words: "Poetry is our mother; eternity is her glory; the universe is her image [*izobrazhenie*]." In an essay initially published under the title "Some Ideas about a Plan for a Journal" (*The Moscow Herald*, which became the organ of this group in 1827) Venevitinov presented the progress of culture (he calls it "enlightenment") as a people's drive toward self-cognition. The Russian people , he said, had as yet made no attempt at self-cognition but had merely imitated the thought and the commitment of other peoples. Therefore they were still "unable to boast of a single monument which would bear the stamp of free inspiration and true passion for knowledge."[23] The difference between Venevitinov's thinking and that of contemporaries like Somov and Vyazemsky was that Venevitinov did not perceive the national spirit (*dukh narodnyi*) as an assemblage of customs, habits, traditions, and local color but as an ideal quality inherent in the character of the people, which every nation would have to bring forth in a process of creative self-expression and self-cognition.

The ideas of the wisdom lovers also found expression in Vladimir Odoevsky's *Russian Nights*, a work published in 1844, although much of it was written and parts of it published in the 1820s. It is similar in structure to E. T. A. Hoffmann's *Die Serapionsbrüder* and shares much of its spirit (Hoffmann, too, was influenced by Schelling's philosophy). Tales of varied content and mode, told by different narrators, alternate with discussions on a variety of subjects. The whole nevertheless conveys a well-defined philosophy, of which Schelling is explicitly identified as the source. Its tenor is antirationalist and antipositivist. The proper avenue to a realization of the unity and harmony of the cosmos is perceived as that of self-realization and self-expression of the human soul. Hence intuitive cognition, especially by the artist, poet, and musician (the musician's being the most potent), is placed above scientific cognition mediated by such rational constructs as mathematical concepts. The affinity of the artist's intuition to religious mysticism is emphasized. The tales in *Russian Nights* are designed to illustrate or corroborate Odoevsky's philosophical ideas.

Stepan Shevyryov, later to become a professor of Russian literature at Moscow University (in 1834) and a major figure in the Slavophile camp, was the leading critic of *The Moscow Herald* in 1827–28 (he went abroad to study from 1829 to 1832). At this stage he was an enthusiastic Schellingian.

Aleksei Khomyakov, who had graduated from Moscow University in mathematics in 1821, was to become a leader of the Slavophile movement and an important theologian. In the 1820s and 1830s he was publishing his poetry in *The Moscow Herald*. His early verses take a lofty view of the poet's calling ("A Dream," 1828), echo Schelling's *Naturphilosophie*, and give some previews of his mature Slavophile ideas ("The Forest Spring," 1835).

Ivan Kireevsky, perhaps the best critical mind among the wisdom lovers, and later

23. D. Venevitinov, *Sochineniya* (Moscow, 1829), 24–33.

among the Slavophiles, was an assiduous student of Schelling, though he also attended Hegel's lectures in 1830. It was through Schelling—the later, conservative Schelling—that Kireevsky found the justification to advance from philosophical idealism to a mystical faith in Russian Orthodoxy. As early as 1830, in his "Survey of Russian Literature in the Year 1829," Kireevsky observed that Europe, having acquired "the one-sidendness of maturity," had stagnated spiritually, so that "all of Europe's hope had shifted toward Russia." Meanwhile Kireevsky's critical assessment of contemporary Russian literature was remarkably astute. His observations on Pushkin's "Poltava" are incisive and judicious. He discerns two schools in Russian poetry: the French (Pushkin and Vyazemsky) and the German (Shevyryov, Khomyakov, Tyutchev, and the anonymous author of *Izborsky*—Küchelbecker, that is). That the future Slavophiles should be listed with the German school is less remarkable than it might seem.

In the essay "The Nineteenth Century," for which his journal, *The European*, was closed in 1832, Kireevsky explicitly declared that Peter the Great's reforms were a mere external innovation which went against Russia's organic development. As for the future, he observed that after an age of destruction (the French Revolution) and political restoration, the time had come for an age of reconciliation, with religion taking the lead. Russia's time was at hand.

Chaadaev

German philosophical idealism was the main source of Russian conservative thought from the wisdom lovers to the symbolists. But it was also one of the sources of Russian progressive (westernizing) thought.

Pyotr Yakovlevich Chaadaev (1794–1856), a wealthy aristocrat and officer in the hussars, resigned his commission in 1821 to study and travel in Europe. He met and corresponded with Schelling and kept abreast of recent European thought, including Hegel. Between 1829 and 1831 Chaadaev wrote his *Lettres philosophiques addressées à une dame*, which was circulated in manuscript. In 1836 a translation of the first letter was published in Nadezhdin's *Telescope*. The journal was closed, Nadezhdin exiled, the censor who had passed the piece dismissed, and Chaadaev declared officially insane and placed under house arrest—hence his subsequent "Apology of a Madman" (1837, published posthumously).

The main idea of Chaadaev's first "philosophical letter" was that Russia was, at the present point in history, an "ahistorical" nation, a nation possessing no permanent and cherished institutions, no unifying traditions, no national ideals, and therefore no meaningful history. Russia, Chaadaev said, was not a legitimate member of the family of Western nations (like Schelling and Hegel, he identified human civilization with Western civilization) since Peter's reforms had remained on the surface and Russians were taking over Western ideas ready-made, without contributing any thought of their own. Chaadaev saw religion as the mainstay of culture and found that whereas the Western church had given structure, direction, and meaning to Western civilization, the Russian Orthodox church had remained ritualistic, lacking an ideal content and having little influence on morality.

Chaadaev's harsh judgment of Russia was accepted in one way or another by progressive westernizers (*zapadniki*) who followed him. Belinsky's interpretation of Gogol's *Inspector General* as a valid representation of the inanity of Russian life and

Turgenev's crushing admission of Russia's cultural inferiority in *Smoke* (1867) were restatements of Chaadaev's conception. Chaadaev's image of Russia remained present in the consciousness of educated Russians well into the twentieth century.[24]

Slavophiles

The Slavophiles (*slavyanofily*), several of whom were former members or associates of the Society of Wisdom Lovers, became a distinct grouping in the late 1830s. In 1835 Shevyryov, Pogodin, Khomyakov, and some others founded the conservative *Moscow Observer*. In 1838 it was run briefly by Bakunin and Belinsky before failing in 1839. *The Muscovite* (1841–56), with Pogodin as publisher and editor, Shevyryov in charge of literary criticism, and Ivan Kireevsky as editor for three issues in 1845, was a reliable outlet for Slavophile ideas, though not an exclusive organ of the movement.

Slavophiles, true to their Schellingian background, believed that philosophy (as well as science) and faith should be governed by identical principles, with the burden being on philosophy (science) to rise to the level of faith. Believers in the "national spirit," they developed a distinct hypostasis of the Russian national spirit and a conception of Russia's historical mission. The Slavophile image of the Russian national spirit was composed of free and spontaneous submission of the individual to the community (sometimes called *roevoe nachalo*, "the principle of the beehive"), religious devotion as a vehicle and the monarchy as symbol of communality, the primacy of moral and religious traditions over formal legality, a spontaneous sense of right and wrong, a preponderance of inner spiritual wisdom

24. See Osip Mandelshtam's essay "Pyotr Chaadaev" (1914–15).

over external rationality, integrity of the family, and a basically rural outlook. Coming from German idealist philosophy, the Slavophiles took pains to place this image into a historical scheme. In an essay of 1839, "In Answer to A. S. Khomyakov," Ivan Kireevsky explained the West's penchant for formal reasoning, legalism, and a separation of faith from reason as vestiges of the pagan classical tradition dominant in the Western church. He noted with satisfaction that the Russian church, untouched by the culture of classical antiquity, had no scholastic philosophy, never felt obliged to prove the dogmas of faith, and had no renaissance to contend with. Russia, having had no part of the West's struggle of faith against reason, developed its traditions "organically" rather than by way of conscious decision making. Russian life had reason, faith, and emotion in balance; it possessed an "inner integrity of self-consciousness."

In two essays of 1845 and 1846, "Foreign Opinions of Russia" and "Russian Opinions of Foreigners," Khomyakov tried to show that post-Petrine Russia's woes were because Russians, "children of a noble race," had chosen "to play the role of foundlings." He said that Russians were trying to be like Europeans instead of being themselves and, falling short of playing that role to perfection, would feel inferior—an attitude that foreigners would naturally applaud, thus enhancing Russia's feeling of inferiority.

Slavophiles believed that life in the West had lost its spiritual component and was devoting all its energies to material values (Kireevsky called this *promyshlennost'*, "industry"). They rejected the bourgeois culture of the West as a whole, and specifically its positivism and materialism, its individualism (even as regards private property), and its legalism. Khomyakov, a staunch Anglophile, found Disraeli's maxim that

"English manners save England from English law" admirably suited to Russian life. The Slavophiles were for the most part well-to-do landowners of good families and tended to be capable managers of their private fortunes who also took an active interest in Russia's national economy.

In their publicism the Slavophiles supported freedom of thought and freedom of the press, emancipation of the peasants, and the establishment of local self-government. They promoted Russian folkways and were industrious students and collectors of Russian folklore, dialectological and ethnographic material, and monuments of pre-Petrine Russian culture. Ivan Kireevsky's brother Pyotr (1808–56) devoted most of his life to collecting Russian folk songs.[25]

The Slavophiles refused to call themselves romantics, although their ideas as well as their poetics were derived from German romanticism.[26] They tended to be Francophobes who deplored the influence of French utopian socialism, George Sand, French positivism, and any trend in Russian literature that was of French origin. They were also Anglophiles, admiring British traditions, conservatism, good sense, and family life. Their thinking was basically utopian, continuing the conservative utopian tradition that had existed in Russia since the eighteenth century. Venevitinov's "Anaxagoras," based on Schelling, envisages a world in which "moral freedom will be a common legacy, all human knowledge will be fused in a single idea of man, all branches

of science will come together in one science of self-knowledge." Ivan Kireevsky wrote a utopian short story, "The Island" (1838), depicting a Slavophile Orthodox paradise. Vladimir Odoevsky wrote several interesting utopian pieces. Even Sergei Aksakov's *Family Chronicle* is a utopia of sorts.

Slavophile criticism was based on the notion that the poet is an organ of the national spirit and of his epoch, and it was guided by the Slavophiles' image of the "true" spirit of the Russian nation. Slavophiles generally took a critical view of Pushkin, finding in him a lack of moral seriousness, religious feeling, and real concern for the people. Lermontov was rejected as rootless and decadent, his Byronism seen as an ephemeral phenomenon with no organic ties to Russian life. Gogol, who had close personal ties to the Aksakovs, Pogodin, and Shevyryov, was perceived as much closer to Slavophile ideals. Konstantin Aksakov (1817–60) reacted to the appearance of *Dead Souls* with an encomiastic essay in which he called Gogol's work a Russian national epopoeia and saw Homeric traits in it. The Westernizer Belinsky responded with a vitriolic putdown.

The Slavophiles responded negatively to the natural school and disputed with its champion Belinsky. Yury Samarin (1819–1876), in an essay, "On Historical and Literary Opinions of *The Contemporary*" (published in *The Muscovite*, 1847), condemned it for its negative image of the Russian people (writers of the natural school saw mainly poverty, brutishness, and apathy where the Slavophiles would see faith, dignity, and native wisdom) and for its indiscriminate adoption of foreign ideas (Belinsky was singled out on this score). Konstantin Aksakov wrote extremely negative reviews of Dostoevsky's first novels, *Poor Folk* and *The Double*, calling them unpoetic, imitative (of

25. *Songs*, collected by P. V. Kireevsky, 10 vols. (1860–74).

26. Russian contemporaries were well aware of this debt. Chernyshevsky said, in his *Essays in the Gogol Period of Russian Literature*, "Slavophilism came to us from the West. There is not a single substantial thought in it (decidedly, *not one*) that was not borrowed from certain second-rate French and German writers."

Gogol), and negative. Other works of the natural school met with a similar response on the part of Slavophile critics. Turgenev's *A Hunter's Sketches*, some parts of which idealize the Russian peasant, was received more favorably.

Stepan Shevyryov (1806–64), a minor poet and competent translator, professor of Moscow University and author of a scholarly *History of Old Russian Literature* (1846–60),[27] was the most important Slavophile critic. He also published theoretical treatises on aesthetic theory and Russian versification. As a critic, he was regularly embroiled in polemics with Bulgarin, Belinsky, and others. He deplored what he saw as growing commercialism and catering to vulgar tastes in the literature of his day. An academic critic, Shevyryov felt that it was the task of criticism to mediate between art and scholarship. Meanwhile, to Russia's youth it was the political message of literature that mattered, as Shevyryov's friend Pogodin wryly observed, and it was Belinsky's social criticism that carried the day. Shevyryov's criticism was not without merit, however. Using the synesthetic metaphors of romanticism, he considered Derzhavin a poet of the "plastic school," Batyushkov and Zhukovsky as poets of the "musical school," and Pushkin as a synthesis of both. Building on his synesthetic metaphor, Shevyryov then visualized Pushkin's oeuvre as a magnificent sketch (*eskiz*) of an unfinished edifice, richly ornamented, with some parts exquisitely finished and with a wealth of precious material ready for resuming its construction, which "the Russian people are destined to work on for many centuries to come and will one day bring to a glorious conclusion." Shevyryov saw Gogol's *Dead Souls* as an

epopoeia of Russian life. But unlike Aksakov, he also saw the verbalism, the caricature, the hyperbole, and the grotesque in it and interpreted these traits, in Hegelian terms, as a just reflection of the incidental absurdities that custom, habit, ritual, and common opinion impart to human life without affecting its holy and serious substance. Belinsky viewed the same traits of Gogol's humor as a attack on the existing order of things. Shevyryov was one of the few to recognize and respect Gogol's mysticism and religious searchings and to defend his *Selected Passages from a Correspondence with My Friends*. Shevyryov's criticism of Lermontov and of the natural school showed little appreciation or understanding of the new realist literature. Good Slavophile that he was, Shevyryov attributed the lack of "true artistry" in the works of Grigorovich, Goncharov, and Turgenev to their "total rejection of the deeply rooted principles of our popular life, that basic essence, that living truth which is ingrained in our people." In other words, these writers were refusing to accept the idealized image of the Russian people in which the Slavophiles believed.

Polevoi, Bulgarin, and Senkovsky

Nikolai Polevoi (1796–1846), the first major literary raznochinets of the nineteenth century, has not received his due, perhaps because he was heartily disliked by Pushkin. (To have been "against Pushkin" is a sin not easily forgiven in the history of Russian literature.) Polevoi, the son of a Siberian merchant, came to Moscow in 1820 and, although he had no formal education, made himself into one of the leading journalists of his age, as well as a competent critic, historian, playwright, and novelist. In his writings we meet an educated man, a European, and a critical spirit in no way inferior to his

---

27. Shevyryov's four-volume work did not, however, leave a major mark on the study or understanding of medieval Russian literature.

noble contemporaries. When the aristocrat Vyazemsky denied Polevoi these qualities, he was taking a narrow and prejudiced view.

Polevoi's journal, *The Moscow Telegraph* (1825–34), addressed to a broad readership, was a commercial success until publication was suspended for a negative review of Nestor Kukolnik's patriotic play "The Hand of the Almighty Has Saved the Fatherland." *The Moscow Telegraph* printed translations of essays by Madame de Staël, Sismondi, Herder, Schelling, the Schlegels, Chateaubriand, Cousin, and Hugo (his programmatic "Preface to *Cromwell*," in 1832). Polevoi made himself the spokesman of progressive romanticism in the spirit of Hugo and Lamartine. But the "high philosophical content" he demanded of literature is never specified, and when moral judgments are made, they follow conventional values. Still, Polevoi's journal built a reputation for liberalism (Pushkin, in a notebook entry, called it Jacobinism) and carried on polemics, not only with the conservative *Herald of Europe*, but even with the progressive but "aristocratic" *Literary Gazette*. The skirmish with *The Literary Gazette* had class overtones.[28] Polevoi made himself notorious by his criticism of Karamzin's *History of the Russian State*, to which he responded with his own *History of the Russian People* (six volumes, 1829–33). Karamzin had been essentially a biographer of royalty, an artist, and a moralist. Polevoi tried to be a historian in the romantic sense, making the Russian people the hero of a narrative moved by the "national spirit."

28. Here is a parodic reaction to Pushkin's ode "To a Magnate" (1830), from the *Moscow Telegraph*: "Like a youthful, virgin eagle, / He struck his golden chords, / soared high above the earth, / sat down in the magnate's antechamber, / And in a rapture of joy / Began to sing wondrous, living songs."

Polevoi's assessment of the major Russian poets was generally intelligent. He appreciated Derzhavin's greatness and recognized Zhukovsky's merits, but called Dmitriev a "non-Russian" poet. Though at times unfair to Pushkin, he made some good observations, too. Polevoi refused to find anything Russian about "Ruslan and Lyudmila" or Pushkin's romantic verse epics, including "The Gypsies," and instead pointed out their Byronic traits. He considered *Boris Godunov* a dramatic failure whose "fate was decided by its dedication to Karamzin." But he had high praise for Pushkin's lyric poetry and saw in him "the fullest expression of his country and his epoch." He applauded the first chapter of *Eugene Onegin*, which met with a cool reception on the part of Pushkin's friends and admirers, such as Bestuzhev and Venevitinov. After 1828, when negative reviews of Pushkin's works became the rule, Polevoi followed the trend. Speaking of the later chapters of *Eugene Onegin*, he noted the fragmentariness of the novel, calling it "an assemblage of separate disconnected observations and thoughts," but failed to see the traits that make it a great work of art.

Polevoi's response to the early Gogol was sensible. He recognized in *The Inspector General* what he called the *tolle Welt* (mad world) of the carnival season, pure comedy that turns the world upside down. Polevoi's response to *Dead Souls* was unimaginative, though not unintelligent. He saw bad grammar, a chaotic lexicon, the absence of a consistent style, unmotivated transitions from the most exalted to the lowest—in a word, "bad taste"—but missed the legerdemain by which Gogol converts all these minuses into pluses. In the 1840s Polevoi the raznochinets, of all people, decried the progressive vulgarization of Russian literature begun by Gogol. It must be said in his defense that after the loss of his journal he was reduced to the state of a literary hack, working for his former enemies, Bulgarin and Grech.

Romantics and classicists, Slavophiles and Westernizers, were active in an ambience in which the loudest and most commonly heard voices were those of critics who belonged to no particular group and whose opinions were guided by mundane advantage rather than by any philosophical or aesthetic principles. In 1832 Count S. S. Uvarov, minister of education and himself a minor poet (in Russian and German), coined the slogan "Orthodoxy, Monarchy, and Nationality" to define an attitude approved by the government. Several journals prospered by assuming this attitude. The criticism of Faddei Bulgarin (1789–1859), publisher of *The Northern Bee* (1825–59), and Nikolai Grech (1787–1867), editor of *Son of the Fatherland* (1812–39), each of whom also coedited the other's journal, was guided by a desire to please the authorities, increase the circulation of their journals, and put down any competition by whatever means would seem expedient. The criticism printed in these journals is generally unworthy of serious attention.

Osip Senkovsky (1800–59), publisher of the *Reading Library* (1834–47), had erudition and common sense, along with a remarkable facility of style, but lacked empathy, seriousness, and real love or respect for Russian literature. His reviews were written to show off the reviewer's shallow ironic wit, rather than to convey an understanding of the work in question. His critical opinions of Pushkin and Gogol may be safely disregarded. But Senkovsky was very successful. His bantering, diffuse, tasteless style was widely imitated and left its mark on Russian journalese.

Gogol

Nikolai Gogol was always underestimated. This goes also for his criticism. Although not voluminous, it contains a wealth of original thoughts. It was Gogol who called Pushkin Russia's national poet (as early as 1835), and it was he who said first much of what Dostoevsky would say in his celebrated "Discourse on Pushkin" of 1880, including that Pushkin, though Russian to the core, could embrace the spirit of every European nation. It was Gogol who saw Pushkin as the poet par excellence, but it was also Gogol who first perceived literature as an organ of social progress—for which he was properly praised by Chernyshevsky.

The pattern of Gogol's aesthetic and critical opinions is one of familiar romantic principles bent to a moral-didactic end, or in other words, romantic practices justified by classicist theory. In an early essay, "Sculpture, Painting, and Music," Gogol in good romantic fashion declares music the most spiritual art form, but also dwells on the ennobling effect of all art and on art's civic function. The arch-romantic "pearl of creation" passage in *Dead Souls* (chapter 7), which defines art as a "quintessence of reality," is part of a sober disquisition on the disadvantage of being a writer who writes about ordinary people. The story "The Portrait," a veritable manual of romantic clichés, features the struggle of good and evil projected into the creative process—a disquieting position of real depth—but also veers off into pedestrian observations on the harmful effects even of minute embellishment of empirical reality.

Gogol had a comprehensive vision of the past, present, and future of Russian literature. His sketch of its past in the essay "What, Then, Is the Essence of Russian Poetry, and What Does Its Special Character Amount To?" (1847) is truly historicist and in fact dialectical (Pushkin is considered a synthesis of Zhukovsky and Batyushkov). The present is seen as an age of ferment, presaging new tasks and new battles. Here Gogol anticipates positions of the *pochven-niki* (men of the soil), Dostoevsky in particular, as he predicts the emergence of a powerful new religious strain in Russian literature. Gogol's symbolic interpretations of his own works were not nearly as far-fetched as his contemporaries took them to be. Of course, he could also be terribly naive, for instance, when he wildly overestimated the importance of Zhukovsky's truly outstanding translation of the *Odyssey*.

Student Circles at Moscow University. Nadezhdin

Moscow University in the 1830s was a hotbed of diverse ideas and the first station in the career of many important literary figures. Some of the students in the Schellingian circle around Nikolai Stankevich joined him in Berlin, where he went in 1837 to study philosophy, and brought back the Hegelian ideas that were to inform Belinsky, among others. Mikhail Bakunin, one of the first to introduce Hegel in Russia, went on to become an anarchist and a revolutionary. Ivan Turgenev, who also studied philosophy in Berlin, remained uncommitted to any particular doctrine, although he maintained a liberal outlook. Mikhail Katkov (1818–87), who brought back the lecture notes of Hegel's course in aesthetics and translated them for Belinsky, turned conservative. Konstantin Aksakov, another member of the circle around Stankevich, went on to become a leading Slavophile ideologue.

The existence of the Stankevich and Her-

zen-Ogaryov student circles coincided with the tenure of Nikolai Nadezhdin (1804–56), who became a professor of the theory of fine arts and archaeology in 1831, and with the publication of the literary journal *The Telescope* (1831–36), which he founded that same year. Nadezhdin, a raznochinets (he was the son of a deacon), had defended a master's thesis on romanticism, *De origine, natura et fatis Poëseos, quae Romantica audit* (1830), in which he discussed Schiller, Bouterwek, Sismondi, and the Schlegels. His historical conception of the evolution of art was in fact Hegelian: classical man was subject to nature, romantic man to the movements of his soul, whereas modern man was about to create a synthesis of both tendencies. Like Hegel, Nadezhdin historicized the theory of genres,[29] which caused him to reject Pushkin's heroic verse epic "Poltava" as an anachronism, and saw the novel as the genre proper to the modern age. He demanded that art be philosophically (socially and politically) conscious and attuned to contemporary reality (*deistvitel'nost'*, "reality," is one of his key terms). Hence he rejected art that was merely playful, like Pushkin's "Count Nulin," but also naturalist art, on the grounds that it lacked an "idea." Nadezhdin's reviews and his programmatic essay "The Contemporary Direction of Enlightenment" (1831) contain much of what was later to be the substance of Russian literary theory as developed by his student Belinsky. After the suspension of the *Telescope* Nadezhdin, briefly exiled to the northeast, was able to start a new career in ethnography and never returned to literature.

29. Hegel taught that art forms (sculpture, painting, music) and literary genres (epic, lyric, drama) were organically linked to the historical process.

Belinsky

The importance of Vissarion Grigoryevich Belinsky (1811–48) in Russian literature is unparalleled for any man of letters who was exclusively a literary critic. A raznochinets, the son of a country doctor, he attended Moscow University but was eventually dismissed in 1832 "for reason of his poor health and limited ability." He was a member of the Stankevich circle and retained active ties with several of its members for the rest of his life. In 1833 Professor Nadezhdin engaged him as a collaborator for *The Telescope*, where he made his debut with a series of essays under the title "Literary Reveries" (1834). After the suppression of *The Telescope* Belinsky worked, in succession, for *The Moscow Observer* (1838–39), the *National Annals* (1839–46), and *The Contemporary* (1846–48). During his only trip abroad, in 1847, Belinsky wrote his celebrated "Letter to Gogol" (first published by Herzen in London in 1855 but widely circulated in manuscript), a response to Gogol's *Selected Passages from a Correspondence with My Friends*. Belinsky's letter, in which he denounced the imperial bureaucracy and the Orthodex church, became a cherished revolutionary document. Soon afterward he died of consumption.

Belinsky was a man of remarkable gifts that made him ideally suited for the profession of a journal critic. His enthusiasm, easily kindled, was tempered by good sense, love of truth, and a capacity for self-criticism. He was well read, though he knew only Russian and French, and was capable of writing literary history as well as his academic contemporaries. In profiling Nikolai Polevoi, Belinsky in effect described himself: "The absence of a systematic education saved him from scholastic prejudice and pedantry, and made him a publicist who addresses not an academic lecture hall but society."

In the course of his career as critic, Belinsky embraced first Fichte, then Schelling, Hegel, French utopian socialism, and left-Hegelianism, and was apparently reverting to a more conservative Hegelian position during the last two years of his life. His opponents charged that he simply went along with the most recent trend, but in retrospect we can see that under the influence of foreign ideas, and stimulated by events of Russian social and literary life, Belinsky developed his own view of the role of Russian literature in the creation of a national consciousness.

Belinsky's achievements are diverse. He produced a huge volume of occasional criticism, reviewing not only innumerable works of imaginative literature, from the greatest to the most trivial, but also books and brochures on any conceivable subject. Some of these reviews became essays on the subject. For example, some of Belinsky's reviews of books for children are in effect essays on education. Belinsky was a knowledgeable theater critic. He wrote a series of annual surveys of Russian literature (1840–47), in which he made many observations of a theoretical and programmatic nature. He also wrote major essays that became a point of departure for all future discussion of the author or topic in question. These include his four essays on Russian folklore (1841), his essay on Derzhavin (1843), and his eleven essays on Pushkin (1843–45).

Belinsky pursued several objectives. He advertised certain tendencies in Russian literature, the natural school in particular, and promoted writers who he felt were of social or aesthetic value: Gogol, whose importance he recognized early ("On the Russian Short Story and the Short Stories of Mr. Gogol," 1836) and whose champion he was until the debacle of *Selected Passages*; Lermontov, to whom he devoted several major essays in 1840 and 1841; and later Herzen, Goncharov, Turgenev, and Dostoevsky.

A Westernizer, Belinsky acted as a mediator between Western culture and the Russian public. He wrote a number of essay reviews of foreign authors, pointing the Russian public in the direction he favored. He wrote a fine essay on *Hamlet* (1838), defended Goethe against his German detractors, helped spread the influence of George Sand, and said some interesting things about Hoffmann, Balzac, Hugo, Dickens, Sue, and others. He always made it explicit that Russia needed the West, whereas the West did not need Russia. He discriminated between different kinds of Western literature reaching Russia, bluntly rejecting commercial trash (Alexandre Dumas), recognizing the social or educational value of some works whose aesthetic value he held to be low (Sue, some works by George Sand), and cherishing the great poets and writers of the West as though they were Russia's own (Shakespeare, Byron, Goethe, Schiller, and —somewhat overenthusiastically—Walter Scott and Fenimore Cooper).

Belinsky was at all times a critic with an ideology and with an aesthetic theory. Although both changed in the course of his career, his basic principles were constant. They soon became anchored in Russian literature as almost universally accepted axioms. Belinsky distinguished three levels of literature: poesy (*poeziya*, in the sense of German *Dichtung*, that is creative literature), belles lettres (*belletristika*), and journalism. Poesy creates permanent values and points the way to the nation's future. Belles lettres convey the ideal values created by poesy to the masses. Journalism, in turn,

applies these ideas to practical life and to current events.

Belinsky's aesthetic is Hegelian. All art forms are perceived as organic manifestations of a nation's vital concerns during a given historical epoch. A work of art is an organic fusion of content and form, where the content is an idea and form is its concrete realization. Hence Belinsky, like Hegel, excluded from the domain of poesy, on the one hand, naturalist and formalist works and, on the other, works whose philosophical, moral, or didactic content was not realized in concrete, individualized symbols (*obrazy*). Satire, though highly valued, was to Belinsky (as to Hegel) "nonart." However, Belinsky stressed that a work of nonart could still have a legitimate social function, more so in fact than some genuine works of art. Herzen's *Whose Fault?* and Goncharov's *Same Old Story* were a case in point. *Whose Fault?* was hardly a work of art but was socially valuable, whereas *The Same Old Story* was an enjoyable masterpiece but of little social relevance.

Belinsky saw art and literature as integral elements of the historical process and of the national spirit. A believer in progress, he thought that literature should be its standard-bearer.[30] Hence his terrible disappointment when Gogol turned "reactionary." Belinsky did not hesitate to call even Pushkin passé, superseded by Lermontov. He felt that Derzhavin, a poet of genius, had fallen short of true greatness because in his

30. There was at least one critic who disagreed with Belinsky on this score, Valerian Maikov (1823–47), brother of the poet Apollon Maikov. Maikov, called by some the first Russian Marxist, engaged Belinsky in a debate, asserting that progress depended on a progressive dilution of national traits and was headed toward a universal literature. Maikov also thought that literature was normally the rearguard rather than the vanguard of progress.

time there was still no Russian national consciousness that he might have expressed, and he placed Pushkin and even his beloved Gogol below their European contemporaries—Lord Byron, Walter Scott, and George Sand—because Russian national concerns had not as yet become universal. Belinsky leaned toward Chaadaev's opinion according to which the Russian national character was still poorly defined, but saw in this a great opportunity for cultural universality, thus anticipating the main thesis of Dostoevsky's "Discourse on Pushkin."

Belinsky never doubted that it was natural for literature to fulfill its aesthetic and its social functions simultaneously and without detriment to either. He believed that Russian literature should mirror Russian reality without any embellishments or illusions. Subsequently, Russian writers and critics tended to follow him in believing in a literature totally committed to social, political, or religious ideas yet true to the autonomy and authenticity of the creative imagination. Belinsky's immense influence was considered beneficial by most of those who embraced his historical, social, and national "organicism." The exception is those who, while retaining his organicist model as a whole, disagreed with Belinsky's westernizing and atheistic view of history and replaced it with a Slavophile model. Apollon Grigoryev and Dostoevsky are cases in point. Belinsky's influence has been branded as harmful by those who take the Kantian view of art, considering art an end in itself, ideally independent of intellectual, social, and political concerns. Aleksandr Blok, in his celebrated last discourse, "On the Poet's Calling," said flatly that Belinsky was more dangerous to poetry than Count Benckendorf, chief of gendarmes and Pushkin's censor: Benckendorf could temporarily stop a poet's work from reaching its public, whereas Belinsky

could divert the poet from his true calling, the creation of harmony and beauty.

Belinsky's nationalism was more moderate than that of the Slavophiles, nor did he succumb to the populist mystique of the generation that succeeded his. He knew that a love for the Russian people entailed no obligation to write edifying tales about idealized Russian peasants. But he did establish the precedent of critical praise for "correct" choice of subject matter and "correctly" placed social sympathy. While ridiculing Shevyryov for asking for more elegant works about the refined life of high society, Belinsky himself commended mediocre works of the natural school for their "honest treatment" of ordinary life among the lower classes and their compassion for the poor and downtrodden. Dostoevsky's *Poor Folk* earned Belinsky's praise on this score, rather than for the virtuosity of its composition and its clever ambiguities. It is largely Belinsky's merit—or fault—that "pure art" never acquired respectability in Russia.

Belinsky's record as a practicing critic is impressive. He accurately sorted out the major and the minor, the meritorious and the worthless writers of his age. His judgment usually stands up well to historical hindsight. Where it does not, as in the case of Pushkin's prose, of which he had a relatively low opinion, his case is not without merit. In some instances he was lucky. He sensed Gogol's greatness but, at least in the case of *Dead Souls*, never found the key to it. He recognized Dostoevsky's talent but saw only its surface, without ever discovering or even suspecting its depth.

The Golden Age of Russian Poetry

The early decades of the nineteenth century, from Zhukovsky to Lermontov, are considered the golden age of Russian poetry. Some of the poets who were a part of it survived and continued to write poetry long after Lermontov's death in 1841. Some did their best work after the golden age was over—Vyazemsky, Glinka, and especially Tyutchev.

The extraordinary flowering of poetry from the 1800s to the 1830s was not unprepared. The poets of the golden age worked in many of the same genres as their predecessors, followed the same rules of versification, treated some of the same ideas, myths, and imagery, and continued some of the debates that had been started by Karamzin and his contemporaries. Some of the members of the generation that preceded the golden age, Krylov for example, survived Pushkin and Lermontov.

Although the golden age continued to produce a good deal of poetry in the classicist manner, it was marked by the influx and eventual dominance of romantic ideas and a romantic sensibility. Throughout the period, however, no single aesthetic theory predominated.

The poetry of the golden age was a product of Russian upper-class culture. Some of its genres, such as the epistle, album verse, and the epigram, were an integral part of the social life of that class. Most of the poets of the golden age were nobles, and many belonged to high society. Thousands of Russian men and women wrote some poetry at the time, but only a few hundred published their poems, and most of those who did were members of the literary ambience of Petersburg and Moscow and knew each other personally. Throughout the golden age the epistle was still a favored genre, and innumerable poems were addressed or dedicated by one poet to another.

Most of the poets of the golden age belonged at various times to one literary circle or another.[31] A group of poets might gather around a journal or almanac, but partisan ideological or social criteria were rarely involved in editorial policy. The poets of the golden age were generally amateurs, although some collected handsome honoraria for their works. In the 1820s a slim volume of lyric poems or a brief verse epic could sell well enough to bring the publisher a profit and the author an adequate fee. Pushkin, however, was the only poet to derive a substantial income from his poetic works.

The poetry of the golden age was still written to be recited before an audience of friends, many of them also poets. There existed a number of literary salons where poets and men of letters gathered for recitals and debates, like the salons of Duchess Zinaida Volkonsky (1792–1862) in Moscow in the 1820s, frequented by Pushkin, Baratynsky, Mickiewicz, Venevitinov, and others,[32] and of Karolina Pavlova, herself a fine poet, in the late 1830s and 1840s.

Zhukovsky

Vasily Andreevich Zhukovsky (1783–1852) is the hero of yet another incredible success story. Born the illegitimate son of a prosperous landowner and a Turkish slave woman brought back to Russia as a war prize, he got his surname and patronymic from a poor hanger-on of his natural father, who had his son educated at a Moscow boarding school. Zhukovsky had the good fortune of possessing not only poetic genius but also the talent to accept gracefully whatever came to him

31. See p. 172.

32. Duchess Volkonsky left Russia for Italy in 1829. Gogol lived in her Roman villa for years. She herself was a writer and a composer.

in life and to meet his betters, equals, and inferiors with equal goodwill, restraint, and dignity. His successes were many. As a young man he became Karamzin's associate and editor of *The Herald of Europe*. Fame as a poet came to him early. His patriotic "Singer in the Camp of Russian Warriors" made him a national figure in 1812. He was considered to be Russia's leading poet until Pushkin gained that distinction. His literary reputation led to a distinguished career at court, beginning as reader to the widow of Paul I, then teaching Russian to Princess Charlotte of Prussia, consort of Grand Duke (later Tsar) Nicholas, and eventually serving as tutor to the future Tsar Alexander II. He thus had·a real influence on the course Russian history would take. Zhukovsky used his considerable credit at court selflessly to help fellow writers and the literary community at large. He was a trusted friend and adviser to Pushkin and Gogol.

Zhukovsky knew adversity as well. His natural niece, Marya Protasova, was the great love of his life. Her mother, Zhukovsky's natural half-sister, sternly vetoed any thought of marriage. Marya married a German professor of the Livonian university of Dorpat and died young, in childbirth. Late in life, while in honorable retirement in Germany, Zhukovsky married a young German woman, who soon became mentally unbalanced. He went blind in his declining years, but overcame this handicap by dictating his last and probably finest work, *Ahasuerus*, to a secretary. Fyodor Tyutchev left a moving and profound poetic appreciation of Zhukovsky the man and the poet:

In truth, he was as pure and whole
In spirit as a dove; though he did not
    despise
A serpent's wisdom, understood it well,

The spirit that moved him was purely
    columbine.

> ("To the Memory of V. A.
> Zhukovsky," 1852)

Zhukovsky was widely considered heir to Derzhavin, though the difference between his genius and Derzhavin's was recognized. Zhukovsky's triumphal and martial odes are much inferior to Derzhavin's or Lomonosov's. His "Singer in the Camp of Russian Warriors" (1812) lacks the energy of their odes. Its symbols and metaphors are the familiar ones, though somewhat worse for wear. Zhukovsky's language and ethos, however, are Karamzin's. The singer is more at ease with harp or lyre than with sword and arrow (still "arrows" rather than "bullets"), and with the civic virtues of "truthfulness, simplicity, and sincerity of manners" than with the martial ones of "valor, a warrior's adornment, firmness, and obedience," with which he credits the Russian warrior. But the versification shows effortless brilliance, and the patriotic pathos has a ring of naive sincerity.[33] Clearly, though, this genre had no poetic future, and it was uncongenial to Zhukovsky. Other efforts in the same vein, like the lengthy "Anniversary of Borodino"

33. "The Singer in the Camp of Russian Warriors" has some seven hundred lines in all, consisting of the singer's twelve-line iambic stanzas and a warriors' chorus repeating four lines at irregular intervals. It is mainly a catalog of Russian heroes to whom the singer raises his cup, starting with the tenth-centry Svyatoslav and ending with officers killed in recent battles against the invading French. The living heroes are arranged hierarchically: first the tsar, then the commander in chief followed by his generals (not in order of their rank) and some leaders of guerrilla detachments, among them the poet Davydov. The singer also finds time to toast revenge, friendship, and love, the muses, inspired poets, "the Russian God," and "true love *here*, a sweet reunion *there*."

(1839), are officious and at times pedestrian.

Zhukovsky was a court poet, too. Some of his poems, although not directly commissioned by his imperial patronesses, were still occasioned by his daily contact with them and were addressed to them. To the amazement of free spirits like Vyazemsky, Zhukovsky's court poems had none of the officiousness or even the prudent discretion of Derzhavin's "Felitsa" cycle. Zhukovsky's poetic persona remains throughout that of an independent but sympathetic friend of the family. Some of these poems are actually among his best.[34]

Like his predecessors, Zhukovsky wrote some religious poetry (for instance, "Stabat mater," 1837), but it is not very distinguished, perhaps because Zhukovsky's poetic sensibility was Goethean[35] and Neoplatonist rather than Deist or traditionally Orthodox. But Zhukovsky succeeded in giving expression to the *Weltgefühl* of German romanticism as eloquently as only Tyutchev among the Russians, and few among the Germans, could. "The Ineffable"

(written in 1819, published in 1827) speaks of those moments when the soul senses the presence of the ineffable, yet "art falls silent, powerless":

> The Holy, palpably descending from the
>   heights,
> The Creator's presence in His creation—
> What language is there for them? Yet the
>   soul soars high,
> As all infinity is compressed into a single
>   sigh
> And silence alone speaks to our
>   understanding.

The "genius of inspiration" was one of Zhukovsky's favorite poetic clichés, and nothing defines his sensibility better than the famous line, "Poesy is God in the holy dreams of this earth."[36]

The genres most congenial to Zhukovsky were the elegy and the occasional lyric, even though much of what he wrote in these genres was translated from the German, English, and French. His translation of Gray's "Elegy Written in a Country Churchyard" was his first published poem, appearing in *The Herald of Europe* in 1802. Zhukovsky used alexandrines in lieu of the original's iambic pentameter. In 1839, after a visit to the site that inspired Gray, Zhukovsky produced a more accurate translation in hexameters, a meter that created an

---

34. For example, "The Pledge Flower" (1819) was written at the suggestion of Grand Duchess Aleksandra Fyodorovna, who had found a flower (*Ländler-Gras*) that in Germany was symbolic of a pledge of undying friendship. In this poem Zhukovsky discreetly introduces his patroness's persona, letting her reminisce about her happy days in the bosom of the royal family of Prussia and have a "sweet premonition" of a glorious future in her new home. Along the way, Zhukovsky produces some marvelous lines and happy conceits. The poem is one of his most melodious.

35. Zhukovsky and other Russian poets, the Moscow wisdom lovers in particluar, eagerly pursued contacts with Goethe, and the great man responded with encouraging comments on Russian poetry, Zhukovsky's in particular. In the poem "To Goethe" (1827) Zhukovsky expresses his gratitude and admiration with quiet dignity. Zhukovsky translated the poem into German and presented it to Goethe on a visit to Weimar.

36. The line comes at the conclusion of Zhukovsky's translation of "Camões" by E. F. Münch-Bellinghausen (pen name Friedrich Halm). Zhukovsky's version (1839) adds to the philosophical content of the original, expressing the Russian poet's own view of poetry: "All that is beautiful, great, and holy on earth, / All that even my inspired imagination could only divine, / All that is ineffable to thought or word, / Assumes thine image in this hour of my death, / And, with the world leaning over the head rest of my bed, / Becomes for me faith, hope, and love. / So thou art poetry: I recognize thee, / Facing my grave, I've grasped thy meaning."

idyllic rather than elegiac mood. Zhukovsky's translation became a Russian classic. His own elegiac poems, such as "To Nina: An Epistle" (1808), addressed to Marya Protasova, are more personal and intimate than Gray's elegy.[37]

Zhukovsky's short occasional poems are mostly translations or adaptations from the German. His original poems are derivative of this tradition. In them he succeeded in creating Russian equivalents of the imagery, the emotions, and the metaphysical concepts of Goethe, Schiller, and the German romantics.[38] Echoes of Zhukovsky's lines often resound in Russian poetry from Pushkin to the twentieth century. For example, Zhukovsky's "Song" (1818) immediately calls to mind Pushkin's famous "To A. P. Kern," and it is as good an imageless poem as Pushkin's. Another reminiscence, Osip Mandelshtam's "Meganom," although close in rhythm and phraseology, shows the difference: Mandelshtam's poem is saturated with concrete images.[39] Zhukovsky's nature poems emphasize mood and vision instead of extensive descriptive detail. Their precision of detail, however, often succeeds in rendering nature romantically animate. Poems like "Evening: An Elegy" or "Spring Is Near" anticipate Tyutchev's and Fet's—who, like many others, owed much to Zhukovsky.

Zhukovsky translated ballads and epic poems by Goethe, Schiller, Ludwig Uhland, Johann Peter Hebel, Walter Scott, Robert Southey, Thomas Campbell, and Thomas Moore. He did three entirely different versions of Gottfried August Bürger's "Lenore," a ballad celebrated for the driving rhythm in which it relates a maiden's nocturnal ride with the ghost of her lover, who was killed in battle. The first version, "Lyudmila" (1808), in trochaic tetrameter and twelve-line strophes, is slightly Russified but remains close to the original. "Svetlana," (1808–12, published in 1813), also in trochaic tetrameter but in fourteen-line strophes, with a strong infusion of Russian folklore and a happy ending (Svetlana's nocturnal ride was only a dream), became Zhukovsky's most famous poem. It is not among his best: its folkloric stylization is homey but rather insipid, the plentiful local color somewhat pale. Its vigorous rhythm cannot compensate for the all too tame action. Zhukovsky dedicated "Svetlana" to Aleksandra Voeikova, née Protasova, Marya's sister, and it meets the standards of poetry for genteel young ladies—hardly the intent of "Lenore." The final version, "Lenora" (1831), is an outright translation in the original meter and shows that Zhukovsky, if he chose to, could be folksy, vigorous, and unafraid of offending gentle sensibilities. In fact, this very ability got him into trouble with the censors more than once. He had great difficulties with the publication of Walter Scott's "Eve of Saint John" (published in 1824), whose cruel pathos and wedding of a

---

37. Here are some lines from "To Nina" "My dear, don't fear the minute of thine end: / As a bearer of peace, with a ray of consolation, / I shall lean over thy deathbed / And alleviate thy last agony / With the sounds of a celestial harp."

38. Zhukovsky's versions of poems by Goethe, Schiller, Uhland, Hebel, Schelling, F.-G. Wetzel, Theodor Körner, Millevoye, Xavier de Maistre, Cottin, and others are eminently singable, and most of them have been set to music, some more than once.

39. Here it semantically and euphonically anticipates Pushkin's poem: "Minuvshikh dnei ocharovan'e, / Zachem opyat' voskreslo ty? / Kto razbudil vospominan'e, / I zamolchavshie mechty?" And a stanza that anticipates Mandelshtam's poem: "Zachem dusha v tot krai stremitsya, / Gde byli dni, kakikh uzh net? / Pustynnyi krai ne naselitsya, / Ne úzrit on minuvshikh let." In both instances a subliminal reminiscence of Zhukovsky's poem must have affected the other poet's imagination.

plot of criminal passion to a religious holiday were deemed intolerable. "The Prisoner of Chillon" (1822) is a masterful piece of translation, but Zhukovsky had to change the emphasis somewhat—from freedom to fraternal love and human suffering. Byron's introductory "Sonnet on Chillon" was omitted entirely, surely on account of its glorification of freedom.[40]

Zhukovsky's translations of German and English ballads and epic poems quickly became a part of Russian literary culture. For generations, many educated Russians knew them by heart—like Dimitry Karamazov, who declaims Schiller in Zhukovsky's translation. Zhukovsky's rendering of the *Odyssey*, done without a knowledge of Greek but with the assistance of a German classical philologist, remains unsurpassed to this day.

Zhukovsky's epic poem *Ahasuerus* (1851–52, published in 1857) was about half finished at the poet's death. Around seventeen hundred lines in blank verse are extant. Ahasuerus tells his story to Napoleon on the island of Saint Helena. It is the story of the gradual awakening of a soul, its struggle with God, and its eventual acquiescence in God's world. It begins with a "defamiliarized" account of the passion of Christ, tells with power and discretion the gruesome story of the siege and destruction of Jerusalem after Josephus Flavius, and lets Ahasuerus witness the martyrdom of early Christians. Along the way, it makes palpable the horror, desolation, and despair of a man damned to live a life not naturally his own, in a world to which he does not naturally belong. It is puzzling that *Ahasuerus* has not enjoyed the fame it deserves. It is a great romantic masterpiece and the noblest and

most profound treatment of the Ahasuerus theme, so prominent in the literature of the romantic age.

Batyushkov and Other Older Poets of the Golden Age

The life of Konstantin Nikolaevich Batyushkov (1787–1855) was indeed romantic, and so were the subjects and modes of his poetry, although his poetic style was closer to classicism. Born the son of a landowner in Vologda in northeastern Russia, he was educated at two Petersburg boarding schools, the first run by a Frenchman, the other by an Italian. He wrote his first extant poem, "Fantasy," an Ossianic meditation on the poet and his inspiration, in 1802 and began to publish regularly in 1805. He served in the army from 1807 to 1810 and again from 1813 to 1816, was wounded in battle, and saw Finland, Sweden, Germany, France, and England. In 1818 he entered the Russian diplomatic service and was stationed in Italy until 1821, when severe depression forced him to take an indefinite leave of absence. He spent the rest of his life as a mental invalid in institutions and with relatives.

Batyushkov's distinctive trait is a romantic nostalgia for the world of the Romance Mediterranean. Fluent in French and Italian, he translated and wrote essays on Petrarch, Tasso, and Ariosto, liked to quote Montaigne and Voltaire, and appeared to be entirely at home in their world. In a dialogue, "An Evening at Kantemir's," he lets the Russian satirist, who was ambassador to France, engage in a debate on the future of Russian literature with an unidentified abbé and Montesquieu (whom Kantemir actually knew). Enamored of the mellifluous grace of Italian verse, Batyushkov strove to give his own lines a smooth and easy flow. Consis-

40. Zhukovsky's interest in Byron began in 1819 when he translated Byron's "Stanzas for Music" under the title "A Song."

tent use of alliteration, assonance, and vowel modulation, along with properly placed caesuras, make Batyushkov's lines among the most melodious in the language.

Batyushkov's splendid talent was equal to the lighter as well as the melancholy genres. The verve and deft touch of his epigrams and parodies are rivaled only by Pushkin's. His "Singer in the Colloquy of Amateurs of the Russian Word" (1813) is a sparkling tour de force: the clumsy rhymesters of Shishkov's Colloquy are made fun of in what is also a sprightly parody of Zhukovsky's "Singer in the Camp of Russian Warriors," whose meter, strophic structure, and phraseology Batyushkov uses to ridicule the "warriors" for the purity of the Russian language. To his contemporaries, Batyushkov was mainly the Russian Parny, a singer of charming Anacreontic songs, idylls, and erotic elegies. Batyushkov's free versions of Tibullus (in alexandrines) are distinguished by a warm pathos and rhetorical brilliance. But he also wrote Ossianic odes and ballads, some confessional elegies, and many epistles to friends. Batyushkov's masterpiece is "The Dying Tasso" (1817), a long elegy in which Batyushkov assumes the persona of Tasso facing the triumph of ascending to the Capitol to be crowned poet laureate, and with it facing death and immortality.

Denis Davydov (1784–1839) described himself in a poem entitled "Response" (1826):

> I am not a poet; I am a partisan, a cossack.
> I've been to Pindus on occasion, but only
>   in a swoop;
>   carefree, helter-skelter,
> I've pitched my independent bivouac at
>   the Castalian spring.

Davydov gained fame twice—as "Anacreon in a dolman," and as commander of a guerril-

la detachment in the campaign of 1812 (the prototype of Denisov in Tolstoi's *War and Peace*). A brave and resourceful man of action, he reached general's rank and would have gone higher but for a reputation as a frondeur, which he earned by some early satirical poems. Davydov was an extraordinarily talented poet and prose writer. His memoirs and military writings ("An Essay in the Theory of Guerrilla Warfare," 1821) are lively and witty, written in a succinct and vigorous style.

As a poet, Davydov worked in the established genres of the elegy, Anacreontic and Horatian odes, romance, fable, epistle, and epigram, using conventional diction and imagery but in a bolder, more offhand way than his contemporaries. He gave the familiar meters a more energetic beat than anyone except Pushkin, who credited Davydov with having provided him with a manly alternative to the mellifluous Batyushkov and Zhukovsky.

The poetic persona that made Davydov famous is that of a warrior poet and lover, a reckless, boisterous hussar, "the flame of whose courage is fed by the fire of love" ("The Hussar," 1822). His missives addressed to a fellow hussar named Burtsov (a profligate notorious for his wild drinking sprees) and other poems exulting in the hard-drinking, hard-riding, daredevil life of a hussar have a certain ingenuous charm, though it may all have been only a pose. Pushkin's ballad "The Hussar," written in Davydov's manner, is wholly tongue in cheek.

Davydov's most frequently quoted poem after his death was the satirical "Contemporary Song" (1836), in which he sardonically ridicules all the things that a well-to-do provincial landowner and retired general would dislike. He also chastises contemporary liberals for their hypocrisy ("that Russian Mirabeau slapping around his old servant because of a rumpled jabot").

Fyodor Glinka (1786–1880) described his experiences fighting in the campaigns of the Napoleonic Wars in *Letters of a Russian Officer* (1815–16) and *Sketches of the Battle of Borodino* (1839). A member of the Decembrist Union of Prosperity, he also served from 1819 to 1825 as president of the Free Society of Amateurs of Russian Letters. His "Lamentation of Captive Jews," published in *The Pole Star* of 1823, was read as a political manifesto. Its concluding lines are, "Slaves who drag their chains behind them do not sing inspired songs!" Although Glinka did not take part in the Decembrist uprising, he was dismissed from military service and exiled to the far north, where he remained until 1830 and wrote his Karelian poems. By the late 1830s Glinka had joined the Slavophile camp and was concentrating on composing religious poetry.

Although Glinka is remembered mostly for a couple of ballads that became popular songs, such as the famous "Troika" (1824), he is in fact one of the few important religious and mystical poets of the nineteenth century. Glinka's *Essays in Sacred Poetry* and *Essays in Allegory and Emblematic Description in Verse and in Prose* (both 1826) are largely exercises on familiar romantic themes, in particular the theme stated in the prose piece "Poverty and Luxury": "Much as a sound elicited from a sleeping player's harp by a passing breath of wind will not disappear into a void but will seek to join the chorus of universal harmony, so the soul, upon its release, seeks out a new existence in the communal life of the universe, in the common harmony of the world." The power of imagination, the progress of the soul, cosmic visions (some of them apocalyptic), the sea as a symbol of the

soul, Platonic anamnesis—all these romantic themes appear, often as palpably as in Tyutchev and, later, in symbolist poetry.[41] In the poem "Another Life" the mystical experience of becoming a disembodied spirit ("without hands, without legs, without head"), "wiped off the face of the earth" and having "escaped the iron cage of time" to float into infinity "like a point, like a monad," is made remarkably plastic.

From these romantic positions, essentially Schellingian *Naturphilosophie* turned into poetic symbols, Glinka moved on to purely religious poetry on biblical themes, taking the Psalter and the prophets as his model. His versions of the Psalms vie with the best of his predecessors.

Late in life Glinka followed in the footsteps of Dante, Milton, Klopstock, and Zhukovsky (all of them mentioned in a preface) in creating a religious epic, *The Mystic Droplet* (1861), loosely attached to a legend according to which the evildoer crucified to the right of the Lord is saved by a drop of Mary's milk, of which he partook as a babe. The epic follows Jesus from the Holy Family's flight to Egypt through the Gospel story and to heaven and hell. Structurally, it is a sequence of separate poems, with the narrator's persona appearing from time to time to advance the story line, provide moral exegesis, and create a sense of drama. Narrative passages alternate with passages in which the voices of prophets, apostles, Satan, choruses of angels and of damned souls, and other allegorical figures are heard. The poetic quality of *The Mystic Droplet* is uneven. It has inspired verses of high lyric pathos, but pedestrian ones as well.

Although Glinka's versification is often careless (he uses blank verse more often

41. A contemporary, the poet and critic Pyotr Pletnyov (1792–1865), actually called Glinka's poetry symbolic (*simvolicheskaya*).

than most Russian poets), the depth of his thought and the wealth and variety of his imagery leave no doubt that he is a major metaphysical poet who has been badly neglected and will perhaps yet come into his own.

Ivan Kozlov (1789–1840) began to write poetry only in the 1820s, after he—almost overnight—found himself blind and without the use of his legs. He was, however, well prepared for a poet's vocation. The scion of an aristocratic family, he was brilliantly educated, well read in several European literatures (he read English literature in the original), and was on friendly terms with many men of letters. Kozlov overcame his disability splendidly: he was much admired by his peers and enjoyed a wide popularity with Russian readers, who knew about his misfortune from his poetry. It appears, however, that Kozlov was no more than an exceptionally able versifier. All his better poems are more or less close translations or imitations—for example, his famous "Evening Bells" (1827, a translation of Thomas Moore's "Those Evening Bells"), his moving "Elegy: A Free Imitation of Saint Gregory of Nazianzus" (1830), and his excellent free versions of Mickiewicz's *Crimean Sonnets* (1828). Kozlov's versions of poems by Petrarch, Tasso, Ariosto, Chénier, Byron, Burns, Walter Scott, and others are generally creditable. His own poems tend to be moving only when the poet's personal anguish and suffering come to the fore, as in "My Prayer" (1833), "Prayer" (1839), and other artless confessional poems. In Kozlov's lifetime his narrative poems, "The Blackfriar" (1824), "Duchess Nataliya Borisovna Dolgoruky" (1827), and "The Madwoman" (1830), were received favorably by critics and readers alike. Although well versified, they are vague, static, and overladen with romantic clichés. A comparison with Kozlov's

competent translation of Byron's "Bride of Abydos" shows up the lack of palpable imagery in Kozlov's own poems.

Pavel Katenin (1792–1853) was a failure in life and in his poetry, but only measured against what he might have been. His promising military career came to a halt in 1822 because his liberal views made him suspect to Tsar Alexander. He was eventually retired with the rank of major general—not bad for most people, but a bitter pill to swallow for a brilliant *grand seigneur*. As a poet, Katenin—erudite, conversant with modern European ideas, and an innovator proven right by history in his poetic instincts—was given a negative and oftentimes derisory reception by his contemporaries and failed to leave a single poem that would be anthologized for other than "historical" interest.

Katenin pioneered the romantic folk-style ballad in "Natasha," "The Murderer," and "The Wood Demon" (all 1815), the first two foreshadowing Pushkin's ballads "The Bridegroom" and "The Drowned Man," the last (even rhythmically) Nekrasov's narrative poems. Katenin's verse epic "A Poet's World" (1822) anticipates Hugo's *Légende des siècles*, presenting a poetic panorama of human history from its dawn to the Middle Ages in some six hundred lines. The poem's warm pathos and poetic invention give the reader a fresh and stirring view of familiar scenes from the Bible, Greek mythology, and ancient and medieval history. "Song about the First Battle of the Russians against the Tatars on the Kalka River, under the Leadership of Mstislav Mstislavich the Brave, Duke of Galicia" (1820), an epic poem on a subject from Russian history, is stylized to elicit associations with the folk epic and the chronicles, its meter shifting throughout from short staccato lines to flowing alexandrines and other long meters. It inevitably brings to mind Blok's "On the Field of Kulikovo."

Katenin wrote poems in a variety of other manners, including elegies, sonnets, a cantata *Sappho* (with translations of Sappho's poems inserted), and versions of passages from *The Cid* and *The Divine Comedy*. His poetic oeuvre warrants asking why Katenin was never recognized as the major poet he would seem to be from today's vantage point, if for no other reason then for his innovative approach to poetic language. Katenin's rough-and-tumble poetic language and imagery appeared coarse and unpoetic to most contemporaries, with the notable exception of Pushkin; his bold metaphors were thought absurd or ridiculous. To be sure, Pushkin met with similar criticism, but his genius swept away the detractors. Readers nowadays may dismiss Katenin for different reasons. If Boris Eichenbaum divided Russia's poets into "musical" (Zhukovsky) and "verbal" (Pushkin), then Katenin is at the farthest edge of verbal. There is not a hint of melody in his verses. His lines are metrically accurate, but his rhythms are ragged and are never foregrounded: the verbal meaning alone has to propel the poem. Poetry of this kind never gained much favor in Russia.

Pushkin

Aleksandr Sergeevich Pushkin (1799–1837) means to Russians what Shakespeare means to the English-speaking world. Beside Peter the Great, he is the only authentic Russian hero in the Carlylian sense. Pushkin's life coincided with the golden age of Russian poetry, and he was the cynosure of what came to be called the Pushkin pleiad of poets. All of them were his friends; some, like Delvig and Küchelbecker, were his schoolmates. Whether older than Pushkin, like Vyazemsky, or a little younger, like Baratynsky, they all recognized the superiority of his genius.

Pushkin's person and his works have become a part of Russia's national mythology. Exhaustively anthologized, especially in schoolbooks, he has also been an influence, reference, and point of departure for a host of major Russian poets and writers in both the nineteenth and the twentieth centuries. Pushkin is by far the most intensively researched author of Russian literature, and many talented scholars, some of them major figures in their own right (Gershenzon, Bryusov, Bely, Akhmatova), devoted years of their lives to him.

This towering position in Russian literature is not matched by Pushkin's reputation in world literature. The reasons for this are to be found both in the nature of his oeuvre and in the difference between a Russian and a non-Russian audience.

Pushkin's brief but eventful life soon became a legend. On his father's side, Pushkin came from a Muscovite family that traced its lineage to the thirteenth century. Pushkin's pride in his ancestry and his chagrin at the lack of respect accorded Russia's ancient families are amply reflected in his works. A Pushkin appears in *Boris Godunov*. The humble hero of "The Bronze Horseman" comes from a venerable family now in decline. Several of Pushkin's satirical poems, such as "My Lineage" (1830), stake the dignity of the poet's ancient nobility against the arrogance of upstart careerists.

Pushkin's mother was the granddaughter of Abram (Ibrahim) Hannibal, a black Abyssinian who served Peter the Great with distinction, reached general's rank, and was made a noble and given the estate of Mikhailovskoe near the Livonian border.

Pushkin was proud of his African ancestry, too. His unfinished story, "The Black Man of Peter the Great," features a much-idealized Hannibal.

Like other youths of his class, Pushkin was brought up by French governesses and tutors. In 1811 he was enrolled in the Lyceum of Tsarskoe Selo (near Petersburg), founded that same year, where he received an excellent liberal education and made several lifelong friends. He entered the literary world brilliantly while still a student, publishing his first poem in *The Herald of Europe* in 1814, and was an active member of the Arzamas group. After his graduation in 1817 Pushkin held a nominal position in the College of Foreign Affairs, lived a life of dissipation as a member of the capital's *jeunesse dorée,* and quickly matured as a poet. The verse epic "Ruslan and Lyudmila," published in 1820, raised him to the summit of the Russian Parnassus. That same year some subversive poems that had come to the tsar's attention earned Pushkin a transfer to the south of Russia, where he saw the Crimea, the Caucasus, Bessarabia, and the seaport of Odessa, continued his dissipated life, and launched his Byronic period as a poet. His first Byronic verse epics were a huge success. In 1824 a letter, intercepted by the censor, in which Pushkin declared himself to be an atheist led to his dismissal from the civil service and indefinite house arrest at Mikhailovskoe, where he lived the life of a country gentleman and continued to grow as a poet. (*Boris Godunov* was written there.)

In the fall of 1826 Tsar Nicholas summoned Pushkin to Moscow, granted him a complete pardon—although Pushkin freely admitted that he would have been with his Decembrist friends during the coup had he been in Petersburg—and promised that he would be the poet's only censor. As it turned out, more often than not Count Benckendorf, chief of gendarmes, substituted for the tsar, and Pushkin's connection with the court brought him more grief than advantages. Some poems in which the poet's reconciliation with the tsar found expression were resented by some of Pushkin's friends, as were his poems supporting the suppression of the Polish uprising of 1830. Pushkin's marriage in 1830 to Nataliya Goncharova, a dazzling beauty, compounded his problems. In order to secure the beauteous Nataliya's presence at his court, Nicholas made Pushkin a *Kammerjunker* (junior chamberlain), an honor to which the poet took exception. Pushkin's literary work gave him a handsome income, and he owned an estate of four hundred "souls," but he lived—and gambled—beyond his means and soon found himself heavily in debt. After 1830 many considered him passé, the leader of a literary aristocracy out of touch with the times.

In the 1830s Pushkin wrote less poetry and concentrated on his prose fiction, historical research (leading to his "History of Pugachov," 1834) and his journalism. In 1836 he received permission to start his own journal, *The Contemporary*, an enterprise that he pursued vigorously. On January 27, 1837, Pushkin was mortally wounded in a duel with Baron Georges D'Anthès, a French nobleman in the Russian service who had made advances to Nataliya. He died two days later. Pushkin was a man of exuberant sanguinic temperament, considerable physical as well as moral courage, and superb intelligence. He was a devoted friend, but reckless at times and impatient with slower minds than his own.

Pushkin was an eminent dramatist, prose writer, and critic, but he is first and foremost

Russia's greatest poet. I believe that his genius is served best if his prose is dealt with separately.[42] His dramatic works, all of which are in verse, will be discussed twice, as dramatic poems in this section, and as plays.[43]

Pushkin's poetical works are commonly divided into three periods: his early Lyceum verse, presented by a conventional classicistic persona; his poetry of the early 1820s, dominated by a romantic poet's persona; and the multiplicity of poetic personas and points of view in the mature period. The first period displays a variety of meters used with a casual carelessness; the second is dominated by iambic tetrameter and a strict adherence to self-imposed rules; and the third again shows more metrical variety and elasticity, but also consummate artistry. Pushkin, at least in his last two periods, was a meticulous craftsman. A poet who worked on paper rather than, like most poets, in his head, he achieved the effortless grace of his verses by rewriting and polishing them interminably. Generations of scholars, starting with Valery Bryusov, have shown how every line of Pushkin's mature verse is crafted rhythmically and euphonically through intricate patterns of alliteration, assonance, and vowel modulation, and how these patterns (his rhymes in particular) support its semantic and emotive content. Pushkin can be melodious like Zhukovsky, but only when this fits the poem's subject. Pushkin's delightfully witty observations on the theory and practice of versification in "The Little House in Kolomna" (1830) demonstrate his keen interest in the technical side of the poet's craft. An eminently conscious craftsman, Pushkin was not the brilliant improviser he describes in "Egyptian

Nights." He was a thoughtful, aesthetically and psychologically sophisticated artist who realized early on that any subject, no matter how mundane or lowly, may be a suitable subject of the poet's imagination.

Almost immediately after his exile to the south, Pushkin developed what has been called his protean quality to adapt his poetic style, his emotional attitude, in fact his poetic persona to his subject. Although this trait induced him to write many pieces in a classicist mode, it is in tune with the principle of romantic aesthetics according to which the relation of content and form is one of unity through dialectic give and take.

Pushkin's Lyceum verses, often delightful though derivative, include Anacreontic verse composed from the familiar motifs of roses, myrtles, doves, nightingales, frothing beakers, wreaths, and lyres, idylls and erotic verse in the manner of French rococo poets, elegies in the manner of the Roman elegists (here Batyushkov's influence is discernible), and odes in several different manners: Ossianic ("Osgar," 1814), Derzhavinian ("Reminiscences in Tsarskoe Selo," 1814, with clear echoes of Derzhavin's "Waterfall"; Pushkin recited this poem at a public examination in Derzhavin's presence), triumphal ("On the Return of Our Sovereign Emperor from Paris in the Year 1815," rather imitative of Zhukovsky), and philosophical ("Unbelief," 1817, understandably gauche, since it was delivered as part of a final examination in Russian literature). Among the many epistles to friends and other poets the most interesting is "To my Aristarch" (Pushkin's teacher, N. F. Koshansky, 1815), a charming self-portrait, which characterizes the young poet as a follower of the light muse of Parny and Gresset but also shows him as very much a professional, keenly aware that he still has a lot to learn technically.

42. See pp. 239–243.
43. See pp. 280–282.

In the Petersburg years before his exile Pushkin produced more poetry in the same vein—some of it unabashedly erotic or outright obscene—the verse epic "Ruslan and Lyudmila," and a number of poems in a civic vein which earned him his "transfer" to the south. The ode "Freedom" (1817) rather luridly celebrates tyrannicide, "To Chaadaev" (1818) espouses republican ideals, and "The Village" (1819) openly attacks serfdom. These and other civic poems are undistinguished artistically, but their pathos is genuine.

"Ruslan and Lyudmila," in iambic tetrameter in six cantos, is not generally considered a romantic work, and it does indeed have traits that point back to the eighteenth century. Its *sujet* owes some details to the Russian chapbooks, and Vladimir of Kiev appears as Lyudmila's father, but other than that "Ruslan and Lyudmila" has little to do with Russian folk poetry. Its plot and manner are those of Ariosto's *Orlando furioso* or Wieland's *Oberon*. Lyudmila is abducted from her wedding couch by a wicked sorcerer and after many adventures is saved by Ruslan, the bridegroom. The tone and details of the narrative are playfully ironic. Its occasional lubricity smacks of the eighteenth century. Much of the suspense is created by threats to the heroine's virginity, each parried by another miracle. "Ruslan and Lyudmila" is poetry as an elegant, sophisticated, and enjoyable game, but it is more than that. It has genuine humor, as the characters who go through these fantastic adventures are in fact ordinary people animated by ordinary feelings. It is also an exercise in romantic irony, as the narrator keeps destroying the reader's illusion by introducing material pointedly extraneous to the story: for instance, when he likens the sorcerer's gardens first to those of Tasso's Armida, then to those of King Solomon, and finally to those of Duke Potyomkin, or when it dawns on the reader that "the wondrous genius of poesy" praised in superlatives is indeed Zhukovsky, "that Orpheus of the north," whose fairy tale in verse "The Twelve Sleeping Maidens" the narrator proceeds first to paraphrase and then to parody. "Ruslan and Lyudmila" is a romantic poem—if E.T.A. Hoffmann's "Golden Pot" is a romantic tale.

Even after 1820 Pushkin refused to call himself a romantic and would say that his sensibility was classical rather than romantic. His involvement with Byron lasted only a few years, and when he looked for a poet with whom to identify, it was André Chénier to whose person and poetry he continually returned. In his large ode "André Chénier" (1825) Pushkin let his own persona merge with the French poet's. Throughout his life Pushkin continued to write some verse in the manner of eighteenth-century classicism. Some of this, though often sparkling with wit, is insignificant: album verse, epigrams, short gnomic poems (often based on a single conceit), and some anthological verse, either translated outright (via the French) or stylized. Pushkin's many epistles, mostly addressed to literary friends like Chaadaev (1821), Yazykov (1827), Delvig (1827), and Gnedich (1832) are on the whole elegant rhetorical exercises.

Pushkin wrote some of his elegiac poems in a classicist rather than a romantic vein even after his departure to the south. The elegy "To Ovid" (1821), composed near the place of Ovid's exile, is one of Pushkin's masterpieces. It paraphrases highlights of Ovid's *Tristia* and juxtaposes them to Pushkin's own, much happier experience. "A robust Slav, I shed no tears, but understand yours," he says, and proceeds to establish a cordial bond between himself and the revered Roman poet. Later elegiac pieces, such as Pushkin's poems occasioned by

Lyceum reunions, are conventionally classicist in their rhetoric and sensibility.

The mature Pushkin continued to cultivate the ode, the classicist genre par excellence, and some of his odes are in the spirit of Derzhavin and other eighteenth-century poets. "To a Magnate" (1830) was greeted by a rather mean parody in Polevoi's *Moscow Telegraph*, which made fun of Pushkin's alleged fawning on the high and the mighty. Pushkin's patriotic odes, such as "The Anniversary of Borodino" (1831) or "Before a Sacred Grave" (1831), resemble Derzhavin's in their lofty solemnity, Horatian imagery (sword, wreath, bloody banner, shadow of the dead hero, Nemesis), and archaizing language.

Among Pushkin's verse epics several are closer to a classicist than to a romantic sensibility. "The Gabrieliad" (1821), a rather insipid, blasphemous and lascivious persiflage of the Annunciation in the manner of Voltaire caused the young poet some unpleasantness. "Count Nulin," dashed off in two days in 1825, is a mildly naughty parodic treatment of the Tarquin-Lucretia theme. It raised a storm of critical indignation, a sign that Pushkin's sensibility was already behind the times: a new, bourgeois sense of propriety was emerging. Although Pushkin did not take the attacks on "Count Nulin" seriously, he was genuinely chagrined at the negative critical reaction to "Poltava" (1828, published in 1829), his only attempt at a heroic epic. Nadezhdin and Belinsky, among others, felt that the heroic epic was an anachronism as a genre and that "Poltava" was an ill-conceived work. They had a point. "Poltava" not altogether successfully combines two themes, loosely connected by the battle of Poltava, in which Peter the Great defeated Charles XII of Sweden and his Ukrainian cohorts under Hetman Mazeppa, known in

the West through Byron's poem "Mazeppa," where the hero is a youth. Mazeppa, an old man now, plays a dual role in Pushkin's epic. He is a traitor to Russia (to Pushkin, the Ukraine is a Russian province), and he is the villain in a melodramatic plot of criminal love and vengeance. The battle scenes recall Derzhavin's, as do their patriotic ardor and hero worship of Peter the Great. The love plot is gothic: seventy-year old Mazeppa's victim is a trusting maiden madly in love with him. Her father tries to save her from his clutches and is beheaded at Mazeppa's behest, and the maiden goes out of her mind. On the whole, the many magnificent verses found in "Poltava" do not make up for its structural and psychological deficiencies.

"Angelo" (1833, published in 1834), a seemingly artless paraphrase in alexandrines of Shakespeare's *Measure for Measure*, was disparaged by the same critics who had showered Pushkin with praise for his earlier Byronic poems. It is classically spare, almost austere, stylized to convey the mode of an old Italian novella or chronicle. It is thus both classical and romantic.

Pushkin's romantic period began on his way south, when friends introduced him to Byron's poetry, which he would later read in the original. The elegy "The light of day is now extinct," written on board ship on the Black Sea in August 1820, has traits that recur in many later poems: it addresses the elements, welcomes the winds that carry the poet away from his lost youth into the unknown, and expresses remorse at "wanton errors of the past." Some of Pushkin's most personal confessional poems—"Recollection," "Premonition," and "Life, Vain and Accidental Gift" (all 1828)—express remorse at a misspent past, anxiety about the present, and a sense of aimlessness for the future. One, the famous "Elegy" (1830), adds a note of hope: inspiration will yet come, and perhaps even love will smile on the poet "amidst the travails and grief of future's stormy seas."

In such poems as "When I stroll along the noisy streets" (1829), "May the Lord not let me lose my mind" (1833), or "I've visited anew that spot on earth" (1835) Pushkin takes stock both of his own life and of the human condition, laying bare his sensitive, impressionable, and vulnerable soul. The pose of Byronic defiance, so prominent in the early verse epics, is absent from Pushkin's elegiac poetry, which also lacks the mystical strains found in Zhukovsky and other contemporaries.

The onset of Pushkin's romantic period affected the ethos of his love lyrics. Like his elegies, they became personal and immediate, eschewing conventional metaphors and imagery. It is no accident that the poem chosen by Formalist critics as the quintessential "imageless" poem is a love poem by Pushkin, "I Loved You" (1829). This and other of his love poems describe disenchantment and separation, "emotion recollected in tranquillity." There are exceptions. Pushkin's most famous poem, "To A. P. Kern" (1825), addressed and actually presented to the object of the poet's enamoration, speaks of emotion rekindled. It, too, is virtually imageless. Its effect is rhetorical and musical, not emotional. "Night" (1823) is perhaps the only poem by Pushkin which speaks of love's happiness.

No subject was more congenial to the romantic ode than Napoleon. In Pushkin's earlier, classicist poetry Napoleon had been a villain, first as Russia's enemy, then as a traitor to the Revolution. Now he was a hero and at the news of Napoleon's death Pushkin in an ode, "Napoleon" (1821), shared the feelings of a generation of romantic poets who lamented the passing of a heroic age. The death of Byron and Pushkin's departure from Odessa occasioned another great romantic ode, "To the Sea" (1824). In saying farewell to the "free element," the poet regrets that he did not follow the call of the sea, fixes his eye on the desolate rock on which Napoleon died, then asks the sea to stir up a storm to celebrate the memory of its bard, Byron, who himself was like the sea, powerful, deep, and somber.

In the late 1820s Pushkin wrote several poems known collectively as his cycle on the poet. All speak of the poet's dual nature. As a man, he may be "Among the worthless children of this world / Perhaps the most worthless of all ("The Poet"). He refuses to be "useful" or to "teach the people bold lessons" ("Poet and Crowd"). But as a poet he is inspired by the deity, ignores the unhallowed crowd, and is "his own supreme judge" ("To a Poet"). None of the poems of this cycle, except perhaps "Arion," is among Pushkin's best. His "Exegi monumentum" (1836) does not compare favorably with Derzhavin's. Yet the cycle on the poet does place Pushkin among the romantics.

Pushkin's stay in the south and a journey to the Caucasus in 1829 produced many romantic seascape and landscape poems. The seascape repeatedly features the figure of a woman outlined against a stormy sea ("The Nereid," 1820; "The nasty day has died," 1824; "Storm," 1825). Pushkin's landscapes of the Crimea ("Who knows the land," 1821) and the Caucasus ("Caucasus" and "Avalanche," 1829) are equally romantic but also are well focussed, precise, and animated. As a landscape painter, however, Pushkin is at his best in his fall and winter renderings of the Russian north. "Winter Evening" (1825), "Winter, what shall we do in the country?" and "Winter Morning" (written on two consecutive days in November 1829) are beautiful winter idylls, as are some scenes in *Eugene Onegin*. They may be compared to Dutch genre paintings. Similarly, "Fall" (1833) is an idyllic yet realistic image of autumn in Russia.

Pushkin wrote a great deal of stylized poetry on exotic themes: free versions of suras from the Koran, Spanish romances, Persian love poems in the manner of Hafiz, a "satirical poem by the janissary Amin-Oglu" ("The giaours are praising Stambul now," 1830), gypsy songs, and even a lenten prayer by Ephraim Syrus, "Hermit Fathers and Virtuous Women" (1836). Many of these stylized pieces are poetic gems.

Pushkin was interested in Russian folklore, recorded some folktales and folk songs, and composed some poems in the manner of the Russian folk song, such as "Tale about a She-Bear" (1830), which is in authentic bylina verse. The plots of Pushkin's "folktales in verse" are taken mostly from foreign sources: "The Bridegroom" (1825) and "Tale of the Fisherman and the Fish" (1833) from the brothers Grimm, "The Golden Cockerel" (1834) from Washington Irving's *Alhambra*, the "Tale of Tsar Saltan" (1831) from the chapbook *Bova Korolevich*. Only the "Tale about the Priest and Balda, His Hired Hand" (1830), featuring a theme also found in the brothers Grimm, is composed in authentic Russian folk verse (*rayoshnik*); the others are mostly in a lively trochaic tetrameter, and "The Bridegroom" is in the Chevy Chase strophe. Miraculously, the tales are not only delightful but also unmistakably Russian. They were almost immediately absorbed by Russian folklore.

Pushkin's "Songs of the Western Slavs" (1834, published 1835), sixteen in all, are styled to resemble the Serbian folk epic, including a reasonable imitation of its meter. Eleven of these are paraphrases of texts from Prosper Mérimée's collection of Illyric poetry, *La Guzla* (1827), two are versions of authentic Serbian songs collected by Vuk

Karadžić, and three are Pushkin's own compositions based on Serbian themes. They are all ingeniously stylized but do not bear the peculiar imprint of Pushkin's serene genius which animates his Russian tales.

Pushkin's ballads and short narrative poems are characterized by a driving rhythm always synchronized with the action, aptly chosen imagery, artfully stylized language, and economy and wit. They range far and wide in time and space—from classical antiquity to the Russian and European Middle Ages, Peter the Great, and contemporary Russia, as well as all over the map of Europe, Russia, and the Orient. Among the most famous are the "Song of Oleg the Wise" (1822), which retells a legend from the Primary Chronicle; "Cleopatra" (1824), eventually incorporated into the unfinished short story "Egyptian Nights"; "The Drowned Man" (1828), a Russian folk tradition; "The Upas Tree" (1828), one of Pushkin's great poems (it has a king send a slave to fetch him the deadly poison of the upas tree for his death-dealing arrows);[44] "The Poor Knight" (1829), a ballad about a knight who falls in love with the Holy Virgin (it plays a role in Dostoevsky's novel *The Idiot*);[45] "The Hussar" (1833), a sprightly ride to a Ukrainian witches' sabbath; and "The Feast of Peter the Great" (1835), Pushkin's futile hint to Nicholas I to pardon the Decembrists: the tsar celebrates a pardon he has granted to those guilty before him and makes peace with his enemies.

Pushkin continued to write risky political verse even after his early rebellious poems

44. The manuscript of this poem has an epigraph from Coleridge's poem "Remorse": "It is a poison-tree that pierced to the inmost / Weeps only tears of poison."

45. In this instance the censor did Pushkin a favor by deleting the last three stanzas, which trivialize the tragic theme of the poem.

had brought him exile. "The Dagger" (1821) is the weapon of the freedom fighter. The collapse of the revolutionary movement in Spain caused him to write the embittered "Sower of Freedom in a Desert" (1823), with the epigraph, "A sower went forth to sow," ironically pointing to the biblical parable. Pushkin sent the poem to his friend A. I. Turgenev as "an imitation of that fable by the moderate democrat Jesus Christ." After the failure of the Decembrist coup, Pushkin, torn between loyalty to his exiled friends and to the tsar, wrote poems expressing conflicting sentiments. The noble "In the Depth of Siberian Mines" (1827) reached the Decembrists in Siberia and elicited a warm poetic response from the Decembrist poet Aleksandr Odoevsky (1802–39). Yet in 1826 Pushkin addressed the tsar in a poem, "Stanzas," published in 1828, in which he wished Nicholas success and likened the start of his reign to Peter the Great's. He then had to defend himself in "Stanzas" (1828), saying, "No, I am no flatterer when I give my free praise to the tsar." Pushkin hailed the suppression of the Polish uprising of 1830 and in a political ode, "To the Slanderers of Russia" (1831), sanctimoniously asked the West to stay out of this argument between two fraternal Slavic nations. Simultaneously, his former friend Mickiewicz, now living in the West, was publishing his anti-Russian political verse. Pushkin responded with "He Lived among Us" (1834), an unpleasantly unctious admonition to the Polish poet to return to his former peaceful and gentle strains. We may not like the message of these pieces, but they are unquestionably masterful.

Pushkin wrote a great deal of poetry having political, moral, and philosophical content. Each piece not only is eloquent but also rings sincere. Yet as a body, these poems hardly allow us to extract a consistent political or moral philosophy. It would seem that Pushkin responded to a given idea, emotion, or insight with the instinct of an artist, perceived it as a theme, and gave it objective expression without projecting onto it any preconceived idea.

Pushkin's Byronic verse epics, "The Prisoner of the Caucasus" (1820–21), "The Fountain of Bakhchisarai (1821–23, published as a separate booklet, with an essay by Vyazemsky, in 1824), and "The Gypsies" (1824, published as a separate booklet in 1827) were huge successes at their appearance. Pushkin himself soon realized that the first two were immature youthful efforts. He was of two minds about "The Gypsies." All three poems have fine descriptive and lyric passages and show Pushkin's iambic tetrameter in its full irresistible power. But their character delineation and plot development are those of simple romantic melodrama. "The Prisoner of the Caucasus" is about a young Russian officer afflicted with Byronic ennui and a Circassian maiden who falls in love with the captive (echoes of Chateaubriand's *Atala*—but Pushkin's prisoner does not love her) and is drowned as he swims to freedom. "The Fountain of Bakhchisarai" tells a somber story of harem intrigue and passion. In "The Gypsies," Aleko, the hero, has joined a band of roving gypsies to flee civilization. But when Zemfira, the gypsy maiden he loves, deserts him for another lover, he murders both. "The Gypsies," a work with many beautiful passages, has been accorded various ingenious interpretations, for example, as a tragic conflict between a desire for anarchic freedom and the inexorable law of fate, which Aleko, civilized man, refuses to accept. Zemfira, like Carmen in Mérimée's novella, accepts it.

"The Little House in Kolomna" (1830) starts with the words "I'm tired of iambic tetrameter." Its octaves are in iambic pentameter. The whole poem of forty octaves is really a tongue-in-cheek literary causerie with a silly plot appended, somewhat like Byron's "Beppo."

"The Bronze Horseman," written in 1833, appeared posthumously in 1837, with some changes made by Zhukovsky: Nicholas I had quibbled about some passages he felt were injurious to his imperial majesty. The poem is a variant of a novel in verse that Pushkin planned and actually started. Like so many great works of art, "The Bronze Horseman" is a paradox. There is a huge disparity between the content of the poem and its plot. The content is the tragic and glorious history of modern Russia; the plot concerns a government clerk whose fiancée is drowned in the disastrous Petersburg flood of 1824. The shock of her death drives him out of his mind. One day, as the poor madman walks by Falconet's equestrian statue of Peter the Great, he has a flash of lucidity and shakes his fist at the tsar whose reckless action— building the new capital on a swamp— caused his misery. The bronze horseman comes to life, and when Evgeny turns and runs, gallops after him in pursuit. Evgeny will never raise his fist at the bronze horseman again.

Pushkin took pains to treat the two levels of the poem with equal sympathy: it is both a paean to the city of Peter, its might, splendor, and martial glory, and a description of the capital's low life: a garret room, a humble cottage in the suburbs, an unpainted fence, and a willow tree. These two levels are carried through in the imagery, the language, the rhythm, and even in the grammar of the poem.[46] The symbolic meaning of

"The Bronze Horseman" has been debated since its appearance. Belinsky saw Evgeny as the regrettable individual victim of the inevitable course of history, symbolized by the galloping horseman. Merezhkovsky perceived the conflict in the poem as symbolic of the struggle between a pagan and a Christian ethos: meek Evgeny stands up to an arrogant pagan idol (the bronze horseman is referred to as "the idol on his bronzen steed"). Soviet critics have interpreted Evgeny's fist shaking as a prophetic gesture pointing toward the revolt of the masses against the monarchy. But Peter the Great was also a revolutionary "who turned the wheel of the ship of state around," and Evgeny is the impoverished scion of an ancient Russian family. Finally, the poem is about an encounter of man (Evgeny) and demon (the bronze horseman), a favorite theme of romantic poetry.

"The Bronze Horseman" is a work defying classification. Some of its passages continue the tradition of the classicist triumphal ode; the ghostly ride of the bronze horseman through the moonlit streets of his city is romantic; and much of Evgeny's story is pure realism. The poem quickly acquired a life of its own in the consciousness of educated Russians. Variations on the theme of the little man shaking his fist at the giant tsar began to appear in Russian literature, as did the image of the tsar "who made Russia rear up at the edge of an abyss."

Eugene Onegin (1823–30) accompanied Pushkin through much of his adult life. He observed that it changed with him as he grew to full maturity as a poet. Successive chapters of the novel appeared before its

---

46. The verbs in the poem that refer to Peter the Great tend to be in the imperfective aspect, a verbal category in Russian indicating perma-nence, whereas the verbs that refer to Evgeny are in the perfective aspect, suggesting a transitory existence, as Roman Jakobson has pointed out.

completion. Many fine strophes (including a whole set of connected stanzas forming "Onegin's Travels," intended for the seventh chapter but eventually becoming an appended ninth chapter) were left out of the definitive version. There is a large body of variants to the text (the manuscripts are extant). Scholars are still debating the question of whether some manuscript pages written in code—they contain politically dangerous material—were part of a projected tenth chapter.

The eight chapters of *Eugene Onegin* are composed in fourteen-line stanzas with a regular rhyme scheme—the so-called Onegin strophe, rather close to sonnet form. Tatyana's letter in chapter 3, a short song of peasant girls in the same chapter, and Onegin's letter in chapter 8 are the only exceptions to this rule. Each stanza is semantically and structurally a complete unit, with the concluding masculine-rhyme couplet always bringing a surprise, a sententious or gnomic statement, or an elegant conceit. The result is a paradox: a pointedly unstructured narrative is pressed into a pointedly structured form.

Eugene Onegin, introduced as Pushkin's good friend, is a Petersbug dandy who at twenty-six has grown tired of a dissipated life and amatory conquests and has retired to his country estate. His neighbor, a romantic poet named Vladimir Lensky, is in love with Olga Larin, the pretty daughter of another neighbor. After a single encounter Olga's sister Tatyana, a quiet sort who has read too many romantic novels, falls in love with Onegin and writes him a torrid love letter. Onegin rebuffs her tactfully, causing her to love him even more. Annoyed, he makes a show of flirting with Olga at Tatyana's name-day party. Lensky challenges Onegin to a duel and is killed. Olga, quickly consoled, is soon married to an officer in the uhlans. Tatyana, too, is married off, to an important general. The narrative resumes some years later when Onegin meets Tatyana at a ball in Petersburg. She has changed from naive country girl to brilliant socialite. It is Onegin's turn to fall in love and write her an anguished letter. Now it is he who is rebuffed, and here the novel ends.

The hourglass pattern of the plot is obscured by the presence of an intrusive narrator, clearly Pushkin himself, and by incessant digressions and intermezzi of a lyric, literary, critical, satirical, anecdotal, or personal nature. As Pisarev was to observe, the story of Onegin and Tatyana (not to speak of Lensky, a *bad* romantic poet, as his verses written on the eve of the duel show) was hardly worthy of a great modern novel. Still, in spite of its brevity, *Eugene Onegin* is a genuine modern novel containing visible elements of several of its subgenres. It is a novel of manners (Belinsky called it an encyclopedia of Russian life), though only of the upper class, a family novel, a love novel, a bildungs- and desillusionsroman, a literary and society roman à clef, and above all an autobiographical novel. It is also a mirror of the poet's search for an identity, a world order, and a mythology. The outcome of this search makes *Eugene Onegin* the saddest of all Russian novels. The world of upper-class Russia, the only one to which the reader is introduced, is empty, trivial, and mindless. It is also heartless. Onegin kills Lensky, a boy of seventeen, only because avoiding a duel would have required an effort of the heart and mind. Tatyana was made, by Dostoevsky and many others, into a mythologized ideal of Russian feminine virtue. Again, Pisarev was right when he debunked this notion. Tatyana's love letter (the author's "translation" of her French original) is touching, but also a potpourri of silly clichés. Her much-admired refusal to become Onegin's mistress, although she still loves him, is the rational reaction of a wiser society matron: there is nothing noble about it.

The exhilarating and inspiring quality of *Eugene Onegin* comes from the triumph that art celebrates over reality without ever denying or suspending it. Pushkin sketches his career as a poet at the beginning of chapter 8. He presents it as encounters with several incarnations of his muse and at the end of the fifth stanza lets her appear as "a provincial miss with pensive sadness in her eyes and a French novel in her hands." At one point in the novel, Vyazemsky, Pushkin's good friend, takes pity on Tatyana, a wallflower at a Moscow ball, and says a few kind words to her. This is characteristic of the romantic irony that permeates the novel: Tatyana, utterly convincing and "real" though she may appear throughout, is still explicitly identified as a figment of the poet's imagination. The poet's magic—as well as his wisdom, understanding, and wit—transform a sad reality into a thing of beauty.

Pushkin never leaves his characters alone with his readers. He makes the readers his confidants, engages them in light banter or shares his worldly wisdom with them. He incorporates a large number of literary titles and figures, anecdotes, quotes, and allusions into his text, but also a number of living people, some mentioned by name (Chaadaev, Yazykov, Delvig, and Vyazemsky, for example), others recognizable according to the reader's familiarity with Petersburg society and the literary world. All of this and the many other elements of which the novel is composed enter into a synthesis of a way of life, a fascinating yet very human personality—Pushkin's own—and consummate art.

None of Pushkin's dramatic works, all of them in blank verse, were ever successful on the stage. Only operatic versions of his plays, like Musorgsky's *Boris Godunov*, have earned permanent places in the repertory. *Boris Godunov*, a romantic drama fashioned after Shakespeare's historical plays, is a remarkable play and will be discussed in the section on drama. It has some scenes that are great poetry in their own right—the monologue of the chronicler Pimen, for example.

Pushkin's "little tragedies," by consensus the pinnacle of his artistry, were inspired by Barry Cornwall's "dramatic scenes." All four have a carefully developed European setting and, though conceived and started at different times, were finished within a few days in the fall of 1830. Each has the length of a one-act play.

The Covetous Knight was published in *The Contemporary* in 1836. The subtitle, *Scenes from Shenstone's Tragicomedy "The Covetous Knight,"* was a mystification, probably devised to defuse the suspicion that the father-son clash in the play reflected the poet's own stormy relationship with his father. The old knight is a usurer with an idea. He fancies that the power of his hoarded gold makes him God-like. In a great monologue, he boasts that it will buy him labor, loyalty, virtue, beauty, talent, and of course crime. His idea has a flaw—death, anticipated even in the monologue, which ends in the knight's wish to return after death as a ghost to guard his treasure.

Mozart and Salieri was performed in Pushkin's lifetime, in 1832. Its plot is based on the rumor that Salieri poisoned his rival, Mozart. Pushkin's Salieri pretends to be in revolt against the injustice that makes the childlike and frivolous Mozart a great genius, whose divine compositions reduce to naught a dedicated craftsman's labors. He poisons Mozart to restore justice. His flaw is that ordinary base envy was the real motive of his action.

The Stone Guest, published posthumously, is a version of the Don Juan theme. Pushkin's hero is the romantic Don Juan of Hoffmann's tale: superior, conquering, full of joie de vivre, and a poet. He, too, has a flaw. By feeling and acting superior to "ordinary" people, he has placed himself outside society. Like a thief, he must wait for nightfall to enter Madrid. When he kills his last victim—in a fair fight, of course—he must dump his body on the crossroads, like a common brigand. The knight commander whom he killed earlier and whose widow he now seduces was a small and puny man, but brave and righteous. The little commander's statue defeats Don Juan's arrogance.

The Feast during the Plague, published in 1831, is a translation of a scene from John Wilson's play *The City of the Plague*. Pushkin inserted his own "Hymn to the Plague," in which the master of revels celebrates the fascinating appeal of death and destruction. The master, like the heroes of the other little tragedies, is defeated: his is the bravado of despair, for he is mad with grief, having just lost his young wife.

Thus, each of the little tragedies presents a different version of human hubris. The old baron arrogates God's power, and Salieri arrogates God's justice; Don Juan defies morality, and the master of revels defies death. They are all defeated. In each case the conflict is a tragic one, since the loser's idea, though ill-conceived, is deeply rooted in the human condition.

In the 1820s Pushkin was a target of all the reactions, positive and negative, that were accorded the new literary trends he represented. In the 1830s he had to hear that he had fallen behind the times. Yet he had also attained the status of Russia's lead-ing poet, which he was never to lose. After his death, his image acquired a life of its own.

In the 1850s and 1860s Pushkin's image underwent several metamorphoses. Apollon Grigoryev resuscitated Gogol's idea that Pushkin was Russia's national poet and developed it to mean that in Pushkin the Russian national spirit had found its fullest incarnation and its direction toward the future. Aleksandr Druzhinin and Boris Almazov created the image of Pushkin the Olympian, the pure artist, the serene beauty and harmony of whose poetry stood above temporal and mundane concerns. To a generation of radicals of the 1850s and 1860s, such as Dobrolyubov and Pisarev, Pushkin was the poet of "little feet" (Russian *nozhki*, an allusion to several passages in his poetry addressed to a beautiful woman's feet), the frivolous bard of an aristocratic life of leisure. Dostoevsky's "Discourse on Pushkin" (1880) once and for all fixed the image created by Gogol and developed by Grigoryev: Pushkin was a perfect and prophetic expression of the Russian national spirit; he had anticipated not only the alienation of the westernized upper class, but also its redemption; Aleko of "The Gypsies" was the first symbolic figure in which the tragedy of the alienated Russian wanderer had found a prophetic expression; Pushkin's universality and the facility with which he dealt with foreign themes were a beacon pointing Russia toward its mission of creating a new, regenerated synthesis of European culture. Tolstoi revived the views of the radicals of the 1860s, adding to them some moral misgivings that had been voiced by some Slavophiles earlier: when all was said and done, Pushkin was an amoral man and his poetry quite incompatible with Christian humanitarian ethics.

The twentieth century has seen Pushkin's

position as Russia's national poet solidified, with the left claiming that he was "for his time" a progressive who sympathized with the aspirations of the oppressed, and the right pointing out the ample evidence for Pushkin's conservative views.

The Golden Age, Continued

The Pushkin Pleiad

The poets discussed earlier in this chapter were at least a decade older than Pushkin and, though from a historical perspective a part of Pushkin's circle, could well be viewed independently of him. The poets to be discussed in this section belong to the Pushkin pleiad in a more narrow, even biographical sense. Their life and works were inseparably linked with Pushkin's.

Toward the end of his life Duke Pyotr Andreevich Vyazemsky (1792–1878) wrote about himself:

Poor man, he was born at the wrong time,
Untimely were his life and death,
And in the lottery of life
He drew a losing number.

Heir to a great name and a great fortune, he used neither to any advantage. He gambled away his fortune, and his liberal leanings excluded him from a career in his younger years. When he did reach high rank late in life, it gave him no satisfaction. A liberal of the 1820s and 1830s, he lived to see himself denounced as a reactionary by the radicals of the 1860s. He survived Pushkin and every other member of the pleiad but could do little to perpetuate their heritage, except through his memoirs (invaluable to scholars). Brilliantly educated, well read, sophisticated and witty though he was, his critical judgment was never profound,

was often beside the point, and was sometimes simply wrongheaded, because he assessed literature by yesterday's standards—essentially Karamzin's. He said nothing particularly revealing about Pushkin, whom he knew intimately. His positive reviews of Gogol's *Inspector General* and *Selected Passages from a Correspondence with My Friends* are to his credit only in their general tenor; they are flaccid and vague in their details. Vyazemsky considered himself a pathfinder of romanticism, but his sensibility, formed under Karamzin's tutelage, was never equal to this task, remaining preromantic.

Vyazemsky was "too clever," as Pushkin once observed in response to Vyazemsky's elegy "To a Woman Who Thinks Herself Fortunate" (1825), and too self-conscious to be a great lyric poet. His best lyric poems belong to his old age, when the somewhat glib restlessness, spleen, and ennui of his younger years had matured to tragic despondency, desolation, and anguish.

The range of a poet whose lyric persona is entirely subjective, as was Vyazemsky's, is naturally narrow. Vyazemsky was a deliberate and skillful versifier. Like Pushkin, he wrote poems on versification ("To V. A. Zhukovsky," 1819, "On Alexandrines," 1853). Since he was also prolific, he was bound to produce some good poems aside from the confessional *senilia*: nature poems (winter is his forte), landscapes and cityscapes gathered during his many travels in Russia, Europe, and Palestine, songs ("Another Troika," 1834), album verse, and many elegant epistles to friends, male and female. Vyazemsky's natural medium was the Juvenalian satire. The rage of an intelligent and honorable man at the stupidity and baseness of the world around him, which one finds in "To Sibiryakov" (1819), "Indignation" (1820), "An Epistle to M. T. Kachenovsky" (1820), and "The Russian God" (1828), is real and eloquent.

Scholars differ in their assessments of Nikolai Mikhailovich Yazykov (1803–1847). To some he was merely a shallow, though exceptionally skillful versifier. To others he was an Epicurean, facile perhaps but nonetheless the best of all Russian Anacreontic poets. Still others see him also as a serious poet, first of a libertarian, later of a religious and Slavophile orientation. Yazykov was at the center of the Russian literary world for a quarter of a century and was personally close to Pushkin and several members of his pleiad, with whom he exchanged missives and carried on an interesting correspondence. In the 1830s and 1840s he was equally close to the leading Moscow Slavophiles and on friendly terms with Gogol.

Yazykov came from the rural gentry, started several different lines of study, and spent seven years (1822–29) at the German university of Dorpat in Livonia without graduating. Later he lived at his country estate, in Moscow and abroad, where he sought a cure for his ill health. In Dorpat Yazykov indulged in all the rambunctious pleasures of the German student fraternities (he himself founded a Russian fraternity, Ruthenia) and wrote many student songs in the German manner, celebrating "wine, freedom, and joy" and easy erotic conquests. During that same period he composed elegies, epistles, ballads (several of them on Livonian themes), romances, and songs, not distinctive in content but having a driving rhythm that becomes an end in itself. Whenever Yazykov chooses a subject also treated by Pushkin, substantial similarities appear. In fact, some of the same phrases, rhymes, and rhythms show up in both independently of

one another. Yazykov's "The Poet" (1825) expresses the same ideas as Pushkin's cycle on the poet. Yazykov's elegies, like Pushkin's, reflect a mood of "emotion recollected in tranquillity" and, like Pushkin's, often include a sense of regret or even remorse.

Yazykov's love poems, many of them addressed in a properly veiled way to Aleksandra Voeikova (the sister of Marya, Zhukovsky's great love and his "Svetlana"),[47] are elegant but too obviously literary. They tend to be imageless, like some of Pushkin's famous love poems. The virtuosity of Yazykov's versification is demonstrated by his ability to versify fluently—by keeping the rhythm generated by his chosen meter in phase with the natural spoken rhythm—even the most prosaic subjects, such as a travelogue ("A Sentimental Journey to Revel," 1822) or a recipe (for ginger lemonade). Yazykov's "Prisoner of Valdai,"[48] a parody of Zhukovsky's translation of "The Prisoner of Chillon," is only mildly amusing, but it duplicates Zhukovsky's rhythms to perfection.

In the 1830s and 1840s Yazykov, while retaining his previous forms (elegy, epistle, ballad) and fluent rhythms, turned to different themes: bittersweet memories of a carefree but misspent youth, prayer ("Imitation of a Psalm," 1844), German and Alpine

47. She and her husband Aleksandr Voeikov (1779–1839), a professor of Russian literature, first in Dorpat and later in Saint Petersburg, presided over one of several literary salons which were foci of the world of letters during the golden age. Voeikov, himself a minor poet, wrote a running satirical commentary on the Russain literature of his age, which circulated widely in manuscript (1814–39).

48. Valdai, a stop on the stagecoach line from Petersburg to Moscow, was notorious for its lewd, aggressive, and thieving women, who preyed on unwary travelers.

landscapes. Now allied to the Slavophiles, Yazykov developed an active interest in Russian folklore and wrote a couple of versified fairy tales, among them "The Firebird" (1836), which is in dramatic form. These pieces contain some rather feeble stabs at romantic irony. Although the versification is sure-handed, they entirely lack the magic of Pushkin's fairy tales in verse. In the 1840s Yazykov, after his own fashion, tried to join the natural school. His satirical tale in verse "The Linden Trees" (1846) told a story of high-level corruption with such venom that it was stopped by the censor with the comment that it should not have been submitted to him in the first place; it was not allowed to appear until 1859.

All in all, Yazykov was a poet of extraordinary talent and no genius. The expressions of his ordinary mind and heart are perhaps the clearest mirror of the sensibility of the golden age reduced to the level of its average personalities.

Baron Anton Antonovich Delvig (1798–1831) is a deceptive figure, too easily dismissed as a minor poet of Pushkin's pleiad. Yet he was well respected by his contemporaries. His output was small, and much of it is conventional and derivative. But there are some real gems, too. In spite of his German name, Delvig knew no German before he entered the Lyceum of Tsarskoe Selo, and his forte as a poet was the Russian folk song. Some lines in Pushkin suggest that Delvig was particularly close to him, but actually it was Küchelbecker, not Pushkin, who gave Delvig's poetry its direction. Notorious for his indolence, Delvig nevertheless edited the most successful literary ventures of the Pushkin pleiad, the almanac *Northern Flowers* (1825–31) and *The Literary Gazette* (1830–31). A placid and sweet-tempered man, Delvig stood up to a rude

Count Benckendorf when called on the carpet for something printed in *The Literary Gazette* and eventually obtained an apology from him.

As a poet, Delvig is remembered most for his Russian songs and romances. "The Nightingale," set to music by Alabyev, is still heard in concert halls all over the world. But he also wrote some of the best sonnets in the language, in particular two sonnets of 1823 whose subject is poetry, "Inspiration" and "To N. M. Yazykov." Most of Delvig's poems are in the manner of rococo Classicism and, though pleasant, are undistinguished. But then there is that delightful idyll in excellent hexameters, "The Bathing Women," which delicately introduces the theme of Leda and the swan. It compares favorably with Baratynsky's rather heavy-handed treatment of the same theme in his "Leda." And yet it is unlikely that Delvig would still be remembered without Pushkin's fond and unforgettable lines to and about his friend.

Evgeny Abramovich Baratynsky (1800–1844) is considered the most important among the poets of the Pushkin pleiad. Pushkin, a friend of his, thought highly of his talent. Baratynsky came from the landed gentry. His youth was overshadowed by his expulsion from the Corps of Pages (for participating in a theft) and resulting service in the ranks. Only in 1825, thanks to Zhukovsky's intervention at court, was he made an officer. He soon resigned his commission, married, and spent the rest of his life as a country gentleman.

In a short poem of 1828, the key reference in Osip Mandelshtam's momentous essay "On the Interlocutor," Baratynsky said that his "gift was poor, and his voice not loud." In other poems devoted to the poet in general and to his own peculiar talent (like Pushkin, he wrote many of these), he said that his muse was hardly a beauty yet "bore an uncommon expression on her face" ("My Muse," 1829) and that for him life on earth paled "before the naked sword of thought" ("All thought and thought, poor artist of the word," 1840).

Baratynsky is a poet of the intellectual conceit. He is never melodious like Zhukovsky and rarely shows Pushkin's driving rhythms or ingenious rhymes. His imagery is pallid and his moods subdued. His many epigrams are clever, not witty. Baratynsky is more clearly a romantic poet than are most members of the pleiad. His early Finnish landscapes and seascapes ("Finland," 1820, "Storm," 1824) have an austere Ossianic air about them, and his later nature poems, even when they speak of springtime, are elegiac ("Spring, Spring!" 1834). Autumnal moods were more congenial to him. The ode "Fall" (1836–37) is among his finest poems. Baratynsky's confessional poetry is pensive, introspective, and melancholy. One of the finest Russian elegists, Baratynsky invariably speaks of departure, separation, disenchantment, regret, and resignation in such poems as "Elegy," "Dissuasion" (both 1821), "To Delia" (1822), "An Admission," "Truth" (both 1823), and "Justification" (1824). "Death" (1828) is in fact a hymn to the "luminous beauty" of death, restorer of peace and harmony, equalizer, and "solution of all riddles, liberation from all chains." (Russian *smert'*, "death," is feminine and hence may appear as gentle, soothing, and motherly.)

The romantic theme of man's paradoxic dual nature, earthbound and divine, appears often in Baratynsky's poetry. It is stated most explicitly in "The Stillborn" (1835), and with great poignancy in the poem's last lines:

> On earth
> I have revived a stillborn creature,
> Departed having never been there:[49]
> Fateful rapid flow of time!
> Your luxury is burdensome to me,
> O meaningless eternity!

Baratynsky's musings on the future of mankind are romantically anti-utopian. "The Last Death" (1827) and "The Last Poet" (1835) assert the ultimate futility of human striving. In the first, death comes to humanity through man's alienation from nature and a wholly manmade intellectual mode of being. In the second, the poet, realizing that the sea alone has remained unconquered by human rapacity, flings himself into the water off Sappho's cliff on the island of Leucas. Having lost its last poet, mankind has forever lost its capacity for communion with the cosmos.

Baratynsky's verse epics, with the exception of the early "Eda" (1824), met with a cool or hostile reception. It may be that Baratynsky's thoughtful psychological approach to the theme of love and betrayal was better suited to prose. A comparison of Baratynsky's "Eda," the sad story of the seduction and betrayal of a simple Finnish girl by a Russian officer, and Pushkin's "Prisoner of the Caucasus" reveals more psychological verity and genuine feeling in "Eda," and much more verve and rhetorical pathos in Pushkin's poem. "The Ball" (1825–28) and "The Gypsy Woman" (1829–31, 1842) also deal with the theme of male betrayal. They are both remarkable for their attention to the heroine's inner life and to details of her emotional reaction to her lover's be-

---

49. An untranslatable pun: *otbyl on bez bytiya*, "he departed without being," where *otbyl*, "departed, went away," and *bytie*, "being," are both derived from the verb *byt'*, "to be."

trayal. Baratynsky's treatment of erotic love as it appears in his verse epics and in his many love poems is less conventional, more analytical, and closer to what one finds later in realist prose fiction than that by the other poets of the Pushkin pleiad—or even by Pushkin himself.

Kondraty Ryleev (1795–1826) would be but a minor figure except for his role in the Decembrist uprising. A leader of the Northern Society (in Moscow and Petersburg) of the conspiracy against Tsar Alexander I, he was one of the five rebels hanged on July 13, 1826. His martyrdom, enhanced by the fact that he was a poet, a gentle soul, and a beloved friend of Pushkin and other poets assured him a place in the pantheon of Russian poets.

Ryleev's fame as a poet is based on his "Meditations," a collection of vignettes from Russian history, each of which is a rather naive exercise in hero worship with a transparently didactic end. Ryleev's verse epic "Voinarovsky" (1823–24, published 1825) testifies to his special love for the Ukraine (several others works of his, too, have themes from Ukrainian history). Its hero is Andrei Voinarovsky, nephew of and briefly successor to Ivan Mazeppa, hetman of the Ukraine, who cast his lot with Charles XII of Sweden against Peter I. In Ryleev's poem, an aged Voinarovsky in his Siberian wilderness exile tells a highly idealized story of his life to Professor Gerhard Friedrich Müller of the Russian Academy, who wrote a history of Siberia. The plot of "Voinarovsky" overlaps with that of Pushkin's "Poltava." Since "Poltava" does not show Pushkin at his best, some lines and scenes of Ryleev's epic can stand comparison with it. Nevertheless, even "Voinarovsky," Ryleev's best effort, is no more than a moderately skillful exercise in romantic commonplaces.

Wilhelm Küchelbecker (1797–1846) is one of the most striking, tragic, and attractive figures in all of Russian literature. The son of a German immigrant who had made a career under Tsar Paul, he came to the Lyceum of Tsarskoe Selo at fifteen, had initial difficulties with the Russian language, but at graduation was challenging Delvig for second place after Pushkin among the Lyceum's young poets. The promise of a successful career as a man of letters was dashed by Küchelbecker's active participation in the Decembrist uprising. He spent ten years in prison and subsequently was never allowed to return from exile in Siberia. He did his best work in prison and exile, however. He was a born romantic, a generous, bold, and fiery spirit, naive and inept in practical things. Beloved by his friends, especially Pushkin, he was also a favorite butt of their raillery. Küchelbecker and his works, most of them published many years after his death, were largely forgotten until Yury Tynyanov's biographical novel *Kyukhlya* (1925) restored him to his rightful place in the history of Russian literature.

Küchelbecker's early poetry is unoriginal and shows him still struggling with language and meter. A journey through Germany, France, and Italy (1820–21) produced some poems in the spirit of romantic nostalgia for the beauty of the Mediterranean south. Some poems, including songs inserted into a historical tale, *Ado* (1824), are devoted to an idyllic Estonia, where Küchelbecker's father owned an estate. Ado is an imaginary Estonian warrior hero fighting for the freedom of his people against German invaders. Küchelbecker, in spite of his German background, shared the sympathy of his Russian friends, such as Bestuzhev, for the oppressed indigenous peoples of the Baltic provinces. But most of his early poetry deals with the familiar themes of the Pushkin pleiad, and more than a few poems are addressed to its members. None of them approaches the level of artistry found in Pushkin, Baratynsky, or Yazykov.

Küchelbecker reached the heights of great poetry only in the years of his imprisonment. A cycle of sonnets devoted to religious holidays, including Nativity, Easter, and Ascension (1832), is comparable to the best in the tradition of the Catholic religious sonnet. Carried by intense religious feeling, they are nobly restrained and perfect in form. In his declining years the poet produced much moving *Erlebnislyrik*. Two sonnets in which he perceives himself as Tantalus seem to anticipate Vyacheslav Ivanov. He has learned to express himself with poignant directness, avoiding poetic commonplaces. In the poem "They will not understand my suffering" (1839), Küchelbecker deplores his fate, which refused him a tragic end and instead tortures him with the petty annoyances of day-to-day existence. The sadness and anguish of these confessional or prayerful poems are tempered by a quiet dignity and noble humility. A sonnet on the poet's loss of his eyesight (1846), in which he lets God address himself, is worthy of a Milton. The language of his late ballads is as folksy and idiomatic as Pushkin's. And when Küchelbecker enters into outright competition with Pushkin with a poem on the Lyceum's anniversary, "October 19, 1837" (1838), he achieves the subdued elegance of his recently deceased friend.

In prison and in Siberia Küchelbecker worked on several verse epics, as well as dramatic works. Here, too, he showed great progress from his first major effort, *Cassandra* (1822–23), in which Byron and Zhukovsky were his obvious mentors. His *David: An Epic Poem Taken from Holy Writ* (1826–29)—ten books and an epilogue, close to five thousand lines, mostly in ter-

cines—combines epic narrative after the First Book of Samuel with versions of the psalms of David, and digressions in which the modern poet speaks in his own name about man, poetry, faith, and God and His creation. It has rousing invocations to love, hope, and faith, and to Sophia, Divine Wisdom. A magnificent essay on man, focusing on man's dual nature ("What is man? A confluence of light and shadow!") and man's incessant struggle to find the good and overcome evil, culminates in presenting Sisyphus as the symbol of the human condition.

Ahasuerus: A Poem in Fragments (1832–46) resembles Zhukovsky's poem of the same title (apparently Zhukovsky had no knowledge of his friend's work). It, too, was to be a panorama of world history. Küchelbecker's poem is pessimistic, lacking Zhukovsky's theme of redemption. In a lofty prefatory meditation, the poet develops a grandiose cosmic vision of the mortality not only of everything under the sun, but of the sun and of the material universe itself. With immortality of the spirit his only hope, he renounces "the deceptions, the phantoms, and the darkness of this earth" and "that inane, melancholy dream, infused with lethal poison, which we in mindless blindness call happiness and glory." In a dialogue with an anonymous "Someone" (the devil), Ahasuerus timidly suggests that "He may have really been the Messiah." But Someone confidently asserts the victory of matter over spirit, and of power over the creative imagination.

These and several other verse epics, including some in the lighter vein of Pushkin's "Little House in Kolomna," were published many years after Küchelbecker's death. They never had the benefit of a contemporary audience and could be appreciated only by a select group of literary historians, particularly since the genre of the romantic verse epic was considered obsolescent even in the 1830s. Moreover, the romantic philosophy and ethos of Küchelbecker's poetry were hardly of a kind that could win an audience once the romantic period was over. The Russian symbolists might have appreciated it, but Küchelbecker was rediscovered only in the Soviet period. At any rate, his "David" and parts of his other verse epics are, by virtue of the depth and originality of their thought, the plasticity of their imagery, the nobility of their language, and the sure touch of their rhythm, the equal of anything in the genre and perhaps of greater intrinsic value than, say, Pushkin's "Gypsies."

Slavophiles, Plebeians, Epigoni

Among Pushkin's contemporaries, some poets were socially, ideologically, or aesthetically distant from the world of the Pushkin pleiad. There were the Moscow "wisdom lovers" and later Slavophiles, whose philosophic views were alien to Pushkin. An emergent strain of plebeian and populist sensibility was hostile to the ambience of the Petersburg salons. The plebeian Koltsov felt more at ease in the company of seminarians and literary raznochintsy like Belinsky than in the presence of a patronizing Zhukovsky or Pushkin. Polezhaev, another plebeian, was a revolutionary, whereas the aristocratic Decembrists were frondeurs. Karolina Pavlova's feminism would have been as alien to Pushkin as her husband's plebeian *ressentiment*. And with Benediktov an entirely new aesthetic sensibility made its appearance—still romantic, but now second-hand, epigonic.

Dmitry Vladimirovich Venevitinov (1805–27) died too early to have developed a distinct intellectual or poetic profile, but he was very talented. His poems, many of which appeared in *The Moscow*

Herald, are amazingly mature technically. They develop the familiar themes of romantic poetry with elegance and restraint. Several poems devoted to the poet ("The Poet," "A Poet and His Friend," "Epistle to R——y," the last with a stirring tribute to Shakespeare's greatness) are worthy companions of Pushkin's poems on the poet, which appeared in *The Moscow Herald* at about the same time and whose image of the poet they share. In his poem "To Pushkin" Venevitinov addresses the older poet as his master and as the equal of Byron, Chénier, and Goethe. Venevitinov, like the other wisdom lovers, revered Goethe and in this poem expresses the hope that the German sage, "his and Pushkin's master," will yet recognize Pushkin before taking leave of this world.

Venevitinov's philosophy of life is at times close to Pushkin's. The poem "Life" has the same resigned message as Pushkin's "Cart of Life." Like Pushkin, Venevitinov has his elegiac moments, with a premonition of an early death. The many instances in which Venevitinov's poetry can be compared to Pushkin's suggest that he was intellectually Pushkin's equal, but perhaps less of a poet.

The wisdom lover and later Slavophile Aleksei Khomyakov was essentially a thinker, ideologue, and publicist whose poems and plays served the expression of his ideas. He was, however, a competent versifier, and his poems, though lacking warmth of pathos, melody, or rhythmic vitality, are often strong on the side of poetic logos. Khomyakov's several early poems on the condition of the poet are artful romantic conceits rather than expressions of personal experience. "The Poet" (1827), for example, conceives of the poet as the organ that gave mute Earth the voice allowing her to join in the music of the spheres. In "A Wish" (also 1827) it is the poet's wish to merge with the phenomena of nature—a star, a cloud, or a bird.

By the 1830s Khomyakov was writing poetry in which the ideas of Slavophilism were stated in explicit or allegorical terms. His "Ode" (1831) on the Polish uprising—like Pushkin, he calls it a mutiny (*bunt*)—resembles Pushkin's "To the Slanderers of Russia" but lacks its rhetorical élan. A year later, "The Eagle" explicitly perceives all Slavdom united under the wings of the Russian eagle. In "A Fantasy" (1834) a cosmic allegory is used to deliver a political message: the West has seen its magnificent streaks of light and glorious rainbows of color but is now obscured by a dark cloud—it is time for the East to awaken. Another allegory, "The Island" (1836), is a hymn in praise of Britain, yet in the last stanza we hear that even her glory will be superseded by that of "another, humble land." The hymn "To Russia" (1839) is addressed to the country that will "embrace all nations with her love, reveal to them the mystery of freedom, and pour out the radiance of faith over them."

Khomyakov wrote a number of religious poems. In what is certainly his most moving poem, "The Laborer" (1858), he sees himself as a plowman patiently pushing his heavy plow though it is getting late and he is very tired. But he will not quit until he has broken the ground for God's seed to be sown.

Aleksei Koltsov (1809–42) is a poet whose fame and importance exceed the intrinsic value of his oeuvre. Koltsov, the son of a wealthy cattle dealer in Voronezh, who stayed in his father's business until the end of his life, came to poetry by natural inclination. He had only a little more than a year of elementary schooling and might have remained an anonymous singer of songs in the manner spread by the chapbooks, a mixture of Russian folksong and European-style romance, had he not been discovered by Nikolai Stankevich in 1830. Stankevich sent Koltsov's poem "The Ring" to *The Literary Gazette*, where it was published with a note by Stankevich. In 1831 Stankevich introduced Koltsov to Belinsky, who became a champion of Koltsov's poetry and, together with Stankevich, helped him bring out a volume of his poems in 1835. Belinsky also wrote a major essay as preface to a posthumous edition of Koltsov's poems in 1846. In his lifetime and after, Koltsov received much publicity as a poet "of the people" and as living testimony to the link that many sought to establish, for various reasons, between Russian literature and the Russian people. Koltsov was also patronized by Zhukovsky and Pushkin, among others.

Koltsov wrote many poems in the familiar manner of his romantic contemporaries. These are derivative and are distinguished only by occasional unintentional bathos. Koltsov's philosophical meditations (*dumy*) on the age-old questions of God, providence, the human condition (of the peasant and the pauper, in particular), the good life, and the poet and the crowd are sometimes moving, so long as they stay on the level of an unsophisticated consciousness ("The Mower," "A Grave," both 1836). They become strained and affected every time the romantic philosophy that Koltsov had learned from his learned friends makes an appearance ("The Realm of Thought," 1837).

Koltsov's "Russian songs" were his lasting contribution. Although literate Russian poets had composed songs in the manner of the Russian folk song before, and some of Koltsov's contempararies excelled in it (Delvig, for example), it was Koltsov who was the first to be remembered exclusively for his Russian songs and established this genre as a permanent fixture of Russian poetry. Koltsov's folksongs are for the most part composed in unrhymed tonic verse, that is, the rhythm is created by a constant number of stresses (two or three) per line. Their imagery and phraseology are the conventional ones of the folk song. The themes are unhappy love, the loss of a loved one, the seasonal cycle of the farmer, an orphan's hard lot, a young lad's swagger or remorse. Some of these poems were set to music and indeed became popular folk songs.

Koltsov was the first in a long line of so-called peasant poets, though he was not a peasant himself: in an epigram of 1830 he wrote, "I am a burgher [*meshchanin*], not a poet," echoing Ryleev's famous line, "I am not a poet, I am a citizen." Koltsov's precarious position between two cultures revealed the gulf between the cultures of the westernized upper class and the uneducated middle class, whose culture was then only beginning to turn away from the popular traditions of folk culture. It also showed that a synthesis of high culture and folk culture was hardly possible.

Aleksandr Polezhaev (1804 or 1805–38), although closer in age to the Pushkin pleiad, belonged in spirit to the generation of Belinsky and Lermontov and in many ways anticipated even the revolutionary poets of the 1860s. The illegitimate son of a wealthy landowner and a serf woman, Polezhaev received a good education and graduated from Moscow University in 1826. That same year his satirical poem "Sashka," which contained many obscenities and a few atheistic and antigovernment sorties, was brought to the attention of Tsar Nicholas, who personally ordered Polezhaev conscripted into the army. Polezhaev spent the rest of his life as a soldier in various garrison towns, on combat duty in the Caucasus, and in military prisons. He died of consumption in a military hospital a few months after having run the gauntlet for desertion and drunk and disorderly conduct and, absurdly, a few weeks after his promotion to officer's rank.

Polezhaev was very talented. His translations of Byron, Lamartine, Hugo, and other French poets are impeccable. He seems to have been particularly attracted to Hugo. The language of his poetry is remarkably modern, with many prosaisms added to the conventional poetic idiom. His rhythms, too, are Lermontovian or even Nekrasovian. The live, colloquial quality of Polezhaev's verse is not the Pushkinian colloquial Russian of the salon, but the Nekrasovian of a student debate or a journal feuilleton. Considering the circumstances of Polezhaev's short life, he left a fairly voluminous corpus of poetry, much of it published in his lifetime (surprisingly) or in a posthumous collection of 1838 (even though cut by the censor), some by Herzen and Ogaryov in London in the 1850s and 1860s, and some only after the October Revolution, when the texts of some poems were found in the archives of the secret police.

Polezhaev's work is quite varied. He does better than most of his contemporaries in the familiar romantic genres: songs and romances, elegies, and symbolic nature poems and mythological conceits like "Endymion" (1835–36) or "The Waterfall" (1830–31), where the waterfall becomes a symbol of freedom. Byronic moods were congenial to Polezhaev. They appear in exotic compositions expressing the poet's own anguished defiance in a veiled form ("Song of a Captive Iroquois," "Song of a Sinking Mariner," both 1828), and in metaphysical meditations full of Byronic desolation and despair ("A Farewell to Life," 1835, "Despair," 1835–36, "Ennui," 1837).

Polezhaev, like Byron and Lermontov, favored the longer poetic genres. His republican verse epics "The Vision of Brutus" (1832–33) and "Coriolanus" (1834) were published with significant cuts by the censor. His lengthy verse narratives describing the Caucasian campaigns in which he participated ("Erpeli," 1830, "Chir-Yurt," 1831–32) approach Lermontov's realistic view of war, as in "Valerik," or Tolstoi's, in his Caucasian sketches. They are rough and diffuse, at times cruelly naturalistic, at times still veering into the conventional rhetoric of martial glory, then again into moody introspection and even into efforts to adopt the mountaineers' view of events. Polezhaev anticipated the natural school in such satirical verse feuilletons as "Kuzma's Tale, or an Evening in Königsberg: A True Story in Verse" (1825), where Königsberg is a German beer hall. Moscow low life is described with naturalistic gusto.

Polezhaev's uniqueness rests with his lyric narrative poems relating to his years of misfortune and suffering: "The Prisoner" (1828, written in the form of an epistle to a friend), "The Hardened One," "The Condemned Man," "The Living Dead" (all 1828), "Prison" (1835–36), and "Consumption" (1837). Here Polezhaev's hatred of the existing order and his sense of utter abandonment speak directly, albeit not without some rhetorical embellishment and sentimental self-pity. Polezhaev's poetic persona is unattractive. Most of his poems are hardly things of beauty. But they often have genuine expressive power.

Karolina Pavlova (née Jaenisch, 1807–1893) was a poet of talent who never quite came into her own. The daughter of a German professor, she was a bright and splendidly educated young woman when she met the Polish poet Adam Mickiewicz in 1828. Her liaison with him ended in frustration but may have induced her to become a poet. In 1837 she married the writer Nikolai Pav-

lov. Her family had come into a substantial inheritance, and the Pavlovs ran a brilliant literary salon frequented by Vyazemsky, Baratynsky, Gogol, Turgenev, Herzen, and especially the Slavophiles Shevyryov, Pogodin, and Khomyakov. The marriage broke up in 1853. Pavlova left Russia in 1856 and spent the rest of her life in Germany.

Pavlova unfortunately split her efforts as a poet and translator among Russian, French, and German. Her translations into Russian are of high quality and much superior to her translations of Russian verse. Her original poems in German are mediocre at best; some of the French are better. Her Russian poetry bears comparison with that of the Pushkin pleiad, which she joined belatedly. Her first extant Russian poem, "The Sphinx," dates from 1831. Most of her better poetry was written in the 1840s and 1850s, when her style had become epigonic, and her political outlook—European and "world-historical," though with a strain of Slavophilism—seemed far removed from the narrow national and populist concerns of the generation that followed hers. Her historical visions in such poems as "A Conversation at Trianon" (1848) in which Count Mirabeau and Count Cagliostro discuss the course of world history, and "A Conversation at the Kremlin" (1854), a survey of Russian history from an Englishman's, a Frenchman's, and a Russian's point of view, are intelligent and eloquently phrased. The elegy "Life Calls Us" (1846), in which Pavlova reminisces about the past and about poets she has known and loved, is less cerebral and more moving.

Pavlova was rediscovered by the symbolists in the 1900s. Valery Bryusov collected and published her works in two volumes (1915). Andrei Bely in his studies on Russian versification called her a master of Russian verse, placing her alongside Zhukovsky,

Baratynsky, and Fet. Today Pavlova is an object of renewed interest on account of her feminist ethos. The poems that are a part of her short novel *A Dual Life*, though conventionally romantic, consistently present a woman's point of view and inner life. "The Quadrille" (1843–59), a set of four confessions in verse with a frame, is among the best of the genre of lyric verse narrative cultivated by Zhukovsky, Glinka, Küchelbecker, Polezhaev, and Lermontov. Each confession tells the story of a woman's debut, heartbreak, and survival in the world of upper-class society. It is the same world as that of *Eugene Onegin*, but one that is not transfigured by the golden glow of Pushkin's serene genius.

Vladimir Benediktov (1807–73), an official in the Ministry of Finance, made his debut in 1835 with a volume of poetry that made him instantly famous. Its forty poems in different meters plus eight sonnets cover a variety of topics but share a common sensibility and style. Benediktov's sensibility is that of the humble clerk of Dostoevsky's "White Nights" (1848), who in his daydreams lives an exciting life of swashbuckling adventure and erotic conquest. Lacking the gentle self-irony that gives so much charm to Dostoevsky's dreamer, Benediktov's fantasies are simply pretentious and easily slide into bathos. When Benediktov tackles the familiar romantic theme of nature as a mysterious hieroglyph whose secret is best left inviolate, he likens it to the chaste pleasures of a lover who will not remove the covers that separate him from the body of his beloved and seals the bathos by rhyming "prism" and "mysticism."

Each of Benediktov's poems is built around a more or less far-fetched yet readily intelligible and often familiar conceit which is developed slowly and methodically toward a spectacular climax. In the most famous of these poems, "My Martial Beauty," a naked sword is introduced as the warrior's mistress. Its action in battle all too explicitly evokes the act of love, and once the sword is sheathed, "it rests silent and gentle at her lover's side" (*sablya*, "sword," is feminine in Russian).

Benediktov uses a great deal of elemental imagery (sun, stars, thunderstorm, rainbow), always as a symbol of human emotions. "The Comet" (a sonnet) is a symbol of freedom in a universe of ironclad laws. A cliff high above the sea becomes a symbol of a potent spirit's superiority over the raging elements. In "Day's Complaint," Day (masculine in Russian), in love with Night (feminine), indulges in an erotic fantasy about being united with her.

Benediktov's love poems are gingerly lascivious. In "The Horsewoman" the description of a young woman riding sidesaddle on a powerful stallion carries a heavy and explicit subtext of erotic excitement. Benediktov's love poems are rich in stilted metaphors and grandiloquent phrases. Such lines as "Burn me in the living fire of your embrace" or "I am the proud enemy of the brilliant plague of vanity" are characteristic of his style.

Benediktov's versification is competent but ordinary. There is little concern for rhythm: these are poems to be read, not recited. Although Benediktov is chronologically a poet of the golden age, his whole manner is alien to it. His romanticism is derivative, second- or thirdhand. His poetry is modern in an artful, cerebral, and contrived way. Some of his poems could be by Valery Bryusov. Benediktov was destroyed by Belinsky, who recognized the artificial quality of his poetry. Other contemporaries, however, like Zhukovsky and Vyazemsky, thought highly of him. In retrospect it appears that even on his own terms, those of an artful versifier of fanciful conceits, Benediktov was only second-rate.

Lermontov

Mikhail Yuryevich Lermontov (1814–41) lost his mother when he was only three. Since she belonged to a rich and prominent family, whereas his father was an army officer and a landowner of modest means, the child was brought up by his maternal grandmother, and was surrounded and spoiled by various female relatives. He developed into a precocious, morbidly self-conscious, and highly sensitive adolescent. Already at thirteen he was writing a great deal of poetry and prose fiction. Lermontov spent two years at Moscow University without getting a degree. But when he left Moscow in 1832 to enroll in the Petersburg School of Cavalry Cadets, he was well read, particularly in Russian, French, German, and English poetry, and had translated Byron, Goethe, Heine, Mickiewicz, and others.

The poetry that Lermontov read and that often served as material for his own was different from that which defined the sensibility of the Pushkin pleiad. There is no residue of classicism in Lermontov's poetic style. Pushkin and his pleiad as well as Byron and Byronism informed much of his oeuvre. Heine and the French romantics (Chateaubriand, Hugo, de Vigny) were also a distinct presence. From his early youth, Lermontov was familiar with Thomas Moore, Walter Scott, Southey, and Wordsworth.

As a cadet, and after receiving his commission in the hussars of the guard in 1834, Lermontov led a dissolute life and wrote little serious verse. But in 1837 he responded to the death of Pushkin with "Death of a Poet," an impassioned outburst of grief and anger. The tsar saw the poem—correctly—as an impertinent attack on the society over which he presided and had Lermontov court-martialed and transferred to a regiment of the line in the Caucasus. When Lermontov was pardoned and restored to the guards a year later, he was lionized by Petersburg society and quickly came into his own as a poet. His contributions were now eagerly sought by literary journals, and he became a mainstay of Kraevsky's journal *National Annals*, founded in 1839.

In 1840 Lermontov fought a duel, over a trivial matter, with the son of the French ambassador. Neither party was hurt, but Lermontov was punished by another transfer to the Caucasus, where he distinguished himself in action. On July 15, 1841, he fought another duel, again over a trivial pretext, and was killed on the spot. He became and for a long time remained something of a cult figure. Young Russians fancied themselves as Lermontovian heroes, or as Lermontov himself. Lermontov was not an attractive person. He compensated for his ungainly appearance by playing the role of a *bretteur* and Don Juan. Turgenev's story "The Bretteur" features Lermontov minus his poetic gift. The *bretteur* Solyony in Chekhov's *Three Sisters* tries to play the role of Lermontov. Belinsky, on the basis of Lermontov's novel *A Hero of Our Time* and a personal interview with the author, saw him as a rebel without a cause, the spokesman of a generation that had repudiated the old order but had not yet found a new ideal to follow.

Lermontov has often been called Russia's second greatest poet, and his popularity bears out the designation. No other poet save Pushkin has been quoted, paraphrased, or alluded to in Russian literature as often as Lermontov.[50] Certainly more of his poems have been successfully set to music and anthologized than those of any poet except Pushkin.

Lermontov left about four hundred poems, though only about eighty from the period between 1836 and 1841. He kept rewriting his poems and consistently used verses once written as material for later works. The vast majority of his poetic output, published posthumously, was in fact raw material. Shevyryov pointed out, as early as in 1841, that even much of Lermontov's published verse was eclectic, put together from echoes, reminiscences, and outright borrowings from the poetry of the Pushkin pleiad and romantic poets of the West, Byron and Heine in particular. In short, most of Lermontov's poetry was still at the stage of pastiche, with the poet's own style still in abeyance. The number of his lyric poems that should be called great is small.

Some of Lermontov's regularly anthologized poems are simple romantic conceits involving the pathetic fallacy: "The Sail" (written in 1832, published in 1841), "Clouds" (1840), and "A Leaf" (1841) all reflect the poet's restless lonely spirit, his nostalgia, and his homelessness. Other equally popular poems express similar moods directly, for instance, "I'm bored and sad, and there's no one to shake hands with" (1840), with the punchline, "Life is such an inane and stupid joke." The brief poem "A Prayer" (1839) strikes a different note, as the wondrous effect of saying a prayer in a moment of travail is gratefully acknowledged. All these poems are catchy and appeal to the common taste, but a sophisti-

cated reader will find serious flaws and little poetic magic in them.[51]

Some other famous poems by Lermontov are skillfully composed and versified, but their effect is rhetorical rather than lyrical, as in "Borodino" (1837, published 1839), in which a veteran of Borodino relives the battle in stirring verses. Like any good romantic, Lermontov paid tribute to Napoleon. The ode "His Last Move" (1841), written on the occasion of the transfer of the emperor's remains to France, is a piece of eloquent publicism. The poem that brought Lermontov his first fame, "Death of a Poet" (1837), a bitter invective in which he accused Petersburg society of Pushkin's death, is vigorous, its pathos genuine, and it has a line that became proverbial: "An empty heart beats evenly, the gun won't tremble in his hand." But it, too, is basically a piece of spirited rhetoric.

Lermontov wrote several poems in which he expressed his disgust with the society of which he was a part. In "Meditation" (1838) he speaks of his lost generation, a generation without identity, joy, goals, or future; it will leave no trace, and the generation that will follow it will insult it with the "bitter sneer of a son defrauded of his inheritance by a bankrupt father." The key image in this poem, recurring elsewhere, is that of a sickly fruit ripe before its time and therefore ignored and useless.

Lermontov's Caucasian war poem "Valerik" (1840), written in the form of a letter to a friend, describes matter-of-factly, without any rhetorical embellishments, a skirmish between a Russian unit and attacking Circassians. The death of a Russian officer is reported in precise, unsentimental detail.

50. There are explicit echoes of Lermontov even in the poetry of such "modernists" as Pasternak, Mandelshtam, and Mayakovsky.

51. The poet Valery Pereleshin gave a demonstration of this in an analysis of Lermontov's "Clouds" (*Novoe russkoe slovo*, January 10, 1971).

Here Lermontov anticipated the manner of Tolstoi's military sketches.

Although Lermontov's poetic talent may not have been of the lyric variety, he still left some poems that are great lyric poetry from almost any viewpoint. "My Homeland" (1841) is a Pushkinian, down-to-earth panorama of the Russian lands. Its lyric point is that the poet's love of his land stirs when he thinks of the unprepossessing Russian landscape, not of Russia's military glory or historical traditions. "The Prophet" (1841), an ironic response to Pushkin's poem of the same title, is in its own right a strong statement of the loneliness of the inspired. In "A Dream" (1841) the poet sees himself "lying dead with a bullet in his chest in the plain of Daghestan" and dreaming of his beloved, who has a vision of him "lying dead with a bullet in his chest in the plain of Daghestan." The rondeau effect of this short poem is achieved naturally and with stunning effect. "I walk out alone onto the highway" (1841) is one of the great lyric poems in the language. In the course of five quatrains the poet recognizes the beauty and majesty of nature, realizes his own alienation from it, and finds the answer to his quest in a dream of love and life. The trochaic pentameter of this poem acquired a magic life of its own, as a host of later poets who happened to approach the theme of a lonely walk or torturous journey found themselves using that meter.[52]

Epic forms were more congenial to Lermontov than purely lyric ones. He wrote some romantic ballads, such as "Tamara" (1841), about a queen who has her lovers flung into the river at the foot of her castle after a night of love. He started a whole series of verse epics in his student years and finished several of them. The few that he produced in his more mature years rival Pushkin's in popularity.

"Boyar Orsha" (1835–36) is a Gothic poem set in the sixteenth century, its subject a lowborn young man's love for the boyar's daughter. *Sashka* (1835–39), a novel in verse in eleven-line strophes of iambic pentameter, resembles Polezhaev's poem of the same title. The work includes biographies of Lermontov's friend, the Decembrist poet Aleksandr Odoevsky (in a lyric address), and of Lermontov himself. Its tone is ironic, bilious, truculent, flippant, occasionally obscene, but too often callow and sophomoric. But there are some stirring stanzas, too.

"A Song about Tsar Ivan Vasilyevich, a Young Oprichnik,[53] and the Valiant Merchant Kalashnikov" (1837) was published in 1840, thanks to Zhukovsky's energetic intervention with the censor. Stylized in the manner of the bylina, it tells the story of a Moscow merchant who avenges the dishonor inflicted on his innocent wife by one of the tsar's oprichniki and manfully meets his death for it. The idea that this plot was a veiled allusion to the tragedy of Pushkin could not have been far from the readers' minds. "A Song about the Merchant Kalashnikov," as it is usually referred to, won unanimous praise for its popular (*narodnoe*) quality. The image it projects of Ivan the Terrible as a stern but just ruler is indeed that of the Russian folk epic, and many of the formulaic phrases and images of the Russian folk song are present. Nevertheless, it is still a stylized work romantic in spirit, not an authentic folk song. It uses its poetic devices much more liberally than the

---

52. It has, however, been pointed out that even this poem is to some extent derivative. It is reminiscent of Heine's "Der Tod, das ist die kühle Nacht," which Lermontov undoubtedly knew.

53. A member of the oprichnina, a special task-force under Ivan the Terrible which was feared for its brutality.

oral poet, tells more of a story faster, and is much more tightly structured.

"The Paymaster's Wife of Tambov" (1837–38), published in *The Contemporary*, an anecdote in the Onegin strophe, relates how a middle-aged paymaster lost his wife to a young uhlan in a cardgame—a trivial and decidedly unfunny piece. "The Fugitive" (c. 1838, published in 1846) is the story of a Circassian warrior who alone escapes from the battlefield when his father and brothers are all killed. He is rejected by everybody, even his mother, and is finally put out of his misery by somebody's dagger. This somber theme was more congenial to Lermontov.

"Mtsyri" (1840), which contains a number of lines from "Boyar Orsha" and other early works, is a lyric monologue in the manner of Byron's "Prisoner of Chillon." The staccato rhythm of its energetic masculine couplets of iambic tetrameter is symbolic of the narrator's condition: he is a dying man, gasping for air and in a hurry to tell his story. "Mtsyri" is about a novice monk who escapes from his monastery and spends a few glorious days of freedom in the mountain wilderness, only to discover, when he collapses in exhaustion, that he has been wandering in circles and is still within earshot of the monastery. He is dying without regret, blaming no one but himself: he was weak and was defeated. He admires the panther he slew in the forest for having looked his killer in the eye.

Exotic nature is beautifully synchronized with the moods of the narrative. The fugitive's exuberant sense of freedom is enhanced by the luxuriant growth of a densely forested mountainside and the many sounds that echo on it as he awakens the morning after his escape. As he crawls through the underbrush to get away from human habitations, he blissfully identifies with the snake

he sees slithering away from him. When a merciless sun burns down on the delirious hero, who is dying of thirst, he dreams that he is at the bottom of a cool river. "Mtsyri" is a masterpiece.

"The Demon," Lermontov's most famous work, is not. The poem is extant in several variants, the first from 1830, the last from 1841. Only fragments were published in the poet's lifetime because of censorship. The full text appeared first abroad, in 1856. "The Demon" is an epic poem in two parts, composed almost entirely in iambic tetrameter. In the first part, the demon has the bridegroom of Tamara, a Georgian princess, killed in an ambush as he leads a rich caravan to his wedding. In the second, the demon seduces Tamara, now a nun. The demon is Lucifer, a fallen angel who "having grown tired of evil" for a moment regains a sense of "the holiness of love, goodness, and beauty." As he approaches Tamara's cell, he senses the pangs of love and "drops a heavy tear which like a flame burns through a stone, still seen nearby today." The demon's impassioned tirades convince Tamara that he has, for the sake of her love, renounced vengeance and pride and "wants to make peace with heaven, to love and pray." He kills her with a burning kiss, but an angel carries her soul to heaven. As the demon tries in vain to pry his victim's soul from the angel, he is again "full of lethal poison and boundless hatred."

"The Demon" has enjoyed huge popularity ever since it first became available to a broad reading public. Anton Rubinstein turned it into a successful opera. Yet it is anything but a great work. It has some beautiful descriptive passages, but Tamara remains a pale and schematic figure, and the demon's lengthy tirades are vapid, prolix, and repetitious. "The Demon" has no philosophical or psychological depth.

The appeal of this work to generations of readers may be explained by the hypnotic effect of its emotion-laden rhetoric and perhaps by the fact that it gives the conflicting emotions and violent passions of late adolescence a sublimated and glamorous expression.

Lermontov's lasting popularity and substantial influence on poets perhaps greater than himself (Blok, for example) forces us to look for the secret of such success. One reason may be that Lermontov was a master of the quotable line, often paradoxical: "But he, the rebel, asks for storm, / As if a storm could bring him peace" ("The Sail"). Flashy lines often appear in otherwise mediocre poems. Another reason may be that Lermontov in a way recapitulated the whole romantic period, Russian as well as European, and stands as a monument to its values, moods, and forms. To later generations unaware of the debt Lermontov owed his predecessors, he conveyed these in a packaged form accessible to a sensibility no longer romantic. The romantic ethos reflected in Lermontov's poetry was enhanced by the reader's inevitable awareness of Lermontov's romantic biography. The charm of Lermontov's decorative exotic detail is another factor. Perhaps most of all, the rhetorical power of Lermontov's style may be responsible for his enduring success.

Tyutchev

Fyodor Ivanovich Tyutchev (1803–73) was a contemporary of Pushkin's. His first poetic effort, an excellent free version of Horace's missive to Maecenas (*Carmina*, 3.29) was published in 1819. He published many of his best poems in Pushkin's journal *The Contemporary*. But he was recognized as a major poet only in 1850—by Nekrasov, of all people, a political antagonist who was then the editor of *The Contemporary*, in an article entitled "Russia's Poets of the Second Rank." Nekrasov, himself a poet of the first rank, devoted most of his article to the anonymous "Poems Sent from Germany," which had appeared in *The Contemporary* fifteen years earlier. Tyutchev's first volume of verse appeared only in 1854.

Nevertheless, Tyutchev belongs to the romantic period. Only the circumstances of his life prevented him from having been a member of the Pushkin pleiad or of the Moscow wisdom lovers. Of ancient nobility, Tyutchev was educated in Moscow, where Semyon Raich (1792–1855), a minor poet and editor, as well as mentor to a small circle of young poets, was his tutor. Tyutchev graduated from Moscow University in 1821 and immediately entered the diplomatic service. He spent the next twenty-two years abroad, holding diplomatic posts in Munich and Turin, then living the last five years in Munich as a private citizen, having been dismissed from his post for dereliction of duty. In 1846 he published a political brochure, *Russia and Germany* (in French), which met with the tsar's approval. Tyutchev was reinstated into the Ministry of Foreign Affairs and served there as a censor of foreign publications until the end of his life. He acquired some influence as a conservative nationalist with strong Slavophile and Pan-Slavic leanings. A habitué of high society, he was famous for his eccentric behavior and brilliant wit (in French). He was a fascinated observer of the European political scene, making penetrating and sometimes prophetic observations about it. In a poem, "Cicero" (1830), he said:

> Blessed is he who visited this world
> In its fateful moments!
> Good gods summoned him to be
> Their companion at a feast.

Tyutchev's private life was marred by several extramarital love affairs, the next to last of which started when he was forty-seven and Elena Denisyeva, a lady of good family, twenty-four. It lingered until Denisyeva's death in 1864 and caused everybody concerned (Tyutchev had grown children by then) unspeakable grief. It also led to his heart-wrenching "Denisyeva cycle" of poems.

For much of his life Tyutchev used Russian only to write poetry. He was twice married, both times to Bavarian noblewomen. His political essays were all written in French, and what little French poetry he wrote is very good indeed. His translations from the French, German, and English are consistently brilliant. His versions of Schiller's "Ode to Joy," passages from Goethe's *Faust*, Shakespeare's "The lunatic, the lover, and the poet," and other pieces by Goethe, Schiller, Hugo, and Lamartine are as magnificent as the originals. Isolated from his Russian contemporaries, Tyutchev developed his poetic style independently. The language of his early poems is closer to Derzhavin's than to Pushkin's. He met Schelling and Heine while in Munich and was well familiar with German romantic philosophy and poetry. Much of his poetry moves within the range of romantic *Naturphilosophie*.

Tyutchev's nature poems have a breath of cosmic feeling. "An Autumn Evening" (1830) ends in the words

> over it all
> A gentle smile of fading,
> Which, in a rational creature, one might call
> The divine reticence of suffering.

Tyutchev has about as many fall poems in a minor key as spring poems in a major key, like the jubilant "A Thunderstorm in Spring" (1828). The excellence of his nature poems comes from a perfect synchronization of precise descriptive detail, euphonic orchestration, mood, and metaphysical intimations.

Tyutchev's *Gedankenlyrik* is imbued with the spirit of German romantic philosophy and permeated by a sense of universal panpsychism:

> Nature is not what you think:
> Not a stencil or a soulless form,
> It has a soul, it has freedom,
> It has love, it has a language.
>
> (1836)

Tyutchev has a pantheistic sense of the identity of human soul and world soul. "Much as the ocean girds the globe" (1830), a poem of rare musical magic, conveys the experience of a consciousness immersed in an ocean of dreams, floating on waves of sound ("borne by an infinity of dark waves"), and surrounded by "the flaming abyss of the firmament." Tyutchev's several seascapes are fusions of real experience at sea and visions of an inner sea, for example, "Dream at Sea" (1828–33).

Nature in Tyutchev is polarized. The light and harmony of day are often contrasted to the chaos of night ("Day and Night," 1839). Cruel, lethal passion is opposed to tender love, heaven to earth, thunder to silence, north to south, east to west. Characteristically, many of Tyutchev's poems consist of two juxtaposed quatrains. Yet in every instance such dualism appears as a dialectic unity, as in "The Fountain" (1836), where the fountain is seen as a symbol of human thought, which rises heavenward but must always return to earth.

In Tyutchev's later years, themes of the "nocturnal side of nature" begin to predominate, and the poet perceives the human soul as discordant and alienated from universal harmony:

Hence and how arose this dissonance?
And why is it that in the universal choir
The soul sings not what the ocean does,
And why does the thinking reed
    murmur?[54]

("There is a song in ocean waves," 1865)

Tyutchev's most famous poem, "Silentium!" (1830), in which the individual consciousness is envisioned as a windowless monad ("a whole world in itself"), while also arch-romantic, is a Fichtean deviation from Tyutchev's generally Schellingian worldview.

Tyutchev's occasional poems, usually though not necessarily romantic, are often small masterpieces. Two poems on Napoleon (1828 and 1840) are romantic and very strong. A poem occasioned by the news of Pushkin's death (1837) is undistinguished, but Tyutchev's memorial to Zhukovsky (1852) is probably the finest poem of this kind in the language. The casual "I remember those golden days" (1834), a portrait of a lovely young woman (the poem is addressed to a Baroness von Krüdener), with a romantic landscape in the background, caused Nekrasov to say that "even Pushkin would not have denied authorship of this poem."

Tyutchev's political and religious poems, poignant and pithy, tended to contradict the views he professed as a political ideologue. His reaction to the Decembrist uprising, "December 14, 1825" (1826) was remarkably perceptive, sober, and pessimistic. "Our Age" (1851) is a strikingly gloomy assessment of Russia's present and future for a Slavophile and staunch supporter of Orthodoxy. It ends with an anguished biblical quotation: "Lord, I believe; help Thou mine unbelief." The much-anthologized poem, "I like the service of the Lutherans" (1834), sees the bare walls of a Lutheran church as a sign that its occupant, faith, is ready to move out.

Tyutchev's many love poems run the gamut from delicate erotic conceits to resigned surrender to the awesome power of love and painful recognition of love's lethal denouement. Unlike Pushkin's love poems, Tyutchev's express a love that still delights and torments the poet. A comparison of Tyutchev's "Yesterday, in charmed dreams" (1836) with Benediktov's "Three Sights," which appears to have triggered Tyutchev's poem, reveals the superiority of Tyutchev's art. Both poems describe a sleeping beauty and her awakening. Benediktov's poem, vulgar and cliché-ridden, though sensuous, evokes no visual image. Tyutchev's subdued, exquisitely tender poem makes the scene palpably real. "Last Love" (1852) wonderfully combines the "bliss and hopelessness" of "love in our declining years" with the image of a lingering ray of light in the evening sky. The poems of the Denisyeva cycle focus on the theme stated poignantly in the first lines of one of them (1854):

Oh, how murderously we love
And in the savage blindness of our
    passions
Destroy the more surely
What is dearest to our heart!

So far as the short lyric genre is concerned, Tyutchev is second to no nineteenth-century Russian poet. If overall he is second to Pushkin, it is because of Pushkin's far-wider range.

Prose Fiction

Prose continued to lag behind poetry until the 1840s, although the 1830s saw some examples of excellent prose fiction. It con-

---

54. An allusion to Pascal's *roseau pensant*.

tinued to develop along the lines established by the end of the eighteenth century. The popular chapbook kept going strong as literacy among the lower classes was gradually increasing. The tradition of lively entertainment for a middlebrow readership, started by Chulkov and others in the eighteenth century, was continued by such writers as Narezhny, Kvitka, Begichev, and Bulgarin. The Karamzinian strain of literature for the genteel reader ("beautiful ladies" in particular) was initially the weaker, because the energies of the literary elite were directed at poetry until about 1830. The society tale became the most significant genre of this strain. The Napoleonic Wars generated a great deal of memoiristic literature, such as Denis Davydov's *Military Notes of the Partisan Denis Davydov* (1834–35). But their reflection in imaginative prose before Tolstoi's *War and Peace* was on the whole appallingly pedestrian and officiously chauvinistic.

The appearance in 1818 of the first eight volumes of Karamzin's *History of the Russian State*, and of translations of as many as six historical novels by Walter Scott that same year, gave a powerful impetus to the development of historical fiction. Starting in the 1830s, Pushkin, Gogol, Zagoskin, Lazhechnikov, and many others wrote historical novels and stories. Other genres of romantic fiction began to appear and indeed flourished in the 1830s: Gothic tales of mystery, horror, and high passion, tales based on Russian folklore, and exotic tales set in the Caucasus or the Orient.

Meanwhile a major part of the Russian reading public's fare was still provided by translations. Literary allusions in Russian works of the period as often refer to foreign as to Russian works, and chapter epigraphs are as often in French, German, English, and Italian as in Russian. At least for the first third of the century, many eighteenth-century writers remained alive to the Russian reader and influenced Russian writers one way or the other: Sterne, Fielding, Richardson, Goldsmith, and Ann Radcliffe among the English; Rousseau, Ducray-Duminil, Léonard, and Louvet de Couvray among the French; Goethe and Vulpius among the Germans. By the 1820s works by virtually every notable contemporary European writer appeared on the pages of Russian journals or in book form. For example, Polevoi's *Moscow Telegraph* (1825–34) published stories or novels (usually in excerpt) by Washington Irving, Walter Scott, Charles Robert Maturin, Fenimore Cooper, Prosper Mérimée, Benjamin Constant, Charles Nodier, Eugène Sue, Victor Hugo, Jules Janin, Alfred de Vigny, Honoré de Balzac, Heinrich Zschokke, Jean Paul Richter, E. T. A. Hoffmann, and many others. When novels by Dickens, George Sand, Dumas père, and Captain Marryat appeared, they were translated almost immediately.

The years 1829–30 signaled the end of the golden age of poetry and the ascendancy of prose fiction. In 1829 Bulgarin's novel *Ivan Vyzhigin* became the first Russian bestseller, and Zagoskin scored a hit with his Scottian historical novel *Yury Miloslavsky*. Pushkin turned to prose in 1830. Aleksandr Bestuzhev began a new career under the pen name Marlinsky in 1830 and soon became Russia's most popular storyteller. Gogol, the first major figure in modern Russian literature to write only prose, launched his meteoric career in 1831. Dahl, Weltmann, Pavlov, and several other writers began theirs at the same time. Belinsky registered the unstoppable march of the short story (*povest'*) in a major survey, "On the Russian Short Story and the Short Stories of Mr. Gogol" (1835). There was now more of a market for prose fiction, as literary journals were eager to publish original Russian works. In several instances writers now published collections of their stories: Pushkin's *Tales of Belkin* (1831), Pogodin's *Tales* (1832), Polevoi's *Dreams and Life: Real Stories and Fiction* (1833–34), Pavlov's *Three Tales* (1835), and others.

The main tendency of Russian prose fiction in the 1830s was romantic. The gothic tale had made its appearance even before 1830, as in "The Poppyseed-Cake Woman of Lefortovo" (1828), by Antony Pogorelsky (pseudonym of Aleksei Perovsky, 1787–1836), and flourished in the 1830s. The tales of Hoffmann inspired Russian writers to write *Künstlernovellen* about an artist's conflict with society or with himself, as well as fantastic tales dealing with themes of romantic philosophy or the "nocturnal aspect" of human nature. Pogorelsky's *The Double, or My Evenings in the Ukraine* (1828) was the first Russian exercise in the Hoffmannesque. The French phrenetic school found immediate imitators. Several of Gogol's Ukrainian as well as Petersburg tales have obvious phrenetic traits.

There was a good deal of transfer of them and moods from the Byronic verse epic to the prose tale of exotic adventure, of which Bestuzhev-Marlinsky was the prime exponent. The interest in folklore and native culture generated by the romantic movement led to the appearance of stories either patterned after the folktale or based on folk traditions. Weltmann is considered the main representative of "romantic folklorism," but Somov, Vladimir Odoevsky, Dahl, and others also wrote in this manner. Regional and dialect tales, Ukrainian in particular, also made their appearance. Several major authors were from the Ukraine—Gogol, of course, but also Somov, Pogorelsky, Kvitka, and Grebenka.

The Russian society tale, patterned after Balzac, Alfred de Musset, George Sand, and Bulwer-Lytton, had several subgenres. The novella of love and intrigue, often culminating in a fatal duel or some other tragic denouement, implicitly carried a message condemning the emptiness and cruelty of high society. The diary or confession form was common, too. Often it had an undercurrent of protest against societal injustices and prejudices. Here the influence of George Sand was great, and several woman writers wrote stories of this type. In some instances the society tale would turn into outright social satire, as in some tales by Vladimir Odoevsky and Sollogub.

Romantic prose fiction coexisted with older traditions, and especially with the picaresque adventure novel, the bildungsroman, the "family novel" of manners, and combinations of these three.

Vasily Narezhny (1780–1825) came from the poor Ukrainian gentry, attended Moscow University (1799–1801), and served in the civil service in the Caucasus and Saint Petersburg. As a student, he wrote some tragedies in the Storm and Stress manner. *Dmitry the Pretender* was published in 1804. *Slavonic Nights* (1809), a collection of tales about the heroes of Kievan Russia, was well received. The first three parts of Narezhny's main work. *A Russian Gil Blas, or the Adventures of Duke Gavrila Simonovich Chistyakov* (1814) were passed by the censor, but the next three were stopped and the first three retroactively suppressed. Undaunted by this misfortune, Narezhny continued to write fiction. *A Black Year, or Mountaineer Dukes*, finished in 1818 but published posthumously in 1829, is a vivid account of the installation of a rapacious colonial bureaucracy in the Caucasus. *Aristion, or Reeducation* (1822) is a spirited satire on modern education. *Two Ivans, or a Passion for Litigation* (1825) is a piece of genre painting à la Teniers, anticipating Gogol's "Tale of How Ivan Ivanovich Quarreled with Ivan Nikiforovich." For a long time Narezhny was best known for his historical novels reviving the Ukrainian past. *A Ukrainian Cossack* and *The Seminarian*, both published in 1824, are ahistorical but still closer to historical reality than is Gogol's *Taras Bulba*.

Contemporary critics castigated Narezhny for lack of taste (read: low subject matter), lack of refinement (read: coarse language), and lack of measure (read: a penchant for grotesque caricature). Narezhny's sensibility and language were those of clerks and seminarians, not of the salons and literary societies of the capitals. He uses a Karamzinian sentimentalist style straightforwardly at times, but also with a parodic edge, and richly laced with Slavonicisms, vulgarisms, chancery jargon, snippets of Latin, and a great deal of verbal clowning and grotesquerie. Narezhny's *Gil Blas* is closer in its sensibility and style to the brutal, burlesque, naturalist Spanish picaresque novels than to the more genteel French *Gil Blas*.

A Russian Gil Blas is written in response to Lesage's work, as Narezhny states in the introduction and again toward the end, when the hero finds himself reading *Gil Blas*. Narezhny's pessimistic message is not that of Lesage. As the narrator observes toward the end, a human being, whether guided by reason or by the heart, will always fall into error. As for virtue, it is entirely its own reward, but also wholly relative to the society that responds to it. Narezhny has no confidence in the ethical rationalism of the Enlightenment. Book 5 features a philippic on the disastrous effects of liberalism and enlightened morals. Narezhny displays no sympathy for Western ideas, and the vignettes he draws of foreigners are savagely

xenophobic. His didactic message is ultimately Orthodox: Chistyakov, born with his native share of goodness, is corrupted by a profoundly sinful world, and only suffering awakens this dormant goodness and returns him to religion, the lone way to salvation.

The censors had ample reason to suppress the novel. All-powerful Duke Latron (from Latin *latro*, "robber"—proper names are suggestive throughout), whose secretary the hero is at one time, is a most uncomplimentary portrait of Duke Potyomkin; Narezhny has barely disguised it by moving the action to Warsaw and calling the royal lady who gives Latron his power a princess (she herself is clearly Catherine). Gadinsky (*gad*, "reptile"), Chistyakov's predecessor as Latron's secretary, lectures the young man on how to get ahead in government service. His advice is: Fawn on your superiors, put the interests of the state behind those of your superiors, divest yourself of your conscience, honor, compassion, and other virtues, and don't hesitate to use your wife or sister to promote your career. The image of Russian lawcourts presented in several episodes is as negative as in Kapnist's *Chicane*. Priests are money-grubbing scoundrels, and even a nunnery turns out to be a den of iniquity. The only character in the whole long novel who is honest, wise, and compassionate is Yanka, a Jewish innkeeper in Chistyakov's home village. His kindness and good sense earn him nothing but hatred and cruel injustice. The scene of Yanka's death and the prayer he says before he dies are deeply moving.

Narezhny's satire lashes out at a variety of targets. At one point Chistyakov becomes a Freemason. His mentor Dobroslavov (*dobro*, "good," *slava*, "fame") may well be Novikov in caricature. In the end it turns out that the Masons are all either crooks or their dupes. Admiral Shishkov and his purist zealots appear in a slapstick episode. Chistyakov, as secretary to Duke Latron, has a "poet" compose an ode in his own honor, a crude but apt parody of the Lomonosovian triumphal ode. The theater gets its share of abuse, too: "As to the French [tragedies], they appear to me as narrow, flat boats, on which puppets of various Achilleses, Agamemnons, Hectors, Alexanders, and Caesars float along a gurgling brook, clothed in court dress coats and wearing seventeenth-century wigs and wig bags." (He then finds some merit in English and German tragedies.)

Structurally, *A Russian Gil Blas* is chaotic. Middle-aged Chistyakov tells the story of his life to different listeners, with many interruptions and digressions. His tale is woven into several frames which have plots of their own and interact and intersect with Chistyakov's narrative. The work is in effect a hybrid of the picaresque novel and the family novel. Many stories and disquisitions are inserted without much motivation, and the whole is therefore very uneven. But there can be no doubt that *A Russian Gil Blas* is a major novel whose satirical power, wealth of invention, and acuity of observation amply make up for its lack of urbanity and measure.

Grigory Kvitka (1778–1843), who used the pen name Osnovyanenko (after his family estate, Osnova), was the first major modern Ukrainian prose writer.[55] Like other Ukrainian writers of the first half of the century, he also wrote in Russian. Unlike them, however, Kvitka did not leave his native province, Kharkov, but devoted his remarkable energy to the social and literary life of Kharkov, where he organized a professional theater, founded a journal, *The Ukrainian Herald* (1816–17), and was the soul of various philanthropic and cultural activities. Kvitka's first Russian works were satirical sketches of local gentry life. His first major work in Russian, the novel *The Life and Adventures of Pyotr Pustolobov* (1834) was initially stopped by the censor, then published in reworked form as *The Life and Adventures of Pyotr, Son of Stepan, Stolbikov* (1841). Kvitka's satirical style, clever in a down-to-earth way, is much smoother than Narezhny's, but it lacks the power of Narezhny's Juvenalian indignation. Kvitka's *Mister Khalyavsky* (1840), a satirical chronicle of the old Ukrainian country gentry, is notable for its easy narrative manner and homespun humor.

Dmitry Begichev (1786–1855), of ancient nobility, had a successful career in the military and civil service. He was governor of Voronezh Province (1830–36) and was appointed senator in 1840. He published his works anonymously. *The Kholmsky Family: Some Traits of the Manners and Way of Life, Married and Single, of Russian Nobles*, in five volumes, appeared in Moscow in 1832. It is a vintage family novel. The Kholmskys and assorted relatives and acquaintances go through various experiences which might have occurred to a real Russian family. The similarity to a modern soap opera is striking. One of the Kholmsky sisters, Elizaveta, marries a rich duke who is not a handsome man and is older than herself. He is wholly absorbed in the management of his estate. She resents this and reacts by being unresponsive and rude. She has a miscarriage, is glad for it, and wants to have no children. Her sister Katerina loves her husband, is a good mother, and is initially happy in her marriage. But then her husband succumbs to his gambling habit, loses his entire fortune, falls in with a band of cardsharpers, and finally becomes an accessory to murder. Katerina dies of a broken

---

55. See p. 275 for Kvitka's plays.

heart. Her brother Aleksei marries the silly and plain daughter of a nouveau riche tax farmer for her money. Another sister, Nataliya, marries an aged and wealthy count, figuring that he will die soon and leave her well provided for. There are innumerable digressions from the main plot line: inserted novellas, anecdotes, character sketches, moral discourses, extensive descriptions (such as of a model estate and of one whose owner ruins himself by foolish investments), and a great deal of worldly wisdom (including ample quotes from Benjamin Franklin!) dispensed by the narrator and assorted characters, as when Mrs. Kholmsky lectures her daughter Elizaveta on how to keep a husband happy and affectionate.

Some chapters have a sharp satirical edge. In one opisode, police officers systematically extort bribes from honest citizens by falsely arresting them as alleged accomplices to actual robberies. They then let the real robbers "escape" to eliminate all evidence. A horror story of judicial corruption is taken directly from Kapnist's *Chicane*. Some noble ladies are vicious scandalmongers, and some gentlemen and members of the club are crooks or bullies. When Colonel Chadsky, who is courting Sofya, one of the Kholmsky girls, kills a hapless rival in a duel, ladies find him "interesting." Marriage, unhappy marriage in particular, is the central topic, but the pros and cons of a woman's single state are also considered. Weddings, births, and funerals are described in detail.

The language of *The Kholmsky Family* is fluent, often colloquial. It is laced with quotations from Russian and French literature and occasional French phrases. The epigraph of each chapter, usually French, but also Russian, English, and German, indicates its moral key. The names of most characters are taken from well-known Rus-

sian plays by Kapnist, Shakhovskoi, Griboedov, and Khmelnitsky, or are blatantly symbolic. An old maid is called Vestalkov, two crooks Zmeikin (from *zmeika*, "little snake") and Vampirov, a dishonest steward Friponenko (from French *fripon*, "crook"), a hypocrite Tartyufov, and so on. *The Kholmsky Family* must have made for entertaining reading in its day. Its importance as an antecedent of *War and Peace* is obvious. Like Tolstoi's novel, it reflects the landed gentry's view of Russian life. The facts relating to the life of the other classes are either filtered out or distorted by a westernized Russian's "European" sensibility shaped largely by Western literature.

Faddei Bulgarin (1789–1859) was born in Belorussia, where his family belonged to the Polish gentry. He was educated in the Corps of Cadets in Petersburg. Subsequently he served in the tsar's army, then in Napoleon's. At the end of the war Bulgarin found himself in Wilno, then a Polish university town, and after 1816 in Petersburg, where he started a career in journalism. In 1822 he founded the journal *The Northern Archive*, and in 1825 the newspaper *The Northern Bee*. As a journalist he was one of the pioneers of the Russian feuilleton and physiological sketch in the manner of Joseph-Étienne Jouy's *L'Hermite de la chaussée d'Antin* and *L'Hermite en province*. Before December 1825 Bulgarin was close to some of the Decembrists; thereafter he was careful to take positions that he assumed to be the government's. He also worked as an informer for the secret police for many years.

Bulgarin's *Ivan Vyzhigin, a Moral-Satirical Novel* (1829) was the first Russian best-seller. Some seven thousand copies sold in 1829, and three years later it had been translated into eight foreign languages, including English. Bulgarin published excerpts from the novel, then called *Ivan Vyzhigin, or a Russian Gil Blas*, starting in 1825. The plan of the novel resembles *Tom Jones* more than it does *Gil Blas*, since the hero, who begins his life as a nameless orphan, is really the natural son of a Duke Miloslavsky. His mother, a rich lady, eventually recognizes him but initially claims that she is his aunt, not his mother.[56] The adventures of Ivan Vyzhigin are even more fantastic than those of Gavrila Chistyakov. Before meeting his "aunt" in Moscow, he is adopted and abused by a landowner in Belorussia, where he later serves a rich Jew. In Moscow the poor orphan turns young gentleman of distinction almost overnight, falls in love, and follows his ladylove to Orenburg, where he is kidnapped by Kirghiz tribesmen. Freed by an old friend, Vyzhigin returns to Moscow. On his way there, he meets various "Russian types," such as an official who takes no bribes. Back in Moscow, he becomes a man about town, is ruined, falls in with a gang of cardsharpers, almost marries the daughter of a merchant, and finally enlists in the army. Wounded in battle, he retires from the military and goes to Petersburg, where he falls in love with a virtuous orphan girl and is unexpectedly thrown in prison. It turns out that this misfortune is due to a plot to deprive him of his inheritance. But these nefarious schemes are foiled. Vyzhigin inherits Duke Miloslavsky's fortune, a million rubles, marries the orphan girl, and retires to his country estate. Inserted into Vyzhigin's story are many anecdotes and several novellas.

Most knowledgeable contemporaries and all posterity were in agreement that *Ivan Vyzhigin* was a bad novel. Its satire is heavyhanded, its moralizing pedestrian, its char-

acters not only unbelievable but also uninteresting. The story line is arbitrarily contrived. Bulgarin's style is that of the newspaper feuilleton. Though momentarily amusing, its smug chattiness becomes insufferable after reading more than a few pages. Nevertheless, *Ivan Vyzhigin* was an epochal event in the history of Russian prose fiction, particularly in view of the fact that Narezhny's vastly superior *Russian Gil Blas* was unavailable to a broad readership. It was the first successful Russian novel and was instantly imitated, even by Bulgarin himself, who wrote a sequel, *Pyotr Ivanovich Vyzhigin* (1831). It was one of the first novels to deal with Russian society, albeit in an oblique and dishonest way. Bulgarin's novel was derived not so much from *Gil Blas* as from the novels *The Adventures of Mikolaj Doświadczyński* (1776) and *Pan Podstoli* (1778–1803), by the Polish writer Ignacy Krasicki (1735–1801), both works characteristic of the Enlightenment. Bulgarin's descriptions of life in the Russian provinces really apply to Polish-Belorussian more than to Russian mores. (This is confirmed by Bulgarin's memoirs, published later, in which he quite frankly reveals his beliefs, convictions, and prejudices, those of an oldfashioned Polish country squire.) But even so, *Ivan Vyzhigin* was a step forward, for earlier fiction was generally based on West European models, still further removed from Russian reality.

Pushkin's Prose

The prose works of Pushkin had no great success in his lifetime, and many of them remained incomplete and unpublished until after his death. Today it is understood that Pushkin's prose was the foundation on which much of the prose fiction of succeeding generations was built—an opinion first

---

56. She recognizes him by a burn mark (*vyzhiga*), whence his assumed name. But *vyzhiga* also means rogue or crook.

stated, with great conviction, by Apollon Grigoryev in the 1850s.

The Tales of the Late Ivan Petrovich Belkin (1831) contains five short stories with an editor's preface, which gives some information about Belkin, revealing that he was not the author of these tales but merely their collector. The editor, though he signs his preface A. P., is not Pushkin speaking in his own voice but the mocking parody of a literary entrepreneur. The stories reflect the personalities of their alleged authors but are also parodies of various directions then current in Russian prose fiction.

"The Shot," told by a Lieutenant Colonel I. L. P., is a romantic novella. There is a single plot line. The hero, Silvio, a Byronic figure, provokes a duel with a hated rival, a young count. The count, who fires first, misses. Seeing that his adversary is not afraid to die, Silvio suspends his own shot. Years later, upon hearing that the count, recently married, now values his life more, he returns to claim his shot. He humiliates his adversary by granting him a second shot before taking his first. When the count misses again, Silvio spares his life, satisfied with his enemy's humiliation. The narrative structure of "The Shot" is intricate. We hear, in turn, the narrator, Silvio, again the narrator, the count, and once more the narrator. "The Shot" has been interpreted as a parodic deflation of the Byronic hero obsessed with the memory of a single traumatic experience, but it is a fine short story even in a straightforward reading.

"The Blizzard," told by a Miss K. I. T., tells the incredible story of Marya Gavrilovna, a country miss, who agrees to elope with her sweetheart Vladimir. She makes it to church through a blizzard, but barely. Vladimir loses his way and never gets there. Another traveler, Burmin, also lost in the snowstorm, accidentally enters the church and is taken

for the bridegroom. The bride, dazed by the drive through the storm, cries out, "Not him!"—but only after the ceremony is over. She then returns home and tries to forget. Some years later, Burmin accidentally meets Marya Gavrilovna, falls in love without recognizing her, and confesses that he is legally a married man. Having heard his account of that night in the blizzard, she exclaims, "So it was you!" as he throws himself at her feet.

"The Undertaker," told by B. V., a steward, is a comic grotesque. Prokhorov, an undertaker, gets drunk at a party and has a nightmare in which a host of his customers pay him a visit. The story features some black humor (foreshadowing Gogol), as we hear such phrases as "A dead man cannot live without his coffin" or "Only those [of the dead] who were by then really incapacitated stayed at home."

"The Stationmaster," told by A. G. N., titular councillor, gives an ironic twist to the sentimental theme of the simple maiden seduced by a frivolous nobleman, as well as to the parable of the prodigal son (pictures relating it hang on the walls in the stationmaster's quarters.) Dunya, the stationmaster's daughter, runs off to Petersburg with Minsky, a dashing young officer, leaving her father heartbroken. He looks up Minsky in Petersburg and begs him to return him his daughter, but in vain. Disconsolate, he returns home and drinks himself to death. The story ends with Dunya, now an elegant lady and mother of three, visiting her father's grave. Perhaps his grief had been groundless after all.

The last story, "The Peasant Miss," is told by Miss K. I. T. and is a Russian version of the hackneyed theme of a young gentleman falling in love with a peasant beauty, who then turns out to be a young lady who had dressed up in peasant garb.

The Tales of Belkin got a lukewarm reception from contemporaries, who saw the stories as no more than passable entertainment. It is now understood that *The Tales* is a parodic anthology of early nineteenth-century fiction. This was not the impression contemporary readers gained from it. Dostoevsky's response to "The Stationmaster" in his own novel *Poor Folk* seems to be based on a straight reading. *The Tales of Belkin* have received extraordinary attention. Generations of critics have infused these stories with meanings not sensed by otherwise perceptive contemporaries. Apollon Grigoryev saw Belkin as the epoch-making prototype of "new Russian man"—the "meek" Russian returning to his "native soil." Every single motif in *The Tales* has literary antecedents. Parodic deconstruction, such as is seen in *The Tales of Belkin*, was a common feature of romantic tales, E. T. A. Hoffmann's and Washington Irving's in particular.

"The Queen of Spades," first published in *The Reading Library* in 1834, was an immediate success. Tchaikovsky's opera, first performed in 1890, made it well known internationally. The narrative features frequent changes of point of view and contains several flashbacks, the first of which sets the plot in motion. Tomsky, a young officer, tells his friends about the secret of three winning cards revealed to his grandmother by the notorious Count Saint Germain sixty years earlier. Among the listeners is Hermann, a young officer in the Corps of Engineers. Magnetically attracted to the old countess's secret, Hermann hits upon the idea of gaining access to her through Liza, her *démoiselle de compagnie*. When Liza invites him to her room one night, Hermann hides in the countess's chamber instead, awaiting the old lady's return from a ball. He pleads with her to reveal to him the secret of the winning cards, and when he gets no

response threatens her with a pistol. She dies of fright. Three days later, Hermann has a vision of the dead countess, who enters his room and names three cards: trey, seven, ace. He proceeds to a gaming house and stakes his entire patrimony, forty-seven thousand rubles, on the trey. He wins, doubles his bet, and wins again, this time on the seven. When he stakes everything on the ace, it wins, too, but he discovers to his horror that the card in his hand is not the ace but the queen of spades, in whom he recognizes the countess. Hermann goes mad and spends the rest of his life repeating the words "trey, seven, ace—trey, seven, queen."

"The Queen of Spades," a fine short story, has been overinterpreted even more than *The Tales of Belkin*. It contains many literary echoes, possibly some coded personal allusions, and certainly a multitude of numbers—mostly ones, twos, threes, and sevens—which has caused some scholars to engage in numerological speculations on the text. Certain scholars believe to have discovered Masonic and other arcane symbolism in the story. "The Queen of Spades" was declared, by Dostoevsky and others, to be the prototype of a new genre, the Petersburg tale. Hermann, with his Napoleonic profile and Mephistophelian airs, has been seen as a template of Raskolnikov and other godless, egotistical, and driven rebels of Russian literature. Even a Freudian interpretation has been attempted: when Hermann stakes his patrimony on a card, he rebels against what his bourgeois German father stood for: hard work, patience, and a planned career.[57]

Pushkin left a number of incomplete

57. Paul Debreczeny, *The Other Pushkin: A Study of Alexander Pushkin's Prose Fiction* (Stanford, Calif.: Stanford University Press, 1983), 232–38.

prose works, most of which are too short and fragmentary to be recognized as either a novel or a short story. The plan of a historical novel to be called *The Black Man of Peter the Great* occupied Pushkin for a long time, at least since 1825.[58] Its principal source was a biography of Abram Hannibal, written in German, which Pushkin received from Pyotr Hannibal, Abram's son, who lived near Mikhailovskoe. This biography embellished the facts, and Pushkin used further poetic license in his version. The novel remained a fragment, but two excerpts were published in Pushkin's lifetime. It begins in Paris, where young Ibrahim (Abram) has a love affair with a French countess, then moves to Russia, where the tsar, who is fond of Ibrahim, acts as his matchmaker. The maiden chosen by the tsar is from a proud boyar family who resent the match but do not resist it. At this point the novel breaks off. Apparently Pushkin planned for Ibrahim's marital problems to provide the dramatic conflict of the work.

The short novel *Dubrovsky* (1832–33) was published posthumously in 1841. It is set in the late eighteenth century. Dubrovsky, a young officer and landowner, turns outlaw when his small estate is wrongfully taken from him by General Troekurov, his rich and powerful neighbor. Impersonating a French tutor, Dubrovsky makes Troekurov's daughter fall in love with him. But when he arrives late to prevent her marriage to a middle-aged duke, she refuses to break her marriage vows. Dubrovsky disappears after having won a pitched battle against government troops. This tale of romantic brigandage is told in Pushkin's succinct and vigorous style, without moralizing or sentimentality. The reason why Pushkin would devote his energy to such a trite and melodramatic story may be found in his preoccupation with the trials to which the freedom and honor of a nobleman were subjected in Russia.

The incomplete "Egyptian Nights," first published posthumously in 1837, is apparently a short story, but it is dominated by the unfinished poem with whose recitation the manuscript ends.[59] The introductory prose portion draws a character sketch of a Russian poet and man of the world. The poet arranges for the performance of a visiting Italian improviser, who recites, first a brief ode on the poet's independence, then a verse epic, "Cleopatra and Her Lovers."

Pushkin's historical novel *The Captain's Daughter* appeared in *The Contemporary* in 1836. It grew in Pushkin's imagination from his archival work in 1833–34 for his *History of the Pugachov Rebellion*, written at the same time but published earlier, in 1834. Pushkin took his historical research seriously. When a negative review of his *History* appeared in *Son of the Fatherland* (1835), he responded with a detailed rebuttal in *The Contemporary* (1836). Pushkin's historical prose, here and in several fragments on various topics (all published posthumously), is terse and to the point, yet anything but artless. The thread of the narrative is carefully maintained, the cadences of its sentences are energetic, and the mot juste is always found. The historian lets the terrible facts of the rebellion speak for themselves. They tell the reader that the Pugachov rebellion was a class war, an uprising of the common people against the gentry, the government, and everything that smacked of the West. Pugachov, an Old Believer, hanged every man, woman, or child wearing "German" garb. The facts also

---

58. The hero is referred to as *le Nègre du czar* in the text.

59. It was eventually finished by Valery Bryusov.

tell the reader that no matter how justified the people's grievances and how much in sympathy a liberal nobleman might be with them, victory of the rebellion meant chaos and a relapse into barbarity. The Pugachov rebellion, as presented by Pushkin, is a fateful clash of two irreconcilable forces. Pugachov, an illiterate and shiftless but bold and clever Don Cossack, appears as an actor of genius in a tragedy he could not fully understand.

Whereas *A History of the Pugachov Rebellion* is a serious work of great importance, *The Captain's Daughter* is a fine novel that has its flaws. A Waverley novel, it is told many years after the event by Grinyov, who as a teenage ensign happened to cross the path of Pugachov. He once gave a nameless tramp his rabbitskin coat for showing him the way in a blizzard. Later, when Grinyov was about to get hanged along with the other officers of his outpost, the tramp, who was none other than Pugachov himself, recognized him and spared his life. Grinyov was now willy-nilly a traitor to his rank as an officer and a gentleman. After some more adventures, he was saved by his fiancée, the captain's daughter, who got the empress herself to pardon him. Pushkin, as "editor" of Grinyov's memoirs, adds a brief postface. The excellence of *The Captain's Daughter* is in the detail of its language and realia. The hero is properly nondescript, like Edward Waverley, and so is the captain's daughter. Pugachov is glamorized à la Rob Roy but appears credible, though he is different from the historical Pugachov in *A History of the Pugachov Rebellion*. The villain of the novel, Shvabrin, is unconvincing and unnecessary. He apparently remained in the novel after Pushkin abandoned the idea to put into the work a historical personage, an ensign named Shvanvich, who joined Pugachov but got away with only mild

punishment. Some minor characters, however, are memorable: Grinyov's faithful old servant Savelyich, Captain Mironov, and especially the captain's wife. The chapters about the lonely outpost on the fringes of the empire, the excitement of the brewing rebellion, and the horror of Pugachov's atrocities are done masterfully. The rest is unremarkable, but still it is told energetically.

Historical Novels

While some short historical fiction (by Karamzin, Fyodor Glinka, Bestuzhev, and others) had appeared earlier, the historical novel came into its own only around 1830. It owed its existence entirely to Walter Scott who, since about 1820 had become as much a part of an educated Russian's consciousness as he did in the English speaking world. Much as elsewhere, he found numerous imitators. James Fenimore Cooper's novels were almost as popular. They had a special appeal because of some similarities between the American and the Russian experience. It is probably because of Cooper's influence that the Cossack Ermak, who conquered much of Siberia for Ivan the Terrible, became a favorite subject of historical fiction and drama.

The first full-fledged Scottian historical novel, *Yury Miloslavsky, or the Russians in 1612*, by Mikhail Zagoskin (1789–1852), appeared in 1829. Zagoskin made an official career as a librarian, then in the management of the imperial theaters, and finally as director of the Moscow Armory Museum. In the 1810s and 1820s he wrote a series of popular comedies. *Yury Miloslavsky* was a huge success. It tells of the adventures of young duke Yury Miloslavsky and his friend Kirsha, a Ukrainian Cossack, toward the end of the Time of Troubles. The book is weak, as historical novels go. Zagoskin never manages to integrate his story with the exciting historical events of the period. At one point the hero gets some fatherly advice from Avraamy Palitsyn, chronicler of the heroic defense of Trinity Monastery, but other than that, historical events and historical personages remain in the background. The story has the familiar treasonous villains, whose plots are miraculously but all too expectedly foiled, and comic relief comes from the misfortunes of a cowardly braggart—Polish, of course. There is a great deal of officious patriotic rhetoric, quite ahistorical, with proper bows in the direction of the Romanovs. What made *Yury Miloslavsky* such a success must have been its fluent language, the introduction of some authentic descriptive detail, and, most of all, Zagoskin's truly modest effort to Russify his Scottian characters. Zagoskin's later novels are even weaker, though they, too, were quite successful in their time. The patriotic rhetoric of *Roslavlev, or the Russians in 1812* (1831), however, was recognized for the sham it was even by many contemporaries.

Ivan Lazhechnikov (1792–1869), the son of a wealthy and progressive-minded merchant, was well educated. He served as an officer in the campaign of 1812 (his *Campaign Notes of a Russian Officer* appeared in 1820). Subsequently he held government posts as a teacher, school principal, school inspector, vice-governor of a province, and finally as a censor in Petersburg. He wrote several plays, but his fame rests on his historical novels. The first of these, *The Last Novice* (1831–33), is set in Livonia at the time of its conquest by Peter the Great. *The Ice Palace* (1835), Lazhechnikov's best novel, is set in the winter of 1740, the last year of the reign of Empress Anna. Its plot rather implausibly weaves a love story into the historical court intrigue that led to the execution of Duke Artemy Volynsky and a

group of courtiers loyal to him in a power struggle against Ernst Biron, duke of Curland, the empress's favorite and lover. Volynsky is idealized and presented as a noble patriot and champion of the Russian people against the depredations of the German Biron and his clique. His fall is partly caused by his involvement with the beautiful Marioritsa, a Moldavian princess and the empress's pet. In good gothic fashion Marioritsa turns out to be the daughter of Mariula, a Gypsy woman, also involved in the court intrigue. Anna's court poet, Trediakovsky, plays a minor and not very attractive role. His ode celebrating the mock wedding of a court jester to a "lady's lady" in a magnificent ice palace erected for the amusement of the court appears in the text. At one point in the novel Lazhechnikov says that he is following in the footsteps of "our grandfather Walter Scott." He does so mainly in descriptive passages and in footnotes, where he parades his historical erudition. The dialogue is only sporadically stylized, the characters engage in some utterly anachronistic rhetoric, and the narrative has many effusive lyric tirades. The lasting success of *The Ice Palace* is due to its subject matter: the grotesque and cruel drama enacted in the year of Anna's death would have been a great story even if told badly, but Lazhechnikov tells it rather well. His later novels, among which *The Infidel* (1838), set in the age of Ivan III, is the best known, are weaker than *The Ice Palace*.

Much as elsewhere, the historical novel became a fixture in the popular literature of Russia. Besides those already mentioned, K. P. Masalsky (*The Musketeers*, 1831), Faddei Bulgarin (*Dimitry the Pretender*, 1830), Nikolai Polevoi (*An Oath by the Holy Sepulchre*, 1832), and others entered this promising market.

Romantic Storytellers

The career of Aleksandr Bestuzhev (1797–1837) was cut in half by the Decembrist revolt of 1825. He was permitted to resume publishing only in 1830, but under a pen name, Marlinsky. His stories were phenomenally successful with the public. "Marlinsky" was divested of his unchallenged position as Russia's foremost prose writer only by Belinsky, who in a series of essays and reviews went out to deflate the romantic school and its leading figure, Bestuzhev. Belinsky's view was that Bestuzhev's stories contained "no truth of life, no reality, such as it is, for all in them is invented, all is determined by a calculus of probability, much as happens in the making or construction of machines." Belinsky further asserted that readers could see the strings and pulleys moving this machine. He did, however, credit Bestuzhev with erudition, intelligence, and "occasionally, excellent thoughts." He also acknowledged that Bestuzhev's style was "original and brilliant, strained though it is." Belinsky was right. Bestuzhev's prose is rhetorical and mannered, but it has verve and vigor. His characters, dashing young officers mostly, speak in conceits, witticisms, and rhetorical flourishes, offering up bons mots (sometimes in French) rather after the fashion of Dumas père. Bestuzhev's narrator draws his readers into his confidence, asks questions of them, enlightens them, and on the whole flatters them.

Bestuzhev's mind and imagination were extraordinarily responsive to his environment. Imprisoned in a fortress in Finland, he responded with a romantic poem, "Finland," a description of that country's austere landscape. Exiled to Yakutia, he wrote a lengthy ballad, "Saltyr," based on a local tradition. Transferred to the Caucasus, Bestuzhev immediately set out to learn the local dialects, and he soon introduced the folklore of the Caucasian mountaineers into his stories—the death songs of the Kabardinians in "Ammalat-Bek," for example.

Bestuzhev had a great facility for acquiring languages and a histrionic ability to impersonate human types. He was well read, had traveled far, and was familiar with different milieus: high society, the army, the navy, and life in the Baltic provinces, Siberia, and the Caucasus. His descriptive passages are vivid and interesting. Both narrative and dialogue feature many expressions and whole phrases from various languages: French in the society tales, English in the sea stories, and Tatar and Persian, properly translated for the reader, in the Caucasian tales.

The structure of Bestuzhev's stories is that of his Western examples: Walter Scott, Captain Marryat, E. T. A. Hoffmann, or the Byronic verse epic. As a rule, they have a frame or master narrative which may or may not be thematically linked to the story (or stories) being told. Such digressions as letters, documents, lines of poetry, or descriptive and essayistic passages often interrupt the flow of the narrative.

Bestuzhev's stories belong to four basic types: society tales, sea stories, gothic tales, and exotic (Caucasian) stories. "The Test" (1830), a society tale, starts with a description of a ball, with scraps of party banter and stale witticisms ever so slightly overdone to turn them into satire. The social criticism implied is moderately liberal. The plot is typical of the society tale. Duke Gremin asks his friend Strelinsky to test the faithfulness of his beloved, the widowed Countess Zvezdich. Strelinsky's flirtation turns into real love, and he proposes marriage to the countess. Gremin, though by then out of love with her, nevertheless feels obliged to challenge Strelinsky to a duel. Only the resolute intervention of Olga, Strelinsky's sister, who loves Gremin, saves both. Bestuzhev's description of Strelinsky's courtship of Countess Zvezdich anticipates Vronsky's courtship of Anna Karenina in some specific details.

"The Frigate *Nadezhda*" (1832) is a mixture of society tale and sea story. Pravin, the skipper of the frigate, has an adulterous love affair with Duchess Vera N. He invites her and her unsuspecting husband to be his guests on a passage to England. When they have disembarked, and he is about to continue his voyage, Pravin cannot resist the temptation of one last tryst with Vera. He leaves for shore in a sloop, although warned by his mate that a storm is brewing. When Pravin returns to take command of his ship, the sloop is smashed against the hull of the frigate, and there is loss of life in both vessels. Pravin himself is gravely injured. Tortured by guilt, and feeling that he has lost his honor, he has no will to live and so dies. Vera dies soon, too, of a broken heart. The theme of a conflict between love and duty is carried over from classicist tragedy, but its treatment here is romantic. The narrator's sympathy is with the adulterous lovers throughout. He portrays Pravin and Vera as morally superior to most members of their social set. It is not objective retribution that kills Pravin, but the turmoil in his soul. The story may be a projection of Bestuzhev's own feelings of guilt. A leader of the Decembrist revolt, he got off relatively lightly by fully cooperating with the authorities after his surrender, whereas some of his friends were executed or served long sentences in Siberia.

Bestuzhev's other sea tales lack the psychological dimension of "The Frigate *Nadezhda*," but they are marked by fine descriptions of the sea and seamanship, as well as the particulars of various types of sailing ships and rigging.

In his gothic tales, some of which are set in Livonia, Bestuzhev follows the example of Ann Radcliffe in that seemingly supernatural events are eventually shown to have a natural explanation. Bestuzhev carefully introduces details that build up a mood of imminent danger and create suspense by holding up the plot at crucial junctures. "A Terrible Fortune-Telling" (1831), a lively and suspenseful story, has strong elements of folklore, specifically various superstitions about divination on New Year's Eve. "The Cuirassier" (1832) has an artfully constructed though quite preposterous plot, in which the frame narrative and the stories within interact to resolve the mysteries of several plot lines.

Bestuzhev's Caucasian tales show him at his best. He does not abandon his romantic manner but combines it with topographic and ethnographic detail. "Ammalat-Bek" (1832) is based on a real character. The brave and honest young chieftain Ammalat-Bek is torn between his tribal loyalties and his friendship with a young Russian officer. Eventually Ammalat-Bek kills his friend, and he himself perishes, a traitor to the Russians but still rejected by his own people. The suspenseful plot is advanced through third-person narrative, less rhetorical than the narrative in most of Bestuzhev's stories, letters, diary pages, monologues, and dialogue. "Ammalat-Bek" is a remarkably cogent treatment of the encounter of a European romantic with a "noble savage," who is shown to be moved by emotions and values that are alien to a civilized European.

"Mulla-Nur" (1836) is a Scottish romance transplanted to the Caucasus. A Caucasian Rob Roy, Mulla-Nur is a brave and crafty outlaw, who generously pays back the story's hero, young Iskander-Bek, for having saved his life. The love story of Iskander-Bek and the beautiful Kichkene is uninteresting, but the story still makes for entertaining reading, mostly because of its plentiful local color and amusing minor characters, like the cowardly braggart and liar Hadji Yusuf and the greedy and treacherous Mulla Sadek.

Aleksandr Veltman (Weltmann 1800–1870) attended the boarding school of Moscow University and the School of Quartermasters in Moscow. He served in the army from 1818 to 1831 and was stationed in Bessarabia, where he became friendly with Pushkin. In 1831 he resigned his commission and entered the civil service. He joined the staff of the Moscow Armory Museum in 1842 and was appointed its director after Zagoskin's death in 1852. In 1854 Veltman was elected a corresponding member of the Academy of Sciences on the strength of his archaeological and historical studies. Veltman was an extraordinarily prolific writer of poetry, fiction, and rather fanciful scholarly works. He began his writing career with some romantic verse epics ("The Fugitive," 1825), a genre which he continued to cultivate even in later years ("Troyan and Angelitsa: A Tale Told to the Clear Moon by the Bright Morning Star," 1846). He came into his own with *The Wanderer* (1831–32),[60] a romantic lyric philosophical novel with many interludes in verse. Its text keeps switching from the "real" experiences of a Russian officer on a march through Bessarabia to an imaginary journey on a map of the region in which the narrator indulges his whimsical fancy. There followed several novels in which Veltman made fantastic excursions into the distant future (*The Year MMMCDXLVIII: A Manuscript of Martin Zadek*, 1833) or the distant past (*Aleksandr Filippovich Makedonsky*, 1836).[61] *Kashchei the Deathless* (1833) is one of Veltman's folkloristic novels. It features a chase after the elusive Kashchei, an evil demon of Russian fairy tales. The hero, a Russian country squire, believes that Kashchei has kidnapped his wife and sets out to rescue her (in fact, she has run away with her lover). The action of the novel keeps moving in and out of the world of the Russian fairy tale, a ploy used by Veltman in several other works as well.

A New Emelya, or Metamorphoses (1845) is a parody of the bildungsroman (Emelya is Russian for Émile, the title character of Rousseau's educational classic). The ingenuous hero gets the worst possible education—and still does fine in life. The action of this novel, too, moves on several different planes, as it features excursions into the world of the Russian bylina and grotesque metamorphoses of recent history. Contemporaries, including Dostoevsky, found *Emelya* "a delight." Veltman concluded his career as a novelist with a five-volume cycle, *Adventures Extracted from the Ocean of Life* (1846–63), the last volume of which remained unpublished. An epic of Russian life in all strata of society, it approaches the manner of the mid-century realist novel. The first volume, *Salomeya*, has a beautiful, enterprising, and energetic heroine who is a selfish and unprincipled adventuress. Her male counterpart, Dmitritsky, is an adventurer of often criminal

60. Veltman's *Wanderer* falls within the genre of the imaginary travelogue initiated by Xavier de Maistre's *Voyage autour de ma chambre* (1794). De Maistre emigrated to Russia, where he made the rank of general. He found several imitators even before Veltman, among them K. N. Batyushkov, *A Walk around Moscow* (1811–12) and *A Walk to the Academy of Fine Arts* (1814), and M. L. Yakovlev, *Sentimental Journeys along Nevsky Boulevard* (1820).

61. The title character, of course, is Alexander the Great, of Macedon.

propensities, but with "noble instincts," which cause him occasionally to punish injustice and help underdogs. The paths of these two cross time and again throughout this long novel, until they are finally united to engage in useful labor. *Salomeya* is a picaresque novel with concessions to an emerging realism. The other four volumes also contain intricate and somewhat contrived plots, have their share of satirical bite, and advance humanitarian attitudes.

In addition to his novels, Veltman wrote many short stories in various romantic styles. "Erotis" (1835) may be an echo of the real-life story of Nadezhda Durova, the "maiden cavalryman." It is the sad tale of an Amazon horsewoman's tragic love, ending in her death in a duel at the hands of the man she loves. Like other stories by Veltman, it may be also read as a spoof. "Roland the Furious" (1835) has a plot resembling that of *The Inspector General*. A half-mad and drunken actor, dressed in a fancy uniform, is taken for the visiting governor general and humored accordingly by local dignitaries, as he declaims incoherent monologues from his tragic repertoire. "A Man from the Provinces, or an Uproar in the Capital" (1841) is a spirited satire on the literary world of Moscow. A mediocre young poet from the provinces accidentally gains admission to the best Moscow society as a budding genius but is soon discarded as other attractions appear on the scene. The story contains many parodic imitations of the poetry of Vladimir Benediktov, who enjoyed great though ephemeral fame in the late 1830s and early 1840s.

Veltman, next to Bestuzhev, was the most popular prose writer of the 1830s and continued as a leading writer through the 1840s. His fame then quickly faded. Veltman's relaxed, digressive, and playful manner went well with his antiquarian and ethnographic erudition. His novels and stories ranged over the whole spectrum of romantic fiction: historical, utopian, gothic, fantastic, adventure, exotic, and satirical. He was willing to incorporate any kind of diction (that of the *Igor Tale*, folktales, chronicles, chapbooks, anecdotes) into his narrative, yet left the door open to romantic irony, casually moving from one point of view to another. Veltman's lively but zigzagging story lines, constant changes of scenery and shifts of focus, frequent digressions, erudition, and stabs at satirical grotesquerie and whimsical humor resemble Sterne and Jean Paul, both of whom surely influenced Veltman directly.

Orest Somov (1793–1833) came to Saint Petersburg from the Ukraine. Best known for his essay "On Romantic Poetry" (1823), Somov published a number of short stories and some Russian and Ukrainian folktales. His tales provide examples of romantic folklorism and ethnographism, reshaping folk traditions and folk superstitions to suit the tastes of his reader. Most of them are rather weak, but "The Witches of Kiev" (1833), essentially the same story as Pushkin's ballad "The Hussar," except for its sad ending, is lively and suspenseful. Somov also wrote some novellas of manners, not all that different from Pushkin's *Tales of Belkin*. Their narrative manner is digressive, ironic, and often stylized, aiming at wit and surprise. But Somov's plots are uninteresting or poorly constructed, his characters schematic and lifeless.

Polish-born Osip Senkovsky (1800–1858), a professor of oriental languages at Petersburg University, began his career in journalism with a Polish newspaper in Saint Petersburg and from 1834 to 1847 was publisher and editor of *The Reading Library*, the most successful "thick journal" of his age. He created the character Baron Brambeus, under whose name he published *The Fantastic Journeys of Baron Brambeus* and a great deal of fiction, essays, feuilletons, and criticism. Senkovsky specialized in oriental tales, based in part on his travels in the Near East and in part on his studies in oriental literatures, as well as on other, more accessible sources, such as Herodotus ("Mikeriya, Lily of the Nile," 1845, is based on the second book of Herodotus). In his satirical society tales Senkovsky freely borrowed from Western authors. For example, "A Grand Outing at Satan's" (1833) was taken from Balzac's "La Comédie du diable." An amateur scientist and inventor, Senkovsky was more original in his science fiction. His fiction tended to slide into the genre of the feuilleton, for he sacrificed the integrity of his narrative to punning, anecdotal digressions, irresponsible humor, and the parading of his scholarly and scientific erudition.

Duke Vladimir Odoevsky (1804–1869) was a man of many talents. He pursued a successful career in public service as a librarian and educator. An amateur composer and competent musicologist, he also dabbled in science and was an inventor. This background is reflected in his fiction. Odoevsky's *Russian Nights* (1844) is the masterpiece of Russian philosophical romanticism. It is patterned after E. T. A. Hoffmann's *Die Serapionsbrüder*. The narrative frame has a group of young Russians read their own stories to each other and discuss their content, as well as some other topics. The stories of *Russian Nights*, some of which were written in the 1820s, range broadly. The lead story, "Opere del Cavaliere Giambattista Piranesi," resembles Hoffmann's "Der Ritter von Gluck." A Neapolitan eccentric dreams of executing Piranesi's fantastic architectural projects, believing that he himself is the cavaliere, much as Hoffmann's eccentric declares that he is the

famous composer. Two of the stories are fictionalized tributes to great composers: "Beethoven's Last Quartet" and "Sebastian Bach." In the latter, an eccentric works on a dictionary of the hieroglyphics of a universal language that is the basis of all art forms. Other stories are gothic fantasies. "The Ball" starts with a triumphant war communiqué, continues with the description of a great ball celebrating the victory, and ends in a vision of a danse macabre of all those killed or maimed in that victorious battle. "A Dead Man's Joke" has a beautiful lady, who abandoned her young lover to marry a middle-aged dignitary, dream first of a brilliant ball, which is routed by the raging floodwaters of the Neva, then of herself astride a coffin whose lid snaps open to reveal the livid features of her dead lover. The lady wakes up to learn that she had fainted at a ball. "The Brigadier" is an amazing preview of Tolstoi's "Death of Ivan Ilyich." Like Tolstoi's story, it starts with the funeral of what must have been a happy and successful man, then lets the dead man tell the true story of his life, which is most proper and rather ordinary if viewed from the outside, but in fact is an ugly tale of sinful waste.

The main interest of *Russian Nights* is with humanity's future. "The Last Suicide" is an avowedly Malthusian fantasy. After terrible overpopulation has brought about a perversion of all moral values, the peoples of the world finally find unanimity in a plan to blow up the globe. "A Nameless City" is another condensed "history" of modern humanity ending in ruin. Here the optimistic economic theories of Adam Smith and Jeremy Bentham are the target of Odoevsky's irony. The stories of *Russian Nights* are challenging philosophically, but they may not be great fiction. Odoevsky achieves greater philosophical depth than does Hoffmann; but he reveals little of Hoffmann's luxuriant imagination in the details of his tales. Odoevsky can tell a good story, and his style is lively, but he lacks the German story-teller's gentle irony, mellow humor, and deft verbal artistry.

Odoevsky wrote a number of stories that did not enter *Russian Nights*. Most of them are very Hoffmannesque, and not very good. But there are also some strong pieces which, like "The Brigadier," anticipate later works of Russian literature. "The Painter" (1839) is a tale of artistic failure such as was earlier attempted by Polevoi in a story of the same title (1833) and brilliantly realized by Dostoevsky in *Netochka Nezvanova* (1848). Odoevsky's painter has real talent; but poverty, a lack of understanding on the part of his customers, and his own stubborn insistence on pursuing his fleeting visions, rather than completing his pictures, cause him to fail. He dies young, leaving a single large canvas covered by many layers of uncompleted paintings. "The Unpassable House" (1842), a tale in the manner of a Russian folk legend, strikingly anticipates Tolstoi's *Tales for the People*. Odoevsky's society tales go a long way toward the psychological novella of Turgenev. "Duchess Mimi" (1834) is a masterful character sketch of an aging spinster, whose spiteful gossip precipitates a hideous tragedy. The portrayals of her victims, though placed into an ingenious and credible plot, remain schematic. "Duchess Zizi" (1839) has an attractive heroine and an intriguing plot. Zizi devotes her life to a seemingly decent and attractive man. When he marries her frivolous sister, she conceals her love for him and is content with the role of house-keeper and governess in her sister's household. When her sister dies, Zizi finally reveals her feelings to her brother-in-law, but soon discovers that he is a scoundrel, who married her sister for her money and will use her similarly. She recovers from this blow, and the end of the story shows her as a charming and wise middle-aged woman who enjoys life.

Lermontov's Prose

Mikhail Lermontov, poet and dramatist, was also a prolific prose writer in all of the romantic genres, including the historical novel. His only mature prose work, though, is *A Hero of Our Time* (1840), a novel. It developed from what were originally separate short stories, three of which—"Taman," "Bela," and "The Fatalist"—had previously appeared. Only "Bela" was initially projected to be part of a cycle, *From an Officer's Caucasian Notebooks*, its subtitle in the journal version of 1839.

In some ways *A Hero of Our Time* resembles *The Tales of Belkin*. It has a hierarchy of narrators, providing a narrative frame, and five stories, each in a different style. The stories of *A Hero of Our Time*, however, are linked by a common hero, Pechorin, whose character is gradually revealed through successive episodes in his life. Boris Eichenbaum has suggested that in Russia, with no real tradition of the novel, it was precisely the cycle of short stories, popular in romantic literature, that led to the novel. The first three great Russian novels, *Eugene Onegin*, *A Hero of Our Time*, and *Dead Souls*, were thus composed, and so were the first novels of Dostoevsky (*Netochka Nezvanova*) and Tolstoi (*Childhood*).

A Hero of Our Time, like *The Tales of Belkin*, has had the benefit of extensive interpretation. This goes particularly for the novel's many connections with other works of Russian and world literature. Pechorin (from Pechora, a northern river) is a pointed challenge to Onegin (from Onega, another northern river). Lermontov's narrative, which starts as a Caucasian travelogue, immediately evokes Pushkin's travelogue "A Journey to Arzrum." Eichenbaum found veiled messages of political protest in various cleverly planted details, such as when Pechorin is reported to be reading Walter Scott's novel *Old Mortality*, which tells of the struggle of Scottish Whigs against the king of England. Eichenbaum also saw a polemical edge aimed at Alfred de Musset's novel *Confession d'un enfant du siècle*. Unlike *The Tales of Belkin*, Lermontov's novel was much appreciated by contemporaries. Belinsky's authority, never seriously challenged by Apollon Grigoryev's charge that Pechorin was an artificial creation not anchored in Russian life, made Pechorin a generic type and the novel a classic.

The lead story, "Bela," is a Caucasian romance à la Marlinsky in which Pechorin, presented by Maksim Maksimych, an honest but simpleminded fellow officer, plays the role of a blasé Byronic hero. The story of an innocent native girl's tragic love for an emotionally burned-out European is framed by a travelogue which twice interrupts the narrative. The narrative is *erlebte Rede* (speech projected through the prism of a listener's consciousness), with Maksim Maksimych's voice projected through the consciousness of a more sophisticated narrator; but Pechorin's voice is also heard, for Maksim Maksimych "quotes" him repeatedly. In spite of its skillful presentation, "Bela" is a trite and predictable variation on an old theme. In the second story, "Maksim Maksimych," the narrator witnesses a chance meeting of Pechorin and Maksim Maksimych, giving him an opportunity to draw a first character sketch of Pechorin. It provides a link to the following stories, as the

narrator now finds himself in possession of Pechorin's notebooks. The next story, "Taman," is a romantic tease. Pechorin's adventures in Taman, a small seaport in the Caucasus, feature a haunted house, an enticing and mysterious young woman, and an uncanny blind boy, but the action resolves itself quite prosaically. "Taman" is a rebuttal of the Rousseauan clichés in "Bela" and a deflation of that story's hero. Viktor Vinogradov has suggested that "Taman" makes a parodic stab at Zhukovsky's "Undina," a versified version of Friedrich de la Motte-Fouqué's famous romantic tale "Undine." Pechorin, cast in the role of a knightly hero, calls the young woman who almost drowns him his *undina*, or mermaid.

The fourth story, "Duchess Mary," is a society tale of illicit love and intrigue, ending in a fatal duel. It is told by Pechorin himself and reveals more of his character. Pechorin's victim, young Grushnitsky, is Pechorin in travesty, as it were, and is as much a projection of Lermontov's personality as is Pechorin. The final story, "The Fatalist," is a conventional romantic tale of suspense, but it also reveals the mainspring of Pechorin's character: without any firm beliefs or principles he follows his impulses and, being naturally brave and vigorous, delights in any challenge, even against heavy odds. Like several of Pushkin's characters, Pechorin fades from the scene without a resolution of his existential impasse.

Pechorin became Onegin's successor in a chain of "superfluous men" in Russian literature. He represented a step forward: a rebel without a cause instead of an aimless sybarite. Lermontov's economical prose style had a considerable influence on the subsequent development of Russian prose fiction. *A Hero of Our Time* has some glaring weaknesses in composition and plot development, but its reputation as one of the great novels of Russian literature has remained largely unchallenged.

Women Writers

In the 1830s there appeared for the first time enough women writers to speak of them as a distinct phenomenon in Russian literature. With no occupation save that of governess open to an educated woman, a career as a writer was particularly attractive to women. In general, women writers were locked into a special compartment of literature, that of innocuous entertainment combined with maudlin edification. There was now a steady demand for children's books, and some women writers, such as Aleksandra Ishimova (1806–1881), specialized in this field. Belinsky, in a review article, "The Works of Zeneida R——va [Elena Hahn]" (1843), pointed out that the example of George Sand had freed women writers everywhere from decorous mediocrity and had made it possible for them to write, as men always could, challengingly and provocatively, advancing new ideas, women's rights in particular. In fact, the women writers of the 1830s and 1840s gave more promise of an emerging feminist literature than was realized by the following generation.

Nadezhda Durova (1783–1866) was the famous "maiden cavalryman." Disguised as a man, Durova, married and the mother of a child, served with distinction in the tsar's cavalry from 1806 to 1816. In 1836 she published her memoirs, *Notes of a Maiden Cavalryman*, and subsequently a novel and a number of short stories appeared in one volume, *Tales and Stories* (1839). Durova's fiction is in the romantic vein of Bestuzhev or Veltman. Her stories tend to have an intricate plot, feature local color, and are told vigorously, though conventionally. Durova's best-known story, "The Sulphur Spring," is a tale of two young lovers. When the man dies in a fight with a huge bear, his beloved loses her mind from grief. The story is set in a Cheremis village and is lent an exotic air by some touches of folklore. Durova was, however, no more than a talented amateur.

Marya Zhukova (1804–55) scored a significant success with her two-volume collection of stories *Evenings on Karpovka* (1838–39). Her *Tales* (1840), also in two parts, was well received. *Sketches of Southern France and Nice* (1844) was also successful. Some of Zhukova's stories are historical novellas, and some are set abroad, with non-Russian characters, quite common in Russian literature during the romantic period. But her main theme is the life of an educated, soulful, but unhappy Russian woman. In "The Medallion" (1838) she is a homely and pensive orphan girl, who must live in the shadow of the beautiful and vivacious natural daughter of her foster parents. As in other works on that theme, Marya is the deeper and more talented of the two, but Sofya always wins the prize with her superficial brilliance. In "The Self-Sacrifice" (1840), Liza, the ward of a rich countess, is in love with Minsky, a distant relative of her benefactress. As the family is taking the waters at a German spa, the countess is having an affair with a French gentleman. When the count surprises the lovers, Liza has the presence of mind to pretend that it is she, not the countess, who is involved in an illicit liaison. Liza has lost Minsky, but the French gentleman is so impressed with her generosity that he asks for her hand. She accepts, but later absolves him of his promise and returns to Russia to open a boarding school for young girls.

Zhukova, taking after George Sand, often

digresses from her narrative to discuss social and moral issues, in particular her thesis that women are capable of having, and ought to be allowed to have, a sphere of activity even outside the family. Her style is Sandian, too—fluent, at times florid, emotional, but without a distinctive personal note. The composition of her stories is awkward. They are not well focused, and the gaps between exposition, inserted flashbacks, and epilogue are sometimes annoying.

Karolina Pavlova's society tale *A Dual Life* (1848) has a simple, familiar plot. Cecilia, a beautiful, pensive, and soulful young lady, has many suitors. Her mother arranges her marriage to an attractive young man who, although somewhat in love with her, really marries her for her money. The reader is made to recognize that Cecilia is about to enter an unhappy marriage and waste her gifts in an aimless life: the bridegroom, at a boisterous bachelor party, makes a bet that he will spend a night with the Gypsies before he has been married a week. Cecilia's lonely meditations are presented in verse, a device motivated by the theme of a dual life: outwardly a radiant society belle, Cecilia has a rich inner life, filled with melancholy forebodings, doubts about the meaning of her life, and a yearning for higher spheres of existence. Pavlova's excellent verses are in tune with the heroine's feelings. Her prose is fluent and elegant, though not very expressive.

Countess Evdokiya Rostopchina (1811–58), a Moscow socialite, was known for her poetry, and especially for her plays of the 1850s, more than for her society tales—which are, however, not significantly inferior to those of her contemporaries, such as Nikolai Pavlov or Zhukova. "Rank and Money" (1838), like so many prose works of this period, is awkwardly structured. It consists of a single long letter from Vadim Svirs-ky, a young man without rank or fortune, to his sister; excerpts from Vadim's diary; and a third-person epilogue, told by Svirsky's sister. The plot is a familiar one. Svirsky falls in love with Vera, a beautiful Moscow debutante whose parents will not allow her to marry him. She is forced instead to marry a middle-aged general. Vadim kills himself, and Vera dies of a broken heart. "The Duel" (1838) begins with a physiological sketch of an army officer's life, then reveals the guilty secret of its melancholy hero. The story he finally tells resembles that of Silvio in Pushkin's "The Shot," with the difference that the other man is killed. A soulful heroine and a Gypsy's prophesy of doom are added, the latter in a rather gauche post-mortem.

Elena Hahn (Russ. Gan, née Fadeeva, 1814–42), who published under the pen name Zeneida R—va, met with instant success and was hailed by some as the Russian George Sand. Several of her stories, such as "The Ideal" (1837), "Society's Judgment" (1840), and "God's Judgment" (1840), deal with her own plight. A well-educated young woman, she was married to an army officer, who was intellectually her inferior, and had to live under the stifling conditions of garrison life in the provinces. Her stories are a cry of anguish over the slow death of a woman's mind and soul in a society that has no use for either. Unlike in some of George Sand's novels, or even in Aleksandr Druzhinin's Sandian novel *Polinka Saks* (1847), the heroine always remains virtuous, and sexual emancipation is not a concern of the author's. Like George Sand, Hahn ventured into exotic settings, as in "Utballa" (1838), where she uses her familiarity with the Kalmyks of the Astrakhan region, or in "Teofania Abbiaggio" (1841), set in Italy. Hahn, a talented writer whose promising career was cut short by an early death, shared some of the virtues, but also some of the faults, of the early George Sand. Her emotionality sometimes becomes sentimental, her fluid style rhetorical, and her sharply drawn characters stereotyped. Yet when Hahn speaks of what were evidently her own experiences—such as when describing the reaction of some officers' wives to the appearance among them of a writer, who also happens to be the wife of a mere captain ("Society's Judgment"), or when venting her outrage at men's callous lack of concern for a woman's ideals ("The Ideal")—her voice rings with genuine pathos.

Avdotya Panaeva (1820–93), the legal wife of Ivan Panaev and common-law wife of Nikolai Nekrasov, actively participated in their work on *The Contemporary*. She launched her career as a writer with the short novel *The Talnikov Family*, printed in *An Illustrated Almanac* in 1848. The almanac was confiscated by the authorities, however, largely on account of Panaeva's contribution, which was declared "subversive of parental authority." Panaeva went on to write several more novels and short stories, as well as important memoirs. *The Talnikov Family* is a family novel in the manner of the natural school, describing the life of an upper-middle class family from the viewpoint of an ugly-duckling daughter, from six years of age to the day of her wedding at seventeen. The picture is a sordid and depressing one. A brutal father and an insensitive mother neglect their children, leaving them to the care of a stupid and cruel governess, or of uncles and aunts who are worse. The children survive because they become callous themselves. The whole story is crassly naturalistic, down to graphic descriptions of whippings and the filth and vermin that infest this genteel home. The narrative is vivid and has the ring of truth, although it is obviously influenced by similar works by Dickens, Sue, and possibly others.

Gogol

Nikolai Vasilyevich Gogol (1809–52) was born in Sorochintsy, a small town near Poltava in the Ukraine, the son of a country squire and Ukrainian "dialect" playwright. He attended school in Nezhin, also in the Ukraine, where he acquired a good humanistic education. Like many young Ukrainians, he went to Petersburg after his graduation in 1828 to make his fortune. He tried teaching and clerking, even auditioned at one of the theaters of the capital (he had considerable histrionic talent and would later be a brilliant reader of his own works), but soon discovered that writing was his best bet. His first published work, "Hans Küchelgarten," an idyll of German life in blank verse, which he published at his own expense, was a failure, although it was no worse than many similar works of the period. But his two volumes of Ukrainian stories, *Evenings on a Farm near the Dikanka River* (1831–32) were a huge success. Two more volumes of Ukrainian tales under the title *Mirgorod* (1835) and two volumes of miscellaneous prose entitled *Arabesques* (1835), containing various essays and the first of his Petersburg tales, established Gogol as Russia's leading prose writer. He was on cordial terms with Zhukovsky and Pushkin and published a story, "The Nose," in *The Contemporary*. Gogol later claimed that he had received the themes of both his *Inspector General* and *Dead Souls* from Pushkin. In 1834–35 Gogol taught medieval history at Petersburg University. Later accounts, by Turgenev and others, of his alleged inadequacy as a professor were probably exaggerated. Some lectures that were included in Gogol's *Arabesques*, though not original, are interesting and eloquent.

On April 19, 1836, Gogol's comedy *The Inspector General* was staged in Saint

Petersburg, with the personal approval of the tsar and in his presence. It was a great theatrical success, but it also elicited vituperative protests from many people who felt that Gogol's satire of provincial mismanagement and corruption was unfair to Russian officialdom and was a gratuitous insult to Russian society at large. Gogol spent the next twelve years abroad, mostly in Rome, which had a substantial Russian colony at the time, returning to Russia for brief visits only. He found patronesses among the expatriate Russian aristocracy and on his visits to Russia met with the hospitality and adulation of the Moscow Slavophiles. Abroad, Gogol rewrote several of his early works, wrote another brilliant comedy, *Marriage*, and finished the first part of *Dead Souls*, which appeared in 1842. Gogol started work on the second part of *Dead Souls* immediately but was never able to complete it to his satisfaction. He destroyed one manuscript in 1846 and another before his death in 1852. He read portions of it to his friends, who were favorably impressed. An early manuscript accidentally survived. Part Two is generally considered much inferior to Part One, although it, too, left deep traces in Russian literature.[62]

In 1847 Gogol published his ill-fated *Selected Passages from My Correspondence with Friends*, a collection of essays and thoughts on a variety of subjects religious, moral, social, and literary. The tenor of the work was conservative, its leitmotiv that individual virtue and self-perfection were the answer to Russia's problems, not any newfangled ideas or social changes. He thus put himself squarely behind the existing order and in fact endorsed serfdom, which he perceived as a patriarchal relationship between landowner and peasant. As for civic virtue, Gogol considered it inseparable from religion and in his essays on literature insisted on the primacy of its religious and moral mission. Accordingly, he gave a narrow moral meaning to his own work, specifically *Dead Souls*. *Selected Passages*, a very uneven book, has some truly edifying pages (such as the essay "Easter Sunday") and some perceptive observations (for example, on Pushkin's position in Russian literature); but it also has some flat, pedestrian, pretentious, and outrageous ones. The response was overwhelmingly negative, even on the part of some of Gogol's Slavophile friends— after all, they were opposed to serfdom, too. Belinsky, Gogol's lifelong champion, felt that Gogol had betrayed the cause of progress, and he responded with his "Letter to Gogol." The book was met warmly by only a few critics, notably Apollon Grigoryev. In retrospect, *Selected Passages* was no artistic success, but it stated with remarkable perspicacity the positions of Russian conservative thought as developed by the generation following Gogol's.

Shattered by the negative response to *Selected Passages*, Gogol went on a pilgrimage to the Holy Land in 1848 and then returned to Russia, where he spent the last years of his life in restless travel. His mind was more than ever preoccupied with the salvation of his soul. He was now under the influence of Father Matvei Konstantinovsky, a narrow-minded religious fanatic, who urged him to abandon his secular writing. Nevertheless, he did continue to work on part 2 of *Dead Souls*. Gogol died in Moscow on February 21, 1852, apparently of exhaustion and collapse of his vital functions due to excessive ascetic practices.

Gogol was a mystery to his contemporaries and has remained so to this day, in part because of his secretive and histrionic

---

62. For example, Goncharov's *Oblomov* is unthinkable without Tentetnikov, the lovable but inert landowner of Part Two of Dead Souls.

nature. His tendency to dissimulate or to withdraw into a shell had deep roots. He was an alien and outsider all his life— ethnically as a Ukrainian to whom Russian was an acquired language, socially as a poor provincial of dubious nobility in a largely aristocratic ambience, intellectually as a man who literally believed in heaven and hell (and devils, too) among enlightened men of letters. Although the fragment "Rome" is Gogol's only mature work set abroad, the fact that he saw the Russia of *Dead Souls* "from his splendid afar," as he put it, is not to be ignored. Furthermore, Gogol, who never married and never was romantically involved with a woman, may have been homoerotically inclined.[63] Gogol apparently suffered from a manic-depressive condition: an entertaining conversationalist and brilliant improviser, he also experienced periods of torpid inactivity and black melancholy.

The literary sources of Gogol's works are manifold. He was well read in Russian and European literatures. His aesthetics and poetics fit within the framework of romantic literature, from which his themes and characters are for the most part derived. He owed a debt to his Ukrainian predecessors Narezhny and Kvitka-Osnovyanenko and took an active interest in Ukrainian folklore, of which he was an avid collector. His Ukrainian tales reflect this interest.

Evenings on a Farm near the Dikanka River is a miscellany of stories loosely connected by a narrative frame: a beekeeper of the town of Mirgorod identifies himself as the author or transcriber of these stories. Some of them are told by a deacon in town, and in one story three narrators are interposed between author and reader—the

63. See Simon Karlinsky, *The Sexual Labyrinth of Nikolai Gogol* (Cambridge, Mass.: Harvard University Press, 1976).

beekeeper, the deacon, and the deacon's late grandfather. An ingenuous narrator "of the people" was a common device of romantic literature, as were local color, folk traditions, and regional dialect, all of which appear in Gogol's tales. Some quotations from the dialect comedies of Gogol's father appear in the text and as epigraphs in some of the stories. The characters are stereotypes of the Ukrainian puppet theater— dashing young Cossacks, pretty maidens, foolish, drunken and henpecked old men, shrewish old women who are not averse to extramarital escapades, and of course the devil. The mood is frankly Ukrainian: Muscovites are baited lustily, as are Jews, Poles, and Catholics.

The stories of *Evenings* are a mixture of romantic genres, styles, and moods. Delicate lyric passages and pathetic tirades alternate with slapstick comedy and racy dialogue, idyllic high style with folksy vulgarisms, and perfectly literate Russian with blatant Ukrainianisms. Occasional pensive observations on the transitoriness of human joy and gladness interrupt the flow of rustic humor that prevails in most of the stories. A passage of this sort concludes the otherwise riotously funny lead story, "The Sorochintsy Fair."

The plots of Gogol's Ukrainian tales range from farce and genre comedy to gothic melodrama. In "The Night before Christmas" Vakula, the village smith, who does some icon painting as a sideline, has angered the devil by making some uncomplimentary likenesses of him. The devil strikes back by causing all kinds of mischief in the village, some of it revolving around the amorous escapades of Vakula's mother, who is the village witch. Meanwhile Oksana, Vakula's ladylove, promises to marry him if he will give her a pair of shoes like the ones the empress herself wears. Vakula hitches a ride on the devil's back and gets the shoes. The episode in Petersburg presents a whimsically estranged vignette of Catherine the Great and her court. Upon his return Vakula gets the blessing of Oksana's wealthy father to marry her. Half a dozen other stories by Gogol are similar to "The Night before Christmas."

In other of Gogol's Ukrainian tales gothic melodrama prevails. "A Terrible Vengeance" has an intricate plot which gradually unravels the secret of an ancient curse. The story contains many of the motifs typical of a gothic tale: horrible dungeons, a cemetery from which the dead arise, the conjuring of spirits, a hint of incestuous passion, a pious hermit, and the murder of an innocent babe. It has some beautiful lyric passages, too, specifically a famous description of the Dnepr River. The gothic themes here and in other stories by Gogol have been traced to E. T. A. Hoffmann, Ludwig Tieck, and other Western writers. "A Terrible Vengeance" also contains some elements of the Ukrainian folk epic, the *duma*, especially in the rhythm of its narrative, the structure of its imagery (triadic arrangement, negative simile), and the style of some lyric passages, such as a lament by Katerina, the story's tragic heroine.

Gogol's second collection, *Mirgorod*, contains some of his finest stories. "Taras Bulba," a historical novella in its *Mirgorod* version, was later expanded into a historical novel (1842), much to the detriment of the work. "Taras Bulba" is set in an idealized Ukraine of an unspecified past. Bulba is a Cossack leader who mounts a campaign against the king of Poland to give his two sons, who have just returned from school in Kiev, a chance to prove their valor. He loses both. The older is captured by the Poles and executed in Warsaw, before his father's eyes. The younger turns traitor and joins the enemy for the sake of his love for a beautiful Polish woman. Bulba kills him when they meet on the field of battle. Bulba is himself killed after having cut a bloody swath through the Polish lands. This story of tragic hubris, guilt, and atonement is embedded in a wildly implausible plot and a monstrously uneven text. There are some excellent lyric and descriptive passages, but also naturalistic accounts of unspeakable atrocities and cruel suffering. The battle scenes, apparently patterned after Virgil, are utterly unbelievable. Crude buffoonery and grotesque hyperbole are found throughout the work. The second version, moreover, features a great deal of pro-Muscovite rhetoric. Both versions, though the second more than the first, are marred by much ugly baiting of Jews and Poles. "Taras Bulba" was greeted by almost everybody as an inspirational patriotic work and has been a recommended school text ever since. It has too many serious flaws to be deserving of its fame.

"The Viy," like "A Terrible Vengeance," is a gothic tale set in the Ukraine of old. A Kiev divinity student rides an old witch to death on a frenzied nocturnal flight and discovers at dawn that the dead woman is a beautiful young maiden. He is summoned by her father, a powerful dignitary, to read the prayers for the soul of the departed over her coffin. He barely survives two spooky nights and is done in on the third by the Viy, a horrible earth spirit, who kills him with his lethal gaze. "The Viy" is a successful fusion of lighthearted genre comedy (analogous to genre painting) and terrifying grotesque. It is one of Gogol's few stories featuring an erotic motif, though it is quickly dismissed. Like some other stories by Gogol, it invites a Freudian reading. Opinions on Gogol's gothic tales vary, from "absurd" and "contrived" to "ingeniously structured" and "psychologically challenging."

Two of the *Mirgorod* stories are acknowledged masterpieces. "Old-Time Landowners" is a *parodie sérieuse* of the Philemon and Baucis theme, explicitly mentioned in the text. What seems to be a rural idyll is slowly undermined by the casual exposure of the terrible sloth, gluttony, and mindlessness of the old couple, then given another turn by the touching story of their death. "The Tale of How Ivan Ivanovich Quarreled with Ivan Nikiforovich," ostensibly a good-natured satire, has hidden depths. It eventually dawns on readers that what they were inclined to take for an absurd grotesque is simply the truth of life. Caricatures of human types turn out to be portraits. Harmless banality is really ugly cruelty. Hyperbole masquerading as realistic description (yet dangerously close to the truth), ludicrous non sequitur, and other forms of verbal clowning, including so-called sound speech (*zvukorech*)—that is, sequences of meaningless but funny or grotesque-sounding words or word combinations—are all ultimately symbolic of an inane and absurd world.

Arabesques contained three important short stories, all set in Petersburg. "The Portrait" is a Hoffmannesque *Künstlernovelle* with an involved plot, combining a serious though hardly original treatment of the familiar theme of the artist's obligation to his talent with an assortment of gothic details, such as a cursed portrait with an "evil eye."

"Nevsky Prospect" is part *Künstlernovelle*, too. It starts with a lively description of Nevsky Prospect, Petersburg's main thoroughfare, traces the path of two young men, an artist and an officer, and ends with another glance at Nevsky Prospect, as "a demon lights the streetlamps only to let everything appear not as it really is." The sensitive artist meets a young woman of great beauty who turns out to be a vulgar prostitute. This gives him such a shock that he goes out of his mind and dies. The officer also follows a beautiful young woman, but she turns out to be the virtuous wife of a German artisan. His attempts at seduction are rewarded by a sound thrashing from Frau Schiller's husband and his friends Hoffmann and Kuntz. He easily shakes off this indignity and that very night is seen dancing the mazurka in the best company. Lieutenant Pirogov became proverbial as the happily mindless Russian.

"Diary of a Madman" is a tour de force: the romantic theme of a dreamer's tragic clash with reality is moved from the world of art (an early version still bore the title "Diary of a Mad Musician") into the drab day-to-day existence of a copying clerk. The hero, Poprishchin (from *poprishche*, "career"), who suffers the plight reserved in romantic literature for painters, poets, and musicians of genius, is an ignorant, stupid, and rather obnoxious fellow. The existential question raised by the story is, how should an ordinary copying clerk, a cog in a soulless machine, realize himself as an individual? Poprishchin does it by imagining that he is the king of Spain. The inevitable corollary is that there is no rational way out of his dilemma. Dostoevsky's novel *The Double* (1846), a spin-off of Gogol's story, makes the point that the copying clerk's attempts to assert his individuality in the "real world" can lead only to a futile replication of his self.

"The Nose" (1836), a comic grotesque, tells of the mysterious disappearance and eventual return of Collegiate Assessor Kovalyov's nose. The loss and recovery of one's nose, as well as other puns and anecdotes about noses, were common in eighteenth- and early nineteenth-century literature. Some readers, even without recourse to Freudian interpretation, would substitute another part of the anatomy for "nose." Since the nose appears in many Russian proverbial expressions, the story is also an exercise in realized metaphor. Letting a miraculous event occur in ordinary trivial surroundings was common in romantic literature (Hoffmann's tales, in particular), as was the way Gogol uses this device to demonstrate the absurdity of "normal" life. The noseless Kovalyov engages the aid of the police, a doctor, and a newspaper advertising agency. It develops that real police work, real medical practice, and real ads are if anything even more absurd than Kovalyov's lost nose. The surrealist plot of "The Nose" has no "key" or resolution and deconstructs itself repeatedly. The initial plot line, which has Kovalyov's barber find a nose in his bread, is soon abandoned. The story is told by a third-person narrator who exudes bonhomie and unconditional solidarity with and solicitude for his hero. "The Nose" is a piece of virtuosic writing. Still, the vast scholarly attention it has received seems excessive.

The same may be said of "The Overcoat" (1842), although it is one of the great short stories in all of literature. Its hero, Akaky Akakyevich Bashmachkin (from *bashmak*, "shoe"), has been a copying clerk for thirty years and lives only for his work. His tailor gives him the bad news that his old overcoat is beyond repair and that he will have to get a new one. Most of the story is devoted to Akaky Akakyevich's efforts to save the money needed for the new coat: he starves himself, quits drinking tea, walks on tiptoes to save the heels of his shoes. When he finally wears his new coat to the office, he is invited to a party to celebrate the occasion. On his way home, the coat is stolen off his back. He makes a desperate effort to get a search for it started, but an "important personage" gives him a tongue-lashing for

bothering him. Heartbroken, Akaky Akakyevich takes ill and dies. His ghost is reported to be haunting the streets of Petersburg and robbing people's overcoats. The important personage, too, becomes a victim of the vengeful ghost. The ghost, by the way, is a tease, a metaphor, and something "real" all at the same time.

The character type that Gogol presented in "The Overcoat" was not new. Dickens's poor clerks and the supernumeraries of Balzac are his close relatives. But Gogol drove the dehumanization of a human being to the limit, creating a man whose only delight is the shape of certain letters and whose only love affair in life is with an overcoat. The story is told in a tone of light banter, only a few times interrupted by some moralizing observations, which caused the message of the story to be taken for one of "sentimental humanitarianism," as Apollon Grigoryev put it. The appearance of the ghost was then a call to rebellion against the "little man's" oppressors. Countless other interpretations have been advanced. According to one of these, first suggested by Belinsky, "The Overcoat" is a study in human existence as it approaches nonexistence. The hero's life is ghostlike, in the sense in which Hoffmann spoke of a "ghostlike philistine existence." Only in death does Akaky Akakyevich acquire a modicum of reality. This interpretation moves "The Overcoat" into that region of romantic fiction which, like Hoffmann's "Master Flea," generates dread by reducing the normal to the subnormal. As Vladimir Nabokov put it, we find in "The Overcoat" shadows "linking our state of existence to those other states and modes which we dimly apprehend in our rare moments of irrational perception."

Dostoevsky, in his first novel, *Poor Folk* (1846), has his hero, another copying clerk, view "The Overcoat" as a libelous attack on the human dignity of the "little man." Vasily Rozanov saw in Akaky Akakyevich a cruel caricature, a travesty of a human being, deprived of his soul. In Boris Eichenbaum's celebrated essay, "How Is Gogol's 'Overcoat' Made?" (1919), "The Overcoat" is conceived as a comic grotesque in which sound effects (iconic use of funny or expressive sound patterns, as in the hero's name and patronymic), verbal clowning, and comic imagery are the real object of the writer's art. F. C. Driessen observed that the story echoes the legend of Saint Akaky (Acacius), the humble servant of a stern elder. When Akaky died, his master, forgetting that his servant was dead, called for him—and Akaky obediently rose from his bier. The story of Akaky Akakyevich's life and death is then a travesty of a saint's life.

Dead Souls, Gogol's most ambitious work, defies classification. Its plot is that of a picaresque novel. The hero, Chichikov, a retired government official, arrives in a provincial town, makes friends with everybody, and soon starts calling on local landowners with the purpose of buying their "dead souls," meaning serfs deceased but still carried on the tax rolls until the next census. He visits the insipid dreamer Manilov, the dense and superstitious widow Korobochka, the drunken braggart and bully Nozdryov, the brutish but shrewd Sobakevich, and the dirty miser Plyushkin. Having acquired some four hundred dead souls, he returns to town to obtain legal title to them. He is at first lionized as a millionaire, but soon suspicions arise, and Chichikov leaves town in a hurry. In a flashback the reader is told the story of Chichikov's past. It reveals that he was twice dismissed from government service for embezzlement and corruption, and that his current scheme is to use his dead souls as collateral for a loan from a government agency. In Part Two, Chichikov con-

tinues to buy dead souls but also gets involved in other crooked schemes. He is caught and thrown in prison, but then saved by a friend who is intent on returning him to the path of righteousness. It was Gogol's plan to follow his hero to the day when he would be fully reformed.

The characters of *Dead Souls* are Russian versions of familiar universal types. But then, too, *Dead Souls* is a satire of Russian life: its targets are not only official inefficiency and corruption but also the crushing banality and utter lack of spiritual or intellectual awareness in Russian life.[64] The very title of the work, demoted to subtitle by the censor,[65] draws attention to the fact that although Chichikov's transactions with dead souls are illegal, the sale of living souls (serfs) is perfectly legal; but at the same time it suggests that the society presented in the work is made up of dead souls.

The narrative is interrupted by many digressions, some of them quite long—causeries with the reader on a variety of topics, character sketches, anecdotes, worldly wisdom, philosophical discourses, Homeric similes, and lyric effusions. Many of these digressions are gems in their own right, like the marvelous description of a "concert" of barking dogs as Chichikov approaches a village in chapter 3. One of several Homeric similes develops in chapter 5 when Chichikov approaches Sobakevich's manor and discerns two faces in a window, the female resembling a cucumber and the male a pumpkin. At this point the narrator veers off into an idyllic vignette on bala-

64. The Russian word *poshlost'*, "banality, tawdriness, paltriness," has been called untranslatable. The poshlost' of Russian life was considered, even by contemporaries, to be the main subject of Gogol's art.

65. The title as it appeared in 1842 was *The Adventures of Chichikov, or Dead Souls: A Poem*.

laikas made from Moldavian pumpkins and strummed by peasant lads courting their lasses. A discourse on the creative writer who raises a scene from humble everyday life to the level of a "pearl of creation" introduces chapter 7. A satirical essay on how a scholarly theory will, like any common rumor, acquire a life of its own and take possession of its creator appears in chapter 9. And then there is the famous troika passage at the conclusion of Part One in which Russia is likened to a troika galloping at full speed into an uncertain future. The longest of the many digressions is the tale of Captain Kopeikin, told by the local postmaster, who suspects that Chichikov is in fact the ex-captain and feared highway robber Kopeikin. The tale is stylized to seem to be told by a naive and awkward narrator, a device called *skaz* (from *skazat'*, "to tell") by Russian Formalist scholars. The postmaster's hunch is absurd, for Kopeikin is known to be a one-legged and one-armed war invalid, but not quite as absurd as some other theories the locals advance regarding Chichikov's identity, one of which has it that he is really Napoleon, escaped from Saint Helena.

The narrative manner of *Dead Souls* is highly diverse, ranging from serious to humorous, from straightforward reporting to tongue-in-cheek banter, from accurate description to poetic or grotesque hyperbole, and from friendly chatting to outright verbal legerdemain, such as when the narrator apologizes for having uttered Chichikov's name too loudly—he might have awakened his hero, whom he had left asleep in his carriage. The narrative also has some traits that are peculiarly Gogolian. It is dominated by what Andrei Bely called the figure of fiction: Things seem solid, then dissolve into a fiction, like Chichikov's southern estate, for which he claims to be

buying all these "souls." Meanwhile, fictions acquire an oppressive reality. After champaign toasts at the police chief's, Chichikov returns to his hotel and orders his servant to line up the souls, whose acquisition he has celebrated, for a roll call. The narrative seems to be realistic and precise, yet on closer scrutiny it turns out that nothing described in the text is real: it cannot be determined from the text what season it really is, or by what route Chichikov gets to the places he visits. The real movement takes place in the narrator's imagination. It follows a manic-depressive pattern, undulating from earthbound heaviness and banality to epic gladness and easy flight of poetic fancy.

The inspired pasasge at the conclusion of chapter 5, on the power of the Russian word—which the narrator utters as it were from a vantage point in the sky, allowing him to see all of Russia spread out below him—is preceded by the description of a peasant carrying a huge log on his shoulder. Another panoramic vision of Russia, early in chapter 11, follows the description of a funeral. The exhilarating troika passage is preceded by some melancholy earthbound observations. This pattern appears throughout. In the process, Gogol uses poetic license in extending imaginative powers to the philistine Chichikov and even to the bearlike Sobakevich. Their fantasizing about dead souls changing owners contrasts with down-to-earth scenes with live souls who appear throughout the narrative.

The epic gladness and plenitude which balance the satirical and grotesque aspects of *Dead Souls* are enhanced by a host of details: loving descriptions of food, drink, and other amenities of life; vignettes of popular life in the manner of the Flemish school; ostentatious exhibition of the wealth of the Russian language through proverbs, sayings, idioms, jargon, and catalogs of words (Gogol's "verbal gluttony"); recurrent symbolic imagery, such as the recurring image of a wheel of Chichikov's carriage or the amusing bear imagery that accompanies Sobakevich; ample name symbolism (for instance, Nozdryov, from *nozdrya*, "nostril") and expressive sound patterning ("That canaille [*kanal'ya*] sings like a canary [*kanareika*]," says Nozdryov in praise of an actress).

The charm of *Dead Souls* lies in its verbal magic, which no reader who is willing to suspend rational analysis of the text can resist. Even some contemporaries pointed out that Gogol's text would not withstand such analysis and that Gogol was not describing any real Russian locale or ambience. But word by word, phrase by phrase, and passage by passage the text is bursting with energy and expressive power generated by a cornucopia of poetic devices. There is no prose work of this length in all of world literature that so consistently keeps the word as such foregrounded through ambiguity, irony, catachresis, pathos, hyperbole and hyperoche, symbolic suggestiveness, metaphoric or metonymic power, and all kinds of parallelism, as well as through its inherent qualities—words that are funny per se because they sound fancy to the Russian ear, because they elicit strange associations, or because they seem to fit their meaning perfectly.[66]

Dead Souls became an instant classic, although critical opinions were divided as to its value. No one could deny that it was immensely entertaining, but detractors shrugged off its humor as mere buffoonery

while finding the lofty lyric passages ludicrous. Belinsky insisted that it was no mere satire but rather a profoundly truthful representation of Russian life. He, too, felt that the lyric passages were out of place. Konstantin Aksakov welcomed it enthusiastically as a Russian epopoeia, kindred in spirit to Homer. Within a generation *Dead Souls* became firmly ingrained in the consciousness of every educated Russian, more so even than *Eugene Onegin*, because of its broader, middle-class sensibility. Its characters became generic, and innumerable phrases from *Dead Souls* entered the language. Quotes from and allusions to *Dead Souls* are ubiquitous in Russian literature.

Gogol was much praised and much abused by his contemporaries. He was misunderstood and underestimated by most, even by his champion, Belinsky. Belinsky's notion that Gogol had introduced realism (he did not use that term but called it "poetry of reality") into Russian literature was made canonical by Nikolai Chernyshevsky's *Essays in the Gogolian Period of Russian Literature* (1855–56). Chernyshevsky believed that Gogol was the first Russian writer to create works that were actively concerned with contemporary Russian life from a social viewpoint.[67] In other words, he considered Gogol to be the father of Russian realism. "We have all come out of Gogol's 'Overcoat,'" an anonymous Russian realist is reported to have said. Vasily Rozanov in the 1890s reversed this view, presenting Gogol as an illusionist who had tricked generations of readers into mistaking his world of soulless puppets for Russian reality. The true father of Russian realism was Pushkin, said Rozanov, and the symbol-

66. Nozdryov calls Chichikov a *fetyuk*. The word is derived from the letter *theta*, Russian *fita* or *feta*, which has the form of the female genitals. It was this kind of verbal curiosity that Gogol would pursue.

67. The critic Valerian Maikov had said this a decade earlier, as he destinguished the "social" writer Gogol from the "psychological" writer Dostoevsky.

ist critics who followed him made "the Gogolian strain of Russian literature" refer to writers who followed Gogol in using an active prose style featuring irony, ambiguity, innuendo, a literary subtext, symbolic imagery, and metaphor—as against writers who wrote straightforwardly and objectively, with metonymy their principal trope. Dostoevsky and Leskov would then be writers in the Gogolian manner, Turgenev and Tolstoi in the Pushkinian. Gogol also became the model for twentieth-century modernist and ornamentalist writers.

The Natural School

At the time of the flowering of the romantic tale, there developed what Belinsky called the tale of real life. The term *natural school* was used at first sarcastically by Bulgarin and then generically by Belinsky and others.[68] The natural school developed under the influence of the French phrenetic school, Dickens, Balzac, and the French *socialisant* roman-feuilleton. Its most typical genre was the so-called physiological sketch, a plotless or nearly plotless description of a particular milieu of Russian life, such as "The Organ Grinders of Saint Petersburg" (1845), by Dmitry Grigorovich (subtitled "A Story," though it has no plot). This genre, too, was of Western origin. Balzac's physiological sketches and Dickens's *Sketches by Boz* were key influences.

The natural school, which flourished until the early 1850s (Tolstoi's early stories are physiological sketches), spawned several other genres. The tale about a poor clerk, of which Gogol's "The Overcoat" is the most famous example, appeared in at least forty

different versions.[69] Social injustice and inequality were the theme of the abolitionist (antiserfdom) story, such as "The Nameday Party" (1835), by Nikolai Pavlov. The anti-serfdom story overlaps with the simple *Dorfgeschichte* (village story) in which the life of the Russian peasantry is presented for its "ethnographic" interest, sometimes in the peasant's own idiom, as in some of Vladimir Dahl's stories. The natural school's tale of a superfluous man exposes the idle, empty, and parasitic existence of the Russian upper classes. Turgenev's "Diary of a Superfluous Man" (1850) is the most famous of these stories.

The natural school developed a peculiar style whose principal trait was a tendency to fuse the narrator's point of view with that of his subject, though often retaining an ironic tension between them. Specifically, the narrator would adopt some of the speech mannerisms of his characters. Self-conscious verbal stylization ("grimacing"), a somewhat forced humor, grotesque exaggeration or understatement, and various types of catachresis (pointedly "incorrect" usage) were also common in works of the natural school.

Opponents of the natural school, such as Bulgarin and Senkovsky, denounced it for making "peasants, janitors, cabmen, etc." the heroes of their stories and presenting such settings as "slum tenements, the refuges of hungry beggars, and all kinds of immorality." In fact, writers of the natural school lowered the mentality of their subjects to a level unheard of before and, moreover, infused their stories with sympathy and compassion for the lowly social underdog. Apollon Grigoryev coined the label "the school of sentimental humanitarianism" for the many

68. Bulgarin, in a review of *A Petersburg Miscellany*, in *Northern Bee*, February 26, 1846; Belinsky, in a review of the same book, in *National Annals* 45. no. 3 (1846).

69. See A. G. Tseitlin, *Povest' o bednom chinovnike (k istorii odnogo syuzheta)* (Moscow, 1923).

writers who had this attitude, singling out the young Dostoevsky as the most talented among them.

In spite of Belinsky's advertising of the new school as one of "the poetry of reality,"[70] most of its works still bore romantic traits, even if their subject was the life of the rural or urban lower classes. Dostoevsky's stories of the 1840s feature lyric intermezzi, romantic irony (as when literary allusions deconstruct the realism of the plot), symbolic detail, and familiar romantic themes, such as a dreamer's clash with reality or an artist's clash with society.

There was some overlap in time between romantic and naturalist fiction. Most of the key figures of naturalism were born around 1820 and began to publish in the 1840s. But there were some who were much older and were already publishing in the 1830s. Nikolai Pavlov (1803–64) was born a serf, but after the manumission of his family in 1811 received a good education. He was the first Russian translator of Balzac and wrote some undistinguished verse before his *Three Tales* (1835) brought him general recognition. Later Pavlov was active mainly as a critic and journalist, without much distinction. His early tales are awkwardly constructed and told in a jerky, self-conscious manner. But they contain flashes of genuine pathos and on occasion have the ring of truth.

"The Dagger" sounds like a real event made into an implausible story. An impetuous young officer, in love with a beautiful young lady, kills a rival in a duel and is demoted to the ranks. His colonel happens to be another of the lady's suitors. The young man refuses to cede her to him, and when the colonel has him flogged for insubordination, stabs him with the dagger that

appears in the title of the story and acts as its "falcon."[71] A description of preparations for the gauntlet, which the soldier will not survive, concludes the story. "The Nameday Party" (*Imeniny*) is an antiserfdom tale. The hero is a serf who was trained to be a musician. His talent gains him admission to elegant drawing rooms, where the guests are unaware that they are being entertained by a serf. He falls in love with a young lady and she with him. He reveals his secret to her and enlists in the army, his only chance to become a free man. Having won a battlefield promotion to officer's rank, he returns to his home province, where he accidentally meets the woman he loved, but as another man's wife. Pavlov's society tales were among the first to feature consistent, though awkward, attempts at psychological motivation, as well as a conscious effort to connect fiction with Russian social reality.

Count Vladimir Sollogub (1813–82) is best known for "The Traveling Cart" (1845), a satire about a journey in which a Slavophile is pitted against a landowner with old-fashioned common sense. He also wrote a number of short stories that were highly thought of in the 1840s. Sollogub came from a family of Polish magnates and belonged to high society, but as a writer he cast his lot with the raznochintsy of the natural school. "A Story of Two Galoshes" (1839) is a künstlernovelle. The hero is a German musician who suffers every kind of misfortune and dies in poverty and despair. The narrative frame is provided, grotesquely and needlessly, by the delivery of two pairs of galoshes, one to the poor musician and one to the

---

70. The term *realism* was first used by Pavel Annenkov in an article in the *Contemporary*, 1849, no.1.

71. After Boccaccio's tale of that title in the *Decameron*. The falcon was used generically by Paul Heyse and other nineteenth-century theorists of the short story to signify a central dominant symbol upon which the plot and the denouement of a story hinge.

official who has married the musician's great love. "The Apothecary's Wife" (1841) also has a German cast, as the plot moves from Dorpat in Livonia (Sollogub had attended the University of Dorpat) to a town in Russia. A young baron meets the woman he had jilted when a student in Dorpat; she is now married to his schoolmate, a provincial apothecary. The baron tries to rekindle their romance but leaves her with a broken heart. "The Lapdog" (1845) is a ferocious satire on provincial corruption. The wife of a police chief takes a fancy to a lapdog belonging to the prima donna of a traveling troupe. When the actress refuses to part with her pet, the police chief closes the theater and declares that he will allow it reopen only when his wife gets the dog and a three-hundred-ruble shawl, and he a thousand rubles. The actors finally have to give in.

Evgeny Grebenka (1812–48) was one of the founders of modern Ukrainian literature. But his Russian stories in the vein of the natural school are also noteworthy. In "The Snipe" (1841), his most renowned story, Petrushka, a house serf, falls in love with Masha, a chambermaid on the neighboring estate. They are not allowed to marry, because their masters have quarreled over hunting rights. Petrushka and Masha make a suicide pact. He shoots her but is stopped from turning the gun on himself. He soon dies in prison. The story delivers its antiserfdom message most effectively, as Grebenka cleverly contrasts a rural idyll with the landowners' callous brutality. He also displays some of his compatriot Gogol's stylistic mannerisms, such as a sly pretense of solicitous solidarity with the detestable landowners and bureaucrats who populate his stories.

Vladimir Dahl (Russ. Dal', 1801–72), the son of a Danish father and a German mother, is best known as a lexicographer, linguist, and collector of Russian folklore. He started his professional life in the navy, then studied medicine, practicing it for some years, and served as an administrator in the eastern provinces of European Russia. His manifold practical, scientific (he was also a busy naturalist), and scholarly activities are reflected in his fiction, published under a pseudonym, Kazak Lugansky (Cossack of Lugansk), mostly in the 1830s and 1840s. A political conservative, Dahl was nonetheless an outspoken critic of the imperial bureaucracy and an astute observer of popular life. His style ranges from sly satire and gentle irony to impersonation of various narrative voices (*skaz*), including peasant dialect. Dahl's ethnographic pieces anticipate Turgenev's *Hunter's Sketches*. For example, "A Ural Cossack" (1842) is a character sketch of Proklyatov, a stalwart Old Believer Cossack warrior, fisherman, and paterfamilias. The final scene is quite moving. The Cossacks are returning from the wars, and when Proklyatov's wife asks the first horseman about her husband, he replies, "Further back." When she hears the same from the next squad, and the next, she knows the truth and breaks into a wail. In many ways Dahl anticipates Leskov. He has a genuine knowledge of and fondness for the Russian people, and reproduces their language without making it sound stylized. He does not conceal or gloss over the dark side of serfdom, exposing as much as the censorship will allow. His sympathy with the underdog is sincere, but unsentimental.

Dahl's naturalist stories are both rural and urban. "Drunken Ravings, Dream, and Reality" (1843) starts with an ethnographic sketch of the life-style of peasants who work as seasonal traveling artisans throughout Russia. It then tells the story of Stepan Voropaev, a carpenter, who kills a highway robber in self-defense and empties the dead man's billfold. His conscience does not bother him until he wakes up one morning, after some heavy drinking, with the recollection of having killed his drinking companion and pushed his body into a river. He remorsefully confesses his crime and is about to be deported, when the "dead" man turns up. Stepan's guilty conscience had caused him to dream of a crime, and drunk as he was, he took the dream for reality. He tries to confess to his actual crime but is laughed out of court. He takes this lesson to heart, though, and becomes a good family man. Among Dahl's urban pieces are some physiological sketches, such as "A Petersburg Janitor" (1844) and tales about a poor clerk. "A Man's Life, or a Walk along Nevsky Prospect" (1843) is about a clerk whose whole life moves, literally, along Nevsky Prospect. Much like Gogol's "Overcoat," the story amounts to the reduction of man to a ludicrously narrow and petty range of experience, leading to his utter helplessness outside his little niche in life and a paralyzing fear of having to leave it. The story has a Gogolian touch of the grotesque, but it is more concrete and closer to reality than "The Overcoat."

Dahl's repertory extends well beyond the natural school. "Pavel Alekseevich Igrivy" (1847) is a fine psychological novella. It begins with a meticulously detailed description of the daily routine of a provincial landowner, apparently a dull-witted recluse. It then tells the story of his life, which shows that he is really a noble, sensitive, loving, and capable man, whose happiness and zest for life were destroyed by several unfortunate accidents. Dahl's psychology is unconventional: his villains are weak and pathetic, although the effects of their villainies are disastrous. The hero anticipates Turgenev's Lavretsky of *A Nest of Gentlefolk*.

Nikolai Nekrasov is known mainly as one of the great poets of the nineteenth century and as the publisher of *The Contemporary*, *The National Annals*, and several important almanacs, including *A Physiology of Petersburg*. Nekrasov began to write for a living when not yet twenty. Much of what he wrote was hastily concocted and clearly derivative. Some of his stories display the mannerisms of the natural school in a particularly obtrusive way. Among these mannerisms are a penchant for the farfetched metaphor or simile (as well as for realized metaphor), a pervasive ironic tone often lapsing into verbal clowning, and frequent apostrophes to the reader. A typical example is "The Life of Aleksandra Ivanovna: A Tale of Four Carriages" (1841), which records the stations of the heroine's slide from the high life of kept woman, who rides in an elegant carriage, to death as a poor washerwoman whose coffin is carted to the cemetery.

Ivan Panaev (1812–62), publisher and editor, with Nekrasov, of *The Contemporary*, was primarily a journalist. He wrote short stories, essays, feuilletons, and reviews. He began publishing his stories in the early 1830s but gained prominence as a leader of the natural school only in the 1840s. Panaev's stories point an accusing finger at the parasitic upper class. "A Lady" (1841) is a physiological sketch describing the various "subspecies" (capital versus provincial, for instance) of the Russian lady. Its centerpiece is the story of Pelageya Petrovna, a Petersburg socialite, whose life is marked by idleness, living beyond her husband's means, and mismanaging her household. Its only meaning is from her always maintaining the status of a lady. "The Onager" (1841) is a harebrained, insipid young gentleman who is wasting his mother's money on high living in Saint Petersburg. When his debts assume menacing proportions, he gets word that his uncle has died, leaving him an estate of twenty-eight hundred souls. The impecunious "onager" has turned into a wealthy gentleman and a brilliant match.[72] He marries a beautiful and refined lady, who is forced by her parents to accept his proposal, although she cannot stand him. "Actaeon" (1842) continues the story of the onager, Pyotr Aleksandrovich, describing how he ruins his affairs through gambling, mismanagement, and general stupidity. The message of the story is that the typical Russian landowner is simply a parasite with no redeeming virtues. This somber picture has a silver lining. Olga Mikhailovna, his wife, is mentally and morally superior to her husband. She eventually dies of a broken heart, but she is clearly the "new woman," and her son's tutor, with whom she is in love, is the "new man," a cultured and sensitive raznochinets.

Yakov Butkov (c. 1820–57) was perhaps the most typical exponent of the natural school. He himself belonged to the world that he described in two volumes of stories published under the title *The Summits* [read: *Garrets*] *of Saint Petersburg* (1845–46). He was a friend of Dostoevsky's during the period (1847–49) when both were regular contributors to *The National Annals*. Butkov's literary career came to a halt with the Petrashevsky affair of 1849. Although he was not directly involved, the censors considered him suspect and he could no longer publish much. He died in a hospital for the poor. Butkov's witty and literate introduction to *The Summits* presents a mock phenomenology of Saint Petersburg in which its inhabitants are classified according to the position, horizontal and vertical, they occupy in the capital city. (This conceit is

72. An onager is a kind of wild ass. In Panaev's time it was also a term for a playboy.

lifted from a passage in Jules Janin's *La Confession*.) Butkov notes that the "lofty people" on the highest rung (the garrets) have received little attention in literature, and he proposes to rectify this situation. He offers to translate the garret dwellers' philosophy of life into the language of those who live on the middle floors of the better quarters of the city.

Butkov's stories are of two kinds: satirical or pathetic. "A Decent Man" (who is a cardsharper) and "A Respected Man" (who organizes charities to line his own pockets) are satires, as is "A Good Position" (which the hero obtains by discreetly staying away from home when His Excellency pays a visit and letting his pretty wife entertain him). Butkov's pathetic tales, such as "A Hundred Rubles," The First of the Month," and "A Hard-Luck Guy" (the titles speak for themselves), resemble Dostoevsky's early stories but are more hopeless, bleak, and cruel. Butkov's hapless clerks, downtrodden, meek, and dullwitted, struggle to maintain their identity as human beings, but barely succeed. Their stories are told with ironic detachment, and they appear as limp puppets on a string rather than as live people. The automaton theme, common in romantic fiction, shows up often, sometimes explicitly. The plot develops around a usually trivial anecdote. In "A Business Suit" the hero misses his chance for a career and happiness because he does not have a proper suit of clothes to wear to a party that may make his fortune. "Nevsky Prospect, or the Travels of Nestor Zaletaev" has a jobless clerk win an elegant carriage in a lottery and impersonate a gentleman for two days. Butkov's style is feuilletonistic, mannered, even whimsical. Altogether, his style is characteristic of the natural school: the subject matter and the author's social attitude are those of realism, whereas his subjective, self-conscious, and often needlessly ironic narrative style are a carryover from romantic fiction.

Ivan Kokorev (1825–53), a Moscow raznochinets, spent most of his literary career with the journal *The Muscovite*. An alcoholic, he died in a hospital for the poor. Kokorev wrote a series of perceptive physiological sketches of Moscow low life and some short stories. "Savvushka," the best of them, was written in 1847, rejected by the censor, and printed only in 1852. It is set in a Moscow slum and follows the life of Savvushka, a tailor, through a series of episodes from adolescence to old age. It is rich in genre scenes, describing the goings-on in a beer parlor, a tailor's shop, and a teeming tenement house. Kokorev lets his characters tell their stories in their own argot, even imitating the lilt of a rhymed folktale (*rayoshnik*). The basic narrative, however, like that of most stories of the natural school, is conducted in the journalese of the 1840s.

Dmitry Grigorovich (1822–99) had the reputation of a major writer throughout his life, but he owes his place in Russian literature entirely to his short stories of the 1840s. A schoolmate of Dostoevsky's and at one time his roommate, Grigorovich launched his literary career before Dostoevsky and was instrumental in his friend's discovery by Nekrasov and Belinsky. Grigorovich's stories of the 1840s stand midway between the sentimental humanitarianism of the natural school and the realism of the 1850s. Their plots are unpretentious and credible. The setting of each tale, although not particularly rich in descriptive detail, is solidly realistic. Grigorovich's narrative style is fluent and basically objective, yet he will steal an occasional self-conscious glance at his reader. The dialogue seems authentic, but without excessive dialectisms.

Grigorovich covered all the main genres of the natural school. His physiological sketch "The Organ Grinders of Saint Petersburg" (1843) became the best-known example of that genre. Grigorovich's tales from peasant life paint a depressing picture of poverty, ignorance, brutality, and needless suffering. "The Village" (1846) tells the story of the orphan Akulina, whose life is all sorrow and suffering. Even her master's well-meant gesture to get her married adds to her misery, for her husband turns out to be a drunken brute who neglects and abuses her. The story ends in Akulina's untimely, lonely, and unlamented death. "Anton Goremyka" (*goremyka* means "hapless fellow"), a long short-story published in 1847, tells of Anton, a poor peasant, and his many misfortunes. Having fallen behind in his rent payments, Anton is forced to take his only horse to market to come up with the money. On the way there the horse is stolen. Desperate, Anton seeks the help of his brother Ermolai, a thief. When Ermolai is arrested, Anton is taken with him. Anton's family is left behind wailing. These and other stories are a stepping stone toward the peasant tales of Turgenev ("The Roadside Inn," 1855) and Tolstoi ("Polikushka," 1863).

The life and literary career of Aleksandr Ivanovich Herzen (1812–70) were intersected by his departure from Russia in 1847. He was born the son of I. A. Yakovlev, a wealthy nobleman, and his German common-law wife. His surname was given to him by his father, whose name he could not legally bear. Herzen attended Moscow University (1829–33), where he was the leader of a student circle that discussed current European ideas, including utopian socialism. In 1834 he and several members of his circle were arrested for alleged subversion. Herzen was sent into exile to northeastern Russia, where he served as a government clerk. Allowed to return to Saint Petersburg in 1840, he was soon exiled again, this time to Novgorod. From 1842 to 1847 he lived in Moscow and devoted himself to his literary activities.

Herzen's novel *Whose Fault?* (1841–46) appeared, with some cuts by the censor, in *National Annals* (1845–46) and as a separate book (1847). It was the first pure social novel of Russian literature. Belinsky observed that it was weak as a work of art, but valuable as a social and psychological analysis of contemporary Russian life. The novel has two parts. In the first, inept and penniless Dmitry Krutsifersky, the son of a country doctor, is hired to tutor the son of Negrov, a retired general and rich landowner, and eventually marries Lyubov, Negrov's illegitimate daughter. In the second, Krutsifersky, now a schoolteacher in a provincial town, and Lyubov are happily married and have a three-year-old child. Their happiness is destroyed when Beltov, a rich and brilliantly educated young landowner, becomes a friend of the family and develops a liaison with Lyubov. Realizing the hopelessness of the situation, Beltov departs for Europe, leaving both Krutsiferskys heartbroken and doomed to an early death. Part One is on the whole a bilious satire exposing the coarseness and utter paltriness of the landowning gentry, precisely because the brutish Negrov and his lazy and lewd wife (she tries to seduce Krutsifersky) are understood to be rather a good sort. Part Two introduces the type of the superfluous man. Beltov, intelligent, kind, and well-intentioned, has all the advantages a Russian could possibly have, but lives an utterly useless and dreary life. He despises the parasitic and corrupt civil service, loathes the country squires who are his neighbors, and, widely traveled in Europe, is "an alien at home and an alien abroad, too." Krutsifersky, an idealistic and

scholarly drudge, drinks himself to death. His beautiful wife, far more intelligent than her husband, must consider herself happy to be a provincial schoolteacher's wife. Herzen deduces from his story a cruel law of supply and demand of manpower: there just is no demand for Russia's superfluous men and women. Throughout the novel Herzen accompanies his narrative by clever psychological observations, as when Lyubov says that "the most self-effacing love is also the most selfish" and that "humility is also terrible pride, hidden cruelty." *Whose Fault?* is an amazingly modern novel for its period. Herzen also wrote a number of short stories. "The Thieving Magpie" (1848) is one of the most powerful antiserfdom stories. It tells the tragedy of a great actress who happens to be a serf belonging to a rich landowner in whose theater she plays. The story is told with the pathos of smoldering indignation.

Belinsky contrasted Herzen's socially beneficial nonart to Ivan Goncharov's socially irrelevant yet artistically superb first novel, *The Same Old Story* (written in 1844–46, published in *The Contemporary* in 1847). Ivan Aleksandrovich Goncharov (1812–91) came from a well-to-do family of merchants but was legally and by upbringing a member of the gentry. He graduated from Moscow University in 1834 and entered the government service in 1835. He advanced steadily through the table of ranks, was a censor at one time, and retired only in 1867. His literary career was cut in half by his participation, as secretary to the admiral in command of the frigate *Pallas*, in an expedition to Japan (1852–55). A cautious man, Goncharov wrote a great deal of poetry and prose beginning in his early youth but published almost nothing before his first novel. It was a great success. In *The Same Old Story* young Aleksandr Aduev comes to Petersburg from the provinces to seek his fortune. He gains the protection of his uncle Pyotr Aduev, a government official on the make. Pyotr finds him a job and becomes his mentor. In the course of a few years Aleksandr lives out all the romantic dreams, infatuations, and disappointments of a young man. He falls in love three times and is disappointed each time, feels betrayed by a friend, tries to become a writer and is told that he has no talent, and cannot make a go of his career because he lacks the assiduousness required of a government official. All along, his uncle dispenses advice in a good-natured way, assuring him that all these disappointments are natural and in fact to the good. After eight years Aleksandr returns to his country estate sad and resigned. But in an epilogue, set four years later, he is back in Petersburg, a collegiate assessor and about to enter into a marriage of convenience to a rich heiress. His uncle is proud of him. But we also learn that Pyotr Aduev, who is about to be promoted to privy councillor and is the owner of a factory that gives him a generous income, has decided to retire prematurely, sell the factory, and retire to Italy, and that he was as much of a romantic in his youth as his nephew.

Belinsky said of *The Same Old Story* that reading it was "like eating cool watermelon on a hot summer day." Goncharov's brilliance derives from a mature sensibility and a knack for the felicitous commonplace and precise detail. *The Same Old Story* is an apotheosis of philistine good sense. Every phrase testifies to the writer's sovereign control of his characters and sure command of his language.

Fyodor Mikhailovich Dostoevsky (1821–81), the principal exponent of sentimental humanitarianism (according to Apollon Grigoryev), was born the son of a doctor in Moscow. His father, a nobleman, came from the southwestern Ukraine, his mother from a Moscow family of merchants. He was educated at a Moscow boarding school and at the Petersburg School of Military Engineers (1837–43). Upon graduation he served in the Corps of Engineers, resigning his commission in 1844 to become a professional writer. His first novel, *Poor Folk*, was a popular success, but the works that followed were not. Nevertheless, Dostoevsky had established himself as a leading writer of the young generation when his literary career was interrupted by his arrest in April 1849 for having participated in the activities of a circle of utopian socialists headed by M. V. Butashevich-Petrashevsky. Dostoevsky was also charged with having read Belinsky's "Letter to Gogol" at a gathering and with possession of two prohibited utopian socialist books. He was counted among the most serious offenders and along with them was sentenced to death by a court-martial. The tsar commuted the death sentence to four years at hard labor in Siberia, with the proviso that the guilty be subjected to a public mock execution. Dostoevsky spent the next ten years in Siberia and disappeared from the literary scene until 1859.

Poor Folk (1846), Dostoevsky's first published work (his translation of Balzac's *Eugénie Grandet* had appeared in 1844), is a remarkably sophisticated, clever, and literate piece of writing. Formally it is a parody of the sentimental epistolary novel. Devushkin (from *devushka*, "maiden") a forty-seven-year-old copying clerk, exchanges letters with eighteen-year old Varenka Dobrosyolova (from *dobroe selo*, "good village"), although they are separated only by the courtyard of a Petersburg tenement house. Their onesided and unconsummated (except for a single kiss) love affair comes to a sudden end when a Mr. Bykov (from *byk*, "bull"), who had earlier seduced and jilted Varenka, comes back to marry her after all.

The text of *Poor Folk* is teeming with parodic echoes of Russian and Western literature. Dostoevsky even has Devushkin read Gogol's "Overcoat" and denounce it as an unfair and untrue portrait of himself. Devushkin, a humanized version of the poor clerk, is Dostoevsky's polemical response to Gogol. *Poor Folk* is also a "physiology"—really, a psychology—of poverty, defined as a disease that is congenital (Devushkin is a born pauper, Varenka is not), chronic (nothing will ever cure Devushkin of his poverty), and contagious ("Stay away from the poor!" says Devushkin). Devushkin's letters are cleverly stylized, creating many funny effects. But *Poor Folk* is also a great tearjerker.

The Double (1846) is a travesty of the romantic novel. The hero, Golyadkin, another copying clerk, goes out of his mind (echoes of Gogol's "Memoirs of a Madman") and, in addition to a host of other symptoms, develops a split personality. He projects his modest dreams of official and social success upon a double, the evil Golyadkin, Jr., who step by step pushes the honest Golyadkin, Sr., out of his rightful position in the world; in the end Golyadkin, Sr., is taken away to an asylum as Golyadkin, Jr., triumphs. The parodic point is that the evil in Golyadkin, Jr., is as trivial as the good in Golyadkin, Sr. Hence it does not matter which of the two prevails. *The Double*, an artistic failure according to Dostoevsky's own admission, has received inordinate critical attention on account of its psychological subtleties, complex style (the third-person narrator alternately assumes the hero's point of view, then ironically distances himself from it), and puzzling plot.

Netochka Nezvanova (1848–49), Dostoevsky's first full-size novel, remained unfinished becauses of his arrest. It has a George Sandian narrator who tells the story of her life, beginning with her childhood. The first of three episodes is a psychological study, perhaps autobiographical, of an artist's tragic failure caused by his misjudgment of his own talent. The fiddler Efimov, Netochka's step father, fancies himself a virtuoso, although he is merely a competent critic of the play of others (Dostoevsky may have felt so about his own talent). In the second episode Netochka experiences a torrid homoerotic love affair with another young girl (this episode was apparently rifled from Eugène Sue's novel *Mathilde*). It also features a profound study of neurotic behavior in a child, Netochka's playmate, a boy named Larya. The third episode, obviously still in the draft stage, has Netochka, a teenager now, get caught up in a somber family tragedy of guilt and jealousy.

These as well as Dostoevsky's other works of the 1840s fit the mold of the natural school, with the exception, perhaps, of "The Landlady" (1847) and "White Nights" (1848), which have strong romantic elements. The narrative structure and style of Dostoevsky's early works show great variety, but all of them may be reduced to a single formula: a romantic character or theme is driven to the limit by being developed in a setting of Petersburg low life. The story "The Landlady" tells of the mad infatuation of Ordynov, a young scholar, with his beautiful landlady, Katerina, the wife of a sinister old man, Murin, who has an inexplicable power over her. A tale of arson, murder, and criminal passion (Murin may be Katerina's natural father) unfolds before a delirious Ordynov. Belinsky rightly said that the story was a mixture of Hoffmann and Marlinsky, with some Russian folklore thrown in for good measure. "The Landlady" is an artistic failure, but it contains the seed of some of Dostoevsky's deepest ideas, including the Grand Inquisitor theme of *The*

Brothers Karamazov. It may have an allegorical subtext inspired by the author's utopian socialist ideas: Murin is autocracy,
Katerina the Russian people, and Ordynov
the revolutionary who seeks to free the
people.[73]

"White Nights" is the loveliest of all of
Dostoevsky's stories. Subtitled "A Sentimental Romance," it is an anonymous
young dreamer's retrospective diary of four
Petersburg summer nights. The dreamer,
who has lived all his life in a world of
Hoffmann and Walter Scott, romantic poetry
and music, meets a beautiful young girl on
the first of these nights and seems to have a
chance at real, rather than imaginary, happiness. But he lets his chance slip by. Now he
has lost his ability to dream and is condemned to live out his life in a bleak reality.
"White Nights" may be read as a regretful
farewell to romanticism, but also, by virtue
of the intrinsic value of the dreamer's fantasies, as an apotheosis of an escapist
imagination.[74]

The young Dostoevsky, in experimenting
with different styles, points of view, and
narrative plans, was responding to his reading of Pushkin, Gogol, Hoffmann, George
Sand, and others. He had not found his own
style yet. But even so, his fiction of the
1840s stood head and shoulders above most
of what his contemporaries had to offer.

Ivan Sergeevich Turgenev (1818–1883)
was born into a gentry family on a large
manorial estate in central Russia. He studied
in Moscow, Petersburg, and Berlin, earning a

master's degree in philosophy. He was on
friendly terms with Nikolai Stankevich and
several members of his circle, including Belinsky and Bakunin. A convinced liberal and
Westernizer, Turgenev was opposed to all
radicalism and violence, however, and stopped short of following Herzen's example
and taking an open stand against the existing
order. In 1843 Turgenev fell in love with the
opera singer Pauline Garcia-Viardot and remained attached to her and her family (he
developed a solid friendship with her husband, too) for the rest of his life. Turgenev
began his literary career as a poet and dramatist, but soon turned to prose fiction. His
early stories show him experimenting with
various styles. "Andrei Kolosov" (1844),
Turgenev's first published story, happens to
be vintage Turgenev, a psychological study
in human weakness. "Three Portraits"
(1846) is a romantic tale of passion and
violence, rather in the manner of Marlinsky. "The Jew" (1847) also has a Marlinskian
flavor, yet it is noteworthy for its theme. The
narrator, a young officer, witnesses the
arrest and execution of a Jew, who is caught
spying on the Russians laying siege to Dan-
zig in the campaign of 1813. The contrast
between what the Russian officer perceives
as the Jew's grotesque behavior and the
human anguish he recognizes in it provides
the message of the story. "The Bretteur"
(1847) is patently derived from Lermontov's *A Hero of Our Time.* Pechorin is
changed into an insensitive bully who lets
his physical courage compensate for his
severe shortcomings in every other respect,
and his victim is morally upgraded. The vain
and callow Grushnitsky becomes a soulful
and high-minded youth. "Petushkov"
(1848) is an unsuccessful attempt at doing a
story in the Gogolian manner. Gogol's
humor is replaced by an unpleasant irony,

73. See Rudolf Neuhäuser, *Das Frühwerk Dos-
toevskijs: Literarische Tradition und gesell-
schaftlicher Anspruch* (Heidelberg: Carl Winter,
1979), 176–89.

74. See Gary Rosenshield, "Point of View and the
Imagination in Dostoevskij's 'White Nights,' " *Slavic and East European Journal* 21 (1977): 191–
203.

making the story of how Lieutenant Petush-kov was ruined by his infatuation with a buxom bakery salesgirl painful and none-too-amusing reading.

"The Diary of a Superfluous Man" (1850) is Turgenev's first successful novella. Writ-ten in the form of a confession, it fixed once and for all the type of the Russian intellec-tual who, by virtue of his morbid self-consciousness and lack of a meaningful occupation, has lost his self-respect and his will to live. Turgenev's Chulkaturin is an important step toward Dostoevsky's "anti-hero" in *Notes from Underground* (1864). The story itself tells of a disastrous love affair experienced by the hero as a young man. Clearly, Chulkaturin is essentially a new ver-sion of the alienated romantic hero (such as Chateaubriand's René) placed into a drab naturalistic setting and deprived of all his glamour.

A Hunter's Sketches appeared in book form only in 1852, but most of the pieces collected in that volume had appeared in *The Contemporary* between 1847 and 1850. Much later, three more were added, including the famous "A Living Relic" (1874). Most of the pieces are plotless phy-siological sketches of country life, combined with character sketches of peasants and landowners. The novelty and implied point of these pieces is that peasants are indi-viduals covering the spectrum of human types and characters. "Khor and Kalinych" introduces a prosperous peasant household headed by the patriarch Khor. Though illiterate, Khor is a shrewd businessman and a skeptic who has an ironic view of life. He knows how to handle people, including his nominal owner (Khor is a serf). Kalinych, his friend, is literate, but poor and shiftless. A dreamer and romantic, he prefers hunting and doing odd jobs to any steady work. He is

close to nature and has a lucky hand with cattle and bees. Kalinych sings and plays the balalaika, and Khor likes to listen to him. "Kasyan of Krasivaya Mecha" introduces a peasant eccentric, whose free spirit, gentle-ness, and Franciscan philosophy of life (he upbraids the hunter for gratuitously killing the creatures of the forest) put the gentle-man hunter to shame. In "Biryuk" (*biryuk* is a dialect word for "wolf") the hunter meets a stalwart gamekeeper who in appearance and character has all the traits of a tragic hero. He lives alone in the forest, hated by the peasant community because he does his job honestly. His life is in constant danger. His wife has abandoned him, leaving him with two children to care for. The "wolf," as the peasants call him, is also a good man who suffers his fate with dignity and without rancor. The gentleman hunter admires him.

Turgenev's landscape descriptions are among the best in the language. His peasant characters are vivid and credible. In their precision and expressiveness the best of the sketches are unsurpassed masterpieces. *A Hunter's Sketches* gained the reputation of an antiserfdom classic. But those of the sto-ries that pursue a definite moral tendency, branding serfdom an evil that corrupts mas-ter and serf alike, are not among the better ones. Neither are the few pieces that are regular short stories with a plot particularly remarkable. Turgenev's unique contribution to Russian literature is the vignette that presents a slice of life, replacing plot development with character study and de-riving its unity from the presence of the narrator's observant and sympathetic con-sciousness. Turgenev's manner of projecting a lyric mood through a landscape became established in Russian fiction (the lyricism of Chekhov was a direct descendant of this trait).

Drama

The eighteenth century had made a solid start for the Russian theater and native drama. The nineteenth century initially showed little that went beyond the achievements of the classicist theater. None of the few plays in the manner of Storm and Stress, the comédie larmoyante, or the middle-class tragedy that appeared after the turn of the century survived long, though some did create a stir at the time of their staging. A tearful play by N. I. Ilyin, *Magnanimity, or the Recruit Draft* (1804), caused a lively discussion on account of its having brought to the stage not only the real plight of real Russian peasants but also their "coarse" language. Likewise, the high emotionality of Ozerov's plays was severely criticized by conservative critics of Shishkov's camp. The years of the Napoleonic Wars produced some patriotic plays by Ozerov, Narezhny, M. V. Kryukovsky (1781–1811),[75] and others, but none of them had more than an ephemeral success. Only the advent of the romantic historical drama, inaugurated by Pushkin's *Boris Godunov*, created new movement on the Russian tragic stage.

Comedy, as Pushkin once said, was more fortunate. Classicist comedy, championed by Shakhovskoi in theory (in his journal, *The Dramatic Herald*) and practice, held the Russian stage until finally displaced by the realist theater of Ostrovsky. Gogol's two great comedies were anomalies, a fact borne out by the difficulties Russian directors and actors had staging them as envisaged by the playwright. In the meantime, however, Russian comedy and vaudeville were meeting the demands of a grateful public with lightweight, conventional, and usually derivative plots and stock characters,[76] often made more interesting by allusions to topics of the day and familiar figures of literary life. Besides the veterans Krylov and Shakhovskoi,[77] several capable though unoriginal playwrights provided the Russian stage with agreeable entertainment.

Nikolai Khmelnitsky (1789–1845), a high-ranking government official (he was at one time governor of Smolensk and Archangel provinces), was also a successful playwright who produced a number of comedies and vaudevilles, most of them adaptations from the French, others original works (*A Social Affair*, 1829). His verse is casual, his language colloquial and aphoristic, not much different from Griboedov's, with whom he collaborated (along with Shakhovskoi) on a comedy, *It's All in the Family, or the Married Bride* (1818).

76. Here, for example, is a plot summary of A. Markov's *Marriage of Alnaskarov: A Comedy in One Act, in Verse, Serving as a Sequel to the Comedy "Castles in the Air," by N. I. Khmelnitsky* (1824). Count Lestov had fallen in love with the portrait of Aglaeva, a young widow. He is on his way to her estate and has stopped at an inn two versts from there. He learns from Ipat, the servant of Aglaeva's aunt, that Midshipman Alnaskarov, a dreamer and adventurer, had momentarily won her heart, as she took him for Count Lestov. Once the misunderstanding became apparent, she promptly stopped preparations for a wedding. Alnaskarov himself now shows up. He is an old friend of Lestov's and once saved his life. Lestov offers to act as his matchmaker. He hands him her aunt's letter, which will identify him as the real count. When Aglaeva, who has received news that she has lost almost her entire fortune, hears this, she has a rapid change of heart and is gladly willing to marry him. Count Lestov now appears and gives the couple his blessings. The whole intrigue is paralleled by the "romance" of Viktor, Alnaskarov's servant, and Sasha, Aglaeva's maid. Both manipulate their masters quite brazenly. Viktor is already dreaming of stealing his master's money, then loaning it to him at a high rate of interest.

75. Pushkin remembered Kryukovsky's play *Pozharsky, or Moscow Liberated* (1807).

77. Even Derzhavin wrote some comedies in his old age.

Mikhail Zagoskin wrote a series of successful comedies, starting with *Comedy against Comedy* and *The Trickster* (both 1815), before he gained fame as a historical novelist. The talented Aleksandr Pisarev (1803–28) took issue with the romantic aesthetics of *The Moscow Telegraph*, defending the position that the theater's primary object is entertainment, not moral education. He therefore rejected Griboedov's *Woe from Wit*. His own comedies and vaudevilles, though derivative, are witty and stagy: *Teacher and Pupil, or They Got Drunk and I Got a Hangover* (1824), *Mr. Bustle, or A Job Fears a Master* (1825), and *A Method to Get Your Daughters Married* (1828). Pyotr Karatygin (1805–79), brother of the great tragic actor Vasily Karatygin, and Dmitry Lensky (stage name of Vorobyov, 1805–60) were fine comic actors (Lensky played Khlestakov in *The Inspector General*) who also wrote many comedies and vaudevilles, mostly adapted to Russian manners from the French. Karatygin's vaudevilles in particular (he wrote a total of seventy plays, forty-six of them vaudevilles) were popular for their topical interest, racy dialogue, and snappy lyrics.

Whereas all these writers, whenever they turned to literary topics, would make fun of either the romantics or the natural school (Karatygin actually had a vaudeville, *The Natural School*, 1847, lampooning it), Fyodor Koni (1809–79), another master of the vaudeville, favored the natural school, lampooned reactionary writers like Bulgarin, and brought the topics of the natural school to the stage (*Petersburg Apartments, A Titular Councillor, A Man of Affairs*).

The comedies of Grigory Kvitka resumed the satirical tradition of Fonvizin. *A Stranger from the Capital, or Uproar in a Provincial Town* (written in 1827, published in 1840) probably provided the plot for Gogol's *Inspector General*. The two parts of *Gentry Elections* (1827–36), *Shelmenko, County Clerk* and *Shelmenko, Orderly* (*Shel'ma* means "rogue"), also have a sharp satirical edge.

In spite of this bustling activity on the comic stage, the lone play to survive the period was *Woe from Wit*, by Griboedov. Aleksandr Sergeevich Griboedov (1795–1829) was born in Moscow. A precocious youth of many talents, he took his first degree (in the humanities) from Moscow University at fourteen, and a law degree two years later. He mastered many languages, including classical Latin and Greek and several oriental languages, and was an accomplished pianist. His progress toward a doctorate in the natural sciences was interrupted by the Napoleonic War of 1812. He served in the cavalry, but saw no action, and after the war joined the foreign service. He was stationed first in Saint Petersburg and later in the Caucasus and in Persia. His career was temporarily halted by his arrest as a suspect in the conspiracy that had led to the Decembrist revolt. He was kept under arrest for months, but was able to exculpate himself and returned to his post in the Caucasus. In 1828 he ably negotiated the peace treaty of Turkmenchai with Persia and took it back to Saint Petersburg for ratification. He was rewarded by a promotion in rank, a generous monetary award, and appointment as ambassador to Teheran. On Jan 30, 1829, an angry mob stormed the Russian embassy and massacred Griboedov and his whole staff. Pushkin on his way to Arzrum crossed paths with the cortege bearing Griboedov's remains.

Most of Griboedov's literary activities date from the period before 1825. He belonged to the Shishkovian camp of Russian men of letters and was in sympathy with the archaist and civic tendencies promoted by

Küchelbecker and Ryleev. He wrote some undistinguished poetry and several comedies and vaudevilles: *A Young Couple* (1815), a free adaptation of *Le Secret du ménage* (1809), by Augustin Creuzé de Lessert; *The Student* (1817), coauthored with Katenin; *It's All in the Family, or the Married Bride* (1818), written with Shakhovskoi and Khmelnitsky; *Simulated Infidelity* (1818), a translation of *Les Fausses Infidélités* (1768), by Nicolas Thomas Barthe; and *Who's Brother, Who's Sister, or Deception after Deception* (first staged in 1824), coauthored with Vyazemsky, who wrote the lyrics for this vaudeville. Fragments and plans for comedies and tragedies are extant.

Woe from Wit, begun in 1820, was completed in 1824 and circulated in many copies. Echoes of it started to appear in contemporary literature before it was first staged in 1831 and published in 1833 (with substantial cuts). Publication of the full text was not allowed until decades later, in 1860. Griboedov was one of the so-called neo-archaists, and *Woe from Wit* is an old-fashioned classicist comedy. Chatsky, a brilliant young Muscovite nobleman, has returned to Moscow after several years of travel abroad to propose marriage to Sofya, daughter of Famusov, an important government official. In his absence, Sofya, who is a bit of a bluestocking, has convinced herself that she is in love with Molchalin (from *molchat'*, "to be silent"), her father's secretary, a young man of limited gifts and base mentality whose ambition goes no higher than modest advancement in the service as a protégé of her father's. He accommodates himself to Sofya's moonstruck moods and on the sly makes passes at Liza, her pert maid. (So does Famusov.) Sofya, who does not appreciate Chatsky's attentions at all, starts the rumor that he has gone out of his mind. Chatsky himself contributes to this opinion

by launching a series of angry tirades against the baseness, banality, and hypocrisy of Moscow society. In the course of a soiree at Famusov's, the audience is given a sampling of Moscow characters: Colonel Skalozub (from *skalit' zuby*, "to show one's teeth, to grin"), who advocates the substitution of marching drills for school wisdom in educational institutions; the windbag Repetilov, whose bragging about his liberal ideas merely reveals their emptiness; the busybody and gossip Zagoretsky; Mme. Khlystova (from *khlyst*, "whip"), who has brought her lapdog and her black servant to the party to keep her company on the way and offers to "show off" the black woman; and so forth. The denouement of the comedy has Sofya overhear Molchalin speaking his mind to Liza, with Chatsky eavesdropping on the whole scene, Famusov joining the resulting commotion, and Chatsky taking his leave with a final bitter tirade.

Woe from Wit is not a dramatic masterpiece, and the verse, rhymed iambic lines of varying length, is at times labored. The main characters are familiar from classicist comedy: Famusov is an old-fashioned raisonneur, Liza the familiar soubrette, and Chatsky himself a Russian version of Alceste. But some of the minor characters are Moscow originals. Chatsky dominates the play with his fiery tirades and is the key to its message—the inability of an idealist to come to terms with the society he is expected to join. Chatsky's wit and intellect are wasted on the people he addresses. Pushkin wryly commented that although Griboedov was very clever, Chatsky was not. Chatsky has been a wonderful challenge to great actors precisely because of the ambiguity of the character: How clever is he really? Is he truly crazy? Is he a ridiculous character or an almost tragic one? How deeply is he in love? Once it could be staged without cuts, *Woe from Wit* became a fixture on the Russian stage and, like *Eugene Onegin* and *Dead Souls*, a part of the consciousness of all educated Russians. Many lines from the play have become a part of common usage and are no longer recognized as quotations from Griboedov.

Gogol's Theater

Gogol's first attempt at drama was *Order of Vladimir, Third Class*, a satirical comedy of manners about bureaucratic intrigue and corruption in Saint Petersburg. He soon realized that this play would have serious problems with the censor and abandoned it in favor of *The Inspector General*, the target of whose satire was less likely to cause trouble. It had some predecessors on the Russian stage: *A Judge's Nameday* (1781), by Ivan Sokolov; *Chicane* (1798), by Kapnist; *An Unheard-of Miracle, or an Honest Secretary* (1803), by Nikolai Sudovshchikov; *Gentry Elections* (1827–36), by Kvitka; and *The Inspectors* (1832), by Polevoi. The theme of a traveler who is taken for a high-ranking government official also had appeared in Russian prose fiction.[78]

The plot of the *The Inspector General* is simple. Skvoznik-Dmukhanovsky, mayor of a provincial town, has received word that a government inspector may soon visit his town. He discusses this contingency with other local officials, revealing the inefficiency and corruption of his administration. When he hears that a young official from Petersburg has stopped at an inn, he jumps to the conclusion that this is the feared inspector general. Meanwhile a young profligate gentleman, Khlestakov, who has no money to pay his bill, is worried that the innkeeper will report him to the mayor and have him sent to prison. When the mayor rushes to the inn to welcome the "inspector," a comic dialogue of the deaf ensues, as it takes the harebrained Khlestakov a long time to realize what is going on. Once he does, he plays his role with abandon, bragging about his power, honors, and accomplishments in Petersburg, courting the mayor's wife and daughter, and "borrowing" substantial amounts of money from all comers. When Khlestakov asks for his daughter's hand, the mayor believes he has triumphed over all his enemies and dreams of a transfer to Petersburg and promotion to the rank of general. Khlestakov quits town, leaving the mayor and his associates in a state of euphoria. This bliss is shattered by the postmaster, who has opened Khlestakov's letter to a Petersburg friend in which he makes lighthearted fun of his hosts. The assembled officials have yet to recover from their shock when a gendarm enters announcing the arrival of the real inspector general. They stand speechless, some frozen still, others grimacing in surprise and agony—for a minute and a half, according to Gogol's stage directions.

The initial reaction to *The Inspector General* was mixed. The tsar guffawed heartily, which saved Gogol from any reprisals. But most people in the Saint Petersburg audience were embarrassed or angry. Reactionary reviewers like Bulgarin and Senkovsky tried to blunt the satirical bite of the comedy by calling it a mere farce. But this was only a holding action. Other reviewers, such as Vyazemsky, objected to the notion that the play's lowly subject matter and absence of positive characters excluded it from being considered a serious work. V. P.

---

78. Kvitka's comedy *A Stranger from the Capital* was written in 1827 but published only in 1840. Gogol, however, may have seen it in manuscript. The false inspector also appears in August Kotzebue's comedy *Die deutschen Kleinstädter* (1803), which was often staged in Russia. See also p. 248 regarding Veltman's story "Roland the Furious."

Androsov of *The Moscow Observer* recognized the "high comedy" of *The Inspector General* in the Hegelian terms of a conflict between the interests of state and family. Belinsky, likewise in Hegelian terms, saw *The Inspector General* as a profoundly true realization of the inanity of Russian life. Gogol himself, in a dramatic dialogue entitled *Denouement of "The Inspector General"* (1846), gave it an allegorical interpretation. The town is the town of the human soul, populated by various vices. Khlestakov is deceptive worldly conscience, which allows men to live comfortably with their vices. The real inspector is the one "who awaits us at death's door." Gogol's suggestion is not as farfetched as most critics have felt (the actor Shchepkin, for whom Gogol wrote the piece, angrily rejected it). It ought to be treated with respect.

What makes *The Inspector General* a great play? Its plot is not very ingenious. It lacks intellectual brilliance. Its characters are hardly attractive. But every line has a prodigious energy generated by Gogol's whimsical imagination. The most absurd notions are put into a context that renders them plausible and true to life. When the mayor asks the local judge to do something about his assessor, who is always reeking of vodka, the judge answer, "He says his nurse bumped him when he was a baby and he has had that slight smell of vodka about him ever since." When Khlestakov observes to an official, "Tell me, please, it seems to me that yesterday you were of somewhat shorter stature than today, isn't it so?", the answer is, "That is certainly possible." Khlestakov is so carried away by his sudden popularity that he proposes marriage to the mayor's wife, who responds, "But I am married, in a certain sense." To which Khlestakov counters with a jumble of non sequiturs

that have become proverbial: "So what? Love knows no distinction, and Karamzin said, 'The law condemns.' We shall retire to the shade of brooks. Your hand, I'm asking for your hand!" If these and many other such repartees were a mere collection of clever gags, *The Inspector General* would be what Bulgarin and Senkovsky believed it to be: excellent entertainment. But they are more. Though absurd, they are also true to the characters who deliver them. Together they produce a world that is wonderfully alive in its absurdity, folly, and quirkiness, as well as in its greed, vanity, and cunning.

Marriage, an Entirely Implausible Occurrence in Two Acts was started in 1833 and completed in 1841. It appeared in Gogol's *Collected Works* in 1842. Opening night in Petersburg, on December 9, 1842, was a disaster: several of the actors played their parts without having understood them at all. In 1843 Sergei Aksakov supervised the Moscow production and the play was a fair success (although Shchepkin was miscast as Podkolyosin). The comedy came into its own slowly, along with Ostrovsky's theater, whose audiences began to appreciate slower, psychologically more complex and subtle action.

Podkolyosin ("Underwheel"), a middle-aged, middle-echelon official, has been persuaded by his friend Kochkaryov that the time has come for him to marry. The prospective bride is Agafya, the plump, thirtyish heiress of her late merchant father's modest fortune. She has the matchmaker Fyokla line up suitors, insisting that the chosen one must be a gentleman, because merchants are indelicate and beat their wives. (Her own father's "bucket-size" hands had shortened her mother's life, we hear in a casual repartee.) Podkolyosin finds himself in competition with three other "gentlemen": a civil servant named Yaichnitsa ("scrambled eggs"), Anuchkin ("put-tee"), a retired army officer, and Zhevakin ("chewer"), retired from the navy. All three are well on in years, physically unattractive, and of brutish manners and low mentality. Yet they consider themselves highly desirable suitors—as does Agafya. It is only through Kochkaryov's energetic efforts that Podkolyosin, the most civilized of the lot, is finally chosen. Everything is ready for the betrothal. Podkolyosin, left alone, starts a monologue welcoming the marital bliss that awaits him. He then begins to have some doubts, works himself into a state of dread, and decides to make his escape through the window. After he has jumped, he is heard hailing a cab. Kochkaryov promises to bring him back, but the more experienced Fyokla says, "If he'd run out the door, maybe, but if he left through a window, forget it!"

Dostoevsky observed (in *The Idiot*), speaking of the typical in art, that although not many men jump out of windows to escape marriage, Podkolyosin was still a recognizable typical figure. In *Marriage* Gogol does brilliantly what he also accomplishes in the best of his stories: he turns the life of his society—its marriage customs, in this case—into a grotesque, then makes us wonder if it is not real life after all that unfolds before our eyes. The dialogue of *Marriage* is not as rambunctious as that of *The Inspector General*, but it is perhaps deeper and more thought-provoking. Its humor is less spirited, certainly blacker, but irresistible. As for the setting, Gogol anticipates the theater of Ostrovsky. The milieu and some traits of Ostrovsky's first comedy, *Bankrupt* (1847), are readily discernible in *Marriage*.

The one-act play *The Gamblers* (1842) is a trifle compared to *Marriage*, though well done. Its plot is the familiar one of a crook victimized by an even smarter crook. *After the Theater* (published in 1842 but conceived after the first night of *The Inspector General*) is formally a skit, but in fact it is one of the finest pieces of literary criticism in all of Russian literature. The "author," hidden behind a column, eavesdrops on what his audience has to say about his play and responds to his "critics" (some of them are easily identified). A lady tells of a "fat man" who screams that "such baseness and villainy does not exist among us" yet is himself "the basest scoundrel, always ready to sell his soul, his conscience, and whatever else you may want." The "fat man" is clearly Bulgarin. Gogol parades all the negative opinions he had heard about his play: that it is a mere farce, that it lacks structure, that it has no positive characters, that it is too sordid, and so forth. There is only one opinion which the author seriously resents: that the play is "just another yarn" (*pobasyonki*), good only for laughs. The author and some of the viewers develop Gogol's own view of art, comedy, and *The Inspector General* in terms of the romantic aesthetic of the age. Art should be an integral element of national and social life, of which the comedies of Aristophanes are an undying example. Comedy is as meaningful as serious drama, since both seek to reveal the truth and bring it to the attention of the public. Hence its effect can only be positive and constructive. As for *The Inspector General*, one viewer observes that its central idea is to assert the need for a positive ideal by presenting a world bereft of such ideals.

Whereas Russian comedy gave a fair account of itself, Russian tragedy had to wait for the height of the romantic period to come to life. Katenin's vigorous translations and adaptations of French classics (*Esther*, *Athalie*, and *Andromaque*, by Racine, and other plays) were unable "to awaken the Russian theater from its sleep," as Pushkin put it. (He also called Katenin's *Andromache* "the best Russian tragedy.") An early tragedy by another neo-archaist, Wilhelm Küchelbecker, might have seconded Katenin's efforts if it had been staged. Küchelbecker's tragedy *The Argives*, written in 1822–23, of which only excerpts were published in his lifetime but which was known to his friends, was in some ways a precursor of Pushkin's *Boris Godunov.* Its plot is taken from ancient history, but its message is clearly modern and republican (Küchelbecker's friends told him that it did not have a chance to pass censorship). It has ample choral interludes but is written largely in blank verse.[79] It retains the peripeteias of classicist tragedy but places more emphasis on psychological motivation. *The Argives* is the tragedy of Timophanes, tyrant of Corinth, who is toppled by a conspiracy headed by his older brother, Timoleon. Its message is that power corrupts even the noblest man, that a tyrant faces "nothing but turmoil, mutiny and executions, sorrow and killings," and that he who fancies himself a god will turn into "a vicious beast." *The Argives*, well constructed and well versified, is a fine play, as classicist tragedies go. It features a noble heroine, Aglaia, Timophanes' spouse, in whose heart love and admiration for her husband struggle with fear that she may get infected by the "mute obsequiousness of the slaves" who surround him. Aglaia is a live and moving character. Still, the play's language and entire sensibility appear hopelessly outdated if compared to Pushkin's *Boris Godunov*, not so much because of the classical setting as

79. *The Argives* is thus the first Russian tragedy in blank verse. Pushkin also mentions *Ventseslav* by Andrei Zhandr, fragments of which were printed in the almanac *Thalia* in 1825. *Ventseslav*, however, was a translation of *Venceslas* (1648), by Jean de Rotrou.

because of the absence of individualized characters and historical color.

Romantic Theater

Pushkin took a lifelong interest in the theater. His early "Notes on the Russian Theater" (c. 1820) show him well acquainted with its repertoire and with its actors and actresses, whose individual styles he discusses with confidence. In another early note Pushkin observes that no genre requires a greater degree of suspension of disbelief than tragedy and suggests that one ought to follow the romantics and jettison classical unities, retaining one, "the unity of interest." Pushkin's notes and correspondence show him to be a convinced proponent of the romantic, by which he means Shakespearean theater. He is keenly aware of the stiltedness of French classicist tragedy, which he blames in part on the fact that its authors stood socially below their public.

Pushkin started *Boris Godunov* in December 1824, after having read volumes 10 and 11 of Karamzin's *History of the Russian State.* It was completed on November 7, 1825. Pushkin had a great deal of trouble with the play's publication and had to make some changes, in which Zhukovsky helped him. The best known of these is the replacement of the last line of the original text, "Long live Tsar Dimitry Ivanovich!" with the stage direction, "The people stand silent."

Pushkin basically followed Karamzin's account and interpretation of the events starting with the elevation of Boris Godunov to tsar in 1598 and ending with the arrival of the "false Dimitry" in Moscow in 1605. He introduced a few minor characters (including an ancestor of his, not mentioned by Karamzin) and invented some minor events. The play remained without a focus, as the action shifts back and forth from tsar to pretender. With the plot determined by history, Pushkin let the tragic tension of the play develop from Godunov's conscience, burdened by the murder of Tsarevich Dimitry. As Polevoi was to point out, the result was that the action amounts to the execution of a condemned criminal. An innocent Godunov (historical evidence for his guilt was anything but conclusive) would have provided a plot more appealing to Polevoi's romantic sensibility. As for the pretender, Pushkin departed from his predecessors, presenting him as an amiable and brilliant adventurer. Marina Mniszek, the pretender's consort, a character who fascinated Pushkin, has but one scene, the only one in the play that features a clash of wills. When Marina, a proud and ambitious woman, contemptuously repulses him (having learned the secret of his true identity), the pretender, though enthralled by her charms, declares in a grand repartee that "the shade of [Ivan] the Terrible has adopted him" and that he will "no longer abase himself before a proud Polish woman." Even if she were to divulge his secret, she could not stop the course of events that will carry him to the Russian throne. No further drama develops from this conflict. *Boris Godunov* is a Shakespearean historical drama, divided into scenes rather than acts. None of the classical unities are observed, as the scene changes from various locations in Moscow to Chudovo monastery, to an inn on the Lithuanian border, to Poland, and then back to Moscow. The structure, mood, and language of *Boris Godunov* are radically different from those of any earlier serious play. The characters are credible human beings with credible passions. Their language, basically modern, is slightly stylized to create a "historical" atmosphere. Two itinerant beggar monks whom the pretender meets at the border inn provide a comic interlude. Pushkin's

vigorous blank verse, alternating with Shakespearean prose scenes, was also an innovation.[80]

Boris Godunov is a fine dramatic poem, but not an effective play. It lacks a dramatic conflict and continuity of action. Unlike Pushkin's little tragedies,[81] *Boris Godunov* does not convey an important idea. The notion, expressed by some critics, that the decisive role played by the common people in "making history" is such an idea seems unwarranted.

Pushkin started several other dramatic works, one of which, *The Water Spirit*,[82] he nearly completed. It was made into a successful opera by Aleksandr Dargomyzhsky.

Among the members of Pushkin's pleiad only Küchelbecker gave any serious attention to the drama. (His tragedy *The Argives* is discussed on p. 280). *Shakespearean Spirits: A Dramatic Farce in Two Acts* (1825) is a delightful potpourri of poetic variations on Shakespearean themes, mostly from *A Midsummer Night's Dream* and *The Tempest*, and assorted allusions to the contemporary literary scene. *Ivan, a Young Merchant* (1833–42) is a whimsical romantic fairy-tale play in the manner of Carlo Gozzi and Ludwig Tieck. Andana, daughter of the khan of Bukhara, falls in love with Ivan, a greedy and cunning Russian merchant of singularly low mentality, and elopes with him to Russia. Along the way they experience all kinds of fantastic adventures. A key role is played by Bulat, a Bukhara strongman whom Ivan bought from bondage for a hundred rubles. Bulat comes to a sad end—he is turned to stone and sold to Lord Elgin as an antique statue—while Ivan goes on to prosper. The action is often

80. See note 79.

81. See pp. 214–215.

82. There is no title in Pushkin's manuscript.

interrupted by interludes in which not only assorted demons, devils, and witches but also a bird, the poet, and the public make their appearance. The dialogue is lively and witty, but the whole thing is altogether too intricate for staging. Küchelbecker's tragedy *Prokofy Lyapunov* (1834) is set in the Time of Troubles and based on events related in volume 12 of Karamzin's *History of the Russian State.*

Pushkin's *Boris Godunov* launched the Russian historical drama on a long streak of dominance on the Russian stage. Along with it came Shakespeare and plays in the Shakespearean manner, Schiller's in particular, all of which rendered the Russian tragic stage of the 1830s and 1840s thoroughly romantic. Among the many exponents of the Russian historical drama of this period, Nestor Kukolnik and Nikolai Polevoi were the most prominent.

Nestor Kukolnik (1809–68), a Petersburg government official who had been Gogol's schoolmate, scored a huge success with his patriotic five-act drama in blank verse, *The Hand of the Almighty Has Saved the Fatherland* (1832, staged in 1834; the title is a line from Ozerov's *Dimitry Donskoi)*. The play is set in 1613, as the Time of Troubles ends with the election of the first Romanov. There is little action, but a great deal of panegyrical rhetoric glorifying Russia. Kukolnik followed with a series of further patriotic plays, including *Duke Mikhail Vasilyevich Skopin-Shuisky*, also set in the Time of Troubles, *Lieutenant-General Patkul*, whose hero is a Livonian nobleman who took Peter's side in the Northern War and was executed as a traitor to King Charles XII of Sweden, and *The Orderly*, set in Moscow in 1722. Kukolnik also wrote several plays featuring the tragic fate of misunderstood or neglected artists:

Torquato Tasso (1830–31), *Giulio Mosti* (1832–33), *Giacopo Sannazaro* (1833), and *Ermil Ivanovich Kostrov* (1853), the last about a Russian poet (1755–96) of humble origins but great promise, who took to drink and died abandoned and destitute. Kostrov had previously been the subject of poems by Pushkin and Küchelbecker. Kukolnik was also a prolific author of historical novels, such as *Alf and Aldona*, set in fourteenth-century Lithuania, *Two Ivans, Two Stepanychs, Two Kostylkovs*, set in the time of Peter the Great, and *Three Periods*, based on the life of the German poet Gottfried August Bürger.

Nikolai Polevoi (1796–1846) was even more prolific than Kukolnik. Between 1837 and the year of his death he wrote more than forty plays, including romantic tragedies, historical dramas, comedies, and vaudevilles. Like Kukolnik, Polevoi took his subjects from European as well as Russian history: *Ugolino* (1838), *Igolkin, a Merchant* (1839), *Lomonosov* (1843). In particular, Polevoi sought to demonstrate the patriotism and loyalty of the Russian merchant class. More important than Polevoi's original efforts was his prose translation of *Hamlet* (1837), which scored a success with the great Pavel Mochalov in the title role (1838). Polevoi also wrote historical novels as well as novels and short stories set in contemporary Russia, Germany, and elsewhere. His activities as an editor and critic have been discussed earlier (see pp. 189–191).

The Slavophile Aleksei Khomyakov's drama *Dimitry the Pretender* (1833) is far more interesting than any of Kukolnik's officiously patriotic plays. The pretender, having admitted to the dowager empress that he is not her son, speaks of his dream to remake Russia in the image of the free and prosperous West, "Where divine fire burns in human hearts/And human hands tame nature/And measure the heavens with shrewd eyes." The empress answers, "He is mad!" Like the pretender, she is caught in a tragic dilemma. Her desire to get her revenge on the Godunovs drove her to lie; now she must live that lie. She is later moved by a holy man to return to the truth. In act 3 Marina lectures the pretender on the futility of his dream: the Muscovites understand Godunov's low cunning and Ivan's bloody terror, but not "noble feelings, high-minded and bold ideas."

Khomyakov's pretender is an attractive and noble young man who has grandiose plans—war against the Turks to free Constantinople. His fatal mistake is that he forgave Shuisky, who conspired against him, and trusted that he would win him over with his generosity. Or is he doomed beforehand because he is a westernizer, like Godunov? Khomyakov's tragedy is well structured, well focused, and well balanced, if compared to Pushkin's *Boris Godunov*. But it is also much less robust, less down-to-earth, too Schillerian.

The pretender's tragedy was a compelling topic for a Slavophile. But Khomyakov was too honest to exploit it fully. The people of Moscow rise against the Poles, not out of any noble patriotic feelings or to defend ideal, but because the Poles are arrogant aliens who do not respect local customs. Shuisky is a schemer, and the other boyars are hardly high-minded patriots. Lyapunov, a wise idealist, remains a marginal figure.

Khomyakov's *Dimitry the Pretender* is a thought-provoking play, though historically anachronistic. As a play *à thèse* it stands up well to Pushkin's *Boris Godunov*. But it is not good theater. Khomyakov's earlier play, *Ermak* (1829), is even worse in this respect,

as Pushkin noted, and lacks the virtues of *Dimitry the Pretender*.[83]

Lermontov wrote six plays, of which only *A Masked Ball* (1835) earned a permanent spot in the Russian repertoire. *Gypsies, The Spaniards, Menschen und Leidenschaften, A Strange Man*, and *Two Brothers* are all very early works and are arch-romantic. (*A Strange Man* is subtitled *A Romantic Drama*.) None of the plays was published or staged in Lermontov's lifetime. *A Masked Ball* was repeatedly rejected by the censor, who felt that it could not be passed even with significant changes. He remarked in his report that the play may have been based on a real event. *A Masked Ball* was finally published in 1842, but attempts to stage it met with stubborn resistance from the authorities. Even Mochalov's efforts were in vain. Only in 1852 did some scenes from the play reach the stage, and the whole play was not produced until 1862. It has been a fixture of the Russian stage ever since.

Although *A Masked Ball* is written in rhymed iambics (mostly pentameter), its language is surprisingly modern, colloquial, and fluent. The dialogue, while emotionally outré, is also remarkably natural. The melodramatic plot is made believable by the genuine passion that animates every line. Arbenin, an ex-gambler and ex–Don Juan, now the jealous husband of a virtuous young wife, is the victim of a fateful accident. His wife loses a bracelet. Baroness Strahl, a woman of easy virtue, finds it, and it winds up in the hands of Duke Zvezdich, a young rake. Arbenin, who suspects his wife of an indiscretion, is led to believe that Zvezdich is her lover. He punishes him by publicly

83. Ermak, the conqueror of Siberia, was a frequent subject of historical drama (Polevoi and Dmitriev, among others, also made him the hero of their dramatic poems) and historical fiction.

declaring him a scoundrel and a card cheat. Zvezdich gets even by intimating that he has indeed cuckolded Arbenin. After some cold-blooded deliberation, Arbenin decides not to kill Zvezdich and instead poisons his wife, who dies protesting her innocence. Zvezdich then confesses that she had indeed rejected his advances. Arbenin collapses in a paroxysm of grief and despair.

The reasons why the censors would suppress the play were obvious. Russian high society is presented as thoroughly depraved. Arbenin and several other characters are jaded immoralists. One of them brazenly preaches an amoral sensualism, and gambling as the essence of human existence. At one point the baroness, referring to George Sand, delivers a monologue protesting against the subjugated condition of women. These and assorted Byronic verities are presented with an intensity and eloquence that are ideally suited for the stage. *A Masked Ball* is not a great work of art, but it is superb theater.

Russian romantic drama, though derived from Western examples even more clearly than Russian romantic fiction, by and large realized little of the spirit of romanticism— its dualistic worldview, its dialectic of the ideal and the real, its symbolic conception of art, and its aesthetic of irony and ambiguity. Flashes of these romantic traits appear in Küchelbecker and Khomyakov. Other dramatists tend to pursue only the external trappings of romanticism—an exalted diction, a penchant for high passion and exotic settings, and an abiding interest in the glories of their nation's past. Russian romanticism started a tradition of historical drama that would remain strong throughout the century and after. Russian historical drama, however, starting even with Pushkin's *Boris Godunov*, was inclined toward a realist rather than romantic view of history.

Chapter 7

The Age of the Novel

The Crimean War of 1855–56, in which France and Britain soundly defeated Russia on its own soil, destroyed the myth of Russian military might, the single remaining item Nicholas I could list to the credit of his reign. Nicholas died before the end of the war. Alexander II (r. 1855–81) continued his father's foreign policy. Like Nicholas, he had to put down an uprising in Poland; and like the Polish uprising of 1830, that of 1863 helped the tsar at home, as even liberals rallied around the monarchy. The Russian Empire continued to expand: the Caucasus was definitely "pacified" by 1860, and vast new territories were conquered in Central Asia during the 1860s. The Russo-Turkish War of 1877–78 was a military success, but the threat of British intervention again forced Russia to withdraw from the Balkans. At home Alexander II pursued a liberal reformist course from the start. Sweeping reforms were prepared and then carried out in the course of the 1860s. The most important of these was the abolition of serfage in 1861. House serfs were freed from any obligation to their masters. Peasant serfs were freed with an allotment of land, on the average about equal to the portion that the landowner retained. The government arranged for bank loans to peasant communes to make redemption payments to the landowner. The "emancipation" was neither an economic nor a social success. As the poet Nekrasov put it, when the chain of serfage snapped, one end hit the landowner and the other the peasant, knocking down both. Many landowners were unprepared for the new situation, although it had been slow in coming, and were soon ruined. The landed gentry now rapidly declined as a class. Many peasant communes were not economically viable, could not keep up their redemption payments, and disintegrated. A new class of landowners, made up of former peasants or merchants, emerged. A large-scale migration of landless peasants to the cities steadily gained momentum. Russian agriculture, still backward, was now beginning to feel the disastrous effects of the deforestation of the Russian heartland and the exhaustion of its soil as a result of inefficient cultivation. The 1860s and 1870s also showed a dramatic increase in alcoholism and violent crime among a pauperized peasantry.

The other reforms of Alexander II were more auspicious. The establishment in 1864 of elected local self-government, the zemstvo, to take charge of elementary schools, public libraries, public health and charity, roads and local transportation, fire insurance, and other public trusts was beneficial, as was the establishment of autonomous city government in 1870. The zemstvos went on to play a vital role in raising the level of literacy, providing medical care, and generating civic initiative. The judicial reform of 1864 established the principle of equality before the law, called for jury trial in criminal cases, abolished corporal punishment, and in general brought European standards to Russian courts of law. It was a boon to the Russian legal profession, which quickly gained in influence, self-assurance, and prestige. The reform of the military culminated in the institution of universal service in 1874, doing away with the privileges of the nobility. Corporal punishment was eliminated and length of service drastically reduced.

The reforms of Alexander II, along with the liberal climate they generated, helped move Russia closer to a Western way of life. The so-called liberal professions—law, medicine, journalism, education, science— now formed the nucleus of educated society and public life. The building of railroads (private as well as government-owned) and the growth of mining and industry, all of which required the services of trained managers and technical personnel, also contributed to the emergence of a Western-style middle class. The conservative merchant class began to adopt Western business methods and Western ways. Although the old class structure was officially retained,

Russian society was de facto rapidly transformed into what was essentially a two-class society of the educated and the uneducated. In the past a majority of the educated came from the landowning or bureaucratic gentry. The new educated class was composed of individuals of mixed origin. Among the collaborators of *The Contemporary* in the 1850s were aristocrats such as Druzhinin, Turgenev, and Tolstoi, seminarians (sons of parish priests who had acquired some of their education at a seminary), including Chernyshevsky, Dobrolyubov, and Pomyalovsky, and men from the merchant class like Botkin and Goncharov. A man's social background did not determine his political stance. Some of the most radical nihilists came from the landed gentry—Pisarev and Sleptsov, for example—whereas some raznochintsy were staunch conservatives.

The political groupings that had emerged in the 1840s developed well-defined contours in the course of the 1850s. The Slavophiles, in particular those of the second generation, such as Ivan Aksakov (1823–86) and Yury Samarin (1819–76), transformed the Slavophile myth of pre-Petrine Russia into a political program. It meant an endorsement of the Orthodox state religion and patrimonial monarchy, but also opposition to the unchecked power of the imperial bureaucracy and the Western values that it enforced. The Slavophiles continued to believe that the communalism (*sobornost'*) inherent in the Russian national character and alive in the Russian peasant commune would, in conjunction with a revival of Orthodox Christian communal worship, become the source of Russia's moral and cultural regeneration. The book *Russia and Europe* (1869), by Nikolai Danilevsky (1822–85), postulated a peculiar "Slavic type" of civilization, most fully expressed in the Russian people. These ideas, combined with the groundwork done by the first generation of Slavophiles, gave Slavophile journalists a political agenda that they pursued vigorously: abroad, support of the Pan-Slavic movement and of Russia's military thrust into the Balkans to free the southern Slavs from the Turkish "yoke"; at home, cultivation of national traditions, opposition to ideas and institutions derived from abroad, and open hostility toward minorities, specifically Jews, Poles, and Germans.

Close to the Slavophiles were the *pochvenniki* (from *pochva*, "soil," hence "men of the soil"), whose Slavophilism was more democratic and down-to-earth than that of the mainstream Slavophiles. Apollon Grigoryev (1822–64) was the initiator of this movement and Fyodor Dostoevsky its most effective proponent. The pochvenniki discounted the romantic mysticism of the Slavophiles as mere theory and sought to develop their own nationalist ideology on the basis of what they thought were the empirical "facts" of Russian life. Like the Slavophiles, the pochvenniki believed that Western civilization was in a state of moral and spiritual decay. They suggested that it would be regenerated by Russian civilization, a creative synthesis of the great national cultures of the West. Dostoevsky's celebrated "Discourse on Pushkin" (1880) is a concise statement of their position.

The government, still anchored in the credo "Orthodoxy, monarchy, and nationality (*narodnost'*)," was now pursuing what were clearly Westernizing policies, so much so that conservative government officials, churchmen, and men of letters felt slighted and persecuted. Nikolai Leskov's novel *Cathedral Folk* (1867–72) expresses these sentiments. Lev Tolstoi's fiction and nonfiction of the 1860s and 1870s take a wholly negative view of "progress" in every area—

social, political, economic, even educational. On the other side, some strong liberals and Westernizers, such as Herzen and Turgenev, sought to expose the government's position as a hypocritical exercise in futility.

The mood of a majority of educated Russians, as mirrored by the Russian press, was moderately liberal and gradualist. Criticism, directed at particular details of public life without an all-out attack on the existing order, was now possible with relatively minor restrictions. Such works as Dostoevsky's *Notes from the House of the Dead* (1861–62), which reports on the ugly reality of a Siberian prison in naturalistic detail, Pomyalovsky's *Seminary Sketches* (1862–63), a lurid account of life in an Orthodox divinity school, or Saltykov-Shchedrin's *Provincial Sketches* (1856–57), describing corrupt and inefficient officialdom—all honest representations of contemporary Russian life—could appear, albeit with some unavoidable cuts.

Even the radical left could now more or less explicitly voice its ideas, which amounted to a rejection of all the values of the existing order. The label "nihilists" pinned on the radicals by Turgenev's novel *Fathers and Sons* (1862) reflected the fact that the radicals rejected religion, the authority of the state, the family (as an institution that enslaves women and children), social conventions, and aesthetic values ("beauty") as deleterious or irrelevant to the well-being of the masses. They advertised their attitude by adopting conspicuously casual dress and hairstyle (men long, women short), wearing dark glasses, and flaunting the rules of ordinary polite behavior. The nihilists recognized only the truths of a materialist science and a positivist sociology. They were also socialists, believing that only socialism could bring universal well-being to Russia. They took for granted that before establishing a rational socialist society built on the principles of science, the old order would have to be destroyed, by force if necessary. The program of the radicals advanced beyond the talking stage in the 1860s, as some underground groups, mostly of students, took to organized anti-government propaganda and terrorist acts. The first attempt on the tsar's life was made by Dmitry Karakozov, a member of a group of conspirators, on April 4, 1866. A series of further attempts followed until the tsar-emancipator was finally assassinated, by terrorists of a group that called itself the People's Will, on March 13, 1881. Although the number of active conspirators remained small, they had many sympathizers, as reflected in the art and literature of the period.

In the 1870s radicalism took a new turn under the name of populism (*narodnichest-vo*, from *narod*, "the people"). The populist ideology moved away from the materialist positivism of the nihilists of the 1860s, replacing it with the idealist moral principles of social justice, social duty, and integrity of the human individual. The populists believed in the duty of the advantaged to help the disadvantaged, that is, the people. In the early 1870s thousands of young people of both sexes participated in a movement called "going to the people" (*khozhdenie v narod*). They dressed up in peasant garb and tried to convert peasants to socialism or urged them to resist the authorities. The movement failed dismally: most peasant communities saw the agitators as troublemakers and ignored them or turned them over to the police. Scores of populists, many of them women, were put on trial for subversion and sentenced to prison and exile. The populist movement survived, however, and eventually became

the Socialist Revolutionary party in the twentieth century.

Relaxed censorship made journalism more rewarding and more attractive to the best minds and pens. Although there were still many annoying restrictions and a periodical could be suspended by administrative fiat, the risk incurred was no longer to one's person. Enough writers and editors would readily challenge the censors to a battle of wits and try to get their message across by using Aesopian language. The new freedom also caused irresponsible and semi-literate scribblers to launch satirical journals and scandal sheets of questionable good taste. The so-called thick journals continued their dominance of the literary scene, covering the spectrum of political opinion.

In the 1850s *The Contemporary*, under the energetic leadership of Nikolai Nekrasov, played the dual role of being the favored outlet for most of the leading writers of the period (Lev and Aleksei Tolstoi, Turgenev, Goncharov, Ostrovsky, and others) and the organ of the radical democratic intelligentsia. The addition to its staff of the radical zealots Chernyshevsky in 1856 and Dobrolyubov in 1857 eventually caused the "liberals," including all of those mentioned, to leave *The Contemporary*, as Nekrasov chose to side with the radicals when it came to a showdown. *The Contemporary* remained strong, though, as it retained the services of Nekrasov himself, Saltykov-Shchedrin, and some capable second stringers like Pomyalovsky, Reshetnikov, and Nikolai and Gleb Uspensky. After Dobrolyubov's death in 1861 and Chernyshevsky's arrest in 1862, the criticism section of *The Contemporary* deteriorated into doctrinaire preaching and indiscriminate vilification of all who disagreed with the radical ideology.

In 1866, in the wake of Karakozov's

attempt on the tsar's life, *The Contemporary* was suspended by the authorities. Nekrasov immediately acquired A. A. Kraevsky's *National Annals*, which had fallen on hard times, and ably assisted by his coeditor, Saltykov-Shchedrin, made that journal into the organ of radical populism. Gleb Uspensky, Vsevolod Garshin, and the populist ideologue and critic Nikolai Mikhailovsky were among its contributors.

The Russian Word (1859–66), which had started as a conservative journal under Apollon Grigoryev and Yakov Polonsky, turned radical in 1860 under the editorship of G. E. Blagosvetlov and became the mouthpiece of the radical critics and essayists Dmitry Pisarev and Varfolomei Zaitsev. It was closed in 1866 along with *The Contemporary*.

In the 1850s *The National Annals* had continued to represent the moderately liberal and westernizing line, publishing works by Pisemsky and Goncharov, among others. But Kraevsky, the journal's publisher, was unable to hold his own against his radical and conservative competitors and was happy to sell his journal to Nekrasov in 1866. *The Herald of Europe* (1866–1918), under the editorship of the historian M. M. Stasyulevich (1826–1911), now became the organ of the middle-of-the-road gradualist liberal intelligentsia. Such liberal writers as Turgenev, Goncharov, and Ostrovsky published their works there.

The Muscovite (1841–56), under the editorship of the Slavophile historian M. P. Pogodin and with Shevyryov, another Slavophile, in charge of criticism, flourished for a few years in the early 1850s, when its so-called young editorial board consisting of Ostrovsky, Pisemsky, and Grigoryev, among others, brought some life to it. But Pogodin's inept leadership eventually caused its demise. The Slavophiles briefly had their own thick journal, *Russian Colloquy* (1856–60), to which all of the Slavophiles as well as some others (Ostrovsky, Marko Vovchok, and even Saltykov-Shchedrin) contributed.

Mikhail Katkov's *Russian Herald* (1856–1906) was by far the most successful of all the thick journals of the period. It started out as a moderately liberal periodical but after 1861 became increasingly more conservative. Katkov, an extraordinarily efficient editor, was able to attract contributions even from writers like Turgenev who disagreed with his conservative nationalist and monarchist views. Many of the great novels of Turgenev, Tolstoi, Dostoevsky, Pisemsky, and Leskov first appeared in The *Russian Herald.*

The journals of the brothers Dostoevsky, *Time* (1861–63) and *Epoch* (1864–65), took a conservative position, but without entirely embracing either the quirky ideas of the Slavophiles or the jingoistic nationalism of Katkov's *Russian Herald*. Their mainstay was Fyodor Dostoevsky himself, who contributed his fiction as well as superb nonfiction.

The political spectrum of the daily and weekly press was somewhat narrower. The venerable *Saint Petersburg News* (1728–1917) was the most liberal paper to cover the entire period. *The Stock Exchange News* of Saint Petersburg (1861–79) was considered a mouthpiece of the progressive liberal bourgeoisie, as was *New Times* (1866–1917), another Petersburg daily. Katkov took over *The Moscow News* (1756–1917) in 1851 and made it into the most influential newspaper of the period. It steered a conservative course and generally supported government policies. Duke V. P. Meshchersky's *Citizen* (1872–1914), a conservative paper (edited by Dostoevsky in 1873–74), was considered semiofficial. The Slavophiles had several newspapers, none of which ran for long: *The Sail* (1859), *Day* (1861–65), and *Moscow* (1867–68). Many other dailies were produced in the capitals as well as in the provinces. All of those mentioned had a regular book review section. A book by a prominent author would commonly be reviewed in as many as thirty different periodicals.

A new dimension was given to Russian journalism and literature by the appearance in London (1855–62) and Geneva (1869) of an annual almanac, *The Pole Star*, published by Aleksandr Herzen and Nikolai Ogaryov. The almanac's cover featured profiles of the five hanged Decembrists, thus stressing its continuity with the *Pole Star* of 1823–25. The new *Pole Star* published many items that could not appear in Russia, such as Belinsky's "Letter to Gogol," the writings of Pyotr Chaadaev, and suppressed poems by Pushkin, Ryleev, Lermontov, and others. Herzen and Ogaryov's newspaper *The Bell*, published irregularly in London and Geneva from 1857 to 1867 (a total of 245 issues) with a circulation of up to three thousand, found its way into Russia and was widely read, even by government officials and, it was rumored, by the tsar himself. *The Bell* reported facts of Russian life that could not be aired in the censored press, as well as printing a variety of essays, memoirs, poems, reviews, and polemical pieces by Russian and foreign authors. Among the former were Herzen, Ogaryov, Bakunin, Annenkov, Dobrolyubov, and Varfolomei Zaitsev, among the latter Proudhon, Michelet, Garibaldi, and Mazzini. In the 1870s some further émigré periodicals appeared, such as the *People's Cause* (1870), organ of the Russian section of the First International, as well as some underground populist papers like *The People's Will* (1879–1885).

The growth of the revolutionary movement in the 1860s and 1870s had the side effect of releasing a steady stream of political emigrants who established an ever-shifting network of revolutionary groupings in the West, often in contact with other national or international socialist or anarchist organizations. Since many of the émigrés were journalists and writers, an émigré literature began to develop. As it was not too difficult or risky to send or take such literature back to Russia, it tended to enter the mainstream of Russian thought almost immediately and found a response in "legal" literature. Among the more prominent émigrés, besides Herzen and Ogaryov, were Pyotr Lavrov (after 1870), Varfolomei Zaitsev (after 1869), Sergei Stepnyak-Kravchinsky (after 1876), Pyotr Kropotkin (after 1876), Mikhail Bakunin (after 1861), and Georgy Plekhanov (after 1880). Since most Russian writers made occasional trips to the West and some lived there for long periods, personal contacts between émigré and mainstream writers were frequent and fruitful.

By mid-century Russian institutions of higher learning had attained a European level and produced scientists of international repute. The Saint Petersburg Academy of Medicine and Surgery (founded in 1798, renamed the Academy of Military Medicine in 1881) became a first-rate research institution. The surgeon N. I. Pirogov (1810–81), the chemist A. P. Borodin (1833–87), and the physiologist I. P. Pavlov (1849–1936) were on its faculty. Other Russian scientists of international stature were the mathematician N. I. Lobachevsky (1793–1856), the physiologist I. I. Sechenov (1829–1905), the chemist D. I. Mendeleev (1834–1907), the neurologist V. M. Bekhterev (1857–1927), and the psychiatrist S. S. Korsakov (1854–1900). Many of Russia's leading scientists published articles in popular journals, spreading their materialist and positivist worldview among the general public. It became fashionable for progressive-minded young men to follow an academic curriculum in the natural sciences even if they had no intention to pursue a scientific career. A definite connection existed between an orientation toward the natural sciences and a "progressive" political outlook. A subject of a running controversy was the government's policy of admitting to university studies only graduates of *gimnazii*, secondary schools whose curriculum was heavily weighted toward a study of the classics, the humanities, and pure mathematics, whereas graduates of the more modern *real'nye uchilishcha*, which taught modern languages and the natural sciences, were allowed to pursue a higher technical education only. A writer's political orientation could be gathered from his position on this issue. For example, Dostoevsky, an engineer by education, supported the government's policy.

Throughout the period the Russian universities were hotbeds of political activity. Many professors were active on the political scene and experienced severe difficulties when in disagreement with the official policies of the moment. Timofei Granovsky (1813–55), a professor of universal history at Moscow University who was famous for his eloquence and was called the Pushkin of Russian history, was continually harassed by the authorities for his liberal ideas derived from German idealism.[1] Aleksandr Pypin (1833–1904), a phenomenally productive historian of literature, resigned his professorship of Russian literature at Saint Petersburg in 1861 in protest against government action

in response to student demonstrations. His election to the Imperial Academy in 1871 was not confirmed by the tsar, and Pypin had to wait until 1898 to become a member. Of course, there were also many professors who supported the government.

From the 1860s on, university students and often secondary school students, too, posed a permanent problem to the government. Many of them were poor raznochintsy, eking out a meager living as tutors, hack writers, translators, or clerks. With no native tradition in parliamentary give and take or political compromise, these young men, to whom young women were added when "higher courses for women" were instituted at Russian universities in the 1860s, were inclined to embrace radical ideas and ideological maximalism. Many became militant atheists, socialists, and, if not active revolutionaries, at least sympathizers, easily swayed by student or outside activists to participate in demonstrations and protests. Many of the activists were the sons of parish priests and themselves ex-seminarians who brought with them a certain doctrinaire arrogance and fanatical conviction in the righteousness of their cause.

Academic study of Russian language and literature was by mid-century well integrated into the international professional community. The methodology of literature and folklore studies followed the development of these disciplines in the West. The mythological school of the brothers Grimm found followers in F. I. Buslaev (1818–97) of Moscow University and A. N. Afanasyev (1826–71), a private scholar.[2] It was superseded by the cultural-historical school, represented by (to mention only the most prominent) A. N. Pypin and O. F. Miller (1833–89), both professors of Saint Peters-

1. Granovsky was the prototype of Stepan Trofimovich Verkhovensky in Dostoevsky's novel *The Possessed.*

2. See p. 3.

burg University, and N. S. Tikhonravov (1832–93), who taught at Moscow University. Almost contemporaneously, a comparatist school also flourished. V. F. Miller (1848–1913) of Moscow University and the brothers Aleksandr (1838–1906) and Aleksei Veselovsky (1843–1918), who taught at Saint Petersburg and Moscow universities, respectively, were among its most renowned exponents. A. A. Potebnya (1835–1891), who taught at Kharkov University, did some work in the theory of verbal art, which was to influence twentieth-century Formalist poetics. Potebnya's basic idea was that the connection between an object and its artistic representation is not objective but symbolic: a work of art is a function of the artist's worldview.

Several of the works and editions produced during this period remained in use well into the twentieth century. Vladimir Dahl's *Reasoned Dictionary of the Living Great Russian Language* (1863–66) is still in use. *Materials toward a Lexicon of the Old Russian Language* (1893–1911), compiled by I. I. Sreznevsky (1812–80) of Saint Petersburg University, was superseded only in the 1980s. Other major achievements were Pyotr Kireevsky's *Songs* (10 vols., 1860–74); collections of byliny by P. N. Rybnikov (1831–85) and A. F. Hilferding (1831–72), both in three volumes, the first 1861–67, the other 1873; A. N. Afanasyev's *Folktales* (1855–64); N. S. Tikhonravov's editions of Russian apocrypha (1863) and the collected works of Gogol (1889–93); and P. V. Annenkov's edition of the collected works of Pushkin (1855).

One area in which Russia made no important original contribution was philosophy. Noteworthy contributions to Russian thought came not from professional philosophers but from writers (Tolstoi and Dostoevsky) or critics (Herzen, Chernyshevsky,

and Mikhailovsky). The one Russian who gained fame as a philosopher was Vladimir Solovyov (1853–1900), son of the historian Sergei Solovyov (1820–79). His mystical philosophy, derived from Schelling and Jakob Böhme, had little social or political effect but would be important for the symbolist movement in early twentieth-century poetry. Nikolai Fyodorov (1828–1903), a Moscow librarian, created a philosophical system that was published posthumously as *The Philosophy of the Common Cause* (1906) but was well known even in the 1870s to Dostoevsky, Tolstoi, Solovyov, and other Russian men of letters. Fyodorov's system combined archaist and mystical thought with modern scientific and sociological principles. It made the common cause of a corporeal "resurrection of the fathers" the ultimate goal of humanity, a goal to be pursued in every conceivable way, including an advance of science to a point of control over nature that would allow this.

The Russian theater received a permanent indigenous repertory from Aleksandr Ostrovsky (1823–86), who wrote some forty plays and translated a number of others from English, Italian, French, and German. Ostrovsky devoted his whole life to the theater, not only as a playwright, but also as a successful fighter for better pay and working conditions for actors and as organizer of a theater guild. He was instrumental in breaking the monopoly of the imperial stage in the capitals. Ostrovsky's realist slice-of-life plays forced the style of Russian acting to shift from the extremes of vaudeville and romantic exaltation to a more subdued "natural" manner. Aleksandr Lensky (1847–1908), a great actor who played some thirty different roles in Ostrovsky's plays, was also a great acting coach who anticipated many of the principles of the Moscow Art Theater of the 1890s and 1900s, specifically the idea that acting should be based on training rather than on intuition.

Since mid-century Russian music and painting, although in living contact with the West, began to assume an independent national character. Russian painting moved away from the academicism of the first half of the century to a socially oriented realism. Many Russian painters were no less socially conscious than Russian writers of the same period, whereas others were equally interested in human psychology. The Society of Mobile Art Exhibitions (1870–1923), popularly called the Itinerants (*peredvizhniki*), took its socially attuned art, which often carried a strong populist message, to people all over the country. Its leader was I. N. Kramskoi (1837–87), who did memorable portraits of Tolstoi and Dostoevsky. Some of the leading Itinerants were V. G. Perov (1833–82), mainly a portrait painter, A. K. Savrasov (1830–97), a landscape painter, V. I. Surikov (1848–1916), famous for his historical paintings, V. M. Vasnetsov (1848–1926), a painter of mythological and fairy-tale scenes, and I. E. Repin (1844–1930), who excelled in all of these genres. Some paintings by the Itinerants, such as Repin's *Volga Barge Haulers* and *Religious Procession*, both eloquent statements about contemporary Russian life, elicited lively discussions in which major writers participated.

A movement analogous to social and psychological realism in art went on in music. Both were championed by the eminent art and music critic Vladimir Stasov (1824–1906). The first musical "realist" was A. S. Dargomyzhsky (1813–1869), whose opera *The Water Spirit* (1856), after Pushkin's play, is still heard. Russian music gained international recognition simul-

taneously with Russian literature. The credit for this belongs largely to the "mighty bunch" (*moguchaya kuchka*), a group of composers formed in Saint Petersburg in the late 1850s. Its guiding spirit was Mily Balakirev (1836–1919), the first Russian to compose program music, noted with displeasure by Tolstoi in *Anna Karenina*. Aleksandr Borodin (1833–87), who was also a prominent scientist, wrote highly original symphonic and chamber music. His opera *Prince Igor* was completed by Rimsky-Korsakov and staged in 1890. Modest Musorgsky (1839–1881), an officer and civil service official, wrote interesting program music and several operas in which he sought to wed the verbal to the musical content. *The Sorochintsy Fair* and *Marriage* were based on works by Gogol, and *Boris Godunov* (1869, staged in 1874) was skilfully adapted from Pushkin's drama. Musorgsky's last opera, *Khovanshchina*, was completed by Rimsky-Korsakov in 1883. The other members of the "mighty bunch" were César Cui (1835–1918), a civil engineer, and Nikolai Rimsky-Korsakov (1844–1908), a naval officer who eventually became the only professional composer of the group. His numerous operas are based on texts by Russian writers. They are still regularly staged in Russia, though rarely in the West. His virtuosically orchestrated symphonic music is heard often in the world's concert halls. Other leading composers were Anton Rubinstein (1829–94), founder (1862) and first head of the Saint Petersburg Conservatory, who composed fourteen operas (*The Demon*, after Lermontov's poem, is the most famous), and Pyotr Tchaikovsky (1840–93), the best-known Russian composer, if perhaps not the greatest or most original. Tchaikovsky's operas *Eugene Onegin* and *The Queen of Spades*, both after Pushkin, helped introduce Russian literature to audiences all over the world.

Although in the course of the nineteenth century the Russian economy and Russian society as a whole remained backward and troubled, every aspect of Russian culture was not only entirely westernized but also reached a level of quality that was in no way inferior to its equivalent in the West. The excellence of Russian fiction was in line with achievements in other fields. That successful works of Russian literature would now be routinely translated into the languages of the West showed that Russia had arrived culturally, though it would take some time until the West realized that *Anna Karenina* (1875–77) was a "European event," as Dostoevsky put it, and that the Russian novel of that period was one of the high points in all literature.

Other developments were running contrary to a rapprochement of Russian culture to the West. The preoccupation of educated Russia with the condition of the Russian masses diverted the attention of the intelligentsia from broader European interests. The positivist and materialist orientation of many educated Russians alienated them from a large part of Europe's—and even Russia's own—cultural heritage. Much of the literature and literary criticism of the period is, compared to the preceding, decidedly provincial. Unlike the poets of the golden age, whose themes, imagery, and sensibilities were largely derived from Western literature, the great Russian novelists entered world literature on their own terms.

Aesthetic Theory and Literary Criticism

From the 1850s until well into the 1890s Russian literary criticism followed Belin-

sky's example, seeing mediatorship between literature and society as its principal concern. There was general agreement that literature had a social responsibility and that its truth content was the decisive criterion of its excellence. An aesthetic based on the concept of beauty and "art for art's sake," still professed by some romantic epigones such as the poet Afanasy Fet, was considered hardly worthy of discussion. Literary criticism, like literature, was politically aligned. A critic's position in the political spectrum tended to determine his theoretical views on art and all too often even his judgment of particular authors and works.

The radical left took a utilitarian view of art and literature, giving priority to "correct thinking." The liberal center sought a compromise, defending the autonomy of art while maintaining its social role. The right put an even stronger emphasis on the autonomy of art and contended that all true art was by nature socially valuable. With everybody wanting literature to be socially relevant, the difference lay in the question: On whose terms, the artist's or the political activist's?

Even in a more direct way, Belinsky's was still a dominant presence during this entire period. Critics of the left venerated him, referred to him profusely, and considered themselves his heirs. Leading liberals such as Annenkov, Botkin, Druzhinin, and Turgenev had had close personal relations with Belinsky and claimed still to be his followers. Even Apollon Grigoryev, the leading critic of the right, explicitly called himself a disciple of Belinsky's, although he rejected some of Belinsky's utilitarian excesses.

Belinsky had often digressed from a discussion of a work under review to observations on Russian society. His successors made this their standard practice. As Grigoryev and Dobrolyubov freely admitted, they wrote their reviews not about but *apropos* of a given work, using it rather as a preacher would use a biblical text for his sunday sermon.

Not only was Russian criticism arranged along a political spectrum from a materialist left to an idealist right. There also were serious disagreements within the left as well as the right. Dmitry Pisarev of *The Russian Word* carried on a spirited polemic with Dobrolyubov and Saltykov-Shchedrin of *The Contemporary*.[3] Apollon Grigoryev and Dostoevsky attacked not only the radicals but also the Slavophiles and the extreme conservatives of *The Russian Herald*. The emergent populists, such as Lavrov and Mikhailovsky, had serious disagreements with the nihilists of the 1860s.

After Belinsky's death the criticism section of *The Contemporary* continued his course. Nekrasov himself, a good judge of poetry, wrote some important surveys and reviews. Among its frequent contributors were Vasily Botkin (1810–69), Pavel Annenkov (1812–87), and Aleksandr Druzhinin (1824–64). All three had been on cordial terms with Belinsky, and Botkin had been a close personal friend. These critics insisted, more emphatically than Belinsky had in his later years, on the autonomy of art. Their reviews of Turgenev, Tolstoi, Pisemsky, Ostrovsky, and other writers discussed their works in terms of Belinskian social criticism, yet with more attention to their formal side.

Botkin, from a wealthy Moscow merchant family, was a Westernizer, traveled widely in Europe (he wrote a travelogue of Spain), and was a connoisseur of music and painting. His critical judgment was widely respected. Turgenev, Pisemsky, Ostrovsky, Nekrasov, and Fet (who was his brother-in-law) all sought his advice. Botkin had introduced Belinsky to left-Hegelian thought and was a political liberal, but he deplored the vulgarization of Russian literature, which had begun with the natural school, and rejected Chernyshevsky's utilitarian aesthetics. In 1856 he tried to have Chernyshevsky replaced by Grigoryev on the staff of *The Contemporary* but failed. He nevertheless stayed with *The Contemporary*, collaborating on some articles with Nekrasov in 1855–56 and in 1857 publishing a major article on Fet.

Botkin's essay on Fet—Dobrolyubov called it "simply stupid"—contains ideas that became the nucleus of the symbolist aesthetic some forty years later. He called Fet's poetry an exhibit of the musical aspect of poetry. There are works, he said, "which we forget along with their content, but whose melody is mysteriously fused with the whole life of our soul and merges into our spiritual organism." In opposition to Chernyshevsky, Botkin declared that art belongs to a sphere of the human spirit that resists rational analysis. He also asserted that empirical reality was irrelevant to art and that it was based, rather, in the subjective subconscious, as well as that art's calling was to serve not the interests of the day but the unchanging basic needs of the human soul. These views made Botkin an "aesthete" in the eyes of the "seminarians" Dobrolyubov and Chernyshevsky. When the conflict between aesthetes and seminarians had become too acrimonious to allow further collaboration, Nekrasov sided with the seminarians, and Botkin left *The Contemporary*.

---

3. Dostoevsky, in an essay, "Mr. Shchedrin and the Schism among the Nihilists" (1864), called the *Russian Word* the organ of the immoderate nihilists, and the *Contemporary* the organ of the moderate nihilists.

Annenkov, a gentleman littérateur, was a friend of Belinsky's and Turgenev's. He also knew Gogol well and met him in Rome. A westernizing liberal, Annenkov had contacts with utopian socialists and left-Hegelians. He knew Marx and Engels personally and corresponded with both. Annenkov's important edition of Pushkin's *Collected Works* (1855–57) was accompanied by a volume, *Materials toward a Biography of A. S. Pushkin*. The image of Pushkin developed in this volume, essentially the one that eventually prevailed in the twentieth century, was fiercely challenged by the radicals. Annenkov took a position according to which the world of poetry had its own laws: the "truth of life" and the "truth of literature" were two different things. However, Annenkov still stood for realist art, and his reviews of Turgenev, Tolstoi, and others took for granted that literature has a social and moral responsibility. His review of *War and Peace* (1868) is still one of the better pieces on that work. Annenkov's memoirs, in particular *The Remarkable Decade: 1838–1848* (1880), are of great importance for the biographies of Gogol, Belinsky, Turgenev, Stankevich, Granovsky, Bakunin, and Dostoevsky.

Druzhinin was the most outspoken of the aesthetes on *The Contemporary*. His early fiction, such as his George Sandian short novel *Polinka Saks* (1847), was in line with Belinsky's "progressive" ideas. In the 1850s Druzhinin concentrated on criticism, essays on French and English literature, and translations of Shakespeare. His article "A. S. Pushkin and the Last Edition of His Works" (1855) develops the conception of Pushkin the Olympian, the objective artist, the poet who transcends his own age with all its conflicts, prejudices, and problems. Pushkin became the rallying point of the beleaguered aesthetes, while their utilitarian

opponents declared him the frivolous bard of sybaritic *savoir vivre*.

In 1856 Druzhinin left *The Contemporary* and took over *The Reading Library* (1856–61), making it the voice of the autonomy of art. He responded to Chernyshevsky's programmatic *Essays in the Gogolian Period of Russian Literature* with "A Critique of the Gogolian Period of Russian Literature and Our Relation to It" (1856), where he set up the Pushkinian tradition as the truly life-affirming and creative one in Russian literature. Druzhinin, by no means an advocate of pure art, approved of Pisemsky's objective realism, and his great hope for the future was his own close friend Lev Tolstoi, who at the time fully shared Druzhinin's views on art and literature. Chernyshevsky responded to Druzhinin's positive review of Pisemsky's peasant tales by suggesting that what Druzhinin had praised was precisely their failing: the lack of a critical attitude and a lack of desire to combat the ills of Russian life.

Druzhinin's criticism has stood up well to time. The deprecatory remarks of his radical opponents were grossly unfair. Druzhinin was no great critic or original thinker. His assets were an excellent erudition in European literature, a recognition of the creative imagination, and respect for the writer's craft.

Druzhinin was not alone in his defense of the autonomy of art. Such critics as Evgeny Edelson (1824–68), Boris Almazov (1827–76), and Efim Zarin (1829–92) consolidated and defended the position, long since established by Belinsky, that attention to form did not imply disregard for content, and that neglect of form could not fail to have an adverse effect on content. In fact, most major writers of the period, including Turgenev, Goncharov, and Dostoevsky, explicitly supported this notion. Only the radical left and, in some instances, the radical right[4] were inclined to equate form with "elegance of execution" and to consider it a hindrance to art's "real" task, that of giving the consciousness of society the "proper" direction.

Nikolai Gavrilovich Chernyshevsky (1828–89) may have had a greater influence on the course of Russian history than any other major figure of Russian literature. The son of a parish priest in Saratov on the Volga, Chernyshevsky earned a scholarship at Petersburg University, where he was a brilliant student. His master's thesis, *On the Aesthetic Relations of Art to Reality* (1855), created a sensation and charted the program of the new literature of the 1860s. His *Essays in the Gogolian Period of Russian Literature* (1856) inaugurated the age of a socially conscious realism in Russian literature, largely by quoting profusely and selectively from Belinsky and by presenting Gogol as a civic-minded writer. A contributor to the *Contemporary* since 1853, Chernyshevsky headed its criticism section until ceding it to Dobrolyubov in 1857 to concentrate on economic, social, and pedagogical matters. In July 1862 he was arrested on suspicion of subversive activities and authorship of an inflammatory revolutionary pamphlet. He was held at Saint Peter and Paul Fortress for two years, during which he wrote his socialist utopian novel *What Is to Be Done?* which was legally published in *The Contemporary*. In May 1864 he was subjected to a public ceremony depriving him of his civil rights and transported to Siberia to serve seven years at hard labor. He was allowed to return to European Russia in 1883. Chernyshevsky was revered as a martyr by the radical Russian intelligentsia, which embraced his materialist, rationalist, and positivist philosophy. His writings (in particular *What Is to Be Done?*) were immensely influential. He has been the subject of as much attention in Soviet literary and historical studies as the greatest figures of the nineteenth century.

Chernyshevsky's worldview may be defined as materialist monism (mental processes are physical processes, subject to known laws of nature and therefore fully determinate), combined with an idealist fervor for social progress. Considering religion and metaphysics to be superstitions plain and simple, he advocated and lived a life of selfless devotion to the cause of socialism. Chernyshevsky was an uncritical believer in human progress, which he perceived as ascending to ever more complete mastery of nature, more rational organization of society, and more perfect happiness. He saw recent Russian history in these terms, too. His anthropology was that of the eighteenth-century Enlightenment: man was a natural egoist, yet capable of pursuing his self-interest rationally and hence of creating a social ambience that would allow him to live in harmony with other humans; man was also possessed of social instincts, and to be engaged in useful labor was his natural condition; unhappiness and disorder in human affairs were caused by unnatural conditions in man's environment and could be remedied by rational action.

Chernyshevsky's aesthetic was based on the premise that healthy art was no more and no less than imitation of nature, a substitute for real objects, useful in case of their absence. He insisted that even the greatest work of art was inherently inferior to the real object it represented. He revived the eighteenth-century idea that instrumental music was inferior to vocal

---

4. Katkov would occasionally lean in that direction.

music by virtue of being an imitation of the human voice, whereas the latter produced firsthand imitations of nature. (He also found Beethoven "incomprehensible and savage" and Mozart's *Don Giovanni* "boring.") Chernyshevsky considered fantasy at best a poor substitute for precise knowledge of real facts, at worst the reflection of an abnormal mental condition. The crux of Chernyshesvky's thesis is what Pisarev was later to call his "abolition of aesthetics." He demonstrated to his own and Pisarev's satisfaction that all aesthetic concepts were readily reduced to ordinary practical experience, the tragic being simply the extraordinarily sad, the sublime the extraordinarily large, and so on. Chernyshevsky defined beauty as "life as it ought to be." Accordingly, he found "a young housewife who has happily furnished her modest three- or four-room apartment more poetic than any Medici or Louvre Venus."

Chernyshevsky saw the role of art in utilitarian terms: "Let art be satisfied with its lofty and beautiful calling: to be in the case of the absence of reality to some extent a substitute for it and to be thus a textbook of life." In particular, he felt that literature was useful in conveying scientific information to those who were not up to reading authentic scientific works. He rejected "art for art's sake" as an unhealthy pastime of the idle rich, never considering the possibility that art might be something other than useful didactic material or hedonistic diversion.

It seems incredible that these opinions were held by a man of excellent academic credentials. Chernyshevsky knew his Plato and Aristotle, as well as his Schelling and Hegel. He acknowledged that his philosophy owed much to Ludwig Feuerbach, a left-Hegelian materialist philosopher. Chernyshevsky was well read in aesthetic theory from Plotinus to Friedrich Theodor Vischer.

He could clearly see the connection between German idealist philosophy and romantic literature, and rejected both as a deplorable reactionary betrayal of the achievements of the Enlightenment. He certainly knew the major works of world literature. He found Homer incoherent, cynical, and lacking in moral feeling. Aeschylus and Sophocles were rude and arid, Goethe's "Hermann und Dorothea" disgusting. Chernyshevsky admired Béranger, George Sand, Heine, Dickens, and Thackeray.

Chernyshevsky, who believed that literature had at all times played a negligible role in the progress of human society, felt compelled to become a literary critic because in Russia, unlike in the West, "literature constituted the whole intellectual life of the nation." To Chernyshevsky, Belinsky was by far the most important figure of Russian literature. He fully recognized Belinsky's Hegelianism and pointed out his progress toward an application of Hegel's ideas to concrete problems of Russian society and a conception of literature as a vehicle of social progress.

"Belinsky had executed Gogol; Chernyshevsky rehabilitated him," Andrei Bely observed. Chernyshevsky unequivocally declared Gogol to have been the father of Russian prose fiction, the originator of the "critical tendency" in Russian literature, the first Russian writer to be independent of Western examples—in a word, the greatest Russian writer and the head of "the only school of which Russian literature can be proud." The "Gogolian period" of Russian literature was to Chernyshevsky the period in which Russian literature developed a growing social concern and began to direct its attention to the ills of Russian life. Chernyshevsky explained Gogol's betrayal of the cause of progress and his espousal of a religious worldview by his upbringing, insufficient education, expatriation and isolation, and the pernicious influence of reactionaries like Zhukovsky and Shevyryov. Gogol's melancholy, he says, was caused by the social ills he discerned in Russian life. As he singles out some passages for particular approval, Chernyshevsky is attracted to episodes in Part Two of *Dead Souls* which have a blatantly moralizing ethos, particularly the governor general's speech toward the end, a piece of unctuous rhetoric. Chernyshevsky, like Belinsky before him, appreciates Gogol for what from today's viewpoint appear to be entirely the wrong reasons.

Chernyshevsky's criticism of his contemporaries was determined by his theoretical views. He gave an entirely negative account of Ostrovsky's *Poverty Is No Vice* (1854), a play that Grigoryev hailed as an expression of the Russian soul and the truth of Russian life. To Chernyshevsky, the play was a false idealization of an obsolescent way of life. But he had high praise for Ostrovsky's play *A Lucrative Position*, an exposé of official corruption.

Chernyshevsky's review article on the works of the young Tolstoi (1856) contained some just observations. He conjectured that Tolstoi's amazing psychological analyses were based on introspection and observed that Tolstoi was interested primarily in "the psychological process itself, its forms, its laws, the dialectics of the soul." Moreover, he credited Tolstoi with "remarkable freshness" owing to the "purity of his moral feeling." Tolstoi was soon to part ways with *The Contemporary*, where he had started his career, because he disapproved of the utilitarian tendency of the journal, for which Chernyshevsky was responsible. In turn, Chernyshevsky criticized Tolstoi for his downplaying of the value of schools for peasant children in Tolstoi's journal *Yasnaya Polyana*. Yet much of what Tolstoi had to say about art—even in *Yasnaya Polyana*, and later in *What Is Art?*—was astoundingly close to Chernyshevsky's aesthetic doctrine.

Chernyshevsky's famous essay "A Russian at a Rendez-Vous" (1858) was occasioned by Turgenev's fine short story "Asya." Chernyshevsky faulted Turgenev for creating heroes who, in spite of their good intentions, would in the end prove too weak for life's challenge. He wanted to see fighters and builders, honest workers who would stand up for their ideals. Annenkov's response to Chernyshevsky, "The Literary Type of a Weak Man" (1858), maintained that Turgenev's types were not only true to life but also positive, in that they bore the seed of progress in them: weren't creative individuals and bearers of ideas more often than not "weak men"?

Chernyshevsky formulated his demands of contemporary Russian literature in a review article, "Could This Be the Beginning of a Change?" (1861), written in response to the *Tales* of Nikolai Uspensky. Chernyshevsky wholeheartedly approves of Uspensky's brutally naturalistic descriptions of the abject poverty, frightening savagery, and abysmal ignorance of the Russian peasantry. What Chernyshevsky wanted were competent case studies, not idealized artistic pieces like Turgenev's *Hunter's Sketches*. He wanted a literature that would tell the reader that the peasants were simply people who needed to be educated and helped. Like Uspensky, Chernyshevsky ignored the religious faith and native culture of the Russian peasant.

Chernyshevsky's ideas in their purest form were fully embraced only by the nihilists of the 1860s. They were modified in the 1870s by the populists and later by

Marxists, Plekhanov in particular. But a residue of these ideas would always remain in the thinking, criticism, and literary practice of the radical left.

Nikolai Aleksandrovich Dobrolyubov (1836–61), like Chernyshevsky and many other radical journalists, was the son of a parish priest and started his education at a seminary, whence he transferred to the Petersburg Pedagogical Institute. He became a permanent member of the staff of *The Contemporary* immediately after his graduation in 1857 and was that journal's chief literary critic until his death of consumption. He enjoyed the respect and admiration of his older colleagues for his unflagging revolutionary zeal, moral purity, and amazing energy and remarkable talent. Having a more complex mind than Chernyshevsky, he wrote poetry and was no stranger to emotional conflict. He had been deeply religious as an adolescent and injected his religious fervor into his revolutionary creed. His manner is less arid, doctrinaire, and self-righteous than Chernyshevsky's, but his style is awkward and prolix, in part because he was writing "around" the censorship, using elaborate circumlocutions and Aesopian language to camouflage his message.

Dobrolyubov's philosophy was the same as Chernyshevsky's. Less learned than Chernyshevsky, he stated it in more graphic terms: "It is time to abandon Platonic dreams and understand that bread is not an empty sign, the reflection of a higher, abstract life force, but simply bread, an object which one can eat."[5] He also rejected

out of hand any intimation of a teleology in history or art. Dobrolyubov shared Chernyshevsky's optimistic anthropology. He declared that "crime is not a consequence of human nature, but a consequence of the abnormal conditions in which a person has been placed by society, and the more abnormal these are, the more often crimes are committed even by decent people." It was this position that was challenged by Dostoevsky, specifically in *Crime and Punishment*. Dobrolyubov also believed that "normal" conditions were preserved more often among the people than among the upper classes.

The people were Dobrolyubov's main concern. Unlike to the Slavophiles or the pochvennik Grigoryev, the people meant to Dobrolyubov the poor and uneducated masses, rural or urban. The prosperous merchant class was not included, as far as he was concerned. The fact that the people had preserved elements of native Russian culture was of little interest to Dobrolyubov. He was disappointed in Afanasyev's *Russian Folktales* (1857) because the mentality he found in them did not correspond to his ideal of an upright and morally superior, though oppressed, people. He was delighted to discover a negative image of pre-Petrine Russia in Kotoshikhin.[6] In his long essay "On the Degree of the Role of *narodnost'* in the Development of Russian Literature" (1858) the people (*narod*) are clearly the poor. The essay is not so much concerned with the popular strain in Russian literature as with the degree to which a work or author will stand up for the true interests of the people, that is, expose the injustice suffered

5. Quoted from Dobrolyubov's programmatic essay, "On the Degree of the Role of *narodnost'* in the Development of Russian Literature" (1858). Dobrolyubov is implicitly attacking the sacred and ritual function of bread. Symbolists

and even the Acmeist Mandelshtam would reverse this position.

6. See pp. 93–94 above.

by the people and voice its grievances. Derzhavin earns no more than a few disparaging remarks. Pushkin comes off badly: owing to his background and social status he was unable to understand the social needs of his day.

Dobrolyubov's last word about literature and the Russian people was a review article, "Traits of a Characterization of the Common Russian People" (1860), occasioned by Marko Vovchok's *Tales from the Life of the Russian People* (1859). In Vovchok's tales Dobrolyubov happily discovered peasant characters, particularly female, who fully met his ideal: intelligent, energetic, eager to win their freedom and willing to make sacrifices to that end. Druzhinin and Dostoevsky were to recognize that Dobrolyubov's enthusiastic effusion ("The people is not dead, it has not lost its energy, the wellspring of life has not run dry in it!") was a projection of his own feelings and that Vovchok's freedom-loving heroines were maudlin fabrications of a liberal "lady writer."

Dobrolyubov saw "the main task of literary criticism in explaining the phenomena of reality which informed the work under review." He would routinely use a text to illustrate some observation regarding the progress of Russian society. He saw major works of literature as catalysts of social progress by virtue of the fact that they helped society become conscious of ongoing social processes and change.

Dobrolyubov's criticism shows a sharp turn away from European concerns and toward a preoccupation with strictly Russian issues—from a narrow, partisan point of view. Dobrolyubov's references to Pushkin presage the disrespectful or even hostile attitude that the "men of the sixties" developed toward the poet whom they saw as a frivolous aristocrat who indulged himself in art for art's sake. He found that Pushkin was "a shallow nature, but lively, easygoing, readily carried away, and at that, as a result of a lack of a proper education, carried away rather by things external." He found fault with Pushkin's conservatism, aestheticism, genealogical prejudices, epicurean tendencies, and "his education under the tutelage of French émigrés." He also thought that Pushkin, while "most impressionable artistically," was "disinclined to think hard and actively." Dobrolyubov's evaluation of Gogol follows Chernyshevsky's. When he gets to review Belinsky's *Collected Works* in 1859, he is for once unreservedly enthusiastic and unabashedly lyrical: "We have waited for it so long and finally it is here! How many happy, pure minutes will these articles give us again!"

"What Is Oblomovitis?" (1859) is the best known of Dobrolyubov's articles and the most characteristic of his method. His thesis is that the story of Oblomov's life is the story of the corruption of the Russian gentry by the idleness and parasitism imposed on it by a social order that deprives it of the freedom to lead an active working life. Dobrolyubov also welcomes the impending demise of Oblomov's class, using a rather awkward parable to make his point. In the parable some people were lost in a jungle, and a few of them climbed tall trees to look for a way out. Since it was dry and safe up there, and since sweet fruits grew in those trees, they stayed aloft and forgot about the people still on the ground struggling to find their way out of the jungle. Then the people decided to clear a path and in the process chopped down the trees on which their pathfinders were perched. In other words, the cultured westernized gentry and become superfluous.

Dobrolyubov's essays on Ostrovsky, "A Dark Kingdom" (1859) and "A Ray of Light in the Dark Kingdom" (1860), have a polemical edge aimed at Apollon Grigoryev's idealized image of traditional Russian society, as derived by Grigoryev from Ostrovsky's plays. Dobrolyubov asks what keeps the "dark kingdom" of the Russian merchant class going, and comes to the conclusion that it is simple inertia and everybody's desire to be materially secure. He stresses that the condition of the dark kingdom is unnatural and that it must be rectified by the light of reason. Along the way Dobrolyubov makes some perceptive remarks about Ostrovsky's plays, as when he defends *The Thunderstorm* against the charge that it violates the unity of action by introducing extraneous characters and details: in real life, he says, people also walk on and off stage at random, and unscheduled things do occur.

The message of Dobrolyubov's essay "When Will It Really Be Day?" (1860), written in response to Turgenev's novel *On the Eve*, went against the author's own interpretation. Dobrolyubov was grateful to Turgenev, who was no longer counted among the progressives, for his having created the type of "a man, consciously and wholly penetrated by a great idea," but faulted him for implying that such a man could not find a suitable field of activity in Russia. Dobrolyubov saw in Turgenev's hero Insarov, a Bulgarian freedom fighter, a Russian revolutionary in disguise.

Dobrolyubov's last major essay, "Downtrodden People" (1860), was devoted to Dostoevsky, whose novel *The Insulted and Injured* was included in his survey. When Dobrolyubov declared that Dostoevsky probably would not mind his saying that this work was "below aesthetic criticism" yet worthy of serious discussion, he must have

meant this almost as a compliment. But he did credit Dostoevsky with belonging to the humanist strain in Russian literature (Dobrolyubov did not live to be disappointed in this opinion) and with a profound understanding of the psyche of the downtrodden. He felt obliged to add, though, that Dostoevsky obviously lacked the talent to suggest a solution to their plight. Dobrolyubov shared the opinion of most of Dostoevsky's contemporaries that *Poor Folk*, "written under the influence of the best side of Gogol and the most vital ideas of Belinsky," was his best work.

Dobrolyubov must not be faulted for opinions that today seem obtuse, superficial, or absurd. Belinsky, too, had read Gogol and Dostoevsky shallowly and, like Chernyshevsky and Dobrolyubov, had a faith in man and in Russia's future that made them overlook ambiguities and ironies that twentieth-century readers would readily perceive.

Dmitry Ivanovich Pisarev (1840–68) was by far the most talented Russian critic of his age and perhaps the most talented ever. Born into the landed gentry, he briefly attended Petersburg University but had to interrupt his studies in 1860 when he had a nervous breakdown, after which he spent some time in a sanitarium. He had begun to publish in *Dawn*, a ladies' journal, in 1859. After his graduation in 1861 he became chief critic of *The Russian Word*. Varfolomei Zaitsev (1842–82) and Nikolai Shelgunov (1824–91), two other radical critics, were also on the staff of *The Russian Word*. In July 1862 Pisarev was arrested for having written a pamphlet that called for the overthrow of the government and the removal of the reigning monarch. He was held for more than four years at the Peter and Paul Fortress, where he was allowed to continue his work for *The Russian Word*. Most of his best criticism, as well as essays on education, economics, history, and social problems, were written in prison. After his release in 1866 Pisarev wrote some articles for the *National Annals* (*The Russian Word* had been suspended). He was drowned in the sea near Riga in July 1868, probably a suicide, for he had been distraught after his release from prison.

Pisarev's first major review (of *Oblomov*, still in *Dawn*) was only moderately "progressive," but his first essays in *The Russian Word*, "Plato's Idealism" and "Nineteenth-Century Scholasticism" (both 1861), are programmatic statements in which Pisarev rethinks morality in terms of "modern scientific views." In a survey article, "Female Types in the Works of Pisemsky, Turgenev, and Goncharov" (1861), he gives the edge to Pisemsky, the least artistic, but the most sober realist of the three.

In a review article on Turgenev's *Fathers and Sons*, "Bazarov" (1862), Pisarev correctly charged that M. A. Antonovich, another critic, was mistaken in seeing the novel as a slanderous attack on the progressive young generation. Instead, he said, it was an intelligent statement by a member of the older generation who had presented the "new man" as he saw him and was asking the younger generation about their ideals and goals. Pisarev went on to identify wholeheartedly with Bazarov's materialism, positivism, and scientism, as well as with his nihilism, that is, his denial of all traditional values.

Of all the progressive critics, Pisarev was the most consistent and uncompromising materialist and positivist. He rejected any historical teleology, any ideals or ideas, and developed a purely utilitarian theory of art. He asked, "What is the value of art?" and came up with the answer that aside from the pleasure it might provide some hedonists,

its only value was to be found in its didactic potential. In a programmatic essay, "Realists" (1864), Pisarev set forth a theory of the economic use of human mental powers. Having quoted Bazarov, who said that nature was "not a temple, but a workshop," Pisarev asserts that using one's mental powers to produce works of art is wasteful and a sign of immaturity. "An aesthete and a realist," he says, "are both egoists, but the aesthete's egoism is like the senseless egoism of a child ready at any time to stuff himself with cake and candy, whereas a realist's egoism is the conscious egoism of a mature person who creates for himself a supply of fresh pleasure for his whole life."

In the essay "The Abolition of Aesthetics" (1865) Pisarev takes the decisive step toward what he calls "consistent realism and the strictest utilitarianism." Taking his point of departure from Chernyshevsky's *Aesthetic Relations of Art to Reality*, he maintains that if the so-called aesthetic categories (the beautiful, the sublime, the tragic, and so on) can indeed be reduced to general psychological terms, as Chernyshevsky had demonstrated, the whole science of aesthetics is redundant, as is aesthetic criticism. The charge raised against Pisarev by Plekhanov and others, that his debunking of Pushkin and Belinsky was based on substituting empirical truth for poetic truth, is thus made invalid.

Pisarev took an even more radically utilitarian approach to literature than the radicals of *The Contemporary*, with whom he engaged in rather acrimonious polemics. In an essay entitled "Flowers of Innocent Humor" (1864) he charged that Saltykov-Shchedrin's satires were insufficiently utilitarian and in fact were leaning toward "pure art." Pisarev's long essay "Pushkin and Belinsky" (1865) is not only witty and entertaining but also makes good sense. His key observation is that Belinsky consistently reads into Pushkin's texts his own noble and humanitarian ideas. Unlike Belinsky—and like Chernyshevsky—Pisarev considers the role of literature in the progress of Russian society to have been minimal and suggests accordingly that one ought not overestimate the importance of the fact that Pushkin did indeed "perfect Russian verse and dared in verse to speak of beer mugs and beaver collars, while his precursors had spoken only of vials and chlamyses."

Quite naturally, Pisarev zeroes in on Pushkin's cycle on the poet and gleefully demolishes Belinsky's attempts to exonerate Pushkin from the charge of aestheticism and social indifference. Pisarev also justly refutes Belinsky's interpretation of *Eugene Onegin*, demonstrating that it is no more and no less than a "vivid and brilliant apotheosis of a most melancholy and senseless status quo." He does all this, Pisarev says, "not to mock the sacred memory of our great teacher Belinsky, but to show our readers how dangerous and pernicious the allure of aestheticism may be even to strong and remarkable minds."

Pisarev's principle according to which a literary critic should at all times relate literature to real life was flawed in that his materialist conception of real life was of course simplistic. In a review of Dostoevsky's *Crime and Punishment* (1867), entitled "The Struggle for Survival," he asserted that poverty was the real motive of Raskolnikov's crime, ignoring the whole complexity of Dostoevsky's text—and the complexity of the human psyche as well. But Pisarev's position was at least consistent, more so than Belinsky's or even Dobrolyubov's. By relinquishing any claim to art's cognitive, prophetic, or symbolic powers, he could gladly release the "aesthetic" aspect of

literature to "aesthetes." A moral puritan like most nihilists, he did so not without a contemptuous sneer. With all this, Pisarev was a lucid thinker, an elegant stylist, and a witty and entertaining writer. In spite of his crude materialism, his whole manner is infinitely more intelligent and urbane than that of any of his fellow critics in the radical camp. Pisarev was later chastised by Marxist theorists, for good reason, since his positivism and "vulgar" materialism were in flagrant contradiction to their historical teleology and dialectical materialism.

Varfolomei Zaitsev (1842–82), Pisarev's colleague on the staff of *The Russian Word* since 1863, was even more intransigent in denouncing the aesthetic domain. He equated "art" with the "artificial" and considered it a waste of time and resources diverted from more useful pursuits. Like Pisarev, he was well educated, having studied law and later medicine at Saint Petersburg University. A keen polemicist, Zaitsev took on all comers: *The Russian Herald, Time, Epoch, The Reading Library, The National Annals*, and even *The Contemporary*. His essay, "Those from Glupov[7] who Got into *The Contemporary*" (1864), triggered by a flippant remark of Saltykov-Shchedrin's regarding *What Is to to Be Done?*, initiated a bitter polemic between *The Russian Word* and *The Contemporary* and gave Dostoevsky occasion to write a gleeful comment, "A Schism among the Nihilists" (1864). Zaitsev emigrated in 1869 and was active in the international socialist movement. He was the prototype of Shigalyov, the fanatical revolutionary theorist in Dostoevsky's *The Possessed*.

With Dobrolyubov and Chernyshevsky

7. An allusion to Saltykov's *The History of a City* (see p. 340).

gone, radical criticism as practiced by Maksim Antonovich, Nikolai Shelgunov, Grigory Eliseev, and others was largely reduced to arid doctrinaire preaching and crude partisan vituperation. But in Mikhail Saltykov, who published under the pen name N. Shchedrin, *The Contemporary* and later *The National Annals* had a publicist, theorist, and critic who combined ideological orthodoxy with intellectual independence, wit, and style. A consistent and radical adherent of a utilitarian view of art, he heartily approved of and himself created frankly tendentious art and was a bitter opponent of "pure art," whose exponents, such as the poet Fet, he pursued with bilious sarcasm. He was an equally bitter opponent of naturalism, Zola's in particular, saying that its sterile objectivity did nothing to advance the cause of progress. In a series of programmatic articles of the late 1860s—"Unnecessary Apprehensions" (1868), "The Daily Needs of Literature" (1869), and "Street Philosophy" (1869)—Saltykov insisted that a "correct worldview" was the decisive criterion of the value of a work of art. "Literature and propaganda are one and the same thing—however old this truth may be, it has so little entered the consciousness of literature itself that it is by no means superfluous to repeat it," he wrote in "Street Philosophy," in which he summarily dismissed Leskov, Pisemsky, Dostoevsky, and other contemporaries on the grounds that their ideas were ambiguous and indistinct, as a result of which their works clouded issues, confusing people and distracting them from the straight path of progress. Saltykov wanted literature to "foresee the laws of the future and to create the image of man of the future," to come up with types that explicitly pointed toward a new social order. Saltykov's theoretical views

were remarkably close to the principles of socialist realism as first professed and practiced by Maksim Gorky.

Several influential critics of the 1870s and 1880s came from the ranks of the populists, who followed the nihilists of the 1860s. The aesthetics and literary criticism of Pyotr Lavrov (1823–1900), whose *Historical Letters* (1870) had a great influence on Russian revolutionary thought, evolved from a Belinskian organicism to a frank utilitarianism and a near denial of the value of art. Aleksandr Skabichevsky (1838–1910), who started his career as a literary critic in the early 1860s, advanced the populist view of art in his *Conversations on Russian Literature* (1876–77). Skabichevsky's is a crude and watered-down version of Chernyshevsky's approach to literature. His style is pedestrian. The populists produced one major critic, Nikolai Mikhailovsky (1842–1904), some of whose reviews and essays cannot be ignored even today. Mikhailovsky began to publish as early as 1860, while still a student of mining engineering. He was a mainstay of *The National Annals* from 1869 to 1884. A leader of the liberal populists, he published mostly in legal periodicals and toward the end of his life polemicized with Russian Marxists, including Lenin.

In a famous essay, "What Is Progress?" (1869), Mikhailovsky advocated a comprehensive development of the human personality and a society that gives it a chance to develop. He saw progress in terms of "stages" and "types" of social organization, the Russian peasant commune being the highest type at a very low stage of development. Mikhailovsky denied the very possibility of so-called pure art, which he considered as simply a camouflaged method to protect the ideals of the ruling class. He therefore rejected the notion that Pushkin was Russia's national poet, suggesting instead that Pushkin was "primarily a poet of the nobility" whose appeal was to an audience of "average noblemen."

Mikhailovsky wrote a series of articles on Lev Tolstoi, the best known of which is "The Right and the Left Hand of Count Lev Tolstoi" (1875). Tolstoi's "right hand" is his honest practical approach to specific issues, his astute and constructive thinking, and his pluralism. His "left hand" is his nihilism, his sweeping pessimistic generalizations, and his false idealization of the simple life. Mikhailovsky later had reason to complain that "the great writer of the Russian lands had turned all left-handed." Mikhailovsky also wrote major articles on Dostoevsky (1882), Turgenev (1883), Gleb Uspensky (1888), Saltykov-Shchedrin (1889), and Chekhov (1890). In the article on Dostoevsky, entitled "A Cruel Talent," Mikhailovsky suggests that Dostoevsky is grossly overestimated by his few admirers, who make a "prophet" and "national leader" out of him. His analysis of Dostoevsky's art also demolishes Dobrolyubov's image of Dostoevsky as a compassionate champion of the "insulted and injured" and advances the thesis that Dostoevsky's art is much more an expression of "some kind of instinctive urge to cause pain to these 'insulted and injured.'" Dostoevsky's "humor," says Mikhailovsky, is like that of a cat who gets excited by its play and soon takes to clawing and biting. No one in all Russian literature, he says, "has ever analyzed the sensations of a wolf devouring a sheep in such meticulous profundity, or with such love, one might say, as Dostoevsky." Mikhailovsky adduces many examples to prove his contention, always ignoring that extra turn of the screw which will turn cruelty into compassion. Mikhailovsky's necrology of Turgenev also concentrates on a negative point, namely,

that Turgenev never did, as so many believed, express the successive stages in the evolution of Russian social consciousness, but always presented "the same type in a different costume." Mikhailovsky was quite negative in his assessment of Chekhov as well. Although he may often have been wrong, his arguments were never unfounded and his judgment was always intelligent. Mikhailovsky was also an eloquent and witty stylist.

Apollon Aleksandrovich Grigoryev (1822–64), the leading critic of the right, was well liked by his contemporaries but never quite taken seriously. After his untimely death he was soon forgotten. Early in the twentieth century he was rediscovered and called by some the greatest Russian critic, but again he was remanded to oblivion after the Revolution. He has begun to come into his own since the 1960s. Grigoryev is hard to pidgeonhole, and the final judgment on him is still pending. The son of a minor but affluent official, Grigoryev grew up in the merchants' quarter south of the Moscow River and took a law degree from Moscow University. He briefly joined the civil service but went to Petersburg in 1844 to devote himself to literature. He had some modest success with his formally ragged poetry, which features Lermontovian ennui, romantic passion, Masonic mysticism (he translated a cycle of Masonic hymns from the German), and social themes. He also wrote some very diffuse verse epics, several undistinguished short stories, and some plays, including translations of *A Midsummer Night's Dream* and *Antigone*. But he soon realized that criticism was his real calling. Starting in 1845 he wrote critical surveys, articles, and reviews for a series of journals and newspapers, including *The Moscow News*, whose theater critic he was in the 1850s, *The Muscovite*, where he published most of his programmatic essays, *The National Annals* (1856–60), *The Russian Word* (1859), and finally *Time* and *Epoch*, the journals of the Dostoevsky brothers. Grigoryev's personal life was untidy—unhappy love affairs, a drinking problem, debtor's prison. But apparently nothing could dampen his enthusiasm for the theater, lofty ideas, music, and literature, or take away from his good nature and joie de vivre.

Grigoryev reminisced about his childhood and youth in his memoirs, *My Literary and Moral Wanderings* (1862–64), dedicated to Mikhail Dostoevsky. Perhaps these memoirs were written in response to Herzen's *My Past and Thoughts*. The aristocrat Herzen saw all that was evil in Russia under Nicholas I—the abuses of serfage, the morass of bureaucratic corruption, the tyranny of the tsar's police state. Grigoryev, a raznochinets, saw the warmth and security of the extended family of which his father's house serfs were a part (his mother was a serf woman whom his father had married). He also saw the stability of Russian middle-class society and delighted in the intellectual ferment of the late 1830s. All along the impression conveyed is one of a robust though easygoing and somewhat chaotic vitality. A surprising trait of Grigoryev's memoirs, as well as of his whole oeuvre and personality, is the effortless way in which he and apparently others in his ambience were able to combine a lively and sophisticated interest in Western ideas with an attachment to traditional Russian values, folkways, and social attitudes. Grigoryev was fluent in French and German, read English and Italian literature in the original, and had a good background in the classics. But he also liked to sing Russian songs, wrote gypsy romances, expertly played the guitar, and loved the easy camaraderie of "philosophical discussions" over a bottle of vodka. His love for Western culture was as genuine as his love for the Russian way of life.

Grigoryev's aesthetic, which he called "organic," was essentially a conservative version of Belinsky's. To Grigoryev, historical sense meant an awareness of the organic unity and continuity of national culture. To Belinsky, it meant being on the side of progress. Like Belinsky, Grigoryev believed in the cognitive power of art and in the poet as a prophet and national leader. As an Orthodox Christian believer, he placed art in the immediate vicinity of religion, not politics. He saw Gogol first and foremost as the bearer of a Christian illumination (*ozarenie*), something he missed in the writers of the natural school. His reaction to Gogol's *Selected Passages* was therefore positive.

Grigoryev was powerfully influenced by Schelling, especially his late studies in mythology and revelation, but was opposed to Hegelian historicism. He was very much attracted to Carlyle's national mystique and vitalism. He had a theory according to which modern Russia had developed two basic human types: the "predatory," restless, grasping, and westernized, had no future; the "humble," firmly rooted in Russian soil, would eventually create a stable national culture. Grigoryev saw Pushkin's Onegin and Belkin as prophetic prototypes of the predatory and the humble Russian.

Grigoryev defined organic criticism as "viewing art as something synthetic, integral, immediate, and as what might be called an intuitive understanding of life, distinct from 'knowledge,' that is, analytical understanding which is gradual, aggregative, and verifiable by data." He knew that this marked the critic's wisdom as second-hand, dependent on his ability to recognize the mysteries of the human soul and of national life revealed in works of art. It was the critic's task to recognize all true and living art, while exposing the sham and falsehood of all that was artificial and stillborn. Grigoryev's theoretical views were thus quintessentially romantic. In some specific details they strikingly anticipate the ideas of Benedetto Croce.

Grigoryev's practicing criticism was, like Belinsky's, basically "philosophical": he would look for the "idea" of a work and then evaluate the efficacy of its expression. He insisted that what might appear as a mere "technical" flaw had to be a signal of a flawed idea. Grigoryev's critical judgment was invariably sensitive, often penetrating, and sometimes profound. His opinions have stood up well to the judgment of time. He was the first to declare Pushkin's prose to be as important as his poetry. He was one of the few to recognize Gogol as a significant conservative political and religious thinker. He asserted that Lermontov's ennui, particularly as expressed in *A Hero of Our Time*, was an ephemeral and not truly organic Russian phenomenon.

Grigoryev's analysis of Turgenev's art was subtle and perceptive. He suggested that Turgenev, in his many and varied subjects, ultimately mirrored his own state of mind and projected his own sensibility onto everything he saw. He likened Turgenev's novel *A Nest of Gentlefolk* to an unfinished canvas, some parts of which were covered with splendid painting, some with barely recognizable outlines of objects and figures, and some entirely blank. Grigoryev's understanding of the young Tolstoi was truly prophetic. He recognized his genius, but also the inner conflicts with which that genius was afflicted, in particular the danger posed by Tolstoi the moralist's corrosive analytical mind to Tolstoi the artist's organic intuitions. Grigoryev saw in Goncharov's

Oblomov a positive Russian type (the "humble" Russian!) and in the landowner Oblomov's marriage to Agafya, a simple woman of the people, a symbolic detail of deep significance.

Much as Belinsky had championed Gogol, often against heavy opposition, so Grigoryev made it his mission to support and promote the theater of Ostrovsky. The fact that Grigoryev and Ostrovsky came from the same quarter of Moscow and from the same social milieu, were colleagues on the "young editorial board" of *The Muscovite*, and were frequent drinking companions may have had something to do with it. They both loved the theater (Grigoryev was a fine theater critic), and both were fond of Russian conviviality and Russian songs and dances—of which there is a lot in Ostrovsky's plays. Grigoryev found that Ostrovsky's sober realism and healthy sense of humor were close to having grasped the essence and direction of Russian life. Grigoryev did not live to see Ostrovsky's later plays, such as *The Dowerless Girl*, which presented a different world, for even Russia's conservative middle class was rapidly becoming westernized.

Grigoryev is one of the most attractive but also one of the more exasperating figures in Russian literature. His conservatism is enlightened and lacks bitterness or malice. His idealism is sincere and his enthusiasm genuine. He is well read in world literature, handles philosophical concepts with a scholar's cogency, and has a consistent aesthetic theory. He is generous and urbane even toward his adversaries, without any of the doctrinaire righteousness of his radical opponents. His essayistic style stands above the journalese of the radicals. But his ideas about Russian society were soon proven to have been wrongheaded.

The link between his theoretical thought and his criticism is often tenuous. The composition of his essays is diffuse: they ramble along and rarely make their point succinctly. His prolix and exclamatory style resembles Carlyle's, who may have influenced him even in this regard. Grigoryev repeated himself interminably, but this is a fault of many journal critics, who are apt to use previously published material when pressed for time. On balance much of Grigoryev's intelligent and thought-provoking criticism has remained more relevant to an understanding of his period and of the authors he discussed than that of any nineteenth-century critic save Belinsky.

Konstantin Leontyev (1831–91), one of the most interesting minds of the nineteenth century, was so far out of the mainstream of Russian thought that his provocative ideas met with little response from his contemporaries. His life was adventurous, strange, and unhappy. He came from a family of landowners, studied medicine at Moscow University and participated in the Crimean War as a military surgeon. He then made a promising start as a writer and critic. His novels, *Podlipki* (1861) and *At Home* (1864), and short stories, all to some extent autobiographical, are strong on psychological analysis, which caused him to be mentioned in one breath with Dostoevsky. In 1863 Leontyev joined the Russian diplomatic service and had a rather stormy career in the Balkans, on the island of Crete, and in Constantinople. In 1871 he fell gravely ill and upon his recovery spent a year at a monastery on Mount Athos in fulfilment of a religious vow. In 1873 he resigned from the diplomatic service and until 1887 devoted himself to journalism. In 1880 he was appointed censor. Leontyev's late fiction is based on his experiences in the Balkans. His

three volumes, *From the Life of Christians in Turkey* (1876), are well told and realistic, but aside from their exotic interest not very distinguished. In 1887 Leontyev joined the Optina Pustyn Monastery and eventually took holy vows.[8]

Leontyev's essays, gathered in two volumes under the title *The East, Russia, and Slavdom* (1885–86), developed a unique philosophy of history. (These volumes included Leontyev's earlier cycle of essays, *Byzantinism and Slavdom*, 1871–72.) Leontyev anticipated Oswald Spengler's biological model of history by postulating that civilizations go through a life cycle which starts with a stage of primitive simplicity, develops into "complex flowering," and declines to secondary simplification, followed by death. By "complex flowering" Leontyev meant a condition of creative struggle in every aspect of life, such as between militant religious and vigorous secular concerns, between a cult of beauty and ascetic disdain for all aesthetic values, between a powerful and harsh authoritarian state and a warm and tender family life. In order for both religion and art to flourish, their struggle must be as fierce as possible: under such conditions religious life will be refined as well as intense, and art will be more spiritual. Leontyev saw this condition realized in Byzantine civilization. "Byzantinism" was for him, however, a universal human attitude rather than a unique historical phenomenon. To Leontyev, flaccid and tolerant European liberalism was an obvious case of a civilization in decline. He warned Russia not to join it. He was confident that socialism—young, vigorous, despotic—

8. This famous monastery played a role in the lives of Dostoevsky and Tolstoi as well. It may be recognized as Father Zosima's hermitage in *The Brothers Karamazov.*

would defeat liberalism and revitalize society by introducing a new "complexity," struggle, violence, and suffering.

Leontyev's values were aesthetically determined and in their immoralism resemble Nietzsche's. Leontyev carried over this emphasis on aesthetic values into his literary criticism. His position was that Russian literature had adopted from German idealism a lofty aesthetic theory but had "in its artistic practice assumed a more or less negative, mocking, venomous, or somber character." Leontyev's emphasis is on style, good form, and propriety. He is strongly opposed to what he sees as the crass naturalism, "the slavering, sputtering, and sniveling" which one encounters at every step in the best Russian writers, such as Tolstoi and Dostoevsky. He finds it odious that Vronsky (in *Anna Karenina*), whom he perceives as a highly positive character, should be shown suffering from a toothache as he takes leave of the reader.

Leontyev appreciated Russia's "lady writers" for their refusal to succumb to "naturalism" and had words of praise for Marko Vovchok's "sweet, musical, fragrant, though liberal-tendentious language." He was opposed to psychologism, the fantastic, the morbid, and the perverse in literature. He disliked Dostoevsky, saying that whereas the tragic in Tolstoi's *War and Peace* was justified because it inculcated in the reader martial heroism and a willingness to make a sacrifice for one's country, the tragic in Dostoevsky's works could please only "certain psychopaths living in poorly furnished rooms." In spite of his aestheticism Leontyev was receptive to the civic function of art. He was the first to point out the importance of *War and Peace* as a "political fact." He was also the first to explicitly perceive Tolstoi and Dostoevsky as antipodes, the former being an "objective-epic,"

the latter a "lyric-subjective," artist.[9] In the essay "Our Rosy Christians" (1882) Leontyev charged, with some justification, that both Tolstoi and Dostoevsky were in violation of the teachings of the Orthodox church by virtue of their overly optimistic, humanist, and secular interpretation of the Gospel.

Leontyev rejected most of the socially engaged literature of the 1860s and 1870s, including Turgenev's novels. But he applauded Turgenev's apolitical works, such as "First Love." Similarly, he rejected the painting of the Itinerants, asking that art produce ideal, elegant, and beautiful images.

Poetry

The end of golden age of poetry did not mean that there was any dearth of poets after the deaths of Pushkin and Lermontov, or even a dearth of good poetry. After a brief interval in the 1840s, the 1850s witnessed a renewed surge of outstanding poetry. Poetry continued to have a broad readership; many post—golden age poems became popular romances or even folk songs. But discounting the civic poetry of the *shestidesyatniki* ("men of the sixties") and specifically the poetry of social compassion by Nekrasov, Nikitin, and other poets of a populist orientation, no new forms, styles, themes, or motifs emerged until the advent of symbolism in the 1890s. The best poems of Aleksei Tolstoi, Polonsky, or Maikov might have been written by any of the better poets of the golden age. Like the historical novelists and dramatists of the second half of the century, most of the poets of that period were epigones of the romantic age. Like the poets of the golden age, they retained

9. Cf. Schiller's dichotomy of "naive" and "sentimental" poetry, where Goethe is a naive and Schiller himself a sentimental poet.

contact with the poetic tradition of the West. Verses echoing or even addressed to Petrarch, Dante, Shakespeare, Goethe, and Schiller continued to occur in their poetry. Those who remained active until the end of the century, like Fet and Polonsky, formed a bridge from the golden age to symbolism in this and other respects.

At the height of materialist-positivist fervor in the 1860s poetry of the kind produced by epigones of the golden age was attacked as a harmful diversion from pragmatic concerns. At the same time civic and satirical poetry flourished and, though received coolly by critical "aesthetes," had a broad and enthusiastic readership. It was precisely Nekrasov's "poetry of compassion" and the racy satirical verse of poets of *The Spark*, a satirical journal of the radicals, that introduced formal innovations which pointed toward the twentieth century. Nekrasov's ternary meters and the virtuosic word play and rhymes of Dmitry Minaev (1835–89) and Vasily Kurochkin (1827–75) would reappear in Mayakovsky and Pasternak.

Nikolai Ogaryov (1813–77), remembered primarily as Herzen's friend and coeditor with him of *The Bell*, was a remarkable romantic poet. He was by talent and temperament quite different from his friend. The private lives of both were scarred by tragedies, which could not break Herzen's spirit but broke Ogaryov's. Herzen was ebullient and an optimist, Ogaryov a melancholy pessimist. Herzen was a man of the world, a political man, and a born leader; Ogaryov was awkward in his personal relations and lacked political tact. Herzen made many enemies, but retained everybody's respect; Ogaryov became pathetic. Herzen's literary talent was rhetorical; Ogaryov was a poet.

Ogaryov's poetry is decidedly depressing.

It expresses all the emotions of Turgenev's "superfluous man"—ennui, despair, self-hate—against a background of desolate autumn or winter landscapes. It is the poetry of a sensitive and gentle soul and a refined intellect, but it lacks the melodious voice of a Tyutchev or the rhetorical vigor of a Lermontov. Ogaryov's political verse is labored and pedestrian. He never completed any of his many narrative poems, most of which are versified notebooks of a deeply sad man torn between his love for Russian nature and the Russian way of life and a loathing for the government and social order of Russia. Much of Ogaryov's poetry deals with foreign landscapes, cities, and traditions—understandably so, since he spent many years abroad even before his emigration.

Count Aleksei Konstantinovich Tolstoi (1817–75) often expressed his alienation from the prevailing mood of his age. His programmatic poem "Against the Current" (1867) states the position of a romantic and lover of pure art, who is isolated and ignored in an age of positivism but knows that he will be vindicated by history. He recalls the premature triumphs of the Pharisees in Jerusalem and of the iconoclasts in Byzantium, and encourages himself to "believe in the wondrous star of inspiration" and to "keep rowing, in the name of Beauty, against the current."

Tolstoi unabashedly indulges in Neoplatonic conceits which might have been Zhukovsky's. "Other worlds" and "another life" are recurrent themes in his poetry:

Wait some more, liberation is near—
Soon we shall all be merged in one love,
One love, vast like a sea
Which no earthly shores could contain!
("A tear trembles in your jealous glance,"
1858)

Or, he will deny that the artist is "the creator of his works" but assert that "they had hovered above the earth, invisible, in all eternity." The influence of German romantic poetry, and of Goethe in particular, is very strong in Tolstoi and extends to his style. His "bad rhymes" and uneven rhythms have a German sound (Tolstoi once noted the "bad rhymes" in Gretchen's prayer in *Faust*), as does his pointed use of poetic clichés and "simple" words. (Tolstoi was a skillful and highly sophisticated craftsman, so it cannot have been mere carelessness.)

Tolstoi's romantic ballads and byliny are among the best in the language. His narrative poem *John Damascene* (1858), a poeticized vita, features the struggle between the untrammeled pantheist mind of the poet and the religious discipline to which he must bow as a saint. "John Damascene" contains some wonderful religious poetry, such as the great troparion of John Damascene, in which Tolstoi equals Derzhavin at his best.

Tolstoi followed the romantic tradition even in his frequent excursions into the Romance world. "The Dragon" (1875), a narrative poem in excellent tercines, is stylized to sound as if "from the Italian." The dragon is a realized metaphor for the Ghibellines invading Italy but is made frighteningly palpable. Another late poem, "In a Desert Monastery near Cordoba" (1870), recalls a painting that shows the martyrdom of a saint who was flayed alive. As Tolstoi likens the poet's own mental torments to the martyr's, he reaches the intensity of Saint John of the Cross:

The covers are torn off my soul,
Its live flesh bared,
And every touch of life to it
Is cruel pain and burning torture.

Tolstoi had everything to make him a major poet, except timing. When the symbolists began to write poetry very much like his, it was—once again—"new." But in Tolstoi's age it was still epigonic.

Yakov Polonsky (1819–98) came from a noble family of modest means, studied law in Saint Petersburg, and was in the civil service in Georgia and Saint Petersburg. Like some other writers, he was a censor at one time. Polonsky was less committed politically than most of his contemporaries. Basically a conservative, he was an editor of *The Russian Word* (1859–60) and published not only in *The Muscovite, Time, Epoch*, and other conservative journals, but also in *The Contemporary* and *The National Annals*. In the 1850s and 1860s he extolled science in enthusiastic verse ("The Realm of Science," for example) and in the late 1860s and 1870s wrote a great deal of "compassionate" poetry ("Hunger," "A Miasm," "The Prisoner") not all that far removed from Nekrasov's, though without an edge of social protest.

Polonsky was an exceptionally prolific poet and writer who worked in almost every conceivable genre; writing novels (in verse and in prose), short stories, plays (in verse and in prose), verse epics (serious, satirical, and humorous), essays, sketches, memoirs, opera libretti, and an autobiographic novel in verse, *Recent Memory* (1861–62). He is remembered, however, only as a lyric poet, as some of his poems have continued to be anthologized and some have become folk songs ("A Gypsy Woman's Song," "The Shut-In"). The range of Polonsky's lyrics is wide: love poems in a variety of moods (both happy and sad), Gypsy romances, landscapes (Russian, Crimean, Caucasian, Mediterranean), anthological poems, idylls, sonnets ("To a New Laura"), album verse, cycles of "Georgian poems," "Tatar songs," "Armenian themes," and biblical themes ("Hagar"), and historical, exotic, and popular ballads. First and foremost, Polonsky cultivated the familiar romantic themes of graveyards, nocturnal visitations, mystic dreams, and encounters with death. All of these poems are competently versified and reflect a cultured and sensitive mind. But in none of them is there a stanza, or even a line, with an individual note or a happy conceit the reader will gratefully remember. We meet the familiar romantic themes of the proud savagery of Caucasian mountaineers ("Agbar"), the mysterious hieroglyphs on the walls of the temple of Isis ("Facing a Sealed Truth"), a ghostly ride through a dark forest ("The Miller"), an exhilarating storm at sea ("Swaying in a Storm"), and so forth. To a reader familiar with the romantic period all these themes have lost their freshness.

Afanasy Afanasyevich Fet-Shenshin (1820–92) lived a life that paradoxically proved his philosophy of art to be correct. A lifelong practitioner and defender of pure art, he was for his utilitarian contemporaries a perennial scapegoat whenever an example was needed of "how a poet should not sing" (Fet's lines, "I don't even know that I shall sing, yet a song is welling up within me," would be quoted with derision). Fet's life was remarkably unpoetic. He was the son of Afanasy Shenshin, a landowner of ancient nobility, and Charlotte Foeth, a lady he had brought back with him from Germany, although she was already married. Fet's mother was pregnant when she left her husband, however, so her son Afanasy was denied the right to bear the name Shenshin (Shenshin later married Charlotte). This denial meant the loss of his nobility and even his Russian citizenship. The court

order to this effect came when Fet was fourteen, and he spent much of his life in an effort to regain his nobility and the family name. He studied the humanities at Moscow University, where he was a bad student but managed to graduate. He roomed with the Grigoryevs at one time and was friendly with Apollon Grigoryev. Fet began to publish his poetry early. In 1842 and 1843 as many as eighty-five poems by him appeared in *The Muscovite* and *The National Annals*. In the hope of regaining his nobility by reaching officer's rank in the military, Fet joined the army in 1845. He wrote and published little during his army years, even though it was then that he experienced his life's great and unhappy love. Fet's military career ended in frustration. Only a few months before he received his commission, it was decreed that only the rank of major should give its holder hereditary nobility. He finally resigned his commission in 1858. In 1857 he had married a Moscow heiress, plain and no longer young, the sister of the critic Vasily Botkin. Her dowry allowed him to make a new start as a landowner, in which capacity he showed extraordinary energy and business acumen. He became a rich man, succeeded in having his name changed to Shenshin, and published articles in which he defended the rights and interests of the landed gentry. Fet's arch-conservative stance alienated his former friends, including Turgenev, with whom he had been close for years. Fet wrote little poetry in the 1860s and 1870s, spending his leisure hours translating Latin verse, including the complete works of Horace, and the writings of Schopenhauer. In those years Fet developed a friendship with Lev Tolstoi, whose estate was not far from his and whose views, like his, were conservative and hostile to the liberal trend of the times. He introduced

Tolstoi to Schopenhauer, who became a significant factor in Tolstoi's thought.

In the 1880s Fet experienced a new creative surge which continued until the end of his life. He wrote much of his best poetry in those years and lived to see it recognized, becoming a living bridge between the romantic period and the emergent symbolist movement. The philosopher Vladimir Solovyov was one of his admirers.

Fet's memoirs and correspondence, and the letters and reminiscences of people who knew him, show a man of singularly unpoetic character. Yet he was one of the great poets of the century and, moreover, a poet of the most purely lyric-musical type. Fet's poetry offers ample illustrations for Verlaine's "L'Art poétique": its logos, if present at all, is indefinite, fragmentary, allusive rather than explicit; its imagery is vague, airy, pastel-colored; its language is never precise or poignant. It speaks to the listener the way music does, even before and without rational comprehension. No wonder that Fet appealed to the symbolists, or to a neoromantic like Pasternak. Fet's faith in the poet's power "to whisper that before which the tongue goes numb" and "to reach for the heavens with wings spread wide," the recurrent theme of a cosmic epiphany where the soul discovers God, infinity, and the blinding light of the sun within itself, endeared Fet to mystics like Solovyov. Some of Fet's cosmic visions reflect Schopenhauer's Buddhist philosophy, for example, "Tortured by life and the perfidy of hope" (1864), which bears an epigraph from Schopenhauer and derives solace from the notion that human consciousness is part of a dream that is dreamed by the whole universe. More often than not, Fet's cosmic moods are nocturnal, hypnotic, and thanatoid. He has a number of very strong poems expressing a death wish, such as "To Death" (two poems of that title, 1856 and 1884) and "Death" (1878), where death is poetically hypostasized and made attractive. In a poem of 1864, "Life flew by without leaving a clear trace," life is likened to the erratic flight of a snowflake driven by the wind and finally coming to rest in a snowbank. A fallen leaf (*opavshii list*, Verlaine's *feuille morte*) is a recurring image and symbol in Fet's poetry. Yet Fet's rich nature poetry is by no means limited to autumnal or winter landscapes but has many vernal and summer landscapes as well. An image characteristic of Fet's vision is that of the starry sky, for instance, in the famous poem "Upon a Haystack on a Southern Night" (1857).

Fet's love lyrics are among the most delicate and chaste in the language. Almost all of them are devoted to dreams of a lost love. The best and the most moving of them were written in Fet's old age. Fet also wrote a great deal of anthological, idyllic, occasional, epistolary, and album verse, only some of it outstanding. He certainly wrote his share of mediocre poems. His poetic translations, mostly from the German, are merely competent. Fet's range, for a great poet, is narrow. His poetry is not rich in ingenious conceits, and his poetic imagination is static. Some of his best-known poems, such as "Whisper, timid breathing" (1850), which Dostoevsky used as an example of pure poetry par excellence in his polemic with Dobrolyubov, are composed entirely (or almost entirely) of nouns and adjectives, with no verbs. Fet's poetic vocabulary and imagery are limited and conventional, and his rhymes are unremarkable. The prosodic rhythm of his poems tends to coincide with the natural phrase rhythm, creating an enhanced melodic effect. In a word, nothing is foregrounded in a poem by Fet except the consonance of mood and rhythm.

Apollon Maikov (1821–97), brother of

the critic Valerian Maikov, was rated higher in his lifetime than he is today. In his youth he was a liberal and close to the Petrashevsky circle, but he soon turned conservative. He had a fairly successful career in the civil service, toward the end of which he reached the rank of privy councillor as a censor of foreign literature. His mature views were close to those of his lifelong friend and correspondent Fyodor Dostoevsky. A believer in the monarchy, Orthodoxy, and the Russian people, Maikov was, like Aleksei Tolstoi, very much a European and critical of the more extreme positions of the Slavophiles. Maikov's poetry is in its themes, ethos, and form almost indistinguishable from that of the golden age. He has many poems on the poet and his divine mission, many impressions of the Mediterranean world, translations and adaptations of the Greek anthological poets, elegies, and some religious poetry, such as the cycle "From Apollodorus Gnosticus" (1877–93).[10] Maikov is at his best in the idyllic genres, as in a delightful long poem in alexandrines, "On Angling" (1855), and songs about haymaking or harvesting. Maikov's verse epics, a couple of which approach being novels in verse, are forgettable. His satirical poetry is of lesser quality than Aleksei Tolstoi's.

Lev Mei (1822–62), a Muscovite of German descent, was basically a skillful versifier of no originality. The quality of his elegiac, idyllic, and nature poetry is a credit rather to the high level of poetic culture reached by Russian literature than to his talent. "To the Departed" (1856), a melancholy and

dignified elegy in alexandrines addressed to a long list of departed family members and friends, reminds one of Zhukovsky. "The Village" (ca. 1858) is a very pleasing idyll. "Will-o'-the-Wisp" (1861) is one of his several picturesque nature poems. But Mei's ballads and byliny in the style of folk poetry, some based on medieval chronicles and saints' lives, are much inferior to Aleksei Tolstoi's. The cycle "From the Ancient World" is weak, the ballad cycle "On Biblical Themes" undistinguished.

Nikolai Shcherbina (1821–69) was a poet of some originality. He came from Taganrog on the Black Sea, where he grew up near a Greek community. His grandmother was Greek, and he was attracted to Greece, ancient and modern, all his life, although he lived mainly in Moscow and Petersburg, holding a middle-echelon position in the Ministry of Education (he got it through Duke Pyotr Vyazemsky, who liked the young man's poetry, wit, and conservative views). Having previously published only a few occasional poems, Shcherbina scored a major success with his *Greek Poems*, which appeared in Odessa in 1850. In many of these poems he succeeded in recreating the naive freshness and grace of ancient Greek poetry in idyllic, erotic, elegiac, and gnomic compositions. He followed with *New Greek Poems* in 1851 and subsequently wrote more poetry in this vein. He also wrote a cycle entitled "Modern Greek Melodies" (1849–59), based on Greek folklore, and two dramatic fragments, also on Greek themes.

Shcherbina's romantic nature poetry and impressions of his travels in the West, Italy in particular, have immediacy and plasticity. His blend of a Russian's indelible memory of the bleak plains and snowdrifts of his country and his impressions of a glorious Mediterranean world is successful in several

10. Apollodorus Gnosticus" is a mystification. The following lines from this cycle became proverbial: "Do not say that there is no salvation, / That you are worn down by grief: / The darker the night, the brighter the stars, / The deeper your sorrow, the nearer God."

instances. Shcherbina's philosophical poetry is never perfect, but it contains occasional felicitous conceits and sometimes expresses genuine sentiment with vigor. "Man" (1847), a Neoplatonic hymn, has several happy conceits, such as when man is defined as "the light of God's face descended to earth."

Shcherbina's civic poetry is undistinguished, his *Satirical Chronicle: Iambs, Xeniae, and Epigrams* (1861–69) bitter, often malicious, and rarely witty. Shcherbina had real talent and deserves more attention than he has commonly received. His ultraconservative political views were long remembered. He was a loner in the world of Russian letters, "half-Greek, half-Ukrainian" among Muscovites, and on friendly terms with almost no one. Tyutchev, in a brief poem, "To N. F. Shcherbina" (1857), said that he understood Shcherbina well and caught the essence of his poetic vision succinctly:

Thus a captive Hellene, asleep,
Oblivious of the steppes around him,
Would dream amidst a Scythian blizzard
Of golden freedom
And the sky of Greece.

The 1850s and 1860s produced a new genre, which may be called the poetry of compassion, verses in which the poet would open his eyes and his heart to the life of the oppressed masses of the Russian people, relive their hardships, and empathize with their sufferings. The people as they appear in this kind of poetry are usually idealized. The populist mystique of the poetry of compassion is found in poets of a Slavophile orientation no less than in poets of the radical camp. One of the first poems in a compassionate populist vein belongs to the Slavophile journalist and ideologue Ivan

Aksakov. His narrative poem "The Tramp" (1852) bears all the marks of this genre.

Nekrasov

Nikolai Alekseevich Nekrasov (1821–78) was a central figure of Russian literature, journalism, and public life for thirty years. The son of a country squire, he went to Petersburg in 1838 to escape a gloomy, oppressive, and stifling life at home, attended the university as an auditor, and quickly learned to stand on his own feet. He started by doing hack work for various newspapers and journals, and wrote a couple of vaudevilles, as well as a great deal of rather superficial fiction in the manner of the natural school. His first volume of poetry, *Dreams and Sounds*, appeared in 1840. As early as 1843 he started a career as publisher and editor. The miscellanies *A Physiology of Petersburg* (1845) and *A Petersburg Miscellany* (1846), which he edited and published, contained works by most of the leading writers of the time, including his own, and became manifestos of the natural school. They were also financial successes. In 1846 Nekrasov and his friend Ivan Panaev took over *The Contemporary* from Pyotr Pletnyov and made it into the organ of the radical intelligentsia and the most successful "thick journal" of the 1850s and 1860s. Nekrasov's own poetry was one of its major attractions. When *The Contemporary* was closed by the authorities in 1866, Nekrasov continued the course he had pursued by acquiring *The National Annals*. Nekrasov was not only an excellent judge of talent, a perceptive critic, and an efficient editor, but also a shrewd businessman and man of the world. His private life was not in accord with his public image as a leader of the puritanical radical intelligentsia and a champion of the oppressed Russian people. He made many enemies but enjoyed the love and admiration of wide circles of the educated public. At his funeral, which attracted a huge crowd, Dostoevsky in his eulogy called him a poet "right next to Pushkin." In response there were shouts from the crowd: "Above!"

Nekrasov, a prolific poet, was a natural versifier who easily produced reems of feuilletonistic, parodic, and satirical verse. Most of it is of course dated and needs to be read with a commentary, for instance, his lengthy series of vignettes of Russian financiers and entrepreneurs, *Contemporaries* (1875). But here and there Nekrasov comes up with satirical conceits that have remained alive through their vigorous language and Juvenalian sense of outrage.

Some early pieces rather straightforwardly express the anger of a very bright young man at the baseness and stupidity of the world around him: "A Moral Person" (1847), "A Government Official" (1844), and "Lullaby" (1845), the last a parody of Lermontov's "Cossack Lullaby," where a mother's bittersweet dream of her son the warrior is replaced by a resigned realization that her son will be a bribe-taking scoundrel like his father. "Riding to the Hounds" (1846) is a satirical idyll: the good clean fun of a country squire's hunting party, described with obvious expertise, is viewed through a prism of bilious contempt for the hunter's mindless brutality. In later years Nekrasov's satire is amused or even melancholy rather than angry. In "Ballet" (1865–66) the reporter asks his reader, What makes all these Russians attending the ballet look so much alike, regardless of whether they are young or old, civilians or military men, bachelors or patresfamilias? The answer is that they all wear the same

expression on their faces, which says, "Where could I possibly borrow some money?"

"The Railroad" (1864) has an epigraph: "*Vanya*: 'Daddy, who built this railroad?' *Daddy* (in a general's uniform): 'Count Pyotr Andreich Kleinmichel!' (Conversation overheard in a railway compartment)." The reporter asks "Good Daddy" to allow him to tell Vanya the truth about who built this railroad—hunger, the hunger that made thousands of landless peasants join the gangs of laborers whose bones lie buried right beside the roadbeds, embankments, and bridges which they built under inhuman conditions. When "Daddy" asks the reporter to show the positive side also, he obliges with an idyllic scene: the work of the Russian laborers is done, skilled Germans are laying the tracks, a potbellied contractor thanks the laborers for their good work, rewards them with a keg of vodka, and, besides, forgives them whatever they may owe him. The laborers gratefully respond by unhitching his horses and, with loud cheers, pulling his carriage as a sign of their devotion. "Could anyone paint a more positive picture, general?"

Nekrasov's unequivocally civic poems, such as "Poet and Citizen" (1855–56),[11] "V. G. Belinsky" (1855), the passages on Belinsky and Granovsky in "The Bearhunt" (1866–67), "The Prophet" (1874), and "To a Poet: To the Memory of Schiller" (1874), offer examples of a sincere and sometimes noble rhetoric. Nekrasov's two long narrative poems dealing with the Decembrists, "Grandfather" (1870) and "Russian Women" (1872), also belong to the civic genre.

---

11. The title echoes Ryleev's famous line, "I am not a poet, but a citizen."

Nekrasov's fame is based on his "poetry of compassion," many short and several long poems in which the observer, implicitly a "repentant gentleman," speaks of the hard lot of the people with deep compassion, at times not without sentimentality. Examples include "A Field Left Unharvested" (1854), "A Wedding" (1855; the bridegroom, a ruddy faced artisan, is the drinking, brawling type; the bride, pale and wan, is pregnant, and her future will be sad), "Children Weeping" (1860, about child labor in a factory), "Red-Nosed Frost" (1862–63; a peasant woman's sad life flashes by in her memory as she freezes to death in the forest where she has gone for firewood after having buried her husband), "Orina, a Soldier's Mother" (1863; a mother tells of the death of her son, who has returned from the army a sick and broken man), and "Peasant Children" (1861, with a famous scene about a six-year-old hauling firewood on a cold winter day). Nekrasov effects a fusion of the observer's consciousness with that of his subjects through his peculiar rhythms. Most of Nekrasov's poems of compassion are composed in ternary meters—anapests, dactyls, or amphibrachs—and often use dactylic rhymes or a dactyl-trochee clausule, which brings them closer to the lilt of the folk song, and to the natural prosody of spoken Russian, than do the iambics which otherwise dominate Russian poetry. Though not really stylized, they nevertheless convey an impression of popular sentiment.

Some of Nekrasov's narrative poems written in the same manner are simply vignettes from the life of the people without moral overtones. "The Peddlers" (1861) tells of the adventures of two peddlers, ending in their murder by a half-wit gamekeeper. In "The Cabbie" (1855) a drunken merchant forgets his purse in Vanya's sled. Vanya never noticed it, and the money is all there when his ride comes back for it. The merchant gives him a fifty-kopeck tip. Vanya hangs himself. Late in life Nekrasov wrote a cycle entitled "Poems Dedicated to Russian Children" (1873), in the same manner.

Nekrasov wrote conventional *Erlebnislyrik* all his life, mostly in an elegiac mode. Some poems of his early period, such as "When I drive in the night down a dark street," "When tormented by violent passion," and "You are always immeasurably beautiful" (all 1847), convey the experience of tragic love with great intensity. "Home" (1846), a somber elegy evoking bitter memories of the Nekrasov family estate and the unhappy people who lived there, projects the same intensity of feeling. Many years later, "Depression" (1874), another elegiac return to the poet's ancestral home, has less intensity as it draws up a balance sheet of his life, reaches a discouraging result, and sees his melancholy mood enhanced by the many changes for the worse all around him.

For the last fifteen years of his life Nekrasov worked on his populist epic "Who Is Happy in Russia?" which remained incomplete and only a part of which was published in his lifetime. The prologue has seven peasants argue about who is happiest in Russia: the landowner, the government official, the priest, the merchant, the tsar's minister, or the tsar himself. They have the good fortune to catch a magic bird that will provide them with a magic tablecloth allowing them to travel all over Russia to find out who is happiest there. In Part One the seven peasants set out and meet various people whom they ask if they are happy. They interview a priest, a landowner, and some other people reported to be happy. Part Two tells the story of an old landowner whom his former serfs keep happy by making him believe they are still his serfs, so he will rent them his hayfields on favorable terms—but he dies, and his heirs will not be fooled. Part Three is devoted to a peasant woman whom her neighbors call "the lucky one." Her story is one of hardship, pain and injustice, all stoically suffered. Part Four (posthumous) is a miscellany of vignettes from Russian life. It ends in a hymn to Russia, "poor, plentiful, downtrodden, powerful Mother Russia." "Who Is Happy in Russia?" is written for the most part in an easy lilting meter; several unrhymed iambic tetrameters ending in a pyrrhic ($xx/xx/xx/xx$) are succeeded by a clausule in iambic trimeter ($xx/xx/xx$). This rhythm, vaguely resembling folk verse, combined with simple language and liberal use of poetic figures of folk poetry, makes "Who Is Happy in Russia?" sound folksy, but it is a stylized folksiness, and the image of the Russian people projected by it is an idealized one. This idealization is authentic, though, in tune with the verbiage of tearful self-pity, cagey swagger, and mocking cynicism with which the Russian social underdog typically tries to assert himself.

Many of Nekrasov's poems became school texts or folk songs and thus a part of the national consciousness. Nekrasov was a poet of great stature, indubitable originality, and immense influence. Yet his iamgination was earthbound, and his verse lacked the musical quality found in Tyutchev or Fet.

Ivan Nikitin (1824–61) was, like Koltsov, to whom he owed a great deal, a native of Voronezh and the son of a fairly prosperous businessman. He did, however, get an education at the local seminary, which he left in 1843 without graduating. Nikitin made his living as an innkeeper, and it was ten years until he dared to submit a poem to a journal under his own name. His first poem, "Russia," appeared in a local journal in 1853. He was invited to join a literary circle in Voronezh, which in turn introduced him to Apollon Maikov and other leading poets.

Much of Nikitin's early poetry was second-rate imitation of Zhukovsky, Pushkin, and Koltsov, but his melancholy Russian landscapes and vivid genre scenes ("Winter Night in the Village," 1853; "Truck Stop," 1854) are genuine. Encouraged by reviews by Chernyshevsky (1856) and Dobrolyubov (1857 and 1860), Nikitin developed his own style, similar to that of Nekrasov's poems of compassion. Nikitin's late poems speak of the nagging pain of hopeless poverty and unrewarded backbreaking labor in a tone of tearful self-pity and in a language close to that of folk poetry. The versification of these poems is often adapted to the rhythm of the Russian folk song: "The Plowman" (1856), "The Plow" (1857), "Ah, Poverty," (1857), "The Beggar" (1857), "The Village Pauper" (1857), "Night in the Village" (1857–58), "The Spinner" (1857–58), "The Old Servant" (1859), and other poems depict the hard lot of country and city poor. The style and manner of these poems became a distinct genre of Russian poetry. They were imitated well into the twentieth century: the poetry of Esenin is still close to Nikitin's. Some of Nikitin's poems became folk songs. His ballad, "A dashing merchant returned from the fair" (1858), one of the most popular of all Russian songs, had a life of its own and was sung in many different variants.

Among many other "compassionate" poets, Vsevolod Krestovsky (1840–95) deserves separate mention. Krestovsky came from an ancient family of Ukrainian gentry. As a student of Saint Petersburg University (1857–60) he was initially close to Pisarev and wrote for *The Russian Word*. His early poetry put him squarely into the radical camp. "Paris, July 1848" has a vision of

Christ on the barricades of Paris. His first major prose work, *The Slums of Petersburg* (1864), still bears a noticeable *socialisant* tendency. But in the mid-1860s Krestovsky changed his political orientation, and his later prose fiction was decidedly anti-nihilist.[12]

Krestovsky's early poetry includes tales, ballads, fables, and legends in the manner of folk poetry. There are also many poems in the vein of Koltsov, such as "Vladimirka" (1858), addressing the road on which convicts were marched to Siberia, or "A Groan of the Earth" (1855), where the earth bewails all the grief and sorrow she must bear. Several of Krestovsky's narrative poems are of Nekrasov's "compassionate" type. In "The Pilgrim Woman" (1860) a mother wanders all over Russia looking for her only son, who was taken into the army. When she finally finds him, he is getting ready to run the gauntlet for desertion. "Death in the Springtime" (1861) is the story of a serf, a fiddler, who after his manumission makes a living as a street musician, together with his little daughter. She dies of consumption, and he plays the fiddle over her grave. The poem is a bitter indictment of serfdom. At the same time, however, Krestovsky wrote many poems in the manner of the golden age and translated Greek and Roman poets, Goethe's *Roman Elegies*, Heine, and others.

Prose Fiction

In the course of the 1850s Russian prose fiction gradually shed the traits of the natural school and moved toward an objective realism. Romantic genres like the historical novel by no means disappeared, but they were no longer in the forefront of the literary scene. Virtually all the big names in Russian literature from the 1850s through the 1880s were those of prose writers. The novel became the principal genre, although the short story and the sketch remained strong. The great novelists of the period also wrote some fine short stories, and Turgenev and Leskov were better short-story writers than novelists. Still, literary life centered on the great novels of the period.

A novel would normally appear in installments in one of the so-called thick journals. Often a writer would still be working on his novel while its installments were appearing in print. Since he would get ample feedback from his readership and critics while still in the process of composing his work, writing a novel was a public event not only in its intent but even in its execution. The journal in which a novel appeared generally signaled the work's political orientation. A typical novel of the period not only addressed itself to topical issues but also incorporated events, ideas, and personalities of topical interest. Polemical sorties and literary allusions were common, as were novels *à clef*. The format of the novel allowed the insertion of various digressions and excursus in response to topical events or problems. Some of the great novelists, such as Dostoevsky and Leskov, were life-long professional journalists, and others wrote a great deal of professional nonfiction, such as Lev Tolstoi in the field of education.

The great novels of the period generally pursued at least a dual purpose. They were, of course, written and perceived as entertainment, but almost always they were also composed and received as bearing a political, social, or religious message of some sort. To many writers and critics a novel was also a work of art. The criticism of the period

12. See p. 342.

generally addressed itself to the ideological argument of a novel, but there were still critics who had a sophisticated understanding of the art of the novel, and the best writers certainly were serious artists. We need only to follow Turgenev's correspondence with his critic friends Botkin and Annenkov, or Dostoevsky's notebooks, to see that we are dealing with conscious craftsmen.

The mid-century point coincided with a noticeable break in the progress of Russian literature. Herzen emigrated in 1847, Belinsky died in 1848, and the Petrashevsky affair of 1849 stopped the careers of several young writers. Zhukovsky and Gogol, the latter inactive since 1847, died in 1852. Goncharov departed for Japan that year, to return in 1854, and Turgenev was banished to his country estate for an innocuous commemorative article devoted to Gogol. Censorship became so unrelenting after the European events of 1848 that literature was frozen in its tracks until the death of Nicholas I. Under the frosty cover fresh shoots were stirring. Goncharov had published "Oblomov's Dream" in 1849 and was working on the complete novel. Turgenev was beginning to establish himself as Russia's leading prose writer. Pisemsky scored his first success with *The Wimp* in 1850. Lev Tolstoi burst on the scene in 1852 with a masterpiece, *Childhood*. After the death of Nicholas I, with censorship relaxed and an optimistic mood rising in the country, Russian prose within a decade produced an amazing array of important works. The masterpieces of this period represented different philosophies, political directions, literary styles, emotional moods, and auctorial personalities. The works of Goncharov, Turgenev, Tolstoi, Pisemsky, Dostoevsky, Leskov, Chernyshevsky, and many others,

which appeared within a few years of one another and often enough simultaneously, referred to contemporary Russian reality, each from its own particular vantage point.

Aksakov and Herzen

The Slavophiles produced a great deal of critical and essayistic prose, did valuable scholarly work, and were active in the gathering and preservation of Russian folk poetry.[13] But the only Slavophile to excel in prose fiction was their patriarch, Sergei Timofeevich Aksakov (1791–1859). Aksakov came from an ancient family of landowners, which he was to describe in his *Family Chronicle*. He attended Kazan University without graduating and subsequently held several civil service posts. In 1843 he retired to his estate, Abramtsevo, near Moscow, which became a gathering point for writers, actors, and artists. Aksakov started his literary career as a theater critic in the late 1820s and published his first piece of imaginative writing, a sketch entitled "Blizzard," in 1834. His *Notes on Angling* (1847) and *A Hunter's Notes on Hunting with a Shotgun in Orenburg Province* (1852) were immediately recognized as masterpieces. The charm of Aksakov's sketches rests with his sure command of language and subject matter: he has the exact term for every detail, every move, and every visual and aural impression. He knows what he is talking about.

Aksakov's *Family Chronicle* (1856) and *The Childhood of Bagrov-Grandson* (1858) are a fictionalized account of Aksakov's own family history and early impressions. Grand-

13. Konstantin Aksakov, for example, was a linguist and grammarian of note, Pyotr Kireevsky a great collector of folk songs, and Aleksei Khomyakov an important theologian.

father Bagrov resettles his serfs from the Volga region to the virgin steppes of Ufa between Volga and the Urals, moves his whole household there, and makes his new home into a prosperous estate. He is a strong patriarch, righteous and generous but given to fits of towering rage. Bagrov-Son (Aksakov's father) lacks his father's heroic qualities. He is kind and gentle, but thoroughly ordinary. Much of the *Family Chronicle* is devoted to the story of his wooing of Sofya Zubova, the daughter of an Ufa government official. He is shy, tongue-tied and something of a country bumpkin. She is well educated, lively, and modern. This is the age of Catherine II, and Sofya is an independent woman. She is bitterly resented by her husband's female relatives. Fortunately, her father-in-law takes her side. *The Childhood of Bagrov-Grandson* is the story of a thoroughly normal and uneventful childhood.

Aksakov's narrative manner is objective, undramatic, matter-of-fact. Aksakov shows the good and the bad of Russia under serfdom with dispassionate precision. A landowner in those days had virtually unchecked power over his serfs and household. The Bagrovs use their power wisely. But one episode of *A Family Chronicle* deals with the villainies of the landowner Kurolesov, a relative by marriage, who abuses his wife, holds wild orgies, cruelly mistreats his houseserfs, and altogether makes his manor into a house of horrors. Kurolesov, by the way, is an efficient manager of his estate, and his peasant serfs have no complaints. *A Family Chronicle* was in fact used as evidence in support of as well as against the old order. It did not conceal the abuses of serfdom. Yet it also showed that old patriarchal Russia had its virtues, too. Aksakov's work remained a classic after it had lost its topical interest.

There could not be a better illustration of the variety of views of the world and of Russia at which members of the upper class could arrive than a juxtaposition of Aksakov's *Family Chronicle* and Herzen's *My Past and Thoughts*.

Aleksandr Herzen, who had established himself as a leading man of letters by his fiction and some popular articles on various philosophical and scientific topics, went abroad in 1847. He sent back to *The Contemporary* a series of challenging essays in which he managed to steer past the censor's crayon some remarkably radical ideas. When revolutions broke out all over Europe in 1848, Herzen and his friend Bakunin openly sided with the revolutionary movement. Bakunin, a leader of uprisings in Paris, Prague, and Dresden, was eventually extradited to Russia. He spent years in prison and Siberian exile, whence he escaped in 1861. He soon joined Herzen in London and plunged into revolutionary activity with renewed vigor. Herzen, having arrived in Paris from Rome in May 1848, was only a passive observer of the June uprising and its suppression by General Cavaignac. In 1851 he set up residence in London, where his friend Nikolai Ogaryov joined him in 1856. Financially independent (he had succeeded in transferring much of his large fortune abroad) and a naturalized Swiss citizen, he devoted his life to causes of social and political progress and played a major role in the international socialist movement. His innumerable essays, articles, pamphlets, and reviews were published in various European languages and in many different periodicals, including his own almanac *The Pole Star* and newspaper *The Bell*. A good many of them reached Russia, where they had a huge influence on public opinion in the late 1850s and early 1860s. Herzen's ideas became part of many major works of the period, including works by his ideological adversaries, such as Tolstoi and Dostoevsky.

Not a great writer of fiction, Herzen was anybody's match as an essayist and memoirist. His style is Gallic, having none of the Teutonic prolixity of his contemporaries Belinsky or Grigoryev. Lucid, vigorously argued, and readable, his essays deliver their message, citing concrete facts and expressing palpable sentiments without pressing them into a structured argument. His logic can be forceful, his irony mordant, and his pathos stirring.

Herzen, Russia's westernizer par excellence, was in many ways a man of the eighteenth century, which he thought was morally and intellectually superior to his own. He was a man of encyclopedic but not specialized learning, a cosmopolitan who was eloquent not only in Russian but in French and German as well, a man of letters to whom a proper style was a sine qua non of public discourse, a man of the world who found the petty amour propre and doctrinaire squabbling of his middle-class fellow émigrés annoying and, as an aristocrat, could not help noticing their bad manners.

Herzen's masterpieces are *From the Other Shore* (1847–50), a series of essays in response to the events of 1848, and *My Past and Thoughts*, memoirs written for the most part between 1852 and 1855 but continued up to 1868. *From the Other Shore* was initially published in German, under the title *Vom anderen Ufer* (Hamburg, 1850). The first Russian edition appeared in London in 1855. It is a profession of faith and a critical assessment of Europe's present and future. Herzen dramatizes the crucial question of his inquiry by quoting a passage from Karamzin in which human progress is likened to the labors of Sisyphus. Has humanity, after its triumph in the preceding

century, reached the top of the hill? Will Western civilization hurtle back into barbarism? Herzen believes that the old order, based on the rule of an aristocratic and clerical elite over an uneducated and mostly wretched working class, has outlived its natural life and can sustain itself only by force and artifice. "Liberal" reforms prompted by the elite's guilty conscience are futile since they address an image of the people which the liberals have themselves created, rather than addressing the people. The condition of Western Europe is essentially that of imperial Rome, with socialism the equivalent of early Christendom. The last essay concludes with the observation that Julian the Apostate may have been right in seeking to preserve the Rome of old, for the Christians were indeed promoting an impossible utopian dream: "But what's the use of having been right? Rome's time was over, the time of the Gospel had started!" Herzen's organicist and cyclic view of history was not determinist, however. He perceived history as a creative process, whose agents are free to develop it in any direction.

Herzen issued from rationalist, positivist, and atheist premises. Christianity was to him an anachronism that fostered hypocrisy. For an example of such hypocrisy he brings up the natural scientist who *"for the sake of propriety* in his preface speaks of the Creator and admires His wisdom." He is equally critical of other myths and abstractions. "Why is it stupid to believe in the heavenly kingdom, but wise to believe in an earthly utopia?" he asks. A cultural relativist, Herzen challenges even Rousseau's dictum that "man is born free yet is everywhere in chains," because values—such as freedom—depend on the subject and are imposed by the elite.

Still, Herzen's attitude is fundamentally

optimistic. He delights in human freedom and is confident that creative individuals will assert themselves in any society, either as doers or as critical observers. He speaks scornfully of the European (in particular the French) bourgeoisie, but with sincere warmth of the French working man.

My Past and Thoughts combines the intimacy of an autobiography with the broad sweep of *Zeitgeschichte*, details of manners and life-styles with sharp social analysis, and studies in portraiture with intellectual discourse. The first half covers Herzen's childhood at the country estate of his father, a wealthy landowner, his years at Moscow University, his arrest and incarceration in 1834, his years of exile as a government official in the provinces (with an intervening period of literary life in Moscow and Petersburg), and his departure from Russia.

The first episode is a disturbing study of serf-holding Russia, a troubled world of unhinged and unhappy people, who happen to be owners of large estates and thousands of serfs. The portrait of Herzen's father provides an almost tragic centerpiece which in striking fashion anticipates old Duke Bolkonsky of *War and Peace*.

The episode at Moscow University covers a key chapter in Russian intellectual history. Among Herzen's fellow students were Belinsky, Bakunin, Stankevich, and others who, like him, were to play major roles in it. This part concludes with the heart-wrenching story of the poet Polezhaev's tragic fate.

Herzen's account of his years in exile are sardonic, even amused: the wealthy aristocrat realizes that what is demeaning drudgery for him is a condition that scores of provincial government clerks have coveted for years. Herzen's sketch of Russian intellectual life during the "marvelous decade" of the 1840s shows him more concerned with the stirrings of political thought, preoccupied

with the inconveniences and indignities of Russian life, and obsessed with his hatred of Nicholas I and his police state than impressed with the amazing surge of Russian prose. To Herzen, Belinsky was a far more interesting figure than Gogol, Goncharov, or Dostoevsky.

In the second part of *My Past and Thoughts*, set in the West, Herzen emerges as a fascinated eyewitness of European history and as an associate, friend, confidant, or adversary of major European figures including Proudhon, John Stuart Mill, Carlyle, Robert Owen, Mazzini, Garibaldi, Marx, Ruge, and Heine (he does not like the last three much, but then he has an aversion to the German émigré community as a whole), Bakunin (his character sketch of him is both fond and exasperated), Vladimir Pecherin (1807–85, a romantic poet who had defected in 1840 and become a Redemptorist monk), and many others. The sad story of Madame Herzen's affair with the German poet and revolutionary Georg Herwegh is told with remarkable detachment.

Along the way Herzen expresses his opinions on virtually everything that would occupy Russian thought for the rest of the century and after. His leitmotif is still human freedom, but the emphasis is now on the individual's freedom from the moral bondage imposed by a tyrannical majority. The United States is given as a recent example. But he also sees the other side of the coin: elitist disregard for the humble concerns of the masses. He deplores the monstrous rift between the Russian people and the ruling class created by Peter the Great's Europeanization of Russia. He still rejects all theories and abstractions: "Nature and history *are going nowhere*, and therefore they are ready to go *anywhere* and wherever they are directed." As far as Russia is concerned, he continues to be a Westernizer: "We [Russians] need Europe as an ideal, a reproach, a good example." On the other hand, he also believes in Russia's future and devoutly hopes that the Russian peasant commune will be the nucleus of a new and better society. He has, however, no precise idea of how this is to come about, and he has no faith at all in the young revolutionaries of the 1860s.[14]

Herzen had the intellect, the experience, and the character to take a critical view of ideas, his own most cherished ideas included. His thoughts were safe enough in his own fertile but critical mind. Once appropriated by others, they could become dangerous.

Goncharov

Having returned from Japan, Goncharov serialized his travelogue *The Frigate Pallas* (1855–57), which has remained a readable classic to this day. A staid, middle-aged bureaucrat, he was disinclined to see anything like romantic adventure in this voyage, although he was reporting some exciting things (he saw China at the time of the Taiping rebellion) and had visited a country almost no Europeans had seen. Goncharov never pretends to observe things from any viewpoint but his own, that of a smug and priggish European. He finds no particular reason why he should be interested in Madeira (he has tried that vintage before), South Africa, or even Japan. But as he happens to be a writer, he reports what he sees conscientiously, with that imperturbable attention to detail that was his forte. It is precisely the utter absence of a romantic strain that gives *The Frigate Pallas* an undying freshness.

Oblomov is a great novel in spite of its obvious flaws—greater, in fact, than its author. One might say that Goncharov, a man of considerable talent but no genius, quite in spite of himself produced a work of genius. He had published the chapter "Oblomov's Dream" in a miscellany of 1849. His work on the novel was interrupted by his trip to the Far East, and *Oblomov* appeared in *The National Annals* only in 1859. It was hailed as a capital work by every major critic, including Dobrolyubov, Grigoryev, Druzhinin, and Pisarev, although their interpretations were much at variance: those of the left saw Oblomov as a negative, those of the right as a positive type. Goncharov, a moderately liberal Westernizer, agreed with Dobrolyubov's one-sided interpretation—evidence that he was indeed smaller than his work.

The story of Ilya Oblomov's life is simple. Raised at Oblomovka, the family estate, he grows up pampered and overprotected. A bright child, he gets a fair education at a private school run by Stoltz, a German, whose son Andrei becomes his lifelong friend. Oblomov joins the civil service but soon quits his job; rents a flat in Petersburg, and lives the carefree life of a bachelor of means, letting a steward manage Oblomovka. He is thirty when young Stoltz, who has become a prosperous man of affairs, shakes him from his lethargy. Oblomov meets and falls in love with Olga Ilyinsky, a beautiful

14. Here is Herzen's characterization of the nihilists: "Their nakedness did not conceal but rather revealed what they were. It revealed that their systematic uncouthness, their rude and insolent talk, had nothing in common with the inoffensive and simplehearted coarseness of the peasant, but did have a great deal in common with the manners of the low-class pettifogger, the shop boy, and the flunky. The people no more considered them as one of themselves than they did a Slavophile in a *murmolka* [a tall Russian hat]. To the people these men have remained alien, the lowest stratum of the enemy's camp, skinny young masters, scribblers out of a job, Russians turned Germans."

and cultured young lady, who reciprocates his feelings. But their romance dies when Oblomov cannot muster the energy to take the practical steps required to make marriage possible. Olga eventually marries Stoltz. Oblomov goes on to live a quiet life on the suburban Viborg side of Saint Petersburg, where his landlady, the widow Agafya Pshenitsyna, barely literate but a great cook, takes good care of him. Eventually he marries her, and they have a son. At one time Oblomov's tranquil existence is threatened by a scheme of Mukhoyarov, Agafya's brother, and Oblomov's old "friend," the crook Tarantyev, who plot to extort most of his income from him; but Stoltz comes to the rescue, and Oblomov continues his contemplative and somnolent life punctuated by good meals. He dies, too young, of a stroke, leaving Agafya disconsolate. She is happy when Stoltz offers to undertake the education of young Oblomov so that he will become, like his father, a gentleman.

Oblomov is composed of heterogeneous elements. There is a love plot involving the triangle Oblomov-Olga-Stoltz. There are elements of a bildungsroman. The chapter "Oblomov's Dream" is an idyll. Some episodes are close to the genre of the physiological sketch, for instance—scenes from the world of Oblomov's servants and Agafya's kitchen. There are several character sketches, specifically a parade of Oblomov's visitors early in the novel, only one of whom, the sponger Tarantyev, will reappear later in the novel. Frequent descriptive passages, bits of the narrator's worldly wisdom, and a good deal of satire make *Oblomov* a novel of manners depicting Russian life on the eve of the reforms of Alexander II.

Oblomov's uncomplicated inner life is laid open all along. The description of Olga

and Oblomov in love is sensitive, though conventional. But Goncharov's description of Agafya's budding attachment to and eventual deep and undying love for Oblomov is masterful and profound. He shows how this simple woman senses the difference between the gait, the mien, the obsequious manners of her late husband, an underling, and the free and open deportment of Oblomov, a gentleman. She "learns the physiognomy of every shirt of his, has counted every worn heel of his stockings," and knows his every taste and habit. When she finally slips into his bed, it comes naturally and without the slightest embarrassment.

It takes the whole first part of the book to get the plot on its way. But after a skillful transition from Oblomov's dream to the appearance of Stoltz, who sets Oblomov and the plot in motion, *Oblomov* becomes a real novel, and from here on, the slow but steady movement of the hero's fortunes is presented masterfully. Transitions are artfully devised. The transition to the unhappy end of Oblomov's romance with Olga is made when Oblomov comes home after his first kiss from Olga and finds waiting for him Tarantyev, his evil spirit, who engineers his moving to the Viborg side. Part Three ends in Oblomov's emotional collapse, but also in the words, " 'Today is Sunday,' he heard a gentle voice say, 'we've baked a pie: wouldn't you care to have a bite?' " The phrase *we've baked a pie* is Agafya's label. There is also a great deal of foreshadowing and significant detail. Medical particulars become more and more ominous as the novel progresses. Sleep in many variations is a recurrent significant detail, and so are Oblomov's Asian silk dressing gown (it is mothballed during his romance with Olga, brought back when it is over), and his fear of the cold outside.

The treatment of time in *Oblomov* is

symbolic. Hours, days, weeks, and years are all alike in their slowness. It takes Oblomov a hundred pages to get out of bed. His courtship of Olga advances with excruciating slowness, and in the end years go by imperceptibly, as Oblomov sleeps away his life under Agafya's tender care. The restraint with which Goncharov maintains his andante throughout the whole novel is admirable.

Oblomov was seen by most as a roman à thèse, a novel about the clash of opposing principles. Stoltz stands for a new, European Russia. He is a self-made man, an entrepreneur, and a gourmet, but cultured and not without a conscience. He is also a social climber and a snob. He cannot understand how Oblomov could live with that "simple woman, in that filthy, stifling air of crude stupidity." The son of a German father and a Russian mother, Stoltz is as much at home in the West as in Russia, whereas Oblomov, who comes from a venerable family of country squires, stands for old Russia. Stoltz and the people of Petersburg live individual, personal lives. They pursue careers. Oblomov is "so imbued with the familial principle that he envisaged even his work in the civil service as some kind of family affair" and thought that a superior was "the father of his subordinates." In Agafya Oblomov finds incarnate "that ideal of an imperturbable tranquillity of life, boundless like the ocean, the image of which had left an indelible trace in his soul in his childhood, in the house of his parents." Agafya, even when her life has become empty after her husband's death, "knew why she had lived and that she had not lived in vain." Oblomov himself, an utter failure in Stoltz's terms, is a good husband and father. Oblomov's ideal is that of Evgeny in "The Bronze Horseman"—the ideal of life outside history, life without change, without individuation.

However unconvincing Stoltz and his ideal may appear, Oblomov's remorse at not having lived up to it are made very real. The moments when he perceives himself as a failure are described with great poignancy. The negative side of old Russia is personified not only in Oblomov, whose parasitic quality is softened by kindness, sensitivity, and thoughtfulness. Oblomov's thieving and drunken servant Zakhar, though devoted to his master, is just as lazy and incompetent, but without Oblomov's redeeming traits. Tarantyev and Mukhoyarov stand for old Russia, too. They hate Stoltz and all "foreigners." They do not understand the new Russia (Mukhoyarov fails miserably as a contractor), but they thrive as parasites in the tsar's bureaucracy, extorting small bribes from peasant petitioners.

Oblomov is a novel rich in symbolic detail. Some details are introduced in a significant binary fashion. Oblomov's dream of old Oblomovka, for example, is counterpointed with his daydreams about what Oblomovka will be like after he "takes care of it." Each major character has metonymic "labels." Oblomov has his bloated though pleasant face, sleepy eyes, and dressing gown and slippers. Zakhar has his huge sideburns, "from which you'd expect any moment two or three birds to fly out." Agafya has that pair of round white elbows that Oblomov loves to watch when she is busy over her kitchen table. Mukhoyarov always wears galoshes, always comes home from work carrying a package, and when pointing out something in a document does it "with his fingernail down." Tarantyev has a voice that sounds like three empty carts rumbling over a bridge.

The first significant event in the novel is when Oblomov is given notice that his lease has been terminated, because "the wreckers are coming." In 1859, with the emancipation of the serfs imminent, this had an ominous ring. Stoltz sees Oblomov's salvation in a trip abroad, which never materializes. As a child, Oblomov is eager to explore the world around him but dares not because of fear instilled in him by folk superstitions. The women in the novel are better and wiser than the men, a detail clearly symbolic of the strength of the feminine component of Russian life. The word *oblomovshchina*, "Oblomovitis," is used generically even in the text. It immediately entered the Russian language.

After *Oblomov* Goncharov wrote one more novel, *The Precipice* (1869). It had a moderate success but is quite undistinguished, presenting a panorama of contemporary Russian life and various characters all of whom by then had appeared in scores of other novels, Turgenev's in particular. Goncharov, who put great stock in *The Precipice*, contended that Turgenev and several other authors had plagiarized the idea and important elements of the novel, whose plan he had conveyed to them in private and excerpts from which he had read before small audiences. So persistently did Goncharov level his accusations that a "court of honor" was convened by fellow writers. It reached a compromise solution, clearing Turgenev of all charges of plagiarism but conceding that Goncharov had had some reason to suspect that it had occurred. Goncharov lived out his life as a lonely bachelor, continuing to publish some not very distinguished essays, reviews, and reminiscences.

Turgenev

In 1852 Turgenev was arrested for a commemorative essay on the death of Gogol which the authorities for no good reason

deemed to be subversive. After a month in the guardhouse he was ordered to return to his estate. He had to wait five years until he would again get a passport to leave Russia and join his lifelong friends, the Viardots. He spent the rest of his life mostly abroad, returning to Russia for brief sojourns. He lived in the fashionable German spa of Baden-Baden until the Franco-Prussian War of 1870–71 and joined the Viardots in Paris when they moved to France after the war. He resided in Bougival near Paris until his death of cancer in 1883. Because of his long absence from Russia, Turgenev was often charged with having lost contact with Russian reality. Some of his works, such as the novels *Smoke* and *Torrents of Spring*, are set in Western Europe. Turgenev was the first Russian writer to have a Western European following and to be consistently translated into all the languages of the West. By the 1870s critics would refer to a "Turgenevian manner" in the works of some German writers. Turgenev owed this success in part to his personal contacts with German, French, and English writers, with many of whom he carried on a stimulating correspondence in all these languages. Among his many German friends were Berthold Auerbach and Theodor Storm. In Paris, he belonged to a circle of writers who met on Sunday afternoons chez Magny. He was close to Flaubert, George Sand, and Zola, among others, and was well liked and much respected by the French literary fraternity. His gentler realism and valiant faith in humanity were set up as an example to counter the misanthropic pessimism of the French naturalists by critics such as Jules Lemaître and Emile Hennequin. Henry James, whom he met in Paris, considered himself a disciple. Turgenev's authority allowed him to persuade his European colleagues to take Russian literature seriously. In particular, he did much to spread Tolstoi's fame.

Whereas Turgenev made only friends in the West, his relations with his Russian *confrères* tended to sour sooner or later. After he had broken with *The Contemporary* in 1858, he published his works in Katkov's conservative *Russian Herald*, later in Stasyulevich's liberal *Herald of Europe*, and invariably met with hostile reviews from the radical left. An inveterate liberal and Westernizer, he was attacked with equal vehemence by the conservative right. Dostoevsky, in particular, who had once been a friend, pursued him with deadly venom. Tolstoi and Turgenev, close friends at one time, quarreled for personal reasons in June 1861 and never renewed their friendship. Tolstoi did not respect Turgenev, and said once that Turgenev was a sad person and that sad people should not write novels. Turgenev, in turn, was annoyed by what he saw as Tolstoi's eccentricities and bigotry. As Fet, another close friend, was turning more and more reactionary, their friendship cooled as well, and their correspondence, once lively, came to a halt. Only the critics Botkin and Annenkov, moderate liberals like Turgenev, remained his friends and were attentive and helpful readers of his manuscripts.

Turgenev felt that the novel was not the natural vehicle for his art and considered his novels really to be novellas. He produced a steady stream of short stories, but his fame rests primarily with a series of short novels, spread over a period of almost a generation, in which he meant to express the moods, hopes, and apprehensions of educated Russia at a given moment of its history. Although Turgenev wrote some stories about peasant life even after *A Hunter's Sketches* ("Mumu," 1854, "The Roadside Inn," 1855), he made it explicit that his viewpoint was at all times that of the educated class.

Turgenev often said that he found Tolstoi's and Dostoevsky's psychologizing annoying. There is little psychological analysis in Turgenev's fiction, and the narrator rarely takes advantage of his privilege to read the characters' minds. Turgenev is also on record having said that his characters were in almost every case based on persons he had met and that his plots were derived from the characters, not vice versa. Turgenev's novels and stories have simple plots. Their momentum is generated by the character of their dramatis personae or by simple accidents. The structure of a Turgenevian novel or novella is that of a stage play. A stranger arrives, intruding into a placid though by no means happy world, creates a stir, but soon leaves without having effected any permanent change. The dramatic unities are observed, discounting flashbacks and an unavoidable epilogue. The main action takes place within a few weeks, mostly at or near one location. There are relatively few characters. Dialogue dominates over narrative.

Although the conventional view of Turgenev's oeuvre, and his own view, was that it developed in step with the progress of Russian society, it seems more correct to see in it mainly a projection of Turgenev's melancholy consciousness and to view its basic mood as that of a weak and voluble soul's yearning for strength and integrity, or to use Mikhail Gershenzon's metaphor, the dream of the earthbound to soar. Turgenev's remarkable essay "Hamlet and Don Quixote" (1860) explains this state of mind: Hamlet, a clever and capable man, cannot but envy Don Quixote, a ludicrous madman, because Don Quixote has the integrity that only faith in an ideal can give. Hamlet's tragedy is that he cannot be Don Quixote.

Rudin (1856), a roman à clef, introduces Russia's "men of the 1840s" as they approach middle age. The plot features a single brief episode in the life of Rudin, a peregrinating liberal intellectual in whom one recognizes Turgenev's friend Mikhail Bakunin. Rudin is a summer guest at the estate of Madame Lasunsky, a patroness of the arts and letters. Now thirty-five, he has an air of failure about him, but he still professes the ideals that once animated a circle of students at Moscow University (evidently Nikolai Stankevich's circle): a striving to find a philosophy of life, a thirst for knowledge and creativity, and faith in humanity. Rudin's eloquence so impresses young Natasha, the daughter of Rudin's hostess, that she offers to elope with him and share his uncertain and perilous life. He has not the strength or the confidence to accept her offer. He leaves hastily to continue his wanderings. In a new edition of 1860, Turgenev let him perish on the barricades of Paris in 1848. *Rudin* might have been even more effective as a play than it is as a novel. Its composition is awkward, as Turgenev has difficulties providing narrative links between his dialogue passages. But the characters are sharply drawn, and Rudin, attractive and pathetic, always hopeful and always frustrated, is very much alive. The plight of Russia's superfluous intellectual, who has no cause to which he can apply his energy, is presented with sympathy. Natasha is the first of "Turgenev's women," who are as idealistic as their male counterparts but are braver, more ready to make a sacrifice and have more integrity. Tolstoi said that whereas Turgenev had created these women in his fiction, they would later actually appear in life.

The long short story "Asya" (1858) is set on the Rhine. Asya is the natural daughter of a Russian landowner, traveling with her half brother, the lawful heir. The narrator falls in love with the beautiful, passionate, and vulnerable Asya, but hesitates to propose marriage—after all, her mother was a serf woman. When he finally dismisses his doubts, it is too late—Asya is gone forever. In "Asya" a narrative stance of regretful and remorseful remembrance, characteristic of Turgenev's narrators, appears with particular poignancy. "Asya" provided the occasion for a spirited debate started by Chernyshevsky's essay "A Russian at a Rendezvous," which made Turgenev's story into an allegory of the Russian intellectual's encounter with the people.

A Nest of Gentlefolk (1859) is a well-constructed novel. Lavretsky, a kind and generous, but shy and ineffectual landowner, is married to a glamorous but shallow woman. She has left him for a French lover and lives in Paris. Lavretsky falls in love with Liza Kalitina, a pure and devout young woman, and she reciprocates his feelings. When news of his wife's death comes from Paris, their road to happiness seems open. But Lavretsky's wife is in fact alive and soon enough returns to Russia, asking him to forgive her. Liza withdraws to a convent, Lavretsky decides to concentrate on doing some useful work managing his farm, and his wife returns to Paris. The moral of the novel, often reiterated by Turgenev, is that man is not destined to be happy and that life punishes those who pursue their personal happiness. *A Nest of Gentlefolk* was the best received of all Turgenev's novels. It particularly pleased the conservative right, mainly on account of Liza Kalitina, who became, next to Pushkin's Tatyana, the most revered symbol of pure Russian womanhood. Even Dostoevsky gave Turgenev credit for her in his "Discourse on Pushkin." Grigoryev welcomed Lavretsky as a proper symbol of the new Russian man: humble, kind, willing to sacrifice himself.

On the Eve (1860) had a catchy title, considering that the reforms of Alexander II were imminent, as was the Russian revolutionary movement. Its hero is Insarov, a Bulgarian freedom fighter living in Moscow but ready to return to Bulgaria as soon as the time is ripe for a national uprising. Elena Stakhova, a high-minded Russian woman, chooses the poor and rather gloomy Insarov over two more promising and pleasant Russian suitors, marries him, and joins him when he leaves for the Balkans. Insarov dies of tuberculosis without ever reaching his destination. Elena continues on her way to join the freedom fighters as a nurse. Turgenev had conceived Insarov as yet another study in the Hamlet–Don Quixote theme. Insarov, not brilliant and perhaps even narrow-minded, towers over his more intelligent and talented rivals because he has an ideal for which he will lay down his life. (Turgenev's hero had a real-life Bulgarian prototype.) The critic Dobrolyubov gave the novel an allegorical reading and saw Insarov as a camouflaged Russian revolutionary. Many readers formed their image of the "new man" and "new woman" on the model of Insarov and Elena Stakhova.

"First Love" (1860) is one of the great short stories in all literature. A middle-aged narrator revives bittersweet memories of his first love. Sixteen-year-old Vladimir falls in love with a beautiful young woman who is surrounded by a crowd of suitors. Her playful attentions make him blissfully happy until he discovers that she is having an affair with his father. From behind the touching but trivial story of his puppy love there emerges the shadowy outline of a tragic love story which destroys the beautiful Zinaida,

who had so casually tormented her adoring suitors, and causes Vladimir's father, a proud and lordly man, to die of a broken heart. The reader, learning only as much as young Vladimir can catch in a few stolen glimpses and from snatches of bitter exchanges between his father and mother, is challenged to imagine how it all happened. In "First Love" Turgenev's art of telling a story by allusion, intimation, and a few significant details appears at its brightest.

Fathers and Sons (1862) became one of the most controversial works of nineteenth-century Russian literature and an example of a work of literature as a public event. Its plot follows a familiar pattern. Arkady Kirsanov, the son of a prosperous landowner, has invited his friend Bazarov, a young physician, to stay with him over the summer. Bazarov's father, a country doctor, lives nearby. It develops that Bazarov is a nihilist, meaning that he recognizes no truths except those of science and rejects all values save that of physical well-being. He considers romantic love, faith, honor, and beauty—in a word, all the values of the old generation—to be mere superstitions stemming from ignorance. When Bazarov expounds his ideas at the Kirsanovs' dinner table, he meets a determined opponent in Arkady's uncle, Pavel Kirsanov, a retired officer. Kirsanov's hostility toward Bazarov is nurtured by the suspicion that Bazarov is trying to seduce Fenechka, his brother Nikolai's young mistress and mother of Nikolai's child. He challenges Bazarov to a duel, which ends in a superficial wound to Kirsanov. Meanwhile Arkady and Bazarov have made visits to several neighbors, on one of which Bazarov meets Madame Odintsova, a young widow, and falls in love with her; Arkady in turn is attracted to Katya, her young sister. Odintsova, though attracted to Bazarov, rejects his advances because she values her freedom too highly to compromise it by marriage. Bazarov, in low spirits, accidently cuts himself while dissecting the corpse of a victim of typhoid fever and neglects to disinfect the wound. Stricken, he returns to his parents' house where he dies after having asked to see Odintsova. Arkady marries Katya, and his father marries Fenechka.

In *Fathers and Sons* Turgenev tried to define the positions of the old generation, the romantic idealists of the 1840s, versus those of the young generation, the matarialists of the 1860s. Only one serious reviewer, Pisarev, appreciated this, finding that Turgenev had done the young generation a favor by spelling out in all frankness what it stood for, at least in his own mind. Other critics, such as Maksim Antonovich, found that Bazarov was a calumny on the idealistic young generation. (It was only to the extent that Bazarov, late in the novel, remarks in a foul mood that it would matter little to him whether Russian peasants of the future lived in neat whitewashed cottages once he was "pushing up daisies.") Whereas Bazarov is, after all, an almost heroic figure, his adversary, Pavel Krisanov, is almost a caricature. This caused critics of the right to charge that Turgenev was siding with the nihilists. Nobody cared to point out that *Fathers and Sons* was an exercise in irony.

In the course of the novel Bazarov embraces every position he had denounced: he falls in love in good romantic fashion, he defends his honor by fighting a duel, and he who had said that nature was "not a temple but a workshop" dies while pursuing "science for the sake of science," much as a poet pursues "art for art's sake." Bazarov the materialist is a de facto idealist, for he is willing to work hard and make sacrifices to make the world a better place. Pavel Kirsanov, by contrast, has lost at love, fights a

duel with a man who has never fired a gun in his life, and is good only at keeping his financial affairs in order and at maintaining the appearance of a gentleman. Bazarov, who would have been a fine doctor, dies, whereas Kirsanov will live out his useless and bored life.

Turgenev was so discouraged by the negative reception of *Fathers and Sons* that he considered retiring from literature. He expressed his chagrin in a lengthy lyric monologue in prose entitled "Enough" (1865), which Dostoevsky would subject to a devastating parody in *The Possessed*. Another work which suffered that fate was the story "Phantoms" (1864), which appeared in Dostoevsky's journal *Epoch*. A fantastic allegory, it is one of Turgenev's weaker pieces. (He wrote many stories of the supernatural, and they are all second-rate.) Dostoevsky's parody had an easy target.

Turgenev's next novel, *Smoke* (1867), also earned him vituperative reviews. Set in Baden-Baden, it is an unsuccessful fusion of a very fine love story and a great deal of venomous political satire. The love story has Litvinov, a Russian landowner engaged to be married to a loving young woman, meet glamorous Irina Ratmirova, the woman he had loved in his student days. She is the wife of a brilliant young general (there is a hint that she was the mistress of an august personage before she became Madame Ratmirova). Irina declares that she still loves Litvinov, and he is so dazzled by her beauty that he breaks his engagement. When it turns out that Irina will only have an affair with him and will not leave her husband, the honest Litvinov finds himself at an impasse. He returns to Russia to win back Tanya's affection, knowing that their love will never be the same again. This love story is cluttered with a satirical gallery of Russian tourists and émigrés and the bitter tirades of Potugin, a character introduced solely for the purpose of voicing some of Turgenev's opinions, specifically that of Russia's moral and cultural inferiority.

"King Lear of the Steppes" (1870), a short story, is different from most of Turgenev's works. It recasts in a Russian setting the theme of a boisterous, generous, larger-than-life father betrayed by his strong, single-minded, and thankless daughters and comes up with a mythical and yet credible story. Obvious borrowings from *King Lear* are counterbalanced by specifically Russian traits. One of Kharlov's daughters becomes a cult figure, venerated as Mother of God by a group of Old Believer sectarians. Turgenev called it a "brutal" story, and indeed there is something Tolstoian about it.

Spring Torrents (1872) showed what Turgenev could do when leaving politics alone. It takes up the plot of *Smoke* and makes it into a perfect novella. Sanin, a young Russian, falls in love with Gemma, a beautiful but simple Italian girl, the daughter of a Frankfurt baker. They are engaged to be married when a dazzling Russian woman, Madame Polozova, appears on the scene. She easily enthralls Sanin, who will spend the rest of his youth as her page. Gemma marries another man and emigrates to America. Sanin is left with bittersweet memories of a happiness that might have been.

Turgenev's last novel, *Virgin Soil* (1877), was a response to the populist movement. Several characters who make an attempt at "going to the people" and stirring up revolutionary activity are introduced. They all fail dismally, as the peasants whom they seek to win over to the cause of the revolution at best do not understand them and at worst turn them over to the police. Nezhdanov, the central character, kills himself. Marianna, a young woman whom he had persuaded to join the movement, marries Solomin, a "gradualist" factory manager. Critics were quick to point out that each and every one of Turgenev's populists was a misfit. Nezhdanov is the illegitimate son of an aristocrat and socially "neither fish nor fowl." Marianna is Polish, an orphan and not pretty. She lives with rich relatives, and Madame Sipyagina, the glamorous lady of the house, lets her feel that she is a recipient of charity. She will do anything to escape this humiliating condition. Other populists are presented as embittered failures, compulsive schemers, vain fools, power-hungry manipulators, or plain drifters. The response from the left was a howl of protest. But Turgenev made everybody else angry, too, for his conservatives (one of them a nasty caricature of the writer Boleslav Markevich) and moderate liberals (Mr. Sipyagin) come off even worse and get none of the populists' saving grace of a misguided idealism. *Virgin Soil* makes good psychological sense, but it is not a good novel. It promotes Turgenev's gradualist message too blatantly. The plot is awkward, and some characters are too obviously inserted merely to make a point.

Turgenev continued writing to the end of his life and dictated his last story to Pauline Viardot in French, but nothing significant came from his pen after *Virgin Soil*. Some of his *Poems in Prose* (1879–83) have been frequently anthologized and are considered classics, but they are not poetry as such but rhetorical prose, sometimes embarrassingly so.

Turgenev is today considered the least of the "big three" Russian novelists, especially in the West, although—or because—his worldview was Western and his thinking more congenial to Western intellectuals than Dostoevsky's or Tolstoi's. His failings, too, were those of his Western confreres: a certain flabbiness, a lack of faith ("from weakness," said Dostoevsky), a melancholy and at times unpleasant skepticism, and a deafness for the cosmic and metaphysical. Yet in his diffident and inconsistent way Turgenev may have loved humanity better than his more forceful rivals, and Merezhkovsky may not have been entirely wrong when he said that Turgenev the agnostic was a better Christian than either. As an artist, Turgenev at his best was as good as anyone, but his worst was very bad indeed.

Works of the fifteen-year period after 1856 can be generally assigned to either the nihilist or the antinihilist camp, with some liberals straddling the fence between them. Nihilist fiction has two basic tendencies: to expose the wretched material and mental poverty of the Russian masses and to advertise the notion that help is on the way from altruistic "new men and women" of the educated classes. Other salient concerns of nihilist fiction are the emancipation of women, a more humane and meaningful education, and a struggle against all kinds of prejudices.

Nikolai Chernyshevsky did not claim to be a novelist. But he believed that a well-educated person with good sense and in possession of the right ideas could certainly write a novel that would convey a useful message to its readership. When held at the Saints Peter and Paul Fortress in 1862–63 he did just that. *What Is to Be Done?* elicited many reactions from friend and foe alike. It became an inspirational text to "progressive" Russian youth and its leading characters became household names. Subtitled "From Tales about New Men and Women," *What Is to Be Done?* is a fictionalized program of the revolutionary intelligentsia. Vera Pavlovna, the heroine, grows up in an upper-middle class family. Her tutor, the

student Lopukhov, opens her eyes to a new and better way of life. They get married, not because they are in love, but to allow her to escape the stifling atmosphere of her home. Once free, Vera Pavlovna educates herself and also engages in useful practical activity. She starts a dress shop, which develops into a producer and consumer cooperative. When she falls in love with Lopukhov's friend Kirsanov, Lopukhov fakes suicide to allow her to marry Kirsanov, and himself goes to America. Lopukhov prospers in America and returns to Russia as Mr. Beaumont, a well-to-do American citizen. He marries Vera Pavlovna's best friend, and they all go on to live in friendship and harmony.

The novel also introduces the ideal of the Russian revolutionary. Rakhmetov, born a nobleman, has decided to devote his life to the people. A man of iron will, he possesses all the virtues of a fighter and leader. In the course of the novel Chernyshevsky develops his entire program: equality of sexes, removal of all social, national, and religious prejudices and conventions, and a socialist utopia achieved by nothing more dramatic than persuasion, the power of reason, and human desire for a better life. The characters of *What Is to Be Done?* are abstract schemes. The didactic message is delivered straightforwardly. It was precisely the simplicity and logic of Chernyshevsky's arguments as well as the ease with which Vera Pavlovna and her friends achieved success in life that appealed to Chernyshevsky's readers. The synthetic revolutionary Rakhmetov impressed and inspired two generations of young Russians because he posed no problems and no doubts. *What Is to Be Done?* was a brilliant vindication of Chernyshevsky's aesthetic theory. His admittedly and pointedly "unartistic" novel accomplished what the artful works of his contemporaries failed to achieve: it had a real effect on the progress of Russian society.

In an essay of 1861, "Could This Be the Beginning of Change?" Chernyshevsky approved of the honest realism of the stories of Nikolai Uspensky, finding that it was exactly what was needed. The life of Uspensky (1837–89) was sad, like that of many other writers of his generation and orientation. The son of a country priest, he studied medicine and later the humanities in Saint Petersburg but never graduated. He became a permanent collaborator of *The Contemporary* in 1861, but soon quarreled with Nekrasov and moved on to teach at Tolstoi's Yasnaya Polyana school. Later he taught at various provincial schools. He failed to catch on with the populists and disappeared from the literary scene in the 1870s. After 1884 he was a tramp; his body was found in a Moscow street in 1889. Uspensky's stories and sketches are of the slice-of-life type, without any message from the commentator. They tend to be gloomy, even brutal. The irony, if there is any, is grim. "Supper" is a sketch of suppertime in a village; the key episode features an orphan child, puny and severely undernourished, who ends up not getting fed at all. "A Christening" details the sad and sordid condition of a sexton's family, punctuated by its wry conclusion: "The baby, thank God, died soon." "A Good Life" has an innkeeper boast of the various ways in which his customers obtain money for vodka; for example, they may catch a thief and force him to pawn all his belongings to buy them drinks. "Brusilov" is one of Uspensky's stories about the desperate poverty of Russian students; as the story ends, Brusilov lies dying. Uspensky's stories are very strong, reminding one of Chekhov's in the 1880s.

Aleksandr Levitov (1835–77), the son of a deacon, attended the Saint Petersburg Academy of Medicine and Surgery (1855–56) but was arrested in 1856 and exiled to Vologda in the northeast. Allowed to return from exile in 1859, he led the unsteady life of a drifter, drank heavily, and died of tuberculosis. Levitov's ambience is the world of tradesmen, hucksters, petty crooks, drunks, and prostitutes. His manner is objective, concrete, obviously firsthand, but literate (there are occasional literary allusions). It differs from the manner of the natural school in that there is no effort at stylization and no ironic distancing from the subject at hand. The facts of life are presented with brutal frankness. The ravages of drunkenness, in particular, are presented in depressing detail. Levitov left an unfinished autobiographical novel, *Dreams and Facts*. A chapter from it, entitled "The Talking Ape," features a dialogue between the hero and a Mr. Alcohol and other hallucinatory interlocutors. This and more than a few other pieces by Levitov suggest that he had great talent.

Nikolai Pomyalovsky (1835–63), the son of a Petersburg deacon, attended a seminary and divinity school in the capital. Though very talented, he finished next to last at graduation and was not recommended for a deaconship. He attended lectures at Saint Petersburg University, tried teaching, and began to submit articles to Petersburg periodicals. "Vukol: A Psychological Sketch" (1859), published in a pedagogical journal, is the story of an intelligent but ungainly orphan boy's progress under the rods of obtuse guardians and educators, until he finally finds a teacher to whose fatherly love he can respond. Pomyalovsky's short novel *Bourgeois Happiness* and its sequel *Molotov* appeared in *The Contemporary* in 1861, making him the most promising writer of the progressive young generation. They tell the story of a poor young plebeian's advance to self-realization and a place in the world. The narrative is accompanied by a running moral commentary in the manner of Chernyshevsky's essays. Molotov sees himself as "a man of no race or tribe, house or home," as one who does not even belong to a particular social class (an orphan, he was brought up by a bachelor professor), "a cosmopolitan without any firm ground under his feet." The family of country gentry whose son he tutors is profoundly alien to him, nor will they ever consider him their equal, though he is a university graduate. He will never wear a civil servant's uniform because it would stifle his freedom. Nadya, the woman he loves, will have to break all ties with her parents, who want her to marry a middle-aged general. The moral, revealed on the last page of *Molotov*, is: "Is it really forbidden to try for simple bourgeois happiness? Do not millions live simply to enjoy life honestly? We are simple people," says Molotov, "people of the masses. Are you willing to accept this?" Nadya answers, "I am yours."

Pomyalovsky then published his sensational *Seminary Sketches* (1862–63), a fictionalized but factual account of his fourteen years as a seminarian. It is an exposé of the mindless drudgery and soulless indoctrination whose products are to be Russia's spiritual leaders. Student-teacher relations are characterized by shameless favoritism, suppression of all independent thought, and the steady monotony of brutal floggings. The internal life of the student body is governed by the law of the stronger fist. The whole atmosphere stifles all the good and brings out the worst in these young boys and adolescents. Pisarev responded to *Seminary Sketches* by reviewing it together with

Dostoevsky's *Notes from the House of the Dead*, under the title "Those Who Are Lost and Those Who Are About to Be Lost,"[15] pointing out that Dostoevsky's account of life in a Siberian prison was more optimistic and gave more reason for hope than Pomyalovsky's work.

After *Seminary Sketches* Pomyalovsky had planned a major novel, *Brother and Sister*, dealing with the life of the lower classes of Saint Petersburg. His death, from gangrene that developed after a minor injury, prevented him from finishing it, but the extant pages show that he was growing as a novelist. He was, however, by then a hopeless alcoholic, with week-long binges in the lowest dives of the capital and several bouts with delirium tremens behind him.

The biography of Fyodor Reshetnikov (1841–71) was similar to that of Levitov, Pomyalovsky, and other seminarians turned radicals. The son of a mailman and former church deacon, he began his literary career in 1861 with a local paper in Perm, in the remote northeast. He came to Petersburg in 1863, and in 1864 created a mild sensation with a short novel, *The People of Podlipnoe*, subtitled "An Ethnographic Sketch," about the Finnish *permyaki* of his home province. *The People of Podlipnoe* reveals the grinding poverty and abject degradation of the villagers of Podlipnoe. Most are so debilitated by undernourishment that they are incapable of strenuous labor. The most enterprising leave the village to beg, or if they are lucky, to work as lumberjacks for minimal wages. The people of Podlipnoe have no religion save the crudest superstition, and their family life lacks affection, as the struggle for survival has killed all human

15. *Pogibshie i pogibayushchie*, where the same verb appears in the past and present participle, an elegant play of words which cannot be duplicated in English.

feeling in them. Reshetnikov's work had a shocking effect on his readers and was grist for the mill of radical critics.

Reshetnikov's three novels, *The Miners* (1866), *The Glumovs* (1866–67), and *Where Is It Better?* (1868), have the distinction of being the first coherent fictional treatment of the emerging Russian proletariat and its nascent class consciousness. The last of these novels features the first description of a strike found in Russian literature. Reshetnikov is the purest exponent of Russian naturalism. His style is awkward, prolix, and repetitious. He often gets bogged down in irrelevant detail and long and pointless dialogue. But his subject matter and his manner of presentation announced a new direction in Russian literature, pointing toward Maksim Gorky. Reshetnikov died of an illness aggravated by acute alcoholism.

Vasily Sleptsov (1836–78), the son of an officer, attended Moscow University (1854–55) but never graduated. He held a job in the civil service from 1857 to 1862 and thereafter devoted himself entirely to writing and social work. In 1860 he made a long trip on foot through the Russian countryside, observing peasant life and gathering folklore and ethnographic material. He published a series of sketches based on this trip, under the title *Vladimirka and Klyazma* (1861), in Countess Salhias de Tournemir's journal *Russian Speech*. Inspired by Chernyshevsky's novel *What Is to Be Done?* Sleptsov in 1863 organized a commune in which he sought to realize the principles of collective labor and equality of the sexes. He dissolved the commune in 1864, apparently fearing official repression, but continued his work, particularly in the cause of equality for women. He played a role in organizing popular-science lectures for women and trade unions of female workers, and in founding a journal, *Women's World*. He also wrote articles, sketches, and stories for newspapers and journals, *The Contemporary* and *The National Annals* in particular. Sleptsov died of tuberculosis, like so many of his contemporaries.

Sleptsov had great talent. His sketches and stories of Russian low life, mostly rural, are masterful, combining precision of descriptive detail with cool ironic detachment. He is also good at creating narrative voices. In "A Night at a Roadside Inn" people tell stories. A peasant relates how he had to pay the local village council a silver ruble so that they would go ahead and give him his flogging for having let the village herd trample the squire's field. They had kept him waiting for four days, and he lost his pay while away from his job. In "The Foster Daughter" a mother is looking for her four-year-old daughter, who has been placed with foster parents. All she has to go by is the misspelled name of a village. Of course she never finds her child. The poor woman's misery is skillfully understated. In "Evening" we hear of life at the manor house from an ex-houseserf's viewpoint. Sleptsov's stories are mostly about suffering and misery, violence, child abuse, wife beating, and disease (particularly in "Scenes at a Hospital"), but also moments of good cheer, fishing, and choir practice, all described in vivid naturalistic detail and with the same cool irony.

Sleptsov's short novel *Hard Times* (1865) has little action but is thoughtful and artfully builds tension, leading to a surprising resolution. Ryazanov, a seminarian and nihilist, is visiting with his friend Shchetinin, a liberal landowner, whose wife, Marya Nikolaevna, falls in love with him as he introduces her to his nihilist philosophy. When confronted by Shchetinin, who accuses him of having "taken everything from him, his energy, his peace, and his family happiness," Ryazanov wryly responds, "The woman wants to live. You and I are merely witnesses in this matter. Our roles are trivial: she needed you to rid herself of her mother, I freed her from you, and she has freed herself from me by herself. Now she does not need anybody—she is her own mistress."

The novel is set in 1863, when all the problems and hardships connected with the emancipation were coming to a head. Shchetinin tries to run his farm with "free labor" and works hard at it. Ryazanov puts him down, saying that it is no use: doing well in a bad cause is like saying, "What a good boil you have on your neck!" Sleptsov tries to get past the censor his conviction that the reforms of Alexander II are a sham, just as the fancy-sounding White Swan is an ordinary pothouse. He expresses this idea in various more or less camouflaged ways. At one point Ryazanov suggests that all statements regarding "schools" should be adjusted to read "skins" instead: "We must make our schools safe" really means "We must save our skins." The point is that schools are installed by the authorities as one of the means by which the ruling class tries to consolidate its hold on the people. Sleptsov also manages to suggest that the people sense that all these liberal measures are really directed against them. One peasant says that all literate peasants will be drafted to become "cantonists," a fate much feared.[16] Sleptsov sees the relations between landowner and peasant as "war"— guerrilla warfare, that is. The peasant who steals Shchetinin's lumber, the one who spends the money entrusted to him on drink, the one who cheats the landowner any way he can—they are all engaged in guerrilla warfare. Shchetinin, the gradualist,

16. Cantonists were peasants drafted to serve in "military settlements," which combined labor with military drill; they were founded under Alexander I and later abolished.

is made attractive to prove that even the best of the liberals are really bloodsuckers and rapacious exploiters of the poor. *Hard Times* is incomparably stronger than most novels of the period that share its subject. (As the critic A. E. Zarin pointed out in a review article in *The National Annals*, three other novels with exactly the same subject were appearing simultaneously with *Hard Times*.) It stands comparison with *Fathers and Sons*. Sleptsov is as intelligent as Turgenev but tougher and more intense. He is desperate where Turgenev is only sad.

Saltykov-Shchedrin

Mikhail Evgrafovich Saltykov (1826–89), who wrote under the pseudonym N. Shchedrin, had a remarkable dual career. His father was of ancient though impoverished nobility; his mother came from a rich Moscow merchant family. An energetic and capable woman, she was the prototype of Arina Petrovna, the matriarch of *The Golovlyovs*. Saltykov attended the Lyceum of Tsarskoe Selo from 1838 to 1844, a generation after Pushkin, and entered the civil service in Saint Petersburg, where he moved in liberal circles. He was close to the critic Valerian Maikov and at one time attended some meetings of the Petrashevsky circle. Saltykov started his literary career with reviews for *The Contemporary* and *The National Annals*. Two stories in the manner of the natural school, "Contradictions" (1847) and "An Involved Affair" (1848), earned him a transfer to Vyatka in 1848 "for harmful thoughts and a detrimental striving to disseminate ideas which have already shaken all of Western Europe." Like Herzen, who had been in Vyatka fifteen years earlier, he served there as a middle-echelon official under the local governor. In 1855 Saltykov was allowed to return to Saint Petersburg, where he resumed his literary career with his highly successsful *Provincial Sketches* (1856–57). As an "official for special projects" of the Ministry of the Interior, he played an active role in the government's preparations for the imminent emancipation of the peasants. Subsequently he served as vice governor in Ryazan and Tver, all the while continuing to be an active contributor to *The Contemporary*. In 1862 he left the civil service to concentrate on his literary work. Saltykov's political radicalism was always diluted by a practical man's and a satirist's common sense, which caused him to make concessions to "immediate needs" at the expense of "remote guiding ideals"— and disparaging remarks about Chernyshevsk͵'s *What Is Be Done*? He developed serious disagreements with his colleagues on the staff of *The Contemporary*, resigned, and rejoined the civil service in 1865, holding responsible posts in several provincial capitals. In 1868, following a complaint by the governor of Ryazan Province, Saltykov was asked to resign, which he did, having reached general's rank. He immediately joined Nekrasov as a partner and coeditor of *The National Annals*, in which position he remained after Nekrasov's death until the journal was closed in 1884. Saltykov continued to publish in other journals and newapapers until the end of his life.

Saltykov was a prolific writer, but most of his writings were journalism rather than literature. To contemporaries, Saltykov was at least as important a figure as his adversary, Dostoevsky, who was also regarded as a publicist more than as a writer of fiction. Saltykov has occupied a position of preeminence during the entire Soviet period, for his ideological position was in almost perfect accord with that of socialist realism. Saltykov's essayistic and satirical writings are for the most part dated and often are difficult to read since they are full of allusions to contemporary events and personages and, moreover, written in an Aesopian language that contemporaries were better equipped to decode. Saltykov's *Provincial Sketches* are physiological sketches of provincial life seen from the viewpoint of an amused outsider, with only a dash of satirical exaggeration. The leitmotif and message of *Provincial Sketches* is that the provincial administration is a foreign body that does nothing for the welfare of the population but interferes with the normal course of life. Saltykov's *Pompadours and Pompadouresses* (1863–74) and *Letters from the Provinces* (1869), sequels to *Provincial Sketches*, were more purely satirical. It was here that Saltykov showed a tendency to be diverted from his civic message to burlesque raillery and light banter, castigated by Pisarev as "flowers of innocent humor." *Pompadour* is a code word for governor, and a pompadouress is a governor's wife or, more often, his mistress. A pompadour leads an army of assistant and subaltern pompadours. Some of these sardonic satirical sketches exposing the bumbling inefficiency, extreme stupidity, and total lack of concern for the public weal of all pompadours, high and low, veer into straight invective. In some others the satire turns burlesque, as in a chapter entitled "Opinions of Prominent Foreigners about Pompadours," where Saltykov exercises his ironic wit in excerpts from "*Impressions de voyage et d'art*, par le prince de la Cassonade, ancien Grand Veneur de S. M. l'Empereur Soulouque I, actuellement, grâce aux vicissitudes de la fortune, garçon en chef au Café Riche à Paris." This and some of the other pieces are laced with "quotes from the French original."

Saltykov's most famous satire is *The History of a City* (1869–70). The "editor" proposes to show how the grand design of Russian history is reflected in the history of the town of Glupov (from *glupy*, "stupid"). The mayors of the age of Biron flogged the citizenry "absolutely," those under Potemkin "explaining the reasons for such measures" and those under Razumovsky urging the citizens to "rely entirely on the valor of their superiors," so that the first would tremble unconsciously, the second tremble while aware of their own advantage, and the third tremble with trepidation elevated to the level of confidence. The mayors of Glupov are transparent caricatures of tsars, tsarinas, and their ministers. Catherine II appears as a "plump, blond German with a high bust, red cheeks, and full lips like cherries, named Amalia Karlovna Stockfisch," whose only claim to authority is that she was once for two months the mistress of some mayor, but who easily seizes power at the head of six drunken soldiers. The satire is savage throughout, but particularly when it reaches the reign of Alexander I. Saltykov's view of Russia is gloomy: it is a place of chaotic social conditions, vicious power struggles, demented and unrealizable projects, and senseless cruelty. Several further cycles of satires are equally gloomy: *Gentlemen of Tashkent* (1869–72), *Well-Intentioned Discourses* (1872–76), *In the Realm of Moderation and Precision* (1874–77), *Sanctuary Monrepos* (1878–79), and others.

Among the large volume of Saltykov's works only his novel *The Golovlyovs* (1875–80) is a work of art of lasting value. Its somber power makes it one of the great novels of the nineteenth century. *The Golovlyovs* is a family chronicle spanning three generations. Its first half is dominated by Arina Petrovna, the grandmother, the second by her son Porfiry Vladimirovich, called Yudushka (Little Judas). Arina Petrov-

na's husband Vladimir Mikhailovich is an alcoholic with a touch of the poet, consumed by fear and hatred for his wife, who despises him. They have four children. Stepan, not a bad sort, is destroyed by his mother, who never calls him anything but "the booby" (*balbes*). He drinks himself to an early grave. Pavel is mentally and emotionally stunted. He also dies young. Anna elopes with her lover, is abandoned by him, and dies having given birth to twin girls, Anna and Lyubov. Porfiry, of low mentality but normal enough, has two sons, Vladimir and Pyotr. Both are destroyed by their father. Anna and Lyubov leave the family estate and join a troupe of traveling actors. Within a few years they are reduced to a choice between starvation and prostitution. Cheerful, fun-loving Lyubov commits suicide. Anna, dreamy and soulful, comes home to live with her uncle and share his decline into black despair and alcoholic stupor.

Arina Petrovna is not an altogether repulsive figure. Active and intelligent, she runs the family estate efficiently, buying more land and increasing her wealth, always "for the family." But she perceives life entirely in material terms and cannot give her family what it needs most: love. Greedy, miserly, and heartless though she is, Arina Petrovna is still a human being. Yudushka is not. He is the Russian Tartuffe, but Saltykov is quick to point out that he does not measure up to his European counterpart. He is a natural slave. Low, cowardly cunning is the best he can muster mentally. He is a hypocrite, not by conscious design, but because the only way he knows how to think is in worn proverbs and pious phrases. He is greedy, stingy, and callous like his mother, but without her healthy business sense. He will throw away a ruble to save a kopeck and fritter away the family fortune pursuing harebrained schemes to increase it. Yudushka destroys everything he touches. His son Vladimir commits suicide. When Pyotr, his other son, comes home to tell him that he has lost three thousand rubles of his regiment's money in a card game and will be court-martialed if he cannot replace it, Yudushka, a rich man, gives him pious phrases about repentance and the beneficial effects of punishment, but no money. Pyotr dies on his way to Siberia. After his wife's death Yudushka takes a deacon's daughter for his live-in housekeeper and mistress. When she bears him a child, he has it committed to an orphanage, where it will die. At last Yudushka, too, succumbs to the curse of the Golovlyovs: alcoholism. The conclusion of the novel is ambiguous. Porfiry utters some phrases that seem to indicate an epiphany of remorse, then says, "I must go out to dear mama's grave to say adieu to her," walks out into a blizzard and freezes to death in a snowbank.

The Golovlyovs remains—in spite of its intensity, which never allows the reader to develop even a spark of disbelief—a roman à thèse whose object is to show that the landed gentry, together with its way of life, is sick and doomed, and that there is no reason to feel sorry for it. All black and gray, without a ray of light in all its gloom, *The Golovlyovs*, is a flawlessly beautiful novel. The utter darkness and total abjection that it so perfectly expresses not only make it a great work of art but also give it a metaphysical quality. In the character of Yudushka Golovlyov the banality of evil, its cosy fellowship with common sense, conventional piety, and hearty sentimentality, and the unholy alliance that evil may enter with language have found an expression equal to anything in world literature. Yudushka Golovlyov became proverbial. When Vladimir Solovyov wanted to denounce Vasily

Rozanov for his essay "Freedom and Faith" (1894), in which Rozanov asserted that the church should not allow any dissent, he entitled his rejoinder "Porfiry Golovlyov on Freedom and Faith."

The antinihilist novel is represented by several famous names: Dostoevsky. Pisemsky, Leskov, and Goncharov. But besides novels like *The Possessed, Troubled Seas, No Way Out*, or *The Precipice* there appeared quite a few works by authors who were soon forgotten. Viktor Ashkochensky (1820–79), a minor journalist, authored the first explicitly antinihilist novel, *An Asmodeus of Our Age* (1858).[17] His nihilist, Pustovtsev (from *pustoi*, "empty, inane"), is well educated and gets a good start in life, but his moral foundations are crumbling:

> It is awful to touch upon the religious views of his lively mind! There was then in fashion the most pitiable, the most stupid and irresponsible unbelief; one rejected everything without even bothering to analyze what it was one rejected; one laughed at everything sacred only because it was inaccessible to one's narrow and obtuse mind. Pustovtsev, however, was not of this school: from the great mystery of the universe to the phenomena of God's power in our own poor age, he subjected everything to a critical examination, asking for nothing but knowledge; but what was above his intellect, that which would not fit into the narrow cells of human logic, he rejected as trivia, as pure nonsense.

Pustovtsev bases his life entirely on rational materialist principles. As a government official, he is a heartless formalist. In society he

17. Asmodeus is an evil spirit in Jewish demonology.

impresses the ladies with his liberal ideas. "He is honest," they say, "but like a heathen." Pustovtsev is honest in money matters and in his official duties, but "the honor of your spouse, sister, or daughter is not safe with him." He seduces innocent Marie, who bears him an illegitimate child. After he finally marries her, she soon dies of a broken heart. Pustovtsev eventually comes to a bad end: he shoots himself.

Mirage (1864), by Viktor Klyushnikov (1841–92), which appeared initially in *The Russian Herald* and later as a separate book, was somewhat less primitive than *An Asmodeus of Our Age. Mirage* is set in the western Ukraine at the time of the Polish uprising of 1863. Rusanov, the hero, fights on the government's side. The heroine, Inna Gorobets, daughter of a Russian general and landowner, is persuaded by Broński, a demonic Polish count, to join the cause of the insurgents. Rusanov sees Broński in London after the uprising is defeated: the proud Pole is now a broken man. Russian nihilists in *Mirage* are merely ridiculous. Kolya, a schoolboy who spouts revolutionary phrases, tries to incite the local peasantry to revolt but fails wretchedly. Altogether, the novel is boring, awkwardly told, and loosely structured. But it had great success as a roman-feuilleton of topical interest and was violently attacked by Pisarev, Zaitsev, Saltykov, and other critics of the radical and liberal camp. *Mirage* started the practice of baiting Poles and Jews, which became a standard trait of the antinihilist novels of the Katkov school. Klyushnikov's later works, which follow the same tendency, went almost unnoticed. Since the 1870s he concentrated on writing for young readers. He also became editor of the popular magazine *The Cornfield.*

Vsevolod Krestovsky, a liberal in the 1850s and early 1860s, changed his political orientation in the mid-1860s. His novel *The Flock of Panurge* (1869) deals with the Polish uprising of 1863 and Russian nihilism in aggressively negative terms. It is, however, well observed and well written. Krestovsky's later works were even more frankly chauvinistic and anti-Semitic.

Boleslav Markevich (1822–84), a high-ranking government official and close friend and collaborator of Mikhail Katkov, publisher of the conservative *Russian Herald*, started his career as a novelist late in life. His first novel, *Marina of Red Horn: A Contemporary Tale* (1873), established the pattern he would follow in subsequent works. His novels have the distinction of making a sympathetic presentation of the world of the Russian upper class, of which one gets only disapproving glimpses in better-known novels like *Anna Karenina, The Idiot*, or *Smoke.* The hero of this novel, Count Zavalevsky, is a sensitive, kindly, and generous aristocrat. His friend and rival for the heroine's affection is the equally positive, though eccentric, Duke Puzhbolsky. Both deplore the decline of the humanities, good manners, and good taste that Russia has witnessed in the past two decades. These aristocrats are honorable men, sincere humanitarians, modest and self-effacing. Their only weakness is a certain good-natured naiveté and trustfulness. They are surrounded by vulgar and cynical nihilists, such as the seminarian Leviafanov, scheming Jewish businessmen, dishonest stewards (Zavalevsky's steward is Marina's stepfather), and brutish peasants. The rot that affects the hero's immediate surroundings has spread even to the administration and to the mood of the whole country. The heroine, however, initially misguided by nihilist tutors of Leviafanov's ilk, slowly comes to realize that she has been in error. The topical features of the novel render the melodramatic and rather implausible plot almost irrelevant. Markevich's psychology is superficial, his style rhetorical, at times florid, strewn with French and some German, English, Latin, and Italian quotations. On the whole, his novels are quite readable. Markevich's political views were not all that different from those of other antinihilist writers. What gave him a bad reputation was the snobbery and affectation that speak from every page of his novels. He insists on the moral and physical superiority of his aristocratic heroes, pointing out not only their breeding but even that they are of a "good race," and intimates that he himself is at home in the world of high society and not far removed from august personages.

Pisemsky

Aleksei Feofilaktovich Pisemsky (1821–81) came from an impoverished noble family in Kostroma Province, northeast of Moscow. He graduated from Saint Petersburg University in mathematics (1844) and subsequently held positions in the civil service in Kostroma and Moscow. Having established himself as a writer and as a member of the "young editorial board" of *The Muscovite*, he quit has post and moved to Petersburg to become a professional writer. From 1857 to 1863 he was at first coeditor (with Druzhinin) and later sole editor of *The Reading Library*. He moved to Moscow in 1863 and continued to write prolifically until the end of his life.

Pisemsky, the least known of the major novelists of his generation, had a distinctive sensibility and style. His imagination was dramatic. He perceived life as a sequence of delusions, fateful mistakes, and guilty desires, all of which overwhelm people imperceptibly, inexorably, and fatefully. His characters are ordinary men and women.

The passions that ruin them are mundane. Love in Pisemsky is carnal. He is more of a pure realist than Goncharov, even more of a pessimist than Turgenev, and a gloomier, less forgiving ironist than Dostoevsky. His evocative power is great, but he does not make for pleasant or inspiring reading. His narrative style is artless, not to say blunt.

Pisemsky's first success came with his short story "The Wimp" (1850), published in *The Muscovite*, which has all the qualities of Pisemsky at his bilious best. It is the story of an unhappy marriage and two bungled lives. Nobody is to blame but the principals themselves. (Pisemsky can be as keen a moralist as Tolstoi.) The "wimp" (*tyufyak*), a flabby young landowner who seems kind but is merely spineless and whose crude manners and intellectual apathy belie his university degree, is cajoled into marrying a beautiful, spirited, and self-willed but dowerless girl. Her father, an impecunious man of the world, is behind the match. The hideous tragedy of the story develops as a matter of course, without fanfare, and almost anticlimactically.

In the early 1850s Pisemsky published, among other pieces, some tales from peasant life. They were hailed by Grigoryev and Druzhinin as the beginning of a new trend supplanting the natural school. These critics observed that Pisemsky was not treating his underdogs with condescending sentimentality, but matter-of-factly, with the irony of a dispassionate observer. Pisemsky concluded his Kostroma period with his three best-known works, the novel *One Thousand Souls* (1858), the play *A Hard Lot* (1859),[18] and the short novel *An Old Man's Sin* (1861). *One Thousand Souls* is a novel of success (*roman de réussite*) with an ironic twist, and thus a novel of disillu-

18. See p. 370.

sionment (*Desillusionsroman*). Its title must be an allusion to *Dead Souls*. Kalinovich, the hero, is an ambitious raznochinets who after graduating from the university comes to a provincial town to assume the position of superintendant of schools. He is intelligent, energetic, and capable; if he is not excessively scrupulous, neither is he outright dishonest. Yet he never gets to earn any of his successes. His novel is published only because a friend puts in a good word with the publisher. He realizes his dream of wealth—being the owner of one thousand souls—by jilting Nastenka, the woman he loves, and marrying an unloved heiress. He rises in the civil service only after his marriage has elevated him to the ranks of the ruling elite. When he has risen to acting governor of the province in which he had started his career, and believes he has exposed the crooked machinations of Duke Ramensky, his erstwhile mentor, he discovers once more that he is powerless by himself. After Ramensky has triumphed and Kalinovich's career has come to an end, Nastenka comes back into his life. Unlike him, she has earned her success, as she is now a well-known and respected actress. But their life together will never be what it might have been. The mood of *One Thousand Souls* is one of grim irony. The reader's worst suspicions invariably turn out to be justified. When local louts smear Nastenka's gate with tar, they do not even know that she has in fact surrendered her virginity to Kalinovich. His betrayal of her is a certainty when he himself does not even suspect it will happen. That Kalinovich is presented as no villain, but as better than most people, is perhaps the greatest irony of the novel. Pisemsky, However, is no cynic: some honest and kind people are also found in this world, though they are powerless and ineffectual. The wise literary critic

who advises Kalinovich to quit literature is modeled after Belinsky.

In *An Old Man's Sin* a government accountant, a lonely "old man" (middle-aged, really) who has been a paragon of righteousness all his life, falls in love with an attractive young woman who has some business with his office and to help her misappropriates a sum of money. His crime is discovered, and when it is revealed that she has a "past" and quite simply used him, he hangs himself. The power of Pisemsky's treatment of what might have easily become a maudlin tearjerker derives from the ruthless ironic detachment with which the story is told.

In the early 1860s Pisemsky, in spite of his continued vigorous denunciations of the ills of the existing order, found himself in the antinihilist camp on the strength of a series of feuilletons and the long novel *Troubled Seas* (1863). Pisemsky's position, bitterly resented by his opponents, was that nihilism and the revolutionary movement were in fact nothing but the mindless antics of an idle and misguided leisure class. In a later novel, *In the Whirlpool* (1871), Pisemsky retreated from this position, allowing his heroine to be a naive idealist, but she is used and manipulated by self-seeking adventurers. Late in Pisemsky's life his disapproval of the direction that Russian society was taking found expression in plays and fiction attacking emergent Russian capitalism and in two novels in which the idealist past of the Russian educated elite is contrasted to the materialist present. In the autobiographical novel *Men of the 1840s* (1869) he looks back fondly to the youth of his generation. One of the characters resembles the poet Katenin, who had been Pisemsky's mentor in the 1840s. Pisemsky's last novel, *The Masons* (1880), is set in the 1830s and creates a sympathetic image of the idealistic

Freemasons. By the 1870s Pisemsky had lost his prominent position in the world of Russian letters. That he has never been considered the equal of his great contemporaries, and has never entered world literature, is to be explained not so much by his inferior powers as by his point of view, which remained at all times Russian—that is, provincial—not only in its concerns but also in its sensibility.

Dostoevsky

Dostoevsky was away from literary life for ten years, serving a four-year sentence at hard labor and subsequently in the military, both in Siberia, until 1859, when he was permitted to return, first to Tver (which he used as the setting for *The Possessed*) and then to Saint Petersburg. In 1857 "A Little Hero," a delightful story about a child who gets involved in an adult love intrigue, written in 1849 while in prison, had appeared anonymously. When Dostoevsky returned from Siberia, married to an attractive but consumptive young widow, he brought with him some half-finished works and ample notes about his life in prison. Within two years he was back at the top of the literary profession. The journal *Time*, which he and his brother Mikhail started in 1861, was a success. But it was suspended in 1863 because of an article by Nikolai Strakhov which the authorities interpreted as being in sympathy with the Polish insurrection. In 1864 the Dostoevsky brothers got permission to start anew under a different title, *Epoch*, but could not make a go of it. Mikhail and Dostoevsky's wife died that year. *Epoch* had to stop publication in 1865, leaving Dostoevsky deeply in debt. Pressed for time by a contract to deliver a novel to his publisher, he hired a stenographer and dictated to her a short novel, *The Gambler*

(1866). Simultaneously he was working on *Crime and Punishment*, which appeared in *The Russian Herald* (1866–67). In 1867 Dostoevsky married his stenographer and went abroad with her to escape his creditors. There his financial condition at first went from bad to worse as a result of his compulsive gambling. Living in Germany, Switzerland, Italy, Austria, and again in Germany, Dostoevsky wrote *The Idiot* (1868–69) and most of *The Possessed* (1871–72). The Dostoevskys returned to Russia in 1871, their finances having improved. In 1873–74 Dostoevsky was editor in chief of *The Citizen*, a conservative weekly, in which he published his *Diary of a Writer*, a miscellany of essays, reviews, notes, reportage, necrologies, and short fiction. After having published *A Raw Youth* (1875) in *The National Annals*, he returned to his *Diary of a Writer*, which he now published independently. His last novel, *The Brothers Karamazov* (1879–80), appeared in *The Russian Herald*. On June 8, 1880, he delivered his celebrated "Discourse on Pushkin" at the unveiling of a monument to the poet. Dostoevsky died seven months later of a pulmonary hemorrhage in Saint Petersburg.

Throughout his career Dostoevsky spent much of his time on journalism. His articles dealt with every question that was in the news at the time: public education, inflation, the "woman question," the "Jewish question," disintegration of the peasant commune, alcoholism, a wave of suicides among young people, child abuse, wife beating, spiritualism, and a variety of other topics, many of which would resurface in his fiction. Dostoevsky was also a capable trial reporter. Several criminal trials on which he reported in *Diary of a Writer* entered the text of his novels. As a writer and journalist, Dostoevsky maintained a keen interest in

European affairs. His travelogue *Winter Notes on Summer Impressions* (1863) presented a Russian tourist's witty and perceptive, though rather hostile, view of France and England. His frequent comments on Western literature were intelligent and appreciative. Dostoevsky was, however, a strong nationalist and shared the attitudes of his right-wing allies—a certain xenophobia, anti-Catholic prejudices, and anti-Semitism. When Russia went to war against Turkey in 1877, he wholeheartedly supported the Russian war effort and saw the capture of Constantinople, the ancient capital of Eastern Christendom, as its ultimate goal.[19] A *pochvennik*, Dostoevsky rejected the legalism, positivism, and scientism of the progressives as a harmful import from the West which interfered with Russia's organic development. Like the Slavophiles, with whom he agreed on many, but not all, issues, Dostoevsky believed that Western civilization was in decline but might be regenerated by Russian spirituality, if only the Russian elite would find a way back to the Christian faith of the simple Russian people. If he were to choose between the truth of science and the truth of Christ, said Dostoevsky, he would choose Christ.[20]

Dostoevsky's nonfiction is good journalism, but no more. His philosophy is all in his fiction. His essays are truly brilliant only when they deal with art and literature. (His critical judgment was excellent: A. L. Bem has called him a "reader of genius.") "Mr. [Dobrolyu] bov and the Question of Art" (1861) is a spirited defense of art against Dobrolyubov's utilitarianism. For the sake of argument, Dostoevsky assumes that a Portuguese poet printed an idyllic love poem (he gives Fet's "Whisper, timid breathing" as an example) the morning after the Lisbon earthquake. The good people of Lisbon, righteously incensed by the poet's callous disregard for the suffering around him, surely would have seized him and strung him up on the nearest lantern post. But— and this is Dostoevsky's point—art would not be at fault here, only the timing of its presentation. Years later, with the calamity forgotten, the people of Lisbon might yet have erected a monument to the poet, grateful for the lovely poem he left them. The gist of Dostoevsky's philosophy of art is that art is an absolute human value, that man needs art as he needs air to breathe, and that art is a direct avenue to truth. An artist is one who has the gift to recognize truth better than most people. He must live in the world and observe it with open eyes. A vision of truth may then arise in his mind— that is "the poet" in him. And he must find an appropriate form for his vision—that is "the artist" in him. All these ideas are characteristic of the organic aesthetics of romanticism.

The poetics of Dostoevsky's fiction is also more romantic than that of any of his major contemporaries. His novels have a significant literary subtext—that is, literary allusions, references, quotations, and polemical sorties—which subverts their realism. Extreme types, situations, and passions abound. Dostoevsky's novels present men and women in moments of high crisis. Detractors would see all this as melodramatic.

A metaphysical dimension is always in evidence, although the supernatural, when-

---

19. Tolstoi declared himself against the war in the last installment of *Anna Karenina*. Katkov refused to publish it in *The Russian Herald*, and it appeared as a separate brochure.

20. "Moreover, if somebody were to prove to me that Christ is outside truth, and if it were *in fact* so that truth were outside Christ, I would still want to stay with Christ, rather than with truth." Letter to N. D. Fonvizina, January-February 1854, in *Polnoe sobranie sochinenii* (Leningrad: Nauka, 1972–88), 28 (1): 176.

ever it appears, may be accounted for even in natural terms. Dostoevsky's faith in the prophetic power of art causes him to project an allegorical subtext into his novels, each of which not only tells a story but also advances a philosophical argument. Each of the great novels carries a Christian message. This message is often delivered obliquely or by characters who are failures in life.

Dostoevsky resumed his career as a writer with two short stories, "Uncle's Dream" and "The Village of Stepanchikovo and Its Denizens." Both were initially meant to become comedies and are structured as such. "The Village of Stepanchilcovo" has been staged often and successfully. Its hero, Foma Fomich Opiskin, a sorry ex-writer who dispenses edifying platitudes to an awed audience, is a cruel caricature of Gogol as he appears in his *Selected Passages*.

The Insulted and Injured (1861) is an entertaining, sentimental, Dickensian potboiler. Dostoevsky acknowledges his debt by calling his child heroine Nelly and making her grandfather an Englishman. In *Notes from the House of the Dead* (1860–62) he fictionalized his prison experience. While presenting all its horrors (cramped quarters, filth and stench, sadistic wardens, brutal floggings, and general degradation) and dwelling at length on the criminal personality (most of his fellow inmates were common criminals), he managed to insert into his journey through a cold and bleak inferno a message of faith in humanity and in the Russian people. *Notes from the House of the Dead* won Dostoevsky the sympathy of progressive circles. He lost it soon afterward with his polemical journalism and *Notes from Underground* (1864), a short novel in which he first stated his philosophy.

The anonymous narrator of *Notes from Underground* is a forty-year-old Petersburg intellectual who in Part One expounds his philosophy and in Part Two reminisces about an episode in his life which may explain his philosophy. This novel is the first of Dostoevsky's multileveled and ambiguous works: a polemical tract, a psychological study in neurotic behavior, a philosophical discourse, and a social satire all at once. Its subject is the modern intellectual. The polemic is directed at Chernyshevsky's anthropological principle. The antihero (Dostoevsky's term) declares—and proves by his actions—that, contrary to that principle, men often act consciously against their rational self-interest, and also that enlightened thought is by no means a guarantee for a kinder and happier humanity. Psychologically the antihero is a neurotic, whose compulsive self-analysis and hyperconsciousness leave him at a moral and intellectual impasse. He has lost his self-respect and has become a hypochondriac, a misanthrope, and a masochist.

As a study in philosophical anthropology, *Notes from Underground* became a cornerstone of twentieth-century existentialism. The antihero vigorously advances the idea that from the viewpoint of the human self it is impossible to deal with the human being as a determinate entity, or to accept the laws of nature and of logic (that twice two equals four) as absolutes. What defines conscious human beings is the fact that they will not be dealt with as "piano keys" but will assert their free will even at the cost of personal disadvantage and suffering. Since the antihero, a weak character, finds it difficult to impose his will on the world around him, he has created for himself a mental world of his own, whose captive he has become.[21]

21. The antihero's voluntarism is neither the optimistic one of J. G. Fichte (1762–1814) nor the pessimistic one of Schopenhauer, but rather the pragmatic one of Max Stirner (1806–56).

Dostoevsky's intent was to suggest an escape from the antihero's absurd world. Yet the antihero only gets as far as saying that he is searching for "something quite different—something I long for but cannot find."[22] This something is faith, of course, as even at least one contemporary reviewer, Saltykov-Shchedrin, realized. Dostoevsky later used the word *underground* generically, to mean any condition that causes people to become alienated from "real life."

Notes from Underground is the best example of what Mikhail Bakhtin called Dostoevsky's "polyphonic" style.[23] It means the presence in a text of two or more distinct voices, as in parody, ambiguity, and irony. In *Notes from Underground* all these elements are present, but also a trait that Bakhtin found peculiarly Dostoevskian, the "inner dialogue" that the antihero carries on in his mind. The distinctive feature of the text is precisely the narrator's refusal to stay put, his constant hedging, his exasperating habit of contradicting himself or of withdrawing a statement just made.

After *The Gambler*, whose hero goes "underground" by substituting the pseudolife at the gaming tables for "real life," Dostoevsky wrote *Crime and Punishment*, an ideological novel that may be read on several different levels. As a psychological novel, it probes a murderer's mind from the moment when he conceives his crime to the moment when he confesses it.[24] On this level it is a crime thriller where the search for the killer is replaced by a search for the motive. Raskolnikov, a student, has carefully

planned the murder and robbery of a pawnbroker, a nasty old woman. But the pawnbroker's half sister, an innocent simple soul, surprises him at the scene. He kills her, too, and manages to make his escape. He soon discovers that he cannot live with the murders on his conscience and, encouraged by Sonya Marmeladova, a saintly young prostitute, confesses his crime to the police. Sonya follows him to Siberia. Why did Raskolnikov, an honest and generous young man, become a murderer? Was it the money, as Pisarev insisted? Was it a self-imposed test of will? Raskolnikov had a theory that "extraordinary" men, the movers of history, were natural criminals—so he would test himself to see if he was an extraordinary man. Was it the thrill of the crime? Was he acting under a compulsion? Was committing a murder a desperate step to escape the "underground" and enter "real life"? All of these and some other motives for the murder are well substantiated by the text. There is no definite answer.

Crime and Punishment may be read as an allegory of the Russian revolution: Raskolnikov is the revolutionary movement, the pawnbroker is capitalism, and her sister the innocent people who will also die in the revolution. As a study in philosophical anthropology, it raises several issues. Is crime compatible with "normal" human nature? What is the effect of crime on the criminal? Are there in fact "ordinary" and "extraordinary" people? On a moral level, *Crime and Punishment* advances the idea that reason is a poor guide in moral matters. Raskolnikov's is a thinking man's crime. In his dreams, with his reason eliminated, Raskolnikov shrinks from going through with his plan. The text makes it clear that the devil works through Raskolnikov's conscious mind. *Crime and Punishment* is a Christian novel. Raskolnikov will be healthy

22. Dostoevsky's correspondence with his brother suggests that the intimation of a Christian epiphany was cut from the text by the censor.

23. Bakhtin's book *Problems of Dostoevsky's Oeuvre* appeared in 1929.

24. Dostoevsky initially wrote the novel in the first-person singular as the murderer's confession.

again only when he has overcome his pride and embraced Sonya's Christian faith, as happens in the epilogue.

Like Dostoevsky's other great novels, *Crime and Punishment* has many dramatic traits. The action is fast, furious, and suspenseful. Space is used symbolically, not to say theatrically. There is a great deal of symbolic detail, much of it Christian. Dostoevsky takes much dramatic license, employing chance encounters and messengers, eavesdropping, and accelerated action. *Crime and Punishment*, set in a teeming Petersburg slum in the month of July, is alive with realistic detail, crowds (literally) of individualized characters who easily blend into the main action, and a whole concert of individual voices. It combines the challenge of an ideological antinihilist novel with the concreteness of a realistic social novel.

The Idiot falls short of the compactness and energy of *Crime and Punishment*. Its hero is Prince Myshkin, a saintly epileptic, who is cast into a world ruled by greed, intrigue, and carnal passion. *The Idiot* is set in upper middle-class Petersburg and has many of the traits of a pleasant family novel, until it ends in a hideous murder and one of the great tragic scenes in all literature: crazed Prince Myshkin and the murderer Rogozhin keeping vigil over the corpse of the beautiful woman they both loved. An allegorical meaning emerges more clearly here than in Dostoevsky's other novels, as a Christ-like Prince Myshkin reenacts the appearance of Christ on earth. On a metaphysical level *The Idiot* deals with the antinomy posed by the presence of death in a world created by an all-good, all-loving, and all-powerful God and by the failure of Christ to effect any changes in the empirical world.

After *The Eternal Husband* (1870), an interesting psychological study in jealousy (a chapter entitled "Analysis" makes the point that all psychological analysis is double-edged), came *The Possessed*, an explicitly political novel. Told by a chronicler, an intelligent local resident who plays a minor role in the action, it details the subversive activities of a group of nihilists in a provincial capital. An anatomy of the Russian revolution, it introduces the various types involved in it: the fanatical zealot, the pedantic theorist, the embittered failure, the quirky eccentric, the starry-eyed idealist, the naive fellow traveler, the cynical opportunist, and the common criminal. It shows these types in action subverting morality, encouraging disrespect for religion and authority, undermining law and order, and fomenting arson and murder. Their success is made easy by the weakness and frivolity of the local authorities and by the absence in educated Russian society of any values to oppose to the nihilists' attractive promise of a society that will make no demands of excellence, talent, or honor on its members.

In an allegorical reading, *The Possessed* (the Russian title, *Besy*, means "devils") is a demonology. Stavrogin, the central character, has Luciferian traits. Pyotr Stepanovich Verkhovensky, a revolutionary organizer, is less glamorous but still intensely diabolical. There are many other devils, some frightening, some petty and impish. The novel has its lighter, satirical side, especially in its strong literary subtext. Karmazinov, "a great writer," who cravenly fawns on the nihilists while liquidating his Russian assets and establishing permanent residence in Germany, is an all-too-explicit caricature of Turgenev. The lop-eared theorist Shigalyov, who has proved "with mathematical certainty" and to the applause of his audience that the society of the future will consist of nine-tenths slaves, equal in mediocrity and degradation, and one-tenth rulers, is patterned after Varfolomei Zaitsev. Stepan Trofimovich Verkhovensky, father of the meanest of the "devils" and tutor of the most terrible, Stavrogin, is one of those romantics of the 1840s who replaced Christianity with an idealist humanism. In Dostoevsky's notebooks he is called Granovsky, one of the leading figures to emerge from Stankevich's circle. There are other characters in the novel who have a literary identity, and the text is teeming with literary allusions.

The Possessed continues an argument started in *Notes from Underground* and in *The Idiot.* Kirillov, one of the nihilists, draws a corollary from God's proven nonexistence. If there is no God, man must take His place. Kirillov, like his predecessor Ippolit Terentyev of *The Idiot,* finds no better way to assert his godhead than to kill himself gratuitously, as a prophet of human free will and a nobler, happier humanity. Kirillov is morally pure and generous, but he is also a madman. He kills himself in a frenzy, from despair rather than from elation. In an eerie way Kirillov's teaching and personality anticipated Nietzsche's. The positive message of *The Possessed* is left to Shatov, a former nihilist who has decided to leave the conspiracy and instead work at rejoining the Russian people in their Christian faith. He is murdered by the conspirators at the very moment when he has made a new start in his life.

The chronicler of *The Possessed* is a witty satirist who shoots off veritable fireworks of amusing persiflage, cruelly apt caricature, and insidious faint praise. Stepan Trofimovich is the butt of many left-handed compliments and appears in one comic situation after another. The parody of Turgenev's works (at least five may be clearly recognized) is deadly. The ludicrous sides of nihilism are presented with Aristophanean

gusto. The local authorities, headed by bumbling governor von Lembke, are made fun of from beginning to end. The chronicler himself is the target of his creator's irony. In spite of his wit and cleverness he is only a gossipy and spineless philistine. The loftier metaphysical meaning of the events that he so vividly describes is beyond him. When the text reaches out toward the metaphysical and the tragic, Dostoevsky relieves his narrator and uses a different voice, a shift that some critics have taken for a violation of the artistic integrity of the text.

A Raw Youth is in its flaws and virtues the most Dostoevskian of Dostoevsky's novels. Its teenage narrator and hero carries on an incessant inner dialogue as he stumbles through a world of adult intrigue which he slowly learns to understand. Young Arkady Dolgoruky ("not Duke Dolgoruky, but the illegitimate son of Versilov, a landowner, and a serf woman," as he sometimes feels obliged to declare) must choose between his natural father, an *homme du monde* of great charm, and his legal father, Makar Dolgoruky, formerly Versilov's serf and now a pious pilgrim. He is fascinated by Versilov, who ultimately turns out to be a man without inner strength or substance. Makar Dolgoruky is one of few major characters in all Dostoevsky's works who are "of the people." Secure in his faith, Makar humbly accepts whatever life brings him. Versilov is complex and and unpredictable. Makar is so simple that he has no psychology. Young Arkady is never quite sure where he is headed. He had started out with a plan to become a Rothschild to avenge himself on the world for his illegitimacy, his clumsiness, and his "slave mentality," but soon he abandons it and goes through a rapid sequence of ideas, friendships, infatuations, temptations, misconceptions, and follies.

A Raw Youth has no unified plot or

discernible structure. It decidedly belongs to the genre of the roman-feuilleton. By conventional standards it is no work of art, but it has that unique Dostoevskian forte—a narrative voice that is vibrantly alive, youthful, naive, embarrassingly effusive and foolish, but also marvelously to the point, clever, and apt.

The Brothers Karamazov was written as an introduction, as it were, to the projected "main novel," whose hero would be Alyosha Karamazov, the youngest of three brothers and the least important in the novel we have. It ends with the fate of all three brothers still in the balance. Set in a small provincial town, it is told by a chatty chronicler, apparently a local resident of mature years and conservative views. On the surface the novel is a murder mystery. Fyodor Pavlovich Karamazov, a bibulous and lecherous fifty-five-year old man of affairs, is murdered in his house. His eldest son Dmitry, an impetuous and reckless sort, is arrested and convicted of the crime on the strength of a slew of evidence. Dmitry and his father had been rivals for the attentions of Grushenka, a handsome young woman of tarnished reputation, and had bitterly argued about Dmitry's patrimony. Karamazov's servant, the epileptic Smerdyakov, who is reputed to be the old man's illegitimate son, is the actual killer, and Ivan, the second son, an intellectual and writer of some note, had guilty knowledge of the crime. Alyosha, a novice monk, could not prevent the crime, for he himself was in a crisis after the death of his beloved mentor, Father Zosima.

On an allegorical level the three sons may well stand for the three faculties of the human soul—Ivan for the intellect, Dmitry for the sensual, and Alyosha for the spiritual. Ivan, proud and capable, fails. Dmitry is in great peril but will be saved. Alyosha re-

mains unscathed and ends the novel on a confident note. On a moral-philosophical level the novel raises the question of divine justice (human justice is discredited by the conviction of Dmitry, an innocent man), linking it to the theme of fatherhood. Ivan asks if the suffering of innocent children (he produces some shocking examples) is compatible with God's fatherhood and answers his question in the negative. Then, in his "poem" (in prose), "The Grand Inquisitor," he develops the idea of a church of wise men who, knowing that there is no God, keep the masses happy in a false faith by following the advice that the devil gave Christ when he tempted Him in the desert. Ivan's position is refuted by the deterioration and eventual disintegration of his personality, ending in a hallucinatory dialogue with the devil. Meanwhile Dmitry discovers that his terrible misfortune has brought him back to God and God's truth. Alyosha experiences a glorious epiphany as a radiant Father Zosima appears to him in a vision inspired by the recital at his bier of the verses on Cana of Galilee.

The Brothers Karamazov has a strong metaphysical subtext, as diabolical and heavenly forces make frequent incursions into the human world. Visions of hell appear in several variations, and diabolical visitations occur throughout the text. (A psychological explanation is at hand in every instance, though.) But signs and visions sent by heaven also appear, and Father Zosima says explicitly that man can live only as long as he has contact "with other worlds" and that whenever such contact ceases man loses his will to live and perishes.

In *The Brothers Karamazov* the traits of Dostoevsky's art are amplified. It has more of a literary subtext than any of his novels. Goethe, Schiller, Shakespeare, Hugo, Pushkin, Gogol, Turgenev, and many others are not only quoted or alluded to but are actually engaged in the novel's argument. Through innumerable biblical quotations and references the novel presents modern life in the mirror of the Gospel. The polyphonic quality of the novel is sustained by the introduction of individualized voices: Ivan's "Grand Inquisitor," the life and teachings of Father Zosima as written down by Alyosha Karamazov, Grushenka's "tale about the onion," the speeches of the prosecutor and the counsel for the defense at Dmitry's trial, and countless other discourses, anecdotes, arguments, and dialogues create a colorful symphony. Although all these voices are independent of the narrative voice, they are still under the control of an inaudible "conductor," who tints the impression produced by each voice to suit his grand design—to exalt his Christian message and discredit its opponents. Deceived by Dostoevsky's conscientious performance as devil's advocate, some readers have failed to hear the false notes and strident chords in the voices of Ivan Karamazov and other characters whom Dostoevsky meant to undercut. Others, lacking the necessary faith and sympathy, find Father Zosima's discourses boring and pointless rather than edifying and moving.

Another peculiar quality of Dostoevsky's fiction is what Bakhtin called the "carnivalesque," meaning the presentation of the work's ideas and insights in a grotesque or even burlesque form to complement their serious or tragic version. Fyodor Pavlovich Karamazov, who likes to play the buffoon, suggests at one point that the nonexistence of hell is a gross injustice, for it allows an inveterate and unrepentant sinner like himself to enjoy the fruits of his sins with impunity. He thus brings up the question of divine justice—in carnivalesque form—even before it is raised seriously by his son

Ivan. Other carnivalesque characters, episodes, and conceits are more plentiful in *The Brothers Karamazov* than in Dostoevsky's other novels.

The somber tragedy and lofty metaphysical argument of *The Brothers Karamazov* are embedded in a world of carnal physicality. The menu of a Sunday dinner at the monastery, Fyodor Pavlovich afterdinner coffee and cognac, or Dmitry's shopping spree for a last fling with Grushenka are handled with as much care as the metaphysical anguish of Ivan Karamazov or the serene spirituality of Father Zosima.

In his lifetime Dostoevsky was generally considered a major figure, but nobody said that he was a great artist. The philosopher Vladimir Solovyov was the first to declare Dostoevsky an important thinker.[25] He was seconded by Vasily Rozanov, whose *F. M. Dostoevsky's Legend of the Grand Inquisitor* (1894), however, misinterpreted Dostoevsky by assuming that Ivan Karamazov's position was Dostoevsky's own. Symbolist critics of the 1900s, such as Merezhkovsky, Vyacheslav Ivanov, and Volynsky, laid the foundation of his reputation as a religious visionary, which soon spread to the West. Later his works were used as exhibits to illustrate the insights of Freudian psychoanalysis, Spenglerian speculations on the decline of the West and the ascendancy of Russia, and, along with Nietzsche and Kierkegaard, the existentialism of Sartre and Camus. Dostoevsky the master novelist was discovered late. The decisive breakthrough came in Mikhail Bakhtin's *Problems of Dostoevsky's Oeuvre* (1929), which established the fact that Dostoevsky should not be judged by the familiar standards of novelistic style and structure; rather, his

25. V. S. Solovyov, "Three Discourses in Memory of Dostoevsky" (1881–83).

novels were to be read as polyphonic compositions featuring a concert of individual voices. Subsequently Russian and Western critics learned to describe the intricacies of Dostoevsky's art in concrete detail.

Tolstoi (to 1880)

Count Lev Nikolaevich Tolstoi (1828–1910) came from a family of ancient nobility. He lost his parents early and was brought up by female relatives at the family estate of Yasnaya Polyana, in Tula Province. He attended Kazan University without graduating (1844–47), then led an aimless and dissipated life in Moscow and Petersburg for a few years before enlisting in the army in 1851. He served in the Caucasus, on the Danube, and in the Crimea, where he fought as an artillery officer in the siege of Sevastopol. He had established a literary reputation with a short novel, *Childhood* (1852), his first published work, and several sketches of military life, all published in *The Contemporary*. His *Sevastopol Stories* (1855–56) made him a national figure. After the Crimean War Tolstoi resigned his commission and spent some time in Saint Petersburg, but he found the literary ambience there uncongenial. He withdrew to Yasnaya Polyana, where he concentrated on his school for peasant children. He had prepared himself for that task by visiting educators during an extensive sojourn in the West (1861–62). In 1862 and 1863 Tolstoi published a pedagogical journal, *Yasnaya Polyana*, reporting on experiences gathered in his teaching practice. Tolstoi's educational philosophy was derived from Rousseau. The pupils of the Yasnaya Polyana school could come and go as they pleased, and all school work was voluntary. They were taught only things of immediate use or interest to them.

Tolstoi refrained from teaching them a scientific worldview or world history, feeling that it was irrelevant to them whether the earth was flat or a globe and that they were interested in history only so long as it nurtured their patriotic feelings. In an essay, "Who Ought to Teach Whom How to Write: We Our Peasant Children, or Our Peasant Children Us?" Tolstoi declared himself for the latter alternative. In an assessment of his work at the Yasnaya Polyana school, he stated that education of the kind that he and his associates (students of Moscow University) had delivered to their pupils had done them little good and had possibly done severe damage to their pure souls. Tolstoi's pedagogical nihilism found severe critics in Chernyshevsky and Mikhailovsky.

In 1862 Tolstoi married Sofya Andreevna Behrs, the seventeen-year-old daughter of a Moscow physician. The marriage was happy at first, but later deteriorated and became the cause of intense anguish for both sides. Sofya Andreevna bore her husband thirteen children. The story of this marriage is reflected in several of Tolstoi's works, *Anna Karenina* in particular. Tolstoi spent the years 1863 to 1869 writing *War and Peace* and 1873 to 1877 writing *Anna Karenina*. Between these two great novels he concentrated on his pedagogical work and produced *A New Primer* and *A Russian Reader*, texts designed for a complete elementary education. Published in 1875, these books gained wide acceptance, and millions of Russian children were brought up on them. In the late 1870s Tolstoi went through an inner crisis. Hinted at in the last chapters of *Anna Karenina*, it found full expression in *Confession* (1882), a spiritual autobiography.

Tolstoi's fiction is marked by several traits that persisted even as his worldview and his style underwent radical changes. His penchant for introspective psychological analysis appears in his first extant work, "A History of Yesterday" (1851, published posthumously). Right from the start Tolstoi developed a habit of working with a strong narrative voice—his own. A preoccupation with moral values is a dominant trait of his first published work, *Childhood*. A habit of subjecting conventional behavior to moral scrutiny is very much in evidence in *Childhood* and its sequels, *Adolescence* (1854) and *Youth* (1857), where a mature narrator passes judgment on his earlier, immature self. Along with this moral orientation comes Tolstoi's lifelong trademark, a trope called "making it strange" (*ostranenie*), which amounts to taking a view of objects and events that strips them of all conventional trimmings. At its simplest, it is achieved by seeing things through the eyes of a child.

In *Childhood* Tolstoi develops a format that he would sustain for the rest of his life. The novel consists of many short chapters, each a finished vignette in which various details are arranged to create a specific effect.[26] In other ways *Childhood*, an inimitable masterpiece, is very different from Tolstoi's later works. It has an air of the eighteenth century about it: a Rousseauan sensibility, a good deal of tearful sentiment, a stable world of unchallenged values, and a crystal-clear, very French style. The singular charm of *Childhood* begins to vanish in *Adolescence* and is gone in *Youth. Childhood* is autobiographical, but only partly so. The marvelous portraits of Nikolenka's father and mother, for instance, are not those of Tolstoi's own parents.

---

26. The Soviet scholar Boris Eichenbaum likened this technique to cinematic montage. Viktor Shklovsky, another Soviet scholar, suggested that Tolstoi had learned it from Sterne.

Tolstoi's years in the army led to a series of physiological sketches of military life, including "The Raid" (1853), "A Woodcutting Expedition" (1855), and the three *Sevastopol Stories* (1855–56). They are directed against the romantic tradition of Bestuzhev-Marlinsky, pointing up the everyday side of war in meticulous detail. Their physiological aspect appears in systematic naturalist analyses, such as of the Russian soldier, who appears in three main types ("fussy," "desperate," and "depraved"), each having its subcategories; or of courage: the commanding general has courage because he owes it to his rank, a seasoned middle-aged captain has courage because it is part of his job, a young junior officer has courage because he has romantic daydreams. In his *Sevastopol Stories* Tolstoi gives some striking examples of his psychological technique. There is one stream-of-consciousness passage, nearly a page long, describing the last moment of an officer who was "killed on the spot."

After his *Sevastopol Stories* Tolstoi tried various other styles. *Family Happiness* (1858–59) is a family novel in the English manner. It tells an unexciting story of courtship, early married bliss, subsequent marital problems, and eventual compromise, all from a young woman's point of view and in the prim, conventionally proper, but perceptive style of a Victorian "lady writer." *Family Happiness* has a certain placid charm, though it does not seem to be by Tolstoi. "Albert" (1858), a *Künstlernovelle* about an alcoholic violinist, tackles the romantic theme, trite by then, of a talented artist's failure in life. "Polikushka" (1861–63) and some other tales from peasant life are well told but hardly go beyond what Grigorovich had done in the 1840s and lack the brutal frankness of Nikolai Uspensky's or Sleptsov's peasant stories.

An irritating moralizing tone gives some of the stories of this period a shrill quality. The vehicle of Tolstoi's moral message is a juxtaposition of "natural," therefore "good," and "unnatural" therefore "bad," individuals and actions. In "Two Hussars" (1856) two hussar officers, father and son, are put into similar situations. Count Turbin, a reckless gambler, bully, and ladies' man, but "natural," seduces a pretty young widow and leaves her with nothing worse than a blissful memory; his son, a "thinking man," bungles the seduction of her daughter, brags about a conquest that was not, and escapes a duel over it through the good offices of a Major Schultz (Tolstoi was never above using nasty little "significant details"—he would give Vronsky of *Anna Karenina* a Polish name along with a bald spot.) In "Three Deaths" (1859) the death of an educated young woman, a coachman, and a tree are juxtaposed. The gentlewoman dies badly, fighting death all the way; the coachman dies matter-of-factly, the tree gently.

In *The Cossacks* (1863) Olenin, a young Russian officer, essentially Tolstoi himself, spends some time in a Cossack village in the Caucasus, where he encounters a society that has not yet emerged from its heroic "natural" state. Uncle Erosha, one of Tolstoi's unforgettable characters, is a stalwart old Cossack who has become the village drunk but is still a great hunter, as well as teller of tales and a philosopher. He is cruel and tender, cunning and naive, a cynical agnostic and a pantheist. Erosha has killed often in his life, but he shoos away night butterflies to save them from flying into his campfire. He teaches Olenin what it means to live with nature and that to do so is bliss. At one point Olenin has a mystic epiphany when hunting in the steamy jungle. As swarms of mosquitoes descend on him, he suddenly feels his consciousness merging with that of the mosquito who is sucking his blood. As the tale draws to a close, Olenin gets orders to move on. The Cossack girl he was in love with will marry a brave young Cossack, and Uncle Erosha, with drunken tears, sobs that his world is coming to an end: the Cossacks, too, are becoming civilized. *The Cossacks* has some glorious landscapes, fascinating ethnographic detail, and a magnificent passage on the freedom of a Russian nobleman. Tolstoi's ideal of natural man has found a credible and attractive incarnation in Uncle Erosha. *The Cossacks* ought to be compared to Fenimore Cooper's Leatherstocking novels, which pursue the same end and create a similar impression. Tolstoi's novel is clearly superior to them in concreteness of detail, character delineation, and precision of language.

War and Peace grew out of one variant of a novel, *The Decembrists*, which Tolstoi started in 1856 and worked on intermittently until 1879, but never finished. There is a hint at the end of *War and Peace* that Pierre Bezukhov, its surviving hero, will become a Decembrist. Tolstoi started *War and Peace* in 1863 and finished it in 1869. The first two parts, under the title *1805*, appeared in *The Russian Herald* in 1865 and 1866. They were reworked substantially at least twice. The first version of the complete novel, entitled *All's Well That Ends Well*, differs from the definitive version in many details of plot. Petya Rostov and Duke Andrei Bolkonsky, for example, both of whom die in the definitive version, here survive. The plan and ethos of the novel also changed as Tolstoi rewrote it time and again. Conceived as a family novel with the thesis that familial, private concerns are at the bottom of what appear to be grand historical developments, it gradually became a historical epopoeia. What was initially an antiwar novel grew into a patriotic epic glorifying the spirit and fortitude of the Russian people. As a result of this change in perspective, Tolstoi's theoretical statements often contradict the practical message delivered in the narrative. Duke Andrei, who often expresses Tolstoi's views, bitterly denounces war and the military class, saying that its essence is "the absence of freedom called 'discipline,' idleness, ignorance, cruelty, debauchery, and drunkenness." But on the practical side, Tolstoi often shows the positive aspects of military life: camaraderie, good humor in adversity, courage, self-sacrifice, and sangfroid under fire. The characters of the heroes also changed. Field Marshal Kutuzov is quite negative in early variants; in the definitive version he is a symbol of wisdom and rectitude.

After the complete text appeared in 1869, it underwent a series of further changes. Reviews had found fault with the pervasive use of French and the philosophical digressions in the novel. Tolstoi threw out all of the digressions in the edition of 1873, converting a part of them into an appendix, but he brought them back in later editions. The so-called fifth edition, aimed at a broad reading public, eliminated the French dialogue altogether. As a result, it is almost impossible to agree on a canonical text of *War and Peace*.

War and Peace follows the fate of several aristocratic Russian families—the Rostovs, Bolkonskys, Drubetskois, and Kuragins[27]—from 1805 until about 1820 and introduces a spate of other characters, some of whom appear only briefly, never to return. The question of historical authenticity was raised immediately. Turgenev, although an admirer of *War and Peace*, felt that the picture of the epoch as painted by Tolstoi was false, if not falsified. He suggested that Tolstoi's "trick" was to create palpable, though imaginary, details of "little history," such as Napoleon taking a cologne bath before the battle of Borodino, that would convince the reader of his reliability as a reporter of major historical facts. The extent of Tolstoi's historical research was queried even by contemporaries and has been debated ever since.[28] Tolstoi himself, in a postscript, "A Few Words about *War and Peace*" (1868), denied that he had misrepresented or idealized the past and asserted that he had studied letters, diaries, and family traditions to create a historically correct picture of the epoch. This was quite true. It is also true, however, that Tolstoi used a limited number of historical sources, mostly Russian, official and patriotic, such as memoirs of Russian participants in the Napoleonic Wars and even the lowbrow historical novels of Rafail Zotov (1795–1871). He used the works of Louis Adolphe Thiers (1797–1877), a Bonapartiste historian, largely as a foil. Tolstoi's ideas in *War and Peace* had their sources in Proudhon's *La Guerre et la paix* (1861),[29] *Soirées de St. Petersbourg* of Joseph de Maistre (1753–1821),[30] the *Historical Aphorisms* (1836) of the Slavophile historian Mikhail Pogodin (1800–1875), and the writings and oral communications of Tolstoi's conservative aristocratic friends, in particular Duke S. S. Urusov (1827–97). Many of Tolstoi's

---

27. Tolstoi did not bother to invent his own names. Bolkonsky stands for Volkonsky, his mother's family, Drubetskoi for Trubetskoi, a prominent Russian family of the nobility, and so on.

28. P. I. Bartenev (1829–1912), a historian who was acquainted with the genesis of *War and Peace*, asserted that "Count Tolstoi has not studied the history of the great epoch at all."

29. Tolstoi had visited Proudhon in Brussels in 1861.

30. Joseph de Maistre had lived in Saint Petersburg as an émigré from 1803 to 1817.

observations have been traced to these sources. He owed to de Maistre much of his philosophy of war, specifically the idea that morale is decisive in the outcome of a war; to Urusov, a soldier and mathematician, the use of scientific metaphors (mass, momentum, velocity) in the discussion of military operations and the notion of a historical calculus; to Pogodin, the conception of historical events as elemental movements of nations.

All in all, *War and Peace* projects a patriotic, anti-French, and conservative position. Tolstoi underplays Napoleon's appeal to libertarian aristocratic circles. He minimizes the seriousness of peasant uprisings ahead of the advancing French. The campaign of 1812 is depicted as a popular patriotic war, which it was in a very limited sense. There is no mention of the cruel reprisals against real or alleged collaborators by Russian "partisan" detachments, as reported by Denis Davydov (who appears in the novel as Denisov). As Konstantin Leontyev was to point out, *War and Peace* was a work of huge political importance. It gave the educated Russian the reassuring image of a strong and unified nation. Russia at the height of serfage appears as a prosperous, stable, and on the whole happy society. Generations of Russians have seen and still see the Napoleonic age in terms of Tolstoi's biased view.

The philosophy of history was a much-discussed topic in the 1860s. Marx had as yet not reached Russia, but the theories of Hippolyte Taine (1828–93) and Thomas Buckle (1821–62) were well known. Tolstoi set out to discredit the notion that the causes of historical events could be determined and the direction of history predicted. This task was made difficult by Tolstoi's rejection of the theory that history is made by great men and by his firm opposition to a romantic cult of Napoleon. He ultimately arrived at a position that has been called historic nihilism, which rejects any causes or principles of historical evolution and puts in question the value of history as a scholarly discipline. Tolstoi concluded that no calculus of power, the mover of history, exists, although it might yet be found.

Whereas Tolstoi's philosophy of history is hardly synchronized with his narrative, his philosophy of life comes through strongly throughout the novel. It amounts to an amoral vitalism which rewards those characters who have a spontaneous and irrational love of life and punishes those who live self-conscious, rational, or theoretical lives. All the members of the Rostov family are natural people and Russian to the core. In young Natasha Rostova these qualities are raised to the level of a mystique.

In Tolstoi's later works peasant characters represent his ideal of the natural human being. In *War and Peace* they show up mostly in the background, with the exception of Platon Karataev, a soldier who with Pierre is held captive by the French. Karataev, a soldier for thirty years, has retained the meekness, good nature, and wisdom that Tolstoi would ascribe to his ideal of the peasant. Karataev tells Pierre a story whose point is that one should accept the good and the bad from God with equal gratitude, for it is all to the good in the end. It expresses the quietist philosophy that Tolstoi would embrace in the 1880s.

Opposed to "natural" man and his intuitive wisdom is the cleverness of "reflecting" man. One of Tolstoi's concerns in *War and Peace* is to demonstrate the futility, falsehood, and evil of such cleverness. Its main exponent is Napoleon. Tolstoi's favorite stylistic device, "making it strange," is used frequently to expose the rhetoric of clever people as bombast or deception. When Napoleon has made another of his strong and pithy statements, Tolstoi continues, "But he nevertheless immediately ran away again, abandoning to its fate the scattered fragments of the army he left behind." It is the word "ran away" (*ubezhal*) that strips the emperor of all his conventional majesty.

War and Peace is also a bildungsroman. Pierre merely grows up, remaining the same man—weak, well-intentioned but ineffectual, and enthusiastic without discretion. Duke Andrei undergoes a difficult evolution. He starts out as an ambitious man of action with a Napoleon complex, but his promising career is cut short by a bullet on the battlefield of Austerlitz. Lying flat on his back and seeing only the sky above him, he asks himself: "How didn't I see that high sky before? And how happy I am that I have finally found it." From here on, each new cycle in Duke Andrei's life is introduced by an epiphanic encounter with nature. The ruin of his ambitious dreams and the death of his young wife cause Duke Andrei to become discouraged and a skeptic. He is still young, however, and capable of a return to vigorous activity, this time in connection with the civic reforms of Alexander I. But he is soon disappointed in this venture. Here Tolstoi produces a clever put-down of Speransky, the engineer of these reforms and a commoner, by viewing him through the critical eyes of Volkonsky, an aristocrat. When Duke Andrei falls in love with Natasha Rostova, he experiences another surge of vitality. After her abortive elopement with the scoundrel Anatole Kuragin, he begins to resemble his father, an embittered, misanthropic eccentric. When the French invade Russia in 1812, Duke Andrei rejoins the army. On the battlefield of Borodino he has his last epiphany, an intense feeling of communion with nature. Mortally wounded,

he finds himself under Natasha's loving care. Before death ends his struggle between love of life and reflection, he catches a glimpse of a third possibility: love and compassion for his fellow human beings. In his dying moment he feels "as if powers till then confined within him had been liberated and a strange lightness would not leave him again." It has been pointed out that Duke Andrei and Pierre are projections of two complementary aspects of Tolstoi's own personality. The whole evolution of Duke Andrei, in particular its final stage, is not well motivated psychologically but is an expression of Tolstoi's intellectual searchings. Pierre is more of a psychological self-portrait. In Freudian terms, Pierre is the ego, Duke Andrei the superego.

Contemporary reviewers observed that *War and Peace* was "not a novel," and Western critics of the nineteenth-century counted it among the "baggy monsters" (in Henry James's phrase) so typical of Russian literature. Tolstoi himself was acutely aware of this.[31] There have been attempts to rescue *War and Peace* even in conventional terms. Its open structure is of course that of life itself. The much-maligned digressions are a legitimate novelistic trait. Although the plot is largely open-ended, various devices give it an inner cohesion: such contrasts as good families versus bad families, good versus bad people (the good are rewarded and the bad punished); fateful chains of coincidences (Natasha's marriage to Duke Andrei fails so that her brother Nicholas can marry Duchess Mary); leitmotifs (whenever Dolokhov, a fascinating and depraved char-

---

31. "What is *War and Peace*? It is not a novel, even less is it a *poema*, and still less a historical chronicle. *War and Peace* is what the author wished and was able to express in the form in which it is expressed." L. N. Tolstoi, "Some Words about *War and Peace*," 1868.

acter unrelated to any of the novel's families, appears, the life and happiness of one of the main characters are in grave danger); and a basic mood of fondness for family values and scorn for the blandishments of high society.

War and Peace has strong epic traits, though it also debunks some of the foundations of the epic (the role of divine intervention, of heroic leaders, of fate). "Space is the lord of War and Peace," said E. M. Forster, not time. Like the *Iliad* or the *Divine Comedy*, *War and Peace* produces a panoramic view of a whole country and of a historical era. Its patriotic attitude, its grateful acceptance of a way of life in its totality, and its loving description of feasts, balls, hunting parties, and battles are epic. The unmotivated introduction of large numbers of characters who never return is epic, and so is the introduction of different levels of action, from the Olympian heights of royalty, to the war council of generals, and down to the battlefield where soldiers fight and die. Tolstoi's ample use of metonymic labels and other significant details may be also considered epic. Kutuzov's flabby cheeks; the short, downy upper lip of Lise, Duke Andrei's wife; Duchess Mary's heavy gait and luminous eyes; Dolokhov's insolent blue eyes; Denisov's uvular *r*'s; Speransky's white hands, "like those of a soldier who has spent a long time in the hospital"—all these act as vehicles of characterization, but also as mnemonic devices. *War and Peace* is rich in Homeric similes. Moscow abandoned by its people is compared to a queenless beehive, and a lengthy description of such a hive follows. The movements of the Russian and French armies during the French retreat from Moscow are likened to a game of blindman's buff, which is then described in detail.

War and Peace is written in a style of its own, even within Tolstoi's own oeuvre.

There is little historical stylization. Its epic narrator takes his time, making sure that nothing remains unsaid, and expects the reader to read slowly and attentively. Not only the theoretical digressions feature long and involved periods. The general impression is one of ponderous power, for every phrase, every embedded subordinate clause, has a genuine meaning and is important. By leaving nothing unsaid, he forces readers to adopt his view of things.

War and Peace was very successful with the public but was not immediately accepted by the critics. Nikolai Strakhov, a pochvennik, was the only critic to give it a wholeheartedly enthusiastic review. The left recognized the novel's conservative message. Nikolai Shelgunov (1824–91), a populist, called it "an apology of well-fed gentility, hypocrisy, bigotry, and depravity." Pisarev's review, entitled "Old-fashioned Gentry" (*Staroe barstvo*), was almost as hostile. The right resented Tolstoi's satirical presentation of high society and his antimilitarist sorties (a General Dragomirov wrote a rebuttal). But within a few years these voices fell silent and *War and Peace* was recognized by all as a national epic.

Anna Karenina is closer to being a typical nineteenth-century novel than is *War and Peace*. Like other novels of its age, it brings up, often explicitly, a variety of topical issues, such as the crisis in Russian agriculture after the emancipation, the decline of the landed gentry, the emergence of a new class of bourgeois entrepreneurs, and of course the "woman question." Before starting *Anna Karenina*, Tolstoi did some serious work toward a historical novel set in the age of Peter the Great. He abandoned the project after he discovered that the historical Peter the Great was a moral monster. The conception of a historical epoch in which a society has lost its bearings as a new order is born was carried over into *Anna Karenina*. Early versions suggest a narrower and more explicit roman à thèse.[32] Anna is less attractive, and her adulterous liaison appears in a context of nihilist ideology. By the time Tolstoi began publishing his novel, nihilism had lost its topical interest. It appears on the fringes of the plot, in an episode that has Lyovin's brother Nikolai, a nihilist, die of consumption, a broken man who has wasted his life.

Anna Karenina remained a roman à thèse, but with a much broader message. A title that Tolstoi considered at one time, "Two Families," describes its structure and its meaning. The two families, one "good," the other "bad," are connected by marriage. The Shcherbatskys are a good Moscow family. Their daughter Dolly, a faithful wife and good mother, is married to Duke Stepan ("Stiva") Oblonsky, a good-natured and charming spendthrift and philanderer. Stiva's sister Anna, a spirited woman of rare beauty, is married to Aleksei Karenin, a high-ranking government official in Saint Petersburg who is much older than her. Kitty, Dolly's sister, marries Konstantin Lyovin, a country squire and close self-portrait of Tolstoi, but not before having been disappointed in her love for Count Aleksei Vronsky, a brilliant guardsman. Vronsky, who was expected to propose marriage to Kitty, instead falls in love with Anna, pursues her, and eventually becomes her lover. After many peripeties Anna, who has lived with Vronsky and has born him a child, throws herself under a train. Vronsky, his career dashed and his spirit broken, goes off to war in the Balkans as a volunteer. Karenin's career, too, has come to a stop,

and he will live out a meaningless life. Stiva, his and his wife's fortunes exhausted, will nevertheless survive as he adapts to the new capitalist order. His name and title will be worth something on the board of a railway company. Lyovin and Kitty are a happy married couple, although everything is not well with Lyovin's inner life. Unlike *War and Peace, Anna Karenina* is a closed novel. An experienced reader realizes that Anna is marked for a fall even as she arrives, all serene virtue, at her brother's house to save his marriage after Dolly has discovered yet another infidelity of his.

Anna Karenina is an attempt to create a world in which a moral order is still present. The epigraph, "Vengeance belongeth unto me, I will recompense, saith the Lord" (Hebrews 10:30), suggests this much. Much as in *War and Peace*, the characters of *Anna Karenina* live "natural" or "unnatural" lives. Kitty is almost wholly natural, Vronsky almost wholly unnatural. Lyovin and Anna are engaged in a struggle to maintain their natural selves against a steady onslaught of unnatural forces. Lyovin is able to maintain a precarious balance to the end. Anna, however, perishes. Her first unnatural act, leaving her son to be with her lover, leads to a long string of other unnatural actions: practicing birth control to remain attractive to her lover, smoking cigarettes, using drugs, and finally committing suicide. Tolstoi injects a rather heavy-handed moral argument into his text by planting a host of significant details. He lets Anna neglect the child she bears Vronsky. He mentions that Vronsky's yardman respects his own (lawful) wife more than Anna, his master's gracious mistress. Tolstoi also introduces a wealth of details by which he seeks to discredit capitalism, industrialization, science (the social sciences in particular), railroads, and even modern music. The railroad plays an

32. There is evidence that Tolstoi may have found the seed of *Anna Karenina* in a fragment by Pushkin that delineates the plot of a novel about a society lady's adulterous love affair.

ominous role throughout the novel. Petersburg high society is depicted as effete, vacuous, and depraved. The efforts of westernizing liberals (Vronsky is one of them) are belittled. Local elections appear to the old-fashioned country squire Lyovin as an absurd exercise in futility. Country life, on the other hand, is presented with love and sympathy. A masterful description of Lyovin mowing hay with his laborers is one of the highlights of the novel.

In spite of its pervasive negativism, *Anna Karenina* conveys a sense of epic gladness, plenitude, and vitality. The Russia of this novel is still a good country to live in. Although Tolstoi heartily disapproves of sumptuous meals, elegant balls, exciting horse races, and the whole life-style of his social class, he still describes them with gusto. Almost all of the characters come off as nice people, and the peasants and servants who appear on the fringes of the narrative seem happy enough. Considering that Russia in the 1870s was in the throes of appalling social and economic difficulties, it is understandable that critics found the novel artistically admirable but socially wrongheaded. Many readers asked why Anna was singled out for such cruel punishment, whereas the secret infidelities of other society matrons, not to mention those of her brother and other men, went unpunished. When asked about the moral message of *Anna Karenina*, Tolstoi aptly responded that the answer was contained in the whole text of his work and could not be abstracted from it.

Anna Karenina has a strain of symbolism embedded in its realist texture. A string of symbolic details punctuates the tragic plot. Early in the novel Vronsky rides in a steeple chase, with all of elegant Petersburg, including the tsar, in attendance. He is leading the race on Frou-Frou, his beautiful thoroughbred mare, when a false move on the last jump causes him to fall, breaking his horse's back, as Anna watches in horror. In an early version the horse's name was Tiny (Vronsky was an Anglophile), and Anna was still Tanya. Even without such an obvious hint, the effect of symbolic foreshadowing will hardly be missed by the reader. The same is true of several other details, including some terrifying symbolic dreams. In fact, such use of symbolic detail was pointed out as a violation of realism by some contemporary critics.

Leskov

Nikolai Semyonovich Leskov (1831–95) lost his father, a minor government official, early in life, had to quit school at fifteen, and went to work as a clerk in the criminal court of his hometown, Orel, in 1847. In 1849 he was transferred to Kiev, where he served as an army recruiting agent and audited some courses at the university. In Kiev Leskov made Polish and Ukrainian friends and learned to speak both languages, which he would later use (especially Ukrainian) in his fiction. In 1857 he resigned from the government service and went to work for an uncle who managed the estates of some large landowners. Leskov assisted in the resettlement of peasant families from central Russia to the eastern provinces and became intimately acquainted with peasant life. The reports he sent back to his uncle found their way into the press. In 1860 Leskov began to publish his sketches and articles on peasant life regularly, and in 1861 he moved to Petersburg to devote himself entirely to literature. As a publicist, Leskov combined a sincere concern for the social underdog with a sense of the possible and a suspicion of utopian or revolutionary schemes. Some of his pieces aroused the ire of the radicals, and soon Leskov found himself in the antinihilist camp. *No Way Out*, his first novel, appeared under a pseudonym in *The Reading Library* in 1864. It was successful with the public and went through several editions as a separate book. A roman à clef, it was bitterly resented by the individuals and groups who recognized themselves in Leskov's caricatures. A literary busybody named the Marquise de Baral is an uncomplimentary portrait of Countess Salhias de Tournemir, alias Evgeniya Tur. Vasily Sleptsov and his commune appear as a character named Beloyartsev and his *domus concordiae*. An unplesant character named Zavulonov, whose "small gray hands and wrinkled gray face gave him a certain unwashably dirty and repulsive look, as if inner dirt were coming out through the pores of his skin," is Aleksandr Levitov. An antinihilist novel first and foremost, *No Way Out* also takes stabs at the Polish resistance movement, scheming Jesuits, and the threat of a "Jewish takeover." Leskov himself appears as Doctor Rozanov, a decent and sensible man whose painful separation from a shallow and hysterical wife was in part a projection of the author's own experience. The "woman question" and the theme of unhappy marriage dominate the plot of this long novel. Its heroine, Liza Bakhareva, an idealistic and enterprising young woman, perishes senselessly, a victim of the turmoil, perverse ideas, and false hopes of her generation.

No Way Out is a typical roman-feuilleton, loosely structured, with many essayistic digressions, literary quotes and allusions, chatty apostrophes to the reader, grotesque satirical vignettes, anecdotes, and curiosities. Some of the dialogue is in Ukrainian and even in Polish. The psychology is superficial, and Leskov's attempts at revealing the inner life of his characters are awkward.

Leskov's later novels of the 1860s were also antinihilist. *Those Passed Over* (1865), in which he explicitly takes on Chernyshevsky's *What Is to Be Done?*, and *At Daggers Drawn* (1870–71), an even sharper attack on the Russian "progressives" than *No Way Out*, are diffuse and feuilletonistic but have merit in some particular details and characters.

Leskov's genius was unsuited to the staged roman à thèse in which Turgenev and Dostoevsky excelled. He was a natural storyteller whose imagination was syntagmatic (focusing on the story line) rather than paradigmatic (focusing on the structure and meaning of the whole). The art of integrating an ideological argument, an allegorical meaning, or metaphysical symbolism into a story line was beyond him. But he had his own assets, which were huge. He was never at a loss for a good story. He controlled a wider range of social types than any of his rivals: peasants, artisans, merchants, clerks, soldiers, priests, students, landowners—he knew them all and could reproduce their language authentically. He was a master of narrative impersonation, known as *skaz*. The author of those flabby, disorganized, and incoherent novels was publishing simultaneously some of the liveliest, most colorful, and most exciting stories in all of Russian literature. Leskov the political novelist was visibly trying too hard to be witty, clever, and profound, but he never found a proper voice for his narrative. Leskov the storyteller would create a narrative voice and let the story speak for itself. "Lady Macbeth of Mtsensk District" (1865), the lurid melodrama of Katerina Izmailova, a staid merchant's beautiful and sex-starved wife, who drifts from adultery to murder and to her own violent end, is credible precisely because Leskov has given it a personalized narrator, a semieducated local official or landowner.[33]

In the 1870s Leskov created his best-known longer works, *Cathedral Folk* (1872), *The Enchanted Pilgrim* (1873), and *The Sealed Angel* (1873). Religion is an important ingredient in all three. Leskov took a lively interest in religious life: even in *No Way Out* some of the best scenes are set in a nunnery. *Cathedral Folk* tells the story of Father Savely Tuberozov, a strong and righteous priest, and his ceaseless troubles with his ecclesiastical superiors and secular authorities. Tuberozov's deacon, Akhilla Desnitsyn, a bear of a man with the mind of a child and a gentle heart to match, provides some warm comedy. In Father Tuberozov Leskov succeeded in creating a beautiful character who is also entirely credible, letting his hero, a loser on every worldly count, be the glorious victor in spirit, whose "vita has begun as his life is coming to an end." Dostoevsky's admiration for this character was well placed. Father Tuberozov has his failings but is pure of heart and generous of spirit. He is no ignoramus and nobody's fool. His faith is firm and profound. But there is a melancholy air of anachronism about him. The world around him refuses to see why the skeleton that the local freethinker, a schoolmaster, has hanging in his study should get a Christian burial, as Father Tuberozov insists. *Cathedral Folk* is presented as a chronicle, with pages from Father Tuberozov's diary and various anecdotes in skaz thrown in. The whole is entertaining, funny, moving, and wholesomely sentimental.

The Enchanted Pilgrim is a picaresque novel narrated by the hero, Ivan Flyagin.

33. The story was made into an opera by Dmitry Shostakovich (1934).

The Russia of Flyagin's adventures is a land of opportunity. Born a serf, Flyagin is not downtrodden, but reckless and exuberant: he will do anything on a dare. He is the epitome of the Russian folk hero who can dish it out with the best, but who can also take an incredible amount of punishment. He gets into a flogging match with a Tatar: the combatants sit on the ground, face to face, and each flails away with a whip at the other's bare back until one gives up. Flyagin wins. Flyagin himself does not know what really moves him, but he has a fatalistic sense that whatever he did was ordained and that he could not help it. In the end he finds peace in a monastery. *The Enchanted Pilgrim* has captured the penchant for reckless daring inherent in the ethos of Russian folk culture that is not often reflected in Russian literature.

The Sealed Angel is a charming story about the tribulations of an Old Believer community whose cherished icon has been confiscated and sealed by the authorities. They finally succeed in retrieving it by guile and trickery. Built into the story is the harrowing message that millions of Russia's most capable and industrious citizens are placed into an adversary relation to the state on account of what are really minor differences in religious ritual.

Leskov's lifelong attraction to religion had a dual effect. His disapproval of the mindless ritualism of the state church led to some satirical tales, such as "The Unbaptized Priest" (1877). His belief in the moral beneficence of true religion, enhanced by his conversion to Tolstoianism in the 1880s, caused him to write a cycle of moral tales based on saints' lives of the Orthodox Synaxary (*Prolog*), rather in the manner of Tolstoi's tales for the people. Like Tolstoi, Leskov late in life developed a pessimistic view of contemporary Russian society. His late stories, though still vibrant and powerful, lack the mellow light that brightens the subdued melancholy of his earlier works.

Leskov's short stories cover an amazing variety of milieus, characters, and situations, past and present. Usually they are told by a personalized narrator whose idiosyncratic speech enhances the story's distinctive atmosphere. In "The Battle-Ax" (1866) a "respectable" procuress pours out her heart about the thanklessness of the women as whose selfless benefactor she presents herself. The trick is to let her tell it in her own language. "The Rabbit Warren" (written 1891–95, published 1917) is Leskov's last tour de force of stylization. Its mad narrator's language is a jumble of officialese, Ukrainian, Slavonic, and just plain lunacy. A former rural policeman, he tells the story of his frantic efforts to earn a commendation by catching a dangerous nihilist, each ending in an absurd *qui pro quo*. Leskov's most famous tale, "Lefty, or a Tale about a One-eyed Left-hander of Tula and a Steel Flea" (1881), offers an example of Leskov's virtuosic stylization. It is about a master craftsman who outdoes the feat of British artisans, who have made a life-size steel flea, by shoeing the British flea with golden shoes. The ragged bravado and superb skill of the left-handed craftsman are mirrored in the virtuosically stylized narrative, done in the manner of a chapbook folktale and with a dazzling array of clever malapropisms.

Leskov's career was not nearly as spectacular as his talent should have warranted. He alienated the left early in his life, and later broke with the right as well by withdrawing his novel *A Decrepit Clan* (1874) from *The Russian Herald* when Katkov, the editor, made some unauthorized changes in the text. His critical attitude toward the

Orthodox church did not help. Nor was Leskov's posthumous fame equal to his achievement. As Tolstoi observed, Leskov's mannerist form, which foregrounded fortuitous details of language, gave his works an ephemeral quality, "so that people no longer read him." The effect of much of Leskov's work is based on local color, another trait that made it age fast. There still remains the wealth of his invention, the great variety of his characters, and that certain élan which animates all of his stories. Leskov's art is in many ways similar to that of Faulkner. His greatness stems from the genius of the language he so completely mastered, which is, unfortunately, untranslatable.

The interest in folkways and folk culture which developed in the romantic period caused many educated Russians to become collectors of folklore, folk art, folk music, and ethnographic material. Their contributions were published not only in scholarly periodicals but also in the "thick journals" of the capitals, as well as in provincial periodicals, official and private. In many instances collectors would move on to using their material in fiction. Dahl, Reshetnikov, Levitov, Sleptsov, Leskov, and others started their literary careers in this fashion. Much as the romantic period had produced the folkloric novel, the age of realism produced the ethnographic novel. Pavel Melnikov (1818–83), who wrote under the pseudonym Andrei Pechersky, was by far its finest exponent. Melnikov came from the gentry of Nizhny Novgorod Province and graduated from Kazan University in the humanities in 1837. He worked as a schoolteacher and journalist in Nizhny Novgorod, where he also published historical, statistical, and ethnographic material. From 1847 to 1866 he served as an official for special projects in that region, concentrating on matters pertaining to Old Believer communities and their suppression. He then retired to his country estate and devoted himself to his literary work. Melnikov published occasional sketches and short stories after 1839, always about life in his home region. He used the same material in his great epic novels, *In the Woods* (1871–74) and *In the Hills* (1875–81), the best examples of the Russian ethnographic novel. His most memorable character is the peasant Chapurin, a capable and resourceful man, who, with the help of some breaks that come his way, gets rich without abandoning his old ways. Melnikov's message is that Russia's future rests with the industrious and enterprising merchant class.

Both novels have gorgeous panoramic landscape descriptions of the region between the Volga and the Urals and ample ethnological flashbacks explaining its present condition. The former population, Finns and Chuvash, would not cut down any of the forest. To the advancing Russians, the forest was "like an enemy": they used it and cut it down ruthlessly. Other flashbacks reach to the age of Ivan the Terrible, to the beginnings of the Old Believer communities, and even to pre-Christian times. Melnikov describes the people of the region—their trades and businesses, holidays and feasts, customs, meals and garb—in meticulous ethnographic detail. The Old Believer communities of the region get a great deal of attention. The basic tone of the novels is optimistic. The people of the region beyond the Volga are hardworking and enterprising, and by and large they live well. There is plenty of superstition and bigotry in their lives, but they are not a dominant trait. Melnikov's command of local peasant speech and his fondness for the ethos of the people are obvious. His novels make for interesting and informative reading while staying well within the framework of a realist novel.

The historical novel continued strong throughout the period, but for the time being it sank from the forefront of serious literature to the level of entertainment, a development that also involved the historical novels of the romantic age. The novels of Walter Scott, Zagoskin's *Yury Miloslavsky*, and Pushkin's *The Captain's Daughter* were still read, but now mostly by adolescents. In the Silver Age, at the turn of the century, the historical novel would again attract the attention of writers at the cutting edge of creative literary endeavor. Among the major writers of the period, Tolstoi and Pisemsky did serious historical research toward some of their works. *War and Peace* and *The Masons*, however, may be called historical novels only marginally, for they relate to an era still in living memory.

Aleksei Tolstoi started his historical novel *Duke Serebryany* as early as 1840. When it appeared in 1862 it was something of an anachronism, but it soon became an immensely popular book for young readers. It helped perpetuate the myth of Ivan the Terrible as a cruel and willful, but generous and mighty, ruler, who laid the cornerstone to Russia's greatness. Grigory Danilevsky (1829–90), a high-ranking government official, turned to the historical novel late in life. He wrote poetry and prose in Ukrainian after 1846, and in the 1860s published several novels from peasant life in Russian. But he gained real fame only with his historical novels, among them *Mirovich* (1879), *Duchess Tarakanova* (1883), and *Moscow Destroyed by Fire* (1886). These novels were based on solid historical research. They paint a vivid picture of the past and are very readable. Count Evgeny Salhias de Tournemir (1840–1908), the son of the writer Evgeniya Tur, was expelled from Moscow University in 1861 for participating in a student demonstration. From 1862 to 1869 he lived abroad, mostly in Spain, and published a Spanish travelogue (1864). He launched a series of successful historical novels with *Pugachov's Men* (1874). His novels, set in various periods and places, are entertaining, use colorful language, and are well told, but they are also rather superficial, and their historical veracity is marginal. Vsevolod Solovyov (1849–1903), son of the historian Sergei Solovyov and brother of the philosopher Vladimir Solovyov, was a more serious writer. A conservative, he also wrote contemporary novels with a political tendency, the Dostoevskian *Temptation* (1879), the anti-Tolstoian *Evil Whirlwinds* (1893), and the anti-Nietzschean *Flowers of the Abyss* (1895). His historical novels, *Duchess Ostrozhsky* (1876), *The Young Emperor* (1877), *The Virgin Tsar* (1878), and a series of novels featuring the history of a noble family, the Gorbatovs, in the eighteenth and early nineteenth centuries are strong on historical and ethnographic detail and have lively plots.

Women Writers

The concern of educated Russian society with the "woman question," women's improved though still woefully inadequate access to education, and the active role played by women in the revolutionary movement provided fertile ground for the emergence of women writers. It is impossible to say anything about women writers collectively because they formed no groups, had no contact with each other except by chance, were not organzied in any way, and belonged to the literary profession as indi-

viduals, not as representatives of their sex. The failure of the period to produce a great woman writer may be considered an accident, for the number of women in literature was now significant and several women were among the more successful writers of the period.

Evgeniya Salhias de Tournemir (1815–92), who wrote under the pen name Evgeniya Tur, came from an aristocratic family and received a superlative education in Russia and France. Professors Nadezhdin and Pogodin tutored her in the Russian language and in history. Her early stories, published in *The Contemporary*, earned her the praise of Turgenev, Ostrovsky, and Grigoryev. *A Mistake* (1849) is a society tale. Aleksandr Mikhailovich Slavin, the hero, has for many years sought his family's permission to marry Olga Nikolaevna, a young lady of modest circumstances. When he finally gets it, various chance events delay their wedding, and Slavin realizes to his dismay that he has fallen out of love. He becomes infatuated with the glamorous but cold Duchess Gorskina and marries her, leaving Olga heartbroken but resigned to her fate. The dialogue of *A Mistake* is quite unrealistic, but the psychology is subtle and credible. *A Niece* (1850) has the same qualities. Tur's novel *On the Boundary* (1859) is more ambitious. A beautiful young widow, Tatyana Ilyinishna Istomina, returns from abroad to take over her huge country estate. She develops a friendship with a young country doctor, Fyodor Pavlovich, as they work together fighting a cholera epidemic. Fyodor Pavlovich is expected to become engaged to Yuliya Ivanovna, daughter of Madame Istomina's steward, but he falls in love with Tatyana Ilyinishna, and she responds. When news of their romance reaches her mother and family, they use every kind of pressure, including threats of violence against Fyodor Pavlovich, to prevent the mésalliance. They succeed. Fyodor Pavlovich, resigned to his fate, says farewell to Yuliya and leaves for the Caucasus, hoping to forget her. *On the Boundary*, still a society tale, carries a strong anti–high society message. Again the dialogue is awkward but the psychology convincing. This novel and some other later works were less successful than Tur's early stories. Subsequently she was active mostly as an essayist and critic. She wrote competent reviews of works by Turgenev, Dostoevsky, Tolstoi, and other Russian writers, as well as of foreign literature. She also wrote books for children.

Nadezhda Sokhanskaya (1823 or 1825–84) wrote under the pen name Kokhanovskaya. The daughter of a country squire in Kharkov Province in the Ukraine, Sokhanskaya wrote numerous stories and plays about provincial life in her home region, some contemporary and some set in the age of Catherine the Great. Her first story appeared in 1844. In 1850 she began to contribute to *The Contemporary*. Such stories as "Visiting after Dinner" (1858), "Kirilla Petrov and Nastasya Dmitrova" (1862), "Encounter in the Distant Past" (1862), and "Old Times" (1862) show her as an expert at describing folk customs and folk traditions. She also has perfect command of her subjects' speech. Her world is that of a middling country squire and her ethos the conservative one of Aksakov's *Family Chronicle*. Her ideal of womanhood was old-fashioned: a woman realized herself in motherhood and in devotion to her husband, virtue, and modesty. After 1863 Sokhanskaya published mostly in Slavophile periodicals.

Marya Aleksandrovna Vilinskaya-Markovich (1834–1907), who published under the pseudonym Marko Vovchok, came from a family of Russian landowners and was educated at a Kharkov boarding school. In 1851 she married A. V. Markovich, a Ukrainian folklorist and ethnographer, and traveled with him in the Ukraine, gathering ethnographic material and studying folk traditions. In 1857 she published a volume of Ukrainian tales, whose Russian translation by Turgenev appeared in 1859. Subsequently she published in both Russian and Ukrainian. Vilinskaya-Markovich lived abroad from 1859 to 1867, associating with Russian and foreign writers (Turgenev, Herzen, Flaubert) as well as with Polish émigrés. Between 1866 and 1871 she published a number of folktales and stories in French in the Parisian journal *Magasin d'éducation et de récréation*. After her return to Russia, Markovich published a series of novels and stories in *The National Annals*. "A Living Soul" (1869), "Marusya" (1871), "A Snug Little Nest" (1873), and other works were all strongly progressive.

Marko Vovchok's stories were hailed by Dobrolyubov and other radical critics as a truthful expression of the sentiments and aspirations of the Russian people and a vigorous indictment of the landed gentry. Less biased critics saw them for what they were—projections of a progressive intellectual's idealized image of the people into melodramatic plots of considerable appeal to unsophisticated readers.

Marko Vovchok creates a synthetic narrative voice belonging to a Ukrainian woman of the people who tells her story in literary Russian, but with a pointedly simple syntax and occasional Ukrainianisms. Whenever a cast of landowner's and peasants appears, the peasants are positive, the landowners (in particular their women) negative. In "The Girl from Finishing School" (1860) a serf relates how her life was ruined when her man was sent away to serve in the army by her spoiled, stupid, and ill-tempered mistress. In "A Worthless Woman" (1861) Nastya, a young serf, takes to drink and to irresponsible behavior because she cannot stand not being free. When papers certifying that she is indeed a free woman finally come through, it is too late. She dies soon afterward "free, but a drunk, a worthless woman." Marko Vovchok's synthetically "artless" style is particularly distinctive when her female narrator tells a story whose hero is male, as in "A Dangerous Man" (1861). Marko Vovchok's narrative manner found imitators, male and female.

Russia had the equivalent of the three Brontë sisters in the three Khvoshchinskaya sisters, Nadezhda, Sofya, and Praskovya. They were the daughters of a provincial government official who was dismissed from the service on a charge of embezzlement of public funds. It took him ten years to clear his name, and his family sank into deep poverty. The girls became writers as a way to relieve the family's poverty. Praskovya (1832–1916), the youngest, who used the pen name Ivan Vesenyev, was the least significant of the three. Sofya (1828–65), who published under the pseudonym S. Zimarova, early made a name for herself and after 1857 published in *The National Annals, The Reading Library*, and other periodicals. Her themes were the degeneracy of the gentry, the plight of the peasantry, and the hypocrisy of progressive liberals. Her short novel *Zernovsky* (1859) and her novels *Town and Country* (1863), *A Domestic Idyll of the Recent Past* (1863), and *A Strange Man* (1861) mainly expose the pettiness and meaninglessness of the life of the educated gentry. They are strong in descriptive detail, have absorbing plots, and occasionally project great intensity of emotion. Sofya Khvoshchinskaya also wrote articles on the "woman question" and other topical issues.

Nadezhda Khvoshchinskaya (1824–89) made a living as a writer all her life. She published her first poems in 1847 and continued to write mostly poetry into the early 1850s, all under her own name. In 1850 she published her first prose work, the short novel *Anna Mikhailovna*, under the pseudonym V. Krestovsky. Later, when Vladimir Krestovsky entered Russian literature, she signed her works "V. Krestovsky—pseudonym." A prolific writer, she published many novels and stories, mostly in *The Contemporary* and *The National Annals*, whose editors were eager to print her contributions, even though Saltykov once observed that she kept writing the same novel over and over again. Khvoshchinskaya's main themes are the "new man" and the "new woman" in revolt against the stifling and unjust old social order, the plight of an educated woman in the provinces, the unfair preference that parents, and mothers in particular, give their sons over their daughters, and the contemptible type of the idle and depraved gentleman parasite. Khvoshchinskaya's prose has immediacy and intensity. She is never at a loss for a plot, though it becomes predictable after one has read a few of her works. Her characters are stereotypes, but the narrator's strong feelings toward them breathe life into them. In "Kid Brother" (1858) a widowed mother and her daughters are at the mercy of Seryozha, the only male in the family, a selfish, spoiled, and utterly worthless young man. They skimp and scrounge so that he can indulge his vanity. The girls give up their dowries and resign themselves to spinsterhood so he can pay his debts, only to be told how grateful they have to be to him for enriching their lives.

In "The Schoolgirl" (1860) Olenka, the heroine, meets Veretitsyn, one of the "new men," who has been exiled to her provincial town. He opens her eyes to the mindlessness of the education she is getting and the stifling narrowness of her family. She leaves for Petersburg and becomes a free-lance writer and artist. There she meets Veretitsyn by accident, and he tells her that her triumph of independence and a satisfying personal life is still less admirable than the work of those women who devote themselves to bringing up a new generation of better human beings. In *Ursa Major* (1871), Khvoshchinskaya's most successful novel, Katya Bagryanskaya recovers from an unhappy love affair with an unworthy married man and becomes a tireless worker for the people, "living like a peasant woman" and teaching children and even adults.

Khvoshchinskaya's perennial villain is the elegant young gentleman who, rotten to the core, secures himself a life of ease and privilege by nepotism, connections, clever play on class prejudice, favoritism, and the weakness of older aristocratic women for his refined manners and good looks. In the short novel *Early Struggles* (1869) she lets Serge, the hero, tell his own story. The son of a hardworking and kind raznochinets, he is brought up and thoroughly spoiled in a rich family as a foster child. He becomes a vain, self-centered, and lazy youth who shamelessly uses everybody, but especially women, around him—and succeeds, because he is handsome, has good manners, and speaks the best French in town. "The Schoolteacher" (1879–80) once more combines Khvoshchinskaya's basic heroine and basic villain. Zinaida Nikolaevna, a young woman who has overcome many hardships in her life, is a dedicated and successful teacher at a rural school. It so happens that a lady who knows the local squire needs to place her good-for-nothing son in a job that would render him exempt from military service (it is the time of the Russo-Turkish War of 1877–78). Young Boris, who has neither the training nor the desire to be a good teacher, gets the job, and Zinaida Nikolaevna is let go. The new teacher's first step will be to get rid of all the girls in school, as he does not believe in education for women. Khvoshchinskaya's many novels and stories follow essentially the same pattern. Almost invariably they reflect anger, bitterness, and outrage at what were no doubt real injustices. The social types presented by her are real, too. All in all, Khvoshchinskaya is not that far removed from the Chekhov of the 1880s.

Avdotya Panaeva-Golovachova (1820–93) was a full-time staff member of *The Contemporary* from 1848 to 1864 and was in charge of its fashion section. Her many stories and novels all deal with the plight of women in contemporary Russian society: "A Careless Word" (1848), "A Monster of a Husband" (1848), "The Watchmaker's Wife" (1849), "An Inadvertent Step" (1850), "Life's Trivia" (1854), "Domestic Hell" (1857). Panaeva's most important novel, *A Woman's Lot* (1862), reflects Chernyshevsky's ideas and introduces "new" men and women. Panaeva's *Memoirs*, published in *The Historical Herald* in 1889, contain a great deal of valuable material on the many literary figures she knew, but it has some inaccuracies of fact.

Drama

Russian drama could not match the successes of prose fiction, or even of poetry. Whereas several major novelists were active during the period, the theater had a single mainstay in Ostrovsky. Several of the major prose writers and poets of the period also wrote some plays—Grigoryev, Turgenev, Pisemsky, Aleksei and Lev Tolstoi, for example—but their main interest was not in the theater. Dostoevsky, all of whose novels have been staged successfully, did not leave a single play. The continued dearth of good Russian drama was caused in part by censorship, which was more severe for the stage than for the printed word, and perhaps also by the greater and more immediate financial reward brought by placing a novel in a major journal than by having a play accepted for staging.

Still relying to a considerable extent on a foreign repertoire, the Russian stage continued to flourish and to grow, both in the capitals and in the provinces. Its financial viability continued to depend on light entertainment, particularly the operettas of Strauss and Offenbach, which superseded the French vaudeville that had dominated the first half of the century.

Ivan Turgenev wrote a number of plays early in his career but, perhaps regrettably, decided that the theater was not his métier. Actually, his plays were ahead of the times in that they were based on atmosphere, mood, and character instead of on plot or even conflict. Their dialogue does not aim at immediate audience response and is rather understated. Much as Turgenev's stories of *A Hunter's Sketches* anticipated the Chekhovian slice-of-life short story, Turgenev's plays, and most of all his comedy *A Month in the Country* (1850, published 1855), anticipated Chekhov's theater. *Impecuniousness* (1846), *Brunch at the Marshal's* (staged 1849, published 1856), *The Bachelor* (1849), and *The House Guest* (1848, published 1857) are short plays, each the equivalent of a short story in the manner of the natural school. *Conversation on the*

Highway (1851) is a strange, almost surrealist one-acter which bears a resemblance to Beckett's *Waiting for Godot*. *The Provincial Lady* (1851) is a spirited short comedy in which the wife of a provincial underling uses her charms on a visiting dignitary from the capital to advance her husband's career. It has been a bravura role for mature Russian actresses for a long time now. *A Month in the Country*, a full-length comedy, is amazingly Chekhovian, though without Chekhov's melancholy nuances and without Chekhov's symbolic devices. It is a play with a pointedly aborted plot of tentative desires, latent passion, and ineffectual self-expression.

Of all the major prose writers of the period, Pisemsky was the most active and most successful as a playwright. His first play, *The Hypochondriac*, appeared in *The Muscovite* in 1852. *A Hard Lot* (1860), a drama in four acts, is one of the best Russian plays. Its plot is simple. The peasant Anany Yakovlev returns from Petersburg after a year's absence and learns that his wife Lizaveta has become the landowner Cheglov's mistress and has born him a child. Lizaveta loves the young landowner and has never loved Anany, who is thirty-six and to whom she was married against her will. Anany is willing to forgive her if she will join him in Petersburg with her child to get away from the dishonor in their home village. Cheglov loves her, too, and is willing to make any financial amends to Anany if he will leave him Lizaveta. But Anany, feeling that he is legally and morally in the right, refuses to listen to his pleas. The conflict is thus between one man's honor and another man's love. It is resolved when Anany kills Lizaveta's child. He refuses to give any explanation for his crime, even when assured that it would earn him "mitigating circumstances." He takes leave of the community, asking everybody's forgiveness, and is removed to face trial and deportation to Siberia. Cheglov is not present at these proceedings: he is ill, apparently having suffered a nervous breakdown. *A Hard Lot* is an old-fashioned tragedy. The conflict between Anany's claim to what he feels is his right and his wife's and her lover's equally sincere love can only have a tragic solution. Pisemsky has fully succeeded in making his tragic hero psychologically convincing. Lizaveta, too, asserts herself forcefully. Cheglov is a kind but weak man; Anany is much the better man, which enhances the poignancy of the tragic conflict. The dialogue is realistic and vigorous. It has nuances which suggest that the inner life of Anany and Lizaveta is anything but simple.

In the 1860s Pisemsky wrote a number of plays, the most interesting of which are *Former Falcons* (1868) and its sequel *Fledglings of the Last Flight* (published posthumously, 1883–86), a tense drama of incestuous passion, which Pisemsky had to rewrite repeatedly before it passed the censor. His three historical plays, two of which are set in the eighteenth century and one at the time of Peter the Great's accession to the throne, are better-than-average theater. In the 1870s Pisemsky wrote several plays in which he tried to expose the evils of Russia's nascent capitalism: *Plunderers* (1873), *Baal* (1873), *An Enlightened Age* (1875), and *A Financial Genius* (1876) are well constructed, though by no means profound. Their characters are melodramatically overstated and their satirical edge theatrical but effective.

Ostrovsky

The importance of Aleksandr Nikolaevich Ostrovsky (1823–86) in Russia is more out of proportion with his international stature than is the case with any other figure of Russian literature. His plays are rarely seen on the world's stages, yet at home they provide, along with Shakespeare, the bulk of the classical repertoire of the Russian stage. Ostrovsky came from Moscow's merchant quarter, where his father was a minor official and solicitor. He attended but did not graduate from Moscow University and worked for years as a law clerk at Moscow's commercial court. After the success of his first plays he devoted himself entirely to the theater, writing close to fifty original plays and translating several more from different languages. The homespun quality of most of Ostrovsky's plays belies his intellectual capacities. Like his friend Apollon Grigoryev, he was well read in all the major Western languages as well as in the classics.

Ostrovsky's career was delayed somewhat by the troubles his first and perhaps best play, a comedy variously entitled *The Insolvent Debtor, Bankrupt,* or *It's All in the Family—We'll Come to Terms,* had with the censor and Tsar Nicholas himself. In the original version, submitted to the censor in 1849, Bolshov ("big"), a wealthy Moscow merchant, decides to retire from business and concocts a scheme by which he will secretly transfer his assets to his trusted steward and son-in-law Podkhalyuzin ("lickspittle") and declare bankruptcy. Podkhalyuzin double-crosses him, leaving him penniless: even his daughter Lipochka agrees with her husband that the old man will do a better job of begging his creditors to settle for "ten kopecks to the ruble" when facing debtor's prison with no hope of relief. The play was widely known even before its publication, and the Moscow business community exerted strong pressure to have it suppressed. It was published, however, in *The Muscovite* in 1850. But then the tsar agreed with the censor that the play was immoral and dirty, vetoed its staging, and ordered that Ostrovsky be investigated. Eventually Ostrovsky gave the play a new ending, which has Podkhalyuzin unmasked and brought to justice. This version was finally cleared for the stage in 1861, by which time Ostrovsky was well established as a playwright.

Most of Ostrovsky's plays are in the manner of *It's All in the Family*: called comedies, they are really slice-of-life realistic "scenes from Moscow life," as some of them are subtitled. Many are set in the merchant quarters of Moscow or of a provincial town, some in the ambience of minor officialdom, some at a country estate of the declining landed gentry. Ostrovsky also wrote eight plays in undistinguished blank verse: several historical plays; a fairy-tale play, *The Snow Maiden* (1873); and *A Seventeenth-Century Comedian* (1873), a comedy with a comedy of Pastor Gregori's theater inserted into its plot, written to celebrate the two hundredth anniversary of the Russian theater.

Ostrovsky's plays are objective representations of a reality that he knew intimately, without a shade of subjective involvement or any attempt at psychological complexity. The verisimilitude of Ostrovsky's simple plots, socially stylized dialogue, and ample ethnographic detail, including a good deal of popular song and dance, is impaired only by the usual conventions of the stage. Ostrovsky's plays have few poetic or rhetorical highlights, and few witty repartees, jokes, or punch lines. What laughs—chuckles, really—they get come from situations where the inherent absurdity of a character's position or opinions becomes too obvious, such as when a matchmaker gets carried away advertising her client—a recurrent situation.

The moral message of Ostrovsky's plays is simple. It is often expressed in a play's catchy title, usually in the form of a Russian proverb, which also serves as a punch line in the play: *Poverty Is No Vice* (1852), *Sit in Your Own Sled* (1853), *Don't Live as You Like* (1854), *It's Not All Shrovetide for the Cat* (1871). Symbolic names like *Bolshov* ("big") and *Dikoi* ("wild"), are fairly common, as are symbolic stage effects for example, the rumbling of thunder in *The Thunderstorm*.

Ostrovsky's characters are for the most part recurrent stereotypes, though sometimes colorful. There is the *samodur*, the one type we may say he created, an obdurate domestic tyrant who keeps his wife and grown children in a state of perpetual fear, and his female counterpart, the selfish, rich, self-righteous old widow or spinster who insists on meddling in the lives of those around her. There is the samodur's cowed young head clerk who does all the work and is rewarded with niggardly wages and constant abuse. He may be in love with the samodur's daughter. There is the beautiful dowerless girl who painfully realizes that she has to sell herself to the highest bidder. There is the worthless and impecunious young man who is out to better himself by an advantageous marriage. Finally, there is the pathetic down-and-out alcoholic who, however, has not lost either his heart or his conscience. Ostrovsky introduced some variety into these characters as he responded to the changes that came with the emancipation of the peasantry, the westernization of the merchant class, and the emergence of Western-style capitalism.

In *A Poor Bride* (1852), beautiful and well-educated but dowerless Marya Andreevna is let down by her more attractive suitors and in desperation marries a middle-aged clerk. She wryly observes, "Some will simply buy me, like some thing; I own property, he says, and you have nothing, so I'll take your daughter for her beauty." The play ends in a betrothal scene during which an onlooker observes, "Look at her crying, the poor thing." Another onlooker answers, "Yes, my dear, she is poor—he's marrying her for her beauty." In *Sit in Your Own Sled*, Vikhorev ("whirlwind"), an impecunious ex-cavalry officer, elopes with the daughter of Rusakov, a rich merchant, but quickly drops her when he realizes that no dowry will be forthcoming; the jilted bride is happy to marry a young merchant of her own estate. *Poverty Is No Vice*, set during the Christmas season, the time for mummery and caroling, features a particularly rich strain of folk song and dance. Gordei ("proud") Tortsov, a well-to-do merchant, almost gives his daughter in marriage to Korshunov ("hawk"), a rich middle-aged factory owner, but is stopped by his brother, Lyubim ("beloved"), a drunken beggar, who recognizes Korshunov as the man who started him on the road to ruin. Gordei Tortsov discovers that he has a heart after all and lets his daughter marry his young head clerk, the man she loves. This play inspired Apollon Grigoryev to compose an effusive panegyric in verse. He and other critics with Slavophile leanings saw in Lyubim Tortsov a quintessential Russian type, a humble man who through all adversity maintains the goodness of his heart and the purity of his conscience.

A Lucrative Position (1856) is a satire on the corruption of the official bureaucracy. Zhadov, an honest young man, enters the civil service with romantic ideas of being an honest public servant but soon learns that this is not what it is all about. *The Thunderstorm* (1860) features the samodur Dikoi and his female counterpart, the widow Kabanova ("boar"), mother-in-law of the heroine, Katerina, who in the absence of her weak and insipid husband commits adultery with Dikoi's gentle nephew Boris. In the end, Katerina is driven to suicide. Dobrolyubov had responded to *It's All in the Family* in an essay entitled "The Dark Kingdom" (1859), an indictment of the self-satisfied bigotry, mindless brutality, and habitual dishonesty of the Russian merchant class. He followed up on *The Thunderstorm* with an essay, "A Ray of Light in the Kingdom of Darkness" (1860), where the ray of light is the rebellion of Boris and Katerina against the old generation. Although another radical critic, Pisarev, soon debunked Dobrolyubov's position as wishful thinking, *The Thunderstorm* gave Ostrovsky, who was actually closest to the conservative pochvenniki, a great deal of credit with the progressives. It became the flagship of Ostrovsky's theater.

It's Not All Shrovetide for the Cat (1871) has another great samodur in Akhov, a sixtyish merchant who wants to marry pretty twenty-year-old Agniya, another dowerless girl. But this time the samodur meets his match in pert Agniya and her youngish, brazen, and resourceful mother. They manipulate the old man into paying his young head clerk Ippolit his full wages for years of faithful service so that he can open his own business and marry Agniya. In the end then, "it isn't all Shrovetide for the cat [the samodur]—there is also a lenten season."

Lumber (1871), one of Ostrovsky's most popular plays, is also the most theatrical. Schastlivtsev ("fortunate") and Neschastlivtsev ("unfortunate"), two itinerant actors down on their luck, stop at the country estate of Miss Gurmyzhsky, a woman in her fifties who is about to marry Bulanov, a good-for-nothing, sniveling high school dropout. The tragedian Neschastlivtsev's real name is Gurmyzhsky: he is a relative of

Miss Gurmyzhsky's and the brother of Aksinya, her much-abused *demoiselle de compagnie*. He poses as a retired officer and lets Schastlivtsev, the comedian, play the role of his valet. With a lot of sound and fury (Neschastlivtsev speaks in snippets from his tragic roles) Neschastlivtsev succeeds not only in straightening out Miss Gurmyzhsky's business affairs, involving the sale of a forest for lumber, but also in wheedling from her a dowry for his sister so that she can marry the young merchant she is in love with. When it is revealed that Neschastlivtsev is no retired officer but only an actor, Miss Gurmyzhsky bids the "comedians" to leave forthwith. Neschastlivtsev gives his famous repartee: "Comedians? No, we are artists, noble artists—it's you who are the comedians."

In *Wolves and Sheep* (1875), the crooks and wheeler-dealers are more modern and more westernized than in the earlier plays. Miss Murzavetsky, a lady of sixty-five, is the owner of a large estate and fancies herself a benefactress of society. She gets involved in some crooked machinations in order to force Madame Kupavina, a rich young widow, to marry her nephew, Ensign Murzavetsky, a drunken good-for-nothing. In the end, Berkutov, a dashing middle-aged man of affairs, saves Madame Kupavina, as he wants to marry her himself, and "the wolves have had their fill and the sheep are still in one piece." *The Dowerless Girl* (1879) is more modern still. Larisa Dmitrievna, the beautiful daughter of a genteel widow who lives on a small pension and her wits, is madly in love with Paratov, a dashing Volga shipowner. When Paratov leaves her, she decides to marry Karandashov ("pencil"), a dull and vulgar government clerk, who will take her to show her off to his betters as a prize. But then Paratov returns, and Larisa

follows him without a moment's hesitation. It develops that Paratov will not marry her, and she learns that two other businessmen have flipped a coin for the chance to succeed him in her favors. Larisa is grateful to Karandashov when he shoots her, wounding her mortally. As Paratov and his friends come rushing to the scene, she says that she did it herself. Her dying words are, "You must live and I must die . . . I'm not accusing anybody, I'm not feeling hurt by anybody . . . You are all good people, I love you all." *The Dowerless Girl* and some other of Ostrovsky's later plays show that he was moving ahead with the times. It reveals not only an altogether different, decidedly westernized and bourgeois ambience, but also greater psychological complexity than *A Poor Bride*, written a generation earlier. *The Dowerless Girl* might pass for a play by Ibsen. The role of Larisa has been an exciting challenge to generations of actresses, including the great Vera Kommissarzhevskaya.

Nevertheless, the question remains: how did it come about that Ostrovsky not only conquered the Russian stage but also earned the praise of critics of indubitable competence, such as Annenkov, Nekrasov, and Grigoryev? (There were a few dissenting voices, Herzen's in particular.) Many critics of the period, certainly Dobrolyubov, were more interested in the facts of Russian life than in art. Ostrovsky gave them enough facts to have a good discussion. But Grigoryev had a sure sense of style, and he found that Ostrovsky's plays had "wholeness," "common sense," a "healthy sense of humor," and, first and foremost, a quality of "Russianness." Apparently Grigoryev fell victim to his personal sympathies. He took Ostrovsky's milieu, which was that of his own youth, to be the mainstream of Russian life and ascribed to Ostrovsky's theater the prophetic quality of great art, whereas in fact it was merely good theater.

Other Dramatists

Aleksandr Sukhovo-Kobylin (1817–1903) came from a family of wealthy landowners. He graduated from Moscow University in 1838, earning a gold medal for his scholarship, and went on to live the life of a habitué of Moscow salons, a dandy, and a Don Juan. He had the reputation of a brilliant wit and serious connoisseur of the theater. An extraordinarily handsome and charming man, Sukhovo-Kobylin also seems to have had a violent streak. In 1850 the battered body of his French mistress was found in a Moscow street. It was soon established that she had been killed in her lover's apartment. The money and influence of Sukhovo-Kobylin's family finally succeeded in having the case against him dropped in 1856. Four of his serfs, who were initially convicted of the crime, apparently after they had confessed to it under torture by the police, were also set free. In 1854, however, Sukhovo-Kobylin spent a few months in prison, where he wrote his play *Krechinsky's Wedding*. He later used the experiences gathered in the course of his protracted trial in the second part of his dramatic trilogy, *The Case* (1861), which concluded with *Tarelkin's Death* (1857–69).

Krechinsky's Wedding is a well-made comedy à la Scribe. Krechinsky, a dashing gentleman gambler of forty, plans to boost his sagging fortunes by marrying naive eighteen-year-old Lidochka Muromsky, whose father, an honest veteran of 1812, is a prosperous landowner. Hounded by aggressive creditors and afraid that Muromsky might not let his daughter marry him if he learned the truth about his finances, Krechinsky concocts a scheme to tide himself over until the wedding. Under a pretext he borrows Lidochka's expensive diamond pin and pawns its paste copy for six thousand rubles. The scheme is foiled at the last moment, and Krechinsky makes his escape. It would seem that Lidochka may now marry the honest Nelkin, who is still in love with her, but whom she had rejected in favor of the more handsome Krechinsky.

The Case shows otherwise. Five years have passed, and the Muromskys are still entangled in legal proceedings which have Lidochka charged with having been an accomplice of Krechinsky's. A whole hierarchy of greedy officials, headed by Varravin, a senior official, and his lieutenant Tarelkin, milks the wealthy Muromsky for all he is worth, threatening to bring additional charges: if Lidochka was Krechinsky's willing accomplice, wasn't she also his paramour (charges of immoral conduct might be brought), and if so, was there perhaps an illegitimate child born of their criminal union? Where is that child? In the end, Muromsky agrees to give Varravin thirty thousand rubles to drop the case. When Varravin tricks him by keeping most of the money, then charging him with attempted bribery by producing an envelope with fifteen hundred rubles, Muromsky collapses and dies of heart failure. Tarelkin, who had hoped to be rewarded for his job of softening up Muromsky for the kill, gets nothing. *The Case* projects an atmosphere of unmitigated, cynical, and triumphant evil. It does so convincingly, since each of the evil officials has a distinctive voice, and their diabolic plot develops quite naturally, step by step. The victims are drawn into its web as inexorably as the hero of a Greek tragedy. *The Case* is a harrowing but fascinating play.

Tarelkin's Death is a black comedy. Tarelkin, at the end of his rope, pursued by hordes of creditors, has decided to "die" and assume the identity of his neighbor, Kopylov, who has recently died away from home. Tarelkin has stolen some incriminating documents from Varravin's file and plans to blackmail him after having established residence at a safe distance. In a series of burlesque scenes Tarelkin learns that his new identity is no better than the old one. In the very first of these he discovers that he is the father of several children. Soon Varravin shows up in disguise to recover the stolen documents. When it develops that Kopylov is in fact dead, the examining magistrate comes to the conclusion that Tarelkin must be a revenant. Varravin sees to it that he is locked up and kept without water, because "water has for these evil creatures an explosive power—no lock or chain will hold them, and a misfortune might happen, he might get away!" Dying of thirst after a few days without water, Tarelkin is ready to meet Varravin's terms. He surrenders the documents for a drink of water. Varravin lets him keep Kopylov's papers and gives him some money so he can have a new start. *Tarelkin's Death* is a remarkably modern play. Its rapid-fire phantasmagorical metamorphoses, grotesque humor (the play begins with Tarelkin ordering his housekeeper to buy a lot of rotten fish to act as a substitute for his corpse), and burlesque or absurd repartees anticipate the theater of Alfred Jarry. The play had trouble with censorship and could only be staged in 1900, and with some changes at that. Vsevolod Meyerhold later staged it brilliantly as a constructivist circus bouffonnade.

Aleksei Potekhin (1829–1908) served as an officer in the army and later in the civil service in Kostroma Province before devoting himself entirely to literature and the theater. He eventually became a theater administrator. Potekhin started with a series of peasant dramas (*muzhitskie dramy*), such as *Human Justice Is Not God's Justice* (1854) and *Goods That Aren't Yours Won't Do You Any Good* (1855), and a novel, *A Peasant Girl* (1853), whose heroine is a peasant girl brought up as a lady. In a sequel, the play *Sheepskin Coat—Human Heart* (1854),[34] the heroine goes on to marry a landowner. In the late 1850s and the 1860s Potekhin wrote several plays with a moderately "progressive" tendency, advocating a fair implementation of the peasant reform (*The Cut-Off Piece,* 1865), exposing bureaucratic corruption (*Tinsel*, 1858), and supporting the emancipation of women (*A Guilty Female*, 1868). Potekhin's plays are well focussed and tightly structured, and the dialogue is competently individualized. But they are also schematic, their tendency is transparent, and they have no real comic or tragic power. Potekhin also wrote a great deal of prose fiction, mostly dealing with peasant life and showing a liberal Slavophile tendency, but theater was his first love. He managed dramatic ensembles in Moscow and Petersburg and was eventually appointed artistic director of the imperial theaters, a position in which he helped to implement much-needed reforms.

Historical Drama

There continued to be some demand for historical drama even after the romantic period, particularly since Russian opera was now coming into its own. Earlier historical plays were made into opera libretti, as were some more recent ones. Lev Mei's historical

---

34. A Sheepskin coat marked its wearer as a member of the lower classes.

plays (in verse) *The Tsar's Bride* (1849) and *The Woman of Pskov* (1860) both became better known as operas by Rimsky-Korsakov, but they have some dramatic merit. The first is based on a true historical episode. Tsar Ivan IV, recently widowed, was looking for a new bride and chose Marfa, daughter of a Novgorod merchant, Vasily Sobakin. She died of a mysterious illness shortly after her marriage. Mei invented a plot of jealous intrigue which leads to the poisoning of the young woman. The dialogue is lively and the action reasonably suspenseful, but the whole thing seems a bit melodramatic and trivial for a historical drama. *The Woman of Pskov* is a dramatization of the tragic fall of the free city of Pskov in 1570, when it surrendered to Ivan IV. The authentic, historically documented sentiments of the citizens of Pskov, who keenly felt the loss of their freedom,[35] come through in several fiery speeches of the play, carrying a topical message to the audience of 1860.

Among the major figures of the period, Pisemsky, Ostrovsky, Konstantin Aksakov, and others wrote historical plays. But only in the case of Aleksei Tolstoi were they the main part of the writer's achievement. Count Aleksei Tolstoi (1817–1875) came from an aristocratic family. His parents separated soon after his birth, and he was brought up by his mother and her brother, the writer A. A. Perovsky (pseudonym A. Pogorelsky). On his mother's side he was descended from the last hetman of the Ukraine, which may in part explain his lifelong sympathy for Kievan Russia and antipathy for Muscovite despotism. He pursued a career first as a diplomat and later at court, and was personally close to Tsar Alexander II. He left the government service

in 1861 and retired to his estate to devote himself entirely to his literary work. Tolstoi started his career as a writer with a Hoffmannesque story, "The Vampire" (1841), and had his greatest success with a historical novel, *Duke Serebryany* (1862). His historical ballads were also very popular, his romantic poetry less so.[36] His main importance, though, is as the best Russian historical dramatist, and this by virtue of his dramatic trilogy, *The Death of Ivan the Terrible* (1866), *Tsar Fyodor Ioannovich* (1868). and *Tsar Boris* (1870).

Tsar Fyodor Ioannovich is a great play and can stand on its own. It is the tragedy of a simple good man who is cast in a role he cannot play and does not want to play. His goodness, simplicity and faith are painfully out of tune with the clever scheming, vicious power struggle, and wholesale deception of the court around him. Yet Tolstoi has succeeded in making Tsar Fyodor Ioannovich the hero of his play. The humble tsar towers over the many strong, clever, and capable men around him. The very fact that he is pathetically ineffectual as a ruler elevates him morally over all of them, and particularly over Boris Godunov, his successor. *Tsar Fyodor Ioannovich* has the same message as Dostoevsky's novel *The Idiot*: a Christian hero's triumph is not of this world.

The Death of Ivan the Terrible is a tense and stagy play. Tolstoi adroitly uses various scenic devices to recapitulate the glory, the horror, and the ultimate defeat of the awesome tsar. In the fourth act the Tsar talks to a hermit who has spent the past thirty years secluded from the world. The hermit asks the tsar one question after another about the men who helped him take Kazan, the last event he remembers, and the answer is that they have all been executed. Mes-

35. See p. 73.

36. See p. 312.

sages of disasters arrive from all sides. On the day soothsayers have prophesied that the tsar will die, he vacillates between despair and arrogance, remorse and fury. As the day nears its end he orders the soothsayers executed. Godunov refuses to carry out the order, for the day is not over. The tsar flies into a rage, collapses, and dies. Godunov confidently takes over in the name of the tsar's weak son, Fyodor.

Tsar Boris is an attempt to improve on Pushkin's *Boris Godunov*, mostly by focusing the whole play on the tsar. The conflict is the same, however. Godunov, who believed that the end of giving Russia a wise and progressive ruler justified the sacrifice of the life of one small child, discovers step by step that he was wrong. Tolstoi achieves a modicum of dramatic tension by never letting Godunov explicitly admit his guilt and by making the murdered tsarevich his invisible antagonist. Unlike in Pushkin's play, the pretender never appears on stage, and his real identity is not made known. On balance, *Tsar Boris* is a well-constructed play which might be scenically effective if it did not have Pushkin's *Boris Godunov* hovering over it, much as Karamzin's text hovers over Pushkin's.

Chapter

The Silver Age

On March 1, 1881, Tsar Alexander II was assassinated in Saint Petersburg. He was succeeded by his son Alexander III (1881–94), who had opposed his father's liberal policies. He took drastic measures to stop revolutionary activity, and terrorist acts were fewer during his reign. They never ceased, however, and they again plagued the government under his son, Nicholas II, the last Romanov. Tsar Alexander III and his adviser, Konstantin Pobedonostsev, a friend of Dostoevsky's, conducted a policy based on the ideas of conserving Russia's "national traditions" and rejecting "European" rationalism and optimistic humanist anthropology. His reign was marked by aggressive Russification in the non-Russian provinces, suspension of higher education for women (1882), withdrawal of autonomy from the universities (1884), and more severe censorship. A side effect of the government's chauvinistic policies was periodic flare-ups of savage rioting (*pogrom*) against Jews in the cities of western Russia, which the authorities did little to prevent.

The tragic reign of Nicholas II, who tried

unsuccessfully to continue his father's policies, saw Russia's humiliating defeat in the Russo-Japanese War of 1904–05; the revolution of 1905, which the tsar and his government survived at the expense of granting Russia a constitution and an elected parliamentary body, the State Duma; World War I, in which the Russian army suffered terrible losses and crushing defeats at the hands of better-equipped German forces, and the February revolution of 1917, which led to the tsar's abdication. Russia's brief spell of political freedom came to an end when Lenin's Bolshevik coup of October 25, 1917, toppled the Provisional Government of Alexander Kerensky and established a "dictatorship of the proletariat," which resulted in the transformation of Russia into the Union of Soviet Socialist Republics. The Soviet regime survived a strong counterrevolutionary backlash in a civil war that cost millions of lives, left the country's economy devastated, and led to the emigration of hundreds of thousands of Russians, mostly members of the educated elite. The Russian Empire also suffered significant territorial losses: Finland, the Baltic states of Estonia, Latvia, and Lithuania, and Poland emerged as independent states, and Bessarabia was ceded to Romania.

Behind these stark political facts, less negative social developments took their course, and the period witnessed an amazing cultural flowering. The population of Russia doubled from 73 million in 1861 to 170 million in 1914. During the same period the urban population tripled and the population of the capitals quadrupled. Tsar Alexander III and his able minister Sergei Witte encouraged Russia's industrialization and the influx of foreign capital. Russian industry, mining, and oil production registered growth rates comparable to those of the United States. By 1890 Russia had some two million industrial workers, and their numbers were expanding rapidly. Wages and working conditions were poor, however, and bitter and sometimes bloody strikes were common after the turn of the century. The revolution of 1905 showed the Russian industrial proletariat to be a formidable political force. It was courted by underground revolutionary organizations, such as the Socialist Revolutionaries, who had emerged from the populist movement of the 1870s, and the Marxist Social Democratic Workers Party, founded in 1898 and led by Vladimir Ulyanov, alias Lenin (1870–1924), whose brother, Aleksandr Ulyanov, had been executed in 1887 for his participation in a plot to assassinate the tsar. The Social Democrats split into two factions in 1903—the radical Bolsheviks, under Lenin, and the less militant Mensheviks, led by Georgy Plekhanov, L. Martov (pseudonym of Yuly Tsederbaum), and Pavel Axelrod. When political parties became legal in 1906 in connection with elections to the State Duma (no fewer than forty different parties nominated candidates for at least one of the four Dumas, the last in 1912), both Bolsheviks and Mensheviks nominated candidates, along with the Socialist Revolutionaries, the liberal Constitutional Democrats ("Cadets"), the more conservative Octobrists, and the conservative Union of the Russian People.

Meanwhile the Russian middle class was growing at a tremendous pace. The cities were beginning to resemble Western cities, with manufacturing, commerce, banking, insurance, public transportation, and communications creating better-paid jobs. In the countryside the old gentry was progressively losing its hold on the land, which it was being forced to sell to middle-class entrepreneurs, peasants, or land developers.

The urban population was now largely literate, and literacy was spreading even in the countryside. Such newspapers and popular magazines as *The Cornfield* (1870–1918) achieved huge circulations—as much as a quarter of a million copies. Mass entertainment was becoming a part of urban life, as theater, circus, and (in the twentieth century) film and sports were becoming accessible even to the working class. The progress of higher education was unstoppable, even though the government was not eager to encourage it. The university population rose from four thousand in 1865 to twenty-two thousand in 1905, and forty thousand in 1912. Thousands of Russians studied abroad, mostly in Germany, Switzerland, and France. In 1912, for instance, 552 Russians were enrolled at the Technical University of Munich. Russian science and scholarship had reached a European level. Russian professors who emigrated after the 1917 revolution generally were able to resume their careers at European or American universities.

Russian intellectual life, once it had recovered from the temporary torpor of the reactionary 1880s, was lively, pluralist, and once again receptive to Western influences. Most educated Russians frequently traveled to Western Europe and were conversant with the latest developments in Europe. Intellectuals of non-Russian ethnic background were playing a progressively greater role in Russian cultural life. Many writers, poets, painters, directors, and actors of the early twentieth century, who wholeheartedly embraced Russian culture, came from Jewish, German, Polish, and other non-Russian families in which they often were the first Russian-speaking generation. The international success of Russian literature, music, and ballet caused Russian culture to be valued on equal terms with that of the nations of Western Europe.

Educated Russian society was more pluralist than ever before. Populist and revolutionary attitudes were still widespread. Many educated men and women of an idealistic bent worked as zemstvo doctors, nurses, schoolteachers, and social workers at low salaries. Their political attitude was generally leftist to liberal. So-called legal populism had its own journal, *Russian Wealth* (1876–1918). In the 1880s it leaned toward Tolstoianism, but in the 1890s, led by Nikolai Mikhailovsky and Vladimir Korolenko, it assumed a more purely populist stance.

Since the 1890s Marxism was a political and ideological force in Russian life, and such Russian radicals as Sergei Kravchinsky (pseudonym Stepnyak, 1851–95), Georgy Plekhanov (1856–1918), Pavel Axelrod, and Vladimir Lenin played a role in the international socialist movement. Kravchinsky, who had assassinated Nikolai Mezentsev, chief of gendarmes, in 1878, escaped abroad, where he published books and articles promoting the cause of revolution. Plekhanov left Russia in 1880 and spent the next thirty-seven years abroad, lecturing and writing prolifically in several languages. He was one of the leaders of the Second International. Marxism as a philosophy appealed even to Russian intellectuals who would later be opposed to its political side—Nikolai Berdyaev and Pyotr Struve, for example. Russian Marxists built a strong organization abroad and, using funds donated by the singer Fyodor Chaliapin and the writer Maksim Gorky, among others, were able to invite twenty young Russian workers to a Communist party school on the island of Capri in 1909. The Marxist Aleksandr Malinovsky (pseudonym Bogdanov, 1873–1928), a physician, developed a quasi-religious humanist version of Marxism,[1] which had working humanity ("the people") acting as a theurgic ("god-building") force, and the Communist party as a quintessential expression of that force. The key to progress was, for Bogdanov, not so much class struggle as the evolution of man to a higher type of individual, an idea embraced earlier by Mikhailovsky and other populists. Accordingly, Bogdanov propagated the idea of a new, proletarian culture that would supersede and surpass bourgeois culture. Anatoly Lunacharsky (1875–1933), a Marxist critic and playwright, who was Bogdanov's brother-in-law, shared his ideas and expressed them in a utopian play, *Faust and the City* (1916). He had earlier dealt with the Faust theme in an essay, "A Russian Faust" (1902), a sharp critique of Dostoevsky's "Grand Inquisitor." In 1911 Lunacharsky founded the Circle for Proletarian Culture in Paris. In addition, Bogdanov,

---

1. Gorky wholeheartedly supported Bogdanov's idea: "I saw the almighty and immortal people . . . and I prayed: Thou art God, and let there be no other gods but Thee in the world, for Thou art the one God who does miracles. This I believe and profess." (Maksim Gorky, "Confession")

Lunacharsky, and Gorky were instrumental in organizing the Capri party school. Lenin was strongly opposed to Bogdanov's and Gorky's god-building ideas. His *Materialism and Empiriocriticism* (1909) was a refutation not only of the neo-Kantian empiriocriticism of Ernst Mach and Richard Avenarius but also of Bogdanov's materialist "empiriomonism."[2]

In the 1890s, while a positivist worldview was still prevalent among the majority of the Russian intelligentsia, various idealist strains began to make a vigorous comeback. The mystical idealism of Vladimir Solovyov, derived from Neoplatonism, Schelling, and Jakob Böhme, did not gain a wide following but, an admirable intellectual achievement in itself, acted as a stimulus to Russian symbolist poetry. Schopenhauer and Nietzsche were widely known, and many Russian writers, including Minsky, Rozanov, Volynsky, Vyacheslav Ivanov, Merezhkovsky, Sologub, and Gorky, reacted to them, each in his peculiar way. Lev Shestov (1866–1938), a thinker of vigorous originality and a brilliant stylist, was the first to recognize the affinity between Nietzsche and Dostoevsky in their existential approach to the great questions of philosophy. His study *Dostoevsky and Nietzsche: The Philosophy of Tragedy* (1903) was to become a classic of existentialism.

Neo-Kantian thought entered Russian intellectual life through academia and had some original ramifications, in the linguistic and poetic theory of Aleksandr Potebnya, for example. The phenomenological principle of dealing with reality solely in terms of the subject at hand, without being compelled to link it to the world at large, led to interest-

ing aesthetic and poetic concepts, specifically that of "the word as such" in Russian futurism.[3]

Religion, though hardly in the traditional Orthodox sense, experienced a strong revival in the 1890s. There was Tolstoianism, which thousands of Russians embraced as a practical religion beginning in the 1880s. Some intellectuals were inclined to follow a form of Christianity not wholly alienated from the Orthodox state church (as was Tolstoianism) yet imbued with a touch of Neoplatonic mysticism and a claim to modernity and cultural sophistication. Such were the intellectuals who participated in the meetings of the Religious-Philosophical Society of Saint Petersburg from 1901 to 1903. The society was organized by Dmitry Merezhkovsky and his wife, Zinaida Hippius. Among those who attended its meetings and contributed to its organ, *The New Path* (1903–05), were Rozanov, Berdyaev, Minsky, Bely, Blok, and Sologub.

Vasily Rozanov (1856–1919) challenged the preoccupation of the Russian intelligentsia with the grand design of things and advocated a more positive attitude toward family life, sexuality, and the little pleasures of daily life, as well as a religion that was less ascetic and abstract, and more joyous and this-worldly, even at the price of being more ritualistic and less spiritual.

Theosophy, which in one form appeared in the philosophy of Vladimir Solovyov, also reached Russia from the West. Some Russian intellectuals became involved in the international theosophical movement, which owed its existence in part to Elena Blavatsky, née Hahn (1831–91), a daughter of the writer Elena Hahn.[4] The symbolists Vyacheslav Ivanov and Andrei Bely were under the sway

---

2. Here the prefix *empirio* is derived from the empiriocriticism of Mach and Avenarius, the suffix *monism* from Ernst Haeckel's identical term signifying a monistic materialist philosophy.

3. See pp. 410–411.
4. See p. 252.

of theosophy at one time, and Bely was for several years a faithful disciple of the Austrian theosophist Rudolf Steiner.

Liberal thought, oriented toward a constitutional monarchy politically, and toward an Aristotelian pluralism philosophically, was exemplified by Pyotr Struve (1870–1944), a leader of the Constitutional Democrats and editor of the journal *Russian Thought* (1907–18). The liberal position was highlighted by a collection of essays entitled *Landmarks* (1909), initiated by the brilliant literary historian Mikhail Gershenzon (1869–1925). Among the contributors to *Landmarks* were Struve, Berdyaev, and Gershenzon. It was their consensus that the radical Russian intelligentsia had reached a state of impotence as a result of profound contradictions between its professed goals and its philosophical beliefs. As Semyon Frank put it, an ideal Russian intellectual was "a militant monk of a nihilistic religion of earthly prosperity." *Landmarks* called on the Russian intelligentsia to abandon its negative attitude toward constructive work in the spirit of the Constitutional Manifesto of October 17, 1905, and to open its minds to spiritual values still cherished by the Russian people. *Landmarks* met with immediate angry rebuttals by the radical left.

The 1880s saw the beginning of a turn from the social realism and utilitarianism of the preceding period to more form-oriented art, and a return of most of the themes, modes, and moods that had been characteristic of romanticism. The great age of the Russian realist novel came to an end with the deaths of Dostoevsky, Turgenev, and Pisemsky and with Tolstoi's decision to abandon the novel. The one novel he wrote after 1880, *Resurrection*, was almost an anachronism. Although many realist novels, some very successful, continued to appear throughout the period, the best prose

fiction, including Tolstoi's, was now concentrated in the short story. The short stories of Garshin, Chekhov, Korolenko, Gorky, and Tolstoi, while retaining their realist subject matter, drifted into a form-conscious impressionism and symbolism. In the early twentieth century the historical novel reappeared as a serious genre, and entirely new symbolist and ornamentalist modes of prose fiction emerged.

In poetry, a new generation of poets, born mostly in the 1860s, rediscovered romanticism and, under the influence of French symbolism and of Nietzsche, moved on to decadence and symbolism. The symbolist movement was pioneered by the philosopher Vladimir Solovyov, the critic Akim Volynsky (pseudonym of Akim Flekser, 1863–1926), Dmitry Merezhkovsky, and Valery Bryusov. Volynsky became editor of *The Northern Herald* in 1891, when it became the first outlet for "decadent" literature. Other landmarks of the emergence of symbolism were Merezhkovsky's treatises *On the Reasons for the Decline and on New Trends in Contemporary Russian Literature* (1893) and *The Mystic Movement of Our Age* (1893), three volumes entitled *Russian Symbolists* (1894–95), edited by Bryusov and A. A. Miropolsky, Aleksandr Dobrolyubov's collection of verse *Natura naturans, Natura naturata* (1895), and the founding in 1900 of the publishing house Skorpion, funded by S. A. Polyakov, a Moscow Maecenas, and managed by Bryusov.

In art, the Itinerants had been largely independent of European art and never were recognized by the West. They perceived art essentially as narrative, as in Repin's political paintings, for example. The paintings of the Itinerants were also open-ended, as the characters and actions depicted implied or pointed to things beyond the frame. In the 1890s Andrei Ryabushkin

(1861–1904), Viktor Vasnetsov (1848–1926), and Mikhail Vrubel (1856–1910) developed a more decorative style, composing scenes that were staged and stylized, and therefore closed. This development paralleled the evolution of Russian prose fiction as it turned toward an impressionist manner of composition, at the expense of straight narrative and an unequivocal social message. Even Tolstoi now wrote "tales for the people," stylized in the manner of the folktale or folk legend.

Art and literature combined to inaugurate the twentieth century in an illustrated magazine, *The World of Art* (1898–1904), funded by Savva Mamontov (1841–1918), an industrialist, and Duchess Marya Tenisheva (1867–1928), wife of another industrialist, both munificent patrons of the arts.[5] Sergei Diaghilev (1871–1929), who would later gain fame as the impressario of the Ballets Russes, was the editor, Dmitry Filosofov (1872–1942), Diaghilev's cousin, was his editorial assistant. The editorial policy and aesthetic sensibility of *The World of Art*

were eclectic. The magazine was cosmopolitan, but it also cultivated a sophisticated version of Russian national culture. It featured the art of Vasnetsov, Alexandre Benois (1870–1960), Lev Bakst (1866–1924), Nikolai Roerich (1874–1947), and Mstislav Dobuzhinsky (1875–1957), among others, and rather indiscriminately introduced the Russian public to contemporary European art, including the work of the pre-Raphaelites, Puvis de Chavannes, and Aubrey Beardsley. It was, however, pointedly critical of both academic art and the Itinerants. Among the literary contributors to *The World of Art* were Merezhkovsky, Hippius, Minsky, Rozanov, Shestov, Bryusov, and Bely. The literary preferences of *The World of Art* ranged widely: E. T. A. Hoffmann, Hans Christian Andersen, Ruskin, Nietzsche, Ibsen, and, among the Russians, Gogol, Dostoevsky, and Vladimir Solovyov —but Tolstoi, too. Some articles in *The World of Art* were decidedly opposed to everything the Russian intelligentsia had stood for since the 1860s. An essay by Balmont on Goya advanced the notion that beauty could be found in the music of the spheres, but also in the paroxysm of horror, for art was no more and no less than the expression of a heightened state of mind. *Dostoevsky and Nietzsche*, whose author, Lev Shestov, was certainly an admirer of Nietzsche, appeared here, as did Merezhkovsky's *Tolstoi and Dostoevsky*, a work biased in Dostoevsky's favor. Articles by Rozanov and Bely challenged the ascetic ideal of Christianity. Occasional manifestations of aestheticism would offend the sensibility of a reader brought up on Chernyshevsky and Pisarev.

Merezhkovsky, Hippius, and some other contributors left *The World of Art* in 1902 to start a new journal, *New Path*, oriented toward literature and philosophical and relig-

5. Patrons of the arts played a large role in late nineteenth- and early twentieth-century Russia. Pavel Tretyakov, an industrialist, was the founder of the Moscow gallery that bears his name. Savva Mamontov bought the Abramtsevo estate near Moscow, formerly property of the Aksakovs, in 1870 and made it a center of the arts. His wife, Elizaveta, founded a museum of folk art there in 1881. A private theater was organized at Abramtsevo in the 1880s, and in 1885 Mamontov founded a private opera in Moscow. Konstantin Alekseev-Stanislavsky, Elizaveta Mamontova's cousin, became the founder of the Moscow Art Theater. Duchess Marya Tenisheva, the wife of another industrialist, established a studio for art students at her estate, Talashkino, near Smolensk. It was directed by Repin from 1895 to 1898. Two Moscow merchants, Sergei Shchukin and Ivan Morozov, brought several hundred French impressionist and post-impressionist paintings to Russia and sponsored Russian avant-garde painters.

ious thought in the spirit of a mystic symbolism. *The World of Art* was succeeded by *The Golden Fleece* (1906–09), funded by N. P. Ryabushinsky (1876–1951), a banker, amateur painter and poet, and patron of the arts. It was the organ not only of symbolist poetry but also of the Blue Rose, a school of innovative painters. *The Golden Fleece* was typographically refined and addressed to a sophisticated readership. At the end of 1907 several symbolists, including Merezhkovsky, Hippius, Bryusov, and Bely, resigned from the editorial board of *The Golden Fleece*, and it became an art magazine more than a literary journal. The leading symbolist journal was *Scales* (1904–09), published in Moscow by another Maecenas, S. A. Polyakov. Like *The Golden Fleece*, it was luxuriously designed and illustrated. It served as a forum for doctrinal disputes between those symbolists who stressed the spiritual mission of symbolism, such as Bely and Vyacheslav Ivanov, and those to whom symbolism was merely an artistic orientation, a view championed by Bryusov.

Russian symbolism was never a monolithic movement, nor would distinguishing between decadence and symbolism help define it. Certain complexes of ideas and sensibility, however, may be readily recognized as symbolist, alien to realism and its age, even though some symbolists never actually embraced one or the other of them. Symbolism also shared some of its traits with other modernist schools. Such was, for example, the symbolists' claim to the mythopoeic power of their art, a point on which acmeists and futurists also insisted. A solar mythology occurs in such diverse authors as Balmont, Bely, Mayakovsky, Kruchonykh, and Gorky. All symbolists agreed on the principle of "correspondences," the notion that all art is symbolic rather than mimetic. A sense of fin de siècle and impending doom is pervasive in symbolism. Its moods are predominantly pessimistic, though occasional bursts of faith in Russia's regeneration and Russian messianism do occur. Symbolist apocalypticism coincided with the revolutionary visions of the radical left. A sense of unreality, a fragile and shadowy world, a penchant for masks, doppelgängers, and other problematic forms of existence are characteristic of all symbolists. A romantic satanism was cultivated by such decadents as Sologub and Hippius, but the demonic is a pervasive trait in all symbolism. Prometheanism, quite in the manner of Goethe or Shelley, is a recurrent complex, appearing in ideological contexts ranging from the mystical idealism of Vyacheslav Ivanov to the Marxist utopianism of Gorky. The modernist composer Aleksandr Scriabin (1872–1915) called one of his major compositions *Prometheus: A Poem of Fire* (1909–10, published 1911). The concept of theurgia, "creating godhead," likewise appears in the mystical symbolists Bely and Ivanov, but also in the Marxist utopianists Bogdanov, Gorky, and Lunacharsky. An avowed aestheticism and sensualism is limited to some of the decadents. A conscious pursuit of explicit correlations between content and form, specifically through sound symbolism and rhythmic devices, was advocated and practiced by some symbolists, such as Bryusov and Balmont, but rejected by others, particularly Ivanov.

Symbolism as an aesthetic, a worldview, and a sensibility coexisted and was in conflict with several other schools, which often attacked one or the other of its positions. A realist conception of art made a vigorous comeback in the 1900s, gathering its forces around the publishing house Knowledge (1898–1913), under the leadership of Maksim Gorky, who joined it in 1900. The acmeists (or Adamists), whose leader, Nikolai Gumilyov, founded and edited the journal *Apollon* (1909–17), professed to be Parnassians who refused to see symbols everywhere and in everything, instead reveling in the beauty and vigor of the world as perceived by the senses and in the power of the word as Johannine logos. Two of the great poets of the century, Anna Akhmatova and Osip Mandelshtam, belonged to this school. Whereas the symbolists leaned toward Teutonic romanticism, the acmeists' orientation was toward the classical Latin world.

The Russian avant-garde—a term not used in Russia with reference to Russian modernist groupings—challenged symbolism more decisively. It consisted of several diverse strains and may be defined only by its opposition to traditional art and literature. Hence the various avant-garde groups of all branches of art were, until about 1920, often referred to collectively as futurists. In fact, there was a good deal of interaction between futurists proper, who were mainly poets, such as Khlebnikov, Kruchonykh, and Mayakovsky, and avant-garde painters of the groups known by the names of their exhibitions—Jack of Diamonds (1910, 1912, 1913), Donkey's Tail (1912), and 0.10 and Tramway V (both 1915). The "opera" *Victory over the Sun* (1913) combined words by Kruchonykh and Khlebnikov, music by the modernist composer Mikhail Matyushin, and sets by Kazimir Malevich.

Paradoxically, one of the notable strains of futurism was the primitivism and tribal archaism of the poet Velimir Khlebnikov, traits that had a parallel in the primitivist painting of Mikhail Larionov and the primitive-archaist music of Igor Stravinsky's ballet suites *The Firebird* (1910) and *The Rite of Spring* (1913). Archaizing and folkloric stylization was practiced by several *World of Art* painters, such as Vasnetsov and Roerich, as well as by many of the symbolist poets, including Blok, Bely, and Vyacheslav Ivanov. Some members of the Russian avant-garde vociferously claimed total independence from any Western modernist schools, even though the influence of Marinetti (on Khlebnikov and Kruchonykh) and of Italian futurist painting (on Larionov's "rayonism," *luchizm*) was rather obvious. Others freely mingled with the international avant-garde. At the second Jack of Diamonds exhibition Picasso, Delaunay, Matisse, and Léger exhibited together with the Russians.

Whereas symbolists and acmeists used mostly conventional poetic language, various futurist groups indulged in more or less radical deformation of the Russian language, ranging from massive use of neologisms and idiosyncratic syntax by both ego-futurists and cubo-futurists to out-and-out "transsense" language (*zaumny yazyk*)—words with no dictionary meaning. Such verbal practices were to a considerable extent inspired by abstractionist painting, one of whose originators was the Russian Vasily Kandinsky. The Russian cubo-futurists, most of whom were painters as well as poets, derived not only their name but also their basic poetic device, deformation (*sdvig*, "shift"), from the Parisian cubists. Their attention to sound texture (*faktura*) also stemmed from the art of canvas painting. Their conception of "the word as such" (*slovo kak takovoe*) in its symbolic, ritual, or magical power was shared by symbolists, acmeists, and futurists alike, albeit in different philosophical contexts.[6]

6. Mikhail Larionov, in his rayonist manifesto of 1913, declared: "We deny that individuality has any value in a work of art. One should only call attention to a work of art and look at it according to the means and laws by which it was created."

Mystical conceptions of the word were paralleled by analogous ideas in the visual arts and in music. Scriabin and Kandinsky believed in a total synthesis of the arts (both composed "color symphonies") and in mystical revelations released by their harmonies.[7] The suprematist paintings of Kazimir Malevich and the trans-sense poetry of Velimir Khlebnikov likewise aspired to higher levels of consciousness and to cosmic vision.

The last stage of Russian modernism was constructivism, whose ascendancy coincided with the 1917 revolution. Its basic principle was not only that art should be utilitarian in a general way but that it should also be applied to specific tasks. Intuition should be replaced by controlled design. Russian constructivism, like other modernist trends, had its Western antecedents, specifically in the German Werkbund and Bauhaus. A constructivist aesthetic made an appearance in all branches of art, including poetry, where the jingles of Agitprop combined with the didactic and agitational cartoons of the Soviet telegraph agency ROSTA's show windows.

Russian drama reflected all of the modernist trends of the world theater and made some major contributions to it. Although some playwrights continued to produce conventional realist plays in the manner of Ostrovsky, Chekhov (as his works were staged by the Moscow Art Theater) created a wholly new impressionist style. Tolstoi

favored the conventional theater, but his one great play, *The Power of Darkness*, became a paradigm for the naturalist stage and at the same time featured some striking symbolist elements. The plays of Maksim Gorky, internationally successful like Chekhov's and Tolstoi's, combined elements of Chekhov's theater with crass naturalism and, at times, with allegorical and symbolist traits. Several of the Russian symbolist poets, Blok and Sologub in particular, wrote plays in the manner of Maurice Maeterlinck's symbolist drama. Plays in various stylized forms, such as the *mystère*, the allegory, the medieval romance, and the monodrama, were produced by symbolists as well as futurists. Diaghilev's Ballets Russes, which starting in 1909 created a sensation in Paris, combined the innovative choreography of Michel Fokine and Leonid Massine with the revolutionary music of Igor Stravinsky and sets by artists of the *World of Art* group— Bakst, Benois, Roerich, and Korovin. The Ballets Russes intermittently exhibited primitivist, archaist, symbolist, allegorical, and modernist tendencies.

Literary Movements, Theory, and Criticism

Aesthetic and literary theory showed greater energy and variety during this period than ever before or since. The tradition of Belinskian social criticism continued unabated, particularly in the writings of critics of a populist orientation, such as Nikolai Mikhailovsky and Aleksandr Skabichevsky. Such critics of the radical left as the Marxists Vatslav Vorovsky and Anatoly Lunarcharsky continued to produce literary criticism in the manner of Saltykov-Shchedrin. A psychological dimension was added to a basically sociohistorical approach by academic scho-

---

The essence of a rayonist painting lay in "color as such"—the degree of its saturation, the intensity of surface treatment, and the relationship between masses of color.

7. Kandinsky's essay "On the Spiritual in Art" was read by Nikolai Kulbin, in the author's absence, at the First All-Russian Congress of Artists in Saint Petersburg in 1911.

lar-critics like Dmitry Ovsyaniko-Kulikovsky (1853–1920) and Semyon Vengerov (1855–1920), who were influenced by the theory of verbal art developed by Aleksandr Potebnya (1835–91), a professor at Kharkov University.

Beginning in the 1890s, an ever-expanding range of ideas enlivened the literary scene, producing a neoromantic renaissance and a rapid sequence of totally new conceptions of the nature and function of art and poetry.

Tolstoi

Lev Tolstoi had expressed strong, and at times contradictory opinions on art and literature since the 1860s. His treatise *What Is Art?* (1897–98), on which he had worked off and on for fifteen years, summarized his post-conversion views. Tolstoi's theory of art dispenses with the concept of beauty—certainly a wise decision. His preliminary definition of art, however, as "a human activity by which one man by way of certain external signs consciously communicates to others his own feelings, in such way that these other people are infected with these feelings and also experience them" is exceedingly broad. Tolstoi develops some further criteria by which he distinguishes art from nonart, and good art from bad art. He says that art should be universal in every conceivable way, that is, intelligible to people of all levels of society and all nations. It should be sincere and spontaneous, free of conventional devices and artifices. It should be inspired, not manufactured or imitative. It should deal with important matters rather than with trivial ones. Bad art, by contrast, is art that infects people with morally bad feelings—jingoistic patriotism or sensuality, for example. Bad art is also art that is reactionary, leading people back to ideals and feelings of the past, such as from Christianity back to paganism.

With all these demands, Tolstoi could only have a low opinion of modern art and literature. According to Tolstoi, most contemporary art is quite unintelligible and irrelevant to the masses. It caters to the petty, perverse, and immoral feelings of the idle rich. It contributes to the moral confusion of the poorly educated and the young, particularly as it substitutes beauty—really, pleasure—for moral values. It often becomes an opiate that diverts people from real life. It wastes time, labor, and resources that might have been devoted to more useful pursuits. Tolstoi's ideal artist is an amateur who lives a normal hardworking life—a peasant singer or teller of tales, for example. A loving and brotherly communion of all people is the only legitimate purpose of human striving and hence of art. All art that serves other ends is either nonart or bad art. Tolstoi's favorite device to discredit modern art—an opera by Wagner, for instance—is to view it through the eyes of a Russian peasant who is of course ignorant of its conventions and therefore cannot but find it absurd.

After *What Is Art?* Tolstoi worked on a treatise, *On Shakespeare and the Drama* (1903–04, published 1906), in which he applied his moralist aesthetics to Shakespeare. He found Shakespeare lacking on every count, although he gave him credit for insightful and forceful presentation of the movements of the human soul. He totally ignored Shakespeare the poet. It may be mentioned that Shaw found merit in Tolstoi's moral observations while rejecting Tolstoi's negative assessment of Shakespeare's craftsmanship. Tolstoi's view of art, and of modern art in particular, was by no means an isolated one. In many ways it coincided with that of the Marxists.

Plekhanov

Georgy Valentinovich Plekhanov (1856–1918) came from the rural gentry. As student at the Petersburg Mining Institute, he led a demonstration organized by the Land and Freedom group on October 6, 1876; subsequently he went underground and in 1880 left Russia. In 1881 he discovered Marxism and became its principal Russian ideologue and propagator. He was one of the leaders of the Second International, later joining Lenin and his Social Democratic Workers Party. He sided with the Mensheviks, against Lenin, in 1903. After the February revolution he returned to Russia, but he had no part in the October revolution.

A prolific political journalist, Plekhanov was also a major literary theorist and critic who sought an aesthetic theory that would fit his Marxist ideology. He arrived at a conception according to which art, though a sui generis human activity, is also a superstructure of the socioeconomic base and therefore subject to the same laws of history. He looked to demonstrate the validity of this theory in a historical study, *French Dramatic Literature and French Painting of the Eighteenth Century from a Sociological Viewpoint* (1905), and in many essays and reviews on Russian and Western literature: "Gleb Uspensky" (1888), "The Literary Views of V. G. Belinsky" (1897), "N. G. Chernyshevsky's Aesthetic Theory" (1897), "The Proletarian Movement and Bourgeois Art" (1905), "A Critique of Decadence and Modernism: Henrik Ibsen" (1906), and "Dobrolyubov and Ostrovsky" (1911). He recapitulated his ideas in *Art and Social Life* (1912–13).

Plekhanov's theory of art is Hegelian—or Belinskian—as he takes Chernyshevsky, Dobrolyubov, and Pisarev to task for an ahistorical approach that would judge Pushkin by the sociohistorical standards of the 1860s and for ignoring the autonomous nature of art. He sees the interaction of art and social life as a dialectical process, rather than as a one-way dependance of art on the socioeconomic base, and rejects a blatantly utilitarian conception of art. He insists, however, on the truth value of art, as well as on objective criteria of art versus nonart: genuine art expresses progressive ideas and finds a form that is adequate to these ideas. There is nothing wrong with "tendentious" art if its "tendency" is progressive. Plekhanov's sociological approach allowed him to dismiss such manifestations of modernist art as formalism, décadence, and mysticism as an expression of the bourgeois artists' despair of, or escape from, a reality that threatened them with the imminent demise of their social class.

Plekhanov's aesthetic views were immensely influential. They were embraced by such Marxist critics as Lunacharsky and Vorovsky even before the 1917 revolution and by critics of the Pereval group in the 1920s. The principles of the sociological school of the 1920s also reflected Plekhanov's ideas, and the "thaw" after Stalin's death caused them to reemerge. Plekhanov was an influential figure even in international Marxist literary theory. Georg Lukács, in particular, owed much to him.

Rozanov

Vasily Vasilyevich Rozanov (1856–1919) graduated from Moscow University in the humanities in 1880 and taught secondary school in the provinces until 1893. He then worked as a free-lance journalist, publishing articles in such newspapers as *New Times* and *The Russian Word* and such journals as *The World of Art* and *New Path*. His first wife was Apollinariya Suslova, who had had a liaison with Dostoevsky in the 1860s. Difficult, unpredictable, and seemingly unprincipled, Rozanov made many enemies and had no real friends. His more perceptive contemporaries, however, did recognize the originality of his mind.

Inspired by an arbitrary interpretation of Dostoevsky, Rozanov developed an existential philosophy that went against the grain of every known strain of Russian thought. In some ways it did hark back to the *pochvennik* ideas of Apollon Grigoryev, for it pursued an organic plenitude of life in the maintenance of national and popular traditions realized in a happy private sphere—family life, sexuality, and the pursuit of individual goals. Much as Grigoryev had promoted the humble Ivan Petrovich Belkin as the prototype of the positive Russian, Rozanov pointed to the unassuming "doer of little things," like Lermontov's Maksim Maksimych and Tolstoi's Captain Tushin, as the positive stuff of Russian literature while condemning the one-sided satirical presentation of the pursuit of private happiness started by Gogol.

In his seminal essay *The Legend of the Grand Inquisitor* (1894) Rozanov correctly recognized that Dostoevsky's worldview hinged on the reality of that "mysterious other world" of which Father Zosima says that no one can live and love without touching. He notes, also correctly, that intrusions from "another world" may be diabolic, too. Rozanov made several other just observations that later became a part of the canon of the interpretation of Dostoevsky's works. He contrasted Tolstoi, the master of life that has assumed stable forms, to Dostoevsky, the analyst of what is still in flux. Rozanov's meticulous and perceptive analysis of the Grand Inquisitor chapter leads to the conclusion that its message is one of "a deep awareness of human weakness, bordering on contempt for man, and at the same time a love for him, a love that is ready to leave God and share man's abjection, beastliness, and stupidity—and with it, his suffering." Moreover, he asserts that mankind, inherently perverse and living a lie, can only be helped by more falsehood and perversion. Rozanov refuses to see that Dostoevsky's position is not Ivan Karamazov's. But his study is nevertheless a contribution of lasting value and is far superior to anything written about Dostoevsky by Rozanov's contemporaries.

In his essay "Pushkin and Gogol" (1894) Rozanov reversed the position of Chernyshevsky's *Essays in the Gogolian Period of Russian Literature*, declaring that it was Pushkin who was the founder of Russian realism, whereas Gogol had created mere caricatures of Russian life and by the magic of his artistry made generations of readers take his soulless puppets for real people, and the landscape of his imagination for Russia.[8]

Rozanov was at his best when writing in fragmentary aphoristic stream of consciousness, not unlike the method of Nietzsche, who had some influence on him. His books *Solitaria* (1912) and *Fallen Leaves* (1913–15) resemble Dostoevsky's *Notes from Underground* in the way the writer pointedly contradicts himself, mixes the profound with the banal, the philosophical with the mundane, the political with the intimate, as he discusses a great variety of topics in a lively feuilletonistic style. These books have a certain unity of emotion, which may be defined as a lonely soul's yearning for the warmth of love and compassion. Rozanov's last book, *The Apocalypse of Our Time* (1917–18), carries a truly tragic pathos.

---

8. This position, too, was to some extent anticipated by Grigoryev and Dostoevsky.

Rozanov's observations on the 1917 revolution show a visionary perceptiveness.

Symbolism

Russian symbolists perceived their movement both as a resumption of what romanticism had stood for and as an antithesis to the realism and positivism of the preceding period. Merezhkovsky's essay *On the Reasons for the Decline and on New Trends in Contemporary Russian Literature* (1893), which marks the beginning of Russian symbolism, was clearly directed against the ideological basis of the prevailing literary and artistic attitudes, sensibility, and style. The symbolists resuscitated the romantic poetry of Tyutchev and Fet and restored Pushkin to a permanent place of honor. E. T. A. Hoffmann was a favorite of theirs, and Vyacheslav Ivanov translated and wrote essays on Novalis.[9] The aesthetic theories of Apollon Grigoryev now received attention (Blok wrote an essay on him), and Dostoevsky's art seemed more congenial than Tolstoi's. In many ways symbolism repeated the development of romanticism. In a reaction to the apparent failure of the preceding age to satisfy the spiritual needs of the educated classes, it returned to an idealist worldview, renewing the search for absolute values and for a religious sensibility. Then, having driven such idealism to an extreme, some symbolists, like some romantics, would negate it through some form of romantic irony or veer into mysticism, escapism, or unchecked fantasy. The political experience of some Russian symbolists also paralleled that of the romantics: they started as near revolutionaries and eventually found themselves in the ranks of conservative opponents of the Soviet regime.

Russian symbolists resembled the romantics in many other ways, too. They tended to be philologically educated and actively interested in various branches of the humanities. Some did important scholarly work—Bryusov, Bely, and Vyacheslav Ivanov, for example. Although the symbolists were culturally cosmopolitan,[10] they developed a peculiar national sensibility and mythology. Like romanticism, too, Russian symbolism was an elitist movement. The reintegration of Russian poetry into Western literature came at the expense of giving up on the idea of *narodnost'* in art. Both romanticism and symbolism, in spite of a fondness for folk traditions and folk poetry, gave little thought to a better life for the people. The symbolists' returning of the individual to a position of absolute value inevitably happened at the expense of literature's social concerns—another repetition of what had occurred in the romantic age.

The poets who considered themselves symbolists not only had their individual styles and temperaments, as well as their particular literary and personal backgrounds, but also disagreed on questions of philosophical and aesthetic principle. Only a definition by negatives, as performed by those who were opposed to it, could make

9. Viktor Zhirmunsky's *German Romanticism and Contemporary Mysticism* (1914) drew attention to the many direct connections between romanticism and symbolism.

10. Nikolai Gumilyov, a critic of symbolism, gave the symbolists credit for this: "The Russian symbolists took upon themselves a difficult but lofty task: to lead Russian poetry from the Babylonian captivity of ideology and preconceived notions in which it had languished for nearly half a century. Beside their creative work they had to plant the seeds of culture, talk about elementary truths, and defend, foaming at their mouths, ideas that were truisms in the West. In this sense, Bryusov may be likened to Peter the Great." *Sobranie sochinenii*, 4 vols. (Washington, D.C.: Victor Kamkin, 1964–68), 4:235.

Russian symbolism a meaningful term. Certain figures, like Mikhail Kuzmin, must be considered marginal to symbolism in that their poetic style and aesthetic views were hardly representative of symbolism, although they were part of the inner circle of symbolists. Others, like Innokenty Annensky, did not belong to that circle at all but were symbolists in their conception of poetry. Some appear minor in retrospect, as do Georgy Chulkov (1879–1939) and Aleksandr Dobrolyubov (1876–1944?). Chulkov's pamphlet *On Mystical Anarchism* (1906) attempted to reconcile freedom with communal life through religious mysticism and ritual, an idea that goes back to the Slavophile Khomyakov. Chulkov was at one time close to Vyacheslav Ivanov, who held similar views. Chulkov, only a second-rate poet and novelist, distinguished himself as a literary historian after the revolution. Dobrolyubov, whose collection of ornate, aliusive, and dreamlike mystical poetry, *Natura naturans, Natura naturata* (1895), was one of the harbingers of symbolism, later became a pious pilgrim in the Russian north and eventually founded his own religious sect.

Russian symbolism had many antecedents and sources besides romanticism. The influence of German idealist philosophy, Schelling's in particular, was great, especially in the form in which it reached symbolist poets through the philosophy and poetry of Vladimir Solovyov. The influence of Schopenhauer and Eduard von Hartmann was also pervasive, as was Nietzsche's. French symbolism was substantial presence: virtually all the Russian symbolists translated French symbolist poetry. The German influence was greater among those Russians who were inclined to mysticism, whereas the aesthetes and decadents leaned toward the French. Some of the mystics were under the spell of Dostoevsky—Merezhkovsky and Ivanov in particular.

In symbolism (and acmeism, too) Russian literature saw a late but impassioned burst of Hellenism—finally, a Russian Renaissance!—and of romantic nostalgia for the Mediterranean. The symbolists perceived themselves as argonauts in pursuit of the Golden Fleece; hence the title of their journal.[11] There is a plenitude of classical themes in the poetry of Solovyov, Bryusov, Vyacheslav Ivanov, Kuzmin, and Voloshin. Mediterranean landscapes abound in their work, as well as in that of Blok and others.

A focal trait of Russian symbolism, shared by all symbolists, though not with equal devotion, was a professed Platonism that made the phenomenal world a mere reflection of a higher, ideal reality. Art was to the symbolists, in good romantic or Neoplatonic fashion, an avenue to grasping that higher reality, as their slogan indicates: *a realibus ad realiora.* Symbolist aesthetics is organic, entirely in the sense in which the romantics or Apollon Grigoryev had understood it. The symbolist poet Balmont put it this way: "How to define symbolist poetry? It is a poetry in which two contents are fused organically, not forcibly: a hidden abstraction and visible beauty flow together as easily and naturally as the waters of a river are harmoniously suffused with sunlight on a summer morning."[12] The emphasis that each symbolist placed upon the metaphysical or even mystical nature of the higher and ideal aspect of reality varied considerably. It could be religious, pantheist, theosophic, erotic, or even populist. Collectively, the Russian symbolists found symbolic corre-

11. Andrei Bely's programmatic poem of that title appeared in *The World of Art* in 1904.

12 Quoted from *Literaturnye manifesty*, ed. N. L. Brodsky (Moscow, 1929), 26.

spondences in any phenomenon of nature and of life. As Vyacheslav Ivanov, receptive to a broader range of correspondences than most symbolists, expressed it in a sonnet, "The Alpine Horn" (1901): "Nature is a symbol, like this horn. She resounds to make an echo. And the echo is God." Symbolist poetry almost never tries to describe mystic visions or the ineffable, actual religious experience. Symbolists are confident that their description or expression of the phenomenal will act as a bridge to a higher, ideal reality.

Symbolism as a whole took the romantic position of claiming intuitive cognitive power for art in general and for poetry in particular. The subject and presumed range of cognition vary greatly from author to author. Vladimir Solovyov and his followers spoke of mystical entities like the World Soul and the Eternal Feminine (*das Ewig-Weibliche*). Merezhkovsky and Hippius thought of themselves as founders of a new church. Bely and Ivanov saw their intuitions as a vehicle of spiritual regeneration and the birth of a higher humanity. The philosopher Nikolai Berdyaev at one time saw in Bely the bearer of "a new cosmic rhythm." Blok and Bely felt that the rhythms of their poems could capture the "music of the age," the rhythm of history, as it were. In the 1880s Solovyov at one time planned to write a treatise on aesthetics under the title "A Free Theurgy." Bely partly realized this plan in an essay, "On Theurgy" (1903). Theurgic creation meant the revelation through art and poetry of the "mystical essence" of phenomena and the promotion of a religious way of life in accord with it. The less mystically inclined among the symbolists avoided identifying the subject of intuitive cognition so precisely, but they, too, assigned real truth value to their creations.

Among the intuitions of the symbolists

were forebodings of an imminent crisis and catastrophe. Themes of utopia and regeneration alternate with eschatological visions and dystopia in Vladimir Solovyov and later in Merezhkovsky, Blok, and Bely. These eschatological moods are at times universal but are usually focused on the fate of Russia.

As with many romantics, music was the highest art form for the symbolists—higher even than poetry. Bely went as far as to say that whereas other art forms created images of phenomenal reality, music—and poetry, insofar as it was musical—reflected the "inner side" of these images, the movement giving them direction. Bely's rationale for this assumption was that the creative energy of a composer of music is untrammeled by the need to choose concrete images for the incarnation of his ideas. Blok perceived human history in terms of the musicality of an age and its culture: "In the beginning there was music. Music is the essence of the world. The world grows in elastic rhythms. This growth may be contained for some time, only to burst forth in a flood. . . . The growth of the world is culture. Culture is musical rhythm" (diary entry, March 31, 1919). Blok goes on to say that when a culture grows stale, it loses its music and becomes mere "civilization." The Russian symbolists' penchant for music was surely in part inspired by the French symbolists, as was their interest in sound symbolism, euphony, and the semantics of rhythm.

The fusion of word and music had to lead to further synesthetic conceptions, particularly because strong ties between music and the visual arts were also being promoted by contemporary composers and painters. Many symbolist—and acmeist—poems, particularly by Annensky, Balmont, Kuzmin, Voloshin, and Mandelshtam, are clearly aimed at creating a synesthetic impression.

Russian symbolism had its decadent side.

Until about 1900 the symbolists actually prided themselves on their decadence, but with Merezhkovsky's turn to religion, he and Zinaida Hippius, and later Vyacheslav Ivanov, drew a line between good and evil—that is, decadent—symbolism. Even the "good" symbolists, however, shared some traits with the decadents.

In its decadent traits, too, symbolism repeated the experience of romanticism and even of the baroque. It also exemplifies Leontyev's conception of "complex flowering": a coexistence of deep religious feeling and flagrant aestheticism, ascetic ideals and sensuality, cruelty and tenderness. Russian symbolists, partly under the influence of French decadence and of Nietzsche, were inclined to share the pessimistic moods of the European fin de siècle. "L'Ennui de vivre" (1902), the title of a poem by Bryusov, is a recurrent theme not only of Bryusov's poetry. The attraction of death and destruction is a pervasive theme, as is a fascination with horror, as in Hippius's poem "Spiders" (1903), and with the beauty of Sodom, of which Solovyov speaks eloquently in his poem "Das Ewig-Weibliche" (1898). Romantic satanism and a rich demonology are ubiquitous in Hippius, Sologub, Bely, Blok, and other symbolists. The romantic theme of the doppelgänger appears frequently. Another return to romantic themes and moods may be seen in symbolism's fondness for masks, the show-booth, and the puppet theater. The stylized reenactment of literary myths—Hamlet and Ophelia, Othello and Desdemona, Don Quixote and Dulcinea—is also a repetition of romantic practices.

The gothic aspect of romanticism has its symbolist equivalent in a turn to urbanism and a fascination with the seamy and nocturnal side of the big city. The aesthetization of life, a focal trait of decadence, also had its romantic antecedents. The philosophies of Schopenhauer and Nietzsche provided theoretical models and a moral justification for it. Bryusov proclaimed it in many eloquent verses.[13] The aestheticism of decadence is often accompanied by playfulness, frank escapism, exoticism, and a pursuit of the quaint, the morbid, and the bizarre—in all, a pointed antirealism. Even in Blok we find elements of a decadent sensibility in details of imagery and atmosphere. Their equivalents in the visual arts are found in Vrubel, Bakst, and other artists of the *World of Art* group. Decadence is marked by stylization but no style, by an escape from the major forms into the miniature, and by an absence of firm moral or aesthetic standards. A genre typical of decadence is the lyric *poema*—plotless, lacking focus, resembling a free stream of consciousness, fragmentary, and polymetric. Balmont, Bryusov, and Blok cultivated this genre.

Solovyov

Vladimir Sergeevich Solovyov (1853–1900) must be considered Russia's foremost professional philosopher, although his philosophical system was hardly original. He was certainly one of Russia's finest essayists. Although he is considered to have been only a minor poet, he did develop a distinctive poetic voice. His humorous skits were a step toward the Russian symbolist theater. Most important, Solovyov gave Russian symbolism a philosophy and an aesthetic theory. Both were inherited from German romantic idealism, but Solovyov gave them an attractive Russian form.

Solovyov was the son of Sergei Solovyov, a prominent historian and rector of Moscow University. A brilliant polyhistor, he de-

13. See p. 420.

fended his master's thesis, "The Crisis of Western Philosophy: Against the Positivists," in 1874 and his doctor's dissertation, "A Critique of Abstract Principles," in 1880. In 1875 and 1876 he traveled to London on a fellowship. While working at the British Museum he had a mystic vision, which caused him to travel to Egypt, where he had another vision. Upon his return to Russia he assumed a teaching assignment at Moscow University. His lectures, subsequently published as *Lectures on Godmanhood*, were a public success. It was in connection with them that Solovyov met Dostoevsky, with whom he undertook a pilgrimage to Optina Pustyn Monastery in 1879. (Solovyov may have been the prototype of Ivan Karamazov.) In 1881 Solovyov was dismissed from his teaching position for having suggested in a lecture that Tsar Alexander III pardon his father's assassins. He continued to publish prolifically, though, and his main concern in *The Spiritual Foundations of Life* (1884) and *The History and Future of Theocracy* (1887) was the introduction of religion into public life. He worked on the idea of a new ecumenical church and in two books advocated a rapprochement between the Catholic and the Orthodox churches: *L'Idée russe* (1888) and *La Russie et l'église universelle* (1889), written in French because they could not be published in Russia.

In the 1880s Solovyov developed friendships with Leontyev, Nikolai Fyodorov, and Fet. His relations with Fet were particularly cordial, in spite of their ideological differences (Fet was an agnostic). By the 1890s Solovyov's dreams of an ecumenical church had come to naught, and he withdrew into his own Neoplatonic-Gnostic religion, formulated in five essays published under the title *The Meaning of Love* (1892–94). An erotic ascetic, Solovyov developed a Platonic notion of eros as the means by which man overcomes self-will. At the same time, Solovyov was turning progressively more pessimistic with regard to Russia's future. Formerly an apologist of Russia as the "third Rome," he now foresaw the fall of the empire and Russia's relapse into Asian barbarity. Solovyov's last years produced some spirited polemical writings. In *The Justification of the Good* (1897) he sought to develop ethics as an autonomous philosophical discipline, rejecting not only Nietzsche's ethics of power and beauty but also Tolstoianism and so-called positive religion. His *Three Conversations on War, Progress, and the End of History* (1900) are a masterful revival of the Platonic dialogue. The main personae are a general who stands for practical religion and defends the use of force in a good cause, a liberal politician who advances the ideals of modern civilization, a Tolstoian who preaches nonresistance to evil, and a Mr. Z, who expresses Solovyov's ideas of an absolute and active Christianity. Solovyov's last work, "A Short Tale of the Antichrist" (1900), is a strangely vivid and detailed account of the end of the world in the twenty-first century. It appears that during the last few years of his life Solovyov experienced diabolical visitations. His poem "Das Ewig-Weibliche: An Admonitory Sermon to Sea Devils" (1898) is testimony to this effect.

Initially, Solovyov's philosophy was largely in accord with Dostoevsky's. They both believed in the possibility of a progressive transfiguration of humanity—its spiritualization, as it were—and in art as one of the vehicles of this process. Solovyov held that mankind could enter the Kingdom of God "through the gates of history," and so did Dostoevsky—a heretical position, as Leontyev pointed out. Solovyov and Dostoevsky also shared a belief in the decisive role of communality (*sobornost'*) in this process of transfiguration. Their conception of communality differs from that of Marxist communism in that it is based on people's moral and spiritual, rather than on their economic, needs.[14] At the time of his association with Dostoevsky, Solovyov also developed a theory of "three powers": the Moslem East which reduces man to nothingness and reveres an inhuman God; the West, which aims at elevating man to godhead; and a third power, which will act as a mediator between God and humanity—the Russian people, who will create a synthesis of East and West in "godmanhood." Essentially the same idea appears in Dostoevsky. There were also, however, some points of disagreement between Solovyov and Dostoevsky. Solovyov's religious mysticism was divorced from the populist mystique, so important for Dostoevsky. Politically, Solovyov was a westernizing liberal. His later move toward Catholicism would have shocked Dostoevsky.

The most striking trait of Solovyov's philosophy is his identification of Sophia, Divine Wisdom, with the Eternal Feminine, and the introduction into it of an erotic element.[15] It was this conception of Sophia that was to inspire the symbolist poets, especially Blok. Solovyov's theosophy, including his conception of Sophia, coincides with that of Jakob Böhme,[16] who was an important source of German romantic philosophy, Schelling's in particular. Solovyov follows Schelling in seeing matter as potential spirit, rather than as a *mē on* hostile to the spirit, which it is to Plotinus and the Gnostics.

Solovyov's aesthetic theory, which he passed on to the Russian symbolists, was Neoplatonic. He developed it under the impression of the lyric poetry of Fet, Polonsky, and Aleksei Tolstoi. In an essay, "On Lyric Poetry: On the Latest Poems of Fet and Polonsky" (1890), Solovyov builds an aesthetic theory from the concrete material of verses by these poets. He defines beauty "from the negative side as pure uselessness, and from the positive as spiritual corporeality." Art creates beauty by transforming matter through the incarnation in it of a spiritual principle. Solovyov's metaphor for this is a diamond made to sparkle by the light that passes through it. In another essay, "The General Meaning of Art" (1890), Solovyov resuscitates the Orphic conception of art and poetry, prominent in romantics like Novalis. His definition of art as "every sensual representation of any object or phenomenon with a view to its ultimate condition or in the light of the world of the future" is a corollary of his basic conceptions of the world engaged in a process of spiritualization and of the Kingdom of Heaven to be realized on earth. In the poem

14. In his *Lectures on Godmanhood* Solovyov developed an anthropology and Christology that one will recognize in Dostoevsky. The Johannine logos is God as active power. It generates *sophia*, ideal humanity or godmanhood. Christ unites in Himself logos and sophia. He is both God and man. Individual human beings partake of this faculty. Human beings, though individually distinct and alienated from one another as a result of the fall from grace, are nonetheless united in essence and strive for total unity and ideal humanity. Solovyov's conception of evil was also similar to Dostoevsky's. He saw self-will, self-assertion, and self-love as its essence.

15. Cf. Novalis, "Sophie, oder über die Frauen (das Ewig-Weibliche)." Its last aphorism reads, "Kunst, alles in Sophien zu verwandeln—oder umgekehrt" (Art—to transform everything into Sophia, or vice versa).

16. See Zdenek Vaclav David, "The Formation of the Religious and Social System of Vladimir S. Solovev (Ph.D. diss., Harvard University, 1960). David demonstrates Solovyov's direct dependance on Böhme.

"Three Feats" (1882) Solovyov assigns three tasks to art, each symbolized by a figure of Greek mythology: liberation of the idea from a block of marble (in the myth of Pygmalion), victory over the savage and chaotic (in the myth of Perseus), and victory over death (in the myth of Orpheus). The idea of the magic power of art occurs in various forms throughout Russian modernism, echoing Solovyov in the theurgic conception of the symbolists Blok, Bely, and Ivanov, in the cult of the living, magic word in the acmeists Gumilyov and Mandelshtam, and in the magic incantations of the futurist Khlebnikov. Solovyov also predicted an art of the future as direct "transfiguration" instead of mere representation of the world, an idea important for twentieth-century avant-garde art.

As a literary critic, Solovyov was interested almost exclusively in lyric poetry. He disliked Tolstoi not only as a thinker but also as an artist, and saw Dostoevsky only as a thinker. His favorite prose work was E. T. A. Hoffmann's "Der goldene Topf"—understandably so, as it is a metaphor of the transfiguration of the mundane into the spiritual. Of all Russian prose writers, Solovyov liked Gogol best, because he resembled Hoffmann most. Solovyov wrote a number of essays on Russian poets: Lermontov, Tyutchev, Aleksei Tolstoi, Polonsky, Sluchevsky, several on Pushkin, and an essay, "Russian Symbolists" (1895). As a critic he reintroduced the principles of romantic organic aesthetics, which had been overshadowed by a utilitarian or naturalist conception of art. Consistent with these principles, Solovyov rejected art for art's sake, the motto of Bryusov and the early decadents. The later symbolists, such as Vyacheslav Ivanov, followed Solovyov even on this point.

Merezhkovsky

Dmitry Sergeevich Merezhkovsky (1865–1941) came from an aristocratic family. His father was a high-ranking government official. Merezhkovsky studied the humanities at Saint Petersburg University (1884–88) and developed an early interest in literature. His first book of verse appeared in 1888. In 1889 he married Zinaida Nikolaevna Hippius. They settled in Saint Petersburg to start a lifelong creative relationship. After an initial populist phase, Merezhkovsky as early as 1885 turned to neoromantic themes under the influence of Baudelaire and Verlaine. A few years later he discovered Nietzsche, who dominated his thinking until the end of the 1890s. Merezhkovsky's book of verse *Symbols* (1892) and his treatise *On the Reasons for the Decline of, and on New Trends in, Contemporary Russian Literature* (1893) made him a leader of a new movement, called "decadent" or "symbolist." In the late 1890s Merezhkovsky, by then more a novelist and critic than a poet, turned from Nietzscheanism to Christianity, a development reflected in his first major critical study, *L. Tolstoi and Dostoevsky*, which appeared in *The World of Art* in 1900–1901. Merezhkovsky, Hippius, and their friend Dmitry Filosofov developed the concept of a "church of the Holy Flesh and the Holy Spirit," in which they sought to integrate the life-affirming traits of Greek paganism into Christian spirituality. Their religious thought also had strong apocalyptic overtones. In 1901 the private gatherings of a small group of intellectuals associated with *The World of Art* became the officially sanctioned Religious-Philosophical Society of Saint Petersburg. *New Path* became its organ in 1903. After the revolution of 1905, which the Merezhkovskys welcomed as a preview of the Second Coming, they moved to France, where they lived from 1906 to 1908. Merezhkovsky was now established as a major writer and critic. Two editions of his *Collected Works* appeared in 1911–13 and 1914, and many of his works were translated into various European languages. The Merezhkovskys were among the first Russian writers to actively oppose the Soviet regime. They fled Russia in 1919 and eventually settled in Paris.

Merezhkovsky's *On the Reasons for the Decline of Russian Literature* was a reassertion of the principles of romantic aesthetics and a critique of the positivism and utilitarianism then reigning in Russian literature. Merezhkovsky denounced the "flight from culture," Western culture in particular, in Russian life and charged that a "shame to be beautiful" vitiated the achievement even of major talents like Nekrasov and Gleb Uspensky. He urged Russian writers and critics to overcome the drabness, banality, and tedium into which they had sunk and not to be afraid of creating Goethean *schwankende Gestalten*—dream images, fleeting impressions, and indistinct symbols.

In *L. Tolstoi and Dostoevsky* Merezhkovsky did much to establish a fixed image of these writers. He saw them as antipodes: Tolstoi, essentially pagan, "Aryan," a great "seer of the flesh"; Dostoevsky, deeply spiritual, with an almost "Semitic" capacity for guilt and atonement. He made many excellent observations on the works of both writers, particularly by suggesting symbolic interpretations. Merezhkovsky's study was biased in Dostoevsky's favor. He later changed his mind on some issues and admitted that he had been unfair to Tolstoi.

In his novel-trilogy *Christ and Antichrist* (1895–1905) Merezhkovsky still saw Christ and Antichrist as opposing principles of equal power. After 1905 he changed this

position. In an open letter to Nikolai Berdyaev, "On New Religious Action" (1905), he declared that the Antichrist could not be an antithesis but only a travesty of Christ. The devil could pervert and debase God's work but had nothing himself to offer. In this, Merezhkovsky followed Dostoevsky. Yet in a treatise devoted specifically to Dostoevsky, *A Prophet of the Russian Revolution* (1906), he found fault with what he thought was Dostoevsky's confusion of state and people, of political-military and religious-moral goals, and with his failure to recognize that the Russian Orthodox church had, like the Western church, fallen into the trap of the devil's third temptation. At this stage Merezhkovsky hoped that a Russian "religious revolution" would sweep away both the "frozen anarchy" of the Russian monarchy and the godless materialism of Western bourgeois civilization.

In a prophetic treatise, *The Coming Boor* (1906),[17] Merezhkovsky speaks of the "yellow peril" that threatens Europe from the inside. Europe, and Russia with her, are turning "Chinese," positivist in principle, abandoning all spiritual values. In Russia the "coming boor" has three faces: the dead positivism of the tsar's police state, the dead positivism of the state church, and the dead positivism of the underclass. They threaten to crush the Russian intelligentsia: only a "coming Christ" can vanquish the "coming boor."

Besides a large number of political, philosophical, historical, and religious essays, reviews, and articles, Merezhkovsky wrote many essays on Russian and world literature. The first installment of a series, *Eternal Companions*, devoted to great figures of

17. *Gryadushchii kham*, In Russian *kham*, the biblical Ham, originally meant slave or serf, but in modern usage acquired a pejorative moral meaning: flunky, boor, lout.

world culture, appeared in 1897, and Mevezhkovsky continued it to the end of his life. Merezhkovsky wrote important studies of several Russian writers. Among the more interesting are his monograph *Gogol and the Devil* (1906) and the article "On Chekhov: Chekhov and Gorky" (1905). The former drew attention to a side of Gogol that had been largely ignored: the presence of cryptic diabolical forces that pull the strings even in those of his works in which personalized or allegorical demons are absent. The latter gave a rather surprising evaluation of two of his leading contemporaries. Merezhkovsky saw the work of Chekhov and Gorky as a retreat from the greatness of Tolstoi and Dostoevsky, accommodating the mood of a public with much-reduced aspirations. Chekhov, a great artist, said Merezhkovsky, had no positive message. The world he depicted was ever more turning into a world of the living dead. Meanwhile Gorky was an ideologue of the lumpen proletariat, an absolute, destructive, aggressive nihilist, a semiliterate follower of Nietzsche, who hated Russian peasants and their faith. Chekhov and Gorky, so Merezhkovsky felt, offered the Russian public object lessons in life without God. Merezhkovsky's literary criticism is opinionated, sometimes extravagant, but always spirited, perceptive, and vigorously argued.

Bryusov

Valery Bryusov's theory of art, literary criticism, and literary scholarship were eclectic. They reflected a lively though not original mind and a sincere love of art. Bryusov, a first-rate Pushkin scholar, patterned not only his poetry but also his theoretical thought after Pushkin. Like Pushkin, he wrote many poems on the theme of the poet, asserting the poet's special standing among people,

his freedom, and the dignity of his mission. Unlike Pushkin, he insisted that the poet's mission was not limited to his moments of inspiration but encompassed his whole life.

The young Bryusov tried to explain symbolism and decadence to the Russian public. In a preface to *Russian Symbolists* he pointed out that the strange and unusual tropes and figures of decadence were not an indispensable element of symbolism. Rather, he said, symbolists might use these, among other devices, "to hypnotize the reader, as it were, through a series of juxtaposed images and to elicit in him a certain mood." Even this early statement indicates that Bryusov's concern was with the art, or even with the technique, not with the content of poetry. He would retain this attitude for the rest of his life. Bryusov conceded that a poet could create the desired impression by presenting anything from "the whole picture" to a "seemingly chaotic assemblage of images." He considered symbolism, however, to be "a poetry of hints." In his essay "On Art" (1899) Bryusov defined art as an effort to make incarnate "a fleeting moment of human existence."

Bryusov's aesthetic was neo-Kantian, in spite of occasional concessions to mysticism, mostly in his poetry.[18] He was consistently opposed to the theurgic and mystical conception of the poet's mission preached by Bely and Vyacheslav Ivanov:[19] he once said, "We accept all religions, all mystical teachings, just to avoid being within reality."[20] In the essay "An Unneeded Truth:

18. "Know that all secrets are within us! / Where there's no thought, there are no centuries, / Light's only where there is an eye" ("To the Tsar of the North Pole").

19. Particularly in his essay "On 'Slavish Language,' in Defense of Poetry" (1910).

20. "Kto vsem, kto ishchet," introduction to A. Miropolsky, *Lestvitsa* (Moscow, 1903), 10–11.

Concerning the Moscow Art Theater" (1902) Bryusov states emphatically that "objective reality" is only material that may be used to express the artist's idea or the movements of the artist's soul: "Imitation of nature is a means in art, not its goal." Hence Bryusov's only commandment to the artist is, "Be sincere." Originality is a condition sine qua non. Imitation is always pseudo-art. Bryusov believed that the new art (symbolism) freed the artist from both the formal restraints of classicism and the romantic demand that art express "the reality of life" (Bryusov considered realism a branch of romanticism).

After 1900 Bryusov often voiced ideas that contradicted the conception of art as an expression of individual experience. In a review article on René Ghil's *De la poésie scientifique* he fully endorses Ghil's notion that poetry should not be afraid to tackle modern and even scientific problems, using its own intuitive approach. In the last years of his life Bryusov himself wrote some didactic poetry on themes of modern science.[21]

Bely

Throughout his life Andrei Bely struggled for an integrated worldview. Yet of all the major symbolists he was least successful in creating order in his own thinking, or even in synchronizing the ideas of his poetry, prose fiction, aesthetic theory, and philological work, all of which were significant.

In his early years Bely was obsessed with creating a philosophically based aesthetic theory of symbolism and devoted a large number of essays to this task. Some of these were collected in the volumes *Symbolism* and *A Green Meadow* (both 1910). Bely perceived symbolism not as a mere school

of poetry, as Bryusov did and as it really was in retrospect, but as a spiritual movement which had significantly expanded the horizons of human cognition and creativity. He refused to see symbolism as a "modernist" school and correctly pointed out that Bryusov had more ties to Pushkin and Baratynsky than to Merezhkovsky, who in turn had more in common with Dostoevsky and Nietzsche than with Blok, whose closest ties were to early romanticism.

In his theory of art Bely frequently refers to Kant, Schopenhauer, Nietzsche, Heinrich Rickert, Hermann Cohen, Herbert Spencer, and other philosophers. He sees the essence of art in "the revelation of an absolute principle by way of one or another aesthetic form."[22] The energy of artistic creation is therefore identical with that of religious experience. Bely admits, however, the possibility of creating a system of arbitrary or conventional symbols forming a fictitious symbolic world which leads away from truth and from reality.[23] In the essay "The Emblematics of Meaning" (1909) Bely establishes a rather Hegelian "ladder of realities" (*lestvitsa deistvitel'nosti*), along which the energy of human creativity advances in revealing progressively higher forms of the absolute. The rungs of this ladder, which starts at chaos and ends in logos, comprise "primitive symbolism," myth, aesthetic creation, religious creation, and theurgy. Each level acts as an emblem of the form next to it in the hierarchy. For example, in aesthetic creation the religious symbol of the Son appears as Dionysus, and Sophia (Divine Wisdom) as the muse.

Bely, like the romantic philosophers,

21. See p. 420.

22. "The Meaning of Art" (1907), in *Symbolism* (1910), 199.

23. "Symbolism and Contemporary Russian Art" (1908), in *Green Meadow* (1910), 29–30.

arranges the art forms hierarchically. His criterion is freedom from the constraints of a three-dimensional reality. He thus obtains the scheme *architecture—sculpture—painting—poetry—music.*

Art is to Bely, as in romantic aesthetics, symbolic by definition, for it is always an effort to capture the absolute—whether one calls it the noumenal (with Kant), "pure contemplation of the world will" (with Schopenhauer), or "a manifestation of the spirit of music" (with Nietzsche)—in terms of the artist's particular experience. Bely calls a symbol in the conventional sense an "emblem" and, like the romantics, insists that an allegory is never a symbol.

Although Bely's basic aesthetic positions were only rediscoveries of familiar romantic clichés, he made some perceptive and pertinent observations on the contemporary scene. In the essay "Lyrics and Experiment" (1909) he anticipated Russian formalism in deploring the incorporation of aesthetics and poetics into sociology, history, and anthropology, and also registered the fact that the emergence of mass art forced people truly devoted to art "to descend to the catacombs," that is, into esoteric art. In "The Magic of Words" (1909), which in many ways anticipates the ideas of Gumilyov and Mandelshtam, Bely perceives all human creativity as essentially verbal: "The word is the only real ship on which we sail from one unknown to the other, amidst unknown spaces called earth, heaven, ether, the void, etc., and amidst unknown times called gods, demons, souls." Verbal creation, though only an "illusion of cognition," is, however, the only way in which man can "defend himself against the onslaught of the unknown." History thus becomes a cyclical development of the flourishing, then decaying, crystallizing, and renewed flourishing of the word.

In "The Art of the Future" (1907) Bely discusses the alienation of modern art from reality and suggests, much as Hegel had said a hundred years earlier, that it is caused by a prevailing emphasis on method instead of substance. In its extreme manifestation this tendency leads to nonobjective art in which method becomes an end in itself. Such art is, in Bely's opinion, tantamount to chaos and disintegration of art as a whole, since each work of art becomes a form in itself, whereas "myth has become frozen or has disintegrated into colors and stones." At the same time art of this kind, no longer intuitive, moves into the domain of science and technology. The old art—a symphony by Beethoven, Nietzsche's dionysiac dithyrambs—becomes, in spite of all its splendor, dead, artfully embalmed art. Modern art faces a fatal crisis. The way out of it will be found by theurgic artists, creators of a new religious worldview.

Bely's attempts to apply his theoretical conceptions to the contemporary literary scene in Russia are mostly vague and, in retrospect, rarely felicitous. This is true of his essay "The Apocalypse in Russian Poetry" (1905), in which he sketches the religious-philosophical genesis of Russian symbolism starting with Vladimir Solovyov's apocalyptic visions and ending in an ecstatic invocation of the Second Coming. It is also true of "Symbolism" (1908), in which he seeks to summarize the ideal essence and the goals of symbolism, and "The Meaning of Art" (1907), in which he tries to characterize his fellow symbolists in terms of his aesthetic categories.

Blok

Aleksandr Blok's aesthetic views were more conventionally romantic than those of his fellow symbolists. Especially in his early phase, he was more directly under the influence of Vladimir Solovyov than they. As a student, he studied Platonic philosophy. Blok's philosophy of art was close to that of Apollon Grigoryev, about whom he wrote an appreciative essay. He was convinced of the cognitive powers of the artist's intuition, which "removes the covers from the truth of life," and considered the argument about "pure" and "didactic" art to be vacuous because the aesthetic and the moral value of a genuine work of art were one. All his life Blok believed that the poet was somehow more closely in touch with "universal life" and history than were other humans. More than the other symbolists, too, Blok lived a "poetic life": to be a poet, he felt, meant to devote oneself entirely to poetry.

Blok, an important innovator and perhaps the most accomplished master of verse rhythm in Russian literature, conceived of the cognitive function of poetry as the poet's perception of the rhythm of life, a notion also embraced by Schiller and Novalis, among others. He said that the experiences and impressions that he tried to express in his poetry were decidedly musical and were perceived by him as rhythmic units. Blok states this explicitly in the preface to his poem *Retribution*. As for lyric poetry, Blok's essay "On Lyric Poetry" (1907) makes it a distinct way to perceive the world rather than a mere literary genre.

Blok's worldview underwent a tortuous transformation. The Solovyovian religious mysticism of his early years gave way to the disillusionment, pessimism, and decadence of the late 1900s. In 1908 Blok wrote several papers in which he discussed the crisis of Russia, of the Russian intelligentsia, and of contemporary art. In "The People and the Intelligentsia" he warns that Russia is on the eve of a catastrophe, a notion he also expressed in several poems of that period. In

"Element and Culture" and "Three Questions" he discusses the alienation of art from the basic concerns of public life. Recalling that there once existed a firm link between art and labor, namely rhythm (in work songs, for example), Blok asks where that link is today, and answers that the oeuvre of Ibsen, for one, "says, sings, shouts that duty is the rhythm of our life." Yet, he continues, there are always few true artists, and there may be none at all today, as the modern artist precariously steers his ship between the Scylla of "an unattainable phantom of *beauty*" and the Charybdis of "the immobile and impenetrable cliffs of the *necessary*." The modern artist's task is to produce a consciousness of beautiful duty; but as things stand, beauty is useless, the useful ugly.

In his essay "On the Contemporary Condition of Russian Symbolism: In Response to V. I. Ivanov's Lecture" (1910) Blok recapitulates his own career as a poet and the course taken by Russian symbolism. The "theurgic stage" inspired by Vladimir Solovyov, a period of faith in mystic visions and absolute truths, is the thesis of this development. Its antithesis arrives with the realization that it is the poet himself who has created and who controls the spirits—and demons—of his visions. This is the period of Blok's *Show-booth* (1906), the period when the poet realizes that the Beautiful Lady, symbol of the Eternal Feminine, is only a doll made by him. A synthesis is produced by the poet's realization that the demons he has created begin to act—as in the impending social upheaval. At this stage Blok resolutely condemns the decadent moods of symbolism, including his own.[24]

24. In a poem of 1885, "The raptures of the soul with calculated deception [he replaced]" (Vostorg dushi raschetlivym obmanom), Vladimir Solovyov had charted with amazing precision the

Blok responded to the events of 1917 at first alertly and with hope, then with despair. After the October revolution Blok writes the poem "The Twelve" and an essay that may be read as a commentary to it, "Intelligentsia and Revolution" (1918). Once again he expresses his idea in musical terms. He says that the intelligentsia used to like "those dissonances, those roars, those ringing bells, those unexpected transitions—in concert." Now the time has come to show if the intelligentsia really loves this music, or merely liked to titillate its nerves with it in music halls. The true intelligentsia must hear and accept the music of the revolution. Blok's "The Twelve" was an attempt to capture this music.

Blok's effort to accept the revolution was short-lived. He soon realized that it had brought with it no "music" at all. In his last public lecture, "On the Poet's Calling" (1921), Blok spoke of Pushkin and the nature of poetry. He returns to his original romantic conception of the poet, whom he declares to be "a son of harmony" and "an immutable entity" whose calling entails three tasks: "The first is to free sounds from their native, chaotic element, the second is to bring these sounds into harmony and to give them shape, and the third, to introduce this harmony into the external world." Who prevents the poet from fulfilling his mission? Censorship may stop him at the third stage. Ideology is more dangerous, for it may divert the poet from his pursuit of harmony and point him toward cacophony. The progressive critic Belinsky was a more dangerous enemy of poetry than Count Benckendorf, Pushkin's censor. Blok's lecture was a frontal attack on the Soviet government's efforts to ideologize literature.

course that Aleksandr Blok would take. A poem by Blok, "When I first saw the light" (Kogda ya prozreval vpervye, 1909) resembles Solovyov's.

Ivanov

Vyacheslav Ivanov, a classical philologist of great accomplishment, was the most learned among the symbolists. His many theoretical articles, gathered in the volumes *Following the Stars* (1909) and *Furrows and Landmarks* (1916), were based on an intimate familiarity with Plato and Neoplatonism, German idealism, Goethe and German romanticism, Dostoevsky, Vladimir Solovyov, and Nietzsche. Like Solovyov and his fellow symbolists, Ivanov believed in the poet as a seer, saw art as inherently symbolic, and condemned art for art's sake as categorically as he rejected the excesses of mimesis. Like Solovyov and Blok, he warned against "illusionism" in poetry—verbal magic with no basis in objective reality. Of course Ivanov's concept of reality included a higher, mystical reality: the artist's task was to advance *a realibus ad realiora*.

Ivanov introduced into the familiar structure of romantic aesthetics several categories which he had found in Nietzsche. The most important is that of Dionysian and Apollonian creation, from which derive further discriminations, such as creation from hunger and from plenitude, male and female creation, as well as creative ascent and creative descent. Apollonian ascent is "a winged victory" over earthly inertia; Dionysian descent goes down to the womb of Mother Earth. Ivanov recognizes manifestations of ascent and descent not only in classical but also in Christian myth: he saw ascent in the soul's yearning for a union with the divine and in an ascetic's renunciation of this world, descent in God's second hypostasis, the Son, in Christ's kenosis, and in the Christian humility of the Russian people.

In an essay of 1913, "On the Limits of Art," Ivanov develops a hierarchy of the creative imagination on a vertical axis of ascent toward an epiphany and subsequent descent to artistic incarnation. The lowest form of art takes the artist to a subjective mirroring of his own consciousness. Objective realist art rises a step higher and is exceeded by "transcendent contemplation of a reality to be overcome," a region of the imagination which Ivanov calls "the desert." Art of "high symbolism" traverses the desert and reaches for "higher realities." On its descent the imagination goes through several stages of "Dionysian excitation," which leads on to incarnation. This model of artistic creation bears a strong resemblance to the vertical topography of a spiritual cosmos in Neoplatonism.

Ivanov, himself an esoteric poet and dramatist, professed in his theoretical writings a traditional social organicism. The artist is a member of the community and must meet its commissions. Dionysian artists are mystifiers who give their public riddles, mysteries, and masks. Aeschylus, Shakespeare, and Goethe were Dionysians. Apollonian demystifiers, like Sophocles, Cervantes, and Tolstoi, tear off masks and reveal the essence of life to the community. In another, hierarchic, arrangement, Ivanov establishes an ascending gradation of the artist's independence: In pandemic art, such as Homer's or Dante's, the creator is submerged in the soul of his people. In demotic art, like that of the great European novelists, he loses some of the plenitude of life but establishes an individual vision of the world. Once he progresses from the "grand" to the "small" forms of "intimate art," his lyric voice is heard by still fewer people but is very much his own. In the last stage, which Ivanov calls the monastic (*keleinoe*, from *kel'ya*, "cell"), the creator, by relinquishing his ties with society, fuses his "I" with the cosmic absolute.

Ivanov applied all these ideas to contemporary literature. He saw the art of Russian

decadence as 'intimate art" but felt that a rebirth of "grand art" was imminent. In particular, he looked for a rebirth of the drama as a pandemic syncretic form in which all art forms would once more be fused. Ivanov deplored the "aesthetic anarchism or eclecticism" of his age, rejected abstractionism because he felt that anthropomorphism is inherent in art, and was critical of any art that abandons life for any sort of riddles, games, or formal exercises.

Consistently with his philosophy, Ivanov also rejected the psychologism characteristic of much of contemporary literature. He wanted dramatic and novelistic characters to be symbols, not individuals. Subjective psychological detail could only detract from the symbolic meaning of art, Ivanov felt. He correctly pointed out that Dostoevsky, though a great psychologist, always insisted that "scientific" psychological analysis was not the correct approach to the secrets of human nature.

Besides his scholarly works in classical philology, Ivanov wrote many articles and essays on Russian and world literature. Whereas his articles on Goethe, Schiller, Novalis, Byron, and other figures of world literature are competent but not particularly original, his essays on Gogol, Dostoevsky, and Tolstoi are highly idiosyncratic and of seminal importance. Starting in 1911, Ivanov wrote several long essays on Dostoevsky which eventually became the basis of a German book, *Dostojewskij: Tragödie—Mythos—Mystik* (1932).[25] Ivanov's reading of Dostoevsky was a major step in the direction of a symbolic, multileveled, and dialogic interpretation of Dostoevsky's novels, widely accepted by Western scholars. He coined the term *novel-tragedy* for Dos-

25. Published in English as *Freedom and the Tragic Life* (1952).

toevsky's novels and read them as religious allegories of the human condition, analogous to the myths of Greek drama. Like Merezhkovsky, Ivanov saw Tolstoi as an antipode of Dostoevsky. In an essay of 1912, "Tolstoi and Culture," Ivanov characterizes Tolstoi as a great simplifier and rationalist, whose "moral utilitarianism" was deeply hostile to Dionysus, art, and spirituality. Ivanov's brilliant essay "Gogol's *Inspector General* and the Comedy of Aristophanes" (1925) advances the thesis that Gogol's comedy harks back to the old comedy, a public spectacle where a community acts, speaks, and is addressed—an interpretation supported by Gogol's own explanation advanced in "The Denouement of *The Inspector General.*"

Acmeism arose in connection with the crisis in Russian symbolism in 1909–10 around the journal *Apollon*, edited by Nikolai Gumilyov and Sergei Makovsky. Some of the leading symbolists published their work in *Apollon* and settled their differences on its pages. Mikhail Kuzmin's essay "On Beautiful Clarity" (1910), which appeared in *Apollon*, attacked the core of symbolist aesthetics by suggesting that clarity and beauty, rather than mysterious vagueness and metaphysical profundity, were the essence of poetry. Gumilyov's essay "The Life of Verse" (also 1910) established the central position of what would be the acmeist aesthetics, namely, that the poetic word was analogous to a living organism and had a complex existence of its own. In a review article of 1910 Gumilyov set up Innokenty Annensky, whose posthumous collection *The Cypress Coffer* was one of the titles under review, as an antithesis to symbolism, calling Annensky's poetry "a catechism of contemporary sensibility." In retrospect however, Annensky was more of a symbolist than an acmeist.

In November 1911, after a clash with Vyacheslav Ivanov, Gumilyov founded the Poets' Guild (*tsekh poetov*), a workshop whose participants would later be known as acmeists. Reviews of and references to symbolism and individual symbolists by Gumilyov and members of the Poets' Guild were civil but bold in criticizing older and well-established poets. Mandelshtam's essay "On the Interlocutor" (1913) was out-and-out disrespectful toward Balmont.

Gumilyov first used the term *acmeism* in his September 1912 review article, which is devoted largely to a fellow acmeist, Sergei Gorodetsky. He defines acmeism as a school whose poets "have repudiated both the excesses of youth and flaccid, senile moderation, who strain all their powers uniformly, who embrace the word in all its dimensions—musical, pictorial, and ideological—and who demand that every creation be a microcosm in itself." In January 1913 two acmeist manifestos, Gumilyov's "Acmeism and the Precepts of Symbolism" and Gorodetsky's "Some Currents in Contemporary Russian Poetry," appeared in *Apollon.* Mandelshtam's "The Morning of Acmeism," written in 1913, appeared only in 1919. Gorodetsky's manifesto gave an alternate name, Adamism, to the movement, defining it as an effort to perceive the world anew, as Adam did on the day of his creation. Programmatic poems by six self-declared acmeists appeared in the March issue of the journal: Gumilyov, Gorodetsky, Mandelshtam, Anna Akhmatova, Vladimir Narbut, and Mikhail Zenkevich.

Acmeism was born of symbolism—Vyacheslav Ivanov's Tower[26] rather than decadence—and shared important traits with it. The acmeists shared the symbolists' "nostalgia for world culture" and incorporated

26. See p. 434.

the mythology and literature of the West into their own creations. They had a similar historical consciousness and like the symbolists thought that their poetic sensibility had an ethical and epistemological dimension. They adhered to a similar organicist aesthetic and believed in "inner form." Acmeism was antithetical to symbolism in its rejection of symbolism's pursuit of the metaphysical, its mysticism, and its vagueness and ambiguity. Acmeism wanted to be poetry of the real, not the allegorical, rose, of the real woman, not of the Eternal Feminine. Acmeism therefore went back from a metaphysical to biological organicism. "A poem, like Pallas Athene, who sprang from the head of Zeus, arises from the poet's soul and becomes a separate organism, and like every living organism it has its anatomy and its physiology," said Gumilyov in an essay, "The Reader" (published posthumously in 1923). Once alive, poems enter human life—some as guardian angels, some as wise leaders, some as dear friends, but some as corrupting and tempting demons.

A good deal of acmeist thought and poetry deals with the conception of "the word as such," the "living word" possessed of a body and a soul, with a life of its own. Gumilyov expressed this notion in a famous poem, "The Word" (published 1921), and Mandelshtam stated it many times in verse and in prose. The acmeists stressed that the logos (conscious meaning) was very much a part of the poetic word, certainly no less than the "music" of the symbolists. When the futurists threw conscious meaning overboard, Mandelshtam said in "The Morning of Acmeism," they were as much in the wrong as their realist predecessors, who thought that logos alone represented the content of a word.

A corollary of the acmeist conception of the poetic word is an understanding of the poet and his audience which Mandelshtam developed in a brilliant essay, "On the Interlocutor." True poetry, Mandelshtam suggests, does not address itself to a concrete interlocutor but rather to an unknown and sometimes a distant one. The difference between poetry and literature is precisely that the former is concrete and deals with the known—how else could an unknown addressee grasp it?—whereas the latter accommodates its message to a known addressee and can afford to take much knowledge for granted. Nadson's poetic self-analysis is boring because he is his own interlocutor and hence the only person really interested in his subject, whereas Sologub's poems, addressed to a distant and vaguely defined interlocutor, are fascinating.

The acmeists opposed to the shadowy, fleeting images of symbolism the ideal of a poetry that reflected an integrated and structured, yet vigorous and dynamic culture. In the essay "François Villon" (1910) Mandelshtam praised Villon's concreteness, which swept away the abstract allegorical edifice of the *Roman de la rose.* Christian culture, the freedom and inspiration which it gives to the artist, is stressed instead of the Neoplatonic speculations of symbolism. It was with this in mind that Mandelshtam devoted some of the best poems of his first collection, *Stone* (1913), to the great edifices of Christendom. The religious attitude of the acmeists—they are no less positive as regards religion than the symbolists—is this-worldly. They see this world not as an obstacle to spiritual life but "as a castle given us by God," as Mandelshtam put it in "The Morning of Acmeism." And whereas the symbolists strove *a realibus ad realiora*, the acmeists were happy with Schelling's law of identity. "A = A—what a beautiful poetic theme," said Mandelshtam in the same article.

Russian futurism subsumes several diverse groups, some of whose members belonged to different groups at different times. There was some rivalry, and a united front of Russian futurism never existed, although close personal and professional ties linked members of different groups. The social, philosophical, and aesthetic beliefs of the Russian futurists were extremely diverse, not to say chaotic, and the one thing that united them was that they all flouted social and literary conventions and were hostile to all past as well as contemporary art and literature, except that of select modernist schools. This hostility was directed especially at the symbolists, although Russian futurism in many instances took over or modified ideas, practices, and devices characteristic of Russian decadence and even mystical symbolism.

Ego-futurism, founded by Igor Severyanin and Konstantin Olimpov in Saint Petersburg in 1911, was proclaimed in a manifesto of January 1912. It was a hodgepodge of theosophy, Max Stirner, Schopenhauer, and Nietzsche—essentially decadence vulgarized to suit the tastes of a middlebrow public. Ego-futurism advocated a cult of the ego, *jouissance de vie*, amoralism, and vitalism. The poetics of Severyanin and the other ego-futurists was only mildly unconventional, but it featured a profusion of (not-too-inventive) neologisms, such as *poeza*, "poem."

In 1913 Vadim Shershenevich (1893–1942) founded the Mezzanine of Poetry, a futurist group close to ego-futurism, in Moscow. It issued three almanacs, *Vernissage, A Feast during the Plague*, and *Crematorium of Common Sense* (all 1913). Shershenevich's treatise *Futurism without a Mask* (1913), followed by *Green Street* (1916),[27] was essentially a restatement of the ideas of the Italian futurist Marinetti, whose works Shershenevich also translated. Shershenevish later became the founder of Russian imagism.

Centrifuge, another futurist group based in Moscow, issued several miscellanies: *Lyrics* (1913), *Brachiopod* (1914), and *A Second Centrifuge Miscellany* (1916). It was connected with avant-garde art groups, and its publications were illustrated by such avant-garde artists as Alexandra Exter and El Lisitsky. The group was headed by Sergei Bobrov (1889–1971) and had among its members Boris Pasternak and Nikolai Aseev. It was less radical than the other futurist groups and feuded with the cubo-futurists and the Mezzanine of Poetry. It leaned toward symbolism and showed some German influence (E. T. A. Hoffmann, Rilke). The Centrifuge group developed no coherent aesthetic, but one of its members, Ivan Aksyonov (1884–1935), advocated an aesthetic theory according to which rhythm was the foundation of all art.

The cubo-futurists were by far the most important group of avant-garde poets. They originated from a circle of poets who called themselves *budetlyane* (from *budet*, "will be") and had contributed to a modernist miscellany, *Studio of Impressionists* (1910), edited by Nikolai Kulbin, an army doctor who sponsored several modernist undertakings. Among the poems in this collection were Velimir Khlebnikov's "Incantation by Laughter" and "Thickets Were Filled with Sound," soon recognized as landmarks of Russian avant-garde poetry. Another miscellany of 1910, *A Trap for Judges*, which had

---

27. "Green Street" is a euphemism for the gauntlet.

pieces by the three Burlyuk brothers, David, Nikolai, and Vladimir, Vasily Kamensky, and Elena Guro, showed the marks of what would soon become cubo-futurism: a pointed anti-aestheticism (it was printed on wallpaper), a good deal of *épatage*, and an assault on the writers connected with *Apollon*. In 1912 the same group, led by David Burlyuk (1882–1967), a professional painter and amateur poet, and now joined by Vladimir Mayakovsky and Aleksei Kruchonykh (1886–1969), published a manifesto, *A Slap in the Face of Public Taste*, which established cubo-futurism as a nuisance at first, and soon as a major phenomenon on the literary scene. The manifesto proposed to "throw overboard from the steamer of contemporary life" not only all of the classics (including Pushkin) but also every known contemporary writer, even some of a decidedly modernist bent like Sologub, Kuzmin, Remizov, and Gorky. Bryusov came in for a particularly vitriolic putdown. On the positive side, the manifesto proposed to create an entirely new literary language and announced the coming of the "self-sufficient word" (*samovitoe slovo*). *A Slap in the Face of Public Taste* was followed by a slew of other futurist publications, mostly short pamphlets. The first cubo-futurist almanac bore the title *Futurists—"Hylaea"—Croaked Moon* (1913).[28] It contained Benedikt Livshits's programmatic essay "The Liberation of the Word." *The Word as Such*, another futurist manifesto, written by Khlebnikov and Kruchonykh,

appeared the same year. The fall of 1913 saw the presentation on alternate nights at Petersburg's Luna Park Theater of Mayakovsky's lyric drama *Vladimir Mayakovsky*, with the poet in the title role, of course, and Kruchonykh's "opera" *Victory over the Sun*, with a prologue by Khlebnikov. Both were done in collaboration with avant-garde painters. *Victory over the Sun*, which has the futurists capture and bring home the sun, was a dig at the solar cult of symbolism, with the sun a symbol of the illusory world of the past.[29] In the winter of 1913–14 the futurists went on a tour of the Russian provinces. They read their poetry and lectured on modern art and the new modernist aesthetic. Their appearances were accompanied and advertised by outrageous publicity stunts and drew large crowds. They featured mainly David Burlyuk, Kamensky, and Mayakovsky, who was quickly turning into the star of the movement. The ego-futurist Severyanin initially participated in the tour but soon quit.

Cubo-futurism, like the other branches of futurism, was apolitical. Mayakovsky, Aseev, Kamensky, and many others discovered their political calling only after the revolution. Livshits declared that the poetry of Futurism "did not seek any relations whatsoever with the world and in no way coordinated itself with it."[30] Mayakovsky in 1914 suggested that "perhaps the whole war was

28. In antiquity Hylaea was the Greek name of the region north of the Black Sea, now part of the Ukraine, whence came the Burlyuk brothers. The name Hylaea was to give the movement a "Scythian" flair, suggesting something primeval and savage, yet dynamic. Primitivism, however, was only one of the components of the futurist sensibility.

29. Symbolism itself had sublated its cult of the sun. In Sologub's *Dragons* (Zmii, 1907), the sun is berated as the source of earthly existence and thus the origin of evil and suffering.

30. Benedikt Livshits (1887–1939) had written some noteworthy poetry before joining the futurists. His memoir, *The One-and-a-Half-Eyed Archer* (1933), is one of the main sources on futurism and Russian avant-garde art. *The One-and-a-Half-Eyed Archer* is also the title of a brilliant cubist painting by Vladimir Burlyuk. The archer is a Scythian, of course.

thought up only so somebody would write one good poem about it." In opposition to symbolism and acmeism, cubo-futurism was deeply antihistorical, though in two drastically different ways: on the one hand, an unconditional cult of urban modernity coupled with a nihilist attitude toward all past culture, and on the other, a return to the prehistorical tribal culture of an imaginary Slavic race. In opposition to symbolism and acmeism, cubo-futurism advocated a formalist aesthetic, with a tendency to reduce art to skill, craftsmanship, and virtuosity. Cubofuturists liked to create effects by means of such mechanical devices as "typographical metaphor" (paper, type, layout, and spelling made to relate to the content of a work), blatant onomatopoeia, persistent sound symbolism, and synesthesia. At the crossroads where man faces the choice between the roads to mangodhood, godmanhood, and a return to pristine innocence, cubofuturism would choose the first or the third: the mangodhood of the perfect machine[31] or the pristine innocence of primitivism. It was no accident that Vasily Kamensky (1884–1961), a leading cubo-futurist, was also one of Russia's first aviators.

Russian cubo-futurism had several distinct sources. There is a strong expressionist strain in Russian modernism, cubo-futurism in particular. Several Russians played an important role in German expressionism. Vasily Kandinsky was one of its leaders. David Burlyuk exhibited with the Blaue Reiter group (so named after a painting by Kandinsky). Expressionism sought bright, loud, bold colors, sharp transitions, jagged outlines—all traits in which it was diametrically opposed to impressionism. Symbolist poetry was largely impressionist, whereas, futurist poetry was expressionist. Expressionism was of two kinds, one colorful and life-affirming, the other painfully aware of the ugliness, cruelty, and horror of life, especially modern urban life. The painters Kandinsky, Larionov, and Goncharova and the poets Pasternak and Aseev belonged to the former type, Burlyuk and Mayakovsky to the latter. Most of the futurist poets were also painters. Burlyuk, Mayakovsky, and Kruchonykh were painters before they became poets. Much impressed with the cubism of Picasso and Braque, they proceeded to apply its principles to poetry. David Burlyuk said that modern art was based on "disharmony, dissymmetry, and disconstruction," and Kruchonykh asserted that the basic elements of art were texture (*faktura*), deformation (*sdvig*), and penetration into regions of trans-sense (*zaum'*). Much as the cubist painter atomizes line, plane, and color, then reassembles these elements to achieve deformation and (through it) transsense penetration, the poet must atomize language into its constituent roots and sounds, then reassemble them to create new, or discover hidden, meanings. Kruchonykh perceived vowels in terms of spatial and temporal functions, consonants in terms of color, sound, and smell. This fanciful notion would be the seed of Roman Jakobson's acoustic phonology of "distinctive features." Khlebnikov developed a theory of language resembling Plato's in *Cratylus*. It makes the "roots" of language absolute entities from which words and languages are created: words, Khlebnikov said, were "of men," their roots "of God." Going back to the primeval Slavic roots of Russian and giving them their "original" (etymological) meaning, Khlebnikov believed, would open up wholly new and profound, even cosmic, aspects of meaning. His "Incantation

31. Not a new idea: Heinrich von Kleist had thought of it in his essay "Über das Marionettentheater" (1811).

by Laughter" was an exercise in creating a poem from variations of a single root, *sme-* (laugh).

The influence of the Italian futurist Filippo Tommaso Marinetti on Russian futurism is indubitable, but it poses some problems. Marinetti's first futurist manifesto, issued February 20, 1909, was printed in the Saint Petersburg newspaper *Evening* on March 8, 1909. Khlebnikov's first "futurist" piece, "A Sinner's Temptation," appeared in the Petersburg modernist magazine *Springtime* in October 1908. Burlyuk falsely claimed that *A Trap for Judges, I* had appeared in 1908. Mikhail Osorgin's *Sketches of Contemporary Italy* (1913) contained the full text of Marinetti's manifesto and ample background information. It was probably the principal source of Shershenevich's version of futurism. Late in 1913 Mayakovsky gave a talk in Moscow on "The Achievements of Futurism," in which he categorically denied any connection between Italian and Russian futurism. When Marinetti visited Russia in the winter of 1914, giving several lectures in French, he was vehemently attacked by Khlebnikov in Saint Petersburg and by Larionov in Moscow. After Marinetti's second lecture in Saint Petersburg (February 4, 1914) the Russian cubo-futurists published a declaration to the effect that they had nothing in common with Italian futurism except its name. Marinetti, however, took it for granted that Russian futurism was derived from his, but felt that the Russian version was too pessimistic and too abstract. The Russian futurists, in turn, found Marinetti to be too much the bourgeois. Marinetti further observed (apparently referring to Khlebnikov) that the Russians engaged in an "archaeologism" quite alien to him and labeled Russian cubo-futurism *sauvagisme*. Still, the influence was there. It appears that Mayakovsky in parti-

cular went through a development from genuine, Kruchonykh-Khlebnikovian cubism to futurism à la Marinetti. Marinetti's fierce nationalism and his racial theory of civilization have an analogue in Russian futurism, as do his glorification of manhood and his misogyny. Striking examples of the latter are found in *Victory over the Sun* and in Mayakovsky's early poetry. Russian modernists certainly learned some stylistic devices from Marinetti, for instance, "montage" of a noun with an analogous noun instead of with an adjective.

The main traits of cubo-futurism were negative. It was anti-Western. It flaunted an anti-aesthetic, antirealist, and antipasséist pose. Among the most memorable lines in *A Slap in the Face of Public Taste* are Burlyuk's: "Poetry is a frazzled wench / And beauty sacrilegious trash." These attitudes find expression in the dehumanization and grotesque exaggeration of the ugliness of the modern city in Mayakovsky's early poems. In a technical sense cubo-futurism introduced a poetics that negated the principles of the poetry that had preceded it. It substituted rhythm for melody and the material for the spiritual. The emphasis on rhythm led to free verse and to ample use of rhythmic cadences and sound effects independently of meter. The cubo-futurists perceived a work of art as construction from a given material, rather than as the realization of an "inner form." Much as modernist painters saw color, line, and shape as self-sufficient entities, cubo-futurist poets perceived the word "as such" (its phonic side in particular) as the stuff of which their work was made. Nature was merely material to be molded into any shape that might please the artist—as were the poetry, art, and music of the past. Trans-sense poems composed of arbitrary morphemes with no dictionary meaning, one-word and even one-letter poems, and poems created for the sake of a pun, a charade, or a certain graphic effect were among the products of this new poetics.

Russian modernist painting developed some significant primitivist strains, such as Goncharova's stylized folk art and Larionov's imitations of sign painting, chapbook illustrations, and children's drawings. Likewise, Russian modernist music went beyond using folk tunes and proceeded to reproducing even the discordant harmonies of folk music. In poetry, Khlebnikov's pursuit of a primitive sensibility and primeval cosmic myth produced some fine verse. Khlebnikov's archaism was also in line with Scythianism (*skifstvo*), an intellectual movement of the 1910s which sought to draw attention to Russia's "Asian" and "barbarian" roots.

Poetry

The 1880s saw a revival of interest in poetry, without producing a new poetic style. The poetry of Apukhtin, Nadson, Minsky, Fofanov, and Lokhvitskaya had great success with the reading public of the 1880s, but it appears in retrospect that it added little to the treasury of Russian verse. Its imagery and poetic vocabulary were well worn. Its ideas and emotions, too, were hardly new. Some of the poets who were successful in the 1880s went on to join the decadents of the 1890s without rising to real prominence.

Aleksei Apukhtin (1840–93) exemplified the nadir Russian poetry had reached in the 1880s. Of ancient nobility and brilliantly gifted, he graduated from the Petersburg School of Jurisprudence, where the composer Tchaikovsky was his classmate. They became lifelong friends. Apukhtin addressed several of his poems to Tchaikovsky, and the

composer set some of his friend's poems to music. A habitué of Petersburg salons, where his ready wit was in demand, Apukhtin was a poetic dilettante who received little attention before the 1880s, when he scored a success with his *Poems* (1886). Apukhtin had talent, but he also had the misfortune to be caught in a rut from which only a talent greater than his, or a powerful outside influence, could have freed him. In his fluent verses the familiar elegiac themes of the golden age are slightly modernized, its imagery, phraseology, and rhythms reduced to banal déjà vu, its "luminous sadness" to torpid depression.

Semyon Nadson (1862–87) had an unhappy childhood, graduated from a military school, and briefly served as an officer in the army until illness forced him to resign his commission. Aleksei Pleshcheev (1825–93), a well-respected minor poet and writer, introduced him to *The National Annals* in 1882, and within the few years that were left him before he died of consumption at the age of twenty-four he acquired a huge following. For years after his death he remained a beloved poet, especially of the young generation. Later he was dismissed, perhaps unfairly, as a minor epigone of Lermontov and Nekrasov.

Nadson's poetry, mostly in flowing conventional meters not broken into stanzas, is an eloquent intimate diary (several poems are entitled "From a Diary") of a young man with a passionate soul and alert mind but an ordinary imagination. It expressed feelings that thousands of Nadson's contemporaries recognized as their own. It has basically two dimensions. First, there are the effusions of a sickly, sad, and lonely young man, disappointed in life and humanity, who weeps about a life that is "narrow and stifling." Scores of poems tell about early death, illness, the ennui of a pointless life, daily drudgery on the job, remorse at wasting what little time is given one, and general weltschmerz. Nadson's sentiments recall those of Ippolit Terentyev in Dostoevsky's *The Idiot*. Like Ippolit, Nadson also dreams of suicide.

The other dimension shows a populist poet whose ideal is the martyr for a great cause and who is fascinated by the early Christians. In "A Dream" (1882–83), dedicated to Pleshcheev, the poet at first indulges in puerile daydreams, fancying himself a famous poet giving a recital to the applause of a huge crowd, climaxed by the queen of his dreams, who hands him the rose from her breast; but as he has matured, he "joins the ranks of fighters for a ravished liberty and becomes a singer of labor, knowledge, and sorrow." In many ringing verses Nadson casts his lot with suffering humanity, "the burning groans of tempestuous suffering, / Bloodshed, and the sharp clanging of chains." Most of these verses are very bad. It must be said to Nadson's credit that on occasion he would admit that all his defiance and rebellious ideas, even his readiness to be "crucified and disgraced" for the sake of a great cause, were only make-believe and that those who indulged in these dreams "would go back to their usual tasks each morning."

That a poet of Nadson's description should have occupied the position he did indicates that Russian poetry had indeed reached a low in the 1880s—not because Nadson's poetry lacked content but because it totally lacked style and a distinctive form or manner. It was poetry reduced to versification of familiar experience, at best, or reiteration of tired clichés, at worst.

Konstantin Fofanov (1862–1911), who came from the merchant class, began to publish poems in 1881 and quickly became famous for his verses of springtime, flowers,

nightingales, and young love, but also of graveyards, consumptive maidens, "incorporeal spirits," and even vampires. He won the praise of his older contemporaries Polonsky and Maikov. In the 1890s the up-and-coming symbolists were eager to have him as a contributor to their almanacs. Critics were kind to him in his lifetime and even after, praising his freshness, joie de vivre, and "genuine gift of song." Many of his poems were set to music and became popular romances. Today, the best explanation for Fofanov's success can only be that his poems were so bad that they were good. Compared to the literate, erudite, and polished verses of the romantic epigones, Fofanov's were frankly sentimental, disarmingly ingenuous, blithely unaware of their own total lack of originality, honestly rhymy and true to their beat. In his choice of words Fofanov would quite unsuspectingly lapse into the most blatant clichés and into bathos and catachresis. Fofanov's numerous narrative poems and ballads, such as "The Poetess: A Novel in Verse," "The Poet and Mephistopheles," and "Baron Klaks: A Tale in Verse," at first appear to be parodies, and amusing ones at that. But as we read on, we realize that they are quite serious.

Nikolai Minsky (pseudonym of Nikolai Vilenkin, 1855–1937) has received little attention because he did not fit neatly into any of the movements of which he was a part. He was the first Jew to become a major figure in Russian literature. (He converted to Orthodoxy only in 1886, after his initial successes as a poet.) Minsky got a law degree from Petersburg University in 1879 but devoted himself entirely to literature. He had begun to publish poetry, much of it in a strongly populist vein and some of it illegally, in 1876. His narrative poem "Last Confession" (1879–85) is a dialogue between a condemned revolutionary and a priest who has come to confess him before his execution. The poem was made famous in a painting by Ilya Repin, which brings out the condemned man's defiance with great poignancy. In another poem of that period, "Execution," the woman executed is also a revolutionary. It ends with the words, "She waited, praying that together with her / Night would expire, and darkness vanish." But as early as in the lyric *poema* "White Nights" (1879) the revolutionary message becomes ambiguous and is muted by a note of decadent pessimism. The poet decides that the sweetness of revenge will not be worth the devastation and bloodshed that the revolution will bring with it. "The Garden of Gethsemane" (1884, published in 1899), a narrative poem, was stopped by the censor but still circulated in many copies. It is thematically related to Dostoevsky's tale of the Grand Inquisitor. The devil shows to a distressed Christ the future of His church: an inquisitor burning heretics with Christ's name on his lips, a lurid scene in which one recognizes the Borgias, and a godless revolutionary (perhaps Robespierre) denouncing Christ and replacing Him with a half-naked woman, the "goddess of reason." Minsky's political meditations are rhetorically strong and have a ring of sincerity, genuine anguish, and humane feeling. Thoughtful rather than rousing, and only moderately eloquent, they have warmth of feeling and honest good sense.

Minsky continued to be associated with the revolutionary movement in the 1900s. He was the editor of the Bolshevik paper *New Life* when Lenin published his article "Party Organization and Party Literature" there in 1905. Minsky's "Workers' Hymn" and other revolutionary poems, all very weak, were also published in *New Life*. After the 1905 revolution Minsky, who had spent some time in prison, was forced to emigrate, and he never returned to Russia. At one time he worked for the Soviet embassy in London.

Minsky's role as a literary theorist was not in accord with his revolutionary biography. In an essay of 1884, "An Ancient Controversy," he denounced positivism and utilitarianism and advocated a mystique of pure beauty. His book of essays, *In the Light of Conscience* (1890), was the first programmatic statement of Russian decadence. He developed a meonic (from Greek *mē*, "not," and *on*, "being") theory of poetry, in which he asserted that poetry should strive for the ideal, impossible, and nonexistent. Minsky was also one of the organizers of the Religious-Philosophical Society meetings in Saint Petersburg (1901–03). Minsky's poetry resuscitates familiar romantic themes: the poet's divine calling ("Song," with the first lines, "I am called Beauty, I am the sister of stern Truth"), "The Fires of Prometheus," "The Prophet," and a whole cycle on Ahasuerus. It is cerebral, sometimes thoughtful, though rarely original, highly literate, and at times elegant, but wholly lacking lyric melos. Minsky is at his best when he is frankly rhetorical or didactic.

Mirra Lokhvitskaya (1869–1905), the daughter of a prominent Moscow lawyer and sister of the writer Teffi,[32] led an uneventful life. She married in 1892, had several children, and died of tuberculosis. In the 1890s she was much admired as the "Russian Sappho" (she wrote several poems derived from Sappho). Her torrid love poems use conventional phraseology ("secret desires and dreams," "luxuriant flower of living love," "your burning gaze excites my blood") and imagery (nymphs, roses, swans, violets, gold and purple), but they are rhythmically alive and well orchestrated euphoni-

32. See p. 536.

cally. A few of Lokhvitskaya's poems are modern and personal. "Learn to Suffer" (1895) boldly asks women to learn to remain silent when "branded for a moment stolen from happiness" and to suffer when "made to drag the yoke of a slave," though "bearing the mark of the elect." Lokhvitskaya reveals herself as a sophisticated and form-conscious poet in poems in which she talks about her own art and that of others. In "To a Rival" (1896–98) she marshals her "singing dactyls," "fiery iambs," "restless anapests," and "radiant swarm of trochees" to rout her beauteous rival. In one of several poems addressed to her good friend Balmont, she describes his art in suggestive metaphors, likening his rhymes to "chimes of crystalline chords," his imagery to "chains of inadvertent and strange, lacelike arabesques," and, for a final effect, wishing "to be his rhyme." In the poem "Lionel" (1898) she gives an apt catalogue of Balmont's (he sometimes signed his poems Lionel) favorite themes and images. Lokhvitskaya, very talented and more famous in her time than her contemporary, Zinaida Hippius, lacked Hippius's originality and power, but some of her feminist poems deserve to be anthologized.

Among the poets who acted as a link between romantic epigones and modernism Konstantin Sluchevsky (1837–1904) is, after Fet, the most extraordinary. The son of a senator, he was educated in the Corps of Cadets and served in the Guards, but he resigned his commission in 1860 and went abroad to study. He earned a doctorate in philosophy from the University of Heidelberg and after his return to Russia in 1866 joined the civil service. He held a high position at court, accompanying royal personages on their travels throughout the empire, which led to the publication of several volumes of geographic and ethnographic notes. In his early years Sluchevsky leaned toward liberal ideas and published some poems in *The Contemporary*. They were greeted with enthusiasm by Apollon Grigoryev and parodied with relish by Dobrolyubov and the satirical poets of *The Spark*. After his return from abroad Sluchevsky published a brochure, "Phenomena of Russian Life under the Criticism of Aesthetics" (1867), in which he deplored the "abolition of aesthetics" effected by radical criticism. It made him odious to radical and even to liberal circles, and when he resumed publication he preferred to remain anonymous; he did not sign his poetry with his full name until 1874. Four thin volumes of his poems appeared in the 1880s, and his collected works, in six volumes, came out in 1898. Toward the end of his life Sluchevsky, now back in fashion, entertained the young symbolists Balmont, Bryusov, and Sologub at his salon. Echoes of Sluchevsky's themes and style are readily found in their poetry, as well as in Blok's and Bely's.

Sluchevsky's style did not change much over the years. A member of the generation of Pushkin's "grandsons," as he called himself in a late poem, "Should There Be Song?" (1903), he wrote poetry that blended readily into "the new spring" of Silver Age verse. He inherited from the romantic age the themes of a dual world and of the doppelgänger ("There Are Two of Us," 1880), a tendency toward Satanism (a whole cycle of "Mephistophelean" poems in the 1880s), and a preoccupation with night and death. The cycle *Posthumous Poems* (1902) calmly lays out the progress of the persona's consciousness before, through, and after death, culminating in a frightening vision of standing naked with the full truth of all one's sinful and shameful actions bared for the world to see. Romantic themes acquire a deeply pessimistic Schopenhauerian coloration. In "On a Theme by Michelangelo" (1880) the theme is Night the liberator, welcome because it removes all walls, so that "prison and world become one." In "Lux aeterna" (1881) life appears as a necropolis in which men flit about like shadows—one has a feeling that "one lived somewhere before, at sometime in the past." Some of Sluchevsky's best poems recall Baratynsky's fascination with sadness ("The Goddess of Sadness," 1898; "It burns, it burns, without soot or smoke," 1902).

Sluchevsky's landscape and cityscape poems are distinctively prosaic, even naturalistic ("Scurvy," "On the Volga," both 1881). They cover Russia, all the way from the Arctic to the Crimea, as well as Western Europe, with some fine Swiss landscapes. Grigoryev recognized Sluchevsky's peculiar talent in one of his first published poems, "The wind struts along the Neva" (1859), a fresh and catchy song of Petersburg.

Some of Sluchevsky's poems challenge the reader with bold conceits, which pedestrian critics found absurd and ridiculous. "In the Graveyard" (1860), which anticipates "Bobok," Dostoevsky's macabre dialogue of the dead, was mercilessly parodied at its appearance. In "After an Execution in Geneva" (1881) the persona imagines himself broken and strung out on the wheel until he feels like a single taut string, strummed by a terrifying old woman as she hums a dirge for the departed. In "Our mind is sometimes like a field after a battle" (1880) the human mind is likened to a battlefield strewn with dead and wounded men—but there, on a bloody bayonet, a bird has perched and is twittering.

Sluchevsky's verse is among the least musical of all major Russian poetry. Even his best poems are rhythmically and euphonically ragged, so much so that one critic called him a stammerer.[33] But the originality of his imagination makes up for this deficiency. In Sluchevsky's narrative poems the dullness of his verse becomes fatal. "Eloa: An Apocryphal Tradition" (1883) is memorable for a powerful apocalyptic vision in the spirit of Vladimir Solovyov. Yet another trait that made Sluchevsky a precursor of symbolism was his strong identification with the ideas of Dostoevsky, to whom he wrote a stirring eulogy, "After the Funeral of F. M. Dostoevsky" (1881).

Russian symbolism produced several major and a host of minor poets. Although it was certainly a school—all the symbolist poets knew each other personally, met frequently at the editorial offices of their journals, at Vyacheslav Ivanov's Petersburg apartment (the famous "Tower") or at the Stray Dog cabaret, and addressed or dedicated poems to one another—it is still a fact that, at least as far as the major symbolists are concerned, no distinctive symbolist poetic style ever existed. The styles of Balmont, Hippius, Sologub, Bely, Blok, and Vyacheslav Ivanov are decidedly more different from one another than, say, the styles of the poets of the Pushkin pleiad. The Russian critic Vladimir Weidlé later suggested that such inability to create a dominant style and the substitution of stylization for style were a sign of decline. Be that as it may, the Silver Age, and symbolism in particular, produced by far the largest number, of any period before or after, of poets with a decidedly distinctive manner. It also produced the first truly major woman poets of Russian literature.

33. D. S. Mirsky, *A History of Russian Literature* (New York, Random House, 1958), 244.

Symbolism as a movement existed for a decade and a half, until about 1910, although some of its leaders survived it by many years and wrote some of their best poetry after the revolution. The poetry of the Silver Age was the product of a social, cultural, and artistic ambience that disappeared with the start of World War I.

Solovyov and Merezhkovsky

Vladimir Solovyov not only gave Russian symbolism its aesthetic theory but also wrote poetry that became a model for some of the symbolists. The reason for the common belief that Solovyov had no genuine poetic talent is that Solovyov's verse, though metrically accurate, is lacking in lyric melos and pathos. It does, in fact, seem cerebral. Yet it also has its own inimitable voice, the voice of a passionate thinker. The metaphysical and aesthetic topoi of Solovyov's philosophy, which are also those of romanticism—a yearning for "other worlds," the dualism that permeates all being, rays and echoes descending to this world from heavenly spheres, the liberating power of art, and the Eternal Feminine—are stated in clear and precise language, creating an effect of mild estrangement.

Solovyov's Erlebnislyrik is Pushkinian in its directness and precision, quite different from the musical vagueness of Fet and the symbolists. The poet's visionary experiences are reported soberly, even with an occasional touch of wry humor, as in "Three Encounters" (1898), an account of Solovyov's three visions of Sophia, or "Das Ewig-Weibliche: An Admonitory Sermon to Sea Devils" (1898).

Solovyov is an inimitable master of nonsense verse and parody. His humorous epitaphs to himself are terrifying—in a left-handed way. Solovyov liked to joke about death. His parodies are brilliant—for example, his parody of the miscellanies of the Russian symbolists (1895), which is so much more remarkable in that Solovyov admired the poetry of Fet and Sluchevsky, to both of whom he addressed fond poems, and he himself wrote poetry which was close in spirit to that of the young symbolists. Solovyov anticipated many of the more specific themes, moods, and images of Russian symbolism: northern landscapes (Solovyov has some fine Finnish landscapes), life as a theater of flitting shadows, Orphic themes, the threat of an Asian invasion, and the vision of a great battle (Blok's cycle "On the Field of Kulikovo" and his famous poem "Scythians" both echo poems by Solovyov).

Dmitry Merezhkovsky, another theorist of Russian symbolism, was a minor poet of considerable skill, though without a distinctive voice. His first collection, *Poems: 1883–1887* (it appeared in 1888) is epigonic, but competent. It has some nature poetry, some *Stimmungslyrik*, and some narrative poems with a philosophical bent. Merezhkovsky's second collection, *Symbols: Songs and Poems* (1892), includes programmatic poems, such as "Morituri" (1891), which introduces the prophets of a new faith who will perish to pave the way to "divine poets of the future."

Later poems reflect the further progress of Merezhkovsky's ideas. "Leonardo da Vinci" (1895), for example, sees Leonardo as "a prophet or demon, or sorcerer, preserving an eternal riddle" and as a symbol of "godlike man who, sovereign himself, holds the gods in contempt." The programmatic "Children of Night" (1896) combines all the slogans of the young symbolist movement: the children of night direct their eyes to the east, awaiting their prophet, "yearning for as-yet uncreated worlds" and hoping "to see the light in whose rays they will die like shadows."

Hippius

Zinaida Nikolaevna Hippius (1869–1945) came from an aristocratic family and was educated by tutors. She married Dmitry Merezhkovsky in 1889, and thereafter they never spent a day of their lives away from each other. Their literary careers proceeded independently, although their political, philosophical, and religious views were in unison. Hippius, who started out as a successful short story writer, developed into one of the great poets of the twentieth century. She was also a first-rate literary critic, publishing under the pen name Anton Krainy.

Hippius's poetry is elegant, masterly, inventive and original in its language, imagery, and conceits, and intellectually brilliant. Her sonnets, though relatively few, are all perfect and seem effortless. Her poetry has great thematic variety but a single, highly idiosyncratic style. Almost all her poems have a male persona. Love poems are usually addressed to a woman. Hippius's decadent poems are more poignant by far than those of any of the other symbolists. Even Sologub's appear tame in comparison.

Hippius creates haunting landscapes of a tormented human soul. In such poems as "Snow" and "Snowflakes" (1894), "Dust" (1897), "Buttercups of the Meadow" and "Pines" (1902), and "Rain" (1904), snowflakes, raindrops, dust, spiderwebs, clouds, birds, trees, and flowers are magically converted into human emotions. In other poems, emotions are hypostatized and become palpable. In "I Don't Know" (1901) a boundless loneliness acquires a physical shape and turns into a "tender, strange monster." The poem "Devastation" (1902) is a desolate landscape of the soul. Spiders spin their stifling webs in the human soul ("Spiders," 1903), and the leeches of sin suck at the soul's "tired, dead slime" ("Leeches," 1902). The soul is grotesquely materialized in several powerful poems. In "She" (1905) we hear of something "gray like dust . . . coarse and prickly . . . cold like a snake . . . dead, black, and terrible"—to learn only in the last word of the poem that this something is "my soul." In "The Waterfall" (1905), dedicated to Aleksandr Blok, the soul is a stream of black water of "seething iciness" and "snowy fire" flowing between frozen riverbanks.

Death, devil, and netherworld are a strong presence in Hippius's poetry, often in strange and paradoxical contexts. An early poem, "Joy" (1889), senses the proximity of death "not in a damp, dark, stifling grave" but as "a breath of wind or ray of sunshine, a pale wave of the sea or shadow of a cloud" that will touch the beloved—and death turns into joy. Her masterful "Sonnet" (1894) is an almost serene welcome to death. But there is also "Fear and Death" (1901) and a ghostly boatride on the river Lethe ("There," 1900). The devil has many faces. He is the insidious corrupter ("Nets," 1902) but also "God's Creature" (1902), for whom the persona prays to God: "I love the devil, for I see in him my suffering." The devil may be the noble Lermontovian demon: "A desolate globe in an empty desert, / Like one of the devil's pensive moods" ("Earth," 1908). He may also be a mean and repulsive imp who worms his way into one's house and heart until he becomes part of one's very nature ("The Imp," 1906).

At the core of Hippius's poetic world there is the Dostoevskian underground, a human being torn by conflicting emotions and irresoluble contradictions. In "Impotence" (1893) the persona feels "close to God, but cannot pray" and "wants love, yet cannot love." "The Limit" (1901), a poem dedicated to Dmitry Filosofov, defines the condition of the underground in a series of antitheses: "We want sounds, but fear harmony, / we are tormented by a vain desire for limits . . . / and die having never reached them." Other poems are literally catalogs of the uncounted ills and evils of the world, of human vices and frailties: "Monotony" (1895, a poem whose impression is enhanced by a monotonous chain of grammatical rhymes), "A Scream" (1896), "What Is Sin?" (1902), and "A Christian's Deathbed Confession" (1902).

Hippius's love poems tend to be addressed to love itself hypostatized. Whenever the object of love is present at all, it is female, as in "The Kiss" (1904), a daintily erotic piece, "To Her" (1905), a poem about the fear and trembling of love, or "A Ballad" (1903), an intensely erotic poem about an affair with a water sprite. "Thou" (1905) is an elegant love poem addressed to a bisexual moon: in Russian there are two words for the moon, one masculine, the other feminine. Hippius's poetry is rich in conceits that generate an impression by giving physical being to a purely verbal construct like "nonlove," in a poem of that title (1907). Other such poems are "The Clock Stopped" (1902), where time becomes eerily palpable, and "Thirteen" (1903), a numerological tour de force.

In opposition to the decadent pole of Hippius's poetry there stand many poems of a positive religious content. They have no less intensity, plasticity, or originality than her decadent poems. In "Annunciation" (1904) the persona is Mary's, the mood simple and serene. In "Accomplices" (1902), dedicated to Valery Bryusov, the persona relives the crucifixion—as an active participant. "The Martyr" (1902) is an intense poem about the joys of torture. Some poems are composed as prayers, for instance, "A Prayer" (1897), "To Christ" (1901), and "Freedom" (1904).

Hippius's talent was not limited to pure lyric poetry. Her ballads, gnomic poetry, and parables are crisp, fluent, and compact. Eventually, she also showed herself as a master of the more rhetorical modes. "December 14" (1909), a solemn address to the memory of the Decembrists, promising to follow in their footsteps, is eloquent and has great rhythmic élan. When the revolution transformed Hippius into a political poet, she revealed her skill at writing versified philippics, stirring in exhortation and stinging in invective.

Bryusov

Valery Yakovlevich Bryusov (1873–1924)—a poet, novelist, and critic of indubitable, though not extraordinary, talent—was the central figure of Russian symbolism. The son of a well-to-do Moscow merchant and grandson of a serf who had bought his freedom, he was a studious youth who developed a serious interest in classical and contemporary poetry, mostly French, while still in secondary school. Like most of the Russian symbolists, he went on to acquire an academic degree in the humanities, graduating from Moscow University in 1899. In March 1894, in collaboration with a schoolmate, A. A. Lang, who wrote under the pseudonym A. Miropolsky, Bryusov published a miscellany, *Russian Symbolists*, which brough him instant notoriety. Shortly thereafter he published a translation of Verlaine's *Romances sans paroles*, and in August 1895 he put out his first independent book of poems, *Chefs d'oeuvre*, to almost unanimous vituperation. Another miscellany, *A Book of Meditations* (1899), in which Balmont, Konevskoi, and Modest

Durnov participated, and Bryusov's own collection *Tertia Vigilia* (1900) received more favorable attention. In 1900 Bryusov became the managing editor of Skorpion, a publishing house funded by the Moscow art patron S. A. Polyakov. It published works by Russian symbolists, including Balmont, Bely, Sologub, Vyacheslav Ivanov, and Zinaida Hippius, five issues of an almanac, *Northern Flowers* (1901–04, 1911),[34] and the literary journal *Scales* (1904–09). Bryusov was now the de facto leader of Russian symbolism. When a reaction set in against symbolism, Bryusov, now an established figure in the world of letters, was often singled out for attack as a stalwart of the "old" literature. He met these attacks with equanimity and actually offered encouragement to such poets of the young generation as Tsvetaeva, Gumilyov, and Mayakovsky. Bryusov's relations with the younger generation of symbolists, and with Andrei Bely in particular (they almost fought a duel once), were unstable, and around 1910 he parted ways with them. Bryusov never accepted the theurgic principle of poetry embraced by Vyacheslav Ivanov and Andrei Bely. He also remained cool to the religious searchings of the Merezhkovskys and their circle.

Bryusov's political position was moderate after 1905. For a while he edited Pyotr Struve's journal *Russian Thought.* Yet he was the only major figure of Russian symbolism to accept the Bolshevik revolution without reservation. He joined the Communist party in 1920 and spent the last years of his life as a functionary of the People's Commissariat of Education, whose literature section he headed. In 1921 he founded the Advanced Institute of Literary Arts, designed to train cadres of young writers. He also lectured on a variety of subjects at Moscow University, the Communist Academy, and other institutions. Bryusov was an important Pushkin scholar and did some pioneering work in the theory of Russian versification. He wrote thoughtful essays on Fet, Tyutchev, and other poets, as well as perceptive surveys of futurism and acmeism. Bryusov is also important as a translator of Virgil's *Aeneid*, a great deal of nineteenth-century French poetry, particularly Emile Verhaeren, and Armenian, Finnish, Latvian, and other poetry previously unavailable in Russian.

Several conflicting traits inform Bryusov's poetic oeuvre. For ten years he was synonymous with symbolism, but in retrospect his poetry is only marginally modernist and clearly belongs to the nineteenth century. The influence of Verlaine and Verhaeren on Bryusov is less pronounced than that of Poe, Hugo, and Baudelaire, is far less significant than that of Tyutchev, Fet, and Baratynsky, and pales before the pervasive presence of Pushkin. Whereas most of the other symbolists struggled for faith or a firm worldview, to Bryusov—as to Pushkin—the world and ideas were no more and no less than material for his poetry.[35] Bryusov's worldview was always eclectic, humanist, and at bottom positivist. He had, like Pushkin, "a yearning for world culture," as Mandelshtam noted. Many of his best poems seek to capture the spirit of an alien culture and its mythology—classical antiquity, most often, but also Egypt, the ancient Hebrews, the Vikings, Holland, and Finland. Bryusov could write a good poem "In the Manner of

---

34. The title commemorated Anton Delvig's almanac (1825–32).

35. An 1899 diary entry reads: "There are many truths, and they often contradict one another. . . . I have always dreamed of a pantheon, a temple of all gods. Let us pray to day and to night, to Mithras and Adonis, to Christ and to the devil."

Eichendorff" (1912), "In the Manner of the Latin Anthology" (1912), and the like. Toward the end of his life he had started to compose a grand cycle of poems called *Mankind's Dreams*, patterned after Victor Hugo's *La Légende des siècles* and René Ghil's *De la poésie scientifique* (1909).[36] Bryusov's late poems include one entitled "The Principle of Relativity" (1922), and another, "The Legend of Years" (1922), mentions Einstein opposite Archimedes.

Whereas the symbolists at large believed in the poet as a seer, Bryusov always considered himself a maker, a versifier (*slagatel' stikhov*).[37] He once said that he was a "utilitarian" among "symbolists." Bryusov's language and imagery, though rich, lack originality and an individual note. Bely observed that Bryusov's rhythms were too "metrical." Bryusov used accentual verse a great deal less than the younger symbolists, and his rhymes, sometimes ingenious, tend to be precise. He recited his verses in a staccato, metallic voice.

The most idiosyncratic trait of Bryusov's poetic message is his insistence on the absolute value of poetry and poetic form. He stated it often, starting with an early "Sonnet to Form" (1894) and the programmatic "To a Young Poet" (1896). In a poem entitled "To a Poet" (1907) he says, "Perhaps all in life is only a means / To brilliant, melodious verses." Such bold assertion of art for art's sake was unprecedented in Russia.

Bryusov's poetry, especially his early

verse, has enough of a decadent strain to account for the scorn with which it was initially met. There are sultry erotic scenes, scandalous to a reader of the 1890s. Grotesque cityscapes appear in such poems as "At Night" (1895): "Moscow's asleep, like the female of a sleeping ostrich, / Her dirty wings spread over its dark ground." There are demons ("The Demon of Suicide," 1910, which in rhythm and setting echoes Blok's "The Stranger"), ubiquitous shadows, and death (for instance, in the cycle "The Breath of Death," 1895). Cosmic themes, "other worlds," the Eternal Feminine, and musical imagery play a lesser, though noticeable, role. Bryusov's utopian-dystopian poems, such as "Approaching Huns" (1904–05), "To the Happy Ones" (1904–05, addressed to an unknown, happier future), and "We Scythians" (1916), express the same apprehensions, fears, and hopes that one finds in other symbolists. Bryusov's revolutionary, civil-war and postrevolutionary poetry is rhetorical and for the most part pedestrian.

The brief narrative or descriptive poem is Bryusov's forte. His reworking of and conclusion to Pushkin's "Egyptian Nights" (1914–16) shows him, though not Pushkin's equal, at least a worthy epigone. Bryusov's entire activity, as well as his poetry, falls in line with the spirit of his age. That the son of a Moscow merchant should have become an adept of French symbolist poetry and devoted the better part of his oeuvre to Western culture was symptomatic of the transformation that was taking place in Russian society at the turn of the century. Pushkin and the poets of his pleiad had participated in European culture by virtue of their privileged social position and upbringing. Bryusov and the poets of his generation did so simply by virtue of being educated, middle-class Russians.

36. Bryusov published essays on Ghil in *Scales* (1904) and *Russian Thought* (1909).

37. In a polemical essay written in response to Balmont, Bryusov stated, "The poet's work is not some sort of uncontrollable ecstasy, but conscious—in the highest sense of that word— labor" ("A Right to Work," *Utro Rossii*, 1913, no. 190, August 18).

Balmont

Konstantin Dmitrievich Balmont (1867–1942) came from a family of provincial gentry in Vladimir Province. He briefly attended Moscow University but decided early to become a professional poet, writer, and translator. He traveled restlessly on all five continents and after 1896 lived in Russia only intermittently. He never returned after leaving Russia on a Soviet passport in 1920. After 1927 he lived mostly in Capbreton in Brittany. A polyglot who knew some forty languages, Balmont introduced many exotic themes into his poetry, particularly Spanish and Mexican, but also Indian, Egyptian, Scandinavian, and many others. English poetry was his first love; his favorite poet was Shelley, whom he translated masterfully, along with Blake, Byron, Tennyson, Wilde, and Poe.

Balmont was a natural improviser who believed in the power of inspiration and refused to polish his verses. He could write as many as ten poems in a single day. His twenty-nine volumes of published poetry contain only a part of his works. He wrote many excellent poems, but his formal facility caused him to write many shallow and banal ones, too. He is one of the masters of the Russian sonnet. Balmont's virtuoso command of rhythm and sound symbolism allowed him to achieve perfect symbolic synchronization of acoustic instrumentation and visual imagery, such as in long lines or rolling ternary meters representing the rhythm of ocean waves (he wrote many sea poems), the flight of a seagull ("The Seagull," 1894), the rustling of leaves ("Fall," 1905), or the swaying of reeds or grass in the wind ("Feather Grass," 1895, "Reeds," 1898). Balmont's play with alliteration and assonance was masterly and at times extravagant ("Song without Words," 1896).

Balmont is at his best in poems that deal explicitly with the elements. He has many fire, wind, and water poems. "White Conflagration" (1900) is a brilliant tour de force on Nietzsche's "Hier stehe ich inmitten des Brandes der Brandung" (Here I stand amidst the conflagration of the surf). There are many solar, lunar, and stellar poems, too. In "Moonlight" (1894), a superb sonnet, moonlight inspires the poet to soar above the strife and suffering on earth into "another world." There is a dithyrambic "Hymn to Fire" (1900) and a similar "Hymn to the Sun" (1903). So ubiquitous, obsessive, and persistent was Balmont's poetic cult of the sun that "Victory over the Sun" became the slogan of Russian futurism when it mounted its attack against symbolism.

Balmont's poetry puts forward all the themes of decadence and symbolism vigorously and in profusion: the human spirit soaring to transcend the mundane (*Let Us Be like the Sun: A Book of Symbols*, 1903), the metaphysical quality of music ("The Birth of Music," 1916), cosmic visions ("Aeons Will Pass," 1896), the attraction of oblivion, shadows, and death ("Belladonna," 1898, "Death," 1894). The early "I was catching fleeting shadows in my dreams" (1894) is one of the programmatic poems of early symbolism: as he pursues the shadows of a waning day, the poet climbs the steps of a tower whence he can perceive luminous mountain peaks, while night spreads out below.

Balmont's religious poetry is dominated by the theme of an earthbound soul yearning to soar heavenward ("Why?" 1894). Significantly, the poem "An Aerial Way" (1903) is dedicated to the memory of Vladimir Solovyov. Balmont is inclined toward the joyful and luminous more than toward the gloomy and depressed. But he gives his due to decadence in a large-enough number of poems. Among Balmont's sea and water poems many veer toward the morbid and threatening. There are underwater poems ("Underwater Plants," 1894, "Amidst Underwater Stalks," 1903) and poems about dead ships (several in the cycle "Quiet," 1898). In the collection *Burning Buildings* (1900) there are some strong poems of horror, despair, and defiance ("The Scorpion," 1899). There are occasional echoes of Nietzsche in epigraphs, occasional references to the superman (*sverkhchelovek*), and outbursts of defiance: "But my soul heard, 'Burn!' " ("The Pledge of Being," 1901). Blamont shares with virtually all modernists the persistent idea of "the word as such," be it living ("Harmony of Words," 1900) or dead ("The Word," 1913).

Balmont wrote a good deal of political poetry, some of it revolutionary. Most of it is undistinguished, though there are some vigorous invectives against the tsar and his regime. Balmont wrote poetry until the end of his life, with no decline in his skill. A late collection, *In the Parted Distance* (1930), is one of his strongest. He also retained an ingenuous enthusiasm, and the spontaneity of youth. He played no major role, however, in the Russian émigré community, although he gave public readings in various European countries.

Sologub

Fyodor Kuzmich Teternikov-Sologub (1863–1927) was the son of a tailor, formerly a serf, who died when Fyodor was four. He was brought up in the house of the family that his mother served as a maid. He graduated from a teachers' institute in Saint Petersburg in 1882 and taught school in the

provinces for ten years. In 1892 he was back in Petersburg teaching mathematics; later he became an assistant principal and a member of the Saint Petersburg Pedagogical Council (1899). Starting in 1892 he published his poetry in *The Northern Herald.* A. V. Volynsky was its coeditor, and Minksy, Merezhkovsky, Hippius, and Balmont were contributors. The editors of *The Northern Herald* gave him his pseudonym, Sologub. Later Volynsky said about his first encounter with Sologub's poetry, "His verses struck me with their clear simplicity, some kind of intangible prosaic quality in the most subtle poetic sense of that term." Volynsky also called Sologub "a kind of Russian Schopenhauer"—a more proper characterization, in view of the pervasive presence of Schopenhaueriana in Sologub's poetry, than Sologub's own persistent identification with the ideas and characters of Dostoevsky.

Besides poetry, Sologub wrote a great deal of prose fiction as well as journalism, particularly in the field of education. Child abuse, a topic that appears both in his poetry and in his prose, was also a major concern of his as a pedagogue. Sologub's political position was rather more leftist than that of other symbolists. It was reflected in the extremely negative picture of contemporary society which he presented in his prose fiction and in some frankly revolutionary poetry, much of it appallingly pedestrian, written during the revolution of 1905. In retaliation, he was asked to resign his position as a school administrator in 1907. After the failure of the revolution he abandoned all immediate concerns with social reality. His symbolist plays of 1907–08 dealt with epiphanies of beauty, love, and death in a way that was wholly detached from topical issues. A separate edition of Sologub's novel *A Petty Demon*, which appeared in 1907, was a major success and quickly went through five editions. His eighth collection of poems, *The Fiery Circle* (1908), was also a triumph. In 1908 Sologub married the writer and critic Anastasiya Chebotarevskaya and with her started a salon which became a meeting place of writers, artists, actors, and journalists. The humble schoolman had become an admired *maître*. Along with Gorky, Kuprin, and Andreev, he was now among the most famous living Russian writers. For a few years Sologub's poetry expressed an attitude prevalent among the Russian intelligentsia and was decidedly popular.

Whereas Sologub's prose never again reached the excellence of *A Petty Demon*, his poetry grew stronger. His late poetry is purer, nobler, almost serene at times, although its themes and basic mode are the same. Sologub greeted the February revolution with enthusiasm and on the whole was willing to cooperate with the Soviet regime. In spite of the shock of his wife's suicide in 1921, he continued to be active until the end of his life. He translated a great deal of poetry, mostly French, producing some masterful versions of Paul Verlaine, a poet who was emotionally close to him.

Sologub's poetry has a distinct individual note, but also bears the decadent traits of the older generation of symbolists. Much of it revives the themes and moods of romanticism. Sologub has a good deal of simple nature poetry, not so different from Fet's. More specifically romantic are the pantheist themes which abound. "God made me from moist clay" (1896) conveys a sense of being a part of everything: as the moist clay of a dirt road, the persona feels the wheels of a cart rolling over it and the feet of a man walking on it. In "I love to wander over a quagmire" (1902) the persona experiences incarnations as a will-o'-the-wisp, a spider, and a horsefly, tormenting other creatures in a frantic effort to cease being himself. In "All

in All" (1896) the poet empathizes with all the suffering in the world. There are many poems on "correspondences," moments of metaphysical epiphany, and the miracle of a spiritual world arising from a "dead and poor nature" ("I do not understand why," 1898). "Other worlds" is a pervasive theme (for example, in the famous cycle "A Star Named Mair," 1898), as are "life is a dream" ("I am painfully disturbed by a terrible dream," 1895–1901), distant unearthly melodies ("I was languishing in lunar magic," 1899), and the world as will and representation. The last occurs quite explicity in several poems, for instance, "I have bewitched all nature" (1902), whose last line has the poet realize that "he himself has created nature."

It is a peculiarity of Sologub's poetry that "correspondences" are often found between the persona and evil or lethal forces. Romantic Satanism is a pervasive trait. Dragon (*zmii*) and snake (*zmeya*) are recurrent symbols in Sologub. In "Dragon, Ruler of the Universe" (1902) the world is perceived as the creation of a "fiery, madly evil" dragon.[38] In "My Life, My Snake" (1907) life itself is called a snake. The devil's presence is taken for granted and grimly acknowledged. In a short ballad of 1902 the poet cries out, as his ship is sinking: "My father, devil, save me, have mercy, I am drowning." The devil saves him, and he will serve him faithfully henceforth:

> Thee, my father, I shall celebrate
> In reproach to iniquitous daylight,
> I shall denounce God's world
> And I shall, by flattery, seduce.

The raucous "Devil's Swing" (1907) is one of Sologub's most famous poems. A perva-

---

38. This vision of the sun as an evil force makes the theme of "Victory over the Sun" in Russian futurism more comprehensible.

sive theme of Sologub's poetry is an invisible but apparently malevolent presence to which the poet is strangely attracted ("Is there somebody standing around the corner?" 1897).

Death is a favorite theme, and a death wish is explicitly stated in many poems. A striking conceit in "The nocturnal match-maker came" (1905) has death appear as a bride. Some of Sologub's most interesting poems deal with the aesthetics of suffering, torture, and death. "The dim verdure of olive trees" (1911) has the poet "savor the charm of mournful Gethsemane." The ballad "The Hangman of Nuremberg" (1907) is, like some other poems, explicitly sadistic. Sologub is stronger perhaps than any other Russian poet in the art of the macabre. His "Horrible Lullaby" (1918) is a spine-chilling *parodie sérieuse* of Lermontov's famous "Cossack Lullaby."[39] "Dream of a Funeral" (1907) is a powerful vision of the cosmos as death and putrefaction: as the persona experiences the horror of its own painful decay and dissolution, the sun, "malodorous evil snake, bloated and blue," is rotting away "like carrion above a silent desert," and "liquefied heat descends from the rotting queen's body."

Not all of Sologub's poems are negative and decadent. His pessimistic Satanism is balanced by silent and grateful contemplation of placid nature ("Reeds Are Swaying," 1898), songs of Dionysian ecstasy ("I would cover my face with a mask," 1895–96), and visions of unearthly love ("I betrayed thee, unearthly one,/ and fell in love with an earthly woman," 1896). His love poems, however, are more often decadent than

metaphysical. Often the woman loved is an enchantress or a witch ("I would burn her, evil sorceress," 1902). A union of love, lechery, torture, and murder is not unknown in Sologub's poetry. A ballad, "Of the Harsh Labor of Executioners" (1904), has a beautiful queen leave her banquet hall and descend to the torture chambers of her castle to wield the executioner's whip. In a poem of 1908, "She Came Back," the lover lies in his grave as his ladylove comes "to excite him for a last time with the desire for a kiss and sinful nakedness."

Sologub's poetry is a poetry of moods in a minor key, moods of futility and lassitude, of vague yearning—the mood of a beggar or captive, or of a barefoot pilgrim whose Jerusalem, still far away, he may never reach ("The Pilgrim," 1896). The persona often feels burdened with a body while reaching for freedom and miracle. In the late poems Don Quixote appears repeatedly. All these moods are translated into light, graceful, hovering musical verse. Sologub achieves such lightness by using simple rhymes, many unstressed syllables in the strong positions of a line (so-called acceleration), and ample assonance and alliteration.

Annensky

Innokenty Fyodorovich Annensky (1855–1909), older than all of the symbolists, entered the Russian Parnassus later than they and never belonged to any of their groupings. He was a symbolist insofar as his poetic sensibility was informed by French symbolism, Mallarmé in particular. Though born in Siberia, Annensky spent virtually all his life in Saint Petersburg, where he graduated from the university in comparative linguistics in 1879 and worked as a teacher of classical and Russian literature, with a three-

39. Nekrasov's parody of the same poem, vitriolic though it is, appears tame in comparison. See p. 317.

year interruption in Kiev, until his death. From 1896 to 1906 he was headmaster of the Tsarskoe Selo gymnasium, where the poet Gumilyov was his student.

Annensky wrote a great deal of poetry early but did not publish any of it until five years before his death, when his collection *Quiet Songs* (1904) appeared anonymously and received almost no attention. Previously he had published only scholarly and pedagogical articles. He began his translation of the complete tragedies of Euripides in the early 1890s. The first volume appeared in 1907, and the project was completed after Annensky's death by his friend, Professor Tadeusz Zieliński. Annensky's own tragedies in the manner of Euripides had appeared earlier: *Melanippa the Philosopher* (1902), *King Ixion* (1904), and *Laodamia* (1906). In 1906 a collection of Annensky's critical essays appeared under the title *A Book of Reflections*, followed by *A Second Book of Reflections* in 1909. Annensky's fame as a poet came posthumously with the publication of his second book of poems, *The Cypress Coffer* (1910). Annensky remained a poet for the few, but in the judgment of connoisseurs he is unequivocally one of the great poets of the Silver Age. He developed a distinctive style, apparently under the influence of the French symbolists Rimbaud, Verlaine, and Mallarmé, whose poetry he translated masterfully.

Annensky's poetry expresses pensive sadness in a great variety of nuances. It is intensely musical in the sense that its subliminal effect is achieved without immediate comprehension of its logos. Like Mallarmé, Annensky consistently uses the pathetic fallacy, "metaphysical"—that is, farfetched —metaphors, a great deal of hypallage, and unusual word combinations which yield the logos of a poem only after careful reading. The following lines from a sonnet, "Luminous Nimbus," are characteristic:

> Hovering dust of the lines of sunset
> Had long spilled over the candles,
> And undulating incense was still pouring
>   forth
> As paling flowers were slowly shrinking.

The symbolist principle *de la musique avant toute chose* is not only practiced but also stated explicitly as "the dreams of music, still unaware of words" ("A Painful Sonnet," 1910). There are many poems dealing with music, two "piano sonnets," for example, in which the keyboard, the pianist's fingers, and the impression evoked by the music—a garden in the moonlight, a mad dance of maenads over the keyboard, crystalline voices accompanied by castanets—blend into a single musical impression of pain and inspiration. "Bow and Strings" (1910) works on a pathetic fallacy which makes the strings of a violin feel as pain what the listener perceives as music. The sounds, colors, and fragrances of nature are synesthetically combined to form musical compositions, for instance, in a cycle of poems devoted to months of the year (1904). In each of these poems it is clear that one is dealing with visionary rather than descriptive poetry: the landscapes, although familiar in their mundane outlines, are metaphysical, often by virtue of a pathetic fallacy, such as when "the black, bottomless ponds of the park have long been ready for mature suffering" ("September").

Annensky's poetry is decidedly modernist. He is not afraid of using such modern words as *asphalt, electric light,* or *locomotive.* Some of the scenes he paints seem to come right out of Toulouse-Lautrec, for instance, "The Tavern of Life" (1904)—Blok might have written this poem. Others recall the turn-of-the-century *Jugendstil*, for example, "Oh, not your figure" (1906). Annensky also participated in the formal innovations of the symbolists: his rhymes are more ingenious and less precise than those of the romantic epigones, and he clearly pursues a more intense instrumentation.

At the same time, there is much about Annensky that is avowedly neoromantic. The two poems that introduce his *Quiet Songs* give a definition of poetry which is cosmic and metaphysical and which places poetry in the vicinity of religion. In searching for it,

> One must flee the arrogance of the temple
> And the priest's encomium,
> To search in the ocean of dim distances,
> In mad anticipation of the sacred,
> For traces of Her sandals
> Among the sanddrifts of the desert.

In the companion poem, entitled "∞," poetry is called "the mysterious one" and likened to a "prone 8," that is, the sign for infinity. "A Third Painful Sonnet," addressed to the verses that have tormented the poet for a long time, ends, "But I love verses— and there is no feeling more sacred: / Thus only a mother loves, and only sick children."

Blok

Aleksandr Aleksandrovich Blok (1880– 1921) came from an academic background. His father, a jurist, was a professor at Warsaw University. His maternal grandfather was A. N. Beketov, a botanist and rector of Petersburg University. Blok's parents were separated soon after his birth, and his mother remarried. He attended school in Saint Petersburg and graduated from Saint Petersburg University in the humanities in 1906. In 1903 he married Lyubov Dmitrievna Mendeleeva, daughter of the famous chemist and industrialist. Their marriage was not a happy one, but she inspired much of his early and some of his later poetry. Blok published his first verses in the symbolist journal *New Path* in 1903. He had attended meetings of contributors to *The World of Art* since 1902 and after the publication of his first verses he developed close relations with the Moscow symbolists Bely, Bryusov, and Balmont. He was personally closest to the poet and theologian Sergei Solovyov, a second cousin of his and a nephew of the philosopher Vladimir Solovyov. Later Blok developed fruitful relations with the symbolists Vyacheslav Ivanov, Georgy Chulkov, Jurgis Baltrušaitis, and with the younger acmeists.

Blok's first collection of verse, *Verses about a Beautiful Lady* (1904), showing the strong influence of Vladimir Solovyov, was only a moderate success. His second collection, *Inadvertent Joy* (1906), and his play *The Showbooth* (1906), staged by Vsevolod Meyerhold at Vera Kommissarzhevskaya's theater, made him famous. He was a professional littérateur for the rest of his life, writing poetry, plays, and many reviews and essays on literary as well as social topics, and frequently giving public readings and lectures. Blok made several extended trips abroad, among which one to Italy in 1909 bore rich poetic fruit. His poem "The Twelve" (1918) was an attempt to come to terms with the October revolution. But he soon became disillusioned with the revolution, and his last poem, "To Pushkin House" (1921), was an assertion of the autonomy of poetry. Soon thereafter he died of a mysterious disease.

Blok's poetry, though intensely subjective, reflects the zeitgeist in its manifold manifestations. Blok himself assessed its essence thus: "All these seemingly different facts have a single musical meaning for me. I have become used to confronting facts from all areas of life, accessible to my vision at a given time, and I am convinced that, together, they create a unified musical impression" (preface to *Retribution*, 1919). Blok believed that the poetic imagination allowed a poet to render the world "close and familiar" and that there ought to be no rift between the personal and the universal:[40]

Oh, I madly want to live:
To eternalize all that is,
To humanize all that's impersonal,
To make the unfulfilled incarnate.
                    ("Iambs," 1914)

Blok's poetic persona is the intellectual of his age, although he may wear the mask of a Lermontovian demon, Hamlet, Harlequin, a modern flaneur or poète maudit, a monk or a medieval knight.[41] Blok's poetry, like that of the other symbolists, is replete with echoes from Zhukovsky, Pushkin, Lermontov,[42] Tyutchev, Grigoryev, Fet, Maikov, Dostoevsky, Vladimir Solovyov, and other Russians, as well as from world literature: Dante, Hamlet and Ophelia, the witches of Macbeth, Don Juan and Doña Ana, Orpheus and Eurydice, Carmen, Pierrot

and Colombina, danse macabre, Novalis, Byron, Hugo, Heine, Ibsen, and Strindberg. He translated Grillparzer, Heine, Byron, Runeberg, Rutebeuf, Isaakian, and others.

Blok's attitude toward Russia and the West is ambiguous. His poetry is imbued with Western culture. His *Italian Verses* (1909) and many other poems show him to be fully a European. But he also deplores the degeneration of Western culture into a mere "civilization" (for instance, in the cycle "Florence," from *Italian Verses*), and a Slavophile sensibility surfaces in many of his poems addressed to Russia, particularly in the cycle "On the Field of Kulikovo" (1908). The famous poem "Scythians" (1918), a defiant gesture dramatizing the rift between East and West and yielding to the then-fashionable impulse to embrace Russia's Asian and barbarian side,[43] is hardly representative of Blok's general attitude.

Some have called Blok Russia's last romantic poet. His poetics is one of symbolic correspondences. The poet's lyric diary is given a mystical, suprapersonal meaning. The metaphysical—theophanic, demonic, or eschatological—reveals itself in the mundane. Religious symbolism, church interiors, and prayerful moods alternate with mordant cynicism and cruel harlequinade. Dualism is the motor of Blok's imagination: the interplay of dream and reality, this world and other worlds, the people and the intelligentsia, and other dichotomies is the lifeblood of his poetry.

Blok's poems convey the flow of immediate impression, rarely structured by paradigmatic editing or deepened by reflection. "The Twelve" was written in two days and printed essentially as first conceived. Rhythm is Blok's great forte. His poetry is basically iambic, but Nekrasovian ternary

---

40. This realization is stated in a poem of 1912, "And again, impetuousness of youth": "The cup of creative inspiration / Has spilled over the brim, / And all is no longer mine, but ours, / And a firm tie with the world has been established."

41. When Blok says, "I am only a knight and a poet, / Descended from a Nordic skald" ("To a Casual Encounter," 1908), this is to some extent personal. He was intensely aware of his "Nordic" ancestry on his father's side.

42. Lermontov is closest to Blok in sensibility and personality. One finds striking parallels between Blok's and Lermontov's verses. For example, "The Demon" (1910) is a variation on Lermontov's poem of the same title, "Autumnal Freedom" (1905) a variation on Lermontov's "I walk out onto the highway."

43. On Scythianism, see pp. 411, 510.

meters appear often. He pioneered accentual verse ("The Nocturnal Violet," 1906), *dol'niki*[44] ("Snowdrifts," 1907) and free verse (the sixth poem in the cycle "The Life of a Friend of Mine," 1914). He also used rhymed folk verse (*rayoshnik*, for example, in "Springtime Creatures," 1905) and *chastushka* ("The Twelve"). Whatever its meter, Blok's poetry has an inimitable, easy, yet always lively and never monotonous lilt. No other poet of the twentieth century is so purely musical. Rhythm is foregrounded in Blok's verses: they are not nearly as effective upon slow, reflective reading as they are in recitation.

Blok's lyric oeuvre is divided into three periods, according to the three volumes of his *Collected Poems* of 1916: 1898–1904, 1904–08, and 1907–1916. (There is some overlap of the second and third periods.) In the first period the persona is variously the devotee of the Beautiful Lady, a seraphic youth, a solitary "son of the earth," and a young monk and visionary; but he is also a jester, Pierrot, or Harlequin, or even a man struggling with the demon within him ("I Love Lofty Cathedrals," 1902). In the second period he may be a flaneur, a habitué of bars and night spots, or a lonely recluse ground into the dust by the cruel city. There are excursions into mythology and fairy tale, into the mind of a child, and into the world of the Russian people. A lonely visionary addressing Russia makes an appearance in some poems—as does Pierrot, a fixture of the first period. In the third period the youth has become an "aging youth" ("The Double," 1909), a "sullen wanderer," a tired and sad man, a sinner in hell who was "on earth under the heavy yoke of joyless passion" ("Song of Hell," 1909, in tercines and entire-

ly in the manner of Dante's *Inferno*), a dead man among the living ("Danses macabres," 1912–14), or even an evil demon ("The Demon," 1916). But there is also the tourist of *Italian Verses* and the bard prophetically addressing Russia in the cycle "My Country" (1907–16).

The first period is dominated by the Beautiful Lady (capitalized, as are pronouns referring to her). In her image a young woman, loved by the poet, and the majestic Eternal Woman of Vladimir Solovyov are fused, rather in the way Novalis had elevated the image of his deceased fiancée, Sophie von Kühn, to an abstract concept of the Eternal Feminine. The image of the Holy Virgin also appears. A poem of 1901 features the Annunciation theme, anticipating "Annunciation" (1909), from *Italian Verses*. Some of the encounters with the Beautiful Lady are set in a "darkened church." Few of the poems of this period are outright love poems. Many more convey a mood of vague anticipation, anamnesis ("Life whispers forgotten words," in a poem of 1902, "Life went slowly"), and "echoes of worlds of the past" ("Evening Twilight," 1901). Indistinct, shadowy visions and phantoms are ubiquitous, as are sunset and twilight.

The second period displays even more thematic variety. Its mood is overwhelmingly gloomy. Its first cycle, "Bubbles of the Earth" (1904–05), with an epigraph from *Macbeth*,[45] is set in a dreamlike, faintly eerie swamp populated by imps, a ghostly little "swamp priest" (shown setting a frog's broken bone), "sorcerers and shaggy witches," and other uncanny denizens. The *poema* "The Nocturnal Violet: A Dream" (1906) is literally the account of a strange and involved dream. The nocturnal violet is

---

44. *Dol'niki* is the Russian term for verse with a variable number of unstressed syllables (almost always one or two) between the downbeats.

45. "The earth hath bubbles as the water has, / And these are of them" (*Macbeth*, I.iii).

a flower that blooms at night, spreading a sweet narcotic fragrance; but it is also "the queen of a forgotten country," as the dreamer turns from "habitué of night spots" into "a brave warrior and singer of Scandinavian sagas." There are other pieces in which an atmosphere of medieval fairy tale prevails. Blok himself credited Victor Hugo's "La Légende du beau Pécopin et de la belle Bouldour" with his attraction to medieval themes, but there was also much interest in the Middle Ages in contemporary art, evidenced by the popularity of Viktor Vasnetsov's historical paintings[46] and of the Pre-Raphaelites, who were well known in Russia.

The cycle "The City" (1904–08) is devoted to a doomed Saint Petersburg, a Sodom before its destruction. It is marked by intrusions of the demonic into drab cityscapes and a great deal of apocalyptic imagery. In "The Last Day" (1904) a couple awakens from a night of venal love to the mad excitement of "the last day," announced by a huge pink cross in the sky. The Beautiful Lady has turned femme fatale, the "stranger" of the poem of that title (1906)—Blok's most famous, though hardly his best. She appears in many other poems, an elegant, alluring, mysterious woman, "nameless," "shamelessly intoxicating and humiliatingly proud," "unattainable and solitary," "smokelike and airy."

"The Snow Mask" (1907),[47] a cycle of some thirty poems, "is subjective in the highest degree, accessible to a small circle only," as Blok later wrote. Its subject is a beautiful woman surrounded by the snow-drifts and storms of winter. Blizzards were a favorite setting of Blok's from beginning to end. This cycle is varied metrically and rich in extravagant conceits: one poem is entitled "On a Pyre of Snow." The poem "A Heart Devoted to the Blizzard" ends with the lines, "Penetrate me, / Winged glance, / With a needle of snowy fire!"

The next cycle, "Faina" (1906–08), continues the love affair started in "The Snow Mask," now in a theatrical setting permeated by an air of heavy sensuality. The lover's persona turns theatrical, too. He sees himself as a medieval knight or as a monk, and in one poem he unexpectedly strikes the pose of an urban lower-class beau serenading his ladylove on the harmonica. Several of the poems of this cycle belong to the genre of the gypsy romance, which Blok assiduously cultivated. Almost all of the thirty poems of "Faina" are pure love poems. Some are direct and banal in their decadent phraseology: "a slender body swathed in silk," "intoxicating fragrance of lilies of the Nile," "come slither to me like a snake," "strangle me with your black braid," and even "whistle, my thin whip" ("Faina's Song"—it is she who wields the whip). But there are also poems where the pangs of love are transfigured into sublime images of impending doom, crucifixion, and the agony of death ("Autumnal Love").

During his second period Blok began to address Russia in a manner suggesting that she had taken the place of the Beautiful Lady. Russia is sad and poverty stricken, but great and mysterious ("Rus," 1906). Blok also begins to discover the touching simplicity of Russian folk religion and "the Russian Christ," rather in the spirit of the paintings of Mikhail Nesterov ("Here He is, Christ, in chains and roses," 1905); "Willow Catkins," 1906; "Saint John's Eve," 1906). "A Tale about a Rooster and an Old Woman" (1906)

---

46. At least one poem, "Gamayun, Wise Bird" (1899), refers directly to a painting by Vasnetsov.

47. Dedicated to the actress Natalya Nikolaevna Volokhova, who also inspired the next cycle, "Faina." She was in the cast of Blok's *The Showbooth* at Vera Kommissarzhevskaya's theater.

is a powerful and terrifying folk ballad. The rooster is the fire that will burn up the poor old woman.

The third period continues the themes and moods of "The City." The cycles "Danses macabres" (1912–14) and "The Life of a Friend" (1913–15) depict a life that is really death. The only remedy for ubiquitous ennui, despair, and madness is a plunge into an abyss of oblivion. "The Demon" (1916) has the demon take his victim to lofty heights, where "the earth will appear as a star," and then fling her into the void. Blok's gypsy romances of this period, such as "I am nailed fast to the bar" (1908), channel despair into alcoholic stupor. But the same period also has Blok's *Italian Verses*, where beauty conquers ennui and the poet's sadness appears in a "haze of light blue mist of Umbrian hills" ("Perugia"). "Annunciation," inspired by a painting by Giannicola Manni of Perugia, returns to the reverent attitude toward the Eternal Feminine so pronounced in the first period.

The cycle "My Country" explicitly resurrects the Eternal Feminine in the image of Russia, perceived as a beautiful woman, her brow darkened by sorrow ("Russia," 1908). In the subcycle "On the Field of Kulikovo," the poet, in addressing Russia, calls her *zhena moya*—where *zhena* is both "wife" and the archaic-poetic word for Solovyov's Sophia and Blok's Beautiful Lady. The poems of "On the Field of Kulikovo" resurrect the apprehensive, solemn, and prayerful mood on the eve of that great battle to express the mood of contemporary Russia, herself on the eve of "inavertible grief" (here Blok echoes lines and sentiments of Vladimir Solovyov). Only in the poem "A New America" (1913) does Blok strike a more optimistic note: in the growth of Russian's industrial might he perceives the seeds of a better future.

Blok's *poema* "Retribution," which he began in 1910 upon returning from his father's funeral, remained a torso. Blok was able to complete the prologue, the first chapter, and parts of chapters 2 and 3; he also left several hundred lines of rough sketches and chapter summaries. "Retribution" was planned as a novel in verse detailing the fate of three generations of a family of the Russian intelligentsia, Blok's own, starting in 1878. It was to get its focus from the idea that each new generation brings retribution to the preceding. The preface to "Retribution" bears an epigraph, "Youth is retribution," from Ibsen's play *Bygmester Solness*. The driving iambic tetrameter of "Retribution" and its entire manner resemble Pushkin's *Eugene Onegin*. It paints a broad panoramic picture of late nineteenth-century Petersburg, then introduces the reader to the Beketovs, the family of Blok's mother. The story of the courtship of his parents follows. The poet's father emerges as the only individualized personage, but even he remains shadowy— a brilliant, handsome, but gloomy and introverted man. The third chapter depicts his decline into a bigoted recluse and miser. Along the way Blok makes critical observations on the society and literature of the period, dispenses worldly wisdom, and as always captivates his reader by the élan of his verse. Nevertheless, there is not enough of "Retribution" to place it alongside the great verse epics of Russian literature.

"The Twelve" is considered Blok's greatest work. It is the first of many masterpieces generated by the revolution. Written in January 1918, it captured the mood of Petersburg immediately after the October revolution. In the bitter cold a howling wind sweeps through the icy, almost deserted streets, patrolled by a squad of twelve Red Guards. What is left of the old world, a cowed bourgeois on the street corner hiding his nose in his collar, a long-haired intellectual muttering something like "Russia's lost," a priest slinking by, trying to make himself inconspicuous—they all resemble the hungry stray dog on that same street corner. A smart sleigh comes racing along; in it are Katya and her soldier boyfriend. Katya used to go with Petya, one of the Red Guards. Petya remembers how he cut her up with his knife and killed the officer he caught her whoring with. Now he takes aim at her and at her boyfriend, who gets away, leaving Katya dead in the snow. The patrol marches on without bothering to pick up the body. Petya feels sorry for himself as he remembers the good times he had with Katya, but consoles himself by thinking of how he will drown his grief in bourgeois blood. The twelve march on through a thickening blizzard, the hungry dog behind them:

> Ahead of them—with blood-red flag,
>   Invisible behind the blizzard,
>   And unhurt by any bullet,
> With dainty steps above the snowbanks
> In a pearly sprinkle of snowflakes,
>   Wearing a wreath of white roses—
>   ahead of them walks Jesus Christ.

This unexpected conclusion to "The Twelve" was immediately objected to by both left and right, who alike declared that Blok had misunderstood the meaning of the revolution. Blok believed that the bloodshed and suffering caused by the revolution were a necessary sacrificial offering to redeem the sins of Russia's past and that Russia would arise from its horrors purified. He lived long enough to see how wrong he was. Aside from the ending, "The Twelve" captured the mood of the times admirably. The flowing, genteel iambs of "Retribution" are replaced by the trochaic staccato rhythms of the cynically irreverent chastushka. Regular

iambs show up briefly in three quatrains—in blatant mockery of the defeated old order:

> The bourgeois stands, just like that
>   hungry dog.
> He stands in silence, like a question mark,
> And the old world, it too, like a stray dog,
> Behind him, with its tail between its legs.

"The Twelve" is a poem about senseless violence and wanton destruction. The victorious Red Guards stand for nothing positive. They march to the tune of defiant swagger and class hatred, raised to a fever pitch by revolutionary slogans. "The Twelve" is more honest and more truthful than the innumerable revolutionary poems of those years that celebrated the idealism of the revolutionary proletariat and perceived the revolution as an event of lofty cosmic proportions.

Blok is a poet whose stature depends not so much on the extraordinary quality of individual poems as on the totality of his work. He gains a great deal when read in whole cycles. As he himself once pointed out, he had difficulty bringing a poem to its conclusion or even sustaining its energy to the end. This, of course, is a quality of all purely lyric poetry. There is no Russian poet who could so directly synchronize atmosphere, mood, and a single dominant emotion with the rhythm of his verses as could Blok.

Bely

As a poet, Andrei Bely, one of the main figures of Russian symbolism and considered a major poet by his contemporaries, has not left a distinct legacy, although he certainly did as a critic and novelist. Bely had the habit of interminably rewriting his poems. On occasion this led to conscious or unintentional self-parody. Much of his lyric oeuvre reflects the process rather than the fruits of poetic creativity. Bely's associative and hence disorienting, jerky composition; his leaps from one idea or image to another, triggered by acoustic, visual, emotional, mnemonic, or etymological associations; and his tendency to isolate phrases (his poems often run whole series of single words separated by pauses) all contribute to this effect. Bely's poems, like his prose works, often have the appearance of an ingenious collage. They take on a mannerist quality by virtue of the poet's conscious effort to activate the formal side of the poem (rhythm, sound patterns) semantically.[48] Bely's poetry is uneven: strong and original lines and stanzas may be followed by banal and uninspired ones.

Bely's first collection, *Gold in Azure* (1904), is Balmontian. It features a great deal of pseudo-mythology à la Wagner, Böcklin and Stuck, a precious vocabulary of precious stones and fancy colors (especially such compounds as lilac-purple, velvety-black, fiery-red, and pale-gold), and mannerist metaphors—"a glacier of frozen tears," "armor woven from sunlight," "the earth is numb from aerial drinking bouts" ("In the Fields," 1904). A Balmontian cult of the sun is reflected in many poems, particularly in the cycles "The Golden Fleece" (1903) and "Sunsets" (1902). A poem, "The Sun" (1903), is dedicated to "the author of *Let Us Be like the Sun.*" *Gold in Azure* reveals Bely's allegiance to symbolism in many ways. Metaphysical themes appear often: "An Image of Eternity" (1903, dedicated to Beethoven), "The World Soul" (1902), "Clairvoyance" (1902). One poem is en-

titled "An Imitation of Vladimir Solovyov" (1902). Some poems are dedicated to other symbolists—Merezhkovsky, Bryusov, Ellis, Blok, Baltrušaitis. The manner of *Gold in Azure* never disappeared from Bely's poetry entirely, returning strongly in *Princess and Knights* (1919) and *The Star* (1922).

Bely's second collection, *Ashes* (1909; revised in 1921, 1925, and 1929) is dedicated to the memory of Nekrasov. Its world is the impoverished, despairing Russia of Chekhov's "Peasants." The setting is the barren Russian countryside, mostly in late fall or in winter, the prevalent mood one of grief and desolation. The subject or poetic persona is often one of the "insulted and injured" ("A Convict," 1906–08, "Prisoners," 1904). The cycle "Spiderweb" has some poems whose persona is a grotesque "monster on crutches" who "looks like a spider" ("The Cripple," 1908, "The Spider," 1908). Some of the poems of *Ashes* are stylized in the manner of the urban folk ditty or the robber song of Russian folklore, where the persona is a thief, a murderer, or an escaped convict. In the poem "The Gallows" (1908) the Villonesque first-person subject describes his own hanging. Some poems feature surprisingly frank sex. "The Priest's Daughter" (1906) and "The Merchant" (1908, a variation on the theme of Nikitin's "A dashing merchant returned from the fair") have all-too-explicit seduction scenes.

The poems of *Ashes*, a panorama of death, prison, poverty, suffering, and madness (as one cycle is entitled), are a restatement of Nekrasov without his warm glow of compassion and relief in tears. Bely's poems addressed to Russia—"My Country" (1908), "Rus" (1908), and others—are not only sad, but also bitter. *Ashes* shows Bely as a poet who could express the carnality, brutality, and banality of life with power, but who failed when he tried to rise to the heights of

48. Bely was aware of this: "My fascination with Dostoevsky, Ibsen, and the symbolists brought poetry and literature into my field of consciousness, but I felt more like a composer than like a poet" ("Andrei Bely about Himself," *Novoe russkoe slovo*, September 3, 1967).

the cosmic or metaphysical, as implicitly but aptly stated in the poem "Life" (1906), dedicated to Vyacheslav Ivanov.[49]

Bely's third collection, *The Urn* (1909), is dedicated to Valery Bryusov, who is addressed in a fine poem, "Magus" (1904, 1908). *The Urn* is Bryusovian in its variety of themes and moods. The most interesting poems of this collection are found in the cycle "Philosophical Sadness," which in elegant language expresses the poet's disenchantment with neo-Kantian philosophy. One of these, "The Tempter" (1908), is addressed to the painter Vrubel. Another, "I" (1907, one of several poems by Bely so entitled), provides an example of Bely's efforts to engage formal elements—rhythm, in this case—semantically:

> You'll quit, you'll sleep—not here, but
>   there.
> Forget the world. Yet it will be.
> There, too, like here, do try to dream:
> In repetitions be recast.

The dualism of human existence is suggested by the sharp caesura that splits the iambic tetrameter exactly in half, in every line of every stanza of the poem.

Bely collected his revolutionary and war poems in the volume *Star* (1922). They are shrill, even hysterical. The most famous of them, "To My Country" (1917, one of several poems of that title), is a hodgepodge of symbolist clichés, cosmic images that were then coming in vogue in revolutionary poetry, Russian messianism, metaphysical conceits,[50] and rhetorically effective sound patterns.

Bely's narrative poems, "Christ Has Risen" (1918) and "First Rendezvous" (1921), relate to Blok and Mayakovsky. The former was seen as a counterpart to Blok's "The Twelve." It is, however, closer to Mayakovsky, both in mood and in form (it is in rhymed free verse). The cruel, grotesque part devoted to the crucifixion is powerful, but Bely's attempt to project the Resurrection on the Bolshevik revolution is a trivial ploy to fuse Mayakovskian rhetoric with symbolist clichés. "First Rendezvous" is a poetic self-portrait and memoir in iambic tetrameter resembling Blok's "Retribution." It is also a recapitulation of Russian symbolism—its ideas, leitmotifs, and images. The poem details Bely's intellectual experiences and searchings through Hindu sages, modern physicists (he predicts that an "atomic bomb" will destroy the world), Nietzsche, the Solovyov family (including an encounter with Vladimir Solovyov), various poets, artists, and musicians, but first and foremost Nadezhda Lvovna Zarina, really Margarita Kirillovna Morozova (1873–1958), wife of M. A. Morozov, a Maecenas who financed the symbolist journal *New Path*. "First Rendezvous" has striking poetic conceits, passages in which sound patterns are explicitly foregrounded (for instance, in a description of a chemical laboratory and of an orchestra's tuning up), and a great deal of euphonic and rhythmic legerdemain. The sparkling, strident, capricious stream of consciousness of "First Rendezvous" is quintessential Bely.

Ivanov

Vyacheslav Ivanov (1866–1949), the *doctus poeta* of Russian symbolism, pursued a career as a classical philologist and historian before he ascended to the Russian Parnassus with his first collection, *Lodestars*, in 1903. His essay "The Hellenic Religion of the Suf-

---

49. Bely wrote at least half a dozen poems of that title.

50. "Dry deserts of shame, / Inexhaustible oceans of tears, / With a ray of a wordless glance, / Christ will descend to warm them." Other passages are at least as shrill and mannered.

fering and Resurrected God" (1904), published in *New Path*, was also a major event. In 1905 Ivanov and his second wife, the writer Lidiya Dmitrievna Zinovyeva-Annibal, with whom he had lived abroad since 1895, settled in Saint Petersburg, where their apartment ("The Tower") became a brilliant literary salon. It flourished until 1907, when Lidiya Dmitrievna died. In the period between 1903 and the revolution Ivanov was prolific as a poet (*Transparency*, 1904; *Eros*, 1907; *Cor ardens*, 1911; *Tender Mystery*, 1912), as translator of Sappho, Alcaeus, Aeschylus, Dante, Petrarch, Novalis, and others, as a dramatist in the classical manner, and as a literary theorist and critic.

Ivanov's prerevolutionary poetry is different from his poetry after 1917. The subjective element of personal experience, which will be present in Ivanov's later poetry, is almost entirely absent. His early verse is an effort to make poetry an avenue to a higher—or deeper—reality; it is not metaphor, but prophecy, cult, ritual, and public function. Ivanov perceived this exalted image of poetry in the poets of ancient Greece, in Dante, and in Goethe and the German romantics, Novalis in particular, all of whom he studied as a scholar and also translated. In his poems on the poet and his craft Ivanov explicitly recognizes the Orphic principle as the foundation of all poetry. In a sonnet, "To the Memory of Scriabin" (1915), he says:

> He was one of those singers (as was
>   Novalis)
> Who in their dreams see themselves as
>   heirs to the lyre
> To which at the dawn of ages obeyed
> Spirit, rock, tree, animal, water, fire, ether.

Greek poetry, mythology, and philosophy are a dominant presence in Ivanov's poetry. He has many poems in classical meters, often using an involute Hellenizing syntax and a great variety of Greek words, names, epithets, and images. Allusions to Greek mythology, often obscure to the uninitiated, are ubiquitous. Pervasive elements of a Dionysian nature religion are fused with Christian themes, theosophy, and occasional excursions into Slavic, Germanic, and even Indic mythology. Many of Ivanov's prerevolutionary poems come across as mannerist and hermetic. Even simple nature poems tend to carry a mythical or symbolic meaning and often relate to Mediterranean or biblical landscapes. In "Scales" (1913) a bright midsummer day is perceived as "a fragile moment of balance" maintained by an invisible woman on her golden scales, where each yellow leaf threatens to tilt the scales "toward the cold grave of light."

The themes of many of Ivanov's poems are derived from his Neoplatonic philosophy: a merging of the human spirit with the cosmos and its elements (air, fire, the sea, or Mother Earth); the ascent of the soul to the heights of purity and freedom ("Spirit," 1903); the descent of the deity as grace or incarnation ("Incarnation," 1903); the divine spark in man's soul ("Night in the Desert," 1903); Platonic anamnesis ("Recollection," 1903); correspondences between natural and spiritual phenomena ("The Realm of Transparency," a cycle of poems of 1904, devoted to the symbolic meaning of precious stones—diamond, ruby, emerald, saphire, and amethyst). The Eternal Feminine appears first in "To an Unknown God" (1903) and then, with particular poignancy, in several cycles from the collection *Cor ardens*, where the image of the poet's deceased spouse merges with Dante's Beatrice, Homer's Andromache, a Dionysian maenad, various hypostases of the Virgin Mary (specifically in the cycle "Golden Sandals"), and a symbolic rose (in "Ghazels on the Rose").

Much of Ivanov's poetry is dominated by elemental imagery—the four elements and the sun, moon, and stars. It also abounds in vertical movement—upward, as anastasis, ascent of the soul, victory over earthly sluggishness, and cosmic striving; or downward, as incarnation, the descent of the deity to earth, or descent to the bowels of Mother Earth to gain strength from her.

A prolific poet in his prerevolutionary period, Ivanov also wrote many more-conventional poems, such as his elegant Italian sonnets, devoted to Italian paintings, edifices, and landscapes (gathered in *Lodestars*), his mordant "Parisian Epigrams" (1891), and the elegiac distichs of "Laeta" (1892), echoing Goethe's *Roman Elegies*. The form of Ivanov's poetry is always perfect, but never foregrounded. He avoids the more obvious, showy play with rhythm and sound patterns found in other symbolists. He is a consummate master of lyric composition, as proven by the excellence of his many sonnets. Nevertheless, if we had only Ivanov's prerevolutionary poetry, he might have stood as merely a remarkable Parnassian poet, too difficult to be appreciated by most lovers of poetry.

The few—no more than a dozen or so—poets who at least at one time considered themselves acmeists have even less in common than the far more numerous symbolists. Even a negative definition does not help much since the acmeist poets, having emerged from symbolism, retained many of its traits even while asserting their opposition to it. Akhmatova's early poetry has decadent traits. Gumilyov's exotic, mythological, and literary themes are also found in Balmont and Bryusov. Mandelshtam's preoccupation with the magical word is symbolist. But the contradictions in the acmeists' theoretical positions, which are obvious even in Gumilyov's programmatic essay "The Legacy of Symbolism and Acmeism" (1913), in no way affected the integrity of their poetry.

Gumilyov

Nikolai Stepanovich Gumilyov (1886–1921) was born in Kronstadt, where his father was then serving as a medical officer in the navy. He attended secondary school in Tsarskoe Selo, where the poet Innokenty Annensky was his headmaster and where he met his future wife, Anna Akhmatova (m. 1910). He graduated as late as 1906, a year after he had published his first volume of verse, *Road of the Conquistadors*. He studied French literature at the Sorbonne in 1907–08 and later continued his studies at Saint Petersburg University, but never graduated. Between 1908 and 1910 Gumilyov made a vigorous entry into Petersburg literary life, becoming coeditor, in 1909, of the new literary journal *Apollon*, where he published his "Letters on Russian Poetry." In 1912 he founded the Guild of Poets, a workshop with a structured program of mutual instruction in poetic technique (it also became the organization of the acmeist group of poets), and a publishing house and journal, *The Hyperborean*. Somehow he found time to travel widely, especially in Africa. Ethiopia, which he visited three times, became one of the favorite locales for his poetry. At the outbreak of war in Europe in 1914 Gumilyov immediately volunteered for active duty. He saw action, was twice decorated, and worked his way up from private to ensign. In 1917 he was sent to France to join the Russian expeditionary corps on the Western front and spent six months in Paris, then several more months in London waiting for an assignment. His adaptations of Chinese and Indochinese poetry, collected in *The China Pavilion* (1918), were done during this period. In May 1918 Gumilyov returned to Russia, where he resumed his literary career. In 1918 he and Anna Akhmatova were divorced. Both remarried, Gumilyov in 1919. In August 1921 he was arrested on a charge of belonging to a counterrevolutionary conspiracy and was shot, along with many others, a few weeks later. His works were not immediately prohibited in the Soviet Union, and a collection appeared in 1923; but they were not again reprinted until the 1980s.

As a poet, Gumilyov was a late bloomer. His first collections, *Road of the Conquistadors* and *Romantic Flowers* (1908), consist of graceless versifications of more or less familiar romantic themes. His many exotic poems, such as "The Hyena," "The Jaguar," and "The Giraffe," recall the paintings of Henri Rousseau. In *Pearls* (1910) and *A Foreign Sky* (1912) Gumilyov's peculiar talent begins to show: given a concrete theme, he can versify it skillfully, at least as well as Bryusov and Balmont. "Portrait of a Man: A Picture by an Unknown Master in the Louvre" (1910) is one of Gumilyov's excellent verbalizations of a painting or sculpture. The cycle "The Return of Odysseus" (1910) is an energetic paraphrase of Homer; "Don Juan" (1910) gives the old theme a new twist, ending in the lines, "No woman ever had a child by me, / No man would ever call me brother." "Margarita" (1912), a variation on a scene in Goethe's *Faust*, has Valentin, her brother, who is slain by Faust, as its hero. To this period also belong the brief epic poems "The Prodigal Son" (1912) and "The Discovery of America" (1910), both vigorously told and versified. *A Foreign Sky* contained several translations from Théophile Gautier, one of the four chosen patrons of acmeism (the others were Shakespeare, Villon, and Rabelais).

Gumilyov's fifth collection, *The Quiver* (1916), shows a mature poet of remarkable versatility. The lead poem, "To the Memory of Annensky, " is a noble tribute to the poet's mentor; the last is an equally inspired "Ode to d'Annunzio: On his Recital in Genoa." The collection includes several war poems: "War," "Offensive," Death," and "A Vision." Gumilyov's persona here is that of a holy warrior fighting in a sacred cause and protected by Saint George. The mood of these poems is solemn and exalted. Gumilyov, who was known to be utterly fearless and to relish and seek out physical danger, was surely sincere in his seemingly anachronistic view of war. *The Quiver* has several poems in an elegiac mode in which the poet takes stock of his life. One of these, "Iambic Pentameters," is perhaps Gumilyov's one great love poem (he wrote many, but they all seem somewhat pale and abstract). In it he wistfully admits the loss of a great love (Akhmatova, of course): "I lost you, as did mad King Nal / Lose Damayanti in a game of dice." *The Quiver* also has several excellent poems about Italy, in no way inferior to Blok's. "Fra Beato Angelico" is yet another beautiful tribute to a painting.

The Pyre (1918) and *A Column of Fire* (1921) contain Gumilyov's finest poems. The former includes "Andrei Rublyov,"[51] a mystical-allegoric interpretation of an icon; "A Small Town," a vivid genre picture à la Boris Kustodiev, delightful painter of a happy turn-of-the-century Russia; a cycle of crisp Scandinavian impressions; and a brief verbalization of the famous Nike of Samothrace: whose rhythm marvelously duplicates the élan of the winged goddess. *Column of Fire* has several unforgettable

---

51. Andrei Rublyov (c. 1370–1430), Russia's greatest icon painter.

poems. "Memory" is an allegorical, idealized, and poeticized autobiography; "The Word" is a hymn to the magical living word of the poet and prophet, concluding in a denunciation of the dead word that serves humans as a mere tool; "Body and Soul" presents a metaphysical dialog whose personas are a melancholy soul grieving for its lost cosmic freedom, a body full of joie de vivre yet aware of its mortality, and God, who conveys His unfathomable essence to body and soul, each "only a faint reflection of a dream that slides along the bottom of His being." "The Sixth Sense," another powerful poem, first praises the five known senses, then seeks to express in three ingenious metaphors the yearning that men sense when they hear immortal verses. "The Runaway Streetcar," Gumilyov's most famous poem, may owe its inception to Rimbaud's "Le Bateau ivre." It is a disoriented, fractured, surrealist ride through space and time on a streetcar that refuses to stop.

The Tent (1921), a collection of Gumilyov's African poems, reads like a versified geography and ethnology of equatorial Africa. Its companion piece is "Mik: An African Poem" (1916), more than a thousand lines of rhymed couplets in iambic tetrameter, slightly stylized to convey the experiences of Mik, an Ethiopian tribesman, who from servitude rises to wealth and honors.

Gumilyov's late collections show that he was still growing and changing as a poet when he died. They also show that he had overcome the technical difficulties and relative lack of literary sophistication that had affected the quality of his early verse. If Gumilyov is considered the third among the acmeists, behind Akhmatova and Mandelshtam, it is probably because he is much inferior to them when not at his best. But in his best work Gumilyov is the equal of any twentieth-century poet.

Akhmatova

Anna Andreevna Akhmatova (1889–1966), the daughter of a naval officer, Andrei Gorenko, was born in Odessa but spent much of her life in or near Saint Petersburg. She was a poet of that city all her life, and even in her early period devoted some poems to Petersburg ("Verses about Petersburg," 1913). She attended secondary school in Tsarskoe Selo, briefly studied law in Kiev, and married the poet Nikolai Gumilyov in 1910. She gained immediate recognition with her collections *Evening* (1912) and *Rosary* (1914) and became a highly visible figure on the Petersburg literary scene. During an extended stay in Western Europe in 1910–11 she met the painter Amedeo Modigliani, who made several drawings of Akhmatova, a strikingly beautiful woman. One more volume of her poetry, *The White Flock* (1917), appeared before the revolution. In 1918 she divorced Gumilyov, by whom she had a son.

Evening, amazingly mature for a first collection, is close to Annensky (a poem of 1911 is entitled "Imitation of I. F. Annensky") but shows an original and inimitable style. Her vision is pointedly feminine, without ever lapsing into the clichés of the modernist woman poets who were her contemporaries. Akhmatova is a purely lyric poet. Each poem expresses a mood, synchronized with a concrete setting. Its subject is most often the many nuances of love—anticipation, playfulness, tenderness, excitement, heartache, dismay, and madness. Each poem is a dramatic moment frozen in time. The setting if realistic, may be Chekhovian, as in "A Song of Our Last

Meeting" and "I clenched my hands under my veil" (both 1911), or, when stylized, symbolist, as in "The Gray-Eyed King" (1910) and "Believe me, not a snake's sharp sting" (1911). A few pieces are stylized in the manner of the modern folk song or chapbook: "The Fisherman," "My husband whipped me with his figured belt," "I have fun with you when you are drunk" (all 1911).

The early poems, more so in *Evening* than in *Rosary*, display many traits of *art nouveau* or *Jugendstil*, much as in Annensky, Kuzmin, or the early Blok. There are Pierrots, Mignons, masks, parrots and Chinese parasols, princes and marquises, velvet, lace, and brocade, lilies and chrysanthemums, sachet, Sèvres figurines, and blue china. The dominant adjectives are of the "svelte" and "languid" family: light, pale, airy, fading, fatigued, light-blue, stifling, lethargic. The willow is the favored tree. These seemingly banal elements form poems of great evocative intensity and haunting beauty, because they are a natural part of the persona's world and reflect the period's sensibility as accurately as does Rachmaninoff's music or Vrubel's paintings, as well as because they are put together with economic precision, controlled understatement, and acmeist palpability. As a contemporary critic, Valerian Chudovsky, pointed out in a 1912 review,[52] Akhmatova's poems have the quality of Japanese art, then in vogue, to create a total picture by presenting a few fragmented impressions, omitting details, and allowing breaks in the composition.

The elements of a gracefully decadent mannerism began to disappear in Akhmatova's second collection, giving way to less decorative, more prosaic settings, and to more poignant, ironic, and even tragic moods. Her style of composition remained the same, however. The third collection introduces the war and entirely new emotions of worry, desolation, and despair over Russia's fate. There are more prayerful moods, and a sense of the disintegration of what had been a compact world. In the decades to come, Akhmatova, a poet and intellect of great depth, would rise to the challenge of adversity and add much to an oeuvre which, even if it had broken off in 1917, would have been impressive.

Mandelshtam

Osip Emilyevich Mandelshtam (1891–1938) was born in Warsaw but spent most of his life in Saint Petersburg, the city that lives in many of his poems. He came from a middle-class Jewish family, but Russian was his native language. His poetic sensibility was oriented toward Christian culture. Mandelshtam attended secondary school in Petersburg. He visited Paris in 1907 and in 1910 spent two semesters in Heidelberg studying old French literature. In 1911 he enrolled in Saint Petersburg University to study Romance and Germanic philology, but never graduated. In 1909 he published his first poems, in *Apollon*, and met Nikolai Gumilyov and Anna Akhmatova, who became lifelong friends. When Gumilyov founded the Guild of Poets, Mandelshtam vigorously participated in the assault of the young acmeists on symbolism. His very first essay in *Apollon* showed him to be a master of that genre.[53]

Mandelshtam was one of those rare poets who needed no apprenticeship. The few poems left from his teenage years are all

52. Valerian Chudovsky, "Apropos the Poetry of Anna Akhmatova," *Apollon*, 1912, no. 5: 45–50.

53. Osip Mandelshtam, "François Villon," *Apollon*, 1913, no. 4: 30–35.

superb. His first book of verse, *Stone* (1913; expanded edition, 1916) reveals a mature poet. The more perceptive among his contemporaries, Voloshin and Georgy Ivanov, for example, immediately recognized his genius. Voloshin called him "a born singer."[54] Indeed, the early Mandelshtam is a poet who distinctly foregrounds the modulations of his vowels. His poems ask for a chanted, sometimes solemn, recitative. An early poem, "There are orioles in the woods, and the length of vowels" (1914), is both an extended metaphor and an exhibit of the poet's awareness of the peculiar music of his verse.

Many of Mandelshtam's early poems are still symbolist: vague, shadowy, mysterious, and musical. In several early poems the link between music and nature is brought out in Orphic conceits. "Silentium" (1910) captures the moment of Aphrodite's birth, exclaiming:

Remain as foam, O Aphrodite,
Let word be music once again,
Let heart be sensitive to heart,
Fused with primeval founts of life.

The Orphic theme, with an allusion to Novalis's blue grotto, appears in "Why is my soul so full of song" (1911). Two of the greatest poems in any language to capture the essence of music in concept, image, and sound metaphor are "Bach" (1913) and "Ode to Beethoven" (1914), the latter with a Nietzschean invocation to "an unknown god" and a hymn to the all-consuming fire and searing white light of creation.

The peculiar traits of an acmeist aesthetics make their appearance even before 1913. They show forth in the plasticity and precision of several early nature poems, still

lives, and interiors, whose objects become magically animate, and in a series of poems that relive in vivid detail the mood of a work of world literature: Homer ("Sleeplessness, Homer, taut sails," 1915), Racine ("I'll never see the celebrated *Phèdre*," 1915), Poe ("We cannot stand tense silence," 1913), Dickens ("Dombey and Son,"1913), Hugo's *Notre-Dame de Paris* ("In the tavern a band of thieves," 1913), and Flaubert and Zola ("L'Abbé," 1914). Acmeism's devotion to Bergsonian *durée*, the endurance and permanence of human creations, and to a humanist universalism[55] is expressed most clearly in several poems addressed to great edifices: "Hagia Sophia" (1912), "Notre Dame" (1912), "The Admiralty" (1913) and other poems devoted to Saint Petersburg, and a whole cycle in praise of the order and permanence of Rome, for instance, "Nature is like Rome, and is reflected in it" (1914).

Mandelshtam the acmeist sides with poetic logos. His poems have a clearly stated meaning and appreciate that quality in the art of others: "But you jubilate like Isaiah, / O most rational Bach!" The hypostatization of the word as a living organism, a key position of acmeism, is expressed in several beautiful poems, such as "Thine Image, Torturous and Vacillating" (1912), with the lines: "The Name of God, like a big bird, / Flew from my Breast." In "To this day, on Mount Athos" (1915) the poet identifies with the heretical sect of the *imyabozhtsy* (from *imya*, "name," and *Bog*, "God"), calling theirs a "beautiful heresy": "The word is pure joy, / It heals human sadness!"

The image of modern culture in the big city was negative whenever it appeared in symbolism. Mandelshtam experiences even modern life with joy and wonder, though

54. Maksimilian Voloshin, "Voices of Poets" (1917).

55. Mandelshtam's early essay "Pyotr Chaadaev" (1915) is an eloquent appreciation of this idea.

with a tinge of amused detachment ("Film," 1913; "Tennis," 1913, "An American Miss," 1913). The title of Mandelshtam's *Stone* is derived from the architectural poems of the collection and more specifically from the poem "I hate the light of monotonous stars" (1912), in which the poet addresses the stone:

Stone, be like lace
And become like a spiderweb:
With a thin needle prick
The empty breast of the sky.

This and many other poems are vivid expressions of acmeist Prometheanism: Man the maker of beautiful things, the builder of cathedrals, composer of musical harmonies, and creator of magical words, proudly competes with Nature.

Russian futurism produced two major poets, Khlebnikov and Mayakovsky, who had little in common. The leader of ego-futurism, Igor Severyanin (pseudonym of Igor Lotarev, 1887–1941), who as late as 1918 was crowned king of poets by frenzied audiences, owed his success more to his skill as a performer, and to the immediate appeal of his verses to his audiences, than to the poetic quality of his work. His grandiloquent and mannered celebrations of sensuality and luxury, gathered in books under such pretentious titles as *Thunder-seething Goblet* (1913), *Golden Lyre* (1914), *Pineapple in Champagne*, and *Victoria Regia* (both 1915), may claim poetic value only if perceived as self-parody. Severyanin's neologisms, uninspired in themselves, established patterns that were followed by other futurists, Mayakovsky in particular. Severyanin made a point of introducing rare meters and exotic strophic patterns without adding thereby to the quality of his verse. Among the other ego-futurists, Vadim Shershenevich, who would later become the leader of the Russian imagists, published several volumes in Severyanin's manner and under titles resembling his. Vasilisk (Vasily) Gnedov (b. 1890), Ryurik Ivnyov (pseudonym of Mikhail Kovalyov, 1891–1981), who later also became an imagist, Ivan Ignatyev (pseudonym of Ivan Kazansky, 1892–1914), and a few other ego-futurists left little of other than historical interest.

Among the cubo-futurists, David Burlyuk, a painter more than a poet, showed his inventiveness mostly in the graphic arrangement of his verses and the typographical extravagances of the futurist miscellanies he edited. Vasily Kamensky (1884–1961), one of the originators of cubo-futurism, was also one of the movement's more active experimenters. In his booklet *Tango with Cows: Ferroconcrete Poems* (1914) he introduced poems whose graphic form was a concrete part of the poem or which were simply graphic arrangements of key phrases. Aleksei Kruchonykh (1886–1969), the most radical of all futurists, left little enduring poetry. He was the most consistently primitivist among the futurists, patterning his poems after crude chapbook ditties and printing them with intentional misprints, bad grammar, and faulty or absent punctuation. His booklets *A Game in Hell* (1912), *Worldbackwards* (1912), and *Hermits* (1913) were provided with likewise primitivist illustrations by Larionov, Goncharova, Tatlin, Malevich, and Olga Rozanova. Kruchonykh also wrote the most notorious trans-sense poetry, specifically in his booklet *Pomade* (1913), illustrated by Larionov.

Khlebnikov

Velimir (pseudonym of Viktor) Vladimirovich Khlebnikov (1885–1922) was born in Astrakhan Province in the Volga delta, where his father was a district administrator.

The family later moved to Volhynia and then to Kazan, where Khlebnikov enrolled in the mathematics department of the university in 1903. He later switched to the natural sciences and took part in several extended field trips. In 1908 he enrolled in the natural sciences department of Saint Petersburg University, but never graduated. In Petersburg he made some literary contacts and attended the Wednesday gatherings at Vyacheslav Ivanov's "Tower." He failed to catch on with any of the established literary journals but as early as 1908 made his debut in the journal *Springtime*, whose editor was Vasily Kamensky, later a fellow futurist. Kamensky introduced him to the modernist composer Mikhail Matyushin and his wife, the writer Elena Guro, through whom he met the avant-garde painter and poet David Burlyuk. From here on Khlebnikov belonged to the nucleus of Russian futurism, as a major contributor to Nikolai Kulbin's *Studio of Impressionists*, the provocative miscellany *A Trap for Judges*, the programmatic *A Slap in the Face of Public Taste*, and several other avant-garde miscellanies. He co-authored, with Kruchonykh, the futurist manifesto *The Word as Such* (1913) and wrote the prologue to Kruchonykh and Matyushin's "opera" *Victory over the Sun*. In April 1916 Khlebnikov was drafted into the army, and he never again had a permanent place of residence, spending time on trains, in hospitals, in prison, and in mental institutions. His travels took him as far as Baku and Iran. He died in a hospital near Novgorod, apparently of general exhaustion, having previously suffered from malaria and several bouts with typhus.

Khlebnikov wrote poetry almost incessantly and rarely polished his poems. He often left them in the hands of friends, David Burlyuk in particular, who would publish them after having edited them without consulting Khlebnikov. Much of his work was published posthumously between 1928 and 1933, and some must have been lost. The bulk of Khlebnikov's surviving work is poetic raw material—though raw material of exceptional quality. Khlebnikov was an eccentric and was obsessed with irrational fixed ideas. He spent much of his time on numerological calculations, by which he meant to find mathematical formulas controlling the course of history, and on glottogonic speculations about the cosmic ties of the sounds of language. These speculations often entered his poetic works, not always to their detriment.

Khlebnikov's poetry is heterogeneous, ranging from hermetic and surrealist free verse to perfectly rational poetry in conventional meter. Examples of the latter are "A Burial Mound" (n.d.), three perfect stanzas about the resting place of a Christian warrior who died in the Mongol invasion, and "Sayan" (n.d.), a beautifully composed landscape of Central Asia centering on a stone monument with a mysterious runic inscription. Only a minor part of Khlebnikov's poetry is simply unintelligible or too rough to have any aesthetic value. But few poems may be considered finished masterpieces. Some are trifles featuring a pun, an exercise in jingling nonsense verse, or a display of the poet's virtuosity, such as "Turnabout" (before 1913), where each of seventeen lines is a palindrome. Others are mainly demonstrations of Khlebnikov's "etymologism," the reduction of language to its roots and the creation of new words and phrases from those roots—the famous "Incantation by Laughter" for example.

Still other of Khlebnikov's poems are devoted to his idea of the intrinsic meaning of the sounds of human speech, such as "Discourse on El" (before 1920), a long poem consisting entirely of phrases whose nucleus is a word starting with the letter *l*. "The word as such" generates the stream of consciousness of many poems through its punning, rhyming, and associative potential. "Iranian Song" (published in 1921) is a good example. Among other curious things that happen in it, an airplane, *samolyot*, "valiant brother of the cloud," appears in the sky— "so where, then, is the magic tablecloth [*skatert'-samobranka*], *samolyot*'s wife? Is she late by accident, or has she been thrown into prison?" The association between *samolyot* (masculine) and *samobranka* (feminine) is grammatical: the prefix *samo* is the Russian equivalent of *auto*.

Many poems by Khlebnikov may be called surrealist, producing irrational, dreamlike associations ("On this day of light-blue bears," 1918). Khlebnikov also has a few trans-sense poems in which artificially created morphemes with no suggestion of a lexical meaning appear, such as the often-quoted "Bobeòbi lips were sung," where *bobeòbi* does not resemble any known Russian word.

Khlebnikov's main genre is the verse narrative, long or short. Its subjects extend from the Stone Age ("I and E: A Tale of the Stone Age," c. 1912) to the present ("Night Raid," 1921). A great deal of it is primitivist, devoted to mythic visions of heroic Slavdom's pagan roots and Asian connections. Regardless of the subject, Khlebnikov's language is only slightly stylized. The whole vocabulary of contemporary Russian, plus archaisms, dialectisms, and Khlebnikov's own neologisms, is thrown into the crucible of his poetic vocabulary. There are no real metric innovations, except for occasional metrically inexact lines. Rhyming is casual: there are many conventional, trite rhymes, but also many inexact and ingenious ones. Nonetheless, Khlebnikov's verses have extraordinary rhythmic vigor and drive.

The distinctive thing about Khlebnikov's narrative poems is his invention of original imaginary worlds. "Maiden of the Forest" (written 1907–08, published 1914) starts as a love idyll of the forest maiden and a singer who charms her with the magic of his songs. Then, as she sleeps, the singer is killed by an intruding warrior, who promptly makes love to the maiden while she has barely awakened. She senses that the lovemaking is different, but only later realizes what has happened and is duly disconsolate. The piece has an ingenuous charm. In "Shaman and Venus" (written no later than 1911–12) Venus, lovely and naked, walks into an old Mongol shaman's cave and asks for shelter: she has been betrayed and abandoned by those who revered her and built temples to her. The shaman meets her without much enthusiasm, smoking his pipe: "You are just cold, and you must have let an affair go sour on you." The two develop a relationship of sorts and she makes the cave into an attractive home. When she finally leaves, they are rather fond of each other. The story is told with disarming, casual freshness. The reader is free to detect a delicate irony between its lines.

Khlebnikov responded to war and revolution with a series of narrative poems which he apparently planned to combine into a single epopoeia of the revolution. In some of these, such as "The Washerwoman or Hot Field"[56] and "The Real Thing," the bitterness and spite of workers, washerwomen, prostitutes, tramps, and all kinds of street people, the exultation of their triumph over their oppressors, and the sweetness of their

---

56. "Hot Field," a dump in Saint Petersburg, was so called because it was always smoking from fires started by spontaneous combustion. The homeless could be seen rummaging through the refuse there.

revenge are expressed with remarkable empathy. In "Night Raid" (1921), a piece of almost hysterical dramatic tension, a squad of Red sailors raids an apartment in which some White Guards are hiding. Having shot their enemies, who meet their killers with cold contempt, the sailors start a drinking bout. As they get drunk, their flippant mockery of their dead victims, of the surviving women, and of an icon of Christ gradually turns into self-pity, pangs of conscience at having killed a mere boy under his mother's eyes, and a no longer flippant, but desperate, challenge to the image of Christ. The poem ends as the sailors realize that the old woman has set fire to the apartment and that there is no escape for them. "Night Raid" is a worthy companion piece to Blok's "The Twelve." Its Christ image is skillfully inserted into the poem as a moral challenge to the revolution. The sailors' revolutionary swagger is carried off well and even more imaginatively than in Blok's poem.

Khlebnikov's poems of the revolution also give occasion to compare him to Mayakovsky, and he comes out well. His poems "Hunger," "Blow your horn, shout, and deliver," and "Three Dinners" (all 1921) are frighteningly graphic and powerful calls for famine relief, a theme also treated by Mayakovsky. The last of these is a grotesque description of sumptuous feasting to contrast with the horrors of famine. Khlebnikov's understanding of the revolution was more immediate, visceral, and Breughelian, as against the more detached, though likewise grotesque, caricatures of Mayakovsky.

The most difficult, but perhaps the most important, aspect of Khlebnikov's poetic oeuvre is the cosmic. He made several attempts to express his vision of the cosmos. The most successful of these, from a poetic standpoint, is "The One Book" (1920), a Whitmanesque vision of a mysterious book of life on earth, read by a cosmic reader. In "A Scratch in the Sky: A Breakthrough into Language" (1922) the sounds of Russian become animate entities in a cosmic drama into which Khlebnikov's numerology also enters. "Break into the Universe" (n.d.) is a surrealist, but graphic, apocalyptic vision, whose focus is "the death of the wise word" as "songs disintegrate, like the flesh of a corpse, into the simplest particles." Khlebnikov's last and most important cosmic poem is *Zangezi* (1922), a poem in prose, verse, dramatic dialogue, etymology, and numerology, in which Khlebnikov's main themes are repeated and synthesized. Khlebnikov himself is Zangezi, something of a Zarathustra, inventor of a "stellar language" and poet of "stellar poems, where the algebra of words is mixed with yardsticks and clocks." The poem ends with an "Amusing Note," which reports Zangezi's suicide after "the destruction of his manuscripts by malicious scoundrels with a large lower jaw" (Burlyuk?). The final words are, "*Zangezi:* 'Zangezi lives, this was an unfunny joke.'" This proved to be correct. Khlebnikov, long neglected, has received much attention in recent years, particularly in the West. He is at this stage a fascinating subject of study and interpretation more than he is a poet accessible to the general reader. But there is no question that a portion of his work stands comparison with the finest poetry of the twentieth century anywhere.

Mayakovsky

Vladimir Vladimirovich Mayakovsky (1893–1930) was born in Georgia, where his father was a forester. After his father's death in 1906 the family moved to Moscow, where Vladimir and his two sisters attended school. Vladimir almost immediately became involved in revolutionary activities. He was arrested three times and in 1909 spent several months in prison for his involvement in a jailbreak. He was eventually released to his mother's custody and went back to school, now to the Moscow School of Painting, Sculpture, and Architecture. He had real talent and became a good portraitist and cartoonist. In 1911 he met David Burlyuk, an older and much more advanced fellow student, to whom he showed some of his poems. Burlyuk told him that he was a genius and recruited him into the budding futurist movement, whose enfant terrible and star performer he soon became. As early as 1913 he scored a succès de scandale with his "tragedy" *Vladimir Mayakovsky*. Of course he played himself, the brazen, provocative, aggressive, brilliant, clairvoyant, tormented, and suffering poet ("I, perhaps the last poet").

Behind the craziness, bravado, and epatage there stood a precocious youth who had a good understanding of modern art and poetry and had perfect control of his verse. Mayakovsky's early essays, especially a couple of short pieces devoted to film, are well informed, intelligent, and perceptive. In 1914 Mayakovsky wrote the first and most famous of his many lyric verse epics, "A Cloud in Trousers." In 1915 he met Osip and Lily Brik, who would be his lifelong companions. Lily, the great love of his life, is the femme fatale of his second *poema*, "The Backbone Flute" (1915). His next two verse epics, "War and the World" (1915–16) and "Man" (1916–17), could only be published after the revolution, on account of some blasphemy in them.

Mayakovsky matured quickly as a poet and almost immediately developed his own style, based on a militantly anti-aesthetic, antisocial, and antihistorical sensibility, coupled with a penchant for virtuosity and ori-

ginality at any cost. He used mostly free verse, a relative novelty in Russian poetry, but rhymed it with inexact yet spectacularly inventive rhymes. Mayakovsky's language encompasses the entire vocabulary of Russian from pompous Slavonicisms to the vilest slang, all used without regard for moral, social, or aesthetic propriety, but always expressively: "I like to see how children die" ("A Few Words about Myself," 1913) or "The street has collapsed, like a syphilitic's nose. / The river is lechery, running to spittle" ("And Yet," 1914). The art, poetry, and culture of the past and present, Russian and Western, are treated with brazen irreverence as so much material for Mayakovsky's puns and witticisms. Mayakovsky's imagery ranges from the lowlife of the city to the religious and cosmic. His metaphors are far-fetched, hyperbolic, and perverse in a baroque way, but often extremely ingenious, such as when a speeding streetcar is perceived as having tracks pulled from its face by a magician, or a steamer's lifeboats are said to be suckling at their iron mother's teats. In one of his earliest poems, "But Could You?" (1913), he brags that he can "paint the ocean's slanting jaws/on a dish of fish jelly/And read The call of new lips/On the scales of a tin fish," and asks, "But you,/ Could you/Play a nocturne/On the flute of drainage pipes?"

The emotions of Mayakovsky's lyrics range from sneering, jeering, swagger, and epatage to hyperbolic and hence parodic self-glorification, plaintive self-pity, unbearable pain, raging despair—all expressed in ingenious and wildly overstated conceits, for example, speaking of the tortures of jealous love: "Tie me to comets, as to horses' tails, / And drag me, / Crash me against the jagged teeth of stars" ("The Backbone Flute"). Most of this is delivered deadpan. Only occasionally is there a suggestion of the tongue-in-cheek grimace that will appear in Mayakovsky's postrevolutionary poetry. "A Cloud in Trousers" and "The Backbone Flute" are mostly furious outbursts of love and jealousy. In "War and the World" the pain and horror of the world war, perceived in a grotesque expressionist manner, are entirely absorbed by the poet's persona, who becomes killer and victim alike. As in most of Mayakovsky's poetry, the poet's ego overpowers even this enormous subject. In "Man"[57] Mayakovsky and his love are again the outright subject. It is in structure and language a saint's life, featuring Mayakovsky's nativity, life, passion, ascension, return to earth, and message "to the ages." The poem ends with these lines: "All will perish, / Come to naught. / And He, / The Mover of Life, / Will have squeezed the last ray from the last suns / Over planets plunged into darkness. / And only / My pain / Sharper: / I stand / Wrapped in fire / On the unextinguishable pyre / Of an impossible love." As is progressively more often the case in Mayakovsky's poems, these lines, though printed as free verse, are actually in perfectly regular, rhymed iambic tetrameter.

The prerevolutionary Mayakovsky is a poet of immense virtuosity and inventiveness. Clever manipulation of language is the essence of his poetry. It confirms the notion expressed by Bely, among others, that modern art has arrived at a point where it is all self-serving intrinsic "form," method and skill, with no significant extrinsic "content." A reader's attempt to extract from Mayakovsky's poetry any philosphical, social, or psychological verities would do it a disservice.

57. Since Russian has neither a definite nor an indefinite article, the Russian title "Chelovek" may also be translated as "A Man" or "The Man."

Among the major poets of the Silver Age there were several who cannot justly be considered in the context of any of the principal schools of the period, even though they associated with symbolists, acmeists, and futurists and their poetry may display traits of one or the other of these groups. Besides the two major figures who will be discussed here, Marina Tsvetaeva, Vladislav Khodasevich, and Georgy Ivanov, who will come up in the next chapter, belong in this category.

Kuzmin

Mikhail Alekseevich Kuzmin (1875–1936), who came from the provincial gentry, studied the humanities at Saint Petersburg University and music with Nikolai Rimsky-Korsakov. He set many of his own poems to music. Kuzmin traveled to Egypt and Italy, but also to Old Believer settlements in the north of Russia. He was personally close to some of the symbolists, Vyacheslav Ivanov in particular. He was a key figure in the Stray Dog cabaret, meeting place of symbolists, acmeists, and futurists in the 1910s. Kuzmin's essay "On Beautiful Clarity" (1910) was seen as a manifesto of acmeism.

Kuzmin's fame as a poet rests largely with his cycle "Alexandrian Songs" (1905–08). These are love poems with different personas, male and female, mostly homoerotic, stylized to reflect the sensibility of Alexandria in the age of Hadrian. One subcycle tells of a Roman soldier enamored of a distant Antinous, whose beauty overwhelms him at first sight. The poems are in unrhymed free verse, one of the few real successes in the writing of Russian free verse. The moods of the Mediterranean metropolis, its sights, sounds, and smells, provide a rich background to ingenuous and mostly serene declarations, confessions, and exultant boasts of love. The whole spirit of "Alexandrian Songs" is a credit to Russian poetry's ability to project a sensibility so totally alien to Russian life.

Kuzmin's poetry is more casual, relaxed, and colloquial, less metaphoric and pictorial than that of the symbolists or even the acmeists, save Akhmatova. It is close in its ethos to the Roman elegists, Tibullus and Propertius. In fact, he has some poems that explicitly imitate their manner, for example, "Gods, what a nasty rain" (1909) or "Why are you teasing me, hiding in the wooded hills?" (1909). Kuzmin's versification is freer, more casual than that of any contemporary, but graceful and pleasing. He often uses free verse and lines of unequal length and does not break his poems into stanzas. When he follows a closed form, as in the sonnet, his mastery is consummate, as in the beautiful winter sonnet "The snows have covered the smooth plains" (1908–09).

Kuzmin's best poems are all love poems, many of them homoerotic. They express the joy and the heartbreak, the elation and the disenchantment of love straightforwardly, without strain or hyperbole. Whenever a conceit is used it is apt and poignant:

> What is my heart? A weedy kitchen garden,
> Trampled as though by a herd of wild horses.
> How shall I live a life that's rent asunder,
> When all my thoughts are only about one?
> (1908–09)

The point of the poem, arrived at after many imprecations, is:

> What gracious saints may I still call upon?
> Who will help me? And who will hear me?
> For it was he who was the gardener here
> Who has himself trampled down his garden.

A poem of 1911, "A Window's Indistinct Outline," graphically describes two lovers after a night of love. It ends with this quatrain:

> May the bluebird of happiness
> Not fly away as we're asleep,
> Let this twilight last forever
> In the window's darkened frame.

Often erotic passion will be allowed to flare up in prosaic surroundings, against the background of a precisely described interior or scenery:

> How I love the smell of leather,
> But I also love the smell of jasmin.
> They do not resemble one another,
> But they have something in common.

The poem then recalls the moment when the poet first saw his beloved riding by as he stood on the Via Calzajuoli in front of the cobbler Tommaso's shop, where a twig of jasmin could be seen in a jar on a shelf—a Proustian moment of precise and intimate recollection.

Kuzmin's heterosexual love poems tend to be parodic, for example, "Letter before a Duel" (1913). But he also easily imitated the ingenuous pastoral poetry of the rococo ("Consolation to Shepherdesses," 1912–13), the romantic verse epic ("A New Rolla," 1908–10, subtitled "An Unfinished Novel in Fragments"), the oriental ghazel ("A Crown of Spring," 1908), and other genres.

Kuzmin can play with ingenious conceits when he so wishes. The title poem of the cycle "Clay Pigeons" (second edition, 1923) is built around an untranslatable pun: "I molded light-blue doves of clay / With my industrious hands." Russian *goluboi*, "light-blue," is etymologically derived from *golub*, "dove, pigeon." But *golubka*, "dove," is also a word of endearment and as a noun means "beloved, ladylove." The point of the poem is that the sculptor would convert his lifeless "doves" into living "loves."

Kuzmin wrote some poems stylized in the manner of a folk song, and in particular many religious poems in the manner of the popular spiritual rime (*dukhovny stikh*), for example, "The Virgin's Descent to the Torments of Hell," "The Hermit and the Lion," "The Last Judgment," and others. In all, Kuzmin's direct and easy, or transparently stylized, poetry offers a welcome change of pace to the intense and demanding poetry of his contemporaries.

Voloshin

Maksimilian Aleksandrovich Kirienko-Voloshin (1877–1932) lost his father early and was brought up by his German mother, an energetic and intellectually active woman to whom he remained close until her death in 1923. In 1893 she bought a lot on the Crimean seashore at Koktebel and built a house there. It later became a colony and refuge of poets and artists during and after the war and revolution. Voloshin devoted an eloquent and moving poem to it, "A Poet's House" (1926). Voloshin studied law at Moscow University but never graduated, owing to troubles with the police because of his involvement in student unrest. In 1900–1901 he spent some time in Central Asia working on the construction of a railway line as a volunteer. Thereafter he resided mostly in Paris until 1916. After his return to Russia he lived in Koktebel almost without interruption. Voloshin was a professional painter of great ability and originality, excelling in watercolors. As a poet, he published in the symbolist magazines *Scales* and *The Golden Fleece*, and later in the acmeist *Apollon*. His whole manner, though, was closer to acmeism. His first independent

book of verse appeared in 1910 and was followed by several others, including a volume of translations from the poetry of Emile Verhaeren (1919).

Voloshin's poetic oeuvre is sharply divided into two periods. In the first he is a Parnassian, influenced by the French Parnassians, particularly Hérédia. In the second he is a powerful civic and philosophical poet. Voloshin the Parnassian stated his view of his craft in a profound and eloquent *ars poetica*, "The Journeyman" (1917). He felt that it was not given him to be a "luminous lyricist" but that he was rather a "smith of stubborn words, who would reveal the taste, smell, color, and measure of their hidden essence." In a poem dedicated to Valery Bryusov, which is part of a cycle, "When Time Has a Stop" (1903), Voloshin sees himself as a poet of cosmic estrangement, a visitor from another world to whom "all that is commonplace to you is so new and full of joy":

> Yes, I remember another world,
> Half-erased, not a good likeness.
> In your world I am a transient,
> Close to all, yet alien to everything.

There is little pathos in Voloshin's Parnassian verses, but their form and imagery are exquisite. He is a master of the sonnet, a form akin to the watercolor, whose technique he projected into it. Many of Voloshin's poems are in fact verbal landscape paintings, where the persona more or less explicitly ("I am all tones of pearly water color," 1903) identifies himself as a watercolorist:

> How near and understandable
> This world of green and blue,
> A world of live transparent patches
> And elastic, supple lines.
>
> (1901 or 1902)

In Voloshin's poetry color in particular is used quite differently than in symbolist poetry, say, Balmont's or Bely's, where it is mostly symbolic. When Voloshin sees "green twilight" ("In a Green Twilight," 1905), saffron fog (no. 13 of the cycle "Cimmerian Twilight"), or "lilac rays" (in a poem of that title, 1907), this is to be taken visually, not symbolically.

Voloshin's landscapes initially were mostly Mediterranean, some from Central Asia. He also has many subtle watercolors in verse of Paris—in the rain, in the springtime, in the fall, in the evening, scenes from the Bois de Boulogne, the Seine, the chestnut trees—as well as reminiscences of Parisian history ("The Head of Madame de Lamballe," 1905–06; "Diane de Poitiers," 1907). Later, in his Cimmerian cycles, the barren pastel-colored hills of Koktebel, its wormwood shrubbery, and the "tired waves lapping the shore of the Euxinus" appear in many poems, rich in nuances of mood and color. The memory of Greek myth is often evoked ("Odysseus in Cimmeria," 1907).

Voloshin's cycle "Rouen Cathedral" (1906–07) anticipates Mandelshtam's poems devoted to great European edifices. It approaches the great cathedral from its "stony roots" and secret crypts, then reaches up to the soaring lacework of its towers blending with the clouds in a moving symphony of aesthetic and religious sentiment. The seventh poem of this cycle, entitled "Resurrection," ends with these lines:

These stones, put together with effort,
Know no fetters and no earthly
    boundaries!
They will suddenly flap their frightened
    wings
And soar heavenward, a flock of doves.

Voloshin's Parnassian poetry features most of the themes found in symbolist poetry. The sun is ever present in his world, more often implicitly, as the source of the various shapes and shades of light, but also addressed directly ("The Sun," 1907) or as Apollo ("The sun will stand in fiery regions," 1909; "Delos," 1909). The dualism of the mundane and the cosmic is a major theme for him, too. A crown of sonnets, "Corona astralis" (1909), revolves around the theme stated in the master sonnet:

In worlds of love we are unruly comets,
And closed to us the paths of regulated
    orbits.
The earth will not destroy the Real in our
    dreams
And midnight suns attract us with their
    light.

The same dualism is brilliantly expressed in a pair of sonnets, "Two Demons" (1911–15), where the key conceit is, "The ray of joy in me is broken / Into seven colors of pain."

War and revolution gave Voloshin's poetry a new direction. He was one of those few poets anywhere who found a way to address the war without martial chauvinism, romantic hysteria, or naturalist cynicism: he perceived it soberly, yet with a sense of tragic pain and fatedness. "Mater Dei of Reims" (1915), inspired by the destruction of Reims Cathedral by the Germans, "Apollyon" (1915), a powerfully estranged panoramic vision of the war in free verse (with an epigraph from Revelation 9:3), and other poems of Voloshin's collection *Anno mundi ardentis* (1916) sustain a noble tragic pathos.

The revolution and civil war, with their unspeakable atrocities, found in Voloshin's cycles *Deafmute Demons* (1919, 1923) and

Verses on Terror (1923) a unique response that combined impassioned civic eloquence with lofty poetic imagination. Such poems as "Peace" (1917), "Kitezh" (1919), and "Red Spring" (1921) are angry philippics castigating the criminal folly, callous brutality, and utter abandonment of shame and human decency that have flung Russia "unto the refuse dump, like carrion." Other poems, like the title poem of *Deafmute Demons*, "Demetrius Imperator, 1591–1613," "Stenka's Judgment" (referring to Stenka Razin), and "Northeast," develop the theme of Russia's curse and redemption. Russia is seen as a nation possessed by cruel demons, walking into the teeth of a howling blizzard, but with a glimmer of hope that "the face of the Lord may break through the darkness of the clouds above." "The Unburnable Bush" (1919, after Exodus 3:2–3), title poem of a collection of 1925, became to Voloshin a symbol of Russia's hope:

We perish without dying,
We bare our spirit to the core...
Lo, a miracle: it burns, but will not burn up,
The unburnable bush.

The stark imagery, driving rhythm, and masterful instrumentation of "Demetrius Imperator" and "Northeast" give those poems exceptional suggestive power. In the former, the horrors of the Time of Troubles are retold by the murdered tsarevich as he assumes the identities of all the impostors who impersonated him. He concludes his narration with the declaration, "And I shall return—in three hundred years." The theme of "Northeast" is compressed in the lines, "In the commissars, the spirit of autocracy, / Explosions of revolution in the tsars."

Voloshin's postrevolutionary years were devoted largely to *The Ways of Cain*, a great philosophical poem in the manner of Lucretius's *De rerum natura*, a cosmogony and history of the earth and of man, seen in Manichaean terms. Cosmic themes had occurred previously in Voloshin's poetry. An early poem, "I walked through the night" (1904), dedicated to the painter Odilon Redon, is one of several that view the earth through the eyes of a cosmic traveler. The cycle "Cosmos" in *The Ways of Cain* develops the idea of cosmic and human evolution as a dialectic of spirit and matter, an admirable exercise in clarity of thought coupled with vigorously conceived metaphor. "Cosmos" is followed by an apocalyptic "Leviathan," ending with a dialogue between God and man in which God justifies His creation. *The Ways of Cain* is pregnant with challenging thoughts and ingenious conceits. It is a worthy addition to a tradition of philosophical-didactic poetry started by Trediakovsky and continued by Zhukovsky, Küchelbecker, and Glinka.

Voloshin was much neglected in the Soviet Union. Only in 1977 could a small collection of his poetry, which omitted some of his finest poems, finally appear. Intellectually more challenging than any of his contemporaries, Voloshin wrote poetry not as immediately captivating as Blok's or as fascinating as Mandelshtam's, but containing great riches that reveal themselves to the attentive reader. Voloshin was among the great poets of the century.

Prose Fiction

The Russian novel by no means died with the end of its golden age. Many of the leading figures and innumerable lesser lights of the Silver Age wrote in the genre, and their novels created as much of a stir as the great ones had in the 1860s and 1870s. Only Sologub's *Petty Demon* and Bely's *Petersburg*, however, eventually entered the historical canon along with the major novels of the preceding period. Most, like Mikhail Artsybashev's *Sanin* (1907), a somewhat pornographic vulgarization of Dostoevsky's *Notes from Underground*, or Lidiya Z'novyeva-Annibal's *Thirty-three Abominations* (1907), the first Russian novel to feature lesbian love, were ephemeral sensations. Some novelists who enjoyed as much success with the reading public as did the leading writers of the 1860s in their day—Anastasiya Verbitskaya and Vasily Nemirovich-Danchenko, for example—faded from the scene without leaving much of a trace. The prose writers of the Silver Age who were read and remembered later in the twentieth century wrote short stories or novels which, like those of Sologub, Bely, and Remizov, were radically different from their predecessors'.

Was the temporary decline of the novel linked to any developments in the society and culture of the period? Osip Mandelshtam suggested that this decline was caused by the death of biography, or more precisely, by a loss of faith in the notion that an individual's biography was a function of social conditions, individual character, and ideas held by the individual and his or her environment. The short stories of Chekhov or the novels of Bely and Remizov deal with situations that are accidental in nature and are part of a more or less chaotic world. This attitude apparently reflected the general sensibility of the Russian intelligentsia of the Silver Age, excepting those few intellectuals who possessed some well-defined ideology. Gorky's novel *Mother*, which presented a determinate world populated by characters with a "revolutionary biography," seemed false to most contemporaries, though it appealed to doctrinaire revolutionaries like Lenin.

The novel of the nineteenth century had been a hybrid art form, open to intrusions of didactic, polemical, and moral subtexts. The major authors of the Silver Age, less concerned with fulfilling a "social commission" or propounding a "moral message" than with creating a work of art, gravitated toward the short story or short novel, forms more apt to be free of serious artistic flaws than was the conventional novel. Such writers as Chekhov, Bunin, Remizov, Sologub, and Bely were more conscious of style than were their predecessors—another reason why they would favor the shorter prose forms, or would be more successful in them. Many of the prose writers of the Silver Age were also important dramatists: Chekhov, of course, but also Andreev, Gorky, Sologub, and Remizov. An association with the drama tends to predispose an author to the short story rather than to the novel. Indeed, the Silver Age was the great age of the Russian short story.

Tolstoi (after 1880)

The connection between Tolstoi's personal life and his literary work, always close, became even closer after he embraced religion in 1877. By 1879 he was working on his *Confession* and related religious works. *Confession* was ready in February 1880. An attempt to publish it failed, as it was blocked by the ecclesiastical censorship. It appeared in Geneva in 1884, and the first complete edition came out in Russia as late as 1906. In *Confession* Tolstoi sketches his path from naive childhood faith to its loss in late adolescence, his attempts to substitute for it various earthly doctrines and beliefs, his arrival at a pessimistic assessment of human life as meaningless suffering followed by the nothingness of death, and efforts to overcome his utter despair by emulating the uneducated Russian peasant's faith in God. *Confession* was, as it were, a preface to several works written in the early 1880s which were the fruit of Tolstoi's intensive study of religion: *A Harmony and Translation of the Four Gospels* (1879–81), *A Study of Dogmatic Theology* (1879–80), *A Brief Exegesis of the Gospel* (1881), and *What I Believe In* (1883–84). Since Tolstoi's understanding of Christianity was heretical, these and some of his other post-1880 works could not be published in Russia, but were printed abroad. These writings were soon translated into many languages and gained Tolstoi worldwide fame and influence. Tolstoi was now a public figure of international stature. He was beginning to have a following among the Russian intelligentsia. Some important literary figures were at least temporarily (Chekhov and Leskov, for example) converted to Tolstoianism.

Tolstoi's interpretation of the Gospels was based on a thorough study of the Greek text and up-to-date biblical scholarship, but it was also dictated by his acceptance of the Sermon of the Mount as the sole correct guide to a Christian life. Tolstoi's understanding of Christ's commands with regard to sexual conduct was particularly severe. He assumed that the phrase "except on the ground of unchastity" in Matthew 5:32 was spurious (with little philological evidence to support this view) and declared that Christ had taught that without exception sexual union should be limited to a single partner in a lifetime, and this as an inferior alternative to celibacy. He also derived from the Sermon of the Mount a doctrine of uni-versal brotherhood of men and nonresistance to evil, as well as a prohibition of taking an oath under any circumstances. Furthermore, Tolstoi interpreted the fifth commandment to mean that human life should not be taken under any circumstances, including in war, in self-defense, or in punishment (execution of criminals). Whereas Tolstoi's moral teaching was maximalist, resembling past and contemporary sectarian doctrines suppressed by the church, his theology was entirely negative. He explicitly challenged the authority of the church and every one of its dogmas, such as the Holy Trinity, the divinity of Christ, and the Immaculate Conception. He declared the ritual of the Orthodox church to be so much mumbo jumbo, and the sacraments crude and useless sorcery.

Tolstoi spent the remainder of his life propagating his religious views and their social, political, and practical corollaries. After 1880 he wrote a great deal more nonfiction than fiction. He outlined his practical program in the tract *What Then Shall We Do?* (1882–86). It begins with a starkly naturalistic description of poverty in a Moscow slum, which Tolstoi had seen as a volunteer census taker in 1882. Its recommendations are nihilist, anarchist, and pacifist. He advocates the abolition of every aspect of modern society and a return to communal subsistence farming. He sees the way to his utopia in passive resistance to draft boards, tax collectors, and all the blandishments of modern civilization. Tolstoi repeated this message in several later works.

Tolstoi's nonfiction was every bit as powerful and fascinating as his fiction, sometimes even more so. He did, however, continue to write some fiction. The 1880s saw "The Death of Ivan Ilyich," one of the great short stories in all literature, "The Kreutzer

Sonata," some twenty moral tales "for the people," almost all of them superior pieces of writing,[58] and a great play, *The Power of Darkness*. "The Devil" and "Father Sergius," masterpieces published only posthumously, joined "The Kreutzer Sonata" to form a trilogy on the evils of sexual passion. "Hadji Murat," a powerful short novel in which Tolstoi returned to the Caucasus of his youth, is among Tolstoi's finest works. Ironically, it was written concurrently with the treatise *What Is Art?* whose precepts it summarily violates. Tolstoi released his long novel *Resurrection* for publication in *The Cornfield* against his artistic judgment, because he wanted to contribute a large sum to the resettlement to Canada of the *dukhobory*, a religious sect persecuted by the Russian government.

When Tolstoi returned to fiction in the mid-1880s, it was unabashedly moralizing, often in a heavy-handed way. But artistically the fiction was no worse for the preaching. If anything, it gained power, since Tolstoi now abandoned his psychologizing and philosophical digressions, adopting the straightforward manner of the parable or chronicle. "Yardstick, the Story of a Horse," a piece Tolstoi had first thought of in 1856, was completed and published in 1885. Yardstick is a great trotter who tells his own story, exposing the stupid cruelty of the human world—matter-of-factly and without rancor. "Yardstick" is a modernized animal fable which gets maximum use out of Tolstoi's favorite device, *ostranenie*, or "making it strange." As in all great animal tales, Yardstick is also sufficiently equine. Tolstoi knew his horses.

58. With the assistance of his disciple Vladimir Chertkov (1854–1936), Tolstoi in 1884 founded a publishing house, Posrednik (Intermediary), to disseminate these tales as well as his other writings.

"The Death of Ivan Ilyich," started in 1881 but finished only in 1886, is an example par excellence of Tolstoi's post-conversion style. The characters are no longer individualized: Ivan Ilyich is Everyman. The narrative brings only essential facts and no picturesque details. The language is lapidary, stern, and unadorned. The story moves from Ivan Ilyich's funeral back through his life, up to the moment of his death. His illness, apparently intestinal cancer, is described in brutal detail. The point of the story is that Ivan Ilyich, a judge, who has been by conventional standards a decent, successful, and happy man, has in fact criminally wasted his life. He begins to live only hours before his death, when he finally accepts death as a part of life and as the business at hand, necessary to relieve his family of his hideously emaciated, screaming and stinking presence. He is rewarded by an epiphany of light as he lapses into a coma. Ivan Ilyich's doctors treat him as their "case," much as he, as a judge, had sought to eliminate all but the legal aspect from his work. The positive message of the story is provided by Gerasim, a peasant lad working in Ivan Ilyich's household. He feels pity for his suffering master and by natural human impulse does his best to help him. "The Death of Ivan Ilyich" is a story whose narrative frame, plot, atmosphere, and idea are perfectly synchronized and accentuated by a wealth of symbolic details, all well disguised as ordinary facts of life.

Tolstoi's "tales for the people" are for the most part based on folktales and folk legends, adjusted to convey a message in accord with Tolstoi's teaching of unconditional nonviolence, meek quietism, and universal brotherhood. Tolstoi hoped that they would provide proper "spiritual nourishment" for the people and an alternative to the commercial trash which was inundating the cheap book market. Although the high artistic quality of Tolstoi's tales was never in doubt, critics raised the question of their value as popular literature. Mikhailovsky asked why Tolstoi, always a realist in his works addressed to an educated public, would introduce angels, devils, and miracles in his tales for the people. Wasn't this unwarranted condescension? Mikhailovsky also found fault with several stories in which Tolstoi made it explicit that a servant's state was preferable to a master's; he pointed out that Tolstoi's message of nonresistance to evil was perversely overstated and that his whole understanding of the human condition was suggestive of "outright contempt for life in all of its complex forms." Mikhailovsky's perceptive criticism was socially valid but aesthetically misplaced. He judged Tolstoi's stylized, allegorical, and symbolist tales by the standards of realist art.

"The Kreutzer Sonata," begun in 1887 and completed in 1889, was vetoed by the censor in 1890 but cleared by Alexander III personally in 1891. By then it was circulating in thousands of manuscript copies and had been translated into several foreign languages. The story is told, in a dark train compartment, by Pozdnyshev, a landowner, who has just been acquitted, for reason of temporary insanity, of the murder of his wife, whom he had suspected of adultery. It is the story of a "normal" marriage that is in fact hell on earth. Woven into the narrative are violent diatribes against carnal love and its glorification through music, poetry, and art. Beethoven's Kreutzer Sonata, the "falcon" of the story,[59] bears much of the guilt: Pozdnyshev's wife was the pianist, her lover the violinist, performing the sonata. The moral of the story, pointed out by Tolstoi in

an afterword and confirmed by an epigraph stating Christ's ascetic view of sex (Matthew 5:28, 19:10–12), is that erotic love and everything connected with it are evil and that a marriage based on it must be unhappy. There is, however, much Schopenhauerian misogynism in it, too. "The Kreutzer Sonata," an inferior work artistically, created a huge controversy, because it brought out into the open problems never before discussed in public. In retrospect, while Tolstoi had some of his details wrong (Chekhov, a physician, noted this with some irritation: no, he said, it is not true that all women find the act of love revolting), his grasp of the conflict in modern marriage was profound. Pozdnyshev wants to control his wife and their married life; she resists and wants to have her own way; their life turns into a battle for control, in which their children are the pawns.

The evils of carnal passion are the subject of two other stories, "The Devil," started in 1889 and finished in 1890, and "Father Sergius," started in 1890 and finished in 1898. Both are powerful, somber, and cruel. In "The Devil" a cultured and kindly landowner is driven to murder (in one version) and suicide (in the other) by his carnal passion for a seductive peasant woman. "Father Sergius" is a modern saint's life. Father Sergius, a hermit revered for his great sanctity, is torn by concupiscence and doubt. One night a provincial society lioness makes a bet that she will seduce the holy man. Father Sergius saves himself by chopping off a finger with an axe. But he falls all the same, with a mentally retarded and physically repulsive girl brought to him by her father to be healed of her afflictions. In commenting on the story, Tolstoi said that if the holy man had sinned with a beautiful and healthy woman, he would have had no justification for it; but here he had the vile excuse of pity

59. See p. 264.

for the girl, for who else would have wanted her? The story goes on, however, and Father Sergius is saved.

"Master and Man," written in 1894–95, is a new variation on the theme of an early story, "Blizzard." The sheer terror of being lost in a snowstorm and sure to freeze to death is turned into a morality: the master, a hard and greedy man, sacrifices his life when he protects his hired man with his own body, keeping him warm until rescue comes. The story offers yet another instance of Tolstoi's preoccupation with an epiphany in the hour of death.

The novel *Resurrection* was first conceived in 1888, following a story Tolstoi heard from the jurist A. F. Koni about a juror who recognized in the accused thief, a prostitute marked by a loathsome disease, the woman he had once seduced. He tried to have her freed, promising to marry her, but she died in prison. Tolstoi worked on the novel in several spurts but was never content with it. It has no satisfactory conclusion, as Chekhov immediately pointed out. The novel's structure is multileveled. It is the story of Duke Nekhlyudov's personal "resurrection" from effete sybaritism as he abandons his earthly possessions and follows Katyusha Maslova, the girl he had seduced as a student, to Siberia. It is also the story of Katyusha's awakening from the mindless cynicism of a still young and healthy prostitute to a social consciousness. It is furthermore a scathing indictment of Russian society, a long journey that takes Nekhlyudov from Moscow to Petersburg and then all the way to Siberia, as well as through all levels of society, from high-ranking officials to lowly convicts. The story of Nekhlyudov's resurrection is unconvincing. Romain Rolland observed that Tolstoi had implausibly put his own mind, that of

a seventy-year-old man, into the body of a thirty-five-year old *viveur*. The story of Katyusha Maslova is more convincing. Her seduction is done *con amore*, quite contrary to Tolstoi's otherwise squeamish attitude toward sex. She is not ashamed of being a prostitute and rather has contempt for working people, but she is ashamed of being a jailbird. That she is converted to revolutionary ideas by Marya Pavlovna, a political prisoner, is plausible. The antigovernment, anticapitalist, antichurch bias in *Resurrection* is so strong that even a Marxist critic must be satisfied. In *Anna Karenina* nobles and government officials could be good types or bad. In *Resurrection* the noble, rich, and powerful are all bad, except those who renounce their class. The legal system is presented as a body that obstructs justice. Maslova is convicted because of an error by the jury: the trial judge, anxious to finish the case quickly so he could rush to an adulterous tryst, had failed to instruct it properly. In prison most convicts are either totally innocent of any wrongdoing or are innocent victims of the system or of social conditions. The church is hit hard, too. The priests encountered are all negative characters. In one scene Tolstoi produces a mockingly estranged, blasphemous description of a church service and the Eucharist. The revolutionaries whom Nekhlyudov meets on his way to Siberia are mostly positive characters. Some are advocates of Tolstoi's own ideas: universal brotherhood and reverence for life, populism, vegetarianism, and celibacy. Technically, *Resurrection* has kept pace with the times. Compared to Tolstoi's earlier works, it is shockingly naturalistic. It amply uses impressionist devices to create the effect of stark contrast between rich and poor that permeates the novel. But on the whole it leaves the reader depressed, *pace*

Viktor Shklovsky, who said that it featured "the victory of the spring of love over the autumn of repentance."

"Hadji Murat," started in 1896 and finished in 1904, is an epic tale and a return to the spirit and manner of *The Cossacks* and *War and Peace*. It begins with the description of a thistle (Russian *tatarin*, literally, Tartar) in the middle of a plowed field, its stalk ripped in half by the plow, its blossom crushed by the horse's hooves—yet it has righted itself and keeps growing. The story ends, "It was this death"—Hadji Murat's—"that the thistle in the middle of a plowed field reminded me of." Hadji Murat was a Caucasian chieftain and a major figure in the resistance of Moslem mountaineers to the conquering Russians. His story is an apotheosis of the will to live, of predatory man, of strength and courage. Hadji Murat's last stand is one of the highlights in all heroic fiction. It takes place in a grove in which the song of several nightingales rings out. When it is over, "the nightingales who had fallen silent during the shooting resumed their song, first one nearby and then others in the distance."

Populist Fiction

The populist movement produced a gallery of writers, born mostly after 1840, who continued the traditions started by the "men of the sixties." Their basic genres were still the sketch of urban or rural low life and the novel, usually short, about "new men" and "new women." But there was now more of an effort to perceive "the people" as individuals. At the same time, the image of the people's "enemy" also changed. With the decline of the landowning gentry, a more ruthless and much greedier entrepreneur from the uneducated lower middle class

often appears as the villain. By the late 1880s the self-image of the progressive intellectual had become clouded by doubt and self-criticism. Nevertheless, a branch of Russian literature devoted to bringing the plight of the Russian masses to the intelligentsia's attention and mobilizing it for the struggle against injustice, prejudice, and indifference continued to exist throughout the period and until the revolution of 1917.

Innokenty Fyodorov (pseudonym Omulevsky, 1837–1884) came from Siberia, where his father was a police officer. He went to St. Petersburg in 1856 and attended the university as an auditor. In the 1860s and 1870s he was popular as a poet in the manner of Nekrasov. His autobiographical novel *Step by Step* (1870), greeted with warm approval by Saltykov-Shchedrin, presents the progress of an idealized "new man" in an aura of optimism. The hero, Svetlov, returns to Siberia after having finished his studies in Petersburg. Svetlov, "step by step," applies the new ideas that he has acquired through his studies in practical work. He will not join the civil service but prefers to found a private school, where he can use modern enlightened methods of instruction. The "woman question" is broached when a friend of Svetlov's refuses to be the "property" of her unworthy husband and leaves him. The concern of the "new man" for social justice is demonstrated in an episode where the workers of a state-owned factory go on strike against its crooked manager. Svetlov is accused of having incited the strike and is put in prison. But he is eventually cleared and continues his good works.

Nikolai Zlatovratsky (1845–1911), the son of a minor government official, studied at the Petersburg Technological Institute but never graduated. He started his literary career in 1866 with a short story published in *The National Annals*, which was to remain his principal outlet. His prolific output of novels, stories, and sketches representative of the populist ideology and ethos was marked by an intimate familiarity with popular life, a faith in the positive qualities and moral virtues of the people, a bias for the rural as against the urban type, and a search for educated Russians, notably raznochintsy, who will help the people find a way to a better life. Zlatovratsky's first success was the short novel *Peasant Jurors* (1874–75), which tells about the journey of eight peasants from the same community traveling into town—on foot, since their horses are needed at home—for jury duty, about their performance as jurors (they find a man guilty of bigamy), and about their return to their home village. One of them, an old man, falls ill and dies. *Peasant Jurors* is a study in "making it strange." The jurors have only a dim notion of what the court proceedings are all about and view them with a sense of profound estrangement. The educated people in the courtroom (the accused is a university graduate) in turn have no idea of the sentiments and concerns of the peasant jurors. They wonder if what they feel was a miscarriage of justice was worth the "enlightening influence" that participating in the judicial process will have on the peasantry. *Peasant Jurors* shows Zlatovratsky and populist realism at their best. His many sketches of rural as well as urban popular life, which appeared under such titles as *Everyday Life in the Village*, *Sketches of Rural Attitudes*, *Sketches of Popular Life*, and *The City of Workers*, are rather inferior to those of Nikolai Uspensky and Sleptsov.

Zlatovratsky's populist ideology shows up clearly in his best-known work, the novel *Foundations*, serialized in *The National Annals* from 1878 to 1883. It was meant to present the "foundations" of Russian popular life, the peasant commune (mir) and the workers' artel, in a positive light, but in effect demonstrated their demise at the hands of entrepreneurs and kulaks. The central figure, Pyotr Volk, a good-natured, bright, and enterprising peasant lad, is corrupted by city life when he goes to work in Moscow. When he rises in the world, he becomes a callous destroyer of the peasant community whence he came. The plot of the novel is diffuse and hardly interesting. But some sketches within the novel, such as one about sickly and retarded children who rarely survive the first decade of life, are memorable. In his later years Zlatovratsky, disappointed in his populist ideas, wrote stories in which his heroes experience such disappointment. He also wrote remarkable memoirs.

Sergei Terpigorev (1841–95) came from a family of Tambov Province gentry. He was a student of law at Petersburg University but was expelled in 1862 for participating in student disorders. Throughout the 1860s and 1870s he published articles, notes, and reportage in various newspapers and journals. *Impoverishment: Sketches, Notes and Meditations of a Tambov Landowner* (1880) made him famous. This work sketches the decline of the gentry after the emancipation in a series of paradigmatic vignettes, each presenting a different way in which a landowner would lose his estate to a merchant, minor government clerk, or ex-serf. The gross ignorance, panic-stricken folly, gullibility, and total incompetence of the landowners make them easy pickings for the ruthless new entrepreneurs. As presented by Terpigorev, these landowners richly deserve their fate. They have few or no redeeming virtues. Terpigorev tells his stories as if he himself were a Tambov landowner and knew all the characters personally. This gives a grim irony to his mournful catalog of uncles, cousins, schoolmates, and neighbors who mismanage their mortgaged estates, squander the redemption payments received from the government, and, having lost their estates, follow the general *Drang nach Petersburg* (Turgenev's phrase), where they join their former house serfs to swell the ranks of unemployed drifters without resources or marketable skills. Terpigorev's view of the emancipation is heavily jaundiced: it destroyed the landed gentry but did not help the peasants, who find themselves in the hands of far more efficient and pitiless exploiters.

Ivan Kushchevsky (1847–76) was born in Barnaul, Siberia, the son of a minor official, and attended the Tomsk gymnasium, also in Siberia. He came to Petersburg in 1866 to enroll in the university, and worked at odd jobs and lived in flophouses for several years. In 1870 he began to write sketches describing his experiences. Kushchevsky died a victim of alcoholism, like so many men of his generation. He was a *homo unius libri*. His novel *Nikolai Negorev, or a Russian Doing Well*, serialized in *The National Annals* in 1871, is an important work, lively, well written, its characters sharply but convincingly delineated, and its ideological bent sufficiently camouflaged by ambiguity. Nikolai Negorev, the son of a middling landowner, tells the story of his progress from age twelve to his arrival at what promises to be the start of a solid career in government service. The novel paints a vivid picture of a provincial gymnasium (dull, drunken teachers, brutal floggings, learning by rote, but also youthful enthusiasm, work on a student newspaper, and pure fun) and of Petersburg University (intellectual ferment, student circles, revolutionary activity, professors who fawn on their liberal students, afraid they will make

trouble in classes). Nikolai Negorev's career in the civil service is compressed into the last chapter. Nikolai's foil, his brother Andrei, is sanguine, brave, and impetuous, but reckless, undisciplined, lacking any ability to conform. There is also Overin, the zealot, who is utterly dedicated to whatever he does: he starts with religious zeal as a schoolboy and ends up as a revolutionary sentenced to fifteen years at hard labor. Malinin, a good-natured and industrious "average man," will make a middle-echelon career. He marries Negorev's sister. There are other characters, including several young women—each sharply and distinctively drawn, each involved in the action. The hero himself is mainly sensible. Some would say he is a scoundrel, because he chooses to be cautious. He keeps out of trouble as best he can, works hard, and does not stick out his neck; but he has normal human feelings, except that they are not strong and he manages to keep them in check. He has his share of reverses like everybody. Surely Kushchevsky meant to make his conservative antihero a despicable type, a disgrace to the Russian intelligentsia. But his artistic tact caused him to present Negorev as a normal human being, with the result that the very message of the novel became ambiguous: maybe Negorev was right and the revolutionary idealists wrong. It is possible that Maksim Gorky modeled his *Life of Klim Samgin* on *Nikolai Negorev*.

Gleb Uspensky (1843–1902), the son of a government official in Tula, studied in Saint Petersburg and Moscow without graduating from a university. He began to write in 1862, influenced by his cousin Nikolai Uspensky. He published his sketches in Tolstoi's *Yasnaya Polyana*, *The Russian Word*, and *The Contemporary*. A series of sketches, *The Manners of Rasteryaeva Street*, began to appear in *The Contemporary* in 1866. Later

Uspensky published mostly in *The National Annals*. In the 1870s Uspensky did journalistic work, which took him abroad (*Letters from Serbia*, 1876). From the early 1880s on, he concentrated on essays and stories about country life (he was now living near Chudovo in Novgorod Province), collected in *The Peasant and Peasant Labor* (1880), *The Power of the Land* (1882), and *Living Numbers* (1888). Thereafter Uspensky was mentally ill and unable to continue his work.

Uspensky was the quintessential populist writer. He sought to relive the life of the people in all its abject misery and abysmal ignorance. He took for granted that its violence, drinking, wife beating, and child abuse were caused by "grief that has lasted too long." This goes even for his policemen, guards, firemen, and other instruments of authority. Disadvantaged (they often come from regions where poverty is endemic), conditioned by cruel military service, and assigned to do a mind-killing job, these men act without understanding and react to any "disorder" with mindless and indiscriminate violence. Uspensky's great specialty is to take wretchedness, apathy, and hopelessness to their limits.

Uspensky's best-known work, *The Manners of Rasteryaeva Street*, is a series of vignettes from the life of a busy street in Tula, a center of Russian metal works. Its leitmotif is grief: "The knock-knock of hammers, the constant singing or cheery joking of the artisans, the idyllic gaiety of the children playing in the street, the good cheer of fighting womenfolk, all going on in broad daylight and right in the street, all these external, public manifestations of life in Rasteryaeva Street would not, however, give an observer any idea of the dark grief that oppresses a dweller of Rasteryaeva Street from cradle to grave." Prokhor Porfirych, a turner who handcrafts all kinds of guns on his lathe, is the central character. The illegitimate son of a "gentleman," he has decided to rise in the world by refusing to fall into the vices of Rasteryaeva Street—idleness, violence, and drinking. Inserted are the stories of other characters living in Rasteryaeva Street. "Petka's Career" is the story of an orphan boy who is on his way to becoming a workingman: he has learned to make matches. His future is visualized as hard work, drinking, fighting, hospital, and prison. "An Exemplary Family" tells about a greedy and domineering mother, her cretinous son, and his browbeaten wife. "Need Makes You Sing Songs" is a vignette about an itinerant magician and illusionist. The mood of all these stories is gloomy, foul, and dreary, without a ray of light anywhere.

Uspensky was much respected, even revered by the radicals of his age and after. His name was often mentioned in one breath with those of Turgenev, Tolstoi, and Chekhov. He deserves credit more for his acute sensitivity to the sufferings of the Russian people and his moral outrage at the injustices inflicted upon them than for his art.

Aleksandr Ertel (1855–1908), the son of a German who managed the estates of rich noblemen, developed a broader view of Russian life than most of the other populists. His peasant tales and stories about the relationship between the intelligentsia and the people are less schematic than most. His panoramic novel *The Gardenins, Their Servants, Friends, and Enemies* (1889) was received with respect and approval by knowledgeable contemporaries, including Tolstoi. The action of the novel is centered in the Gardenins' huge estate and famous stud farm in Voronezh Province. A plethora of characters, from the aristocratic Gardenins down to peasants and hired hands, is introduced. This is post-reform Russia, with a great deal of upward social mobility: there now exists a new class of educated Russians who have no ties to the landed gentry and its culture. The son of the Gardenins' stable-master, Efrem Kapitonov, is a student in Saint Pétersburg. Nikolai Rakhmanny, a steward's son, develops a friendship with the heiress, Elise Gardenina. It defines the difference between the aristocrat and the raznochinets: Elise believes in the imagination, Nikolai in reason and science. To Nikolai, Elise seems terribly ignorant, because she does not even know who Dobrolyubov was. She is fascinated by Dostoevsky, who means little to him.

Korolenko

Vladimir Galaktionovich Korolenko (1853–1921) came from the Ukraine, where his father was a judge. His mother was the daughter of a Polish landowner. Elements of his Ukrainian background often appear in his works. Korolenko's studies of agronomy and mining in Petersburg were twice interrupted by arrest and exile for participating in student protests. In 1881 he was exiled to Yakutia. When he returned from exile in 1885 he settled in Nizhny Novgorod. There Korolenko, a well-known writer by then, helped Maksim Gorky launch his career. In 1893 Korolenko made a trip to the United States, an experience reflected in one of his longer stories, "Without Language" (1895). In 1896 he moved to Saint Petersburg, where he was coeditor, with Nikolai Mikhailovsky, of the populist journal *Russian Wealth*. He spent the last years of his life in Poltava in the Ukraine, still active as a writer and journalist.

Korolenko began to publish his stories in 1879. He scored his first success with the collection *Notes of a Siberian Tourist* (1885) and subsequently produced a steady flow of stories, sketches, essays, and articles. He also wrote ethnographic sketches, essays on Russian literature (Tolstoi, Chekhov, Garshin, and others), and during the last sixteen years of his life worked on his memoirs, *A History of A Contemporary of Mine* (published posthumously in 1922), in the manner of Herzen's *My Past and Thoughts*. Korolenko, a populist, was a sincere humanist, a kindly, modest, and very admirable human being. As a writer, he took a sober but optimistic view of the human race and of life at large. He was not a great artist. His stories lack structure and drama, and his narrator is dominated by his material. His success therefore depends on whether he has a good story to tell—and Korolenko had many good ones. He was intimately acquainted with many milieus: a Ukrainian manor, a country inn, a Siberian hovel, the station houses along the way to Eastern Siberia, prison, factories, and more. On his wanderings throughout Siberia he had met many unusual types: political exiles, convicts, dangerous criminals on the loose, tramps, and hermits. Back home he knew not only the manor house but also the peasant village and the Jewish shtetl. When he has a good story—and he often does—Korolenko may not tell it all that well, but the kindness and goodwill that speak from it make it memorable. In "Frost" (1900–1901) two mountain goats try to cross the Lena River, leaping from ice floe to ice floe, and make it against all odds, to the delight of a crowd of rough-and-tough Siberians—as well as a huge dog who courteously steps out of the goats' way as they jump ashore. The second half of the story has man matched against the Siberian winter. It ends in a double tragedy but asserts the courage and high-mindedness of which human beings are capable.

Korolenko's stories about the underdogs

and outcasts of society—an armless man who earns a living for himself and his companion by demonstrating his prowess with his feet ("A Paradox," 1894), a man born blind ("The Blind Musician," 1886–98), a mad Jewish philosopher in a Siberian prison ("Yashka," 1880), a proud young noblewoman being transported as a political prisoner ("A Strange One," 1880)—all affirm the inalienable dignity of man. In this, and in his interest in drifters, tramps, and criminals, Korolenko anticipated Gorky.

In "Without Language" (1895, 1902) Korolenko describes the life of Ukrainian and Jewish immigrants in the United States with a fine appreciation of the positive changes that the American way of life brings about in their perception of the world. The Ukrainian peasant discovers a wholly n_w attitude toward his Jewish fellow immigrant. A Jewish rabbi finds himself to be the equal of Protestant ministers and promptly preaches to his congregation that it is all right to work on the Sabbath if necessary to hold a job: did not the Maccabees, after all, tell the Jewish people that they would have to fight on the Sabbath if they wanted to survive? The Ukrainian peasant discovers, painfully enough, that the rules by which he was raised are not valid in America, but also that America is a land of opportunity and of a freedom he had not known before. In a way, the story of Matthew Lozinsky's experiences in New York City are a variation on the theme of Korolenko's most famous story, the early "Makar's Dream" (1883), where a wretched Yakutian peasant asserts his humanity, and his desire for justice and a good life, before a stern heavenly judge in the last dream of his life, as he is freezing to death in a snowbank after having consumed a bottle of vodka to celebrate Christmas. Matthew's quest is the same: it is, like

Makar's, dreamlike, for America appears to him as a dream and an occasional nightmare.

The emergence of an educated middle class, alien to the declining landed gentry, willing to work for progress under the existing system but unwilling to embrace the revolutionary creed, was mirrored in many works that depicted Russian life critically, but without advertising an ideology, and tackled its ills without condemning it as a whole. Chekhov was of course the principal exponent of this attitude, but he by no means stood alone.

Dmitry Mamin (pseudonym Sibiryak, 1852–1912), the son of a priest, came from the Urals, started his education at a seminary, and later studied medicine and law without graduating. He returned to the Urals in 1877 and lived there until 1891, when he settled in Saint Petersburg. Mamin, who started his career as a writer under the influence of populism, soon departed from its ideology. In his epic novels about life in the industrial and mining towns of the Urals he presents things from the viewpoint of both entrepreneurs and workers, without introducing any bias of his own. He sees the coming of a complex capitalist economy without deploring the passing of a simpler patriarchal society or dreaming of an ideal socialist one. His novels, *The Privalov Millions* (1883), *A Mountain Nest* (1884), *The Gordeev Brothers* (1891), *Gold* (1892), and *Grain* (1895), as well as many short stories and sketches, show a wealth and precision of factual detail and a sober positivism. They lack the zest and color of Melnikov-Pechersky's panoramic novels but probably give a more accurate picture of Russia between the Volga and the Urals.

Aleksei Lugovoi (pseudonym of Aleksei Tikhonov, 1853–1914), of merchant background, began to publish in 1884. He was editor of *The Cornfield* from 1895 to 1897. His plays and novels enjoyed great popularity in the 1890s. He also wrote epigonic Nekrasovian poetry. His novel *Facets of Life* (1894) is typical of the developing bourgeois attitude toward business, the landed gentry, and the people. The heroine, Lidiya Aleksandrovna Neramova, having graduated from finishing school, refuses to marry the rich middle-aged suitor chosen by her widowed father, a landowner proud of his ancient lineage, and goes to Petersburg to become a governess. After some initial difficulties, she gets a job as a lady's companion. She meets Egor Dmitrievich Sarmatov, who becomes a faithful friend and eventually her husband. The educated and wellborn heroine decides to become a couturière; she borrows money from Sarmatov to start her salon, and prospers. Her brother, an officer with aristocratic airs, who has claimed and spent every penny of his inheritance— Lidiya Aleksandrovna has received nothing —breaks off all relations with her. Only after their father's death, when it turns out that he died penniless and leaving three children from a leech of a peasant woman who cajoled him into marrying her, does he deign to contact his sister, begging her to help take care of the orphans. The novel is entertaining and well told. But its many discourses on the "woman question" and other issues are banal, the characters are stereotypes, plot construction is awkward, and the narrative style is facile.

Vasily Nemirovich-Danchenko (1844–1936), older brother of writer and director Vladimir Nemirovich-Danchenko, was a journalist, war correspondent, world traveler, memoirist, and writer of great versatility. Amazingly prolific, he claimed in his day at least as many readers as did Tolstoi and Chekhov. His novels and short stories dealt with all the current issues—the "woman question," social inequality, criminal justice, education, even the "Jewish question"— which qualified them as serious reading. His characters were stereotypical enough for readers to recognize in them themselves or people they knew. He wrote a fluent, not too taxing prose and conveyed to his reader an air of good sense, sympathy for the underdog, and moderate liberalism.

In *The Slastenov Millions* (1893) Vasily Gerasimovich Slastenov, a poor Petersburg student, learns that his uncle, a millionaire, has died without leaving a will; hence his nephew is made his sole heir. Slastenov has great difficulties adjusting to his good fortune. He marries Praskovya Yakovlevna, a rich heiress, but is not up to being the husband of this strong, vibrant woman. She leaves him and he falls into the hands of crooks who make him invest in a phony Caspian-Black Sea Canal scheme. The principal villain is Gottlieb Gottliebovich Kurz-von-Galopp, alias Bogolyub Bogolyubovich Korotkov-Bystrov, formerly Vershek Kurz-galopp—a Jew of Berdichev, now a Russified German and Lutheran. He is seconded by one Isaak Yakovlevich Plyus. When a huge apartment house built on Slastenov's money collapses, killing scores of workers, Slastenov decides to renounce his fortune. It also turns out that the inheritance really is not his—Plyus had concealed the will, which left the entire fortune to another uncle. Kurz-von-Galopp murders Plyus but fails to make his escape from the scene of his crime and is arrested. Slastenov decides to join his uncle's company and work his way up in the business. His wife returns to him, and they will live happily ever after. The novel is lively, entertaining, and contains some good descriptive passages and psychological sketches. But it is facile and superficial, obviously catering to the tastes and sensibilities of a middle-brow mass audience.

Confession of a Woman (1900) is a short novel whose action takes place in various exotic and attractive places (Milan, Monza, the Caucasus, Petersburg, Bad Ems, Lugano). The heroine tells the story of her marriage to a kind and honest professor, who neglects her and does not take her intellectual, artistic, and emotional aspirations seriously, and of an adulterous affair which, after brief happiness, leads to separation and a lonely exile. She soon dies of consumption, not yet thirty. The novel is sympathetic to the plight of a talented and active woman's predicament in a conventional marriage, but its whole manner is banal, cliché-ridden, and predictable. The same theme is treated more concretely and more subtly by Chekhov and Hippius, among others.

Nemirovich-Danchenko's short stories invite comparison with those of his contemporaries—Chekhov, Garshin, Andreev—whose world was the same as his. "Egorka" (1891) is the heart-warming story of an orphan boy and his dog. Egorka will beg but not steal, as he remembers what his onetime foster father, a village priest, had taught him. The horrors of poverty are described realistically, but Nemirovich-Danchenko fudges the issue by always letting Egorka and his dog escape the worst. In the end Egorka can look forward to a bright future. "Egorka" ought to be seen in the context of such stories as Gleb Uspensky's "Petka's Career" or Chekhov's "Vanka," which face the issue squarely. In "He Shot Himself" (1891) young Aleksandr has flunked his Latin exam and decides to commit suicide. He writes suicide notes to his parents and to his Latin teacher and is getting ready to pull the trigger when he falls asleep. His parents find the note and save him. The psychology here is not bad, but it is superficial. Again, a comparison with Chekhov's "Volodya" or Andreev's "In the Fog," which also deal with teenage suicide, demonstrates the inferiority of Nemirovich-Danchenko's treatment of this theme.

Anastasiya Verbitskaya (1861–1928) came from the gentry but became a professional writer early. She started her career as a political journalist in 1883 and turned to fiction in 1887, with great and almost immediate success. She also wrote several plays. Prolific like Nemirovich-Danchenko, Verbitskaya was as popular as he (perhaps even more popular), and for much the same reasons. She created characters with whom the average reader could identify and placed them in situations that reflected readers' concerns. She was a master at expressing the moods of the day in a language that the middlebrow reader could understand. Her sympathies were with the underdog, and her ideas were liberal—particularly as regards the role of women in society—but without any outright revolutionary tendencies. Verbitskaya reacted to the events and ideas of the day and often referred to contemporary literature, Russian as well as Western, but her main topic was still the love life of the educated Russian woman, with which she dealt in a great variety of "real-life" plots. Her love scenes were remarkably bold for her age, and at times she could be shockingly "immoral." In "Nadenka," a short story of 1899, a pretty governess is propositioned by an officer who is the lover of her mistress. Nadenka realizes that the lady already knows and will surely dismiss her the next day—so she will at least make love to him.

The heroines of Verbitskaya's novels typically project a contemporary educated woman's image of herself, slightly glamorized and in a light halo of self-pity and noble resignation. Manya, the heroine of

Keys of Happiness: A Contemporary Novel (1909–13), is a sensitive, headstrong, and idealistic girl. She is brilliant and misses getting a gold medal at her graduation only because of her defiant behavior. She has three lovers: Jan, a gentle student with a touch of the poet; Baron Steinbach, a Jewish millionaire and man of the world; and Neli-dov, a young landowner. In all of these relationships Manya shows herself proud, high-minded, and recklessly passionate. In her love life she follows her irrational in-stincts—even her sense of smell: Jan smells sweet and innocent, Steinbach "repulsive and fascinating." Verbitskaya was a writer of talent. Her best short stories deserve to be anthologized next to the best work of her contemporaries—Korolenko, Hippius, Solo-gub, and Andreev.

Pyotr Boborykin (1838–1921) was born in Nizhny Novgorod, the son of a wealthy landowner. He studied law at Kazan Uni-versity, then the natural sciences at the Uni-versity of Dorpat. A cultured man, fluent in several languages, and a writer of great facil-ity, Boborykin started his literary career as a playwright in 1860. He published his first novel, the autobiographical *On My Way*, in installments between 1862 and 1864, was editor and publisher of *The Reading Library* from 1863 to 1865, and went to Paris as a correspondent for *The National Annals* in 1871. He wrote many articles and sketches on economic and social developments in Russia ("A Russian Sheffield," 1877). From the early 1890s on, Boborykin lived abroad. He died in Lugano, Switzerland. The author of many plays, novels, stories, sketches, and essays, he also published articles on the history of Russian and Western literatures and a book, *The European Novel of the Nineteenth Century* (1900). A moderate liberal, Boborykin was often maligned by his contemporaries for the matter-of-fact way in which he accepted modern capitalism and the westernization of Russian social and eco-nomic life. Boborykin's narrative manner is naturalist à la Zola. Critics accused him of describing people he—and some of his readers—knew well, rather than "types," and of depicting social conditions from the vantage point of an observer without a social theory or ideal.

The novels *Solid Virtues* (1870), *Wheeler-Dealers* (1872–73), *Kitai-Gorod* (1882), *Vasily Tyorkin* (1892), and *Watershed* (1894), among other works, deal with the emergence of a capitalist economy in Russia. *Kitai-Gorod*, the best known of these, fol-lows the lives of several characters, male and female, in Kitai-Gorod, the business district of Moscow. Some of his characters are gentlemen and gentlewomen who are forced to adapt to the business world; others are men and women of the merchant class who aspire to the status of nobles. Old-fashioned Russian ways of doing business and the patriarchal family clash with Euro-pean business practices and more liberal Western mores. The two pivotal figures are Paltusov, a nobleman and ex-officer, who works his way up in the business world at the cost of much of his pride, some of his honor, but not all of his conscience; and Madame Stanitsyna, the wife of a rich businessman who prefers to squander his fortune in Paris, letting her manage it. Madame Stanitsyna, herself the owner of a large textile plant, eventually divorces her worthless husband and marries Paltusov, af-ter the latter has been chastened by a nasty brush with the law on charges of misappro-priation of funds, which land him temporarily in prison. *Kitai-Gorod* is good entertain-ment. Its descriptive details—there are many more of meals and interior furnishings than of productive work or business deal-ings—are colorful and attractive. Its characters are alive, though in a superficial way. Psychological motivation is straightforward. The plot is lively but based entirely on accident—adultery, disease, business failure, various intrigues, suicide. In fact, it resembles the modern television soap opera. The general impression left by *Kitai-Gorod* and Boborykin's other works is that capitalist society, with all its shortcomings, is vibrant, dynamic, and full of promise.

Boborykin's later novels continued to deal with the further development of Russian economic and political life from the viewpoint of a liberal observer, equally critical of jingo patriotism, cynical opportunism, and doctrinaire populism and Marxism. *New Men* (1887) attacks reactionary nationalism. *On the Wane* and *He Got Wise* (both 1890) deal with a disillusioned and unprincipled new generation and those "men of the sixties" who abandoned their progressive ideals and joined the reaction under Alexander III. *Another Way* (1897) and *Draft* (1898) capture the inception of the struggle between fading populism and rising Marxism for control of the masses. Boborykin reacted to the 1905 revolution in a family chronicle, *The Great Wreck* (1908), an unequivocally counterrevolutionary work.

Boborykin, Nemirovich-Danchenko, Lugovoi, and Verbitskaya, prolific and read by more readers than the more artistic and demanding writers of their age, are important as a mirror of the sensibility and worldview of their readership, the educated middlebrow Russian around the turn of the century. It is useful to compare them to their predecessors, such as Chulkov in the eighteenth century, Narezhny in the 1800s, Bulgarin and Begichev in the 1830s, and Krestovsky and Khvoshchinskaya in the 1860s and 1870s.

Garshin

Vsevolod Mikhailovich Garshin (1855–88), the son of an officer, attended secondary school and the Mining Institute in Saint Petersburg. His studies were interrupted in 1877, when he volunteered for army service at the outbreak of the Russo-Turkish War. He marched in the Balkan campaign as a private, was wounded in action, and was promoted to officer's rank at the conclusion of the war. He soon resigned his commission and devoted himself entirely to literature (he had previously published some newspaper articles, particularly reviews of art exhibitions, mostly in *The National Annals*). His promising career was cut short by mental illness. He committed suicide while under treatment at a mental hospital.

Garshin's short fiction marks a transition from the naturalism of the 1860s to the impressionism, even pointillism, of Chekhov. The unity of his stories is that of mood and atmosphere. Garshin's narrators (he likes first-person narrators) are, like Chekhov's, never opinionated, bitter, or ironic, but let their significant details speak for themselves. Garshin's best stories advance their humanitarian message unobtrusively, by implication or by understated and casual comments. This may be explained, in part, by the necessity to write around the censorship, but Garshin does it so masterfully that it is also aesthetically effective. In the story "Artists" (1879) the voices of two artists, a happy landscape painter and a tormented painter committed to social themes, are introduced. In describing the subjects of the latter artist's work—he is clearly alluding to the Itinerant movement in Russian art —Garshin manages to introduce an indictment of the inhuman working conditions in Russian machine shops and to advance the thesis of the artist's duty to society.

Garshin's military tales are more than objective accounts of his personal experience. They put across—in a sober, understated way—the message that most of the men who die in the war have no interest in or awareness of its political or other ends. Garshin does not conceal the hideous horrors of war. In the first of his war stories, "Four Days" (1877), based on a real experience (not Garshin's own), a Russian soldier, incapacitated by his wounds, lay in thick shrubbery for four days next to the decomposing body of a Turkish soldier he had killed before being wounded himself; he is finally rescued. Garshin also brings out the callous brutality with which officers treat their soldiers. But Garshin's general message, nonetheless, is upbeat, not unlike that of the early Tolstoi: war brings men closer to one another and brings out the best in them. Captain Ventsel, a character in "From the Memoirs of Private Ivanov" (1883), is an efficient officer and a man of some culture, but he brutally beats his men on slight provocation and seems cold and heartless. At the end of the story Captain Ventsel five times leads his company into a hail of Turkish fire to take a key position. The last lines of the story have him sobbing uncontrollably, stammering "Fifty-two, fifty-two," the number of men he has lost—half his company. This hard and arrogant German cared more about his men than about credit for a successful engagement.

"An Incident" (1878) and "Nadezhda Nikolaevna (1885) have the same heroine, an educated young woman forced by circumstances into prostitution. She is also the femme fatale in the life of a young man. Both stories are told, alternatively, by several narrators, a device that enhances their strained, melodramatic quality. "Nadezhda Nikolaevna," the stronger of the two stories, is made more credible by the introduction of details of two paintings: one of Charlotte Corday, for which Nadezhda Nikolaevna sits as a model, and the other of Ilya Muromets, hero of heroes of the Russian folk epic, turned hermit; its subject is clearly Tolstoi's doctrine of nonviolence. In spite of their strained quality these two stories have real pathos—a pathos that inspired Chekhov to write one of his finest stories, "A Nervous Breakdown."

Garshin's most famous story, "The Red Flower" (1883), is set in an insane asylum. The hero, a patient, develops an idée fixe that all the evil and bloodshed in the world comes from three red poppies—the narrator observes that the notion of the evils of opium may have triggered this mania—which grow in the hospital yard. He uses all his remaining strength and madman's cunning to break his straitjacket, bend the iron bars on his window, and jump to the ground to tear out the last of the flowers. He dies happy. The story's theme, a suicidal struggle for an impossible goal, appears in several other pieces, quite explicitly in "Attalea princeps" (1879), the story of a palm tree which, reaching for freedom, breaks the glass roof of the hothouse in which it grows, ignoring warnings that it will freeze to death outside. It is then cut down and burned, as a special glass cupola would cost too much—and the tree would outgrow that, too.

Garshin's stories have at least as much concreteness and precision of descriptive and psychological detail as the best pieces of the naturalists of the 1860s, but they are also animated by ideas that arise naturally from the narrative. They have a point, but it is unobtrusive, and the reader is never quite sure whether the point should be understood positively or negatively. In "An Encounter" two schoolmates meet in a seaport on the Black Sea, where one of them has been employed as a harbor engineer for some years. He makes sixteen hundred rubles a year but has built himself a thirty-thousand-ruble aquarium, which he proudly shows to his friend, who is horrified by the cynicism with which he reveals the source of his wealth: the building and maintenance of a seawall that exists on paper only. The point of the story is made as the two friends watch the aquarium: a small fish barely escapes the jaws of a big fish—only to be snatched up by another, more alert predator. The harbor engineer sees this as the law of life by which he lives. His friend disagrees. Readers will make their own judgments.

Chekhov

Anton Pavlovich Chekhov (1860–1904) was born in the southern seaport of Taganrog, the son of a grocer. His grandfather had been a serf before he bought his freedom. In 1876 his father went bankrupt and moved to Moscow. Anton stayed in Taganrog until his graduation from secondary school in 1879. He entered the medical school of Moscow University that year and graduated in 1884. As early as 1878 he started writing humorous short stories and feuilletons for various satirical journals and under various pseudonyms to support himself and his family (he had four brothers, two of them minor writers, and a sister). In 1882 he started an association with the Petersburg satirical journal *Fragments*, whose publisher, Nikolai Leikin (1841–1906), was himself a popular humorist. In 1884 Chekhov published his first collection of stories; it was followed by many more at short intervals. Starting in 1886 he began to write for the large circulation newspaper *New Times*, and its pub-

lisher, Aleksei Suvorin, became a close friend. In 1890 Chekhov traveled to the island of Sakhalin to report on the living conditions of convicts and exiles held there (*The Island of Sakhalin*, 1893–94). In 1892, by now a celebrity and financially secure, Chekhov bought a country estate near Moscow, where he dispensed free medical aid to local peasants, actively participating in famine relief in 1892 and fighting the cholera epidemic of 1892–93. In the late 1890s Chekhov resumed his work as a playwright, which had met with little success in the late 1880s. The triumph of *The Seagull* at the Moscow Art Theater in 1898 was followed by three more successful plays. In 1898 Chekhov, now suffering from virulent tuberculosis, moved to Yalta, in the Crimea, where he often met with Tolstoi, Gorky, Bunin, and other writers and artists. In 1901 he married Olga Knipper, a young actress of the Moscow Art Theater. He died at the German spa of Badenweiler, where he had gone to seek relief from his illness.

Chekhov's career as a short story writer may be divided into three periods: early (until 1888), during which he wrote several hundred stories, sketches, and feuilletons, many of them humorous trifles, although some of Chekhov's most famous stories are among them, too; middle (1888–94), when he developed a severely objective style and the distinctive manner of the "Chekhovian" short story; and late (1895–1904), when a certain subjective mellowing and a tendency toward social analysis made an appearance. The Chekhovian short story was not without antecedents. Turgenev was an example and an influence. He, like Chekhov, had given a lyric component to his stories and often let them derive their unity from mood and atmosphere rather than from a conventional plot. Contemporaries noticed the affinity between Chekhov's manner and that of Guy de Maupassant, whom Chekhov admired.

Chekhov was very much a part of the literary life of his age. Many of his stories have a polemical edge that today's reader may not see. In particular, Chekhov felt compelled to debunk the rebirth of romantic mysticism in the 1890s ("The Black Monk," 1894). Almost a Tolstoian at one time, Chekhov grew disenchanted with Tolstoianism after 1890, and his story "Ward No. 6" (1892) clearly challenges Tolstoi's quietism and doctrine of nonresistance to evil. "Vanka" (1886), a prosaic Christmas story with an ironic twist, is a response to edifying romantic Christmas tales like Dostoevsky's "The Boy at Christ's Christmas Party." "The Lady with a Lap Dog" (1899) was probably a polemical response to a story by V. Mikulich (pseudonym of V. I. Veselitskaya), "Mimochka at the Spa," which had a conventional message. Although Chekhov was pointedly apolitical and refused to be identified with any ideology, some of his early stories had a satirical edge and were perceived as barbs pointed at bureaucratic inefficiency and corruption, police brutality, and other such public ills.

Chekhov's stories offer a rich panorama of Russian life in the city and in the country, at all levels of society except high society. A remarkable array of professions, social conditions, and circumstances are represented. Young and old, male and female characters appear as memorable individuals, although individualized speech is not Chekhov's forte and his psychology is straightforward and deterministic: his personages act in character.

"Peasants" (1897), one of Chekhov's longer stories, deals with rural poverty and blight. The peasants are shiftless, prone to drunkenness, wife beating, and crude superstition. Their desperate poverty is at least in part of their own doing. But they are human beings in all their feelings and in their suffering. Chekhov was attacked by the populist Mikhailovsky and others for presenting such a hopeless picture of the Russian countryside. "In the Ravine" (1900), which deals with the lower middle class in a small company town, is even more negative: greed, dishonesty, and heartlessness are pervasive in this milieu, which sees no less human suffering than the peasant village. The picture is equally somber on every other level of Russian society. In "A Doctor's Visit" (1898) a doctor summoned to examine the heiress to a large factory finds her no less miserable than the workers whose wretched existence is the foundation of her fortune. None except the smug, the callous, and the heartless seem to be happy in Russia. People "live badly" (a favorite phrase of Chekhov's). Marriages are mostly unhappy, as in "A Nameday Party" (1888), a remarkably modern story: change the names, and it could be set in affluent Westchester County. Businesses fail, as in "Misfortune" (1887). Education is deadening drudgery under the guidance of tired, gray, and timid schoolmasters, as in "The Man in a Case" (1898). Even good people realize the futility of their strivings, as in "A Tedious Story" (1889), about a famous professor of medicine at the end of his career—another story that elicited indignant protest.

Chekhov's world is the world of the great novelists brought down to the level of the ordinary, familiar, and predictable. But he views this world from a moral standpoint entirely his own and quite different from those of his predecessors or contemporaries. His moral concern is with the petty venial sins that lack the glamour of mortal sin but make human life hard: selfishness, inconsiderateness, disloyalty, untruthfulness, pretentiousness, bad temper. Chekhov's anger against these sins burns with a steady flame, though it never explodes. "Rothschild's Fiddle" (1894) is a good example of a steady undertow of anger at the hero's callous selfishness and meanness. Chekhov saw these moral ills as a consequence of human unfreedom. In a famous letter to Suvorin (January 7, 1889) he said that he had had to "squeeze the slave out of myself drop by drop." He felt an equal—perhaps even a stronger—anger against the aesthetic aspect of the slave mentality: vulgarity. In a passage of the story "At Christmas time" (1900) this anger reaches the boiling point: "This was vulgarity itself, coarse, arrogant, invincible vulgarity, proud that it was born and raised in a pothouse." Chekhov's positive values are freedom, charity, and truthfulness. Freedom is the quality of being oneself, not playing the role assigned by others. Chekhov's characters are unhappy because they haven't the strength to be themselves. Charity, a minor virtue since it requires no sacrifice or self-effacement, is a major concern, brought out explicitly in "Gooseberries" (1898). A man who through callous meanness has reached his life's goal, to become a landowner and eat his own gooseberries, thinks that his life is a good one. The narrator inserts that whenever someone feels like the happy eater of his own gooseberries, "a man with a small hammer" should give a knock and remind him of all the unhappy people in the world.

Chekhov's moral code often clashed with conventional morality. His sympathy is with the adulterers in "About Love" (1898) and "The Lady with the Lap Dog." In the latter story, Gurov leads a double life, and his carefully concealed adulterous affair is the real and the better one. In "The Darling" (1899) the heroine is a woman who is happy when she is totally absorbed in the

man in her life. Chekhov treats her with faint irony. Tolstoi chided him for this, feeling that "the darling" was an ideal woman.

Chekhov was out of the mainstream of Russian literature in that he did not insist that art and beauty were linked to progress or morality. He will interrupt an otherwise depressing narrative to depict a moment of beauty. In "Peasants," among a wealth of naturalistic detail of untidy poverty, we come across the description of a glorious sunset. When young Fyokla comes home in the middle of night, having been stripped naked by some men with whom she has been partying, the narrator observes, "She was shivering with cold and her teeth were chattering, and in the bright light of the moon she appeared very pale, beautiful, and strange. The shadows and the moonlight on her skin created a striking impression and her dark eyebrows and young, firm breasts stood out with particular poignancy." In "Gusev" (1890) Chekhov recounts the torturous voyage home of some sick and dying soldiers returning to Russia from the Far East. Some, including Gusev, do not make it. But the story ends in the description of a fantastic tropical sunset over the Indian Ocean.

Chekhov believed that the essence of life lies not in flashes of high passion or mystic epiphany but in the minutiae of day-to-day living. He therefore shuns the metaphysical; but it enters some of his finest stories through the back door, as beauty or as art transcending ordinary life (in "Rothschild's Fiddle," for example), but also as religious experience. In "The Student" (1894) religious feeling is triggered by the reading of the passion of Christ from the Gospels. In "The Bishop" (1902), another Easter story, the churchman's love for his ministry and its ritual is presented with edifying sympathy.

Chekhov was an eminently conscious and

deliberate artist, although he followed no specific system in composing his stories. He liked to discuss writing technique and to give advice to young writers, and felt that his scientific training had an important and beneficial influence on his writing. He justified his peculiar way of storytelling by suggesting that he was doing his best to express honestly the truth of life. Chekhov's stories may be assigned to a variety of subgenres: the long short story (*povest'*), such as "In the Ravine," the short story (*rasskaz*), such as "The Student," the novella with a philosophical or moral point ("The Grasshopper," 1892), the confession ("A Tedious Story"), the character sketch ("The Darling"), the social study ("Peasants"), the animal tale ("Kashtanka," 1887, the story of a mongrel dog's adventures), the sketch ("Sergeant Prishibeev," 1885), the seasonal tale ("At Christmas Time"), the satire ("The Chameleon," 1884), the humoresque ("A Horsey Name," 1885), and some others. Many of them fit the conventional mold of the given subgenre. But often the best do not. Chekhov tears up the old contract between writer and reader, canceling its time-honored rules: he substitutes an open-ended slice-of-life narrative for a closed plot; replaces drama and story line with unity of consciousness, mood, or atmosphere; tells his story objectively, without apparent bias; introduces static characters (only age may effect a change, as in "Ionych," 1898); and forgoes giving his story a point.

Chekhov at his best replaces the old obligations of the storyteller with new ones, creating a difficult syncretic form of fiction combining epic, dramatic, and lyric traits. He introduces into his texts an arsenal of lyric devices: metaphor, symbolic and decorative imagery, rhythmic phrase structure, alliteration and assonance, even sound symbolism. Occasional unmotivated lyric intermezzi appear. At the same time he takes advantage of all the devices of an epic narrator: descriptive precision, clarity, and metonymy. This occurs especially in those stories which are in effect novels condensed to the length of a short story: "Ionych," "The Lady with a Lap Dog," "Ariadna" (1895), and "My Life" (1896). The old novella of action has been defined as "drama narrated." Chekhov's stories of situation are in fact narrated versions of a Chekhovian play.

Merezhkovsky, as early as 1892, called Chekhov an impressionist—as did Tolstoi—without a hint of disapproval. Other contemporaries, who failed to understand Chekhov's art, spoke of his formlessness, incompleteness, fragmentariness, and randomness. Starting with "The Steppe: The Story of a Trip" (1888), Chekhov generally replaces the continuous story line with strings of seemingly random details which enhance the desired effect. He pays careful attention to colors, sounds, and smells. "Gooseberries," one of Chekhov's finest stories, seems at first sight to be a haphazard sequence of details. Two hunters walking through the countryside, in the rain, come to the yard of a mill and estate where work is in full swing. A sketch of the owner—a pleasant, educated man—follows, as he greets his guests, then washes the dust and grime from his face in the millpond, and all have a delightful swim under a warm rain. Then the scene shifts to the manor house. We get two or three glimpses of a strikingly beautiful maid. After dinner, someone tells a story about a happy man who would eat his own gooseberries at the cost of a lifetime of wretched miserliness—on his own estate, by his own brook, though its water is brown, polluted by a tannery upstream. Then comes an intermezzo about a man with a little hammer who ought to remind every happy person that there are unhappy people in the world. There is a description of the living room where the three men relax. Then it is bedtime; the smell of tobacco will not let one of the guests fall asleep; and at the end, again, is the rain. "Gooseberries," one of three stories of a cycle ("The Man in a Case" and "About Love" are the other two), is about the good and the bad life. The good life is associated with positive symbols, the bad with negative ones—the clean, refreshing water of the millpond at the good man's place, the dirty, polluted stream at the bad man's. The bad man's gooseberries are hard and sour, though he pretends that they are delicious. At the good man's place tea and sweet jam are served by that smiling, incredibly beautiful maid. The good man is genuinely glad to see his unexpected guests; the bad man lives alone. The good men are themselves; the bad man, once he has become a landowner, pretends to be somebody he is not. Chekhov refuses to explain connections, using instead casual details, hints, and fragments of thought.

The randomness of real life extends to every level of the narrative: story line, moral message, descriptive detail, characters, and language. There is little psychological analysis in Chekhov. Like Turgenev, he works by suggestion rather than by analysis. His characters are drawn with a few haphazard strokes or in bare outline, and critics charged him with incompleteness and carelessness. But what is given is in fact carefully chosen to steer the reader's imagination in the right direction.

Chekhov once gave this advice to another writer: "Tear up the first half of your manuscript, adjust a few things in the second half—and you have yourself a story." Chekhov generally does away with the exposition, though he often uses a conventional frame. The early stories generally

have a conventional finale, often with a surprising climax or anticlimax. "Sleepy" (1888), the story of a teenage baby-sitter tormented by long hours of sleeplessness over a crying child, ends abruptly, as the hallucinating girl "strangles the baby, quickly stretches out on the floor, laughs happily that she can now sleep, and in another moment is sound asleep." Later, Chekhov gets away from surprise endings and looks for subtler and more varied means "to condense for the reader an impression of the entire work," as he put it in a letter to the writer A. N. Pleshcheev (September 30, 1889). A common practice is an antifinale, where the reader is made to realize that the story is far from over. The concluding lines of "The Lady with a Lapdog," which tells the story of an adulterous liaison, may serve as an example: "And it seemed to them that in a little more time a solution would be found, and then a new and beautiful life would begin; and it was clear to both that the end was still far, far off and that the most complicated and difficult part was only beginning." A concluding nature image may invite the reader to think about the meaning of life in a broader context ("Gusev," "Gooseberries," "In the Ravine").

The point or message of a story is often signaled by some detail that may seem extraneous to its subject. Chekhov was delighted when the veteran writer Grigorovich noticed his description of the fresh white snow in "A Nervous Breakdown" (1888), a story about a visit by some students to the Moscow red-light district. Of course the clean snow functions as a contrast to the sordid, hideous scenes that cause one of the students to have a nervous breakdown. The galoshes that the schoolmaster Belikov wears in fine weather or foul ("The Man in a Case") are another such "significant detail": the man is hopelessly encased in his proprieties, prejudices, and fears—just as everything around him must be kept safely in a case. The sour berries in "Gooseberries" are another example. In other instances a detail will help create the story's atmosphere without being really a symbol—the ubiquitous dirty yellow color in "A Doctor's Visit" or the green and black shadows on the ceiling in "Sleepy," the bells in "The Bishop" or the noises of the steppe in "The Steppe."

Chekhov is an artist who derives the utmost in effects from nature. Nature creates atmosphere (the somber, menacing landscape in "Murder," 1895), sets the stage for the story (the blizzard in "On Official Business," 1899), acts as contrast ("A Nervous Breakdown") or as symbol ("The Steppe"). It may be integrated into the story or presented in a lyric intermezzo.

Point of view is not Chekhov's forte. An objective writer, he finds an individualized point of view uncongenial to his style. Moreover, Chekhov's language is not very distinctive. Of all the great Russian writers, he loses least in translation. "The Midas touch of a golden sadness" (Yuly Aikhenvald) which he imparts to whatever he touches is, however, inimitable. In Russia, a "Chekhovian mood" came to mean life without an ideal, without hope, bogged down in the frustrations of day-to-day living. Some critics have credited Chekhov's all-encompassing sympathy and pity with the deep effect he has had, and continues to have, on his readers. But this point should not be overemphasized: it may in fact reflect a shallow reading of Chekhov. There is also plenty of anger and bitterness in his stories. Many of his contemporaries—Rozanov, Shestov, Merezhkovsky, and Hippius, for example—saw him as a pernicious influence

on the morale of Russian society. But no serious critic in touch with the times denied his extraordinary artistry, which soon found many imitators in Russia and abroad.

Gorky

The publishing house Knowledge, founded in 1898 as an outlet for popular science and educational material, soon became the focus of a neorealist movement antithetical to symbolism and other "modernist" trends. Maksim Gorky, who joined it in 1900, led a pleiad of prose writers who strove to emulate the literature of the 1860s and 1870s, combining an honest analysis of Russian life and a progressive, though not necessarily revolutionary, attitude toward its problems with a solid realism. Among the writers of the Knowledge group were Aleksandr Kuprin, Leonid Andreev, Ivan Bunin, Vikenty Veresaev, Mikhail Prishvin, Ivan Shmelyov, and Aleksandr Serafimovich. In retrospect, little of the work done by these writers has survived, except what was saved by Gorky's authority and Bunin's Nobel Prize.

Maksim Gorky (pseudonym of Aleksei Maksimovich Peshkov, 1868–1936) was born in Nizhny Novgorod, later renamed Gorky in his honor. He lost his father early and was raised in his grandparents' family, who were lower middle class but sliding toward poverty. He went to work at eleven and moved through a variety of jobs—dishwasher on a Volga steamer, apprentice icon painter, baker, stevedore. He would later describe those years in an autobiographical trilogy. He read voraciously and, encouraged by the writer Korolenko, whom he met in Nizhny Novgorod in 1889, wrote his own stories and poetry. His first short story appeared in a Tbilisi newspaper in 1892. Soon afterward he became a professional writer, publishing stories, articles, feuilletons, and reviews in several newspapers in the Volga region. By 1895 his stories had begun to appear in the capitals, and a two-volume collection of 1898 made him an instant celebrity, first in Russia and then abroad. Around the turn of the century Gorky developed several important associations. One was with the Marxist journals *Life* and *New Word*; another with the Moscow Art Theater, which staged his first plays, *Burghers* and *The Lower Depths*; a third with the publishing house Knowledge, whose director and main shareholder he soon became; and last with Tolstoi and Chekhov, about whom he would later writer perceptive reminiscences. Gorky actively supported the revolution of 1905 and left the country in 1906 to escape arrest. He traveled to America, where he wrote his most famous novel, *Mother* (1906). Late in 1906 Gorky settled in Italy, where he joined the Marxist group of Aleksandr Bogdanov and took part in the work of the Capri party school. The amnesty of 1913 allowed him to return to Russia, where he founded the journal *Chronicle* in 1915. Gorky was not involved in the October 1917 revolution and had serious disagreements with Lenin all along. In the years following the revolution he used his authority to save lives and cultural values as best he could.

Gorky's oeuvre is inseparable from the role that fell to him as the only prerevolutionary Russian writer of stature to support the Social Democratic Workers Party and to be personally close to Lenin. Gorky is rightly considered the father of socialist realism. His novel *Mother* was to serve as a model for countless works of that school, in Russia and elsewhere, and established its moral and aesthetic canon. *Mother* is, however, hardly typical of Gorky's general style.

Gorky started writing in a literary manner which, in deference to his later position as dean of Soviet literature, has been dubbed revolutionary romanticism. It is best exemplified by his poems "Song of the Falcon" (1895) and "Song of the Stormy Petrel" (1901). The falcon would rather soar high and perish than live like the snake, who finds a safe and snug place at the bottom of a ravine, where it is "warm and damp." The stormy petrel rejoices in the approaching storm, while "the stupid penguin timidly hides his fat body in the cliffs." Such neoromantic Byronism is also found in a number of Gorky's early stories dealing with tragic love in exotic—Tatar, Gypsy, Moldavian—settings.

Gorky's more realistic stories owed their success to his discovery of a milieu which had hardly figured in Russian literature before, that of the lumpen proletariat—thieves, tramps, drifters, and other outcasts of society, some of whom had seen better days. This milieu, combined with a Nietzschean contempt for the security of organized society, fascinated Russian readers, who found in it a spirit of freedom and adventure that contrasted with the gray drabness of Chekhovian and populist Russia. "Chelkash" (1894) is about a professional thief who plies his trade in the port of Odessa. He needs a helper for a job on a docked steamer and hires himself a sturdy peasant lad down on his luck and desperate. The robbery proceeds smoothly, and after the merchandise is sold, Chelkash flashes a bankroll which seems so huge to his accomplice that he is tempted to kill Chelkash. When Chelkash sees the peasant's naked greed, he disdainfully throws him the money and walks away. Gorky's early stories ("Grandpa Arkhip and Lyonka," 1893; "My Fellow Traveler," 1894; "Once in Fall," 1895; "In the Steppe," 1897; "The Tramp," 1898) are strong in their descriptive detail but trail off into melodrama or rhetoric when they move beyond it. This is true even of "Twenty-six and One" (1899), Gorky's most famous story. It tells of twenty-six overworked, surly bakers, collectively in love with a pretty lass. Their tenderness turns to angry vituperation when she takes a lover. The best of the early stories are those that have little or no plot and are essentially sketches.

The limitations of Gorky's talent show in his novels. His first novel, *Foma Gordeev* (1899), in which he develops a theme he was to tackle again in several later novels— that of a young man in rebellion against his bourgeois family and environment—is no masterpiece. Gorky's novels are static and lack drama. The famous *Mother* has these shortcomings, too. It is the story of Pavel Vlasov, a factory worker turned revolutionary, and Nilovna, his mother. The novel begins with a convincing description of the life of a working-class family in a typical company town. The rest of this long novel is made up of a series of disconnected episodes, telling of clandestine revolutionary activities, a strike, workers' demonstrations, clashes with the police, the murder of an informer, and a trial at which the revolutionaries are allowed to make fiery speeches. What story line there is rests with Nilovna's growth from a timid, submissive, and devoutly religious housewife to a brave, dedicated, and enlightened revolutionary. *Mother* develops traits that had appeared in "progressive" literature since the 1860s into a closed system. A character's moral qualities are determined by his or her social class. Capitalists, bosses, judges, government officials, and policemen are evil, corrupt, brutish, old, and even physically repulsive. Workers are noble, intelligent, selfless, young, and attractive. Even young revolutionaries, male and female, of bourgeois or upper-class background are morally inferior to Nilovna, Pavel, and other workers. Revolutionaries are superior human beings. Pavel will devote his whole life to the revolution. He will not marry the woman he is attracted to, because having a family will take away from his effectiveness as a revolutionary. The revolutionary creed is explicitly declared to supersede Christianity. Nilovna herself exemplifies this transition. The industrial proletariat is the unchallenged vanguard of the revolution. A peasant type is introduced to demonstrate the weakness of the undisciplined, "elemental" revolt of the peasantry, which interferes with the disciplined work of the proletarian revolutionaries. In spite of its revolutionary pathos, *Mother* is not an optimistic book. It concedes that the revolution will cause rivers of blood to flow, and it grimly foresees the huge problems that the peasantry will pose to a revolutionary regime. The novel's characters are allegorical figures with no individual identity. *Mother* was found to be artistically weak even by knowledgeable Marxist critics like Plekhanov. But Lenin considered it good propaganda. He was right: a young worker might well see in Pavel Vlasov a realization of his own dreams; and as Gorky would put it later, Nilovna, though still nonexistent in real life, might help this type to come into existence.

During his exile in Italy, Gorky wrote several more plays and a great many more stories, gathered in a collection, *Through Russia* (1912–16). His satirical *Russian Fairy Tales* (1912) were directed against reactionary phenomena of Russian life, such as *décadence. Fairy Tales about Italy* (1911–13) is mostly about the revolutionary movement in Italy, and of the several novels Gorky wrote while there, *The Life of Matvei Kozhemyakin* (1910–11), a dreary tale of provincial stagnation, is the most notable. Gorky reached the apogee of his creative powers in his autobiographical trilogy, *Childhood, In the World* and *My University Years* (this title is ironical: Gorky tried to enroll in Kazan University but was never admitted), a magnificent panorama of Russian lower and lower middle-class life. In vignette after vignette from his own life, Gorky is at his best, as he deftly shifts the center of attention from himself to the situation and people he faces. The writer's personal involvement in the situation acts as a control, restraining him from veering into needless philosophizing or misplaced pathos: he is too busy reliving the episode to comment on it.

Vikenty Veresaev (pseudonym of Vikenty Smidovich, 1867–1946) was next to Gorky the most important writer whose sympathies were decidedly Marxist. His most successful book was the semiautobiographical *A Doctor's Notes* (1901), in which he subjected medical education in Russia to sharp criticism (Veresaev was himself a physician). Veresaev's novel-trilogy, *No Way* (1895), *Pestilent Air* (1897), and *The Turning Point* (1902), sketches the progress of a young doctor, Chekanovsky, and a student, Natasha, from a vague though dedicated populism to a firm Marxism.

Aleksandr Kuprin (1870–1938) was in the period between 1900 and the revolution among the most successful Russian writers. Like Gorky, he owed much of his success to his subject matter. His stories are topical, interesting, colorful, exciting, and sentimental. "A Bracelet of Garnets" (1911) is a tearful story of undying but unrequited love. "Gambrinus" (1907) tells of a Jewish fiddler in Odessa who delights sailors with his catchy tunes until his hands are crippled when he is viciously beaten in a pogrom. But he comes back undaunted, with a penny whistle on which he can still play all the same tunes. "Staff Captain Rybnikov" (1906) is a spy thriller, for Rybnikov is a Japanese master spy who is unmasked when a prostitute hears him mutter in his sleep the one Japanese word she knows: *banzai.* "Anathema" (1913) tells of a deacon who refuses to read the anathema of Tolstoi in his church and instead reads a eulogy. The artistic quality of these and scores of other stories is low. Kuprin is a writer of the obvious idea, the ordinary emotion, and the familiar expression, but without the naiveté that alone can make these qualities attractive.

Even more than his short stories, Kuprin's longer works, each of which created a minor sensation, owed their success to their subject matter. *The Duel* (1905) is an exposé of army life. *Moloch* (1896) castigates the evils of capitalism and explores the revolutionary ferment among the working class. *The Pit* (Part One, 1909, Part Two, 1914–15) is a graphic but overly sentimental study of life in a brothel. All three works lack narrative structure and narrative objectivity. The narrator is swayed by his own emotions, which he projects onto his characters. Having lost their topical interest, these works are now barely readable.

Bunin

Ivan Alekseevich Bunin (1870–1953), of ancient but impoverished nobility, came to literature via journalism. He traveled a great deal and wrote many stories on non-Russian and exotic themes, such as the celebrated "Gentleman from San Francisco" (1916). The objective manner of his impressionistically composed short stories conceals a deep pessimism and preoccupation with death and lethal passion.

The Village (1909–10), a short novel, established Bunin as a major writer. Like Chekhov's "Peasants," it rudely destroys the populist mystique by presenting popular life without any Tolstoian Platon Karataevs (in fact, Platon Karataev, a character from *War and Peace*, is dealt with rather irreverently in *The Village*). Like Chekhov's peasants, "the people" of *The Village* are mostly brutish, ignorant and shiftless, but they are all individuals, each very different from the other. The action is set at the time of the revolution of 1905: peasants are burning or pillaging manor houses, and landowners are fleeing to the cities. A Gorkian component may be seen in a massive introduction of various forms of deviant or deranged types, scenes of shocking brutality and coarse sex. *The Village* has no real plot. It has two central characters, the brothers Tikhon and Kuzma Krasov, who have both risen from the peasantry to the urban middle class. Tikhon, a wheeler-dealer businessman, gets so prosperous he buys what is left of a local squire's estate. Yet his life is a failure. His wife bears him only stillborn girls, and being a landowner brings him only worry and fear. Kuzma, self-taught and dreaming of becoming a writer, stumbles through a long series of menial white-collar jobs. The closest he comes to realizing his literary ambitions is placing some articles on the grain trade in the local newspaper while working for a grain dealer in Voronezh. He does publish a book of bad poetry à la Koltsov, at his own expense. The peasant-*intelligent* (Kuzma at one time even converts to Tolstoianism) is as miserable as the peasant-capitalist. The impression left of provincial life in the Russian heartland is one of pervasive unhappiness, unrest, and impending doom. As in Chekhov, people "live badly."

"Sukhodol" (1911), a *povest'*, one of Bunin's strongest works, has the misfortune of inviting comparison with Saltykov-Shchedrin's *The Golovlyovs*. It comes out second to it on every score. Like *The Golov-*

lyovs, "Sukhodol" tells of the decline of a family of the old rural gentry over three generations. Violence, folly, eccentricity, madness and alcoholism wipe out the Khrushchov family, masters of Sukhodol. Whereas Saltykov-Shchedrin's novel has the inexorable logic of tragedy, "Sukhodol" is composed of a series of anecdotal episodes—perhaps more true to life, as Bunin was reporting specific details of his own family history. The story of the Khrushchovs is as gloomy as that of the Golovlyovs; but the touching story of Natalya, a serf in love with her master, who is the pivotal character of "Sukhodol" relieves its bitterness, though at the risk of drifting into sentimentality. Bunin, however, finds concrete details that give the story credibility. Love-lorn Natalya steals her young master's silver hand mirror. She is discovered and punished by having her hair cut off and being banished to a remote farm to work as a cowgirl. The point is that to her master this was a case of simple theft, whereas to her it was a spontaneous act born of an urge to possess and admire a piece touched by her master, whom she adores.

Andreev

Leonid Nikolaevich Andreev (1871–1919) in his lifetime enjoyed the reputation of a major writer and playwright in Russia and abroad. His stories are still reprinted in Russia and occasionally anthologized in translation, but their importance has been downgraded in the Soviet Union on ideological grounds; and even artistically they appear second-rate. Andreev, who earned a law degree from Moscow University in 1897, started his literary career as a court reporter for *The Moscow Herald* and from 1898 on produced a steady stream of short stories published in various periodicals. He was also a successful playwright,[60] a witty feuilletonist, and a perceptive theater critic. Andreev's first collection of stories was published by the Knowledge publishing house, headed by Maksim Gorky, with whom Andreev developed a rather tempestuous friendship. Andreev started out from positions close to those of Gleb Uspensky but gradually moved toward the right: he supported the Russian war effort in World War I and emigrated to Finland after the revolution.

Andreev's stories range from light feuilleton to somberly nightmarish pieces, from mild social satire to apocalyptic visions, and from Chekhovian impressionism to a heavy-handed symbolism. A writer of extraordinary verbal facility but ordinary imagination, Andreev took much of his material from current events and from his experiences as a court reporter. By dramatizing them and inventing a plausible psychological motivation for the actions of his characters, he achieved an effect of verity and social relevance, which caused some of his stories to became the subject of public controversy. The story "In the Fog" (1902) brought a storm of protest. In it a teenage boy from a good family catches a loathsome disease from a prostitute, after much mental self-torture murders another prostitute in an agony of despair, and then kills himself. Countess Tolstoi wrote an outraged letter to the editor of *New Times*, in which she asserted that Andreev "derived enjoyment from the very baseness of the phenomena of human depravity that he described." Others came to his defense. Lev Tolstoi, in private, said that Andreev had presented the subject "correctly, though somewhat crudely."

Another story that created a sensation, "The Life of Vasily Fiveisky" (1903), is a cruel travesty of a saint's life. Father Fiveisky

is a parish priest who is pursued by misfortune after misfortune but persists in his faith. In the end he goes mad and persuades himself that his faith is strong enough to raise a man from the dead. When he fails, he storms out of his church in despair and collapses dead. The story's transparent message is that faith in a beneficent deity is incompatible with the actual condition of the world. The story is hysterically overwritten, undercutting the tragic potential of its theme and leaving a painfully unpleasant impression. "Red Laughter" (1904), written in response to the Russo-Japanese War, is an impassioned indictment of war, which it perceives as madness. Composed in the form of an officer's diary, it is intolerably melodramatic, with many emotional tirades but few hard facts. Here and in other instances where Andreev may by compared to Garshin, he comes out much the inferior artist.

"The Tale of the Seven Who Were Hanged" (1908), Andreev's most famous story, reflects the suppression of revolutionary activity after 1905. Five of the seven are terrorists, arrested in a failed attempt to assassinate a minister of the tsar; two are common criminals—murderers both—introduced to contrast with the noble revolutionaries. Each of the revolutionaries, three men and two women, is presented as a sharply defined character. The revolutionaries—the two young women in particular—are implausibly idealized. The account of how they prepare for and meet their death is hardly convincing psychologically. Contemporary Marxist critics felt that Andreev was anachronistically projecting the mentality of the populists of the 1870s onto the contemporary scene. The story is told with a sympathy so strong that it lapses into sentimentality. It is a flashy piece, but on repeated reading it shows its flaws. Andreev's last major story, the posthumous

60. See p. 495.

novel-length "Satan's Diary" (1921), which has Satan enter the body of a Chicago billionaire and launches into a satire of capitalist society, is decidedly weak.

Andreev wrote some stories in which he used biblical themes, trying to give them a psychological twist and a modern symbolic message. In "Eleazar" (1906) the subject is Lazarus, the man whom Christ raised from the dead; in "Judas Iscariot" (1907) Judas is made into a complex and tormented version of a trickster.

Remizov

Modernism came to Russian prose fiction from various sources. There was Chekhov, of course, who found many imitators. There was symbolism, which transferred the poetics of lyric poetry into prose fiction. There was futurism, with its poetics of surrealist stream of consciousness and "the word as such" (*slovo kak takovoe*), applicable to poetry as well as prose. Modernism in prose fiction meant a shift toward form over content—that is, toward imagery, style, and expression. It meant a foregrounding of "the word as such," both as object and as symbol. The most original, many-sided, and accomplished modernist prose writer was Aleksei Remizov, a writer who at best would score a *succès d'estime* with a select public and never gained international recognition.

Aleksei Mikhailovich Remizov (1877–1957) came from a Moscow family of prosperous and cultured merchants. He graduated from a commercial secondary school but soon decided to become a writer. In 1897 he was arrested in connection with student disorders and spent the next six years in exile in northern Russia. His novel *The Pond* (1902–03) is a deformed and intensified reflection of the early period of his life. Remizov lived in Saint Petersburg from 1905 to his emigration in 1921. He was on cordial terms with Blok, Bely, and other contemporaries, but remained independent in his creative ways. Remizov, like other modernists, excelled in two art forms: literature and graphic art. He prepared some of his works calligraphically and with his own illustrations. He was also musical, but his extreme myopia prevented him from developing that talent.

The distinguishing trait of Remizov's prose is the foregrounding of the word as an object "as such," which made him a precursor of the symbolist prose fiction of Bely, the expressionist prose of Mandelshtam, Babel, and Olesha, and the ornamentalism of Pilnyak. Remizov's prose style is always adapted to the subject matter. It may be folkloric, as in a cycle of lyric prose vignettes, "Following the Sun" (1906). It may imitate the manner of the chapbook, as in a series of popular tales, such as "Melusine" and "Bruntsvik," retold by Remizov, or in some of the "Prohibited Tales"—prohibited on account of their obscenity. It may use an archaizing idiom imitating the language of sacred literature, as in *Limonarium: A Spiritual Meadow* (1906–11), a collection of legends and religious folk traditions. It may use the language of the nursery in tales addressed to children. But even when Remizov deals with contemporary life from the viewpoint of an educated Russian, his language in pointedly different. Elements of spoken language appear pervasively in word order and in frequent syntactic solecisms (anacolutha, asyndets, and aposiopesis). Remizov's choice of words shows a conscious effort to find the striking and memorable: rare and dialect words, extraordinarily long words, tongue twisters, words whose sound structure is suggestive of the action described. Paronomasia (the same or similar word root appearing in two different words of the same phrase) and polyptoton (one noun or verb appearing in various forms), both familiar figures of folk poetry and the spoken vernacular, occur often. Word play, motivated and unmotivated, is a constant feature, and hyperbole and metaphor are also frequent. Remizov's narrative often veers into rhythmic prose with occasional metrical passages, syntactical parallelism, exclamatory phrases, rhetorical questions, and staccato and glissando sequences.

Remizov holds the reader's attention by various devices of estrangement, retardation, and "making it difficult" (*zatrudnenie*), such as laconicism; mixing of the tragic with the comic; sudden change of perspective from one character to another; confusion of dream, fiction, and reality; and outright stream of consciousness. His stories are composed rather than narrated. Remizov himself talked of their "symphonic" or "musical" structure, obtained through the use of leitmotifs, recurrent images and epithets, situational rhyme, and programmed introduction and clausule.

Those of Remizov's stories that are set in contemporary Russia are marked by meticulous detail of everyday life (*byt*), holiday customs, church services, traditional Russian games, and folktales, all reported with sure-handed linguistic precision. Remizov could also be unsentimentally graphic in descriptions of filthy poverty and of the goriest and most cruel details of violence, illness, death, and suicide.

Remizov's prose style was well suited only to the short prose forms, as he himself would admit. His first major work, the autobiographical novel *The Pond*, has two parts, each consisting of twenty-five short vignettes, each a complete short story in itself. It is about the life of two merchant families, the immensely rich Ogorelyshevs and their poor in-laws, the Finogenovs. One Finogenov brother, Aleksandr, works his way up to become heir apparent to the fortune and power of Arseny Ogorelyshev, head of an industrial and banking empire. Aleksandr's brother Nikolai, the central character of the novel and the author's alter ego, grows up from an unruly child to a spirited and rebellious youth in part One. A large portion of part Two is devoted to Nikolai's experience as a political prisoner and exile. It ends in a nightmarish scene in which Nikolai strangles Arseny Ogorelyshev, possibly to avenge the death of his mother, Arseny's sister, who hanged herself after a wretched life ruined by a loveless marriage, the cold neglect of her three rich brothers, and her alcoholism. *The Pond* is quite different from all earlier—and later—novels with a similar subject not only in its abruptly discontinuous structure. No personalized narrator is allowed to show himself, as the most grossly naturalistic scenes are presented with cool detachment. It is the manner in which each detail is presented that is foregrounded: the reader's reaction is not, "My God, the poor woman killed herself!" But rather, "My God, what a way to relate this!" The inner life of the characters is presented in an estranged way, from ever-shifting points of view. Even in this early work the question is never as to whether it is well written, but whether it is overwritten.

Remizov's other longer work of the early period, the short novel *The Clock* (1903–04), is a strange, somber, and powerful creation. It is the story of the disintegration of the Klochkov family and the failure of its jewelry and clockmaker's shop. Its central character is Kostya, the owner's cretinous brother, among whose duties it is to wind the clock on the cathedral tower. Kostya lives in a world of fears, hatreds, and schizophrenic fantasies, one of which is the central theme of the novel: by controlling time through the clock by which the city does its business, Kostya dreams of gaining mastery over the people who have insulted and tormented him as long as he can remember and, by stopping time altogether, stopping death and becoming master of all life. *The Clock* is even more discontinuous than *The Pond*, as the action rapidly shifts from one character to another, from dream or fantasy to waking reality, all without any real sense of time.

Remizov's short stories are equally mannered. They often deal with ordinary characters (priests, clerks, schoolboys) and situations in a quaint, estranged or quirky style. Remizov's stories leave an impression of wonder, uneasiness, and perplexity. Life as he presents it seems remote, strange, difficult to understand.

Symbolist Prose

Although the leading symbolists are known primarily as poets, most of them also wrote prose fiction. Merezhkovsky, Sologub, and Bely won more fame with their prose than with their poetry, and Hippius and Bryusov wrote a great deal of substantial prose fiction. In general, each author's prose corresponds to his or her image as a poet and literary theorist.

Dmitry Merezhkovsky was a prolific writer of historical fiction. His European fame rests primarily on his trilogy of historical novels, *Christ and Antichrist*, which reflects the evolution of his philosophy of history. In *Julian the Apostate* (1896) Merezhkovsky is still the Nietzschean, sharing Nietzsche's nostalgia for the world of classical antiquity and seeing Christ as another incarnation of the suffering god, Dionysus. In *Leonardo da Vinci* (1901) the Greek gods are reborn in the splendor of Renaissance art and rise to

challenge the Christian ideal. *Antichrist: Peter and Alexis* (1905) reflects a turnabout in Merezhkovsky's philosophy as he abandons Nietzsche and joins Dostoevsky. The Antichrist is no longer Christ's complementary alter ego but a usurper, fiend, and corrupter. The central idea is that it will be in Russia that the decisive battle between Christ and Antichrist will be fought. The pagan revolution launched by Peter the Great sets the stage for it. The novel is based on ample research, with some sections directly lifted from historical documents—diaries, letters, sermons, government records. There are many naturalistic descriptions of executions, tortures, and wild drinking bouts, but also of day-to-day living. Peter is presented objectively, in his good and in his bad moments. He is a strong and immensely capable ruler, but also a man possessed, cruel and violent. His son, Alexis, is a weak, impressionable, forever vacillating young man of limited mental and moral capacities. The real heroes of the novel are the persecuted Old Believers, who choose to burn themselves alive rather than submit to Peter, the Antichrist. In the next to last (ninth) book Merezhkovsky introduces a Solovyovian myth of a luminous Sophia,[61] allowing it to merge with the Mother Earth cult of Russian folk religion and Orthodox veneration of the Virgin. A hermit nun named Sophia inspires the faithful to "a fiery baptism, eternal sun, a red death." The apocalyptic mood of the Old Believers is linked to universal history by the figure of Tikhon, a runaway student who has joined the Old Believers. He recognizes in their feverish apocalyptic ravings the ideas of Isaac Newton's commentary on the Apocaly-

---

61. Saint Sophia is portrayed with a solar crown in Russian icons.

pse. In the last book, "Father and Son," the doomed tsarevich becomes the hero. He prophesies that his blood will come upon the heads of all successive members of his father's house. An explicit prediction of the fall of the monarchy is made. The hypocrisy, treachery, and baseness of the tsar's henchmen is exposed: they declare that the tsarevich, who was tortured to death, died of a stroke. In an epilogue, Tikhon vacillates between the Old Believers and the new order, as Feofan Prokopovich takes him under his wing. In the end he decides that the new religion of reason is a dead one and rejoins the people. *Antichrist: Peter and Alexis* may be artistically flawed, but it is a novel of indubitable power and much greater historical integrity than any other work about Peter the Great.

Fyodor Sologub published sixteen volumes of short stories, altogether nearly a hundred pieces, between 1896 and 1921. Some of these collections have symbolic titles: *The Sting of Death* (1904) is focused on life *sub specie mortis*; *Moldering Masks* (1907) concerns the theme of overcoming the forces of evil by tearing off their masks; *A Book of Enchantments* (1909) features the miracle of fantasy and the metamorphosis of fancy into reality. Sologub's stories are conventionally structured—they have a plot, a focus, and a point—and are patterned after Hoffmann and Poe, though they lack Hoffmann's graceful romantic irony and only a few match Poe's power of invention. Sologub shares Hoffmann's interest in children and a child's world of fantasy and magic, and defenseless, suffering children are a special concern of his. Sologub often uses Poe's device of telling a fantastic story in a deceptively sober manner. In "A Little Man" the hero buys a potion to reduce the size of his huge wife, drinks it himself by mistake,

and shrinks out of existence. In "The Red-Lipped Guest" the Christ child saves the hero from imminent death at the lips of a voluptuous vampire. In "Turandina" a beautiful young woman steps out of a fairy tale, becomes the wife of a young lawyer, bears him two children, then disappears without leaving a trace. Some of Sologub's stories are transparent political allegories. "Beyond the Meirur River" tells of a people whose object of religious veneration is revealed to be a bloodthirsty wild beast. Some stories deliver their message even more directly. "The Mounted Policeman" is about a schoolmaster who enjoys flogging his pupils and finds his proper calling when he changes his civil service uniform to that of a mounted policeman wielding a Cossack whip. Sologub's stories are often clever and always well told, but they lack real depth or originality.

Sologub wrote several novels, all except one of little significance. The first, *Heavy Dreams* (1896), was a rather awkward, more autobiographical preview of *The Petty Demon* (1907). The trilogy *A Created Legend* (1914), which tried to fuse social realism with utopian fantasy, and several others were failures. *The Petty Demon*, however, was a huge success. Its hero, the schoolmaster Peredonov, became proverbial. It still stands as one of the more remarkable novels of the twentieth century. *The Petty Demon* is a clinically precise study of the mental deterioration and eventual lapse into murderous paranoia of Peredonov, a base, dull-witted, and sadistic teacher of Russian at a provincial secondary school. It is also a scathing satire on the manners of the so-called educated class, the torpor of whose life is relieved only by petty intrigues, envious gossip, and moments of perverse erotic excitement. *The Petty Demon* is modern in its structure and texture. It derives its unity not from a plot or story line, but from leitmotifs, recurrent images, and a multitude of symbols. Its texture is isomorphic to its content. A nervous and sketchy third-person narrative generates a chaotic kaleidoscope of impressions, flashes of innocence and beauty amidst ubiquitous filth and banality, intrusions of the uncanny and diabolic into an otherwise stiflingly tedious reality, and all of it gradually sliding toward the oppressive yet insufferably banal hallucinations of the mad Peredonov.

Zinaida Hippius, a great poet and astute critic, was also a fine short story writer. She published six volumes of stories between 1898 and 1912. Her stories at first sight resemble Chekhov's. They tell of ordinary people under ordinary circumstances and maintain a solid psychological verisimilitude. What makes them different is their religious undercurrent and antipositivist and antiliberal tendency, often artfully camouflaged. "The Madwoman" (1906) is on the surface a psychological study of an intelligent and sensitive woman chafing under the constraints of a marriage to a hopelessly mediocre, though kind and forbearing husband, but toward the end of the story it becomes clear that the cause of her suffering is her husband's godlessness. She would rather live in an insane asylum than be stifled by his smug positivist humanism. "Luna" (1898) makes the point that true love is only love in Christ, inseparable from religion. In "An Ordinary Event" (1908) the death of a teenage boy is a meaningless though traumatic event to his father, a liberal, freethinking professor, but a meaningful event, sanctified by religion and its rites, to his mother, a believer, and to their devout maid. Hippius's short stories deserve more attention than they have received to date.

Valery Bryusov published a volume of outstanding short stories (1907) and several novels. An excellent prose stylist, he was in his prose fiction as in his poetry a follower of Pushkin. He tells a good story thoughtfully and economically, choosing the proper language for its subject. Bryusov's short stories are pessimistic; two of them are presented as medical case histories of mental derangement. "The Republic of the Southern Cross," the best known of Bryusov's stories, is an anti-utopia foreshadowing Zamyatin's *We*. "The Last Martyrs" is even gloomier. The last martyrs are the world's poets, artists, and thinkers, collectively condemned to death by the Central Committee of the Revolution.

The Fiery Angel was serialized in *Scales* in 1907 and came out as a separate book in 1908. It was translated into many languages (English, 1930) and was made into an opera by Prokofyev (1927). A historical novel (readers familiar with the details of Bryusov's biography will see the personal subtext), it is told by the hero, Ruprecht, a German humanist and adventurer of the early sixteenth century, who meets various historical personages, some well known (Doctor Faustus, Cornelius Agrippa of Nettesheim), and reacts to the works and reputation of many others (Erasmus, Luther, Ulrich von Hutten, Paracelsus). The plot centers around Ruprecht's fateful love for Renate, a beautiful woman whose life is dominated by visions of a "fiery angel." She is eventually put on trial for witchcraft and tortured; she dies in Ruprecht's arms. *The Fiery Angel* is based on ample and judicious historical study and paints a fascinating picture of Germany at the time of the Reformation. The narrative is expertly stylized and rich in concrete detail. *The Fiery Angel* shows to what extent Russian literature had embraced European history and culture and felt at home in it.

Bely

Andrei Bely is considered by many the most important innovator of twentieth-century Russian prose. Basically, he extended the principles of lyric poetry, as he saw them, to prose fiction. "The word as such," in addition to its dictionary meaning, acquires a function by virtue of its sound structure, chance associations (as in punning), repetition, or symbolic power. Bely's prose is built on the principle of a "symphonic" view of verbal art, where the musical aspect of language provides the deepest level of meaning. Planes of meaning are deliberately fused, point of view shifts continually, the border line between waking, hallucinatory, and dream reality is fluid. Bely's prose fiction is structured paradigmatically, through leitmotifs, literary echoes, recurrent imagery, dominant colors, situational rhyme, and other such devices, as much as syntagmatically through plot development.

Bely first developed his idiosyncratic prose style in four "Symphonies" (1900– 1908), following these with a fantastic though formally conventional novel, *The Silver Dove* (1909), set in a community of sectarians who practice orgiastic rites. He then worked for years on *Petersburg* (1913–22), his masterpiece, extant in several versions. The novel is set in contemporary Saint Petersburg, and its action centers on a bomb concealed in a sardine can. A group of revolutionaries has entrusted Nikolai Apollonovich Ableukhov, a student, with the bomb to blow up his father, Apollon Apollonovich, a high-ranking government official. Various other characters move in and out of the text: revolutionaries, police agents, some male and female friends of

Nikolai Apollonovich's. From an incoherent and unpredictable stream-of-consciousness narration there emerge a gruesome murder, a botched suicide, and some wild chases before the bomb finally explodes— harmlessly. The tone of the narrative shifts continually, ranging from mock seriousness and flippant small talk to tragic pathos. The treatment of time is nonlinear, surrealist. The whole text is best understood as "cerebral play" (Bely's term) of the author's consciousness: the author frequently enters the text in his own voice, and details are often demonstratively generated at his whim. The novel is alive with transparent literary echoes, mainly from works set in Petersburg—most spectacularly from Pushkin's "Bronze Horseman" but also from his "Queen of Spades," Dostoevsky's *The Possessed* and *The Double*, and even Tolstoi's *Anna Karenina*. Vladimir Solovyov's Sophia appears in travesty. The narrative manner resembles that of Gogol's Petersburg tales. Not only thoughts, dreams, cosmic visions, and hallucinatory experiences assume a palpable and autonomous reality, but purely verbal entities as well. A Mr. Shishnarfne, alias Enfranshish, enters the novel as a three-dimensional though hallucinatory figure, then begins to lose dimensionality and ends up a dot.

Bely's Petersburg is Dostoevsky's nightmarish city of drunks, dreamers, and madmen, into which the author projects his own preoccupations and fantasies: Kant and Nietzsche, the frustrations of a failed intellectual, an unfortunate father-son relationship, Satanism, apocalyptic fears, the threat of masses of workers from the islands pouring across the bridges into the city's administrative center, the ubiquitous presence of Asian details and intimations of a "yellow peril" (the Ableukhovs are themselves of Tatar descent), contrasting with the imperial city's geometric design and glossy interiors.

Petersburg is hardly a novel in the nineteeth-century sense. Its composition is an attempt to fuse subjective stream of consciousness with an objective plot, some guiding ideas, and a vision of the city as a living entity. Bely's stream of consciousness has exuberant wealth of imagination, lyric power, and verbal invention, but its links to the objective plot and to the living city are tenuous. All its magnificent sound and fury, all its Breughelian grotesquerie, all its verbal legerdemain are like Horace's mountain that labors to give birth to a mouse. The novel's title promises something the text does not deliver. The only live character in the novel is the author, and its story boils down to a rather sordid and petty family affair. Bely went on to write several more novels, but they did not reach the intensity of *Petersburg*.

Mikhail Kuzmin, a remarkable poet, also wrote a great deal of somewhat less remarkable prose fiction. His most famous prose piece, the short novel *Wings*, which first appeared in the symbolist journal *Scales* in 1906, was the first work of Russian literature to deal explicitly with homosexual love. *Wings* follows young Smurov from Petersburg to an Old Believer monastery on the Volga and then to Italy, as he gradually discovers the nature of his sexuality. Artfully intertwined with the story are many perceptive observations on old and new literature, art and music, and an eloquent apology of homoeroticism, whose key idea is that it is not the quality of the physical act that matters in love, or in anything else, but the emotion behind it. *Wings* and Kuzmin's other stories have a certain facile and sometimes flippant charm, a quality not often found in Russian literature.

Homosexual motifs surface in other works by Kuzmin. In another short novel, *Sailing Travelers* (1923), interwining loves and love affairs of several married and single men are reported with amused detachment. But then young Lavrik, the central figure, is jolted from the world of his adolescent heterosexual dalliances when he observes two grown men—one in a riding habit, the other in officer's uniform—kissing, after one of them exclaims in a paroxysm of joy, "How can people live without having known such moments?!"

Futurism

Russian futurism, unlike symbolism, did not produce much exceptional prose fiction. Bely's *Petersburg* is as close to a realization of a futurist poetics in prose fiction as any futurist work before the revolution.

Elena Guro (pseudonym of Eleonora von Notenberg, 1877–1913), wife of the modernist composer Mikhail Matyushin and herself a professional painter, wrote some interesting modernist poetry but is more important as the first futurist prose writer. Her booklet *The Hurdy-Gurdy* (1909) contains poetry, drama, and prose. The prose pieces are plotless, impressionistic sketches of city and country life, some of which are close to pure stream of consciousness. Guro's dominant idea is a sense of the communion of all living things. She uses the device of estrangement often by presenting the world through the eyes of children. Her posthumous booklet *Baby Camels of the Sky* (1914) contains lyric prose miniatures alternating with poems, mostly in free verse. The unity of the book is one of style and mood, established by the first piece, "A Newspaper Ad" about catching baby camels in the sky, good-natured and clumsy things that are shorn of their fluff, which is used to make shirts, and then set free.

Guro's primitivist stream of consciousness was imitated by her sister, Ekaterina Nizen, whose piece "Spots" appeared in *A Trap for Judges, II*, along with much of what would later be Guro's book *Baby Camels of the Sky*.

Vasily Kamensky wrote a good deal of prose fiction that he believed to be futurist. It tended to be less futurist than simply disorganized, banal, and in bad taste. *The Mud Hut* (1910) is an anti-urbanist novel whose hero rejects the city and finds happiness in the primitive life in a mud hut in the bosom of nature. *The Mud Hut* is a feeble piece of impressionist prose mixed with free-verse poetry. Kamensky's "Winter and May" (1916), a short story about a love affair between an old man and a fourteen-year-old girl, is notable only for its many neologisms.

Velimir Khlebnikov's prose claims the same privileges as his poetry. Its punning, associative, surrealist manner allows no plot or structure of a conventional kind to develop. In effect, Khlebnikov's short prose pieces are surrealist poems in prose. There are a few exceptions. "Nikolai" is a quite ordinary character study whose subject is a "lone wolf" hunter.

As early as 1907 Khlebnikov wrote a brief prose piece, *Pesn' miryazya* (Song of *miryaz'*, a neologism formed from *mir*, "world, cosmos, peace," and rhyming with *knyaz'*, "prince, duke," and *vityaz'*, "hero, warrior"). In this and several pieces that followed, the principle of James Joyce's *Finnegan's Wake* is largely anticipated. The text is composed of grammatical phrases, but much of the vocabulary, and specifically key nouns and significant adjectives, are neologisms whose meaning can be only guessed by the reader, although they are derived from familiar Russian roots. The whole piece generates a vague impression of a forest idyll.

Recently Khlebnikov's story "Ka" (1916) has received a great deal of scholarly and critical attention. Ka, the Egyptian word for soul, is immediately introduced as "shadow of the soul, its double, its envoy, with those people about whom a snoring gentleman dreams." Ka knows no boundaries of time, moving from dream to dream, traversing time to reach "the bronze of time." Ka comes from the Egypt of Pharaoh Amenophis IV, to which he returns toward the end of the tale. En route he meets a host of strange characters—historical, literary, and imaginary, from Egypt, Arabia, China, Japan, Mexico, and India. In the fractured world through which Ka moves, one also recognizes Khlebnikov's preoccupations with language, numerology, and time. One character says, "I also wage war—not for space, but for time. I sit in my trench and capture a strip of time from the past." "Ka" features many striking conceits like this and makes for challenging reading.

Drama

The Russian theater of the Silver Age developed in more fruitful interaction with Russian literature than ever before, even if a majority of plays staged at many theaters were still foreign. The domestic repertoire of Russian opera and ballet was growing by leaps and bounds. Leading Russian artists, first of the *World of Art* group and then of the avant-garde, were actively involved in theatrical productions. Leading writers and poets took more of an interest in the theater, beyond writing plays for it, and for the first time the relation between literature and the theater became a subject of debate.

The end of the monopoly of the imperial

theaters in the capitals in the 1880s did not immediately lead to a flowering of private theaters. The Aleksandrinsky of Saint Petersburg and the Moscow Maly continued to establish the style practiced by theaters all over the country until the end of the century and even after. But the road was now open for a wave of private theaters large and small, most of them ephemeral but some to stay until the revolution and after. The Moscow millionaire Savva Mamontov founded a private opera in 1896, which competed with the imperial theaters. A year later the Moscow Art Theater was founded by another Moscow millionaire, Konstantin Alekseev, who was to become famous under his stage name, Stanislavsky.

The old drama of communication, represented by Ibsen, a powerful presence on all Russian stages, continued to flourish. Plays by Tolstoi, Gorky, and Andreev delivered a strong social message. Its strongest exponent was the Moscow Art Theater, which gave its first performance in 1898. Its naturalist style had its parallels in the Paris Théâtre libre, founded in 1887, and the Freie Bühne of Berlin, founded in 1889, both of which staged Tolstoi's *Power of Darkness* before it was allowed to be performed in Russia. As an antithesis to it, there appeared the symbolist theater of noncommunication, whose master, Maurice Maeterlinck, was ever-present on Russian stages. His manner found imitators among the Russian symbolists, and Russian directors, headed by Vsevolod Meyerhold, Nikolai Evreinov, and Fyodor Kommissarzhevsky, delighted in staging them at the risk of rejection by an uncomprehending public. Symbolist theater had its origins in the Théâtre d'Art of Paris and the Munich theater of Georg Fuchs, whose book *Schaubühne der Zukunft* (1906) contained many of the ideas employed by Russians in their productions.

The theater of Vera Kommissarzhevskaya (1864–1910), founded in Saint Petersburg in 1904, which had Meyerhold (1906–07), Evreinov (1908–09), and her brother Fyodor as directors, was the principal outlet of symbolist drama, though the Moscow Art Theater and even the Imperial theaters did not entirely spurn it. Along with symbolist theater came various forms of stylized theater, often performed at small private theaters: the harlequinade, the morality play, the medieval romance à la Maeterlinck's *Pelléas et Mélisande*, and the grotesque nonstop farce of the commedia dell'arte. The Ancient Theater of Saint Petersburg (and later Moscow), founded by Evreinov in 1907, staged *Le Jeu de Robin et Marion*, by Adam de la Halle (1230–88), and other medieval plays. Several cabaret-type theaters in Petersburg and Moscow specialized in short satirical and parodic pieces. Such were Evreinov's Crooked Mirror (1910–17) in Petersburg and Nikita Baliev's Bat (1908 until after the revolution) in Moscow. Private experimental theaters proliferated in the capitals and even in the provinces. The large established theaters like the Moscow Art Theater supported studio theaters, which provided opportunites for experimental performances.

The Russian theater of the Silver Age followed the example of European avant-garde theater in becoming dominated by directors. The Moscow Art Theater's two founders, Konstantin Stanislavsky (1863–1938) and Vladimir Nemirovich-Danchenko (1858–1943), were also innovative directors. Stanislavsky, himself a great actor, was responsible for the technical side, Nemirovich-Danchenko, a successful novelist and dramatist, for the artistic side. The guiding principle of the Moscow Art Theater was "to take the theater out of the theater," making the action onstage a slice of real life. Declamation, false pathos, and theatrical gestures were out. Another principle of the Moscow Art Theater was, "Today Hamlet, tomorrow a minor role," meaning that there were no stars, only an ensemble, tightly controlled by the director. Stanislavsky insisted that acting should be based on scientific study, training, and discipline instead of intuition. Some established actors resented this "dictatorship of the director," but the Moscow Art Theater compensated for it by providing them a pleasant environment behind the stage (comfortable dressing rooms, for example) and a modern stage with the most modern technical equipment. The Moscow Art Theater launched the dramatic works of Chekhov and Gorky. It also staged a number of other contemporary Russian plays, by Evgeny Chirikov, Sergei Naidyonov, and others, as well as the Russian classics and many foreign plays.

Vsevolod Meyerhold (1874–1940) played Treplyov in *The Seagull* and Tusenbach in *Three Sisters* at the Moscow Art Theater before leaving it in 1902, intent upon having his own theater. He took to the road with his own company for a few years and in 1906–07 directed several plays at Vera Kommissarzhevskaya's theater, among them Blok's *Showbooth*, Andreev's *Life of Man*, and Sologub's *Triumph of Death*. In 1908 Meyerhold went to the Aleksandrinsky, where he staged Sologub's *Hostages of Life* (1912) and Hippius's *Green Ring* (1915), among other plays; his lavish production of Lermontov's *A Masked Ball* (1917) became quite famous. Meyerhold went on to be the leading theatrical figure of the Soviet period. Meyerhold was a compulsive experimenter and innovator. His impulse was to make a theatrical performance a spectacle, with the

actors a part of the show and blending in with the setting.[62] As a result, Meyerhold's plays tended to turn into pantomimes, with the spoken word pushed into the background. In some of his productions Meyerhold eliminated the background from the stage so that the actors would move as if in a bas-relief. Meyerhold's other challenge to Stanislavsky's naturalism was that he liked to stage the unreal, to distort life by refracting it through a prism of free fantasy or mystic vision. A great admirer of E. T. A. Hoffmann, he too had a penchant for the grotesque.

Nikolai Evreinov (1879–1953) was a playwright before becoming a director, although he then continued to write plays. He also wrote a great deal about the history of the Russian theater and the theory of drama. He developed a theory of monodrama, whose essence was that the plot and dramatis personae of a play should be relayed to the audience through the subjective vision of a single central character. Evreinov went even further than Meyerhold, a lifelong rival, in advocating the theatricalization not only of the theater but of life as well, meaning that a joyful vitality, a dreamlike fantasy, and an enchanted world of make-believe should penetrate all life. Evreinov stressed that the roots of theater were in the very instincts of universal human nature. In theatrical practice this meant a move toward audience participation and elimination of a fixed boundary between stage and audience.

62. Meyerhold, for example, stylized Maeterlinck's *Sister Beatrice* at Kommissarzhevskaya's theater (with her in the title role) à la Botticelli, Memling, and other old masters. He brought reproductions of their paintings to the theater and asked actors to study gestures and facial expressions. The production thus became an exercise in Pre-Raphaelite art.

In 1914 Aleksandr Tairov (1885–1950) opened the Chamber Theater in Moscow. His theater followed no particular ideological line but insisted on theater as an art in its own right—not as imitation of life, allegory, or political forum. Tairov wanted his actors and actresses to be handsome, graceful, and musical—like ballet dancers. He believed in giving a performance a rhythmic dimension and liked to inject as much music as possible into his plays. Among Tairov's early productions was Innokenty Annensky's Euripidean tragedy *Thamyras Citharoedus* (1916), billed as a "satyr drama." Tairov staged it as a symphony of two conflicting rhythms: the delicate and noble Apollonian of the tragic musician Thamyras and the savagely sensuous rhythm of choruses of satyrs and maenads.

Fyodor Kommissarzhevsky (1874–1954), brother of the great actress Vera Kommissarzhevskaya, was a producer and director of talent and inventiveness. He took the middle road between the naturalism of Stanislavsky and the mechanical puppet theater of Meyerhold, proposing instead a theater of ideas that were to illuminate the ensemble and the audience. He saw the director's task in recognizing the governing idea of a play and seeing to it that it was properly expressed. Kommissarzhevsky produced Remizov's *Devil's Comedy* (1907), with sets by Dobuzhinsky and music by Kuzmin, Andreev's *Black Masks* (1908), and Sologub's *Vanka the Butler and the Page Jehan* (1909). Kommissarzhevsky left Russia after the revolution and enjoyed success abroad.

The innovative theater of the 1900s created a climate of controversy in which prominent figures of both literature and theater participated. One subject of controversy was Stanislavsky's thesis that the new theater should replace theatricality with "real life." In an article, "Unneeded Truth: On the Moscow Art Theater," published in *The World of Art* in 1902, Valery Bryusov charged that the naturalism of the Moscow Art Theater was a misdirected and ultimately futile effort, a pretense to reality that inevitably had to fall short of its goal. Moreover, far from being "the theater of the future," it merely perfected what the old theater of Ostrovsky had been trying to do all along. Theater, as all art, Bryusov said, is by nature conventional. The task of the actor is not to be "like everybody else," but to express ideas and emotions through his or her art.

The relation between literature and the theater, author and actor, was another subject of controversy. Playwright-directors like Evreinov complained that the theater had all too long been in the hands of literary men who had little understanding of the theater as a public spectacle. They demanded that the theater return to the traditions of Shakespeare and Molière, who were actors and understood the theater. Evreinov, Meyerhold, and their disciples rode roughshod over classical dramatic texts, adjusting them to their theatrical purposes. Some writers thought the exact opposite. Sologub, in his essay "The Theater of the Single Will" (1908), suggested that since "the drama is the product of a single conception in the same way as the universe is the product of a single creative thought," the actor should be no more than a device whose function is to read the lines of the play. The text is the thing—sets, lighting, and all other stage effects are only distractions. Sologub was seconded by the critic Yuly Aikhenvald (1872–1928) who in the essay "A Rejection of the Theater" (1910) said that staging was a coarse materialization of drama. Meyerhold's "dematerialization" of the actor and his transformation into a device to express the director's single will was a practical application of Sologub's conception.

A great deal of theorizing went on along the lines of a new theater addressed to a participating audience and having an important public function. The new theater was envisaged as a synthesis of all art forms in the spirit of Wagner's *Gesamtkunstwerk*, both by those who conceived of it as a vehicle of religious mythopoeia (Vyacheslav Ivanov, for instance) and by those like Lunacharsky who saw its possibilities as a form of political indoctrination.

Even after Ostrovsky the Russian theater continued to experience a dearth of original Russian plays, a condition that had plagued it since its inception. Plays by French, English, German, Italian, and Scandinavian plyawrights (Ibsen, Strindberg, Hauptmann, Wedekind, d'Annunzio, Maeterlinck, Verhaeren, Wilde) provided a significant part of the contemporary repertoire. Stage versions of well-known Russian novels, Dostoevsky's in particular, were established as a permanent feature of the Russian stage by the Moscow Art Theater and other theaters of the period.

After Ostrovsky's death several minor dramatists continued to provide the Russian stage with slightly updated versions of Ostrovskian plays. *Winter Crop*, by Aleksei Lugovoi, staged in 1890, is typical. Bocharov, a wine merchant, is plotting to drive Koryukhin, a grain merchant, into bankruptcy so that he can take over his business. He also wants his oafish son, Ivan, to marry Koryukhin's beautiful and educated daughter, Lyubov. When Lyubov realizes that her father will go to debtor's prison if she refuses, she agrees to marry Ivan, who loves her dearly, and Bocharov gives Koryukhin more time to pay his bills. A year later, Lyubov is married to Ivan and they have a child. Bocharov has tightened the noose

around Koryukhin's neck. He calls in all the bills due him, and when Koryukhin cannot pay promptly, has him thrown in prison. A stormy scene ensues. Ivan says he will leave home if his father refuses to release his father-in-law, and asks Lyubov to get up when she falls to her knees pleading for her father. At that moment Bocharov suddenly collapses and dies. The dialogue is realistic, the action lively. *Winter Crop* is an entertaining play, though cliché-ridden and altogether predictable.

Tolstoi

The Russian stage received a major contribution from a quite unexpected source, Lev Tolstoi. In the early 1860s Tolstoi had worked on a couple of comedies with a topical political slant, but had abandoned them. In the 1880s he returned to the drama, now with remarkable success. A short morality play, *The First Distiller, or How the Imp Earned His Slice of Bread* (1886), is a dramatization of one of Tolstoi's tales for the people. It was first played before an audience of factory hands in Saint Petersburg in 1886. Tolstoi later wrote two more such pieces. *The Power of Darkness, or Once a Claw Is Stuck, the Whole Bird is Lost* (1886), also conceived as a morality play, became a full-fledged drama. It tells the story of the farmhand Nikita, a village Don Juan, who abandons Marina, the girl who loves him dearly, and gets involved with Anisya, the wife of his employer, Pyotr, a rich peasant. Nikita's mother, Matryona, incites Anisya to poison her husband so that Nikita can marry her and take over the farm. One crime leads to another. Nikita has seduced Akulina, Pyotr's daughter from his first marriage, and kills her newborn child so she can be married off. At Akulina's wedding, when things seem to be going his way,

Nikita, encouraged by his poor but righteous father, Akim, goes down on his knees and publicly confesses his crimes. *The Power of Darkness* combines a stark naturalism, which caused it to be stopped by the censorship until 1895, with heavy symbolism. The characters are symbolic figures. Evil Matryona is clever in the world's ways, but ignorant of God's. Akim is a fool before men, but wise before God. Nikita and the three young women of the play are Everyman and Everywoman in the clutches of the devil of lust. The dialogue is straightforward and to the point, without ornamental or psychological refinements. The moral message is delivered in the bluntest possible way. *The Power of Darkness*, a great play, was successful on European stages even before it was finally staged at the Moscow Maly Theater.

The Fruits of Enlightenment, a comedy started in 1886 and finished in 1890, was first staged at the Maly in 1892. It is a caustic satire on educated Russian society. Its effects were obtained largely by Tolstoi's favorite device, "making it strange": the activities of the mistress of the house (having her morning coffee, practicing the piano) are described to visiting peasants by the lady's cook—of course they all find her doings absurd and sinful. In the play a clever chambermaid rigs a spiritualist séance so that the master of the house will sell the peasants the land they need on terms advantageous to them. The bias of the play is blunt and transparent, as a result of which its humor is a bit grim.

Tolstoi did not approve of Chekhov's theater. He wrote *A Living Corpse* in 1900 in response to a performance of *Uncle Vanya*, which Tolstoi found outrageous. The plot was based on a real court case, and Tolstoi refused to release the play for staging or publication to avoid causing the family involved any more grief. First staged by the Moscow Art Theater in 1911, *A Living Corpse* became a staple of the Russian repertory. The hero, Fyodor (Fedya) Protasov, has abandoned his wife, Liza, for Gypsy music, Gypsy women, and drink. When Viktor Karenin, an old friend who has always loved Liza, begs him to give her a divorce, Fedya instead sends him a suicide note and fakes suicide. Karenin marries Liza. But a year later Fedya, while drunk, tells the story to a friend, who tells the police. The case comes to trial, and when it looks bad for Karenin and Liza, Fedya shoots himself. *A Living Corpse*, like Tolstoi's other plays, is a play with an obvious tendency. To justify his drinking, Fedya says that there are three ways to come to terms with life: to live the shameful life of the idle rich, robbing the people; to take a stand against it; or to take to drink. Tolstoi projected onto Fedya his own desire to escape the life to which he was tied by his family.

And the Light Shines in the Darkness, a play on which Tolstoi worked intermittently beginning in the 1880s, remained incomplete. The content of the last act is available only in a brief synopsis. The play was published, however, in 1911 and has occasionally been staged. Its subject is Tolstoi himself, his difficulties with his family, and his responsibility for the movement he launched. In the play, young duke Boris Cheremshanov, converted to Tolstoianism by Nikolai Ivanovich Saryntsev, clearly an alter ego of Tolstoi, refuses to swear allegiance to the tsar when called up to serve in the army and instead preaches the Tolstoian gospel to officers, priests, policemen, and doctors who try to make him change his mind. His mother implores him to relent and begs Saryntsev to induce Boris to be reasonable, but to no avail. Boris is sent to serve in a penal battalion, where he is sure to perish.

In the last act Duchess Cheremshanova was to shoot Saryntsev. *And the Light Shines in the Darkness* is a cruel satire whose targets are Tolstoi himself and the society whose very foundations he proposed to destroy. The crushing message of the play is that young Boris's sacrifice is just as useless as Saryntsev's efforts, in his old age, to learn a joiner's trade. Society will not listen to Boris, and one more joiner will only mean less much-needed work for others.

Chekhov

Anton Chekhov, the great innovator of the short story, not only gave the Russian stage a new direction but also put Russian drama on all the stages of the world.

Chekhov had histrionic talent and a life-long love for the theater and any kind of playacting, as several humorous skits of the 1880s, such as "The Bear" (1888), reveal. Chekhov's serious plays of that period, however, were failures, because the Russian stage was not yet ready for Chekhov's new theater. Chekhov's innovative theater had its antecedents, though. Gogol's *Marriage* and Turgenev's *A Month in the Country* are quite Chekhovian, and even Ostrovsky used Chekhovian symbolic detail in some of his plays. Chekhov felt all along that the Russian stage had reached an impasse and that it was time to relieve it of its conventions and canons. First and foremost, he believed that more realism was in order. (Chekhov never got rid of some of the most blatant "unrealistic" conventions of the theater, however, such as eavesdropping, the aside, and the monologue.)

Chekhov's early plays, *Platonov*, *Ivanov*, and *The Wood Demon*, the last of which was later reshaped into *Uncle Vanya*, were condemned by all critics for precisely the qualities that are basic to Chekhov's new theater: plotlessness and the absence of a central hero and of clearly delineated relations between characters—in a word, failure to transform "life" into "drama." When Chekhov's late plays became hits ten years later, the success of Ibsen, Hauptmann, and Strindberg certainly had something to do with it. Nevertheless, Chekhov's manner was even then perceived as unorthodox; it met with much negative criticism and elicited many vitriolic parodies. Many leading actors and directors, however, were intrigued and saw Chekhov's theater as a welcome challenge. The Moscow Art Theater made Chekhov's *Seagull* its emblem, blessing the tears of its enraptured audiences with the self-satisfied smile of success—both unfailing marks of vulgarity in Chekhov. The great Vera Kommissarzhevskaya was enthusiastic. Vsevolod Meyerhold interpreted Chekhov as a symbolist but never came up with a truly outstanding production of a Chekhov play.

The basic traits of Chekhov's theater are analogous to those of his late short stories. The course of events in the play is determined by *byt*, the contingencies of day-to-day living, not by plot. Characters tend to be simple; they do not develop but merely reveal themselves (Natasha in *Three Sisters* is a good example of this). There are no thematically focused "dramatic" scenes; rather, they are replaced by the ordinary course of everyday life. Instead of being continuous, the dialogue is often gratuitously interrupted, and more than one dialogue may be heard onstage simultaneously. Scenic composition is aimed at enhancing lyric and emotional effects. Chekhov's theater of atmosphere is ideally suited for Stanislavsky's director-dominated theater. The drift and mood of the play are obtained not from the text, but rather from a subtext whose interpretation is left to the director's discretion. Whether a given line is sad, moving, or funny is a constant question. Trofimov's speech in *The Cherry Orchard*, "Forward! Do not lag behind, friends!" to which Anya responds, "How well you speak!" is a good example. It is moving in itself, but the context makes it potentially laughable. The director must decide which side to emphasize. Or, how should Masha, in *The Seagull*, intone her famous line, "I am in mourning for my life"?

Mood is created by a variety of devices: obvious symbols, such as the gratuitously killed seagull or the cherry orchard felled in the final scene; suggestive sets, such as the nostalgic nursery in *The Cherry Orchard*; sounds coming from offstage—a shot in the distance, the howling of a dog, the thud of axes; nature, as in the change of seasons in *The Seagull*; offstage characters, such as the professor's first wife in *Uncle Vanya*; and literary quotes and allusions—Solyony in *Three Sisters* plays Lermontov, Arkadina and Treplyov in *The Seagull* recite lines from *Hamlet* (a case of Sophoclean irony, since they do not suspect how close they are to Hamlet and Gertrude). It is generally thought that Chekhov's plays, like Tchaikovsky's music, are in a minor key, corresponding to the mood of the period. Chekhov himself, however, felt that Stanislavsky's emotional staging overdid the melancholy and insufficiently brought out comic aspect of his plays.

The first night of *The Seagull* at the Aleksandrinsky on October 17, 1896, created a scandal and got a devastating critical response. People found it offensive that a play ending in a suicide should be billed as a comedy. *The Seagull* is about art and passion and their mutual relations, its plan concealed behind a random and asymmetric cast and an assortment of inconsequential trivia. From the opening curtain it is also a play about the theater. The sets of Treplyov's outdoor stage are so arranged and the performance of his play so timed that the moon rises above the lake in the background: nature becomes a prop of art. The play within the play, really a monologue by a feminine World Soul speaking after all life has become extinct on earth, may be viewed as a parody of symbolist drama. Treplyov, the "new" dramatist, and his actress, Nina Zarechnaya, project themselves into their art. Their antipodes—the realist writer Trigorin (a self-portrait of Chekhov) and Irina Nikolaevna Arkadina, Treplyov's mother and a famous actress—use life to create art. Trigorin seduces and abandons Nina, but he will put her into a story about a tragic young woman and a seagull killed for no reason. Treplyov's suicide, too, will become material for one of Trigorin's stories. Throughout the play the trivial appears side by side with the fateful. The tragic scene between Treplyov and Zarechnaya just before his suicide is preceded by a game of lotto, and the laughter of Arkadina and Trigorin is heard in the background during the scene. The drama of *The Seagull* is created by the emotional relations between its characters, but unlike in the old drama, no resolution is achieved. The motive for Treplyov's suicide is by no means clear. There is no real hierarchy of characters, and the presence of some minor characters is not motivated by any obvious function they may have in the play. Doctor Dorn provides the exception: he has Chekhov's other profession, and he is the only one to appreciate Treplyov's play. It is he who draws Trigorin aside, after a shot is heard in the background, and speaks the final lines of the play: "Take Irina Nikolaevna away somewhere. The thing is that Konstantin Gavrilovich has shot himself."

Uncle Vanya was staged in the provinces

in 1898—99, with great success. Only after the triumph of *The Seagull* at the Moscow Art Theater did Chekhov allow *Uncle Vanya* to be staged at the Moscow Maly. Critics, approvingly now, noticed its plotlessness and actionlessness, its naturalism and its modernity. The play is about a rebellion of the meek and unhappy against the arrogant and happy. Ivan Petrovich Voinitsky (Uncle Vanya) has managed, for many years, the estate that his deceased sister brought into her marriage to Aleksandr Vladimirovich Serebryakov, a professor of literature, now retired. Sonya, Serebryakov's daughter from his first marriage, has been his helper. Their selfless labors have allowed the professor, a smug and pompous sort, to lead a carefree life with his young and beautiful second wife, Elena Andreevna. When Serebryakov announces his intention to sell the estate and move back to the city, leaving Voinitsky and Sonya without a place to stay, Uncle Vanya rebels and actually tries to shoot Serebryakov. He misses. When Serebryakov relents—to the extent that he will move back to the city but let Uncle Vanya continue to manage the estate, providing a decent income for the professor— everything returns to what it was before.

The play is also about waste: Uncle Vanya, now middle-aged, has wasted his life supporting the professor, whose many writings, he now realizes, are utterly worthless. Elena Andreevna's great beauty is wasted on an old and infirm husband. She is also a fine pianist, but her husband will not allow her to play, because it might disturb him. The love of Sonya, a good woman, for Doctor Astrov is wasted, because she is not pretty and he is in love with the beautiful Elena Andreevna, who rejects his advances. Astrov is preoccupied with the waste of natural resources all around, especially the destruc-

tion of the land by deforestation at the hands of desperate peasants intent on just surviving another day. The moral of it all, given in Sonya's monologue at the end of the play, is that the best one can do with one's life is to get some work done, even if it serves no useful purpose. *Uncle Vanya* is the least pleasant and most bitter of Chekhov's plays. Vanya's—and Chekhov's—hatred for the smug Serebryakov and his profession burns with a steady glow. The pathetic futility of the other characters, while pitiful, is also irritating. There are some exchanges in the play that angered conservatives, liberals, and radicals alike. It has a smaller cast than the other great plays and presents an almost closed private world. Still, *Uncle Vanya* is not atypical of Chekhov: some stories of his are in a similar mood.

Three Sisters (1901) may be viewed as a classical tragedy—in travesty. It is the story of the fall of a great house, the late general Prozorov's. Most of the men onstage are officers of Prozorov's regiment. The classical suggestion is established by the set: "A parlor with columns, behind which a large hall is visible." In classical mythology, "three sisters" are the Parcae, who control human fate. Here, three noble and beautiful sisters, Olga, Masha, and Irina, are at the mercy of fate. They lose the house of their father to the vulgar upstart Natasha, who marries their weak brother. Olga teaches school; Irina works at the telegraph office; Masha is married to a bore of a Latin teacher. *Three Sisters* is a play about time and its many faces. It starts with a temporal statement: "Father died exactly one year ago." Attention is drawn to the theme of time throughout the play—by clocks onstage, by references to the time of day in the dialogue, by recurrent wistful recollections of a happy past, and by speeches by several characters, including Olga's at the conclusion of the play, which cast a glance into a more or less utopian future. Baron Tusenbach, who will die in a duel with the odious bully Solyony, makes a prophetic speech about "a healthy, powerful storm that is approaching and will soon blow away from our society laziness, indifference, prejudice against labor, and rotten boredom."

Chebutykin, an old army doctor, acts as the chorus of the drama. A sometimes cheerful, sometimes sentimental cynic, he inserts tired clichés, self-deprecatory tirades, assorted absurdities, and a hummed *tarara-boomdee-ay* into the dialogue throughout the play. Chebutykin could have stopped the duel between Solyony and Tusenbach. But he only says, "The baron is a good man, but one baron more or less, isn't it all the same? Let them. It's all the same."

The scenic composition of *Three Sisters* interwines the humdrum and sometimes sordid world of a provincial town and the lyric effusions of the three sisters, Baron Tusenbach, who is Irina's fiancé, and Lieutenant Colonel Vershinin, Masha's lover. In *Three Sisters* the peculiarities of Chekhov's theater appear in profusion: the weather, music, and various physical details are all attuned to the mood of the moment; the banal is mixed with the tragic; there is plenty of multiple dialogue and symbolic foreshadowing; and there is a leitmotif, "to Moscow," where the three sisters futilely hope to recover their lost happiness.

Chekhov initially wanted to make *The Cherry Orchard* (1904) a pure comedy. In fact, he was angry with Stanislavsky for turning it into a lachrymose drama and wished that it would be played at a much more rapid tempo. Several of the play's characters are outright vaudeville figures, good for easy laughs, and the more serious characters have their comic moments as well. The central character, Lyubov Andreevna Ranevskaya, owner of the estate whose famous cherry orchard will be sold at auction unless she can come up with a plan to satisfy her creditors, is also the pivot of the question of comedy or tragedy. She is both a shallow, frivolous, spoiled woman and a loving, generous soul touched by tragedy: her little son Grisha was drowned some years earlier. Either side of her may be foregrounded. When a middle-aged woman "with a past" produces a lyric effusion starting with the words "Oh my childhood, my purity!" the scene may be made moving, but it is also open to bathos. The same is true of her brother Gaev's speech addressed to a hundred-year-old bookcase: it is ludicrously pompous, but the stage directions say that Gaev has tears in his eyes. A psychological angle suggests itself: Ranevskaya and Gaev are emotionally retarded—they have remained children (Gaev also sucks sweets all the time and keeps playing an imaginary game of billiards).

In a Marxist interpretation, *The Cherry Orchard* is a satirical comedy of manners about the demise of the landowning gentry and the ascendancy of the bourgeoisie. The merchant Lopakhin buys the cherry orchard and has it cut down to parcel it out into lots for summer homes. Gaev will get a job as a bank clerk. Ranevskaya will go back to Paris and her French lover to squander what is left of her fortune. The manor house is abandoned, with an old servant, whom everybody has forgotten, left inside to die. He mutters, "Life has passed by as though one hadn't even lived." The concluding stage directions contradict a sober positivist interpretation: "A remote sound, coming as if from the sky, the sound of a broken string, dying slowly, sadly, is heard. Silence sets in, and one can only hear the thud of axes hitting trees."

Gorky

Maksim Gorky's spectacular success on Russian and international stages is to be explained, like the success of his stories, by his subject matter; but he also gave audiences, receptive to Chekhov's theater, plays in which Chekhovian principles and techniques were applied to a lower social milieu. Chekhov's plays were about the Russian upper middle class, with lower-class characters appearing at the fringes. Gorky's first play, *Burghers* (1901),[63] presents a "slice of life" from a milieu that Chekhov had often described in his stories but not in his plays. Vasily Vasilyich Bessemyonov, an uneducated but well-to-do provincial businessman (he contracts for house-painting jobs), has raised a son, Pyotr, a student currently suspended for participating in a demonstration; a daughter, Tatyana, a schoolteacher; and a foster son, Nil, a machinist, all of whom live in his house. In the course of the play, Nil declares that he will marry Polya, the penniless daughter of a drunken catcher of songbirds (a version of Ostrovsky's Lyubim Tortsov),[64] whereupon Tatyana, who has been in love with Nil, tries to poison herself. Pyotr will marry an attractive but loose young widow, which will mean an end to his studies. The tension—and constant bickering—in the play is caused by a generation gap. Bessemyonov thinks he is a good husband and father and a solid citizen, yet he

gets no respect from the young generation. His revenge will be that the young people, who hold his values in contempt but have none of their own, will as they grow older fall back on his. The play is very Chekhovian, but the drabness and banality of the life it represents are not relieved by those moments of wry humor and golden lyricism that add a dimension of poetry to Chekhov's plays.

The Lower Depths (1902), Gorky's most famous play, is a melodramatic, disorganized sequence of scenes of jealousy, plotting, murder, and suicide with the distinction of a setting not previously seen on the Russian stage: a flophouse. The characters are day laborers, thieves, cardsharps, prostitutes, drunken derelicts, and a single devout pilgrim, Luka. Kostylyov, the owner, is a fence. He enjoys the protection of a policeman who is the uncle of his young wife, Vasilisa. The truth of life that emerges from the play is that people live badly, mostly through their own fault. Pepel, a thief, was born a thief's son and had little chance in life, but he wants out: "I feel no remorse. I don't believe in conscience. But I do feel one thing: one must live differently. One must live better, so that one can respect oneself." In the end he goes to Siberia, though, for the murder of Kostylyov, whereas Vasilisa, who put him up to it, gets away with it. Throughout the action various characters deliver themselves of sententious statements about life, humanity, and values. Pepel says, "Work, if you like it. What is there to be proud of? If people were to be valued for their work, a horse would be better than any man." When Pepel offers the baron, a pathetic derelict, a bottle of vodka if he will go down on all fours and bark like a dog, the baron observes, "What satisfaction can you get out of this when I know myself that I am now rather worse than you? You ought to

---

63. Russian *meshchanin* (burgher, city dweller) was the official designation of the class of urban artisans and shopkeepers who were not members of the merchant class. It had a pejorative connotation and must sometimes be translated as "philistine."

64. See p. 373.

have tried to make me walk on all fours when I wasn't like you." Satin, a gambler down on his luck, has some famous lines, obviously echoing Nietzsche: "I know what a lie is. He who is faint of heart and lives off the juices of others, he needs lies. . . . Lies are the religion of slaves and masters. Truth is the god of freemen." And later: "*Man!* That is magnificent! That sounds proud!*" This assertion, like the others, is ambiguous, for it comes from the mouth of a man who has reached the depths of human existence. The message of humility, compassion, and forgiveness preached by Luka was rendered equally ambiguous by Gorky's own suggestion, made after 1917, that the introduction of this character was a mistake, which caused some performers of this role to present the pious pilgrim as a cunning charlatan.

Gorky wrote some fifteen plays altogether. Some of them are better than *The Lower Depths*, but none had its success. *Vacationers* (1904) is about the split in the Russian intelligentsia into those who turn bourgeois and those who embrace the ideals of the revolution. *Children of the Sun* (1905) carries the message that free science and creativity are impossible in bourgeois society. *Barbarians* (1905) advances the thesis of the moral barbarity of the bourgeoisie, and that any progress of backward Russia will come through social liberation, not through capitalist progress. *Enemies* (1906), a play with much talk and little action, is noteworthy for its explicit definition of the social situation in Russia as class war. As one of the capitalists in the play puts it, "It is not class struggle; it is a struggle of races—white and black!" *Enemies* is set in a provincial town during a bitter confrontation between management and workers. During a demonstration a worker kills one of the owners with the latter's gun. The

defenders of the existing order are all negative: cold, arrogant, hypocritical, cruel, insensitive, and stupid. The workers and their sympathizers are sensitive, courageous, noble, and wise. They are also confident of their victory.

Evgeny Chirikov (1864–1932), who also had some success with his realist prose fiction, scored several hits as a topical dramatist. His play *Jews* (1904) dealt with the worst blot on imperial Russia's record: the pogrom. *Ivan Mironych* (1905) is a satire on a stagnant educational system; *Peasants* (1906) is yet another piece dealing with the hopeless plight of the Russian countryside. Chirikov viewed the manifold social problems of Russian with humane sympathy, though with a certain pessimism, but certainly without Gorky's doctrinaire intolerance.

Andreev

Leonid Andreev wrote close to thirty plays within ten years and was phenomenally successful with many of them. Most of his plays faded from the repertoire after his death, but some have been revived in Russia as well as in the West, with moderate success. Andreev started with a series of symbolist plays, then moved on to a more realistic psychological manner. *The Life of Man*, staged at the Moscow Art Theater and at Vera Kommissarzhevskaya's theater in 1907, is an Everyman allegory in five acts with a prologue (a somewhat pompous argument of the play), delivered by He, otherwise identified as "someone in gray," who subsequently serves as an occasional commentator. The five acts present man's birth, love and early poverty, wealth, misfortune, and death. The birth is a difficult one, but a baby boy is born, strong and healthy. He becomes an architect who at first cannot sell his plans.

He and his wife are poor but happy: they laugh and dance. Success is just around the corner. Wealth brings luxury, envy, enemies, all shown at a grand ball given by the now-famous architect. Then comes loss of fortune and loss of the couple's son; finally, death in misery and degradation.

Black Masks (1908), *King Hunger* (1908), which depicts the revolt of the masses driven to despair and blind fury, and *Anathema* (1909) were also symbolist morality plays. Anathema is the diabolic principle with traits of Cain, Manfred, and the Nietzschean superman. His antagonist is David Leiser, a poor little Jew, who embodies kindness, compassion, and self-effacement. Their encounters are staged in various allegorical locales, terrestrial as well as celestial. Andreev's psychological plays, such as *Anfisa* (1909), *Gaudeamus* (1910), and *Ekaterina Ivanovna* and *Professor Storitsyn* (both 1912), deal with lust and passion, as well as death and the futility of life, through melodramatic overstatement. They were, in their own time, effective theater.

He Who Gets Slapped: A Performance in Four Acts (1915) is Andreev's most famous play. A circus play, it has great potential for atmosphere. An anonymous gentleman applies for a job with Briquet, director of a provincial circus. He finally gets hired as He Who Gets Slapped, a clown. He falls in love with Consuelo-Veronica, a trick rider. She is the adopted daughter of Count Mancini, an impoverished aristocrat who likes little girls. Mancini is trying to arrange her marriage to Baron Regnard, a fat millionaire. Other circus characters are interested parties to these proceedings: Zinida, Briquet's wife, who is a lion tamer; Jim Jackson, a clown; Alfred Bezano, a jockey; and others. Moreover, an anonymous shadowy gentleman shows up. He apparently has stolen He's book, a huge success, and He's wife and family. The gen-

tleman is He's shadow, the crowd who vulgarizes and debases everything great and noble. In the end He poisons Consuelo, the baron shoots himself, and He takes poison. The melodrama of *He Who Gets Slapped* is good but forgettable theater. Andreev, in his fiction and his drama, is the most striking example in Russian literature of a flashy but second-rate talent rising quickly to fame and fortune, sustaining success for a brief time, then fading into oblivion. Gorky, incidentally, considered himself much inferior to Andreev in talent.

Symbolism and Futurism

Russian symbolist theater carried the dualism of the symbolist vision over onto the stage. Georgy Chulkov, himself a symbolist poet, called Blok's *Showbooth* a "mystic satire" and spoke of Blok's "mystic skepticism."[65] The mood of the Russian symbolist theater is deeply ambiguous. It rejects the old religion and the new religion of positivism alike, and reaches out for an as yet unknown god in whom it will not dare but would passionately like to believe. Such ambiguity was often extended to the plot structure of symbolist plays, for instance, in Blok's *Showbooth*, Sologub's *Triumph of Death*, Annensky's *Thamyras Citharoedus*, and Remizov's *Devil's Comedy*. In Remizov's *Tragedy of Judas, Duke of Iscariot*, the hero's tragedy is counterpointed by the bizarre antics of Zif and Orif. In Kuzmin's *Venetian Madcaps*, tragedy invades commedia dell'arte.

Hippius, Merezhkovsky, Balmont, and other symbolists wrote for the theater, but only Blok and Sologub among the major symbolists wrote plays that were a significant component of their oeuvre. *The Show-*

65. Review of *The Showbooth, Molodaya zhizn'*, 1906, no. 4 (December 27).

booth (1906), staged by Meyerhold at Vera Kommissarzhevskaya's theater, is an allegory of multiple ambiguities. The lyric simpleton Pierrot and his more worldly double, Harlequin, conduct a dialogue—largely of the deaf—with a group of mystics. Its subject is whether a beautiful young woman clad in white is Pierrot's fiancée, Colombina, or death.[66] In the end, Harlequin casually reveals that theirs is a "cardboard fiancée." In Meyerhold's staging, the mystics too were projected as cardboard figures. The action is repeatedly interrupted by the Author, who rushes on stage to complain that his idea of a nice realistic boy-meets-girl play is being perverted. The second scene shows three enamored couples at a masked ball exchanging opaque subtleties. The scene ends in Harlequin's monologue expressing his desire to leave this sad make-believe world for "a happy spring festival" visible through a picture window. He leaps through the window, which turns out to be made of paper. The torn paper reveals the figure of death, with Pierrot walking toward her. As he approaches her, she slowly turns into a live Colombina. The Author now bursts on the scene and welcomes the happy ending, but at this point the props on stage become airborne, the masks scatter in panic, and the Author follows their example. Pierrot is left onstage alone to lament the loss of his cardboard fiancée. *The Showbooth* got a mixed reception. Whistles and catcalls were drowned out by applause. People debated the play's meaning and suggested different interpretations. Some thought that Colombina was the long-awaited but elusive Russian constitution. In retrospect, the symbolic meaning of the play is fairly obvious. It

coincides with the conception, frequently expressed in Blok's poems of that period and anticipated by Solovyov, of the poet who, abandoned by his native inspiration, creates a make-believe world that may "deceive the fools" but leaves him bereft of the ability to communicate with "other worlds." Pierrot is Blok, faithful knight of the Beautiful Lady, who like Harlequin discovers that she is made of cardboard. The symbolist mystics who give her a metaphysical meaning are themselves cardboard figures. This realization leaves Blok-Pierrot heartbroken. In spite of some beautiful lines of poetry, *The Showbooth* is mostly satire, and as such it is quite dated.

The King on the Square (1906) is a short three-act play in which the impending revolution is presented in disguise, along with conventional allegorical figures—the king, the jester, the poet, the builder. The play seems terribly mannered and stilted today. *The Stranger* (1906) is thematically close to the famous poem of the same title. Among its dramatis personae are a poet and an astronomer. In the first scene, there is some talk about "the stranger." In the second, the stranger materializes from a bright star, while the poet changes into the Light-Blue One, a starry-eyed visitor from heaven. The stranger reveals that her name is Maria. In the third scene, Maria appears as a guest at a party. The astronomer is there, announcing the fall of the star Maria. At this point the stranger disappears, and through a window the star shines in renewed splendor. *The Stranger* could not be staged, as the censor found it blasphemous on account of obvious hints at the stranger's identity with the Virgin. It saw several private performances before the revolution. *Song of Fate: A Dramatic Poem* (1908–19) is another dreamlike sequence of "visions." Herman, the hero, leaves his loving wife, Elena, for the myste-

---

66. The *qui pro quo* is partly based on an untranslatable pun. Russian *kosa* is Colombina's braid and death's scythe.

rious and elusive Faina. His pursuit of her ends on a barren snowswept plain, where Faina leaves him. The play has many explicit echoes from the cycles "Faina" and "The Snow Mask," as well as from the Kulikovo cycle. This play has possibilities, and both Vera Kommissarzhevskaya and Meyerhold offered to stage it. But Blok offered it to Stanislavsky, who eventually rejected it.

Rose and Cross (1912–13), set in Languedoc in the thirteenth century, has a real plot. Bertrand, nicknamed the Knight of Misfortune, is a faithful vassal of Count Archimbaut and secretly in love with beautiful Izora, the countess. When she orders him to find the trouvère whose song has left her enthralled, he finds him, but Gaetan (the trouvère) is an old man. As Izora listens to his song, she inadvertently rests her head on the shoulder of her handsome page Aliscan and faints. Soon the castle is attacked by rebellious Albigensians; it is saved only by the heroics of the faithful Bertrand, who suffers a grievous wound. When the countess engages his services to arrange a tryst with Aliscan, he meekly obliges, promising to stand guard and drop his sword to warn the lovers if anybody approaches. When he does drop it in the morning, he is found dead. *Rose and Cross* was sought by Tairov for the Chamber Theater, but Blok gave it to Stanislavsky, who started rehearsals but never got around to producing it.

Aleksei Remizov wrote three original plays: *Devil's Comedy* (1907), *The Tragedy of Judas, Duke of Iscariot* (1098), and *The Comedy of George the Valiant* (1910). He also reworked the folk drama *Tsar Maksimilian* (1918). *Devil's Comedy*, based on a medieval morality play on the struggle between Life and Death, was performed at Kommissarzhevskaya's theater in December 1907 and created a scandal—much as did Blok's *Showbooth. The Tregedy of Judas* was

prepared for staging, but the censor stopped it. It is based on an apocryphal tale that has nothing to do with the biblical Judas. Rather, it is a version of the Oedipus myth set in Pontius Pilate's Jerusalem.

After 1907 Fyodor Sologub wrote several plays, all of them symbolist and well suited to the style of Meyerhold, a friend and kindred spirit. *The Triumph of Death* (1907) is the first of several plays about the ambiguity of life and death. It was Meyerhold's last production at Kommissarzhevskaya's theater. In a prologue, Dulcinea, a serpent-eyed enchantress who is the peasant wench Aldonza to some and Queen Ortruda to others, complains that "spectacle will remain spectacle," failing to become mystery, but announces that she will continue "to fulfill her eternal design" in the play that follows. The play is based on the medieval legend *Berthe au grand pied*. The sorceress Malgista substitutes her beautiful daughter, Algista, for Queen Bertha in King Clodoveg's bedchamber. Lame and pockmarked Bertha is banished from the king's court as the servant girl Algista. But the deception is discovered, and Algista and her son are killed, as Bertha takes her rightful place at the king's side. In the last act Malgista brings Algista and her child back to life. Algista implores Clodoveg, in the name of their mutual love, to undo the evil he has done to her, to leave Bertha and his kingdom behind, and to follow her "to a life of freedom and joy." But the king's self-righteousness prevails over his love. He refuses to follow Algista, who dies a second death, while "King Clodoveg and those around him have turned to stone."

The Gift of the Wise Bees (1907), a version of the myth of Laodamia and Protesilaos (also treated by Annensky in a tragedy, *Laodamia*), is a parable of the triumph of creative imagination over death. The play was banned by the censor on account of a too explicitly homoerotic episode introduced—gratuitously—by Sologub. *Vanka the Butler and the Page Jehan*, a dramatization of the itinerant anecdote about the love of princess and servant, presented two parallel versions, one set in eighteenth-century France, the other in Russia. It was produced by Fyodor Kommissarzhevsky in 1909. Sologub added a third, contemporary, version in 1915. *Hostages of Life*, produced by Meyerhold at the Aleksandrinsky in 1912, was Sologub's greatest theatrical success. It demonstrated that what is beyond "suspension of disbelief" in prose fiction may come off onstage. The play combines Chekhovian realist drama with purely symbolic characters, something Sologub also tried in his novel *Created Legend*. Sologub wrote several more plays, none of which seem to be significant.

Nikolai Evreinov, an innovative director and theorist of the theater, was also a prolific playwright, mostly in the symbolist manner. *A Merry Death* (1908, staged 1909) is a charming Harlequinade and another exercise in the ambiguity of death. Harlequin spends his last hours cheerfully, satisfied that he has gotten all out of life that was to be had: the cup of life is empty.

Evreinov's exercises in "monodrama" are interesting, but were difficult to stage and met with little success. In *Theater of the Soul: A One-Act Monodrama with Prologue* (1910) "the action takes place in the Soul within a span of thirty seconds." The conflict is between three aspects of the Soul, S_1 (the rational), S_2 (the emotional), and S_3 (the subconscious); its object is whether to yield to an impulse to follow the pretty songstress or remain faithful to one's wife. Wife and songstress each have two conflicting images, one that attracts and one that repels the Soul. *Theater of Love* is also set in the mind.

The protagonist is "I." There is also "an inner voice" called "She! She!" and a villain, "my rival." As the mood of "I" changes, the other personas respond by changing accordingly. Lighting and musical effects must be synchronized with these changes, a difficult task. Evreinov's most successful play, *The Main Thing*, was produced after the revolution.

Mikhail Kuzmin was associated with experimental theaters much of his life. A composer of music as well as a poet, he wrote the music for Blok's *Showbooth* and for other plays, including his own. His play *Venetian Madcaps*, staged at a private residence in 1914 (published in 1915), is one of the best symbolist plays and is also another play in which Eros and Thanatos meet. The play is set in eighteenth-century Venice. It has Count Stello's lover, Narcisetto, fall in love with the comedienne Finette, while Finette, who is Harlequin's wife, plans to seduce the unapproachable count. Narcisetto and Stello participate in a pantomime dressed as Harlequin and Colombina. Narcisetto stabs the count and flings his body into a canal to remove the obstacle to his love for Finette. She asks him if he did it for love of her. He answers Yes, but when she says, "You love me, then?" his response is, "I love no one but the count." Finette tells Harlequin of the murder. He addresses the public explaining that the troupe must leave quickly. Finette sings a warm farewell song. The count had had a premonition of death all along. He had said that beauty is found everywhere, whereupon Narcisetto had asked, "Even in death?" The count responded: "Oh my gentle sister Death, uninvited, but always a welcome guest!"

The revival of Greek tragedy in four plays by Innokenty Annensky and two by Vyacheslav Ivanov was an accident in that two major poets of the period happened to be classical philologists. The approach to tragedy is quite different in Annensky and Ivanov. Annensky, the translator of Euripides, chose subjects that had been treated by Euripides and produced very Euripidean tragedies. *Laodamia* (1906) is the best. Laodamia was the bride of Protesilaos, the first Greek killed before Troy. He had left for Troy before he could consummate his marriage, and the gods granted him a return to earth—as a shadow. In Annensky's play, Laodamia burns herself to death to join her husband in Hades. *Thamyras Cytharoedus* (completed 1906, published 1913), a weaker play, did enjoy a scenic success, albeit brief, when staged by Tairov in 1916.

Ivanov's tragedies were a projection of his aesthetic thought, influenced by Nietzsche. Both are classical tragedies in that the hero is destroyed by hubris. But this *hubris* is perceived in terms of Nietzschean aesthetic categories. *Tantalus* (1905) was conceived as a tragedy of plenitude and surfeit, *Prometheus* (1919) as a tragedy of hunger. The plots of both are built on a vertical of ascent and descent. Annensky's tragedies seem less stilted and stylized than Ivanov's, more lyrical and less structured as well. Their verse is fluent and at times it rises to lyric warmth. But on the whole they lack real power, either as drama or as poetry. Ivanov's tragedies are admirable in a cold, academic way but are not suited for the stage.

Futurist drama would have great opportunities in the new medium of film, as Mayakovsky realized in an early article and had occasion to demonstrate after the revolution. The principles of futurist theater were realized, also after the revolution, by Vsevolod Meyerhold. Prerevolutionary futurist theater was limited to four nights at the Petersburg Luna Park Theater, when Mayakovsky's "tragedy" *Vladimir Mayakovsky* and Kruchonykh-Matyushin's

"opera" *Victory over the Sun* were presented to packed houses in December 1913.

Vladimir Mayakovsky, in which Mayakovsky himself played the lead, is a lyric monologue in two acts, the first act set in a hysterically desperate present and the second in a liberated future, with a mocking prologue and an anticlimactic epilogue. The hero, who expresses the moods of the young Mayakovsky's lyric poetry—rebellious swagger, flippant mockery, insufferable boredom, abysmal despair, and oracular melancholy—is supported by a cast of allegorical characters, such as "a man without an eye and a leg," "a man without an ear," "a man without a head," and "an old man with black dry cats (several thousand years old)." The last of these is an inside joke: Mayakovsky liked to say in his public lectures that the ancient Egyptians knew that they could produce electric sparks by stroking dry black cats but had not put electricity to use—much as pre-futurist poets had used some futurist devices without arriving at the real truth of futurism. Some of the allegorical figures deliver long monologues or act as a chorus. "Women with tiny, ordinary, and huge tears" carry together a pile of tears that Mayakovsky gathers up in a suitcase to take to "where in the clutches of infinite grief/a fanatical ocean/eternally/tears his breast/with the fingers of waves." *Vladimir Mayakovsky*, even as theater, was superior to most modernist plays of the period. It was not taken seriously by its audience because it was staged ineptly: the extras were all volunteers who had barely had time to rehearse their roles.

Victory over the Sun, also in two acts, had the advantage of Kazimir Malevich's brilliant abstract sets. Matyushin's music was perceived as off-key Verdi. Kruchonykh's text was more thoroughly absurd, fractured, and incomprehensible than Mayakovsky's. It lacks Mayakovsky's lyric vibrancy and is insufferably flat most of the time. In the first act, futurist heroes proclaim their power and demonstrate it by stabbing and then capturing the sun. The second act, like Mayakovsky's, is set in the future, as mankind adjusts to the strength and lightness of its new condition. The optimistic hubris of *Victory over the Sun* goes with a great deal of heavy-handed grotesquerie and silly language games (in the world of the future all nouns are masculine, so that feminine nouns lose their final *a* and neuter nouns their *o*), all of which is counterproductive to the futurist pathos of the play, as it turns into buffoonery. *Vladimir Mayakovsky* and *Victory over the Sun* were not entirely forgotten: their manner was revived by the *oberiuty* of the 1920s.

Chapter 9

The Soviet Period

Lenin's coup d'état of October 1917 triggered a social revolution that quickly engulfed the country as local soviets (councils) of workers and soldiers, led by Bolshevik activists, seized power throughout Russia. The Bolshevik government, whose trump card was a promise of immediate peace, ceded vast territories to Germany in the peace treaty of Brest-Litovsk, signed March 3, 1918. Upon the collapse of Germany in November 1918, local separatist movements seized control over most of these territories. The republics of Finland, Poland, Lithuania, Latvia, and Estonia successfully declared their independence. Separatist movements also held sway in the Ukraine, Belorussia, and the Caucasus. Counterrevolutionary offensives supported by the Western allies, had the Soviet government teetering on the brink several times, but in the end the Bolsheviks prevailed. Their success was due to the energy with which they implemented "war communism," a program of expropriation of private industry, commerce, housing, and other resources placed in the service of their war effort. Cadres of revolutionary workers were dispatched to the countryside to requisition forcibly grain and other foodstuffs to supply the Red Army and workers of key industrial plants.

The civil war was conducted with great ferocity by both sides. Indiscriminate executions were common. By the time the war was over in 1920, hundreds of thousands of Russians, mostly members of the educated elite, found themselves abroad, in Manchuria, Turkey, Czechoslovakia, Poland, and the Baltic countries, as well as in Western Europe and the Americas. They almost immediately formed communities with political and cultural organizations, journals, and newspapers. Many of these émigrés were to make important contributions to their host countries—the airplane designer Igor Sikorsky, composers Rachmaninoff, Stravinsky, Prokofiev, and Glazunov, painters Larionov, Goncharova, Chagall, and Kandinsky, linguists Nikolai Trubetskoi and Roman Jakobson, the sociologist Pitirim Sorokin, the historian Mikhail Rostovtsev, and Sergei Diaghilev and his Ballets Russes, to name but a few.

Within an amazingly short time the Soviet

regime established a new life-style, morality, and sensibility, at least in the cities. It crushed the Orthodox church, pillar of the old society, closing most churches, confiscating all church property, arresting many priests, and launching an unrelenting antireligious propaganda campaign. The family likewise was weakened by laws making both marriage and divorce perfunctory and by policies that encouraged women to join the work force, leaving their children in the care of a day nursery. Voluntary agencies promoting culture, welfare, and education were abolished and replaced by organs of the Soviet state. And of course the Soviet government never neglected to emphasize, by word and by deed, that it was protecting the interests of the working class, the peasantry, and the "working intelligentsia," in that order, and that all other classes of people, such as clergy, merchants, and kulaks, were "class enemies." Along with this fundamental reorganization of Russian society came an unprecedented reassessment of values. Poverty was now a virtue, as were godlessness, scoffing at the old morality, old customs, holidays, and the whole traditional way of life. New forms of public celebration and public spectacles were introduced. Mass demonstrations with marchers bearing placards and shouting communist slogans, along thoroughfares decorated with red flags, posters, and banners, became a fixture on November 7 (the anniversary of the Bolshevik revolution) and May 1. Other festivals, such as Aviation Day or national and international congresses of the party and its affiliated organizations, offered occasions for similar celebrations. A special form of the mass spectacle was the theatrical reenactment of the October revolution by large groups of people before even larger crowds. "The Storming of the Winter Palace," enacted on November 7,

1920, with thousands of participants and a hundred thousand spectators, was the most famous of these.

The new order brought with it a revolution in the Russian language, as the Marxist political jargon of *class struggle, class enemy, dictatorship of the proletariat, vestiges of capitalism*, and hundreds of other such clichés became common usage. The daily routine of party work added hundreds more. A mushrooming new bureaucracy created a spate of acronyms—SSSR, GPU, Cheka (the political police), Narkom ("people's commissar"), Politruk ("political counselor"), Komsomol ("communist youth organization"), and kolkhoz ("collective farm")—which created an impression of strange futuristic modernity. The new regime made a vigorous effort to fight illiteracy, and millions of Russian adults became literate in the first years of the Soviet regime. With no traditional schooling in the literary language, they proceeded to speak and write the jargon of communist indoctrination as their idiom of social intercourse.

The Sovietization of Russian life brought with it, on the one hand, a set of Western ideas and terms, as well as a modern technological utopia and a frenzied cult of the machine. But on the other hand, it soon nailed shut the window to Europe that the Romanovs had opened. The capital was immediately moved to Moscow and kept there. Foreign travel, tolerated to some extent in the early 1920s, become progressively more difficult and virtually stopped in the 1930s. Russians educated under the Soviets would no longer know foreign languages, unless they were trained specialists. The importation of foreign books and periodicals was gradually reduced to almost nil, and many works of modern Western literatures remained untranslated for decades.

The New Economic Policy (NEP), instituted by Lenin in 1921, was a step back from war communism. While industry, communication, and transportation remained nationalized, a modicum of private enterprise was given legal sanction and administrative toleration in farming, handicrafts, the service industries, and retail trade. The NEP was a relative success in that it restored day-to-day living to almost prewar conditions, except for a terrible housing shortage in the cities. Stabilization of the ruble as a negotiable internal currency was a significant achievement. Foreign trade was also resumed, though in a severely limited way.

The NEP created a new intellectual climate. The Soviet regime was there to stay and felt inclined to engage the services of those who, though not among its natural supporters, were willing to cooperate with it. These included, for the time being, middle peasants (*serednyaki*), artisans who worked with their own tools, and intellectuals—artists, actors, filmmakers, musicians, and writers. In describing these people, Leon Trotsky, who took an active interest in literature and commented on it perceptively, though from a narrow doctrinaire viewpoint, coined the term "fellow travelers" (*poputchiki*) of the revolution. The Soviet government really had no choice but to tolerate their activity, for it could hardly function without the cooperation of those engineers, economists, physicians, scientists, accountants, agronomists, teachers, and other trained professionals who had not left the country. In the course of the 1920s many of them resumed their work in their former positions. This was also true of secondary school teachers and university professors. Soviet universities and technical schools were asked to train many thousands of men and women who gained admission by virtue of their "social background" or their work in the party or the Komsomol,

but subject matter and quality of instruction remained essentially unchanged, although at least lip service to Marxism was expected in the humanities and social sciences. The quality of Russian literary and linguistic scholarship remained high into the 1930s. As for literature, the Soviet regime, in a "resolution" of the press section of the Central Committee of the Communist party dated July 1, 1925, declared itself uncommitted to any particular grouping and willing to offer help and guidance to any deserving group or individual.

The NEP period witnessed the coexistence of a relatively broad spectrum of literary groupings, all of which professed to be loyal to the Soviet regime but held divergent views on the relation between art and society. Avant-garde groups like Lef (Left Front of the Arts) offered to put revolutionary modernist art at the service of the social revolution. Radical proletarian groups like October and Smithy, heirs to the Proletkult (Proletarian Culture) movement of the war communism years, insisted on seeing literature primarily as a tool of ongoing class struggle and felt that literature should seek the guidance of the party in all questions of ideology and topical political issues. Pereval (Divide, or Watershed), a less radical group, took the Plekhanovian position that a genuine artist's intuition could be trusted to mirror reality correctly and that an honest representation of reality was in the best interest of the people, the victorious proletariat, and the party. Pereval welcomed works by writers of nonproletarian background, provided they faced Soviet reality without a counterrevolutionary bias. Peasant writers had their own organization, the All-Union (or All-Russian) Association of Peasant Writers (it changed its name several times), whose membership was second only to that of the Russian Association of Proletarian Writers (RAPP). Its journal, *Land of the Soviets*, was allowed to exist until 1932.

Among several more informal groupings of writers, the Serapion Brothers stand out. Evgeny Zamyatin was the mentor of the group, and of the ten Serapions, Konstantin Fedin, Vsevolod Ivanov, Venyamin Kaverin, Mikhail Zoshchenko, Lev Lunts, and Nikolai Tikhonov went on to become major figures in Soviet literature. Formed early in 1921, the Serapion Brothers, so named after E. T. A. Hoffmann's *Die Serapionsbrüder*, professed their dedication to creative individuality and excellence of craftsmanship. Their program was singularly unsuited to the times, and they disbanded before the decade was over.

Equally informal, ephemeral, and rich in talent was the so-called Formal school, a group of linguists, literary scholars, and writers who concentrated on the study of literary theory and the creative process. It, too, ceased to exist by 1930. In the 1920s informal circles of intellectuals of an openly nonconformist mentality still existed, such as Petrograd's Resurrection (1917–28), which at one time had no fewer than two hundred members. Its professed concern was to attempt a fusion of religion and communism after the Christian Socialist tradition of Lamennais. The historian and religious thinker Georgy Fedotov (1886–1951), who edited the circle's journal *Free Voices* (1918), emigrated to France in 1925 and eventually to the United States, where he left a rich corpus of works on Russian religion and spirituality. Most of the other members of the group were arrested in 1928 or 1929 on charges of having plotted the "resurrection" of the tsarist regime and disappeared in the prison camps of the Stalin era.

Stalin's launching of his first five-year plan

in 1928 and forced collectivization of agriculture in 1929 augured the end of the relative autonomy of Soviet intellectual life under the NEP. The enthusiastic support that the proletarian writers of RAPP and the avantgarde of Lef gave to Stalin's projects did not prevent him from decreeing the abolition of all independent groupings, regardless of their professed loyalty, and their replacement by a single Union of Soviet Writers on the strength of a resolution of the Press Section of the Central Committee of the Communist Party, dated April 23, 1932. This meant that proletarians, peasants, and fellow travelers were now on an equal footing. It also meant an end to all independent publishing houses and journals.

The first All-Union Congress of Soviet Writers, in August 1934, witnessed the institution of socialist realism as the sole correct method in literature. It remained the official doctrine and only sanctioned method of Soviet art and literature for the next fifty years. Soviet literature became a de facto organ of the government. Members of the Union of Soviet Writers enjoyed such privileges as a secure and relatively high income, a chance to win the munificent Stalin Prize and other state prizes, comfortable club facilities in major cities, and attractive vacation homes. In return, they were obliged to tailor their works to the requirements of party policies and refrain from undue formal experimentation. On those occasions when their work, commonly owing to changes in the party line, would find itself in conflict with the party's position, they would have to go through a ritual of abject "self-criticism," rewrite the offending texts, or submit to substantive editorial changes. The rigid regimentation of Soviet literature caused some of the leading writers and poets to withdraw from creative writing and concentrate on translation, literature for children, scholarship, and hackwork for the press or film. Akhmatova, Mandelshtam, Pasternak, Olesha, Babel, and Bulgakov were cases in point.

Stalin's purges of the 1930s hit the literary community hard, Since victims were chosen by a variety of different criteria, writers of all social and ideological colorations were affected. Many peasant poets—Nikolai Klyuev, Sergei Klychkov, Pavel Vasilyev, Pyotr Oreshin—perished because they were suspected of being kulak sympathizers. Proletarian poets, Old Bolsheviks, and activists of the October group were charged with "leftist deviationism" and Trotskyism. Aleksandr Tarasov-Rodionov, one of the organizers of the October group, Aleksandr Voronsky, editor of *Red Virgin Soil*, Leopold Auerbach, editor of *On Literary Post*, the journal of RAPP, and G. Lelevich (pseudonym of Labori Gilelevich Kalmanson), one of the more radical ideologues of the October group, all died in the purges. The casualty rate was also high among the avant-garde. Sergei Tretyakov, Vsevolod Meyerhold, Daniil Kharms, and Aleksandr Vvedensky were among the victims. Other major figures who perished were Isaak Babel, Osip Mandelshtam, Boris Pilnyak, Ivan Kataev, and Vladimir Kirshon. Some survived years of imprisonment and lived to see at least their partial rehabilitation: Nikolai Zabolotsky, literary theorist Valerian Pereverzev, critic and scholar Yulian Oksman, and a few others. Some writers whose social background, political past, and writings might have seemed anything but auspicious for survival not only survived but flourished under Stalin. They include Aleksei Tolstoi, who had emigrated after the revolution but returned in 1923; Ilya Ehrenburg, of bourgeois background, with "decadent"

leanings and a record of shuttling back and forth between the Soviet Union and the West; and Nikolai Tikhonov, a onetime member of the Serapion Brothers.

The German invasion in June 1941 had a mixed effect on Russian literature. Russian writers for once had a cause with which they could honestly identify. Censorship was relaxed during the war. Many writers worked as war correspondents, and some were killed in the war: Aleksandr Afinogenov, Arkady Gaidar, Evgeny Kataev, Yury Krymov. Some were displaced to the West as part of the "second wave" of emigration. The war provided material for a generation of poets and writers and became a subject of controversy, when controversy became possible, after Stalin's death.

The war was barely over when Stalin ordered a halt to the relaxation of restrictions on writers. His aide, Andrei Zhdanov, who had directed the Congress of Soviet Writers in 1934, now cracked down on deviations from socialist realism and made an example of the journals *Leningrad* and *Zvezda*, singling out the poet Akhmatova and the satirist Zoshchenko as the objects of his ire. The editors of the journals were removed, and Akhmatova and Zoshchenko were expelled from the Union of Soviet Writers.

The years between the end of the war and Stalin's death in 1953 were the darkest in all the history of modern Russian literature. With large parts of the country in ruins, its economy unable to convert from military to civilian needs, much of the rural population living in bleak poverty, and millions of citizens languishing in prison camps, the party line had it that socialism had been fully attained in the Soviet Union, which was now on its way to communism. A corollary of this absurd position was so-called conflictless literature, which celebrated the achievements of Stalin and the party in what amounted to literary Potemkin villages. Authors were rewarded with generous Stalin prizes, but their novels lay unread on the shelves of bookstores or libraries and their plays were staged to half-empty theaters. As Aleksandr Tvardovsky later put it, in the poem *Distance beyond Distance* (1960), "And all of it so like or similar/To that which may or ought to be,/But as a whole so nauseating,/It makes you scream at the top of your voice." This situation acquired a potential for permanence even beyond Stalin's reign, for almost the entire generation of writers to enter Russian literature in the decade after Stalin's death were alumni of the Gorky Literary Institute, which prepared promising young writers for their profession. This explains why even writers who eventually developed into "dissidents"— Yury Trifonov, for example—began their careers with works of orthodox socialist realism.

The last years of Stalin's tyranny were marked by the cold war, a tightening of the iron curtain between East and West, and a campaign against "kowtowing before the West" and "rootless cosmopolitans," that is, anyone who in his work or private life had developed any ties with the West. Often "rootless cosmopolitan" was simply a code name for "Jewish intellectual." In the study of literature, the denunciation of kowtowing before the West discouraged all comparative studies that might suggest any Western influence in Russian literature. The historical-comparative school of Aleksandr Veselovsky (1838–1906), who ten years earlier had been celebrated as a great Russian scholar, was now declared to be the main progenitor of kowtowing before the West. Such venerable scholars as Eichenbaum, Zhirmunsky, and Propp were forced to re-

nounce publicly Veselovsky's ideas and the "mistakes" committed in their own works.

The thaw after Stalin's death had its ups and downs. Its first stage, starting in 1953, was marked by the publication of several articles and pieces of fiction directly or indirectly calling for more sincerity in literature. Among these, an essay by Vladimir Pomerantsev (b. 1907), "On Sincerity in Literature," which appeared in the December 1953 issue of *Novy mir*, and a short novel, *The Thaw* (1954), by Ilya Ehrenburg, received the widest attention. The first thaw lasted for only a year, as the new leadership of the party put a stop to it. Aleksandr Tvardovsky, editor of *Novy mir*, whose journal was a beacon of liberal tendencies throughout the post-Stalin years, was fired in 1954. (He was reinstated as editor in 1958.) The second thaw was triggered by Khrushchev's "secret speech" of February 25, 1956, at the Twentieth Party Congress, in which he exposed some of Stalin's crimes. It opened up, albeit slowly, the topic of innocent people executed or detained in prison camps and the return of survivors to a new life. Tvardovsky's *Distance beyond Distance* (1950–60), Viktor Nekrasov's *Kira Georgievna* (1961), and other works that brought up this topic did so warily. The most significant work of the second thaw, the novel *Not by Bread Alone* (1956), by Vladimir Dudintsev (b. 1918), was in every respect a good socialist realist novel (the plot revolves around a new process in the production of drainage pipes), yet it had for its villains not class enemies or foreign agents but high-ranking functionaries of scientific and government institutions. The second thaw was cut short by the Hungarian uprising of November 1956. The new freeze caused the reversal of a decision concerning publication of Boris Pasternak's novel *Doctor Zhivago*, which then appeared in the

West in 1957, creating an international incident. The third thaw was initiated by the Twenty-second Party Congress, in October 1961, which marked a new start in Khrushchev's effort to free Soviet society of the legacy of Stalinism. This time a new generation of writers and poets, born in the 1930s and without an adult memory of the horrors of war or Stalin's reign of terror, made a decisive break with the canon of socialist realism. Abandoning the heroic and celebratory manner of the Stalin era, the young poets and writers of the early 1960s turned to moods of pensive introspection, inquisitive contemplation of nature and society, and a critical attitude toward the axioms of communist ideology. A miscellany of sketches, stories, poetry, and essays, *Pages from Tarusa* (1961), edited by Konstantin Paustovsky, acted as a manifesto of a "quiet school" that turned away from the blustering rhetoric of socialist realism.

The most significant work of the period, Aleksandr Solzhenitsyn's *One Day in the Life of Ivan Denisovich*, a short novel that appeared in *Novy mir* in November 1962, is set in a prison camp. (Solzhenitsyn himself had served eight years in a camp.) This work and a few other short pieces that Solzhenitsyn was allowed to publish made the point not only that the inmates of Soviet prison camps were for the most part innocent of any crime, but also that official Soviet policies contradicted the innate moral sense of an honest Russian man or woman.

Beginning in the 1960s, most but not all writers who had perished in Stalin's purges were "posthumously rehabilitated," and their works, in some cases, were again made available. Works that had never appeared in the Soviet Union but were known in the West were now published, often after much bureaucratic wrangling. The publication of memoirs in which these writers were freely and fondly mentioned, such as Ehrenburg's *People, Years, Life* (1961–65), contributed to the process of rehabilitation. The third thaw ended with Khrushchev's fall in 1964. That year Iosif Brodsky, a young poet, was arrested and tried for "parasitism," although his poetry, while not socialist realist, was quite apolitical. In 1965 writers Yuly Daniel and Andrei Sinyavsky were arrested and put on trial for having published works in the West under the pseudonyms Nikolai Arzhak and Abram Tertz, respectively. All three served time in labor camps. In 1966 dissident writer Valery Tarsis (b. 1906), who had been committed to a mental hospital in 1962 after he had asked to be allowed to emigrate, was stripped of his citizenship and permitted to leave the Soviet Union. Subsequently a host of other writers, including Solzhenitsyn, Sinyavsky, Brodsky, Nekrasov, and Aksyonov, were either deported from the Soviet Union or allowed to leave, signaling a new episode in the history of Russian literature, the third wave of emigration. Once again, many of Russia's leading writers were in exile.

Literary Theory, Criticism, Schools, and Groupings

The period of revolution, civil war, and the NEP was dominated by politically oriented ideas. It also however, saw a carryover of several movements that had started before the revolution. Some of these, like futurism and constructivism, jumped on the bandwagon of the revolution, assuming that their aesthetic radicalism could be synchronized with the political radicalism of the Bolsheviks. Others, like imagism, were clearly irrelevant to the large-scale events sweeping the country. Still others, like the Formal and Sociological schools of literary studies, believed that they were in step with the ideology of the Soviet regime, but were stopped in their tracks as the regime turned against them.

There were also ideas and groups that were obviously incompatible with Soviet ideology and could only lead a brief and precarious existence. Scythianism, for example, was based on the notion that Russia is defined by being half-Asian and half-European. This idea had cropped up variously in the works of Vladimir Solovyov, the symbolists (Bely in particular), and the futurists (especially Khlebnikov). Scythianism meant an affirmation of Russia's Asian identity—savage, chaotic, but dynamic. In an essay, "Scythians" (1918), Evgeny Zamyatin defined the Scythian as an eternal nomad in permanent revolt against the constraints of civilization and hence a born revolutionary. In 1917 and 1918 a group of writers whose theorist was the critic R. V. Ivanov-Razumnik (1878–1946) called themselves Scythians. Andrei Bely, Sergei Esenin, and Nikolai Klyuev belonged to the movement at one time. Two volumes of an almanac, *Scythians*, appeared in 1917 and 1918. The image of the Russian revolution as an eruption of elemental, chaotic powers, as presented in some works of the early 1920s, reflected Scythian ideas. These ideas were aired among Russian émigrés in the 1920s, who saw the Soviet regime as a manifestation of the "Asian" component of Russian culture. A "Eurasian" theory of Russian civilization, as embraced by critic Dmitry Svyatopolk-Mirsky (1890–1939), linguist Nikolai Trubetskoi, historian Georgy Vernadsky, and others, was another version of Scythianism.

Cosmism, another ephemeral strain, was close to the leftist avant-garde and the Proletkult movement of the war communism years, though cosmic moods and cosmic imagery were prominent even in mystic symbolism and in cubo-futurism. Cosmism came into its own in the revolutionary poetry of the first years of the Soviet regime, when proletarian poets like Ivan Filipchenko (1887–1939), Vasily Aleksandrovsky (1897–1934), and Mikhail Gerasimov (1889–1939) celebrated the revolution as a cosmic event, using appropriate solar and stellar imagery in their dithyrambic effusions. The initiator of cosmism as a school was Vadim Bayan (pseudonym of Vladimir Sidorov), a minor ego- and cubo-futurist, who was later immortalized as the "bard" Oleg Bayan in Mayakovsky's *Bedbug*.

The program of Russian imagism was developed for the most part by Vadim Shershenevich (1893–1942), a well-read, intelligent, and industrious littérateur, though only a second-rate poet. Shershenevich was initially associated with ego-futurism, writing the first comprehensive survey of futurism, *Futurism without a Mask* (1913). He was a key figure in the short-lived Mezzanine of Poetry and one of the few Russian futurists to welcome Marinetti on his visit to Russia in 1914. He translated Heine, Verlaine, Laforgue, Rilke, and Marinetti and was intensely committed to a "modernist" view of poetry. Late in 1918 he became the founder and main theorist of a group of poets and artists who called themselves *imazhinisty* (apparently derived from the Italian *immagine*). Among its members were the "peasant poet" Sergei Esenin, Anatoly Marienhof, Ryurik Ivnyov, formerly an ego-futurist, and playwright Nikolai Erdman. The group issued a declaration that appeared in the newspaper *Land of the Soviets* in February 1919. Subsequently Shershenevich published a programmatic essay, $2 \times 2 = 5$ (1920), which stated the positions of imagism vigorously, though somewhat inchoately. Esenin's essay "The Keys of Mary," which also appeared in 1920, is dated 1918 and seems to have been pre-imagist. "Mary" is a metaphor for "soul," current in folk poetry. Esenin's rather confused essay advances the view that the pristine mythology of a nation, expressed in its songs and ornaments, should remain the foundation of its art and poetry. In an essay of 1921, "Living [*byt*] and Art," Esenin warned his fellow imagists against becoming virtuosi divorced from life. But his concern with the image (*obraz*) in its various manifestations is distinctly imagist. Marienhof published a volume of essays, *Rowdy Island: Imagism* (1920). The imagists put out four issues of a journal, *Hotel for Travelers in the Beautiful* (1922–24), and their publishing house, Imagists, produced several miscellanies.

The imagists denounced every modernist group that had preceded them and vigorously attacked the aesthetics of both the leftist avant-garde and Proletkult, the former for surrendering art to political utilitarianism, the latter for artistic banality and lack of originality. Imagism prided itself on being apolitical, classless, and universal. The imagists stressed their individualism as against the futurists' collectivist mentality. The theory of imagism is based largely on Marinetti's aesthetics of power and speed, energy-laden chaos, and simultaneity (the contraction of movement into a blurred stasis, as in the "simultaneous" paintings of the cubists and Malevich). In imagist poetics this meant metaphors based on the similarity of wholly unrelated objects, such as Esenin's "Like a golden frog, the moon/Lies sprawling on the quiet waters./Like apple blossoms, the white/Has spilled all over my father's beard." ("I've left my native home," 1918). It also meant, in some imagist poems (Shershenevich's in particular), direct juxta-

position of images without a syntactic bond, cultivation of noun phrases, and the "destruction of grammar" (elimination of inflection). The central concept of imagist poetics is the the "word-image," a word that elicits rich sensual representations while ignoring logos, metaphysics, and even the transsensual meaning pursued by the futurists. Imagism wants none of the symbolists' "inner vision." A word-image should be not so much a symbol of the world as a part of it. A poem should be an uninterrupted sequence of images, as Marinetti had taught. A consequence of this view was the reduction of poetry to a static art form, analogous to the romantic view of architecture as frozen music.

Imagism insisted on the independence of art from, and its superiority to, real life. "A poet," said Shershenevich, "is a madman who finds himself sitting in a blazing skyscraper and calmly sharpens his crayons so he can make a drawing of the conflagration. As soon as he takes to helping those who are trying to put out the fire he becomes a citizen and ceases being a poet."[1] Hence imagism was determined to "sweep form clean of the dust of content," that is, of any intellectual or moral message. Obviously this program had no future in the land of the Soviets.

Russian constructivism initially developed in architecture and the visual arts. Its principal exponent was the painter, sculptor, architect, and designer Vladimir Tatlin (1885–1953). The basic principle of constructivism was emphasis on economy, simplicity, and expediency in art. Constructivist art was functional. Though aesthetically attractive, it meant to serve a practical

1. "Timely Meditations," *Hotel for Travelers in Beauty*, no. 4 (1924).

purpose. Constructivist artists designed furniture, clothing, footwear, and other consumer goods. The artists' main concern was to utilize their materials—steel, wood, textiles, leather—as efficiently as possible. The contructivist aesthetic quickly spread to poetry, theater, and film. Mayakovsky, Aseev, Kamensky, and many others enthusiastically produced pointedly utilitarian verse. Mayakovsky affirmed the utilitarian nature of his art many times, in verse and in prose. In one of his finest poems, "Brooklyn Bridge," a paean to modern technology, he welcomes the ascendancy of "construction" over "style." In the theater, Meyerhold's principle of biomechanics applied the ideas of constructivism to the stage. In film, the central role assigned to the technique of montage was a response to the same principles.

Lef, the journal of the leftist avant-garde, became the principal outlet for the new utilitarian aesthetic theory and its practical application. *Lef* theorists Viktor Shklovsky, Osip Brik, and Boris Arvatov believed that imaginative fiction had outlived its usefulness and that the future belonged to "literature of fact" (the title of a *Lef* miscellany of 1929) and to "factographic" genres such as reportage, travelogue, diary, and popular science, all of which were cultivated brilliantly by Shklovsky. Filmmakers associated with *Lef*, such as Sergei Eisenstein and Dziga Vertov, promoted the documentary and the newsreel and advertised the propaganda value of film, much as Mayakovsky and Tretyakov took for granted that the theater should be an organ of political debate and of consciousness raising. Their plays were written as vehicles of indoctrination and political polemic. Meyerhold was delighted to stage Mayakovsky's *Mystery-Bouffe* (1918), clearly a piece of *agitprop* (agitation and propaganda). He allowed the walls

of his theater to be covered in posters enhancing the political message of Mayakovsky's *Bathhouse* (1929). Obviously he and Mayakovsky agreed that the performance was a political as well as a theatrical event.

A constructivist literary theory emerged in the mid-1920s, in connection with the formation of the Literary Center of Constructivists, whose theorist was Kornely Zelinsky and among whose members were the poets Eduard Bagritsky, Ilya Selvinsky, and Vera Inber. In its "Declaration" (1924) the Center stated its positions vis-à-vis *Lef* as well as more conservative populist and nationalist tendencies. Subsequently it published several miscellanies under such titles as *Gosplan of Literature* (1925)[2] and *Business* (1929).[3] The constructivists advocated "Soviet Westernism" and "Americanism," seeing progress in terms of a rational technological utopia. Their positive values were speed, precision, intensity, and expediency. The poetics of constructivism was based on the idea that poetry should be a tool for reducing the complexities of a modern world to simple terms accessible to the masses. Poetry was to be one way to transform the world into a manageable structure and an instance of the triumph of technology over nature. The poetics of constructivism had two branches. One, advanced and practiced mainly by Aleksei Chicherin, emphasized the principle of "constructive distribution of material and maximal charge of utilization per unit," leading to a highly compressed style and "dematerialization" of verse, that is, frequent replacement of natural language by graphic symbols. The other, whose principal exponent was Ilya Selvin-

2. *Gosplan* means "state plan."
3. In the original, *Biznes*, transliterated from the English.

sky, advocated and practiced an iconic approach to the form of poetry, meaning that the lexicon, sound structure, and rhythm of a literary text should be isomorphic to its meaning. For example, Selvinsky's poem "The Thief" is composed entirely in thieves' cant.

Constructivism lasted until 1930, when Zelinsky published "The End of Constructivism," an article in which he cravenly denounced his earlier positions.[4] Chicherin had withdrawn from the Literary Center of Constructivists even earlier. Both went on to become successful literary scholars and critics.

Revolutionary enthusiasm generated the Proletkult movement, whose ideological father was Aleksandr Bogdanov.[5] Its guiding principle was that the victorious proletariat should replace the old bourgeois culture with its own proletarian culture. Groups of workers under the leadership of communist activists formed literary workshops, art studios, and theatrical ensembles to realize this idea. Established poets such as Bely, Bryusov, and Khodasevich volunteered to act as instructors. Members of the Proletkult worked as war correspondents and on the staff of frontline newspapers during the civil war. Ivan Kataev's novella *The Poet* (1929) tells the story of one such activist of the Proletkult.

The Proletarian Culture movement produced a school of so-called proletarian poetry with a distinctive style.[6] Some proletarian poets proclaimed the triumph of the proletariat in terms of a demand for the abolition of the old culture and its art.

Raphael, a favorite target of the "men of the 1860s," was again singled out for destruction.

Even though the program of Proletarian Culture largely coincided with that of the leftist avant-garde (Mayakovsky called for the "shooting" of Rastrelli, architect of the Petersburg Winter Palace, partly because it was good for a pun: *rasstrelyat'* means "shoot"), relations between the two movements were strained from the outset. The sophisticated professionals of the avant-garde belittled the Proletkultists' conventionally pedestrian craftsmanship, asserting that a revolutionary content required a revolutionary form. The Proletkultists, in turn, pointed to the bourgeois origins of their opponents and charged that they represented an effete and perverse bohemianism rather than the honest working masses. Surprisingly, the leadership of the party turned against the Proletarian Culture movement, without by any means endorsing the avant-garde. In a decree, "On Proletkult Groups," of December 1, 1920, its activities were branded "deviationist" violations of party discipline. The reasons for this action were twofold. There were Lenin's old disagreements with Bogdanov and Bogdanov's idea of establishing a communist religion, and there was the assumption among the party's leadership, Trotsky in particular, that the dictatorship of the proletariat preceding socialism would be too short to warrant the building of a proletarian culture. A further, pragmatic consideration was that the Proletkult had eighty thousand activists at work without any direct control by the party. Some activists of the Proletkult founded independent radical groups such as the Smithy (1920–32) and October (1922–32) and eventually resurfaced in RAPP. Many joined the ranks of disgruntled old Bolsheviks who

4. Published in *On Literary Guard*, no. 20 (1930).

5. See p. 381.

6. See p. 540.

were turned off by the NEP and the government's courting of fellow travelers. The official biographies of Proletkult poets tend to end in the words, "Unlawfully repressed in the 1930s, posthumously rehabilitated."

October was formed in 1922 in Moscow by a group of communists who believed in a literature that would reflect the viewpoint and interests of a class-conscious proletariat. Since its members were also active members of either the party or the Komsomol, they believed that they deserved the undivided support of the party. The group founded two journals, *On Guard* (1923) and *October* (1924). *On Guard* became the ideological and critical organ of the October group. The "on-guardists" (*napostovtsy*), led by the journal's editors, G. Lelevich (1901–45), Semyon Rodov, and Boris Volin, carried on a running battle with *Lef* and *Red Virgin Soil*, organ of the Pereval group. They took the position that only proletarian writers should be given a voice in Soviet literature and that fellow travelers, particularly those with a bourgeois bohemian past like the futurists of *Lef*, should not be trusted. When a resolution of the Press Section of the Central Committee of the Communist party (July 1, 1925) condemned this position, chiding the on-guardists for their "factionalism" and instructing communist organizations to facilitate the integration of deserving fellow travelers of peasant and intelligentsia origins into Soviet cultural life by meeting them with "tact and understanding," the October group split in two. A majority decided to abide by the party's decision and founded a new journal, *On Literary Guard*, in 1926. Its editorial board included Leopold Auerbach (Averbakh), Vladimir Kirshon, Aleksandr Fadeev, Yury Libedinsky, and Vladimir Ermilov. *On Literary Guard* met the issue that had been the Achilles' heel of proletarian

literature since its inception, that of poor craftsmanship, by calling for more attention to literary form, more-sophisticated psychological motivation, and selective use of the cultural heritage of the pre-Soviet past. The art of Lev Tolstoi was singled out as an example to young Soviet writers. Such works of the October group as *The Rout* by Fadeev or *Birth of a Hero* (1930) by Libedinsky were products of this new attitude. *On Literary Guard*, however, as an organ of RAPP (1928–32), also remained true to its proletarian identity. The baiting of Voronsky and the Pereval group continued, as did the campaign against *Lef* (now *New Lef*). RAPP was well on its way to eliminating all rival groups in 1930 when *Lef* folded and Mayakovsky applied for membership in RAPP. In his suicide note Mayakovsky regretted not to have "slugged it out with Ermilov," one of RAPP's more obtuse ideologues. Meanwhile the radical left wing of the October group, known as Litfront, led by Lelevich, Rodov, and Aleksandr Bezymensky, persisted in its intransigent attitude, although the policies of the party were pointing toward abandoning the world revolution in favor of "building socialism in one country," the Soviet Union.

The abolition of all independent literary groupings and the creation of the Union of Soviet Writers in 1932 put an end to all debate. The journal *October* became the organ of the Union of Soviet Writers. Some members of RAPP—Fadeev and Ermilov, for example—went on to flourish as functionaries of the literary establishment under Stalin. Others, like Kirshon, Auerbach, and Lelevich, perished in the purges of the 1930s. Traits of what might be called a proletarian mystique, however, continued to be a factor in the literature of socialist realism. The principle of socialist realism that made the moral character of a novel's or play's dramatis personae depend on their social class, and their plot on a conflict of social classes such as kulak versus landless peasant, was a legacy of the proletarian movement.

Pereval developed in the winter of 1923–24 around the journal *Red Virgin Soil* and published its last miscellany, *Contemporaries*, in 1932. A manifesto of Pereval published in *Red Virgin Soil* in 1927 was signed by fifty-six writers, among them Eduard Bagritsky, Andrei Platonov, Mikhail Svetlov, Artyom Vesyoly, Ivan Kataev, Mikhail Prishvin, Anna Karavaeva, Abram Lezhnev, and Aleksandr Voronsky. Most of them were members of the Communist party or the Komsomol. Many, like Voronsky, Vesyoly, Bagritsky, and Platonov, were Old Bolsheviks and veterans of the civil war. The guiding principles of Pereval were formulated by the critics Aleksandr Voronsky (1884–1943), Abram Lezhnev (pseudonym of Abram Gorelik, 1893–1938), and Dmitry Gorbov (b. 1894). As professed Marxists, the theorists of Pereval assumed that "consciously or unconsciously a scholar or artist fills orders which he has been given by his social class" (Voronsky), but they also joined Belinsky and Plekhanov in believing in the cognitive powers of an artist's intuition. They had faith in the new art of their age and its ability to grasp the "new truth of life," rejecting RAPP's position according to which literature needed the guidance of the party. The theorists of Pereval also rejected the constructivist aesthetics of Lef. Pereval's historical optimism had it that an objective approach to reality served the interests of a young and victorious proletariat better than the shrill hyperbole of Mayakovsky's propaganda "odes," RAPP's doctrinaire class consciousness, or the futuristic "goal-directedness" (*tseleustremlyonnost'*) of both.

As the NEP approached its end, it became clear that Pereval would be among the losers under Stalin. Voronsky was dismissed from his post as editor of *Red Virgin Soil* in 1927 and by 1928 members of Pereval had begun to defect to RAPP. Many, including Kataev, Lezhnev, Vesyoly, and Voronsky, perished in the purges of the 1930s. The principles of Pereval experienced a renaissance after Stalin's death. Victims of the purges were rehabilitated and some of their works reprinted.

Many Russian avant-garde writers and artists welcomed the 1917 revolution in the belief that the social and political upheaval would release a powerful revolution in the arts and letters. There arose a movement that identified itself as Left Art (*levoe iskusstvo*). The Academy of Arts was abolished in April 1918 and the Fine Arts Division (IZO) of the Soviet Commissariat of Education supported spontaneously formed studios of the Left Art movement, such as Art of the Young (IMO), the Petrograd Free Studios (Svomas), the Moscow Higher Technical-Artistic Studios (Vkhutemas), and Vsevolod Meyerhold's State Theatrical Institute (Gitis), as well as a group of futurist poets who contributed their work to *Art of the Commune* (1918–19), organ of IZO. Such avant-garde artists as Vasily Kandinsky, Marc Chagall, Kazimir Malevich, Vladimir Tatlin, and Lyubov Popova enthusiastically participated in the work of these groups. In 1920 the communist leadership withdrew its support from Left Art. Avant-garde art and theater, which under adverse material conditions had produced innovative art of remarkable quality, were on the wane from here on. Chagall, Kandinsky, and other first-rate artists left Russia.

In 1922 Left Art reconstituted itself as the Left Front of Art (Lef), a loose association of futurist poets, formalist critics, and constructivist artists, whose organs would be the journals *Lef* (1923–25) and *New Lef* (1927–28). Among the members of this group were poets Vladimir Mayakovsky, Nikolai Aseev, Vasily Kamensky, Semyon Kirsanov, and Boris Pasternak, critics and theorists Osip Brik, Nikolai Chuzhak, Boris Arvatov, Boris Eichenbaum, and Viktor Shklovsky, playwrights Sergei Tretyakov and Nikolai Erdman, filmmakers Dziga Vertov and Sergei Eisenstein, theater director Vsevolod Meyerhold, and artist Aleksandr Rodchenko. Lef embraced a utilitarian aesthetic emphasizing the conception of literature as a craft in the service of Soviet society and frankly advocating and practicing poster art. Significantly, members of the Left Art movement cultivated the most modern media of the day: film, radio, and billboard advertising. It was opposed to the "psychologism" of RAPP writers such as Gladkov and Fadeev, asserting that it was the task of the new art to communicate facts and progressive ideas as directly as possible, but it also combatted the degeneration of party slogans and indoctrination into tired clichés.

In spite of Lef's wholehearted support of Stalin's five-year plan and collectivization of agriculture, it was clear by 1929 that its days were numbered. Mayakovsky tried to salvage the independence of Left Art by founding a new group, Ref (Revolutionary Front of Art), but in vain. In 1930 he joined RAPP, whose functionaries welcomed him coldly, suggesting that he would have to prove himself a worthy member of their organization. Little of the aesthetic of Lef survived the 1920s, although Mayakovsky was soon declared a Soviet classic. The socialist realism of the Stalin era meant a return to conservative literary and artistic forms in Soviet literature, theater, film, and art. The struggle of Left Art against the customary, the pretty, and the flabby, and for a lean, pointed, and rational art proved futile, ulti-

mately not because of Stalin's conventional tastes or the reactionary policies of the party but because the Soviet masses were not ready for the art of the avant-garde.

The basic traits of Khlebnikovian cubo-futurism were revived by a group of young avant-garde poets in Leningrad toward the end of the NEP. After several abortive efforts to organize what was left of a radical avant-garde, Daniil Kharms and Aleksandr Vvedensky formed OBERIU (an acronym standing for Association of Real Art) late in 1927. Other members were Nikolai Zabolotsky, Konstantin Vaginov, Nikolai Oleinikov, and Yury Vladimirov. A manifesto of OBERIU insisted on freedom of formal experimentation and advocated the liberation of verbal art from conventional associations of objects and words.[7] Like the cubo-futurists, the oberiuty believed that fragmentation and imaginative reconstitution of objects and verbal units could provide an avenue to deeper strata of meaning. True or not, this assumption led the oberiuty to write poetry and prose of estranged, often childlike freshness. They were the only Russian group of poets whose aesthetics and sensibility resembled those of dada, French surrealism, German expressionism, and the abstractionist art of Malevich and Filonov. Some of the oberiuty also wrote trans-sense poetry.

The oberiuty were able to stage a few theatrical performances and poetry readings in 1928 and 1929 but had difficulty publishing their works. Some of them found a suitable outlet in literature for children, where their estranged and fractured short prose pieces and naively concrete poetry were not perceived as out of the ordinary. Zabolotsky and Vaginov, moderate exponents of the OBERIU sensibility, were able to

7. The manifesto appeared in *Posters of the House of Poets*, no. 2 (1928).

publish their works, to increasingly hostile reactions by officious party critics. OBERIU disbanded in 1930 after a particularly vicious attack labeled them "class enemies." Few of the oberiuty survived the purges of the 1930s unscathed. The group was so totally forgotten that it had to be literally discovered by scholars of the 1960s. Many of the works of the oberiuty were first published in the West in the 1970s and 1980s.

What later became known as the Formal school (*formal'naya shkola*) in Russia and as Russian formalism in the West started as two circles of young scholars interested in linguistic and poetic theory, the Moscow Linguistic Circle, organized in 1915 by Roman Jakobson (1896–1982), then a student at Moscow University, and the Petersburg OPOYAZ (the Society for the Study of Poetic Language), which was formed by a group of students of Petersburg University on the eve of World War I. OPOYAZ published three collections of essays between 1916 and 1919. It disbanded in 1923. Some of the members of the Moscow Linguistic Circle were also futurists (Mayakovsky was a member) and some members of both groups were later active in Lef: Viktor Shklovsky (1893–1984), Boris Eichenbaum (1886–1959), Osip Brik (1888–1945), and Grigory Vinokur (1896–1947). Some worked at the State Institute of Art History in Petrograd: Boris Tomashevsky (1890–1957), Yury Tynyanov (1894–1943), and others. Although the Formal school never had its own journal or a steady gathering place, the formalists were recognized as a school by the scholarly and the literary community as well as by the political authorities.

Philosophically and in some instances personally close to Russian futurism, the formalists saw their work as antithetical to conventional attitudes in literary criticism and scholarship. They saw literature, and poetry in particular, primarily as a linguistic phenomenon, whereas it had been viewed as a sociopolitical phenomenon by Russian critics since Belinsky. Much like the futurists, who were fascinated by "the word as such," the formalists took a phenomenological approach to literature, seeking to understand it in its own terms. As Jakobson put it, they looked for the literary (*literaturnost'*) in literature. In an early essay, "Art as Device," Shklovsky sought to reduce the essence of verbal art to a set of well-defined devices. Translated into the language of Left Art constructivism, this meant that the writer was a skilled craftsman who needed no inspiration, epiphany, or inner vision to produce his works. Instead of perceiving a work of literature as the realization of an integral idea or vision (*obraz*), the formalists, and specifically Boris Tomashevsky in his *Theory of Literature* (1925), analyzed it as an aggregate of themes or motifs. Vladimir Propp (1895–1970), in his *Morphology of the Folktale* (1928), sought to reduce the structure of all folktales to a limited number of motifs and functions. Shklovsky (*The Theory of Prose*, 1925), Eichenbaum ("How Gogol's 'Overcoat' Was Made," published in 1924, though written in 1918), Tynyanov ("Gogol and Dostoevsky: On the Theory of Parody," 1921), and other formalists extended this approach to more complex forms of narrative prose. The formalists also insisted on writing the history of literature in terms of the continuity, rivalry, and substitution of themes, genres, styles, and literary devices rather than in terms of literature's role in social and political history (Tynyanov, "On Literary Evolution," 1927; Shklovsky, *Knight's Move*, 1923).[8] Furthermore, they tended to separate the work from its author,

8. The title is a metaphor suggesting that literary styles are passed on obliquely, not from father to son, but from uncle to nephew.

or emphasize the literary aspect of an author's biography. Eichenbaum, who devoted a lifetime to the study of Lev Tolstoi, presented that writer's life in terms of a search for ever-new forms of expression instead of as a struggle for faith and an integral worldview.

The formalists Eichenbaum, Tomashevsky, Brik, Tynyanov, and Zhirmunsky developed the study of versification into an exact science by doing meticulous statistical studies of Russian verse. They succeeded in establishing specific rhythmic patterns characteristic of different periods and different poets. They were able to determine, for example, precisely how the iambic tetrameter of an eighteenth-century poet differed from that of a Golden Age poet, how the latter differed from the iambic tetrameter of Tyutchev, and so on.

Viktor Shklovsky, the most exuberant of the formalists and himself a brilliant novelist and memoirist, coined several literary terms that survived the heyday of Russian formalism and are in common usage even today. Making it strange, or defamiliarization (*ostranenie*), is the device by which a phenomenon is taken out of its conventional context so that it may once again be *seen*, not merely *recognized*.[9] Presenting a phenomenon in the language of a foreigner, child, or animal is a common way of making it strange. Defacilitation (*zatrudnyonnaya forma*) is any device—semantic, syntactic, or phonological—that forces the reader or listener to follow the text with an intense conscious effort and to wonder about its meaning. Retardation (*zamedlenie*) is effected by any device, such as redundancy, repetition, tautology, parallelism, and willful

concealment of information, that sacrifices efficiency of communication to the requirements of literary form. Laying bare the device (*obnazhenie priyoma*) is a gesture on the part of the author by which he, ingenuously or disingenuously, invites the reader or listener to peek into his or her bag of tricks. Since defamiliarization encompasses the other devices, Shklovsky was inclined to consider it the essence of all art: seeing the world anew, in one way or another, was the purpose of art.

In spite of their progressive philosophical and political views, the formalists soon met with the displeasure of the party, whose functionaries preferred familiar Belinskian organic aesthetics and traditional poetics to their innovative ideas. Shklovsky recanted his formalist views in 1930, but after Stalin's death he returned to write several brilliant books in his former manner. Eichenbaum, Zhirmunsky, and Tomashevsky withdrew to more conventional academic teaching and scholarship. Jakobson, who had gone to Czechoslovakia in 1920 with a Soviet Red Cross mission, did not return to the Soviet Union and eventually became a famous linguist in America. Statistical analysis of poetic texts was resumed by Soviet scholars only after Stalin's death.

Bakhtin

Mikhail Mikhailovich Bakhtin (1896–1975) was known until the 1960s as the author of a single book, *Problems of Dostoevsky's Oeuvre* (1929). He spent much of his life teaching at a provincial pedagogical institute. After republication of his book in 1963 and publication of a book on Rabelais in 1965 he was finally recognized as a major scholar. His posthumous fame as a philosopher of language, enhanced by the publica-

9. The German romantic Novalis used *fremdmachen* in exactly the same sense, as a synonym of *poetisieren*.

tion of two volumes of his essays in 1975 and 1979, soon outstripped his earlier reputation as a historian of literature.

Bakhtin's thought has three main foci: the dialogic nature of discourse, the universal social function of carnival and the carnivalesque in art, and a phenomenological theory of the novel. According to Bakhtin's theory all discourse (*slovo*), including literary discourse, is set in a specific situation in time and space, is directed at an interlocutor, and is usually perceived in a concrete context. Bakhtin saw in Dostoevsky's fiction striking examples of dialogic (or "polyphonic") discourse, where multiple individual voices, inner dialogue, parody, intertextual echoes, irony, and ambiguity interact dialogically, independently of a controlling monologic narrative voice.

Bakhtin's observations regarding a universal human impulse toward carnival as a revolt against and reversal of fixed values and its reflection in folk culture are concentrated in his study of Rabelais. (*Rabelais and His World*). His conception of the novel as an open "antigeneric" form in permanent flux and ready to sublate any existing canon leads to the concept of "novelization" as another universal impulse. Bakhtin's writings are but one example of intense intellectual activity that went on in Stalin's Russia without a chance to be communicated to an audience at home, much less abroad.

Since Marx, Engels, and Lenin had left only a few casual observations regarding art and literature, Georgy Plekhanov, though suspect as a Menshevik, was the only theorist besides Aleksandr Bogdanov (also of dubious authority owing to his differences with Lenin) to whom a Marxist theory of literature could look for guidance. The so-called sociological school, which sought to create a Marxist methodology of literary studies in the 1920s, had few adherents. Its views were declared to be in error and branded "vulgar sociologism" as early as 1930. The key position of the sociological school was that class consciousness is a dominant factor in forming the content of artistic creation. Pavel Sakulin (1868–1930), a first-rate literary scholar, suggested in his "Theory of Literary Styles" (1928) that a work of literature is formed by three different forces: the writer's creative personality, the social conditions of his age, and long-range historical processes. In his *History of Russian Literature*, written for publication in German, Sakulin organized his material along class lines: the literature of the gentry, the literature of the bourgeoisie, and so on. Vladimir Friche (1870–1929), more radical than Sakulin, argued in a series of programmatic treatises (*Plekhanov and Scientific Aesthetics*, 1922; *Outline of a Sociology of Literary Styles*, 1923; *The Sociology of Art*, 1926) that literary styles are representative of specific class interests and that the history of literature should be seen in terms of class struggle as reflected in literary styles. Valerian Pereverzev (1882–1968) took the position that a writer's consciousness is determined by his social position and the various forms of class struggle in which he is involved, consciously or subconsciously. He said, for instance, that Dostoevsky's "dualism" was a function of a struggle between a petit bourgeois plebeian's inferiority complex and his ambition to rise in the world. Pereverzev's *Study of Literature* (1929) caused a fierce debate, which led to charges of deviationism and his eventual arrest. Pereverzev survived eighteen years in a prison camp and lived to see his official rehabilitation.

Only in the 1930s was a first attempt—

apparently inspired by the Hungarian critic Georg Lukács, who was then living in Soviet Russia—made to gather systematically the statements in the "classics of Marxism" regarding aesthetic and literary theory. A chrestomathy, *K. Marx and F. Engels on Art*, edited by M. A. Lifshits, appeared in 1933. Lifshits also was the first to try to integrate the opinions of Marx and Engels with the principles of socialist realism.

In spite of drastic purges in the Academy of Sciences and in the universities, the period between 1925 and 1933 was one of vigorous activity in literary scholarship, highlighted by Academy of Sciences editions of the collected works of Dostoevsky (1926–30), Tolstoi (1928–58), and Chekhov (1930–33). Important theoretical and historical studies also appeared during this period, for example (besides works mentioned earlier), Yury Tynyanov's *Archaists and Innovators* (1929), Boris Tomashevsky's *Theory of Literature* (1925) and *The Writer and the Book: An Outline of Textual Study* (1928), Viktor Zhirmunsky's *Problems of Literary Theory* (1928), and Boris Eichenbaum's *Lev Tolstoi* (1928, 1931).

Socialist Realism

The principles of socialist realism were developed in concert with the party's decision to make the transition to a socialist economy and a classless society in the course of the second five-year-plan (1933–37). The term "socialist realism," as well as the principles, emerged in the course of meetings in April and May 1932 of a five-man commission appointed by the Politburo of the Central Committee of the Communist party. Stalin himself sat on this commission. Implementation of the commission's decisions was left to the organizing committee of the

Union of Soviet Writers. Ivan Gronsky, editor of *Izvestiya*, was appointed its chairman and Valery Kirpotin, head of the Literary Divison of the Central Committee, secretary.

Socialist realism amounted, in theory, to a presentation of objective reality with emphasis on its historical development, that is, the ascendancy of socialism in the Soviet Union and eventually throughout the world. In practice, this meant faithful adherence to the party line of the moment. The theory of socialist realism was based on literary precedent, the few statements on art and literature that could be found in the "classics of Marxism," and the current exigencies of political reality as determined by the communist leadership. Literary precedent was provided by Gorky's *Mother* and some works of the 1920s, such as Furmanov's *Chapaev* and Gladkov's *Cement*, works unquestionably loyal not only to the communist cause but also to the party. A letter by Friedrich Engels to Margaret Harkness (April 1888) provided the authority for a demand that realist literature describe typical characters under typical circumstances. A "theory of reflection," credited specifically to Lenin, which revived Chernyshevsky's naturalist theory of art, was amplified by the assumption that Marxist-Leninist ideology provided a reliable tool for a correct understanding of objective reality. Lenin's article "Party Organization and Party Literature" (1905) was interpreted to say that literature should be a vehicle for the propagation of party ideology. The conflict between the realist component of socialist realism and its mission of projecting a socialist future was removed by a quotation from Lenin suggesting that literature should not only reflect reality but also help change it.

The key terms of socialist realist aesthetics and criticism were "realism" ("critical" for prerevolutionary literature, "socialist" for Soviet literature); "party-mindedness" (*partiinost'*), meaning the quality of being in accord with the doctrines and policies of the party; *ideinost'*, the quality of being inspired by lofty and correct ideas; "historicism," meaning a correct understanding of the historical background of events presented; *narodnost'*, meaning accessibility to popular understanding and sentiment; "humanism," meaning faith in humanity's progress toward communism through the power of human reason; and *khudozhestvennost'* (from *khudozhestvennyi*, "artistic"), the quality of meeting all of these requirements at large. The arsenal of negative terms included "pseudo-objectivism," the opposite of *partiinost'*; "naturalism," meaning an absence of *ideinost'*; "antihumanism," meaning any idea not in accord with humanity's progress toward communism; and *antinarodnost'*, or reactionary elitism.

While socialist realist theory paid lip service to Stalin's slogan "socialist in content, national in form," Russian patriotism became the norm in the 1930s. The literature of the 1930s and 1940s featured historical novels that glorified military successes of the tsars. Historical films celebrated not only revolutionary heroes like Shchors and Chapaev but also Alexander Nevsky, a saint of the Orthodox church, Peter the Great, and General Aleksandr Suvorov, who won his laurels against French and Polish revolutionary armies in the 1790s.

In the mid- and late-1920s some writers of the Lef and RAPP groups had launched a literature of "social commission," which implied that a writer would spend some time at a production site, building project, collective farm, transportation center, or research institute, ideally as a worker and political activist, and would then translate his or her experience into journalism or fiction. In the new genres of the production novel and production drama both were often combined, as the plot was either accompanied by or based on elaborate technical details. In the 1920s pieces of production literature appeared sporadically. In the 1930s a flood of production novels and plays quickly established a genre that soon became the centerpiece of socialist realist literature. The conflict would hinge on the success or failure of a Soviet enterprise, such as the construction of a power plant (*Energy*, 1932–38, by Fyodor Gladkov; *Hydrocentral*, 1931, by Marietta Shaginyan) or a metallurgical plant (*Time, Forward!* 1932, by Valentin Kataev). The hero and heroine—of working-class background, assisted by positive characters some of whom might belong to the intelligentsia, and guided by the party—would overcome a series of obstacles in the form of natural disasters, technical problems, and sabotage by enemies of the Soviet regime and lead the project to a successful conclusion. Saboteurs would be unmasked and get their just deserts. There might be some victims among the positive characters, but the conclusion of the novel or play would be unequivocally upbeat.

Leaving aside the question of artistic merit, the socialist realist production novel was a genuinely innovative form by virtue of a shift of plot, substance, and interest from private and human to social and industrial concerns, a wealth of technical information conveyed to the reader, and strict determination of the moral character of its dramatis personae by social class. A narrowly defined genre, the production novel generated a great deal of hackwork. The question remains whether even such masterful examples of the genre as *Time, Forward!* were inherently flawed by the counterfeit quality of their realism and the disingenuousness of their socialist optimism.

The tendency of successful socialist realist writers like Panfyorov, Ehrenburg, and Grossman, to name but a few, to take advantage of the thaw after Stalin's death to present an altogether different picture of the same ambience suggests that socialist realist fiction was on the whole an exercise in mutual deception performed by writers, editors, and those in power. It is also significant that most of the writers who stood in the forefront of the dissident literature of the thaw were alumni of the Gorky Literary Institute, which trained beginning Soviet writers to become socialist realists.

Emigré Literature

In the nineteenth and early twentieth centuries such major writers as Gogol, Herzen, Turgenev, Ogaryov, Kropotkin, Bakunin, Plekhanov, Gorky, and Minsky either chose or were forced to live and work abroad. Important works by some of these authors (and by some who remained in Russia—Lev Tolstoi, for example) appeared in the West before they could be published in Russia. Nevertheless, the bulk of Russian literature was accessible to the Russian reader, as even writers in exile found ways to communicate with the Russian public. The revolution created an unprecedented situation of two separate literatures.

Among the writers who left or were expelled from Russia within a few years after the revolution were Mark Aldanov, Konstantin Balmont, Andrei Bely, Ivan Bunin, David Burlyuk, Evgeny Chirikov, the satirist Sasha Chorny, Nikolai Evreinov, Dmitry Filosofov, Maksim Gorky, Zinaida Hippius, Georgy Ivanov, Vyacheslav Ivanov, Vladislav Khodasevich, Aleksandr Kuprin, Sergei Makovsky, Dmitry Merezhkovsky, Irina Odoevtseva,

Mikhail Osorgin, Aleksei Remizov, Igor Severyanin, Viktor Shklovsky, Ivan Shmelyov, Nadezhda Teffi, Aleksei Tolstoi, Marina Tsvetaeva, and Boris Zaitsev. Some of these eventually returned to Russia: Bely, Gorky, Kuprin, Shklovsky, Aleksei Tolstoi, and Tsvetaeva. Among major figures of intellectual life who left Russia were Nikolai Berdyaev, Father Sergei Bulgakov, Georgy Fedotov, Semyon Frank, Nikolai Lossky, Pavel Milyukov, Lev Shestov, and Pyotr Struve. Among critics and literary scholars who continued their work abroad were Georgy Adamovich, Yuly Aikhenvald, Alfred Bem (Boehm), Pyotr Bitsilli, Pyotr Bogatyryov, Roman Jakobson, Konstantin Mochulsky, Marc Slonim, Fyodor Stepun, Dmitry Svyatopolk-Mirsky, Nikolai Trubetskoi, and Vladimir Weidlé.

Together with the death of many major figures of intellectual and literary life (Andreev, Blok, Bryusov, Gumilyov, Khlebnikov, Korolenko, Plekhanov, and Sologub) within a few years after the revolution, this mass exodus caused a profound break in Russian literature. While prerevolutionary movements, themes, and styles faded in the Soviet Union, émigré literature continued to cultivate ideas, themes, and forms carried over from prerevolutionary Russia and, unlike Soviet literature, soon began to show the influence of contemporary Western literatures. Whereas earlier Russian literature in exile consisted mainly of works by authors who had left Russia after having started their literary careers, the new émigré literature was produced by a generation of authors who wrote their first works in emigration and developed styles that were independent of what went on in the Soviet Union.

The Russian diaspora spawned several colonies large enough to allow organized cultural activities, such as newspapers and journals, publishing houses, theatrical groups, literary circles, and poetry readings. Emigré writers often moved from one of these centers to another. Berlin became the first cultural center of Russian emigration in the early 1920s, when it was the site of several Russian publishing houses, including Epokha, Petropolis, and Skify (Scythians), periodicals like *The Socialist Herald* (1921–41, continued in New York, 1941–68), which featured reviews and essays by the eminent critic Vera Aleksandrova (1895–1966), and Russian cultural organizations, such as a house of the arts and a writers' club, as well as several Russian schools. Berlin remained a major center of Russian literary activity throughout the years of the Weimar Republic. A good deal of cultural interaction between the Russian and the German avant-garde took place in those years. Russian avant-garde art, theater, and film left a mark on German intellectual life, whose highlights, including expressionism, Freudian psychoanalysis, and a popular version of Einstein's theory of relativity, reached Russia and were reflected in Russian literature of the 1920s.

In the mid-1920s Paris became the capital of Russia in exile. It had two major Russian newspapers, *Late News* and *Renaissance*, whose literary critics were Georgy Adamovich and Vladislav Khodasevich (beginning in 1927), respectively. Over the years, a host of Russian journals appeared there, including *Contemporary Notes* (1920–40), the only "thick journal" of émigré literature.

Prague, the site of the Russian National University, was also a center of literary activity, organized and led by the eminent Dostoevsky scholar Alfred Bem. In Belgrade, where many émigrés found haven through the patronage of the Russophile king Alexander, the Yugoslav Academy of Sciences published a series, *A Russian Library*, featuring

new works by émigré writers. Riga, the capital of Latvia, which had a strong Russian minority population, boasted an excellent Russian daily, *Today*, and over the years saw several literary journals, such as the weekly *Chimes* (1925–28), edited by Boris Zaitsev. Other centers of Russian literary activity were Warsaw, Sofia, Helsinki, Tallinn, Harbin, New York, San Francisco, and Buenos Aires, all of which at one time or another supported literary journals, literary circles, and poetry and prose readings by émigré authors.

After World War II, New York, with a daily, *The New Russian Word*, which had an excellent literary section, and a literary journal, *The New Review*, founded by Mark Aldanov and M. O. Tsetlin in 1942, became next to Paris the most important center of Russian cultural life, a development connected with the immigration in the 1940s and 1950s of many Russian émigrés of the first and second wave. The third wave of the Brezhnev era would make New York a major center of Russian cultural life second only to Moscow and Leningrad. The second wave of emigrants after World War II, most of whom found themselves in Germany, sparked considerable Russian cultural activity in Frankfurt and Munich. The Frankfurt publishing house Posev and the journals *Bridges* and *Facets* played a major role in publishing Soviet dissident, as well as postwar émigré, literature.

The publishing ventures of the émigré community tended to be short-lived and financially unstable, allowing few Russian writers to continue as professional littérateurs. Those who did (Balmont, Bunin, Remizov, Georgy Ivanov, Khodasevich, Merezhkovsky, Hippius) often lived in poverty. Only a few were able to gather an international following: Aldanov, Bunin, Evreinov, Merezhkovsky. There was practically no chance for an émigré writer to be published in the Soviet Union. Mercurial Ilya Ehrenburg, who managed to be equally at home in Paris and in Moscow, and of course Maksim Gorky were exceptions.

The émigré community presented a broad spectrum of political opinion. There was the Change of Landmarks (Smena vekh) group, so named after a miscellany of that title published in Prague in 1921 (the title was a challenge to the Landmarks group of 1909, most of whose members were fellow émigrés). A journal, *Change of Landmarks*, also appeared in Paris in 1921–22. The smenavekhovtsy advocated a reconciliation of the Russian intelligentsia with the Bolsheviks and, in the name of Russian unity, urged émigrés to return to Russia. Most of the returnees soon found themselves in Soviet prisons. "Eurasian" circles, whose journal was the Paris-based *Milestones*, were sympathetic to the ideas of the Change of Landmarks group, for they saw Bolshevism as an "Asian" phenomenon consistent with Russia's destiny. Two of the editors of *Milestones*, the brilliant literary historian and critic Dmitry Svyatopolk-Mirsky and writer Sergei Efron (husband of Marina Tsvetaeva), eventually returned to the Soviet Union, where both perished in the purges.

Some émigré littérateurs were former Mensheviks or Socialist Revolutionaries (SRs). Mark Vishnyak, editor of one of the more successful émigré periodicals, the Paris-based *Contemporary Notes*, and a former SR, was an inveterate opponent of the Change of Landmarks movement. On the other hand, E. E. Lazarev's journal, the Prague-based *Will of Russia*, a SR organ, displayed a conciliatory attitude toward the Soviet regime and consistently reviewed recent Soviet publications.

Pyotr Struve, a leader of the constitutional democrats and member of the Landmarks group, took his journal, *Russian Thought*, from Russia to Sofia (1921), to Prague and Berlin (1922–24), and to Paris (1927). A liberal, he understandably took a negative view of the "national Bolshevism" propagated by the Change of Landmarks group.

Conservative groups also had their periodicals. Writers with strong Orthodox beliefs gathered around the Paris Theological Institute (Bogoslovskii institut) and the journal *The Path* (1925–40), edited by philosopher Nikolai Berdyaev (1874–1948). Dmitry Merezhkovsky and Zinaida Hippius were among the most implacable enemies of Bolshevism. They had no journal of their own but vigorously continued their publicistic activities after they settled in Paris in 1920. The literary circle Green Lamp (Zelyonaya lampa), which they organized in 1927, became a high-powered forum of literary, philosophical, and political discussion.

Poetry workshops and literary discussion circles were formed in many cities with substantial Russian colonies. In Paris, several such groups existed at different times. Encampment (*Kochev'e*), organized by Marc Slonim (1894–1976) in 1928, was a workshop in which young poets gathered for poetry readings, discussions, and talks by established authors. Many of the poems read here were later published in émigré periodicals. The group existed until 1938. A similar group, called Crossroads (*Perekryostok*), was headed by Vladislav Khodasevich. Studio franco-russe (1929–31) featured monthly debates in which a French and a Russian speaker would present his view on a topic of common interest, such as "Spiritual Renewal in France and Russia." Among the French participants were Paul Valéry, André Malraux, François Mauriac, Georges Bernanos, Charles Péguy, and André Maurois; among the Russian, Bunin, Berdyaev, Fedotov, Tsvetaeva, Zaitsev, Teffi, and Slonim.

The condition of émigré literature favored the short genres—lyric poetry, the short story, and the sketch—whose principal outlet was the many more or less ephemeral journals and almanacs of the Russian diaspora. There were few outlets for the novel, and fewer still for drama. In lyric poetry, émigré poets made significant contributions to Russian literature, which continued until the arrival of the third wave caused a burst of activity even in the other genres. Several poets of the prerevolutionary period modified their poetic style in exile; others rose to greater maturity and eminence. Some of Konstantin Balmont's late poems have an unaffected simplicity alien to his earlier work. The ego-futurist Igor Severyanin, who lived in Estonia after the revolution, now wrote simple gnomic and nature poetry using a conventional vocabulary and ordinary versification. Vyacheslav Ivanov, who lived in Italy after his emigration in 1924, wrote relatively little poetry. An eminent scholar, he published many articles and essays in German and Italian. His superb "Roman Sonnets," written in 1924 but published in *Contemporary Notes* only in 1936, are classically lucid, while his long philosophical-religious poem "Man," published in 1939 but written in 1915–16, is complex and esoteric after the fashion of his early symbolist poetry. Ivanov experienced a wonderful burst of creativity late in life. The limpid simplicity, immediacy of feeling, and pious wisdom of his "Roman Diary" cycle of 1944, consisting of short poems quite different from Ivanov's magnificently erudite mannerism of earlier years, have a unique charm and testify to the depth of Ivanov's genius. Zinaida Hippius,

like Ivanov, wrote little poetry in exile, but her late collection *Radiances* (1938), as well as her posthumous poems, show that she, too, had lost none of her creative powers.

Some poets who had made an auspicious start before the revolution reached full maturity in exile: Vladislav Khodasevich, Marina Tsvetaeva, and Georgy Ivanov. Some minor poets, such as Nikolai Otsup (1894–1958), like Ivanov a member of Gumilyov's Guild of Poets, and Antonin Ladinsky (1896–1961), whose poetic style was close to acmeism, also wrote their best verse in exile.

Khodasevich

Vladislav Felitsianovich Khodasevich (1886–1939) was born in Moscow into a middle-class Polish family. His mother was a convert to Russian Orthodoxy from Judaism. He never made much of his Polish origins, although he did translate some Polish poetry. He developed an interest in Jewish culture late in life, when he also translated some Jewish poetry. In a poem of 1923 ("I Was Born in Moscow") he writes, "I am Russia's stepson, and Poland's—/ I don't know myself what I am to Poland." He goes on to say that his "whole motherland is in eight slim volumes"—of Pushkin, as we hear in the last stanza. Khodasevich attended school in Moscow. Valery Bryusov's younger brother, Aleksandr, was his schoolmate, and Khodasevich soon developed intimate ties with the Moscow symbolists. In 1906 Valery Bryusov was best man at his wedding to Marina Ryndina, his first wife, who divorced him in 1907 and married Sergei Makovsky, coeditor of *Apollon*. Khodasevich later married Anna Chulkova, sister of symbolist poet Georgy Chulkov. Andrei

Bely, at first a close friend, became an enemy of Khodasevich's after 1923.

Khodasevich published his first volume of poetry, *Youth*, in 1908 and a second, *A Happy Little House*, in 1913. Neither attracted much attention, but Khodasevich was considered more than a minor poet by most. He soon won respect as a critic and Pushkin scholar, and was feared for his mordant wit. His third and fourth collections, *Grain's Way* (1920) and *Heavy Lyre* (1922), established him as a leading poet. Khodasevich left Russia in 1922, spent some time in Berlin and then with Gorky in Sorrento, and in 1927 assumed editorship of the literary section of the Paris Russian daily *Renaissance*, to which he contributed many articles and reviews. His *Collected Verse* (1927) made him the leading poet of émigré Russia. He wrote little poetry after 1927, but some late poems, such as the profound "To the Memory of Murr the Cat" (1937),[10] published posthumously, suggest that his creative powers were undiminished. Khodasevich wrote a brilliant biography of Derzhavin (1931), some fine essays on Pushkin (collected in *About Pushkin*, 1937), and a fascinating volume of memoirs, *Necropolis* (1939). As a critic, Khodasevich demanded intellectual honesty, clarity, tidiness of form, and respect for culture. He believed that there was good and bad art, and his discriminations were, in retrospect, correct or at least well founded. Khodasevich suffered from various illnesses since his childhood and was not a happy man. He never, however, let his misfortunes distract him from his work.

Khodasevich's poetry is Pushkinian (perhaps, in the early stages, Pushkinian in Bryusov's manner): formally unassuming,

10. Murr is the hero and co-author of E. T. A. Hoffmann's novel *Kater Murr*.

pointedly foregrounding logos and suppressing melos, and avoiding any show of flashiness or virtuosity. Much as Pushkin, Khodasevich was a poet of controlled emotions. His power was that of a strong, hard, and bold mind. Like Pushkin, he always had control of his language, never letting it control him. In one of his last poems, "Should in tetrameter iambic" (1938), Khodasevich ends his paean to the form in which the greatness of Russian poetry was cast in the words, "It has only one law: freedom, / In its freedom lies its law."

Khodasevich's first collection, *Youth*, dedicated to Marina, is decadent in the manner of Zinaida Hippius. *A Happy Little House*, dedicated to his wife, Anna, is acmeist in the manner of Akhmatova and Mandelshtam. In "Rain" (1908) the poet watches from a window as his former ladylove walks by in a rainstorm and is glad when she seeks shelter under someone else's doorway, shaking the raindrops from her coat and turning over her umbrella. "To a Dear Friend" (1911) is addressed to a cricket. "Mice" (1913), a cycle of three poems, projects the atmosphere of a warm home protected by "small deities," where prayers are made to domestic Lares and a mouse's god of cheese. There are echoes here of Pushkin's early poem "To a House Spirit" (1819). "Jenny's Voice" (1912) is a takeoff on Jenny's song in Pushkin's *Feast during the Plague*. Jenny looks down from heaven on her native village, urging her beloved Edmund to live and love an earthly life such as theirs had been. In "The Return of Orpheus" (1909) a despondent Orpheus finds it beyond his powers to sing after his return from Hades.

The lead and title poem of *Grain's Way* is a meditation on John 12:24. It ends in the lines, "For there's a single wisdom given us: / All living things must go grain's way." The poems of this collection and the next,

Heavy Lyre, are close in their ethos to Sologub. They are preoccupied with death always desired, *le poète maudit*, and hints of epiphanies that will never materialize because they are only metaphors of the poet's own creation. Here Khodasevich develops his specialty, the totally unexpected, concrete, and apt image that gives a metaphysical conceit a palpable reality. In "Oh, if in that hour of long-desired rest" (1915) the poet imagines himself laid out on his bier. He concludes the poem by letting Chloe "change the bag of ice on his chest timidly, with a solicitous hand." In a poem of 1922, "It almost isn't worth it to live or sing," the poet speaks of the few moments when he believes he hears "the beat of an altogether different existence," then concludes the poem by likening his experience to that of a pregnant woman who "lovingly puts her excited hand on her heavy, bulging belly."

Khodasevich's poems on the poet often feature ingenious conceits. In "The Acrobat" (1914–21) a crowd is gawking at an acrobat who walks a tightrope from rooftop to rooftop. The poet observes that his trade is the same as the acrobat's—echoes of *Thus Spake Zarathustra*. In the first of two sonnets entitled "About Myself," the poet is likened to a garden spider who knows not the meaning of the cross it bears on its hairy back, and in the second, to a man who mirrors himself in the water under a starry sky, burying his mundane image in the water and giving himself an aura of stars.

Khodasevich's fifth and last collection, *European Night* (it appeared as part of his *Collected Verse* of 1927), is his most idiosyncratic. A poem of 1923, "Springtime babble will not soften my sternly compressed verses," was called Khodasevich's *ars poetica* by the critic Vladimir Weidlé. It is a poem in praise of violent cacophony, "the screeching clangor of a chainsaw," "the tre-

mor that makes your skin crawl," and "the cold sweat of terror." Its ending is characteristic of Khodasevich's later poetry:

> Or in a dream, where I, who once was
>   one,
> Explode, torn into flying fragments,
> Like mud, splattered by a tire,
> Into alien spheres of existence.

"God lives / Sensible, not trans-sensible[11] / I walk amidst my verses" (1923) is another strong statement about the "severe freedom" of the poet. It ends in an amazing couplet:

> Oh, if I could but clothe my dying groan
> In a neatly structured ode!

Khodasevich practiced what he preached. He has a series of cruel expressionist scenes of postwar Berlin, Parisian poems full of anger at people's acquiescence to the ugly reality that surrounds them, and sharp satirical pieces on the Russian revolution, the Soviet regime, and the NEP. His late poems ask the great questions about god, man, life, and death concretely, as applied to modern life in a big city.

In spite of his conventional forms and classical clarity Khodasevich was a thoroughly modern poet. The structure of his "Sorrentine Photographs" (1926) is a clever conceit based on the analogy of a double exposure. A glorious Italian landscape blends with the bleak memory of a pauper's funeral in Moscow. A motorcycle ride on the road from Sorrento to Naples is double-exposed with a recollection of the Peter and Paul Fortress reflected in the green waters of the Neva, "ominous, fiery, and somber." True to his unswerving devotion to Pushkin, Khodasevich was at least as much a European as a Russian poet. His poetic profile

---

11. The Russian is, *umen, a ne zaumen.*

was that of a European poet of his age. Khodasevich deserves to be mentioned in one breath with T. S. Eliot or Gottfried Benn.

Tsvetaeva

Marina Ivanovna Tsvetaeva (1892–1941) was the daughter of a professor of art history at Moscow University. Her mother, of German-Polish background, was a fine pianist. Tsvetaeva attended boarding schools in Switzerland and Germany (1903–05), where her mother was taking treatments for the lung condition that caused her death in 1906. Tsvetaeva was fluent in French and German, and her attachment to Germany and German culture persisted through her whole life. In 1909 she traveled to Paris alone to attend lectures at the Sorbonne. Her first book of verse, *Evening Album* (1910), attracted favorable attention. Maksimilian Voloshin, an established poet and critic, responded with a warm welcoming poem, paid a visit to her, introduced her to literary society, and invited her to his Crimean residence at Koktebel. There, in 1911, she met Sergei Efron, a young would-be writer, whom she married in 1912. She published two more volumes of verse before the outbreak of the war, *Magic Lantern* (1912) and *From Two Books* (1913), and continued to write and publish her poetry through the years of war and revolution. In 1916 she made a trip to Petrograd (as Saint Petersburg was renamed in 1914), where she met Kuzmin, Sologub, Esenin, and Mandelshtam. Her friendship with Mandelshtam led to an exchange of poems. In 1917 she was stranded in Moscow, alone with her two daughters, as her husband, an officer, had joined the Whites. Her younger daughter died of malnutrition in 1920. In 1922 Tsvetaeva emigrated and rejoined her husband,

after her collections *Mileposts* (1921) and *Mileposts, Book One* (1922) had appeared in Moscow. The Efrons lived in Prague from 1922 to 1925 and then moved to Paris. Tsvetaeva now wrote her best poetry and a great deal of excellent prose. She experienced, however, more than an émigré writer's usual difficulties. Her poetry was becoming more unconventional and therefore difficult to place. Her political views were not unequivocally anti-Soviet. Worse, her husband had developed pro-Soviet sympathies and was rumored to have become a Soviet agent. Sergei Efron departed for Republican Spain in 1937 and eventually returned to the Soviet Union, where he was soon shot. In 1939, desperate and under pressure from her daughter and teenage son, Tsvetaeva returned to the Soviet Union. Ignored by the Soviet literary community, destitute and helpless, she committed suicide at Elabuga, a town in the Tatar Autonomous Republic.

Tsvetaeva's early poetry impressed her mature readers with its fresh immediacy. A self-willed, very self-conscious, and unusually energetic young woman was expressing herself not in the clichés of contemporary poetry but in imaginative conceits of her own invention—a language that refused to stay within the boundaries of conventional poetry—and in nervous staccato rhythms of accentual verse. One of her favorite conceits is to imagine herself dead. In "The Day Will Come" (1916) she sees herself laid out as "the late Boyarynya Marina,"[12] on whose face the glow of sainthood is beginning to shine through her earthly features (an untranslatable play on words from the same root, *litso* and *lik*, the first signifying the

12. Apparently an allusion to Boyarynya *Morozava*, sainted martyr of the Old Believers.

mundane, the second the spiritual aspect of the human face).

Tsvetaeva had from the outset an amazing ability to express herself in brief, poignant, energy-laden lines, as in the first stanza of a poem of the cycle "Insomnia" (1916):

I love to kiss
Hands, and I love
To give out names.
And also, to open
Doors!
Wide open, in the middle of a dark night!

Early on, too, she developed a tendency to use the vocabulary and phrasing of the folk song and folk ditty—some would say not to the advantage of her poetry, since her sensibility was hardly that of an uneducated Russian. Still, her stylized pieces, such as the cycle "Stenka Razin" (1917),[13] are as good as anything in this manner by her symbolist contemporaries.

Tsvetaeva's lifelong love affair with Pushkin found expression in such early poems as "An Encounter with Pushkin" (1913). Another "love affair" led to a remarkable cycle, "Verses to Blok" (she had met him briefly), begun in 1916 and completed in 1921, after Blok's death. The first of these poems plays with the sound of the poet's name, calling it "a bird in one's hand," "a piece of ice on one's tongue," and observing that "a stone, flung into a quiet pond, will make a sobbing splash of your name":

Your name is—oh, I shouldn't!—
Your name is: a kiss on the eyes,
On the delicate cool of motionless lids.
Your name is a kiss on the snow,
A gulp of icy, light-blue well water.
With your name, sleep is deep.

13. Stephen Razin, leader of an uprising against Tsar Alexis in the 1670s.

The other poems of the cycle are as breathlessly ecstatic. The inventiveness of Tsvetaeva's imagery makes these poems eminently worthy of their addressee.

Tsvetaeva's cycle "To Akhmatova" (1916) shows an acute awareness of the difference of their sensibilities: "I am the convict, you the guard. Our fate is one. We have been given the same travel papers through vacuous emptiness." Tsvetaeva sees Akhmatova as the graceful, generous, giving spirit, and herself as the humble, devoted, and grateful recipient of her largesse. Unlike the detached and disciplined Akhmatova, the subjective and effusive Tsvetaeva never hesitated to hypostatize herself as the subject of her poetry. She even used the etymology of her name, Marina, to present herself as "foam of the sea" ("Some are made of Stone and some of clay," 1920) or as "born not of a mother's womb, but of the sea" ("Two Songs," 1920).

Like her symbolist and acmeist contemporaries, Tsvetaeva incorporated a great deal of world literature into her poetry. As Manon, she addresses the Chevalier de Grieux ("Chevalier de Grieux, 1917), as Ophelia, Hamlet (in two poems of 1923), and as Phaedra, Hippolytus (in two poems of 1926). Psyche, Orpheus, and Aphrodite make repeated appearances. Some of Tsvetaeva's most moving verses are devoted to poetry, which she loved more than anything else: "Every verse is a child of love, born illegitimate" ("If a soul was born winged," 1918).

During the years of revolution and civil war, Tsvetaeva wrote much anti-Soviet political verse, in particular the cycle "Demesne of the Swans," which she took with her to the West, where she was able to publish six collections of her poetry by 1928. In the 1920s and 1930s Tsvetaeva continued to write short poems of the gnomic and personal type as well as more tributes to other poets ("To B. Pasternak," 1925; a cycle, "Verses to Pushkin," 1931), but she concentrated on longer epic and lyric-epic poems. These poems feature accentual verse, usually not broken into stanzas, inexact but ingenious rhymes, and staccato rhythms generated by short lines and nominal phrases, such as, "Heart sank: What's with him?/Brain: A signal!" ("Poem of the End," 1924). Vocabulary and syntax are colloquial, and the syntagmatic structure tends to be that of a stream of consciousness, generated by unpredictable and often irrational associations. The text may appear hermetic on first reading, proper awareness of context and background reveals it as not surrealist but merely intimate. Thus, "A New Year's Poem" (1927), addressed to Rainer María Rilke, who had died on December 29, 1926, becomes a heart-wrenching dirge and jubilant eulogy, quite understandable in the light of the correspondence between Rilke and Tsvetaeva, published only many years after Tsvetaeva's death. Similarly, "Essay of a Room" (1926) seems hermetic but becomes clear when read in the light of the poet's biography, literary reminiscences, and the theatrical controversy about the "fourth wall" (whose absense reveals the theatricality of all stagecraft).

"The Maiden Tsar" (1920), nearly a hundred pages and written in a variety of meters, retells, with many embellishments and digressions, a well-known Russian fairy tale from Afanasyev's collection. It is vigorous, lively, and racy from beginning to end.

"On That Red Horse" (1921), a two-hundred-line poem in a mixture of free verse and accentual verse in quatrains, is a wild chase after a fiery red horse—Pegasus of course, who springs from the fire of the poet's soul. The allegory has echoes of

Bürger's "Lenore" but also of Mayakovsky, whose style Tsvetaeva sometimes approaches in her long poems.

In "Poem of a Hill" (1924) the hill is Petřina Hora, a Prague working-class suburb, and it doubles as the poet's Parnassus. There is also some play on Russian *gora* (hill), and *gore* (grief), which coincide in some case forms. The poetic estrangement of the poem is achieved by turning the hill into a sentient subject: "The hill grieved [*gora gorevala*] that what was now / Blood and heat would turn to mere sorrow."

"Poem of the End" (1924) is about life in the face of death, about departure and separation, and about one last bridge to cross. It is also about a condemned man awaiting to be shot at four in the morning, and about "wanting to go home" when there is no home: there is no hope of an afterlife. Life is defined as "that place where one can't live, the Jewish quarter," from which it follows that one might as well become Ahasuerus, go to the island of lepers, or to hell—anywhere, only not to a life that "tolerates only renegades and sheep," for "In this most Christian of worlds / Poets are Jews!" "Poem of the End" has great intensity and a Juvenalian power of honest outrage. It is rich in ingenious conceits.

The long poem (more than two thousand lines) "The Ratcatcher: A Lyric Satire" (1925) uses the legend of the piper of Hameln as an allegory of the poet's encounter with society. The piper frees the town from rats (the cares of day-to-day living), but then the mayor refuses to keep his promise of giving his daughter (the soul) to the piper. A satire of small-town philistinism blends with dreamy lyricism, very much in the spirit of German romanticism.

"Poem of a Stairway" (1926) is an angry satire on Parisian poverty as seen, heard, and smelled on the back stairs of a tenement.

Each landing has its own kind of cough. Walking up the stairs is like perusing a menu, each floor emitting its own fetid smell. The poem then veers into an angry catalog of crimes committed by man the destroyer and abuser of nature—and of ways in which nature and things get back at man. Finally, the poem gets around to "things owned by the poor": they are in fact "simply souls, because they burn so cleanly." The poem ends as a poor mother leaves her children with a box of matches to play with and the tenement goes up in smoke.

Tsvetaeva, an expressionist who works with the extremes of the human condition, jagged contours of black and white, and extravagant mannerist metaphor, is more accessible to translation than most of her contemporaries, except those whose style was similar to hers, like the early Mayakovsky. Tsvetaeva is beginning to be recognized as one of the great poets of the century.

Tsvetaeva's remarkable prose was written mostly in the 1930s. It consists of highly subjective literary portraits, autobiographical sketches, and essays on Pushkin, Goethe, and other poets. Her prose falls in line with that of other great poets of her generation, like Mandelstam and Pasternak. It is a lyric poet's prose, elaborate in its choice of words, careful about descriptive detail, composed rather than told. Each vignette has its leitmotifs, verbal and visual. There is a great deal of poetic estrangement, as the narrator speaks as if of an immediate encounter rather than of a reminiscence, for instance, when she describes Voloshin's visit to her in Moscow or her first meeting with Kuzmin. The pieces dealing with her childhood preserve much of the child's point of view. Tsvetaeva's literary judgment, though subjective, is excellent. She correctly assesses the importance, absolute and relative, of each of her contemporaries.

Georgy Ivanov

Georgy Ivanov (1894–1958) joined the Petersburg ego-futurists in 1911 but soon afterward moved on to Gumilyov's Guild of Poets. In 1921 Ivanov married Irina Odoevtseva (1901–90), another talented member of the Guild of Poets. They emigrated in 1923 and settled in Paris, where Ivanov soon established himself as a major poet, critic, and memoirist. His memoirs, *Petersburg Winters* (1928; 2d ed., 1952), were taken to task for the introduction of episodes, deceptively in character with a person's image, that could not withstand critical scrutiny and were recognized as manifest fabrications.

Ivanov's early ego-futurist verses are a schoolboy's exercises. His five acmeist collections, which appeared from 1914 to 1922, show steady growth, but without developing an individual style. They feature many landscapes and cityscapes, still lifes, and some outright verbalizations of paintings ("Claude Lorrain," "In lithographs of ancient masters," "Green background, somewhat dim," all 1921). Poems that echo impressions also found in Gumilyov and Mandelshtam (there are many) suggest that Ivanov, though a mature poet, was at this stage their inferior.

In the collection *Roses* (1931) Ivanov finally found his own, highly idiosyncratic style. He uses a small and conventional vocabulary with a number of recurrent key words (rose, ice, blue, dawn and sunset, sky, stars, world), frequently nominal syntax, and laconic and elliptical phrasing. The metrical structure is regular, the rhymes unspectacular, so that form, while impeccable, is never foregrounded. Typically, a cosmic vision or the hint of a mystic epiphany is presented with intense feeling yet is often undercut by an intrusion of the mundane ("and I realize / That my neighbors in the streetcar / Look at me with strange eyes.") The lead poem may serve as an example:

> Above sunsets and roses—
> All the rest does not matter—
> Above solemn stars
> Our bliss lights up
>
> Bliss to torture and be tortured
> To be jealous and forget.
> Our bliss God-given,
> Our bliss long-awaited,
> Nor can there be another.
>
> All the rest is only music,
> Reflection, magic—
> Or blue, cold,
> Infinite, sterile,
> Cosmic celebration.

The ethos of *Sailing to the Island of Cytherea* (1937) signals a metamorphosis of the metaphysical themes of *Roses*, repeating the pattern of Blok's transition from *Verses about a Beautiful Lady* to *The Showbooth*. Ivanov's cosmic moods have lost their exaltation, turning subdued, somber, even desperate:

> I no longer need music.
> I no longer hear music.
>
> Let it rise toward the stars
> Like a black wall, let it.
>
> Let it scatter like a black wave
> With a muffled roar.
>
> That which only weeps and jingles,
> Blurs and recedes into the night,
>
> Cannot change anything,
> Cannot help anything.

In *Portrait without a Likeness* (1950), Ivanov's last collection to appear in his lifetime, the poet's metaphysical visions have become a bitter memory. The persona is now entirely alone, completely free, and utterly desperate. The poet has come to believe, "Not in the invincibility of evil, / But only in the inevitability of defeat, / Not in the music that burned up my life, / But in the ashes left from its burning." In the poems of his last years, published posthumously in 1958, Ivanov deepens these moods of existential despair, presenting them against a background of wistful reminiscences from the Russia of his youth and echoes from Russian literature. Death is now omnipresent, quite explicitly in the poet's "Posthumous Diary" (1958). The imagery that introduces death is, however, of tantalizing variety, ranging from the sublime to the grotesque. There is this image of universal, solemn nuclear death:

> Then a transparent, all-forgiving, gentle cloud of smoke
> Will tenderly engulf the world.
> And He, who could have helped but did not,
> Will stay in His primordial solitude.

But there is also the hideous death of a lonely beggar who "wanted to pray, but could not," then, "having checked if the noose would hold, flung himself into darkness." The suicide's last thought belongs, "Not to what makes this earth beautiful, / But to a dirty Moscow tavern, / A candle stump, a corridor, / Two white zeroes on a door."

Ivanov's late poetry is a series of powerful exercises in existential philosophy. It asks the "accursed questions" that tormented Dostoevsky's heroes, in an urgently personal way. Ivanov's answers are born of truly metaphysical despair. Few poets in all literature have succeeded in giving so poignant an expression to the Heideggerian conception of human existence as *Dasein zum Tode*, "being there to die."

Ivanov was the most important exponent of the "Parisian note," a school whose leader was Georgy Adamovich (1884–1972), a minor poet but important critic. Adamovich taught that poetry should concern itself with the eternal and universal themes of the human condition—mortality, evil and suffering, God—and deal with them in an honest and artless manner. This meant no to any foregrounding of formal elements, escape into mysticism or sentimentality, adoption of an aestheticizing cult of world culture, or surrender to a surrealist subconscious—in a word, to any of the poetic attitudes adopted by Adamovich's contemporaries. Accordingly, the style of poets representing the Parisian note is spare, even austere, although formally impeccable. Among its exponents besides Ivanov, Anatoly Shteiger, Lidiya Chervinskaya, Anna Prismanova, and Igor Chinnov deserve mention. Each of them added an individual timbre to the Parisian note.

Anatoly Shteiger (1907–44), a Swiss citizen born in Russia, lived in Paris most of his life. He died of tuberculosis in a Swiss sanatorium. His poetry, formally unpretentious, concise, and restrained, reflects the experience of a lonely soul facing an incomprehensible world. Its elegiac sadness comes from a sense of deep alienation yet is animated by a yearning for love and a search for God.

The poetry of Lidiya Chervinskaya (b. 1907) is marked by a sense of loss, of impasse, of falling silent. Ellipsis and aposiopesis, which also occur in Shteiger's

verses, are characteristic of her style. Like Shteiger's, too, her poems often read like notes from an intimate diary, though hers tend to have a dreamy quality that is absent in Shteiger's. Chervinskaya's imagery is urban, sometimes specifically Parisian, always subdued, muffled, and vague. Chervinskaya, though narrow in range, is a poet with a voice of her own.

The same is true of Anna Prismanova (1898–1960), who differs from other poets of the Parisian note in that her poetic world tends toward concrete yet absurdist imagery and alogical, though seemingly familiar, relationships. Igor Chinnov (b. 1909) was born in Riga and lived in Paris and Munich before coming to the United States in 1962, where he taught Russian literature at several universities. His early poetry, eventually gathered in the collections *Monologue* (1950) and *Lines* (1960), is vintage Parisian note. It projects a humanist's resigned pessimism, a skeptic's deep reverence for religion, and a sober realist's gratitude for rare moments of illumination. Chinnov went on to experiment with other styles after he came to the United States.

The Chamber of Poets (Palata poetov), a Parisian group of poets independent of the Parisian note, had among its members Boris Poplavsky, Dovid Knut, Aleksandr Ginger (the husband of Anna Prismanova), and Serge Charchoune (Sergei Sharshun), the last better known as a painter. Among these, Boris Poplavsky (1903–1935) was the most notable. He knew modern French poetry well and was influenced by the French symbolists, Apollinaire, and surrealism. Poplavsky personally felt closest to Blok's visionary poetry. He published a single volume, *Flags* (1931), in his lifetime; most of his poetry and prose were published posthumously. Formally ragged though musical, his poetry is graphic in a hallucinatory way. His apocalyptic visions of a perishing Europe are hauntingly vivid. Poplavsky's place in twentieth-century Russian poetry is still to be determined.

Dovid Knut (pseudonym of David Fiksman, 1900–55), unlike other Russian poets of Jewish parentage, actively stressed his Jewishness, concentrated on Jewish themes, and drew on the Old Testament for his imagery. His best poems are meditations of a modern man seeking to find his God, and of a Jew pondering the fate of his people. Knut's poetry is remarkable even formally, as its rhythmic structure is pointedly synchronized with the flow of its emotions.

Several poets of talent and originality were active away from the major centers of the diaspora, although they always maintained contact with Paris. Yury Ivask (1907–86) was born in Moscow but lived in Estonia between the two world wars. Displaced to Germany in 1944, he immigrated to the United States in 1949, where he taught Russian literature at several universities. A prolific scholar, he published studies on Leontyev, Rozanov, and Dostoevsky, as well as many critical essays and reviews. Ivask's early poetry, gathered in the volumes *Northern Shores* (1938) and *Imperial Autumn* (1953), reveals a *doctus poeta*, whose poems abound in vivid echoes of Russian and Western history, art, architecture, and literature. Like several other poets of the second generation of émigrés, Ivask developed an astonishing capacity for change and growth in his mature years. In the 1960s and 1970s he developed an idiosyncratic manner in which he successfully fused themes of pre-Petrine and folk culture with an erudite and sophisticated Western consciousness, eventually creating a unique sensibility by which he transformed mundane reality into a paradise

(*rai*) of gladness, plenitude, and marvels. His collections *Glory* (1967) and *Cinderella* (1970) and his verse epic *Homo ludens* (1973) made him a major poet.

Valery Pereleshin (pseudonym of Valery Salatko-Petryshche, b. 1913) was born in Irkutsk. He was educated in Harbin, later lived in several cities in China, and since 1953 has resided in Rio de Janeiro. He has translated Chinese poetry into Russian and Russian poetry into Portuguese (Kuzmin's "Alexandrian Songs"), and vice versa. Pereleshin, like Ivask and Chinnov, started with formally impeccable but conventional verse: *On the Road* (1937), *A Good Beehive* (1939), and *Star over the Sea* (1941). Masterful sonnets and crowns of sonnets were a part of his poetic repertoire from the beginning. In the 1960s and 1970s he developed an individual style based on an impassioned dialogue between ardent religious feeling and violent homoerotic passion: *Southern House* (1968), *Swing* (1971), and *Ariel* (1976).

Lidiya Alekseeva (1909–89) spent her childhood in the Crimea, lived in Yugoslavia from 1920 to 1942, and came to the United States in 1949. Her first poems appeared in the 1930s. She published her first collection, *Forest Sun*, in Frankfurt in 1954 and several more collections in the United States, starting with *On the Road* (1959). Alekseeva has a voice and vision distinctly her own. She is adept at finding God, beauty, and joy in the details of ordinary life. A masterful painter of psychologically charged landscapes, she finds objects of fascination even in the cityscape of a New York slum. Even her elegiac sadness radiates light and gratitude.

The second wave of émigrés from the Soviet Union added several outstanding poets to the Russian Parnassus in exile: Dmitry Klenovsky (1893–1976), Ivan Elagin (1918–87), Nikolai Morshen (pseudonym of Nikolai Marchenko, b. 1917), Olga Anstei (1912–85), and others. Among them, Klenovsky is probably the most significant. He had published a volume of verse in Russia in 1917, but nothing more until displaced to Germany by the Second World War. His ten volumes published in exile, starting with *A Trace of Life* (1950) and ending with *Last Poems* (1977), published posthumously after his death in Traunstein, Bavaria, are formally marked by the disciplined poetics of acmeism. Klenovsky's poetic world is, however, far from the serenity and joie de vivre of the acmeists. Rather, his philosophical meditations tend toward a futile search for the absolute, which leads to the only certainty, that of death.

Emigré prose fiction could rely on established writers like Bunin, Zaitsev, Kuprin, Shmelyov, Teffi, Osorgin, and Chirikov, all of them basically practitioners of the shorter prose genres—novella, short story, sketch, and reminiscence. Ivan Bunin's fictionalized autobiography, *Arsenyev's Life* (1930–39) is essentially a suite of lyric prose sketches of Russian life, remembered through a haze of nostalgia. Bunin's short stories of the postrevolutionary period tend to be exercises in the fateful affinity of love and death. Like "Sunstroke" (1925), one of Bunin's most memorable stories, they tell of erotic encounters cut short by death or by a fateful event just short of death. Bunin's preoccupation with violent erotic passion and sudden death, both of which he could make palpably real, is exceptional for a Russian writer. A master at creating a mood or atmosphere, Bunin was not a deep thinker or explorer of the human mind and soul. He saw the obvious and reacted to it with predictable emotions. When Bunin became the first Russian to win a Nobel Prize in literature (1933), this was, though not undeserved,

anticlimactic from the vantage point of Russian literature as a whole. In Russian émigré circles it was expected that Merezhkovsky, not Bunin, would get the prize. Bunin also published a volume of reminiscences (1950). An interesting though incomplete book on Chekhov appeared posthumously (1955).

Kuprin, Hippius, and Merezhkovsky did not produce any important fiction after the revolution. Whereas Kuprin's autobiographical novel *Cadets* (1928–33) and some short stories, nostalgic recollections of the writer's youth, are of slight literary value, Hippius's reminiscences, *Living Faces* (1925) show her at her witty, perceptive, and mordant best. Merezhkovsky continued to work on his Eternal Companions series of biographies of great men and women.

Boris Zaitsev (1881–1972) had established himself as a writer in the manner of Turgenev before he left Russia in 1922. In Paris he developed into a writer of varied interests and great versatility. As a novelist and storyteller, Zaitsev retained a Turgenevian mood of melancholy resignation and an equally Turgenevian emphasis on the self-conscious individual and his struggle for inner freedom. His first major work in exile, *Golden Design* (1926), is set in prerevolutionary Russia, although it leads up to the catastrophe of world war and revolution. Zaitsev's later fiction is set in Russia (*Gleb's Journey*, 1937, a fictionalized account of the writer's childhood) or abroad (*The House in Passy*, 1935). Besides fiction, Zaitsev wrote some literary biographies (*The Life of Turgenev*, 1932; *Zhukovsky*, 1951; *Chekhov*, 1954), several volumes of memoirs, sketches of his travels in Russia and the West, and works of religious content, such as *The Life of Saint Sergius of Radonezh* and *Alexis, Man of God* (both 1925). Zaitsev was a master of stylized and lyric prose who skillfully adapted his language to the topic at hand.

Aleksei Remizov reacted to the revolution with anguish. His lament in rhythmic prose, "The Lay of the Ruin of the Russian Land,"[14] and his poem "Red Banner" (both 1917) portrayed the revolution as a terrible calamity. He emigrated in 1921 and spent the rest of his life in France, living in poverty much of the time. In the 1920s he wrote a series of impressionistic and highly idiosyncratic sketches of Russia torn by war, ruin, and fear: *Sounds of the City* (1921), *Specter* (1922), *Russia in a Whirlwind* (1927), and *Along the Cornices* (1929). He also continued to write adaptations of apocrypha, saints' lives, and legends. Remizov could publish only little in the 1930s. After the war, although in ill health and going blind, he did some of his best writing while also continuing to work as a calligrapher and graphic artist. *Dancing Demon* (1949) is a quaint vision of Russia's orgiastic roots. In *With Clipped Eyes* (1951) scenes from Remizov's childhood and adolescence are turned into a suite of surrealistic vignettes. *Martyn Zadeka: A Book of Dreams* is a collection of Remizov's own dreams, while *The Fire of Things* (both 1954) deals with dreams in Russian literature. *In a Rosy Light* (1952) is the continuation of a biography of the writer's wife, begun as *Olya* in 1927. Remizov's late work confirms his importance as one of the most original prose writers in all of Russian literature.

Ivan Shmelyov (1873–1950) began his career as a writer with Gorky's publishing house Knowledge, though he was from the outset interested in the religious life of the Russian people, its traditions and its shrines. He left Russia in 1922 and settled in Paris in 1925. He had witnessed the horrors of the civil war in the Crimea and described them in a series of stories, sketches, and reminiscences collected under the title *Sun of the Dead* (1926). Thereafter Shmelyov's stories dealt mostly with the travails of simple Russian people under Soviet rule and in exile, described with warm empathy and close attention to the details of everyday life: *Citizen Ukleikin: Tales* (1923), *The Wall: Tales* (1928), *About an Old Woman: New Tales about Russia* (1927), and *Entering Paris: Tales about Russia Abroad* (1929). Shmelyov, a writer in the Gogolian manner, uses *skaz*, lyric, rhythmic, and declamatory diction, hyperbole, dream logic, estrangement, and other devices that make for an ornamental style resembling that which appears in the work of some of his Soviet contemporaries, such as Boris Pilnyak. In his later years Shmelyov again wrote a number of works devoted to religious themes, including *Heavenly Ways* (1931–38) and *A Pilgrimage* (1935).

Nadezhda Teffi (pseudonym of Nadezhda Buchinskaya, née Lokhvitskaya, 1872–1952), sister of the poet Mirra Lokhvitskaya, was an immensely popular feuilletonist even before the revolution. After her emigration in 1919 she settled in Paris, where she soon resumed the role she had played in Petersburg. The subject of her many stories, sketches, and one-act plays is Russian émigrés, bewildered and unhappy in their new and unfamiliar environment, and the many comic and tragicomic situations in which they find themselves because of a conflict between their (often imaginary) past and precarious or humdrum present. In a way, Teffi's humbled émigrés are an inverted mirror image of Zoshchenko's budding Soviet philistines.

The crop of prose writers who established themselves in exile was less impressive than

---

14. The title alludes to the thirteenth-century *Orison on the Ruin of the Russian Land.*

that of émigré poets, but it was far from negligible. Mark Aldanov (pseudonym of Mark Landau, 1886–1957), a research chemist by profession, was known mostly as a literary critic before his emigration in 1919. He lived in Paris from 1924 until moving to New York in 1940, where he became cofounder (with M. O. Tsetlin) of *The New Review* in 1942. In exile, Aldanov soon established a reputation as a major novelist and eventually gained international recognition. Two books written in French, *Lénine* (1919) and *Deux révolutions: La Révolution française et la révolution russe* (1920), became points of departure for two cycles of novels, a tetralogy set in the period of the French Revolution and a trilogy about the Russian revolution. The novels of the first, *Saint Helena, a Small Island* (1922), *The Ninth of Thermidor* (1923), *Devil's Bridge* (1925), and *The Conspiracy* (1927) explore the meaning of the French Revolution. The novels of the latter, *The Key* (1930), *Escape* (1932), and *The Cave* (1934–36), seek to make sense of the chaotic events which wreak havoc in the lives of people who witness the 1917 revolution in Russia. Aldanov's later novels, some historical, such as *The Tenth Symphony* (1931) or *A Night at Ulm: The Philosophy of Chance* (1953), some contemporary, such as *The Beginning of the End* (1938) or *Live as You Wish* (1952), are in effect philosophical essays about the human condition, history, and modern man. Aldanov's favorite device is to juxtapose the fate of an ordinary individual to the grand design of history of which he is quite unaware, or to present a great man—Beethoven for example, in *The Tenth Symphony*—as he is viewed by his contemporaries. Aldanov's novels are logically structured, his psychology pragmatic, and his style lucid, all of which makes his novels very readable. His consistent rationalism, skepticism, and rejection of all religious solutions to human suffering place Aldanov in the tradition of Herzen and liberal Westernism and make him rather unique among Russian novelists. Aldanov was also a brilliant essayist and critic.

Not all the successes in émigré literature were earned by artistic or intellectual quality. It had its share of works that found readers by virtue of their sensational or tendentious quality. General Pyotr Krasnov (1869–1945), a minor amateur writer before the revolution, scored a major hit with a long epic novel, *From Double-Headed Eagle to Red Banner* (1921–22), the biography of a Russian officer that coincides with the reign of Nicholas II, developed against a broad panoramic background. The novel gives a simplistic interpretation of social and political developments that led up to the revolution and is primitive in its construction and psychology, but it projected views held by many émigrés, as well as by right-wing Western readers, particularly in Germany. General Krasnov, who had played a major role in the civil war, resumed his political and military activities in World War II, on the German side. Extradited to Soviet authorities by the Western Allies at the end of the war, he was executed in Moscow.

Nabokov

Vladimir Vladimirovich Nabokov (1899–1977) published his Russian works under the pseudonym Sirin. Like Aldanov, he gave Russian literature some first-rate fiction set in the West. Nabokov studied in Cambridge; he lived in Berlin from 1922 to 1937, then in Paris until 1940, when he went to America and abandoned Russian as his literary medium in favor of English. He had by then established himself as one of the top writers of émigré literature. Nabokov's Russian oeuvre consists of nine short novels, a number of short stories, two plays, poetry, some essays and reviews, and memoirs. His English oeuvre is of a different order from the Russian and must not be viewed as its continuation. Nabokov, like Aldanov, owed little to any Russian writer. Russia only appears in the background. Most of his novels and stories are based on the life of the Russian diaspora. Nabokov's personal interests—chess, tennis, and lepidoptera—show up on occasion.

Nabokov's novels and stories are marked by ingenious plots, precision of detail and phrasing, incisive but unambiguous psychological analysis, a pointedly unsentimental narrator, and a clear moral stance that emerges without even a semblance of moralizing. Nabokov's Russian fiction is also remarkable for its lack of any ideological tendency. None of the plots of Nabokov's novels resembles any other, but they all have heroes who are captives of an obsession, an illusion, or a deception from which there is no escape. *The Spy* (1930) uses a split consciousness syndrome to create a baffling yet logical plot. The plot of *Luzhin's Defense* (1930) is based on parallelism between a chess game and the hero's fate (Luzhin is a chess master). *Despair* (1936) is a crime thriller whose plot is generated by the narrator's—he is also the murderer—deranged mind. *The Gift* (1937–38) is the story of a young writer's growth; laced with provocative opinions on Russian history and literature, it also contains a ruthless deflation of Chernyshevsky, presented as a study by the novel's hero. *Invitation to a Beheading* (1938) is an allegory reminiscent of Kafka's *The Trial*. Its hero, Cincinnatus, is awaiting execution for what appears to be the crime of being "different." He keeps a diary in which he puts down his intuitions

about his true home. When the executioner's ax falls, the cardboard world of the novel disintegrates and Cincinnatus is on his way home.

Nabokov's art goes against the grain of the entire tradition of Russian fiction. His plots are composed of random events and allow for no positive philosophical message. His characters are individuals, not types. Ideas found in his works are not a part of any system. The moral principle that dominates all his works is that of an uncompromising honesty. The only other value that emerges from them is art. But even art is of a precarious worth: Luzhin's defense, a brilliant work of art, turns out to be flawed after all.

The other prose writers of the younger generation, Irina Odoevtseva, Nina Berberova, Yury Felzen, Gaito Gazdanov, and Vasily Yanovsky, to mention the more notable, did not come close to Nabokov either in the quality of their works or in their success. Gaito (Georgy) Gazdanov (1903–1971) was hailed as a major talent on the strength of his first novel, *An Evening with Claire* (1930), but it soon developed that he had his limitations. Like so many of his contemporaries, Gazdanov had difficulty developing a sustained narrative. Strong pages alternate with manifestly indifferent ones. His strength, which comes out in his stories and later novels—*The Story of a Journey* (1938), *Night Roads* (2d ed., 1952), *The Awakening* (1965–66), *Evelyne and Her Friends* (1968–71)—lies in creating vivid episodes in which intense inner experience is synchronized with setting and external detail. The final judgment on Gazdanov is still out.

Discursive literary prose was well represented by several philosophers, critics, and essayists of European stature. Nikolai Berdyaev (1874–1948), a philosopher and critic of Russian thought (*The Russian Idea*, 1946), also wrote an important book on Dostoevsky (*Dostoevsky's Worldview*, 1923) and essays on other Russian writers. Lev Shestov (1866–1938), who had published ground-breaking studies on the philosophy of Tolstoi, Dostoevsky, and Turgenev before the revolution, now produced several books in which he expounded his existential philosophy: *In Job's Balance* (1929), *Kierkegaard and Existential Philosophy* (1936), and *Athens and Jerusalem* (1938). The vigorous and lucid prose of these books has few peers in Russian literature.

Vladimir Weidlé (1895–1979), art historian, essayist, literary critic and theorist, published in several languages besides Russian. He speculated about the direction in which Western civilization was headed and argued that the romantic period marked the beginning of its decline (*The Death of Art: Meditations on the Fate of Literary and Artistic Creativity*, 1937). Weidlé rephrased his ideas in a prize-winning work written in French, *Les abeilles d'Aristée: Essai sur le destin actuel des lettres et des arts* (1954). As a theorist of art, Weidlé rejected not only the formalist method of abstracting the aesthetic (or literary) component of a work of art, on the grounds that it leads to an irreversible separation of understanding from appreciation, but also the "modernist" tendency to make art independent of a structured medium. A brilliant essayist, Weidlé also wrote elegant verse drawing on his impressions as a traveler and a connoisseur of art.

Among critics of the second wave, Boris Filippov (b. 1905), who has lived in Germany and the United States (since 1950), deserves mention for his tireless work in making available the works of poets who were banned in the Soviet Union. Together with Gleb Struve, he prepared editions of Klyuev, Mandelshtam, Gumilyov, Akhmatova, Pasternak, and Zabolotsky; and together with E. V. Zhiglevich, editions of Zoshchenko, Leontyev, Remizov, Zamyatin, and Shkapskaya. His introductory essays to these editions are invariably perceptive, lively, and eloquent.

Poetry in the Soviet Union

The revolution was a watershed even in the history of Russian poetry. It inspired a great deal of poetry, yet it also caused some existing schools of poetry to fall silent. Russian symbolism ceased to exist after the death of Blok and Bryusov and the emigration of Vyacheslav Ivanov, Balmont, Merezhkovsky, and Hippius. Acmeism lost its founder and leader, Gumilyov, and was renounced by its other founder, Sergei Gorodetsky. Several members of the Guild of Poets (Georgy Ivanov, Irina Odoevtseva, Nikolai Otsup) emigrated. The futurists lost Khlebnikov through death, Burlyuk through emigration, and abandoned much of their avant-garde aesthetic as they joined the Left Art movement. The rise of imagism, cosmism, constructivism, and OBERIU coincided with the first years of the Soviet regime by accident. Their rapid fall, though, was at least in part due to the regime's hostility to these schools. In the few years given them they produced some remarkable poetry. The 1920s also witnessed the best work of such independent "inner émigrés" as Voloshin, Sologub, Mandelshtam, and Pasternak. Altogether, the first decade of the Soviet regime saw more great poetry than any comparable period of Russian literature.

The revolution was a powerful poetic stimulus that caused spontaneous and unpredictable reactions. Voloshin's civic cycles, Blok's "The Twelve," Khlebnikov's poems about the revolution, Hippius's poems of political invective, and Mayakovsky's revolutionary manifestoes all broke the mold of the poet's previously established poetic ethos. Other major poets responded to the revolution in a manner consistent with a previously established style. Mandelshtam, who could hear the "music" of the revolution as clearly as anybody, was able to arrange it so as to transform even chaos, fear, and slaughter into pure poetry. Klyuev's dirges about the ruin of Russian peasant culture under the blows of the revolution are held in the very style that celebrated the gladness and plenty of old.

The revolution stimulated the birth of several distinctive poetic styles. One of these developed in the workshops of the Proletarian Culture movement immediately after the revolution. In conventional meters and strophic forms, with little rhythmic or euphonic finesse, the poetry of Proletkult expressed revolutionary enthusiasm, boundless devotion to the cause of the world proletariat, and dreams of a future of ease and plenty, to be attained by the power of human reason and machines invented by man. The imagery and language of this poetry were vehemently, and in retrospect ludicrously, hyperbolic. The revolution was perceived not only as the dawn of a new age but as an event of cosmic proportions, whose repercussions were felt in the whole stellar universe. Heavy machinery, locomotives, factory whistles, and other symbols of industrial progress were used in profusion, both directly and metaphorically. The hero of Proletkult poetry is the factory worker, a "man of iron" at one with the machines he services. He is the "new man." His whole being is rational, mechanized, and coordinated. In his breast beats a "collective heart."

The leading poets of Proletkult were Vasi-

ly Aleksandrovsky (1897–1934), a leader of the Moscow studio of Proletkult and later of the Smithy; Aleksei Gastev (1882–1941), the most intelligent, original, and imaginative poet of the school; Mikhail Gerasimov (1889–1939), an Old Bolshevik who resigned from the party in 1921 in protest against the NEP but continued to write for the Smithy; Vladimir Kirillov (1890–1943), a leader of Proletkult and one of the founders of the Smithy, who in a poem, "We" (1917), proclaimed: "In the name of our tomorrow we shall burn Raphael, destroy the museums, trample underfoot the flowers of art", and Vasily Knyazev (1887–1937), an Old Bolshevik and member of the Red Guard, some of whose poems became revolutionary songs. All of these poets perished in Stalin's purges. Vasily Kazin (b. 1898), unlike his peers of Proletkult and the Smithy, managed to make the transition to poet of the party line and panegyrist of Stalin. Some of his poems poeticizing the artisan's (a bricklayer's, carpenter's, or tinsmith's) labor have a certain ingenuous appeal.

The "democratization of art" professed by Left Art, and by Mayakovsky and his fellow futurists in particular, meant a direct and active involvement of the artist and poet in current affairs. The novelty of this position lay with the readiness of first-rate artists and poets to engage in menial utilitarian work such as delivering the news in accord with the party line, acting as a vehicle of political propaganda and indoctrination, and formulating public service messages so they would catch the public's attention. In volunteering to become an organ of agitprop, the poet declared that he was willing to adapt his art to the mentality of a mass audience. Whereas the aesthetically naive poets of Proletkult tried, no matter how clumsily, to raise the consciousness of an uneducated audience to the level of high poetry, the sophisticated poets of avant-garde Left Art descended to the level of a semiliterate public. The principal outlet of Mayakovsky and other poets of the avant-garde during the years of the civil war was the show windows of ROSTA, the Soviet telegraph agency. Their medium was the jingle, ditty (*chastushka*), or ballad, often illustrated by appropriate cartoons: "A soldier who deserts the Red Army is his own worst enemy!" "Peasants, if you don't want the landowners back, don't hoard your grain, but deliver it to Soviet requisitioning teams, or the workers in the cities won't be able to provide arms for the Red Army!" "Why are the Mensheviks our enemies? Because they have betrayed us to Western capitalists!" "Distilling vodka from much-needed grain is a heinous crime!" ROSTA window poetry, especially Mayakovsky's, is often spirited, witty, and formally masterful. It is also outrageously crude, brazenly mendacious, and absurdly simplistic. It deals in grotesquely deformed stereotypes: capitalists are enormously fat, wear a top hat, and chomp on huge cigars; landowners make peasant women suckle the pups of their hounds. The effectiveness of avant-garde ROSTA window poetry as propaganda is questionable. Party leaders doubted it. Lenin and particularly Trotsky much preferred the less imaginative and virtuosic, but snappy propaganda jingles of Demyan Bedny (Demyan "the Poor," pseudonym of Efim Pridvorov, 1883–1945). An Old Bolshevik, Bedny also wrote catchy songs for the Red Army and blasphemous antireligious tracts, such as *New Testament, without Flaw, of Demyan the Evangelist* (1925). Bedny had a sharp ear for the lilt of folk verse and liked to build his pieces around popular sayings and proverbs. Bedny, like many Old Bolsheviks, fell upon hard times under Stalin, but survived.

Mayakovsky

Mayakovsky, who never became a party member, was nevertheless from its first days an active supporter of the Soviet regime. He published, mostly in the daily press, innumerable pieces, long and short, celebrating Lenin and the party, denouncing the regime's enemies, explaining government policies, fighting social ills such as drunkenness and absenteeism, encouraging good habits such as brushing one's teeth regularly, and pushing the products of government-owned industries. As he put it in his last poem, "At the Top of My Voice" (1930), he "stepped on the throat of his own songs" to become a "latrine cleaner and bard of boiled water." Mayakovsky's utilitarian poetry boasts the qualities that are the best part of his genuine poetry: ingenious rhymes, clever puns, striking imagery, and spirited whimsy. There is no denying that his "Verses about My Soviet Passport" (1929), pure propaganda, is a brilliant piece of versified rhetoric.

Mayakovsky was active on many fronts. He wrote perhaps ten film scenarios and played the lead in a couple of his films. He wrote several important plays. He traveled all over the Soviet Union lecturing and reading his poetry. He gave radio talks for the government's antireligious propaganda program. He went abroad frequently (to America in 1925) and reported about his travels in witty and informative prose and verse, never forgetting to lace it with communist propaganda. He was the heart and soul of *Lef*, the journal of the Soviet avant-garde. His incessant attacks on bureaucratic arrogance, inefficiency, and complacency made him enemies, though, and in 1929 and 1930 he experienced some professional and personal difficulties. Still, his suicide on April 14, 1930 came as a surprise to everybody. Some years after Mayakovsky's death, Stalin declared him to have been the greatest Soviet poet, with the result that for the next twenty years and more Mayakovsky received greater exposure on every level, from academia to grammar school, than any other modern Russian poet. His influence on his younger contemporaries and the poets who began their careers in the 1950s was immense.

Even after the revolution, the lyric verse epic in the manner of his early "A Cloud in Trousers" remained Mayakovsky's favorite genre. Some of these poems, such as "Vladimir Ilyich Lenin" (1924, nearly three thousand lines) and "Good! A Poem of the October Revolution" (1927, more than three thousand lines), are a regrettable waste of much ingenious and polished versification—"Lenin" entirely so. "Good!" does have a few genuinely fine episodes: that of the storming of the Winter Palace and the fall of the Provisional Government, told with somber exuberance, is a piece of magnificent epic narrative in irresistably driving verse. The episode following it tells of a meeting (surely imaginary) between Mayakovsky and Blok one night on the banks of the Neva:

> Blok stood and stared
>   and Blok's shadow
> Stared, too,
>   rising on a wall . . .
> As though
>   both
>   were waiting for Christ
> To come walking across the water.
> But Christ
>   had no intention
>   to show Himself to Blok.

Here Mayakovsky mockingly alludes to the conclusion of Blok's "The Twelve." But much of the rest of "Good!" is no more than versified political indoctrination.

"150,000,000: A Poem" (1920–21), more interesting and original than Mayakovsky's other political verse epics, met with the irritated disapproval of Lenin himself. It combines utopian allegory, political satire, and whimsical grotesque in an epic about a mythic Armageddon in which the giant Ivan—that is, 150,000,000 cold, hungry, and desperate Russians—vanquish an enormously fat Woodrow Wilson, ruler of the capitalist world. In a great battle the animal world, things, and the whole cosmos take sides. Racehorses join Wilson, dray horses join Ivan; similarly, limousines oppose trucks, decadents oppose futurists, and constellations oppose the Milky Way. "150,000,000" is a superbly modern poem. Its imagination is that of an animated cartoon. Realized metaphor is its key device. It was hardly good communist propaganda (Lenin was right in his own terms, calling it preposterous and stupid), but it was an exhilarating tour de force of futurist poetics wed to revolutionary enthusiasm.

"About That" (1923), where "that" is love, is an apotheosis of the poet's love affair with Lily Brik, expressed in a kaleidoscopic sequence of frenzied emotional outbursts and whimsical conceits. As in his prerevolutionary poems, Mayakovsky makes liberal use of world literature as material for his puns and conceits. The title of Part One, "A Ballad of Reading Gaol" (written in Wilde's meter), alludes to Mayakovsky's confinement to his own flat after a lovers' tiff with Lily. When he walks up the stairs to her place, he feels "like Raskolnikov when he went back to ring that bell," and at one point he finds himself at the site of Lermontov's fatal duel. In the course of the poem the lovesick poet undergoes some fantastic metamorphoses, mostly via a realized metaphor. One of these turns him into a polar bear. In the end he finds himself shot to pieces until only a tattered red flag is left of him flying over the Kremlin. Above, the sky sparkles with lyric stars, and Ursa Major, the Great She-Bear, takes to "troubadouring" as sister of the polar bear, who keeps bawling his verses on his flight to the stars. "About That" has little redeeming social value, aside from a suggestion made toward its end that the tribulations of love will be a thing of the past in the communist future, as lovers will become comrades. It is, however, entertaining throughout and in places brilliant.

Mayakovsky wrote many shorter poems (even his "shorter" poems tend to have a hundred lines or more) whose poetic effect is not spoiled by a too-grating communist propaganda message. The cycle "Verses about America" (1925–26) contains some twenty poems presenting a vivid panorama of America in the Roaring Twenties. It combines the futurist's admiration for the marvels of American technology and approval of the dynamic American way of life with a communist propagandist's efforts to find fault with American middle-class bigotry, prudishness, and greed. The most famous of these poems, "Brooklyn Bridge," is an ode to human skill and ingenuity. But it also has unemployed workers jump to their death from the bridge. "Camp Nit Gedajge", devoted to a summer camp of young Jewish communists on the Hudson river, is a stirring tribute to man's victorious struggle against time, but it also lets the young communists' song "make the Hudson flow into the Moscow River."

Upon his return from America, Mayakovsky wrote his famous poem "To Sergei Esenin" (1926), whose genesis he described in his equally famous essay "How to Make Verse?" (1926). It was a response to Esenin's suicide poem, specifically its last lines: "In this life it is not new to die, / But then, to live isn't any newer either." Mayakovsky's last lines were seemingly optimistic, but in retrospect ominous: "In this world it is not difficult to die— / To make a life is considerably more difficult." Here "make a life" means make a life that is livable. The entire poem, with all its wit and bravado, paints a terribly bleak picture of the contemporary scene as it investigates the possible reasons why Esenin should have put an end to his life.

Several poems of Mayakovsky's last years show the poet defending himself and his domain against a new, decidedly Soviet philistinism. In "Conversation with a Tax Collector about Poetry" (1926) he protests against being taxed at a private entrepreneur's high rate, pointing out how difficult and strenuous his craft is: Is not the end of a line like an IOU requiring payment in the form of a rhyme? Is not poetry like the mining of radium?—thousands of tons of verbal ore must be sifted through to obtain a single gram of poetry. And does not the poet have travel expenses, having ridden to death a dozen Pegasuses? What about amortization, especially "that most terrible of amortizations, the amortization of heart and soul"? In "A Letter to Comrade Kostrov from Paris, on the Nature of Love" (1928), Mayakovsky, who had fallen in love with a beautiful young émigrée, apologizes to Comrade Kostrov, editor of *Young Guard*, who had commissioned some suitably edifying political verse, for wasting lines on so frivolous a subject as love; and in "A Letter to Tatyana Yakovleva" (the lady in question), he tries to persuade her to forego a life of effete luxury for the creative rigors of

Soviet life. "At the Top of My Voice" (1930), Mayakovsky's "Exegi monumentum" and apology *pro domo sua*, ends in the words, "When I appear/before the CCC [Central Committee of the Communist party]/of the bright years/of the future,/I shall raise high over a band/of poetic racketeers and crooks /my Bolshevik party membership card:/all hundred volumes/of my/party books." (The point is that Mayakovsky, not a party member, is more loyal to the party than his card-carrying detractors.) The poem presents the poet as one who has sacrificed himself and his art to the cause of socialism, instead of "scribbling/romances,/like others did,/more profitable and prettier"— a disingenuous and unjustified assertion, for Mayakovsky gained more worldly fame and more material rewards than any of the major poets who were his contemporaries.

Paradoxically, Mayakovsky, the most utilitarian of all major Russian poets, was in retrospect a poet's poet, whose verses are, aside from their historical interest as period pieces, valuable only as pure poetry. What thought or emotion they purport to express is either banal or terribly dated. But their sheer verbal, phonic, and rhythmic inventiveness makes them aesthetically appealing and fascinating, especially to the reader familiar with the subtleties of poetic technique.

Nikolai Aseev (1889–1963), a friend of Mayakovsky's, was another poet who successfully made the transition from avant-garde to officially sanctioned poetry. Aseev, who started his poetic career in 1911 with the modernist journal *Springtime*, edited by Vasily Kamensky, was a member of the Centrifuge group in 1914 but then developed a style that was closer to cubo-futurism. Even after he had retreated from his position that "a stream of sounds may generate thoughts

but will never be governed by them,"[15] he retained a futurist penchant for farfetched and realized metaphors, etymologism, and even verbal cubism. After joining *Lef* in 1922, Aseev became Mayakovsky's trusted collaborator and a successful practitioner of ideologically edifying poetry "for the people." Several of his poems became popular songs and school texts: "Budyonny's March,"[16] "My Rifle," and "Five-Pointed Star." The revolutionary romanticism and folksy diction of his verse epics "Budyonny" (1923), "Twenty-Six" (1925) and "Semyon Proskakov" (1928) appealed to rank-and-file readers. They are characterized by lively accentual verse, inexact but rich rhymes, and strident consonantal sound patterns— a somewhat tamer, less ebullient, more relaxed version of Mayakovsky. After Mayakovsky's death, Aseev spent years on a verse epic, *Incipit Mayakovsky* (1937–50), an attempt to write literary history in verse. The work not only contains numerous direct allusions to Mayakovsky's works but also consistently echoes Mayakovsky's rhythms, stylistic mannerisms, and rhyming technique.

Aseev was only one of several poets to emulate Mayakovsky as a poet with a "social commission" and to cultivate a style similar to his. Semyon Kirsanov (1906–1972), a native of Odessa, joined *Lef* in 1925 and toured the country with Mayakovsky. Like Mayakovsky, Kirsanov devoted his talent to versified publicism, such as the *poema* "Five-Year Plan" (1932). Kirsanov's style has many Mayakovskian traits: frequent use of the first-person singular, whimsical imagery,

15. From Aseev's preface to his collection *Letorei* (1915), where *letorei* is a futuristic neologism formed from *leto* (summer, year) and *reyat'* (to soar).

16. Semyon Budyonny, commander of the First Cavalry in the war against Poland in 1920.

puns and conceits, symbolic patterning of sound and syntax. His poetic persona, however, is warmer and more humane than Mayakovsky's, his poetic temper thoughtful rather than aggressive. His voice lacks the stridency of Mayakovsky's. Kirsanov's versified utopian and science fiction ("A Last Contemporary," 1930; "The Golden Age," 1933; "Atom under Siege," 1933; "Poem about a Robot," 1934) is intelligent and thought-provoking. His personal poetry, as in the cycles "Groaning in My Sleep" and "The Last of May" (both 1937), expresses emotional suffering in a genuinely tragic tone. During the war Kirsanov produced his share of patriotic verse. Kirsanov's active role in the "thaw" after Stalin's death was not out of character: his utopian *poema* "Seven Days of the Week" (1956) is an allegory of the ultimate triumph of goodness and honesty in Soviet life. Toward the end of his life Kirsanov turned toward philosophical meditations in free verse, in the manner of romantic *Naturphilosophie*.

Aleksandr Bezymensky (1898–1973), an activist of the Proletarian Culture movement and later of VAPP and RAPP, unlike many of his peers chose to follow the example of Lef and concentrated on publicistic verse, scrupulously adhering to the party line of the moment. He thus came to practice socialist realism even before it was officially introduced. Bezymensky's verse drama *The Shot* (1930) earned Stalin's praise by presenting the typical plot of a production novel with a strong dose of heroic optimism while blaming wreckers and bureaucrats for temporary setbacks. The difference between Bezymensky's work and Mayakovsky's contemporaneous play *The Bathhouse* was that the latter placed the triumph of communism into a mythical future, while Bezymensky's, in good socialist realist fashion, let it be a certainty of the present. Bezymensky went on to flourish throughout Stalin's reign.

There were many other poets who chose to sing of the heroic struggle on the road to socialism and the glorious and happy life "under the sun of Stalin's Constitution." They included Aleksandr Surkov (1899–1983), a mediocre versifier who reached high rank in the party and succeeded Aleksandr Fadeev as first secretary of the Union of Soviet Writers, Stepan Shchipachov (1898–1979), Mikhail Isakovsky (1900–1973), Vasily Lebedev-Kumach (1898–1948), Mikhail Svetlov (1903–64), and Iosif Utkin (1903–44). They not only dutifully sang of heroic labor, martial valor, and boundless devotion to Stalin and the Soviet motherland but also adroitly followed the new line of the mid-1930s, which encouraged old-fashioned Russian patriotism, made concessions to petit bourgeois sentimentality, and pretended that life in the Soviet Union was joyous, full of love and happy laughter. A quatrain of "Song of the Motherland" by Lebedev-Kumach, which for years had the status of an unofficial national anthem, said:

A wind of springtime blows across the
  land,
Life's getting happier every day,
And no one in the whole wide world
Can love and laugh better than we can.

In Isakovsky's popular "Katyusha" a Soviet soldier at a faraway frontier post "guards the motherland and lets [his girl] Katyusha guard their love." Shchipachov devoted fiery lines to the "Palace of the Soviets," planned as the world's tallest building by Stalin but never built. Most, if not all, poems of this type were insincere fabrications: poets wrote genuine poetry before or after the Stalin years which bore no resemblance to the effusions that won them Stalin prizes.

Examples are Nikolai Tikhonov (1896–1979), who wrote excellent acmeist verse in the 1920s and whose appallingly pedestrian propaganda poetry earned him a career as a literary functionary, and Aleksandr Yashin (1913–68), who won a Stalin Prize for his *poema* "Alyona Fomina" (1949), which describes village life in rosy hues, but after 1956 became one of the most outspoken critics of Soviet life.

The 1930s saw the first crop of poets who had grown up entirely under the Soviet system. The most remarkable of them was Aleksandr Tvardovsky (1910–71), the son of a middle peasant who perished as a kulak during collectivization. (Tvardovsky acknowledged his guilt before his father in a late poem, "By Right of Memory," 1968.) Tvardovsky's early narrative poems *The Road to Socialism* (1931) and *The Land of Muraviya* (1934–36, awarded a Stalin Prize), are products of an effort, honest in a misguided way, to come to terms with collectivization. The hero of *The Land of Muraviya*, Nikita Morgunok, refuses to join a collective farm and goes on a search for a mythical land of Muraviya where he can farm his own plot. After many travails and disappointments the hapless Morgunok decides that returning to his home kolkhoz is still his best bet. The moral of the poem is thus the "correct" one, but there is little doubt that many readers sympathized with Morgunok and other characters doomed to extinction in the land of the Soviets: kulaks driven from their homesteads, an itinerant priest, an old man who still believes in God—all are equally pathetic. *The Land of Muraviya* compares favorably with its obvious model, Nekrasov's *Who Has a Good Life in Russia?* Its verse has the easy lilt of the country ditty. Dialogue and narrative are racy, whimsical, and at times pithy. It is, however, the undercurrent of latent heart-break below the surface of the poem's ethnographic realism and folksy humor that makes *The Land of Muraviya* a work of genuine poetry.

During the war Tvardovsky published serially his epic poem *Vasily Tyorkin* (1942–45), which records the experiences of a spunky Russian foot soldier all the way from the difficult early stages of the war to victory in Germany. In *Vasily Tyorkin*, too, Tvardovsky found a felicitous combination of optimism and faith in the common Russian people together with a healthy realism and wry humor. (It won him a second Stalin Prize.) Russian soldiers recognized in Tyorkin the better part of their own selves. *Vasily Tyorkin* became immensely popular and later gave Tvardovsky a modicum of immunity against reprisals when he became a dissident. This started with his epic *Distance beyond Distance* (1950–60), really a suite of poetic impressions and meditations on Russian life, past and present, occasioned by a journey on the Trans-Siberian railroad. In one episode the author meets an old friend who is returning from Siberia after seventeen years in a prison camp. Tvardovsky sadly observes that his friend was a better man than himself and others who were spared his ordeal, and he asks why this injustice had to happen, but has no answer. *Distance beyond Distance* is even formally an astonishing work. Its title, *Za dal'yu dal'*, is a brilliant conceit (*dal'* is an abstract noun related to the adjective *dal'nii*, "distant, faraway") that recurs throughout the poem in different versions: "Beyond the Urals, Transuralia," "Beyond Lake Baikal, Transbaikalia," and so forth. The driving rhythm of the poem's iambic tetrameter conveys the movement of the streaking train, the monotony of the landscape, and the vastness of the country.

In 1963 Tvardovsky published a shorter

satirical poem, "Tyorkin in the Other World," where Tyorkin discovers that hell is a lot like everyday life in the Soviet Union. Tvardovsky's place in Russian literature is enhanced by his editorship of *Novy mir*, which he held from 1950 to 1954 and from 1958 to 1970, when it led the liberalization movement in Soviet literature and published many politically progressive works. Tvardovsky's fate exemplified the tragic conflicts of his generation, of which his poetry gave but an oblique and distant echo transfigured by the irresistible lilt of his verse.

Pavel Vasilyev (1910–37), a talented poet who like Tvardovsky leaned toward the verse epic and themes of peasant life, was not as fortunate as Tvardovsky. Of Siberian Cossack stock, Vasilyev led an adventurous life as a student of oriental languages, sailor, gold miner, instructor of physical education, and journalist, all the while writing a great deal of poetry. He perished in Stalin's purges. Vasilyev was at his best in verse epics about the life of Siberian Cossacks before and after the revolution: "Song of the Fall of the Cossack Commonwealth" (1929–30), "The Salt Rebellion" (1933–34), "Kulaks" (1933–34), and "Sinitsyn & Co." (1934). Written in varied, quickly changing energetic rhythms, they are full of colorful imagery, often taken from folk poetry, vigorous colloquial language, and a fondness for the gladness and plenitude of life in the villages of Siberia. They bear some resemblance to Klyuev and on occasion to the primitivist verse of Khlebnikov. Like Klyuev, Vasilyev was accused of seeing the civil war and collectivization from a kulak's rather than a landless peasant's point of view. When he found it difficult to get his poems printed after a first arrest in 1932, he published some gnomic verse posing as a Kazakh poet, Mukhan Bashmetov, in Russian translation. Like other victims of Stalin's purges, Vasilyev was "posthumously rehabilitated."

Olga Berggolts (1910–75) lived her whole life in Leningrad. She graduated from Leningrad University with a degree in in philology in 1930. Her first volume of verse appeared in 1934 and was followed by several more, all noteworthy for a restrained and thoughtful treatment of the problems of her generation, mainly an intellectual's difficulties in bending to the discipline of a collective mentality. Berggolts won fame with the poems of her lyric diary of the siege of Leningrad (1941–44), during which she worked for Leningrad radio. Her volumes *A Leningrad Notebook* (1942), *Leningrad* (1944), and *Your Road* (1945) contain reactions to daily events and the progress of the war, vignettes of human interest, and some private thoughts, but also stirring assertions of faith in the heroism of the defenders and paeans to the greatness of their city, all in simple, even subdued language. Berggolts and Vera Inber (1890–1972), a onetime constructivist poet, whose long poem *Pulkovo Meridian* (1942–46) is a poignant evocation of the cruel suffering she witnessed and shared during the siege,[17] wrote the most genuine and moving lyrics about the war, far more convincing than Nikolai Tikhonov's *Kirov Is with Us* (1941), in which the spirit of Kirov, the Leningrad party chief assassinated in 1934, inspects the defenses of the city, or the patriotic effusions of Surkov, Simonov, Shchipachov, and countless other male poets.

The modernist strain in Russian poetry lasted for a decade after the revolution. Much as in the visual arts and in music, the common denominator of various modernist groups was a radical turn away from the

17. Pulkovo is an astronomical observatory near Leningrad.

subject-oriented art of the past to an art that would satisfy the artist's creative and innovative urge through the potentialites inherent in his medium. A resulting orientation toward form produced, in imagism, poetry that exploited the effect of juxtaposing sharply contrasting or otherwise striking shapes, colors, and images; in constructivism, poetry that foregrounded expressiveness and palpability; in OBERIU, poetry that struck the listener by an apparent incompatibility of subject matter and form or by absurdly arbitrary arrangement and combination of words and things. These schools, at least implicitly, shared a belief in the native power of language and the absolute meaning of words and objects outside contextual associations, a belief that had also been central to the aesthetics of prerevolutionary futurism.

Among the imagists, Vadim Shershenevich progressed from two early collections of a symbolist and acmeist hue to several versions of futurism (he was one of its leading organizers and theorists from 1913 to 1916) and on to imagism, which he launched in 1919. During the civil war Shershenevich worked with Mayakovsky for the windows of ROSTA. After the imagists disbanded, he worked for the theater and cinema, mostly as a translator. Shershenevich's poetic theories were largely derivative and not especially fruitful. As for his poetry, his penchant for formal experimentation got the better of his power of evocation. His three imagist volumes, *Just a Horse* (1920), *Cooperatives of Happiness* (1921), and *Taking Stock* (1926), as well as his *poema* "Crematorium" (1919), are more remarkable for their anti-aesthetic radicalism and manhandling of Russian grammar than for their poetic expressiveness. Shershenevich was for most of his relatively brief career a poet whose

poetry was essentially applied theory, experimentation for its own sake, and hence meaningful only in the context of its peculiar literary ambience.

Anatoly Marienhof (1897–1962) came to Moscow from the provinces in 1918 to work for a government publishing house. Together with Shershenevich and Esenin (he was linked to the latter by an ostentatiously intimate friendship), he formed the nucleus of the imagist group of poets. He wrote poetry, drama, and criticism in the spirit of imagism until the imagists disbanded in 1927. Thereafter he wrote several novels and plays. *A Novel without Lies* (1927) is a fictionalized memoir of the years of the imagist *bohème*, with Esenin its central character. Marienhof's favorite genre was the lyric *poema*, his favorite persona the tragic clown, and his main themes the nightmare of the modern city and the chaos that was Russia in revolution.

Esenin

Sergei Aleksandrovich Esenin (1895–1925) came from a peasant family in Ryazan Province. He attended a training school for elementary school teachers, and when he and his father moved to Moscow in 1912 he was able to find clerical work and eventually got a job as proofreader with a major press. He wrote poetry all along and began to publish it as early as 1914. He belonged to a circle of beginning poets and musicians named in honor of Ivan Surikov, a nineteenth-century peasant poet, and attended lectures at Russia's first "people's university," an evening school that charged no tuition. In the winter of 1915 Esenin moved to Petersburg, where he, a "rural *intelligent*" rather than a peasant, successfully cultivated the image of a peasant poet and, quite unexpectedly for himself, became famous overnight. He enjoyed the support and friendship of Blok, the acmeist Gorodetsky, and the peasant poet Klyuev, who became his friend, mentor, and probably his lover. Esenin welcomed the revolution, although he never belonged to any radical group. Rather, he was close to the Scythians and, after 1919, belonged to the imagist group. His programmatic essays "The Keys of Mary" and "*Byt* and Art"[18] reflect his searchings for a style beyond the glossy Russian landscapes he had mastered. Esenin's life was by then marred by drinking and rowdy behavior. In 1922–23 he traveled through Europe and America with the famous American dancer Isadora Duncan, whom he had married in May 1922. He returned to Russia in August 1923, and they were soon divorced. Esenin's drinking sprees, which were getting worse, were reflected in a cycle of poems entitled "Moscow of the Taverns" (1924). In the last two years of his life Esenin produced some of his best work, much of it in his familiar manner, though more intense and more tragic. The cycle "Persian Themes," however, features love poems in a major key. Esenin also wrote a poignant farewell poem addressed to Isadora Duncan ("A Letter to a Woman," 1924), and several narrative poems about the revolution. Esenin's suicide in 1925 was an act of desperation whose motives must have been complex.

Esenin's early poems, such as "The Birch" (1913), the cycle "Russia" (1914), and "The Bird-Cherry Tree" (1915), stylize the Russian countryside as in a picture postcard. They are written in correct conventional meters and use just enough clichés of folk poetry to give them a touch of sentimental folksiness. Their lilting rhythm, idyllic na-

ture imagery, and easy charm made Esenin the darling of several genrations of less than sophisticated Russian readers. He continued to write some poems of this type until the end. Another pervasive theme is that of pained compassion for suffering humanity and all living things. "In the Land where Yellow Nettles Grow" (1915) tells of the Vladimirka, the road along which convicts were marched to Siberia. "Song of a Dog" (1915), "A Cow" (1915), and "The Fox" (1916) tell of the misery inflicted on animals by people. "A Song about Bread" (1921) depicts the process by which ears of corn, "cut down the way swans' necks are cut," are made into bread and other "tasty dishes" as a series of murders committed by a murderous breed of men.

The poems of "Moscow of the Taverns" are dominated by wistful memories of a happy life in the poet's native village and by a sense of being hopelessly trapped in the quagmire of the big city:

My low house has caved in without me,
My old dog is long dead.
In the crooked streets of Moscow,
God, it seems, has willed me to die.
      ("Yes! Now it is certain," 1922–23)

In a revolutionary utopian poem, "Inoniya" (1918), Esenin declares himself "the prophet Sergei Esenin" (the poem is dedicated to the prophet Jeremiah) and proceeds to challenge, debunk, and blaspheme the sacred beliefs of Muscovite Russia, showing a far-ranging familiarity with Old Russian literature, folk traditions, and Scriptures. He promises the country a new world, the city of Inoniya (from *inoi*, "other"), "where the God of the living lives." It will be brought about by "a new Savior," by "someone with a new faith, / Without cross or torture, / Who has strung a rainbow / Across the

18. *Byt* here means "the culture of daily life."

sky like a bow." While politically naive, "In-oniya" is imaginative and lively, comparing favorably with the many other cosmic uto-pias of the revolutionary period. Esenin's other poems about the revolution are weaker.

Esenin's suicide poem helped establish a legend that Mayakovsky's attempted re-futation, "To Sergei Esenin," could only enhance. Esenin's poems expressed the feelings of millions of Russians who saw their rural past through a haze of golden nostalgia and their urban present as condu-cive to alcoholic despair. His poems, catchy as any in the language, are easily memorized. Whenever Esenin departed from the familiar language and imagery that he used so suc-cessfully, he would usually turn awkward and slide into bathos. But he was a great poet nevertheless, not so much by virtue of having written any particular great poem or poems, but because he gave perfect expres-sion to a distinctive sensibility.

Klyuev

Far less popular than Esenin, but more ori-ginal and more genuinely close to the Rus-sian soil, was Nikolai Alekseevich Klyuev (1887–1937), Esenin's friend and mentor. Klyuev came from a literate peasant family of Olonets Province, in the Russian north, which was never reached by serfdom and still retained the old peasant culture. The family was Orthodox, but Old Believer tradi-tions were strong in the community. Young Klyuev traveled throughout Russia and be-came intimately familiar with the sectarian underground. He also read voraciously and began to write poetry early. His first poems were published in 1904 in an obscure pro-vincial journal. In 1907 he succeeded in starting a correspondence with Blok, who

was then, like other symbolists, eager to establish contact with "the people." Bely, Kuzmin, and Merezhkovsky also took a great interest in Russian sectarians. Blok helped Klyuev get published in leading journals like *The Golden Fleece*, and when Klyuev made his appearance in the literary world of Mos-cow and Petersburg in 1911 he was lionized everywhere, even in the Stray Dog cabaret. He became the coryphaeus of a group of peasant poets who were then entering the Russian Parnassus: Sergei Esenin, Pavel Radi-mov, Pimen Karpov, Sergei Klychkov, and others. Klyuev welcomed the October rev-olution with enthusiasm and wrote serious poems under such titles as "A Red Song," "Comrade," and "Commune." But by 1921 he realized the hostility of the Soviet regime to his world, and even though collected under the title *Lenin* (1924), his poems of these years were really dirges over the death of the peasant culture he loved. Klyuev's last collection, "Hut in the Field," appeared in 1928 to unequivocally hostile reviews, which noted its reactionary and kulak qua-lity. Klyuev continued to write poetry in the 1930s but could no longer publish it. He was arrested in 1933 and died in Siberia, of heart failure, according to official records.

Klyuev's first collections, *Chimes of Firs* (1911), *Brotherly Songs* and *Forest Tales* (1912), were welcomed especially by the Scythian avant-garde and by all those who were eager to see any form of art that came "from the people." Klyuev was self-educated, but he could and did write liter-ary Russian and flawless syllabotonic verse when he wanted. He was well read in Rus-sian and world literature. His poetry has echoes not only of Koltsov and Nekrasov but also of Blok and other modern poets. Some of his poems could be Blok's, for instance, the Gypsy romance "I love those

Gypsy camps" (1914). Other poems resemble Khlebnikov's, such as "Sound is the angel's brother, and the incorporeal ray's" (1917). Since most of Klyuev's poetry in the manner of the folk song or folk epic was written late in his career, whereas most of his early work is in conventional verse, it would seem that his folk verse is no less stylized than Blok's.

Klyuev wrote many fine conventional poems in which the Russian village and countryside are presented in a nostalgic idyll, the manner Esenin adopted with huge success. Klyuev added an extra dimension to this genre by using symbols of religious ritual, wedding and funeral, prayer and liturgy, to depict Russian nature. The mysteries of crucifixion and resurrection are seen as enacted in nature. In "Hillsides" (1915) fall is a funeral service: the hazy smoke of forest fires is incense billowing over the corpse of nature laid out in a coffin and watched over by autumn, a pale and wan nun. In "Like a Bishop's Grave" (1917) the forest in fall is likened to a bishop's grave, where gold and purple are mixed with earth and putrefaction. A poem of 1915 begins, "The forest twilight is a monk / Over an illuminated book of hours." In some poems Klyuev's visions incorporate the mythology of Russia's heretical sectarians, sometimes with explicitly orgiastic overtones. The image of Christ the bridegroom is made physically graphic, as is that of an eschatological wedding night of Mother Earth. A poem of 1919 is devoted to the glories of eunuchism ("O eunuchism, crown, golden-hearted city!").[19]

Klyuev did his best and most original work after the revolution, when he took his

lonely stand against the wave of mechanization, collectivization, and Westernization that swept away the nature religion, the art, and the songs of the northern peasantry. He speaks of "the gramophone that mocks a Suzdal chapel" ("My country, I am guilty, guilty," c. 1924), "headless gnomes who live in iron, / spin fetters and weave shrouds" ("Iron," 1926), and "the fringe of Babylon's sheets / that grows and spreads over Russia" ("Russia Weeps over Conflagrations," 1924). "The placards of Soviet summer" are a sign of renewed persecution of the Old Faith ("The Psalter of Tsar Alexis," 1924). In many poems of this period Klyuev tries an escape into exotic worlds of "lion bread" (the title of a poem and cycle of 1921–22), baobabs, the Sphinx and the Sahara, Siam and China, confounding their images with the imagery of his native north in a manner reminiscent of Khlebnikov.

Klyuev's lyric verse epics of the Soviet period are the summit of his oeuvre. "The Fourth Rome" (1922), with an epigraph from Esenin ("Now I walk in my top hat / and patent leather shoes!"), asserts Klyuev's resolve to remain true to his origins and create a "fourth Rome" of poetry from Russia's native resources.

"Mother Sabbath" (1922) is a celebration of "the angel of simple human works"—the works of the plowman, the spinner of yarn, the icon painter. This long poem, introduces a wealth of symbolic imagery from Russian iconography and religious folklore. "Mother Sabbath" is a symbol of hope of resurrection after the crucifixion (*subbota*, Sabbath, is feminine in Russian). "Zaozerye" (literally, "land beyond the lake," a place name; 1927) is a versified calendar of saints and holidays, from Saint George's Day (April 23) to Easter, with the meaning, rites, and celebrations of each presented in warm and colorful im-

---

19. The *skoptsy*, who practiced self-castration, were a Russian sect.

ages. This poem did appear in a Soviet journal in 1927. "The Village" (1926) praises Russia's past glory and laments her present sorry condition:

You Russia, Russia, my mother-in-law,
You have put way too much salt in our
  soup,
You have buttered our porridge with
  blood—
Enough to fill our bellies for good.

"Pogorelshchina" (1926; the title is derived from *pogorelets*, one who has lost all his possessions in a fire), a verse epic in rhymed accentual couplets, circulated in many manuscripts, one of which Klyuev gave to the Italian Slavist Ettore Lo Gatto on a visit to the Soviet Union. "Pogorelshchina" first paints an idyllic picture of life in the village of Sigovy Lob in the forest and lake country of the north—its wealth, the skill of its craftsmen, and its faith in harmony with nature and in a communal religion. Then the bad news of changes in the country arrive, carried by a magpie in her beak. The final message is, "Get ready to die." All nature, even the sun, joins in the community's grief. As the old faith dies, everything dies with it, not only in Sigovy Lob but in all of Holy Russia: "October, lean she-wolf,/Gnaws at the forest iconostasis." Soon the people of Sigovy Lob are reduced to dire need, famine, and cannibalism. The old tradition of self-immolation by fire is revived. A sad catalog of the woes of Mother Russia follows. Toward the end of the poem, the poet takes leave of his songs and the garden of Russian poetry.

Klyuev is a difficult poet. He uses many dialect words and often alludes to folk legends and traditions, as well as to religious ritual, both Orthodox and sectarian. The quality of his work is uneven, mostly be-

cause he was creating his own style and sometimes veered into the maudlin and mannered, or into outright bad taste. His cycle "Dirge on the Death of Esenin" (1926) is a case in point. At his best, Klyuev is a poet of great power and originality.

The Literary Center of Constructivists counted among its members several excellent poets, among them Eduard Bagritsky, Vera Inber, Vladimir Lugovskoi, and Ilya Selvinsky. Of these, only Selvinsky consistently applied the theoretical ideas of constructivism to his poetry.

Ilya (born Karl) Selvinsky (1899–1968) led an eventful life. Early on he worked at odd jobs, including as a stevedore, circus wrestler, and fur farmer. He participated in a polar expedition in 1933, served as an officer in World War II, and traveled widely, all the while publishing prolifically in verse and in prose. Selvinsky viewed poetry as a rational, goal-directed activity and his varied practical pursuits as research toward it. In *A Poet's Notebooks* (1928) he has the poet's "autobiography" and theoretical views precede a collection of his verse. Selvinsky followed the constructivist principle of integrating every aspect of his work with its intended message and used local color to give it concreteness. This meant that the language of a given work was to be an accurate reflection of the ambience described therein. Selvinsky's colorful, often outlandish and strange poetry revealed the wealth of his experience. He studied and used slang, technical jargon, and thieves' cant, as well as Jewish, Gypsy, and other dialects according to his subject. Verse narrative and verse drama were his favorite genres. His best-known verse epic, "The Ulyalaev Uprising" (written in 1924, published in 1927), described the rout of a counterrevolutionary peasant uprising. Selvinsky wrote a new version of this work in 1956. Reacting to criticism that the kulak rebel Ulyalaev was a more interesting character than the communist heroes, he now made Lenin the central figure of his epic. "Fur Business" (1929) is noteworthy for being a production novel in verse. Its hero, an honest communist administrator, victoriously battles wreckers and self-seeking bureaucrats. In the 1930s Selvinsky wrote mostly plays, always with a proper ideological message. He continued to write lyric poetry until the end of his life and gathered his views on the art of poetry in a volume, *Studio of Verse* (1962).

Eduard Bagritsky (pseudonym of Dzyubin, 1899–1934), born and educated in Odessa, enthusiastically joined the revolution, fought with a Bolshevik guerrilla group in the civil war, and wrote revolutionary poetry. He came to Moscow in 1925, where he joined Pereval, then the constructivists, and finally RAPP. In 1926 he wrote his best known work, "The Lay about Opanas." Opanas is a Ukrainian peasant who joins the wrong side in the civil war and pays for it with his life. He is not the hero of the "Lay"; a Bolshevik commander is. The "Lay" is written in lively free rhythms that give it a popular air. The revolutionary romanticism of the "Lay" carried over into Bagritsky's first volume of verse, *Southwest* (1928). After joining RAPP in 1930, he began to address himself to the contemporary scene and to the first five-year plan in particular. His verse in this period retained the ingenuous freshness and emotional abandon of his revolutionary poetry. Bagritsky's poetry displays a verse rhythm close to that of live speech, familiar yet imaginatively arranged imagery, and a poetic persona with a touch of a free spirit. It contrasts favorably with

that of other loyal supporters of the Soviet regime. Somehow even his propaganda poetry has a ring of sincerity.

There were some fine poets among the oberiuty, though only Nikolai Zabolotsky received wider attention. Aleksandr Vvedensky (1904–41), a poet of great originality, became known only in the 1970s. He was born in Saint Petersburg, where he studied oriental languages and worked in the linguistics section of the State Institute of Artistic Culture (GINKhUK) from 1923 to 1926. He belonged to several radical Left Art groups, including the *zaumniki* (from *zaum'*, "trans-sense"), who continued the cubo-futurists' pursuit of the roots of a universal language. Vvedensky joined the OBERIU group in 1928 and became one of its most visible members, reciting his provocative verses at public poetry readings and defending them in ensuing debates. He could publish only a few poems, however, before OBERIU disbanded in 1930. He found haven at Detgiz, the state publishing house for children's literature, whose editor, poet Samuil Marshak (1887–1964), took several oberiuty under his wing. Vvedensky published a great deal of poetry and prose for children in book form as well as in magazines for children. He was arrested in 1941 and died soon afterward of unknown causes. He was "rehabilitated" after Stalin's death, but only some of his children's books were reprinted. Collections of his works for adults appeared in the West in the 1970s and 1980s. Vvedensky is closest of all Russian poets to dada and surrealism. The form of his poems tends toward primitivism; their imagery is often grotesque and their semantics absurdist. They are also devoid of emotion, which gives them a strange schizophrenic quality. He was perhaps the only Russian poet to join modernist painters like Filonov in exploring the deeper regions of the subconscious.

Zabolotsky

Nikolai Alekseevich Zabolotsky (1903–58) spent his childhood and youth in remote rural areas of the northeast, graduaed from the Leningrad Pedagogical Institute in 1925, and began to publish his verse as a student. Like other oberiuty, he earned his living by working for Detgiz, both doing original work and adapting classics for young readers.

Zabolotsky's collection of verse *Columns* (1929) was welcomed by connoisseurs but met with a hostile reception from party critics. His *poema* "A Celebration of Agriculture" (1929–30, published in *Zvezda*, 1933) and his *Second book of Verse* (1937) were viciously attacked by the entire official press, including *Pravda*. In 1938 Zabolotsky was arrested on absurd charges of membership in a terrorist organization and spent the next eight years in various prison camps. When released in 1946, he was a sick man. He went on to write some more good poetry, though he never recovered the verve and originality of his early work.

In *Columns* Zabolotsky shows several different faces, each of them fresh, original, and vigorous. He depicts the bleak world of a Soviet philistine in sonorous Pushkinian iambs, then stops to observe that it is this world of cluttered backyards where "his youth is hung up to dry." He describes the hideous horrors of a Soviet city under the NEP—like a quadruple amputee who makes his living playing a penny whistle in a street orchestra—in a brazenly cheerful, insouciant manner, as if all were well in the world. He impersonates the strangest kinds of consciousness—infantile, retarded, whimsical, absurd—with a perfectly straight

face and in a tone of matter-of-fact communication. He will also speak of human destiny, immortality, humanity and nature in disarmingly naive terms, as though he had only discovered these topics "yesterday, as I was meditating about death." All these different voices are wonderfully alive.

Zabolotsky's "Celebration of Agriculture" was taken by party critics to be a lampoon of collective farming, which in fact it may have been on one level of meaning. More clearly, though, it is an expression of man's desire to be a friend and brother of all creatures and an invitation to abandon the obtuse materialist dogmatism that perceives nature as an enemy and leads to its rapacious exploitation by man. Instead, a free and loving transfiguration of man and nature is envisaged, a world of wise animals, rational machines, and lucidly reasoning men and women.

Zabolotsky's late poetry tends toward an almost Pushkinian classicism. It is still concerned with people and nature, good and evil, death and immortality, but now in a more conventional, though always noble and imaginative language. Zabolotsky is without doubt one of the great poets of the twentieth century. Like other victims of Stalin's terror, he came into his own only posthumously.

Acmeism continued to exist, if not as an organized group, then at least as a style, even after the second Guild of Poets, formed in 1920, disbanded following the arrest of its leader, Nikolai Gumilyov. The acmeists, younger than the symbolists, were about to reach maturity in the 1920s. Some did so in the style established by the Guild of Poets; others went on to create a new style. Anna Akhmatova and some lesser poets, such as Mikhail Lozinsky (1886–1955) and Sofya Parnok (1885–1933) in Russia and Nikolai Otsup and Irina Odoevtseva abroad, stayed with the acmeist poetics. Osip Mandelshtam and Georgy Ivanov went beyond it. Konstantin Vaginov, a member of the Guild of Poets who had published two acmeist collections, went on to join OBERIU and concentrate on prose fiction.

Mandelshtam

Osip Mandelshtam continued to grow and change until his tragic death in a prison camp in 1938. He was able to bring out three collections of his poetry after the revolution, the last in 1928. Thereafter he could publish only occasional poems, the last in 1932. A large part of his poetic oeuvre, including some of his greatest poems, was preserved in manuscript by his widow, Nadezhda Mandelshtam, and published posthumously. The first posthumous edition of his poetry appeared in 1955, the first edition of his collected works in 1964–71, both in the United States. The first posthumous collection of his poems in the Soviet Union appeared in 1973. Russian readers may have been so long deprived of perhaps the greatest poet of this century because of a single satirical poem with an uncomplimentary likeness of Stalin, which earned the poet a three-year exile to Voronezh (1934–37) and subsequent arrest and deportation.

Mandelshtam's poetry after *Stone* continued his acmeist excursions into world culture, with Italian themes now preponderant (aside from an Armenian cycle of 1931). He also continued to explore "the nature of the word." His impressionist style, however, became more fragmented, allusive, and on occasion opaque, challenging the reader's erudition and imagination. For instance, realizing his conception of the word as a living entity, Mandelshtam creates the image of a word-soul. A forgotten word is "like a blind swallow" and must descend to the realm of shadows ("I forgot the word I wanted to say," 1920). "Tristia," title poem of Mandelshtam's collection of 1922, takes its cue from Ovid's elegy on his last night in Rome before his departure into exile and goes on to a vision of Tibullus's Delia running barefoot to meet her returning lover. Mandelshtam quotes a complete line from a poem by Akhmatova and presents other poetic reminiscences illustrating the poem's thesis: "All's been before, all will return anew,/ And recognition is our only joy." In "Master of those guilty glances" (1934), a superb love poem, he develops the theme of dangerous illicit love in a series of picturesque conceits hinging on the reader's recognition of the story of an odalisque and her janissary lover caught in adultery and drowned in the Bosporus. Mandelshtam now develops a private vocabulary of key words, such as *apple, salt, dragonfly, transparent*, and *tender*, which acquire a symbolic power that goes far beyond their dictionary meaning. Yet he never abandons the acmeist principle of giving a poem its logos, that is, a rational meaning.

In his postrevolutionary poetry Mandelshtam develops an acute sense of time—its movement, its duration, its music, and its emotional charge—as a friend or as a foe, to be feared or to be pitied:

> He who has kissed time's tormented
>   brow,
> Will later on, with filial tenderness,
> Remember how time went to sleep
> In a wheaten snowdrift under the
>   window.
> Whoever lifted the inflamed eyelids of his
>   age[20]
> —Two somnolent large apples—

---

20. There is a pun here: *veki* (eyelids) and *vek* (age, epoch).

Will hear forever the noise of roaring
rivers
Of times deceitful and numb.

("January 1, 1924," 1924)

To the early Mandelshtam time had been a
friend, creator of values of human culture,
recognized in joyful encounters. In the
Soviet period Mandelshtam's perception of
time becomes complex and ambivalent,
as in the most challenging of his poems,
the great "Slate-Pencil Ode" (1923), nine
octaves of variations on "The River of
Time," Derzhavin's last poem, left in a slate-
pencil autograph. Derzhavin's theme is
joined by an echo of Lermontov's line, "And
one star talks to another," from "I walk out
alone onto the highway,"[21] and leads to
themes of cosmic discourse and disci-
pleship, lessons to be learned from the encounter of running water and flintstone in
a mountain stream, the rivalry of day and
night, and the union of ring and horseshoe,
symbols of permanence and fleeting fortune.
A highlight of all Russian poetry (also available in a magnificent German version by
Paul Celan), "Slate-Pencil Ode" has the
quality of a lofty flight of the imagination
coupled with fascinating strangeness and a
compactness of expression that puts a
panoramic landscape, a multitude of allegorical conceits, and a whole network of
enigmatic and provocative images into a
mere seventy-two lines. Late into the Soviet
period time becomes an enemy, a destroyer,
and eventually falls silent: "Like Rembrandt,
martyr of chiaroscuro, / I have receded deep
into time grown mute" (1937).

As early as 1918 Mandelshtam responded
to the revolution with a prophetic poem,
"Twilight of Freedom." Later he perceived
life in Soviet Russia with a growing sense of
alienation and despondency. The wintery

21. See p. 229

gloom of the verses of his Voronezh exile is
relieved only by the memory of "the hills of
Tuscany," "the honeysuckle of France," or
"the theta and iota of a Greek flute." Even
the stark despair of some of Mandelshtam's
late poems, however, is transfigured by a
noble and imaginative diction, as in the
lines:

Unfortunate is he who is frightened
By his own shadow, by a barking dog,
Bowled over by the wind. And poor is he
Who, half-alive himself, begs a shadow for
alms.

("You have not died as yet," 1937)

Mandelshtam is a poet's poet. No lapses
into prose, no poetic clichés, and no infelici-
ties ever mar his poetry. Each line is unique
and unpredictable. Each image is palpable,
yet strange and fascinating. Each poem
leaves an indelible impression, like a painting by a great master. The melos of Mandelshtam's poetry shows tremendous
variety. There are measured classical meters
in *Stone*, intoxicating melodious compositions in *Tristia*, and nervous, shrill, even
hysterical rhythms in the poems of the
Voronezh years. Mandelshtam is rarely easy;
he addresses an educated European audience. His poems can be translated because
they have a solid logos, because rarely are
his themes peculiarly Russian, and because
melos is relatively less important in his
poetry than, for example, in Blok's or
Annensky's.

Akhmatova

Anna Akhmatova brought out two volumes
of verse after the revolution, *Plantain*
(1921) and *Anno Domini MCMXXI* (1922),
but thereafter could no longer publish her
poetry, except for some verse translations in
the 1930s. Some of her research on Pushkin

appeared in 1933 and 1936. In 1940 she was allowed a comeback, as a collection of her poetry appeared, including her sixth book of verse, *Willow* (later changed to *Reed*). Akhmatova was evacuated from Leningrad during the siege of the city and spent the war years in Tashkent. An unfinished cycle about Central Asia does not show the poet at her best. Her patriotic war poems are no more than competent rhetoric. Upon her return to Leningrad, she had the misfortune to be singled out, together with Mikhail Zoshchenko, as a principal target in Andrei Zhdanov's attack on two journals that had published her poetry. In 1949 her son Lev, who had been arrested twice in the 1930s, was rearrested. In 1950 Akhmatova was able to place a cycle of poems, "Glory to Peace" (read: glory to Stalin), in the popular magazine *Ogonyok*. This abject act did not help her son (he was released only in 1956). At about the same time Akhmatova wrote a short poem, "Imitation, from the Armenian" (published in 1966), in which the poet dreams she is a black ewe who inquires of the padishah if he had found her son to be a tasty meal. After Stalin's death Akhmatova was once again acclaimed as a major poet, and she developed a following among young poets of the post-Stalin generation. Her cycle "Requiem" about the Great Terror appeared in the West in 1963. She was allowed to travel abroad to receive a literary prize in Italy (1964) and an honorary degree from Oxford University (1965).

Akhmatova's collections of 1921 and 1922 are still mostly about love, but now about a tragic, fated, or lost love: "I gave my life to you, but my sadness/I shall take with me to my grave" ("Icefloes Drifting By," 1918). The poet presents herself as humbled, wiser, resigned to her fate, but also as compassionate and willing to forgive. There are poems about fear, calamity, and death:

> And in the West an earthly sun still shines,
> The roofs of cities sparkle in its rays,
> But here the White one marks houses
>   with crosses
> And calls the ravens, and the ravens fly."
>   ("Why is this age worse?", 1919)

The poems that appeared in 1940 and thereafter show a new Akhmatova. She now writes noble tributes to the poets who were her friends ("Boris Pasternak," 1936; "Voronezh," 1936, to Mandelshtam; "To the Memory of M[ikhail] B[ulgakov], 1940). Akhmatova's later poems contain many echoes explicit as well as subliminal, of Aleksandr Blok. Her several poems on the art of poetry show her imagination and intellect at their fullest. "The Muse" (1924, published in 1940) is astounding in its splendid succinctness:

> When I await her coming in the night,
> Life, it would seem, hangs by a thread.
> Pray, what are honors, youth, and
>   freedom
> Before this dear guest, flute in hand?
>
> And here she enters. Throwing back her
>   hood,
> She gives me an attentive glance. And I
> To her: "Did you dictate to Dante
> The lines of his Inferno?" And she
>   answers: "Yes."

In the great sonnet "To an Artist" (also 1924, published in 1940) the artist is God. "Creation" (1936) describes the birth of a poem. The crucial moment is, "But in this sea of whispers and clangors/There arises one sound, conquering all."

Other great poems also testify to the poet's mature powers. "Three Autumns" (1943) combines dynamic nature description with metaphysical depth. The first autumn is "wet, colorful, and bright," a happy season. The second is somber, passionless, and makes everything look "pale and older." Then it is the turn of the third:

> But a gust of wind, and all's flung wide
> open.
> There can be no doubt: the drama is over
> And this is no third autumn, but death.

The poems of Akhmatova's last years deal with the poet, life, and death with mellow wisdom. In "The Poet" (1959) Akhmatova observes that being a poet is "to hear something in music and claim it is yours in jest." "The Last Poem" (1959) speaks of various ways in which a poem may occur to a poet. The last poem is the one that will never become incarnate "and without which I die." "Death of a Poet" (1960) is a sublime tribute to Boris Pasternak. In "There are Four of Us" (1961), with epigraphs from Mandelshtam, Pasternak, and Tsvetaeva, Akhmatova hears the voices of these three coming to her on "aerial ways."

"Requiem" (1935–40, published in 1963–64), a cycle of poems about the horror of the Great Terror and her son's arrest, occupies a special place in Akhmatova's oeuvre. The subject even today is so frought with emotion it is difficult to assess the aesthetic value of the poem. It has an immediacy that both transcends and falls short of poetry:

> I learned how quickly faces become
> sunken,
> How fear peers from behind dropped
> eyelids,
> How suffering will carve its harsh
> Cuneiform pages into cheeks,
> How hair, from black or ashen,
> Will turn to silver overnight,
> How smiles will fade on docile lips
> And fright will tremble in a dry little
> chuckle.

Akhmatova worked on her "Poem without a Hero" from 1940 to 1962. She believed she had finished it several times, but then would come back and add more to it. The poem, altogether about eight hundred lines, is in three parts: "1913: A Petersburg Tale"; an intermezzo, "Tails" (as in heads or tails); and an epilogue. Only Part Two is organized into stanzas (of six lines). "Poem without a Hero" is in lines of eight to ten syllables, rhymed mostly *aabccb*; the meter is anapestic with the third foot usually reduced to an iamb. A typical line scans, $xx\acute{x}/xx\acute{x}/xx\acute{x}/x$ ("All in flowers, like *Spring*— Botticelli's," line 336). This meter, rare in Russian poetry,[22] creates an irresistible, intoxicating rhythm. There is no plot, only allusions to a sad story of 1913: a young dragoon, also a poet, committed suicide. He had been courting an actress friend of Akhmatova's who appears often in her poems and in "Poem without a Hero" is shown dancing "goat-footed" a mad, drunken, devilish jig.

"Poem without a Hero" is a surrealistic suite of impressions from Akhmatova's life. It is also a poem about the death of Dostoevskian, "possessed" Petersburg. Details of Petersburg literary, theatrical, and musical life abound: the Stray Dog cabaret, Anna Pavlova's dancing, Meyerhold-Dapertutto's staging of Molière's *Don Juan*, Shalyapin's singing. These impressions are integrated by a pervasive sense of fatedness, of fin de siècle, and of loss: the poet is the only survivor to see the "*real* twentieth century," all the other faces and masks are ghosts. The poem is full of echoes of poets who were Akhmatova's contemporaries, some of whom are identified by epigraphs from their works: Klyuev, Annensky, Mandelshtam, and

---

22. A major work written in this meter is Nikolai Klyuev's "The Village" (1926).

Vsevolod Knyazev, the dragoon who killed himself. The most constant presence, though, is Blok's, allusions to whose poems and person appear throughout. Pushkin and Dostoevsky also play a prominent role. In the second and third parts the siege of Leningrad and the Great Terror that preceded it enter the poem, as the poet addresses the city in her own name. "Poem without a Hero" will be a challenge to its interpreters for some time yet as they strive to decipher its subtext and intertext, and some aspects of the poem will probably remain obscure.

There were a few other poets who during the period of the NEP and Stalin's tyranny remained independent and uncommitted. Mariya Shkapskaya (1891–1952) received some favorable attention in the 1920s, but she was reduced to writing five-year plan reportage after the early 1920s, and her creative work was rediscovered in the West only in the 1970s. Shkapskaya, a sophisticated intellectual with a degree from the University of Toulouse, published several volumes of highly idiosyncratic poetry devoted almost entirely to a woman's experience as a lover, wife, and mother. Sexuality, conception, abortion, pregnancy, giving birth, and the death of a child are her themes, always approached in the presence of God: how does a mother face God when He has allowed her child to die? Shkapskaya deals with her womanhood concretely, even carnally, yet also with a deep spirituality.

Leonid Martynov (1905–80) published mostly in Siberian journals for many years and became better known only after 1956. Since then he has been considered a major poet. Martynov created a mythical world from the historical past and the traditions of the Russian north, a world that he eventually expanded to embrace all humanity in mythic and cosmic visions. Martynov was also a prolific translator from several European languages.

Pasternak

The main figure among Russian poets of this period, whose poetry was formed by a private and idiosyncratic vision rather than by any school or any extrinsic factors, was Boris Leonidovich Pasternak (1890–1960). Pasternak was born in Moscow, where he spent most of his life. His father was a successful painter, his mother a concert pianist. As a youth he met Tolstoi, the composer Scriabin, and the German poet Rilke. Musically gifted, he studied composition for six years but then abandoned music in favor of philosophy, which he studied at the universities of Moscow and Marburg. In 1913 he abandoned philosophy, too, to devote himself entirely to poetry. He belonged to the Centrifuge group of Moscow futurists, along with Nikolai Aseev and Sergei Bobrov, and published two futurist collections of verse, *Twin in Clouds* (1914) and *Above the Barriers* (1917) without getting much attention. His collections *My Sister Life* (published in 1922, although written in 1917) and *Themes and Variations* (1923) immediately placed him among Russia's leading poets. In the 1920s Pasternak, though close to Lef, never embraced its utilitarian aesthetics and remained true to his idiosyncratic style, both in several verse epics of the 1920s ("High Malady," "Lieutenant Schmidt," "1905," and "Spektorsky," the last an unfinished novel in verse) and a new collection of verse, *Second Birth* (1932). In the 1930s Pasternak had difficulties publishing his original poetry and concentrated on translating Shakespeare, Goethe, Schiller, Kleist, Verlaine, Rilke, and others. The relaxation of censorship during World War II allowed him to publish two further collections, *On Early Trains* (1943) and *Expanses of Land* (1945). Pasternak published ten poems from the cycle of Yury Zhivago's poems in the journal *Znamya* (Banner) in 1954. The publication abroad of his novel *Doctor Zhivago* in 1957 and awarding of the Nobel Prize to him in 1958 led to his ostracism by the Soviet literary establishment. He was forced to decline the prize, but the poems that entered his last collection, *When the Weather Clears* (1956–59), were published soon after his death in his *Collected Poems* (1961).

The poems of Pasternak's first two collections are mostly baffling, as his poeticized colloquialisms and prosaic imagery, vaguely suggestive of something deeper, seem opaque or pointless. In *My Sister Life* the distinctive traits of Pasternak's poetry attain their full power. He uses conventional meters and stanzaic structure with inexact and often ingenious rhymes. He relies on consonants to create intricate patterns of alliteration while not avoiding strident consonant clusters. Pasternak's rhythms are rapid and have the lilt of animated, excited, or even breathless colloquial discourse. Mandelshtam observed, "To read Pasternak's verses is to clear your throat, to refresh your lungs: such verses ought to be a remedy against tuberculosis." Pasternak's language is colloquial, yet rich in rare, long, and decidedly unpoetic words. It is never stylized.

In an autobiographical prose work, *Safe Conduct* (1931), Pasternak said that "art is a recording of the displacement of reality effected by emotion." His poetry reflects the poet's encounters with reality—nature, daily life, great literature, a woman loved—with a strikingly personal immediacy, an unfailing sense of wonder, and a devout and grateful acceptance of life. There is

an astoundingly refreshing randomness and concreteness about Pasternak's settings, scenery, moods, and metaphors. Nature or life itself seems to create the poem. In a poem entitled "A Definition of Poetry" (1922) he says:

> It is a steeply rising whistle.
> It is the clicking of crushed icicles.
> It is a night that makes ice-coated leaves.
> It is a duel of two nightingales.

These are no mere metaphors, as we see in lines from a poem entitled "Poetry" (1922):

> The rainstorm's sprouts stick in thick
> clusters
> And long, long, till the break of dawn
> They drip their acrostic from gables,
> Letting the bubbles form their rhymes.

The pathetic fallacy, organized to form a worldview, is at the basis of much of Pasternak's poetry. Unlike Tsvetaeva and Mayakovsky, who speak to the world, Pasternak lets the world speak to him. A garden really weeps ("The Weeping Garden," 1922), stars "guffaw" ("A Definition of Poetry"), "a forest is embraced by a sunset of dreams" ("In the Forest," 1917), water works "all night without catching its breath" ("Roosters," 1923). Pasternak understands that the identity of the work of art and its subject is the very essence of art:

> Thus, in his time, Chopin inserted
> The living miracle
> Of farms, parks, groves, and graveyards
> Into his études.
> ("In everything I want to reach,"
> 1956–59)

In *My Sister Life* Pasternak conveys an atmosphere of revolutionary excitement and anticipation, but it is projected entirely onto nature. Letting nature do the talking—

and the feeling, as well—persists even in Pasternak's poems about World War II. In one of his last poems, "Beyond the Bend," he expects the future to emerge after a bend in the path through a thick forest.

Pasternak's concrete images do, however, reach for the absolute and the eternal, for "that great god of details,[23] that all-powerful god of love" ("Let us spill words," 1922). Pasternak often stresses the high seriousness of poetry, for instance, in a famous poem of 1931 that begins:

> Oh, had I known that this might happen,
> When I first chanced to get my start,
> That lines of verse draw blood and kill
>   you,
> Go for the throat and do you in.

In the late poems this seriousness turns into an explicitly religious attitude, as in several poems of the Zhivago cycle or in the poem "In the Hospital" (1957), where a man dying of heart failure praises the Lord and the perfection of His works. After 1930 Pasternak's language becomes more transparent, simpler, although it retains its idiosyncratic immediacy:

> Convinced of the kinship of all that is,
> And well conversant with the future,
> One can't but fall, like into heresy,
> Into an unheard-of simplicity.
>
> ("Waves," 1931)

Although for himself Pasternak explicitly rejected romanticism in terms of a poetic life such as was lived by Esenin or Mayakovsky, he was a quintessential romantic. As a poet, he felt closest to Blok among poets of his own century. *My Sister Life* and *Themes and Variations* are replete with epigraphs

and echoes from Shakespeare, Pushkin, Lermontov, Byron, Poe, Lenau, Heine, and Wagner. The idea and practice of art and poetry as a "second nature," the axiomatic conception of art as a symbol of nature (or vice versa), the appearance of the metaphysical in the mundane, and a pervasive cosmic vitalism—all characteristic of Pasternak's poetic vision—are arch-romantic. He is, however, quite unique in his ebullient freshness, vigor, and optimism. If Pasternak is not the greatest Russian poet of the twentieth century—he may be—he is certainly the most appealing, life-affirming, and straightforwardly attractive.

When the first thaw set in after Stalin's death, a generation of young poets, most of whom were born in the 1930s, took advantage of it to publish poetry in which they attempted to express their concerns and sensibility with more sincerity than would have been possible before, though still within the conceptual and rhetorical framework that had developed during the preceding quarter century. During the Khrushchev years public poetry readings, sometimes before thousands and even tens of thousands of people, became a major outlet for the sentiments of this generation. Still loyal to the ideals of socialism and the Soviet way of life, the young generation refused to accept uncritically every official pronouncement or every fact of Soviet reality. Most simply and most commonly, poets like Evgeny Vinokurov (b. 1925) and Rimma Kazakova (b. 1932) dealt with real human problems— grief, alienation, loneliness—thoughtfully and sincerely, in terms free of ideology and officious pathos. Some poets, such as Aleksandr Galich (pseudonym of Aleksandr Ginzburg,1918–77), Bulat Okudzhava (b. 1924), Novella Matveeva (b. 1934), and Vla-

---

23. An allusion to an aphorism of the art historian Aby Warburg, "Gott steckt im Detail."

dimir Vysotsky (1938–80), set their verses to music and sang them to a guitar accompaniment, often before huge audiences. Songs that could not be published were spread by private tape recordings. The common denominator of their art was an estrangement from the official version of Soviet reality, sometimes mild, sometimes profound, expressed in wryly satirical, bittersweetly sentimental, or even darkly tragic phrases. In the songs of these poets the persona is a self-conscious individual who refuses to see himself or herself as any of the stereotypes of socialist realism.

Some poets, like Evgeny Evtushenko (b. 1933), Boris Slutsky (b. 1919), and Robert Rozhdestvensky (b. 1932), engaged in versified publicism, after the fashion of Mayakovsky, in which they stood up against the legacy of Stalinism (Evtushenko's "Stalin's Heirs," 1962; Slutsky's, "The Boss" and "God," written in 1954–55, published in 1962), against latent anti-Semitism (Evtushenko's *poema* "Baby Yar," 1961), and for more open relations with the world outside the Soviet Union. Andrei Voznesensky (b. 1933) and others concentrated on fanciful conceits (*Antiworlds*, 1964), farfetched metaphors, and unorthodox formal devices, such as graphic or figured verse. Some, like Bella Akhmadulina (b. 1937), asserted their individuality by indulging in dreamlike fantasies and imaginary states of being. Viktor Sosnora (b. 1936), among those who turned to archaic themes and styles, went back to medieval Russia in his poems "The Year 1111" (1965) and "Horsemen" (1969). Nikolai Rubtsov (1936–1971) and others withdrew into life with nature and into a regional and rural sensibility reminiscent of nineteenth-century Slavophilism. The Russian north, traditionally a bastion of conservatism, became a symbol of the values and virtues believed to be lost elsewhere.

Soviet Prose Fiction

Revolution and civil war remained the main topic of Soviet literature for several decades. It was approached from different positions. The viewpoint of the communist activist appears in works by Furmanov, Fadeev, and Libedinsky, that of a fellow traveler in works by Fedin, Aleksei Tolstoi, and Leonov, among others. Some saw the revolution as a historical event accessible to rational understanding, others as an eruption of incomprehensible, dark, chaotic forces. Marxist writers like Furmanov, Fadeev, and Sholokhov viewed it as a series of events readily explained in terms of class struggle and the progress of history. Most fellow travelers, but some Old Bolsheviks, too, emphasized the elemental, spontaneous, and irrational aspects of the revolution—Pilnyak, Platonov, and Vesyoly, for example.

The NEP produced new themes and characters. The heroic, tragic, or romantic moods of the revolutionary era yielded to a satirical, comic, or critical manner. The rapid emergence of a new society and "Soviet man" posed a formidable yet enticing challenge. The period also saw a great deal of utilitarian prose fiction produced by writers who perceived their fiction as a vehicle of education and indoctrination. This orientation later became dominant in the production novel of socialist realism.

The revival of Russian patriotism in the 1930s brought forth a host of historical novels. The Second World War became, next to the revolution, the most important theme of Soviet literature. When it receded into the past, the next challenge to Soviet literature was twofold. On the one hand, the terrible legacy of Stalin and Stalinism had to be dealt with. On the other, it was inevitable that after nearly half a century of almost exclusive concern with society and the grand scale of things Russian literature should again develop an interest in individual and private life. The first of these challenges was difficult to meet not only because of continued censorship but also because it asked for an admission that the nation as a whole had made terrible sacrifices and had assented to unspeakable crimes, only to create a society that resembled the nightmare of anticommunist satires like George Orwell's *1984*. The return to a concern with the individual was easier. The late 1950s and the 1960s saw the emergence of a new school of writers—short-story writers, for the most part—who would deal with the fate of a particular, unique person rather than with socially determined types. Whereas the socialist realist production novel gravitated toward the city and large industrial plants, the new prose of the post-Stalin years, such as that of Yury Kazakov, Vladimir Tendryakov, Vasily Belov, and Vasily Shukshin, tended to deal with life in the villages and small towns of remote (mostly northern) regions of the Soviet Union.

The prose of the first decade after the revolution showed great diversity, as well as much experimentation. The prose style of Zamyatin, Pilnyak, Babel, Kharms, Ehrenburg, Shklovsky, Vaginov, and Olesha was original and innovative. The rest of the Soviet period offered a rich variety of subject matter and of socially and intellectually diverse voices, but little formal experimentation and innovation. In fact, the language and style of some major works of the 1920s, such as Sholokhov's *The Quiet Don*, Gladkov's *Cement*, and Leonov's *The Thief*, were standardized and purged by their authors of dialectisms, vulgarisms, and other unconventional traits at the insistence of editors of the Stalin era.

The number of established prose writers who stayed in the Soviet Union after the revolution was not great, and even among them, Gorky and Bely did leave the country temporarily and Zamyatin emigrated in 1931. Other writers who stayed to establish themselves as major Soviet writers were Aleksandr Serafimovich, Mikhail Prishvin, Vyacheslav Shishkov, Olga Forsh, and Sergei Sergeev-Tsensky.

Maksim Gorky's reaction to the October revolution was ambivalent. It found expression in a series of articles, "Untimely Thoughts" (1917–18), published in the Menshevik newspaper *New Life*. Gorky was willing, however, to collaborate with the Soviet regime and actively participated in several of its publishing projects. He preserved many cultural values and even saved lives, both by direct intervention and by the authority of his humane opinions. He left the country in 1921 and settled in Sorrento, where he lived until 1931, with visits to the Soviet Union in 1928 and 1929. He never broke with the Soviet regime, continued to publish his works in the Soviet Union, and stayed aloof from émigré circles, although on cordial terms with some émigré writers, Khodasevich in particular. After his return to the Soviet Union he became a captive of Stalin and his henchmen. He traveled widely in the Soviet Union and published sketches of his impressions, always supportive of Stalin's five-year plans. He also supported the official position at the First Congress of Soviet Writers in 1934. When he died in 1936, he was given a magnificent state funeral, and his native city of Nizhny Novgorod was renamed Gorky in his honor.

Gorky continued to be productive to the end of his life. His literary reminiscenes, particularly of Tolstoi (1919), are remarkable for their robust plasticity and their penetration of the subject's character. His best novel, *The Artamonov Business* (1925), follows the Artamonovs through three generations, from the uneducated grandfather, a strong and enterprising, lusty patriarch who starts a small factory and builds it into a major industrial plant, to a grandson, an intellectual and revolutionary whose generation will see the end of the Artamonov business. Gorky's main work, *The Life of Klim Samgin*, begun in 1925, remained unfinished. It suffers from the faults of all his longer works—absence of a steady plot, no distinctive narrative voice, many tedious passages—yet deserves the attention it has received in the Soviet Union. The novel follows Klim Samgin, a colorless and spineless bourgeois intellectual, from childhood into middle age, focusing on the revolutions of 1905 and 1917. Samgin, selfish and self-centered, never commits himself to any ideology, preferring to remain an interested observer. Soviet criticism has rationalized Gorky's choice of this central character by suggesting that it unmasked those bourgeois historians who asserted that they were writing objective history whereas they were only defending their selfish class interests. But there is no reason why the novel cannot be read simply as an intelligent, pragmatic inquiry into the causes and the social significance of the revolution. In retrospect, *The Life of Klim Samgin* may not be a great novel, but its truth value is as high as that of any major novel about the period it covers.

Andrei Bely initially welcomed the revolution but soon became disillusioned and left Russia in 1921. He returned, however, in 1923 and spent the rest of his life writing prolifically, as before. His autobiographical novel *Kotik Letaev* and its sequel, *The Baptized Chinaman* (both 1922), depict the emergence of consciousness and its development into self-consciousness in a child. Even more than in *Petersburg*, Bely's interest here centers on the strange dialectical patterns of the symbolic world created by the mind. The novels of Bely's Moscow trilogy, *A Moscow Eccentric* (1926), *Moscow under Siege* (1926), and *Masks* (1931), are further exercises in Bely's self-consciously foregrounded and reflective narrative style. Much as in *Petersburg*, their plots are in themselves lively, but appear unreal and seem to be generated by the narrator's "cerebral play."

Bely's four volumes of memoirs, *Recollections of A. A. Blok* (1922), *At the Turn of the Century* (1930), *The Beginning of the Century* (1933), and *Between Two Revolutions* (1934), share the virtues and faults of his fiction. They are largely products of Bely's mind rather than an objective record of facts. Although brilliant and fascinating, they are unreliable. Bely also continued his scholarly work. His study *The Art of Gogol* (1934) is stimulating and perceptive, but also arbitrary in projecting Bely's personal vision into Gogol's texts.

Zamyatin

Evgeny Ivanovich Zamyatin (1884–1937), the son of a priest, joined the Bolshevik party while a student at the Saint Petersburg Polytechnic Institute. He suffered prison and exile in 1905, but graduated in 1908 and worked as a naval engineer while gaining recognition as a writer. His short novels *A Provincial Tale* (1913) and *Out in the Sticks* (1914) and several short stories dealt with provincial tedium, ignorance, and brutishness, his moral indignation concealed by grotesque imagery, sardonic humor, and skaz.

After the revolution Zamyatin lectured on the craft of writing at workshops for young writers and became the mentor of the Serapion Brothers. His postrevolutionary prose was a model of the ornamentalism in vogue at the time. In such stories as "Mamai" (1921), "The Cave" (1922), "The Nursery" (1922), "The Yawl" (1928), and "The Flood" (1929) an elliptical style, frequent nominal phrases, massive and at times paradigmatic use of symbolic imagery, and foregrounding of sound symbolism and phrase rhythm create impressions of haunting intensity. In a lighter vein, Zamyatin wrote satirical sketches of Soviet life in which he deflated the heroic verbiage of official pronouncements. He also wrote some brilliant essays and several successful plays.

Zamyatin's international fame rests with his novel *We* (1924, published in translation before it ever appeared in Russian), a dystopia that in some ways anticipated Aldous Huxley's *Brave New World.* Unlike Orwell's *1984,* which was in part inspired by Zamyatin's work, *We* had little immediate relevance to contemporary reality. It underestimated the potential of technological progress while overestimating society's power to change human nature. Zamyatin's society of the future is on the verge of conquering outer space but has almost succeeded in reducing its members to the status of robots. The hero and narrator, an engineer working on the construction of the spaceship *Integral,* drifts into rebellion against the rational society of which he has been a model member when his latent imagination is awakened by a spark of feeling for a touchingly vulnerable female, the sex partner assigned to him by the state. In the end, the rebel's imagination is surgically removed and everything returns to normal.

The charm of *We* is in its narrative style. The hero's regression from a strangely remote, abstract, and cerebral consciousness to simple human feeling is done with great subtlety. In a way, the hero's tragedy projects Zamyatin's own fate. The world of *We,* however, is so distant from twentieth-century reality that its polemical edge is directed not so much at the actual condition of Soviet society or the policies of the Soviet government as against the communist utopia in the minds of Soviet intellectuals, who were celebrating the end of imaginative creativity and welcoming their own transformation into efficient machines in the service of the state.

Toward the end of his life Zamyatin was working on a historical conception equating the present state of European civilization with that of the Roman Empire on the eve of the great migrations. Attila the Hun is its central character. Zamyatin's unfinished novel *Scourge of God* (1939) is a last echo of the Scythian episode in Russian literature.

Communist Novels of the Revolution

Convinced Bolsheviks saw the revolution not only as a victory of the proletariat, engineered by their party, but also as a rational and necessary step in the progress of world history. They had to struggle, however, with the problem posed by the need to synchronize the rational doctrines of the party with the chaotic developments of which they were witnesses and participants.

Dmitry Furmanov (1891–1926) was a political commissar with the Twenty-fifth Division of the Red Army during the civil war. He fictionalized his experiences in a novel, *Chapaev* (1923), which became a classic of Soviet literature; it has been reprinted in huge editions and made into a famous film. Chapaev, legendary leader of

Red guerrillas, is juxtaposed with Klychkov, his political commissar. Chapaev, a peasant, stands for the spontaneous, elemental power of the people. He is strong and valiant, but reckless, ignorant, and undisciplined. Klychkov, a proletarian, provides the circumspect, goal-directed leadership and class-conscious ideology that Chapaev lacks. Chapaev perishes, but Klychkov will carry on and lead the struggle to a victorious end. The novel is composed in the "factographic," artless style of Left Art, and its ideological message is made amply explicit. *Chapaev* is a documentary whose ideological slant so strongly affects selection of facts and delineation of character that it becomes fiction—and not very good fiction at that.

The Iron Flood (1924) by Aleksandr Serafimovich (1863–1949), a member of the Knowledge group, who had had some success with stories and sketches in the manner of Gorky, is more romantic and flamboyant than *Chapaev.* It tells the typical story of how a heroic Bolshevik leader transforms a disorganized mass of humanity, united only by their hatred of their oppressors and a dream of a better life, into a disciplined fighting force.

Some writers dealt with the same theme less schematically. *A Week* (1922), by Yury Libedinsky (1898–1959), who like Furmanov was a political commissar in the Red Army, tells of a peasant uprising against local Soviet government in the course of which most of the communists perish. The style of *A Week*, like that of *The Iron Flood*, is lyrically effusive, but the Bolshevik activists are presented as human beings whose genuine idealism is blunted by personal weaknesses. At this early stage, Bolshevik writers tended to perceive the road to victory as arduous and the fate of Bolshevik activists as tragic. This attitude appears with particular clarity in the works of some writers of the Pereval

group. The proletarian poet and communist activist who is the hero of Ivan Kataev's short novel *The Poet* (1929) is a tragic figure. Artyom Vesyoly (pseudonym of Nikolai Kochkurov, 1899–1939), in his novel *Russia Drenched in Blood* (1929–32) and in several of his stories that preceded it, perceives the revolution as an elemental, chaotic, and cruel event. Andrei Platonov, who like Furmanov, Libedinsky, and Vesyoly was a real communist, went on to view the revolution not only as a tragedy but also as a tragic failure.

A tragic vision appears as well in *The Rout* (1927), the first novel of Aleksandr Fadeev (1910–56). Fadeev grew up in the Far East, where he fought on the side of the Reds in the civil war. A political activist, he combined a party career with his literary work. *The Rout* tells of the changing fortunes of a Red guerrilla detachment in the Far East, ending with its rout in a Cossack ambush. A more sophisticated work than *The Iron Flood* or *A Week*, *The Rout* is told in a cool, business like manner. As in other works of the RAPP school, the influence of Tolstoi is apparent. Characters are presented as individuals, and their minds are explored by the author, with an implied interest in their moral qualities. *The Rout* also introduces an entirely new, Bolshevik morality and a class-oriented psychology. The proletarian members of the detachment have little respect for private property, and their sexual mores are fairly loose, but they are fiercely loyal to their cause and to their comrades, and they take good care of their horses and weapons. The rout of the Red guerrillas is caused by a mistake in judgment of their leader, Levinson, a Jewish intellectual, who has the wrong man, Mechik, ride in front as his detachment passes through a forest. A youth of middle-class background, Mechik has joined the guerrillas but has not shed the habits of his social class. He does not take proper care of his horse and neglects to clean his rifle. He dreams of glory instead of doing his job. When Mechik turns a corner on the forest trail and finds himself face to face with the enemy, he slides off his horse and dashes for cover, forgetting to fire a warning shot. The proletarian Morozka, who rides next after him, does fire one, paying for it with his life. But the warning comes too late, and Levinson's detachment is wiped out; only nineteeen men escape. Levinson knows the rout was his fault, but will carry on with the men left to him. Mechik may be in some sense a self-portrait of Fadeev, with whom he shared a common background.

The Rout, a work of talent, promised more than Fadeev was able to deliver. His unfinished epic novel *The Last of the Udege* (1929–40), also about the revolution and the early days of the Soviet regime in the Far East, is marked by an energetic narrative style and some strong detail, but it lacks coherence and its plot never gets going.[24] Fadeev went on to make a brilliant career, though, heading the Union of Soviet Writers from 1946 to 1954. In 1956 he shot himself, despondent about having reached a dead end as a writer and blamed by many for his role in Stalin's purges.

Fyodor Gladkov (1883–1958), a schoolteacher of peasant background, was active in the revolutionary movement beginning in 1906, served in the Red Army in the civil war, and belonged to the Smithy group in the 1920s. He became famous overnight in 1925 with his novel *Cement*, next to Gorky's *Mother* the most important milestone on the road to socialist realism. It relates how Gleb Chumalov, a veteran of the Red Army, returns from the civil war to find his

workplace, a large cement plant, laid idle. Overcoming a formidable array of obstacles, he returns it to full productive capacity. Chumalov and his wife, Darya, like him a political activist, sacrifice their private happiness to the cause of building socialism (their marriage fails and their little daughter dies of neglect in a public nursery). The novel's "revolutionary romanticism," praised by Gorky, was branded as false by Lef critics, who claimed that Gladkov's attempt to create an inspirational character of heroic proportions, although the author endowed him with individual psychological traits, was ill-advised. *Cement* was a popular success, in part on account of some graphic violence and sex, the latter toned down in subsequent editions. Gladkov, like Fadeev, never got close to duplicating his first success.

Sholokhov

By far the best work of what may be termed the RAPP school came from a young, little-known writer, Mikhail Aleksandrovich Sholokhov (1905–84). Sholokhov, himself not a Cossack, was born and spent his youth in the Don Military Region, the scene of his works. His formal education ended when he was thirteen. He was too young to fight in the civil war but witnessed the Cossack uprising against the Bolsheviks in 1919 and its eventual collapse. After the war he worked for the Soviet regime in various capacities and took part in operations against White guerrillas. In 1922 he went to Moscow, where he joined the Young Guard, a group of Komsomol writers, publishing his first story in 1923. In 1924 he returned to the Don region, where he stayed for the rest of his life. Between 1923 and 1927 he published some thirty stories, most of them dealing with the civil war and the bitter

24. The title alludes to James Fenimore Cooper's *Last of the Mohicans*. The Udege is a Siberian tribe.

class struggle in the villages of the Don region. Man's inhumanity to man is a dominant theme, and many stories end in violent death. The ethos of these stories, especially their humor, is distinctly that of an uneducated though intelligent and extraordinarily perceptive person. In 1925 Sholokhov started what would become his epic novel, *The Quiet Don* (1928–40), another masterpiece of Russian literature unexpectedly produced by an unlikely author. When the first of the novel's four parts appeared in 1928, some critics immediately asserted that Sholokhov was not the real author. These charges resurfaced when Sholokhov was awarded the Nobel Prize in 1965. It appears, however, that they were groundless.

The Quiet Don follows life in a Cossack village on the Don from about 1912 to 1920, in a way reminiscent of Tolstoi's *War and Peace.* The action centers on the fortunes of the Melekhov family—a hardworking, well-to-do farmer, his wife, two grown sons, and a younger daughter. Several other families are introduced through their various relations with the Melekhovs. More characters enter the picture as the Melekhov boys, Grigory and Pyotra, go off to war, and still more when the civil war sweeps through the Don region. Several communist activists make an appearance but remain on the fringes of the main plot, as do some historical personages, among them General Krasnov, who was to write his own epic novel of the the period.[25] The main hero is Grigory Melekhov, a brave, intelligent, and honest man, who after some indecision chooses the wrong side and ends up as the leader of a counterrevolutionary band of guerrillas fighting in a lost cause. The novel's plot as dictated by the course of history intertwines with the tragic love

25. See p. 537.

story of Grigory Melekhov and Aksinya Astakhov, the wife of the Melekhovs' neighbor. There is no communist bias. The Cossacks, archenemies of the revolution, are depicted as crude and violent, but also as good farmers and brave soldiers. Red and White atrocities are described with the same epic calm. Misha Koshevoi, a landless Cossack turned Bolshevik who runs things in the village when the war is over, is a nonentity. Grigory Melekhov is much the better man, but the future belongs to Koshevoi. Dunya Melekhov marries him, although she knows that he killed her brother Pyotra.

The Quiet Don has some unique qualities. Whereas characters drawn from the upper classes appear schematic and remote, the inner life of uneducated people is treated with sympathy and understanding, and without condescension. Cossack women in particular are presented with tact and fond respect. The feelings of the four characters involved in the love tragedy—Grigory Melekhov's wife loves him dearly despite his infidelity, and Astakhov, a hard and violent man, is destroyed by the loss of his wife—are described simply, believably, and without sentimentality. Episodes showing the Cossacks farming, fishing, and feasting are magnificent, as are Sholokhov's many nature descriptions, which blend harmoniously into the narrative, conveying an epic sense of gladness and love of life. Sholokov's dialogue is lively and authentic, his narrative colorful and colloquial, laced with lyric passages and figurative speech. Hundreds of dialectisms, vulgarisms, and details felt to be offensive, including some that were deemed too negative with regard to the communist characters in the novel, were deleted from later editions of *The Quiet Don.*

While the vocabulary and imagery of folk poetry show up frequently in *The Quiet Don*, it is still a realist novel. Sholokhov's epopoeia is true to the actual course of history. It shows how a stable society, which though coarse and violent has great vitality, is sucked into a cauldron of hatred, brutality, and mass murder. When the bloody nightmare is over, the former plenitude of life is gone and a bleak future seems in store for the survivors. This was hardly the message Soviet authorities wished to hear, but Stalin liked the novel, and Sholokhov, who became a party member only in 1932, was spared the fate of so many of his contemporaries.

Sholokhov may have bought the integrity of *The Quiet Don* at the price of concessions to political expediency in his second novel, *Virgin Soil Upturned* (1932–60), started before *The Quiet Don* was finished. The first volume of this novel describes the collectivization of agriculture—or more precisely, the "liquidation of kulaks as a class"—in a Don Cossack village. It does so with a wary eye on the official position, relying on the message of Stalin's article "Dizzy with Success," which had conceded that activists of the collectivization drive had in some instances been overly zealous. *Virgin Soil Upturned* is, however, not a pure socialist realist novel. The principal villain is properly a former Cossack officer, hence a "class enemy," but he gets help from some poor Cossacks who have done well farming their private plots under the NEP and others who simply feel sorry for the dispossessed, abused, and deported kulaks. The kulaks themselves are presented as human beings, though not necessarily attractive ones, and the local communist activists are not idealized. *Virgin Soil Upturned* has none of the tragic pathos of *The Quiet Don*, possibly because of the nature of its subject matter. The civil war, bloody and cruel though it was, was fought over a real issue: it was a war of poor against rich. The collectivization of agriculture, just as cruel, was a

senseless administrative measure. *Virgin Soil Upturned* is not a beautiful novel, because it presents its subject with external truthfulness yet without exposing its hideous inner meaning.

Sholokhov's career after 1940 was anticlimactic. His unfinished war novel *They Fought for the Fatherland* (1943–44) is second-rate, as is the second volume of *Virgin Soil Upturned.* During the last twenty years of his life Sholokhov wrote little fiction and deteriorated, becoming a fixture of the Soviet literary establishment who was used to endorse the official policy of the moment. He was nevertheless a great writer, and his greatness is enhanced by his having reached it without assuming the sensibility of an educated man, as Gorky had done.

Fellow Travelers of the Revolution

Boris Andreevich Pilnyak (pseudonym of Boris Vogau, 1894–1937), the son of a veterinarian, spent his youth mostly in provincial towns of the Moscow region and graduated from the Moscow Commercial Institute in 1920. He published some short stories beginning in 1915 and became one of the leading Soviet writers overnight with his novel *The Naked Year* (1921), a diffuse potpourri of episodes and impressions from life in a provincial town soon after the revolution. This novel and Pilnyak's stories of the early 1920s, such as "The Blizzard" (1921), "The Third Capital" (1922). and "Black Bread" (1923), seem plotless, and their narrative is lyrically mannered, highstrung, or tending toward a studied primitivism. Along with the short novel *Machines and Wolves* (1924), they are typical of Pilnyak's ornamentalist manner, a mixture of Bely and Remizov, which was in vogue for a brief time after the revolution. In the mid-1920s Pilnyak reverted to a more conventional realist style. He traveled widely in the Soviet Union, Europe, and the Far East and in 1931 spent some months in the United States. Many of his works reflect his travel experiences, for instance, his largely negative impressions of America in *O.K.: An American Novel* (1932).

Pilnyak, who had enjoyed excellent relations with the Kremlin in the early 1920s, lost favor when Stalin got the upper hand in the power struggle with Trotsky. His story "The Tale of the Unextinguished Moon" (1926) was, probably rightly, perceived as a Trotskyite provocation, accusing Stalin of the murder of M. V. Frunze, a popular Red Army commander. It was immediately suppressed. In 1929 Pilnyak's story "Mahogany," published by the émigré publishing house Petropolis in Berlin, was fiercely attacked as sympathetic to the defeated Trotskyite faction of the party and to the kulaks then being liquidated. The novel *The Volga Falls into the Caspian Sea* (1930)[26] was seen, perhaps unfairly, as an attempt by Pilnyak to regain the good graces of the party. Pilnyak perished in Stalin's purges.

The verdict on Pilnyak's position and stature in the literature of his age is still out. According to one view, Pilnyak's works are a montage of random material, arbitrarily and superficially organized through repetition of themes, images, and even sound patterns. But another view has it that Pilnyak's seemingly confused texts are in fact allegories that allow a perceptive reader to recognize a "pattern in the rug." The focal question that Pilnyak seeks to answer may have been whether the turbulent events witnessed by his generation had the direction and meaning that his Marxist contemporaries took for

26. The title is a Russian phrase exemplifying a truism.

granted and that he, as time went on, apparently grew to doubt.

Vsevolod Ivanov (1895–1963) was born in Siberia, the son of a teacher. He left home early and supported himself as a laborer, sailor, actor, and circus performer. He began publishing in 1915 and subsequently belonged to the cosmists and to the Serapion Brothers. Ivanov's trilogy about the civil war in Central Asia, *Guerrillas* (1921), *Armored Train No. 14–69* (1922, made into a play in 1927), and *Colored Winds*, displays the ornamentalist style. A sequence of brief, striking episodes takes the place of a coherent narrative. The horrors of war—made worse by the fact that the native population, to whom the issues of the civil war do not even exist, suffers as much as the fighting Russians—are presented graphically, with estranged and laconic objectivity. For example, we are told without comment that the native women lie down whenever they see a Russian soldier, expecting to be raped. The narrative is supported by assorted documentary and illustrative material, which increases the fragmentary nature of the whole but also makes it vivid. The dialogue is earthy and realistic. Ivanov's later fiction, among which the autobiographic novel *Adventures of a Fakir* (1934–35) is the most interesting, lacks the zest and color of his early works.

Leonid Leonov (b. 1899), who was to become one of the pillars of socialist realism, started his career in the experimental manner of Pilnyak and other ornamentalists. Leonov was born in Moscow. His father was a self-educated poet and journalist who was exiled to Archangel in 1910. Leonov, though educated in Moscow, retained an affection for the Russian north all his life. Having briefly worked on his father's newspaper and served in the Red Army, Leonov did not join any of the proletarian groupings. His early works, although vaguely sympathetic to the Soviet regime, reflect the viewpoint of an intellectual fellow traveler.

Leonov's early stories about the revolution and its impact on various classes of people indicate that he was consciously looking for a style. He soon decided that Dostoevsky's was more congenial to him than any other. The best of his early stories, "The End of a Petty Man" (1924), greatly resembles the early Dostoevsky.

The plot of Leonov's first novel, *The Badgers* (1924), concerns a peasant revolt against Soviet grain requisitioning (the "badgers" are a band of counterrevolutionary guerrillas), but its more interesting episodes are set in the old trading quarter of Moscow. The conflict, spearheaded by two feuding brothers, is not so much between revolution and counterrevolution as between city and country. The novel is loosely structured and episodic, with many digressions, told in the diffuse and expansive manner of ornamentalism.

Leonov's second novel, *The Thief* (1927), for which he is mainly known in the West, is an ambitious but unsuccessful attempt at adapting Dostoevskian novelistic devices, types, and psychology to Soviet reality under the NEP. The hero, Mitya Vekshin, a veteran of the civil war, cannot get over his feelings of guilt about the gratuitous killing of a White officer and sinks to the bottom of Moscow's underworld, where he becomes the leader of a band of thieves. His self-hate and self-laceration eventually have a salutary effect, and he is reformed to become a Bolshevik activist. The novel has several other characters who, like Vekshin, are straight out of Dostoevsky. The writer Firsov accompanies the action as the author's alter ego, responding to anticipated criticism.

Although *The Thief* has some good details and strong pages, it does not jell, and it leaves the reader unconvinced not only of the reality of its characters but also of the author's sincerity. Leonov hurts himself, too, by inviting comparison with Dostoevsky. Leonov's socialist realist novels, however, show him capable of further development.

Konstantin Fedin, one of the Serapion Brothers, (1892–1977), was a student in Germany when the war broke out in 1914. He was interned as an enemy civilian and could return to Russia only after the war. His first novel, *Cities and Years* (1924), showed him a writer of talent and originality. Like other Serapion Brothers, he went on to make a career under Stalin but never quite realized the promise of his first novel.

Cities and Years is an autobiographical work. It tells the story of an educated young Russian interned in Germany who falls deeply in love with a German woman but returns to Russia, where he perishes, having failed to come to terms with the revolution, which shocks him by its cruelty. *Cities and Years* has an interesting structure: its chronological time sequence is pointedly and aptly disturbed, and fragmentary episodes are arranged so as to enhance the impression of time out of joint. *Cities and Years* avoids the shrill stridency common in the prose of the period. Rather, its mood is one of tragic resignation.

Aleksei Nikolaevich Tolstoi (1883–1945) made the most unlikely career of all fellow travelers. As a student at the Saint Petersburg Technological Institute in the 1900s, he wrote symbolist poetry, but he soon switched to prose without developing a style of his own. A war correspondent in World War I, he left Russia after the revolution but returned in 1923. He brought back with him two fine short novels, *Nikita's*

Childhood (1920) and *The Sisters*; the latter became the first part of his epic of the revolution, *A Tour of Hell* (1921–40).[27] Tolstoi then wrote some utopian and science fiction, and in 1929 he published the first part of his historical novel *Peter the First*. As a historical novelist and dramatist he became Stalin's favorite, earning the highest awards and honors, and was pronounced a Soviet classic. *A Tour of Hell* starts as a relatively narrowly conceived novel about upper middle-class Petersburg society, with some excursions into the literary ambience Tolstoi knew well. Aleksandr Blok and other familiar figures appear, thinly disguised. As the action moves toward and beyond the revolution, the novel's framework broadens, extending from Petersburg all over Russia. What is initially a tightly controlled, closely observed, and psychologically convincing study of Tolstoi's own milieu gradually expands into a superficial, though fluently narrated panoramic epic that introduces many characters from various walks of life. Gone, too, is the author's initial objectivity, as he now tries to assume an unequivocally positive attitude toward the Soviet regime. Nevertheless, *A Tour of Hell* is, next to Pasternak's *Doctor Zhivago* and Bulgakov's *White Guard* (1924), the most successful attempt to embody the Russian intelligentsia's tour of the hell of revolutionary upheaval.

Babel

Isaak Emmanuilovich Babel (1894–1941) came from an middle-class Jewish family in Odessa. The teeming polyglot seaport became with Babel's generation a focus of

27. *Khozhdenie po mukam*, the novel's title, is borrowed from the medieval apocrypha about the Virgin's tour of hell. See p. 22. In English the novel is known under the title *The Road to Calvary*, not an apt translation.

literary activity, which produced a genre of its own, the Odessa tale. Bagritsky, Selvinsky, Inber, Olesha, Paustovsky, and the Kataev brothers were other "Odessa writers." Babel grew up trilingual, attending a Russian secondary school but living in a Yiddish-speaking community and receiving a traditional rabbinical education in Hebrew. A Jewish religious, cultural, and linguistic strain appears throughout his oeuvre. Babel also learned to speak French early and as a youth tried to write French stories after Guy de Maupassant. In 1915 Babel moved to Saint Petersburg, where he published a few articles and his first stories. He volunteered for service in the Red Army immediately after the revolution and held assignments with food-requisitioning expeditions and the Cheka, finally working as a war correspondent and propagandist with the Red Cavalry of Semyon Budyonny in the war against Poland in 1920. The thirty-four stories of the cycle *Red Cavalry* are based on notes taken during that campaign. Babel's Odessa tales, published individually between 1921 and 1923 and in book form in 1927, and the stories of *Red Cavalry*, gathered into a book in 1926, made him famous but also caused him a great deal of trouble: Marshal Budyonny protested against what he saw as a slanderous depiction of his men. Babel published only a few stories in the 1930s but was active as an editor, journalist, and screenwriter. Apparently he had some difficulty adapting to socialist realism. Babel was arrested in 1939 and died in prison. He was "posthumously rehabilitated" in 1956.

Babel was a meticulous worker who rewrote his stories interminably. His collected works amount to no more than two volumes. The bulk of his stories, all brief, belongs to three cycles: *Red Cavalry*; Odessa tales about Ben-Zion (Benya) Krik, a flamboyant Jewish gangster; and bittersweet reminiscences of the writer's childhood in Odessa. The stories of *Red Cavalry* have a personalized narrator, Lyutov (Babel's actual nom de guerre), whose voice might well be Babel's own, that of a leftist Jewish intellectual vacillating between Marxism, a Nietzschean cult of power and beauty, and reverence for the gentle pacifism of Hasidic sages. *Red Cavalry* also has several pieces in skaz, told by semiliterate soldiers. The stories about Benya Krik and a play, *Sunset* (1928), about the Krik family, have a delightful flavor of Yiddish in their ethos and cadences. Other stories are told in a vibrant lyric prose.

Babel's art is expressionist. The peculiar charm of his stories derives from their language and composition. Image follows image, usually striking, colorful, even gaudy: the moon rolls down the sky like a lopped-off head, the long legs of a dashing Red commander in tall riding boots look like two prim young ladies in close fitting black dresses up to their necks, the breasts of a buxom Cossack woman move like an animal in a sack. The images of which a story is composed are put together jerkily, often with jarringly dissonant transitions from the sublime to the coarse, from the noble to the sordid. Viktor Shklovsky said that Babel would speak in the same tone about heroism and gonorrhea. Babel's art resembles that of Marc Chagall, whose Jewish shtetls are also the scene of the stories of *Red Cavalry*. There is little narrative or dialogue in Babel's stories, but what there is, is vigorous, poignant, and dramatic. The main event is often presented in a single lapidary sentence.

The stories of *Red Cavalry* feature such traditional epic themes as the sweetness of revenge, the triumph of victory, death in battle, and the cruel sufferings of innocent noncombatants through rape and pillage. In one tour de force after another, Babel fuses high pathos with cool realism, unafraid of the shocking and the sordid. Familiar epic themes are travestied. A young warrior's first triumph features an unlikely hero, Kolesnikov, a bowlegged peasant lad who has risen from platoon to division commander within a few weeks. But Kolesnikov is for real: he fights for glory and after his first victorious command displays "the superb indifference of a Tatar khan." The tragic encounter of father and son on the epic field of battle becomes an account of two brutal executions. The father, a policeman under the tsar, kills his son, whom he catches fighting on the Red side, and himself is killed by another son when captured by the Reds. The story is told by a third son, with a touch of stupid bravado and without a trace of sorrow. The epic ride to a foe's castle to take revenge for past injustices appears as the story of Pavlichenko, a Red commander, who rides to the manor of his former master and tramples him to death—shooting the old man would not have given him the satisfaction he gets from stomping on his foe for a whole hour.

The implied author of *Red Cavalry* is on the side of the revolution, even though he is painfully aware of its cruelties and injustices. In fact, Lyutov feels inferior to those Bolsheviks who follow the party line unquestioningly. He has no love for kulaks, landowners, and priests (Catholic or Orthodox) and his favorite hero is a rabbi's son turned Bolshevik. Babel does not seem to have anticipated the inevitable crisis that Russian Jewry would face under the Soviet regime.

Some moral ambiguities permeate Babel's entire oeuvre. In the story "Line and Color" myopic Kerensky, a loser, refuses to wear glasses because objects, and women in particular, look more beautiful as vague shapes to be realized by the imagination. Bespectacled Trotsky, a winner (when the story was written), only cares to see the cruel line of action. The aesthetic values of power and grace are found in Cossack warriors and gangsters like Benya Krik and Froim Grach, the moral values of kindness, charity, and compassion in gentle Jewish eccentrics. Babel has sympathy for both sides, but on the whole he seems to lean toward power and grace. Lyutov's proudest moment comes when he can say at the end of the last story of *Red Cavalry* that the Cossacks no longer take notice of him as he rides by: he now rides his horse like a Cossack. Babel's position in the conflict between an intellectual's cerebral dreams and a simple man's carnal immediacy is equally ambivalent. The greatness of Babel's art does not hinge on the presence, much less on a resolution, of these ambiguities. It lies almost entirely in the sensuous power of his imagery, the vigorous concision of his language, and a successful fusion of a ruthless realism with a romantic's belief in beauty, high-mindedness, and valor.

Pasternak

Boris Pasternak's novel *Doctor Zhivago* was a belated but important monument to the Russian intelligentsia's "tour of hell" of the revolution. Prose fragments that Pasternak had published between 1918 and 1939 were steps toward the great autobiographical novel, on which Pasternak worked for nearly twenty years and which he finished in 1955. He submitted it to *Novy mir* in 1956, but at the last moment the decision went against publication. When the novel appeared in the West the following year and earned Pasternak the Nobel Prize in 1958, it became a cause célèbre. The Soviet literary establishment reacted with trumped-up

accusations and the West contributed to the furor by making an apolitical work into a political headliner.

Doctor Zhivago follows the panoramic scheme of a nineteenth-century social novel as it pursues events witnessed by Yury Zhivago—a physician, Pasternak's contemporary, and like him a poet—from his boyhood to his death in 1929. Although the presence of a central character gives the plot a certain continuity, much of the novel consists of isolated episodes, accidents of fate, and chance encounters. A large number of characters is introduced, many never to reappear. Yet there develops a pattern of strange coincidences that play a decisive role in Yury Zhivago's life. Apparently all these traits reflect Pasternak's view of the human condition. A unique feature, at least for a modern novel, is the addition of a cycle of poems, each of which relates to a particular episode in the novel. The lead poem, "Hamlet," offers an allegorical key to the meaning of Zhivago's life. An impressionable, imaginative, artistic soul, an observer rather than a doer, he is an actor sent onstage to play Hamlet. He does not feel up to it and, like Christ at Gethsemane, begs that this cup may pass him by:

> But the action of the play has been
>   apportioned,
> And the end of the road is duly marked.
> I stand alone. All is swamped in
>   pharisaism.
> To live a life is not like crossing a field.

The last line is a Russian proverb meaning that life is not easy. The poems of Yury Zhivago give meaning and purpose to the difficult life of a weak man inept at shaping his own fate and dependent on the strength of the three women in his life.

Doctor Zhivago is the confessional novel of a poet, but it is also a novel about the

Russian intelligentsia. Yury Zhivago, Pasternak's alter ego, is also a symbol of its creative spirit. His antipode is Pasha Antipov, who becomes a Bolshevik commander. Lara, Antipov's wife, who may be perceived as a symbol of ideal Russian womanhood, deserts the strong Antipov for the weak Zhivago. It is Lara who sees that the Russian intelligentsia's tragic mistake was to believe that it was nobler to fight and die for an idea unquestioningly than to examine it critically. Antipov's eventual suicide is symbolic of the futility of that attitude.

The grand scheme of *Doctor Zhivago* is magnificent, but its execution is open to criticism. The narrator never develops a distinct voice or a consistent point of view. The narrative lacks vigor but has great lyric highlights. What little dialogue there is lacks spark, but the novel is rich in challenging disourses, attributed to Zhivago and various other characters, on art, the Russian intelligentsia, Jewishness, and other topics. Character delineation is vague; even Zhivago remains remote. These apparent flaws are amply offset by a wealth of concrete physical and psychological detail. The very randomness with which they are presented projects Pasternak's understanding of the artist's mission. He believed that the artist should be like a sponge, sucking up the details of life, rather than like a mirror, seeking to reflect the whole of it.

The NEP invited a different response from that to the revolution. To be sure, plenty of writers followed the example of Gladkov's *Cement* and continued to present life in an upbeat or even heroic mode. Among them were Anna Karavaeva (1893–1979), whose novel *The Sawmill* (1928) depicted the coming of industry to the Soviet countryside, and Lidiya Seifullina (1889–1954), whose short novel *Virineya* (1924) told the story of a peasant woman's struggle for emancipation. Fyodor Panfyorov's (1896–1960) lengthy novel *Bruski: A Story of Peasant Life in Soviet Russia* (1928–37) featured the tenacious struggle of a communist activist to bring the Soviet order to his home village. Another novel dealing with progress in rural Russia, *Milk* (1930), by Ivan Kataev (1902–39), may have cost the author his life. In it a community of flourishing dairy farms under the NEP is described fondly and in careful detail. Kataev, a communist with good credentials, made the mistake of presenting his model dairy farmers as peasants who not only own as many as five cows but are, moreover, religious sectarians. They are depicted as hardworking, resourceful, and receptive to technical progress. Kataev's novel was immediately branded a provocation and an infamous attempt to promote the fortunes of kulaks. Kataev perished in the purges of the 1930s.

Olesha

By far the most interesting work to present Russia under the NEP in a positive light was *Envy* (1927), a short novel by Yury Karlovich Olesha (1899–1960). Olesha came from a middle-class Polish family. He grew up in Odessa and studied law at the University of Novorossiysk. In 1919 he enlisted in the Red Army, breaking with his parents, who eventually emigrated to Poland. He was soon assigned to work as a journalist-propagandist and after his discharge found himself in Moscow on the staff of the Soviet railroaders' journal *The Whistle.* Other staff members were the brothers, Valentin and Evgeny Kataev, Ilya Ilf, Eduard Bagritsky, and Isaak Babel—all, like Olesha, from Odessa. Olesha's spirited satirical verse did its share to make *The Whistle* popular far beyond its professional readership. Olesha published two collections of verse in 1924 and 1927. After the success of *Envy*, he made the novel into an even more successful play, *Conspiracy of Feelings* (1929). "Three Fat Men" (1928), a modern fairy tale about revolution in an imaginary country, also appeared in a stage version (1930) and later in several screen and radio versions. In addition, Olesha published some thoughtful and whimsical short stories.

Envy and *Conspiracy of Feelings* were initially greeted as endorsements of party ideology. But soon it dawned on orthodox critics that Olesha's works were in fact ambiguous and that many readers might identify with their losers rather than with their winners. Olesha prudently abandoned his provocative style and after 1932 did mostly hackwork, writing screenplays and doing translations. He left a great many unpublished fragments, from which a posthumous selection, *No Day without a Line: From the Notebooks*, was published in 1965.

Envy contrasts a positive and a negative Soviet type under the NEP, each represented by two generations. There are two middle-aged brothers, Andrei and Ivan Babichev. Andrei, an Old Bolshevik, is a high-ranking functionary working on creating a chain of restaurants, called The Quarter, that will offer a nourishing meal for twenty-five kopeks. The idea is to take Soviet women out of their kitchens and put them to work on the factory assembly line. Ivan is a brilliant ne'er-do-well, a dreamer and big talker reduced to playing the buffoon in Moscow beer parlors. Kavalerov, in his twenties, lives with Andrei Babichev, who literally picked him up from the gutter. Like Ivan Babichev, he is bright and well educated, but shiftless and chronically unemployed. His antipode is Volodya, his predecessor as Andrei's house guest. Volodya is a member of the Komsomol, an engineering student, and the goalie on a top soccer team. Volodya's ideal is to

make himself into a perfect machine serving Soviet society. An ambiguity is introduced into this scheme of things by virtue of the action's being seen through the eyes of the two negative characters—hence envy as the title and leitmotif of the novel. Kavalerov eagerly looks for flaws in his benefactor's past and present, and indeed does find some. Andrei Babichev, a diligent worker, is obese and a glutton. Although kind and well intentioned, he has a shallow mind. Ivan scores some points, too. He demonstratively carries a pillow with him as a symbol of the warmth and intimacy of the home, threatened by his brother's project. Yet Kavalerov and Ivan Babichev are then discredited not only by their idleness, drunkenness, and other bad habits but also by the sterility of their dreams. Ivan, who fancies himself a modern miracle worker, can do no better than turning wine into water, Kavalerov no better than dreaming of how his individuality would flourish if he lived in France.

A soccer game between a Soviet club of dedicated team players and a foreign professional club of individualistic money players provides a key to the novel's ambiguities. Though the foreign club leads 1–0 at halftime, the Soviet team, which will play the second half with the wind, ought to win—but no victory is explicitly reported. Similarly, The Quarter is only a project. Several subliminal Freudian symbols in the text suggest that Andrei Babichev, the Soviet activist, is as sterile as the shirker Kavalerov.

Envy is the most modern of all Russian novels. It is lively and fascinating as discourse, rather than by virtue of story line or plot, of which there is little. It has surrealist episodes and features some Freudian symbols and paradigmatic color symbolism in the manner of Andrei Bely (green, the color of envy shows up with regularity). Cinematic devices, such as stills, accelerated motion, zoom, and isolated and angled shots, create a sense of estrangement that forces the reader literally to see things. *Envy*, a work of great originality, has retained its freshness over the years.

The return of private enterprise and private wealth under the NEP caused much bitterness among communists, who felt that their cause had been betrayed. Such sentiments were voiced in Gladkov's *Cement*, in Leonov's *The Thief*, in Yury Libedinsky's novels *Tomorrow* (1923), *Commissars* (1925), and *Birth of a Hero* (1930), and in Ilya Ehrenburg's novels *On the Make* (1925) and *In Running Lane* (1927), among others. Libedinsky's novels in particular were frankly Trotskyist, as they deplored the end of the "permanent revolution" and the decline of revolutionary fervor among Russian communists.

The ideological relaxation of the NEP period allowed satire to return to Russian literature. Party policies could not be discussed, but the contrast between the verbiage of organs of the Soviet state and the reality of daily life in the Soviet Union was an inviting subject that could be approached, albeit with discretion.

Satirists

Mikhail Mikhailovich Zoshchenko (1895–1958) came from a cultured family and was educated in Saint Petersburg. A law student, he volunteered for military service soon after the outbreak of the war. He saw duty in the front line, where he was wounded and gassed. He volunteered for the Red Army in 1918, but in 1919 received a medical discharge. Zoshchenko began writing stories in 1920. He joined the Serapion Brothers and brought out his first collection in 1921. His stories soon became immensely popular in the Soviet Union as well as in the émigré diaspora. In the 1930s Zoshchenko's satire was no longer tolerated, and he adopted a different style of writing: ideologically proper works, some of them for children, which many readers may have read as satire far deadlier than the stories of the NEP period; and pieces of literary inquiry, where a theoretical argument is illustrated by fictional case histories, also pregnant with latent parody. For example, "Youth Restored" (1933), a purported treatise on fighting senescence by willpower, is illustrated by the story of an aging professor who is so successful at it that he runs off with his neighbor's young wife. Zoshchenko's last piece of literary research, *Before Sunrise* (1943), explored the causes of his own chronic depression in a series of brief episodes. Publication of *Before Sunrise* was stopped when the authorities belatedly noticed that it was a piece of outrageous "subjectivism" and "psychologism" (Freud was one of the authorities consulted) unfit for publishing while the nation was fighting the "Great Patriotic War." Its conclusion appeared only in 1972. In 1946 Zoshchenko was singled out, along with Anna Akhmatova, as a noxious anti-Soviet element on the literary front and expelled from the Union of Soviet Writers. Rehabilitation after Stalin's death came slowly.

Zoshchenko's satire exposes the various incongruities of Soviet urban life. In his tales, city dwellers have accommodated themselves to the clichés of communist ideology but are still as selfish, greedy, aggressive, inconsiderate, dishonest, lazy, and drunken as before. Most of all, they are trying to survive under trying conditions, like the awful housing shortage. "Sleep more quickly, comrade," are the words that one man, who with his family lives in the bathroom of a communal apartment, hears each morning as his housemates knock on the bathroom door. The standard of living is low. The writer happily reports that by working hard he has earned enough to buy himself "a bed to sleep on and an overcoat to cover himself with." The quality of available goods is terrible. A child knocks himself out with a toy—it is made of heavy wood instead of soft, light rubber. The beginnings of a planned economy make themselves felt: one is embarrassed to sit on a toilet under four-hundred-watt light bulbs, the only kind available because the factory's quota was figured in wattage, not units. The new marriage and divorce laws are having their effect: when Borya wins a tidy sum in the state lottery, he divorces his wife within hours and moves in with the blonde next door. The campaign to liquidate illiteracy is not quite the success it claims to be. Workers who sign their name on the payroll with a cross are counted as literate because they were incapacitated by drunkenness at the time. There is no question this is now a workers' state. When a theater electrician is not given good seats for his two girlfriends, he turns off all the lights until he gets his way. "I'll show you 'technical personnel,'" he boasts. There is a new elite—again, there are people who have personal chauffeurs. Foreigners are in a class by themselves: a Soviet citizen can only marvel at their wealth and refined manners.

The language of Zoshchenko's stories is that of a Soviet citizen who identifies himself as a "person of culture [*chelovek kul'turnyi*], semi-intellectual [*poluintelligentnyi*]," where "person of culture" suggests one who is not often drunk and disorderly and "semi-intellectual" means "semieducated" or "semiliterate."[28] This

28. Russian *intelligentnyi* means "educated, cultured," rather than "intelligent"; an *intelligent* is a member of the *intelligentsia*.

narrator is ostensibly loyal to the regime, but takes no interest in politics. He reports only what goes on around him. All this is camouflage, of course. Andrei Zhdanov said in 1946 that Zoshchenko was guilty of brazen mockery of the Soviet order, and he was right.

The team of Ilya Ilf and Evgeny Petrov (pseudonyms of Ilya Fainzilberg, 1897–1937, and Evgeny Kataev, 1903–1942) rivaled Zoshchenko in popularity. The two met in Moscow in 1925 when both were on the staff of *The Whistle*. In 1927 Evgeny's elder brother Valentin Kataev facetiously challenged them to write a novel together and gave them the theme for *Twelve Chairs*. They responded and in 1928 scored a huge success with their satirical novel, whose picaresque hero, Ostap Bender, became proverbial. Several film versions of *Twelve Chairs* were also successful in the Soviet Union and in the West. The story of *Twelve Chairs*, a hunt for a treasure hidden in one of twelve stuffed chairs, each of which was sold to a different party, allowed Ilf and Petrov to draw a series of satirical sketches of provincial Russia under the NEP, in the manner reminiscent of Gogol's *Dead Souls*. Ostap Bender is a crafty, cynical, and superbly intelligent rogue, who meets various dull philistines, gullible provincial party functionaries, and greedy "vestiges of capitalism" with supercilious nonchalance and condescending irony.

Ilf and Petrov continued their collaboration with a series of feuilletons and satirical stories in which they lampooned the ossification of the Soviet order and the degeneration of Russian literature into a clumsy juggling of meaningless clichés. In 1931 they scored their second hit with *The Golden Calf*, for which they resuscitated Ostap Bender, who had been killed by a fellow treasure hunter in *Twelve Chairs*. In *The*

Golden Calf Bender decides to become a millionaire and reasons that the simplest avenue to the attainment of that goal is to find a multimillionaire and relieve him of one of his millions. Sure enough, he finds a middle-echelon industrial bureaucrat who has discovered a way to milk the plant at which he works for millions of rubles. The rest is easy. Along the way, the Soviet Union of the heroic five-year plan production novels is presented with satirical estrangement. *The Golden Calf* was received coldly by the literary establishment. In 1935–36 Ilf and Petrov made a six-month automobile trip across the United States, which they described in an intelligent and entertaining travelogue, *One-Storey America* (1936). They obviously liked many things about the United States, even their negative comments are perfunctory and good-natured.

The satirical novels and stories of Panteleimon Romanov (1885–1938) were less spirited than those of Ilf and Petrov or Zoshchenko but were also popular. The sexual revolution of the 1920s figured prominently among his topics, but he also exposed the ignorance and boorishness of the new proletarian bureaucrats and the cowardice and cynicism of their fellow-traveler toadies. Best known among his works are *Without Cherry Blossoms* (1926) and *Comrade Kislyakov* (1930, known in English as *Three Pairs of Silk Stockings*).

Valentin Kataev (1897–1986), one of the most talented writers of the Soviet period, started his literary career in his native Odessa and came to Moscow in 1922 to work for *The Whistle*. Kataev's oeuvre moved along with the times. In the 1920s he was mainly a satirist, after his early work had dealt with the revolution and civil war. During the Stalin era his work was a mainstay of socialist realism. In the 1960s he turned to an introspective and even experimental

memoirist prose. Kataev's short novel *Embezzlers* (1927) tells of the adventures of two Moscow government clerks who have absconded with a substantial sum of embezzled money, and in the process he paints an intriguing picture of the seamy side of Soviet society under the NEP. Kataev's satire is apt and robust, the narrative lively, and the dialogue racy. His somewhat facile manner, however, lacks the exuberance of Ilf and Petrov or the sense of the absurd that elevates Zoshchenko's best stories above the ephemeral.

A unique satirical novella, immortalized by Sergei Prokofyev's music, is Yury Tynyanov's "Lieutenant Kizhe" (1927). Set in the reign of Tsar Paul, but readily applicable to the present, it tells the story of a nonperson, born of a scribe's error (*kizhe* is a grammatical suffix with a plural ending plus a conjunction meaning "and"), who is kept alive, promoted, and even married by timorous bureaucrats afraid to admit the error to the tsar.

Venyamin Kaverin (pseudonym of Venyamin Silber, b. 1902), another Serapion Brother, studied Russian and foreign literatures at Petrograd University, graduating in 1924. He wrote essays and critical studies as well as fiction. His study of Osip Senkovsky (1926), reworked into a book, *Baron Brambeus* (1966), is a piece of solid scholarship. Kaverin, who became the chronicler of the Serapion Brothers, was in his own work closer to Hoffmann's "Serapiontic principle" and literary manner than any of the other Serapions. An approach to life through art, aesthetic and poetic theory as a theme of fiction, an appreciation of the symbolic significance of plot, and artful manipulation of time and space are characteristic of Kaverin's works. Kaverin was one of the few Soviet writers who never succumbed to the pressure of socialist realism. His first collection of stories, *Masters and Journeymen* (1923), is Hoffmannesque in its whimsical distortion of time, space, and perception. Kaverin's novels *The Troublemaker* (1928), *Artist Unknown* (1931), and *Wish Fulfillment* (1934–35) all deal with the condition of the creative individual and the intellectual community in Soviet society, often pointing directly to specific groupings like the formalists, events like the decoding of the so-called tenth chapter of *Eugene Onegin*, and fellow writers—Aleksei Tolstoi, for example—all under transparent disguises. The crisis of the humanities in a technologically oriented society, the rapid decline of the Soviet elite into a crowd of cultural barbarians, the rout of the formal school, and the aggressive pressure for organic—that is, socially relevant—art are registerred with the keen eye of a sophisticated critic of culture.

Kaverin's novels also have other traits that distinguish them from most other works of the period. They spotlight the early stages in the life of a gifted young man whose dreams remain unfulfilled—a pattern reminiscent of the romantic novel of disillusionment. In *Wish Fulfillment*, which follows the careers of two young men, a philologist and a natural scientist, the former fails but the latter succeeds—another pattern familiar from romantic literature. A pattern of parallel development also appears in another novel, *Two Captains* (1934–44), where an elaborate invention allows Kaverin to connect the fate of a prerevolutionary explorer, who was lost in the Arctic, with a young Soviet aviator of the 1930s. Kaverin actively participated in the revival of Russian literature after Stalin's death.

The novels of Konstantin Vaginov (pseudonym of Konstantin Vagingeim, 1899–1934) drew an even more somber picture of the decline of Russian culture

under the Soviet regime than those of Kaverin. Vaginov had started out as a member of the Guild of Poets and had published two collections of acmeist verse. In 1927 he joined the OBERIU group and concentrated on his prose fiction. His novel *The Goat Song* (1928; the title is a pun on Greek *tragoidia*, from *tragos*, "goat," and *oidē*, "song") paints a bleak picture of Leningrad as a cultural necropolis, populated by faceless Soviet philistines who, burdened by petty day-to-day cares and squabbles, have forgotten that they were once Russian intellectuals. The cultural heritage of the city is relegated to the novel's subtext.

Platonov

Andrei Platonovich Platonov (originally Klimentov, 1899–1951), one of the most original writers of the century, was a proletarian and dedicated communist. He produced a more profound refutation of Soviet ideology than any anticommunist author in the Soviet Union or abroad. Platonov was born in Voronezh into a working-class family, went to work on the railroad at fifteen, and served in the Red Army in the civil war. After the war he attended a polytechnical institute, earning his diploma in 1924, and worked for several years as a land reclamation and electrical engineer. All along he published professional articles, science fiction, and poetry in regional journals. In 1927 he won national attention with a collection of stories, *The Sluices of Epiphany*, entitled after the lead story, which tells of Bertrand Perry, a Scottish engineer hired by Peter the Great to build a waterway connecting the Baltic, Black, and Caspian seas. The tsar lets him have all the peasant manpower he needs. Perry eventually realizes that the project is not technically feasible and also that he will never see his native country again. He dies a horrible death in a Russian prison. The story develops one of Platonov's favorite themes, the tragic clash between human hubris and the inertia of nature. Humanity is divided into "clever" leaders and "dumb" workers; the schemes of the former ultimately amount to criminal folly, because they invariably aim at violating nature; in the end, the instinctive wisdom of the "dumb" people will prevail.

In the stories "Secret Man" (1928) and "The Origins of a Master" (1929) Platonov developed another key idea. Secret man is a human being who has an urge to renounce his individuality and merge with the universal life of nature and humanity, and hence a desire to sacrifice himself for a cause or for humanity. His sacrifice is, however, as futile as the ambitious schemes of "clever" leaders.

"The Origins of a Master" is the first part of a novel, *Chevengur*, which was not published in Platonov's lifetime and came out only in 1972, in the West. His next novel, *The Foundation Pit*, written around 1930, also first appeared in the West, in 1973. Meanwhile Platonov was able to publish some short stories and essays. The stories of his collection *Potudan River* (1937) are gloomy, with an undercurrent of doom uncharacteristic of the officious optimism of the Stalin era. Satirical stories in which Platonov brought out the absurd incongruities between official phraseology and the true mentality of the people ("Doubting Makar," 1929; "Benefit," 1931) were also published, causing official displeasure.

Platonov worked as a war correspondent during the Would War II. An innocuous story, "Ivanov's Family" (1946), about the difficulties of a veteran returning to civilian life, seems to have evoked Stalin's ire, and Platonov's name disappeared from print. He was allowed to work for the publishing house Detgiz, rewriting folktales for children. Platonov's "rehabilitation" after the death of Stalin came slowly, but by the 1960s he was generally recognized as a great writer.

In Platonov's novels *Chevengur* and *The Foundation Pit* tragic allegory is successfully wed to intensity of feeling and immediacy of expression. *Chevengur*, set in 1921, is the story of a quixotic quest by a handful of "inspired men" (*odukhotvorennyi*, "inspired," is another key word of Platonov's) for a city where true brotherhood and gladness reign in a land of victorious communism. Chevengur, an imaginary city where, it is said, communism is being built at an accelerated pace, is their destination. Their dreams of universal happiness are mixed with necrophilic obsessions. They welcome the death of imperfect human beings, even their own, because it will make room for a more perfect generation that will march on into the communist millennium. Later, all will be resurrected by an omnipotent new humanity. (Here the ideas of Nikolai Fyodorov enter the picture.) One of the seekers is obsessed with the idea that there is still time to reverse the decay of the corpse of the damsel of his dreams, Rosa Luxemburg, a communist leader murdered in Berlin in 1919, by a worldwide victory of the proletariat. The glorious tomorrow of Chevengur is a chimera. Together with Chevengur communism, the youngest member of the group, a child, also dies in the end, a sign that there will be no generation of "new men" and no communist future. In spite of its fantastic plot and strange characters, *Chevengur* has an eerie air of historical verity about it. The years immediately after the revolution produced an atmosphere of mad dreams and hysterical exaltation, which *Chevengur* captured to perfection.

The Foundation Pit is set in the late

1920s, at the start of Stalin's campaign to "liquidate kulaks as a class." Its allegorical meaning thus relates not only to the revolution but also to Stalin's "building of socialism in one country." The "building of socialism" is symbolized by a group of workers who have gathered to build a huge edifice that is to house the entire proletarian collective of the region. The pathos of this allegory is generated by the cruel incongruity between the enthusiasm and good faith of these men and the utter absurdity of their dream. All they can accomplish with their picks and shovels is to dig an ever-deepening hole in the ground. It will be their graveyard. The digging of the foundation pit overlaps with the collectivization of agriculture, an equally senseless undertaking. Misha, a bear, and as good a proletarian as any, is mercilessly overworked and underfed by a kulak smith. Misha gets his revenge with a single slap of his paw and is entrusted with running the village smithy, with predictable results. The collectivized horses of the village now consume their meager hay rations communally, which does not make them last longer. The kulaks are all put on a raft that floats down to the Arctic Ocean, if they will get that far. As in *Chevengur*, all hope dies with the death of a child, a little girl who said that she had begun to live only with the revolution. In *The Foundation Pit* and some other works, too, Platonov re-creates the deformation of the Russian language caused by the revolution, which destroyed the people's traditional concepts and values, giving them a new social consciousness—foreign, artificial, and largely absurd. The simple men in the foundation pit are hopelessly trapped in the web of this new language.

Nowhere in Russian literature has the futility of the effort that created Soviet society been revealed with such honesty and penetration as in *The Foundation Pit*. The simple people digging the pit are real characters. All the fantastic things that happen in the novel are painfully real, in an ordinary as well as in a higher sense. *The Foundation Pit* also has the virtue of representing the simple people's point of view straightforwardly, without condescension, false show of solidarity, or irony. This quality, along with the language of the novel, makes it difficult for Western readers to appreciate what may be the most profound work of Soviet literature.

Factography

The aesthetics of Left Art asked for a literature linked to contemporary life more directly than realist fiction. It encouraged the writer to turn reporter, sociologist, historian, memoirist, educator, and propagandist. Literary investigations, a mixture of the documentary and the imaginative modes, became a substantial genre among Soviet writers. Viktor Shklovsky, one of the main theorists of Left Art, was also the most active practitioner of "factography." His essays on the theory of literature, theater, and film, his many books on historical and literary figures, and his memoiristic works, such as *A Sentimental Journey: Memoirs 1917–1922* (1923), are crammed with facts, full of provocative ideas, and very entertaining. Shklovsky developed an idiosyncratic, aphoristic prose style, with brief and poignant phrases, sudden changes of subject, and "defamiliarization" through assuming an estranged point of view. Other notable examples of imaginative factography were provided by Pasternak, Mayakovsky, Mandelshtam, Bely, Livshits, Marienhof, Chukovsky, and Tynyanov.

Mayakovsky's essay "How to Make Verse" (1926), his American travelogue "My Discovery of America" (1925–26), and other prose pieces are remarkable for their concision, perceptive professionalism, and vigorous language. Pasternak's autobiography *Safe Conduct* (1931) consists of a series of episodes and encounters that he felt played a decisive role in his growth as a poet, with digressions into the theory of art and the psychology of creativity, all presented in unorthodox metaphorical and estranged language.

Mandelshtam, one of the most brilliant essayists in the language, produced eloquent and imaginative formulations of the acmeist aesthetic ("On the Nature of the Word," 1922), insightful profiles of his contemporaries (Blok, Mayakovsky, and Khlebnikov), profound critiques of culture ("The Word and Culture," 1921; "The Nineteenth Century," 1922), and a major synthesis of his philosophy of poetry, "Discourse on Dante" (1933, published posthumously). *The Noise of Time* (1923), a collection of autobiographical sketches, is a marvelously evocative record of Mandelshtam's own *éducation sentimentale* and of the intellectual atmosphere of Saint Petersburg in the 1900s. The travelogue "Journey to Armenia" (1931–32) offers strong parallels to Pushkin's "Journey to Arzrum." Like the latter, it tells of an escape from a stifling capital city into the fresh air of the mountains of the Caucasus and an exotic country with an ancient culture, still untouched by Muscovite regimentation. The brief vignettes of Mandelshtam's "Fourth Prose" (1928–30) are temperamental statements of Mandelshtam's precarious position in the world of Russian letters.

The memoirs of Andrei Bely, though factually unreliable, are brilliant and entertaining. The memoirs of Benedikt Livshits, *The One-and-a-Half-Eyed Archer* (1933), about the beginnings of Russian futurism, are thoughtful as well as reliable. Anatoly Marienhof's *A Novel without Lies* is an unreliable, though most interesting chronicle of the imagist *bohème*.

The historical novels of the literary scholar and theorist Yury Tynyanov—*Kyukhlya* (1925), about Wilhelm Küchelbecker, and *The Death of Vezeer-Mukhtar* (1927–28), about Aleksandr Griboedov, are a happy combination of fiction and valuable historical research. Kornei Chukovsky (pseudonym of Nikolai Korneichukov, 1882–1969), a versatile critic, translator, scholar, and editor, devoted a part of his prodigious energy to literature for children and to the study of child psychology. His *From Two to Five*, first published under the title *Small Children* (1928), went through many editions and was translated into many languages. An expert translator, particularly from English, Chukovsky also wrote a classic study, *The Art of Translation (1930).* Anton Makarenko (1888–1939), a professional educator, was for many years principal of a school for juvenile delinquents. In 1933–35 he serialized his experiences under the title *A Pedagogical Poem* (known in English under the title *The Road to Life*). The book was a huge success and was followed by several more works in the same manner.

Prose of the Stalin Era

Soviet prose under Stalin was dominated by the socialist realist production novel. Its most widely publicized work was, however, an autobiographical novel, *How the Steel Was Tempered*, serialized in 1932–34, by Nikolai Ostrovsky (1904–36). Ostrovsky, an activist in the Ukrainian Komsomol from the age of fifteen, was afflicted with an incurable illness that left him paralyzed and blind. Encouraged by Anna Karavaeva, editor of *The Young Guard*, he dictated the story of his life. It is told in the third person, and the hero is named Pavel Korchagin. It was published as a novel, printed in millions of copies, and translated into every major language of the world; for decades it was required reading for secondary-school students in the Soviet Union and throughout the communist world. *How the Steel was Tempered* is almost plotless, cliché-ridden, and awkwardly narrated. Its virtues are the author's boundless devotion to communism and utter lack of doubt about his values, as well as the sympathy that a story of unflinching courage in the face of cruel adversity evokes in readers.

Only in a few instances, such as in the case of Gladkov or Karavaeva, can a continuity between an author's earlier work and his or her socialist realist novels be observed. More often there was a sharp break between a writer's work under the NEP and his or her socialist realist creations. The satirists Valentin Kataev and Mikhail Zoshchenko are cases in point. Zoshchenko wrote "The Story of a Reforging" (1934), in which a criminal is transformed into a useful citizen while digging the White Sea–Baltic Canal, Stalin's most senseless and most murderous project. The classic production novel is Kataev's *Time Forward!* (1932), whose title is taken from Mayakovsky's "March of the Shock Brigades." *Time Forward!* describes a single shift on the construction site of the Magnitogorsk metallurgical plant in the Urals. The action is generated by the hourly progress of a brigade of cement casters, and suspense mounts concerning whether the brigade will break the world record in units cast, recently set by a team of American construction workers in Chicago. The record is broken, of course, and this in spite of every conceivable natural or human obstacle. An American engineer

makes a solid contribution toward it. He is dead of his own hand before the day is over as he gets news that his life's savings have been wiped out by a bank failure in America. *Time Forward!* vividly conveys the excitement of "socialist competition" between brigades of shock workers staged by Soviet authorities during Stalin's five-year plans. It does not conceal the fact that the shock workers work and live under appallingly primitive conditions, but the mood on the construction site is presented as one of determination, confidence, and good cheer. On balance, *Time Forward!* is as successful a compromise between half-truth and brazen propaganda as may be found in socialist realism.

Ilya Ehrenburg had started his career as a prose writer with anarchist satirical grotesques like *The Extraordinary Adventures of Julio Jurenito and His Disciples* (1922) and *Trust D. E.* (1923, where D. E. stands for "Destruction of Europe," plotted by an American tycoon) and had produced novels of sharp social criticism during the NEP period. Now he made his contribution to five-year-plan literature with such titles as *The Second Day* (1933; the title equates the second five-year plan with the second day of Creation) and *Without Pausing to Catch a Breath* (1937).

Marietta Shaginyan (1888–1982) had started out as a symbolist poet with a penchant for exotic themes (*Orientalia*, 1912). In the 1920s she wrote experimental fiction of diverse genres. In her successful series *Mess Mend* (1923–25), published under the name of "Jim Dollar, and American living in Russia," she replaced the bourgeois sleuth of the Western detective novel with brave and ingenious proletarians who thwart the evil machinations of capitalist tycoons and their henchmen. Her novel *Hydrocentral*

(1931), based on extended and conscientious on-site research, is one of the more honest production novels.

Leonid Leonov, regarded as a fellow-traveler writer of ornamentalist fiction in the 1920s, became the leading novelist, as well as one of the leading dramatists, of socialist realism. His first production novel, *Sot'* (1930), deals with the construction of a paper factory in the forests of the Russian north. The struggle against nature and against saboteurs provides the action. *Skutarevsky* (1932) is set at a research institute. Skutarevsky is a world-famous physicist, pro-Soviet in principle, but an individualist and a loner. The conflict of the novel is generated by a crisis in Skutarevsky's personal life, when his son, also a scientist, becomes involved with a gang of saboteurs and the project that was to crown his long career fails. In the end, the saboteurs are exposed and a chastened Skutarevsky is finally ready to do his work as a loyal member of a Soviet scientific collective. *Road to the Ocean* (1935) has an intricate structure, with several different stories and many characters centering on the operation of a railroad junction. It is a bit too gloomy to be good socialist realism. The main hero, an Old Bolshevik and party functionary, is terminally ill and spends the last months of his life dreaming of "the road to the ocean," his private code for a communist utopia.

The Russian Forest (1953) is set on the eve of World War II but reaches back to the years before the revolution, when the hero and the villain, both professors of forestry, were students. Vikhrov devotes all his energy to conservation; Gratsiansky advocates the reckless exploitation of Russia's forests. Gratsiansky is being blackmailed by foreign agents who know about a youthful indiscretion by which he betrayed a group of revolu-tionaries to the tsar's police. He secretly indulges in decadent pastimes and is in fact writing a treatise on suicide. In the end, Gratsiansky is unmasked and the cause of conservation triumphs, as it had to in accordance with the official position of the moment. In almost every other way, too, the novel scrupulously follows the canon of socialist realism. Vikhrov is of humble origins; Gratsiansky is the son of a professor of theology. The party properly plays a decisive positive role. The novel features long technical discussions about forestry and conservation. Nevertheless, Leonov's professed allegiance to Dostoevsky's poetics shows in his treatment of the villain, who is the pivotal figure of the novel. As a young intellectual before the revolution, Gratsiansky is vain, self-centered, and weak-willed, but also capable of genuine affection and idealism, artistically inclined, and possessing genuine intellectual curiosity: in a word, he is a type common in Western literature. Leonov then shows what life under the Soviet regime will do to this type. Gratsiansky, who might have developed into a positive character in a free society, withdraws into a shell, gradually sheds all positive qualities, develops a death wish, and eventually commits suicide. Although the originality of Leonov's conception in *The Russian Forest* must not be overestimated—the moral deterioration of a weak-willed and self-centered intellectual is one of the clichés of socialist realism—the character and story of Gratsiansky, in their meticulous detail, are for once an achievement worthy of a disciple of Dostoevsky.

Leonov presents a melancholy example of how the Soviet regime could cripple a writer of talent but little integrity of character. When the thaw came along and Leonov, by then a figure of authority with little to fear, had a chance to refashion his novels and plays, the changes he made for the edition of his collected works (1960–62) were generally in the direction of more, not less, socialist realism.

Konstantin Fedin's first two novels, *Cities and Years* (1924) and *The Brothers* (1928), had dealt with the alienated intellectual at odds with the revolution and Soviet mentality. In the 1930s, he tried to make his transition to socialist realism with *The Rape of Europe* (1934–35) and *Sanatorium "Arcturus"* (1936), but these efforts were neither artistically nor ideologically satisfying. After some worrisome years Fedin found his niche in Soviet literature, and toward the end of his life he held the post of first secretary of the Union of Soviet Writers. He established a reputation as a stalwart Soviet writer with a trilogy of novels, *Early Joys* (1946), *No Ordinary Summer* (1948), and *The Bonfire* (1961), in which he takes his hero from the eve of World War I to the "Great Patriotic War," letting three crucial moments of his life coincide with as many pivotal events of Russian history. In these novels Fedin skillfully uses enough palpable details of "little history" to create an aura of credibility for his blatantly falsified presentation of the grand scheme of things. Fedin was a sensitive and intelligent man; the process by which this talented writer betrayed his honest self and turned himself into a tool of Stalin's propaganda machine must have been a painful one.

Writers born around 1910 started their careers with production novels in the 1930s, and some of them would continue to produce them for the next three decades. Boris Polevoi (pseudonym of Boris Kampov, 1908–81), like some other writers of his generation an engineer by training, started his literary career as a journalist and re-

tained a documentary style even when he went on to write fiction. His fiction is vintage inspirational socialist realism, produced on the basis of on-site research at various industrial plants. *Hot Shop* (1939) celebrates the enthusiasm and ingenuity of factory workers who come up with wonderful ideas to increase productivity. This and similar works were essentially a projection of the Soviet government's wishful thinking. Polevoi continued to produce works of this kind after the war and even after Stalin's death.

Vasily Grossman (1905–64), a chemical engineer in the Donets Basin, published his first story from the life of coal miners in 1934. Another story caught the attention of Maksim Gorky, who encouraged Grossman to become a writer. Grossman's four-part novel *Stepan Kolchugin* (1937–40) follows the hero, a young worker, through years of struggle against the tsarist regime, the civil war, and the building of a socialist society in conventional socialist realist fashion. Grossman went on to become a major critic of Stalin's regime after the war.

Yury Krymov (1908–41), an engineer by profession, was killed in World War II. He began to write fiction in the early 1930s. His novel *Tanker "Derbent"* (1938) tells how a communist activist transforms a sullen and disorganized crew into a disciplined and efficient collective. *Tanker "Derbent"* was reprinted in millions of copies, translated into many languages, and made into a film.

Boris Gorbatov (1908–54) romanticized the Komsomol (*The Cell*, 1928), communist activism (*Our Town*, 1930), the Red Army (*Expedition in the Mountains*, 1930–31), Soviet workers (*Masters*, 1933), and the exploits of Soviet arctic expeditions (*Everyday Arctic*, 1937–40) in novels, stories, and sketches. He went on to even greater glory and several Stalin prizes during and after the war.

Not all successful socialist realist novels were of the production type. *Our Friends* (1936), the first novel of Yury German (1910–68), tells the story of a woman's progress through various mistakes (two bad marriages, crime) to a fulfilled life and a happy marriage to an officer of the GPU (the secret police), who is a model of rectitude and compassion. *Our Friends* was well received by the public because it presented ordinary people in familiar situations, and it was praised by the critics for properly advocating a strong work ethic and consciousness raising through indoctrination.

The reorientation from class struggle to patriotism, national unity, and pride in Russian achievements of the past, which started in the mid-1930s, encouraged the writing of historical fiction. Before and during World War II hundreds of historical novels appeared and the heroes of the romantic period—Peter the Great, Ivan the Terrible, Dimitry Donskoi, Alexander Nevsky, Minin and Pozharsky of the Time of Troubles—were brought back. Rebels against the tsars—Ivan Bolotnikov of the Time of Troubles, Stepan Razin under Tsar Alexis, Emelyan Pugachov under Catherine the Great, and the Decembrists—received special attention. Historical fiction also attracted writers because it was less prone to be immediately affected by a change in the party line than works dealing with contemporary reality. This tendency became so pronounced that Andrei Zhdanov, in a speech of 1946, warned Soviet writers against further withdrawal from the contemporary scene.

Even in historical fiction, though, a writer had to be on guard against a "false" interpretation of history. Stalin was known to identify with both Peter the Great and Ivan the Terrible, and hence a negative presentation of these cruel despots was inadvisable. Aleksei Tolstoi, the leading historical novelist of the Stalin era, radically changed the image of Peter the Great that he had created in an early story, "Peter's Day" (1918), when he went on to write his masterpiece, *Peter the First* (1929–45). Tolstoi's blatant idealization of the tsar's image perversely earned him the praise of Soviet historians for having restored Peter the Great to his rightful status as a great historical figure. *Peter the First* was made into a monumental film that drove the glorification of the tsar even further.

Nonetheless, *Peter the First* is a fine historical novel. Tolstoi creates, as did his namesake in *War and Peace*, a semblance of historical verity by introducing a multitude of credible invented characters, a wealth of anecdotal detail of "little history," and a modicum of stylized language. Whereas Lev Tolstoi had stayed mostly with characters of his own social class, Aleksei Tolstoi lets characters from all walks of life participate in the drama of a great age: a wretched convict driving piles into the swampy bank of the Neva River; the peasant Brovkin, who gets rich servicing the tsar's army; the impoverished nobleman Volkov, eager to make a career under the new order and happy to marry one of the Brovkin girls, who has turned into a fine lady. If the reader is willing to ignore the presence of Stalin casting its shadow over *Peter the First*, it is a lively, entertaining, and even inspiring novel. Readers who are familiar with the historical Peter or have read Merezhkovsky's *Peter and Alexis* will find it difficult to go along with Tolstoi's falsification of history.

Olga Forsh (1873–1961) was, along with

Yury Tynyanov, the most outstanding exponent of the fictionalized biography of Russian writers and poets, a genre represented by scores of Soviet novels. Forsh's trilogy *Jacobin Ferment* (1932), *A Landed Lady of Kazan* (1934), and *A Fateful Book* (1939) gives an account of the life of Aleksandr Radishchev and his age. *Firstborn of Freedom* (1950–53) is a chronicle of the Decembrists. Olga Forsh was also an intelligent chronicler of her own age. *Hot Shop* (1926) covers the revolution of 1905; *Crazy Ship* (1931) tells of the Petrograd House of the Arts, a refuge for artists and writers in the early 1920s, and *The Raven* (1933) recreates the literary ambience of the 1910s.

Yury Dombrovsky (1909–78), who spent years of his life in labor camps and exile, has gained posthumous recognition as a writer who inserted the moral issues of his own time, specifically the plight of a lone intellectual facing an oppressive power structure, into his historical fiction. His works deal with both the distant past, as in *Fall of the Empire* (1938) and *Derzhavin* (1939), and the recent past, as in *The Ape Returns for His Skull* (1959), set in Hitler's Germany.

Vyacheslav Shishkov (1873–1945), an engineer by profession, was employed in Siberia and started his literary career with sketches of Siberian life. He became a professional writer after the revolution. Shishkov's Siberian tales are a blend of stark naturalism, raw passion, and a "progressive" social tendency, all rather in the manner of Gorky, whose influence on Shishkov is noticeable. They tend to be more dramatic than Korolenko's Siberian tales, set in the same milieu and similar in ethos, but lack Korolenko's mellow humanity. The best known of these, "Vanka Khlyust" (1914), typical of the populist tale about the sufferings of the poor, is also a striking example of

the Russian folk theme of an underdog's cruel revenge justified by tearful self-pity. Vanka tells his own story. A wild and vile-tempered lad who hated his abusive father and the whole world, he lost both hands to frostbite and ensuing gangrene when a domineering priest made him drive him through a blizzard: poor Vanka wears a thin parka and leather gloves while the priest sits snug in a thick fur coat. Vanka's girl left her crippled lover, apparently for another man, but then drowned herself in an icehole. Vanka, too, tried to kill himself but failed, then continued life as a roving beggar. As he reaches the end of his story, Vanka, who has been drinking all the while, unexpectedly confesses that he set fire to the priest's house and that it was he who pushed his girl into the icehole. His interlocutor, a wise old man, wonders if this is true but, at any rate, sides with Vanka against all who wronged him. Late in his career Shishkov wrote two long panoramic historical novels, *Grim River* (1933), about the colonization of Siberia, and *Emelyan Pugachov* (1941–47), a broadly based story of the Pugachov rebellion. Both stand out among the many works of this genre.

Sergei Sergeev-Tsensky (1875–1958) published poetry and prose beginning in 1898. HIs twelve-volume epic cycle *The Transfiguration of Russia* (1914–58) is a fictionalized chronicle of Russian life as it approaches the revolution. Its unifying conception is that of the inevitability of the transformation of individual and social life that culminates in the establishment of the Soviet order. Sergeev-Tsensky's three-volume historical novel *The Ordeal of Sevastopol* (1937–39), about the siege of Sevastopol in 1854–55, became an instant classic.

Aleksei Novikov-Priboi (1877–1944) served in the tsar's navy. His ship was sunk in the battle of Tsushima and he was captured by the Japanese. After the revolution Novikov used his naval experience to write many sea tales. His novel *Tsushima* (1932–35), a fictionalized account of the naval battle, was widely acclaimed and was translated into many languages.

Aleksei Chapygin (1870–1937), of peasant background, followed in the footsteps of Gorky and Korolenko, writing stories about peasant life, especially about peasants displaced to the city. After the revolution he concentrated on historical fiction. His three-part novel *Razin Stepan* (1926–27) became the model for many later works about popular uprisings against the tsars.

Literature and World War II

World War II mobilized the entire literary community. Many writers became war correspondents; others wrote patriotic articles or suitably inspirational fiction. Most of these efforts, too obviously strained and made to order, were hardly appreciated by Soviet fighting men. Tvardovsky's unheroic *Vasily Tyorkin* was by far the most popular work of those years. The contributions of established writers like Sholokhov, Tolstoi, Vsevolod Ivanov, Karavaeva, Panfyorov, and Gorbatov were decidedly forgettable. Leonov's short novel *The Taking of Velikoshumsk* (1944) is more creditable. It skillfully orchestrates the description of the battle for the town of Velikoshumsk by presenting it from synchronized vantage points—that of the commander of the tank corps which takes the town, that of a tank crew which takes part in the final assault, and some civilians who witness the action.

Aleksandr Fadeev produced one of the better war novels, *The Young Guard* (1945), which tells the story of an under-

ground resistance group of young communists in the Ukrainian town of Krasnodon. The young communists are properly idealized, the Germans properly repulsive, and the action suspenseful. In 1946 Fadeev won a Stalin Prize for the novel, but soon afterward some reviewers charged that he had failed to credit the party properly for its leadership of the resistance movement. Thereupon Fadeev rewrote parts of the novel, and the definitive version of 1951 gives the party more than its due. Boris Polevoi's novel *The Story of a Real Man* (1946), a fictionalized documentary about a Soviet airman who lost both legs when shot down but retrained himself to fly a combat plane again, also won a Stalin Prize.

Vasily Grossman served as a war correspondent and published a series of sketches and stories, among them "Direction of the Main Strike" and "The People Are Immortal" (both 1942). His novel *In a Good Cause* (1952), an epic of the war, was well received initially, but then its second part was suppressed as ideologically flawed. It was allowed to appear only after Stalin's death, in 1954. Grossman had toned it down to a reasonable degree of ideological conformity, so it was hailed by some reviewers as a Soviet *War and Peace* and won him an important decoration. Its sequel, *Life and Fate*, completed in 1960, far closer to the spirit of *War and Peace*, was rejected by Soviet editors and appeared in the West only in 1980. A panoramic epic of the war centering on the battle of Stalingrad, it not only reports on the progress of the war from both the Russian and the German sides but also describes life and death both in a German concentration camp and in a Soviet gulag. Anti-Semitism in the Soviet Union is frankly discussed. Grossman paints a very negative picture of Stalin and of the condition of Soviet society under his rule. *Life and Fate* is an honest, perceptive, and well-informed book, though it is hardly the great novel it has been hailed to be by some Western critics. Grossman's last work, *Everything Flows*, begun in 1955 and completed shortly before the writer's death, is part novel, part meditation on Russian history. A bitter indictment of the Soviet system, it charges not only Stalin but also Lenin with the ills and evils of Soviet society.

Several writers launched their careers with novels or stories about World War II. Emmanuil Kazakevich (1913–62), an engineer by profession, was active in the Autonomous Jewish Region of Birobidzhan in the Far East until the war. His early writings were in Yiddish. He served with distinction in the war and made his wartime experiences the subject of a series of works in Russian. His stories, such as "The Star" (1947), "Two in the Steppe" (1948), "Heart of a Friend" (1953), and "In the Light of Day" (1961), deal with moral conflict under extreme stress. Kazakevich was criticized for excessive "naturalism' and "psychologism" but won a Stalin Prize with his novel *Spring on the Oder* (1949), in which he avoided those traits.

Grigory Baklanov (pseudonym of Grigory Fridman, b. 1923) also fought in the war. A 1951 graduate of the Gorky Literary Institute, he was one of the first Soviet authors to take an honest view of the war. His short novels, *South of the Main Strike* (1958), *An Inch of Ground* (1959), and *There Is No Shame for the Dead* (1961),[29] tell of heroism and self-sacrifice, but also of selfishness and faintheartedness. Yury Bondarev (b. 1924), also a war veteran and, like Baklanov, a 1951 graduate of the Gorky Literary Institute, similarly dealt with moral issues

brought on by critical situations under fire. His short novels *The Battalions Ask for Fire* (1957) and *The Last Volleys* (1959) give incisive descriptions of a combatant's emotional states under fire. Bondarev would later become one of the writers to deal with the legacy of Stalin's purges.

Konstantin Simonov (1915–79), another graduate of the Gorky Literary Institute (1938), worked as a war correspondent and both during the war and after was the most successful writer to present the official view in a form that was palatable to the average reader. A prolific lyric poet, dramatist, and novelist, Simonov also played a key role in the politics of Soviet literary life and was at different times editor of several leading journals. He won a slew of Stalin and Lenin prizes and was made a deputy of the Supreme Soviet. Simonov's novel *Days and Nights* (1943–44), the first of many Soviet works to deal with the battle of Stalingrad, is facile and conventional as fiction but gives a vivid and fairly accurate account of the battle. Simonov's gifts were limited to those of a competent journalist.

Viktor Nekrasov (b. 1911), who fought at Stalingrad, launched his career with the novel *In the Trenches of Stalingrad* (1946), which won him a Stalin Prize in 1947. His novel makes the point that the battle was won by unheroic men in an unheroic manner, as it describes the battle from the viewpoint of the enlisted men and junior officers who did the actual fighting. Nekrasov's narrative is journalistic and matter-of-fact, his dialogue realistic. *In the Trenches of Stalingrad* is not a great novel, but it has the qualities of an honest and competent documentary. After Stalin's death, Nekrasov became one of the leading dissident writers. His novella "Kira Georgievna" (1961) was one of the first works to deal with the prob-

29. The title is a proverb.

lems of a person returning home after years in a prison camp. Nekrasov was forced to emigrate in 1974.

Vera Panova (1905–73) established herself as a major writer with her war novel *Fellow Travelers* (1946, published in English as *The Train*), set in a hospital train. It won her a Stalin Prize in 1947. It differs from the routine Soviet war novel in that it is concerned not with battle heroics but with the private lives and personal problems of the soldiers on the train. The mood of the novel, however, is properly upbeat and no questions about the grand scheme of things are raised. The private life of ordinary Soviet citizens seen from the inside of their minds remained Panova's subject in works that followed, such as *The Factory Town* (1947) and *Span of the Year* (1953). She perceives people's problems honestly but lets them look for solutions entirely within the existing scheme of things. Panova is at her best in stories in which the world is seen through the eyes of a child. The effect of estrangement in such stories as "Seryozha" (1955), however, does not go beyond a mild critique of adult foibles.

A critical view on a grand scale of the Soviet war effort became possible only in the third thaw period. Aleksandr Solzhenitsyn's story "An Incident at Krechetovka Station" (1963) was the first work in which the incompetence of the Red Army command, resulting in chaos in the supply lines of the rear, and the prevailing atmosphere of suspicion and denunciation created in the army by Stalin's purges were pointed out unequivocally. The war stories of Vasily Bykov (b. 1924), who writes in Belorussian and Russian, deal with these matter's as well as with the utter disregard for truth that obtained in the society molded by Stalin's reign, all of which caused the Red Army to suffer crushing defeats and terrible losses early in the war. Bykov began to publish his stories in the 1950s. "The Cry of the Cranes" (1956) was the first to attract critical attention. Only in the 1960s, however, could he publish stories that went beyond individual episodes and attacked the deeper issues of the Soviet war effort and military ethics: "The Dead Feel No Pain" (1966), "Cursed Height" (1968), and "Kruglyansky Bridge" (1969).

The Thaw

The thaw after Stalin's death was almost as clear a divide as the first five-year plan. Many of the writers of the Stalin era were still active, but their work did not matter much anymore, except in those instances where a writer would radically change tune, admitting implicitly that he or she had been dissimulating during all those years. Fedin, Leonov, Libedinsky, Sholokhov, Polevoi, Simonov, and others continued as ranking members of the literary establishment, but times had clearly passed them by. Some other established writers, like Ehrenburg, Kaverin, and Panfyorov, figured more or less prominently in the movement to reinstall an honest critical realism in Russian literature. A new generation, however, of writers carried most of the burden of this task.

The Thaw (1954), a short novel by Ilya Ehrenburg that helped label the new period, was first to break the ice. It is a conventional production novel, except for the fact that things at the factory town where it is set are not rosy and apparently will take a long time to get better. Workers' living conditions are terrible, and management's excuse that their fathers had it even worse is no longer acceptable. The message is that something will have to give, although it is not said what.

Fyodor Panfyorov's last novel, *Mother Volga* (1960), came as a surprise to those readers who knew his Stalin prize–winning *Bruski*. The collective farmers of *Mother Volga* are far from prosperous. In fact, they often go hungry and the outlook for the future is bleak. Panfyorov's novel introduced a string of works in which life on a collective farm is presented as harsh and joyless. Venyamin Kaverin's novel *An Open Book* (1956) and his stories "A Piece of Glass" (1960) and "Seven Pairs of Dirty Ones" (1962),[30] each in a different way, deal with the terrible incongruity between an individual's humanity and the condition of Soviet society under Stalin.

A newcomer, Vladimir Dudintsev (b. 1918), produced a milestone of the thaw with his novel *Not by Bread Alone* (1956). It, too, is a production novel; but the villain is the system itself, and high-ranking bureaucrats and middle-echelon apparatchiks are equally guilty of the persecution of a talented inventor whom they see as a troublemaker. Their self-serving complacency is presented as deeply ingrained in Soviet institutions. In earlier socialist realist novels, villains, failings, and abuses had been shown as something alien to Soviet society—in fact, often as something undermining it from the outside. Dudintsev was violently attacked by orthodox critics, but Nikita Khrushchev eventually took his side when he embarked on his program of de-Stalinization.

Solzhenitsyn and Country Prose

The thaw under Khrushchev reached its apogee in a short novel by Aleksandr Solzhenitsyn (b. 1918), *One Day in the Life of Ivan Denisovich*, published in *Novy mir* in

30. An allusion to Mayakovsky's *Mystery-Bouffe*. See p. 599.

1962 with Khrushchev's personal approval. Solzhenitsyn, an artillery captain, had served with distinction from the beginning of the war until his arrest in February 1945 when a letter from him containing disparaging remarks about Stalin was intercepted by censors. He served eight years in various prison camps and spent three more years in exile. Allowed to return to European Russia in 1956, he worked as a mathematics teacher. He had begun to write after his release from prison and in 1961 submitted *One Day in the Life of Ivan Denisovich* to *Novy mir*.

Ivan Denisovich, a peasant, is serving a ten-year sentence in a prison camp for having surrendered to the enemy in the war, though he had escaped his captors almost immediately and had rejoined his unit. A cold winter day at a prison camp is described in terse documentary style, largely through the eyes of Ivan Denisovich. The worst of the truth about the prison camps is omitted (no violence is reported), but even the normal routine is brutal. It is life on the edge of survival, as half-starved prisoners work under inhuman conditions in the arctic winter. Most of them are, like Ivan Denisovich, innocent of any real crime. Nevertheless, the message of the novel is upbeat. Ivan Denisovich is a survivor, not because he will steal from or inform on his fellow prisoners, but because he has retained his self-respect and human dignity. He does not consider prison his home. He does an honest day's work on his work detail, because that is the only way he knows how to work. He will not demean himself for a mouthful of food or a puff on a cigarette. The message is that Stalin's regime did a terrible wrong to millions of good Russian people like Ivan Denisovich. *One Day in the Life of Ivan Denisovich* remained for a long time the only work printed in the Soviet Union to deal with this legacy of Stalin's regime. Solzhenitsyn would go on to become the most important Russian writer of his generation, winning the Nobel Prize in 1970. He was also expelled from the Union of Soviet Writers in 1969 and from his country in 1974.

The age of Stalin was dominated by the long novel. The thaw period saw a changeover to the short story and the sketch. Many of the leading young writers now chose rural settings, often of the remote north, instead of the industrial or mining sites of the production novels. In the Russian countryside they discovered not only backwardness and misery but also vestiges of the old peasant culture, its moral values, and its religion. Nature, in particular the unspoiled nature of the north, which had been a niche occupied by a few writers such as Mikhail Prishvin even during the Stalin years, now became a favorite subject. The thaw also brought along a shift toward an interest in the single individual independently of his social function. Solzhenitsyn's short story "Matryona's House" (1963) is typical of this trend. It draws a picture of the depressing bleakness, poverty, and moral degradation of life in a Russian village. Against this background there emerges the figure of Matryona, an elderly peasant woman in whom the author recognizes, in the concluding line of the story, "the righteous one without whom, according to the proverb, no village can stand, nor any city, nor our whole land," alluding to the Lord's words to Abraham in Genesis 18:24–33.

Other writers to deal with the Russian countryside in a similar spirit were Sergei Antonov, Vladimir Soloukhin, Vladimir Tendryakov, Aleksandr Yashin, Vasily Belov, Vasily Shukshin, Sergei Zalygin, Yury Nagibin, Yury Kazakov, and Valentin Rasputin.

Sergei Antonov (b. 1915), who began to publish in 1947 and won a state prize in 1951, devoted most of his stories to life on the collective farm. With the thaw his stories began to give an honest picture of the economic and spiritual poverty of the Russian countryside. Antonov's stories are distinguished by careful craftsmanship reminiscent of Chekhov. His several theoretical essays, such as *Letters about the Short Story* (1964), are intelligent and knowledgeable.

Vladimir Soloukhin (b. 1924), a poet as well as prose writer, became an early exponent of a neo-Slavophile trend in Russian cultural life. Starting with *Country Roads of Vladimir* (1953), a journal of a hiking trip through his native region of Vladimir, east of Moscow, Soloukhin in numerous articles, sketches, and stories conducted a campaign to preserve Russia's native culture, churches, religious art, and pre-Petrine literature. In the process Soloukhin would at times cast nostalgic glances at the past integrity of the Russian people's worldview and deplore its passing.

Aleksandr Yashin (pseudonym of Aleksandr Popov, 1913–68) came from the Vologda Region in the northeast. In the 1930s and 1940s he wrote mostly poetry celebrating the happy life of the peasantry of his native north under the new order and was rewarded by a Stalin Prize. In 1956 Yashin published a story, "Levers," in which the whole system of collective farming, run by "levers" of the party, is exposed as a giant fraud, whose victims are the peasants of Vologda.

Vladimir Tendryakov (1923–84), also from Vologda, graduated from the Gorky Literary Institute in 1951 and became editor of the journal *Literaturnaya Moskva* in 1958. Tendryakov's stories of the 1950s are set in the forests, villages, and small towns of the remote north and deal with human choices between good and evil by juxtaposing a traditional sense of right and wrong to that of the new communist morality. In "Potholes" (1956), for example, the choice is between a human life and a tractor. Tendryakov's consistent interest in education is reflected in several of his stories. "Beyond the Present Day" (1959), for example, raises grave doubts about Soviet education. Tendryakov was a careful craftsman much in the tradition of Chekhov. The tendency of his stories emerges from the flow of the narrative without any undue strain.

Vasily Belov (b. 1932), also from Vologda, began to publish in 1956 and soon became one of the leading exponents of country prose. Belov's stories, such as "That's How Things Are" (1966), set in his native Vologda, probe deeply into the effects of collectivization, urbanization, and the destruction of old ways, including religion, on simple Russian people. Their message is that the Russian peasant may still harbor values which though incompatible with the official ideology are worth preserving. Belov uses a good deal of local color, dialect, and folklore, but his art is modern and sophisticated.

Vasily Shukshin (1929–74), who came from Siberia, was a successful filmmaker who doubled as a short-story writer. His first story, "Two on a Cart," appeared in 1958, his first volume of short stories, *Country Folk*, in 1963. Shukshin's stories and films often deal with country folk who have been left outside the mainstream of Soviet society, uprooted, alienated, and aimless, drifting toward crime and alcoholism.

The stories of all these writers had a decided social and moral tendency. In the stories of Yury Kazakov and Yury Nagibin, also often set in the country, impressionist nuances of human emotions are dominant. Their art is a return to the impressionistic lyric manner of Bunin. Yury Kazakov (1927–83) studied and later taught music at the Moscow Conservatory. He also graduated from the Gorky Literary Institute in 1957. He began to publish in 1952 and was soon recognized as a leader of the "quiet school" of writers and poets, who turned from socialist realism to nature, the lone human individual, and art. A native Muscovite, Kazakov placed many of his stories in the rural north. Nostalgic vacation trips to the Russian north, where vestiges of peasant culture were still extant, became popular among Moscow and Leningrad intellectuals of his generation. Kazakov's heroes are often lonely, alienated individuals, social misfits in search of truth, beauty, and a meaningful life. Some of them are rewarded by an epiphany: an unhappy painter in "Adam and Eve" (1962), for example, finds inspiration in the severe beauty of a northern island.

Yury Nagibin (b. 1920) began his career with undistinguished war stories and conflictless stories about life on a collective farm. With the thaw he developed into one of the best writers of the quiet school. His Meshchora (a region east of Moscow) cycle of stories (1963) revived the tradition of Turgenev's *Hunter's Sketches* in describing the unspectacular charm of a Russian landscape, observing the latent tension between rural and urban Russia, and sympathizing with the plight of the Russian village. Nagibin, like Kazakov, introduces a variety of people, most of them quite ordinary, at a moment when they experience an epiphany of some sort and understand themselves and the world in a new way.

Outside the Mainstream

It was characteristic of Soviet literature under Stalin, and even after, that some of its serious writers gravitated toward themes or genres not immediately exposed to the vicissitudes of ideological change: the more distant historical past, nature, childhood, and the world of outright fantasy. Readers, too, were inclined to favor works that gave some relief from the constant bombardment by ideological indoctrination in socialist realism. Mikhail Prishvin and Konstantin Paustovsky were popular with a remarkably large readership for works that were far from meeting the demands of socialist realism yet were hardly likely to attract a broad audience.

Mikhail Prishvin (1873–1954), the son of a wealthy merchant from Russia's north, held a degree in agronomy but spent much of his life traveling throughout Russia, Central Asia, and the Far East, pursuing his interest in languages, ethnography, and folklore. He was also an eager and expert hunter, angler, and bird-watcher. Prishvin's first book of sketches and stories about the nature of the Russian north, *In the Land of Unfrightened Birds and Animals* (1907), was well received. It was followed by many more similar works, such as *Calendar of Nature* (1935) and *The Sun's Storehouse* (1945). The posthumous *Tsar's Road* (1957) tells of the dragging overland of Peter the Great's fleet from the White Sea to the Baltic. Prishvin's observations about the terrible cost in human lives on this venture clearly allude to Stalin's Baltic-White Sea Canal, dug by forced labor. For the last thirty years of his life Prishvin worked on an autobiographical novel, *The Chain of Kashchei* (from Kashchei, or Koshchei the Deathless, a mythical figure of Russian folklore—hence "The Chain of Life"), which he published serially. Prishvin's prose style and choice of subject matter recall Sergei Aksakov. There is little action in his works, but his descriptions are precise and aptly phrased. Somehow they seem to be in step with the slow rhythm of the seasons and the circular movement of time in nature. Prishvin's philosophy is a pantheist *reverentia vitae*, a

serene acceptance of the goodness and plenitude of life, but also of its pain and loss. Prishvin maintained his personal and artistic integrity throughout the Stalin era, never departing from the style he had earlier made his own.

Konstantin Paustovsky (1892–1968) was born in Moscow and studied at Kiev and Moscow universities. He published his first story in 1912 but became well known only in the 1930s. After Stalin's death he served as model and mentor of a new generation of writers, including Kazakov and Nagibin. His work resembles Prishvin's, but has a broader range. Like Prishvin, he traveled widely and recorded his impressions in his stories and sketches. Paustovsky's first book of short stories was *Sea Sketches* (1925). An outdoorsman like Prishvin, he wrote a cycle of stories and sketches about recreational fishing, *Summer Days* (1937). And like Prishvin, he devoted much of his life to a leisurely told autobiography, *Story of a Life* (1945–63). *The Golden Rose* (1955), a book of meditations about the creative process, the nature of art, literary craftsmanship, and the writer's position in society, was a low-key but effective challenge to the content-oriented aesthetics of socialist realism and an invitation to a more form-conscious art. Paustovsky's historical and exotic fiction of the 1920s and early 1930s and his few attempts at socially oriented fiction were less convincing. He was at his best in descriptive prose, where he would find the astonishing in the ordinary and give it a nuanced lyric expression.

Literature for children attracted more first-rate writers and poets than in the West. Antonov, Aseev, Valentin Kataev, Kaverin, Mayakovsky, Prishvin, Olesha, Tikhonov, and Zoshchenko all wrote works for children. The ultramodernist prose and poetry of the oberiuty, in particular, found its way into print only through Detgiz, the publishing house for children's literature. Daniil Kharms (pseudonym of Daniil Yuvachev, 1905–42), who wrote the most radically surrealist and fractured prose among the oberiuty, made his living by writing for children throughout the 1930s, until his arrest in 1941. His short prose pieces of the 1920s follow a surrealist antilogic. Characters change drastically without apparent reason, anything can happen at any moment, and what happens is likely to be outrageous or trivial: animals and inanimate objects may talk, and the style and even the grammar of the text are fractured. In the 1930s Kharms moved toward a simpler and more realistic description of happenings, where events from everyday life are reported—pointlessly, it seems, but with a sense of metaphysical unrest lurking in the background. Kharms was rediscovered only in the 1960s, and a collection of his works appeared in the West between 1978 and 1980.

Lev Kassil (1905–70), who started his career as a writer with *New Lef*, had scientific training and in the 1930s covered recent developments in the sciences for the government newspaper *Izvestiya*. Simultaneously, he developed a lifelong association with the children's magazine *The Pioneer* (the Pioneers are the Soviet Union's Boy Scouts) and eventually concentrated on writing for children, moving from stories depicting the coming of the Soviet order through the eyes of a child to tales explicitly addressed to children. His stories skillfully mix fantasy with reality and deliver their moral message with gentle humor. Yet some of Kassil's fairy tales for children may be and were read as bold satires aimed directly at Stalin. In one of these tales the formerly happy kingdom of Sinegoriya (Blue Moun-

tain) comes under the rule of stupid and wicked King Fanfaron (Windbag), master of all the winds. Fanfaron's winds blow into every nook and corner of Sinegoriya and report to him his subjects' every word. Sinegoriya had prided itself on its gardeners, mirror makers, and tinsmiths. Fanfaron orders the gardeners to grow nothing but dandelions (Russian *oduvanchik* "dandelion," literally means "blow away") and prohibits the making of mirrors so that people cannot see their misery and Fanfaron his own ugly face. Tinsmiths are ordered to make nothing but weather vanes so that everybody can always tell what way the wind is blowing. People who disobey Fanfaron are thrown into a fan, where they are thoroughly "ventilated." Such stories made it into print only because editors and censors were reluctant to acknowledge that they could see the satirical subtext.

The fantastic, in the form of utopian and science fiction, had enjoyed a long association with socialist thought in Russia and elsewhere. Aleksandr Bogdanov, the father of Proletarian Culture, wrote two utopian novels, and utopian, dystopian, and apocalyptic themes were common in the literature of the 1920s. H. G. Wells was one of the most popular writers of the period in Russia. Aleksei Tolstoi, Mayakovsky, Olesha, Valentin Kataev, and Ehrenburg were major writers who wrote utopian fiction or drama. Zamyatin's *We* and Mikhail Bulgakov's "Fatal Eggs" (1924) and "Heart of a Dog" (written in 1925, published posthumously in the West) are examples of dystopian fiction of the 1920s. Also in the 1920s, several journals devoted entirely to science fiction were founded, establishing science fiction as a permanent fixture in Soviet literature. A majority of the science fiction novels and stories that appeared before the 1950s were adventure stories with some pseudo-science built into the plot and were of little social or literary value. Only with the onset of the thaw did the science fiction novel become a vehicle of utopian and dystopian speculation and of ethical or political thought. The immensely successful novel *Andromeda Nebula* (1956), by Ivan Efremov (b. 1907), set in the distant future of intergalactic travel, pioneered the use of science fiction along these lines. The Strugatsky brothers, Arkady (b. 1925) and Boris (b. 1933), became the main exponents of science fiction as an instrument of political and moral satire.

Bulgakov

Mikhail Afanasyevich Bulgakov (1891–1940) was born in Kiev, where his father was a professor at the Kiev Theological Academy. He got his medical degree from Kiev University in 1916 but practiced medicine only briefly. He went to Moscow in 1921 to work as a journalist nd lived there until the end of his life. His first literary works are feuilletons and sketches, many of them autobiographical, such as "Extraordinary Adventures of a Doctor" (1922) and "Notes of a Young Country Doctor" (1926–27). His first novel, *White Guard* (1924), was also largely based on personal experience. In 1925 Bulgakov began his eleven-year association with the Moscow Art Theater. *The Days of the Turbins*, a stage version of *White Guard*, premiered on October 5, 1926 and quickly became a mainstay of the Russian theater. For the rest of his life Bulgakov was known mostly as a playwright. Several more plays by him were successfully staged, and some others were stopped by censorship. Bulgakov emerged as a major novelist only in 1966–67, when

his novel *The Master and Margarita* was published in the Soviet Union (in abridged excerpts) and in the West (in a more complete version).

The action of *The Master and Margarita*, in a throwback to the romantic novel à la Hoffmann, develops on three distinct levels: the banal reality of Moscow in the 1930s; Jerusalem at the time of Christ's crucifixion, introduced as excerpts from a novel by the master; and a metaphysical cosmic region to which the novel's protagonists escape in the end. *The Master and Margarita* thus combines the two main aspects of a utopian novel: satire of contemporary life and a vision of an ideal place reachable through faith and imagination. In good Hoffmannesque fashion, the seemingly predictable reality of a materialistic society is rocked by violent intrusions of diabolic forces at the same time as a vision of a higher mode of existence emerges. The three regions of existence are marked by different narrative styles. The satirical exposé of contemporary Moscow's crude materialism and the dishonesty, hypocrisy, and cowardice of its intellectuals are presented with blunt black humor. The tragedy of Yeshua and Pontius Pilate is recorded in a tone of subdued solemnity, and the metaphysical flight of fancy toward the end is a tour de force of exhilarated excitement. *The Master and Margarita* is yet another masterpiece that came at an unexpected time from an unexpected source. It greatly transcends the rest of Bulgakov's admirable oeuvre.

After the revolution, and especially after the end of the NEP, Russian readers experienced a dearth of literature of pure entertainment and unrestrained fantasy. The flow of romances, exotic and adventure stories, detective novels, and other forms only marginally related to contemporary reality, as well as the mass of pulp literature, soon was reduced to a trickle. The continued demand for such literature was satisfied largely by a few translations from the English, French, and German. Some of the major writers of the period, such as Viktor Shklovsky, Vsevolod Ivanov, Valentin Kataev, Venyamin Kaverin, and Marietta Shaginyan, produced a few pieces in which they tried to combine the adventure story with loyalty to Soviet ideology, all in all a negligible part of their literary work.

One Soviet writer managed to devote all his energies to the creation of a fantasy world. Aleksandr Grin (pseudonym of Aleksandr Grinevsky, 1880–1932) was the son of a Polish revolutionary exiled to the north of Russia and was himself an active Socialist Revolutionary before 1917. As a writer, he was outside the mainstream from the beginning. In his novels and stories he created an enchanting world of swashbuckling adventure in sun-drenched southern seaports. *Crimson Sails* (1923), *Radiant World* (1923), *The Golden Chain* (1925), *Gliding along the Waves* (1928), and *The Road to Nowhere* (1930) form a cycle of sorts, united by a common exotic landscape, emotional atmosphere, and names of cities and characters. Grin's lively plots cannot be assigned to any concrete period, country, or nationality. The ethos of his fiction is one of a dream of exuberant activity and joie de vivre tempered by an undercurrent of pensive melancholy. Grin's works met with hostile criticism, but unlike most of his conformist contemporaries he retained a faithful readership after his death.

Soviet Drama

Russian theater saw a great deal of experimental activity in the years immediately after the revolution. Vsevolod Meyerhold wholeheartedly embraced the communist cause and promoted the idea of a revolutionary theater with his usual energy. In his Moscow workshop he developed "biomechanics," a training system that would prepare the actor to give direct physical expression, by movement and gesture, to the action of a play. In agreement with the antimimetic aesthetics of Left Art, which demanded not representation of reality but effective communication of ideas, Meyerhold developed a style marked by overstatement, grotesque, and "circusization." His 1922 staging of Sukhovo-Kobylin's black comedy *Tarelkin's Death* at the experimental Gitis Theater brilliantly brought out the play's potential by presenting it in the style of a circus bouffonade with clown routines and acrobatics. Meyerhold also applied his expressionist manner of overstatement, distortion, and extreme stylization to such classics as Gogol's *Inspector General* and Griboedov's *Woe from Wit*. He collaborated enthusiastically with avant-garde playwrights Mayakovsky, Tretyakov, Erdman, and Olesha, staging their plays in a spirit of uproarious farce or reckless grotesque. After 1923, when even the liberal commissar of education, Lunacharsky, declared that it was time to go back to Ostrovsky, Meyerhold and avant-garde theater met with increasing hostility on the part of the communist establishment. Meyerhold lost his theater in 1938, was arrested in 1939, and died in prison.

The Moscow Art Theater, still under Stanislavsky and Nemirovich-Danchenko, continued to cultivate its realist style, with some slight concessions to a "progressive" interpretation of the classics, including Chekhov. The first Soviet plays added to its repertoire were Bulgakov's *Days of the Turbins*, in 1926, and Vsevolod Ivanov's *Armored Train 14-69*, in 1927. In the 1930s a number of Soviet propaganda plays by Nikolai Pogodin and others were staged by the Moscow Art Theater. Nevertheless, the theater maintained its style and its high artistic standards.

Aleksandr Tairov's Chamber Theater also continued in the style established before the revolution, using music, creative costumes, and constructivist sets. In the 1920s Tairov relied largely on a foreign repertoire, which included Eugene O'Neill, but in the 1930s he followed the example of the Moscow Art Theater and staged some Soviet propaganda plays, like Vishnevsky's *Optimistic Tragedy* in 1933. On the whole, Russian theater under Stalin remained technically on a high level and was, when the thaw set in, ready to resume experimentation. In the 1950s and 1960s several directors in Leningrad and Moscow, such as Nikolai Okhlopkov (1900–1967), Nikolai Akimov (1901–1968), Georgy Tovstonogov (b. 1915), and Yury Lyubimov (b. 1917) developed their distinctive styles.

Soviet film was innovative until the early 1930s. Directors like Lev Kuleshov, Sergei Eisenstein, Dziga Vertov, and Vsevolod Pudovkin were closely allied with Lef and the avant-garde theater of Meyerhold. Avant-garde writers, such as Mayakovsky, Aseev, Olesha, Tretyakov, and Erdman, wrote film scenarios and used cinematic devices in their fiction or stage plays. In the 1930s Soviet film fell in line with the demands of socialist realism and then with the wave of Russian patriotism in the late 1930s and 1940s. The thaw had a liberating effect on Soviet film no less than on literature and the theater.

Even in the 1920s Soviet drama lagged behind the other genres of literature, and Soviet theaters had to stage mostly prerevolutionary or foreign plays. Gorky's prerevolutionary plays were staged often, even though they had lost their topical edge. This was true even of Gorky's later plays, such as *Egor Bulychov and Others* (1931), whose hero, a strong-willed and capable merchant, has come to despise his own class and has lost his faith in God, as he lies dying and the revolution begins. Staging dramatized versions of well-known novels also was a standard practice that has continued to the present. One of the greatest hits of the Soviet stage was Evgeny Zamyatin's *The Flea* (1925), a dramatization of Nikolai Leskov's story "Lefty." The few interesting plays came from Lef and fellow travellers close to it.

Mayakovsky

Mystery-Bouffe (1918), staged by Meyerhold to celebrate the first anniversary of the October revolution, was an early experiment, jointly undertaken by Mayakovsky and Meyerhold, in the "circusization" of the theater. In fact, a new version was staged at the Moscow Circus in 1921. A travesty of a morality play, it combined the spirit of Aristophanean political comedy with the rhythms of the barker, the ditty, and the jibing and jeering of the carnival parade. The prologue to the 1921 version has this argument of the play:

> Everybody is on the run before the flood of the revolution. Seven clean couples and seven dirty couples, that is, fourteen pauper-proletarians and fourteen bourgeois gentlefolk, and among them with his pair of tear-stained cheeks a little Menshevik. The North Pole is all awash. The last refuge is about to go under. So all start building an ark, a very big ark, in fact. In Act Two folks are en route in their ark: here you have your monarchy and your democratic republic. At last, overboard, the menshevik's wails notwithstanding,

the clean ones are flung head first. In Act Three it is shown that workers don't have to be afraid of anything, not even the devils in hell. In Act four—laugh louder!—the halls of paradise are shown. In Act Five economic ruin, opening its huge mouth, destroys and devours things. Though we had to work on an empty belly, we still defeated economic ruin. In Act Six you have the commune, so everybody sing along at the top of your voice! Look out, then!

Symbolist theater had provided Mayakovsky with the foil for his travesty of biblical themes (the Flood, the new Jerusalem, heaven and hell). Cubo-futurism provided the precedent for animated things, word and sound fetishism, and indiscriminate mixing of semantic levels. The list of dramatis personae has allegorical figures (a "man of the future"); social types, such as an Indian rajah or a Russian black market operator among the "clean ones," and smith, machinist, and laundress among the "dirty ones"; political caricatures (Clemenceau, Lloyd George, and others); "saints" (Methusalah, Jean-Jacques Rousseau, Tolstoi); devils; angels; and assorted "things." *Mystery-Bouffe* is good folk theater and surely more entertaining than most of the plays whose manner it parodies. It is, however, hopelessly dated.

Mayakovsky's late plays, *The Bedbug* (1928–29) and *The Bathhouse* (1930), were written for Meyerhold's theater, and based on the notion that theater should not present simulations of real life but make statements about it. These plays were well suited to the nimble "puppets" of Meyerhold's "biomechanics." They would fall flat in a conventional psychological staging.

The Bedbug: A Fantastic Comedy in Nine Pictures has two acts. The first is a Soviet version of *Le Bourgeois gentilhomme*. Ivan

Prisypkin, a proletarian purged from the party but with a genuine union card, has changed his name to Pierre Skripkin ("Fiddle"), jilted his proletarian girlfriend, Zoya, and is about to marry Elzevira Renaissance, who works as a manicurist in her parents' privately owned hairdressing salon. He is rapidly turning into a Soviet bourgeois. At the wedding party, somebody starts a brawl, a blazing gasoline stove is overturned. The Renaissance Salon goes up in flames, and firemen cannot save a single member of the wedding party. It is winter, and the site of the fire soon resembles a skating rink. Act Two is set fifty years later, in 1979. Prisypkin's body has been discovered frozen in a block of ice. He is resurrected, along with a bedbug on his shirt collar. The world of 1979 is that of a communist utopia: sanitized, orderly, and passionless. Bedbugs are a long-extinct species. Prisypkin soon infects the people of 1979 with the ills of 1929. Some beer, which has been brewed for him to ease his transition into the new world, sends scores of people to the hospital with acute poisoning. His guitar strumming and mawkish romances cause hundreds of young citizens to develop a pathological condition called love, and many of them go through horrible contortions while locked in a tight embrace: Prisypkin has taught them the foxtrot. The local administration is forced to take drastic measures to isolate Prisypkin. After a pathetic speech to the assembled citizenry—and to the audience in the theater—he is remanded to the local zoo as a specimen of *Philistinus vulgaris*, "a terrible humanoid simulator and most amazing parasite."

The Bedbug is a deeply ambiguous play. The utopia of 1979 seems boring and inane, but so too is the reality of Soviet life under the NEP, and the world of 1979 is at least free of bedbugs and NEP profiteers. But then 1979

relapses into 1929 with ridiculous ease, and Prisypkin, an obnoxious and worthless character in 1929, becomes human in 1979. *The Bedbug* features many funny gags, racy dialogue, and entertaining characters, such as Prisypkin's mentor, the "poet" and landlord Oleg Bayan ("Bard"), who at Prisypkin's wedding makes a speech celebrating the union "by the bonds of Hymen, of Labor, obscure yet grandiose, and of Capital, dethroned yet ever so charming" and otherwise lampoons everything the revolution had fought for.

The Bedbug, undoubtedly a great play, met with only moderate success. *The Bathhouse*, on the other hand, failed badly. It is more satirical allegory than play (the title is allegorical, too: it suggests that Soviet society needs a bath badly). What there is of a plot is provided by a time machine that transports people into the age of communism—the year 2030, to be exact—and back. The invention explodes, literally, into a world of smug do-nothing bureaucrats, careerists, and toadies, a world that is hardly ready for communism. The only party genuinely interested in the time machine is Mr. Pont Kitsch, a foreign capitalist. In the end, the train of time that departs for the communist future throws off all undesirables, as one of them wails, "I've been run over by time!" *The Bathhouse*, which features a rousing "March of Time," is characteristic of Mayakovsky's consuming preoccupation with time and his pursuit of an ever-receding future. He was the most enthusiastic and eloquent advocate of "the five-year plan in four years," Soviet man's triumph over nature and over time.

The Bathhouse was a spectacle rather than a play. Mayakovsky's last play, *Moscow on Fire (1905): A Mass Spectacle with Songs and Words*, commissioned for a celebration of the twenty-fifth anniversary of the revolution of 1905, was strictly a spectacle. It was staged at the Moscow Circus a week after Mayakovsky's death, with a cast of five hundred, including teams of clowns and barkers, exploding bombs, fireworks, and various gimmicks, such as a giant worker (on stilts) dwarfing capitalists and the tsar's police. A huge film screen was used to make the spectacle more graphic. The spectacle addressed itself to the present as much as to the past, promoting the collectivization of Soviet agriculture as well as attacking kulaks and denouncing their foreign supporters, such as Ramsay MacDonald and the pope. The whole show catered to the lowest possible taste. Mayakovsky's active participation in rehearsals for the spectacle shows that he was genuinely interested in this venture.

Other Dramatists

Mayakovsky's friend Sergei Tretyakov (1892–1939), the last editor of *New Lef*, was a strong proponent of constructivist poster art. Tretyakov, who held a law degree from Moscow University, was initially close to the ego-futurists but after the revolution collaborated with David Burlyuk, Nikolai Aseev, and Nikolai Chuzhak in a futurist group, Creation (Tvorchestvo), in the Far East. In 1924 Tretyakov went to China, where he taught Russian literature. As a dramatist, he was associated with the Moscow Proletkult theater and with Meyerhold. His plays *Are You Listening, Moscow?* (1923) and *Gas Masks* (1924) combine the manner of German expressionism with that of the agitational skit (*agitka*). Tretyakov's most successful play, *Roar, China!* (1926), which reflects his impressions of China crudely but effectively, was designed to build a mood of anti-imperialist sentiment and revolutionary upheaval. Tretyakov's next play, *I Want a Child* (1927), went into rehearsal at Meyerhold's theater but never got permission to open. After the demise of *New Lef* Tretyakov traveled in the West and translated several foreign plays, including some by Bertolt Brecht. Tretyakov perished in the purges of the 1930s.

Nikolai Erdman (1902–70), another friend and associate of Mayakovsky's, is known mainly for his two satirical comedies, *The Mandate* and *The Suicide*. *The Mandate*, a riotous lampoon of the new Soviet bureaucracy, staged by Meyerhold in 1925, was a huge success. *The Suicide*, an equally hilarious black comedy, went into rehearsal at the Moscow Art Theater and Meyerhold's theater in 1932 but was not allowed to open. It was too transparent a lampoon of the incongruity between the blithely celebratory rhetoric of Stalin's propaganda machine and human misery everywhere. A refrain of "life is wonderful" accompanies the gyrations of the would-be suicide and the sly machinations of those who are to gain from his demise. Subsequently Erdman was reduced to doing minor film work. *The Mandate* returned to the Soviet stage only in 1956.

Mikhail Bulgakov's somewhat tamer comedies, *Zoika's Apartment* (staged in 1926), about the housing shortage and sex for hire, and *Crimson Island* (staged in 1928), about the absurdities of thought control, were banned in 1929. Bulgakov's *a Cabal of Hypocrites* (or *Molière*), written in 1930, had a brief run in 1936 but was taken off the boards after a negative review in *Pravda*. It too obviously reflected Bulgakov's own troubles with the chicaneries of censorship. Meanwhile, Valentin Kataev's *Squaring the Circle* (1928), a comedy in a lighter vein about marital problems under conditions of Moscow's catastrophic housing shortage, enjoyed long runs all over the Soviet Union

and was staged with some success even abroad.

Lev Lunts (1901–24), author of the manifesto of the Serapion Brothers, "Why We Are Serapion Brothers" (1922), emigrated to Germany in 1923, where he died suddenly of an embolism. His play *Outside the Law* (1920) was scheduled for production in Petrograd in 1923 but was not allowed to be staged because of its ambivalent presentation of communism. *Outside the Law* and Lunts's other plays, *Bertran de Born* (1922), *The Apes Are Coming* (1923), and *The City of Truth* (1924), are marked by a fine sense of the theater as an outlet for the irrational strain in a structured and familiar world, obtained through time-honored but cleverly used techniques, such as play within a play and simultaneous action on three different stages.

The *oberiut* Daniil Kharms gave Russian literature a genuinely surrealist and absurdist play, *Elizaveta Bam*, written in December 1927 and performed at the Leningrad House of the Press in 1928. An experiment in nonrepresentational theater, it had no chance to be admitted to the regular stage and remained forgotten until the rediscovery of OBERIU in the 1960s.

The revolution and civil war did not find quite the echo in Russian drama that they found in poetry and prose fiction. By far the most successful play about the revolution was Bulgakov's *The Days of the Turbins* (1926), which presented it from the viewpoint of intellectuals caught up in the turmoil of the civil war and undecided about which side to take. Another play by Bulgakov, *Flight* (1927), went into rehearsal but was never staged in his lifetime. Its subject was those Russian intellectuals who chose emigration, their condition rendered unreal by the use of light effects that make their experiences appear as dreams.

Other featured plays about the revolution and civil war were *Storm* (1924), by Vladimir Bill-Belotserkovsky (1884–1970), *Lyubov Yarovaya* (1925), by Konstantin Trenyov (1876–1945), *Breakup* (1927), by Boris Lavrenyov (1891–1959), *Armored Train No. 14–69*, by Vsevolod Ivanov, *City of Winds* (1929), by Vladimir Kirshon (1902–38), and two plays by Vsevolod Vishnevsky (1900–1951), *First Cavalry* (1929) and *Optimistic Tragedy* (1933). All these plays are loosely constructed, resembling Bertolt Brecht's "epic theater." The action is episodic, and characters are stereotypical; rousing mass scenes play a great role, as do striking sound and light effects. The most celebrated of these palys, Vishnevsky's *Optimistic Tragedy*, also features a narrator and a chorus who explain the action to the audience. The heroine of the play is a political commissar whose inspiring leadership turns a ragged band of sailors into disciplined soldiers of the revolution who lay down their lives for the cause. Vishnevsky's *First Cavalry* was meant to be a rebuttal of Babel's *Red Cavalry*: Vishnevsky depicts Budyonny's Cossacks as model communists.

In drama the fundamental contradiction inherent in socialist realism was even more obvious than in prose fiction, because a realistic staging of a story that the audience knew to be a dishonest fabrication could only enhance the impression of false pretenses. Nevertheless, socialist realism produced a number of competently contrived plays. Nikolai Pogodin (pseudonym of Nikolai Stukalov, 1900–1962), the leading dramatist of the Stalin era, came up with such plays as *Tempo* (1929), about the construction of the Stalingrad tractor plant, and *Aristocrats* (1935), about the digging of the Baltic-White Sea Canal, where a band of convicts, identified in the playbill as "bandits,

thieves, prostitutes, fanatics, kulaks, etc.," is converted into a disciplined work force under the leadership of dedicated guards, identified as *chekisty*, officers of the political police. Among Pogodin's other plays, his trilogy on Lenin and the revolution, *A Man with a Rifle* (1937), *Kremlin Chimes* (1941), and *The Third Pathétique* (1959), earned him generous official praise and state prizes. Pogodin had a sense for the theater and was certainly one of the more dexterous sycophants of Stalin's regime.

Vladimir Kirshon, who perished in the purges of the 1930s, worked on the front of industrialization (*The Rails are Humming*, 1927; *A Miraculous Alloy*, 1934) as well as forced collectivization (*Bread*, 1930). A member of RAPP, he favored greater psychological realism than could be found in the "monumental drama" of Vishnevsky's and Pogodin's revolutionary romanticism.

Aleksandr Afinogenov (1904–41) was active with the Moscow Proletkult Theater from 1926 to 1929 and, like other writers associated with the Proletkult, had his troubles with the party, which he had joined in 1922. He was expelled in 1937 but, unlike many others, was allowed to continue writing. He died in an air raid on Moscow. Afinogenov wrote twenty-six plays, the most successful of which, *Dalyokoe* (Distant Point, a place name), staged in 1936, is the record of twenty-four hours at a small Siberian railway depot and extols the dedication of Soviet railwaymen. Afinogenov's first production play was *The Oddball* (1929), about the five-year plan in a paper factory. Perhaps his best and certainly his most interesting play is *Fear* (1931), set at an institute for psychological research. Some clever saboteurs, who have wormed thier way onto the staff of the institute, develop a theory according to which fear is the basic drive controlling human behavior. They are unmasked, of course, but the atmosphere of the play rather supports their theory. Afinogenov's last play, *On the Eve* (1941), finished shortly before his death, is one of the better Soviet war plays.

Leonid Leonov wrote more than ten plays, several of which were dramatic versions of his novels (*The Badgers*, 1927; *Skutarevsky*, 1934). Leonov's plays, like his novels, are attempts at integrating psychologically plausible human conflicts with the standard topics of socialist realism (internal enemies of the Soviet state, as in *The Wolf*, 1938; corrupt bureaucrats, as in *Blizzard*, 1939). As in Leonov's novels, his negative characters are sometimes interesting and the motives for their actions complex; as a result, he had frequent problems with censorship. He had to rewrite his best-known play, *The Orchards of Polovchansk* (1936–38), several times before it could be staged. Like his novels, Leonov's plays feature a great deal of Chekhovian and Ibsenian symbolic detail, another trait that elicited criticism from orthodox defenders of socialist realism.

Aleksei Arbuzov (1908–86), like Afinogenov, started his career as an actor, director, and playwright with a theater of the Proletkult (in Leningrad), for which he wrote his first agitational skits while still in his teens. He scored his first success with *Tanya* (1939), the story of a woman's growth from callow student to mature physician. Long intervals of time between successive episodes are a common trait in Soviet plays, and Arbuzov's in particular. Arbuzov's many plays, though ideologically conformist, are sometimes theatrically innovative. A man of the theater, Arbuzov was not afraid of melodramatic effects, psychological surprises, or atypical situations. His best-known play, *An Irkutsk Story* (1959), follows the story of a conventional love triangle against the grandiose background of the construction of a giant power plant. The action is commented upon by a chorus and features unusual visual and sound effects. In the 1960s and 1970s Arbuzov would move on to a "neotheatrical" style influenced by Evreinov and Tairov.

Historical drama continued throughout the Soviet period. After sporadic efforts in the 1910s and 1920s—such as Nikolai Gumilyov's *The Poisoned Tunic* (1918), on a theme from Byzantine history, or Evgeny Zamyatin's *The Fires of Saint Dominic* (1923), set in Inquisition Spain, and *Attila* (1928)—the revival of Russian patriotism in the 1930s and 1940s caused major figures like Aleksei Tolstoi and Ilya Selvinsky to turn to historical drama. Some lesser lights also produced a slew of plays about Russian military exploits, literary figures, and rebels against the tsars. The most successful among them was Vladimir Solovyov (b. 1907), with such plays as *Field Marshal Kutuzov* (1939), *The Great Sovereign* (1943–55), and *Denis Davydov* (1953–55). The principal merit of all these plays is that they give their audience a properly slanted awareness of national history. Tolstoi's historical trilogy *Ivan the Terrible* (1941–43) is an embarrassment considering his indubitable talent.

Literature for children as an escape route for fantasy and as a vehicle of satire found an amazing parallel in the theater of Evgeny Shvarts (1896–1958). Shvarts was associated with Detgiz, Nikolai Akimov's Leningrad Theater of Comedy, and the Leningrad Children's Theater. He was also on the staff of two magazines for children. He began his career with works that were unequivocally aimed at young readers. His first play, *Underwood* (1929), was about a young girl who foils the theft of a student's typewriter (the brand name Underwood was then as good as a generic term). He went on to produce three plays based on familiar fairy tales which could be easily understood as caustic satires aimed at Stalin, at cowed Soviet society, and at the absurd ideology to which it was paying lip service. *The Naked King* (1934) and *The Shadow* (1940) were based on tales by Hans Christian Andersen, *The Dragon* (1943–44) on the legend of Lancelot and the dragon. *The Naked King* was staged only in 1960, but the other two plays were actually performed in Stalin's lifetime, although they were taken off the boards after a short run: censors would not dare to recognize the satire for what it was until the reaction of adults in the audience forced their hand. Allusions to Soviet reality in these plays are massive and hardly equivocal. The dragon, who has the power to appear in human shape, has some of Stalin's mannerisms—his fondness for enthusiastic statistics, for example—and the good burghers in the plays behave exactly like Soviet citizens under Stalin. Even without their satirical subtext Shvarts's plays are immensely entertaining, and their wry humor stands up independently of their political meaning. They were staged with great success before adult audiences after Stalin's death.

Soviet playwrights contributed their share to the Soviet war effort. Most Soviet war plays, like Afinogenov's *On the Eve* (1941), Leonov's *Invasion* (1942) and *Lyonushka* (1943), and Simonov's *Russian People* (1942), are contrived to demonstrate the self-effacing heroism of simple Russian people, making them melodramatic and predictable. A more interesting play was *The Front* (1942), by Aleksandr Korneichuk (b. 1905), a Ukrainian playwright whose works were regularly staged in Russian as well as Ukrainian. *The Front* is a tragic grotesque with a real conflict, namely that between the old and new generations of Red Army commanders. Its message was that the aging heroes of the civil war were no match for the job at hand and had to be replaced by new leaders—as in fact happened.

The postwar years were as bleak for Soviet drama as they were for Soviet literature at large. The plays of that period were essentially cautious exercises in translating the party line of the moment into a semblance of drama. The tireless Simonov led these efforts with such plays as *The Russian Question* (1947) and *An Alien Shadow* (1949). In the first he shows how all honest opinions about the Soviet Union are brutally suppressed in America. In the second, a Soviet scientist who believes that his discovery belongs to all humanity and should be communicated to his Western colleagues comes to realize that he was wrong, because the enemy will use this information not to save but to destroy lives.

The thaw released the same tendencies in the Soviet theater as in prose fiction: a more honest and unheroic picture of Soviet reality, so long as the playwright chose to stay within a socialist realist framework, but also a return to plots based on private life, such as stories about growing up and socialization, love, marital problems, and conflicts between generations. There was also a decided tendency toward a return to Chekhov's theater of mood and atmosphere. Among the leading dramatists of the thaw period were Aleksei Arbuzov, Viktor Rozov (b. 1913), and Leonid Zorin (b. 1924). The thaw also saw a revival of plays that had long been banned. Mayakovsky's *Bedbug* and Erdman's *Mandate*, for example, saw triumphant revivals. The most significant development of the thaw was, however, a return to an experimental theater and a new theatricalization of the theater.

Epilogue

Most of the authors mentioned here are still active, and it is too early to assess the importance of their work. Therefore, only general trends are discussed, and no assessment of the aesthetic value of an author's work is made.

The reaction that set in after Khrushchev's fall failed to stop the libertarian tendencies that had begun to sprout in Russian intellectual life. With repression less brutal than under Stalin, and with a new generation of intellectuals who had not experienced Stalin's terror, a running battle between the establishment and a dissident movement (a term coined in the West) went on throughout the Brezhnev years. Although apparatchiks remained in control of most journals and censorship remained rigid until the advent, under Gorbachev, of *glasnost'* (from *glasnyi*, an adjective describing something open to public scrutiny), more and more of the writers who mattered drifted toward either latent opposition through pointed use of Aesopian language and selection of subject matter[1] or open defiance through publication in *samizdat* (from *sam*, "self," and *izdatel'stvo*, "publishing house," formed after *gosizdat*, "state publishing house") or *tamizdat* (*tam*, "over there," that is, in the West), and toward eventual exile.

The dissident movement was by no means homogeneous. It pursued different goals according to different orientations, from a Trotskyite left or "socialism with a human face" to a neo-Slavophile or Orthodox Christian right. Professional writers played a major role in the dissident movement. As had happened before in Russia, some dissidents who might have otherwise chosen a different forum became writers. The dissident movement addressed itself to human rights,[2] independent social and political thought, religious rebirth,[3] revelations

1. For example, the books of Arkady Belinkov (1921–70) on Yury Tynyanov and Yury Olesha, ostensibly literary biographies, were in fact political statements, as readers used to reading between the lines could easily gather. Belinkov defected to the West in 1968.
2. Particularly through the bulletin *Chronicle of Current Events* (1968–).
3. As in the samizdat periodical *Veche* (1971–74), edited by Vladimir Osipov. Its title is derived

607

about Stalin's crimes—in particular the truth about the labor camps—and protest against current abuses. It also encompassed experimental prose and poetry, as well as modernist art, reviving modernist works of the 1910s and 1920s and embarking upon experiments of its own.

Literary scholarship began to recover from the torpor of the Stalin era. An approach to literature that was independent of the rigid political determinism and chauvinism of those years emerged under the label of a "scientific," "quantified," or "structural" approach to the literary text. Statistically based studies of versification were resumed by M. L. Gasparov, A. N. Kolmogorov, and others in a manner more sophisticated mathematically than the studies done by the formalists in the 1920s. Yu. M. Lotman, D. M. Segal, V. N. Toporov, and others applied the principles of information theory to the analysis of poetic texts. A structural school, with centers in Tartu and Moscow, headed by Lotman, Toporov, B. A. Uspensky, V. V. Ivanov, and others, developed an approach to literature that sought to combine the phenomenological tradition of the formalists with a Hegelian-Marxist conception of society as an integrated organic structure in constant dialectical flux.

Samizdat literature, disseminated in typescript (private possession of duplicating machines was illegal), had existed sporadically even under Stalin. It became a movement in the late 1960s. Some individuals now worked for samizdat full-time and created whole samizdat libraries. Government reaction was unpredictable—sometimes harsh, at times indifferent. In searches, il-

legal religious material, would sometimes be ignored as harmless, while legitimate Soviet publications might be seized. *Magnitizdat* (from *magnitofon*, "tape recorder") disseminated the songs of dissident poets and balladeers, such as Vladimir Vysotsky (1937–80), Aleksandr Galich (pseudonym of Aleksandr Ginzburg, 1919–77), and Bulat Okudzhava (b. 1924).

Tamizdat, which began with Pasternak's *Doctor Zhivago* and the Daniel-Sinyavsky case, took off in a big way in the late 1960s. Russian journals active in the West, such as *Facets* in Frankfurt, *The New Review* in New York, and *The Herald of the Russian Christian Movement* in Paris, routinely published smuggled works by Soviet authors. In many instances a writer would publish both legally in the Soviet Union and in tamizdat. Important works by deceased Soviet writers— Platonov, Bulgakov, Grossman—also appeared in the West, as did works by writers still living in the Soviet Union whose publication had been stopped for some reason.

Beginning in the late 1960s, a growing number of Russian writers found themselves in the West; some left the Soviet Union voluntarily, and others were expelled. Among the more prominent were Anatoly Kuznetsov (1929–79), in 1969; Iosif Brodsky (b. 1940), in 1972, Andrei Sinyavsky (b. 1925), in 1973; Vladimir Maksimov (b. 1932) and Viktor Nekrasov (b. 1911), in 1974; Nataliya Gorbanevskaya (b. 1936), in 1975; Anatoly Gladilin (b. 1935), in 1976; Aleksandr Zinovyev (b. 1922), in 1978; and Vasily Aksyonov (b. 1932) and Vladimir Voinovich (b. 1932), in 1980. Only the expulsion of Aleksandr Solzhenitsyn in 1974 made headlines. The emigres of this so-called third wave developed an energetic literary life, with centers in New York, Paris, and Israel, and founded a number of periodicals, such as *Continent* (1974) and

from the medieval popular assembly, or *veche*, in Novgorod and Pskov.

Syntaxis (1978). Once again, as in the 1920s, a significant part of Russian literature was being published in exile. The American publishing house Ardis, in Ann Arbor, Michigan, published many texts by dissident and exiled writers. In 1979, for instance, Ardis published the symposium *Metropolis* (a collection of miscellaneous short works, mostly fiction, by twenty-three authors, several of whom subsequently left the Soviet Union) after its publication had been blocked by the Union of Soviet Writers in 1978.

Samizdat and tamizdat accounted for much of the best in Russian literature of the Brezhnev era. Many works dealt with the legacy of Stalin's terror. Solzhenitsyn's novels *Cancer Ward* and *The First Circle* and his "experiment in literary investigation," *The Gulag Archipelago*, Varlam Shalamov's *Kolyma Tales*, Lidiya Chukovskaya's *Going Under* and *The Deserted House*, Evgeniya Ginzburg's *Journey into the Whirlwind* and *Within the Whirlwind*, and Nadezhda Mandelshtam's *Hope against Hope* and *Hope Abandoned* were all widely known and acclaimed in the West but accessible to only a small audience of samizdat readers in the Soviet Union. Likewise, the works of Akhmatova, Mandelshtam, Bulgakov, Tsvetaeva, Zabolotsky, and others were available in excellent editions in the West and had been translated into many languages before finally reaching the general reader in the Soviet Union.

The Brezhnev years saw a gradual movement away from socialist realism even in officially sanctioned literature. The country prose of Valentin Rasputin, Vasily Belov, Fyodor Abramov (1923–80), Sergei Zalygin (b. 1913), and others unequivocally presented the condition of the Russian countryside as bleak, without any of the reassuring silver lining seen in conformist socialist realist works. Rasputin's *Farewell to Matyora*

(1976) presents the damming of a Siberian river not as a glorious achievement, as it would have been in socialist realism, but as a calamity that has befallen the people, who are being relocated because their homes will be flooded. Some of the leaders of country prose were also spokespeople for conservation, preservation of architectural landmarks, and the maintenance of a demographic and economic balance between urban and rural Russia. Rasputin and Zalygin played a major role in blocking the project of diverting the course of Siberian rivers.

Urban prose by Yury Trifonov (1925–81), Irina Grekova (b. 1907), and Andrei Bitov (b. 1937), among others, ignored the concerns and master plot of socialist realism and went back to a Chekhovian concern with the venial sin, the petty failings, betrayals, and cruelties of ordinary people in day-to-day living. Like Chekhov, these writers cannot but observe that people "live badly." A short novel by Venedikt Erofeev (b. 1938), *Moscow-Petushki* (published in the West in 1977), takes this direction to the limit, not merely presenting an alcoholic's view of the world, but also developing an alcoholic worldview.

The best satirical works could only appear in samizdat. *The Life and Adventures of Private Ivan Chonkin* (published in the West between 1975 and 1979), by Vladimir Voinovich, is a sardonic deflation of what was perhaps more sacred to the established order than even building socialism: the glory of the Red Army. *Yawning Heights* (1976), by Aleksandr Zinovyev, is a caustic dystopia of the Soviet order. *Faithful Ruslan* (first published in *Facets*, 1975), by Georgy Vladimov (b. 1931), illustrates the mentality that produced and tolerated the labor camps presenting it through the consciousness of a guard dog.

Various attempts at experimental prose

were also largely confined to samizdat and tamizdat. Vasily Aksyonov, who wrote rather innocuous satirical prose while still in the Soviet Union, moved on to fantastic, grotesque, and absurdist writing after his emigration in 1980. Sasha Sokolov (b. 1943) emigrated in 1975, and in 1976 his first novel, *School for Fools*, appeared in the West. It views the world through the consciousness of a retarded boy. Eduard Limonov (b. 1943) and Yuz Aleshkovsky (b. 1929), both of whom emigrated and published their works abroad, broke the long-standing taboo against explicit sex and obscene language.

The best and most original poetry was also confined to samizdat—such as in *Syntaxis*, edited by Aleksandr Ginzburg, and *Phoenix*, edited by Yury Galanskov—or appeared abroad. A group of Leningrad poets who gathered around Anna Akhmatova included Iosif Brodsky (b. 1940) and Dmitry Bobyshev (b. 1936), both of whom eventually found themselves in the United States, where Brodsky developed into the finest Russian poet of his generation, winning the Nobel Prize in 1987.

The Gorbachev era brought with it a revolution in literature. Many authors whose names had disappeared from the Soviet version of the history of Russian literature were again discussed and new editions of their works were scheduled for publication. This included even such sworn enemies of the Soviet regime as Dmitry Merezhkovsky and Vladislav Khodasevich. Foreign authors, like Joyce and Kafka, who had long remained untranslated, were made available in Russian. Works that had languished in desk drawers for decades or had appeared only abroad could now be published in the Soviet Union: Pasternak's *Doctor Zhivago*, Solzhenitsyn's *The Gulag Archipelago*, Anatoly Rybakov's *Children of the Arbat*, and others. Foreign travel was greatly facilitated, and Soviet writers and literary scholars who traveled to the West were now unafraid to voice their opinions in public. Faculty and student exchanges became fairly common. Russian society, culture, and literature were beginning to return to a relation with the West that had prevailed before the revolution. It is possible that in the future, émigré writers will become Russian writers who choose to live abroad, whether temporarily or permanently. Some émigré writers, such as Sokolov, Limonov, and Sinyavsky, have said that living and writing abroad means freedom from having to be politically relevant, in a literature which has been and still is compulsively seeking political relevance.

Select English Language Bibliography

Bibliographic and Encyclopedic Works

Bédé, Jean-Albert, and William B. Edgerton, eds. *Columbia Dictionary of Modern European Literatures*. 2d ed. New York: Columbia University Press, 1980.

Gibian, George. *Soviet Russian Literature in English: A Checklist Bibliography: A Selective Bibliography of Soviet Russian Literary Works in English and of Articles and Books in English about Soviet Russian Literature*. Ithaca, N.Y.: Cornell University Press, 1967.

Lewanski, Richard C., comp. *The Literatures of the World in English Translation*. Vol. 2, *The Slavic Literatures*. New York: New York Public Library, 1967.

MLA International Bibliography of Books and Articles on the Modern Languages and Literatures. New York: Modern Language Association of America, 1921–.

Moody, Fred, ed. *Ten Bibliographies of Twentieth-Century Russian Literature*. Ann Arbor, Mich.: Ardis, 1977.

Proffer, Carl R., comp. *Nineteenth-Century Russian Literature in English: A Bibliography of Criticism and Translations*. Ann Arbor, Mich.: Ardis, 1989.

Terras, Victor, ed. *Handbook of Russian Literature*. New Haven, Conn.: Yale University Press, 1985.

Terry, Garth M. *A Subject and Name Index to Articles on the Slavonic and East European Languages and Literatures, Music and Theater, Libraries and the Press, Contained in English-Language Journals, 1920–1975*. Nottingham: University Library, University of Nottingham, 1976.

Weber, Harry B., et al., eds. *The Modern Encyclopedia of Russian and Soviet Literature*. Gulf Breeze, Fla.: Academic International Press, 1977–.

Zenkovsky, Serge A., and David L. Armbruster. *A Guide to the Bibliographies of Russian Literature*. Nashville, Tenn.: Vanderbilt University Press, 1970.

Anthologies

Alexander, Alex E. *Russian Folklore: An Anthology in English Translation*. Belmont, Mass.: Nordland Publishers, 1975.

Bowra, C. M., ed. *A Book of Russian Verse*. Translated into English by various hands. London: Macmillan, 1943.

Brown, Clarence, ed. *The Portable Twentieth-Century Russian Reader*. New York: Penguin Books, 1985.

Glad, John, and Daniel Weissbort, eds. *Russian Poetry: The Modern Period*. Iowa City, Iowa: University of Iowa Press, 1978.

Guerney, Bernard Guilbert. *The Portable Russian Reader: A Collection Newly Translated from*

Classical and Present-Day Authors. New York: Viking Portable Library, 1947.

Karlinsky, Simon, and Alfred Appel, Jr., eds. *Russian Literature and Culture in the West: 1922–1972*. 2 vols. *TriQuarterly* 27–28 (Spring-Fall 1973).

Lawton, Anna, ed. *Russian Futurism through Its Manifestoes, 1912–1928*. Translated by Anna Lawton and Herbert Eagle. Introduction by Anna Lawton. Afterword by Herbert Eagle. Ithaca, N.Y.: Cornell University Press, 1988.

Luker, Nicholas, ed. *From Furmanov to Sholokhov: An Anthology of the Classics of Socialist Realism*. Ann Arbor, Mich.: Ardis, 1988.

Luker, Nicholas, ed. and trans. *An Anthology of Russian Neo-Realism: The "Znanie" School of Maxim Gorky*. Ann Arbor, Mich.: Ardis, 1982.

MacAndrew, A. R. *Nineteenth-Century Russian Drama*. Prefaces by Marc Slonim. New York: Bantam Books, 1963.

———. *Twentieth-Century Russian Drama*. New York: Bantam Books, 1963.

Meerson-Aksenov, Michael, and Boris Shragin. *The Political, Social and Religious Thought of Russian "Samizdat": An Anthology*. Belmont, Mass.: Nordland Publishers, 1977.

Noyes, George Rapall, ed. and trans. *Masterpieces of Russian Drama*. 2 vols. New York: Dover Publications, 1960–61.

Pachmuss, Temira, ed. and trans. *Women Writers in Russian Modernism*. Urbana, Ill.: University of Illinois Press, 1978.

Proffer, Carl R., et al., eds. *Russian Literature of the Twenties: An Anthology*. Ann Arbor, Mich.: Ardis, 1987.

Proffer, Carl R., and Ellendea Proffer, eds. *The Ardis Anthology of Recent Russian Literature*. Ann Arbor, Mich.: Ardis, 1975.

———. *The Ardis Anthology of Russian Futurism*. Ann Arbor, Mich.: Ardis, 1980.

Reeder, Roberta, ed. and trans. *Down along the Mother Volga: An Anthology of Russian Folk Lyrics*. With an introductory essay by V. Ja. Propp. Philadelphia: University of Pennsylvania Press, 1975.

Russian Fairy Tales. Translated by Norbert Guterman, from the collection of Aleksandr Afanas'ev. Folkloristic commentary by Roman Jakobson. New York: Pantheon Books, 1975.

The Russian Symbolist Theater: An Anthology of Plays and Critical Texts. Translated by Michael Green. Ann Arbor, Mich.: Ardis, 1986.

Rydel, Christine, ed. *The Ardis Anthology of Russian Romanticism*. Ann Arbor, Mich.: Ardis, 1984.

Segel, Harold B., ed. and trans. *The Literature of Eighteenth-Century Russia: An Anthology of Russian Literary Materials of the Age of Classicism and the Enlightenment*. 2 vols. New York: Dutton, 1967.

Yarmolinsky, Avrahm, ed. *Russians, Then and Now: A Selection of Russian Writing from the Seventeenth Century to Our Own Day*. New York: Macmillan, 1963.

Zenkovsky, Serge A., ed. and trans. *Medieval Russia's Epics, Chronicles, and Tales*. Rev. and enl. ed. New York: Dutton, 1974.

Histories of Russian Literature

Auty, Robert, and Dimitrii Obolensky, eds. *An Introduction to Russian Language and Literature*. Companion to Russian Studies, vol. 2. New York and Cambridge: Cambridge University Press, 1977.

Mirsky, D. P. *A History of Russian Literature from Its Beginnings to 1900*. Edited by Francis J. Whitfield. New York: Vintage Books, 1958.

Moser, Charles A., ed. *The Cambridge History of Russian Literature*. New York and Cambridge: Cambridge University Press, 1989.

Folklore

Sokolov, Yu. M. *Russian Folklore*. Translated by C. Ruth Smith. Introduction and bibliography by Felix J. Oinas. Hatboro, Pa.: Folklore Associates, 1966.

Pre-Petrine Literature

Brown, W. E. *A History of Seventeenth-Century Russian Literature*. Ann Arbor, Mich.: Ardis, 1980.

Fedotov, George P., ed. and comp. *A Treasury of Russian Spirituality*. Belmont, Mass.: Nordland Publishers, 1975.

Fennell, John. *Early Russian Literature*. Berkeley and Los Angeles: University of California Press, 1974.

Tschižewskij, Dmitrij. *History of Russian Literature from the Eleventh Century to the End of the Baroque*. The Hague: Mouton, 1971.

The Eighteenth Century

Brown, W. E. *A History of Eighteenth-Century Russian Literature.* Ann Arbor, Mich.: Ardis, 1980.

Cross, Anthony G., ed. *Russian Literature in the Age of Catherine the Great: A Collection of Essays.* Oxford: Meews, 1976.

Drage, C. L. *Russian Literature in the Eighteenth Century: The Solemn Ode, the Epic, Other Poetic Genres, the Story, the Novel, Drama: An Introduction for University Courses.* London: Published by the author, 1978.

The Nineteenth Century

Brown, W. E. *A History of Russian Literature of the Romantic Period.* 4 vols. Ann Arbor, Mich.: Ardis, 1986.

Čiževskij, Dmitrij. *History of Nineteenth-Century Russian Literature.* Vol. 1, *The Romantic Period.* Vol. 2, *The Realistic Period.* Edited by Serge A. Zenkovsky. Translated by Richard Noel Parker. Nashville, Tenn.: Vanderbilt University Press, 1974.

Hingley, Ronald. *Russian Writers and Society in the Nineteenth Century.* 2d rev. ed. London: Weidenfeld & Nicolson, 1977.

Todd, William Mills, III. *Fiction and Society in the age of Pushkin: Ideology, Institution, and Narrative.* Cambridge, Mass.: Harvard University Press, 1986.

Todd, William Mills, III, ed. *Literature and Society in Imperial Russia, 1800–1914.* Stanford, Calif.: Stanford University Press, 1978.

The Twentieth Century

Brown, Deming B. *Soviet Literature since Stalin.* New York and Cambridge: Cambridge University Press, 1978.

Brown, Edward J. *Russian Literature since the Revolution.* Cambridge, Mass.: Harvard University Press, 1982.

Hingley, Ronald. *Russian Writers and Soviet Society.* New York: Random House, 1979.

James, C. V. *Soviet Socialist Realism.* New York: St. Martin's Press, 1973.

Lowe, David. *Russian Writing since 1953.: A Critical Survey.* New York: Ungar, 1987.

Markov, Vladimir. *Russian Futurism: A History.* Berkeley and Los Angeles: University of California Press, 1968.

———. *Russian Imagism, 1919–1924.* 2 vols. Bausteine zur Geschichte der Literatur bei den Slaven, 15. Giessen: Wilhelm Schmitz, 1980.

Mirsky, D. P. *Contemporary Russian Literature, 1881–1925.* New York: Knopf, 1926.

Struve, Gleb. *Russian Literature under Lenin and Stalin, 1917–1953.* Norman, Okla.: University of Oklahoma Press, 1971.

Williams, Robert C. *Artists in Revolution: Portraits of the Russian Avant-Garde, 1905–1925.* Bloomington, Ind.: Indiana University Press, 1977.

Poetry

France, Peter. *Poets of Modern Russia.* Cambridge Studies in Russian Literature. New York and Cambridge: Cambridge University Press, 1983.

Poggioli, Renato. *The Poets of Russia, 1890–1930.* Cambridge, Mass.: Harvard University Press, 1960.

Fiction

Clark, Katerina. *The Soviet Novel: History as Ritual.* Chicago: University of Chicago Press, 1981.

Freeborn, Richard Harry. *The Rise of the Russian Novel: Studies in the Russian Novel from "Eugene Onegin" to "War and Peace."* New York and Cambridge: Cambridge University Press, 1973.

Gifford, Henry. *The Novel in Russia: From Pushkin to Pasternak.* London: Hutchinson, 1964.

Hosking, Geoffrey A. *Beyond Socialist Realism: Soviet Fiction since Ivan Denisovich.* New York: Holmes and Meier, 1979.

Mersereau, John, Jr. *Russian Romantic Fiction.* Ann Arbor, Mich.: Ardis, 1983.

Moser, Charles A., ed. *The Russian Short Story: A Critical History.* Boston: Twayne Publishers, 1986.

O'Toole, L. Michael. *Structure, Style and Interpretation in the Russian Short Story.* New Haven, Conn.: Yale University Press, 1982.

Drama

Karlinsky, Simon. *Russian Drama from Its Beginnings to the Age of Pushkin.* Berkeley and Los Angeles: University of California Press, 1985.

Segel, Harold B. *Twentieth-Century Russian Drama: From Gorky to the Present.* New York: Columbia University Press, 1979.

Varneke, Boris V. *History of the Russian Theater, Seventeenth through Nineteenth Century.* Revised and edited by Belle Martin. Translated by Boris Brasol. New York: Macmillan, 1951.

Criticism and Cultural History

Baran, Henryk, ed. *Semiotics and Structuralism: Readings from the Soviet Union.* White Plains, N.Y.: IASP, 1976.

Billington, James H. *The Icon and the Axe: An Interpretive History of Russian Culture.* New York: Vintage Books, 1966.

Erlich, Victor. *Russian Formalism: History, Doctrine.* New Haven, Conn.: Yale University Press, 1981.

Erlich, Victor, ed. *Twentieth-Century Russian Literary Criticism.* New Haven, Conn.: Yale University Press, 1975.

Fedotov, George P. *The Russian Religious Mind.* 2 vols. Belmont, Mass.: Nordland Publishers, 1975.

Leatherbarrow, W. J., and D. C. Offord, eds. and trans. *A Documentary History of Russian Thought from the Enlightenment to Marxism.* Ann Arbor, Mich.: Ardis, 1987.

Moser, Charles A. *Esthetics as Nightmare: Russian Literary Theory, 1855–1870.* Princeton, N.J.: Princeton University Press, 1989.

Rabinowitz, Stanley, ed. and trans. *The Noise of Change: Russian Literature and the Critics (1891–1917).* Ann Arbor, Mich.: Ardis, 1986.

Seyffert, Peter. *Soviet Literary Structuralism: Background, Debate, Issues.* Columbus, Ohio: Slavica, 1983.

Stacy, Robert H. *Russian Literary Criticism: A Short History.* Syracuse, N.Y.: Syracuse University Press, 1974.

Terras, Victor. *Belinskij and Russian Literary Criticism: The Heritage of Organic Aesthetics.* Madison, Wisc.: University of Wisconsin Press, 1974.

Tschižewskij, Dmitrij. *Russian Intellectual History.* Translated by John C. Osborne and Martin P. Rice. Ann Arbor, Mich.: Ardis, 1978.

Walicki, Andrzej. *A History of Russian Thought from the Enlightenment to Marxism.* Translated from Polish by Hilda Andrews-Rusiecka. Stanford, Calif.: Stanford University Press, 1979.

Wellek, René. *A History of Modern Criticism.* Vols. 1–4, 7. New Haven, Conn.: Yale University Press, 1955–65, 1991.

Index